Fourth Canadian Edition
Volume 2

INTERMEDIATE ACCOUNTING

INTERMEDIATE ACCOUNTING

Fourth Canadian Edition
Volume 2

Donald E. Kieso Ph.D., C.P.A.
KPMG Peat Marwick Professor of Accounting
Northern Illinois University
DeKalb, Illinois

Jerry J. Weygandt Ph.D., C.P.A.
Arthur Anderson Alumni Professor of Accounting
University of Wisconsin
Madison, Wisconsin

Canadian Edition prepared by

V. Bruce Irvine Ph.D., C.M.A., F.C.M.A.
University of Saskatchewan
Saskatoon, Saskatchewan

W. Harold Silvester Ph.D., C.P.A., C.A.
University of Saskatchewan
Saskatoon, Saskatchewan

John Wiley & Sons
Toronto   New York   Chichester   Brisbane   Singapore

DEDICATED TO

Marilyn	Viola
Lee-Ann	Susan
Cameron	Dianne
Sandra	Daniel

Canadian Cataloguing in Publication Data

Kieso, Donald E.
   Intermediate Accounting

4th Canadian ed. / prepared by V. Bruce Irvine,
W. Harold Silvester.
Includes bibliographical references and index.
ISBN 0-471-64094-8 (v. 1)   ISBN 0-471-64095-6 (v. 2)

1. Accounting. I. Weygandt, Jerry J. II. Irvine,
V. Bruce. III. Silvester, W. Harold. IV. Title.

HP5635.K54 1994   657'.044   C94-930183-3

Production Credits

Design: JAQ
Cover Design: Selwyn Simon
Cover Photo Credits: Victor Last
Typesetting: Compeer Typographic Services
Film: Compeer Typographic Services

Printed and bound by Metropole Litho Inc.
10 9 8 7 6 5 4 3 2 1

ABOUT THE AUTHORS

CANADIAN EDITION

V. Bruce Irvine Ph.D., C.M.A., F.C.M.A., is a professor of Accounting at the University of Saskatchewan. He received his Ph.D. in accounting from the University of Minnesota. Among his publications are articles and reviews in such journals as *C.M.A. "The Management Accounting Magazine," CA Magazine, Managerial Planning,* and *The Accounting Review.* Designated "Professor of the Year" several times, Dr. Irvine has extensive teaching experience in financial and managerial accounting and has been instrumental in establishing innovative pedagogical techniques and instructional materials at the University of Saskatchewan. He has had considerable involvement with practising accountants through serving on various local, provincial, national, and international committees and boards of the Society of Management Accountants. Additionally, Dr. Irvine has served in various executive committee positions of the Canadian Academic Accounting Association.

W. Harold Silvester Ph.D., C.P.A., C.A., received his doctorate from the University of Missouri, Columbia, and is Professor of Accounting at the University of Saskatchewan. In his teaching capacity, he has played a key role in introducing pedagogical improvements at the University of Saskatchewan and in developing instructional materials for the Accounting program there. He has been named "Professor of the Year" in recognition of his substantial contributions to the College of Commerce. An important contribution has been the development of materials to integrate computers with accounting instruction. Articles by Professor Silvester have appeared in *CA Magazine* and other academic and professional journals.

U.S. EDITION

Donald E. Kieso, PH.D., C.P.A., received his doctorate in accounting from the University of Illinois. He has served as chairman of the Department of Accountancy and is currently the KPMG Peat Marwick Professor of Accountancy at Northern Illinois University. He has public accounting experience with Price Waterhouse & Co. (San Francisco and Chicago) and Arthur Anderson & Co. (Chicago) and research experience with the Research Division of the American Institute of Certified Public Accountants (New York). He has done postdoctorate work as a Visiting Scholar at the University of California at Berkeley and is a recipient of NIU's Teaching Excellence Award and has twice received the Executive MBA Golden Apple Teaching Award. Professor Kieso is the author of other accounting and business books and is a member of the American Accounting Association, the American Institute of Certified Public Accountants, the Financial Executives Institute, and the Illinois CPA Society. He has served as a member of the Board of Directors of the Illinois CPA Society, the AACSB Accounting Accreditation Committee, the Board of Governors of the American Accounting Association's Administrators of Accounting Programs Group, the State of Illinois Comptroller's Commission, as Secretary-Treasurer of the Federation of Schools of Accountancy, and as Secretary-Treasurer of the American Accounting Association. Professor Kieso is currently serving as a member of the Accounting Education Change Commission, the Board of Directors of Aurora University, as the chair of the Accounting Education Change Liaison Committee of the American Accounting Association, and on committees of the Illinois CPA Society. In 1988 he received the Outstanding Accounting Educator Award from the Illinois CPA Society.

Jerry J. Weygandt, Ph.D., C.P.A., is Arthur Anderson Alumni Professor of Accounting at the University of Wisconsin-Madison. He holds a Ph.D. in accounting from the University of Illinois. Articles by Professor Weygandt have appeared in the *Accounting Review*, *Journal of Accounting Research*, the *Journal of Accountancy*, and other professional journals. These articles have examined such financial reporting issues as accounting for price-level adjustments, pensions, convertible securities, stock option contracts, and interim reports. He is a member of the American Accounting Association, the American Institute of Certified Public Accountants, and the Wisconsin Society of Certified Public Accountants. He has served on numerous committees of the American Accounting Association and as a member of the editorial board of the *Accounting Review*. In addition, he is actively involved with the American Institute of Certified Public Accountants and has been a member of the Accounting Standards Executive Committee (AcSEC) of that organization. He has served as a consultant to a number of businesses and state agencies on financial reporting issues and served on the FASB task force that examined the reporting issues related to "accounting for income taxes." Professor Weygandt has received the Chancellor's Award for Excellence in Teaching; he also served as Secretary-Treasurer of the American Accounting Association. In 1991, he received the Wisconsin Institute of CPA's Outstanding Educator's Award.

PREFACE

The fourth Canadian edition of *Intermediate Accounting* discusses in depth the traditional (intermediate) financial accounting topics as well as the recent developments in accounting recognition, measurement, and disclosure practices promulgated by the leading professional accounting organizations and applied by practitioners in public accounting and industry. Explanations and discussions of financial accounting theory are supported and illustrated by examples taken directly from practice and authoritative pronouncements.

Continuing to keep pace with the complexities of the modern business enterprise, we have included a comprehensive set of topics supported by numerous illustrations and judiciously selected appendices. The appendices are concerned primarily with complex subjects, lesser-used methods, or specialized topics.

The text is organized into six major parts:

1. Financial Accounting Functions and Basic Theory (Chapters 1 to 6)
2. Assets: Recognition, Measurement, and Disclosure (Chapters 7 to 12)
3. Liabilities: Recognition, Measurement, and Disclosure (Chapters 13 to 14)
4. Shareholders' Equity, Dilutive Securities, and Investments (Chapters 15 to 18)
5. Issues Related to Selected Topics (Chapters 19 to 22)
6. Preparation and Analysis of Financial Statements (Chapters 23 to 25)

An Appendix to the book explains and illustrates various time value of money concepts and provides present and future value tables.

After careful consideration and discussion with instructors, we have decided to offer the fourth Canadian edition in two separate volumes. Volume 1 contains Chapters 1-12 (dealing with assets) and Volume 2 contains Chapters 13-25 (dealing with liabilities, shareholders' equity, and other topics). Both volumes contain the Appendix on "Accounting and the Time Value of Money" as well as the table of contents and index for the entire book.

Benefiting from the comments and recommendations of adopters of our third revised edition, we have made significant revisions. Explanations have been expanded where necessary, complicated discussions and illustrations have been simplified, realism has been integrated to heighten interest and relevancy, and new topics and coverage have been added to maintain currency. We have deleted some third revised edition coverage and condensed the coverage of other topics.

We have attempted to balance our coverage so that the discussion of underlying concepts of accounting and their practical application are mutually reinforcing. The study of concepts develops an understanding of procedures, and the performance enriches an understanding of the concepts. Accountants must think as well as act; therefore, we have given equal emphasis to **why** and **how**.

We believe that a full understanding of generally accepted accounting principles (which includes the conceptual framework of financial accounting) is necessary for an individual to appropriately account for transactions and other events affecting a business. From this understanding, and given a comprehension of the economic consequences of transactions and events as well as an appreciation for the behavioural impact of information on users, an individual is likely to exercise more informed judgement when making decisions affecting the financial statements. Additionally, as the preparer of financial statements, an accountant must know how these decisions are incorporated into the accounting record-keeping system.

Within this context, an accountant may face ethical dilemmas. As a new feature in this edition, we have identified this as an aspect of an accountant's life (Chapter 1) and have included some questions, cases, and exercises in various chapters to emphasize that doing accounting requires appropriate consideration for ethical behaviour.

NEW FEATURES

Significant changes in this edition of *Intermediate Accounting* occur as the result of incorporating *CICA Handbook* additions and revisions, recent *Exposure Drafts* of the Accounting Standards Board (AcSB) and Canadian accounting studies. As such, the contents reflect Canadian generally accepted accounting principles and issues to June 1993. Additionally, excerpts from recent financial statements of many Canadian companies are included to illustrate contemporary financial reporting practice.

Numerous new features have been added to the fourth Canadian edition:

1. **The sequence of chapters has changed**. Chapter 19 (Revenue Recognition) in the third revised edition has been moved to Chapter 6 of the fourth edition to reflect the importance of this topic to the entire accounting function. Chapter 6 (Accounting and the Time Value of Money) of the third revised edition has been condensed into an appendix located at the end of the book.

2. A **two-colour presentation** to more clearly distinguish section headings as well as a coloured sidebar to mark the location of end-of-chapter material.

3. A **description of each case, exercise, and problem** is provided for the first time to draw attention to the nature of the issues being addressed.

4. **Financial reporting problems** have been developed and placed as the last item of the homework-assignment material. Most of these financial reporting problems require reference to and analysis and interpretation of Moore Corporation Limited's financial statements and accompanying notes (see Appendix 5A).

5. **Ethical issues** have been addressed in the form of text discussion and assignment material to sensitize students to the ethical considerations, situations, and dilemmas encountered by practising accountants.

6. **"Perspectives . . ."** have been added to stress the relevance of accounting topics to the realities of Canadian business. These interviews occur at the end of each Part. Because these interviews contain considerable accounting content and are relevant to an accountant's professional development, they can serve as a basis for classroom discussion.

7. **Learning objectives** are presented in the side margins throughout the book as aids to readers.

Throughout the book, we have attempted to improve the pedagogy and simplify complex presentations. Also, many new questions, cases, exercises, and problems have been incorporated and those retained have been modified.

Chapter 1 emphasizes that one must be concerned with the "whys" of accounting as well as what is done. This chapter contains a discussion of the nature of financial accounting, the environmental factors influencing and influenced by financial accounting, Canadian generally accepted accounting principles (as defined in the *CICA Handbook*), the nature and importance of judgement, and ethical aspects of making accounting decisions.

In Chapter 2, a conceptual framework for financial accounting is examined based on the contents and definitions in Section 1000 of the *CICA Handbook* and other sources. Chapter 3 is a review of the accounting process. Chapters 4 and 5 concentrate on issues related to the content and presentation of the income statement, statement of retained earnings, balance sheet, and statement of changes in financial position. Chapter 6 examines and illustrates revenue recognition and fully incorporates the *CICA Handbook* material on the topic.

Cash and accounts and notes receivable are examined extensively in Chapter 7. Coverage of inventories in Chapters 8 and 9 emphasize methods most frequently used by businesses in Canada. Such issues as "capitalization of interest cost" and "special sale agreements" are included and implications regarding *CICA Handbook* material on revenue recognition are considered.

CICA Handbook material regarding accounting for capital assets, non-monetary transactions, and captalization of interest cost is included in Chapters 10 and 11, which examine the acquistion, disposition, and amortization of property, plant, and equipment. Issues concerning the determination of acquisition cost, and accounting for expenditures subsequent to acquisition and asset disposal are the focus of Chapter 10. Chapter 11 includes discussion of accounting for natural resources as well as traditional methods of accounting for depreciation, capital cost allowance, and investment tax credits. Chapter 12 covers issues related to intangible assets, incorporating material on amortization drawn from the *Exposure Draft* on capital assets.

Current and contingent liabilities are examined in Chapter 13. Chapter 14 examines bonds and other long-term payables and considers some of the accounting implications of financial mechanisms such as interest rate swaps and in-substance defeasance. A new appendix has been added to Chapter 14 that considers issues related to complex financial instruments. Specifically, issues concerning recognition of substance over form, off-balance-sheet financing, and troubled debt restructuring are discussed, based on material in the AcSB's *Exposure Draft* on "Financial Instruments."

Chapters 15 and 16 on shareholders' equity include a discussion of the related provisions of the Canada Business Corporations Act and current developments regarding the increasing difficulty of distinguishing some financing instruments such as debt or equity. Chapter 17 contains a thorough explanation and illustration of the earnings per share requirements of the *CICA Handbook*. Chapter 18 deals with issues associated with accounting for investments in bonds, shares, and funds and has been organized to provide increased and improved coverage of investments in marketable securities.

Chapter 19 on corporate income tax accounting examines accounting for permanent and timing differences between accounting and taxable income. Alternative approaches are considered with concentration being on the comprehensive deferral method. In addition to interperiod tax allocation, intraperiod tax allocation is addressed.

Coverage of pension costs in Chapter 20 has been written to incorporate an integrated approach. This allows readers to reconcile various account balances in the employer's books with amounts in the pension fund accounts. Chapter 21 on leases provides a complete coverage of Section 3065 of the *Handbook*. Topics in this chapter include "guaranteed and unguaranteed residual values," "bargain purchase options," and "initial direct costs."

Chapter 22 on accounting changes and error analysis has been amended to reflect changes to Section 1506 of the *Handbook*.

Chapter 23 on the statement of changes in financial position presents a work sheet approach to the preparation of this statement. In accordance with Section 1540 of the *Handbook*, this chapter focuses on cash and cash equivalents. An appendix to the chapter illustrates the T-account method for those who prefer this approach.

Basic financial statement analysis is covered in Chapter 24 in which new material regarding aspects of uncertainty and risk have been included. Chapter 25 on "full disclosure" contains numerous examples from the financial statements of influential Canadian firms. The appendix to Chapter 25 contains information on accounting for changing prices that has been appropriately changed to reflect the removal of Section 4510 from the *Handbook*.

The Appendix at the end of the book provides material covering the basics of compound interest, annuities, and present value for those wishing to study or review these topics in preparation for understanding their use in various financial accounting topics covered throughout the book. This material includes compound interest tables.

QUESTIONS, CASES, EXERCISES, AND PROBLEMS

At the end of each chapter, there is a comprehensive set of review and homework material consisting of questions, cases, exercises, and problems.

The questions are designed for review, self-testing, and classroom discussion purposes as well as homework assignments. The cases generally require descriptive as opposed to quantitative solutions; they are intended to confront the reader with situations calling for conceptual analysis and the exercise of judgement. They challenge the reader to identify problems and evaluate alternatives. Typically, an exercise covers a specific topic and requires less time and effort to solve than cases and problems. Problems are more challenging to solve than the exercises. They require a more in-depth understanding of material, are more complex, and often integrate topics in the chapter(s) and necessitate understanding of concepts underlying particular accounting treatments or methods.

Probably no more than one-fourth of the total case, exercise, and problem material need be used to cover the subject matter adequately; consequently, problem assignments may be varied from year to year.

SUPPLEMENTARY MATERIALS

Accompanying this textbook is an expanded package of supplements consisting of instructional aids for students and instructors. The following supplements are available for students: (1) A Student Companion Volume prepared by Irene Wiecek of the University of Toronto and (2) a Checklist of Key Figures.

The Student Companion Volume contains chapter overviews and focus points to give additional insights into the key concepts of the text. As well, review questions and solutions are given to allow the student to gain a better understanding of the material. Problems and worked solutions expose students to the fundamental calculations required for that topic. Finally, cases with full solutions help students develop skills in problem-identification and problem-solving within the context of financial reporting. As well, these cases aid the student in coping with uncertainty and developing sound professional judgement. A special chapter is also included on case analysis.

The following supplements are available exclusively for instructor use: (1) a comprehensive Solutions Manual for the end-of-chapter material, (2) an Instructor's Manual containing lecture outlines, an annotated bibliography, and other enrichment material, and (3) selected solutions on Transparency Masters. New to this edition is a Test Bank (printed and computerized), which contains multiple choice questions, exercises, and problems for class testing.

ACKNOWLEDGEMENTS FOR THE FOURTH CANADIAN EDITION

We thank the many individuals who contributed to the book through their comments and constructive criticism. Special thanks are extended to the primary reviewers of our manuscript:

Jim Allen
  Mohawk College

Peter Cunningham
  Bishop's University

Brian Duggan
  University of Manitoba

David Fleming
  George Brown College

Margaret Forbes
  Lakehead University

Bruce Hazelton
  Sheridan College

Selwyn James
  Centennial College

Michelle Pierce
  Seneca College

Wendy Roscoe
  Concordia University

John Varga
  George Brown College

Nora Wilson
  Humber College

Walter Woronchak
  Sheridan College

Gerry Woudstra
  N.A.I.T.

We would also like to thank those who did preliminary reviews in preparation for the writing of this edition:

Dave Carter
    University of Waterloo

Ann Clarke-Okah
    Carleton University

Peter Cunningham
    Bishop's University

Brian Duggan
    University of Manitoba

Janet Falk
    University College of Fraser Valley

David Ferries
    Algonquin College

Leo Gallant
    St. Francis Xavier University

Richard Marshall
    McGill University

Tom Shoniker
    Ryerson Polytechnical University

Ken Sutley
    private practice

Irene Wiecek
    University of Toronto

Gerry Woudstra
    N.A.I.T.

Appreciation is also extended to our colleagues at the University of Saskatchewan who worked on and examined portions of this work and who made valuable suggestions. These include Jack Vicq, Daryl Lindsay, George Murphy, John Brennan, Mardell Vols, Judy Janson, and Maureen Fizzell.

We are most grateful to the staff at John Wiley & Sons Canada Limited: Bill Todd, Edward Ikeda, Diane Wood, Madhu Ranadive, and Karen Bryan. As well, we would like to acknowledge the editorial contributions of Kim Koh, June Trusty, and Claudia Kutchukian.

Sincere appreciation is also extended to the following who provided the authors with excellent services regarding word-processing, research, and proofing: Evadne Merz, Pam Morrell, and Kirsten Jewitt.

We appreciate the cooperation of the Canadian Institute of Chartered Accountants in permitting us to quote from their pronouncements. We also wish to acknowledge the cooperation of the many Canadian companies from whose financial statements we have drawn excerpts.

If this book helps teachers instill in their students an appreciation for the challenges and limitations of accounting, if it encourages students to evaluate critically and understand financial accounting theory and practice, and if it prepares students for advanced study, professional examinations, and the successful pursuit of their careers in accounting and business, then we will have attained our objective.

Suggestions and comments from users of this book will be appreciated. A student reply card has been inserted at the back of the text for this purpose.

Saskatoon, Saskatchewan   V. Bruce Irvine
                                                     W. Harold Silvester

TABLE OF CONTENTS

CHAPTER 3

CHAPTER 4

CHAPTER 12

CHAPTER 13

CHAPTER 14

Long-Term Liabilities 676

Nature of Long-Term Liabilities 676 Bonds Payable 677 Types and Characteristics of Bonds 677; A Bond Issue's Life and Related Accounting 678; Valuation of Bonds Payable: Discount and Premium 679; Accounting for Bonds Payable 681; Effective Interest Method 684; Balance Sheet Presentation of Unamortized Bond Discount or Premium 688; Costs of Issuing Bonds 689; **Extinguishment of Debt 689** Reacquisition of Debt 690; Legal and In-Substance Defeasance 691; **Long-Term Notes Payable 693** Notes Issued Solely for Cash 693; Notes Exchanged for Cash and Some Right or Privilege 694; Notes Issued in Noncash Transactions 694; Imputing an Interest Rate 695; Mortgage Notes Payable 695; Short-Term Obligations Expected to be Refinanced 696; **Reporting Long-Term Debt 696 Fundamental Concepts 698**

Appendix 14A: Complex Issues Regarding Accounting for Long-Term Liabilities 699

Recognition of Substance Over Form 699 Subordinated Perpetual Debt 700; Term Preferred Shares 700; Convertible Bonds 701; Concluding Comment 702; **Off-Balance-Sheet Financing 702** Interest Rate Swaps 702; Project Financing Arrangements 704; Rationale for Off-Balance-Sheet Financing 705; **Troubled Debt Restructuring 705** Settlement of Debt at Less Than Its Carrying Amount 706; Continuation of Debt 706

Appendix 14B: Serial Bonds: Amortization and Redemption Before Maturity 709

Amortization of a Premium or Discount on Serial Bonds 709 Straight-Line Method 709; Bonds Outstanding Method 709; Effective Interest Method 711; **Redemption of Serial Bonds Before Maturity 712** Straight-Line Method 712; Bonds Outstanding Method 712; Effective Interest Method 712

Questions 713; Cases 714; Exercises 718; Problems 722

Perspectives: On Standard Setting 730

PART 4 SHAREHOLDERS' EQUITY, DILUTIVE SECURITIES, AND INVESTMENTS 733

CHAPTER 15

Shareholders' Equity: Issuance and Reacquisition of Share Capital 734

The Nature of Shareholders' Equity 734 Sources of Shareholders' Equity 735; What is Capital? 735; Terminology 736; **The Corporate Form of Entity 736** Corporate Law 737; Share Capital or Capital Stock System 738; Variety of Ownership Interests: Common and Preferred Shares 739; Liability of Shareholders 740; Formality of Profit Distribution 740; **Characteristics of Preferred Shares 741** Nature of Rights in Preferred Shares 741; Debt Characteristics of Preferred Shares 742; **Disclosure of Share Capital 743 Accounting for the Issuance of Shares 743** Accounting for Shares Without Par Value 743; Shares Sold on a Subscription Basis 745; Shares Issued in Combination with Other Securities (Lump Sum Sales) 747; Shares Issued in Noncash Transactions 748; Costs of Issuing Shares 749; **Reacquisition of Shares 749** Reacquisition and Retirement 750;

CHAPTER 18

PART 5 ISSUES RELATED TO SELECTED TOPICS 939

CHAPTER 19

3

Liabilities: Recognition, Measurement, and Disclosure

Current Liabilities and Contingencies

——■——

The credit quality of many corporations has substantially declined. For many Canadian corporations, liabilities have increased in relation to shareholders' equity and interest payments as a proportion of pretax income has also increased. The reason is that Canadian corporations, like the federal government, went on an unprecedented debt binge. Companies borrowed money to expand in a booming economy and, in some cases, to fend off takeovers by other companies. As a result, both investors and the accounting profession now have to pay more attention to liabilities.

WHAT IS A LIABILITY?

Until recently, most accounting thought and analysis have been directed toward the determination of debit, the valuation of assets, or the charge to expense, with related liabilities being handled as an afterthought. Although it is true that all liabilities have credit balances, it is debatable whether all credits appearing above the shareholders' equity section in published balance sheets are liabilities, or whether all liabilities have been recorded.

The question "What is a liability?" is not easy to answer. The acquisition of goods or services on credit terms gives rise to liabilities. But it seems clear that liabilities include more than debts arising from borrowings. Liabilities also result from the imposition of taxes, withholdings from employees' wages and salaries, dividend declarations, and product warranties.

To illustrate the complexity of this issue, one might ask whether preferred shares represent a liability or an ownership claim. The first reaction is to say that preferred shares are, in fact, an ownership claim and should be reported as part of shareholders' equity. In fact, preferred shares often have many elements of debt as well.[1] The issuer (and in some cases, the holder) often has the right to call the shares within a specific period of time, thus making it similar to a repayment of principal. The dividend is in many cases almost guaranteed (cumulative provision) and it looks like interest. Moreover, preferred shares are but one of many financial instruments that are difficult to classify.[2] But, assuming that the preferred shares are cumulative, nonparticipating, and callable by the issuer at any time, are they a liability or a part of shareholders' equity? Or, to go even one step further, let us assume that the preferred shares are cumulative, nonparticipating, and callable by either issuer or holder on demand. Would the preferred shares in this case be a liability? This and

---

[1] It should be noted that this illustration is not just a theoretical exercise. In practice, a number of preferred share issues have all of the characteristics of a debt instrument, except that they are called and legally classified as preferred shares. In some cases, Revenue Canada has even permitted the dividend payments to be treated as interest expense for tax purposes. This issue is discussed further in Chapter 15.

[2] As examples of the diversity within preferred shares, companies now issue (1) mandatorily redeemable preferred shares (redeemable at a specified price and time), (2) Dutch auction preferred shares (holders have the right to change the rate at defined intervals through a bidding process), and (3) increasing rate (exploding rate) preferred shares (holder receives an increasing dividend rate each period, with the issuer having the right to call the shares at a certain date in the future). In all three cases, the issuer either has to redeem the shares per the contract or has strong economic reasons for calling the shares. These securities are more like debt than equity. The CICA released an *Exposure Draft*, "Financial Instruments," in September 1991 that addresses the problem of distinguishing debt and equity instruments.

other similar questions are difficult to answer in the absence of precise definitions. For decades, the official definitions of liabilities have been conceptually deficient. As a result, the liability section of the balance sheet has degenerated into a catch-all for all leftover credit balances, some of them ill conceived.

The Accounting Standards Committee, as part of the Financial Statement Concepts project, defined liabilities as *"obligations of an enterprise arising from past transactions or events, the settlement of which may result in the transfer of assets, provision of services or other yielding of economic benefits."*[3] In other words, a liability has two essential characteristics:

1. It is an obligation to others that entails settlement by future transfer or use of cash, goods, or services on a determinable date or on the occurrence of some specified event.

2. The transaction or other event obligating the enterprise must have already occurred.

Although this definition may be subject to differing interpretations, it is a welcome addition to the professional literature, especially given past definitions developed by professional bodies.[4]

Because liabilities involve future disbursements of assets or services, one of the most important features is the date on which they are payable. Currently maturing obligations represent a demand on the current assets of the enterprise—a demand that must be satisfied promptly and in the ordinary course of business if operations are to be continued. Liabilities with a more distant due date do not, as a rule, represent a claim on the enterprise's current resources and are in a slightly different category. This feature gives rise to the basic division of liabilities into (1) current liabilities and (2) long-term debt.

WHAT IS A CURRENT LIABILITY?

For many years, payment within one year was the characteristic that distinguished a current liability from a long-term debt. But this one-year rule, although simple to follow, produced some unreasonable results when the operating cycle of a business exceeded one year. Under the currently acceptable practice, both current liabilities and current assets are defined in terms of the operating cycle of the individual enterprise.

> **Objective 1**
>
> Define current liabilities and describe how they are valued.

The **operating cycle** is the period of time that elapses between the acquisition of goods and services involved in the manufacturing process and the final cash realization resulting from sales and subsequent collections. Industries that manufacture products requiring an aging process and certain capital-intensive industries have an operating cycle of considerably more than one year; on the other hand, most retail and service establishments have several operating cycles within a year.

Current liabilities *"should include amounts payable within one year from the date of the balance sheet or within the normal operating cycle, where this is longer than a year."*[5] This definition has gained wide acceptance because it recognizes operating cycles of varying lengths in different industries. Implicitly, the period used (operating cycle or year) should be the same as that used for classifying current assets.

VALUATION OF CURRENT LIABILITIES

Theoretically, liabilities should be measured by the present value of the future outlay of cash required to liquidate them. But, in practice, current liabilities are usually recorded in accounting records and

---

[3] *CICA Handbook* (Toronto: CICA), Section 1000, par. .28.

[4] For definitions that are similar to the CICA definition, see: "Elements of Financial Statements of Business Enterprises," *Statement of Financial Accounting Concepts No. 6* (Stamford, CT: FASB, 1980); Maurice Moonitz, "The Changing Concept of a Liability," *The Journal of Accountancy* (May 1960), pp. 41–46; Eldon S. Hendricksen, *Accounting Theory*, 3rd ed. (Homewood, IL: Richard D. Irwin, Inc., 1977), p. 451; and American Accounting Association, *Accounting and Reporting Standards for Corporate Financial Statements* (Sarasota, FL: AAA, 1957), p. 16.

[5] *CICA Handbook*, Section 1510, par. .03.

reported in financial statements at their full maturity amount. Because of the short time periods involved, frequently less than one year, the difference between the present value of a current liability and the maturity value is not usually large. The slight overstatement of liabilities that results from carrying current liabilities at maturity is accepted as immaterial.

DIFFERENCES IN CURRENT LIABILITIES

Liabilities are obligations arising from past transactions. But liabilities also possess characteristics that lend themselves to categorization. *All liabilities, because they are probable future sacrifices, involve an element of uncertainty.* The differences in uncertainty related to liabilities are the dissimilarities that allow us to discuss current liabilities as (1) determinable current liabilities and (2) contingent liabilities.

DETERMINABLE CURRENT LIABILITIES

Objective 2
Identify type of determinable current liabilities.

The types of liabilities discussed in this category can be precisely measured. The amount of cash that will be needed to discharge the obligation and the date of payment or discharge are reasonably certain. There is nothing uncertain about (1) the fact that the obligation has been incurred and (2) its amount. The primary problem is one of discovery, which arises from the possibility of omitting these liabilities. In contrast to long-term debts, which are normally large in amount and supported by documentary evidence consisting of contracts, authorization, and correspondence, current liabilities may result from unwritten extensions of credit or unrecorded accruals, and may be small. Once these liabilities are discovered, however, the amount is readily determinable.

Accounts Payable

Accounts payable, or **trade accounts payable**, are balances owed to others for goods, supplies, and services purchased on open account. Accounts payable arise because of the time lag between the receipt of services or acquisition of title to assets and the payment for them. This period of extended credit is usually found in the terms of the sale (e.g., 2/10, n/30 or 1/10, E.O.M.) and is commonly 30 to 60 days.

Most accounting systems are designed to record liabilities for the purchase of goods when the goods are received or, practically, when the invoices are received. Frequently there is some delay in recording the goods and the related liability on the books. If title has passed to the purchaser before the goods are received, the transaction should be recorded at the time of title passage. Attention must be paid to transactions occurring near the end of one accounting period and at the beginning of the next to ascertain that the record of goods received (the inventory) is in agreement with the liability (accounts payable) and that both are recorded in the proper period.

Measuring the amount of an account payable poses no particular difficulty because the invoice received from the creditor specifies the due date and the exact outlay in money that is necessary to settle the account. The only calculation that may be necessary concerns the amount of cash discount. See Chapter 8 for illustrations of entries relating to accounts payable and purchase discounts.

Notes Payable

Obligations in the form of written promissory notes that are classified as current liabilities are usually (1) trade notes, (2) short-term loan notes, or (3) current maturities of long-term debts.

Trade Notes. Trade notes payable represent the unpaid face amount of promissory notes owed to suppliers of goods, services, and equipment. In some industries and for certain classes of customers, promissory notes are required as part of the transaction in lieu of the normal extension of open account or verbal credit. Normally, both the due date and the amount of the outlay necessary to discharge the note are contained on the note. The only calculation that is commonly involved is the calculation of interest if the note is interest bearing.

Short-Term Loan Notes. Short-term promissory notes payable to banks or loan companies represent a current liability and generally arise from cash loans. When these notes are interest bearing, it is necessary to record and report in financial statements any accrued interest payable and to carry the note payable as a liability at its *face value* (also called *principal amount*).

If a *noninterest-bearing note* is issued, the bank or loan company *discounts* the note and remits the proceeds to the borrower. To illustrate, assume that on October 1 the Airfrate Company has its $100,000, one-year, noninterest-bearing note discounted at 9% at the Corner Brook National Bank. The Airfrate Company will receive the proceeds of $91,000 and will assume the obligation to pay $100,000 to the bank in 12 months. It should be apparent that the Airfrate Company has borrowed $91,000 for a period of one year at a cost of $9,000. Although the *stated discount rate* was 9%, the *effective interest rate* is 9.89% ($9,000/$91,000) because the full $100,000 is not available to the Airfrate Company during the year. A loan under these terms is recorded on the date the loan is completed in the following manner:

Cash	91,000	
Discount on Notes Payable	9,000	
Notes Payable		100,000

The balance in the Discount on Notes Payable account would be deducted on the balance sheet from Notes Payable. Interest expense would be recorded in monthly increments of $750 by reducing Discount on Notes Payable through the following entry (assuming straight-line amortization approximates the effective interest method of amortization):

Interest Expense	750	
Discount on Notes Payable		750

Thus, a balance sheet prepared at December 31 would show the following.

Current Liabilities		
Notes payable	$100,000	
Less: Discount on notes payable	6,750*	
		$93,250

*$9,000 − (3 × $750)

The interest expense of $2,250 for the three-month period would be reported in the income statement.

Current Maturities of Long-Term Debts. The portion of bonds, mortgage notes, and other long-term indebtedness that matures within the next fiscal year is reported as a current liability. When only part of a long-term debt is to be paid within the next 12 months, as in the case of serial bonds that are to be retired through a series of annual instalments, the *maturing portion of the long-term debt is reported as a current liability*. The balance is reported as a long-term debt.

Long-term debts maturing currently should not be included as current liabilities if they are (1) to be retired by assets accumulated for this purpose that properly have not been shown as current assets, (2) to be refinanced or retired from the proceeds of a new debt issue (see next topic), or (3) to be converted into share capital. The plan for liquidation of such a debt should be disclosed either parenthetically or by a note to the financial statements.

However, a liability that is due on demand (callable by the creditor) or will be due on demand within a year (or operating cycle, if longer) should be classified as a current liability. Liabilities often become callable by the creditor when there is a violation of the debt agreement. For example, most debt agreements specify that a given level of equity to debt be maintained, or specify that working capital be of a minimum amount. If an agreement is violated, classification of the debt as current is required because it is a reasonable expectation that existing working capital will be used to satisfy the debt. However, if it can be shown that the violation will *probably* be cured (satisfied) within the grace period usually given in these agreements, then the debt can be classified as noncurrent.

Short-Term Obligations Expected to Be Refinanced

Objective 3

Explain the classification issues of short-term debt expected to be refinanced.

Short-term obligations are those debts that are scheduled to mature within one year after the date of an enterprise's balance sheet or within an enterprise's operating cycle, whichever is longer. Some short-term obligations are expected to be refinanced on a long-term basis and, therefore, are not expected to require the use of working capital during the next year (or operating cycle).[6]

At one time, the accounting profession generally supported the exclusion of short-term obligations from current liabilities if they are "expected to be refinanced." Because the profession provided no specific guidelines, however, the determination of whether a short-term obligation was expected to be refinanced was usually based solely on management's *intent* to refinance on a long-term basis. A company may sell short-term commercial paper to finance new plant and equipment, intending eventually to refinance on a long-term basis. Or it may obtain a five-year bank loan but, because the bank prefers it, handle the actual financing with 90-day notes, which it must keep turning over (renewing). So is it long-term debt or current liabilities?

The accounting profession requires the exclusion of short-term obligations from current liabilities "to the extent that contractual arrangements have been made for settlement from other than current assets."[7] Professional judgement must be used to determine whether the particular contractual arrangement is adequate to permit classification of the short-term obligation as noncurrent. The following conditions in the agreement would help to substantiate its adequacy:

1. The agreement should be noncancellable as to all parties.

2. It should extend beyond the normal operating cycle of the company or one year, whichever is longer.

3. At the balance sheet date and the date of issuance of the financial statements, the company must not be in violation of the agreement.

4. The lender or investor should be financially capable of honouring the agreement.

The amount of short-term debt that may be excluded from current liabilities:

1. Should not exceed the amount available for refinancing under the agreement.

2. Should be adjusted for any limitations or restrictions in the agreement that indicate that the full amount obtainable will not be available to retire the short-term obligations.

3. Should not exceed a reasonable estimate of the *minimum* amount expected to be available, if the amount available for refinancing will fluctuate (that is, the most conservative estimate should be used).

If any of these three amounts cannot be reasonably estimated, the entire amount of the short-term debt should be included in current liabilities.

As an illustration of a fluctuating amount (item 3 above), consider the following:

Yorkton Casket Limited enters into an agreement with the Royal Bank to borrow up to 80% of the amount of its trade receivables. During the next fiscal year, the receivables are expected to range between a low of $900,000 in the first quarter and a high of $1,700,000 in the third quarter. The minimum amount expected to be available to refinance the short-term obligations that mature

---

[6] *Refinancing a short-term obligation on a long-term basis* means either replacing it with a long-term obligation or with equity securities, or renewing, extending, or replacing it with short-term obligations for an uninterrupted period extending beyond one year (or operating cycle, if longer) from the date of the enterprise's balance sheet.
[7] *CICA Handbook*, Section 1510, par. .06.

during the first quarter of the next year is $720,000 (80% of the expected low for receivables during the first quarter). Consequently, no more than $720,000 of short-term obligations may be excluded from current liabilities at the balance sheet date.

An additional question relates to whether a short-term obligation should be excluded from current liabilities if it is paid off after the balance sheet date and subsequently replaced by long-term debt before the balance sheet is issued. To illustrate, Marquardt Company pays off short-term debt of $40,000 on January 17, 1995 and issues long-term debt of $100,000 on February 3, 1995. Marquardt's financial statements dated December 31, 1994 are to be issued March 1, 1995. Because repayment of the short-term obligation *before* funds were obtained through long-term financing required the use of *existing* current assets, the short-term obligation should be included in current liabilities at the balance sheet date (see graphical presentation below).

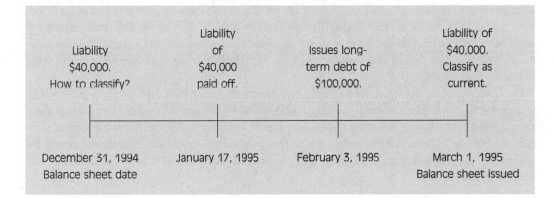

Disclosure. If a short-term obligation is excluded from current liabilities because of refinancing, the note to the financial statements should include:

1. A general description of the financing agreement.

2. The terms of any new obligation incurred or to be incurred.

3. The terms of any equity security issued or to be issued.

When refinancing on a long-term basis is expected to be accomplished through the issuance of equity securities, it is not appropriate to include the short-term obligation in owners' equity. The obligation is a liability and not owners' equity at the date of the balance sheet.

Dividends Payable

A **cash dividend payable** is an amount owed by a corporation to its shareholders as a result of an authorization by the board of directors. At the date of declaration, the corporation assumes a liability that places shareholders in the position of creditors in the amount of dividends declared. Because cash dividends are normally paid within one year of declaration (generally within three months), they are classified as current liabilities.

Accumulated but undeclared dividends on cumulative preferred shares are not a recognized liability because **preferred dividends in arrears** are not an obligation until formal action is taken by the board of directors authorizing the distribution of earnings. Nevertheless, the amount of cumulative dividends unpaid should be disclosed as a note or it may be shown parenthetically in the share capital section.

Dividends payable in the form of additional shares are not recognized as a liability. Such **stock dividends** (as discussed in Chapter 16) do not require future outlays of assets or services and they are revocable by the board of directors at any time prior to issuance. Even so, such undistributed stock dividends are generally reported in the shareholders' equity section because they represent retained earnings in the process of transfer to contributed surplus.

Returnable Deposits

Current liabilities of a company may include returnable deposits received from customers and employees. Deposits may be received from customers to guarantee performance of a contract or service or as guarantees to cover payment of expected future obligations. For example, telephone companies often require a deposit on installation of a phone. Deposits may also be received from customers as guarantees for possible damage to property left with the customer. Some companies require that their employees make deposits for the return of keys or other company property. The classification of these items as current or noncurrent liabilities is dependent on the time between the date of the deposit and the termination of the relationship that requires the deposit.

Liability on the Advance Sale of Tickets, Tokens, and Certificates

Transportation companies may issue tickets or tokens that can be exchanged or used to pay for future fares; restaurants may issue meal tickets that can be exchanged or used to pay for future meals; and retail stores may issue gift certificates that are redeemable in merchandise. In such cases, the businesses have received cash in exchange for promises to perform services or to furnish goods at some indefinite future date.

The sale of these tickets, tokens, and certificates is recorded by a debit to Cash and a credit to a current liability account usually described as Deferred or Unearned Revenue. The balance sheet should reflect the obligation for any outstanding instruments that are redeemable in goods or services; the income statement should reflect the revenues earned as a result of performances during the period. As the claims are redeemed, the liability account is debited and an appropriate revenue account credited.

Sales Taxes

Sales taxes on transfers of tangible personal property and on certain services must be collected from customers and remitted to the proper governmental authority. A liability is set up to provide for the taxes collected from customers but not yet remitted to the tax authority. The Sales Tax Payable account should reflect the liability for sales taxes due the government. The entry below is the proper one for a sale of $3,000 when a 4% sales tax is in effect:

Cash or Accounts Receivable	3,120	
Sales		3,000
Sales Taxes Payable		120

When the sales tax collections credited to the liability account are not equal to the liability computed by the governmental formula, an adjustment of the liability account may be made by recognizing revenue or a loss on sales tax collections.

In many companies, however, the sales tax and the amount of the sale are not segregated at the time of sale; both are credited in total in the Sales account. To reflect correctly the actual amount of sales and the liability for sales taxes, the Sales account must be debited for the amount of the sales taxes due the government on these sales and the Sales Taxes Payable account credited for the same amount.

As an illustration, assume that the sales account balance is $150,000 and includes sales taxes of 4%. Because the amount recorded in the sales account is equal to sales plus 4% of sales, or 1.04 times the sales total, the sales are $150,000 divided by 1.04, or $144,230.77. The sales tax liability is $5,769.23 ($144,230.77 $\times$ 0.04; or $150,000 − $144,230.77), and the following entry would be made to record the amount due the taxing unit:

Sales	5,769.23	
Sales Taxes Payable		5,769.23

Goods and Services Tax

Most businesses in Canada are subject to a goods and services tax (GST). The GST is a tax on the value added by each taxable entity. The amount payable is determined by deducting the amount of GST paid to suppliers on goods and services purchased from the amount of GST collected on sales to customers.

Accounting for GST involves setting up a liability account that is credited with GST charged on sales. This account is debited for the amount of GST paid to suppliers. Normally, the amount collected on sales exceeds the amount paid on purchases and the account will have a credit balance until a remittance is made. Since GST is paid on purchases of fixed assets, it is possible that the GST Payable account will have a debit balance. In these instances, a claim for reimbursement is made to Revenue Canada.

Purchases of taxable goods and services are recorded by debiting the GST Payable account for the amount of GST and debiting the appropriate account(s) for the purchase price. Since the amount of GST paid is a recoverable amount, the cost of items acquired should not normally include this tax.

Accounting for GST involves accumulating the amounts collected and paid in an account (generally a current liability) called GST Payable. Remittances to the Receiver General are debited to the account. The balance in the GST Payable account will normally be the net amount owing at the balance sheet date.

Property Taxes

Local governmental units generally depend on property taxes as their primary source of revenue. Such taxes are based on the assessed value of real and personal property and become a lien against property at a date determined by law. This lien is a liability of the property owner and is a cost of the services of such property. The accounting questions that arise from property taxes are:

1. When should the property owner record the liability?

2. To which income period should the cost be charged?

The accounting profession, in considering the various periods to which property taxes might be charged and how the liability should be reported, contends that generally, the most acceptable basis of providing for property taxes is monthly accrual on the taxpayer's books during the fiscal period of the taxing authority for which the taxes are levied. Charging the taxes to the period subsequent to the levy relates the expense to the period in which the taxes are used by the governmental unit to provide benefits to the property owner.

Assume that Seaboard Limited, which closes its books each year on December 31, receives its property tax bill in May each year. The fiscal year for the city in which Seaboard Limited is located begins on January 1 and ends on the following December 31. Property taxes of $36,000 are levied against Seaboard Company for the 1994 calendar year. However, the tax notice is sent out in May and is payable in equal instalments on July 1 and September 1. Prior to receipt of the tax notice, the company estimates the 1994 taxes at $33,600. Entries to record the liability, monthly tax charges, and tax payments for the 1994 property taxes are shown on page 640.

Prepaid property taxes of $12,600 on July 1 represent a prepayment and $12,400 on September 1 represent a four-month prepayment. At December 31, both the prepaid property tax and property taxes payable will have zero balances.

Some accountants advocate accruing property taxes by charges to expense during the fiscal year ending on the lien date, rather than during the fiscal year beginning on the lien date (the fiscal year of the taxing authority). In such instances, the property tax for the coming fiscal year must be estimated and charged monthly to Property Tax Expense and must be credited to Property Tax Payable. Under this method, the entire amount of the tax accrued by the lien date and the expense is therefore charged to the fiscal period preceding payment of the tax. Justification for this method

January 31 to April 30

Property Tax Expense	2,800	
Property Tax Payable		2,800

May 31 and June 30, 1994 (monthly expense accrual):

Property Tax Expense	3,100	
Property Taxes Payable		3,100

July 1, 1994 (first tax payment):

Property Taxes Payable	17,400	
Prepaid Property Taxes	600	
Cash		18,000

July 31, 1994 (monthly expense accrual):

Property Tax Expense	3,100	
Prepaid Property Tax		600
Property Taxes Payable		2,500

August 31, 1994:

Property Tax Expense	3,100	
Property Tax Payable		3,100

September 1, 1994 (second tax payment):

Property Taxes Payable	5,600	
Prepaid Property Tax	12,400	
Cash		18,000

Sept. 30, Oct. 31, Nov. 30, and Dec. 31, 1994 (monthly expense accrual):

Property Tax Expense	3,100	
Prepaid Property Taxes		3,100

exists when the assessment date precedes the lien date by a year or more, as is the case in some taxing units. In such instances, since the amount is estimated and accrued by the property owner before receipt of the tax bill, it is proper to categorize property taxes as an estimated current liability rather than as a determinable current liability.

Recognizing that special circumstances may suggest the use of alternative accrual periods, it is important that the period chosen be consistent from year to year. The selection of any of the alternative periods mentioned is a matter of individual judgement.

Income Taxes Payable

Any federal or provincial income tax varies in proportion to the amount of annual income. Some accountants consider the amount of income tax on annual income as an estimate because the computation of income (and the tax thereon) is subject to Revenue Canada review and approval. The meaning and application of numerous tax rules, especially new ones, are debatable and often dependent on a court's interpretation. Using the best information and advice available, a business must prepare an income tax return and compute the income tax payable resulting from the operations of the current period. The taxes payable on the income of a corporation, as computed per the tax return, should be classified as a current liability.

Unlike a corporation, the proprietorship and the partnership are not taxable entities. Because the individual proprietor and the members of a partnership are subject to personal income taxes on their share of the business's taxable income, income tax liabilities do not appear on the financial statements of proprietorships and partnerships.

Most corporations make periodic tax payments based on estimates of the current year's income tax. As the estimated total tax liability changes, the periodic contributions also change.

If in a later year an additional tax is assessed on the income of an earlier year, Income Taxes Payable should be credited. The related debit should be charged to current operations unless the criteria for treating it as a prior period adjustment are met.

Most Canadian companies will have differences between taxable income under the tax laws and accounting income under generally accepted accounting principles. Because of these differences, the amount of income tax payable to the government in any given year, based on taxable income, may differ substantially from the amount of income tax that relates to the income before taxes, as reported on the financial statements. Chapter 19 is devoted solely to the problems of accounting for income tax matters and presents an extensive discussion on this complex and controversial problem.

Employee-Related Liabilities

Amounts owed to employees for salaries or wages at the end of an accounting period are reported as a current liability. In addition, the following items related to employee compensation are often reported as current liabilities:

Objective 4

Identify types of employee-related liabilities.

1. Payroll deductions.

2. Post-retirement benefits.

3. Compensated absences.

4. Bonuses.

Payroll Deductions. The most common types of payroll deductions are taxes and miscellaneous items such as insurance premiums, employee savings, and union dues. To the extent that the deductions have not been remitted to the proper authority at the end of the accounting period, they should be recognized as current liabilities.

Canada (Quebec) Pension Plan. The Canada and Quebec pension plans are funded through the imposition of taxes on both the employer and the employee. All employers are required to collect the employee's share of this tax. They deduct it from the employee's gross pay and remit it to the government, along with the employer's share. Both the employer and the employee are taxed at the same rate, currently 2.5% (1994) based on the employee's gross pay up to a $33,400 annual limit. The amount of unremitted employee and employer CPP and QPP contributions should be reported by the employer as a current liability.

Unemployment Insurance. Another payroll tax levied by the federal government provides a system of unemployment insurance. This tax is levied on both employees and employers. Employees must pay a premium of 3% (1994) of insurable earnings, while the employer is required to contribute 1.4 times the amount of employee premiums. Insurable earnings are gross wages above a prescribed minimum and below a maximum amount. Both the premium rates and insurable earnings are adjusted frequently.

Income Tax Withholding. Federal income tax laws require employees to withhold from the pay of each employee an amount approximating the applicable income tax due on those wages. The amount of income tax withheld is computed by the employer according to a government-prescribed formula or a government-provided income tax deduction table, and is dependent on the length of the pay period and each employee's wages, marital status, and claimed dependants.

Illustration. Assume a weekly payroll of $10,000 entirely subject to CPP (2.5%), unemployment insurance (3%), income tax withholdings of $1,320, and union dues of $88. The entry to record the wages and salaries paid and the employee payroll deductions would be:

Wages and Salaries	10,000	
Employee Income Tax Deductions Payable		1,320
CPP Contributions Payable		250
UI Taxes Payable		300
Union Dues Payable		88
Cash		8,042

The entry to record the employer payroll taxes would be:

Payroll Tax Expense	670	
CPP Contributions Payable		250
UI Taxes Payable		420

The employer is required to remit to the Receiver General for Canada its share of CPP (QPP) contributions and UI taxes, along with the employer's share of these payroll taxes. All unremitted employer CPP (QPP) contributions and UI premiums should be recorded as payroll tax expense and payroll taxes payable. In a manufacturing enterprise, all of the payroll costs (wages, payroll taxes, and fringe benefits) are allocated to appropriate cost accounts, such as Direct Labour, Indirect Labour, Sales Salaries, Administrative Salaries, and the like. This appreciated and somewhat simplified discussion of payroll costs and deductions is not indicative of the volume of records and clerical work that may be involved in maintaining a sound and accurate payroll system.

Post-Retirement Benefits. Accounting and reporting for post-retirement benefit payments is complex. These procedures relate to two different types of post-retirement benefits: (1) pensions and (2) post-retirement health care and life insurance benefits.[8]

Pensions. A pension plan is an arrangement whereby an employer provides benefits (payments) to employees after they retire. Pension accounting follows accrual accounting, which necessitates measurement of the obligation to provide future benefits and accrual of the cost during the years that the employee provides the service. As a result, at the end of an accounting period, it is possible that a liability for pensions will appear on the balance sheet because the liability is not fully funded. If part of the liability is due in the next accounting period, it would be classified as current.

Other Post-Retirement Benefits. Companies providing post-retirement benefits such as health, dental, or life insurance commonly use one of three alternative accounting methods. These methods are (1) pay-as-you-go, (2) current accrual, and (3) accrue the liability at the time the employee retires. Under the pay-as-you-go approach, benefit costs are recognized as expenses as they are incurred. This fails to match costs with the periods benefiting from employee services. However, if the amount and timing of the benefits cannot be determined with reasonable precision or if the amount of the employer's liability is not material, then the pay-as-you-go method may be appropriate.

The current accrual method, mandatory in the United States, accomplishes better matching of costs with benefits and a more realistic portrayal of the firm's liabilities. Under this approach, companies record as a current expense each year a portion of the expected future cost of the post-retirement benefits.

A compromise between the above two methods involves estimating the amount of the company's obligation for post-retirement benefits at the date an employee retires. This amount is then recognized as an expense and reported as a liability.

Disclosure of the accounting policy followed is required by Section 1505.09 of the *CICA Handbook*. In addition, a general description of the nature of the post-retirement benefits should be provided in a note to the financial statements. An example of such note disclosure by Imperial Oil Limited follows.

---

[8] These issues are discussed extensively in Chapter 20.

Note 12 Other Post-Employment Benefits

The company shares the cost of certain health care and life insurance benefits for almost all retired employees and surviving spouses. The liability for this cost has been recorded for employees' service to date and for retirees. The annual charge to earnings is based on service provided in the year; cash payments are charged to the liability.

In 1991, other post-employment benefits expense was $17 million (1990: $21 million; 1989: $14 million).

Amounts recognized at December 31

millions of dollars	1991	1990
Long-term liability (Note 6)	172	165
Current liability	9	10

Compensated Absences. Compensated absences are absences from employment, such as vacation, sick leave, and holidays, for which it is expected that employees will be paid. Employers are required under provincial statutes to give each employee an annual vacation of a stipulated number of days or compensation in lieu of the vacation. As a result, employers have an obligation for vacation pay that accrues to the employees. Usually this obligation is satisfied by paying employees their regular salary for the period that they are absent from work while taking an annual vacation.

Vested rights exist when an employer has an obligation to make payment to an employee even if his or her employment is terminated; thus, vested rights are not contingent on an employee's future service. **Accumulated rights** are those that can be carried forward to future periods if not used in the period in which earned.

For example, assume that you have earned four days of vacation pay as of December 31, the end of your employer's fiscal year. In a province where vacation pay is prescribed by statute, your employer will have to pay you for these four days even if you terminate employment. In this situation, your four days of vacation pay are considered vested and should be accrued. Now assume that your vacation days are not vested, but that you can carry the four days over into later periods. Although the rights are not vested, they are accumulated rights for which the employer should provide an accrual, allowing for estimated forfeitures due to turnover.

Entitlement to **sick pay** varies considerably among employers. In some companies, employees are allowed to accumulate unused sick pay and take compensated time off from work even though they are not ill. In other companies, employees receive sick pay only if they are absent because of illness. In the first case, sick pay benefits vest, while in the second case, the benefits do not vest and may or may not accumulate. When benefits vest, accrual of the estimated liability is recommended. However, if the sick pay benefits are paid only when employees are absent from work due to illness, *CICA Handbook* Section 3290 should be applied. Under this section, accruals are required only if the probability of occurrence is high and the amount can be reasonably estimated.[9] Thus, if the actual amount of sick pay payable in future periods as a consequence of services rendered in the current period can be reasonably estimated, accruals should be recorded. Otherwise, a note to the financial statements would be sufficient.

The expense and related liability for compensated absences should be recognized in the year in which earned by employees. For example, if new employees receive rights to two weeks' paid vacation at the beginning of their second year of employment, the vacation pay is considered to be earned during the first year of employment.

After it is determined in what period the employee earned the right to the vacation, an issue arises as to what rate should be used to accrue the compensated absence cost—the current rate or

---

[9] *CICA Handbook*, Section 3290, par. .12.

an estimated future rate. It is likely that companies will use the current rate rather than the future rate, which is less certain and raises issues concerning the discounting of the future amount.

To illustrate, assume that Amutron Limited began operations on January 1, 1993. The company employed 10 individuals who were paid $480 per week. A total of 20 vacation weeks were earned by all employees in 1993, but none were used during this period. In 1994, the vacation weeks were used when the current rate of pay was $540 per week for each employee. The entry at December 31, 1993 to accrue the accumulated vacation pay was as follows:

Wages Expense	9,600	
Vacation Wages Payable		9,600*

*($480 × 20)

At December 31, 1993, the company would report on its balance sheet a liability of $9,600. In 1994, the vacation pay related to 1993 would be recorded as follows:

Vacation Wages Payable	9,600	
Wages Expense	1,200	
Cash		10,800*

*($540 × 20)

In 1994, the vacation weeks were used; therefore, the liability was extinguished. Note that the difference between the amount of cash paid and the reduction in the liability account was recorded as an adjustment to Wages Expense in the period when paid. This difference arose because the liability account was accrued at the rates of pay in effect during the period when compensated time was earned. The cash paid, however, was based on the rates in effect during the period in which compensated time was used. If the future rates of pay were used to compute the accrual in 1993, then the cash paid in 1994 would be equal to the liability.

Bonus Agreements. For various reasons, many companies give a bonus to certain or all officers and employees in addition to their regular salaries or wages. Frequently, the bonus amount is dependent on the company's yearly profit. From the standpoint of the enterprise, **bonus payments to employees** may be considered additional wages and should be included as a deduction in determining the net income for the year.

Drawing up a legal document such as a bonus agreement is a task for a lawyer, not an accountant, although accountants are frequently called on to express an opinion on the agreement's feasibility. In this respect, one should always insist that the agreement state specifically whether income taxes and the bonus itself are expenses deductible in determining income for purposes of the bonus computation.

It should be apparent that no entry can be made for a profit-sharing bonus until all other adjusting entries, except the one for accrued taxes on income, have been made and the income before bonus and tax has been calculated. This calculation can be accomplished through the use of a work sheet or by some other method. Once the income before bonus has been calculated, it is possible to make the bonus calculation and to record it by means of an adjusting entry. Assuming that the amount of the bonus is $10,714.29, the adjusting journal entry will be as follows:

Employees' Bonus Expense	10,714.29	
Accrued Profit-Sharing Bonus Payable		10,714.29

Later, when the bonus is paid, the journal entry will be:

Accrued Profit-Sharing Bonus Payable	10,714.29	
Cash		10,714.29

The expense account should appear in the income statement as an operating expense. The liability, accrued profit-sharing bonus payable, is usually payable within a short period and should be included as a current liability in the balance sheet.

Similar to bonus arrangements are contractual agreements covering rents or royalty payments that are conditional on the amount of revenues earned or the quantity of product produced or extracted. Conditional expenses based on revenues or units produced are usually less difficult to compute than the bonus arrangements just illustrated. For example, if a lease calls for a fixed rent payment of $500 per month and 1% of all sales over $300,000 per year, the annual rent obligation will amount to $6,000 plus $0.01 of each dollar of revenue over $300,000. Or, a royalty agreement may accrue to the patent owner $1.00 for every tonne of product resulting from the patented process, or accrue to the owner of the mineral rights $0.50 on every barrel of oil extracted. As each additional unit of product is produced or extracted, an additional obligation, usually a current liability, is created.

CONTINGENCIES

Contingent liabilities are obligations that are dependent on the occurrence or nonoccurrence of one or more future events to confirm either the amount payable or the payee or the date payable or its existence. That is, determination of one or more of these factors is dependent on a contingency. A contingency is defined in Section 3290 of the *CICA Handbook* as "an existing condition or situation involving uncertainty as to possible gain or loss to an enterprise that will ultimately be resolved when one or more future events occur or fail to occur."[10] A liability incurred as a result of a loss contingency is by definition a contingent liability.

Objective 5

Identify the criteria used to account for and disclose contingent liabilities.

Accounting for Contingent Liabilities

When a loss contingency exists, the likelihood that the future event or events will confirm the incurrence of a liability can range from highly probable (likely) to only slightly probable (unlikely). The *CICA Handbook* uses the terms "likely" and "unlikely" to identify two areas within that range and assigns the following meaning:

> **Likely**: The chance of occurrence (or nonoccurrence) of the future event is high.
> **Unlikely**: The chance of the occurrence (or nonoccurrence) of the future event is slight.

An estimated loss from a loss contingency should be accrued by a charge to income and a liability recorded only if both of the following conditions are met:

1. Information available prior to the issuance of the financial statements indicates that it is likely that a future event will confirm that an asset had been impaired or a liability incurred as of the date of the financial statements.

2. The amount of the loss can be reasonably estimated.

Neither the exact payee nor the exact date payable need be known to record a liability. *What must be known is whether it is likely that a liability has been incurred.*

The second criterion indicates that an amount for the liability can be reasonably determined; otherwise, it should not be accrued as a liability. To determine a reasonable estimate of the liability, such evidence may be based on the company's own experience, experience of other companies in the industry, engineering or research studies, legal advice, or educated guesses by personnel in the best position to know.

The following excerpt from the annual report of First Marathon Inc. is an example of disclosure of a loss contingency.

---

[10] *CICA Handbook*, Section 3290, par. .2.

10. Contingent Liabilities

The Company has been reassessed in respect of its 1986 taxation year and has been advised by Revenue Canada, Taxation, of its intention to reassess the Company in respect of its 1987 and 1988 taxation years, claiming that certain expenses relating to two specific transactions are non-deductible. Based upon the advice of its tax advisers, the Company believes that its income tax filings were proper and correct in all respects and that it should be successful in contesting any such reassessments. In the event that Revenue Canada's position is fully upheld, the Company will be liable for taxes and interest aggregating approximately $27 million of which all but approximately $3 million for each of 1991 and 1990 will be charged to retained earnings as a prior period adjustment. The Company believes that its ongoing business activities would not be materially affected by these reassessments in any event.

The application of the terms "likely" and "unlikely" as guidelines for classifying contingencies involves judgement and subjectivity. The items below are examples of loss contingencies and the general accounting treatment accorded them.

Accounting Treatment of Loss Contingencies

Loss Related to:	Usually Accrued	Not Accrued	May Be Accrued*
1. Collectibility of receivables	X		
2. Obligations related to product warranties and product defects	X		
3. Premiums offered to customers	X		
4. Risk of loss or damage of enterprise property by fire, explosion, or other hazards		X	
5. General or unspecified business risks		X	
6. Risk of loss from catastrophes assumed by property and casualty insurance companies, including reinsurance companies		X	
7. Threat of expropriation of assets			X
8. Pending or threatened litigation			X
9. Actual or possible claims and assessments**			X
10. Guarantees of indebtedness of others			X
11. Obligations of commercial banks under stand-by letters of credit			X
12. Agreements to repurchase receivables (or the related property) that have been sold			X

*Should be accrued when both criteria are met (likely and reasonably estimable).

**Estimated amounts of losses incurred prior to the balance sheet date but settled subsequently should be accrued as of the balance sheet date.

The accounting concepts and procedures relating to contingent items are relatively new and unsettled. Practising accountants express concern over the diversity that now exists in the interpretation of "likely" and "unlikely." Current practice relies heavily on the exact language used in responses received from lawyers (such language is necessarily biased and protective, rather than predictive). As a result, accruals and disclosures of contingencies vary considerably in practice.

Litigation, Claims, and Assessments

The following factors, among others, must be considered in determining whether a liability should be recorded with respect to **pending or threatened litigation** and actual or possible claims and assessments:

1. The *time period* in which the underlying cause for action occurred.

2. The *probability* of an unfavourable outcome.

3. The ability to make a *reasonable estimate* of the amount of loss.

To report a loss and a liability in the financial statements, the event giving rise to the litigation must have occurred on or before the date of the financial statements. It does not matter that the company is not aware of the existence or possibility of the lawsuit or claims until after the date of the financial statements but before they are issued. To evaluate the probability of an unfavourable outcome, consider the nature of the litigation, the progress of the case, the opinion of legal counsel, the experience of your company and others in similar cases, and any management response to the lawsuit.

The outcome of pending litigation, however, can seldom be predicted with any assurance. And, even if the evidence available at the balance sheet date does not favour the defendant, it is hardly reasonable to expect the company to publish in its financial statements a dollar estimate of the probable negative outcome. Such specific disclosures could weaken the company's position in the dispute and encourage the plaintiff to intensify its efforts. A typical example of the wording of such a disclosure is the following note to the financial statements of Rogers Communications Inc., relating to its pending litigation.

Note 17. Contingent Liabilities

a) In January 1991, a claim was filed against Cantel alleging default under an offer to lease office space, claiming damages in the amount of approximately $56,225,000, which amount includes all future rental and operating costs over the term of the lease to August 31, 1999. The Company disputes this claim and has filed a defence and counterclaim for damages of $900,000 plus pre-judgment interest. The plaintiffs' claim does not reflect a reduction for the present value of the rent and operating costs claimed or a reduction to reflect the claimant's legal obligation to mitigate any alleged damages. The plaintiffs have filed a defence to the counterclaim. The probable outcome of this litigation cannot be determined at this time.

With respect to **unfiled suits** and **unasserted claims and assessments**, a company must determine (1) the degree of *probability* that a suit may be filed or a claim or assessment may be asserted and (2) the *probability* of an unfavourable outcome. For example, assume that Nawtee Company is being investigated by the federal government for possible violations of anti-combines legislation, and enforcement proceedings have been instituted. Such proceedings may be followed by private claims. In this case, Nawtee Company must determine the probability of the claims being asserted *and* the probability of damages being awarded. If both are likely, the loss reasonably estimable, and the cause for action dated on or before the date of the financial statements, the liability should be accrued.

Disclosure of Loss Contingencies

A loss contingency and a liability are recorded if the loss is both likely and estimable. But if the loss is *either probable or estimable but not both*, the following disclosure in the notes is required:

1. The nature of the contingency.

2. An estimate of the possible loss or a statement that an estimate cannot be made.

3. How the resulting settlement will be accounted for.[11]

Presented below is a disclosure note (taken from the financial statements of Donohue Inc.) which shows that although actual losses have not been charged to operations, a liability possibly exists and no estimate of this liability is possible.

Donohue Inc.

16. Litigation

a) Normick Perron Inc. instituted an action in nullity against Donohue Inc. and Donohue Normick Inc. to cancel the issue of 1,400,000 common shares of Donohue Normick Inc. to Donohue Inc. in connection with the financing of $20,000,000 for construction cost overruns of Amos newsprint mill. The issue of these shares increased Donohue's ownership in this subsidiary from 51% to 58.1%.

Donohue Inc. and Donohue Normick Inc. are contesting this action and maintain that the common shares, which are the subject of the litigation, were issued by Donohue Normick Inc. to Donohue Inc., in accordance with the agreements entered into by Donohue Inc. Normick Perron Inc., Donohue Normick Inc. and the lenders of the first mortgage bonds of Donohue Normick Inc. As a result of an interlocutory injunction and a court order, these shares are under judicial sequestration.

In the event of an unfavourable judgment for the company, retained earnings would be reduced by an estimated $7,300,000.

b) Normick Perron Inc. instituted an action for a declaratory judgment requesting that the Court give its interpretation of the Newsprint sales contract dated June 30, 1980 and entered into by Donohue Inc., Normick Perron Inc. and Donohue Normick Inc. regarding the calculation of the selling price of newsprint, the sales made to a certain category of customers and the reimbursement of certain sales expenses for the years 1982 through 1989 inclusively.

Donohue Inc. and Donohue Normick Inc. maintain that the sales of newsprint were calculated in accordance with the terms and conditions of the Newsprint sales contract and intend to justify their position in defence of this action.

In event of an unfavourable judgment, retained earnings would be reduced by an estimated $3,100,000.

The Company believes that its legal position is sound in each of the litigations mentioned above. In the event of unfavourable judgments, the financial statements would be adjusted retroactively.

Contingencies involving an unasserted claim or assessment need not be disclosed when no claimant has come forward unless (1) it is considered *likely* that a claim will be asserted *and* (2) it is *likely* that the outcome will be unfavourable.

Certain other contingent liabilities that should be disclosed even though the possibility of loss may be remote are as follows:

1. Guarantees of indebtedness of others.

---

[11] *CICA Handbook*, Section 3290, par. .15.

2. Obligations of commercial banks under stand-by letters of credit.

3. Guarantees to repurchase receivables (or any related property) that have been sold or assigned.

Disclosure should include the nature and amount of the guarantee and, if estimable, the amount that could be recovered from outside parties. Midland Walwyn Inc. disclosed its guarantees of indebtedness of others and its possible obligation under outstanding letters of credit in the following note.

Midland Walwyn Inc.

Note 14: Contingent Liabilities

(a) The Company has lodged bank letters of credit in the amount of $18,700,000 with recognized depositories and clearing corporations.

(b) The company has guaranteed employee share purchase loans totalling $12,679,000 at December 31, 1991 and has lodged securities in the amount of $2,500,000 in support of its guarantees.

(c) The company is involved in certain lawsuits and claims which, in the opinion of management, are in the ordinary course of business and will not have a material effect on the Company's financial position or operating results.

Management is of the opinion that adequate provision has been made for potential losses resulting from the above matters.

Guarantee and Warranty Costs

A **warranty (product guarantee)** is a promise made by a seller to a buyer to make good on a deficiency of quantity, quality, or performance of a product. It is commonly used by manufacturers as a sales promotion technique. Automakers, for instance, recently hyped their sales by extending their new-car warranty to seven years or 115,000 kilometres. For a specified period of time following the date of sale to the consumer, the manufacturer may promise to bear all or part of the cost of replacing defective parts, to perform any necessary repairs or servicing without charge, to refund the purchase price, or even to "double your money back." Warranties and guarantees entail future costs, frequently significant additional costs, which are sometimes called "after costs" or "post-sale costs." Although the future cost is indefinite as to amount, due date, and even customer, a liability does exist and should be recognized in the accounts if it can be reasonably estimated. The amount of the liability is an estimate of all the costs that will be incurred after sale and delivery and that are incident to the correction of defects or deficiencies required under the warranty provisions. Warranty costs are a good example of a loss contingency.

Objective 6

Explain the accounting for different types of contingent liabilities.

Cash Basis. There are two basic methods of accounting for warranty costs: (1) the cash basis method and (2) the accrual method. Under the **cash basis method,** warranty costs are charged to expense as they are incurred; in other words, warranty costs are charged to the period in which the seller or manufacturer complies with the warranty. No liability is recorded for future costs arising from warranties, nor is the period in which the sale is recorded necessarily charged with the costs of making good on outstanding warranties. Use of this method—the only one recognized for income tax purposes—is frequently justified for accounting on the basis of expediency when warranty costs are immaterial or when the warranty period is relatively short. The cash basis method is required when a warranty liability is not accrued in the year of sale either because:

1. It is not likely that a liability has been incurred; or

2. The amount of the liability cannot be reasonably estimated.

Accrual Basis. If it is likely that customers will make claims under warranties relating to goods or services that have been sold, and a reasonable estimate of the costs involved can be made, the accrual method must be used. Under the **accrual method,** warranty costs are charged to operating expense in the year of sale. It is the generally accepted method and should be used whenever the warranty is an integral and inseparable part of the sale and is viewed as a loss contingency. We refer to this approach as the **expense warranty approach.**

Expense Warranty. To illustrate the expense warranty method, assume that the Denson Machinery Company begins production on a new machine in July 1994, and sells 100 units at $5,000 each by its year end, December 31, 1994. Each machine is under warranty for one year and the company has estimated, from past experience with a similar machine, that the warranty cost will probably average $200 per unit. Further, as a result of parts replacements and services rendered in compliance with machinery warranties, the company incurs $4,000 in warranty costs in 1994 and $16,000 in 1995.

Sale of 100 machines at $5,000 each, July through December 1994		
Cash or Accounts Receivable	500,000	
Sales		500,000
Recognition of warranty expense, July through December 1994		
Warranty Expense	4,000	
Cash, Inventory, or Accrued Payroll		4,000
(Warranty costs incurred)		
Warranty Expense	16,000	
Estimated Liability Under Warranties		16,000
(To accrue estimated warranty costs)		

The 12/31/94 balance sheet would report Estimated Liability Under Warranties as a current liability of $16,000, and the income statement for 1994 would report Warranty Expense of $20,000.

Recognition of warranty costs incurred in 1995 (on 1994 machinery sales)		
Estimated Liability Under Warranties	16,000	
Cash, Inventory, or Accrued Payroll		16,000
(Warranty costs incurred)		

If the cash basis method was applied to the facts in the Denson Machinery company example, $4,000 would be recorded as warranty expense in 1994 and $16,000 as warranty expense in 1995, with all of the sale price being recorded as revenue in 1994. In many instances, application of the cash basis method does not match the warranty costs relating to the products sold during a given period with the revenues derived from such products. Where ongoing warranty policies exist year after year, the differences between the cash and the expense warranty basis probably would not be so great.

Sales Warranty. A warranty is sometimes *sold separately from the product.* For example, when you purchase a television set or VCR, you will be entitled to the manufacturer's warranty. You will likely be offered an extended warranty on the product at an additional cost.[12]

---

[12] A contract is separately priced *if the customer has the option to purchase* the services provided under the contract for an expressly stated amount separate from the price of the product. An extended warranty or product maintenance contract usually meets these conditions.

In this case, the seller should recognize the sale of the television or VCR with the manufacturer's warranty and the sale of the extended warranty separately. This approach is referred to as the **sales warranty approach**. Revenue on the sale of the extended warranty is deferred and is generally recognized on a straight-line basis over the life of the contract. Revenue is deferred because the seller of the warranty has an obligation to perform services over the life of the contract. Only costs that vary with and are directly related to the sale of the contracts (mainly commissions) should be deferred and amortized. Costs such as employees' salaries, advertising, and general and administrative expenses that would have been incurred even if no contract were sold should be expensed as incurred.

To illustrate, assume that you have just purchased a new Buick Electra automobile from Sundre Auto for $20,000. In addition to the regular warranty on the auto (all repairs will be paid by the manufacturer for the first 60,000 kilometres or three years, whichever comes first), you purchase an extended warranty that protects you for an additional three years or 60,000 kilometres at a cost of $600. The entry to record the sale of the automobile (with regular warranty) and the sale of the extended warranty on January 2, 1994 on Sundre Auto's books is as follows:

Cash	20,600	
Sales		20,000
Unearned Warranty Revenue		600

The entry to recognize revenue at the end of the fourth year (using straight-line amortization) would be as follows:

Unearned Warranty Revenue	200	
Warranty Revenue		200

Because the extended warranty contract does not start until after the regular warranty expires, revenue is not recognized until the fourth year. If the costs of performing services under the extended warranty contract are incurred on other than a straight-line basis (as historical evidence might indicate), revenue should be recognized over the contract period in proportion to the costs expected to be incurred in performing services under the contract.

Premiums, Coupons, and Air Miles Offered to Customers

Numerous companies offer (either on a limited or on a continuing basis) premiums to customers in return for box tops, certificates, coupons, labels, or wrappers. The **premium** may be silverware, dishes, a small appliance, a toy, or other goods. Also, **printed coupons** that can be redeemed for a cash discount on items purchased are extremely popular. A more recent marketing innovation gaining popularity is the **cash rebate**, which the buyer can obtain by returning the store receipt, a rebate coupon, and Universal Product Code (UPC label) or bar code to the manufacturer. Offering free **air miles** (or kilometres) is another rapidly developing method of promoting sales. Premiums, coupon offers, air miles, and rebates are made to stimulate sales, and their costs should be charged to expense in the period of the sale that benefits from the premium plan. At the end of the accounting period, many of these premium offers may be outstanding and, when presented in subsequent periods, must be redeemed. The number of outstanding premium offers that will be presented for redemption must be estimated in order to reflect the existing current liability and to match costs with revenues.[13] The cost of premium offers should be charged to Premium Expense and the outstanding obligations should be credited to an account entitled Estimated Premium Claims Outstanding.

Premium offers are not included in the CICA's list of loss contingencies. The authors believe that *premium offers result in an existing condition that involves uncertainty as to a possible loss to an enterprise that is likely to occur and can be reasonably estimated in amount and, therefore, are a loss contingency* within the guidelines of *Handbook* Section 3290.

---

[13] In 1987, more than 13 billion coupons with a total value of $6.24 billion were distributed. However, only about 5% were redeemed.

The following example illustrates the accounting treatment accorded a premium offer. The Fluffy Cakemix Company offers its customers a large nonbreakable mixing bowl in exchange for 25 cents and 10 box tops. The mixing bowl costs the Fluffy Cakemix Company 75 cents, and the company estimates that 60% of the box tops will be redeemed. The premium offer begins in June 1994 and results in the following transactions and entries during 1994:

1. To record purchase of 20,000 mixing bowls at 75 cents each:

Inventory of Premium Mixing Bowls	15,000	
Cash		15,000

2. To record sales of 300,000 boxes of cake mix at 80 cents:

Cash	240,000	
Sales		240,000

3. To record redemption of 60,000 box tops, receipt of 25 cents per 10 box tops, and the delivery of the mixing bowls:

Cash (60,000 ÷ 10) × $0.25	1,500	
Premium Expense	3,000	
Inventory of Premium Mixing Bowls		4,500

(60,000 ÷ 10) × $0.75 = $4,500

4. To record estimated liability for outstanding premium offers:

Premium Expense	6,000	
Estimated Premium Claims Outstanding		6,000

Computation:

Total boxes sold in 1994	300,000
Total estimated box top redemptions (60%)	180,000
Box tops redeemed in 1990	60,000
Estimated future redemptions	120,000
Cost of estimated claims outstanding	

(120,000 ÷ 10) × ($0.75 − $0.25) = $6,000

The December 31, 1994 balance sheet of Fluffy Cakemix Company will report an Inventory of Premium Mixing Bowls of $10,500 as a current asset and Estimated Premium Claims Outstanding of $6,000 as a current liability. The 1994 income statement will report a $9,000 Premium Expense among the selling expenses.

Environmental Liabilities

Estimates to clean up existing toxic waste sites in Canada run into billions of dollars. In addition, the cost of cleaning up our air and preventing future deterioration of the environment is estimated to cost even more. These costs will increase when one considers the trend to more stringent environmental laws and their enactments.

Effective December 1, 1990, firms are required to accrue future site restoration costs if the amounts are reasonably determinable.[14] Rio Algom Limited reports a liability of $108 million ($28 million current and $80 million long term) to provide for expected costs to restore mine sites. The accompanying note explaining this procedure follows.

---

[14] *CICA Handbook*, Section 3060, par. .39.

> **Rio Algom Limited**
>
> **Accounting Policies**
> **Site Restoration and Related Obligations**
> The Corporation accounts for site restoration, abandonment and closure costs by systematic charges to cost of production over the expected life of the mine to a maximum of thirty years. In determining expected costs, recoveries to be made at the time of shutdown are estimated and taken into account. The process of cost estimation is a continuous one, subject to changing regulations, regulatory approvals and other external factors. As such, the site restoration costs are based upon best estimates.

Risk of Loss Due to Lack of Insurance Coverage

Uninsured risks may arise in a number of ways, including **noninsurance** of certain risks or **co-insurance** or **deductible clauses** in an insurance contract. But the absence of insurance (frequently referred to as self-insurance) does not mean that a liability has been incurred at the date of the financial statements. For example, fires, explosions, and other similar events that may cause damage to a company's own property are random in occurrence and unrelated to the activities of the company prior to their occurrence. The conditions for accrual stated in *CICA Handbook* Section 3290 are not satisfied prior to the occurrence of the event because until that time there is no diminution in the value of the property. However, if a company lacks adequate insurance coverage against a material risk it may be desirable to disclose this fact.[15]

Exposure to risks of loss resulting from uninsured past injury to others, however, is an existing condition involving uncertainty about the amount and the timing of losses that may develop, in which case a contingency exists. A company with a fleet of vehicles would have to accrue uninsured losses resulting from injury to others or damage to the property of others that took place prior to the date of the financial statements (if the experience of the company or other information enables it to make a reasonable estimate of the liability). However, it should not establish a liability for expected future injury to others or damage to the property of others, even if the amount of losses is reasonably estimable.

DISCLOSURE OF CURRENT LIABILITIES IN THE FINANCIAL STATEMENTS

The current liability accounts are commonly presented as the first classification in the Liabilities and Shareholders' Equity section of the balance sheet. In some instances, current liabilities are presented as a group immediately below current assets, with the total of the current liabilities deducted from the total current assets to obtain Working Capital or Current Assets in Excess of Current Liabilities.

Objective 7

Indicate how current liabilities are disclosed.

Within the current liability section, the accounts may be listed in order of maturity, in descending order of amount, or in order of liquidation preference. The authors' review of published financial statements in 1989 to 1990 disclosed that a significant majority of the companies examined listed Notes Payable first (sometimes called "commercial paper," or "bank loans," or "short-term debt"), regardless of relative amount, followed most often with Accounts Payable, and ended the current liability section with Current Portion of Long-Term Debt.

Detailed and supplemental information concerning current liabilities should be sufficient to meet the requirement of full disclosure. Secured liabilities should be identified clearly and the related assets pledged as collateral indicated. If the due date of any liability can be extended, the details should be disclosed. Current liabilities should not be offset against assets that are to be applied to their liquidation. Current maturities of long-term debt should be classified as current liabilities.

---

[15] *CICA Handbook*, Section 3290.

A major exception exists when a currently maturing obligation is to be paid from assets classified as long term. For example, if payments to retire a bond payable are made from a bond sinking fund classified as a long-term asset, the bonds payable should be reported in the long-term liability section. Presentation of this debt in the current liability section would distort the working capital position of the enterprise.

Existing commitments that will result in obligations in succeeding periods that are material in amount may require disclosure. For example, commitments to purchase goods or services, as well as for construction, purchase, or lease of equipment or properties, may require disclosure in notes accompanying the balance sheet.

Presented below is an example of a published financial statement that is a representative presentation of the current liabilities with appropriate notes, as found in the reports of large corporations.

Potash Corporation of Saskatchewan Inc.

(Dollars in thousands) December 31	1991	1990
Current Liabilities		
Short-term debt (Note 8)	$28,790	$49,980
Accounts payable and accrued charges (Note 9)	34,299	42,378
Current obligations under capital leases (Note 11)	6,947	6,179
	70,036	98,537

Note 8 Short-Term Debt

Short-term debt consists of unsecured bank loans.
The Company has lines of credit for short-term financing in the amount of $125,000 at December 31, 1991 (1990: $125,000).

Note 9 Accounts Payable and Accrued Charges

Trade accounts	$20,386	$29,133
Accrued interest	1,513	2,050
Accrued payroll	5,012	4,215
Dividends	7,388	6,980
	$34,299	$42,378

FUNDAMENTAL CONCEPTS

1. Liability recognition entails identifying three essential characteristics: (1) a likely future transfer of assets is involved, (2) a duty or responsibility of the enterprise exists, and (3) the obligation is a result of past transactions or events.

2. Current liabilities are obligations whose liquidation is reasonably expected to require the use of existing resources properly classified as current assets or the creation of other current liabilities.

3. For some current liabilities (referred to as determinable) there is nothing uncertain about the existence or the amount of the obligation. Examples of determinable current liabilities are accounts and notes payable, current maturities of long-term debts, dividends payable, returnable deposits and advances from customers, and various taxes payable (sales, payroll, property, and income).

4. Short-term obligations can be excluded from current liabilities if the enterprise has made contractual arrangements to refinance the obligation on a long-term basis and it can demonstrate the ability to consummate the refinancing.

(Continued)

5. Contingent liabilities are dependent on the occurrence or nonoccurrence of one or more future events to confirm the amount payable, the payee, the date payable, or the obligation's existence.

6. For a loss contingency to be accrued as an expense and recognized as a liability, it must be likely that a liability has been incurred and that the amount of the loss can be reasonably estimated.

7. Contingent liabilities include those that are typically accrued (uncollectible accounts, product warranties, sale premiums), those that are not accrued (risk of fire and other casualties, general and unspecified business risks), and those that may or may not be accrued depending on the circumstances (threat of expropriation, pending or threatened litigation, claims and assessments, guarantees of indebtedness of others).

8. Loss contingencies that are either indeterminable as to the probability of occurrence or amount of loss are not accrued but must be disclosed in the notes to the financial statements.

9. Although the future cost of warranties and guarantees is indefinite as to amount, due date, and even customer, a liability is probable in most cases and should be recognized if it can be reasonably estimated.

10. Premium offers result in the probable existence of a liability at the date of the financial statements, can be reasonably estimated in amount, are contingent on the occurrence of a future event (redemption), and, therefore, are loss contingencies (often referred to as "estimated liabilities") requiring expense accrual and liability recognition.

QUESTIONS

1. Distinguish between a current liability and a long-term debt.

2. Assume that your friend, who is a music major, asks you to define and discuss the nature of a liability. Assist her by preparing a definition of a liability and by explaining to her what you believe are the elements or factors inherent in the concept of a liability.

3. Why is the liability section of the balance sheet of primary significance to bankers?

4. How are current liabilities related by definition to current assets? How are current liabilities related to a company's operating cycle?

5. How is present value related to the concept of a liability?

6. What is the nature of a discount on notes payable?

7. How should a debt callable by the creditor be reported in the debtor's financial statements?

8. Under what conditions should a short-term obligation be excluded from current liabilities?

9. (a) What conditions must be present in a refinancing agreement in order to permit classification of a short-term obligation as current?
   (b) When a financing agreement is relied on to demonstrate ability to consummate refinancing, what amount of short-term debt may be excluded from current liabilities?

10. Discuss the accounting treatment or disclosure that should be accorded a declared but unpaid cash dividend, an accumulated but undeclared dividend on cumulative preferred shares, and a stock dividend distributable.

11. How does deferred or unearned revenue arise? Why can it be classified properly as a current liability? Give several examples of business activities that result in unearned revenues.

12. What are compensated absences?

13. Under what conditions should an employer accrue a liability for the cost of compensated absences?

14. What are post-retirement benefits? What is the proper reporting for post-retirement benefits?

15. Under what conditions should an employer accrue a liability for sick pay?

16. Over which two periods of time is the property tax most commonly allocated? Under what circumstances might each of these periods be justified as the period of expense?

17. What is the nature of a conditional payment? How is a conditional payment unlike the other liabilities presented under the classification of determinable current liabilities? List three examples of conditional payment liabilities.

18. Define (a) a contingency and (b) a contingent liability.

19. Under what conditions should a contingent liability be recorded?

20. Distinguish between a determinable current liability and a contingent current liability. Give two examples of each type.

21. How are the terms "likely" and "unlikely" related to contingent liabilities?

22. Contrast the cash basis method and the accrual method of accounting for warranty costs.

23. How does the expense warranty treatment differ from the sales warranty method?

24. Aeromaybe Airlines Inc. awards members of its Flightline program a second ticket at half price, valid for two years anywhere on its flight system, when a full-price ticket is purchased. How would you account for the full-fare and half-fare tickets?

25. Cessna Airlines Co. awards members of its Frequent Fliers Club one free round-trip ticket, anywhere on its flight system, for every 50,000 miles flown on its planes. How would you account for the free ticket award?

26. Should a liability be recorded for risk of loss due to lack of insurance coverage? Discuss.

27. What factors must be considered in determining whether or not to record a liability for pending litigation? For threatened litigation?

28. Within the current liability section, how do you believe the accounts should be listed?

29. When should liabilities for each of the following items be recorded on the books of an ordinary business corporation?
    (a) Acquisition of goods by purchase on credit.
    (b) Officers' salaries.
    (c) Special bonus to employees.
    (d) Dividends.
    (e) Purchase commitments.

--------- CASES ---------

C13-1 **(NATURE OF LIABILITIES)** Presented below is the current liability section of Maymont Corporation Ltd.

	($000)	
	1994	1993
Current Liabilities		
Notes payable	$ 68,713	$ 7,700
Accounts payable	179,496	101,379
Compensation to employees	60,312	31,649
Accrued liabilities	158,198	77,621
Income taxes payable	5,486	21,491
Current maturities of long-term debt	16,592	6,649
Total current liabilities	$488,797	$246,489

Instructions

Answer the following questions.

(a) What are the essential characteristics that make an item a liability?

(b) How does one distinguish between a current liability and a long-term liability?

(c) What are accrued liabilities? Give three examples of accrued liabilities that Maymont might have.

(d) What is the theoretically correct way to value liabilities? How are current liabilities usually valued?

(e) Why are notes payable reported first in the current liability section?

(f) What might be the items that comprise Maymont's liability for Compensation to Employees?

(CURRENT VS. NONCURRENT CLASSIFICATION) Klingon Corporation Ltd. includes the following **C13-2** items in their liabilities at December 31, 1994:

1. Notes payable, $20,000,000, due June 30, 1995.

2. Deposits from customers on equipment ordered by them from Klingon, $5,000,000.

3. Salaries payable, $3,000,000 due January 14, 1995.

Instructions

Indicate in what circumstances, if any, each of the three liabilities above would be excluded from current liabilities.

(CURRENT VS. NONCURRENT CLASSIFICATION) The following items are listed as liabilities on the **C13-3** balance sheet of Foster Company on December 31, 1994:

Accounts payable	$ 280,000
Notes payable	500,000
Bonds payable	1,500,000

The accounts payable represent obligations to suppliers that were due in January 1995. The notes payable mature on various dates during 1995. The bonds payable mature on July 1, 1995.

These liabilities must be reported on the balance sheet in accordance with generally accepted accounting principles governing the classification of liabilities as current and noncurrent.

Instructions

(a) What is the general rule for determining whether a liability is classified as current or noncurrent?

(b) Under what conditions may any of Foster Company's liabilities be classified as noncurrent? Explain your answer.

(CMA adapted)

(REFINANCING OF SHORT-TERM DEBT) Guess Corporation Ltd. reflects in the current liability sec- **C13-4** tion of its balance sheet at December 31, 1994 (its year end), short-term obligations of $15,000,000, which includes the current portion of 12% long-term debt in the amount of $10,000,000 (matures in March 1995). Management has stated its intention to refinance the 12% debt, whereby no portion of it will mature during 1995. The date of issuance of the financial statements is March 25, 1995.

Instructions

(a) Is management's intent enough to support long-term classification of the obligation in this situation?

(b) Assume that Guess Corporation Ltd. issues $12,000,000 of 10-year debentures to the public in January 1995 and that management intends to use the proceeds to liquidate the $10,000,000 debt maturing in March 1995. Furthermore, assume that the debt maturing in March 1995 is paid from these proceeds prior to the issuance of the financial statements. Will this have any impact on the balance sheet classification at December 31, 1994? Explain your answer.

(c) Assume that Guess Corporation Ltd. issues common shares to the public in January and that management intends to entirely liquidate the $10,000,000 debt maturing in March 1995 with the proceeds of this equity securities issue. In light of these events, should the $10,000,000 debt maturing in March 1995 be included in current liabilities at December 31, 1994?

(d) Assume that Guess Corporation Ltd., on February 15, 1995, entered into a financing agreement with a commercial bank that permits Guess to borrow at any time through 1996 up to $15,000,000 at the bank's prime rate of interest. Borrowings under the financing agreement mature three years after the date of the loan. The agreement is not cancellable except for violation of a provision with which compliance is objectively determinable. No violation of any provision exists at the date of issuance of the financial statements. Assume further that the $10,000,000 representing the current portion of long-term debt does not mature until August 1995. In addition, management intends to refinance the $10,000,000 obligation under the terms of the financial agreement with the bank, which is expected to be financially capable of honouring the agreement. Given these facts, should the $10,000,000 be classified as current on the balance sheet at December 31, 1994?

C13-5 **(REFINANCING OF SHORT-TERM DEBT)**   Heartbreak Inc. issued $9,000,000 of short-term commercial paper during the year 1993 to finance construction of a plant. At December 31, 1993, the corporation's year end, Heartbreak intends to refinance the commercial paper by issuing long-term debt. However, because the corporation temporarily has excess cash, in January 1994 it liquidates $3,000,000 of the commercial paper as the paper matures. In February 1994, Heartbreak completes an $18,000,000 long-term debt offering. Later during the month of February, it issues its December 31, 1993 financial statements. The proceeds of the long-term debt offering are to be used to replenish $3,000,000 in working capital, to pay $6,000,000 of commercial paper as it matures in March 1994, and to pay $9,000,000 of construction costs expected to be incurred later that year to complete the plant.

Instructions

(a)   How should the $9,000,000 of commercial paper be classified on the balance sheets of December 31, 1993, January 31, 1994, and February 28, 1994? Give support for your answer and also consider the cash element.

(b)   What would your answer be if, instead of a completed financing at the date of issuance of the financial statements, a financing agreement existed at that date?

C13-6 **(LOSS CONTINGENCIES)**   George Duval Company is a manufacturer of toys. During the present year, the following situations arise:

(a)   A safety hazard related to one of its toy products is discovered. It is considered probable that liabilities have been incurred. On the basis of past experience, a reasonable estimate of the amount of loss can be made.

(b)   One of its small warehouses is located on the bank of a river and can no longer be insured against flood losses. No flood losses have occurred after the date that the insurance became unavailable.

(c)   This year, Duval begins promoting a new toy by including a coupon, redeemable for a movie ticket, in each toy's carton. The movie ticket, which costs Duval $3, is purchased in advance and then mailed to the customer when the coupon is received by Duval. Duval estimates, based on past experience, that 60% of the coupons will be redeemed. Forty percent of the coupons are actually redeemed this year, and the remaining 20% of the coupons are expected to be redeemed next year.

Instructions

(a)   How should Duval report the safety hazard? Why?

(b)   How should Duval report the noninsurable flood risk? Why?

(c)   How should Duval account for the toy promotion campaign in this year?

(AICPA adapted)

C13-7 **(GAIN AND LOSS CONTINGENCIES)**

(a)   What is the meaning of the term "contingency" as used in accounting?

(b)   Contrast accounting for a gain contingency that is never accrued in the accounting records and accounting for a loss contingency.

(c)   How should the following situations be recognized in the calendar year-end financial statements of Industrial Chemical Company? Explain.

   1. Pending in a provincial court is a suit against Industrial Chemical. The suit, which asks for token damages, alleges that Industrial has infringed on a 15-year-old patent. Briefs will be heard on March 31.

2. The TUF Union, sole bargaining agent of Industrial's production employees, has threatened a strike unless Industrial agrees to a proposed profit-sharing plan. Negotiations begin on March 1.

3. A recently completed (during the calendar year in question) government contract is subject to renegotiation. Although Industrial suspects that a refund of approximately $175,000 may be required by the government, the company does not wish, for obvious reasons, to publicize this fact.

4. Industrial has a $200,000, 9% note receivable due next May 1 from Markov Company, its largest customer. Industrial discounted the note on December 20, with recourse, at the bank to raise needed cash. Markov Company has never defaulted on a debt and possesses a high credit rating. (Treated as a sale on December 20.)

(LOSS CONTINGENCIES AND ACCOUNTING PRINCIPLES) The two basic requirements for the **C13-8** accrual of a loss contingency are supported by several basic concepts of accounting. Three of these concepts are: periodicity (time periods), measurement, and objectivity.

Instructions

Discuss how the two basic requirements for the accrual of a loss contingency relate to the three concepts listed above.

(AICPA adapted)

(LOSS CONTINGENCIES) On February 1, 1994, one of the huge storage tanks of Power Manufacturing **C13-9** Company exploded. Windows in houses and other buildings within a two-kilometre radius of the explosion were severely damaged, and a number of people were injured. As of February 15, 1994 (when the December 31, 1993 financial statements were completed and sent to the publisher for printing and public distribution), no suits had been filed nor claims asserted against the company as a consequence of the explosion. However, the company fully anticipated that suits would be filed and claims asserted for injuries and damages. Because the casualty was uninsured and the company considered at fault, Power Manufacturing would have to cover the damages from its own resources.

Instructions

Discuss fully the accounting treatment and disclosures that should be accorded the casualty and related contingent losses in the financial statements dated December 31, 1993.

(LOSS CONTINGENCY) Presented below is a note disclosure for Witco Corporation Ltd.: **C13-10**

Litigation and Environmental: The Company has been notified, or is a named or a potentially responsible party in a number of governmental (federal, provincial, and municipal) and private actions associated with environmental matters, such as those relating to hazardous wastes, including certain Canadian sites. These actions seek cleanup costs, penalties, and/or damages for personal injury or to property or natural resources.

In 1993, the Company recorded a pretax charge of $51,229,000, included in the Other Expense (Income): Net caption of the Company's Consolidated Statements of Income, as an additional provision for environmental matters. These expenditures are expected to take place over the next several years and are indicative of the Company's commitment to improve and maintain the environment in which it operates. At December 31, 1993, environmental accruals amounted to $63,931,000, of which $56,535,000 were considered noncurrent and included in the Deferred Credits and Other Liabilities caption of the Company's Consolidated Balance Sheets.

While it is impossible at this time to determine with certainty the ultimate outcome of environmental matters, it is management's opinion, based in part on the advice of independent counsel (after taking into account accruals and insurance coverage applicable to such actions) that when the costs are finally determined, they will not have a material adverse effect on the financial position of the Company.

Instructions

Answer the following questions.

(a) What conditions must exist before a loss contingency can be recorded in the accounts?

(b) Suppose that Witco Corporation could not reasonably estimate the amount of the loss, although it could establish with a high degree of probability the minimum and maximum loss possible. How should this information be reported in the financial statements?

(c) If the amount of the loss were uncertain, how would the loss contingency be reported in the financial statements?

C13-11 (LOSS CONTINGENCIES)   The following three independent sets of facts relate to (1) the possible accrual or (2) the possible disclosure by other means of a loss contingency.

Situation I. Subsequent to the date of a set of financial statements but prior to the issuance of the financial statements, a company enters into a contract that will likely result in a significant loss to the company. The amount of the loss can be reasonably estimated.

Situation II. A company offers a one-year warranty for the product that it manufactures. A history of warranty claims has been compiled and the probable amount of claims related to sales for a given period can be determined.

Situation III. A company has adopted a policy of recording self-insurance for any possible losses resulting from injury to others by the company's vehicles. The premium for an insurance policy for the same risk from an independent insurance company would have an annual cost of $3,000. During the period covered by the financial statements, there were no accidents involving the company's vehicles that resulted in injury to others.

Instructions

Discuss the accrual or type of disclosure necessary (if any) and the reason(s) why such disclosure is appropriate for each of the three independent sets of facts above. Complete your response to each situation before proceeding to the next situation.

(AICPA adapted)

C13-12 (WARRANTIES AND LOSS CONTINGENCIES)   The following two independent situations involve loss contingencies:

Part 1. Panther Company sells two types of merchandise, Type A and Type B. Each carries a one-year warranty.

1. Type A merchandise: Product warranty costs, based on past experience, will normally be 1% of sales.

2. Type B merchandise: Product warranty costs cannot be reasonably estimated because this is a new product line. However, the chief engineer believes that product warranty costs are likely to be incurred.

Instructions

How should Panther report the estimated product warranty costs for each of the two types of merchandise above? Discuss the rationale for your answer. Do not discuss deferred income tax implications, or disclosures that should be made in Panther's financial statements or notes.

Part 2. Barbara Company is being sued for $3,000,000 for an injury caused to a child as a result of alleged negligence while the child was visiting a Barbara Company plant in March 1994. The suit was filed in July 1994. Barbara's lawyer states that it is probable that Barbara will lose the suit and be found liable for a judgement costing anywhere from $300,000 to $1,500,000. However, the lawyer states that the most probable judgement is $600,000.

Instructions

How should Barbara report the suit in its 1994 financial statements? Discuss the rationale for your answer. Include in your answer the disclosures, if any, that should be made in Barbara's financial statements or notes.

(AICPA adapted)

(WARRANTIES)   Presented below is the current liability section and related note of the Toro Company.   C13-13

	1994	1993
	(Dollars in thousands)	
Current liabilities:		
Current portion of long-term debt	$ 15,000	$ 10,000
Short-term debt	2,668	405
Accounts payable	29,495	42,427
Accrued warranty	16,843	16,741
Accrued marketing programs	17,512	16,585
Other accrued liabilities	35,653	33,290
Accrued and deferred income taxes	6,206	7,348
Total current liabilities	$123,377	$126,796

Notes to Consolidated Financial Statements

1 (In part): Summary of Significant Accounting Policies and Related Data:

Accrued Warranty: The Company provides an accrual for future warranty costs based on the relationship of prior years' sales to actual warranty costs.

Instructions

Answer the following questions.

(a)   What is the difference between the cash basis and the accrual basis of accounting for warranty costs?

(b)   Under what circumstance, if any, would it be appropriate for Toro Company to recognize deferred revenue on warranty contracts?

(c)   If Toro Company recognized deferred revenue on warranty contracts, how would it recognize this revenue in subsequent periods?

(WARRANTIES)   During 1994, Hot-Rod Engine Company sells 45,000 high-compression engines under a C13-14 three-year warranty that requires the company to replace all defective parts during the warranty period at no cost to the purchaser. These engines constitute nearly all of the company's 1994 business.

Instructions

(a)   Name two basic methods of accounting for the warranty costs.

(b)   What accounts would be used for each of the two methods?

(c)   What effect would each method have on net income during the period of the warranties?

(d)   In your opinion, which of the two methods is more appropriate for Hot-Rod Engine Company?

————— EXERCISES —————

(BALANCE SHEET CLASSIFICATION OF VARIOUS LIABILITIES)   How would each of the following E13-1 items be reported on the balance sheet?

(a)   Estimated taxes payable.

(b)   Employee payroll deductions unremitted.

(c) Unpaid bonus to officers.

(d) Gift certificates sold to customers but not yet redeemed.

(e) Accrued vacation pay.

(f) Premium offers outstanding.

(g) Personal injury claim pending.

(h) Service warranties on appliance sales.

(i) Current maturities of long-term debt to be paid from current assets.

(j) Discount on notes payable.

(k) Notes receivable discounted.

(l) Cash dividends declared but unpaid.

(m) Deposit received from customer to guarantee performance of a contract.

(n) Dividends in arrears on preferred shares.

(o) Loans from officers.

(p) Sales taxes payable.

E13-2 (ACCOUNTS AND NOTES PAYABLE) The following are selected 1994 transactions of Fergie Limited:

Sept. 1 Purchased inventory from Kerr Company on account for $60,000. Fergie records purchases gross and uses a periodic inventory system.

Oct. 1 Issued a $60,000, 12-month, 10% note to Kerr in payment of account.

Oct. 1 Borrowed $60,000 from the North Bank by signing a 12-month, noninterest-bearing $66,000 note (discounted by bank).

Instructions

(a) Prepare journal entries for the selected transactions above.

(b) Prepare adjusting entries at December 31.

(c) Compute the total net liability to be reported on the December 31 balance sheet for:

1. The interest-bearing note.

2. The noninterest-bearing note.

E13-3 (REFINANCING OF SHORT-TERM DEBT) On December 31, 1994, Slim Down Company had $1,500,000 of short-term debt in the form of notes payable due February 2, 1995. On January 21, 1995, the company issued 25,000 of its common shares for $49.50 per share, receiving $1,225,000 in proceeds after brokerage fees and other costs of issuance. On February 1, 1995, the proceeds from the share issue, supplemented by an additional $275,000 cash, were used to liquidate the $1,500,000 debt. The December 31, 1994, balance sheet was issued on February 23, 1995.

Instructions

Show how the $1,500,000 of short-term debt should be presented on the December 31, 1994 balance sheet, including note disclosure.

(REFINANCING OF SHORT-TERM DEBT)   On December 31, 1994, Chapman Company has $8,000,000 **E13-4** of short-term debt in the form of notes payable to the Royal Bank, due periodically in 1995. On January 18, 1995, Chapman enters into a refinancing agreement with the Royal Bank that will permit it to borrow up to 60% of the gross amount of its accounts receivable. Receivables are expected to range between a low of $5,000,000 in May to a high of $7,000,000 in October during 1995. The interest cost of the maturing short-term debt is 15%, and the new agreement calls for a fluctuating interest at 1% above the prime rate on notes due in 2002. Chapman's December 31, 1994 balance sheet is issued on February 15, 1995.

Instructions

Prepare a partial balance sheet for McInnes at December 31, 1994, showing how its $8,000,000 of short-term debt should be presented, including note disclosures.

(COMPENSATED ABSENCES)   McInnes Company began operations on January 2, 1993. It employs nine **E13-5** individuals who work eight-hour days and are paid hourly. Each employee earns 10 paid vacation days and 6 paid sick days annually. Vacation days may be taken after January 15 of the year following the year in which they are earned. Sick days may be taken as soon as they are earned. Additional information is as follows.

Actual Hourly Wage Rate		Vacation Days Used by Each Employee		Sick Days Used by Each Employee	
1993	1994	1993	1994	1993	1994
$12.00	$14.00	0	9	4	5

McInnes Company has chosen to accrue the cost of compensated absences at rates of pay in effect during the period when earned and to accrue sick pay when earned.

Instructions

(a)   Prepare journal entries to record transactions related to compensated absences during 1993 and 1994.

(b)   Compute the amounts of any liability for compensated absences that should be reported on the balance sheet at December 31 of both 1993 and 1994.

(COMPENSATED ABSENCES)   Assume the facts in the preceding exercise, except that McInnes Company **E13-6** has chosen not to accrue paid sick leave until used, and has chosen to accrue vacation time at expected future rates of pay without discounting. The company uses the following projected rates to accrue vacation time.

Year in Which Vacation Time Was Earned	Projected Future Pay Rates Used to Accrue Vacation Pay
1993	$13.80
1994	15.20

Instructions

(a) Prepare journal entries to record transactions related to compensated absences during 1993 and 1994.

(b) Compute the amounts of any liability for compensated absences that should be reported on the balance sheet at December 31 of both 1993 and 1994.

E13-7 (ADJUSTING ENTRY FOR SALES TAX) During the month of June, Jane's Boutique had cash sales of $243,800 and credit sales of $137,800, both of which include the 8% sales tax that must be remitted to the province by July 15.

Instructions

Prepare the adjusting entry that should be recorded to fairly present the June 30 financial statements.

E13-8 (PAYROLL TAX ENTRIES) The payroll of the Tilley Company for September 1994 is as follows:

1. Total payroll $500,000, of which $120,000 represent amounts paid in excess of the maximum pensionable and insurable earnings of certain employees.

2. Income taxes in the amount of $95,000 are withheld, as are $10,500 in union dues.

3. The current CPP contribution rate is 2.5% for employees and 2.5% for employers.

4. The rate for employee unemployment insurance deduction is 3% and the employer's share is 4.2%.

Instructions

Prepare the necessary journal entries if the wages and salaries paid and the employer payroll taxes are recorded separately.

E13-9 (PAYROLL TAX ENTRIES) Yosemite Hardware Company's payroll for August 1994 is summarized below.

		Amount Subject to Payroll Taxes	
Payroll	Wages Due	CPP	Unemployment Insurance
Factory	$112,000	$112,000	$40,000
Sales	58,000	32,000	4,000
Administrative	12,000	12,000	4,000
Total	$182,000	$156,000	$48,000

At this point in the year, some employees have already received wages in excess of those to which payroll taxes apply. Assume that the unemployment insurance rate for employees is 3% and 4.2% for employers. The CPP rate is 2.5% for both employee and employer. Income tax withheld amounts to $14,000 for factory, $7,000 for sales, and $1,500 for administrative.

Instructions

(a) Prepare a schedule showing the employer's total cost of wages for August by function.

(b) Prepare the journal entries to record the factory, sales, and administrative payrolls, including the employer's payroll taxes.

(WARRANTIES) Deighton Sales Company sold 200 copier machines in 1994 for $6,250 apiece, together with **E13-10** a one-year warranty. Maintenance on each machine during the warranty period averaged $500.

Instructions

(a) Prepare entries to record the sale of the machines and the related warranty costs, assuming that the expense warranty accrual method was used. Actual warranty costs incurred in 1994 were $80,200.

(b) On the basis of the data given, prepare the appropriate entries, assuming that the cash basis method was used.

(WARRANTIES) Otokoks Equipment Company sold 1,000 Rollomatics during 1994 at $6,000 each. During **E13-11** 1994, Otokoks spent $60,000 servicing the two-year warranties that accompany the Rollomatics. All applicable transactions were on a cash basis.

Instructions

(a) Prepare 1994 entries for Otokoks using the expense warranty treatment. Assume that Otokoks estimates the total cost of servicing the warranties will be $240,000 for two years.

(b) Prepare 1994 entries for Otokoks using the sales warranty treatment. Assume that of the sales total, $320,000 relates to sales of warranty contracts. Otokoks estimates the total cost of servicing the warranties will be $240,000 for two years. Estimate revenues earned on the basis of costs incurred and estimated costs.

(LIABILITY FOR RETURNABLE CONTAINERS) Wastenot Company sells its products in expensive, **E13-12** reusable containers. The customer is charged a deposit for each container delivered and receives a refund for each container returned within two years after the year of delivery. Wastenot accounts for containers not returned within the time limit as being sold at the deposit amount. Information for 1994 is as follows:

Containers held by customers at December 31, 1993, from deliveries in:	1992	$170,000	
	1993	480,000	$650,000
Containers delivered in 1994			870,000
Containers returned in 1994 from deliveries in:	1992	$110,000	
	1993	280,000	
	1994	314,000	704,000

Instructions

(a) Prepare all journal entries required for Wastenot Company during 1994 for the returnable containers.

(b) Compute the total amount Wastenot should report as a liability for returnable containers at December 31, 1994.

(c) Should the liability computed in (b) above be reported as current or long term?

(AICPA adapted)

(PREMIUM ENTRIES) Washer Company includes one coupon in each box of soap powder that it packs, **E13-13** and 10 coupons are redeemable for a premium (a kitchen utensil). In 1994, Washer Company purchased 8,800 premiums at 80 cents each and sold 110,000 boxes of soap powder at $3.30 per box; 45,000 coupons were presented for redemption in 1994. It is estimated that 70% of the coupons will eventually be presented for redemption.

Instructions

Prepare all the entries that would be made relative to sales of soap powder and to the premium plan in 1994.

E13-14(CONTINGENCIES)   Presented below are three independent situations. Answer the question at the end of each situation.

1. On October 1, 1994, Hooker Chemical was identified as a potentially responsible party by the provincial Environmental Protection Agency. Hooker's management and its legal counsel have concluded that it is probable that Hooker will be responsible for damages, and a reasonable estimate of these damages is $5,000,000. Hooker's insurance policy of $9,000,000 has a deductible clause of $750,000. How should Hooker Chemical report this information in its financial statements at December 31, 1994?

2. Forrest Inc. had a manufacturing plant in Kuwait that was destroyed in the Gulf War. It is not certain who will compensate Forrest for this destruction, but Forrest has been assured by governmental officials that it will receive a definite amount for this plant. The amount of the compensation will be less than the fair value of the plant, but more than its book value. How should the contingency be reported in the financial statements of Forrest Inc.?

3. During 1994, Arnold Inc. becomes involved in a tax dispute with Revenue Canada. Arnold's attorneys have indicated that they believe Arnold will probably lose this dispute. They also believe that Arnold will have to pay Revenue Canada between $900,000 and $1,400,000. After the 1994 financial statements are issued, the case is settled with Revenue Canada for $1,100,000. What amount, if any, should be reported as a liability for this contingency as of December 31, 1994?

E13-15(PREMIUMS)   Presented below are three independent situations:

1. Marshall Company has sold 600,000 boxes of pie mix under a new sales promotional program. Each box contains one coupon that, submitted with $5.00, entitles the customer to a baking pan. Marshall pays $6.00 per pan and $0.50 for handling and shipping. Marshall estimates that 70% of the coupons will be redeemed, even though only 200,000 coupons were processed during 1994. What amount should Marshall report as a liability for unredeemed coupons at December 31, 1994?

2. Moleski Stamp Company records stamp service revenue and provides for the costs of redemption in the year in which stamps are sold to licensees. Moleski's past experience indicates that only 80% of the stamps sold to licensees will be redeemed. Moleski's liability for stamp redemption is $12,000,000 at December 31, 1993. Additional information for 1994 is as follows:

Stamp service revenue from stamps sold to licensees	$8,000,000
Cost of redemption (stamps sold prior to 1/1/94)	5,500,000

If all the stamps sold in 1994 were presented for redemption in 1995, the redemption cost would be $4,500,000. What amount should Moleski report as a liability for stamp redemptions at December 31, 1994?

3. In packages of its products, Selzer Inc. includes coupons that may be presented at retail stores to obtain discounts on other Selzer products. Retailers are reimbursed for the face amount of coupons redeemed plus 10% of that amount for handling costs. Selzer honours requests for coupon redemption by retailers up to three months after the consumer expiration date. Selzer estimates that 60% of all coupons issued will ultimately be redeemed. Information relating to coupons issued by Selzer during 1994 is as follows:

Consumer expiration date	12/31/94
Total face amount of coupons issued	$700,000
Total payments to retailers as of 12/31/94	240,000

What amount should Selzer report as a liability for unredeemed coupons at December 31, 1994?

(AICPA adapted)

E13-16(FINANCIAL STATEMENT IMPACT OF LIABILITY TRANSACTIONS)   Presented below is a list of possible transactions:

1. Purchased inventory for $70,000 on account (assume perpetual system is used).

2. Issued a $70,000 note payable in payment on account (see item 1 above).

3. Recorded accrued interest on the note from item 2 above.

4. Borrowed $101,000 from the bank by signing a six-month, $110,000, noninterest-bearing note.

5. Recognized four months' interest expense on the note from item 4 above.

6. Recorded cash sales of $63,600, which includes 6% sales tax.

7. Recorded wage expense of $32,000. The cash paid was $22,000; the difference was due to various amounts withheld.

8. Recorded employer's payroll taxes.

9. Accrued accumulated vacation pay.

10. Recorded accrued property taxes payable.

11. Recorded bonuses due to employees.

12. Recorded a contingent loss on a lawsuit that the company will likely lose.

13. Accrued warranty expense (assume expense warranty treatment).

14. Paid warranty costs that were accrued in item 13 above.

15. Recorded sales of product and related warranties (assume sales warranty treatment).

16. Paid warranty costs under contracts from item 15 above.

17. Recognized warranty revenue (see item 15 above).

18. Recorded estimated liability for premium claims outstanding.

Instructions

Set up a table using the format below and analyse the effect of the 18 transactions on the financial statement categories indicated.

#	Assets	Liabilities	Owners' Equity	Net Income
1				

Use the following code:

I: Increase   D: Decrease   NE: No net effect

(ETHICAL ISSUES: BONUS COMPENSATION)   Alberta Can Company has a bonus arrangement that **E13-17** grants the financial vice-president and other executives a $10,000 bonus if net income exceeds the previous year's by $1,000,000. Noting that the current financial statements report an increase of $950,000 in net income, vice-president Anand Bailey asks Bill Watkins, the controller, to reduce the estimate of warranty expense by $60,000. The present estimate of warranty expense is $500,000 and is known by both Bailey and Watkins to be a fairly "soft" amount.

Instructions

(a) Should Watkins lower his estimate?

(b) What ethical issue is at stake? Is anyone harmed?

(c) Is Bailey acting unethically?

E13-18 **(ETHICAL ISSUES: CONTINGENT RENT EXPENSE)** Fidelity Insurance Company, the owner of East Acres Mall, charges Toys For Kids a rental fee of $500 per month plus 5% of yearly profits over $500,000. Harry Grant, the owner of the toy store, directs his accountant, Samantha Byers, to increase the estimate of bad debt expense, warranty costs, and depreciation on the computerized inventory system in order to keep profits at $475,000.

Instructions

(a) Should Byers follow her boss's directive?

(b) Who is harmed if her estimates are increased?

(c) Is Grant's directive unethical?

E13-19 **(ETHICAL ISSUES: ENVIRONMENTAL CONTINGENCIES)** On January 2, 1994, Darby Steel Company receives notice from the Environmental Protection Agency that the Muddy Lake Toxic Disposal Site needs to be cleaned up and that Darby Steel will be assessed 1/25 of the $25,000,000 cost. The cleanup will begin in 1997 and will take an estimated five years. Darby Steel has been using this disposal site for several decades. The vice-president and the controller discuss the proper recording of the environmental liability. Vice-president Sarah Evenson advocates recording the entire liability in 1994. Controller Tim Collins suggests footnote disclosure at most and prefers nondisclosure until cleanup begins in 1997.

Instructions

(a) What is the appropriate manner of reporting?

(b) Is there an ethical issue involved in this discussion?

(c) Who is harmed by nondisclosure?

———— **PROBLEMS** ————

P13-1 **(CURRENT LIABILITY ENTRIES AND ADJUSTMENTS)** Described below are certain transactions of Flicker Corporation Ltd.:

1. On February 2, the corporation purchased goods from Potter Company for $60,000, subject to cash discount terms of 2/10, n/30. Purchases and accounts payable were recorded by the corporation at net amounts after cash discounts. The invoice was paid on February 26.

2. On April 1, the corporation bought a truck for $37,000 from Chrysler Company, paying $6,000 in cash and signing a one-year, 12% note for the balance of the purchase price.

3. On May 1, the corporation borrowed $80,000 from the Royal Bank by signing a $90,800 note due one year from May 1.

4. On June 30 the corporation partially refunded $50,000 of its outstanding 10% note payable made one year ago to the Bank of Nova Scotia by paying $50,000 plus interest of $5,000. Flicker obtained the $55,000 by using $21,000 of its own cash and signing a new one-year, $40,000 note discounted at 15% by the bank.

5. On August 1, the board of directors declared a $220,000 cash dividend that was payable on September 10 to shareholders of record on August 31.

Instructions

(a) Make all the journal entries necessary to record the transactions above, using appropriate dates.

(b) Flicker Corporation Ltd.'s year end is December 31. Assuming that no adjusting entries relative to the transactions above have been recorded at year end, prepare any adjusting journal entries concerning interest that are necessary to present fair financial statements at December 31. Assume straight-line amortization of discounts.

(CURRENT LIABILITY ENTRIES AND ADJUSTMENTS) Listed below are selected transactions of **P13-2** Mitsukoshi Department Store for the current year ending December 31:

1. On December 5, the store received $2,000 from the Townhouse Players as a deposit to be returned after certain furniture to be used in a stage production was returned on January 15.

2. During December, sales totalled $861,000, which included the 5% sales tax that must be remitted to the province by the fifteenth day of the following month.

3. On December 10, the store purchased three delivery trucks for $86,000 in cash. The trucks were purchased in a province that applied no sales tax, but the store was located in and must register the trucks in a province that applied an education and health tax of 5% to nonsaleable goods bought outside of the province.

4. The store followed the practice of recording its property tax liability on the lien date and amortizing the tax over the subsequent 12 months. Property taxes of $72,000 became a lien on May 1 and were paid in two equal instalments on July 1 and October 1.

5. During the year, the store estimated that its annual income tax would be $620,000. At year end, income tax expense (for both accounting and tax return purposes) was determined to be $650,000. (Estimated taxes paid quarterly.)

Instructions

Prepare all the journal entries necessary to record the transactions noted above as they occurred and any adjusting journal entries relative to the transactions that would be required to present fair financial statements at December 31. Date each entry.

(PAYROLL TAX ENTRIES) Sies Company pays its office employee payroll weekly. Below is a partial list of **P13-3** employees and their payroll data for August. Because August is their vacation period, vacation pay is also listed.

Employee	Earnings to July 31	Weekly Pay	Vacation Pay to Be Received in August
Manny Toba	$ 5,600	$180	—
Brent Williams	4,650	150	$300
Karen Hobart	4,650	150	300
Al Berta	7,750	250	—
Ken Kornwall	10,200	330	660

Assume that the federal income tax collected is 10% of wages. Union dues collected are 3% of wages. Vacations are taken the second and third weeks of August by Williams, Hobart, and Kornwall. The unemployment insurance rate is 3% for employees and 1.4 times the employee rate for employers, both on a $6,000 monthly maximum. The CPP rate is 2.5% for employee and employer on an annual maximum of $33,000 per employee.

Instructions

Make the journal entries necessary for each of the four August payrolls. The entries for the payroll and for the company's liability are made separately. Also make the entry to record the monthly payment of accrued payroll liabilities.

(PAYROLL TAX ENTRIES) Following is a payroll sheet for King Export Company for the month of Sep- **P13-4** tember 1994. The unemployment insurance rate is 3% and the maximum monthly amount per employee is $96.85. The employer's obligation for unemployment insurance is 1.4 times the amount of employee deductions. Assume a 10% income tax rate for all employees and a 2.5% CPP premium charged on both employee and employer on a maximum of $33,400 annual earnings per employee.

Name	Earnings to Aug. 31	September Earnings	Income Tax Withholding	CPP	Unemployment Insurance
C. Kirk	$ 5,400	$ 700			
D. Spock	4,900	500			
B. Lauver	6,200	800			
V. Mosso	13,600	1,700			
A. Brown	120,000	15,000			
E. Wyatt	120,000	16,000			

Instructions

(a) Complete the payroll sheet and make the necessary entry to record the payment of the payroll.

(b) Make the entry to record the payroll tax expenses of King Export Company.

(c) Make the entry to pay the payroll liabilities created. Assume that the company pays all payroll liabilities at the end of each month.

P13-5 (**WARRANTIES, ACCRUAL, AND CASH BASIS**)   Thiel Corporation Ltd. sells portable computers under a two-year warranty contract that requires the corporation to replace defective parts and to provide the necessary repair labour. During 1994, the corporation sells 300 computers for cash at a unit price of $2,500. On the basis of past experience, the two-year warranty costs are estimated to be $90 for parts and $135 for labour per unit. (For simplicity, assume that all sales occurred on December 31, 1994.)

Instructions

(a) Record any necessary journal entries in 1994, applying the cash basis method.

(b) Record any necessary journal entries in 1994, applying the expense warranty accrual method.

(c) What liability relative to these transactions would appear on the December 31, 1994 balance sheet and how would it be classified if the cash basis method is applied?

(d) What liability relative to these transactions would appear on the December 31, 1994 balance sheet and how would it be classified if the expense warranty accrual method is applied?

In 1995 the actual warranty cost to Thiel Corporation Ltd. was $12,440 for parts and $18,660 for labour.

(e) Record any necessary journal entries in 1995, applying the cash basis method.

(f) Record any necessary journal entries in 1995, applying the expense warranty accrual method.

P13-6 (**EXTENDED WARRANTIES**)   Speedy Typing Inc. sells electric typewriters for $800 each and offers to each customer a three-year warranty contract for $90 that requires the company to perform periodic services and to replace defective parts. During 1994, the company sells 300 typewriters and 250 warranty contracts for cash. It estimates the three-year warranty costs as $20 for parts and $50 for labour and accounts for warranties on the sales warranty accrual method. Assume that sales occur on December 31, 1994, profit is recognized on the warranties, and straight-line recognition of revenues occurs.

Instructions

(a) Record any necessary journal entries in 1994.

(b) What amounts relative to these transactions would appear on the December 31, 1994 balance sheet and how would they be classified?

In 1995, Speedy Typing Inc. incurred actual costs relative to 1994 typewriter warranty sales of $1,600 for parts and $4,000 for labour.

(c) Record any necessary journal entries in 1995 relative to 1994 typewriter warranties.

(d) What amounts relative to the 1994 typewriter warranties would appear on the December 31, 1995 balance sheet and how would they be classified?

(WARRANTIES, ACCRUAL AND CASH BASIS)   Grant Wood Company sells a machine for $10,000 under **P13-7** a 12-month warranty agreement that requires the company to replace all defective parts and to provide the repair labour at no cost to the customers. With sales being made evenly throughout the year, the company sells 650 machines in 1994 (warranty expense is incurred half in 1994 and half in 1995). As a result of product testing, the company estimates that the warranty cost is $325 per machine ($110 parts and $215 labour).

Instructions

Assuming that actual warranty costs are incurred exactly as estimated, what journal entries would be made relative to these facts:

(a) Under application of the expense warranty accrual method for:

   1. Sale of machinery in 1994?

   2. Warranty costs incurred in 1994?

   3. Warranty expense charged against 1994 revenues?

   4. Warranty costs incurred in 1995?

(b) Under application of the cash basis method for:

   1. Sale of machinery in 1994?

   2. Warranty costs incurred in 1994?

   3. Warranty expense charged against 1994 revenues?

   4. Warranty costs incurred in 1995?

(c) What amount, if any, is disclosed in the balance sheet as a liability for future warranty cost as of December 31, 1994 under each method?

(d) Which method best reflects the income in 1994 and 1995 of Grant Wood Company? Why?

(PREMIUM ENTRIES)   To stimulate the sales of its Tasti Krunch breakfast cereal, the Hapi Company places **P13-8** one coupon in each box. Five coupons are redeemable for a premium consisting of a children's hand puppet. In 1994, the company purchases 40,000 puppets at $1.00 each and sells 400,000 boxes of Tasti Krunch at $3.25 a box. From its experience with other similar premium offers, the company estimates that 40% of the coupons issued will be mailed back for redemption. During 1994, 95,000 coupons are presented for redemption.

Instructions

Prepare the journal entries that should be recorded in 1994 relative to the premium plan.

P13-9 (PREMIUM ENTRIES AND FINANCIAL STATEMENT PRESENTATION) Smackers Candy Company offers a cassette tape as a premium for every five chocolate bar wrappers presented by customers together with $2.00. The chocolate bars are sold by the company to distributors for 30 cents each. The purchase price of each cassette tape to the company is $1.75; in addition, it costs 40 cents to mail each tape. The results of the premium plan for the years 1993 and 1994 are as follows (all purchases and sales are for cash).

	1993	1994
Cassette tapes purchased	250,000	330,000
Chocolate bars sold	2,895,400	2,743,600
Wrappers redeemed	1,200,000	1,500,000
1993 wrappers expected to be redeemed in 1994	290,000	
1994 wrappers expected to be redeemed in 1995		350,000

Instructions

(a) Prepare the journal entries that should be made in 1993 and 1994 to record the transactions related to the premium plan of the Smackers Candy Company.

(b) Indicate the account names, amounts, and classifications of the items related to the premium plan that would appear on the balance sheet and the income statement at the end of 1993 and of 1994.

P13-10 (WARRANTY, BONUS, AND COUPON COMPUTATION) Empira Inc. must make computations and adjusting entries for the following independent situations at December 31, 1994:

1. Its line of amplifiers carries a three-year warranty against defects. On the basis of past experience, the estimated warranty costs related to dollar sales are: first year after sale: 2% of sales; second year after sale: 3% of sales; and third year after sale: 4% of sales. Sales and actual warranty expenditures for the first three years of business are as follows.

Year	Sales	Warranty Expenditures
1992	$ 800,000	$ 7,600
1993	1,100,000	31,500
1994	1,200,000	67,000

Instructions

Compute the amount that Empira Inc. should report as a liability in its December 31, 1994 balance sheet. Assume that all sales are made evenly throughout each year, with warranty expenses also evenly spaced relative to the rates above.

2. Empira Inc.'s profit-sharing plan provides that the company will contribute to a fund an amount equal to one-fourth of its net income after taxes each year. Income before taxes and before deducting the profit-sharing contribution for 1994 is $1,150,000. The applicable income tax rate is 40%, and the profit-sharing contribution is deductible for tax purposes.

Instructions

Compute the amount to be contributed to the profit-sharing fund for 1994.

3. With some of its products, Empira Inc. includes coupons that are redeemable in merchandise. The coupons have no expiration date and, in the company's experience, 40% of them are redeemed. The liability for unredeemed coupons at December 31, 1993 is $18,000. During 1994, coupons worth $46,000 are issued and merchandise worth $16,000 is distributed in exchange for coupons redeemed.

Instructions

Compute the amount of the liability that should appear on the December 31, 1994 balance sheet.

(AICPA adapted)

(LOSS CONTINGENCIES, ENTRIES, AND ESSAY) On November 24, 1994, 26 passengers on Paper **P13-11** Airlines Flight 901 were injured on landing when the plane skidded off the runway. Personal injury suits for damages totalling $8,000,000 were filed on January 11, 1995 against the airline by 18 injured passengers. The airline carried no insurance. Legal counsel studied each suit and advised Paper that it could reasonably expect to pay 60% of the damages claimed. The financial statements for the year ended December 31, 1994 were issued February 17, 1995.

Instructions

(a) Prepare any disclosures and journal entries required by the airline in preparation of the December 31, 1994 financial statements.

(b) Ignoring the November 24, 1994 accident, what liability due to the risk of loss from lack of insurance coverage should Paper Airlines record or disclose? During the past decade, the company had experienced at least one accident per year and incurred average damages of $5,000,000. Discuss fully.

(ENTRIES FOR LIABILITIES AND LOSS CONTINGENCIES) Andrew Wynard Inc., a publishing com- **P13-12** pany, is preparing its December 31, 1994 financial statements and must determine the proper accounting treatment for each of the following situations:

1. Wynard sells subscriptions to several magazines for a one-year, two-year, or three-year period. Cash receipts from subscribers are credited to Magazine Subscriptions Collected in Advance, and this account has a balance of $2,400,000 at December 31, 1994. Outstanding subscriptions at December 31, 1994 expire as follows:

    During 1995: $600,000
    During 1996:   500,000
    During 1997:   800,000

2. On January 2, 1994, Wynard discontinues collision, fire, and theft coverage on its delivery vehicles and becomes self-insured for these risks. Actual losses of $50,000 during 1994 are charged to delivery expense. The 1993 premium for the discontinued coverage amounts to $80,000, and the controller wants to set up a reserve for self-insurance by a debit to delivery expense of $30,000 and a credit to the reserve for self-insurance of $30,000.

3. A suit for breach of contract seeking damages of $1,000,000 is filed by an author against Wynard on July 1, 1994. The company's legal counsel believes that an unfavourable outcome is likely. A reasonable estimate of the court's award to the plaintiff is in the range between $300,000 and $700,000. No amount within this range is a better estimate of potential damages than any other amount.

4. During December 1994, a competitor company files suit against Wynard for industrial espionage, claiming $1,500,000 in damages. In the opinion of management and company counsel, it is reasonably possible that damages will be awarded to the plaintiff. However, the amount of potential damages awarded to the plaintiff cannot be reasonably estimated.

Instructions

For each of the situations above, prepare the journal entry that should be recorded as of December 31, 1994, or explain why an entry should not be recorded. Show supporting computation in good form.

(AICPA adapted)

(LOSS CONTINGENCIES, ENTRIES, AND ESSAYS) Meister Corporation Ltd., in preparation of its **P13-13** December 31, 1994 financial statements, is attempting to determine the proper accounting treatment for each of the following situations:

1. As a result of uninsured accidents during the year, personal injury suits for $100,000 and $350,000 have been filed against the company. It is the judgement of Meister's legal counsel that an unfavourable outcome is unlikely in the $100,000 case and that an unfavourable verdict approximating $225,000 will probably result in the $350,000 case.

2. Meister Corporation Ltd. owns a subsidiary in a foreign country that has a book value of $5,700,000 and an estimated fair value of $8,800,000. The foreign government has communicated to Meister its intention to expropriate the assets and business of all foreign investors. On the basis of settlements that other firms have received from this same country, Meister expects to receive 40% of the fair value of its properties as final settlement.

3. Meister's chemical product division, consisting of five plants, is uninsurable because of the special risk of injury to employees and losses due to fire and explosion. The year 1994 is considered one of the safest (luckiest) in the division's history because there is no loss due to injury or casualty. Having suffered an average of three casualties per year during the rest of the past decade (ranging from $100,000 to $800,000), management is certain that the company will probably not be so fortunate next year.

Instructions

(a) Prepare the journal entries that should be recorded as of December 31, 1994 to recognize each of the situations above.

(b) Indicate what should be reported relative to each situation in the financial statements and accompanying notes. Explain why.

P13-14 (WARRANTIES AND PREMIUMS) Tonedeaf Music Company carries a wide variety of musical instruments, sound reproduction equipment, recorded music, and sheet music. Tonedeaf uses two sales promotion techniques—warranties and premiums—to attract customers.

Musical instruments and sound equipment are sold with a one-year warranty for replacement of parts and labour. The estimated warranty cost, based on past experience, is 2% of sales.

A premium is offered on the recorded and sheet music. Customers receive a coupon for each dollar spent on recorded music or sheet music. Customers may exchange 200 coupons and $20 for a cassette player. Tonedeaf pays $35 for each cassette player and estimates that 60% of the coupons given to customers will be redeemed.

Tonedeaf's total sales for 1994 were $7,200,000—$5,400,000 from musical instruments and sound reproduction equipment and $1,800,000 from recorded music and sheet music. Replacement parts and labour for warranty work total $120,000 during 1994. A total of 6,500 cassette players used in the premium program are purchased during the year and 1,200,000 coupons were redeemed in 1994.

The accrual method is used by Tonedeaf to account for the warranty and premium costs for financial reporting purposes. The balances in the accounts related to warranties and premiums on January 1, 1994 are as shown below:

Inventory of Premium Cassette Players	$41,125
Estimated Premium Claims Outstanding	48,000
Estimated Liability From Warranties	68,000

Instructions

Tonedeaf Music Company is preparing its financial statements for the year ended December 31, 1994. Determine the amounts that will be shown on the 1994 financial statements for the following:

1. Warranty Expense.

2. Estimated Liability From Warranties.

3. Premium Expense.

4. Inventory of Premium Cassette Players.

5. Estimated Premium Claims Outstanding.

(CMA adapted)

——— FINANCIAL REPORTING PROBLEM ———

Refer to the financial statements and other documents of Moore Corporation Limited presented in Appendix 5A and answer the following questions:

1. What are Moore's current portions of long-term debt at December 31 of both 1990 and 1991? What are the amounts of the remaining scheduled maturities of long-term debt for the years 1993 to 1996?

2. How are contingencies reported in Moore's financial statements? What is management's rationale for its reporting practice for these contingencies?

3. Is Moore likely to experience a bank overdraft? Explain.

14

Long-Term Liabilities

■

"**L**et us all be happy and live within our means, even if we have to borrow the money to do it with"[1] appeared to be a motto of the 1980s. Companies and consumers took on increasing levels of debt to finance expansion, take over companies, satisfy consumption needs, and obtain advantages of favourable financial leverage.[2]

Debt, however, brought with it obligations. There had to be cash flows to pay the interest and principal. Restrictions were written into agreements to lower the risk to providers of debt financing. Such restrictions included limiting dividends or level of debt relative to equity, setting up special funds to repay the debt, and maintaining at least a minimum ratio of current assets to current liabilities. Recession in the 1990s resulted in many companies with a high debt load finding it difficult or impossible to survive given these obligations.

While the accounting for debt was not the cause of these economic problems, their occurrence provided a stimulus for accountants to pay more attention than had been given in the past to issues regarding the recognition, measurement, and disclosure of debt in financial statements. Additionally, the emergence of a variety of creative ways to obtain financial capital resulted in criticism of what was or was not being reported in financial statements regarding debt obligations. Off-balance-sheet financing arrangements and failure to report substance over form for some financial instruments (i.e. showing something as equity when, in substance, it was debt) were significant causes of this criticism.

The objectives of this chapter are to consider the nature of long-term debt and to examine the related basic accounting issues regarding recognition, measurement, and disclosure requirements. Bonds payable are the basic instrument used to demonstrate the underlying concepts. Long-term notes and mortgages payable are also considered. Pensions and leases are other important sources of long-term liabilities which are given in-depth coverage in Chapters 20 and 21 respectively. Issues regarding some of the more complex issues associated with accounting for liabilities—recognition of substance over form, off-balance-sheet financing, and troubled debt restructuring—are considered in Appendix 14A. In Appendix 14B, the accounting for serial bonds is examined.

NATURE OF LONG-TERM LIABILITIES

Objective 1

Understand the nature of long-term liabilities.

A **long-term liability** is an *obligation of an entity arising from past transactions or events for which settlement will not take place within the next operating cycle of the business, or within a year if there are several operating cycles within a year*.

Incurring long-term debt is often accompanied by considerable formality. For example, bylaws of corporations often require approval by the board of directors and shareholders before bonds can be issued or other long-term debt arrangements can be contracted.

Generally, long-term debt is issued subject to various **covenants** or **restrictions** for the protection of the lenders. The covenants and other terms of the agreement between the borrower and the lender are stated in the **bond indenture** or **note agreement**. Items often mentioned in the indenture or agreement include the amounts authorized to be issued, interest rate, due date or dates,

---

[1] A comment by Artemus Ward in *Investment Vision*, September/October, 1990.
[2] Favourable financial leverage means that a company has borrowed funds and is earning a return from the use of these funds which exceeds their cost (interest). This notion is examined in Chapter 24.

property pledged as security, sinking fund requirements, working capital and dividend restrictions, and limitations concerning the assumption of additional debt. When these stipulations are important for a complete understanding of the financial position and the results of operations, they should be described in the body or notes of the financial statements (*CICA Handbook*, Section 3210). In many cases, the loan instrument or contract is held by a trustee, usually a financial institution, which acts as an independent third party to protect the interests of the lender(s) and the borrower.

The distinction between long-term debt and equity financing can become hazy. Basically, a **debt instrument** *usually has a maturity date* when the face value (principal amount) must be repaid to the lender. Additionally, a debt instrument *confers no voting rights*, but *usually bears interest that must be paid periodically* (usually annually or semiannually). An **equity instrument**, conversely, generally *does not have a maturity date*; therefore, it need not be redeemed by the issuing corporation. *Voting rights may or may not attach* to an equity security, and *dividends are paid at the discretion and direction of the issuing corporation's board of directors*.

BONDS PAYABLE

A bond arises from a contract known as an **indenture** and represents a promise to pay (1) a sum of money at a designated maturity date, plus (2) periodic interest at a specified (fixed or variable) rate on the maturity amount (face value). Individual bonds are evidenced by a certificate and typically have a face value of $1,000. Bond interest payments are usually made semiannually, although the interest rate is generally expressed as an annual rate.

An entire bond issue may be sold to an investment banker. In such arrangements, investment bankers may either underwrite the entire issue by guaranteeing a certain sum to the corporation, thus taking the risk of selling the bonds for whatever price they can get (firm underwriting), or they may sell the bond issue for a commission to be deducted from the proceeds of the sale (best efforts underwriting). Alternatively, the issuing company may choose to sell the bonds directly to a large institution, financial or otherwise, without the aid of an underwriter (private placement).

Types and Characteristics of Bonds

Various terms are used to describe characteristics that may be associated with a bond. The following are some of the more common characteristics. Note that a single bond may have a variety of these characteristics associated with it (e.g., the bond may be secured, term, convertible, and registered).

> **Objective 2**
>
> Identify various types and characteristics of bonds.

Secured and Unsecured Bonds. Bonds may be **secured** (e.g., mortgage bonds which have a claim on real estate, and collateral trust bonds which have securities of other corporations as security) or **unsecured** (e.g., debenture bonds). A "junk bond" is unsecured and also very risky, and therefore pays a high rate of interest. These bonds are often used to finance leveraged buyouts.

Term and Serial Bonds. Bond issues that mature on a single date are called **term bonds**, and issues that mature in instalments are called **serial bonds**. The accounting for serial bonds is illustrated in Appendix 14B.

Convertible Bonds. If bonds are convertible into other securities of the corporation (e.g., preferred or common shares), they are called **convertible bonds**. Accounting for bond conversion is discussed in Appendix 14A and Chapter 17.

Registered and Bearer Bonds. Bonds issued in the name of the owner are **registered bonds** and require surrender of the certificate and issuance of a new certificate to complete a sale. **Bearer bonds,** however, are not recorded in the name of the owner and may be transferred from one owner to another by mere delivery. Coupons attached to such bonds are submitted by the holder to receive interest payments.

In addition to the types of bonds mentioned above, **income bonds** may be issued. Their interest payments depend upon the issuing company having income. **Revenue bonds** are called such because the interest on them is paid from specified revenue sources. If the issuer has the right to call and retire the bonds prior to maturity, they are **callable or redeemable bonds**.

While bonds incorporating these characteristics have existed for a long time, new characteristics have been developed in an attempt to attract capital in a tight money market. The following serve to exemplify some of the more recent developments in this regard.

Retractable bonds provide the holder with the right to sell the bonds back to the company at his or her option. Exercise of this right is typically restricted to specified time periods and prices. AMCA International Limited and British Columbia Telephone Company have retraction rights in some of their long-term debt instruments.

Extendable bonds allow the holder, at his or her option, to extend the date of maturity under specified terms and conditions. British Columbia Telephone Company is an example of a Canadian company which has an extension right for some of its bonds.

Commodity-backed bonds (also called **asset-linked bonds**) are redeemable in measures of a commodity, such as barrels of oil, tons of coal, or ounces of rare metal. For example, in the 1980s Sunshine Mining, a silver mining producer, sold two issues of bonds redeemable with either $1,000 in cash or 50 ounces of silver (or the cash equivalent), whichever is greater at maturity. Both issues are due in 1995 and have a stated interest rate of 8½%. The accounting problem is one of projecting the maturity value, especially since the price for silver has fluctuated greatly since their issuance.

Deep-discount bonds or **zero-interest bonds** pay very low or no stated interest. When no interest is paid, the price received when the bonds are sold is simply the market's determination of the present value of the face amount to be received at maturity. Therefore, the buyer's total interest payoff is at maturity (the amount of interest being the difference between the maturity amount and the price for which the bonds were sold). A unique version of a zero-interest bond (with overtones of a commodity-backed bond) was proposed by Caesar's World Inc., a Las Vegas/Lake Tahoe gambling casino operator. Caesar's World was to issue 5,000 of $15,000 face amount bonds that would entitle each bondholder to spend two weeks a year at its Lake Tahoe resort in lieu of interest on the bond.[3] In Canada, **stripped bonds**, also known as **zero-coupon bonds**, are a fairly recent phenomena. Basically, such bonds are created by detaching (or stripping) the interest coupons from a coupon bond and selling the stripped bond as a contract in itself.[4] For example, Nova Scotia Power Corp.'s bonds maturing in 2014 are sold by brokers as stripped bonds. Marketing names such as "Cats," "Cougars," and "Tigers" have been used in Canada to describe some deep-discount bonds.

In summary, bonds have many different features and vary in level of risk. The main purpose of bonds is to borrow from the general public or from institutional investors for the long term when the amount of capital needed is too large for one lender to supply. By issuing bonds in $1,000 or $10,000 denominations, a large amount of long-term indebtedness can be divided into many small investing units, thus enabling more than one lender to participate in the loan.

A Bond Issue's Life and Related Accounting

Objective 3

Understand events and transactions associated with bonds.

Figure 14-1 shows the events and transactions associated with bonds. As indicated, planning and making several important decisions occur prior to the issuance of bonds, the action that initiates accounting activities.

---

[3] "Caesar's World May Try Bond Issue Paying in Vacations," *The Wall Street Journal*, January 22, 1982, p. 32.

[4] The stripped coupons are sold to investors, separate from the bond. As such, investors concerned about obtaining a steady flow of income may buy the coupons, while the investor interested in a longer term return of capital (for Registered Retirement Savings Plan purposes, for example) would be willing to buy the stripped bond. The effective interest rate or yield could, of course, differ between the two investment forms.

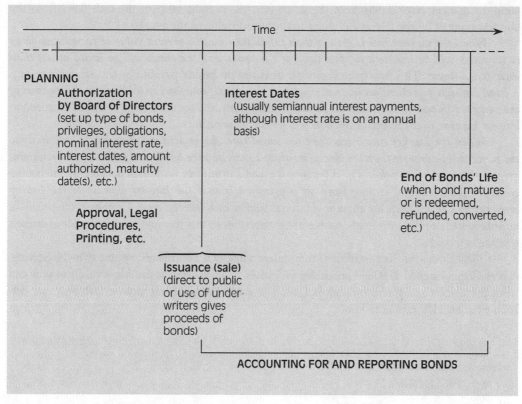

Figure 14-1 Events and Transactions Related to Bonds

When accounting for bonds, there are a multitude of complexities which relate to such things as the proceeds received, the issuance date, the company's year end, interest calculations, and the method of retiring the bonds. While the mechanics involved are fairly complicated, an understanding of them may be enhanced by keeping the following basic purposes of accounting for bonds in mind:

1. To measure the liability appropriately for balance sheet purposes.

2. To report expenses appropriately in the income statement.

Valuation of Bonds Payable: Discount and Premium

The issuance and marketing of bonds is not an overnight happening—it takes time, often weeks or months. Approval must be obtained, audits and issuance of a prospectus may be required, certificates must be printed, and underwriters must be arranged. Frequently, the terms in a bond indenture are established well in advance of the sale of bonds. Between the time the terms are set and the bonds are sold, the market conditions and the financial position of the issuing corporation may change significantly. Such changes affect the marketability of the bonds and thus their selling price.

The selling price of a bond issue is set by such familiar economic phenomena as supply and demand of buyers and sellers, relative risk, market conditions, and the state of the economy. *The investment community values a bond at the present value of its future cash flows, which consist of (1) interest and (2) principal.* The interest rate used to compute the present value of these cash flows is the market rate that provides an acceptable return on an investment, commensurate with the issuer's risk characteristics and consideration for inflation.

The interest rate written in the terms of the bond indenture and ordinarily appearing on the bond certificate is known as the **stated, coupon, or nominal rate**. This rate, which is set by the issuer of the bonds, is expressed as a percentage of the **face value**, also called the **par value, principal amount, or maturity value** of the bonds. If the rate employed by the buyers (called the **effective**

yield, or **market rate**) differs from the stated rate, the present value of the cash flows from the bonds computed by the buyers will differ from the face value of the bonds.[5]

When the market rate is greater than the stated rate, the present value of future cash flows to the buyer will be less than the face value of the bonds, and the bonds will be issued at less than their face amount. This difference is called a **discount on bonds payable** by the issuing company. A *bond discount represents an interest expense to the issuing company in addition to the amount of interest paid in cash at each interest period.* Consequently, the total discount must be amortized to interest expense over the life of the bonds in a systematic manner.

When the market rate is less than the stated rate, the present value of future cash flows to the buyer will be greater than the face value of the bonds, and the bonds will be issued at an amount greater than their face value. The difference is called a **premium on bonds payable** by the issuing company. The *result of issuing bonds at a premium is that the interest expense to the issuing company will be less than the amount of interest paid at each interest date.* Therefore, the premium must be systematically amortized over the life of the bonds so that the appropriate amount of interest expense is recorded.

To illustrate the computation of the present value of a bond issue, assume that the Servicemaster Corp. issues $100,000 in bonds due in 5 years with 9% interest payable annually at year end when the market rate for such bonds is 11%. The actual principal and interest cash flows are discounted at an 11% rate as follows.

Present value of the principal:
$a(p_{\overline{5}|11\%}) = \$100,000\ (.59345)^*$ $59,345.00

Present value of the interest payments:
$R(P_{\overline{5}|11\%}) = \$9,000\ (3.69590)^{**}$ 33,263.10

Present value (selling price) of the bonds   **$92,608.10**

*Interest factor for present value of $1 amount received in 5 periods at 11%, as presented in Table A-2 in the Appendix at the end of the book.

**Interest factor for the present value of an ordinary annuity of $1 received for 5 periods at 11%, as presented in Table A-4 in the Appendix at the end of the book.

By paying $92,608.10 at the date of issue, the investors will realize an effective rate or yield of 11% over the 5-year term of the bonds. These bonds would, therefore, be sold at a *discount* of $7,391.90 ($100,000 − $92,608.10).[6]

When bonds sell below face value, it means that investors demand a rate of interest higher than the stated rate. The investors are not satisfied with the stated rate because they can earn a greater rate on alternative investments of equal risk. They cannot change the stated rate, so they refuse to pay the face value for the bonds and, thus, by changing the amount invested earn the effective rate of interest. Inasmuch as the investors receive cash equal to (1) the stated rate computed on the face value at specified interest dates plus (2) the face value at maturity, they are earning an effective rate that is higher than the stated rate because they paid less than face value for the bonds.

---

[5] Companies frequently set the stated rate of interest on bonds in precise fractions (such as 10⅞%). They also usually attempt to align the stated rate as closely as possible with the market or effective rate. Nevertheless, because the stated rate is set prior to the sale of the bonds, it often still differs from the market rate at the time of sale. The magnitude of the difference tends to be small. For deep-discount or zero-interest bonds, however, the difference is substantial.

[6] The price at which bonds sell is typically stated as a percentage of the face or par value of the bonds. For example, the Servicemaster Corp. bonds sold for 92.6 (92.6% of par). If Servicemaster had received $102,000, we would say the bonds sold for 102 (102% of par).

Had the market rate been 8%, the present value of future cash flows to investors would be $103,992.39 as shown below.

Present value of the principal:	
$a(p_{\overline{5}|8\%}) = \$100,000\ (.68058)$	$ 68,058.00
Present value of the interest payments:	
$R(P_{\overline{5}|8\%}) = \$9,000\ (3.99271)$	35,934.39
Present value (selling price) of the bonds	**$103,992.39**

In this situation, the bonds would sell at a *premium* of $3,992.39 ($103,992.39 − $100,000). Investors would be willing to pay such a premium because they will receive cash interest payments based on the stated rate of 9% as well as the face value at maturity.

Accounting for Bonds Payable

As indicated in Figure 14-1, accounting for bonds is concerned with recording measured amounts related to the date of issuance, interest dates and year ends, and maturity or extinguishment dates, as well as reporting bond-related items appropriately in the financial statements. How this is done is examined in the following paragraphs, which consider the various circumstances that may exist regarding a bond issue.

Bonds Issued at Par on an Interest Date. When bonds are issued on an interest payment date at par (face value), no interest has accrued and no premium or discount exists (the effective interest rate equals the stated rate). The accounting entry is made simply for the cash proceeds and the face value of the bonds. To illustrate, if 10-year term bonds with a par value of $800,000, dated January 1, 1994, and bearing interest at an annual rate of 10% payable semiannually on January 1 and July 1, are sold on January 1 at par, the entry on the books of the issuing corporation would be:

Cash	800,000	
Bonds Payable		800,000

The entry to record the first semiannual interest payment of $40,000 ($800,000 × .10 × 1/2) on July 1, would be:

Bond Interest Expense	40,000	
Cash		40,000

If the year end is December 31, then six months' accrued interest would be recorded on that date as follows:

Bond Interest Expense	40,000	
Bond Interest Payable		40,000

On January 1, the interest would be paid and recorded (assuming no reversing entry) as shown below:

Bond Interest Payable	40,000	
Cash		40,000

Bonds Issued at a Discount or Premium on an Interest Date. If the $800,000 of bonds illustrated above were sold on January 1, 1994 at 97, the issuance would be recorded as follows:

Cash ($800,000 × .97)	776,000	
Discount on Bonds Payable	24,000	
Bonds Payable		800,000

Objective 5

Know how to account for bonds payable and related interest expense when they are sold at par, a discount, or a premium on an interest date or between interest dates.

Because of the relation of the Discount on Bonds Payable to interest as previously discussed, *the discount is amortized and charged to interest expense over the period of time that the bonds are outstanding.* The discount (or premium) may be amortized using the straight-line method or the effective interest method.[7]

Under the **straight-line method**, the amount amortized each year is a constant amount. For example, using the above bond discount of $24,000, the amount amortized to interest expense each year for 10 years is $2,400 ($24,000/10 years) and, *if amortization is recorded annually*, the December 31 adjustment for the discount would be:

Bond Interest Expense	2,400	
Discount on Bonds Payable		2,400

At the end of the first year, 1994, as a result of the above amortization entry, the unamortized balance in Discount on Bonds Payable account is $21,600 ($24,000 − $2,400). The Interest Expense for the year would be $82,400 ($40,000 on both July 1 and December 31 as shown previously plus the $2,400 debit to Interest Expense resulting from the discount amortization).

If the bonds were dated and sold on November 1, 1994 with interest dates of November 1 and May 1, and the fiscal year of the corporation ended on December 31, the discount amortized for 1994 would be only 2/12 of 1/10 of $24,000, or $400. Amortization of this amount and recognition of the accrued interest payable of $13,333 ($800,000 × .10 × 2/12) would result in interest expense of $13,733 for 1994 which would be recorded on December 31 as follows:

Bond Interest Expense	13,733	
Bond Interest Payable		13,333
Discount on Bonds Payable		400

If no reversing entries are made, the entry on May 1, 1995 for the first interest payment (*assuming the amortization of the discount is recorded on the interest date*) would be:

Bond Interest Expense	27,467	
Bond Interest Payable	13,333	
Cash		40,000
Discount on Bonds Payable		800

Premium on Bonds Payable is accounted for in a manner similar to that described for Discount on Bonds Payable. If the 10-year bonds of a par value of $800,000 are sold on January 1, 1994 at 103, then the cash proceeds are $824,000 ($800,000 × 1.03).

The entry to record this is:

Cash	824,000	
Bonds Payable		800,000
Premium on Bonds Payable		24,000

Given interest dates of July 1 and January 1, the company's year end being December 31, and that amortization of the premium is recorded on interest dates, the following entries would be made:

July 1, 1994

Bond Interest Expense	38,800	
Premium Bonds Payable	1,200	
Cash		40,000

(Continued)

---

[7] Although the effective interest method is preferred for amortization of a discount or premium, we have chosen to use initially the straight-line method to emphasize the concepts by avoiding complex calculations. The straight-line method is acceptable if the results obtained are not materially different from those produced by the effective interest method. The effective interest calculations are examined shortly.

December 31, 1994

Bond Interest Expense	38,800	
Premium on Bonds Payable	1,200	
Bond Interest Payable		40,000

January 1, 1995

Bond Interest Payable	40,000	
Cash		40,000

As is evident from these examples, ***bond interest expense is increased by amortization of a discount and decreased by amortization of a premium.***

Bonds Issued Between Interest Dates. Bond interest payments are usually made semiannually on dates specified in the bond indenture. When bonds are issued on other than an interest payment date, buyers of the bonds will pay the seller the interest accrued from the last interest payment date to the date of issue. The purchasers of the bonds, in effect, pay the bond issuer in advance for that portion of the full six-month interest payment to which they are not entitled, not having held the bonds during this period. The purchasers will receive the full six-month interest payment on the semiannual interest payment date.

To illustrate, if 10-year bonds of a par value of $800,000, dated January 1, 1994 and bearing interest at an annual rate of 10% payable semiannually on January 1 and July 1, are issued at ***par plus accrued interest on March 1, 1994,*** the entry on the books of the issuing corporation is:

Cash	813,333	
Bonds Payable		800,000
Bond Interest Expense ($800,000 × .10 × 2/12)		13,333

The purchaser advances two months' interest, because on July 1, 1994, four months after the date of purchase, six months' interest will be received from the issuing company. The company makes the following entry on July 1, 1994:

Bond Interest Expense	40,000	
Cash		40,000

The expense account now contains a debit balance of $26,667, which represents the appropriate amount of interest expense, four months at 10% on $800,000.[8]

The above illustration was simplified by having the January 1, 1994 bonds issued on March 1, 1994 *at par*. If, however, these bonds were issued at 102 (excluding the accrued interest), the entry on March 1 on the books of the issuing corporation would be:

Cash	829,333	
Bonds Payable		800,000
Premium on Bonds Payable		16,000
Bond Interest Expense		13,333

---

[8] Note that instead of creating Bond Interest Expense on March 1, a Bond Interest Payable account could have been credited for the $13,333. Had this been the case, the July 1 debit to Bond Interest Expense would be for $26,667 and the Bond Interest Payable account would be debited for $13,333. When bonds are issued at other than on interest date, the amount of interest accrued may be credited to either Bond Interest Expense or Bond Interest Payable. The subsequent entry to record the first interest payment for the period would have to appropriately link to the method chosen to account for the accrued interest when the bonds were issued. Recognizing this, the authors have chosen to base their examples on the assumption that the accrued interest to the issuance date is credited to Bond Interest Expense.

Since these bonds would mature on January 1, 2004, the period over which the premium would be amortized is 118 months. Therefore, the entry on July 1, 1994 for the interest payment and premium amortization would be:

Bond Interest Expense	39,458	
Premium on Bonds Payable	542	
Cash		40,000

The premium is amortized on a straight-line basis ($16,000 × 4/118 = $542.37, rounded to $542). This amount is deducted from the cash paid to derive the debit amount to interest expense. Considering both the March 1 and July 1 entries, the net amount charged to interest expense for the four months is $26,125 (the July 1 debit for $39,458 less the March 1 credit for $13,333).

Effective Interest Method

The straight-line method for amortizing a premium or discount results in a *constant amount* being charged to interest expense for each full year during the life of the bonds. Charging an equal amount to interest expense each year is not conceptually correct. This is because the relationship of the interest expense to the **carrying value** or **book value** (face value less discount or plus the premium) of the bonds results in an apparent decrease (in the case of discounts) or increase (for premium situations) in the interest rate for successive years. This phenomenon occurs because, although the interest expense is constant, the carrying value increases each year for discounted bonds and decreases for bonds issued at a premium.

The **effective interest method** overcomes this problem. Under the effective interest method:

1. Bond interest expense is computed first by multiplying the carrying value of the bonds at the beginning of the period by the effective interest rate.

2. The bond discount or premium amortization is then determined by comparing the bond interest expense with the interest to be paid.

The computation of the amortization is depicted as follows.

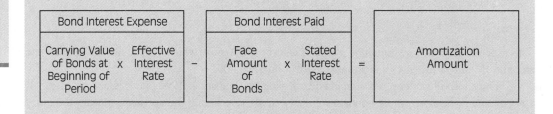

The effective interest method produces a periodic interest expense equal to a *constant percentage of the carrying value of the bonds*. Since the percentage is the effective rate of interest incurred by the borrower at the time of issuance, the effective interest method results in a better matching of expenses with revenues than the straight-line method.

Both the effective interest and straight-line methods result in the same total amount of interest expense over the term of the bonds, and the annual amounts of interest expense are generally quite similar. However, *when the annual amounts are materially different, the effective interest method is preferred.*[9]

---

[9] At the time of writing, there was no Canadian standard requiring the use of the effective interest method when discount or premiums are large. The *Exposure Draft* on "Financial Instruments" (Toronto: CICA, September 1991), however, did contain a proposed recommendation (par. .068) that the effective interest method (called the present value method) be used if the resulting interest expense is materially different from that determined under the straight-line method. In the United States the effective interest method is required in such cases.

Objective 6

Know how to account for bonds payable and interest expense using the effective interest method in various circumstances.

Bonds Issued at a Discount. To illustrate amortization of a discount using the effective interest method, assume that Evermaster Corp. issued $100,000 of 8% bonds on January 1, 1994, due on January 1, 1999, with interest payable each July 1 and January 1. Because the investors required an effective interest rate of 10%, they paid $92,278 for the $100,000 of bonds, creating a $7,722 discount. The $7,722 discount was calculated as follows.[10]

Maturity value of bonds payable		$100,000
Present value of $100,000 due in five years		
at 10%, interest payable semiannually:		
$100,000 × .61391 from Table A-2	$61,391	
Present value of $4,000 interest payable semiannually		
for five years at 10% annually:		
$4,000 × 7.72173 from Table A-4	30,887	
Proceeds from sale of bonds		92,278
Discount on bonds payable		**$ 7,722**

The five-year amortization schedule appears below.

Schedule of Bond Discount Amortization
Effective Interest Method: Semiannual Interest Payments
5-Year, 8% Bonds Sold to Yield 10%

Date	Credit Cash	Debit Interest Expense	Credit Bond Discount	Carrying Value of Bonds
1/1/94				$ 92,278
7/1/94	$ 4,000[a]	$ 4,614[b]	$ 614[c]	92,892[d]
1/1/95	4,000	4,645	645	93,537
7/1/95	4,000	4,677	677	94,214
1/1/96	4,000	4,711	711	94,925
7/1/96	4,000	4,746	746	95,671
1/1/97	4,000	4,783	783	96,454
7/1/97	4,000	4,823	823	97,277
1/1/98	4,000	4,864	864	98,141
7/1/98	4,000	4,907	907	99,048
1/1/99	4,000	4,952	952	100,000
	$40,000	$47,722	$7,722	

[a]$4,000 = $100,000 × 0.08 × 6/12
[b]$4,614 = $92,278 × 0.10 × 6/12
[c]$614 = $4,614 − $4,000
[d]$92,892 = $92,278 + $614

The entry to record the issuance of Evermaster Corp.'s bonds at a discount on January 1, 1994 follows.

---

[10] Because interest is paid semiannually, the interest rate used is 5% (10% × 6/12). The number of periods is 10 (5 years × 2).

Cash	92,278	
Discount on Bonds Payable	7,722	
Bonds Payable		100,000

The journal entry to record the first interest payment and amortization of the discount on July 1, 1994 is:

Bond Interest Expense	4,614	
Discount on Bonds Payable		614
Cash		4,000

The journal entry to record the interest expense accrued at December 31, 1994 (year end) and amortization of the discount is:

Bond Interest Expense	4,645	
Bond Interest Payable		4,000
Discount on Bonds Payable		645

Bonds Issued at a Premium. If the market had been such that investors were willing to accept an effective interest rate of 6% on the bond issue described above, they would have paid $108,530 or a premium of $8,530, based on present value computations. The applicable five-year amortization schedule appears below.

Schedule of Bond Premium Amortization
Effective Interest Method: Semiannual Interest Payments
5-Year, 8% Bonds Sold to Yield 6%

Date	Credit Cash	Debit Interest Expense	Debit Bond Premium	Carrying Value of Bonds
1/1/94				$108,530
7/1/94	$ 4,000[a]	$ 3,256[b]	$ 744[c]	107,786[d]
1/1/95	4,000	3,234	766	107,020
7/1/95	4,000	3,211	789	106,231
1/1/96	4,000	3,187	813	105,418
7/1/96	4,000	3,162	838	104,580
1/1/97	4,000	3,137	863	103,717
7/1/97	4,000	3,112	888	102,829
1/1/98	4,000	3,085	915	101,914
7/1/98	4,000	3,057	943	100,971
1/1/99	4,000	3,029	971	100,000
	$40,000	$31,470	$8,530	

[a]$4,000 = $100,000 \times 0.08 \times 6/12$
[b]$3,256 = $108,530 \times 0.06 \times 6/12$
[c]$744 = $4,000 - $3,256$
[d]$107,786 = $108,530 - 744

The entry to record the issuance of the Evermaster bonds at a premium on January 1, 1994 is:

Cash	108,530	
Premium on Bonds Payable		8,530
Bonds Payable		100,000

The journal entry to record the first interest payment and amortization of the premium on July 1, 1994 follows.

Bond Interest Expense	3,256	
Premium on Bonds Payable	744	
Cash		4,000

Bonds Issued Between Interest Dates. When using the effective interest method on bonds issued at a premium or discount between interest dates, the accounting question concerns the measurement of the premium or discount to be amortized from the issuance date to the first interest payment date. The answer is that *the amount amortized will equal the difference between the amount received for the bonds (excluding accrued interest) and the present value of the bonds at the first interest date following their issuance.* In the following periods, the amount to be amortized is based on an amortization schedule starting with the carrying value of the bonds after the first interest payment.

To illustrate, refer to the Schedule of Bond Premium Amortization for the immediately preceding illustration of Evermaster Corp. Rather than assuming the bonds were sold on January 1, 1994 for $108,530 as in that example, assume the bonds were sold for $108,282[11] on March 1, 1994. As previously discussed, the buyers would also pay accrued interest of $1,333 from the previous interest date of January 1 ($100,000 $\times$ .04 $\times$ 2/6). The following entry would be made on March 1:

Cash	109,615	
Bonds Payable		100,000
Premium on Bonds Payable		8,282
Interest Expense		1,333

On July 1, 1994, the first interest payment date after issuance of the bonds, the following entry would be made:

Interest Expense	3,504	
Premium on Bonds Payable	496	
Cash		4,000

The debit to the Premium account is the difference between the $108,282 received for the bonds and their present value of $107,786 on July 1 after the interest payment (see carrying value of these bonds for 7/1/94 in the amortization schedule). *Amounts in entries* to recognize the premium amortization, interest expense, and cash paid or payable *after the first interest payment would be the same as those applicable to the situation of the bonds being issued on an interest date.*

Interest Dates Do Not Coincide With Year End. In our previous examples, the interest payment dates and the date the financial statements were issued were the same. For example, when Evermaster sold bonds at a premium on January 1, 1994 (page 686), the January 1 interest payment date coincided with the financial reporting date (December 31). However, what happens if Evermaster wishes to report financial statements at the end of February 1994? In this case, the premium is prorated by the appropriate number of months to arrive at the appropriate interest expense shown on page 688.

The journal entry to record this accrual is as follows:

Interest Expense	1,085.33	
Premium on Bonds Payable	248.00	
Interest Payable		1,333.33

---

[11] To determine the price received for bonds sold at other than an interest date: (1) determine the present value of the bonds on the interest dates immediately before and after the issuance using the effective rate at date of issuance, and (2) interpolate the price based on the time of issuance between the dates. For the Evermaster Corp.:

(1) Present value of bonds January 1, 1994 = $108,530
   Present value of bonds July 1, 1994 = $107,786

(2) Since the bonds were issued two months into this six-month period, interpolation results in the following value on March 1, 1994:
   $108,530 − 2/6 ($108,530 − $107,786) = $108,282.

Computation of Interest Expense

Interest accrual ($4,000 × 2/6)	$1,333.33
Premium amortization ($744 × 2/6)*	(248.00)
Interest expense (Jan.–Feb.)	**$1,085.33**

*The premium amortization for the six-month period during which the year end falls, based on the effective interest method, is allocated within that period on a straight-line basis.

If the company also prepared interim financial statements six months later, the same procedure is followed; that is, the premium amortized would be determined as follows.

Premium amortized (March–June) ($744 × 4/6)	$496.00
Premium amortized (July–August) ($766 × 2/6)	255.33
Premium amortized (March–August, 1994)	$751.33

The computation is much simpler if the straight-line method is employed. For example, in the Evermaster situation the total premium of $8,530 is allocated evenly over the five-year period. Thus, premium amortization per month is $142.17 ($8,530 ÷ 60 months).

Balance Sheet Presentation of Unamortized Bond Discount or Premium

Objective 7

Understand how unamortized bond discount or premium may be reported in a balance sheet.

Discount on Bonds Payable is not an asset because it does not provide any future economic benefit. The enterprise has the use of the borrowed funds, but for that use it must pay interest. A bond discount means that the company borrowed less than the face or maturity value of the bond and therefore is faced with an actual (effective) interest rate higher than the stated (nominal) rate. Conceptually, Discount on Bonds Payable is a liability valuation account, that is, a reduction of the face or maturity amount of the related liability. As such it would be reported as a **contra** account to the maturity value of the related bonds payable.

Premium on Bonds Payable is not itself a liability—it has no existence apart from the related debt. A lower interest cost results because the proceeds of borrowing exceed the face or maturity amount of the debt. Conceptually, Premium on Bonds Payable is a liability valuation account, that is, an addition to the face or maturity amount of the related liability. It would be reported as an **adjunct** account to the maturity value of the related bonds payable.

In practice, the unamortized portion of a Discount on Bonds Payable has frequently been shown on the balance sheet under Deferred Charges (a separate category under assets or as an item under the heading "Other Assets"). Correspondingly, an unamortized Premium on Bonds Payable has frequently been shown as a deferred credit item under liabilities. This practice tends to obscure the **effective liability** of the bonds by separating the maturity value and the related discount or premium into different parts of the balance sheet. Consequently, the conceptually correct approach as identified above overcomes this criticism. In the United States, *APB Opinion No. 21* requires that bond discounts be reported on the balance sheet as a direct deduction from the face amount of the bonds and premiums as a direct addition to the face amount of the bonds. No such decree exists in Canada although the *CICA Handbook* (in Section 3070, par. .02 on Deferred Charges) states that "major items among the deferred charges should be shown separately, e.g. debt discount and expenses, . . ." As such, the *Handbook* recognizes the acceptability of showing bond discounts as deferred charges. One may, however, choose to show discounts and premiums as valuation accounts directly to the face amount of the bonds, a practice preferred by the authors.

When a corporation has numerous bond issues outstanding, each with its own related discount or premium, the total unamortized discount or premium may be shown net at the bottom of a schedule of listed bond issuances.

Costs of Issuing Bonds

The issuance of bonds involves engraving and printing costs, legal and accounting fees, commissions, promotion expenses, and other similar charges. One practice is to *merge these items with the discount or premium on bonds*, increasing the balance of the discount or decreasing the balance of the premium account. As such, the debt issue costs increase the effective interest rate and interest expense when they are accounted for as part of the amortization of the discount or premium.

Alternatively, it is acceptable to debit debt issue costs to a **deferred charge** account such as Unamortized Bond Issue Costs and amortize them over the life of the debt. This account would appear in the asset section of the balance sheet under the category "Deferred Charges" or "Other Assets." The acceptability of this approach is implied in Section 3070 of the *CICA Handbook*, which indicates that "debt expenses" are an example of Deferred Charges. This procedure is called for in *APB Opinion No. 21* governing U.S. financial reporting. In Canada, however, the choice of balance sheet presentation remains, although the tendency is to treat such costs as deferred charges.

To illustrate the accounting for costs of issuing bonds as a deferred charge, assume that Microchip Inc. sold $20,000,000 of 10-year bonds for $20,795,000 on January 1, 1994 (also the date of the bonds). Costs of issuing the bonds were $245,000. The entries at January 1, 1994 and December 31, 1994 for issuance of the bonds and amortization of the bond issue costs would be as follows:

Objective 8

Appreciate how bond issue costs can be accounted for.

	January 1, 1994	
Cash	20,550,000	
Unamortized Bond Issue Costs	245,000	
Premium on Bonds Payable		795,000
Bonds Payable		20,000,000

	December 31, 1994	
Bond Issue Expense	24,500	
Unamortized Bond Issue Costs		24,500
(To amortize one year of bond issue costs, straight-line method)		

While the bond issue costs could be amortized using the effective interest method, the straight-line method is generally used in practice because it is easier and the results are not materially different.

EXTINGUISHMENT OF DEBT

How is the payment (often referred to as the extinguishment) of debt recorded? If the bonds (or any other form of debt security) are held to maturity, the answer is relatively straightforward—no gain or loss is computed because the amount of cash required to retire the debt will be equal to its carrying amount. Any premium, discount, or issue costs will have been fully amortized at the date the bonds mature. As a result, the carrying amount will be equal to the maturity (face) value of the bonds at that time.

The problems, however, become more complex when the debt is extinguished prior to maturity. Two types of extinguishment are:

1. Reacquisition of debt.

2. Legal defeasance and in-substance (or economic) defeasance.

Reacquisition of Debt

Objective 9

Know how to account for debt extinguishment by various means of reacquisition.

A **reacquisition of debt** can occur either by payment to the creditor or by reacquisition in the open market. A reacquisition could be for all or any portion of the bonds outstanding. *At the time of reacquisition, an unamortized premium or discount and any costs of issue applicable to the bonds must be amortized up to the reacquisition date.*

The amount paid on extinguishment or redemption before maturity, including any call premium and expense of reacquisition, is called the **reacquisition price**. The **net carrying amount** of the bonds on any specified date is the amount payable at maturity adjusted for unamortized premium, discount, and cost of issuance. The difference between the net carrying amount and the reacquisition price is the **gain** or **loss** from extinguishment.

To illustrate, assume that General Bell Corp. issued bonds of a par value of $800,000 due in 20 years, on January 1, 1994 at 97. Bond issue costs of $16,000 were incurred. Ten years after the issue date, the entire issue is redeemed at 101 and cancelled. The loss on redemption is computed as follows (straight-line amortization is used for simplicity).

Reacquisition price ($800,000 × 101/100)		$808,000
Net carrying amount of bonds redeemed:		
Face value	$800,000	
Unamortized discount ($24,000* × 10/20)	(12,000)	
Unamortized issue costs ($16,000 × 10/20)		
(both amortized using straight-line basis)	(8,000)	780,000
Loss on redemption		**$ 28,000**

*$800,000 × (1 − .97)

The entry to record the reacquisition and cancellation of the bonds is:

Bonds Payable	800,000	
Loss on Redemption of Bonds	28,000	
Discount on Bonds Payable		12,000
Unamortized Bond Issue Costs		8,000
Cash		808,000

Had only one-quarter of the bonds been reacquired, the accounts in the above journal entry would be the same but the amounts would be one-quarter of those shown. The accounting for the remaining bonds would be done in the normal manner.

In some cases, bonds may be reacquired by the issuing corporation or its agent or trustee but not formally cancelled. These are known as **treasury bonds** for the issuing corporation. If the above bonds had been required to be held in treasury, the entry to record the transaction is the same as shown except the debit to Bonds Payable would be to an account titled Treasury Bonds. The treasury bonds would then be shown on the balance sheet at their face value as a deduction from the bonds payable issued to arrive at a net figure representing bonds payable outstanding. When they are sold or cancelled, the Treasury Bonds account would be credited.

It is sometimes advantageous for a corporation to acquire its entire bond issue outstanding and replace it with a new bond issue bearing a lower rate of interest. The replacement of an existing issuance with a new one is called **refunding**. If refunding takes place prior to the maturity date of a bond issue, a difference between the fair market value of the new bonds issued and the net carrying amount of the refunded issue is likely to result. When this occurs, there are three alternative approaches to accounting for the amount of the difference:

1. Treat it as a gain or loss on bond refunding in the current year's income statement.

2. Amortize it over the remaining life of the bonds that have been refunded.

3. Amortize it over the life of the new bonds issued.

In Canada, the choice of approach is left to judgement as the *CICA Handbook* contains no recommendations regarding a preferred method. In the United States, only the first alternative is permitted and, therefore, a gain or loss resulting from early extinguishment of a debt may not be amortized to future periods. This conclusion is based on the opinion that differing reasons for early redemption or differing means by which the bonds are redeemed should have no bearing on how to account for the loss or gain.[12]

Legal and In-Substance Defeasance

Reacquisition of debt results in removing the obligation from the books because the company buys the debt back through payment to the creditor either directly or through the market. *Another means of debt extinguishment is to have the company provide for the future repayment of one or more of its long-term debt issues by placing cash or purchased securities in an irrevocable trust, the principal and interest of which are pledged and are sufficient to pay off the principal and interest of its own debt as it matures.*

There are several reasons for arranging such an extinguishment. *First,* the debt may be removed from the balance sheet without actually being repurchased. Actual purchase is sometimes a problem because (1) it may be costly if a high call premium is required to be paid or (2) much of the debt may be publicly held and may therefore be difficult to buy back in large quantities. In addition to these sound economic reasons, elimination of debt from the balance sheet by such arrangements may be advantageous in terms of contractual commitments (such as meeting a specified debt to equity ratio), reducing interest expense reported in the income statement, or obtaining favourable terms on issuance of new debt. *Second,* because the cost of the purchased securities is usually less than the carrying value of the company's debt (as interest rates rise, the fair value of the outstanding debt falls below carrying value), the company records a gain on its income statement.

Accounting for such arrangements, particularly regarding the issue of whether or not the debt and related interest expense should be removed from the financial statements, is controversial. The arguments regarding various accounting treatments focus on whether the terms of the arrangement result in legal defeasance or in-substance defeasance.

> *Objective 10*
>
> Understand legal and in-substance defeasance as a means of extinguishing debt and recognize the accounting issues involved.

Legal Defeasance. Legal defeasance means the *debtor is released from all legal liability as a result of the arrangement.* This would occur when (1) the party receiving the cash or securities (e.g., the trustee) agrees to assume the debtor's obligations and (2) the creditors agree that the trustee will be responsible for paying the principal and interest. In such situations "it is appropriate for the debtor to remove the liability from its balance sheet since it has fully discharged its contractual obligations and the creditor has not retained any right of recourse against the debtor."[13] Consequently, a legal defeasance would be accounted for in a manner similar to that illustrated for reacquisition of debt except that the carrying value of any securities provided to the trustee would be removed from the company's assets.

To illustrate, assume that PanCan Inc. deposited government securities which had cost $252 million in an irrevocable trust to solely satisfy the scheduled interest and principal requirements on a long-term debt carried at $269 million. The arrangement satisfies the requirements of a legal defeasance. As such PanCan would make the following entry:

Long-Term Debt Payable	269,000,000	
Investment in Securities		252,000,000
Gain from Legal Defeasance		17,000,000

---

[12] "Early Extinguishment of Debt," *Opinions of the Accounting Principles Board No. 26* (New York: AICPA, 1972), par. 20.

[13] "Financial Instruments," *Exposure Draft of the Accounting Standards Board* (Toronto: CICA, September 1991), par. .37.

In-Substance Defeasance. When a company deposits cash and securities in an irrevocable trust which is to be used to pay the principal and interest obligation on a debt of the company, *but the creditor is not a party to the arrangement and may not even know it exists*, a legal defeasance does not occur. It is argued, however, that the end result is, in substance, economically the same as a legal defeasance. Hence, such an arrangement is called an **in-substance defeasance**. The fact that the creditor has not released the obligation of the debtor to pay the principal and interest may not be considered as a material risk because the assets placed in trust are sufficient to cover known payments contracted for in the future. Consequently, many conclude that an in-substance defeasance should be accounted for like a legal defeasance (i.e. as a debt extinguishment), with appropriate disclosure of a contingent, but remote, liability.

Air Canada has applied this accounting treatment to its in-substance defeasances as is indicated by the following excerpt.

**From the notes to the December 31, 1992
financial statements of Air Canada (in millions of dollars)**

5. Long-Term Debt (millions of dollars)

b) In 1990 and 1989, the Corporation concluded agreements with a substantial U.S. financial institution where, upon payment by the Corporation, the financial institution assumed liability for scheduled payments relating to certain long-term obligations in amounts of $98 in 1990 and $107 in 1989 and interest thereon. These obligations (which amount to $92 and $100 respectively at December 31, 1992) are considered extinguished for financial reporting purposes and have been removed from the Corporation's statement of financial position. Until the assumed liabilities have been fully discharged by the financial institution, the Corporation remains contingently liable for such obligations.

While in-substance defeasances occur, accounting for them has not yet been covered in the *CICA Handbook*. Air Canada's accounting treatment follows *Statement No. 76* issued by the FASB in the United States.[14]

Statement No. 76 is controversial and has been subjected to much criticism. Dissenters believe that gain or loss recognition should not be extended to situations wherein the debtor is not legally released from being the primary obligor of the debt obligation. They contend that "the setting aside of assets in trust does not, in and of itself, constitute either the disposition of assets with potential gain or loss recognition or the satisfaction of a liability with potential gain or loss recognition."[15] In other words, committing specific assets to a single purpose might ensure that the debt is serviced in a timely fashion, but that event alone just matches up cash flows; it does not satisfy, eliminate, or extinguish the obligation. For a debt to be satisfied, the creditor must be satisfied. This is not the case in an in-substance defeasance.

The AcSB's *Exposure Draft* on "Financial Instruments" agreed with the opinions of the dissenters of the FASB's *Statement No. 76* by concluding an in-substance defeasance is *not* a debt extinguishment.[16] Since the debtor is not released from the obligation to pay principal and interest, the risks associated with the obligation have not been transferred. Therefore, the assets deposited in trust and the debt obligation they are pledged to service should be reported separately as an asset and liability respectively.

---

[14] "Extinguishment of Debt," *Statement of Financial Accounting Standards No. 76* (Stamford, CT: FASB, 1983).
[15] *Ibid.*, p. 5.
[16] *Exposure Draft*, "Financial Instruments," par. .038.

The "Financial Instruments" *Exposure Draft* contains many complex and controversial recommendations. If and when its provisions become part of the *CICA Handbook*, accounting for insubstance defeasance as done by Air Canada would no longer be acceptable.

LONG-TERM NOTES PAYABLE

The difference between a current note payable and a long-term note payable is the maturity date. As discussed in Chapter 13, short-term notes payable are expected to be paid within a year or the operating cycle, whichever is longer. Long-term notes are similar in substance to bonds in that both have fixed maturity dates and carry either a stated or implicit interest rate. However, notes do not trade as readily as bonds in the organized public securities markets. Noncorporate and smaller corporate enterprises issue notes as their long-term instruments, while larger corporations issue both long-term notes and bonds.

Accounting for notes and bonds is quite similar. Like a bond, a note is valued at the present value of its future interest and principal cash flows with any discount or premium being amortized over the life of the note. Whenever the face amount of the note does not reasonably represent the present value of the consideration given or received in the exchange, the arrangement must be carefully evaluated to appropriately record the exchange and the subsequent interest. This is most apparent when the note is noninterest bearing or when the note has a stated interest rate that is different from the rate of interest appropriate for the transaction at the date of issuance.

Accounting for long-term notes will be examined under the following headings:

1. Notes issued solely for cash.

2. Notes issued for cash, but with some right or privilege also being exchanged. For example, a corporation may lend a supplier cash that is receivable five years hence with no stated interest, in exchange for which the supplier agrees to make products available to the lender at lower than prevailing market prices.

3. Notes issued in a noncash exchange for property, goods, or services.

As one might expect, accounting for long-term notes payable parallels accounting for long-term notes receivable as presented in Chapter 7.

Notes Issued Solely for Cash

When the effective interest on a note is equal to its stated rate, the note sells at its face value. When the stated rate is different from the effective interest (e.g., the note is noninterest bearing or has an unrealistic stated rate), the cash proceeds will be different from the face value of the note. As indicated earlier, the difference between the face value and the cash proceeds received is a discount or a premium that should be amortized over the life of a note.

When a note is issued solely for cash, the total interest expense is equal to the interest paid based on the stated rate times the face amount plus any discount or minus any premium. In such situations, the effective interest rate is that rate which equates the present value of future interest and principal amounts to be paid with the cash proceeds received from the issuance of the note.

An example of such a transaction was Beneficial Corporation's offering of $150 million of zero-coupon notes maturing in eight years. With a face value of $1,000 each, these notes sold for $327—a deep discount of $673 each. Beneficial amortized the discount over the eight-year life of the notes, using an effective interest rate of 15%. The present value of each note was the cash proceeds of $327. The 15% effective interest rate was calculated by determining the rate that equates the $1,000 maturity value to be received in eight years to these proceeds.[17]

> *Objective 11*
>
> Understand the nature of long-term notes payable, know various circumstances resulting in their issuance, and be able to apply the appropriate accounting.

---

[17] Derived using the present value of an amount of 1 in Table A-2 of the Appendix:

$327 = $1,000 $p_{\overline{8}|i}$

$P_{\overline{8}|i}$ = $327/$1,000 = .327

.327 = 15% column interest rate at the 8 year row.

Notes Exchanged for Cash and Some Right or Privilege

Sometimes when a note is issued, additional rights or privileges are given to the recipient of the note. For example, a corporation may receive cash and issue a face value noninterest-bearing note payable that is to be repaid over five years with no stated interest. In exchange it agrees to sell merchandise to the lender at less than the prevailing prices. In this circumstance, the difference between the present value of the payable (determined using a market rate of interest applicable to the issuer) and the amount of cash received could be recorded by the issuer of the note (borrower/supplier) simultaneously as a discount (debit) on the note and as unearned revenue (credit) on the future sales. The discount would be amortized as a charge to interest expense over the life of the note. The unearned revenue, equal in amount to the discount, reflects a partial prepayment for sales transactions that will occur over the next five years. This unearned revenue would be recognized as revenue when sales are made to the lender over the next five years.

To illustrate, assume that a company receives $100,000 cash in exchange for a five-year, non-interest-bearing note with a face or maturity value of $100,000. The appropriate rate of interest is determined to be 10%. The conditions of the note provide that the recipient of the note (lender/customer) can purchase $500,000 of merchandise from the issuer of the note (borrower/supplier) at something less than regular selling price over the next five years. To record the loan, the issuer records a discount of $37,908, the difference between the $100,000 face amount of the note and its present value of $62,092 ($100,000 × .62092 the present value for an amount of $1 received in five years using 10%). As the supplier of the merchandise, the issuer also records a credit to unearned revenue of $37,908. The issuer's journal entry is:

Cash	100,000	
Discount on Notes Payable	37,908	
Notes Payable		100,000
Unearned Revenue		37,908

The Discount on Notes Payable is subsequently amortized to interest expense using the effective interest or straight-line method. The Unearned Revenue is recognized as revenue from the sale of merchandise and is prorated on the basis that each period's sales to the lender-customer bear to the total sales to that customer for the term of the note. In this situation, the write-off of the discount and the recognition of the unearned revenue are at different amounts.

Notes Issued in Noncash Transactions

The third type of situation involves the issuance of a note for some noncash consideration, such as property, goods, or services. When this occurs in a bargained transaction entered into at arm's length, the stated interest rate is presumed to be fair unless:

1. No interest rate is stated, or

2. The stated interest rate is unreasonable, or

3. The face amount of the note is materially different from the current cash sales price for the same or similar items acquired or from the current market value of the debt instrument.

In these circumstances, the present value of the debt instrument can be measured as the fair value of the property, goods, or services or by an amount that reasonably approximates the market value of the note. *The implicit interest element, other than that evidenced by any stated rate of interest, is the difference between the face amount of the note and the fair value of the property, goods, or services received.*

For example, assume that Scenic Development Corp. sold land having a fair market value of $200,000 to Health Spa Inc., in exchange for Health Spa's five-year, $293,860 noninterest-bearing note. The $200,000 represents the present value of the $293,860 note discounted at 8% for five years. If the transaction is recorded on the sale date at the face amount of the note, $293,860, by both parties, Health Spa's land account and Scenic's sales would be overstated by $93,860, the interest for five years at an effective rate of 8%. Interest revenue to Scenic and interest expense to Health Spa for the five-year period correspondingly would be understated by $93,860.

The difference between the fair market value of the land and the face amount of the note represents interest. Therefore, the transaction should be recorded at the exchange date as follows.

Entries for Noncash Note Transactions

Health Spa Inc. Books			Scenic Development Corp. Books		
Land	200,000		Notes Receivable	293,860	
Discount on Notes			Discount on Notes		
Payable	93,860		Receivable		93,860
Notes Payable		293,860	Sales		200,000

During the five-year life of the note, Health Spa amortizes annually a portion of the discount of $93,860 as a charge to interest expense. Scenic Development would record interest revenue totalling $93,860 over the five-year period by also amortizing the discount. The effective interest method is appropriate, although the straight-line method may be used if the results obtained are not materially different.

Imputing an Interest Rate

In each of the previously illustrated situations, the effective or real interest rate was evident or determinable by other factors involved in the exchange, such as the fair market value of what was either given or received. If, however, the fair value of the property, goods, or services is not determinable and if the debt instrument has no ready market, the problem of determining the present value of the debt instrument is more difficult. To estimate the present value of a debt instrument under such circumstances, an applicable interest rate is approximated that may differ from the stated interest rate. This process of interest rate approximation is called **imputation,** and the resulting interest rate is called an **imputed interest rate.** The imputed interest rate is used to establish the present value of the debt instrument by discounting, at that rate, all future payments on the debt. Once this information is determined, accounting for the debt would follow in the usual manner (i.e. as previously illustrated).

The choice of a rate requires the exercise of judgement, considering such factors as the credit standing of the issuer, restrictive covenants, collateral, payments and other terms pertaining to the debt, and the existing prime interest rate. *Determination of the imputed interest rate is made at the time the debt instrument is issued; any subsequent changes in prevailing interest rates are ignored.*

Mortgage Notes Payable

The most common form of long-term note payable is a mortgage note payable. A **mortgage note payable** is a promissory note secured by a document called a mortgage that pledges title to property as security for the loan. Mortgage notes payable tend to be used more frequently by proprietorships and partnerships than by corporations, as corporations usually find that note and bond issues offer advantages in obtaining large loans.

On the balance sheet, the liability should be reported using a title such as "Mortgage Notes Payable" or "Notes Payable—Secured," with a brief disclosure of the property pledged in notes to the financial statements.

Mortgages may be payable in full at maturity or in instalments over the life of the loan. If payable at maturity, the mortgage payable is shown as a long-term liability on the balance sheet until

Objective 12

Appreciate what a mortgage is and how it is reported in the financial statements.

such time as the approaching maturity date warrants showing it as a current liability. If it is payable in instalments, the current instalments due are shown as current liabilities, with the remainder shown as a long-term liability.

Short-Term Obligations Expected to Be Refinanced

Some short-term obligations are often expected to be refinanced on a long-term basis. While an enterprise may intend to refinance the obligations on a long-term basis and can demonstrate an ability to consummate the refinancing, the *CICA Handbook* requires that *a contractual arrangement must exist regarding the refinancing before such items can be reported as noncurrent liabilities.*[18]

REPORTING LONG-TERM DEBT

Objective 13

Know the requirements for disclosure of long-term debt in financial statements and how they are met.

Section 3210 of the *CICA Handbook* includes the following recommendations regarding presentations of long-term debt in the financial statements:

- For bonds, debentures, and similar securities, the title of the issue, the interest rate, the maturity date, the amount outstanding, and the existence of sinking fund, redemption, and conversion provisions should be disclosed. For mortgages and other long-term debt, similar particulars should be provided to the extent practical.

- The aggregate amount of payments estimated to be required in each of the next five years to meet sinking fund or retirement provisions should be disclosed.

- Any portion of long-term debt obligation payable within a year out of current funds should be included in current liabilities.

- Any of the company's own securities purchased and not yet cancelled should be shown separately as a deduction from the relative liability.

- If any of the liabilities are secured, they should be stated separately and the fact that they are secured should be indicated.

- The details of any defaults of the company in principal, interest, sinking fund, or redemption provisions with respect to any outstanding obligation should be disclosed.

- The income statement should distinguish interest on indebtedness initially incurred for a term of more than one year (including the amortization of debt discount or premium and issue expenses).

Companies that have numerous types of long-term debt usually report only the total amount in the balance sheet and support this with comments and schedules in the accompanying notes. Note disclosures generally meet and often exceed the requirements of the *Handbook*. The illustration drawn from financial statements of Donahue Inc. shown on page 697 provides an example of such reporting. Also, see note 7 on long-term liabilities in the financial statements of Moore Corporation Limited presented in Appendix 5A. The note disclosing long-term liabilities can be very long and complex for companies such as Air Canada and Alcan Aluminium Limited, which have many long-term debt instruments and utilize a variety of financing arrangements (e.g., variable rates, foreign sources, swaps, defeasances).

The variety and complexity of long-term debt arrangements have grown considerably with the consequence that many accounting and reporting problems are emerging. Many believe that resolving accounting issues related to new types of financial instruments and the use of off-balance-sheet financing are major financial reporting issues facing the profession today (discussed in Appendix 14A). Likely many other problems associated with long-term debt will come forth. Resolving such issues will not be easy, as our understanding of long-term financing and the components of a con-

---

[18] *CICA Handbook*, Section 1510, par. .06.

From the notes to the 1992 financial statements of Donahue Inc.

6. Long-term Debt (thousands of dollars)

	Effective interest rates	Years of maturity	1992	1991
First mortgage bond (a)				
in US currency ($15,187 US)				
($60,416 US in 1991)	9.3%	1993–1997	$ 19,304	$ 70,088
in CAN currency			—	13,125
Bank term loans			—	81,302
Bank revolving credit facility (b)				
($100,000 US) ($70,000 US in 1991)	5.9%	1994–1999	127,110	81,207
Debentures payable	6%	1993–1997	12,500	15,000
Notes payable	4.7%	1993–1997	48,000	55,000
Loan, noninterest bearing		1994–2004	3,500	3,500
Other	various	1993–1994	264	1,302
			210,678	320,524
Long-term debt due within one year			19,498	44,451
			$191,180	$276,073

(a) The first mortgage bond is secured by a specific charge on fixed assets, rights and contracts of a subsidiary and by a floating charge on all other assets. In addition, the Trust Deed governing this bond contains certain restrictions including conditions relating to the payment of dividends.

(b) The bank revolving credit facility will become a bank term loan at the end of the renewal period on June 30, 1994. The Company may, with the agreement of its lenders, extend the renewal period on an annual basis. The credit agreement contains usual covenants such as maintaining specific financial ratios and certain conditions relating to the payment of dividends.

The annual instalments on long-term debt payable for the next five years under the actual terms of the long-term debt, assuming that the bank revolving credit facility is not extended, are:

1993	$ 9,673	CAN and	$ 7,729	US
1994	$ 9,741	CAN and	$17,458	US
1995	$ 9,650	CAN and	$20,000	US
1996	$ 9,650	CAN and	$20,000	US
1997	$22,650	CAN and	$20,000	US

ceptual framework to guide accounting are sufficiently imprecise that arguments can always be made for accounting for a financial instrument in a particular manner or, perhaps, not accounting for it at all. Therefore, sound judgement must continue to prevail in deciding on such things as "substance over form" when reporting relevant and reliable information to users of the financial statements.

FUNDAMENTAL CONCEPTS

1. Long-term debt consists of obligations of an entity arising from past transactions or events for which settlement will not take place within the next operating cycle, or within a year if there are several operating cycles within a year.

2. A long-term debt usually has a specified maturity date, at which time the face value must be paid. Such debt normally bears an interest cost that must be paid periodically. A debt instrument confers no voting rights on the owner in most circumstances. These characteristics distinguish long-term debt financing from ownership equity financing, although the differences can become hazy in some situations.

3. Bonds payable can have a variety of characteristics. The particular characteristics of an issue are specified in a contract known as a bond indenture. Such characteristics are concerned with security provided, term to maturity, conversion rights, transferability, interest rates and dates, and call privileges.

4. Considerable time, effort, and cost may be incurred in order to plan and prepare bonds for issuance. Accounting for and reporting of bonds begin at the time of issuance, flow through the life of the bonds in terms of interest payments and accruals, and end when the bonds mature or are otherwise extinguished.

5. Issuance of bonds requires appropriate recognition of the liability, any discount or premium, and any accrual of interest since the last interest date.

6. Interest expense related to bonds is recorded on each interest date and at year end, if other than an interest date. Determination of the interest expense reflects an appropriate amortization of any premium or discount on the bonds. The effective interest method for amortizing a premium or discount is theoretically superior to the straight-line method because it results in interest expense being a constant rate multiplied by the carrying value of the debt. Additionally, this method results in the carrying value of the debt on the balance sheet being equal to the present value of future cash payments discounted at the effective interest rate on the issuance date. The straight-line method is simpler and can be used if its results do not differ materially from those of the effective interest method.

7. Extinguishment of debt results in the removal of the liability and any related accounts from the records. At this time, any discount, premium, or issue costs applicable to the debt should be amortized up to the extinguishment date. Removal of the liability and related accounts may result in a gain or loss which would likely be shown on the income statement as a component of income before extraordinary items.

8. Long-term notes payable are similar in substance to bonds in terms of having a fixed maturity date and an interest rate. As such, they are accounted for in a similar manner. This chapter illustrated particular situations involving the issuance of notes for cash, cash and some future right or privilege, and in noncash exchanges. Mortgages are a common type of long-term notes payable.

9. Reporting of long-term debt in financial statements requires an indication of the nature of the liabilities, maturity dates, interest rates, call provisions, conversion privileges, restrictions imposed by the borrower, and assets pledged as security. Disclosure of such information is usually done in the notes. Long-term debt that matures within one year should be reported as a current liability, unless retirement is to be accomplished with other than current assets. If the debt is to be financed, converted into shares, or is to be retired from a bond retirement fund, it should continue to be reported as noncurrent and accompanied with a note explaining the method to be used in its liquidation.

10. Discussion of the nature of, and problems of accounting for, some unique financial instruments, off-balance-sheet financing, and troubled debt restructuring is presented in Appendix 14A. In Appendix 14B the complexities of accounting for serial bonds are examined, which can serve as an additional and review illustration of the basic procedures applied when accounting for bonds.

APPENDIX 14A
Complex Issues Regarding Accounting for Long-Term Liabilities

Bonds, mortgages, and notes have been traditional liability instruments used by organizations to obtain long-term financing. While accounting issues related to their recognition, measurement, disclosure, and extinguishment are important, they have been basically resolved in the manner described in this chapter. In the past decade, however, there has been a significant increase in the variety of financial instruments and arrangements being used by Canadian companies. Examples include bonds that are convertible into shares, bear no interest, are issued in perpetuity, or have variable interest rates depending on some formula and base; shares that have no voting rights but are redeemable by the investor and carry specific preferential rights for dividends; defeasance arrangements; interest rate swaps; and restructuring of debt arrangements for a troubled loan situation. Such instruments and arrangements provide unique accounting challenges for which there is little specific guidance provided in the *CICA Handbook*. At the time of writing this book, however, the AcSB had issued an *Exposure Draft* dealing with accounting for financial instruments.[19] This document proposed some fairly complex treatments for resolving accounting issues associated with complex financial instruments and arrangements.

The purpose of this appendix is not to examine the details of the *Exposure Draft*. Rather, the objective is to identify three of the many important issues contained in the *Exposure Draft* in order to provide an understanding of some critical and current problems facing the accounting profession regarding the recognition, measurement, and disclosure of long-term liabilities. The three issues are:

1. Recognition of substance over form.

2. Off-balance-sheet financing.

3. Troubled debt restructuring.

RECOGNITION OF SUBSTANCE OVER FORM

A primary quality of accounting information identified in the conceptual framework (see Chapter 2) is *reliability*. A component of reliability is representational faithfulness, which means that a transaction or event affecting an entity is presented in the financial statements in a manner that is in agreement with the underlying economic consequences of the transaction or event. This concept was highlighted in the *Exposure Draft* on financial instruments which stated that the "substance of a financial instrument, rather than its form, governs its balance sheet classification."[20] Consequently, the appropriate classification would depend on the instrument's form being consistent with the definition of a financial liability or an equity instrument.

The *Exposure Draft* defined these terms as follows:

A **financial liability** is any liability that is a contractual obligation:
 i) to deliver cash or another financial asset to another entity; or
 ii) to exchange financial instruments with another entity under conditions that are potentially unfavourable.
An **equity instrument** is any contract that evidences a residual interest in the assets of an entity after deducting all its liabilities.[21]

In essence, a financial liability exists when there is a contractual requirement to pay interest and maturity value on specified dates. An equity instrument, in its simplest form, has no such requirement; dividends may be paid at the discretion of the board of directors and capital invested may be returned to the investors on dissolution of the corporation only if assets are available after all liabilities have been paid.

---

[19] *Exposure Draft*, "Financial Instruments".
[20] *Ibid.*, par. .044.
[21] *Ibid.*, par. .005.

Classification as a liability or equity is not always straightforward. This is because some financial instruments may be of the legal form of debt or equity but their economic substance is that of equity or debt respectively. Additionally, a financial instrument may be compound in that its substance consists of both debt and equity components. When financial instruments such as these exist, several interesting and challenging accounting issues result. For illustrative purposes, three examples are considered: subordinated perpetual debt, term-preferred shares, and convertible bonds.

Subordinated Perpetual Debt

Air Canada is an example of a company that has issued **subordinated perpetual debt**. The principal is not secured, is payable only when the corporation is liquidated, and is paid only after all other debt has been paid. Interest is at a specified rate but is subordinated to all interest on other corporate debt.

While the form of this financial instrument is that of a debt (liability), the question is whether or not it is, in economic substance, an equity instrument. It is called "debt" and bears an interest rate. However, the principal has no due date except in the event of corporate liquidation, is unsecured, and is paid only when holders of liabilities are paid in full. These characteristics are similar to traditional preferred shares in terms of being a residual interest in the assets of the corporation. Also, because the interest is subordinated to the payment of interest on other financial liabilities and is not guaranteed, it may be regarded like a stated dividend on preferred shares. Given this thinking about the economic substance of subordinated perpetual debt, it is possible to conclude that it is appropriate to present it as an equity instrument in the financial statements, particularly given the direction in the *Exposure Draft* on financial instruments.

If this occurred, the subordinated perpetual debt could be shown in the shareholders' equity section of the balance sheet, like preferred shares. Alternatively, it may be shown as something between the long-term liabilities and shareholders' equity classifications as is sometimes done with items called "minority interest" and "deferred income taxes" (see Chapter 19).

An even more intriguing accounting issue is how to report any related interest cost. If the arguments that subordinated perpetual debt is an equity instrument are followed through, it would seem that the interest would be appropriately classified as a distribution of earnings, like dividends, and reported in the statement of retained earnings. There would, consequently, be no interest expense reported in income statement. This is the recommended treatment in the *Exposure Draft*.[22]

As the *Exposure Draft* recommendations were not yet required GAAP in Canada, Air Canada, in its 1992 financial statements, disclosed its subordinated perpetual debt as a line item between liabilities and shareholders' equity and treated the interest as an expense in the income statement.

Term-Preferred Shares

The example regarding subordinated perpetual debt considered the situation where a financial instrument had the legal form of a liability but contained provisions which make it, in substance, equity. The reverse can also occur. Term-preferred shares provide an example of a financial instrument which has the legal form of equity, but which carry provisions that may lead to the conclusion that its economic substance is that of a liability.

As will be examined in Chapter 15, preferred shares are considered to be a residual interest (shareholders' equity item) in the assets of a corporation. Various rights, privileges, and restrictions can accompany a particular issue of preferred shares. While traditional preferred shares are sold to provide a perpetual source of financing until the corporation liquidates, some preferred shares are issued for a limited period of time. Forms of such limitation on their life occur when the company can buy them back from holders (redeemable), when the holder can require the company to buy them back (retractable), and when the company is required to retire all or a specified proportion of the shares on some future date. Because such shares are limited in the term of their lives, they are referred to as **term-preferred shares**. In essence, they carry a contractual provision to deliver cash to the owner. This feature suggests they be treated as a financial liability and not as an equity instrument according to definitions provided in the *Exposure Draft* on financial instruments. Term-

---

[22] *Ibid.*, par. .049.

preferred shares may also entitle holders to specified dividends which, if not declared in a given year, are carried forward to the next year before any dividends can be paid to common shareholders (i.e. they are cumulative). Therefore, it may be argued that these dividends are akin to interest on liabilities. Consequently, judging such shares to be of the nature of financial liabilities would be further enhanced.

If term-preferred shares were considered financial liabilities in substance, then they would be presented accordingly on a balance sheet. Additionally, the dividends would become an expense, like interest, on the income statement and would not be shown in the statement of retained earnings as a distribution of income.

The accounting recommendations proposed in the *Exposure Draft* on financial instruments were not Canadian GAAP at the time of writing this book. Consequently, corporations have treated term-preferred shares as an equity instrument in their financial statements.[23]

Convertible Bonds

A **convertible bond** allows the holder to convert the bond into other securities (e.g., preferred or common shares) of the issuing corporation. Conversion rights specify when the bond may be converted and the number of shares into which it may be converted.

Traditionally, the proceeds from sale of convertible bonds are linked entirely to the bond liability. As indicated in this chapter, any difference between these proceeds and the bonds' maturity value results in a premium or discount. The discount or premium is then amortized to interest expense. When the bonds or a portion of them are converted, their carrying value is removed from the bond liability and transferred to the appropriate share capital account.

The *Exposure Draft* on financial instruments recommends a substantially different recognition, measurement, and disclosure approach for such bonds. This different approach is based on the principle of accounting for substance over form. The *Exposure Draft* appropriately argues that a convertible bond comprises two components: a financial liability (a contractual arrangement to deliver cash) and an equity instrument (the right to convert to share equity).[24] Consequently, each component should be accounted for and reported separately.

To do this, the proceeds received for the instrument as a whole must be apportioned between the liability and equity component. This may be done by determining the present value of the maturity value and scheduled interest payments on the bond using the market rate of interest prevailing at the issuance date for similar liabilities which do not have an associated equity instrument.[25] Generally, bonds with a conversion right can be sold bearing an interest rate less than a bond without such a right. Therefore, the determined present value (using a market rate of interest for bonds without the conversion right) would likely be lower than the actual proceeds received. The difference between the proceeds and the determined present value would be assigned to the conversion right.

On issuance, the Bonds Payable account would be credited for the maturity value and any difference between the determined present value and the maturity value would be recorded as a discount or premium. Once this has been determined, the bonds would be accounted for as demonstrated in the chapter.

Also, on issuance of convertible bonds, the difference between the proceeds and determined present value of the bonds would be recognized as a credit to the equity instrument. This account could be called Conversion Rights and would be shown as a component of shareholders' equity (possibly Contributed Capital) in the balance sheet.

To illustrate these notions, assume ED Inc. issued 7% convertible bonds with a maturity value of $1,000,000. The company received proceeds of $1,050,000. If these bonds did not have the conversion feature, an effective interest rate of 8% would have to be paid. The present value of the 7% stated interest payments and maturity value discounted at 8% is $978,000. Therefore, the entry to record the liability and equity components of this financial instrument would be as follows.

---

[23] Treatment of term-preferred shares as an equity instrument was recommended in *Term-Preferred Shares, Accounting Guideline* (Toronto: CICA, December 1977). This document recognized many conceptual issues needed to be addressed before a final conclusion was reached but provided guidance in order to enhance conformity of reporting term-preferred shares by companies. *Financial Reporting in Canada— 1991* (Toronto: CICA, 1991) indicates that term-preferred shares were disclosed by 40 surveyed companies in 1990, 47 in 1989, and 49 in 1988 and 1987. These shares were disclosed as part of share capital in shareholders' equity, but set out separately from other classes of share capital.

[24] *Exposure Draft*, "Financial Instruments," par. .029.

[25] *Ibid.*, par. .030.

Cash		1,050,000	
Discount on Bonds Payable		22,000	
Bonds Payable			1,000,000
Conversion Rights			72,000

When conversion takes place, the appropriate carrying value (maturity value less applicable discount) of the converted bonds and the conversion rights would be transferred to the applicable Preferred or Common Shares account.

Concluding Comment

The examples presented illustrate the underlying issues related to being able to recognize substance over form when accounting for financial instruments. Only three types of instruments were considered. Many more and complex instruments exist. These examples, however, are hopefully helpful in recognizing a fundamental concept in the *Exposure Draft* which will have to be applied in accounting for a variety of specific financial instruments. Clearly, professional judgement will be a major determinant of accounting decisions made in particular circumstances.

Because many financial instruments are complex, it is important that their nature be disclosed in the notes to financial statements. Appropriate disclosure is a key part of recommendations proposed in the *Exposure Draft*.

OFF-BALANCE-SHEET FINANCING

Off-balance-sheet financing is an attempt to borrow monies in such a way that the obligations are not recorded or reported in the balance sheet.[26] It is an issue of extreme importance to accountants as well as general management. As one writer sarcastically noted, "The basic drives of humans are few: to get enough food, to find shelter, and to keep debt off the balance sheet."

We have already discussed some off-balance-sheet financing techniques. In Chapter 7, for example, transfers of receivables to third parties with recourse may be either reported as sales of the receivable or as a borrowing, depending on the facts. When it is deemed to be a sale, no liability is recorded on the balance sheet. In this chapter, in-substance defeasance is viewed as an off-balance-sheet financing transaction when the consequence is that the debt is not reported on the balance sheet even though it is not legally retired.

Two additional off-balance-sheet approaches are considered below:

1. Interest rate swaps.

2. Project financing arrangements.

In subsequent chapters, other off-balance-sheet financing transactions (leasing and pensions) are examined.

Interest Rate Swaps

Comments similar to the following continue to appear in the financial press:

> With today's volatile interest rates, you can be certain of one thing. Nothing is certain. However, you have one option that could considerably lessen the risks involved.

> Hedging flourishes as rates fluctuate.

> If you're confused about the timing of economic recovery and how that affects the nation's credit markets, you might want to hedge your bet. Whether interest rates are headed up or down, diversify now, and you can ride out the storm safely.

As these comments indicate, interest rates are volatile and companies often want protection against their fluctuations. As a result, many companies use sophisticated types of financial instruments such as interest rate futures, forward rate agreements, and interest rate swaps to hedge their bets.

---

[26] James L. Goodfellow, "Now You See Them, Now You Don't," *CA Magazine*, December 1988, pp. 16–23, provides an interesting insight into the motivation for off-balance-sheet financing and the accounting problems related to reporting substance over form.

A corporation in the early 1980s went to its investment banker and presented the following problem: It wanted to borrow at a fixed rate for protection, but either such borrowing was too expensive or no suitable market existed. The investment banker found a borrower who had a fixed-rate loan but wanted a floating rate. The match was made, the two companies swapped interest payments, and the **interest rate swap** was born.

Many companies find interest rate swaps a convenient way to manage interest rate exposure. A company with a substantial amount of variable rate debt may wish to swap into fixed-rate debt to limit its exposure to rising interest rates. Second, some companies with lower credit ratings often cannot borrow in the fixed-rate market but can swap into it.[27]

Swap participants only report on their balance sheets their original borrowings. As a result, swaps as well as many other types of financial instruments give rise to off-balance-sheet financing because the right to receive interest payments and the obligation to make interest payments by the swap agreement is not reported on the balance sheet. These rights and obligations are related to performance in the future, not past completed economic transactions. As such, swap agreements are a form of unexecuted contract.

At the time of writing this book, no specific guidance on how to recognize and disclose interest rate swaps existed in the *CICA Handbook*. Consequently, the general provisions regarding disclosure of contractual obligations (Section 3280 of the *Handbook*) would apply. For arrangements such as interest swaps, this disclosure would require a note regarding the particulars of obligations that are significant because they can govern the level of a certain type of expenditure (i.e. interest) for a considerable period into the future.[28]

The *Exposure Draft* on financial instruments did address interest rate swap accounting and disclosure in a fair amount of depth. While many of the specifics are beyond the scope of this book, it is likely that if the concepts in the *Exposure Draft* are adopted into the *CICA Handbook*, the type of disclosure for financial instruments and arrangements with off-balance-sheet risk would be in the form of a note including the following:

1. The face, contract, or notional principal amount.

2. The nature and terms of the instruments and a discussion of their credit and market risk, cash requirements, and related accounting policies.

3. The accounting loss the entity would incur if any party to the financial instrument failed completely to perform according to the terms of the contract and the collateral or other security, if any, for the amount due proved to be of no value to the entity.

4. The entity's policy for requiring collateral or other security on financial instruments it accepts and a description of collateral on instruments presently held.

These disclosures will become even more important as new and different types of financial instruments continue to be developed.

The following excerpt from the notes to the 1992 financial statements of Abitibi-Price Inc. provides an example of disclosures made regarding interest rate swaps.

From the notes of Abitibi-Price Inc.'s December 31, 1992 financial statements.

12. Long-term debt
(b) Interest is at a rate approximating LIBOR. The loan is secured by an Abitibi-Price Inc. Series L Debenture. The Company has entered into interest rate swap agreements, covering the period to 1994, for a principal amount of U.S. $150 million at an average fixed interest rate of 8.9%. In the event of nonperformance by the other parties to the interest rate swap agreements, the Company would be exposed to floating interest rates.

---

[27] It was estimated by the International Swap Dealers Association that more than $1.4 trillion of interest swaps occurred in 1990 in the international market.

[28] *CICA Handbook*, Section 3280, par. .01(d).

Project Financing Arrangements

Project financing arrangements arise when (1) two or more entities form another entity to construct an operating plant that will be used by both parties, (2) the new entity borrows funds to construct the project and repays the debt from proceeds received from the project, and (3) payment of the debt is guaranteed by the companies that formed the new entity. The advantage of such an arrangement is that the companies that formed the new entity do not have to report the liability on their books. To illustrate, assume that PanCanadian Petroleum and Imperial Oil each put up $1 million and form a separate company to build a chemical plant to be used by both companies. The newly formed company borrows $48 million to construct the plant. This arrangement is illustrated below.

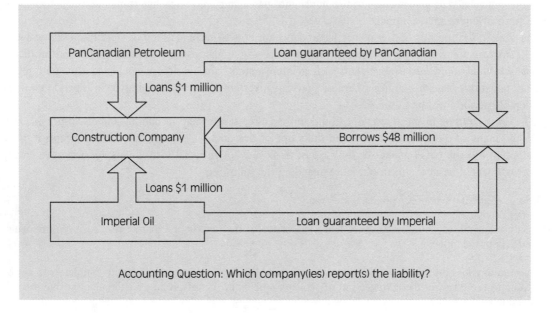

Accounting Question: Which company(ies) report(s) the liability?

In this way neither PanCanadian nor Imperial reports the debt on their balance sheet. Their only disclosure is that they guarantee debt repayment if the project's proceeds are inadequate to pay off the loan.[29]

In some cases, these project financing arrangements become more formalized through the use of a variety of contracts. In a simple **take-or-pay contract,** a purchaser of goods signs an agreement with a seller to pay specified amounts periodically in return for an option to receive products. The purchaser must make specified minimum payments even if delivery of the contracted products is not taken. Often these take-or-pay contracts are associated with project financing arrangements. For example, in the illustration above, PanCanadian and Imperial sign an agreement that they will purchase products from this new plant and that they will make certain minimum payments even if they do not take delivery of the goods.

Through-put agreements are similar in concept to take-or-pay contracts, except that a service instead of a product is provided by the asset under construction. Assume that PanCanadian and Imperial become involved in a project financing arrangement to build a pipeline to transport their various products. An agreement is signed that requires each to pay specified amounts in return for transportation of the product. In addition, these companies are required to make cash payments even if they do not provide the minimum quantities to be transported.

In practice, inconsistent methods have been used to account for and disclose the unconditional obligation in a take-or-pay or through-put contract involved in a project financing arrangement. In general, many companies have attempted to develop these types of contracts to "get the debt off the balance sheet."

---

[29] *CICA Handbook*, Section 3290. It should also be noted that, by the nature of particular agreements, such arrangements may, in fact, become joint ventures, in which case the recommendations of Section 3055 of the *Handbook* would apply.

Rationale for Off-Balance-Sheet Financing

There are several reasons for companies to arrange for off-balance-sheet financing. First, many believe that removing debt enhances the quality of the balance sheet and permits credit to be obtained more readily or at less cost.

Second, loan covenants often impose a limitation on the amount of debt a company may have. As a result, off-balance-sheet financing is used because these types of commitments might not be considered.

Third, it is argued by some that the asset side of the balance sheet is severely understated. For example, companies that use LIFO costing for inventories and depreciate assets on an accelerated basis will often have carrying amounts for inventories and plant and equipment that are much lower than their current values. As an offset to these lower values, some managements believe that part of the debt does not have to be reported. In other words, if assets were reported at current values, less pressure would exist for off-balance-sheet financing arrangements.

Whether these arguments have merit is debatable. The general idea "out of sight, out of mind" may not be true. Many users of financial statements indicate that they factor off-balance-sheet financing into their conclusions when assessing debt to equity relationships. Similarly, many loan covenants do attempt to factor in these complex arrangements. Nevertheless, many managers believe that benefits will accrue to the company if these obligations are not reported on the balance sheet.

The *Exposure Draft* on financial instruments recommends increased note disclosure requirements for off-balance-sheet financing arrangements. This conclusion is consistent with an "efficient markets" philosophy: the important question is not whether the presentation is off-balance-sheet or not but whether the items are disclosed at all.[30]

TROUBLED DEBT RESTRUCTURING

Depressed economic conditions, mismanagement, and other reasons are causes of financial hardship for various companies, provinces, and countries. Such hardship is typically reflected in serious cash flow problems which results in some debtors having difficulty in meeting their obligations to pay interest and/or principal amounts. Well-publicized Canadian examples are Campeau Corp. and companies in the Reichmann's Olympia & York Developments Ltd. group or the Edper Bronfman real estate empire.

While bankruptcy and corporate liquidation may be the eventual result of such problems, organizations may be able to recover by negotiating with debt holders regarding the debt obligations. Successful negotiations result in a troubled debt restructuring.

Troubled debt restructuring occurs when "the creditor for economic or legal reasons related to the debtor's financial difficulties grants a concession to the debtor that it would not otherwise consider."[31] For example, a financial institution such as a bank recognizes that granting some concessions (i.e. restructuring of the debt in a troubled loan situation) is more likely to maximize recovery than forcing the debtor into bankruptcy.

Troubled debt restructuring involves one of two basic types of transactions:

1. **Settlement of debt** at less than its carrying amount.

2. **Continuation of debt** with a modification of terms.

Whether the troubled debt restructuring is a "settlement of the debt" or a "continuation of the debt with a modification of terms," concessions granted to the debtor (borrower) by the creditor (lender) generally will result in a ***gain to the debtor*** and a ***loss to the creditor***.[32] Such a gain or loss would, if material, be separately disclosed in the income statement.

---

[30] It is unlikely that implementing the recommendations in the *Exposure Draft* will reduce off-balance-sheet transactions. Financial information is the "Holy Grail" of financial institutions. Developing new financial instruments and arrangements to sell and market to customers is not only profitable but also adds to the prestige of the investment firms that create them. Thus, new financial products that will test the AcSB's ability to develop appropriate accounting standards will continue to appear.

[31] "Accounting by Debtors and Creditors for Troubled Debt Restructurings," *Statement of Financial Accounting Standards No. 15* (Stamford, CT: FASB, 1977), par. 1.

[32] While the restructuring may result in the recognition of no gains or losses by either debtor or creditor, it is the nature of a troubled debt situation that the creditor cannot have a gain and the debtor cannot have a loss from restructuring.

It would not be identified as extraordinary under Canadian GAAP because it resulted from decisions or determinations of management or owners.[33] Also, the nature of the restructuring would be disclosed in a note.

Settlement of Debt at Less Than Its Carrying Amount

A transfer of noncash assets (real estate, receivables, or other assets) or the issuance of the debtor's shares can be used to settle a debt obligation in a troubled debt restructuring. In these situations, *the noncash assets or equity interest given should be accounted for at their fair market value*. The debtor is required to determine the excess of the carrying amount of the payable over the fair value of the assets or equity transferred (gain). Likewise, the creditor is required to determine the excess of the receivable over the fair value of those same assets or equity interests transferred (loss). The debtor recognizes a gain equal to the amount of the excess and the creditor normally would charge the excess (loss) against Allowance for Doubtful Accounts. In addition, the debtor recognizes a gain or loss on disposition of assets to the extent that the fair value of those assets differs from their carrying amount (book value).

To illustrate a transfer of assets, assume that City Bank has loaned $20,000,000 to Mortgage Company. Mortgage Company in turn has invested these monies in residential apartment buildings, but because of low occupancy rates it cannot meet its loan obligations. City Bank agrees to accept from Mortgage Company real estate with a fair market value of $16,000,000 in full settlement of the $20,000,000 loan obligation. The real estate has a recorded value of $21,000,000 on the books of Mortgage Company. The entry to record this transaction on the books of City Bank (creditor) is as follows:

Real Estate	16,000,000	
Allowance for Doubtful Accounts (Loss on Restructured Debt)	4,000,000	
Note Receivable from Mortgage Company		20,000,000

The real estate is recorded at fair market value, and a charge is made to the Allowance for Doubtful Accounts to reflect the bad debt write-off. If no allowance were available to absorb the charge of $4,000,000, the debit would be to a loss account.

The entry to record this transaction on the books of Mortgage Company (debtor) is as follows:

Note Payable to City Bank	20,000,000	
Loss on Disposition of Real Estate	5,000,000	
Real Estate		21,000,000
Gain on Restructuring of Debt		4,000,000

Mortgage Company has a loss on the disposition of real estate in the amount of $5,000,000, the difference between the $21,000,000 book value and the $16,000,000 fair market value. In addition, it has a gain on restructuring of debt of $4,000,000, the difference between the $20,000,000 carrying amount of the note payable and the $16,000,000 fair market value of the real estate.

Continuation of Debt

In some cases, a debtor will have serious short-run cash flow problems that lead the debtor to request one or a combination of the following modifications:

1. Reduction of the stated interest rate.

2. Extension of the maturity date of the face amount of the debt.

3. Reduction of the face amount of the debt.

4. Reduction or deferral of any accrued interest.

When a troubled debt is so restructured, the *Exposure Draft* on financial instruments recommends that:

> ... the debtor removes its previously recognized financial liability from its balance sheet and recognizes a new liability at an amount based on currently prevailing market interest rates and the rescheduled future cash flows. A troubled debt

---

[33] *CICA Handbook*, Section 3480, par. .02. In the United States, any gain to the debtor on the restructure is considered extraordinary under *FASB Statement No. 15*.

restructuring results in a gain or loss equal to the difference between the carrying amounts of the old and new liabilities. . . . The gain or loss is separately classified in the income statement and the nature of the restructuring is disclosed when the amount of gain or loss is material.[34]

Under this proposed recommendation, the new liability of the debtor or asset of the creditor would be measured at the present value of the future payments required. The consequence of this recommendation is that the restructuring would be accounted for in a manner similar to a refunding or refinancing of a bond payable as identified in this chapter.

To illustrate the accounting, assume that on December 31, 1994, Canadian Bank enters into a debt restructuring agreement with Resorts Development Ltd. The bank restructures a $10,000,000 note issued at par by:

1. Reducing the principal obligation from $10,000,000 to $9,000,000.

2. Forgiving $500,000 of accrued interest due December 31, 1994, which has been recorded by the bank and Resorts.

3. Extending the maturity date from December 31, 1994 to December 31, 2000.

4. Reducing the interest rate from 12% to 8%, with interest payments being due on December 31. The current prevailing market rate is 9%.

The amounts related to the note and accrued interest on the debtor's and creditor's records at December 31, 1994 and the determination of the present value of the restructured note are shown below.

	Resorts Development Ltd. (debtor) liabilities December 31, 1994	Canadian Bank (creditor) receivables December 31, 1994
Principal of note	$10,000,000	$10,000,000
Accrued interest	500,000	500,000
Total	$10,500,000	$10,500,000
Present value of future payments under the restructure arrangement:		
Principal of $9,000,000 discounted for 6 years at 9%, the prevailing market rate $9,000,000 × .59627 (Table A-2)		$5,366,430
Annual interest payments at 8% for 6 years discounted as an annuity at 9% $9,000,000 × .08 × 4.48592 (Table A-4)		3,229,862
Total present value		$8,596,292*

*Since the maturity value of the note is $9,000,000, a discount of $403,708 results.

Based on this analysis, the journal entries on page 708 illustrate the accounting for the debtor and the creditor. Resorts Development Ltd. and Canadian Bank would continue to account for the respective liability or receivable from the 8% note in the normal manner.

---

[34] *Exposure Draft*, "Financial Instruments," par. .090. In the United States, *FASB Statement No. 15* requires a substantially different treatment. Unless the carrying amount at the time of restructure exceeds the *undiscounted* total future cash flows, the debtor will not change the carrying amount of the payable and the creditor will not change the recorded investment in the receivable. But when the carrying amount of the debt at the time of restructure is greater than the *undiscounted* total future cash flows, both the debtor and the creditor adjust the carrying amount. The debtor recognizes a gain, the creditor recognizes a loss, and neither recognizes interest as part of the future payments or receipts. This treatment is based on the argument that a troubled debt restructuring by modification of terms is a continuation of the existing debt arrangement.

Entries for Troubled Debt Restructuring:
Continuation of Debt With Modification of Terms

Resorts Development Ltd (Debtor)		
Note Payable (12%)	10,000,000	
Interest Payable	500,000	
Discount on 8% Note Payable	403,708	
Note Payable (8%)		9,000,000
Gain on Restructuring		
of Debt		1,903,708

Canadian Bank (Creditor)		
Notes Receivable (8%)	9,000,000	
Loss on Restructuring		
a Note Receivable	1,903,708	
Note Receivable (12%)		10,000,000
Discount on 8%		
Note Receivable		403,708
Interest Receivable		500,000

APPENDIX 14B

Serial Bonds: Amortization and Redemption Before Maturity

A serial bond issue may be sold as though each series were a separate bond issue or it may be sold as a package. Whether sold separately or as a package, only one account for the total premium or discount is usually used in the general ledger for that serial issue. The total premium or discount to be amortized, whether computed for each series separately or for the entire issue, is entered as one amount in the Premium or Discount on Bonds Payable account. *The straight-line, bonds outstanding, or effective interest methods may be used to amortize the premium or discount.* These methods and accounting for the redemption of serial bonds before maturity under them are illustrated in this appendix.

AMORTIZATION OF A PREMIUM OR DISCOUNT ON SERIAL BONDS

A serial bond issue in the amount of $1,000,000, dated January 1, 1994, bearing 8% interest payable at December 31 each year, is sold by Yorkville Inc. to yield 9% per annum; the bonds mature in the amount of $200,000 on January 1 of each year beginning in 1995. The bond price and discount are computed as follows.

		Selling Price	Discount
Bonds due 1/1/95 (one year away):			
Principal: $200,000 × 0.91743 (Table A-2)	$183,486		
Interest: $16,000 × 0.91743 (Table A-4)	14,679		
		$198,165	$ 1,835*
Bonds due 1/1/96 (two years away)	Computations	196,482	3,518
Bonds due 1/1/97 (three years away)	similar to	194,937	5,063
Bonds due 1/1/98 (four years away)	those for	193,522	6,478
Bonds due 1/1/99 (five years away)	1/1/95 bonds	192,220	7,780
Total price for all series		$975,326	
Total discount on all series			$24,674

*$1,835 = $200,000 minus $198,165

Straight-Line Method

The straight-line method of amortization may be used if the results are not materially different from those of the effective interest method. The total discount for the Yorkville issue would be apportioned for each series over the five years as shown at the top of page 710.

Bonds Outstanding Method

When the entire issue of serial bonds is sold to underwriters at a stated price, the discount or premium is frequently amortized by the **bonds outstanding method,** since the discount or premium on each series is not definitely determinable. *The bonds outstanding method is an application of the straight-line method to serial bonds and assumes that the discount applicable to each bond of the issue is the same dollar amount per bond per year.*

The total discount for the Yorkville issue would be apportioned over the five years as shown in the second schedule on page 710. The effect of the column for Bonds Outstanding During the Year is to convert all the bonds into terms of bonds outstanding for one year, or a total of $3,000,000 for five years. Accordingly, during 1994 the premium to be amortized would be $1,000,000/$3,000,000 × $24,674, or $8,224. Similarly, during 1997 the premium to be amortized would be $400,000/$3,000,000 × $24,674, or $3,290.

Amortization Schedule: Straight-Line Method

| Series Due Jan. 1 | Total Discount | Term | | Periodic Amortization | | Apportioned to | | | | |
					1994	1995	1996	1997	1998
1995	$ 1,835	÷ 1 year	=	1,835	$1,835				
1996	3,518	÷ 2 years	=	1,759	1,759	$1,759			
1997	5,063	÷ 3 years	=	1,688	1,688	1,688	$1,687		
1998	6,478	÷ 4 years	=	1,619	1,619	1,619	1,620	$1,620	
1999	7,780	÷ 5 years	=	1,556	1,556	1,556	1,556	1,556	$1,556
	$24,674				$8,457	$6,622	$4,863	$3,176	$1,556

Amortization Schedule: Bonds Outstanding Method

Year Ending Dec. 31	Bonds Outstanding During the Year	Proportion of Bonds Outstanding During the Year to Total of Bonds Outstanding Column		Total Discount to Be Amortized		Discount to Be Amortized During Each Year
1994	$1,000,000	10/30	×	$24,674	=	$ 8,224
1995	800,000	8/30		24,674		6,580
1996	600,000	6/30		24,674		4,935
1997	400,000	4/30		24,674		3,290
1998	200,000	2/30		24,674		1,645
	$3,000,000	30/30				$24,674

An amortization schedule should be prepared for serial bonds in the same manner as the amortization schedule for single-maturity bonds, except that the maturity value of each series must be deducted from the total carrying amount of the bonds when the series is paid. The schedule shown below illustrates the amortization of the discount and the reduction in carrying amount for the serial bond issue described above using the bonds outstanding method.

Schedule of Bond Discount Amortization: Serial Bonds
Bonds Outstanding Method

Date	Credit Cash	Credit Bond Discount	Debit Interest Expense	Debit Bonds Payable	Carrying Value of Bonds
1/1/94					$975,326
12/31/94	$ 80,000[a]	$ 8,224[b]	$ 88,224[c]	—	983,550[d]
1/1/95	200,000	—	—	$ 200,000	783,550
12/31/95	64,000	6,580	70,580	—	790,130
1/1/96	200,000	—	—	200,000	590,130
12/31/96	48,000	4,935	52,935	—	595,065

(Continued)

Date	Credit Cash	Credit Bond Discount	Debit Interest Expense	Debit Bonds Payable	Carrying Value of Bonds
1/1/97	200,000	—	—	200,000	395,065
12/31/97	32,000	**3,290**	35,290	—	398,355
1/1/98	200,000	—	—	200,000	198,355
12/31/98	16,000	**1,645**	17,645	—	200,000
1/1/99	200,000	—	—	200,000	—
	$1,240,000	$24,674	$264,674	$1,000,000	

a$80,000 = $1,000,000 × 0.08   c$88,224 = $80,000 + $8,224
b$8,224 = $1,000,000/$3,000,000 × $24,674   d$983,550 = $975,326 + $8,224

Note: Interest expense is a function of the stated interest rate plus a pro rata share of discount amortization or less a pro rata share of premium amortization.

A schedule with similar debit and credit columns could be prepared using the data from the straight-line amortization schedule. The credit to Bond Discount on December 31, 1994 would be $8,457 using the straight-line data.

Effective Interest Method

Application of the effective interest method to serial bonds is similar to that illustrated in the chapter regarding single-maturity bonds. Interest expense for the period is computed by multiplying the effective interest rate times the carrying amount of bonds outstanding during the period. The amount of amortization of bond discount or premium is the difference between the effective interest expense for the period and the actual interest payments. Under this method, the interest expense is at a constant rate relative to the carrying amount of the bonds outstanding. The following schedule illustrates the amortization of discount and the reduction in carrying amount for the Yorkville serial bond issue using the effective interest method.

Schedule of Bond Discount Amortization: Serial Bonds
Effective Interest Method
8% Bonds Sold to Yield 9%

Date	Credit Cash	Credit Bond Discount	Debit Interest Expense	Debit Bonds Payable	Carrying Value of Bonds
1/1/94					$975,326
12/31/94	$ 80,000a	$ 7,779b	$ 87,779c	—	983,105d
1/1/95	200,000	—	—	$ 200,000	783,105
12/31/95	64,000	**6,479**	70,479	—	789,584
1/1/96	200,000	—	—	200,000	589,584
12/31/96	48,000	**5,063**	53,063	—	594,647
1/1/97	200,000	—	—	200,000	394,647
12/31/97	32,000	**3,518**	35,518	—	398,165
1/1/98	200,000	—	—	200,000	198,165
12/31/98	16,000	**1,835**	17,835	—	200,000
1/1/99	200,000	—	—	200,000	—
	$1,240,000	$24,674	$264,674	$1,000,000	

a$80,000 = $1,000,000 × 0.08   c$87,779 = $975,326 × 0.09
b$7,779 = $87,779 − $80,000   d$983,105 = $975,326 + $7,779

Note: Interest expense is a function of the effective interest rate times the book carrying amount outstanding during the period.

The journal entries that would be recorded for the payment of the interest, amortization of the discount, and retirement of each series of bonds can be determined from the column headings in the amortization schedule.

REDEMPTION OF SERIAL BONDS BEFORE MATURITY

If bonds of a certain series are redeemed before maturity date, it is necessary to compute the amount of unamortized discount or premium applicable to those bonds and to remove it from the Discount or Premium on Bonds Payable account.

Straight-Line Method

Assume that on January 1, 1996, $200,000 of the Yorkville serial bonds due January 1, 1999 are redeemed for $201,000. The unamortized discount on the $200,000 of bonds due on January 1, 1999 is $4,668 ($1,556 + $1,556 + $1,556; the discount apportioned to 1996, 1997, and 1998, respectively) as determined from the straight-line amortization schedule on page 710. The loss on early redemption of these bonds is computed as follows.

Purchase price of bonds redeemed	$201,000
Carrying value of 1/1/99 series bonds:	
($200,000 − $7,780 + $1,556 + $1,556) or	
($200,000 − $4,668)	195,332
Loss on bond redemption	**$ 5,668**

Bonds Outstanding Method

Using the same data, the computation of the applicable unamortized discount under the bonds outstanding method is as follows.

$$\frac{3 \text{ (number of years before maturity)} \times \$200,000 \text{ (par of bonds)} \times \$24,674 \text{ (total discount)}}{\$3,000,000 \text{ (total of bonds outstanding column)}} = \$4,935$$

Expressed a little differently, the discount to be amortized each year for each $200,000 of bonds is $200,000/$3,000,000 × $24,674, or $1,645. Therefore, if $200,000 of bonds are retired three years before maturity, the discount to be eliminated is 3 × $1,645, or $4,935.

Under the bonds outstanding method of amortization, the loss on early retirement of these bonds is computed as follows.

Purchase price of bonds redeemed	$201,000
Carrying value of 1/1/99 series bonds:	
($200,000 − $4,935)	195,065
Loss on bond redemption	**$ 5,935**

Effective Interest Method

Under the effective interest method, the carrying value of all the serial bonds outstanding at the time of an early retirement must be reduced by the present value of the bonds being retired. Reference to the effective interest amortization schedule shows that the carrying value of all the Yorkville bonds still outstanding at January 1, 1996 is $589,584. The present value of the bonds being retired is computed as follows (three years at 9%).

Present value of principal ($200,000 × .77218)	$154,436
Present value of interest payments ($16,000 × 2.53130)	40,501
Carrying value of bonds to be retired	$194,937

The entry to record the early redemption using the effective interest method would be as follows on January 1, 1996:

Bonds Payable	200,000	
Loss on Redemption of Bonds	6,063	
Discount on Bonds Payable ($200,000 − $194,937)		5,063
Cash		201,000

The gain or loss on redemption is the difference between the carrying value of the bonds ($194,937) and the cost to retire the bonds ($201,000); in this example, the loss is $6,063.

Note: All **asterisked** questions, cases, exercises, and problems relate to material contained in the appendices to this chapter.

QUESTIONS
---

1. (a) From what sources might a corporation obtain funds through long-term debt?
   (b) What is a bond indenture? What does it contain?
   (c) What is a mortgage?

2. Differentiate between term bonds, mortgage bonds, collateral trust bonds, debenture bonds, income bonds, callable bonds, registered bonds, bearer bonds, convertible bonds, commodity-backed bonds, and deep-discount bonds.

3. Distinguish between the following interest rates for bonds payable:
   (a) Yield rate.
   (b) Nominal rate.
   (c) Stated rate.
   (d) Market rate.
   (e) Effective rate.

4. Distinguish between the following values relative to bonds payable:
   (a) Maturity value.
   (b) Face value.
   (c) Market value.

5. Under what conditions of bond issuance does a discount on bonds payable arise? Under what conditions of bond issuance does a premium on bonds payable arise?

6. How should an unamortized discount on bonds payable be reported in the financial statements? An unamortized premium on bonds payable?

7. What are the two methods of amortizing a discount or premium on bonds payable? Explain each.

8. Breezy Corp. sells its bonds at a premium and applies the effective interest method in amortizing the premium. Will the annual interest expense increase or decrease over the life of the bonds? Explain.

9. How should the costs of issuing bonds be accounted for and classified in the financial statements?

10. Where should treasury bonds be shown on the balance sheet? Would treasury bonds be carried at face value or at reacquisition cost?

11. Why would a company wish to reduce its bond indebtedness before its bonds reach maturity? Indicate how this can be done and the accounting treatment for such a transaction including the possibility of any gain or loss.

12. What is in-substance defeasance? What are the advantages of this technique?

13. What must the accountant do to record a transaction involving the issuance of a noninterest-bearing long-term note in exchange for property?

14. How is the present value of a noninterest-bearing note computed?

15. What is an imputed interest rate, why may it have to be determined, and what factors should be considered in its determination?

16. Under what conditions may a short-term obligation be classified as a long-term debt?

*17. Give an example of a financial instrument which has the legal form of a debt (liability) but which is, in economic substance, an equity instrument.

*18. What arguments can be made for classifying term-preferred shares as a long-term liability?

*19. In the *Exposure Draft* on financial instruments it is recommended that proceeds from the issuance of convertible bonds be apportioned between the liability and equity components of the instrument. If $100,000 maturity value convertible bonds with a stated annual interest of 7% were issued for proceeds of $110,000, but similar bonds without the conversion right would have been sold for $97,000, what is the journal entry to record the issuance of the convertible bonds?

*20. What is off-balance-sheet financing? Why would a company engage in such financing?

*21. Max Inc. recently became involved in an interest rate swap. What is an interest rate swap and how is it reported in the financial statements?

*22. What are project financing arrangements? What are take-or-pay contracts and through-put contracts?

*23. In a troubled debt situation, why might the creditor grant concessions to the debtor? What type of concessions might a creditor grant the debtor?

*24. Lodi Bank agrees to restructure Green Company's troubled debt situation by reducing the interest rate from 14% to 8% and extending the maturity date of the debt by five years. Explain how Green Company should account for this modification of terms in the restructuring of its debt to Lodi Bank following the proposed treatment in the *Exposure Draft* on financial instruments.

*25. (a) Describe the bonds outstanding method of premium or discount amortization for serial bonds.
    (b) Describe the effective interest method of bond premium or discount amortization for serial bonds.

––––––– CASES –––––––

C14-1 **(VARIOUS LONG-TERM LIABILITY CONCEPTUAL ISSUES)** The Good Tire Company has completed a number of transactions during 1994. In January the company purchased under a contract a machine at a total price of $1,000,000, payable over five years with instalments of $200,000 per year. The seller is accounting for the transaction using the instalment method with the title transferring to Good Tire at the time of the final payment.

On March 1, 1994, Good Tire issued $10 million of general revenue bonds priced at 99 with a coupon rate of 10% payable July 1 and January 1 of each of the next 10 years. The July 1 interest was paid and on December 30 the company transferred $1,000,000 to the trustee, Country Trust Company, for payment of the January 1, 1995 interest.

Due to the depressed market for the company's common shares, Good Tire purchased $500,000 maturity value of its 6% convertible bonds for a price of $450,000. Management expects to resell the bonds when the share price has recovered.

As the accountant for Good Tire Company, you have prepared the balance sheet and have presented it to the president of the company. The president then asked you the following questions:

1. Why has depreciation been charged on the machine purchased under the long-term instalment contract? Title has not passed to the company and, therefore, it is not our asset. Why shouldn't the company just show only the amount paid to date on the asset side of the balance sheet instead of showing the full contract price with the unpaid portion on the liability side?

2. What is a bond discount? As a debit balance, why shouldn't it be classified among the assets?

3. Bond interest payable is shown as a current liability. Did we not pay our trustee the full amount of interest due this period?

4. Treasury bonds are shown as a deduction from bonds payable issued. Why should they not be shown as an asset, since they can be sold again? Are they the same as bonds of other companies that we hold as investments?

Instructions

Provide answers to these questions including a brief explanation to justify your conclusions.

(EFFECT OF MARKET CONDITION ON BOND ISSUE)   The following paraphrases and condenses an   **C14-2**
article in a business newspaper:

Bond Markets

Provincial Telephone Corporation Issue Hits Resale Market With $70 Million Left Over

SASKATOON—Provincial Telephone Corporation's slow-selling new 5¼% bonds were tossed onto the
resale market at a reduced price with about $70 million still available from the $200 million offered
Thursday, dealers said.

The utility's bonds originally had been priced at 99.803, to yield 5.3%. They were marked
down yesterday the equivalent of about $5.50 for each $1,000 face amount, to about 99.25, where
their yield jumped to 5.45%.

Instructions

(a)   How will the development above affect the accounting for the utility's bond issue?

(b)   Provide several possible explanations for the markdown and the slow sale of the bonds.

(BOND THEORY: BALANCE SHEET PRESENTATIONS, INTEREST RATE, PREMIUM)   On Jan-   **C14-3**
uary 1, 1994, Central Corp. issued for $1,075,230 its 20-year, 13% bonds that have a maturity value of $1,000,000
and pay interest semiannually on January 1 and July 1. Therefore, the yield rate was 12%. Bond issue costs were
not material in amount. Below are three presentations of the long-term liability section of the balance sheet that
might be used for these bonds at the issue date:

1. Bonds payable (maturing January 1, 2014) $1,000,000
    Unamortized premium on bonds payable   75,230
       Total bond liability $1,075,230

2. Bonds payable—principal (face value
       $1,000,000 maturing January 1, 2014) $ 97,220[a]
    Bonds payable—interest (semiannual payment $65,000)   978,010[b]
       Total bond liability $1,075,230

3. Bonds payable—principal (maturing, January 2014) $1,000,000
    Bonds payable—interest ($65,000 per period for 40 periods)   2,600,000
       Total bond liability $3,600,000

[a]The present value of $1,000,000 due at the end of 40 (6-month) periods at the yield rate of 6% per period.
[b]The present value of $65,000 per period for 40 (6-month) periods at the yield rate of 6% per period.

Instructions

(a)   Discuss the conceptual merit(s) of each of these date-of-issue balance sheet presentations.

(b)   Explain why investors would pay $1,075,230 for bonds that have a maturity value of only $1,000,000.

(c)   Assuming that a discount rate is needed to compute the carrying value of the obligations arising from a bond issue at
      any date during the life of the bonds, discuss the conceptual merit(s) of using for this purpose:

      1. The coupon or nominal rate.

      2. The effective or yield rate at date of issue.

(d)   If the obligations arising from these bonds are to be carried at their present value computed by means of the current
      market rate of interest, how would the bond valuation at dates subsequent to the date of issue be affected by an
      increase or a decrease in the market rate of interest?

(AICPA adapted)

C14-4 (BOND THEORY: PRICE, ISSUE COSTS, PRESENTATION, AND RETIREMENT)   On March 1, 1994, Pueblo Corp. sold its 5-year, $1,000 face value, 6% bonds dated March 1, 1994 at an effective annual interest rate (yield) of 7%. Interest is payable semiannually and the first interest payment date is September 1, 1994. Pueblo uses the effective interest method of amortization. Bond issue costs of a material amount were incurred in preparing and selling the bond issue. The bonds can be called by Pueblo at 101 at any time on or after March 1, 1995.

Instructions

(a) 1. How would the selling price of the bonds be determined?

2. Specify how all items related to the bonds would be presented in a balance sheet prepared immediately after the bond issue was sold.

(b) What items related to the bond issue would be included in Pueblo's 1994 income statement, and how would each be determined?

(c) Would the amount of bond discount amortization using the effective interest method of amortization be lower in the second or third year of the life of the bond issue? Why?

(d) Assuming that the bonds were called in and retired on March 1, 1995, how should Pueblo report the retirement of the bonds on the 1995 income statement?

(AICPA adapted)

C14-5 (IN-SUBSTANCE DEFEASANCE)   Following is a footnote presented in the 1993 annual report of Megus Corporation:

On December 30, 1993, the Company entered into agreements with a trustee which facilitated in-substance defeasance of its 5% and 5¼% capital note issues. Government securities costing $10,063,000 were deposited in an irrevocable trust, the principal and interest of which will be sufficient to pay the scheduled principal and interest on the 5% and 5¼% capital note issues of the Company. Proceeds from the sale of certain short-term liquid assets of the Company were used to purchase these securities. The 5% capital notes require principal payments of $500,000 on January 1 in each of the years 1994 through 2000 and the balance of $7,500,000 in 2001. The 5¼% capital notes require principal payments of $262,500 in each of the years 1994 through 2002 and the balance of $1,750,000 due in 2003. Interest on both issues is payable on January 1 and July 1 of each year that the notes remain outstanding. In December 1993, the Company prepaid the principal and interest payments on both issues due January 1, 1994. The Company recognized a gain in the 1993 income statement as the excess of the current principal outstanding on the note issues over the cost of the securities placed in the defeasance trusts, plus related trustee costs. The gain on the in-substance defeasance of both note issues of $2,732,000 is equivalent to a gain of $0.57 per common share.

Instructions

(a) What is in-substance defeasance?

(b) Discuss alternative accounting methods that might be used for this type of transaction.

(c) If proposed accounting for in-substance defeasance as presented in the AcSB's *Exposure Draft* on financial instruments is adopted, how would Megus Corporation have to account for such an arrangement?

*C14-6 (FINANCIAL STATEMENT PRESENTATION OF A COMPLEX FINANCIAL INSTRUMENT)   In its December 31, 1992 financial statements Noranda Inc. reported an outstanding issuance of $150 million of convertible, unsecured, subordinated debenture bonds due in 2007. These bonds bear an interest rate which is the greater of 5% or 1% plus the percentage that two times the common share dividend paid in the previous six months is of the conversion price. Subject to certain conditions, Noranda may satisfy the interest requirement through the issue of common shares. These debentures are convertible at the holder's option into common shares at a conversion price of $35 per common share on or before the last business day prior to the maturity date of the debentures or the last business day prior to redemption. Noranda has the option of redeeming the debentures for common shares.

Instructions

Based on the concepts in the AcSB's *Exposure Draft* on financial instruments, provide your recommendations as to how these debentures and any related interest should be reported in Noranda Inc.'s financial statements. Provide justification for your recommendations.

(OFF-BALANCE-SHEET FINANCING: INTEREST RATE SWAPS)   Interest rate swaps have been iden- ***C14-7** tified as a form of off-balance-sheet financing. Below is an extract from the note on long-term debt in the 1992 financial statements of Canadian Pacific Forest Products Limited regarding interest rate swaps:

> The Corporation has entered into an interest rate swap agreement with one of its bankers which converts the US $100 million syndicated floating rate loan to a fixed rate debt of 9.71% up to 1999. The Corporation has also entered into several interest rate swap agreements with its bankers which convert the US $225 million 9.25% debentures into floating rate debt until June 1995.

Instructions

(a)   What is meant by off-balance-sheet financing and why would a company engage in such financing?

(b)   What is an interest rate swap, why is it a form of off-balance-sheet financing, and why would Canadian Pacific Forest Products Limited make an interest rate swap?

(TROUBLED DEBT RESTRUCTURING: ALTERNATIVE TREATMENTS)   Chrysis Corp. has ***C14-8** recently fallen into financial difficulties. To help Chrysis avert bankruptcy, Dominion Bank has given Chrysis a break. Chrysis owes Dominion Bank $2,000,000, payable in 10 years. The interest rate on this loan is 10%. Dominion, wishing to minimize its losses, has agreed to reduce the interest rate to 5% per year.

Mr. Walters, Dominion's controller, sees no need for making any journal entries to record this deal. Since Chrysis still owes $2,000,000 he feels that there is no need for a write-down of this loan and a recognition of a loss. Likewise, he would see no need for a journal entry on the books of Chrysis in recognition of this event.

Mr. Mocha, controller for Chrysis, however, would not do it this way. He points out that the $1,385,544 present value of Chrysis's restructured obligations to Dominion (discounted at the currently prevailing 10% market interest rate for similar loans) is considerably less than the $2,000,000 present value of the obligation before the interest rate was reduced. He feels that this provides a basis for recognition of a gain by Chrysis and, correspondingly, a loss by Dominion.

Instructions

(a)   What are possible arguments that you might expect from Dominion Bank and Chrysis Corp. to support their respective views on how the loan restructure should be accounted for?

(b)   What entries would be recorded regarding the recognition of the loan restructure on the books of each company under the accounting treatment preferred by (1) Dominion Bank and (2) Chrysis Corp.?

(c)   Under the proposals of the AcSB's *Exposure Draft* on financial instruments, which accounting treatment would be acceptable?

———— **EXERCISES** ————

E14-1 **(CLASSIFICATION OF LIABILITIES)** Presented below are various accounts and related information for a December 31, 1994 year end:

1. Unamortized premium on bonds payable, of which $1,500 will be amortized during the next year.

2. Bank loans payable due March 10, 1997. (The company's product requires aging for five years before sale.)

3. Serial bonds payable, $500,000, of which $100,000 are due each July 31.

4. Dividends payable in common shares of the company on January 20, 1995.

5. Amounts withheld from employees' wages for income taxes.

6. Notes payable due January 15, 1996.

7. Credit balances in customers' accounts arising from returns and allowances after collection in full of account.

8. Bonds payable of $900,000 maturing June 30, 1995.

9. Overdraft of $500 in a bank account. (No other accounts are carried in this bank.)

10. Deposits made by customers who have ordered goods.

Instructions

Indicate whether each of the items above should be classified on December 31, 1994 as a current liability, a long-term liability, or under some other classification. Consider each one independently from all others; that is, do not assume that all of them relate to one particular business. If the classification of any of the items is doubtful, explain why.

E14-2 **(ENTRIES FOR BOND TRANSACTIONS)** Coldcut Corp. issued $500,000 of 10%, 20-year bonds on January 1, 1994 at 102. Interest is payable semiannually on July 1 and January 1. Coldcut Corp. uses the straight-line method of amortization for bond premium or discount.

Instructions

(a) Prepare the journal entries to record:

1. The issuance of the bonds.

2. The accrual of interest and the premium amortization on June 30, 1994.

3. The accrual of interest and the premium amortization on December 31, 1994.

(b) If the effective interest method of amortization for bond premium or discount was used, what would be the (1) interest expense reported on June 30, 1994 and (2) premium amortization for the six-month period July 1 to December 31, 1994? Assume an effective interest rate of 9.75%.

E14-3 **(ENTRIES AND QUESTIONS FOR BOND TRANSACTIONS)** On June 30, 1994, Potter Corp. issued $3,000,000 face value of 13%, 20-year bonds at $3,225,690, a yield of 12%. Potter uses the effective interest method to amortize bond premium or discount. The bonds pay semiannual interest on June 30 and December 31.

Instructions

(a) Prepare the journal entries to record the following transactions:

1. The issuance of the bonds on June 30, 1994.

2. The payment of interest and the amortization of the premium on December 31, 1994.

3. The payment of interest and the amortization of the premium on June 30, 1995.

4. The payment of interest and the amortization of the premium on December 31, 1995.

(b) Show the presentation for the liability for bonds payable on the December 31, 1995 balance sheet.

(c) Provide answers to the following questions:

1. What amount of interest expense is reported for 1995?

2. Will the bond interest expense reported in 1995 be the same as, greater than, or less than the amount that would be reported if the straight-line method of amortization were used?

3. Determine the total cost of borrowing over the life of the bond.

4. Will the total bond interest expense be greater than, the same as, or less than the total interest expense if the straight-line method of amortization were used?

(DETERMINING AMOUNTS IN ACCOUNT BALANCES) Presented below are three independent situations: **E14-4**

(a) Conley Corporation incurred the following costs in connection with the issuance of bonds: (1) printing and engraving costs, $12,000; (2) legal fees, $37,000; and (3) commissions paid to underwriter, $60,000. What amount should be reported as Unamortized Bond Issue Costs and where should this amount be reported on the balance sheet?

(b) Rodriguez Co. Ltd. sold $2,000,000 of 10%, 10-year bonds at 103 plus accrual interest on March 1, 1994. The bonds were dated January 1, 1994 and pay interest on July 1 and January 1. If Rodriguez uses the straight-line method to amortize bond premium or discount, determine the amount of interest expense to be reported on July 1, 1994 and December 31, 1994.

(c) Oakcrest Inc. issued $480,000 of 9%, 10-year bonds on June 30, 1994 for $450,000. This price provided a yield of 10% on the bonds. Interest is payable semiannually on December 31 and June 30. If Oakcrest uses the effective interest method, determine the amount of interest expense to record if financial statements are issued on October 31, 1994.

(BOND ISSUANCE AND INTEREST WITH ISSUANCE AT OTHER THAN AN INTEREST DATE) Carrie Inc. issued $500,000 par value 8% bonds on March 1, 1994 for proceeds of $462,414 plus accrued interest. The bonds were dated January 1, 1994 from which date they had a five-year life. Interest is payable semiannually on June 30 and December 31. The effective interest rate on the issue date was 10%. **E14-5**

Instructions

Give the necessary journal entries to record the issuance of these bonds and interest costs to be recorded on June 30 and December 31, 1994 assuming the discount is amortized on (1) the straight-line basis and (2) the effective interest basis. (**Hint**: To help determine the discount amortization from March 1 through June 30 under the effective interest method, calculate the present value of the bond obligations at June 30 using the effective interest rate.)

(ENTRY FOR RETIREMENT OF BOND; BOND ISSUE COSTS) On January 2, 1989, Spring Corporation issued $1,500,000 of 10% bonds at 96 due December 31, 1998. Legal and other costs of $24,000 were incurred in connection with the issue. Interest on the bonds is payable annually each December 31. The $24,000 issue costs are being deferred and amortized on a straight-line basis over the 10-year term of the bonds. The **E14-6**

discount on the bonds is also being amortized on a straight-basis over the 10 years (straight-line is not materially different in effect from the effective interest method).

The bonds are callable at 101 (that is, at 101% of face amount), and on January 2, 1994, Spring called $900,000 face amount of the bonds and retired them.

Instructions

Ignoring income taxes, compute the amount of loss, if any, to be recognized by Spring as a result of retiring the $900,000 of bonds in 1994 and prepare the journal entry to record the retirement.

(AICPA adapted)

E14-7   **(ENTRIES FOR RETIREMENT AND ISSUANCE OF BONDS)**   Winter Inc. had outstanding $6,000,000 of 11% bonds (interest payable July 31 and January 31) due in 10 years. On July 1, it issued $9,000,000 of 10% 15-year bonds (interest payable July 1 and January 1) at 97. A portion of the proceeds were used to call the 11% bonds at 102 on July 31. Unamortized bond discount and issue cost applicable to the 11% bonds were $90,000 and $30,000, respectively.

Instructions

Prepare the journal entries necessary to record the refunding of the bonds.

E14-8   **(ENTRIES FOR RETIREMENT AND ISSUANCE OF BONDS)**   On June 30, 1985, Moon Chemical Inc. issued 12% bonds with a par value of $700,000 due in 20 years. They were issued at 98 and were callable at 104 at any date after June 30, 1993. Because of lower interest rates and a significant change in the company's credit rating, it was decided to call the entire issue on June 30, 1994 and to issue new bonds. New 10% bonds were sold in the amount of $800,000 at 102; they mature in 20 years. The company uses straight-line amortization. Interest payment dates are December 31 and June 30.

Instructions

(a)   Prepare journal entries to record the retirement of the old issue and the sale of the new issue on June 30, 1994.

(b)   Prepare the entry required on December 31, 1994 to record the payment of the first six months' interest and the amortization of the premium on the bonds.

E14-9   **(ENTRIES FOR RETIREMENT OF BONDS BY TRUSTEE)**   Under the terms of its 9% bonds (interest payable June 30 and December 31), Fall Corp. must pay $2,000,000 to a trustee each year. The funds are to be used to retire as many bonds as possible in the open market. (**Hint**: Establish a bond retirement fund.)

On July 1, 1994, the company paid $2,000,000 to the trustee, who used the money to purchase $2,200,000 par value of bonds. Unamortized bond discount applicable to the bonds purchased was $50,000.

Instructions

Record the payment and the purchase of the bonds on Fall Corp.'s books.

E14-10   **(ENTRIES FOR NONINTEREST-BEARING DEBT)**   On July 1, 1994, Autumn Inc. makes the two following acquisitions:

1.   Purchases land having a fair market value of $200,000 by issuing a five-year noninterest-bearing promissory note in the face amount of $337,012.

2.   Purchases equipment by issuing a 6%, eight-year promissory note having a maturity value of $180,000 (interest payable annually).

The company has to pay 11% interest for funds from its bank.

Instructions

(a) Provide the journal entries that should be recorded by Autumn Inc. for the two purchases on July 1.

(b) Record the interest at the end of the first year (July 1, 1995) on both notes using the effective interest method.

(NONINTEREST-BEARING DEBT: WITH RIGHTS) Presented below are two independent situations: **E14-11**

(a) On January 1, 1994, Coral Corp. borrowed $4,000,000 (face value) from Holly Co. Ltd., a major customer, through a noninterest-bearing note due in four years. Because the note was noninterest bearing, Coral agreed to sell furniture to this customer at lower than market price. A 10% rate of interest is normally charged on this type of loan. Prepare the journal entry to record this transaction and determine the amount of interest expense to report for 1994.

(b) On January 1, 1994, Tel-Data Inc. purchased land that had an assessed value of $325,000 at the time of purchase. A $500,000 noninterest-bearing note due January 1, 1997 was given in exchange. There was no established exchange price for the land, nor a ready market value for the note. The interest rate charged on notes of this type is 12%. Determine the amount at which the land should be recorded on January 1, 1994 and the interest expense to be reported in 1994.

(LONG-TERM DEBT DISCLOSURE) To secure a long-term supply, Tiger Corp. entered into a take-or- **E14-12** pay contract with an aluminum recycling plant on January 1, 1993. Tiger is obligated to purchase 40% of the output of the plant each period while the debt incurred to finance the plant remains outstanding. The annual cost of the aluminum to Tiger will be the sum of 40% of the raw material costs, operating expenses, depreciation, interest on the debt used to finance the plant, and return on the owner's investment. The minimum amount payable to the plant under the contract, whether or not Tiger is able to take delivery, is $6 million annually through December 31, 2012. Tiger's total purchases under the agreement were $7 million in 1993 and $7.5 million in 1994. Funds to construct the plant were borrowed at an effective interest rate of 9%. Tiger's incremental borrowing rate was 10% at January 1, 1993 and is 11% at December 31, 1994. Tiger intends to disclose the contract in the notes to its financial statements at December 31, 1994.

Instructions

Assuming that the contract is an "unconditional purchase obligation," prepare the note disclosure for the contract at December 31, 1994.

(DEBTOR/CREDITOR ENTRIES FOR SETTLEMENT AND FOR CONTINUATION OF TROU- *****E14-13** BLED DEBT)**

Part I. Tanner Co. Ltd. owes $180,000 plus $19,800 of accrued interest to Zimmer Inc. The debt is a 10-year, 11% note. Because Tanner is in financial trouble, Zimmer agrees to accept some property and cancel the entire debt. The property had a cost of $75,000 to Tanner but its fair market value is now $120,000.

Instructions

(a) Prepare the journal entry on Tanner's books for the debt restructure.

(b) Prepare the journal entry on Zimmer's books for the debt restructure.

Part II. Damon Corp. owes $200,000 plus $24,000 of accrued interest to First Trust Co. Inc. The debt is a 10-year 12% note due December 31, 1994. Because Damon Corp. is in financial trouble, First Trust agrees on December 31, 1994 to forgive the accrued interest, extend the maturity date to December 31, 1996, and reduce the interest rate to 5% with the interest to be paid annually on December 31. The currently prevailing market rate of interest is 10%.

Instructions

(a)   Prepare the journal entry on Damon's books on December 31, 1994 regarding the debt restructure.

(b)   Prepare the journal entries on First Trust's books on December 31, 1994 regarding the debt restructure.

Note: Apply the accounting treatment recommended in the *Exposure Draft* on financial instruments as discussed in Appendix 14A.

*E14-14 (RESTRUCTURE OF NOTE UNDER DIFFERENT CIRCUMSTANCES)   Downunder Corporation is having financial difficulty and therefore has asked Second Canadian Bank to restructure its $3 million note outstanding. The present note has three years remaining and pays a current rate of interest of 10%. The currently prevailing market rate for a loan of this nature is 12%. The note was issued at its face value.

Instructions

Presented below are four independent situations. Prepare the journal entry that Downunder would make for each of these restructurings:

(a)   Second Canadian Bank agrees to take an equity interest in Downunder by accepting common shares valued at $2,500,000 in exchange for relinquishing its claim on this note.

(b)   Second Canadian Bank agrees to accept land in exchange for relinquishing its claim on this note. This land had a cost of $1,900,000 on Downunder's books but its current fair value is $2,300,000.

(c)   Second Canadian Bank agrees to modify the terms of the note, indicating that Downunder does not have to pay any interest on the note over the three-year period.

(d)   Second Canadian Bank agrees to reduce the principal balance due to $2,000,000 and require interest to be at a rate of 12%.

*E14-15 (PREMIUM AMORTIZATION FOR SERIAL BONDS: BONDS OUTSTANDING METHOD)   Murphy Inc. sells a 10% serial bond issue in the amount of $1,000,000 to underwriters for $1,040,000. The bonds are dated January 1, 1990 and mature in the amount of $200,000 on January 1 of each year beginning January 1, 1992.

Instructions

Compute the premium to be amortized during each of the years in which any of the bonds are outstanding, using the bonds outstanding method.

————— **PROBLEMS** —————

P14-1 (ANALYSIS OF AMORTIZATION SCHEDULE AND INTEREST ENTRIES)   The amortization and interest schedule on page 719 reflects the issuance of 10-year bonds by Lane Inc. on January 1, 1994 and the subsequent interest payments and charges. The company's year end is December 31, and financial statements are prepared annually.

Instructions

(a)   Indicate whether the bonds were issued at a premium or a discount and how you can determine this fact from the schedule.

(b)   Indicate whether the amortization schedule is based on the straight-line method or the effective interest method and how you can determine which method is used.

(c)   Determine the stated interest rate and the effective interest rate.

(d) On the basis of the schedule, prepare the journal entry to record the issuance of the bonds on January 1, 1994.

(e) On the basis of the schedule, prepare the journal entries to reflect the bond transactions and accruals for 1994.

(f) On the basis of the schedule, prepare the journal entries to reflect the bond transactions and accruals for 2001.

Amortization Schedule

Year	Cash	Interest	Amount Unamortized	Carrying Value
1/1/94			$5,651	$ 94,349
1994	$11,000	$11,322	5,329	94,671
1995	11,000	11,361	4,968	95,032
1996	11,000	11,404	4,564	95,436
1997	11,000	11,452	4,112	95,888
1998	11,000	11,507	3,605	96,395
1999	11,000	11,567	3,038	96,962
2000	11,000	11,635	2,403	97,597
2001	11,000	11,712	1,691	98,309
2002	11,000	11,797	894	99,106
2003	11,000	11,894		100,000

(ENTRIES FOR BONDS ISSUED AT DISCOUNT; BONDS ISSUED AT PAR WITH PREMIUM AT **P14-2** **MATURITY PROVISION)**   In 1993, Jasper Tent Co. Ltd. was considering the issuance of bonds as of January 1, 1994, as follows:

Plan 1: $2,000,000 par value 11%, first mortgage, 20-year bonds, due Dec. 31, 2013, at 95, with interest payable annually.

Plan 2: $2,000,000 par value 11%, first mortgage, 20-year bonds, due Dec. 31, 2013, at 100, with provision for payment of a 5% ($100,000) premium at maturity, interest payable annually.

Costs of issue such as printing and lawyers' fees may be ignored for the purpose of answering this question. Discount or premium is to be allocated to accounting periods on a straight-line basis.

Instructions

Give two separate sets of journal entries with appropriate explanations showing the accounting treatment that the foregoing plans of bond issues would necessitate, respectively:

(a) At time of issue.

(b) Yearly thereafter.

(c) On payment at date of maturity.

(AMORTIZATION SCHEDULES; STRAIGHT-LINE AND EFFECTIVE INTEREST)   Hydro Corp. **P14-3** sells 10% bonds having a maturity value of $1,500,000 for $1,391,862. The bonds are dated January 1, 1994 and mature January 1, 1999. Interest is payable annually on January 1. (**Hint:** The effective interest rate or yield must be computed.)

Instructions

(a) Set up a schedule of interest expense and discount amortization under the straight-line method.

(b) Set up a schedule of interest expense and discount amortization under the effective interest method.

P14-4 **(ISSUANCE AND RETIREMENT OF BONDS; INCOME STATEMENT PRESENTATION)** Seek Inc. issued its 9%, 25-year mortgage bonds in the principal amount of $5,000,000 on January 2, 1979 at a discount of $200,000, which it proceeded to amortize by charges to expense over the life of the issue on a straight-line basis. The indenture securing the issue provided that the bonds could be called for redemption in total but not in part at any time before maturity at 104% of the principal amount, but it did not provide for any sinking fund.

On December 18, 1993, the company issued its 11%, 20-year debenture bonds in the principal amount of $6,000,000 at 101, and the proceeds were used to redeem the 9%, 25-year mortgage bonds on January 2, 1994 (15 years after their issuance). The indenture securing the new issue did not provide for any sinking fund or for retirement before maturity.

Instructions

(a) Prepare journal entries to record the issuance of the 11% bonds and the retirement of the 9% bonds.

(b) Indicate the income statement treatment of the gain or loss from retirement and any accompanying note disclosure. Assume: 1994 income before the gain or loss, extraordinary items, and income taxes of $3,200,000; a weighted-average number of shares outstanding of 1,500,000; and an income tax rate of 40%.

P14-5 **(COMPREHENSIVE BOND PROBLEM)** In each of the following independent cases the company closes its books on December 31:

1. Blacken Corp. sells $250,000 of 10% bonds on February 1, 1993. The bonds pay interest on February 1 and August 1. The due date of the bonds is August 1, 1996. The bonds yield 12%. Give entries through December 31, 1994.

2. Blue Ltd. sells $600,000 of 12% bonds on June 1, 1993. The bonds pay interest on June 1 and December 1. The due date of the bonds is June 1, 1997. The bonds yield 10%. On September 1, 1994, Blue Ltd. buys back and cancels $120,000 maturity value of bonds for $126,000 (includes accrued interest). Give entries through December 1, 1995.

Instructions

For the two cases, prepare all of the relevant journal entries from the time of sale until the date indicated. Use the effective interest method for discount or premium amortization (construct amortization tables where applicable). Amortize premium or discount on interest dates and at year end. Assume that no reversing entries are made. (Round to the nearest dollar.)

P14-6 **(ISSUANCE OF BONDS BETWEEN INTEREST DATES, STRAIGHT-LINE, RETIREMENT)** Presented below are selected transactions of B. Good Corporation:

May 1, 1993   Bonds payable with a par value of $700,000, which are dated January 1, 1993, are sold at 105 plus accrued interest. They are coupon bonds, bear interest at 12% (payable annually at January 1), and mature January 1, 2003. (Use the Interest Expense account for accrued interest for the four months from the bond date. Note that this results in a total premium amortization period of 116 months.)

Dec. 31   Adjusting entries are made to record the accrued interest on the bonds and the amortization of the premium. (Use straight-line amortization.)

Jan. 1, 1994   Interest on the bonds is paid.

April 1   Bonds of par value of $420,000 which were sold May 1, 1993 are purchased at 102 plus accrued interest, and retired. (Bond premium is to be amortized only at the end of each year.) *up to date of retirement.*

Dec. 31   Adjusting entries are made to record the accrued interest on the bonds and the amount of premium amortized.

Instructions

Prepare journal entries for the transactions above.

(ENTRIES FOR LIFE CYCLE OF BONDS) On April 1, 1993, Beck Inc. sold 12,000 of its 12%, 15-year, **P14-7** $1,000 face value bonds at 97. Interest payment dates are April 1 and October 1, and the company uses the straight-line method of bond discount amortization. On March 1, 1994, Beck took advantage of favourable prices of its shares to extinguish 3,000 of the bonds by issuing 100,000 of its no-par value common shares. The company's shares were selling for $31 each on March 1, 1994.

Instructions

Prepare the journal entries needed on the books of Beck Inc. to record the following:

(a) April 1, 1993: issuance of the bonds.

(b) October 1, 1993: payment of semiannual interest.

(c) December 31, 1993: accrual of interest expense.

(d) March 1, 1994: extinguishment of 3,000 bonds.

(ANALYSIS OF AMORTIZATION SCHEDULE, ISSUE COSTS, RETIREMENT) On January 1, 1991, **P14-8** Brock Inc. sold $150,000 (face value) of bonds. The bonds are dated January 1, 1991 and will mature on January 1, 1996. Interest is paid annually on December 31. The bonds are callable after December 31, 1993 at 101. Issue costs related to these bonds amounted to $3,000, and these costs are being amortized by the straight-line method. The following amortization schedule was prepared by the accountant for the first two years of the life of the bonds.

Date	Cash	Interest	Amortization	Carrying Value of Bonds
1/1/91				$139,186
12/31/91	$15,000	$16,702	$1,702	140,888
12/31/92	15,000	16,907	1,907	142,795

Instructions

On the basis of the information above, answer the following questions (round your answers to the nearest dollar or percent):

(a) What is the nominal or stated rate of interest for this bond issue?

(b) What is the effective or market rate of interest for this bond issue?

(c) Present the journal entry to record the sale of the bond issue, including the issue costs.

(d) Present the appropriate entry(ies) at December 31, 1993.

(e) Present the disclosure of this bond issue on the December 31, 1993 balance sheet. Balance sheet subheadings are to be given.

(f) On June 30, 1994, $100,000 of the bond issue was redeemed at the call price. Present the journal entry for this redemption. Amortization of the discount is recorded only at the end of the year.

(g) Present the effects of the bond redemption on the 1994 income statement and any note disclosure. The income tax rate was 40%. Income from operations before income taxes was $40,000, and the weighted-average number of common shares outstanding during the year was 18,000. Working capital funds were used to redeem the bonds.

P14-9 (ENTRIES FOR LIFE CYCLE OF BONDS: TRUSTEE PAYS INTEREST) Here are transactions of Gucci Leather Inc.:

Jan. 1, 1993   Bonds payable (coupon bonds) in the amount of $1,500,000, and bearing interest at the rate of 10% payable semiannually on January 1 and July 1, due January 1, 2009 (i.e. 16 years from issuance date), are issued at 96.

June 15   The Commerce Bank has been engaged as trustee to handle the payment of interest to individual bondholders. A cheque for the interest due July 1, 1993 is sent to the trustee. (**Note**: Transfer from the Cash account to a Bond Interest Fund until bondholders have been paid.)

     30   Record the interest expense for the first six months of 1993. Bond discount is to be amortized only at the end of each year by the straight-line method.

July 20   The trustee returns to the company cancelled interest coupons paid in the amount of $68,000 and reports that trustee's expenses charged against the account amounted to $645.

Dec. 15   A cheque for the interest due January 1, 1994 and for the July 20 reported expenses is sent to the trustee.

     31   Record the interest expense for the six months ended December 31, and amortize the discount for the year.

Jan. 21, 1994   The trustee returns to the company cancelled interest coupons paid in the amount of $73,000.

Mar. 1   Bonds of par value of $200,000 are bought on the market at 95 plus accrued interest and retired. All interest coupons dated before July 1, 1994 have been removed.

Instructions

(a) Prepare journal entries on the books of Gucci Leather Inc. for the transactions given above. Present answers to the nearest dollar amount.

(b) What will be the amount of the cheque to the trustee for the interest for the first six months of 1994?

(c) What will be the amount, to the nearest dollar, of the discount amortized on December 31, 1994?

P14-10 (ENTRIES FOR NONINTEREST-BEARING DEBT) On December 31, 1993, Waterloo Inc. acquired computers from Laurier Corporation by issuing a $400,000 noninterest-bearing note, payable in full on December 31, 1997. Waterloo's credit rating permits it to borrow funds from its several lines of credit at 10%. The computers are expected to have a five-year life and a $40,000 residual value.

Instructions

(a) Prepare the journal entry for the purchase on December 31, 1993.

(b) Prepare any necessary adjusting entries relative to depreciation (use straight-line) and amortization (use effective interest method) on December 31, 1994.

(c) Prepare any necessary adjusting entries relative to depreciation and amortization on December 31, 1995.

P14-11 (ENTRIES FOR NONINTEREST-BEARING DEBT; PAYABLE IN INSTALMENTS) Swift Clean Inc. purchased machinery on December 31, 1992, paying $10,000 down and agreeing to pay the balance in four equal instalments of $30,000 payable each December 31. An assumed interest of 12% is implicit in the purchase price.

Instructions

Prepare the journal entries to record the purchase of the machine on December 31, 1992 and the payments and interest on December 31, 1993 through 1996.

(COMPREHENSIVE PROBLEM; ISSUANCE, CLASSIFICATION, DEFEASANCE, REPORTING) P14-12
Presented below are five independent situations:

(a) On March 1, 1994, Red Dye Corp. issued at 104 plus accrued interest $3,000,000, 9% bonds. The bonds are dated January 1, 1994 and pay interest semiannually on July 1 and January 1. In addition, Red Dye Corp. incurred $27,000 of bond issuance costs. Compute the net amount of cash received by Red Dye Corp. as a result of the issuance of these bonds.

(b) On January 1, 1993, Electric Co. Ltd. issued 9% bonds with a face value of $500,000 for $469,280 to yield 10%. The bonds are dated January 1, 1993 and pay interest annually. What amount is reported for interest expense in 1993 related to these bonds, assuming that Electric used effective interest method for amortizing bond premium and discount?

(c) Cherub Corp. has a number of long-term bonds outstanding at December 31, 1994. These long-term bonds have the following requirements for sinking fund balances and to pay bond maturities for the next six years.

	Sinking Fund	Maturities
1995	$100,000	$100,000
1996	200,000	250,000
1997	300,000	100,000
1998	200,000	—
1999	200,000	150,000
2000	200,000	100,000

Indicate how this information should be reported in the financial statements at December 31, 1994.

(d) Bip Inc., on February 1, 1991, issued 12%, $4,000,000 face amount, 10-year bonds at 98 plus accrued interest. The bonds are dated November 1, 1990, and interest is payable on May 1 and November 1. On May 1, 1994, Bip decided to defease (legally, not in-substance) this debt because interest rates had dropped, and the bonds are defeased at a cost of $3,650,000. Ignoring the income tax effect, at what amount and where would Bip's defeasance be reported on the financial statements? (Use straight-line amortization.)

(e) In the long-term debt structure of Happy-time Inc., the following three bonds were reported: mortgage bonds payable $10,000,000; collateral trust bonds $5,000,000; bonds maturing in instalments, secured by plant equipment $4,000,000. Determine the total amount, if any, of debenture bonds outstanding.

(COMPREHENSIVE LIABILITY PROBLEM; BALANCE SHEET PRESENTATION) Moonbeam Inc. P14-13 has been producing quality children's apparel for more than 25 years. The company's fiscal year runs from April 1 to March 31. The following information relates to the obligations of Moonbeam as of March 31, 1994.

Bonds Payable
Moonbeam issued $5,000,000 of 11% bonds on July 1, 1988 at 96, which yielded proceeds of $4,800,000. The bonds will mature on July 1, 1998. Interest is paid semiannually on July 1 and January 1. Moonbeam uses the straight-line method to amortize the bond discount.

Notes Payable
Moonbeam has signed several long-term notes with financial institutions and insurance companies. The maturities of these notes are given in the schedule that follows. The total unpaid interest for all of these notes amounts to $210,000 on March 31, 1994.

Due Date	Amount Due
April 1, 1994	$ 200,000
July 1, 1994	150,000
October 1, 1994	150,000
January 1, 1995	150,000
April 1, 1995–March 31, 1996	500,000
April 1, 1996–March 31, 1997	500,000
April 1, 1997–March 31, 1998	700,000
April 1, 1998–March 31, 1999	400,000
April 1, 1999–March 31, 2000	500,000
	$3,250,000

Estimated Warranties

Moonbeam has a one-year product warranty on some selected items in its product line. The estimated warranty liability on sales made during the 1992–1993 fiscal year and still outstanding as of March 31, 1993 amounted to $84,000. The warranty costs on sales made from April 1, 1993 through March 31, 1994 are estimated at $200,000. The actual warranty costs incurred during the current 1993–1994 fiscal year are as follows:

Warranty claims honoured on 1992–1993 sales	$ 84,000
Warranty claims honoured on 1993–1994 sales	95,000
Total warranty claims honoured	$179,000

Other Information

1. **Trade payables.** Accounts payable for supplies, goods, and services purchased on open account amount to $350,000 as of March 31, 1994.

2. **Payroll related items.** Outstanding obligations related to Moonbeam's payroll as of March 31, 1994 are:

Accrued salaries and wages	$150,000
CPP and UI payable	18,000
Income taxes withheld from employees	25,000
Other payroll deductions	5,000

3. **Taxes.** The following taxes incurred but not due until the next fiscal year are:

Income taxes	$305,000
Property taxes	125,000
Sales taxes (not offset by input credits)	182,000

4. **Miscellaneous accruals.** Other accruals not separately classified amount to $75,000 as of March 31, 1994.

5. **Dividends.** On March 15, 1994 Moonbeam's Board of Directors declared a cash dividend of $.40 per common share on its 3,000,000 outstanding shares. This dividend was to be distributed on April 12, 1994 to the common shareholders of record at the close of business on March 31, 1994.

Instructions

Prepare the liability sections of Moonbeam Inc.'s March 31, 1994 balance sheet and appropriate accompanying notes.

(CMA adapted)

(ENTRIES FOR SERIAL BONDS: BONDS OUTSTANDING METHOD) On December 31, 1991, *P14-14 Emma Ltd. sold an 11% serial bond issue in the amount of $3,200,000 for $3,402,116. The bonds mature in the amount of $400,000 on December 31 of each year, beginning December 31, 1992 and interest is payable annually. On December 31 of both 1992 and 1993, the company retired the $400,000 of bonds due on these dates and in addition, on December 31, 1993, purchased at 102 and retired bonds in the amount of $200,000 which were due on December 31, 1995. (**Hint**: the unamortized premium on the $200,000 retired bonds was $5,614.33 at December 31, 1993.)

Instructions

(a) For 1992, prepare entries to record the payment of interest, amortization of the premium for the year using the bonds outstanding method, and redemption of $400,000 of bonds.

(b) Prepare entries to record the redemption of the bonds of $600,000 that were retired on December 31, 1993.

(c) Discuss the disclosures that are required relative to the bond transactions in 1993.

(d) What amount of premium would be amortized for the year 1994 under the bonds outstanding method?

(e) Prepare entries for 1992, 1993, and 1994 to record the transactions above using the effective interest method, assuming the bonds were sold for $3,419,127 to yield 9%.

(PRESENT VALUE AND EFFECTIVE INTEREST ON SERIAL BONDS) On January 1, 1992, Brave *P14-15 Corporation issued $1,000,000 in 5-year, 11% serial bonds to be repaid in the amount of $200,000 on January 1, 1993, 1994, 1995, 1996, and 1997. Interest is payable at the end of each year. The bonds were sold to yield a rate of 12%.

Instructions

(a) Prepare a schedule showing the computation of the total amount received from the issuance of the serial bonds. Show supporting computations, rounded to the nearest dollar.

(b) Assume the bonds were originally sold at a discount of $23,253. Prepare a schedule of amortization of the bond discount for the life of the issuance, using the effective interest method. Show supporting computations.

(AICPA adapted)

PERSPECTIVES

ON STANDARD SETTING

Carol E.A. Loughrey

Carol E.A. Loughrey, FCA, the Comptroller of the Province of New Brunswick, becomes the Chair of the Board of Governors of the 55,000 member Canadian Institute of Chartered Accountants (CICA) in June 1994. She is the first woman to assume this role. Carol has enjoyed a varied career since 1972, when she earned her CA designation. Aside from time devoted to public practice, motherhood, furthering her education, the family business, university teaching and administration, and to the Deputy Minister level chief accountant and internal auditor responsibilities associated with her current position, Carol has been extremely active in the profession.

How did you decide on a career in accounting?

I always enjoyed accounting in university. And on graduating with a business degree in 1970, the one area where there were relevant jobs for females in Fredericton was in accounting. I wanted to continue learning and the accounting route allowed me to do this.

Why a CA?

My exposure had been to chartered accountants. I knew CAs from our family business and my professors in university were CAs. I had developed considerable respect for the designation.

How does standard setting work in Canada?

Since the 1970s, legislation has directed that the accounting and auditing standards of the CICA are to be followed in the preparation of and reporting on financial statements issued to shareholders. The CICA spends $6.4 million of its members' fees in out-of-pocket costs each year on this activity and Institute members contribute approximately that much again in volunteer time.

We use task forces to work on specific issues that need to be addressed, and the Accounting Standards Board, the Auditing Standards Board, and the Public Sector Accounting and Auditing Standards Board have oversight responsibilities. There is an enormous amount of consultation with various interested groups and their opinions are actively sought before the standards are published.

What are some of the major financial accounting issues facing Canadian business today?

Reporting on risk and uncertainty is a major issue. What is the best way to report on the risk associated with the numbers we report, for values assigned to assets in the real estate industry, for example? This is an interesting area where we have spent a lot of time on developing

standards that hopefully will be published in 1994.

The environment is another area. A CICA task force has just reported on the accounting and auditing implications related to environmental issues, and extra funds are being devoted to the development of standards in this area.

Recession-driven asset write-downs, going concern disclosure, accounting for post-employment benefits, off-balance-sheet financing, especially for instruments used in the financial services industry, and increasing pressure for more cash flow reporting, are some of the hot issues.

There is a growing interest in ethics in business today. Do you see this influencing the standards being issued?

Ethics in business is so much a part of what a chartered accountant is all about. A respected management guru recently said that the 90s would be the decade of the accountants because of their concern for ethics and ethical behaviour. Accountants are working with client firms to develop codes of behaviour.

What are the primary influences on standard setting?

The dynamic forces of change.

What do you mean by this?

Changes in the structure of the economy result in new types of business. Look at the information age companies. What are their assets? How do you measure the value of software being developed? How do you get a bank loan when there are no concrete assets?

Another issue is determining the best way to present information. Because of technological advances, we are inundated with data. The more data you have, the less information you have, but the demands are for more and better information for decision making.

Another influence is the development of international accounting standards.

Are there differences in U.S. and Canadian standard-setting processes?

Yes, some major differences exist. Three different organizations in the U.S. carry out what is handled by the CICA.

Accounting standards are set by the Financial Accounting Standards Board (FASB), which is funded by donations from public accounting firms, corporations, and individuals. The standard setters are full-time, paid staff and all meetings and deliberations are public. The Securities and Exchange Commission has a significant oversight function.

Auditing standards are issued by the American Institute of Certified Public Accountants (AICPA). The committees are volunteer, but the members tend to represent their firms rather than sit as individuals as in Canada.

The Government Accounting Standards Board (GASB), funded by the government, is primarily concerned with state-level reporting.

The resulting U.S. standards tend to be more detailed and "cookbook" in nature than the Canadian standards, which allow for the use of much more professional judgement.

Your particular interest is the development of accounting standards for public sector reporting. Are the standards very different from those for the business sector? What is happening in this area?

Interestingly, the accounting is not that different from that for business. A major exception is the expensing of fixed assets, and there is now pressure to change that. Another concerns the recommendation for governments to book the entire unfunded pension liability, directly increasing net direct debt. This is controversial, especially as business is permitted to amortize the unfunded liability over time.

Most issues relate to areas where there is no private sector equivalent and in resolving these, we repeatedly go back to accounting basics, to accrual accounting and matching.

Can you give some examples?

The fact that the federal government adjusts the amount of equalization payments the provinces eventually receive presents a problem of how to account for the change. In a business, past experience helps you decide what you are likely to collect. Last year, after the books were closed, New Brunswick was advised that it would receive approximately $93 million less than anticipated for 1993 and prior years. This is a major adjustment. Is it an extraordinary item? A prior period adjustment? An adjustment to current revenue?

A government lends funds to an outside party, with an agreement to advance funds annually to the organization in the future to repay the loan. Should this be reported as a receivable on the government's financial statements?

How should payments made under the medicare system be reported? Include them as transfer payments to individuals on the basis that the payments were made on behalf of the individual being treated? Or report them as payments for services rendered to the province?

There are no right or wrong answers. It is important to go back to the basics, and I think I did more of this while on the Public Sector Accounting and Auditing Board than I did in 11 years of teaching!

Setting public sector standards is a fascinating area. There is no legal requirement to apply the standards that are issued, so the Board must rely on general acceptance. It is incredible what has been achieved.

Shareholders' Equity, Dilutive Securities, and Investments

■

CHAPTER 15

Shareholders' Equity: Issuance and Reacquisition of Share Capital

■—■—■

In your first exposure to financial accounting you were probably taught that the equity side of the balance sheet represents the sources of enterprise assets. Liabilities represent the amount of assets that were financed by borrowing, and shareholders' equity represents (1) the amount that was contributed by the shareholders and (2) the portion that was earned and retained by the enterprise.

In recent years the creation of a variety of financial instruments together with innovative investment practices have blurred this simple distinction between liabilities and equities. As a result, the AcSB had, at the time of writing, issued an *Exposure Draft* on financial instruments.[1] An important part of this document is its attempt to clarify the distinction between financial liabilities and equity instruments (see Appendix 14A).

The distinction between liabilities and ownership equities is more than a matter of form. Obviously, whether a particular financial instrument is classified as a liability or an equity affects the content of the balance sheet and the ratios of assets to equity and of debt to equity. But, more critically, the line between liabilities and equity affects the measurement of income. Income is defined to include changes in equity during a period other than those resulting from transactions with owners of an enterprise's equity instruments. Income is a return *on* equity capital and includes only inflows in excess of the amount needed to maintain capital. Without a distinction between the claims of creditors and those of owners, measurement of income is not possible.

The coverage in Chapters 15 and 16 is based on current definitions of liabilities and ownership equity with this essential distinction: *a liability embodies an obligation to sacrifice future economic benefits*—due dates for principal and interest—*whereas an equity instrument does not*. Like several other areas of financial accounting, the equity/liability distinction has become more complicated and is under study. Thus, in the near future the basic distinction between these two elements could change.

THE NATURE OF SHAREHOLDERS' EQUITY

Objective 1

Understand the nature of shareholders' equity and know its key components or sources.

The owners of an enterprise bear the ultimate risks and uncertainties and receive the benefits of enterprise operations. Their interest is measured by the difference between the assets and the liabilities of the enterprise. *Owners' or shareholders' interest in a business enterprise is a residual interest*. It ranks after liabilities as a claim to or interest in the assets of an enterprise. Shareholders' equity represents the cumulative net contributions by shareholders plus recorded earnings that have been retained. As a residual interest, shareholders' equity has no existence apart from the assets and liabilities of the enterprise—shareholders' equity equals net assets. Shareholders' equity is not a claim to specific assets but a claim against a portion of the total assets. Its amount is not specified or fixed; it depends on the enterprise's profitability. Shareholders' equity grows if the enterprise is profitable and shrinks or may disappear entirely if the enterprise is unprofitable.

---

[1] "Financial Instruments," *Exposure Draft of the Accounting Standards Board* (Toronto: CICA, September 1991).

Sources of Shareholders' Equity

Accounting for shareholders' equity is greatly influenced by tradition and corporate law. Although the legal aspects of equity must be respected and disclosed, legal requirements need not be the only accounting basis for classifying and reporting the components of equity. *The two primary sources from which owners' equity is derived are (1) contributions by shareholders and (2) income (earnings) retained by a corporation.* These two components should be accounted for and reported by every corporation. The diagram below depicts the two major sources of changes in total shareholders' equity.[2]

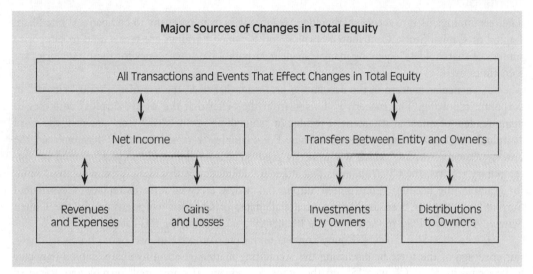

Changes in total shareholders' equity may also occur by conversion of debt into equity and through capital donations to a corporation. In addition, changes within components of, but not the total of, shareholders' equity are brought about by stock dividends and conversion of preferred shares into common shares. Comprehensive revaluation of assets and liabilities (e.g., a financial reorganization) can result in a change in both the components and total of shareholders' equity. These types of changes are examined in Chapters 16 and 17.

What Is Capital?

To this point, the authors have used the term "shareholders' or owners' equity" to denote the total of ownership capital of an enterprise. It is important to understand the many different meanings attached to the word **capital**, because the word often is construed differently by various groups. *In corporation finance,* for example, capital commonly represents the total assets of the enterprise. *In law,* capital is considered that portion of shareholders' equity that is required by statute to be retained in the business for the protection of creditors. Generally, **legal capital (stated capital)** is the full price received for shares issued as specified by the Canada Business Corporations Act and most provincial incorporation acts. In some jurisdictions ownership shares may have a par value, in which case that amount is considered to be the legal capital.

Accountants for the most part define capital more broadly than legal capital but more narrowly than total assets. *When accountants refer to capital they usually mean shareholders' or owners' equity.* They then subclassify shareholders' equity into various components, the primary ones being Share Capital, Contributed Surplus, and Retained Earnings. **Share Capital** (or **Capital Stock**) represents the legal or stated capital of a corporation as defined in the previous paragraph. **Contributed Surplus** includes items such as donations from owners and other sources, gains on forfeited shares,

---

[2] Adapted from "Elements of Financial Statements of Business Enterprises," *Statement of Financial Accounting Concepts No. 3* (Stamford, CT: FASB, 1980), p. 23.

credits arising when shares are reacquired and cancelled at a cost less than their issue price, and amounts received in excess of par value when such shares are issued. *Share Capital and Contributed Surplus constitute* **contributed capital**. **Retained Earnings** represents the **earned capital** of an enterprise and consists of all undistributed income that remains invested in the enterprise. A comprehensive illustration of the shareholders' equity section of a balance sheet is given in Chapter 16 on page 791, which shows how these categories may be presented and provides examples of what they may include.

Terminology

The terminology used to report shareholders' equity varies from company to company. While Share Capital or Capital Stock, Contributed Surplus, and Retained Earnings are terms used to categorize sources of shareholders' equity by many Canadian corporations, other names for these categories are sometimes used.[3]

A particular concern of the accounting profession has been the use of the term "surplus" in corporate reporting. The concern is derived from the belief that the word "surplus" connotes to many readers of financial statements a residue or "something not needed." Consequently, the word "surplus" has been eliminated in most cases. For example, "retained earnings" has replaced the heading "earned surplus," which was formerly used. Whenever the word "surplus" is used in contemporary reports, the CICA suggests that it be in conjunction with a descriptive adjective,[4] as in, for example, the heading "Contributed Surplus." A widely accepted term to replace "Contributed Surplus" has not yet been used in financial statements of Canadian corporations. In the United States, "Additional Paid-In Capital" is the frequently used heading for this category.

Given that Shareholders' Equity consists of various components, we have chosen to divide our coverage of the topic by discussing the accounting matters relating to Share Capital (issuance and reacquisition) in Chapter 15 and the other components (Contributed Surplus and Retained Earnings) in Chapter 16. Additional aspects that can have an impact on shareholders' equity (convertible debt, stock purchase warrants, and stock options) are covered in Chapter 17. But first, in order to account for shareholders' equity, one must understand the corporate form of entity.

THE CORPORATE FORM OF ENTITY

Objective 2

Know and be able to discuss the characteristics of the corporate form of organization.

Of the *three primary forms of business organization—the proprietorship, the partnership, and the corporation*—the corporate form is dominant. In terms of the aggregate amount of resources controlled, goods and services produced, and people employed, the corporation is by far the leader. Nearly all of the largest business organizations are corporations. Although the corporate form has a number of advantages (as well as disadvantages) over the other two forms, a principal factor contributing to its present dominant role is the ability to attract and accumulate large amounts of capital.

Various types of corporations exist, distinguished by the nature of their ownership, their purpose, and the type of legislation under which they have been created. The following are common in Canada.

---

[3] *Financial Reporting in Canada—1991* (Toronto: CICA, 1991) indicated that in 1990: (a) Share Capital was used by 91 of 300 companies surveyed and Capital Stock was used by 162 companies, while other headings used were Capital (8 companies), Stated Capital (8); (b) Contributed Surplus was used by 63 of 70 companies reporting such items, while the remaining companies used such headings as Premium on Shares Issued (3), Capital Surplus (2), Paid-in Capital (2); (c) Retained Earnings was used by 239 of the 300 companies, Deficit by 43, while other headings included Earnings Retained, Reinvested Earnings, Retained Income, and Earnings Reinvested; (d) Shareholders' Equity was used by 282 companies as the title for the balance sheet section with 7 using Common Shareholders' Equity, and 11 using different titles.

[4] *CICA Handbook* (Toronto: CICA), Section 3250, par. .02.

1. **Profit-seeking corporations** engage in activities with the intent of making a financial return for their owners. Ownership may be widely traded and distributed (often called **publicly held corporations**) or held by a small number of shareholders with restrictions on the transferability of shares (often referred to as **privately held corporations**).

2. **Not-for-profit corporations** are created to provide educational, charitable, recreational, or similar services for its members or society in general.

3. **Crown corporations** are created by special government statutes to provide services to the public, such as the Canadian Broadcasting Corporation and Canada Post.

The profit-seeking corporation is the type examined in this book.

Among the special characteristics of the corporate form that affect accounting are:

1. Influence of corporate law.

2. Use of the share capital or capital stock system.

3. Development of a variety of ownership interests.

4. Limited liability of shareholders.

5. Formality of profit distribution.

Corporate Law

In Canada, a corporation may be established provincially or federally by submitting the required documentation to the appropriate government office. If incorporated provincially, the company would be subject to the requirements and provisions of the respective province's business corporations act. Federally incorporated companies are created and operated under the provisions of the **Canada Business Corporations Act** (CBCA). While the provisions of most business corporation acts are reasonably similar, differences do exist. These differences create difficulties when trying to make generalizations in a discussion of shareholders' equity. Consequently, the CBCA will be the focal point when discussing legal aspects of accounting for shareholders' equity in this book.

Under the CBCA, one or more individuals over 18, of sound mind and not bankrupt, are entitled to incorporate. To do so, incorporators develop, sign, and send **articles of incorporation**[5] to the Director, Department of Consumer and Corporate Affairs. The Director, who is responsible for the administration of the CBCA, will issue a **certificate of incorporation** after ensuring that the incorporating documents are appropriately completed. Incorporation is essentially a right under the CBCA because the Director has no discretion to refuse documents that are in order. When a certificate of incorporation is issued, the resulting business becomes a separate legal entity which may act in the capacity of a natural person when conducting its affairs. As with any person, it is bound by the laws of the country. In addition, the corporation (unless a particular exemption is explicitly granted) must act in accordance with all of the provisions of the CBCA. These provisions have significant implications regarding accounting for corporations in general and for shareholders' equity in particular, as will be discussed throughout this and the next chapter.

First, however, one important accounting aspect of the CBCA should be emphasized: the *CBCA Regulations state that financial statements are to be prepared in accordance with the standards set out in the* **CICA Handbook**. This provision gives the *Handbook* a legal status, a fact which significantly contributes to the self-regulating nature of the Canadian accounting profession, as the

---

[5] The articles of incorporation must specify such things as the name of the company (which must use either the words "incorporated" or "limited" or their abbreviation or a French equivalent as part of the name), place of registered office, classes and any maximum number of shares authorized, restrictions on rights to transfer shares, number of directors, and any restrictions on the corporation's business.

authors of the *Handbook* are primarily members of the accounting profession. This privilege and responsibility of the profession does not exist in most other countries in which governmental influences are significant to the determination of accounting practices and standards.[6]

Share Capital or Capital Stock System

The share capital of a corporation is generally made up of a large number of units or shares. For a given class of shares (stock), each share is exactly equal to every other share. Each owner's interest is determined by the number of shares possessed. If a company has but one class of stock divided into 1,000 shares, a person owning 500 shares controls one-half the ownership interest of the corporation; one holding 10 shares has a one-hundredth interest.

Each share has certain rights and privileges that can be restricted only by provisions in the articles of incorporation. In the absence of restrictive provisions, each share carries the following **basic or inherent rights**:

Objective 3

Identify the rights of shareholders.

1. To *share proportionately in profits and losses*.

2. To *share proportionately in management* (the right to vote at shareholder meetings).

3. To *share proportionately in corporate assets upon liquidation*.

In addition to these three rights, the CBCA allows a corporation to assign a **pre-emptive right** to any or all classes of shares through appropriate specification in the articles of incorporation. A pre-emptive right means that existing shareholders of a class of shares have a right to acquire additional shares of any new issue of that class in proportion to their existing holdings before the new issue of shares can be offered to others.

The pre-emptive right protects existing shareholders from involuntary dilution of ownership interest. Without this right, shareholders with a given percentage interest might find their interest reduced by the issuance of additional shares without their knowledge and at prices that were not favourable to them. Because assigning the pre-emptive right makes it inconvenient for a corporation to make large issuances of additional shares, as is frequently done when acquiring other companies, it has not been used by many corporations.

The great advantage of the share system is the ease with which an interest in the business may be transferred from one individual to another. Generally, *individuals owning shares in a corporation may sell them to others at any time and at any price without obtaining the consent of the company or other shareholders*. Each share is the personal property of the owner and may be disposed of at will. All that is required of the corporation is that it maintain a list or subsidiary ledger of shareholders as a basis for dividend payments, issuance of share rights, voting proxies, and the like. Because shares are frequently transferred, it is necessary for the corporation to revise the subsidiary ledger of shareholders periodically, generally in advance of every dividend payment or shareholders' meeting. As the number of shareholders grows, the need may develop for a more efficient system that can handle large numbers of share transactions. Also, the major stock exchanges require controls that the typical corporation finds uneconomic to provide. Thus **registrars and transfer agents** who specialize in providing services for recording and transferring shares are usually used.

While a corporation's shares may be continuously traded in the stock market, only the amount received by the corporation when the shares were originally issued is reported on the financial statements as part of shareholders' equity.

---

[6] Chapter 1 examined the process by which Canadian accounting standards in the *CICA Handbook* are developed and considered some of the implications to the profession resulting from the legal status conferred on the *CICA Handbook*.

Variety of Ownership Interests: Common and Preferred Shares

Corporations may issue shares of various classes. Each class would have specified rights, privileges, restrictions, and conditions attached to it as stated in the company's articles of incorporation. The CBCA simply refers to the possible existence of classes of shares without specifying what they should be called. Consequently, the name corporations give to different classes of shares can be varied.

Typical practice is to identify classes by a letter (i.e. Class A, Class B, etc.) followed by a brief description of the nature of rights or restrictions that attach to the shares in the class. However, the rights and restrictions of Class A shares for one corporation can be quite different from those of Class A shares of another corporation. Therefore, the only means by which one can identify the rights and restrictions of a class of shares for a particular corporation is to examine the description that applies to that class. We will be using the terms "common shares" and "preferred shares" in this book as a means to differentiate between basic ownership interest shares and shares which have specific privileges or restrictions regarding the rights identified in the previous section.

In every corporation, one class of shares must represent the basic ownership interest. This class is called common shares. **Common shares** are the residual corporate interest that bears the ultimate risk of loss and receives the benefits of success. They are guaranteed neither dividends nor assets upon dissolution. But common shareholders generally control the management of the corporation and tend to profit most if the company is successful. In the event that a corporation has only one authorized issue of shares, that issue is considered to be common shares, whether so designated or not.

To appeal to all types of investors, corporations may offer two or more share classes, each with different rights or privileges. The preceding section emphasized that each share of a given class has the same rights as other shares of the same class and that there are three rights inherent in every share (to share in profits, management, and assets upon liquidation). By specification in the articles of incorporation, certain of these rights may be sacrificed, usually in return for other special rights or privileges. Thus special classes of shares are created. Because they have certain preferential rights, they will be referred to as **preferred shares**. In return for special preference, the preferred shareholder will sacrifice some of the inherent rights.

Preferred shareholders typically have a prior claim on earnings. They are assured a dividend, usually a stated amount, before any dividend may be distributed to the common shareholders. In return for this preference, the preferred shareholders may sacrifice the right to a voice in management or the right to share in profits beyond the stated amount.

A company may accomplish a variety of objectives by issuing more than one class of shares. For example, one company created two classes, A and B, when it decided to issue shares to the public several years ago. Both Class A and Class B participate equally (per share) in all dividend payments and have the same claim on assets on dissolution. The differences are that Class A is voting and Class B is not; Class B is traded publicly while Class A, which is "family owned," must be sold privately; and Class A shares are convertible, one for one, into Class B shares but not vice versa. By issuing two classes of shares, the Class A owners obtained a ready market for the company's shares and yet provided an effective shield against outside takeover.[7]

An additional example of the variety of shares that may be issued is provided by Rogers Communications Inc. which has six series of preferred shares (which vary in terms of such factors as redemption, retraction, conversion, and dividend amounts) and two classes labelled as common shares (Class A, with voting rights, and Class B, without voting rights but which are to receive a minimum dividend before dividends may be paid on Class A shares).

---

[7] Ironically, the voting class (which would necessarily be concerned about an unfriendly takeover) often gains the most if an acquisition does take place. That is, the acquirer is willing to pay a substantial premium for the voting shares, but not for the nonvoting ones.

Liability of Shareholders

Shareholders of a corporation contribute cash, other property, or services to the enterprise in return for ownership shares. The amount invested in the enterprise is the extent of a shareholder's possible loss. That is, if the corporation sustains losses to such an extent that remaining assets are insufficient to pay creditors, no recourse can be held by the creditors against the personal assets of the individual shareholders. In a partnership or proprietorship, personal assets of the owners can be called upon to satisfy unpaid claims against the enterprise. Ownership interests in a corporation are legally protected against such a contingency; *the shareholders may lose their investment but they cannot lose more than their investment*.[8]

While the corporate form of organization grants the protective feature of limited liability to the shareholders, it also requires that withdrawal of the amount of shareholders' investment represented by amounts in share capital accounts not occur unless all prior claims on corporate assets have been paid. The corporation must maintain this capital until dissolution. Upon dissolution, it must satisfy all prior claims before distributing any amounts to the shareholders. In a proprietorship or partnership, the owners can withdraw amounts at will because all their personal assets may be called on to protect creditors from loss.

Under the CBCA, all shares must be *without a nominal or par value*. This simply means that all proceeds from the corporation's issuance of shares must be credited to the appropriate share capital account.

Prior to the implementation of the CBCA, federally incorporated companies could have **par value shares** and some provincial acts continue to permit par value shares to be issued. Par value is simply an amount per share determined by the company's incorporators and stated as such in the articles of incorporation. From an accounting point of view, par value is the amount credited to the appropriate share capital account when shares are issued. This par value amount represents legal capital, an amount which cannot be used as a basis for dividend distributions. As an arbitrary amount designated by incorporators, par value has little to do with the market value of shares issued. Because shares with par value are a rapidly diminishing phenomenon for companies incorporated in Canada, the accounting for shares without par value is the focus of this book. However, since par value shares continue to have limited applicability in Canada and are common in many other countries, matters related to them are covered in Appendix 15A at the end of this chapter.[9]

Formality of Profit Distribution

Generally, the directors of an enterprise (elected by shareholders) determine what is to be done with profits realized through operations. Profits may be left in the business to permit expansion or merely to provide a margin of safety, or they may be withdrawn and divided among the owners. In a proprietorship or partnership, this decision is made by the owner or owners informally and requires no specific action. In a corporation, however, profit distribution is controlled by certain legal restrictions.

First, *no amounts may be distributed among the owners unless the corporate capital is maintained intact*. This reflects the presumption that sufficient security must be left in a corporation to satisfy the liability holders after any dividends have been distributed to shareholders. Various tests of corporate solvency have been used over the years. Under the CBCA, dividends may not be declared or paid if there are reasonable grounds for believing that (1) the corporation is, or would

---

[8] While share ownership in a corporation does provide limited liability, this advantage may be lost, particularly for smaller private corporations which have a single or few shareholders, because of contractual agreements. For example, a bank usually requires the owner of an owner-operated corporation to personally guarantee any loans by the bank to the corporation.

[9] *Financial Reporting in Canada—1991* reported that 21 of 300 companies surveyed disclosed the existence of a par value or stated value (similar to par value) for one class of shares issued, often in circumstances where a company had many share classes outstanding. The United States is an example of a country which uses par value shares extensively.

be after the dividend, unable to pay its liabilities as they become due, or (2) the realizable value of the corporation's assets would, as the result of the dividend, be less than the total of its liabilities and stated (legal) capital for all classes of shares.

Second, *distributions to shareholders must be formally approved by the board of directors and recorded in the minutes of their meetings.* As the top executive body in the corporation, the board of directors must make certain that no distributions are made to shareholders that are not justified by profits. Directors are generally held liable to creditors if liabilities cannot be paid because company assets have been illegally paid out to shareholders.

Third, *dividends must be in full agreement with the capital shares provisions as to preferences, participation, and the like.* Once the corporation has created specific stipulations regarding the rights of various classes of shareholders, these stipulations must be observed.

CHARACTERISTICS OF PREFERRED SHARES

As previously stated, preferred shares are a special class of shares because they possess certain preferences or restrictions not possessed by common shares. The following characteristics are most frequently associated with preferred share issues:

Objective 4

Describe and understand the major features of preferred shares.

1. Preference as to dividends (rights regarding priority, and whether or not they are cumulative and/or participating).

2. Preference as to assets in the event of liquidation.

3. Convertible into common shares.

4. Callable (redeemable) at the option of the corporation.

5. Retractable at the option of the shareholder.

6. Nonvoting.

Nature of Rights in Preferred Shares

A corporation may attach whatever preferences or restrictions in whatever combination it desires to a preferred share issue so long as it does not violate its incorporation law. Also, more than one class of preferred shares may be issued by a company. The features that distinguish preferred from common shares may be of a more restrictive and negative nature than preferences; for example, the preferred shares may be nonvoting, noncumulative, and nonparticipating. Unless specifically prohibited, however, all of the inherent rights of ownership apply to preferred shares.

A **dividend on shares without par value** is usually expressed as a **specific dollar amount per share**. A *preference as to dividends is not an assurance that dividends will be paid*; it is merely assurance that the stated dividend applicable to the preferred shares must be paid before dividends can be paid on common shares.

In addition to a preference as to the priority of payment of dividends, various other features that may be attributed to a class of preferred shares are as follows:

1. **Cumulative.** Dividends not paid in any year must be made up in a later year before any dividends can be distributed to common shareholders. If the directors fail to declare a dividend at the normal date for dividend action, the dividend is said to have been "passed." Any passed dividend on cumulative preferred shares constitutes a **dividend in arrears.** *Because no liability exists until the board of directors declares a dividend, a dividend in arrears is not recorded as a liability but is disclosed in a note to the financial statements.* (In common law, if the corporate articles are silent about the cumulative feature, preferred shares are considered to be cumulative.) Because a passed dividend is lost forever on noncumulative preferred shares, they are not attractive to investors and, consequently, are seldom issued.

2. **Participating.** Holders of participating preferred shares share proportionately with the com-

mon shareholders in any profit distributions beyond the prescribed amount. That is, $5 preferred shares, if fully participating, will receive not only their $5 return but also, after a proportional amount per share is paid to common shareholders, additional dividends at the same level as those paid to common shareholders. Also, participating preferred shares may not always be fully participating as described, but partially participating. For example, provisions may be made that $5 preferred shares will be participating up to a maximum total amount of $10 per share, after which they cease to participate in additional profit distributions. Although participating rights are not used very often, Rogers Communications Inc.'s Class B shares are entitled to an annual dividend of $.35 per share and then participate equally in dividends with Class A shares after the Class A shares have also been paid a $.35 per share dividend.

3. **Convertible.** The shareholders may, at their option, exchange their preferred shares for common shares at a predetermined ratio and specified time. The convertible preferred shareholder not only enjoys a prior claim on dividends but also has the option of converting into a common shareholder with unlimited participation in earnings. Convertible preferred shares have been widely used in the past two decades, especially in consummating business combinations, and are favoured by investors who are attracted by the preferred dividend feature and the possibility of sharing in the long-term success of the company. The accounting problems related to convertible securities are discussed in Chapter 17.

4. **Callable (redeemable).** The issuing corporation can call or redeem at its option the outstanding preferred shares at specified future dates and at stipulated prices. Many preferred issues are callable. The call or redemption price is ordinarily set slightly above the original issuance price. The callable feature permits the corporation to use the capital obtained through the issuance of such shares until the need has passed or it is no longer advantageous. The existence of a call price or prices tends to set a ceiling on the market value of the preferred shares unless they are convertible into common shares. When cumulative preferred shares are called for redemption, any dividends in arrears must be paid. For many decades some preferred share issues contained provisions for redemption at some future date through sinking funds or other means. More recently, some preferred share issues have provided for mandatory redemption within five or ten years of issuance.

5. **Retractable.** Holders of retractable preferred shares may, at their option, have the issuing company buy them back, usually at a specified price and at a specified time.

Preferred shares are often issued instead of debt because a company's debt-to-equity ratio has become too high. In other instances, issuances are made through private placements with other corporations at a lower than market dividend rate because the acquiring corporation receives some tax advantages.

Debt Characteristics of Preferred Shares

With the right combination of features (i.e. fixed return, no vote, redeemable), preferred shares may possess more of the characteristics of debt than of ownership equity. Preferred shares generally have no maturity date, but the preferred shareholder's relationship with the company may be terminated if the corporation exercises its call privileges. Despite these debt characteristics, preferred shares have traditionally been accounted for as an ownership equity instrument and reported in the shareholders' equity section of the balance sheet. This accounting emphasizes the legal form of such securities in that they do not have priority over claims of unsecured creditors, and payments to owners are likely to be governed by legal restrictions related to the solvency position of the corporation.

The AcSB's *Exposure Draft* on financial instruments, however, contained proposed recommendations which would require companies to present financial instruments based on their economic substance rather than legal form. As such, preferred shares having the same characteristics as debt would have to be presented in the balance sheet as debt not shareholders' equity. Correspondingly, dividends on such shares would become an interest expense reported in the income statement. For a more detailed consideration of these notions, see Appendix 14A under the heading "Recognition of Substance Over Form."

DISCLOSURE OF SHARE CAPITAL

The *CICA Handbook* recommends that various disclosures be made regarding a corporation's share capital. Basic disclosures regarding *authorized* share capital, *issued* share capital, and *changes in* share capital since the last balance sheet date are required.[10] Note disclosure is the usual means of meeting these requirements. In such notes, each share class is described in terms of (1) the authorized number of shares (or stating there is no authorized limit), (2) the existence of unique rights (e.g., dividend preference and amount of such dividends, redemption and/or retraction privileges, conversion rights, whether or not they are cumulative), (3) the number of shares issued and the amount received, (4) if they are no-par value or par value shares, (5) the amount of any dividends in arrears, and (6) amounts and other details about changes during the year (e.g., new issuances, redemptions, conversions).

> **Objective 5**
>
> Know the requirements regarding disclosures for share capital.

Page 744 provides an example of note disclosure regarding share capital. This note was cross-referenced to the Capital Stock section of Shareholders' Equity in Loblaw's balance sheet which simply contained two line items—one for total preferred shares and the other for total common shares.

ACCOUNTING FOR THE ISSUANCE OF SHARES

From the preceding discussion it can be seen that a corporation obtains funds from its shareholders through a series of events and transactions. After establishing the authorized classes of shares in the articles of incorporation, the shares would be offered for sale, contracts for sale would be entered into, amounts received for shares would be collected, and the shares issued. The accounting involved in this process is discussed under the following topics:

> **Objective 6**
>
> Know how to account for issuance of shares for cash, on a subscription basis, in combination with sale of other securities, and in noncash transactions.

1. Accounting for shares without par value.

2. Accounting for shares sold on a subscription basis.

3. Accounting for shares issued in combination with other securities.

4. Accounting for expenses related to issuance.

Accounting for Shares Without Par Value

The CBCA requires that almost all authorized shares issued by companies incorporated under it be without par or nominal value.[11] **Authorized shares** simply represent the classes and nature of shares which a company is entitled to issue. These would be specified in its articles of incorporation. The CBCA allows but does not require a corporation to specify a number of authorized shares for each class.

Assume that Video Electronics Ltd. is incorporated under the CBCA with 10,000 authorized common shares without par value. No entry, other than a memorandum entry, need be made for the authorization as no economic transaction is involved. A memorandum entry or notation simply means that a Common Shares account would be created and the number of shares authorized (10,000) and their nature (without par value) would be noted. Entries into this account would be made as share transactions between the company and investors take place. By having such a notation in the account,

---

[10] *CICA Handbook*, Section 3240, pars. .01–.04.

[11] The CBCA, in Section 26, subsection 1.2, states that, after November 8, 1977, shares issued in non-arm's-length transactions (in the meaning of that term in the Income Tax Act) may have the whole or any part of the consideration received in exchange added to the stated capital amounts for the shares of the class. As such, assigning an amount less than that deemed to be received for shares is possible under this Act, but the circumstances under which such a treatment would be permitted pertain to tax issues and occur infrequently. When this does happen, the excess of the amount received over the value assigned to the shares would be credited to a Contributed Surplus account.

From the notes to the 1992 financial statements of
Loblaw Companies Limited

Note 8. Capital Stock

	Number of shares issued			Paid-up-capital (in millions of dollars)		
	1992	1991	1990	1992	1991	1990
First preferred shares						
First series	439,652	439,652	439,652	$22.0	$22.0	$22.0
Second series	290,798	299,048	307,273	9.6	9.9	10.1
	730,450	738,700	746,925			
Second preferred shares						
Third series	1,515,700	1,515,700	3,000,000	37.9	37.9	75.0
Fourth series	120	120	120	60.0	60.0	60.0
Fifth series		110	110		55.0	55.0
	1,515,820	1,515,930	3,000,230			
Junior preferred shares	2,200	11,375	14,125	.2	1.1	1.4
Total preferred shares				129.7	185.9	223.5
Common shares	78,932,026	78,381,416	72,621,007	222.8	218.2	110.6
Total capital stock				$352.5	$404.1	$334.1

Share Description

First preferred shares (authorized – 1,000,000)

First series – $2.40 cumulative dividend redeemable at $50. Second series – $3.70 cumulative dividend redeemable at $70. Subject to certain exceptions, in each fiscal year, the Company is obligated to apply $400,000 to the retirement of these shares.

Second preferred shares (authorized – unlimited)
Third series – $1.825 cumulative dividend redeemable at $25, retractable at the option of the holder on September 1, 1993.
Fourth series – cumulative dividend with a fixed rate of 7.75% to March 1, 1995 and a floating rate thereafter, redeemable at $500,000 each on or after March 1, 1995.
Fifth series – cumulative dividend with a fixed rate of 7.75% to March 1, 1995. These shares were redeemed according to their terms at $500,000 each on March 1, 1992.

Junior preferred shares (authorized – unlimited)
Third and fourth series – cumulative dividend with floating rate equal to two-thirds of average bank prime rate plus ¾%. 9,175 third and fourth series shares were converted into 220,510 common shares in 1992. The 2,200 fourth series, redeemable after May 16, 1993 at $100, are convertible into 34,510 common shares (11,375 third and fourth series convertible into 255,020 common shares in 1991).

Common shares (authorized – unlimited)
In June, 1991, the Company issued 5,000,000 common shares for cash consideration of $101,250,000.
In 1992, the Company issued 220,510 (1991 – 43,136) common shares for a consideration of $917,500 (1991 – $275,000) on conversion of 9,175 junior preferred shares.
In 1992, the company issued 330,100 (1991 – 717,273) common shares for cash consideration of $3,631,827 (1991 – $6,078,224) on exercise of employee stock options.
As at January 2, 1993, there were outstanding stock options, which were granted at the market price on the day preceding the grant, to purchase 2,295,711 common shares at prices ranging from $9⅛ to $18½ with a weighted average price of $15⅛. Options expire on dates ranging from January 27, 1993 to December 16, 1999, with 333,690 expiring in 1993.
The exercise of the conversion privileges and stock option would not materially dilute earnings per share.

one can readily determine the number of unissued but authorized shares by deducting the number issued from the authorized number.

__When shares without par value are issued, the full amount of the proceeds received is credited to the appropriate share capital account.__ If 500 common shares of Video Electronics Ltd. are sold for cash at $10 each, the entry would be:

Cash	5,000	
Common Shares		5,000

If another 500 shares are sold at a later date for $11 per share, the entry would be:

Cash	5,500	
Common Shares		5,500

The price received for a share is governed by the marketplace. In determining market price, investors assess the share relative to other shares and financial instruments in terms of rights, future earnings, and risk.

Entries for the sale of preferred shares without par value are of the same nature as illustrated previously for common shares except that a Preferred Shares account would be credited. The accounts titled Common Shares or Preferred Shares may alternately be titled Common Stock or Preferred Stock, or Class A Shares or Class B Shares if so designated.

Shares Sold on a Subscription Basis

The preceding discussion assumed that the shares were sold for cash, but they may also be sold on a subscription basis. Placer Dome Inc. and Canada Development Corporation serve as examples of companies which have had subscription issues. When shares are sold on a subscription basis, the full price is not received immediately. Normally only a partial payment is made initially, and the shares are not issued, nor rights associated with the shares given, until the full subscription price is received.

Accounting for Subscribed Shares. Two new accounts are used when shares are sold on a subscription basis. The first, **Common (or Preferred) Shares Subscribed**, indicates the corporation's obligation to issue shares upon payment of final subscription balances by those who have subscribed. This account thus signifies a commitment against the unissued capital shares. Once the subscription price is fully paid, the Common (or Preferred) Shares Subscribed account is debited and the Common (or Preferred) Shares account is credited. *Shares Subscribed accounts are presented in the shareholders' equity section below the respective Common or Preferred Shares accounts.*

The second account, **Subscriptions Receivable**, indicates the amount yet to be collected before subscribed shares will be issued. Controversy exists concerning the presentation of Subscriptions Receivable on the balance sheet. Some argue that Subscriptions Receivable should be reported in the current asset section (assuming that payment on the receivable will be received within the operating cycle or one year, whichever is longer). They note that it is similar to Trade Accounts Receivable, but that it differs in conception. Trade Accounts Receivable grow out of sales transactions in the ordinary course of business; Subscriptions Receivable relate to the issuance of a concern's own shares and represent capital contributions not yet paid to the corporation.

Others argue that Subscriptions Receivable should be reported as a deduction from Common (or Preferred) Shares Subscribed in the shareholders' equity section. Their reasoning is based on a concern that doing otherwise may result in users of financial statements misunderstanding the share capital accounts (i.e. not realizing that some shares are only partially paid for), and the fact that subscribers cannot be forced to pay the unpaid balance of a subscription receivable.

It should be emphasized that there is no "right" answer to this classification issue. Judgement must therefore be exercised. In the United States, practice generally follows the contra-equity approach, which is required in reports to the Securities Exchange Commission. A similar rule does not exist in Canada.

The journal entries for handling shares sold on a subscription basis are illustrated by the following example. Lakehead Corp. offers 500 no-par value common shares on a subscription basis at a price of $20 per share. Various individuals accept the company's offer and agree to pay 50% down and the remaining 50% at the end of six months. At the date the subscriptions are received, the entries are:

Subscriptions Receivable	10,000	
Common Shares Subscribed		10,000
(To record receipt of subscriptions for 500 shares)		
Cash	5,000	
Subscriptions Receivable		5,000
(To record receipt of first instalment representing		
50% of total due on subscribed shares)		

When the final payment is received and the shares are issued, the entries are:

Cash	5,000	
Subscriptions Receivable		5,000
(To record receipt of final instalment on		
subscribed shares)		
Common Shares Subscribed	10,000	
Common Shares		10,000
(To record issuance of 500 shares upon receipt of		
final instalment from subscribers)		

Assuming that Lakehead Corp. had 10,000 common shares authorized, and had previously issued 5,000 shares for a total of $75,000, the receivable and subscribed accounts after the subscription was received could be shown as follows using the contra-equity approach.

Lakehead Corp.
Partial Balance Sheet

Shareholders' Equity		
Share Capital		
Common shares, no-par value,		
10,000 authorized, 5,000 issued.		$75,000
Common shares subscribed (500 shares)	$10,000	
Less: Subscriptions receivable	(5,000)	5,000
Total share capital		$80,000

Alternatively, the $5,000 subscription receivable could be shown as a current asset and the Common Shares Subscribed amount would be shown at the gross amount ($10,000) in Shareholders' Equity.

Defaulted Subscription Accounts. Sometimes a subscriber is unable to pay all instalments and defaults on the agreement. The question is then what to do with the balance of the subscription account as well as the amount already paid in. The answer depends on the terms of the subscription contract, corporate policy, and any applicable law of the jurisdiction of incorporation. The possibilities include returning the amount already paid by the subscriber (possibly after deducting some expenses), treating the amount paid as forfeited and therefore transferred to a Contributed Surplus account, or issuing shares to the subscriber equivalent to the number that previous subscription payments would have paid in full.

For example, assume that a subscriber to 50 Lakehead Corp. common shares defaulted on the final payment. If the subscription contract stated that amounts paid by a defaulting subscriber would be refunded, Lakehead Corp. would make the following entry when the default occurs (assume the cash is paid at a later date):

Common Shares Subscribed	1,000	
Subscriptions Receivable		500
Due to Defaulting Subscriber		500
(To record default on 50 shares subscribed for		
at $20 each and on which 50% had been paid for		
which the subscriber is given a refund)		

If the amount paid by the subscriber was forfeited, there would be a $500 credit to a Contributed Surplus—Forfeited Shares account instead of to the Due to Defaulting Subscriber account.

Shares Issued in Combination With Other Securities (Lump Sum Sales)

Generally, corporations sell classes of shares separately from one another so that the proceeds relative to each class, and even relative to each lot, are known. Occasionally, two or more classes of securities are issued for a single payment or lump sum. It is not uncommon for more than one type or class of security to be issued in the acquisition of another company. The accounting problem in a lump sum issuance is to determine the allocation of the proceeds between the various classes of securities. The two methods of allocation available for accountants are (1) the proportional method (also called the relative market value method) and (2) the incremental method.

Proportional Method. If the fair market value or another sound basis for determining relative value is available for each class of security, the *lump sum received is allocated between the classes of securities on a proportional basis*—that is, the ratio of each to the total. For instance, if 1,000 common shares having a market value of $20 each and 1,000 preferred shares having a market value of $12 each are issued for a lump sum of $30,000, the allocation of the $30,000 between the two classes would be as determined below.

Fair market value of common (1,000 × $20)	=	$20,000
Fair market value of preferred (1,000 × $12)	=	12,000
Aggregate fair market value		$32,000
Allocated to common: $\dfrac{\$20,000}{\$32,000} \times \$30,000$	=	**$18,750**
Allocated to preferred: $\dfrac{\$12,000}{\$32,000} \times \$30,000$	=	**$11,250**
Total allocation		$30,000

Incremental Method. In instances *where the fair market value of all classes of securities is not determinable, the incremental method may be used*. The market value of the securities is used as a basis for those classes that are known and the remainder of the lump sum is allocated to the class for which the market value is not known. For instance, if 1,000 common shares having a market value of $20 each and 1,000 preferred shares having no established market value are issued for a lump sum of $30,000, the allocation of the $30,000 to the two classes would be as follows.

Lump sum receipt	$30,000
Allocated to common (1,000 shares × $20 fair market value)	20,000
Balance allocated to preferred	$10,000

If fair market value is not determinable for any of the classes of shares involved in a lump sum exchange, the allocation may have to be arbitrary. If it is known that one or more of the classes of securities issued will have a determinable market value in the near future, the arbitrary basis may be used with the intent to make an adjustment when the future market value is established. If a market value is unlikely to be determinable for any of the share classes in the near future, the shares involved may be left in a single account until a separate market value can be established.

Shares Issued in Noncash Transactions

It is not uncommon for a corporation to issue shares in exchange for property, services, or any form of asset other than cash. Accounting for the issuance of shares for property or services may involve a problem of valuation. *The general rule to be applied in such situations is that the property or services be recorded at either their fair market value or the fair market value of the shares issued, whichever is more clearly determinable.*

If the fair market value of only the property or services received or the shares issued is determinable, it is used as the basis for recording the exchange. If both are readily determinable and the transaction is the result of an arm's-length exchange, there will probably be little difference in their fair market values. In such cases it should not matter which value is regarded as the basis for valuing the exchange. If the fair market value of the shares being issued and the property or services being received are not readily determinable, the value to be assigned is generally established by management or the board of directors, usually with the assistance of independent appraisers. The use of book values as a basis of valuation for these transactions should be avoided, if at all possible.

When shares are issued for personal services provided by employees or outsiders, the fair value of the services as of the date of the contract for such services, rather than the date of issuance of the shares, should be the basis for valuation because the contract is viewed in an accounting sense as a subscription. In these exchanges, however, the fair market value of the shares issued may be more readily determinable.

The following illustrates how to record the issuance of 10,000 common shares for a patent under various circumstances:

1. The fair market value of the patent is not readily determinable but the fair market value of the shares is known to be $140,000.

Patent	140,000	
Common Shares		140,000

2. The fair market value of the shares is not readily determinable, but the fair market value of the patent is determined to be $150,000.

Patent	150,000	
Common Shares		150,000

3. Neither the fair market value of the share nor the patent is readily determinable. An independent consultant values the patent at $125,000, and the board of directors agrees with that valuation.

Patent	125,000	
Common Shares		125,000

In corporate law, the board of directors is granted the power to set the value of noncash transactions. In some instances, this power has been abused. The issuance of shares for property or services has resulted in cases of overstated corporate capital through intentional overvaluation of the property or services received. The overvaluation of the shareholders' equity resulting from inflated asset values creates what is referred to as **watered stock**. The "water" can be eliminated from the corporate structure by writing down the overvalued assets.

If, as a result of the issuance of shares for property or services, the recorded assets are undervalued, **secret reserves** are created. A secret reserve may also be achieved by excessive depreciation or amortization charges, by expensing capital expenditures, by excessive write-downs of inventories or receivables, or by any other understatement of assets or overstatement of liabilities. An example of a liability overstatement is an excessive provision for estimated product warranties that correspondingly results in an understatement of owners' equity, thereby creating a secret reserve.

Costs of Issuing Shares

The costs associated with the acquisition of corporate capital resulting from the issuance of securities include attorneys' fees, public accountants' fees, underwriters' fees and commissions, expenses of printing and mailing certificates and registration statements, clerical and administrative expenses of preparation, and costs of advertising the issue.

In practice there are at least three methods of accounting for initial issue costs. *The first and predominantly used method treats issue costs as a reduction of the amounts paid in*. In effect, this treatment has the result of simply reducing the amount received for issued shares. This treatment is based on the premise that issue costs are unrelated to corporate operations and thus are not properly chargeable against earnings from operations; issue costs are viewed as a reduction of proceeds of the financing activity.

The second method treats issue costs as an organization cost that is charged neither to current earnings nor to corporate capital; such costs are capitalized and classified as a deferred charge. They would be amortized over an arbitrary time period not to exceed 40 years. This treatment is based on the premise that amounts paid in as invested capital should not be violated, and that issue costs benefit the corporation over a long period of time or so long as the invested capital is used.

The third method charges issue costs directly against retained earnings. Therefore it accomplishes the objectives of maintaining the total amount received for shares in share capital accounts and not charging issue costs against earning from operations.

In addition to the costs of issuing shares, corporations annually incur costs for maintaining the shareholders' records and handling ownership transfers. These recurring costs, primarily registrar and transfer agents' fees, should be charged as expense to the period in which incurred.

REACQUISITION OF SHARES

It is not unusual for corporations to buy back their own shares. Corporations first obtain approval for such action from the stock exchange on which the shares are listed and then proceed to purchase their own shares. In recent years, *The Globe and Mail* has reported that over 250 companies have obtained approval from the Toronto Stock Exchange and more than 150 of these companies eventually reacquired their own shares. Maclean Hunter Limited, Bombardier Inc., Canada Packers Inc., and Du Pont Canada Inc. are examples of corporations that have reacquired their own shares through buybacks.

Corporations purchase their outstanding shares for a variety of reasons. Rogers Communications Inc. bought a total of 14.2 million shares to reduce its foreign ownership so that it would not lose its eligibility for Canadian broadcasting licences. More general reasons for buybacks include:

Objective 7

Identify the major reasons for reacquiring shares.

1. To have enough shares on hand to meet employee stock option contracts.

2. To reduce the shares outstanding in hopes of increasing earnings per share.

3. To buy out a particular ownership interest.

4. To attempt to make a market in the company's shares.

5. To contract the operations of the business.

6. To meet the share needs of a potential merger.

7. To change the debt-to-equity ratio.

8. To settle a debt.

9. To provide a psychological boost to shareholders.

10. To fulfil the terms of a contract.

11. To satisfy a claim of a dissenting shareholder.

12. To change from public to private corporation status.

Whether or not a corporation may purchase its own shares and what it may do with them depends on the terms and conditions of its articles of incorporation, the legal constraints imposed by the Act under which it is incorporated, and the stock exchange on which its shares are registered.

Assuming that a corporation may purchase or otherwise reacquire its own shares, they may either be (1) retired (cancelled) or (2) held in treasury for reissue.

Reacquisition and Retirement

The CBCA and acts of various provinces permit a corporation to purchase or redeem its shares by special resolution of its board of directors as long as such an action would not result in the insolvency of the corporation. Insolvency (under the CBCA) would result if, after reacquisition, the corporation were unable to pay its liabilities or if the realizable value of its assets were less than its liabilities and stated capital. *The CBCA generally requires that reacquired shares be cancelled or, if the articles have an authorized limit on the number of shares, restored to the status of authorized but unissued shares.*

When shares are purchased or redeemed by the issuing corporation it is likely that the price paid will differ from the amount received for the shares when they were issued. It would be incorrect to treat any differences as a gain or loss shown in the income statement, owing to the capital nature of the transaction.[12] Consequently, when shares are purchased or redeemed and cancelled, shareholders' equity accounts are adjusted. The accounts adjusted and the nature of the adjustment are specified in the *CICA Handbook* as follows:

> Where a company redeems its own shares, or cancels its own shares that it has acquired, and the cost of such shares is equal to or greater than their par, stated or assigned value, the cost should be allocated as follows:
>
> (a) To share capital, in an amount equal to the par, stated, or assigned value of the shares;
>
> (b) Any excess, to contributed surplus to the extent that contributed surplus was created by a net excess of proceeds over cost on cancellation or resale of shares of the same class;
>
> (c) Any excess, to contributed surplus in an amount equal to the pro rata share of the portion of contributed surplus that arose from transactions, other than those in (b) above, in the same class of shares;
>
> (d) Any excess, to retained earnings.[13]
>
> In the case where the cost to purchase shares is less than the par, stated, or assigned value, the cost would be allocated as follows:
>
> (a) To share capital in an amount equal to the par, stated, or assigned value of the shares;
>
> (b) The difference, to contributed surplus.[14]

These specifications are written to apply to both par and no-par value shares. *For shares without par value, the amount of the cost of reacquisition to be charged against the share capital account is an* assigned value *equal to the average per share amount in the account for that class of shares at the date of the reacquisition of the shares.*[15]

For no-par value shares, reacquisition and cancellation at a cost in excess of assigned value would, following the steps in the *Handbook*, normally result in simply debiting the share capital (step a) and retained earnings (step d). An exception to this procedure would occur if a prior can-

---

[12] *CICA Handbook*, Section 3240, par. .06.

[13] *Ibid.*, par. .15.

[14] *Ibid.*, par. .17.

[15] *Ibid.*, par. .18.

Objective 8

Know how to account for a reacquisition of shares resulting in the shares being cancelled or restored to the status of being authorized but unissued.

cellation of some shares of this class had resulted in the creation of contributed surplus; that is, if the cost of the shares purchased was less than their assigned value at that earlier time. In such a case, purchase for cancellation at a cost in excess of assigned value would result in a reduction of the Share Capital account for the assigned value (step a), the Contributed Surplus account created by the prior transaction (step b), and of the Retained Earnings account if necessary (step d).

To illustrate the application of the accounting procedures for the purchase and cancellation of no-par shares, assume the following composition of shareholders' equity for Waterloo Corp. as a starting point.

Waterloo Corp.
Shareholders' Equity
December 31, 1993

Share Capital:

Class A, 10,500 shares issued and outstanding no-par value	$ 63,000
Class B, 50,000 shares issued and outstanding, no-par value	100,000
Total Share Capital	$163,000
Retained Earnings	300,000
Total Shareholders' Equity	$463,000

On January 30, 1994, Waterloo Corp. purchased and cancelled 500 Class A shares at a cost of $4 per share. The required entry would be:

Class A Shares [500 ($63,000/10,500)]	3,000	
Cash		2,000
Contributed Surplus—Excess of Assigned Value Over Reacquisition Cost		1,000

This entry is derived by following the allocation procedure when the cost to purchase is less than the assigned value of shares cancelled.

On September 10, 1994, the company purchased and cancelled an additional 1,000 Class A shares. The purchase cost was $8 per share. This transaction would be recorded as:

Class A Shares [1,000 ($60,000/10,000)]	6,000	
Contributed Surplus—Excess of Assigned Value Over Reacquisition Cost	1,000	
Retained Earnings	1,000	
Cash		8,000

This entry is derived by following the steps for the situation where the cost of the shares purchased is greater than their assigned value. Specifically, the procedure would be as follows:

Step (a): Remove from share capital the assigned value of the Class A shares cancelled. The assigned value is the amount in the Class A shares account ($60,000, which is the $63,000 on December 31 less the $3,000 debit for the reacquisition on January 30) divided by the number of shares issued and outstanding (10,000, which is the 10,500 on December 31 less the 500 reacquired on January 30) at the date of the reacquisition.

Step (b): If there is any contributed surplus arising from previous cancellations of the same share class (i.e. when the cost of purchased shares was less than their assigned value), it would be removed by a debit to that account. The amount would be the lesser of the account's total balance or the amount by which the purchase cost exceeds the assigned value of the cancelled shares. From the cancellation of Class A shares on January 30, 1994, such a Contributed Surplus account resulted in a $1,000 balance. Since the purchase cost of the present cancellation was $2,000 greater than the assigned value, the full $1,000 balance in this Contributed Surplus account is debited.

Step (c): If, after steps (a) and (b), there is still an excess of cost to be accounted for, this excess is to be charged against any Contributed Surplus account—other than that in (b)—that arose from transactions in the same class of shares. The maximum that can be charged to such accounts is based on a pro rata share allocation of the account balance. A pro rata share allocation is determined by dividing the number of shares reacquired by the number of shares issued prior to the reacquisition and multiplying the result by the balance in the Contributed Surplus account. There are no such Contributed Surplus accounts in this example, and they would be rare in the case of no-par value shares (Contributed Surplus on Forfeited Shares would be an example). Such accounts exist for par value shares in which the proceeds received in excess of par value are credited to a Contributed Surplus account.

Step (d): Since there is still an excess of $1,000 of the cost over allocations made in the previous steps, this amount is charged against Retained Earnings.

While this example has illustrated calculations associated with all steps in the process, it would not be necessary to continue through steps beyond those required to allocate the total purchase cost of the shares cancelled. For example, if the cost had been only $6,700, the full amount would be accounted for by debiting the Class A Shares for $6,000 and the Contributed Surplus—Excess of Assigned Value Over Reacquisition Cost account for $700. If there are no accounts in Contributed Surplus arising from transactions in the class of shares involved, steps (b) and (c) would be omitted.

Treasury Shares

Objective 9

Appreciate what treasury shares are and how to account for them under the single-transaction method.

Treasury shares or treasury stock are a company's own shares that have been repurchased but have not been cancelled—they are being held for reissue.

While Canadian corporate law has allowed companies to issue redeemable preferred shares for some time, it was not until 1971 that corporations were permitted to purchase other types of their own shares. At that time, Ontario's incorporation act allowed for such transactions for the first time in a Canadian jurisdiction. Since then, the CBCA and provincial acts have allowed corporations to reacquire their own shares. Legislation varies, however, in terms of what companies may do with such shares. As previously stated, the CBCA requires that repurchased shares be cancelled and, if the articles limit the number of authorized shares, be restored to the status of authorized but unissued shares. Two exceptions allowed by the CBCA are (1) when acting in the capacity of a legal representative not receiving any beneficial interest from the shares and (2) when such shares are held as security for purposes of ordinary business transactions that involve the lending of money.

Consequently, with rare exception, there can be no such thing as treasury shares for companies incorporated under the CBCA. Alternatively, many countries (e.g., the United States) and some provincial jurisdictions do permit such treasury shares to exist.[16] Clearport Petroleums Ltd. is an example of a Canadian company that has disclosed treasury shares. When a corporation holds treasury shares, voting rights and dividend declarations do not usually apply to these shares.

The *CICA Handbook* states that the **single-transaction method** should be used to account for treasury shares.[17] The presumption underlying this method is that the purchase and sale of

---

[16] *Financial Reporting in Canada—1991* reported that of the 300 companies surveyed, 38 in 1990, 28 in 1989, 27 in 1988, and 17 in 1987 disclosed the acquisition of their own common shares. Also, it was reported that of these companies, 34 in 1990, 24 in 1989, 21 in 1988, and 14 in 1987 disclosed cancellations of common shares purchased.

[17] *CICA Handbook*, Section 3240, pars. .10 and .11. Another method, called the **two-transaction method**, exists and is an acceptable alternative to the single-transaction method in other countries (e.g., the United States). The presumption associated with the two-transaction method is that the purchase by a company of its own shares terminates the relationship between the company and the shareholder. Such an acquisition therefore represents a completed, independent transaction in terms of the company's capital. Essentially, the acquisition of shares under this method is recorded as if the shares were retired. A subsequent resale of the acquired shares is also viewed as a separate, independent transaction. Therefore, these two transactions (purchase and sale of shares) would be recorded independently of each other.

treasury shares are essentially two parts of a single procedure being used by a corporation. In essence, the acquisition of treasury shares is the initiation of a transaction that is consummated when the shares are resold. Consequently, the holding by a company of its own shares is viewed as a transition phase between the beginning and end of a single activity.

When shares are purchased under the single-transaction method, the total cost is debited to a Treasury Shares account. There are no direct reductions of any Shareholders' Equity accounts. The balance in the Treasury Shares account is shown as a deduction from the total of the components of Shareholders' Equity in the balance sheet.[18] An example of such disclosure is as follows.

Shareholders' equity:	
Common shares, no-par value; authorized	
24,000,000 shares; issued 19,045,870 shares	
of which 209,750 are in treasury	$ 27,686,000
Retained earnings	253,265,000
Total	$280,951,000
Less: Cost of treasury shares (209,970 shares)	(7,527,000)
Total shareholders' equity	$273,424,000

When the shares are sold, the Treasury Shares account is credited for their cost. If they are sold for more than their cost, the excess is credited to a Contributed Surplus account. If they are sold at less than their cost, the difference is debited to any balance in a Contributed Surplus account resulting from previous sales or cancellations of treasury shares and any remaining difference is charged against Retained Earnings.[19]

To illustrate the accounting entries under the single-transaction method, assume as a starting point the information regarding the shareholders' equity of Waterloo Corp. as at December 31, 1993 (page 751). Now assume that on January 15, 1994, the company reacquired as treasury shares 1,000 Class A shares paying $7 per share. This would be recorded as follows:

Treasury Shares	7,000	
Cash		7,000

On February 15, 1994, all treasury shares were sold for $8 per share. The journal entry would be:

Cash	8,000	
Treasury Shares		7,000
Contributed Surplus—Excess of Sale Price		
of Treasury Shares Over Cost		1,000

If treasury shares recorded under the single-transaction method are subsequently retired (cancelled), then the procedure for cancelling shares is applied, with the balance in the Treasury Shares account being eliminated. For example, if instead of selling the treasury shares on February 15, Waterloo Corp. cancelled them, the entry would be:

Class A Shares	6,000	
Retained Earnings	1,000	
Treasury Shares		7,000

---

[18] *Ibid.*, par. .11.
[19] *Ibid.*, par. .20.

BASIC RECORDS RELATED TO SHARES

A share or stock certificate book and a share or stock transfer book are included among the special corporate records involved in accounting for shares. A share certificate book is similar to a chequebook in that printed share certificates are enclosed. A share transfer book simply tells who owns the shares at a given point in time. Obviously the corporation must be able to obtain at any time a list of the current shareholders so that dividend payments, notices of annual shareholder meetings, and voting proxies may be sent to the appropriate persons.

Many corporations avoid the problems concerned with handling share capital sales and transfers by engaging an organization that specializes in this type of work to serve as a **registrar and transfer agent**. Trust companies frequently serve in this capacity, keeping all the necessary records. The corporation is provided, upon request, with a list of registered shareholders for such purposes as mailing dividend cheques or voting proxies.

FUNDAMENTAL CONCEPTS

1. Shareholders' equity represents the ownership interest in a corporation. It is the difference between total assets and liabilities (i.e. the net assets). Shareholders have a residual interest in an enterprise in the sense that they rank after liability holders in claim to assets.

2. Direct contributions by shareholders and earnings retained by a corporation are the primary sources from which ownership equity is derived. Direct contributions by shareholders are generally subclassified on the balance sheet as Share Capital and Contributed Surplus. Share Capital is that portion of equity that is required by statute to be retained in the business for the protection of creditors. Contributed Surplus represents additional amounts received from shareholders or others, such as donations. Retained Earnings is the undistributed income that remains invested in the enterprise.

3. Canadian companies may be incorporated under the Canada Business Corporations Act (CBCA) or a provincial incorporation act. This book has concentrated on the CBCA, although it should be realized that acts of different jurisdictions may vary. A major aspect of the CBCA is that it confers legal status on the *CICA Handbook*; that is, regulations under this Act require that financial statements be prepared in accordance with the recommendations in the *Handbook*.

4. Ownership interests are represented by share certificates. Basic ownership rights are to share in profits, to share in management (vote at shareholder meetings), and to share in corporate assets upon liquidation. Shares possessing all of these basic rights have been called "common shares." Common shareholders bear the ultimate risks of failure and benefits of success. Other types of shares (called "preferred shares") may exist. Various rights, privileges, restrictions, and conditions attach to preferred shares and differentiate them from common shares. The particulars regarding preferred shares would be specified in an enterprise's articles of incorporation. While the CBCA simply states that shares may be of different "classes" (i.e. A, B, C, etc.), the authors have used the terms "common" and "preferred" to represent the existence of these differences.

5. Preferred shares may have various rights, privileges, or restrictions assigned in terms of dividends or distribution of assets on liquidation, may be convertible, callable, redeemable, or retractable, and usually are nonvoting. In some cases a preferred share has the economic characteristics of a liability even though it has the legal form of being equity. Such circumstances create a dilemma for accountants in terms of classification questions.

6. Accounting for share capital involves recognition, measurement, and disclosure issues with regard to issuance of shares without par value for cash and noncash items, in combination with issuing different equity securities, and on a subscription basis. Accounting issues and procedures related to costs incurred for issuing shares also exist. Although the notion of par value remains an aspect of accounting for share capital, its importance is rapidly diminishing in Canadian financial reporting. See Appendix 15A for the accounting for par value shares.

7. A corporation may purchase its own shares for various reasons. Such reacquired shares are not an asset of the enterprise because a corporation may not own part of itself.

(Continued)

8. While permitting reacquisition of shares, the CBCA requires, in most circumstances, that such shares be retired (cancelled) or restored to the status of authorized but unissued shares. Reacquisition and retirement of shares without par value is accounted for by removing the average amount received for the shares (assigned value) from the appropriate Share Capital account and charging any excess amount paid to a Contributed Surplus account if such exists from previous similar transactions and then to Retained Earnings, if necessary. If the cost of reacquisition is less than the assigned value, the difference is credited to a Contributed Surplus account.

9. In some cases, the jurisdiction of incorporation may permit reacquisition without requiring cancellation. These shares are called treasury shares. The *CICA Handbook* recommends that the single-transaction method be used to account for treasury shares.

APPENDIX 15A
Accounting for Par Value Shares

As indicated in the chapter, par value is an arbitrary amount per share determined by the incorporators of a company and stated as such in the articles of incorporation. When a par value exists, it is usually very low ($1, $5, $10 per share), which contrasts dramatically with the situation in the early 1900s when practically all shares had a par value of $100. The reason for having low par values is to permit the original sale of shares at low amounts per share and to avoid the contingent liability of shareholders associated with shares sold below par. Shares with a low par value are rarely, if ever, sold by the issuing company below par value (i.e. at a discount). Indeed such an action is generally not permitted in Canadian jurisdictions allowing for par value shares. A par value has nothing to do with the market value of the share. The accounting significance of par value is that it is the amount per share issued that is credited to the Share Capital account. Amounts received above par value are charged to other accounts, as will be illustrated shortly.

Par value shares were common in Canada prior to the mid-1980s. In 1975, the Canada Business Corporations Act (CBCA) decreed that par value shares were no longer permitted for companies incorporated under it. Such enterprises had five years from January 1, 1976 to file for continuance under the CBCA—that is, to switch from the requirements of the predecessor Canada Corporations Act to those of the CBCA. Most provincial incorporation acts followed the example of the CBCA in requiring that share capital would be of no-par value. The development of consistent regulations across all Canadian jurisdictions and the necessary conversion by companies from old to new requirements has taken considerable time. *Financial Reporting in Canada—1991* indicated that in 1990, of the 300 companies surveyed, 118 disclosed that all share classes were without par value, 21 disclosed a par value (or a stated value) for at least one class of shares, 27 indicated no-par value for one share class with no reference to other classes, and 134 made no reference to either par or no-par value. The large number making no reference to par or no-par value was stated to be a reflection of the fact that certain corporations acts require all shares to be without par value. Consequently, it would appear safe to conclude that Canadian corporations predominantly issue shares without par value, although some still have par value shares.

While the authors have chosen to follow the CBCA requirements regarding the issuance of shares without par value throughout this book, they recognize that some may wish to consider the accounting aspects related to par value shares to a greater extent than is possible from the limited references to it in the chapter. Also, a more comprehensive examination of such accounting may be beneficial to understanding financial statements which incorporate par value shares (i.e. those of companies that are operating in jurisdictions permitting par value, or are incorporated in countries such as the United States which permit par value shares). For these reasons, the material in this appendix is presented. The accounting for par value shares will be examined under the following headings:

- Issuance of par value shares for cash.

- Par value shares sold on a subscription basis.

- Reacquisition and retirement of par value shares.

- Treasury shares having a par value.

ISSUANCE OF PAR VALUE SHARES FOR CASH

To show the required information for issuance of par value shares, accounts must be kept for each class of shares as follows:

1. **Preferred Shares or Common Shares.** Reflects the par value of the corporation's issued shares. These accounts are credited for the par value when the shares are originally issued. No additional entries are made in these accounts unless additional shares are issued or shares are retired.

2. **Contributed Surplus in Excess of Par** or **Premium on Common** (or **Preferred**) **Shares.** Indicates any excess over par value paid by shareholders in return for the shares issued to them. Once paid, the excess over par becomes a part of the corporation's contributed surplus and the individual shareholder has no greater claim on the excess paid than all other holders of the same class of shares.

To illustrate how these accounts are used, assume that Hamilton Corporation sold 100 common shares with a par value of $5 per share for $1,100. The entry to record the issuance is as follows.

Cash	1,100	
Common Shares		500
Contributed Surplus in Excess of Par		600
(or Premium on Common Shares)		

While this entry reflects the receipt of cash for the shares, such shares could be issued in combination with other securities (lump sum sales) or for noncash items. In such situations, the basic issue is to determine the amount (fair value) received for the shares. Solutions to these issues are the same as those stated in the chapter regarding shares without par value. Once the amount received for par value shares has been determined, the par value is credited to the appropriate Share Capital account and any excess goes to a Contributed Surplus account.

PAR VALUE SHARES SOLD ON A SUBSCRIPTION BASIS

The journal entries for handling par value shares sold on a subscription basis are illustrated by the following example. Mercury Ltd. offers 500 common shares of $5 par value on a subscription basis at a price of $20 per share. Various individuals accept the company's offer and agree to pay 50% down and the remaining 50% at the end of six months.

At date of subscription

Subscriptions Receivable	10,000	
Common Shares Subscribed		2,500
Contributed Surplus in Excess of Par		7,500
(To record receipt of subscriptions for 500 shares)		
Cash	5,000	
Subscriptions Receivable		5,000
(To record receipt of first instalment representing		
50% of total due on subscribed shares)		

When the final payment is received and the shares are issued, the entries are:

Six months later

Cash	5,000	
Subscriptions Receivable		5,000
(To record receipt of final instalment on		
subscribed shares)		
Common Shares Subscribed	2,500	
Common Shares		2,500
(To record issuance of 500 shares upon receipt of		
final instalment from subscribers)		

REACQUISITION AND RETIREMENT OF PAR VALUE SHARES

To illustrate accounting procedures for the purchase and cancellation of par value shares, the Waterloo Corp. example presented in Chapter 15 regarding reacquisition and retirement of no-par value shares will be drawn upon (see page 751). This will allow for comparison of accounting between par value and no-par value shares. Two modifications to the original shareholders' equity section are made: Class A shares issued for $63,000 had a $5 par value and this resulted in a Premium on Class A Shares which is a Contributed Surplus account. Therefore, the starting point for this par value shares illustration is as shown on page 754.

On January 30, 1994, Waterloo Corp. purchased and cancelled 500 Class A shares. The purchase cost was $4 per share. The required entry would be:

Class A Shares	2,500	
Cash		2,000
Contributed Surplus—Excess of Par Value Over		
Reacquisition Cost (Class A)		500

Waterloo Corp.
Shareholders' Equity
December 31, 1993

Share Capital	
Class A, 10,500 shares issued and outstanding, $5 par value	$ 52,500
Class B, 50,000 shares issued and outstanding, no-par value	100,000
Total Share Capital	$152,500
Contributed Surplus	
Premium on Class A Shares	10,500
Retained Earnings	300,000
Total Shareholders' Equity	$463,000

This entry is derived by following the *CICA Handbook* allocation procedure as identified in Chapter 15 when the cost to purchase is less than the par value of shares cancelled.

On September 10, 1994, the company purchased and cancelled an additional 1,000 Class A shares at a cost of $8 each. This transaction would be recorded as:

Class A Shares	5,000	
Contributed Surplus—Excess of Par Value Over		
Reacquisition Cost	500	
Contributed Surplus—Premium on Class A Shares	1,050	
Retained Earnings	1,450	
Cash		8,000

This entry is derived by following the steps in the *CICA Handbook* for the situations where the cost of the shares purchased is greater than their par or assigned value. Specifically, the procedure would be as follows:

Step (a): Remove from share capital the par value of the Class A shares cancelled. This is equal to the par value ($5) multiplied by the shares purchased (1,000).

Step (b): If there is any contributed surplus arising from previous cancellations of the same share class (i.e. when cost of purchased shares was less than its par value), it would be removed by a debit to that account. The amount would be the lesser of the account's total balance or the amount by which the purchase cost exceeds the par value of the cancelled shares. From the cancellation of Class A shares January 30, 1994, such a Contributed Surplus account resulted in a $500 balance. Since the purchase cost of the present cancellation was $3,000 greater than the par value, the full $500 balance in this Contributed Surplus account is debited.

Step (c): If, after steps (a) and (b), there is still an excess of cost to be accounted for, this excess is to be charged against any Contributed Surplus account—other than that in (b)—that arose from transactions in the same class of shares. In this example, Premium on Class A Shares is such an account. The maximum that can be charged to such accounts is based on a pro rata share allocation of the account balance. A pro rata share allocation is determined by dividing the number of shares purchased (1,000) by the number of shares issued prior to the purchase (10,500 from December 31 less 500 retired on January 30 equals 10,000) and multiplying the result (0.1) by the balance in the Premium account ($10,500). The maximum pro rata share allocation of $1,050 is debited to the Premium on Class A Shares account, because there is an excess of cost over allocations made in steps (a) and (b) of $2,500.

Step (d): Since there is still an excess of $1,450 of the cost over allocations made in steps (a), (b), and (c), this amount is charged against Retained Earnings.

If the cost to reacquire the shares had been only $5,300, the full amount would be accounted for by debiting the Class A Shares for $5,000 and the Contributed Surplus—Excess of Par Value Over Reacquisition Cost account for $300.

TREASURY SHARES HAVING A PAR VALUE

The basic concepts of accounting for treasury shares under the single-transaction method were specified in Chapter 15 and continue to apply for par value shares. Again, for purposes of comparison between par value and no-par value shares accounting, we will use the example of the shareholders' equity section of Waterloo Corp. as at December 31, 1993 as a starting point. The events related to treasury shares transactions are:

January 15, 1994—The company acquired treasury shares of 1,000 Class A $5 par value shares by paying $7 per share.

February 15, 1994—The treasury shares were sold for $8 per share.

Using the single-transaction method, the following entries would be made:

	January 15		
Treasury Shares		7,000	
Cash			7,000
	February 15		
Cash		8,000	
Treasury Shares			7,000
Contributed Surplus—Excess of Sale Price			
of Treasury Shares Over Cost			1,000

If, instead of selling the treasury shares bought on February 15, Waterloo Corp. used the single-transaction method to record the purchase and then decided to cancel them, the entry at the time of that decision would be:

Class A Shares	5,000	
Premium on Class A Shares	1,000*	
Retained Earnings	1,000	
Treasury Shares		7,000

$$*\text{Pro rata share allocation} = \frac{1,000 \text{ shares}}{10,500 \text{ shares}} \times \$10,500$$

$$= \$1,000$$

Note: Any **asterisked** questions, cases, exercises, and problems relate to material in the appendix of the chapter.

——— QUESTIONS ———

1. Distinguish between share capital, contributed surplus, contributed capital, and retained earnings as sources of shareholders' equity.

2. Differentiate between capital in a legal sense, capital in a corporate finance sense, and capital in an accounting sense.

3. Distinguish between the following types of corporations:
   (a) Profit-seeking corporations.
   (b) Publicly held corporations.
   (c) Privately held corporations.
   (d) Not-for-profit corporations.
   (e) Crown corporations.

4. Discuss the special characteristics of the corporate form of business that have a direct effect on accounting for owners' equity.

5. In the absence of restrictive provisions, what are the basic or inherent rights of shareholders of a corporation?

6. Distinguish between common and preferred shares.

7. Explain each of the following terms: authorized share capital, unissued shares, issued shares, outstanding shares, subscribed shares, and treasury shares.

8. Why is it important to know the legal jurisdiction under which a company is incorporated?

9. What are the legal restrictions that control the distribution of profit of a corporation?

10. What features or rights may be associated with preferred shares?

11. Neptune Inc. has issued $4 no-par value preferred shares and $4 no-par value participating junior preferred shares. Both are cumulative and have priority as to dividends up to the $4 specified per share. The participating preferred shares share equally with the company's common shares in any dividend distribution in excess of $4 per share to all share classes. What do the terms nonparticipating, partially participating, participating, and cumulative mean as applied to preferred shares?

12. (a) In what ways may preferred shares be more like a debt security than an ownership equity security?
    (b) How would preferred shares which are, in substance, debt instruments be presented in financial statements under proposals in the AcSB's *Exposure Draft* on financial instruments?

13. Describe the accounting regarding subscription for, and eventual issuance of, no-par value common shares.

14. Where might a Subscriptions Receivable account be classified in a balance sheet? Provide arguments supporting each possibility.

15. Explain the difference between the proportional method (relative market value method) and the incremental method of allocating the proceeds of lump sum sales of shares.

16. How are shares valued when they are issued for assets other than cash?

17. Describe the three methods of accounting for share issue costs. Which do you support and why?

18. When shares are purchased and cancelled, how is the cost of the shares assigned to the various shareholders' equity accounts under *CICA Handbook* recommendations?

19. For what reasons might a corporation purchase its own shares?

20. What is the presumption underlying the single-transaction method of accounting for treasury shares? Describe how to account for the acquisition and sale of treasury shares using the single-transaction method.

21. Discuss the propriety of showing:
    (a) Treasury shares as an asset.
    (b) "Gain" or "loss" on sale of treasury shares as additions to or deductions from income.
    (c) Dividends received by the corporation on its own shares held in treasury being treated as income.

22. Brownie Corp. had the following accounts and related balances at December 31, 1994. From this information prepare the Shareholders' Equity section of the company's balance sheet.

Treasury Shares (1,500 common shares)	$ 45,000
Common Shares, no-par value, no authorized limit, 50,000 shares issued, 48,500 shares outstanding	1,250,000
Retained Earnings	2,000,000
Preferred Shares, $5 dividend, no-par value, 10,000 shares authorized, issued, and outstanding	750,000

*23. What is meant by par value, and what is its significance to shareholders?

*24. Describe the accounting regarding subscription for, and eventual issuance of, common shares at a price in excess of their par value.

*25. Telephone Canada Inc. purchases 10,000 shares of its own previously issued $5 par common shares for $280,000. Assuming the shares are held in the treasury with intent to reissue and accounted for by the single-transaction method, what effect does this transaction have on (a) net income, (b) total assets, (c) total contributed surplus, and (d) total shareholders' equity?

--------- CASES ---------

C15-1 **(PRE-EMPTIVE RIGHTS AND DILUTION OF OWNERSHIP)** Neat Computer Ltd. is a small, closely held corporation. Eighty percent of the issued shares are held by Jan Grant, President; of the remainder, 10% are held by members of her family and 10% by Lori Ask, a former officer who is now retired. The balance sheet of the company at June 30, 1994 was substantially as shown on page 761.

Additional authorized share capital of 15,000 no-par value shares had never been issued. To strengthen the cash position of the company, Ms. Grant issued 5,000 shares to herself and paid $100,000 cash. At the next shareholders' meeting, Ms. Ask objected and claimed that her interests had been injured. All shares previously issued were for the same price of $20 per share.

Assets		Liabilities and Shareholder's Equity	
Cash	$ 22,000	Current liabilities	$150,000
Other	600,000	Share capital	300,000
		Retained earnings	172,000
	$622,000		$622,000

Instructions

(a) What shareholder's right may have been ignored in the issue of shares to Ms. Grant?

(b) How may any damage to Ms. Ask's interests be repaired most simply?

(c) If Ms. Grant offered Ms. Ask a personal cash settlement and they agreed to employ you as an impartial arbitrator to determine the amount based only on the information provided, what settlement would you propose? Present your calculations with sufficient explanation to satisfy both parties.

(REDEEMABLE PREFERRED SHARES)   C15-2

Alone Industries Inc.

	1994	1993
	(in thousands)	
Series A first preferred shares—subject to mandatory redemption ($4,062,500 liquidation value in 1994 and 1993); no-par value; authorized 100,000 shares; issued 40,625 shares in 1994 and 1993 (note 6)	$ 3,250	$ 3,250
Common shareholders' equity:		
Common shares, no-par value; authorized 20,000,000 shares; issued 5,522,602 shares in 1994 and 5,280,602 in 1993	552	528
Contributed surplus	463	460
Retained earnings	34,610	20,891
Common shareholders' equity	$35,625	$21,879

Notes to Consolidated Financial Statements

6. Redeemable Preferred Shares:

The Company's preferred shares consist of 250,000 authorized shares of no-par value First Preferred Shares of which 40,625 shares of Series A First Preferred Shares were outstanding at December 31, 1994. The Series A First Preferred Shares, which were not convertible, were sold for $80.00 per share. The shares are entitled to cumulative dividends of $12.70 annually ($3.175 per quarter) per share and must be redeemed at 10% per year commencing on December 31, 1997 at $100.00 per share plus accrued and unpaid dividends. The Company, at its option, may, in 1995 or any subsequent year, redeem any number of shares at that price plus a premium amounting to $3.55 per share. This premium would decline proportionately in each year after 1995 through 2003 after which there will be no premium.

Instructions

From the information provided, answer the following questions:

(a) Do the Series A preferred shares have characteristics more like equity or like debt? Explain.

(b) What are the present (i.e. prior to incorporation into the *CICA Handbook* of any recommendations proposed in the AcSB's *Exposure Draft* on financial instruments) GAAP requirements for the presentation of preferred shares which have the substance of debt but the legal form of equity?

(c) How would preferred shares having the characteristics of debt be reported under proposed recommendations in the *Exposure Draft* on financial instruments?

C15-3 **(SECRET RESERVES AND WATERED STOCK)**   It has been said that (1) the use of the FIFO inventory method during an extended period of declining prices and (2) the expensing of all human resource costs are among the accounting practices that help create "secret reserves."

Instructions

(a) What is a secret reserve? How can secret reserves be created or enlarged?

(b) What is the basis for saying that the two specific practices cited above tend to create secret reserves?

(c) Is it possible to create a secret reserve in connection with accounting for a liability? If so, explain and give an example.

(d) What are the objections to the creation of secret reserves?

(e) It has also been said that "watered stock" is the opposite of a secret reserve. What is watered stock?

(f) Describe the general circumstances in which watered stock can arise.

(g) What steps can be taken to eliminate "water" from a capital structure?

(AICPA adapted)

C15-4 **(EQUIPMENT PURCHASE WITH PAYMENT BY FUTURE DELIVERY OF SHARES)**   Ritz Inc. purchased $160,000 worth of equipment in 1994 for $100,000 cash and a promise to deliver an indeterminate number of common shares having a market value of $20,000 on January 1 of each year for the next four years. Hence, $80,000 in "market value" of shares will be required to discharge the $60,000 balance due on the equipment.

Instructions

(a) Discuss the propriety of recording the equipment at:

  1. $100,000 (the cash payment).

  2. $160,000 (the cash price of the equipment).

  3. $180,000 (the $100,000 cash payment + the $80,000 market value of the shares that must be transferred to the vendor in order to settle the obligation according to the terms of the agreement).

(b) Discuss the arguments for treating the balance due as:

  1. A liability.

  2. Common shares subscribed.

C15-5 **(ISSUANCE OF SHARES FOR PROPERTY, DONATED SHARES, REASSESSMENT OF VALUE)**   In connection with your first audit of Expos Pennant Inc., you note the following facts concerning its share capital transactions:

  1. Authorized capital consists of 8,000,000 common shares of no-par value.

2. All 8,000,000 shares were issued initially in exchange for certain timber properties, which were recorded at an amount of $16,000,000.

3. Soon thereafter, owing to the need for additional working capital, 3,000,000 of the shares were donated to the company and immediately sold for $4,500,000 cash, which resulted in a credit to contributed surplus for this amount.

Instructions

(a) Describe, in order of preference, alternative methods of accounting for the receipt and immediate disposition of donated shares.

(b) 1. What values should be assigned to the timber properties and the shareholders' equity? Discuss.

2. What adjustment, if any, would you recommend?

*(c) Assume the shares had a $1 par value each. Give the journal entries to record the initial issuance, the receipt and sale of the donated shares, and any adjustments regarding the original value assigned to the timber properties and the shareholders' equity accounts given the information in point 3. (Answering this part of the case requires use of material in Appendix 15A.)

(AICPA adapted)

(STRUCTURING SHARE CAPITAL TO REFLECT AN AGREEMENT) Lakeview Powerboat Limited **C15-6** (LPL) is a privately owned Canadian powerboat manufacturer which makes fibreglass powerboats ranging in size from 5 to 10 metres. LPL was federally incorporated in 1978 by three brothers, John, Mark, and Harry Smith. Each brother initially contributed $200,000 in return for a ⅓ interest in the voting common shares. The $600,000 was used to purchase land, a building, and some equipment.

The partner in charge at Simon & King, a public accounting firm, convinced the brothers several years ago that they needed a shareholders' agreement to allow for the retirement of the original owners and the succession of control. The brothers agreed unanimously that control should pass to John Smith's son, Bill, who has expressed an interest in owning and running LPL. Bill is young and aggressive and has some exciting plans for LPL.

The shareholders' agreement was drawn up by a lawyer and signed by the brothers. In addition to specifying that control will pass to Bill, the agreement provides for a buy/sell arrangement regarding the repurchase of shares from any of the brothers. On September 30, 1994, Harry Smith formally notified LPL in writing that he wanted LPL to repurchase his common shares by January 15, 1995.

The Smith brothers have decided that the time has come to hand over the reins to Bill. He will take over as president in mid-November. John and Mark will stay on as managers for five more years, and then they will retire. After several discussions attended by LPL's lawyers, John, Mark, and Bill signed a letter of intent in October 1994 which contains the following agreement in principle:

1. John and Mark will "freeze" the value of their equity, measured in accordance with the shareholders' agreement, based on the financial statements for the fiscal year ended September 30, 1994.

2. All subsequent appreciation or depreciation in the value of LPL will accrue to Bill Smith.

3. John and Mark are flexible as to the form which their equity interest will take, but they insist on retaining voting control until their equity is withdrawn from LPL in the form of cash. The withdrawal shall take place no sooner than October 1, 1999.

4. John and Mark will continue to receive their salary from LPL until their retirement at the end of the 1999 fiscal year.

Instructions

Advise the Smith brothers on how to achieve the spirit of the above agreement through share capital structuring (i.e. classes and rights of shares).

(CICA UFE adapted)

————— **EXERCISES** —————

E15-1 **(RECORDING THE ISSUANCE OF COMMON AND PREFERRED SHARES)** Earlville Corporation was organized on January 1, 1994. It was authorized to issue 10,000 shares of $8 dividend, no-par value preferred shares, and 500,000 no-par common shares. The following share transactions were completed during the first year.

Jan. 10 Issued 80,000 common shares for cash at $3 per share.

Mar. 1 Issued 5,000 preferred shares for cash at $104 per share.

Apr. 1 Issued 24,000 common shares for land. The asking price of the land was $90,000; the fair market value of the land was $80,000.

May 1 Issued 80,000 common shares for cash at $4 per share.

Aug. 1 Issued 10,000 common shares to attorneys to pay their bill of $50,000 for services rendered in organizing the company.

Sept. 1 Issued 10,000 common shares for cash at $6 per share.

Nov. 1 Issued 1,000 preferred shares for cash at $105 per share.

Instructions

Prepare the journal entries to record the above transactions.

E15-2 **(SHARES ISSUED FOR NONMONETARY ASSETS)** Cudly Products Inc. was formed to operate a manufacturing plant in Smalltown. The events for the formation of the corporation include the following:

1. 5,000 shares of no-par common were issued to investors at $21 per share.

2. 8,000 common shares were issued to acquire used equipment which had a depreciated book value to the seller of $120,000.

3. In order to attract the manufacturing plant to Smalltown and stimulate employment in the area, the town council agreed to convey title to land and a building to Cudly. In return, Cudly agreed to sign an $80,000 mortgage contract for these assets. The fair market value of the land was $40,000 and $90,000 for the building.

Instructions

Prepare journal entries for the above transactions.

E15-3 **(SUBSCRIBED SHARES WITH DEFAULTING SUBSCRIBER)** On January 1, 1994, Siskel Inc. received authorization to issue an additional 40,000 common shares of no-par value. Subscribers have contracted to purchase all the shares at the subscription price of $100 per share with terms of 30% down in cash and the remaining 70% at the end of six months.

Instructions

(a) Give Siskel's journal entry for the situation described on the date of subscription.

(b) Assume that Bob Glue has subscribed to 100 of the shares but defaults after paying his 30% down payment. Assume also that the subscription contract affords the subscriber the right to receive shares on a pro rata basis in the event of default. Give Siskel's journal entry for the disposition of the balances in the accounts related to Mr. Glue.

(SUBSCRIBED SHARES WITH DEFAULTING SUBSCRIBER) Ebert Corp. is authorized to issue **E15-4** 300,000 no-par value common shares. On November 30, 1993, 60,000 shares were subscribed at $24 per share. A 40% down payment was made on the subscribed shares. On January 30, 1994, the balance due on the subscribed shares was collected, except for a subscriber of 5,000 shares who defaulted on his subscription. The 5,000 shares were sold on February 10, 1994 at $36 per share and the defaulting subscriber's down payment was returned.

Instructions

Prepare the required journal entries for the transactions above.

(LUMP SUM SALE OF SHARES WITH BONDS) Lake Corp. sells units of its equity. Each unit consists **E15-5** of a $500 maturity value, 12% debenture bond, and 10 of the company's common no-par shares. Lake has issued 10,000 units. The investment broker has retained 400 units as the underwriting fee. The remaining 9,600 units were sold to investors for cash for $950 per unit. Prior to this sale the two-week asking price of common was $40 per share. The 12% interest is a reasonable yield for the debentures.

Instructions

(a) Prepare the journal entry to record the above transaction:

1. Employing the incremental method.

2. Employing the proportional method using the price quotes on the common shares.

(b) In your opinion, which is the better method? Explain.

(LUMP SUM SALE OF COMMON AND PREFERRED SHARES) Dax Corp. was organized with 50,000 **E15-6** preferred shares of no-par value, $9 dividend, and 100,000 no-par value common shares. During the first year, 1,000 preferred shares and 1,000 common shares were issued for a lump sum price of $180,000.

Instructions

What entry should be made to record this transaction under each of the following independent conditions?

(a) Shortly after the transaction described above, 500 preferred shares were sold at $120. *not relevant*

(b) The market value per common share was $95.

(c) At the date of issuance, the preferred shares had a market price of $140 each and the common shares had a market price of $40 each.

(SHARE ISSUANCES, ISSUANCE COSTS, AND REPURCHASE) Concert Corporation is authorized **E15-7** to issue 50,000 no-par value common shares. During 1994, Concert took part in the following selected transactions.

1. Issued 5,000 shares at $45 per share, less costs related to the issuance of the shares totalling $8,000.

2. Issued 1,000 shares for land appraised at $50,000. The shares were actively traded on a national stock exchange at approximately $47 per share on the date of issuance.

3. Purchased 500 shares at $43 per share and restored them to the status of authorized but unissued shares. The shares purchased had an assigned value of $41 per share.

Instructions

(a) Prepare a journal entry to record transaction 1:

    1. Treating the issue costs as a reduction of amounts paid in for the shares.

    2. Treating the issue costs as organization costs.

(b) Prepare a journal entry to record transaction 2.

(c) Prepare a journal entry to record transaction 3.

(d) Discuss the subsequent accounting treatment of the organization costs recorded in (a) 2.

E15-8 **(SUBSTANCE OF A PREFERRED SHARE ISSUE)** Colgate Corporation acquired all of the common shares of Brush Inc. through the issuance of Series A preferred shares. The Series A indenture provides the following: no-par value, dividends $35 per share payable annually. The issue is cumulative, nonparticipating, preferred over common shares and other preferred share series as to both dividends and assets. The shares are nonvoting and not convertible to common but are callable at the discretion of the board of directors and must be redeemed at $400 plus any cumulative dividends in arrears by the end of year 10.

Instructions

(a) Briefly evaluate the economic nature of this preferred share issue.

(b) Draft a memorandum presenting your opinion as to the appropriate disclosures for this security in the body of, and notes to, the financial statements in the annual report.

E15-9 **(REACQUISITION AND SUBSEQUENT SALE OF SHARES)** Vogue Ltd. has outstanding 35,000 common shares of no-par value, all of which had been issued at $35 per share. On July 5, 1994, Vogue repurchased 1,000 of these shares at $36 per share.

Instructions

(a) Assuming the company is incorporated under the Canada Business Corporations Act, what entry would be made on July 5 to record the reacquisition?

(b) Assuming the reacquired shares were to be held as treasury shares, what entry would be made on July 5 using the single-transaction method?

(c) Vogue Ltd., after having repurchased its shares on July 5, 1994 and accounted for them as in (b), sold the shares on July 30, 1994. What entries would be made under the single-transaction method if these treasury shares had been sold for $40 per share? For $30 per share?

E15-10 **(DONATION OF SHARES)** On November 15, 1994, Chris Cross, a wealthy shareholder of Baden Publishing Inc., donates 5,000 of Baden's no-par common shares to the corporation. All shares were originally issued at $25 each and are now selling for $37 each in the marketplace.

Instructions

(a) Prepare Baden's journal entry to record the donation assuming the shares were restored to the status of authorized but unissued.

(b) Assume that Baden resells the shares on December 20, 1994 when the market value is $36 per share. Prepare Baden's journal entries for the resale.

(BALANCE SHEET PRESENTATION OF SHAREHOLDERS' EQUITY) Environmental Products **E15-11** Inc.'s articles authorized 100,000 common shares of no-par value, and 50,000, $8 dividend, cumulative, and nonparticipating preferred shares of no-par value. Environmental Products engaged in the following share transactions through December 31, 1994: 40,000 common shares were issued for cash of $470,000 and 12,000 preferred shares for machinery valued at $1,450,000. Subscriptions for 4,500 common shares have been taken, and 30% of the subscription price of $16 per share has been collected. The shares will be issued upon collection of the subscription price in full. Treasury shares consisting of 1,000 common shares have been purchased for $16 each and accounted for under the single-transaction method. The Retained Earnings balance is $208,000, on which there is a restriction in terms of availability for dividends in an amount equal to the cost of treasury shares.

Instructions

Prepare the shareholders' equity section of the balance sheet as at December 31, 1994.

(PAR VALUE SHARES: SUBSCRIPTION THROUGH ISSUANCE) Cavandish Co. Ltd. intends to sell ***E15-12** common shares to raise additional capital to allow for expansion in the rapidly growing service industry. The corporation decides to sell these shares through a subscription basis and publicly notifies the investment world. The shares have a $10 par value and 30,000 shares are offered at $30 each. The terms of the subscription are 40% down and the balance at the end of six months. All shares are subscribed for during the offering period.

Instructions

Give the journal entries for the original subscription, the collection of the down payments, the collection of the balance of the subscription price, and the issuance of the common shares.

(REACQUISITION AND SUBSEQUENT SALE OF PAR VALUE SHARES) On November 15, 1994, ***E15-13** Country Leisure Corp. acquires 4,000 of its own $10 par value common shares in the market at a cost of $40 per share. All shares issued by the company had originally sold for $32 each.

Instructions

(a) Prepare Leisure's journal entries to record this acquisition as treasury shares under the single-transaction method.

(b) Assume that Leisure sells the reacquired shares on December 20, 1994 for the market price of $48 per share. Prepare the journal entries to reflect this sale under the single-transaction method.

(c) Prepare the journal entry to record (1) the reacquisition of shares being treated as a cancellation and restoration to the status of authorized but unissued shares, and (2) the sale of the reacquired shares for $48 each.

--------- PROBLEMS ---------

(EQUITY TRANSACTIONS AND STATEMENT PREPARATION) On January 5, 1994, Lotsa Fun Cor- **P15-1** poration began operations with authorized capital of 5,000 preferred shares of no-par value, $8 dividend, cumulative, and nonparticipating, and 50,000 common shares of no-par value. It then completed the following transactions.

Jan. 11   Accepted subscriptions to 20,000 common shares at $17 per share; 40% down payments accompanied the subscription.

Feb. 1   Issued to Joyful Corp. 4,000 preferred shares for the following assets; machinery with a fair market value of $50,000; a factory building with a fair market value of $200,000; and land with an appraised value of $190,000.

Mar. 16   Other machinery, with a fair market value of $210,000, was donated to the company. (Assume credited to Contributed Surplus—Donated Machinery.)

Apr. 15   Collected the balance of the subscription price on the common shares and issued them.

May 21   Reacquired 1,800 of its own common shares at $19 per share and restored them to the status of authorized but unissued shares.

Aug. 10   Sold 1,800 common shares at $14 per share.

Aug. 26   Declared a 10% stock dividend on the common shares. The shares were selling at $16 each on the day of the declaration and this amount is used to record the stock dividend (the increase in common shares to be issued as a stock dividend is charged to Retained Earnings and credited to a Common Stock Dividend Distributable account until distributed).

Sept. 15 Distributed the stock dividend.

Dec. 31   Declared a $0.25 per share cash dividend on common and declared the required preferred dividend.

Dec. 31   Closed the Income Summary account. There was a $129,000 net income.

Instructions

(a)   Record the journal entries for the transactions listed above.

(b)   Prepare the shareholders' equity section of Lotsa Fun's balance sheet as of December 31, 1994.

P15-2   **(SHARE TRANSACTIONS)**   Streams Corporation's charter authorized issuance of 100,000 common shares of no-par value, and 50,000 preferred shares of no-par value. The following transactions involving the issuance of shares were completed. Each transaction is independent of the others.

1.   Issued a $10,000, 9% bond payable for the par value and gave as a bonus one preferred share, which was selling for $90 a share at that time.

2.   Issued 500 common shares for machinery. The machinery had been appraised at $7,000; the seller's book value was $6,200. The most recent market price of the common shares was $15 each.

3.   Issued 375 common shares and 100 preferred shares for a lump sum amounting to $15,300. The common had been selling at $14 and the preferred at $105.

4.   Issued 200 common shares and 50 preferred shares for furniture and fixtures. The common had a fair market value of $16 per share and the furniture and fixtures were appraised at $6,200.

Instructions

Record the transactions listed above in journal entry form.

P15-3   **(SUBSCRIBED SHARES WITH DEFAULTING SUBSCRIBER)**   Share transactions of Xavier Corp. are as follows:

Apr. 1   Subscriptions to 500 common shares of no-par value are received, together with cheques from the various subscribers to cover a 40% down payment. The shares were subscribed at a price of $120 per share. The remainder of the subscription price is to be paid in three equal monthly instalments.

May 1   First instalments are collected from all subscribers.

June 1   Second instalments are received from all subscribers except Lee Smith, who had subscribed for 100 shares.

        5   In reply to correspondence, Mr. Smith states that he is unable to complete his instalment payments and authorizes the company to dispose of the shares subscribed for by him.

      17   The shares subscribed for by Mr. Smith are sold for cash of $105 each. Expenses of $125 were incurred in disposing of these shares. Expenses and deficiencies between the subscription price and amounts received are charged against the amount due to the subscriber and the subscriber is then given a refund.

      25   A cheque is mailed to Mr. Smith equal to the refund due him.

July 1   The final instalments are collected on all open subscription accounts and the shares are issued.

Instructions

Prepare entries in general journal form for these transactions and events.

(SHARE REACQUISITION AND BALANCE SHEET PRESENTATION)   The shareholders' equity sec- **P15-4**
tion of the CanAir Inc. balance sheet at December 31, 1993 was as follows:

Common shares—no-par value; 50,000 authorized;	
15,000 shares issued and outstanding	$1,500,000
Contributed Surplus—Donated Land	150,000
Retained Earnings	210,000
	$1,860,000

On January 2, 1994, the company had idle cash and repurchased 1,000 of its outstanding shares for $112,000. These shares were handled in the manner specified in the Canada Business Corporations Act, the legislation under which the company was incorporated. During the year, CanAir sold some of these shares, as they had been restored to the status of authorized but unissued shares. The first such sale was on April 15, at which time the company received $117 per share for 200 shares. The second sale was made on August 13 when another 200 shares were sold for $110 per share.

Instructions

(a)   Prepare the journal entries for the transactions identified for 1994.

(b)   Assuming net income for 1994 was $55,000, prepare the shareholders' equity section of CanAir's balance sheet as at December 31, 1994.

(REACQUISITION OF SHARES: CANCELLATION VERSUS TREASURY SHARES)   Weird Enter- **P15-5**
prises Inc. (WEI) is a closely held toy manufacturer. You have been engaged as the independent public accountant to perform the first audit of WEI. It is agreed that only current-year (1994) financial statements will be prepared.
      The following shareholders' equity information has been developed from WEI records on December 31, 1993:

Common shares, no-par value:	
authorized 30,000 shares; issued 9,000 shares	$405,000
Retained earnings	220,000

The following transactions took place during 1994:

1. On March 15, WEI issued 7,000 common shares to Bart Simpson for $55 per share.

2. On March 31, WEI reacquired 4,000 shares from Mik Rooney (WEI's founder) for $60 per share. These shares were cancelled and retired upon receipt. For the year 1994, WEI reported net income of $112,000.

Instructions

(a) How should the shareholders' equity information be reported in the WEI financial statements for the year ended December 31, 1994?

(b) How would your answer to (a) be altered if WEI had treated the reacquired shares as treasury shares under the single-transaction method?

P15-6 (REACQUISITION AND CANCELLATION OF SHARES: EQUITY SECTION PREPARATION)
Hamilton Co. Ltd. has the following shareholders' equity accounts at December 31, 1993:

Common Shares—no-par value, authorized 8,000,	
issued 4,800	$480,000
Retained Earnings	294,000

Instructions

(a) Prepare journal entries to record the following transactions, which took place during 1994:

1. 240 of the issued shares were reacquired for $96 per share and restored to the status of being authorized but unissued.

2. A $20 per share cash dividend was declared.

3. The dividend declared in No. 2 above was paid.

4. Sold 240 common shares for $102 per share.

5. 500 common shares were reacquired for a total of $51,500 and restored to the status of being authorized but unissued.

6. 120 additional outstanding shares were reacquired at $97 per share and restored to the status of authorized but unissued.

7. 330 common shares were sold for $96 per share.

(b) Prepare the shareholders' equity section of Hamilton Co. Ltd.'s balance sheet after giving effect to these transactions, assuming that the net income for 1994 was $82,000.

P15-7 (COMPREHENSIVE SHAREHOLDERS' EQUITY: WORK SHEET) Gander Corporation is a publicly owned company. At December 31, 1993, Gander had 25,000,000 common shares of no-par value authorized, of which 15,000,000 shares were issued and outstanding.

The shareholders' equity accounts at December 31, 1993 had the following balances:

Common shares	$230,000,000
Retained earnings	50,000,000

During 1994, Gander had the following transactions:

On February 1, a secondary distribution of 2,000,000 common shares was completed. The shares were sold to the public at $18 per share, net of offering costs.

On February 15, Gander issued at $110 per share, 100,000 preferred shares of no-par value, $8 cumulative dividend.

On March 1, Gander reacquired 20,000 common shares for $18.50 per share and they were restored to the status of authorized but unissued.

On March 15, when the common shares were trading for $21 per share, a major shareholder donated 10,000 shares to the company.

On March 31, Gander declared a semiannual cash dividend on the common shares of $0.10 per share, payable on April 30, to shareholders of record on April 10.

On April 30, employees exercised 100,000 options that were granted in 1992 under a stock option plan. When the options were granted, each option entitled the employee to purchase one common share for $20. On April 30, the market price of the common shares was $20 each. Gander issued new shares to settle the transaction.

On May 31, when the market price of the common shares was $20 per share, Gander declared a 5% stock dividend distributable on July 1 to shareholders of record on June 1. The stock dividend is recorded using the market price with the increase in the common shares being charged to the Retained Earnings account.

On June 30, Gander sold 300,000 common shares for $25 per share.

On September 30, Gander declared a semiannual cash dividend on the common shares of $0.10 per share and the yearly dividend on preferred shares, both payable on October 30, to shareholders of record on October 10.

Net income for 1994 was $50,000,000.

Instructions

Prepare a work sheet to be used to summarize, for each transaction, the changes in Gander's shareholders' equity accounts for 1994. The columns on this work sheet should have the following headings:

> Date of transactions (or beginning date)
> Common shares—number of shares
> Common shares—amount
> Preferred shares—number of shares
> Preferred shares—amount
> Contributed Surplus*
> Retained Earnings

> *While there may be several individual accounts that would be recognized in Contributed Surplus, use
> this column to record the effects of transactions on the total amount of Contributed Surplus.

Show supporting computations in good form.

(AICPA adapted)

(PAR VALUE SHARE TRANSACTIONS AND EQUITY SECTION PREPARATION)   Transactions of *P15-8
Pinnochio Co. Ltd. are as follows:

1. The company is incorporated with authorized capital of 15,000 preferred shares of $100 par value and 15,000 common shares with a par value of $10.

2. 8,000 common shares are issued to founders of the corporation for land valued by the board of directors at $220,000.

3. 4,200 preferred shares are sold for cash at $115 each.

4. 600 common shares are sold to an officer of the corporation for $30 a share.

5. 300 of the preferred shares outstanding are purchased for cash at par and immediately restored to the status of authorized but unissued.

6. 400 of the preferred shares outstanding are purchased for cash at 98 and held as treasury shares accounted for using the single-transaction method.

7. 500 of the common shares outstanding are purchased at $35 a share and held as treasury shares accounted for using the single-transaction method.

8. 200 of the repurchased preferred shares in treasury are reissued at 102.5.

9. 2,100 preferred shares are issued at 103.

10. 400 of the reacquired common shares in treasury are reissued for $30 a share.

11. 200 common shares are repurchased for $33 a share and restored to the status of authorized but unissued.

Instructions

(a) Prepare journal entries to record the transactions listed above. No other transactions affecting the share capital accounts have occurred. (Round to the nearest dollar where necessary.)

(b) Assuming that the company has retained earnings, except for the effect of these transactions, of $112,000, prepare the shareholders' equity section of its balance sheet after considering all the transactions given.

*P15-9 (PAR VALUE SHARES AND SHAREHOLDERS' EQUITY CLASSIFICATIONS)   The following information is drawn from the records of the Québec Company Limited as at December 31:

Preferred shares authorized ($100 par value)	$750,000
Common shares authorized ($10 par value)	500,000
Unissued preferred shares	300,000
Unissued common shares	180,000
Subscriptions receivable, common	18,000
Subscriptions receivable, preferred	21,500
Preferred shares subscribed	30,000
Common shares subscribed	45,000
Treasury shares, preferred (1,200 shares at cost)	120,540
Contributed surplus (Excess of amount paid in over par value of common shares)	153,400

Instructions

Use the above information to determine the following:

(a) Total authorized share capital.

(b) Total unissued share capital.

(c) Total issued share capital.

(d) Share capital subscribed.

(e) Share capital available for sale.

(f) Total share capital and contributed surplus.

Shareholders' Equity: Contributed Surplus and Retained Earnings

■

The following three categories most frequently appear as part of shareholders' equity in a corporation's financial statements:

1. Share Capital or Capital Stock (legal or stated capital).

2. Contributed Surplus.

3. Retained Earnings or Deficit.

The first two categories, Share Capital and Contributed Surplus, constitute **contributed capital**. Retained Earnings represents the **earned capital** of the enterprise. The distinction between contributed capital and earned capital has a legal origin, but at present it serves the useful purpose of indicating the different sources from which a corporation has obtained its **equity capital**.

The first category—Share Capital—was discussed in Chapter 15. The objective of this chapter is to examine the accounting for and disclosure of the other categories of shareholders' equity. Within the discussion of Retained Earnings this chapter will cover the accounting for various types of dividends and examine the nature of and accounting for restrictions on, or appropriations of, Retained Earnings. While these three categories represent the most common components of shareholders' equity, other categories may appear. Examples would be Treasury Shares accounted for using the single-transaction method (discussed in Chapter 15) and a Revaluation Adjustment or an Appraisal Increase Credit resulting from a financial reorganization (considered at the end of this chapter).

CONTRIBUTED SURPLUS

The *CICA Handbook* states that there can be only two sources of realized surplus within a corporation, these being amounts received by way of contributions and amounts earned in the conduct of the business. In order to provide readers of financial statements with an adequate view of a company's affairs, it is necessary to report information as to these two basic sources separately.[1]

Contributed Surplus may be derived from a variety of transactions and events as indicated in account form on page 774.[2]

An interesting aspect of the **Canada Business Corporations Act** (CBCA) is that, because of its requirements to have no-par value shares and to cancel reacquired shares, it eliminates most contributed surplus items. However, companies incorporated under acts permitting these or that had

Objective 1

Know the nature of Contributed Surplus, sources from which it may be derived, and how it is reported on the balance sheet.

---

[1] *CICA Handbook* (Toronto: CICA), Section 3250, par. .04. "Surplus" is used in the accounting sense of being the excess of net assets over the total share capital of a corporation (Section 3250, par. .01).

[2] *Ibid.*, par. .05, serves as the basic source of the items listed. Each item represents a potential source for a debit or credit to a control account Contributed Surplus. In most situations there is a subsidiary account kept for each item in which a record of the transactions and events affecting the item is maintained.

Contributed Surplus

1. Discounts on capital shares issued.*
2. Sale of treasury shares below cost under the circumstances and to the extent described in Chapter 15.
3. Absorption of a deficit in a financial reorganization.
4. Distribution of a liquidating dividend.
5. Retirement of shares at a cost in excess of par* or assigned value.

1. Premiums on capital shares issued.*
2. Sale of treasury shares above cost.
3. Additional capital arising in a financial reorganization.
4. Additional assessments on shareholders.
5. Conversion of convertible bonds or preferred shares.*
6. Capital donations from non-shareholders and shareholders.
7. Retirement of shares acquired by purchase at a cost less than par* or assigned value or through donations.

*Items relate to shares having a par value (see Appendix 15A for further explanation).

these items in their accounts before filing for continuance under the CBCA could carry the items forward.[3]

No operating gains or losses or extraordinary gains and losses may be debited or credited to Contributed Surplus. The profession has long discouraged bypassing net income and retained earnings through the write-off of losses (e.g., write-offs of bond discount, goodwill, or obsolete plant and equipment) to contributed surplus accounts or other capital accounts.

In balance sheet presentation, only one account (Contributed Surplus) and one amount (which is the net balance of all of these possible transactions) need appear. A subsidiary ledger or separate general ledger accounts may be kept of the different sources of contributed surplus. Furthermore, maintaining such separate records would greatly facilitate disclosure of changes in contributed surplus during a period as is required by the *CICA Handbook*.[4]

RETAINED EARNINGS

Objective 2

Know the more common causes of changes in Retained Earnings.

The basic source of retained earnings is income from operations. Shareholders assume the greatest risk in enterprise operations and bear any losses or share in any profits resulting from enterprise activities. Any income not distributed among the shareholders becomes additional shareholders' equity. Net income is derived from a variety of sources. These include the main operations of the enterprise (such as manufacturing and selling a given product); any ancillary activities (such as disposing of scrap or renting out unused space); financing decisions (interest income); the results of discontinued operations; and extraordinary items. The more common items that either increase (credit) or decrease (debit) the Retained Earnings account are expressed in account form on page 775.

In Chapter 4, it was pointed out that, under the modified all-inclusive concept of income reporting, the results of unusual and extraordinary transactions should be placed in the income statement, not directly into the retained earnings statement. Prior period adjustments and retroactive adjustments resulting from changing accounting policies or error corrections should be reported as

---

[3] *Financial Reporting in Canada—1991* (Toronto: CICA, 1991) reported that of the 300 companies surveyed, 69 in 1990, 72 in 1989, and 74 in 1988 disclosed the existence of contributed surplus items. In more than 90% of these cases, the items were labelled simply as Contributed Surplus in shareholders' equity.

[4] *CICA Handbook*, Section 3250, par. .13. *Financial Reporting in Canada—1991* indicated that where contributed surplus changed in a period, the nature of the change was predominantly disclosed in notes to the financial statements. Other means of disclosure were by a statement of changes in contributed surplus or inclusion of the change in a statement of changes in shareholders' equity.

Retained Earnings	
1. Net loss.	1. Net income.
2. Prior period adjustments and retroactive adjustments that may result from changes in accounting principles or error corrections.	2. Prior period adjustments and retroactive adjustments that may result from changes in accounting principles or error corrections.
3. Cash dividends.	
4. Stock dividends.	
5. Property dividends.	
6. Transactions involving share reacquisitions as discussed in Chapter 15.	

adjustments to beginning retained earnings, bypassing completely the current period's income statement.

DIVIDEND POLICY

When retained earnings exist within a corporation, there are two possible alternatives regarding its disposition: the credit balance can be (1) reduced by a distribution of assets (a dividend) to the shareholders, or (2) left intact and the off-setting assets used in the operations of the business.

Very few companies pay dividends in amounts equal to the retained earnings legally available for dividends. The major reasons for this are as follows:

1. Lack of sufficient cash.

2. Agreements (bond covenants) with specific creditors to retain all or a portion of the earnings (in the form of assets) to build up additional protection against possible loss for those creditors.

3. Desire to retain assets that would otherwise be paid out as dividends, to finance growth or expansion. This is sometimes called internal financing, reinvesting earnings, or "ploughing" the profits back into the business.

4. Desire to smooth out dividend payments from year to year by accumulating earnings in good years and using such accumulated earnings as a basis for dividends in bad years.

5. Desire to build up a cushion or buffer against possible losses.

6. Legal restrictions included in the acts under which a company is incorporated. For example, a dividend may not be paid if it would render a corporation insolvent even if retained earnings existed. Also, in circumstances permitting treasury shares, the law may require that retained earnings equivalent to the cost of such shares be restricted against dividend declarations.

No particular explanation is required for any of these except the last. The laws of most jurisdictions require that the corporation's stated capital (legal capital) be restricted from distribution to shareholders so that it may serve as a protection against loss to creditors. If, for example, the corporation buys its own outstanding shares, it has reduced its stated capital and distributed assets to shareholders. Therefore, the corporation could, by purchasing shares at any price desired, return to the shareholders their investments and leave creditors with little or no protection against loss. Consequently, restricting dividends to the extent that retained earnings will not fall below the cost of the reacquired shares is a way to overcome this problem.

If a company is considering declaring a dividend, two preliminary questions must be asked:

1. Is the condition of the corporation such that a dividend is **legally permissible**?

2. Is the condition of the corporation such that a dividend is **economically sound**?

Objective 3

Describe the factors to consider when determining if dividends are to be distributed.

Legality of Dividends

The legality of a dividend can be determined only by reviewing the applicable incorporation law. Even then the law may not be clear, and a decision may require recourse to the courts. Usually, to reduce the possibility of legal misinterpretation, the company's lawyer is consulted. For most general dividend declarations, the following guidelines are adequate:

1. Retained earnings, unless legally restricted in some manner, is usually the correct basis for dividend distributions.

2. In some jurisdictions, contributed surplus may be used for dividends.

3. Deficits must be eliminated before the payment of any dividends.

4. In most jurisdictions that allow treasury shares, dividends may not reduce retained earnings below the cost of treasury shares held.

The CBCA prohibits the declaration or payment of dividends if there are reasonable grounds for believing that such an action would (1) result in the corporation being unable to pay its liabilities when they become due, or (2) result in the realizable value of the corporation's assets being less than the total of its liabilities and stated (legal) capital of all share classes. Adhering to the legal requirements associated with dividends is critical to a corporation's directors because, if such requirements are judged to have been violated, the directors can be held jointly and severally liable for the entire debts and obligations of the company.

Financial Condition and Dividend Distributions

Dividend distributions generally require that a corporation has a credit balance in retained earnings. From the standpoint of good management, attention must be given to other conditions as well. Particularly important is the liquidity of the corporation. If we assume an extreme situation such as the following, these considerations become apparent.

Balance Sheet

Plant assets	$500,000	Share capital	$400,000
		Retained earnings	100,000
	$500,000		$500,000

This company has a retained earnings credit balance and, unless it is restricted, can declare a dividend of $100,000. However, because all its assets are plant assets and used in operations, payment of a cash dividend of $100,000 requires the sale of plant assets or borrowing.

Even if we assume a balance sheet showing current assets, there is still the further question of whether those assets are needed for other purposes.

Balance Sheet

Cash	$100,000	Current liabilities		$ 60,000
Plant assets	460,000	Share capital	$400,000	
		Retained earnings	100,000	500,000
	$560,000			$560,000

The existence of current liabilities implies very strongly that some of the cash is needed to meet current debts as they mature. Furthermore, day-by-day cash requirements for payroll and other expenditures not included in current liabilities will also require cash.

Thus, before a dividend is declared, management and directors must consider the ***availability of funds to pay the dividend***. Other demands for cash should be identified, perhaps by preparing a cash forecast. A dividend should not be paid unless both the present and future financial position appear to warrant the distribution.

Directors and management must also consider the effect of inflation and replacement costs on reported income. During a period of rising prices, some costs charged to expense under historical cost accounting are understated in a comparative purchasing power sense. Income is thereby "overstated" because certain costs have not been adjusted for inflation. As an example, at one time a company reported historical cost net income of $179 million but, when it was adjusted for inflation, net income was $68 million. Yet the company paid cash dividends of $72 million. Were cash dividends paid excessive? This subject is discussed in Chapter 25.

The conclusion regarding a decision to declare a dividend is clear. While the existence of available retained earnings is a necessity, many other factors are important. No corporate director should ever recommend a dividend based on the existence of retained earnings alone. The legal requirements as well as the present and expected future financial position must also be considered.

TYPES OF DIVIDENDS

Dividend distributions are based either on accumulated profits—that is, retained earnings—or, in some cases, contributed surplus accounts. The natural expectation of any shareholder who receives a dividend is that the corporation has operated successfully and that he or she is receiving a share of its profits. Any dividend not based on retained earnings (a liquidating dividend) should be adequately described in the accompanying message to the shareholders so that there will be no misunderstanding of its source. Dividends can be of the following types:[5]

> **Objective 4**
>
> Identify the various forms of dividend distributions and know how to account for them.

1. Cash dividends.

2. Property dividends.

3. Scrip dividends (issuance of a note payable for dividends).

4. Liquidating dividends.

5. Stock dividends.

Dividends are commonly paid in cash but occasionally in stock, scrip, or some other asset. ***Any dividend other than a stock dividend reduces the shareholders' equity in the corporation***. The equity is reduced either through an immediate or promised future distribution of assets. When a stock dividend is declared, the corporation does not pay out assets or incur a liability. It issues additional shares to each shareholder and nothing more.

Cash Dividends

The board of directors votes on the declaration of dividends, and if the resolution is approved, the dividend is declared. Before it is paid, a current list of shareholders must be prepared. For this reason there is usually a time lag between declaration and payment. A dividend approved at the January 10 (**date of declaration**) meeting of the board of directors might be declared payable February 5 (**date of payment**) to shareholders of record on January 25 (**date of record**).

---

[5] *Financial Reporting in Canada—1991* indicated that for 1990, 77% of the 300 survey companies disclosed the declaration or payment of a dividend, predominantly a cash dividend.

The period from January 10 to January 25 gives time for any transfers in process to be completed and registered with the transfer agent. The time from January 25 to February 5 provides an opportunity for the transfer agent or accounting department, depending on who does this work, to prepare a list of shareholders as of January 25 and to prepare and mail dividend cheques.

A declared dividend, except for a stock dividend, is a liability and, because payment is generally required soon, it is usually a current liability. The following entries are required to record the declaration and payment of a dividend payable in cash. This example assumes that on June 10 a corporation declared a cash dividend of 50 cents a share on 1.8 million shares, payable July 16 to all shareholders of record on June 24.

At date of declaration (June 10):

Retained Earnings (Cash Dividends Declared)	900,000	
Dividends Payable		900,000

At date of record (June 24):

    No entry

At date of payment (July 16):

Dividends Payable	900,000	
Cash		900,000

To keep track of the amount of dividends declared during the year, an account called Cash Dividends Declared might be debited instead of Retained Earnings at the time of declaration. This account is then closed to Retained Earnings at the end of the year.

Dividend declarations are made as a stated amount per share for no-par value shares issued and outstanding.[6] If a company holds treasury shares or donated shares, or has shares subscribed for but not fully paid, dividends do not apply to these.[7]

Dividend policies vary among corporations. Some older, well-established companies take pride in a long, unbroken string of quarterly or annual dividend payments. They would lower or pass the dividend only if forced to do so by a sustained decline in earnings or a critical shortage of cash.

The percentage of annual earnings distributed as cash dividends ("payout ratio") depends somewhat on the stability and trend of earnings, with 25% to 75% of earnings being paid out by many well-established corporations. "Growth companies," on the other hand, pay little or no cash dividends because their policy is to expand as rapidly as internal and external financing permit. For example, the following statement appeared in the preliminary prospectus (August 1988) regarding common shares of Air Canada and, accordingly, Air Canada has not yet paid any dividends on its common shares.

Dividend Policy

Air Canada has no current plans to pay dividends on its Common Shares. Its present dividend policy is to retain earnings to finance its capital expenditure program. Air Canada's dividend policy will be reviewed periodically depending on the Corporation's cash flow, earnings, financial position and on other factors.

Shareholders in companies which pay small or no dividends hope the price of their shares will appreciate so that they will realize a profit when they sell the shares.

Knowledge of a dividend policy for a particular corporation may be gained from an analysis of its successive financial statements. While no explicit recommendation regarding disclosure of dividend policy exists in Canada, in the United States the SEC encourages companies to disclose

---

[6] For par value shares, dividends may be declared as a certain percentage of the par value.

[7] *CICA Handbook*, Section 3240, par. .22.

their dividend policy in their annual report. For example, companies that (1) have earnings but fail to pay dividends or (2) do not expect to pay dividends in the foreseeable future are encouraged to report this information. In addition, companies that have had a consistent pattern of paying dividends are encouraged to indicate whether they intend to continue this practice in the future.

Property Dividends

Dividends payable in assets of the corporation other than cash are called **property dividends** or **dividends in kind.** Property dividends may be in whatever form the board of directors designates; for example, merchandise, real estate, or investments. Because of the obvious difficulties of divisibility of units and delivery to the shareholders, the usual property dividend is in the form of securities of other companies that the distributing corporation holds as an investment.

A property dividend is a nonreciprocal transfer[8] *of nonmonetary assets between an enterprise and its owners.* Prior to the early 1970s, the accounting for such transfers was based on the carrying amount (book value) of the noncash assets transferred. This practice was based on the rationale that there is no sale or arm's-length transaction on which to base a gain or loss and that only this method is consistent with the historical cost basis of accounting. This practice changed, however, following the issuance of *APB Opinion No. 29* in the United States which provided guidance in the absence of any Canadian standard until 1989 when Section 3830 on "Non-monetary Transactions" was incorporated into the *CICA Handbook.* Under both this guidance and the recommended treatment in the *Handbook, a property dividend is recorded at the fair value of the asset given up.*[9]

The **fair value** of the nonmonetary asset distributed is the amount that would be agreed upon by informed parties dealing at arm's length in an open and unrestricted market.[10] Such amount could be determined by referring to estimated realizable values in cash transactions of the same or similar assets, quoted market prices, independent appraisals, and other available evidence.

The failure to recognize the fair value of nonmonetary assets transferred may both misstate the dividend and fail to recognize gains and losses on assets that have already been earned or incurred by the enterprise. Recording the dividend at fair value permits future comparisons of dividend rates. If cash must be distributed to some shareholders in place of the nonmonetary asset, determination of the amount to be distributed is simplified.

When a property dividend is declared, the corporation should restate at fair value the property to be distributed, recognizing any gain or loss as the difference between the fair value and carrying value of the property at the date of declaration. The declared dividend may then be recorded as a debit to Retained Earnings (or Property Dividends Declared) and a credit to Property Dividends Payable at an amount equal to the fair value of the property to be distributed. Upon distribution of the dividend, Property Dividends Payable is debited, and the account containing the distributed asset (restated at fair value) is credited.

For example, Inuit Inc. transferred some of its investments in marketable securities costing $1,250,000 to shareholders by declaring a property dividend on December 18, 1993, to be distributed on January 30, 1994 to shareholders of record on January 15, 1994. At the date of declaration the securities had a market value of $2,000,000. The entries are as follows.

---

[8] A nonreciprocal transfer is a transfer of assets or services in one direction, either from an enterprise to its owners or another entity or from owners or another entity to the enterprise.

[9] *CICA Handbook*, Section 3830, par. .05. An exception to this accounting treatment occurs when a corporation's shareholders are given the shares of a subsidiary of the corporation. Such an event is called a **spin-off** in that the shareholders now become the direct holders of ownership in the subsidiary company, rather than exercising control through the corporation giving them the shares. While a spin-off results in giving property (i.e. the corporation's investment in the subsidiary) to the corporation's shareholders, the transfer is to be measured at the carrying value, not the fair value, of the shares distributed according to *CICA Handbook* recommendations (Section 3830, par. .11).

[10] *Ibid.*, par. .04.

At date of declaration (December 18, 1993)		
Investments in Securities	750,000	
Gain on Appreciation of Securities		750,000
Retained Earnings (Property Dividends Declared)	2,000,000	
Property Dividends Payable		2,000,000
At date of distribution (January 30, 1994)		
Property Dividends Payable	2,000,000	
Investments in Securities		2,000,000

Scrip Dividends

A dividend payable in scrip means that the corporation, instead of paying the dividend now, has elected to pay it at some later date. *The scrip issued to shareholders as a dividend is merely a special form of note payable.* Scrip dividends may be declared when the corporation has a sufficient retained earnings balance but is short of cash. The recipient of the scrip dividend may hold it until the due date, if one is specified, and collect the dividend or may sell (discount) it to obtain immediate cash.

When a scrip dividend is declared, the corporation debits Retained Earnings (or Scrip Dividend Declared) and credits Scrip Dividend Payable, reporting the payable as a liability on the balance sheet. Upon payment, Scrip Dividend Payable is debited and Cash credited. If the scrip bears interest, the interest portion of the cash payment should be debited to Interest Expense and not treated as part of the dividend.

As an example, Berg Canning Co. Ltd., when short of cash, avoided missing its eighty-fourth consecutive quarterly dividend by declaring on May 6, 1994 a scrip dividend in the form of two-month promissory notes (from the date of record) amounting to 80 cents a share on 2,545,000 shares outstanding. The date of record was May 27, 1994 and scrip notes were sent to shareholders on May 30. The notes had an interest rate of 10% per annum with a maturity (payment) date of July 27. The entries related to this scrip dividend are as follows:

At date of declaration (May 6, 1994):		
Retained Earnings (Scrip Dividend Declared)	2,036,000	
Notes Payable to Shareholders ($.80 × 2,545,000)		2,036,000
At date of payment (July 27, 1994):		
Notes Payable to Shareholders	2,036,000	
Interest Expense ($2,036,000 × 61/365 × .10)[a]	34,026	
Cash		2,070,026

[a]The interest runs from the date of record to the date of payment.

Liquidating Dividends

Some corporations have used contributed surplus as a basis for dividends. Without proper disclosure of this fact, shareholders may erroneously believe the corporation has been operating at a profit. A further result could be subsequent sale of additional shares by the corporation at a higher price than is warranted. This type of deception, intentional or unintentional, can be avoided by providing a clear statement of the basis of dividends accompanying the dividend cheque.

Dividends based on other than retained earnings are sometimes described as liquidating dividends, thus implying that they are a return of the shareholder's investment rather than of profits. In fact, the distribution may be based on contributed surplus that resulted from donations by outsiders or other shareholders and not be a return of the given shareholder's contribution. But, in a more general sense, *any dividend not based on earnings must be a reduction of corporation capital and, to that extent, it is a liquidating dividend.* We noted in Chapter 11 that companies in the extractive industries may pay dividends equal to the total of accumulated income and depletion. The portion of these dividends in excess of accumulated income represents a return of part of the shareholder's investment.

For example, McChesney Mines Inc. issued a "dividend" to its common shareholders of $1,200,000. The cash dividend announcement noted that $900,000 should be considered income and the remainder a return of capital. The entries are:

At date of declaration:

Retained Earnings	900,000	
Contributed Surplus	300,000	
Dividends Payable		1,200,000

At date of payment:

Dividends Payable	1,200,000	
Cash		1,200,000

Stock Dividends

A **stock dividend** occurs when the board of directors of a company declares that a dividend will be paid to shareholders in the form of a company's own shares (of the same or different class).[11] This may occur because the board wishes to capitalize (i.e. reclassify amounts from earned to contributed capital) part of the earnings and thus retain earnings in the business on a permanent basis. Alternatively, a stock dividend may be declared because the board, unwilling or unable to pay a cash dividend, may still desire to provide the shareholders with something tangible for their interest in the company. Many would argue, however, that a stock dividend, while it may provide some psychological benefit to the shareholder, does not provide any real economic benefits. This is because, in a stock dividend, *no assets are distributed*, and *each shareholder has exactly the same proportionate interest in the corporation and the same total book value after the stock dividend as before the dividend*. Of course, *the book value per share is lower because an increased number of shares are outstanding*.

> **Objective 5**
>
> Understand the nature of stock dividends and know how they are accounted for.

Accounting for a stock dividend of no-par value shares results in transferring an amount from retained earnings to the appropriate share capital account. The question to be answered is "What amount should be transferred?" The *CICA Handbook* does not contain a recommendation regarding this. The CBCA states that, for stock dividends, the declared amount of the dividend shall be added to the stated capital account. The CBCA does not allow shares to be issued until they are fully paid for in an amount not less than the fair equivalent of money that the corporation would have received if the shares had been issued for cash. Therefore, *the fair market value must be used* for companies incorporated under it.

Ordinarily, *fair value to be used is the market price of the shares on the date of the dividend declaration*. This is reasonable given the assumption that the market price will not change materially as the result of the stock dividend. When the market price is significantly affected (e.g., when a relatively large number of shares are being issued), it would be more appropriate to account for the event as a stock split (as described later), even though it may be called a stock dividend.

While the corporation issuing a stock dividend transfers the fair value of the no-par value shares issued from retained earnings to appropriate share capital accounts, an interesting question is whether the persons receiving the stock dividend should consider it as income, as they would consider a cash dividend.[12] Conceptually, the answer would be no. The stock dividend is not income to shareholders because it merely distributes the recipient's equity over a larger number of shares. Theoretically, while the number of shares held increases, the underlying worth of the total number

---

[11] *Financial Reporting in Canada—1991* indicated that of the 300 surveyed companies, there were 23 in 1990, 28 in 1989, 29 in 1988, and 33 in 1987 that disclosed the distribution of a stock dividend in a note to their financial statements or in the retained earnings statement.

[12] For Canadian income tax purposes, at the time of this writing, the recipient of a stock dividend had to treat it in the same manner as a cash dividend, with the amount being equal to the "paid up capital" (legal capital, which would be the fair market value for no-par shares) of the shares received. As such, the stock dividend would be taxable, an aspect that may contribute to corporate decisions to not issue stock dividends.

of shares held has not changed because the net assets of the corporation have not changed. If, however, the market price per share does not decline in direct proportion to the increased number of shares now issued (i.e. the market does not respond perfectly), the recipients of the stock dividend could be better off. To realize their gain, however, they would have to sell their shares.

Given the direction in the CBCA, this chapter will illustrate the *accounting for stock dividends using the market value of the shares issued at the date of declaration as the appropriate amount involved*.

Entries for Stock Dividends. Assume that a corporation has outstanding 1,000 common shares of no-par value issued for $100,000 and a retained earnings balance of $50,000. If it declares a 10% stock dividend, it issues 100 additional shares to present shareholders. Assuming that the fair market value per share was $130 at the time of the stock dividend declaration, the entry would be:

Retained Earnings (Stock Dividend Declared)	13,000	
Common Stock Dividend Distributable		13,000

Note from the entry above that *no asset or liability has been affected*. The entry merely reflects a reclassification in shareholders' equity. If a balance sheet is prepared between the dates of declaration and distribution, the Common Stock Dividend Distributable account should be shown in the shareholders' equity section as an addition to share capital (whereas cash or property dividends payable are shown as current liabilities).[13]

When the shares are issued the entry would be:

Common Stock Dividend Distributable	13,000	
Common Shares		13,000

No matter what the fair value is at the time of the stock dividend, each shareholder retains the same proportionate interest in the corporation. The illustration on page 783 shows that the total net worth of each shareholder (A, B, and C) has not changed as a result of a stock dividend, and that each shareholder owns the same proportion of the total shares outstanding after as before the stock dividend.

Stock Splits

If a company has not distributed earnings over several years and a sizeable balance in retained earnings has accumulated, the market value of its outstanding shares is likely to increase. Shares that were issued at prices less than $50 can easily attain a market value in excess of $200 a share. The higher the market price of a share, the less readily shares can be purchased by most people (particularly given that shares are sold in lots, not individually). The managements of many corporations believe that for better public relations, broad ownership of a corporation's shares is desirable. They wish, therefore, to have a market price sufficiently low to be within range of the majority of potential investors. To reduce the market value of shares, the device of a stock split may be employed.[14] For example, when IBM's common shares were selling at $304 each, the company split these shares four-

---

[13] Some would argue that no entry need be made at date of declaration since court decisions have allowed for stock dividends to be revoked after declaration. Nevertheless, the declaration should be disclosed in financial statements. Journalizing at the time of declaration and disclosing in the statements as indicated is appropriate. A note could also be used.

[14] *The DH&S Review*, May 12, 1986, page 7, listed the following as reasons behind a stock split:
1. To adjust the market price of the company's shares to a level where more individuals can afford to invest in the shares.
2. To spread the shareholder base by increasing the number of shares outstanding and making them more marketable.
3. To benefit existing shareholders by allowing them to take advantage of an imperfect market adjustment following the split.

Before dividend:

Share Capital, 1,000 common shares of no-par value	$100,000
Retained Earnings	50,000
Total shareholders' equity	$150,000

Shareholders' interests:

A—400 shares, 40% interest, book value	$ 60,000
B—500 shares, 50% interest, book value	75,000
C—100 shares, 10% interest, book value	15,000
	$150,000

After declaration but before distribution of 10% stock dividend:

If fair market value per share ($130) is used as the basis for entry

Share Capital, 1,000 shares	$100,000
Common Stock Dividend Distributable, 100 shares	13,000
Retained Earnings ($50,000 − $13,000)	37,000
Total shareholders' equity	$150,000

After declaration and distribution of 10% stock dividend:

If fair value ($130) is used as the basis for entry

Share Capital, 1,100 shares	$113,000
Retained Earnings ($50,000 − $13,000)	37,000
Total shareholders' equity	$150,000

Shareholders' interests:

A—440 shares, 40% interest, book value	$ 60,000
B—550 shares, 50% interest, book value	75,000
C—110 shares, 10% interest, book value	15,000
	$150,000

for-one. The day after IBM's split (involving 583,268,480 shares) was effective, the shares sold for $76 each, exactly one-quarter of the price per share before the split. IBM's intent was to obtain a wider distribution of its shares by improving their marketability.[15] Bombardier Inc. and Quartex Corp. are examples of companies which have recently had stock splits.

From an accounting standpoint, *no entry is recorded for a stock split*; a memorandum note, however, may be made to indicate that the number of shares outstanding has increased.[16] The absence of any other changes in shareholders' equity information is indicated in the following illustration for a two-for-one stock split on 1,000 no-par value common shares.

---

[15] Some companies use reverse stock splits. A **reverse stock split** reduces the number of shares outstanding, which increases the per share price. This technique is used when the share price is unusually low or when management wishes to take control of the company. For example, MTC Electronic Technologies Co. Ltd. had a one-for-four reverse split. As a dramatic example of the use of a reverse split, two officers of Metropolitan Maintenance Co. took control of the company several years ago by forcing a 1-for-3,000 reverse stock split on their shareholders. But anyone who had fewer than 3,000 shares received only cash for his or her shares. Only the two officers owned more than 3,000 shares, so they now own all the shares. A nice squeeze play! (*Forbes*, November 19, 1984, p. 54.)

[16] If shares have a par value, the memorandum note would indicate that the par value had changed as well as the number of shares outstanding.

Shareholders' Equity Before 2-for-1 Split		Shareholders' Equity After 2-for-1 Split	
Common, **1,000 shares**, no-par value	$100,000	Common, **2,000 shares**, no-par value	$100,000
Retained earnings	50,000	Retained earnings	50,000
	$150,000		$150,000

Stock Splits and Stock Dividends Differentiated

Objective 6

Distinguish between stock splits and stock dividends.

A stock split is distinguished from a stock dividend in that *a stock split results in an increase* (or decrease in a reverse stock split) *in the number of shares outstanding with no change in the share capital or retained earnings amounts, whereas a stock dividend results in an increase in both the number of shares outstanding and the share capital amount and a decrease in retained earnings. Neither,* however, *results in any change to total shareholders' equity*.

A stock dividend, like a stock split, may be used to increase the marketability of the shares, although marketability is often a secondary consideration. If the stock dividend is so large that the principal consideration appears to be a desire to reduce the price of the shares, the action results in a stock split, regardless of the form it may take. The AICPA Committee on Accounting Procedures stated that *whenever additional shares are issued for the purpose of reducing the unit market price, then the distribution more closely resembles a stock split than a stock dividend. This effect usually results only if the number of shares issued is more than 20% or 25% of the number of shares previously outstanding*.[17] While no such guidelines have been specified for the Canadian practitioner, the U.S. standard is useful when one is required to exercise judgement regarding accounting for substance over form.

Summary of the Accounting Consequences of Cash Dividends, Stock Dividends, and Stock Splits

The following table summarizes and compares the different accounting consequences regarding cash dividends, stock dividends, and stock splits. The accounting consequences of property or scrip dividends on shareholders' equity accounts are the same as for a cash dividend.

	Declaration and Payment of a Cash Dividend	Declaration and Distribution of	
Effect on:		Stock Dividend	Stock Split
Net assets (Assets − Liabilities)	Decrease	–0–	–0–
Share capital	–0–	Increase[a]	–0–
Retained earnings	Decrease	Decrease[a]	–0–
Total shareholders' equity	Decrease	–0–	–0–
Number of shares outstanding	–0–	Increase	Increase

[a]Market value of shares issued

[17] *Accounting Research and Terminology Bulletin No. 43*, par. 13. The U.S. SEC has added more precision to the 20–25% rule. Specifically, the SEC indicates that distributions of 25% or more should be considered a "split-up effected in the form of a dividend." Distributions of less than 25% should be accounted for as a stock dividend.

DIVIDEND PREFERENCES

In Chapter 15, it was indicated that various rights and privileges may be given to particular classes of shares. In most cases, these rights and privileges pertain to dividends and reflect various combinations regarding cumulative and participating arrangements. The examples given below illustrate the effect of various provisions on dividend distributions to common and preferred shareholders. Assume that $50,000 is to be distributed as cash dividends, and that outstanding share capital consists of $400,000 received for 8,000 common shares of no-par value and $100,000 received for 1,000, $6 dividend, preferred no-par value shares. Dividends would be distributed to each class according to the assumptions stated for each situation.[18]

Objective 7

Know how to determine dividend distributions between preferred and common shareholders when the preferred shares are cumulative and have participation rights.

1. Assumption—the preferred shares are noncumulative and nonparticipating.

	Preferred	Common	Total
$6 × 1,000 shares	$6,000		$ 6,000
The remainder to common		$44,000	44,000
Totals	$6,000	$44,000	$50,000

2. Assumption—the preferred shares are cumulative and nonparticipating, and dividends have not been paid on them in the preceding two years.

	Preferred	Common	Total
Dividends in arrears, $6 × 1,000 shares for two years	$12,000		$12,000
Current year's dividend, $6 × 1,000 shares	6,000		6,000
The remainder to common		$32,000	32,000
Totals	$18,000	$32,000	$50,000

3. Assumption—the preferred shares are noncumulative and fully participating. Participation is in terms of the proportionate (percentage) relationship of the amounts paid for the shares (i.e. the amounts in the share capital accounts). Participation takes place after the stipulated preferred dividend is satisfied and common shareholders have been allocated an equal rate on their share capital.

	Preferred	Common	Total
Current year's dividend	$ 6,000	$24,000	$30,000
Participating dividend	4,000	16,000	20,000
Totals	$10,000	$40,000	$50,000

(Continued)

---

[18] The terms and bases for determining participating dividends can be different from those shown in illustrations 3 and 4. The specific details related to how participating dividend amounts are determined would be described in the issuing corporation's articles of incorporation. For example, Canadian Utilities Limited has Class A nonvoting shares and Class B common shares which share equally, on a share for share basis, in all dividends declared by the company.

The amounts are determined as follows:

Current year's dividend
  Preferred ($6 × 1,000 shares) $ 6,000
  Common (Preferred rate × common share capital)
    [($6,000/$100,000) × $400,000]   24,000 $30,000

Amount available for participation $ 20,000
Total share capital ($100,000 + $400,000)   500,000
Rate of participation
  $\dfrac{\text{Amount available}}{\text{Total share capital}} = \dfrac{\$20{,}000}{\$500{,}000}$ 4%
Participating dividend
  Preferred (4% × $100,000) $ 4,000
  Common (4% × $400,000)   16,000
                                                                                      $20,000

An alternative to calculating these amounts would be: *— not in class.*

(a) Determine the percentage of the total amount available for dividends to total share capital:
$$\frac{\$\,50{,}000}{\$500{,}000} = 10\%$$

(b) If this rate is greater than the rate committed to preferred for the year (6% = $6,000/$100,000) then it can be applied to the share capital for each class to determine their respective total dividend:
  To preferred (10% × $100,000) $10,000
  To common (10% × $400,000)   40,000
    Total $50,000

(c) If the rate is less than the rate committed to preferred, the preferred are given their full amount ($6,000) if available, with the remainder, if any, going to the common shareholders.

4. Assumption—the preferred shares are cumulative and fully participating, and dividends have not been paid in the preceding two years. In this case, the dividends in arrears would be allocated to the preferred shareholders and the balance available would be allocated according to the procedures shown in illustration 3. Therefore, the distribution would be as follows.

	Preferred	Common	Total
Preferred dividends in arrears			
(2 years × $6 × 1,000 shares)	$12,000		$12,000
Current year's dividend			
(6% of share capital)	6,000	$24,000	30,000
Participating dividend			
($8,000/$500,000) × share capital	1,600	6,400	8,000
Totals	$19,600	$30,400	$50,000

RESTRICTIONS ON THE DISTRIBUTION OF RETAINED EARNINGS

In general, the balance of retained earnings is considered to be available for distribution as dividends. For various reasons, however, *restrictions may be placed on retained earnings so that a specified amount is not available for dividend distribution.* The causes for such restrictions arise from:

1. ***Statutory or contractual obligations***. For example, a bond indenture may contain a requirement that a specified minimum amount of retained earnings be maintained by a company over the life of the bond.

2. ***Discretionary action by management and the board of directors***. For example, management may have intentions for future plant expansion to be financed internally. As a consequence, an amount of retained earnings may be voluntarily excluded from being available for dividend distribution. Other reasons for such voluntary restrictions may be because of possible future losses (e.g., for declines in inventory prices or from lawsuits or unfavourable contractual obligations), a desire to maintain a strong working capital position, or to provide for general contingencies.

Objective 8

Understand the reasons for restrictions on retained earnings and know how to use notes and/or appropriations to disclose them in financial statements.

While the first cause represents a legal requirement that cannot be avoided, the necessity for formally establishing discretionary restrictions is debatable. Establishing and disclosing a discretionary restriction does reflect a legitimate attempt to inform statement users that, for a particular reason, part of retained earnings is not available for dividends. A consequence, however, may be that such users wonder why the unrestricted retained earnings have not been distributed as dividends. In a sense, all earnings not distributed as dividends are "implicitly restricted" for a variety of reasons. Generally, perhaps to help avoid confusion or because there is no need to do so, companies seldom establish discretionary restrictions.

The ***existence of a contractual or discretionary restriction on retained earnings in no way results in the automatic creation of a cash fund to be available for use for the reasons related to the restriction*** (e.g., to pay bonds or to carry out a plant expansion). Should such a cash fund be required or desired, actions apart from restricting retained earnings must be taken. Also ***restricting retained earnings is not a substitute way to account for loss contingencies*** (discussed in Chapter 5).

When there is a condition restricting or affecting the distribution of retained earnings, the details should be disclosed.[19] This may be accomplished through notes to the financial statements or a more formal accounting procedure for recognizing appropriations of retained earnings.

Disclosure of Restrictions in Notes

Most restrictions on the distribution of retained earnings are disclosed by note.[20] Parenthetical notations are sometimes used, but restrictions imposed by bond indentures and loan agreements commonly require an extended explanation. Notes provide a medium for more complete explanations and free the financial statements from abbreviated notations. The type of detail revealed by such notes could include identification of the source of the restriction, pertinent provisions, and the amount of retained earnings subject to restriction, or the amount not so restricted. The Westcoast

---

Westcoast Energy Inc.

18. Dividend Restrictions
The First Mortgage and the indentures relating to the Company's long term debt contain restrictions as to the declaration or payment of dividends, other than stock dividends, on common shares. Under the most restrictive provision, the amount available for dividends at December 31, 1991 is $213,000,000 (December 31, 1990—$190,000,000, December 31, 1989—$164,000,000).

---

[19] *CICA Handbook*, Section 3250, par. .10.

[20] *Financial Reporting in Canada—1991* stated that in 1990, 41 of the 300 surveyed companies made such disclosures (38 giving details). In 1989 there were 36, in 1988 there were 35, and in 1987 there were 42 of the companies disclosing such restrictions. For the period 1987–1990, only two surveyed companies disclosed restrictions by formally establishing an appropriation or reserve of retained earnings. Previous issues of *Financial Reporting in Canada* indicated greater existence of appropriations—perhaps their use will soon be eliminated in favour of note disclosure.

Energy Inc. and Canadian Utilities Limited examples from annual reports illustrate note disclosure relating to restrictions on retained earnings and dividends.

Canadian Utilities Limited

8. (in part) Retained Earnings
The bond and debenture indentures place certain limitations on the Company which include restrictions on the payment of dividends on Class A and Class B shares. Consolidated retained earnings in the amount of $136,718,000 was free from such restrictions.

When there is more than one type of restriction relating to a particular contract, disclosure of the amount of retained earnings so restricted would be based on the most restrictive covenants. This is sufficient because restrictions seldom, if ever, pyramid in amount.

Appropriations of Retained Earnings

Appropriations (also called reserves[21]) of retained earnings are nothing more than reclassifications of retained earnings, temporarily or perhaps even permanently established to reflect restrictions on the availability of retained earnings for dividends. *Appropriations are created by transferring amounts from the unappropriated retained earnings account to an appropriated retained earnings account. When the appropriation is no longer necessary, the appropriated amount should be returned to unappropriated retained earnings.* The purpose of an appropriation is to show in the body of the balance sheet that a portion of retained earnings is not available for dividend distributions.

The act of appropriating retained earnings is a policy matter requiring approval by the board of directors. According to the *CICA Handbook*, the appropriation of retained earnings is acceptable practice, provided that it is shown within the shareholders' equity section of the balance sheet and is clearly identified as to the source from which it was created.[22]

Recording Appropriations of Retained Earnings

As soon as the board of directors has approved an appropriation of retained earnings, it becomes necessary to record the appropriation in the accounts. The amount of the appropriation is recorded as a debit to Retained Earnings and a credit to an appropriately named account that itself is just a subdivision of retained earnings. If the appropriation merely augments one previously established, the account already in use should receive the credit. For example:

(a) An Appropriation for Plant Expansion is to be created by transfer from Retained Earnings of $400,000 a year for five years. The entry for each year would be:

Retained Earnings	400,000	
Retained Earnings Appropriated for Plant Expansion		400,000

(b) At the end of five years, the appropriation account would have a balance of $2,000,000. If one assumes that the expansion plan has been completed, the appropriation is no longer required and can be returned to retained earnings by making the following entry:

Retained Earnings Appropriated for Plant Expansion	2,000,000	
Retained Earnings		2,000,000

---

[21] The term "reserve" has been used instead of "appropriation" in account titles reflecting a restriction on retained earnings. The authors, however, do not condone this practice because it results in confusion and misunderstanding owing to the public's general interpretation of the term and its diverse use by accountants in the past (e.g., Reserve for Depreciation, Reserve for Uncollectible Accounts, which are contra-asset items). Some of this confusion has been eliminated by the *CICA Handbook*, which limits the use of the term "reserve" to appropriations of retained earnings or other surplus (Section 3260, par. .01).

[22] *CICA Handbook*, Section 3260, par. .04.

Return of such an appropriation to retained earnings has the effect of increasing unappropriated retained earnings without affecting the assets or current position. In effect, over the five years the company has expanded by reinvesting assets acquired through the earnings process.

Reporting appropriations in financial statements is accomplished simply by categorizing total retained earnings into two components: appropriated and unappropriated. For example, if total retained earnings consisted of $800,000 appropriated for plant expansion and $2,200,000 unappropriated, this would be reported in the shareholders' equity section of the balance sheet as follows.

Total Liabilities			$ 500,000
Shareholders' Equity:			
Share Capital		$1,000,000	
Retained Earnings:			
Appropriated for plant expansion	$ 800,000		
Unappropriated	2,200,000	3,000,000	
Total Shareholders' Equity			4,000,000
Total Liabilities and Shareholders' Equity			$4,500,000

While such reporting of the appropriation may be sufficient, more complex reasons for appropriations may be disclosed in a cross-referenced note.

Disclosures for Self-Insurance

A company may insure against many contingencies such as fire, flood, storm, and accident by taking out insurance policies and paying premiums to insurance companies. Some contingencies, however, are not insurable or the rates may be judged as being prohibitively high in the circumstances. In such situations, some companies may adopt a policy referred to as **self-insurance**. Self-insurance appears especially valid when a company's physical or operating characteristics permit application of probability analysis as used by insurance companies. Whenever the risk of loss can be spread over a large number of possible loss events that individually would be small in relation to the total potential loss, self-insurance is a temptation. It is based on the belief that the losses will cost fewer dollars over an extended period of time than the premiums that would be paid to insure against such losses. The company thus avoids paying the insurance company's overhead costs including the insurance agent's commission. Examples of self-insurance situations are a car rental company with hundreds of cars in different locations or a grocery chain with many stores scattered geographically.

Accounting for self-insurance could take one of at least three forms:

Record Losses as Incurred. Under this approach no accounting recognition is given to the fact that self-insurance is the mode of operation and that uninsured losses may have to be absorbed in some future period. Losses are charged against revenues of the period in which it is likely that an asset has been impaired or a liability has been incurred at the date of the financial statements and the amount of loss can be reasonably estimated.[23] *This approach would be permitted under GAAP*.

Appropriate Retained Earnings and Record Losses as Incurred. This approach also charges uninsured losses against revenues in the period in which the losses are sustained. Recognition is given to contingent losses in periods other than their incurrence, however, by appropriations of retained earnings. The amount of the annual appropriation may approximate the premium cost of adequate insurance covering the risk, or it may be a prorated allocation of an estimated and

> **Objective 9**
>
> Appreciate the accounting issues regarding disclosures of self-insurance.

---

[23] *CICA Handbook*, Section 3290, par. .12.

anticipated future loss. The balance of the appropriation account normally does not exceed the maximum expected loss at any one time and is never charged with actual losses. The effect of this and the first method is a varying charge for actual losses instead of a stable charge to expense that would result from premium payments to an insurance company. *This approach also would be permitted under GAAP*.

Accrue Expense. This approach avoids the erratic effects on net income resulting from irregularly occurring uninsured losses and makes the income statement of a company that does not insure appear to be comparable to those of firms carrying insurance. This method accrues the estimated losses by charging operations each year with a hypothetical amount of insurance expense and crediting a similar amount to a liability account titled Liability for Self-Insured Risks or Liability for Uninsured Losses. When the casualty losses occur, they are charged against the liability account. The liability account absorbs the impact of the loss; each year's income statement absorbs only a portion of the loss. *This approach is not permitted under GAAP*.

Self-insurance is no insurance, and any company that assumes its own risks puts itself in the position of incurring expenses or losses as the casualties occur. The improper application of the accrual method (third method) to self-insurance obscures a fundamental difference in circumstances between companies that transfer risks to others through insurance and those that do not. There is little theoretical justification for the establishment of a liability based on a hypothetical charge to insurance expense. This is "as if" accounting.[24] Can there be an expense in advance of the actual occurrence of a casualty, or a liability to incur a casualty loss in the future? The *CICA Handbook*'s answer to this question is:

> Fires, explosions and other similar perils are random in their occurrence and, since no impairment of an asset or incurrence of a liability can exist prior to the occurrence of such an event, accrual is inappropriate. Where, however, an enterprise lacks adequate insurance against a material risk that is normally insured, disclosure of this fact may be desirable.[25]

The following provides an example of note disclosure which describes a company's self-insurance and its accounting treatment.

Adolph Coors Company

Note 4: Commitments and Contingencies
It is generally the policy of the Company to act as a self-insurer for certain insurable risks consisting primarily of physical loss to corporate property, business interruption resulting from such loss, employee health insurance programs, and workmen's compensation. Losses and claims are accrued as incurred.

STATEMENTS PRESENTING CHANGES IN RETAINED EARNINGS, CONTRIBUTED SURPLUS, AND SHARE CAPITAL

The *CICA Handbook* recommends that changes in each of retained earnings and contributed surplus during the period should be disclosed.[26] Also, disclosure of the details of transactions affecting share

---

[24] A commentary in *Forbes* (June 15, 1974, p. 42) stated its position on this matter quite succinctly: "The simple and unquestionable fact of life is this: business is cyclical and full of unexpected surprises. Is it the role of accounting to disguise this unpleasant fact and create a fairyland of smoothly rising earnings? Or, should accounting reflect reality, warts and all—floods, expropriations, and all manner of rude shocks?"
[25] *CICA Handbook*, Section 3290, par. .16.
[26] *CICA Handbook*, Section 3250, par. .13.

capital is required.[27] Notes to the financial statements or statements of changes in these shareholder equity categories may be presented to accomplish this. The basic format for presenting this information is:

1. Balance at the beginning of the period.
2. Additions.
3. Deductions.
4. Balance at the end of the period.

The following examples from financial statements indicate how such disclosure may be accomplished.

Doman Industries Limited
From the Balance Sheet—in Shareholders' Equity (in $000's)

	1992	1991
Share capital (note 9)	$209,876	$ 44,377
Retained earnings	19,142	3,305

Consolidated Statement of Retained Earnings (in 000's)

	1992	1991
Retained Earnings, beginning of year	$ 3,385	$ 56,665
Net earnings (loss)	27,213	(46,537)
	30,598	10,128
Deduct		
Share issue expenses (net of deferred income taxes of $716)	916	—
Premium on common and non-voting shares purchased and cancelled	—	32
Dividends	10,540	6,711
Retained earnings, end of year	$ 19,142	$ 3,385

Note 9 (part e) Changes in Issued Shares

(i) Preferred Shares

	Number of Shares				
	Class A				
	Series 2	Series 3	Series 4	Total	Amount
					($000's)
Balance, December 31, 1990 and 1991	573,553	—	—	573,553	$ 14,339
Issued to extinguish an obligation	—	964,660	1,281,526	2,246,186	112,309
Balance, December 31, 1992	573,553	964,660	1,281,526	2,819,739	$126,648

(Continued)

[27] *CICA Handbook*, Section 3240, par. .04.

Objective 10

Appreciate how to prepare statements presenting changes in retained earnings, contributed surplus, share capital, or total shareholders' equity.

(ii) Common and Non-Voting Shares

	Number of Shares			
	Class A	Class B, Series 2	Total	Amount
				($000's)
Balance, December 31, 1990	6,456,911	12,682,028	19,138,939	$28,651
Issued as stock dividends on common and non-voting shares	—	254,276	254,276	1,399
Purchased and cancelled	(3,000)	(5,000)	(8,000)	(12)
Conversions	(63,400)	63,400	—	—
Balance, December 31, 1991	6,390,511	12,994,704	19,385,215	30,038
Issued for cash	—	4,000,000	4,000,000	26,500
Issued to extinguish an obligation	—	2,936,470	2,936,470	20,000
Issued as stock dividends on common and non-voting shares	—	994,117	994,117	6,690
Conversions	(320,337)	320,337	—	—
Balance, December 31, 1992	6,070,174	21,245,628	27,315,802	$83,228

Senchura Inc.
From the Balance Sheet—in Shareholders' Equity (in $000's)

	1992	1991
Share capital (note 10)	$ 508	$ 3,874
Contributed surplus (note 11)	46,438	39,993
Deficit	(40,733)	(41,004)

Consolidated Statement of Retained Earnings (in $000's)

	1991	1990
(Deficit) retained earnings—beginning of year	$(41,004)	$ 7,355
Net earnings (loss) for the year	271	(22,372)
Dividends	—	(25,987)
Deficit—end of year	$(40,733)	$(41,004)

(Continued)

Note 10. Share capital

	Authorized	Issued and fully paid 1991	
	Number of Shares*	Number of Shares	$000
Class A Special Shares	Unlimited	306,468	508
Class B Non-Voting Shares	Unlimited	—	—
Class C Preferred Shares	Unlimited	—	—
		306,468	508

	Authorized	Issued and fully paid 1990	
	Number of Shares*	Number of Shares	$000
Class A Special Shares	Unlimited	306,664	508
Class B Non-Voting Shares	Unlimited	2,055,820	3,366
		2,362,484	3,874

*All of no par value

In January 1991 the Class B Non-Voting Shares were purchased and cancelled by the Company for $0.01 each pursuant to the resolutions passed by the shareholders at the general meeting of January 25, 1991. The total cost of the purchase of the Class B Non-Voting Shares was $20,558 which has been deducted from the issued capital value of the Class B Non-Voting Shares. The difference of $3,345,694 has been transferred to contributed surplus. The total number of issued and outstanding Class A Special Shares is 306,468 and there is no other class of shares in issue following the reorganization of 1991.

[This note continues with an explanation of the rights attributable to the share classes.]

Note 11. Contributed surplus (in $000's)

	1991	1990
Balance, beginning of year	$39,993	$ 7,416
Contribution to surplus	300	32,577
Transfer from share capital on purchase and cancellation of Class B Non-Voting Shares	3,346	—
Surplus arising on the redemption of Preference Shares held by Senchura Investments Limited	2,799	—
Balance, end of year	$46,438	$39,993

In order to disclose the changes in all shareholder equity items a **columnar format** report can be very useful. Such a format is illustrated in the following example.

Blue Company Limited
Statement of Changes in Shareholders' Equity
(Dollars in millions)

| | Common Shares | | Contributed | Retained |
	No. Shares	Amount	Surplus	Earnings
Balance, December 31, 1993	10,000,000	$ 95.6	$8.2	600.0
Net income for 1994				12.0
Cash dividends paid in 1994				(15.0)
Common shares reacquired and cancelled	(25,000)	(.24)	(.7)	
Common shares issued for cash	1,300,000	16.9		
Common shares issued as stock dividends	500,000	6.2		(6.2)
Donated land			1.0	
Balance, December 31, 1994	11,775,000	$118.46	$8.5	$590.8

APPRAISAL INCREASE CREDITS

The *CICA Handbook* generally requires that all capital assets be recorded at cost.[28] Prior to the inclusion of the new Section 3060 in the *Handbook* in 1990, assets could be written up to an appraised value above their cost in limited circumstances (e.g., a reorganization or to recognize discovery value). When an asset's appraisal value was in excess of its book value and this fact was to be recognized in the accounts, the credit would be made to a shareholders' equity account such as Excess of Appraised Value of Fixed Assets Over Cost (or Depreciated Cost when appropriate) or simply Appraisal Increase. Such appraisal increase credit accounts which existed prior to the new Section 3060 were, and continue to be, shown as a separate item in shareholders' equity.[29] An appraisal increase account balance could remain indefinitely or be amortized to retained earnings each period in amounts not greater than the realization of the appreciation through sale or depreciation provisions.[30]

COMPREHENSIVE ILLUSTRATION OF A SHAREHOLDERS' EQUITY SECTION

The presentation on the following page is an example of a shareholders' equity section of a balance sheet. It includes most of the equity items discussed in Chapters 15 and 16 (notes that would normally provide more details on the items have been omitted).

FINANCIAL REORGANIZATION

A corporation that consistently suffers net losses accumulates negative retained earnings, or a **deficit**. Corporate laws typically provide that no dividends may be declared and paid so long as a corporation's contributed capital (share capital and contributed surplus) has been impaired by a deficit. In these cases, a corporation with a debit balance of retained earnings must accumulate sufficient profits to offset the deficit before dividends are possible.

---

[28] *CICA Handbook*, Section 3060, par. .18. Excluded from coverage by this Section (par. .02) of the *Handbook* are goodwill and special circumstances when a comprehensive revaluation of all assets and liabilities occurs (e.g., a financial reorganization).

[29] *CICA Handbook*, Section 3060, par. .64.

[30] When appraisal increases are recorded, depreciation of the asset would be based on the appraisal value. *Financial Reporting in Canada—1991* reported that of the 300 companies surveyed, 7 in 1990, 8 in 1989, 10 in 1988, and 11 in 1987 had included appraisal increases as a separate item in the shareholders' equity section.

Model Corporation
Shareholders' Equity
December 31, 1994

Share Capital:
Class A, preferred, $9 dividend,
  cumulative, no-par value,
  30,000 shares authorized, issued
  and outstanding .... $ 3,150,000
Class B, common, no-par value, no authorized
  limit, 400,000 shares issued and 398,000
  outstanding as 2,000 are in treasury 4,000,000
Class B common stock dividend
  distributable, 20,000 shares 200,000
    Total share capital .... $ 7,350,000

Contributed Surplus:
Excess of assigned value over
  cost of common shares
  purchased and cancelled .... $ 10,000
Donated land 830,000
    Total contributed surplus 840,000
Retained Earnings:
Appropriated for plant expansion $2,100,000
Unappropriated 2,160,000
    Total retained earnings 4,260,000
    Total share capital, contributed
      surplus, and retained earnings $12,450,000
Excess of Appraised Value of
  Fixed Assets Over Depreciated Cost 100,000
    Total $12,550,000
Less cost of treasury shares (2,000 Class B
  common shares) .... (80,000)
    Total shareholders' equity $12,470,000

This situation may be a real hardship on a corporation and its shareholders. A company that has operated unsuccessfully for several years and accumulated a deficit may have finally "turned the corner." Development of new products and new markets, a new management team, or improved economic conditions may promise much improved operating results. But, if the law prohibits dividends until the deficit has been replaced by earnings, the shareholders must wait until such profits have been earned, which may take a considerable period of time. Furthermore, future success may depend on obtaining additional funds through the sale of shares. If no dividends can be paid for some time, however, the market price of any new share issue is likely to be low, if such shares can be marketed at all.

Additionally, if a corporation in financial difficulty has non-equity interests (e.g., bondholders), it is quite likely that meeting interest and/or principal payments is in jeopardy.

Thus, a company with every prospect of a successful future may be prevented from accomplishing its plans because of past financial difficulties which created the deficit, although present management may have had nothing whatever to do with the years over which the problems occurred. To permit the corporation to proceed with its plans might well be to the advantage of all interests in the enterprise; to require it to eliminate the deficit through profits might actually force it to liquidate.

Objective 12

Know what a
financial reor-
ganization is
and how it is
accounted for
and disclosed
in financial
statements.

A procedure which enables a company that has gone through financial difficulty to proceed with its plans without the encumbrance of having to recover from a deficit is called a **financial reorganization**. A financial reorganization is defined as *a substantial realignment of the equity and non-equity interests of an enterprise such that the holders of one or more of the significant classes of non-equity interests and the holders of all of the significant classes of equity interests give up some (or all) of their rights and claims upon the enterprise.*[31]

A financial reorganization results from negotiation and the reaching of an eventual agreement between non-equity and equity holders in the corporation. These negotiations may take place under the provisions of a legal act (e.g., Companies' Creditors Arrangement Act) or a less formal process.[32]

Accounting for a Financial Reorganization

When a financial reorganization occurs and the same party does not control the company both before and after the reorganization, the assets and liabilities of the company are comprehensively revalued.[33] Additionally, the deficit is eliminated from the books. The consequence is that the company is given a "fresh start" (as if it were a new entity) for purposes of financial reporting.

To account for a financial reorganization, the following occur:[34]

1. The balance in the Retained Earnings (deficit) account is brought up to the date of the reorganization. In addition to closing any open income statement accounts (i.e. the reorganization date is not the same as the year end), any asset write-downs related to circumstances that existed prior to the reorganization must be accounted for (see Chapter 11).

2. The updated balance of retained earnings (deficit) is reclassified to either share capital, contributed surplus, or a separately identified account within shareholders' equity. Consequently, the company's retained earnings account is given a "fresh start" (i.e. starts with a zero balance) from the date of the financial reorganization.

3. The assets and liabilities of the enterprise are comprehensively revalued. This means that values for assets and liabilities established in the negotiations among the equity and non-equity interests (or fair values if no negotiated values are established) become the new costs to be accounted for subsequent to the reorganization. The difference between the carrying values before the reorganization and these new values is accounted for as a **revaluation adjustment**. The revaluation adjustment and any costs directly incurred to carry out the financial reorganization are accounted for as capital transactions and recorded as either share capital, contributed surplus, or a separately identified account within shareholders' equity.

To illustrate, consider the following.[35]

Hopeful Co. Ltd.
(in 000s)

	Balance Prior to Financial Reorganization	Adjustments to Reflect Write-Downs Before Reorganization	Revaluation Adjustment From Reorganization	Balance After Financial Reorganization
Assets:				
Current assets	$1,000			$1,000
				(Continued)

[31] *CICA Handbook*, Section 1625, par. .03.
[32] *Ibid.*, par. .15.
[33] *Ibid.*, pars. .04 and .05. If the same party controls the corporation before and after the reorganization, it is assumed that substantial realignment of non-equity and equity interests has not occurred and, therefore, comprehensive revaluation is not appropriate (par. .16).
[34] *Ibid.*, pars. .39–.49. If the result is a negative total shareholders' equity, share capital is disclosed as a nominal amount and the balance is disclosed as a Capital Deficiency Resulting From Financial Reorganization.
[35] *Ibid.*, appendix, provides a framework for this example.

Property, plant, & equipment	5,000	$(400)	$(600)[2]	4,000
Goodwill	300	(300)		—
Patents	—		100[2]	100
	$6,300	$(700)	$(500)	$5,100
Liabilities and Shareholders' Equity:				
Current liabilities	$2,400			$2,400
Bonds payable	1,000		($500)[2]	500
Preferred shares				
• 4,000 no-par, $20 dividend, two years in arrears	400		(400)[2]	—
Common shares				
• issued prior to reorganization 100,000 shares	4,000			
• issued on financial reorganization to bondholders, 60,000 shares and to preferred shareholders, 45,000 shares			(2,200)[1] 400[2]	2,200
Deficit	(1,500)	(700)	2,200[1]	—
	$6,300	$(700)	$(500)	$5,100

This work sheet reflects the following accounting consequences of a financial reorganization which resulted in:

(a) Property, plant, and equipment to be written down by $400,000 and the $300,000 goodwill to be eliminated in order to reflect circumstances that existed prior to the reorganization. These write-downs relate to income of the period prior to the reorganization and are, therefore, sources for additions to the deficit prior to the reorganization. The work sheet column, "Adjustments to Reflect Write-Downs Before Reorganization," shows the results of the write-downs on balance sheet accounts. The following journal entry would incorporate these write-downs in the accounting records:

Deficit	700,000	
Property, Plant, and Equipment		400,000
Goodwill		300,000

The Deficit account balance prior to the reorganization would now be $2,200,000. This would be reclassified as share capital, contributed surplus, or a separately identified account within the shareholders' equity section. The following entry reclassifies the deficit to share capital, as is shown in the work sheet (coded by a 1):

Common Shares	2,200,000	
Deficit		2,200,000

(b) Comprehensive revaluation of assets and liabilities such that Property, Plant, and Equipment is to be reduced by $600,000 (i.e. after the write-down for circumstances prior to the reorganization), and Patents developed by the company are to be recorded at $100,000. Bondholders agreed to give up one-half of their bonds for 60,000 common shares and preferred shareholders relinquished all their shares and dividends in arrears in exchange for 45,000 common shares. The entry to recognize these facts, with the resulting revaluation adjustment being recorded as share capital is as follows (coded by a 2 in the work sheet column "Revaluation Adjustment From Reorganization").

Patents	100,000	
Bonds Payable	500,000	
Preferred Shares	400,000	
Property, Plant, and Equipment		600,000
Common Shares (revaluation adjustment)		400,000

Financial Statement Disclosure of a Financial Reorganization

Given that comprehensive revaluation of assets and liabilities has taken place as the result of a financial reorganization, the *CICA Handbook* requires that certain disclosures be made.

In financial statements for the period in which the reorganization took place, the date of the reorganization, a description of the reorganization, and the amount of change in each major class of assets, liabilities, and shareholders' equity resulting from the reorganization must be disclosed.[36] Financial statements for at least three years after the reorganization must disclose the date of reorganization, the revaluation adjustment amount and the shareholders' equity account in which it was recorded, and the amount of retained earnings (deficit) reclassified on the reorganization as well as the account to which it was reclassified.[37] Additionally, the measurement bases used to revalue assets and liabilities should be disclosed for as long as the revalued amounts are significant.[38]

FUNDAMENTAL CONCEPTS

1. The basic categories of shareholders' equity are Share Capital (Chapter 15), Contributed Surplus, and Retained Earnings. Other categories such as Appraisal Increase Credits, Treasury Shares, or Revaluation Adjustments from a financial reorganization may sometimes appear.

2. Contributed Surplus comes from a variety of sources that represent amounts contributed by shareholders and others to a corporation. Donations, sale of treasury shares above cost (single-transaction method), excess of assigned value of shares reacquired and cancelled over the cost, and forfeited shares are examples of sources of Contributed Surplus.

3. Retained Earnings is the sum total of all income earned by a corporation less the dividends declared.

4. Dividends are established by a resolution in the minutes of the meeting of the board of directors on the date of declaration which, in addition to specifying amounts, specifies the date of record and the date of payment.

5. Dividend declaration decisions are governed by the corporation having sufficient retained earnings available and assets to distribute so that payment will not result in insolvency. Present and future financial position are important aspects of such decisions.

6. Various types of dividends exist—cash, property, scrip, liquidating, and stock dividends.

7. Preferences as to dividends may exist between classes of shares in terms of priority for dividend distribution, cumulative rights, and participation rights. Various combinations of preferences may exist.

8. Restrictions may exist regarding the availability of retained earnings for dividends. These may be the result of statutory or contractual commitments, or a discretionary decision of the board of directors. Disclosures of such restrictions is necessary and may be accomplished through notes to the financial statements and/or the establishment of an appropriation account.

9. Disclosure of changes in shareholders' equity accounts during a period is required in the financial statements. This may be accomplished in the basic financial statements, in separate statements designed to accomplish this objective, or through notes.

10. In some circumstances, appraisal increase credits (the excess of an appraisal value over the historical cost book value of an asset) may occur. These are to be shown as a separate item in shareholders' equity.

(Continued)

---

[36] *Ibid.*, par. .50.
[37] *Ibid.*, par. .52.
[38] *Ibid.*, par. .51.

11. A financial reorganization requires formal approval by non-equity and equity holders and essentially enables a company to get a fresh start. This process results in a comprehensive revaluation of assets and liabilities and eliminates an accumulated deficit. The deficit is eliminated by reclassifying it as share capital, contributed surplus, or a separately identified account in shareholders' equity. A revaluation adjustment resulting from comprehensive revaluation is recorded as share capital, contributed surplus, or a separately identified shareholders' equity account.

QUESTIONS

1. Distinguish among: contributed capital, earned capital, and equity capital.

2. List the possible sources of contributed surplus.

3. What are some of the common items that increase or decrease retained earnings?

4. What factors influence the dividend policy of a company?

5. Very few companies pay dividends in amounts equal to their retained earnings legally available for dividends. For what reasons might earnings be retained in a business?

6. What are the principal considerations of a board of directors in making decisions involving dividend declarations? Discuss briefly.

7. It has been noted that on a price-level basis (adjusted for specific prices), dividends paid can exceed profits earned. As a result, some companies are in effect undergoing gradual liquidation. Explain what this statement means.

8. Dividends are sometimes said to have been paid "out of retained earnings." What is the error in that statement?

9. Distinguish among: cash dividends, property dividends, scrip dividends, liquidating dividends, and stock dividends.

10. Describe the accounting entry for a stock dividend. Describe the accounting entry for a stock split.

11. Stock splits and stock dividends may be used by a corporation to change the number of its shares outstanding.
    (a) What is meant by a stock split effected in the form of a dividend?
    (b) From an accounting viewpoint, explain how the stock split effected in the form of a dividend differs from an ordinary stock dividend.
    (c) How should a stock dividend which has been declared but not yet issued be classified in a statement of financial position (balance sheet)? Why?

12. This comment appeared in the annual report of Whatso Inc.: "The Company could pay cash or property dividends on the Class A common shares without paying cash or property dividends on the Class B common shares, but if the Company pays any cash or property dividends on the Class B common, it would be required to pay at least the same dividend on the Class A common." What is a property dividend and how is it accounted for in the financial records?

13. Betafax Corporation has consistently reported a significant amount of income and has accumulated a large balance of retained earnings. At a recent shareholders' meeting, the company's policy of declaring little or no dividends caused some controversy.
    (a) Why might Betafax Corporation establish such a conservative dividend policy?
    (b) What steps might Betafax take to reduce the amount of retained earnings available for dividends?

14. Cactus Corp. had 5,000, $2 dividend, no-par value preferred shares and 12,000 no-par value common shares outstanding throughout 1994.
    (a) Assuming that total dividends declared in 1994 were $85,000, and that the preferred shares are not cumulative but are fully participating on a per share basis after common shares have been given a per share dividend equal to that stated for preferred for the year, what amount of 1994 dividends should each common share receive?
    (b) Assuming that total dividends declared in 1994 were $78,000, and that the preferred shares are fully participating (as in (a)) and cumulative with preferred dividends in arrears for 1993, what amount of 1994 dividends should preferred shareholders receive?
    (c) Assuming that total dividends declared in 1994 were $30,000, that cumulative nonparticipating preferred shares were issued on January 1, 1993, and that $5,000 of preferred dividends were declared and paid in 1993, what amount of 1994 dividends should common shareholders receive?

15. For what reasons might a company appropriate a portion of its retained earnings?

16. How should appropriations of retained earnings be created and written off?

17. Indicate the misuse and the accepted use of the term "reserve" from a financial reporting perspective.

18. Is there a duplication of charges to current year's costs or expenses when a reserve is created for fixed-asset replacement as well as there being accumulated depreciation with respect to the fixed assets? Briefly explain your answer.

19. What is self-insurance? What are two acceptable forms of accounting for self-insurance?

20. What is a financial reorganization?

21. Outline the steps involved in accounting for a financial organization.

22. What financial statement disclosures are required regarding a financial reorganization for years subsequent to the reorganization?

―――――― CASES ――――――

C16-1 (CONCEPTUAL ISSUES: EQUITY)   *CICA Handbook*, Section 1000 on "Financial Statement Concepts," sets forth financial accounting and reporting objectives and concepts that are to be used by the Accounting Standards Board in developing standards. Included in Section 1000 are definitions of various elements of financial statements.

Instructions

Answer the following questions based on Section 1000 of the *CICA Handbook*.

(a) Define and discuss the element "equity."

(b) What transactions or events change owners' equity?

(c) Define "investments by owners" and provide examples of this type of transaction. What financial statement element other than equity is typically affected by owner investments?

(d) Define "distributions to owners" and provide examples of this type of transaction. What financial statement element other than equity is typically affected by distributions?

(e) What are examples of changes within owners' equity that do not change the total amount of owners' equity?

C16-2 (STOCK DIVIDENDS AND SPLITS)   The directors of Mystery Co. Ltd. are considering the issuance of a stock dividend. They have asked you to discuss the proposed action by answering the following questions.

Instructions

(a) What is a stock dividend? How is a stock dividend distinguished from a stock split from an accounting standpoint?

(b) For what reasons does a corporation usually declare a stock dividend? A stock split?

(c) Discuss the amount, if any, of retained earnings to be capitalized in connection with a stock dividend.

(d) Discuss the case *against* considering a stock dividend as income to the recipient.

(AICPA adapted)

C16-3 (SELF-INSURANCE)   Crest Inc., a large retail chain store company, has stores throughout Canada. Due to the stores' many different locations, the president thinks it would be advantageous to self-insure the company's stores against the risk of any future loss or damage from fire or other natural causes. From past experience and by applying appropriate statistical and actuarial techniques, the president feels the amount of future losses can be predicted with reasonable accuracy.

Instructions

The president has asked you how Crest should record this type of contingency and on what basis the current period should be allocated a portion of the estimated losses. What would you tell the president?

(RESTRICTED, APPROPRIATED, AND UNAPPROPRIATED RETAINED EARNINGS) The **C16-4** retained earnings section of Home Products Inc.'s balance sheet was presented as follows:

Retained Earnings	
Appropriation for plant expansion	$8,000,000
Appropriation for contingencies	4,000,000
Appropriation regarding bond indenture contract	2,000,000
Total appropriated	$14,000,000
Unappropriated (see note 7)	16,000,000
Total retained earnings	$30,000,000

Note 7: The board of directors has restricted $7,000,000 of this amount, given that there are presently litigation proceedings against the company claiming this as a maximum amount for damages.

Pat Green, a common shareholder in the company, was recently quoted as saying, "I think appropriations mean that dividends can't be declared out of such amounts. Unfortunately, something must have gone wrong with the company's accounting because a special cash account for each of these appropriations was not shown in the asset section of the balance sheet. Also, I don't really understand why an appropriation was not set up for the $7,000,000 regarding litigation proceedings. The fact this was disclosed by a note must mean that the restriction is of a second-class nature to the listed appropriations. Furthermore, at the next shareholders' meeting, I think we should really get after management as they don't appear to want to give us our fair amount of dividends. Even accepting the appropriations and restriction as being reasonable, that leaves $9,000,000 that should have been paid as dividends because management has given no reasons why it should be kept in the company."

Instructions

Discuss Mr. Green's points regarding his understanding of the reported information.

(FINANCIAL REORGANIZATION) Quantum Leap Co. Ltd., a medium-sized manufacturer, has experi- **C16-5** enced losses for the five years it has been doing business. Although the operations for the year just ended resulted in a loss, several important changes resulted in a profitable fourth quarter, and the future operations of the company are expected to be profitable. The treasurer, Helen Smith, suggests that there be a financial reorganization to (1) eliminate the accumulated deficit of $650,000, (2) write up the $700,000 carrying value of operating land and buildings to their fair value, and (3) set up an asset of $120,000 representing the estimated future tax benefit of the losses accumulated to date as they could be offset against future income thereby reducing future taxes payable. Quantum Leap Co. Ltd. has the following liabilities and shareholders' equity items at this time:

Current liabilities	$ 50,000
Long-term notes payable	75,000
Preferred shares	200,000
Common shares (widely held)	1,000,000
Deficit	650,000

Instructions

(a) What is the purpose of a financial reorganization?

(b) Identify the requirements and accounting necessary for a financial reorganization to result in a "fresh start" accounting for the company.

(c) Identify and discuss issues regarding the treasurer's proposals to:

1. Eliminate the deficit of $650,000.

2. Write up the $700,000 carrying value of the operating land and buildings to their fair value.

3. Set up an asset of $120,000 representing the estimated future tax benefit of the losses accumulated to date.

———————— **EXERCISES** ————————

E16-1 **(CLASSIFICATION OF EQUITY ITEMS)**   Shareholders' equity on the balance sheet is composed of three major sections. They are: A. Share Capital; B. Contributed Surplus, and C. Retained Earnings.

Instructions

Classify each of the following items as affecting one of the three sections above or as D, an item not to be included in shareholders' equity.

1. Retained earnings appropriated.

2. Accumulated depreciation—buildings.

3. Sinking fund.

4. Subscriptions receivable.

5. Contributed Capital—forfeit of cash received on preferred shares subscribed but not paid for in full.

6. Net income.

7. Common shares subscribed.

8. Stock split.

9. Donated building.

10. Cash dividends declared.

11. Preferred shares.

E16-2 **(EQUITY ITEMS ON THE BALANCE SHEET)**   The following are selected transactions that may affect shareholders' equity:

1. Recorded accrued interest earned on a note receivable.

2. Declared a cash dividend.

3. Paid the cash dividend declared in item 2 above.

4. Recorded an increase in value of an investment that will be distributed as a property dividend.

5. Declared a property dividend (see item 4 above).

6. Distributed the property dividend to shareholders (see items 4 and 5 above).

7. Recorded accrued interest expense on a note payable.

8. Declared a stock dividend.

9. Distributed the stock dividend declared in item 8.

10. Recorded the expiration of insurance coverage that was previously recorded as prepaid insurance.

11. Declared and distributed a stock split.

12. Recorded a retained earnings appropriation.

Instructions

In a table like the following, indicate the effect each of the 12 transactions has on the financial statement elements listed. Use the following codes:

$$I = Increase$$
$$D = Decrease$$
$$NE = No\ effect$$

Item	Assets	Liabilities	Shareholders' Equity	Share Capital	Retained Earnings	Net Income
1						
2						
etc.						

(CASH DIVIDEND AND LIQUIDATING DIVIDEND) Atlantic Corporation has 10 million common **E16-3** shares issued and outstanding. On June 1 the board of directors voted a $1.25 per share cash dividend to shareholders of record as of June 14, payable June 30.

Instructions

(a) Prepare the journal entry for each of the dates above assuming the dividend represents a distribution of earnings.

(b) How would the entry differ if the dividend were a liquidating dividend?

(PREFERRED DIVIDENDS) Fluffy Co. Ltd.'s ledger shows the following balances on December 31, 1994: **E16-4**

Preferred shares—no-par value, $0.70 dividend, outstanding 20,000 shares	$ 200,000
Common shares—no-par value, outstanding 30,000 shares	3,000,000
Retained earnings	630,000

Instructions

Assuming that the directors decide to declare total dividends in the amount of $366,000, determine how much each class of shares would receive under each of the conditions stated below. Dividends on the preferred shares have not been paid in the previous year.

(a) The preferred shares are cumulative and fully participating based on the proportion of capital share amounts for each class. Participation occurs only after common shareholders have been given a dividend on their invested capital equal to the rate paid to preferred shareholders on their invested capital.

(b) The preferred shares are noncumulative and nonparticipating.

(c) The preferred shares are noncumulative and are to participate in distributions in excess of 10% of the common share capital to common shareholders. Participation is based on the proportion of the number of each class of shares outstanding to the total number of shares outstanding for both classes.

E16-5 (PREFERRED DIVIDENDS) The outstanding share capital of Robin's Cookie Corporation consists of (1) 2,000 preferred shares with no-par value and with a stated dividend of $8 for which $200,000 was received when all were sold and (2) 5,000 common shares of no-par value for which $250,000 was received.

Instructions

Assuming that the company has cash and retained earnings of $95,000, all of which is to be paid out in dividends, and that preferred dividends were not paid during the two years preceding the current year, state how much each class of shares would receive under each of the following conditions:

(a) The preferred shares are noncumulative and nonparticipating.

(b) The preferred shares are cumulative and nonparticipating.

(c) The preferred shares are cumulative and participating, with participation based on the proportion of capital share amounts for each class.

E16-6 (ENTRIES FOR STOCK DIVIDENDS AND STOCK SPLITS) The shareholders' equity accounts of Snow Company Inc. have the following balances on December 31, 1994:

Common shares, no-par value, 400,000 shares issued and outstanding	$4,000,000
Contributed surplus	1,200,000
Retained earnings	5,600,000

Shares of Snow Company Inc. are currently selling on the Pacific Stock Exchange at $34 each.

Instructions

Prepare the appropriate journal entries for each of the following independent events:

(a) A stock dividend of 5% is declared and issued.

(b) A stock dividend of 100% is declared and issued.

(c) A two-for-one stock split is declared and issued.

E16-7 (DIVIDEND ENTRIES) The following data were taken from the balance sheet accounts of Day Corporation on December 31, 1993:

Current Assets	$540,000
Investments	624,000
Common shares, no-par value, no authorized limit, 50,000 shares issued and outstanding	500,000
Contributed Surplus—Donations	150,000
Retained Earnings	840,000

Instructions

Prepare the required journal entries for the following unrelated items:

(a) A 10% stock dividend is declared and distributed at a time when the market value of a share is $38.

(b) A scrip dividend of $100,000 is declared. *180*

(c) The shares are split five-for-one. *183 - no entry - memo.*

(d) A property dividend is declared January 5, 1994, and paid January 25, 1994, in bonds held as an investment; the bonds have a book value of $100,000 and a fair market value of $110,000. *179-780*

(RETAINED EARNINGS APPROPRIATIONS AND DISCLOSURES) At December 31, 1993, the   **E16-8**
retained earnings account of Deep Purple Inc. had a balance of $520,000. There were no appropriations at this time. During 1994, net income was $235,000. Cash dividends declared during the year were $50,000 on preferred and $60,000 on common. A stock dividend on common shares resulted in a $70,000 charge to retained earnings. At December 31, 1994, the board of directors decided to create an appropriation for contingencies of $100,000 because of an outstanding lawsuit that did not meet the criteria for accrual.

Instructions

(a) Prepare the journal entry to record the appropriation at December 31, 1994.

(b) Prepare a statement of unappropriated retained earnings for 1994.

(c) Prepare the retained earnings section of the December 31, 1994 balance sheet.

(d) Assume that in May 1995, the lawsuit is settled and Deep Purple agrees to pay $91,000. At this time, the board of directors also decides to eliminate the appropriation. Prepare all necessary entries.

(e) Assume in (a) that Deep Purple decided to disclose the appropriation through a note at December 31, 1994 instead of preparing a formal journal entry. Prepare the necessary note.

(COMPUTATION OF RETAINED EARNINGS) The following information has been taken from the   **E16-9**
ledger accounts of Gold Corporation:

Total reported income since incorporation	$300,000
Total cash dividends paid	90,000
Proceeds from sale of donated shares	40,000
Total value of stock dividends distributed	45,000
Retroactive adjustment to correct an error in	
undercalculation of depreciation in a prior period	20,000
Unamortized discount on bonds payable	32,000
Appropriated for plant expansion	70,000

Instructions

Determine the current balance of unappropriated retained earnings.

(APPROPRIATIONS FOR SELF-INSURANCE) L. Dykstra, president of Porche Inc., has decided against **E16-10**
purchasing casualty insurance to cover the company's four plants. Recognizing the possibility of casualty losses, he has appropriated $50,000 a year as a reserve for such contingencies; the first appropriation was made in 1991. In 1994 a fire completely destroys one of his plants. The plant had a 30-year life, no salvage value, and an original cost of $300,000 when it was constructed 12 years ago (straight-line depreciation). After the fire in 1994, Dykstra changes his mind, buys insurance and pays an annual premium of $30,000 on January 2, 1995, and eliminates his casualty reserve.

Instructions

Prepare the entries to journalize the insurance and casualty transactions and events of 1991, 1994, and 1995.

E16-11 **(PARTICIPATING PREFERRED, STOCK DIVIDEND, AND SHARE REACQUISITION)** The following is the shareholders' equity section of Mendenhal Corp. at December 31, 1994:

Common shares, no-par, authorized 200,000 shares;	
issued 90,000 shares	$ 3,600,000
Preferred shares,* no-par, authorized 100,000 shares;	
issued 15,000 shares	750,000
Total share capital	$ 4,350,000
Contributed surplus	150,000
Total share capital and contributed surplus	$ 4,500,000
Retained earnings	6,213,000
Total shareholders' equity	$10,713,000

*Each preferred share has a $6 dividend, is cumulative, and is participating in any distribution in excess of 15% of the common share capital to common shareholders. Participation is based on the proportion of share capital for each class of shares.

Instructions

(a) No dividends have been paid in 1992 or 1993. On December 31, 1994, Mendenhal wants to pay a cash dividend of $4.00 a share to common shareholders. How much cash would be needed for the *total amount paid* to preferred and common shareholders?

(b) Instead, Mendenhal will declare a 10% stock dividend on the outstanding common shares. The market value is $60 per common share. Prepare the entry on the date of declaration.

(c) Instead, Mendenhal will acquire and restore to the status of being authorized but unissued 7,500 common shares. The current market value is $65 per share. Prepare the entry to record the reacquisition, assuming the contributed surplus arose from previous reacquisitions of common shares.

E16-12 **(DIVIDENDS AND SHAREHOLDERS' EQUITY SECTION)** Foreman Co. Ltd. reported the following amounts in the shareholders' equity section of its December 31, 1993 balance sheet:

Preferred shares, $10 dividend, no-par, 10,000 shares	
authorized, 2,000 shares issued	$200,000
Common shares, no-par, 100,000 shares authorized,	
20,000 shares issued	200,000
Contributed surplus	25,000
Retained earnings	450,000
Total	$875,000

During 1994, Foreman took part in the following transactions concerning shareholders' equity.

1. Paid the annual 1993 $10 dividend on preferred shares and a $1 dividend on common shares. These dividends had been declared on December 28, 1993.

2. Issued 500 preferred shares at $105 each.

3. Declared a 10% stock dividend on the outstanding common shares when they were selling for $40 each.

4. Issued the stock dividend.

5. Declared the annual 1994 $10 dividend on preferred shares and a $2 dividend on common shares. These dividends are payable in 1995.

6. Appropriated retained earnings for plant expansion, $200,000.

Instructions

(a) Prepare journal entries to record the transactions.

(b) Prepare the December 31, 1994 shareholders' equity section. Assume 1994 net income was $310,000. Provide note disclosure regarding changes in share capital during 1994. Support the retained earnings amount by a statement of retained earnings for the year.

(SHAREHOLDERS' EQUITY SECTION) Hyasaki Corporation's post-closing trial balance at December **E16-13** 31, 1994 was as follows.

Hyasaki Corporation
Post-Closing Trial Balance
December 31, 1994

	Dr.	Cr.
Accounts payable		$ 310,000
Accounts receivable	$ 470,000	
Accumulated depreciation—building and equipment		185,000
Allowance for doubtful accounts		30,000
Appropriated retained earnings—plant expansion		130,000
Bonds payable		300,000
Building and equipment	1,550,000	
Cash	190,000	
Common shares		800,000
Contributed surplus		350,000
Dividends payable on preferred shares—cash		4,000
Inventories	460,000	
Land	400,000	
Preferred shares		500,000
Prepaid expenses	40,000	
Retained earnings		501,000
Totals	$3,110,000	$3,110,000

At December 31, 1994, Hyasaki had the following number of no-par value common and preferred shares.

	Common	Preferred
Authorized	600,000	60,000
Outstanding	160,000	10,000

The dividend on a preferred share is $4 cumulative. In addition, a preferred share has a preference in liquidation of $50 per share.

Instructions

Prepare the shareholders' equity section of Hyasaki's balance sheet at December 31, 1994.

(AICPA adapted)

(FINANCIAL REORGANIZATION: ENTRIES) The condensed balance sheets of Turnaround Co. Ltd. **E16-14** immediately before and one year after it had completed a financial reorganization follow.

	Before Reorganization	One Year After			Before Reorganization	One Year After
Current assets	$ 300,000	$ 415,000	Common shares		$2,400,000	$1,545,000
Plant assets (net)	1,700,000	1,290,000	Contributed surplus		260,000	
			Retained earnings		(660,000)	160,000
	$2,000,000	$1,705,000			$2,000,000	$1,705,000

For the year following the financial reorganization, Turnaround reported net income of $190,000 which included depreciation expense of $80,000, and paid a cash dividend of $30,000. No purchases or sales of plant assets and no share transactions occurred in the year following the financial reorganization.

The company wrote down inventories by $125,000 in order to reflect circumstances that existed prior to the reorganization. Also, the deficit and any revaluation adjustment based on fair value was accounted for by charging the amounts against contributed surplus until it was eliminated, with any remaining amounts being charged against the common shares. The common shares are widely held and there is no controlling interest.

Instructions

(a) Prepare all the journal entries made at the time of the financial reorganization.

(b) Provide the note to the financial statements regarding the required disclosure for the year in which the financial reorganization took place.

E16-15 **(FINANCIAL REORGANIZATION: BALANCE SHEET)**   Groom Inc. has just undergone a financial reorganization. Immediately prior to the reorganization, the company had the following balances in its accounts.

Cash	$ (5,000)	Accounts payable	$ 450,000
Accounts receivable	320,000	Notes payable	605,000
Inventory	450,000	Taxes and wages	60,000
Equipment	860,000	Mortgage payable	150,000
Accumulated depreciation	(525,000)	Common shares	50,000
Intangibles	80,000	Retained earnings	(135,000)
Total	$1,180,000	Total	$1,180,000

The non-equity and equity holders accepted the following financial reorganization agreement. Revaluation of the assets by the following amounts:

Accounts receivable	$ 80,000 write-down
Inventory	$170,000 write-down
Intangibles	$ 80,000 write-off
Equipment	$100,000 write-up

The trade creditors (accounts payable) will reduce their claim by 30%, accept one-year notes for 50% of the amount due, and retain their current claim for the remaining 20%. The bank overdraft, tax, wage, and mortgage claims will remain unchanged. The current common shares will be surrendered to the corporation and cancelled. In consideration thereof, the current shareholders shall be held harmless from any possible personal liability. The current holder of the note payable shall receive 1,000 shares of no-par common stock in full satisfaction of the note payable. The deficit will be eliminated and, after the accounting for the revaluations, the only shareholders' equity item will be the 1,000 common shares held by the former holder of the note payable.

Instructions

Prepare a classified balance sheet that reflects the financial position of the company immediately after the financial reorganization.

──────── PROBLEMS ────────

(CORRECTION OF EQUITY ITEMS)   As the newly appointed controller for McBerger Inc., you are inter-   **P16-1** ested in analysing the Additional Capital account of the company in terms of what it includes and its appropriateness. Your assistant, Roger Hare, who has maintained the account from the inception of the company, submits the following summary.

Additional Capital Account:

	Debits	Credits
Cash dividends—preferred	$ 120,000	
Cash dividends—common	350,000	
Net income		$ 780,000
Appraisal increase credit for land, appropriately recognized prior to 1990		430,000
Additional assessments of prior years' income taxes	91,000	
Extraordinary gain		22,500
Donated building		270,000
Extraordinary loss	98,500	
Correction of a prior period error	55,000	
	$ 714,500	$1,502,500
Credit balance of additional capital account	788,000	
	$1,502,500	$1,502,500

Instructions

(a) Prepare a journal entry to close the Additional Capital account and establish appropriate accounts. Indicate how you derive the balance of each new account.

(b) If generally accepted accounting principles had been followed, what amount should have been shown as net income?

(EQUITY SHORTAGE AND SETTLEMENT BY REACQUIRING SHARES)   The balance sheet of **P16-2** Phantom Inc. shows $400,000 share capital, consisting of 4,000 common shares, and retained earnings of $148,000. As controller of the company, you find that O. Ghost the assistant treasurer is $83,000 short in his accounts and has concealed this shortage by adding the amount to the inventory. He owns 740 of the company's shares and, in settlement of the shortage, offers these shares at their book value. The offer is accepted; the company pays him the excess value and distributes the 740 shares thus acquired to the other shareholders. Assume that the addition to the Inventory account took place after the income had been properly calculated and closed to the retained earnings.

Instructions

(a) What amount should Phantom Inc. pay O. Ghost?

(b) By what journal entries should the foregoing transactions be recorded? (Assume the acquired shares were restored to the status of authorized but unissued and that their redistribution was as a stock dividend with the market value equal to the book value.)

(c) What is the total shareholders' equity after the share distribution?

P16-3 (PREFERRED AND COMMON SHARE DIVIDENDS)   Money Inc. began operations in January 1990 and had the following reported net income or loss for each of its five years of operations:

1990	$ 225,000	loss
1991	140,000	loss
1992	180,000	loss
1993	390,000	income
1994	1,500,000	income

At December 31, 1994, the company's share capital accounts were as follows:

Common, no-par value, authorized 100,000 shares, issued and outstanding 50,000 shares	$ 750,000
$8, nonparticipating, noncumulative preferred, no-par value, authorized, issued, and outstanding 5,000 shares	500,000
$6, fully participating, cumulative preferred, no-par value, authorized, issued, and outstanding 10,000 shares	1,500,000

Money has never declared a cash or stock dividend. There has been no change in the share capital accounts since Money began operations. The incorporation law permits dividends only from retained earnings given their payment will not result in insolvency. For the $6 participating preferred, the participation formula states that common shareholders first receive a dividend to bring them up to the same dividend rate on their share capital as is given to the preferred shareholders on their share capital. Then the $6 preferred and common shareholders participate in additional dividends based on the proportion of each one's share capital to the total share capital provided by each.

Instructions

Prepare a work sheet showing the retained earnings amount available for dividends on December 31, 1994 and how it would be distributable to the holders of the common shares and each of the preferred shares. Show supporting computations in good form.

(AICPA adapted)

P16-4 (STOCK DIVIDEND INVOLVING EXCHANGEABLE SHARES AND CASH IN LIEU OF FRACTIONAL SHARES)   On December 1, 1994, the board of directors of Campbell Corp. declared a 4% stock dividend on the outstanding no-par value common shares of the corporation, payable on December 28, 1994, to the holders of record at the close of business December 15, 1994. They stipulated that cash dividends were to be paid in lieu of issuing any fractional shares. They also directed that the amount to be charged against Retained Earnings should be equal to the market value per share on the declaration date multiplied by the total of (a) the number of shares issued as a stock dividend, and (b) the number of shares on which cash is paid in place of the issuance of fractional shares. The following facts are given:

1. At the dividend date:

   (a) Shares of common issued and outstanding   3,047,650

   (b) Shares of common included in (a) held by persons who will receive cash in lieu of fractional shares   222,750

   (c) Shares of predecessor company that are exchangeable for Campbell common at the rate of 1¼ shares of Campbell common for each share of predecessor company (necessary number of shares of Campbell common have been reserved but not issued). Provision was made for a cash dividend in lieu of fractional shares to holders of 180 of these 1,320 shares.   1,320

2. Values of Campbell common were as follows.

Market value at December 1	$25
Book value at December 1	$14

Instructions

Prepare entries and explanations to record the payment of the dividend. (**Hint:** For the predecessor company shares, the dividends are recorded like a regular stock or cash dividend except the related common shares and cash are not yet distributed.)

(AICPA adapted)

(STOCK AND CASH DIVIDEND ENTRIES)   The books of Elvis Inc. carried the following account bal-   **P16-5** ances as of December 31, 1993:

Cash	$ 289,600
Preferred shares, $.60 cumulative dividend,	
nonparticipating, no-par value, 60,000 shares issued	600,000
Common shares, no-par value, 300,000 shares	
issued, no authorized limit	1,500,000
Retained earnings	250,000

The preferred shares have dividends in arrears for the past year (1993).

The board of directors, at their annual meeting on December 21, 1994, declared the following: "The current year dividends shall be $.60 per share on the preferred and $.50 per share on the common; the dividends in arrears shall be paid by issuing one common share for each 10 shares of preferred held."

The preferred is currently selling at $11 per share and the common at $6 per share. Net income for 1994 is estimated at $60,000.

Instructions

(a) Prepare the journal entries required for the dividend declaration and payment, assuming that they occur simultane-ously. (**Hint:** Assume that all preferred dividends are paid before payment is made to holders of common shares.)

(b) Could Elvis Inc. give the preferred shareholders two years' (1993 and 1994) dividends and common shareholders a $.50 per share dividend, all in cash? Explain the factors to be considered in reaching your decision.

(PREFERRED STOCK DIVIDENDS)   Copper Co. Ltd. has outstanding 2,500 preferred shares of no-par   **P16-6** value, $6 dividend, which were issued for $250,000, and 15,000 common shares of no-par value for which $150,000 was received. The schedule below shows the amount of dividends paid out over the last four years.

Instructions

Allocate the dividends to each class of shares under assumptions (a) and (b). Express your answers in per-share amounts.

		Assumptions			
		(a) Preferred, noncumulative, and nonparticipating		(b) Preferred, cumulative, and fully participating*	
Year	Paid out	Preferred	Common	Preferred	Common
1991	$10,000				

1992	$26,000				
1993	$60,000				
1994	$72,000				

*After common shares have been given a ratable amount (i.e. same percentage on their share capital as the percentage given to preferred shareholders on their share capital), each class participates in additional distributions based on the proportion of their respective share capital to total share capital.

P16-7 **(STOCK AND CASH DIVIDENDS)**   Rubic Inc. has these shareholders' equity accounts:

	Issued Shares	Amount
Preferred shares, no-par value	2,200	$220,000
Common shares without par value (at issue price)	3,600	126,000
Retained earnings		200,000

In view of the large retained earnings, the board of directors resolves: (1) "to pay a 20% stock dividend on all shares outstanding, capitalizing amounts of retained earnings equal to the issue price of the preferred and common shares outstanding," respectively, and thereafter (2) "to pay a cash dividend of $6 on preferred shares and a cash dividend of $3 a share on common."

Instructions

(a)   Prepare entries in journal form to record the declaration of these dividends.

(b)   Prepare the shareholders' equity section of a balance sheet for Rubic Inc. after declaration but before distribution of these dividends.

P16-8 **(ENTRIES FOR SHAREHOLDERS' EQUITY TRANSACTIONS)**   Some of the account balances of Young Corp. at December 31, 1993 are shown below:

Common, no-par, 100,000 shares authorized, 50,000 issued	600,000
Unappropriated Retained Earnings	304,000
Retained Earnings Appropriated for Contingencies	75,000
Retained Earnings Appropriated for Fire Insurance	100,000

The price of the company's common shares has been increasing steadily on the market; it was $21 on January 1, 1994, advanced to $23 on July 1, and $27 at the end of 1994.

Instructions

Give the journal entries for each of the following transactions or events in 1994:

(a)   The company incurred a fire loss of $60,000 to its warehouse.

(b)   The company declared a property dividend on April 1. Each Young Corp. common shareholder was to receive one Akes & Panes Ltd. share for every 10 shares held. Young Corp. owned 8,000 Akes & Panes Ltd. shares (2% of total outstanding shares) which were purchased as an investment in 1991 for $68,400. The market value of Akes & Panes Ltd. shares was $16 each on April 1. Record appreciation only on the shares distributed.

(c)   On July 1, the company declared a 5% stock dividend to the common shareholders, payable in common shares.

(d)   The city of Brandon, in an effort to persuade the company to expand into that locality, donated to Young Corp. some land with an appraised value of $40,000.

(e)   At the annual board of directors' meeting, the board resolved to set up an appropriation of retained earnings for the future construction of a new plant. Such appropriation will be $125,000 per year. Also, it was resolved to increase the appropriation for contingencies by $25,000 and to eliminate the appropriation for fire insurance and begin purchasing such insurance from Safety Insurance Company.

(EQUITY ENTRIES AND RETAINED EARNINGS STATEMENT)   The shareholders' equity section of **P16-9** Julie Corp.'s balance sheet on January 1 of the current year is as follows:

Share Capital		
Common shares, no-par, 20,000 shares		
authorized, 10,000 shares issued		$1,400,000
Retained Earnings		
Unappropriated	$300,000	
Appropriated for plant expansion	120,000	
Total retained earnings		420,000
Total shareholders' equity		$1,820,000

The following selected transactions occurred during the year:

1.   Paid cash dividends of $2 per share on the common shares. The dividend had been properly recorded when declared last year.

2.   Declared a 10% stock dividend on the common shares when the shares were selling at $115 each in the market.

3.   Made a prior period adjustment to correct an error of $70,000 (net of tax) which overstated net income in the previous year. The error was the result of an overstatement of ending inventory. The applicable tax rate was 30%.

4.   Issued the certificates for the stock dividend.

5.   The board appropriated $40,000 of retained earnings for plant expansion, and declared a cash dividend of $1.70 per share on the common shares.

6.   The company's net income was $225,000 for the year (incorporating the inventory error referred to in 3).

Instructions

(a)   Prepare journal entries for the selected transactions above.

(b)   Prepare a statement of unappropriated retained earnings for the current year.

(EQUITY ENTRIES AND BALANCE SHEET PRESENTATION)   On December 15, 1993, the directors **P16-10** of Glad Corporation voted to appropriate $100,000 of retained earnings and to retain in the business assets equal to the appropriation for use in expanding the corporation's factory building. This was the fourth of such appropriations; after it was recorded, the shareholders' equity section of Glad's balance sheet appeared as follows:

Shareholders' equity:		
Common shares, no-par value, 300,000 shares		
authorized, 200,000 shares issued and outstanding		$5,600,000
Retained earnings—		
Unappropriated	$1,800,000	
Appropriated for plant expansion	400,000	
Total retained earnings		2,200,000
Total shareholders' equity		$7,800,000

On January 9, 1994, the corporation entered into a contract for the construction of the factory addition for which the retained earnings were appropriated. On November 1, 1994, the addition was completed and the contractor was paid the contract price of $379,000.

On December 14, 1994, the board of directors voted to return the balance of the Retained Earnings Appropriated for Plant Expansion account to Unappropriated Retained Earnings. They also voted a 25,000 share stock dividend distributable on January 23, 1995 to the January 15, 1995 shareholders of record. The corporation's shares were selling at $46 in the market on December 14, 1994. Glad reported net income for 1993 of $550,000 and for 1994 of $625,000.

Instructions

(a) Prepare the appropriate journal entries for Glad Corporation for the preceding information (December 15, 1993 to January 23, 1995, inclusive).

(b) Prepare the shareholders' equity section of the balance sheet for Glad Corporation at December 31, 1994.

P16-11 (ENTRIES REGARDING, AND STATEMENT OF, RETAINED EARNINGS) The following accounts and balances appear in Logan Corporation's ledger after closing but before considering the consequences resulting from the resolutions at the last board of directors' meeting:

Land Held for Investment	$ 60,000 dr.
Retained Earnings Appropriated for Possible Decline of Inventory Prices	146,000 cr.
Retained Earnings Appropriated for Contingencies	200,000 cr.
Retained Earnings	490,000 cr.
Income Summary	250,000 cr.

The following resolutions were passed by the board of directors of Logan Corporation at their last meeting for the year 1994:

1. A Retained Earnings Appropriated for Possible Additional Income Tax Assessments of Prior Years is to be created in the amount of $50,000.

2. The Retained Earnings Appropriated for Contingencies is to be increased by $80,000.

3. The present Retained Earnings Appropriated for Possible Decline of Inventory Prices that was set up as a charge against Retained Earnings in 1992 is to be written off as no longer required.

4. A decline in the value of land purchased for investment is to be recorded. As measured by the sales value of other property in the area, the value of Logan's land has decreased 20% since date of purchase.

5. A Retained Earnings Appropriated for Future Plant Expansion is to be established equal to 30% of the balance of the Retained Earnings account, after all transactions for the year noted above have been recorded.

6. A stock dividend of 10% on the common shares (5,000 no-par shares had been issued and are outstanding) is declared and issued. The market price of the shares on the date of declaration was $110 each.

Instructions

(a) Prepare entries in general journal form to record the board of directors' resolutions.

(b) What is the amount of retained earnings apparently available for dividends?

(c) What is the amount of retained earnings actually (legally) available for dividends?

(STOCK AND CASH DIVIDENDS)   Media Corp. has outstanding 2,000,000 common shares of no-par value P16-12 which were issued at $10 each. The balance in its Retained Earnings account at January 1, 1994 was $24,000,000. During 1994 the company's net income was $5,600,000. A cash dividend of $0.60 a share was paid June 30, 1994, and a 6% stock dividend was distributed on December 30 to shareholders of record at the close of business on December 15, 1994 (declaration date was November 30). You have been asked to advise on the appropriate accounting treatment for the stock dividend.

The existing shares of the company are quoted on a stock exchange. The market price per share has been as follows:

October 31, 1994	$31
November 30, 1994	33
December 15, 1994	38
December 31, 1994	37
Average price over the past two-month period	35

Instructions

(a)   Prepare a journal entry to record the cash dividend.

(b)   Prepare a journal entry to record the stock dividend.

(c)   Prepare the shareholders' equity section (including a schedule of retained earnings) of the balance sheet of Media Corp. for the year ended December 31, 1994, on the basis of the foregoing information. Draft a note to the financial statements setting forth the basis of the accounting for the stock dividend and provide appropriate comments or explanations regarding the basis chosen.

(FINANCIAL REORGANIZATION)   On June 30, 1994, the shareholders' equity section of the balance sheet P16-13 of Phoenix Company Inc. appears as follows:

Shareholders' equity			
$8, cumulative preferred shares			
Authorized and issued,			
3,000 shares, no-par value	$300,000		
Common shares			
Authorized 30,000 shares of no-par value,			
issued, 13,600 shares	680,000	$980,000	
Retained earnings (deficit)		(400,000)	$580,000

A note to the balance sheet points out that preferred share dividends are in arrears in the amount of $96,000.

At a shareholders' meeting on July 3, 1994, a new group of officers was voted into power, and a financial reorganization plan proposed by the new officers to be effective July 1 was accepted by the shareholders. The short-term creditors position was not to be changed and the company had no long-term debt. The terms of this plan were as follows:

1.   Preferred shareholders are to cancel their claim against the corporation for dividends in arrears.

2.   Certain depreciable properties and inventories owned by the company are to be revalued downward $90,000 and $30,000, respectively, to reflect circumstances that existed prior to the reorganization.

3.   The company owned a patent on a new product it had just developed. It was not shown as an asset on the June 30, 1994 balance sheet. However, it was to be recorded at its fair value of $60,000 as a result of a comprehensive revaluation of assets and liabilities regarding the financial reorganization.

4.   The deficit prior to the reorganization was to be reclassified to common share capital and any revaluation adjustment

was to be accounted for through common share capital.

Instructions

(a) Assuming that the various steps in the financial reorganization plan are effectively carried out as of July 1, 1994, prepare journal entries to record the reorganization.

(b) Assuming that the company earned a net income of $40,000 and paid the preferred share dividend for the year ended June 30, 1995, prepare the shareholders' equity section of the balance sheet as of that date. Provide an appropriate note regarding required disclosure of the financial reorganization.

P16-14 **(PREPARATION OF RETAINED EARNINGS STATEMENT AND EQUITY SECTION)**   River Co. Ltd.'s shares are traded on the over-the-counter market. At December 31, 1993, River had 5,000,000 authorized common shares of no-par value, of which 1,500,000 shares were issued and outstanding. The shareholders' equity accounts at December 31, 1993 had the following balances:

Common shares	$15,000,000
Retained earnings	6,700,000

Transactions during 1994 and other information relating to the shareholders' equity accounts were as follows:

1. On January 5, 1994, River issued at $110 per share, 100,000, $8, cumulative preferred shares. River had 600,000 authorized preferred shares. The preferred shares have a liquidation value of $100 each.

2. On February 1, 1994, River reacquired 20,000 common shares for $16 per share. These shares were restored to the status of authorized but unissued.

3. On April 30, 1994, River sold 500,000 common shares to the public at $18 per share.

4. On June 18, 1994, River declared a cash dividend of $1 per common share, payable on July 12, to shareholders of record on July 1, 1994.

5. On November 10, 1994, River sold 10,000 common shares for $21 per share.

6. On December 14, 1994, River declared the yearly cash dividend on preferred shares, payable on January 14, 1995, to shareholders of record on December 31, 1994.

7. On January 20, 1995, before the books were closed for 1994, River became aware that the ending inventory at December 31, 1993 was understated by $300,000 (after-tax effect on 1993 net income was $180,000). The appropriate correction entry was recorded.

8. After correcting the beginning inventory, net income for 1994 was $4,100,000.

Instructions

(a) Prepare a statement of retained earnings for the year ended December 31, 1994. Assume that only single-period financial statements for 1994 are presented.

(b) Prepare the shareholders' equity section of River's balance sheet at December 31, 1994.

(AICPA adapted)

P16-15 **(ANALYSIS AND CLASSIFICATION OF EQUITY TRANSACTIONS)**   The Scrooge Co. Ltd. was formed on July 1, 1992. It was authorized to issue 300,000 common shares of no-par value and 50,000 preferred shares, $0.60 dividend, no-par value, and cumulative. Scrooge has a July 1–June 30 fiscal year.

The following information relates to the shareholders' equity accounts of Scrooge Co. Ltd.:

Common Shares

Prior to the 1993–1994 fiscal year, Scrooge had 105,000 common shares outstanding, issued as follows.

1. 95,000 shares were issued for cash on July 1, 1992 at $30 per share.

2. On July 24, 1992, 5,000 shares were exchanged for a plot of land which cost the seller $70,000 in 1986 and had an estimated market value of $155,000 on July 24, 1992.

3. 5,000 shares were issued on March 1, 1993; the shares had been subscribed for $32 per share on October 31, 1992.

During the 1993–1994 fiscal year, the following transactions regarding common shares took place:

October 1, 1993   Subscriptions were received for 10,000 shares at $40 per share. Cash of $80,000 was received in full payment for 2,000 shares and share certificates were issued. The remaining subscription for 8,000 shares were to be paid in full by September 30, 1994, at which time the certificates were to be issued.

November 30, 1993   Scrooge purchased 2,000 of its own shares on the open market at $38 per share. These shares were restored to the status of authorized but unissued shares.

December 15, 1993   Scrooge declared a 2% stock dividend for common shareholders of record on January 15, 1994, to be issued on January 31, 1994. Scrooge was having a liquidity problem and could not afford a cash dividend at the time. Scrooge's common shares were selling at $43 per share on December 15, 1993.

June 20, 1994   Scrooge sold 500 common shares for $21,000.

Preferred Shares

Scrooge issued 30,000 preferred shares for $15 each on July 1, 1992.

Cash Dividends

Scrooge has followed a schedule of declaring cash dividends in December and June with payment being made to shareholders of record in the following month. The cash dividends which have been declared since inception of the company through June 30, 1994 are shown below.

Declaration Date	Common Shares	Preferred Shares
12/15/92	$.10 per share	$.30 per share
6/15/93	$.10 per share	$.30 per share
12/15/93	—	$.30 per share

No cash dividends were declared during June 1994 due to the company's liquidity problems.

Retained Earnings

As of June 30, 1993, Scrooge's Retained Earnings account had a balance of $800,000. For the fiscal year ending June 30, 1994, Scrooge reported net income of $50,000.

In March of 1994, Scrooge received a term loan from the Dominion Bank. The bank requires Scrooge to establish a sinking fund and restrict retained earnings for an amount equal to the sinking fund deposit. The annual sinking fund payment of $100,000 is due on April 30 each year; the first payment was made on schedule on April 30, 1994.

Instructions

Prepare the shareholders' equity section of the balance sheet, including appropriate notes, for Scrooge Co. Ltd. as of June 30, 1994.

(CMA adapted)

(RETAINED EARNINGS AND DIVIDEND POLICY) Howat Corporation is a publisher of children's **P16-16** books. The company was started as a family business in 1949 and is still closely held. For its fiscal year ended May 31, 1994, Howat had net income of $850,000 on sales of $10,625,000. The net income included a loss of

$350,000, net of tax, that resulted from the discontinuance of a segment of the business. The Board of Directors of Howat will be meeting on June 25, 1994 to review the company's financial condition. One of the agenda items for this meeting is to re-examine Howat's dividend policy and draft the dividend plans for the 1994–1995 fiscal year.

Debra Sondgeroth, Assistant Controller of Howat Corporation, is responsible for the preparation of the company's financial statements for both internal and external reporting purposes. She is also responsible for preparing any reports and statements to be reviewed by the Board of Directors. Of the material specifically requested by the Board for its June 25 meeting, the only report not yet prepared is the Statement of Retained Earnings. To assist in this preparation, Sondgeroth listed the account balances for Howat's equity accounts as of May 31, 1993 and gathered, from the Corporation's books, pertinent information that affected Howat's equity accounts during the 1993–1994 fiscal year. These data are presented below:

Account Balances as of May 31, 1993

Unappropriated retained earnings	$1,575,000
Appropriation for plant expansion (appropriation is 100% of cost)	350,000
Appropriation for bond sinking fund	275,000
Preferred shares, $8, cumulative, no-par value, 20,000 shares authorized, 10,000 shares issued and outstanding	1,040,000
Common shares, no-par value, 220,000 shares authorized, 190,000 shares issued and outstanding	3,420,000
Contributed surplus—donated equipment	11,000

Additional Information

1. Dividend activity for the year was as follows:
   — A cash dividend of $.50 per share was paid June 10, 1993. The dividend was declared May 10, 1993 to all common shareholders of record May 25, 1993.
   — A cash dividend of $1.25 per share was declared on November 1, 1993 to all common shareholders of record on November 15, 1993. This dividend was paid on November 25, 1993.
   — A 10% stock dividend was declared May 15, 1994 to all common shareholders of record on May 25, 1994. This dividend was to be paid from authorized but unissued common shares on June 15, 1994. The per share market price on May 15, 1994 was $27.
   — The required preferred dividend was paid on May 31, 1994 to all preferred shareholders of record.

2. On June 1, 1993, Howat sold an additional 5,000 preferred shares at $102 per share.

3. The fiscal year addition to the bond sinking fund and the appropriation for the sinking fund was $25,000.

4. On January 1, 1994, 10,000 common shares were sold for $24 each.

5. Howat's plant expansion program was now 60% complete, and a proportionate share of the appropriation for this purpose was to be returned to retained earnings at May 31, 1994.

6. During the year, depreciation expense for the fiscal year ended May 31, 1993 was discovered to be understated by $20,000. This was considered an error that required an adjustment to the previous year's earnings.

7. Howat Corporation was subject to an effective income tax rate of 30% for the fiscal years ended May 31 of both 1993 and 1994.

Instructions

(a) Howat Corporation's Board of Directors requested the Statement of Retained Earnings in order to determine the retained earnings available for dividends as of May 31, 1994. Prepare the Statement of Retained Earnings for the year ended May 31, 1994, showing:

    1. Total (appropriated and unappropriated) retained earnings as of May 31, 1993.

2. Adjustments, additions, and deductions that occurred during the 1993–1994 fiscal year.

3. Total (unappropriated and appropriated) retained earnings as of May 31, 1994.

4. Appropriations of retained earnings by restriction as of May 31, 1994.

5. Retained earnings available for dividends as of May 31, 1994.

(b) Discuss how each of the following items would have an impact on the Board of Directors' decision regarding Howat Corporation's dividend policy:

1. The disposal of the segment during the 1993–1994 fiscal year that resulted in a $350,000 net-of-tax loss.

2. The forecasted earnings for the next three fiscal years.

3. The declaration of the stock dividends to all common shareholders of record that took place on May 15, 1994, and the declaration of any additional stock dividends to common shareholders in the future.

(c) Explain why many companies do not distribute all their available retained earnings.

CHAPTER 17

Dilutive Securities and Earnings-Per-Share Calculations

The urge to merge that dominated the business scene in the 1960s developed into merger mania in the 1980s. One consequence of heavy merger activity is an increase in the use of dilutive securities such as convertible bonds, convertible preferred shares, share purchase warrants, and contingent shares. **Dilutive securities** are defined as securities that are not common shares in form but enable their holders to obtain common shares on exercise or conversion. A reduction (dilution) in earnings per share often results when these securities become common shares.

During the sixties, corporate officers recognized that the issuance of these types of securities in a merger did not have the same immediate adverse effect on earnings per share as the issuance of common shares. In addition, executives found that issuance of convertible securities did not seem to upset common shareholders, even though the common shareholders' interests were substantially diluted when these securities were later converted or exercised. For these reasons, terms such as "funny money" were coined to indicate the peculiar nature of these types of securities and the unusual tricks that could be played on the uninformed investor.

There were many reasons for merger mania in the 1980s: (1) the federal government's attitude was not hostile to mergers, (2) financial institutions had developed sophisticated means of providing credit for acquisitions, (3) many owners of privately held companies wished to sell to acquire personal liquidity, and (4) there was a belief that it was cheaper to buy rather than build, particularly when corporate equity securities were considered undervalued.

As a consequence of this step-up in merger activity during the 1980s, the presence of dilutive securities on corporate balance sheets is now very prevalent. The use of stock option plans, which are dilutive in nature, also increased. These option plans are used mainly to attract and retain executive talent and to provide tax relief for executives in high tax brackets.

The widespread use of different types of dilutive securities has led the accounting profession to examine accounting in this area closely. Specifically, the profession has directed its attention toward accounting for these securities at date of issuance and to the presentation of earnings-per-share figures that recognize their effect. The following discussion includes consideration of convertible securities, warrants, stock options, and contingent shares.

SECTION 1: DILUTIVE SECURITIES AND COMPENSATION PLANS
ACCOUNTING FOR CONVERTIBLE DEBT

If bonds can be converted into other corporate securities during some specified period of time after issuance, they are called convertible bonds. A *convertible bond combines the benefits of a bond with the privilege of exchanging it for shares at the holder's option*. It is purchased by investors who desire the security of a bond holding—guaranteed interest, plus the added option of conversion if the value of the shares appreciates significantly.

Corporations issue convertibles for two main reasons. One is the desire to raise equity capital that, assuming conversion, will arise when the original debt is converted. To illustrate, assume that a company wants to raise $1,000,000 at a time when its common shares are selling at $45 each. Such an issue would require sale of approximately 22,222 shares (ignoring issue costs). By selling 1,000 bonds at $1,000 par, each convertible into 20 common shares, the enterprise may raise $1,000,000 by committing only 20,000 common shares. Most studies of convertible bonds indicate that the main purpose of issuing these securities has been to obtain common share financing at cheaper rates.

A second reason why many companies issue convertible securities is that they can issue debt only at high interest rates unless a convertible covenant is attached. The conversion privilege entices the investors to accept a lower interest rate than would normally be the case on a straight debt issue. To illustrate, a company might have to pay 12% for a straight debt obligation but it can issue a convertible at 9%. For this lower interest rate, the investor receives the right to acquire the company's common shares at a fixed price until maturity, which is often 10 to 20 years. Accounting for convertible debt involves reporting issues at the time of (1) issuance, (2) conversion, and (3) retirement.

At Time of Issuance

The method of recording convertible bonds *at the date of issue follows that used in recording straight debt issues.* Any discount or premium that results from the issuance of convertible bonds is amortized assuming the bonds will be held to maturity because it is difficult to predict when, if at all, conversion will occur. The accounting for convertible debt as a straight debt issue is controversial and is discussed more fully later in this chapter.

At Time of Conversion

If bonds are converted into other securities, the principal accounting problem is to determine the amount at which to record the securities exchanged for the bond. For example, Hilton Limited has issued at a premium of $60 a $1,000 bond convertible into 10 no-par common shares. At the time of conversion, the unamortized premium is $50, the market value of the bond is $1,200, and the shares are quoted on the market at $120. Two possible methods of determining the issue price of the shares could be used:

1. The *market price* of the shares or bonds, $1,200.

2. The *book value* of the bonds, $1,050.

Market Value Approach. Recording the shares issued using its *market price* at the issue date is a theoretically sound method. If 10 common shares could be sold for $1,200, share capital of $1,200 should be recorded. Since bonds having a book value of $1,050 are converted, a $150 ($1,200 − $1,050) loss on the bond conversion occurs. The entry would be:

Bonds Payable	1,000	
Premium on Bonds Payable	50	
Loss on Redemption of Bonds Payable	150	
Common Shares		1,200

Using the bond's market price can be supported on similar grounds. If the market price of the shares is not determinable but the bonds can be purchased at $1,200, a good argument can be made that the shares have an issue price of $1,200.

Book Value Approach. From a practical point of view, if the market price of the shares or the bonds is not determinable, then the *book value* of the bonds offers the best available measurement of the issue price. Indeed, many accountants contend that even if market quotations are available, they should not be used. The common shares are merely substituted for the bonds and should be recorded at the carrying amount of the converted bonds.

Supporters of this view argue that an agreement was established at the date of issuance to pay either a stated amount of cash at maturity or to issue a stated number of shares of equity securities. Therefore, when the debt is converted into equity in relation to pre-existing contract terms, no gain

Objective 1

Describe the accounting for issuance, conversion, and retirement of convertible securities.

or loss is recognized on conversion. To illustrate the specifics of this approach, the entry for the foregoing transaction of Hilton Limited would be:

Bonds Payable	1,000	
Premium on Bonds Payable	50	
Common Shares		1,050

The book value method of recording convertible bonds is the method used in practice[1] and should be used in homework unless the problem specifies otherwise.

Induced Conversions

Sometimes the issuer wishes to induce prompt conversion of its convertible debt into equity securities to reduce interest cost or improve its debt to equity ratio. As a result, the issuer may offer some form of additional consideration (cash, common shares)—a "sweetener"—to *induce conversion*. An amount equal to the fair value of the additional securities or other consideration given should be reported as an expense of the current period.

Assume that Helloid Ltd. has outstanding $1,000,000 par value convertible debentures convertible into 100,000 no-par value common shares. Helloid wishes to reduce its interest cost. To do so, Helloid agrees to pay the holders of the convertible debentures an additional $80,000 if they will convert. Assuming conversion occurs, the following entry is made:

Debt Conversion Expense	80,000	
Bonds Payable	1,000,000	
Common Shares		1,000,000
Cash		80,000

The additional $80,000 is recorded as an expense of the current period and not as a reduction of equity. Some argue that the cost of a conversion inducement is a cost of obtaining equity capital. Others believe that since the transaction involves both the issuance of equity and also the retirement of debt, it should be reported as an expense.[2]

Retirement of Convertible Debt

The retirement of convertible debt can be considered a debt transaction or an equity transaction. If it is treated as a debt transaction, the difference between the carrying amount of the retired convertible debt and the cash paid should result in a charge or credit to income; if it is an equity transaction, the difference should presumably go to Contributed Surplus.

The method for recording the *issuance* of convertible bonds follows that used in recording straight debt issues. Specifically, this means that no portion of the proceeds should be attributable to the conversion feature and credited to Contributed Surplus. Although theoretical objections to this approach can be raised, to be consistent, a gain or loss on **retiring convertible debt** needs to be recognized in the same way as a gain or loss on **retiring debt** that is not convertible. For this reason, differences between the cash acquisition price of debt and its carrying amount should be reported *currently in income as a gain or loss*.[3] Material gains or losses on extinguishment of debt are not considered extraordinary items because they are a result of management decisions.

---

[1] Convertible bonds have become less desirable recently because leveraged buyouts diminish the bondholders' rights. In addition, issuance of bonds may place excessive demands on the issuer's cash flow, which may depress share prices and discourage conversion.

[2] "Induced Conversions of Convertible Debt," *Statement of Financial Accounting Standards No. 84* (Stamford, CT: FASB, 1985).

[3] This method has been adopted as a standard in the United States by "Early Extinguishment of Debt," *Opinions of the Accounting Principles Board No. 26* (New York: AICPA, 1972).

Nevertheless, failure to recognize the equity feature of convertible debt when issued creates problems on early extinguishment. Assume that URL issues convertible debt at a time when the investment community attaches value to the conversion feature. Subsequently, the price of URL shares decreases so sharply that the conversion feature has little or no value. If URL extinguishes its convertible debt early, a large gain develops because the book value of the debt will exceed the retirement price. Many accountants consider this treatment incorrect because the reduction in value of the convertible debt relates to its equity features, not its debt features, and therefore an adjustment to Contributed Surplus should be made. However, present practice requires that a gain or loss be recognized at the time of early extinguishment.

CONVERTIBLE PREFERRED SHARES

The major difference in accounting for a convertible bond and a convertible preferred share at the date of issue is that convertible bonds are considered liabilities, while convertible preferreds (unless mandatory redemption exists) are considered a part of shareholders' equity.

> **Objective 2**
>
> Explain the accounting for convertible preferred shares.

In addition, when preferred share conversion privileges are exercised, there is no theoretical justification for recognition of a gain or loss. No gain or loss is recognized when the entity deals with its shareholders in their capacity as business owners. *The book value method is employed:* Preferred Share Capital is decreased and Common Share Capital is increased by the same amount.

Assume Host Enterprises issued 1,000 no-par common shares on conversion of 1,000 no-par preferred shares that were originally issued for $1,200. The entry would be:

Convertible Preferred Shares	1,200	
Common Shares		1,200

If part of the original issuance price of the convertible preferred shares had been credited to other shareholders' equity accounts, such as Contributed Surplus, these related amounts should be cleared in the entry to record the conversion.

STOCK WARRANTS

Warrants are certificates entitling the holder to acquire shares at a specified price within a stated period. This option is similar to the conversion privilege because warrants, if exercised, become common shares and usually have a dilutive effect (reduce earnings per share) similar to that of the conversion of convertible securities. However, a substantial difference between convertible securities and stock warrants is that, on exercise of the warrants, the holder has to pay a certain amount of money to obtain the shares.

> **Objective 3**
>
> Contrast the accounting for stock warrants and stock warrants issued with other securities.

The issuance of warrants or options to buy additional shares normally arises under three situations:

1. When issuing different types of securities, such as bonds or preferred shares, warrants are often included to make the *security more attractive*, to provide an "equity kicker" as an inducement for investors.

2. On the issuance of additional common shares, existing shareholders may have a *pre-emptive right to purchase common shares* first. Warrants may be issued to evidence that right.

3. Warrants, often referred to as stock options, are given as *compensation to executives and employees*.

The problems in accounting for stock warrants are complex and present many difficulties—some of which remain unresolved.

Stock Warrants Issued With Other Securities

Warrants issued with other securities are basically long-term options to buy common shares at a fixed price. Although some perpetual warrants are traded, generally their life is five years, occasionally ten.

Here is an illustration of the way a warrant works: Tenneco offers a unit comprising one share and one detachable warrant exercisable at $24.25 per share and good for five years. The unit sells for 22¾ ($22.75) and, since the price of the common the day before the sale is 19⅞ ($19.88), it suggests a price of 2⅞ ($2.87) for the warrants.

In this situation, the warrants have an apparent value of 2⅞ ($2.87), even though it would not be profitable at present for the purchaser to exercise the warrant and buy the shares, because the price of the shares is much below the exercise price of $24.25.[4] The investor pays for the warrant to receive a possible future call on the shares at a fixed price when the price has risen significantly. For example, if the price of the shares rises to $30, the investor has gained $2.88 ($30 − $24.25 − $2.87) on an investment of $2.87—a 100% increase! But if the price never rises, the investor loses the full $2.87.[5]

The proceeds from the sale of debt with **detachable stock warrants** should be allocated between the two securities.[6] Two separable instruments are involved, that is, (1) a bond and (2) a warrant giving the holder the right to purchase common shares at a certain price. Warrants that are detachable can be traded separately from the debt and, therefore, a market value can be determined. The two methods of allocation available are (1) the proportional method and (2) the incremental method.

Proportional Method. AT&T's offering of detachable five-year warrants to buy one common share at $25 (at a time when a share was selling for approximately $50) enabled it to price its offering of bonds at par with a moderate 8¾% yield. To place a value on the two securities one would determine (1) the value of the bonds without the warrants and (2) the value of the warrants. For example, assume that AT&T's bonds (par $1,000) sold for 99 without the warrants soon after they were issued. The market value of the warrants at that time was $30. Prior to sale, the warrants will not have a market value. The allocation is based on an estimate of market value, generally as established by an investment dealer or on the relative market value of the bonds and the warrants soon after they are issued and traded. The price paid for 10,000, $1,000 bonds with the warrants attached was par, or $10,000,000. The allocation between the bonds and warrants would be made in the following manner.

Fair market value of bonds (without warrants) ($10,000,000 × .99)		=	$ 9,900,000
Fair market value of warrants (10,000 × $30)		=	300,000
Aggregate fair market value			$10,200,000
Allocated to bond:	$\frac{\$9,900,000}{\$10,200,000} \times \$10,000,000$	=	$9,705,882
Allocated to warrants:	$\frac{\$300,000}{\$10,200,000} \times \$10,000,000$	=	294,118*
Total allocation			$10,000,000

*Rounded

[4] Later in this discussion, it will be shown that the value of the warrant is normally determined on the basis of a relative market value approach because of the difficulty of imputing a warrant value in any other manner.

[5] Trading in warrants is often referred to as licensed gambling. From the illustration, it is apparent that buying warrants can be an "all or nothing" proposition.

[6] A detachable warrant means that the warrant can sell separately from the bond. *APB Opinion No. 14* makes a distinction between detachable and nondetachable warrants, because nondetachable warrants must be sold with the security as a complete package; thus, no allocation is permitted.

In this situation, the bonds sell at a discount and are recorded as follows:

Cash	9,705,882	
Discount on Bonds Payable	294,118	
Bonds Payable		10,000,000

In addition, the company sells warrants that are credited to Contributed Surplus. The entry is as follows:

Cash	294,118	
Contributed Surplus—Stock Warrants		294,118

The entries may be combined if desired; they are shown separately here to indicate that the purchaser of the bond is buying not only a bond but also a possible future claim on common shares.

Assuming that all 10,000 warrants are exercised (one warrant per one share), the following entry would be made:

Cash (10,000 × $25)	250,000	
Contributed Surplus—Stock Warrants	294,118	
Common Shares		544,118

If one assumes, however, that the warrants are not exercised, Contributed Surplus—Stock Warrants is debited for $294,118 and Contributed Surplus From Expired Warrants is credited for a like amount. The contributed surplus reverts to the former shareholders and would be recorded as follows:

Contributed Surplus—Stock Warrants	294,118	
Contributed Surplus—Expired Warrants		294,118

Incremental Method. In instances where the fair values of either the warrants or the bonds are not determinable, the incremental method used in lump sum security purchases (explained in Chapter 15) may be used. That is, the security for which the market value is determinable is used and the remainder of the purchase price is allocated to the security for which the market value is not known. For example, using the AT&T case, assume that the market price of the warrants was known to be $300,000 but the market price of the bonds without the warrants could not be determined. In this case, the amount allocated to the warrants and the shares would be as shown below.

Lump sum receipt	$10,000,000
Allocated to the warrants	300,000
Balance allocated to bonds	**$ 9,700,000**

Conceptual Questions. The question arises whether the allocation of value to the warrants is consistent with the handling accorded convertible debt, in which case no value is allocated to the conversion privilege.[7] The features of a convertible security are *inseparable* in the sense that choices

---

[7] Under the standards proposed in an *Exposure Draft* issued in September 1991, it would be mandatory to account for convertible debt in the same manner as debt with detachable warrants. That is, the proceeds from issuance of convertible debt would be allocated between the debt and equity components. The amount assigned to debt would be the fair value of the debt instrument without a conversion feature. The residual would then be assigned to Contributed Surplus.

are mutually exclusive: The holder either converts or redeems the bonds for cash, but cannot do both. No basis, therefore, exists for recognizing the conversion value in the accounts. However, the issuance of bonds with **detachable warrants** involves two securities, one a debt security, which will remain outstanding until maturity, and the other a warrant to purchase common shares. At the time of issuance, separable instruments exist and, therefore, separate treatment is justified. **Nondetachable warrants**, however, do not require an allocation of the proceeds between the bonds and the warrants. The entire proceeds are recorded as debt.

Many argue that the conversion feature is not significantly different in nature from the call represented by a warrant. The question is whether, although the legal forms are different, sufficient similarities of substance exist to support the same accounting treatment. Some contend that inseparability per se is not a sufficient basis for restricting allocation between identifiable components of a transaction. Examples of allocation between assets of value in a single transaction are not uncommon. Transactions such as allocation of values in basket purchases and separation of principal and interest in capitalizing long-term leases indicate that the accountant has attempted to allocate values in a single transaction. Critics of the current accounting for convertibles say that to deny recognition of value to the conversion feature is to merely look to the form of the instrument and not deal with the substance of the transaction.

The Accounting Standards Board issued an *Exposure Draft*[8] that proposes more stringent standards in accounting for complex securities. The necessity to communicate the substance of transactions and events rather than legal form is specifically emphasized.[9] If the proposed standards are adopted, accountants will have to measure the debt and equity features of a convertible bond and report the individual amounts under liabilities and shareholders' equity, respectively.

Rights to Subscribe to Additional Shares

If the directors of a corporation decide to issue new shares, the existing shareholders generally have the right (pre-emptive privilege) to purchase newly issued shares in proportion to their holdings. The privilege, referred to as a **stock right**, saves existing shareholders from suffering a dilution of voting rights without their consent, and it may allow them to purchase shares somewhat below their market value. The warrants issued in these situations are of short duration, unlike the warrants issued with other securities.

The certificate representing the stock right states the number of shares the holder of the right may purchase, as well as the price at which the new shares may be purchased. Each share ordinarily gives the owner one stock right. The price is normally less than the current market value of such shares, which gives the rights a value in themselves. From the time rights are issued until they expire, they may be purchased and sold like any other security.

No entry is required when rights are issued to existing shareholders. Only a memorandum entry is needed to indicate the number of rights issued to existing shareholders and to ensure that the company has additional unissued shares registered for issuance in case the rights are exercised. No formal entry is made at this time because no shares have been issued and no cash has been received.

If the rights are exercised, usually a cash payment of some type is involved. The appropriate Share Capital account is credited with the amount of cash received.

Objective 4

Differentiate between compensatory and noncompensatory stock compensation plans.

STOCK COMPENSATION PLANS

Another form of the warrant arises in certain methods used to pay and motivate employees. A common type is a **stock option plan** where *selected* employees are given the option to purchase common shares at a given price over an *extended period of time*. Other types of options also exist,

---

[8] "Financial Instruments," *Exposure Draft of the Accounting Standards Board* (Toronto: CICA, September 1991).
[9] *Ibid.*, par. 044.

such as the right to receive cash or shares if certain performance criteria are met in the future. In addition, a common type of warrant develops in a **stock purchase plan**, where *all* employees are given the option to purchase shares at a given price over a *short period of time*.

For accounting purposes, stock option plans are usually considered compensatory and stock purchase plans are usually classified as noncompensatory. **Compensatory** means that the plan was intended to compensate the employees; **noncompensatory** means that the primary purpose was not intended to compensate the employees, but rather to allow the employer to secure equity capital or to induce widespread ownership of an enterprise's common shares among employees. Noncompensatory plans should have the following characteristics:

1. Participation by all employees who meet limited employment qualifications.

2. Equal offers of shares to all eligible employees.

3. Limitation to a reasonable period of the time permitted for the exercise of an option or purchase right.

4. Discount from the market price of the shares no greater than would be reasonable in an offer of shares to shareholders or others.[10]

For example, IBM has a share purchase plan under which employees who meet minimal employment qualifications are entitled to purchase IBM shares at a 15% reduction from market price for a short period of time. Such a reduction from market price is not considered compensatory because the employer's objectives appear to be either to raise additional equity capital or to expand ownership of the enterprise's shares among the employees as a means of enhancing loyalty to the enterprise. This position is debatable because the employee is receiving a valuable fringe benefit. However, because it is difficult to determine the company's objectives, in practice, the foregoing type of stock purchase plan is considered as noncompensatory if the discount is in the amount of 10% to 15% of the market price. *It should be emphasized that plans that do not possess all of the above-mentioned four characteristics should be classified as compensatory.*

Accounting for Stock Compensation Plans

Accounting for noncompensatory plans poses no practical difficulties for accountants because compensation expense is not recorded by the employer corporation. The exercise of the option to purchase shares is simply accounted for as the normal share issue, with shareholders' equity increased by the amount of the option price. Compensatory plans, however, present more difficulties. The following three questions must be resolved:

1. How should compensation expense be determined?

2. Over what periods should compensation expense be allocated?

3. What types of plans are used to compensate officers and key executives?

Determination of Compensation Expense. Total compensation expense is computed as the difference between the market price of the shares and the option price on the **measurement date**. The measurement date is the first date on which are known both (1) the number of shares that an individual employee is entitled to receive and (2) the option or purchase price. The measurement date for many plans is the date an *option is granted* to an employee. The measurement date may be later than the date of grant in plans with variable terms (either number of shares or option price or both

> **Objective 5**
>
> Describe the accounting for various types of stock-based compensation plans.

---

[10] Specific standards for classifying stock compensation plans have not been established in Canada. These criteria have been quoted from "Accounting for Stock Issued to Employees," *Opinions of the Accounting Principles Board No. 25* (New York: AICPA, 1972), par. 7.

not known) that depend on events after date of grant. Usually the measurement date for plans with variable terms is the *date of exercise*.

Allocation of Compensation Expense. Compensation expense is recognized in the period(s) in which the *employee performs the services* (often referred to as the service period). The total compensation expense is determined at the measurement date and allocated to the appropriate periods benefited by the employee's services. In practice, it is often difficult to specify the period of service, and considerable judgement is exercised in this determination. The general rule followed is that any method that is systematic and rational is appropriate, if the periods of service cannot be clearly defined. Assuming the measurement date is the date of grant, many enterprises recognize the compensation expense over an arbitrary period; others amortize it from the grant date to the date the option may be first exercised; and others record it as a current expense.

Types of Plans. Many different types of plans are used to compensate key executives. In all these plans, the amount of the reward is dependent on future events. Consequently, continued employment is a necessary element in almost all types of plans. The popularity of a given plan usually depends on prospects in the stock market and tax considerations. For example, if it appears that appreciation will occur in the price of a company's shares, a plan that offers the option to purchase shares is attractive to an executive. Conversely, if it appears that price appreciation is unlikely, then compensation might be tied to some performance measure, such as an increase in book value or earnings per share. Three common plans that illustrate different accounting issues are:

1. Stock option plans.

2. Stock appreciation rights plans.

3. Performance-type plans.

Stock Option Plans

To illustrate the accounting for a stock option plan, assume that on November 1, 1993, the shareholders of Scott Company approve a plan that grants the company's five executives options to purchase 2,000 shares each of the company's no-par value common shares. The options are granted on January 1, 1994 and may be exercised at any time within the next 10 years. The option price per share is $60, and the market price of the shares at the date of grant is $70 per share. The total compensation expense is computed below. (Note that January 1, 1994 is the measurement date because the number of shares each executive can purchase and the option price are known on this date, which coincides with the beginning of the fiscal period.)

Market value of 10,000 shares at date of grant ($70 per share)	$700,000
Option price of 10,000 shares at date of grant ($60 per share)	600,000
Total compensation expense	**$100,000**

The value of the option should be recognized as an expense in the period(s) in which the employee performs services. In the case of Scott Company, assume that documents associated with issuance of the options indicate that the expected period of benefit is two years, starting with the grant date. The entry to record the total compensation expense at the date of grant is as follows:

Deferred Compensation Expense	100,000	
Contributed Surplus—Stock Options		100,000

The deferred compensation expense (a contra-shareholders' equity account) then is amortized to expense over the period of service involved (two years).[11] The credit balance in the Contributed Surplus—Stock Options account is treated as an element of shareholders' equity. On December 31, 1994 and on December 31, 1995, the following journal entry is recorded to recognize the compensation cost for the year attributable to the stock option plan:

Compensation Expense	50,000	
Deferred Compensation Expense		50,000

At December 31, 1994, the shareholders' equity section would be presented as follows, assuming that 1,000,000 no-par value shares were issued.

Shareholders' equity		
Common shares, no-par value, 1,000,000 shares		
issued and outstanding		$1,000,000
Contributed surplus—stock options	$100,000	
Less: Deferred compensation expense	**50,000**	50,000
Total shareholders' equity		$1,050,000

If 20% or 2,000 of the 10,000 options were exercised on June 1, 1996 (three years and five months after date of grant), the following journal entry would be recorded:

Cash (2,000 × $60)	120,000	
Contributed Surplus—Stock Options (20% of $100,000)	20,000	
Common Shares		140,000

If the remaining stock options are not exercised before their expiration date, the balance in the Contributed Surplus—Stock Options account should be transferred to a more properly titled contributed surplus account, such as Contributed Surplus From Expired Stock Options. The entry to record this transaction at the date of expiration would be as follows:

Contributed Surplus—Stock Options (80% of $100,000)	80,000	
Contributed Surplus From Expired Stock Options		80,000

The fact that a stock option is not exercised does not nullify the propriety of recording the costs of services received from the executives and attributable to the stock option plan. Compensation expense is, therefore, not adjusted on expiration of the options. However, if a stock option is forfeited because an *employee fails to fulfil an obligation* (i.e. leaves employment), the estimate of compensation expense recorded in the current period should be adjusted (as a change in estimate). This change in estimate would be recorded by debiting Contributed Surplus—Stock Options and crediting Compensation Expense, thereby decreasing compensation expense in the period of forfeiture.

Stock Appreciation Rights

In a **stock appreciation rights** (SARs) plan, the executive is given the right to receive **share appreciation**, which is defined as the excess of the market price of the shares at the date of exercise over

---

[11] The rationale for using a contra-equity account is that deferred compensation expense represents an unearned compensation amount and is better reported as contra equity than as an asset. An alternative to this entry is to record no formal entry at the date of grant but to accrue compensation expense at the end of each period as incurred. We will use the approach illustrated above for problem material because this method formalizes in the records the compensation element of these plans.

a pre-established price. This share appreciation may be paid in cash, shares, or a combination of both. The major advantage of SARs is that the executive often does not have to make a cash outlay at the date of exercise, but receives a payment for the share appreciation that may be used to pay related income taxes. Unlike a stock option plan, the shares that constitute the basis for computing the appreciation in a SARs plan are not issued; only cash or shares having a market value equivalent to the appreciation is awarded to the executive.

As indicated earlier, the usual date for measuring compensation related to stock compensation plans is the date of grant. However, with SARs, the final amount of cash or shares (or a combination of the two) to be distributed is not known until the date of exercise and, therefore, total compensation cannot be measured until this date. Thus, the measurement date is the *date of exercise*.

How then should compensation expense be recorded during the interim periods from the date of grant to the date of exercise? Such a determination is not easy because it is impossible to know what the total compensation cost will be until the date of exercise, and the service period will probably not coincide with the exercise date. The best estimate of total compensation cost for the plan at any interim period is the difference between the *current market price* of the shares and the *option price*, multiplied by the number of stock appreciation rights outstanding. This total estimated compensation cost is then allocated over the service period to record an expense (or a decrease in expense if market price falls) in each period. At the end of each interim period, total compensation expense reported to date should equal the percentage of the total service period that has elapsed, multiplied by the estimated compensation cost.

For example, if at an interim period the service period is 40% complete and total estimated compensation is $100,000, then total compensation expense reported to date should equal $40,000 ($100,000 × 40%). As another illustration, in the first year of a four-year plan, the company charges one-fourth of the appreciation to date; in the second year, it charges off two-fourths or 50% of the appreciation to date less the amount already recognized in the first year. In the third year, it charges off three-fourths of the appreciation to date less the amount recognized previously, and in the fourth year it charges off the remaining compensation expense. We will refer to this method as the **percentage approach** for allocating compensation expense.

A special problem arises when the exercise date is later than the service period. In the previous example, if the SARs were not exercised at the end of four years, it would be necessary to account for the difference in the market price and the option price in the fifth year. In this case, compensation expense is adjusted whenever a change in market price of the shares occurs in subsequent reporting periods until the rights expire or are exercised, whichever comes first.

Increases or decreases in the market value of these shares between the date of grant and the exercise date, therefore, result in a change in the measure of compensation. Some periods will have credits to compensation expense if the quoted market price of the shares falls from one period to the next; the credit to compensation expense, however, cannot exceed previously recognized compensation expense. In other words, *cumulative compensation expense arising from the plan cannot be negative.*

To illustrate, assume that Bigger Hotels Ltd. establishes a SARs program on January 1, 1994, which entitles executives to receive cash at the date of exercise (anytime in the next five years) for the difference between the market price of the shares and the pre-established price of $10 on 10,000 SARs; the market price on December 31, 1994 is $13 per share, and the service period runs for two years (1994–1995). The schedule on page 831 indicates the amount of compensation expense to be recorded each period, assuming that the executives hold the SARs for three years, at which time the rights are exercised.

In 1994, Bigger Hotels would record compensation expense of $15,000 because 50% of the $30,000 total compensation cost estimated at December 31, 1994 is allocable to 1994. In 1995, the market price increases to $17 per share; therefore, the additional compensation expense of $55,000 ($70,000 − $15,000) is recorded. The SARs are held through 1996, during which time the share price decreases to $15. The decrease is recognized by recording a $20,000 credit to Compensation Expense and a debit to Liability Under Stock Appreciation Plan. Note that after the service period

Stock Appreciation Rights
Schedule of Compensation Expense

	(1)	(2)	(3)	(4)	(5)	(6)			
						Cumulative			
			Pre-established	Cumulative		Compensation			
		Market	Price	Compensation	Percentage	Accrued	Expense	Expense	Expense
	Date	Price	(10,000 SARs)	Recognizable[a]	Accrued[b]	to Date	1994	1995	1996
Dec. 31/94		$13	$10	$30,000	50	$ 15,000	$15,000		
						55,000		$55,000	
Dec. 31/95		17	10	70,000	100	70,000			
						(20,000)			$(20,000)
Dec. 31/96		15	10	50,000	100	$ 50,000			

[a]Cumulative compensation for unexercised SARs to be allocated to periods of service.
[b]The percentage accrued is based on a two-year service period (1994–1995).

ends, since the rights are still outstanding, the rights are adjusted to market at December 31, 1996. Any such credit to compensation expense cannot exceed previous charges to expense attributable to that plan.

As the compensation expense is recorded each period, the corresponding credit should be to a liability account if the stock appreciation is to be paid in cash. If shares are to be issued, then a more appropriate credit would be to Contributed Surplus. The entry to record compensation expense in the first year, assuming that the SAR ultimately will be paid in cash, is as follows:

Compensation Expense	15,000	
Liability Under Stock Appreciation Plan		15,000

The liability account would be credited again in 1995 for $55,000 and debited for $20,000 in 1996, when the negative compensation expense is recorded. The entry to record the negative compensation expense is as follows:

Liability Under Stock Appreciation Plan	20,000	
Compensation Expense		20,000

At December 31, 1996, executives receive $50,000; the entry removing the liability is as follows:

Liability Under Stock Appreciation Plan	50,000	
Cash		50,000

Because compensation expense is measured by the difference between market price of the shares from period to period, multiplied by the number of SARs, compensation expense can increase or decrease substantially from one period to the next.

Many accountants are disturbed by the accounting for SARs because the amount of compensation expense to be reported each period is subject to fluctuations in the stock market. "Shouldn't earnings determine share prices, rather than share prices determine earnings?" ask some accountants. Even with this drawback, though, this type of plan is gaining in popularity because executives are required to make little, if any, cash outlay under these programs.

SARs are often issued in combination with compensatory stock options (referred to as **tandem** or **combination plans**) and the executives must then select which of the two sets of terms to exercise, thereby cancelling the other. The existence of alternative plans running concurrently poses additional problems from an accounting standpoint because the accountant must determine, on the basis of the facts available each period, which of the two plans has the higher probability of exercise and then account for this plan, and ignore the other.

Performance-Type Plans

Many executives have become disenchanted with stock compensation plans whose ultimate payment depends on an increase in the market price of the common shares. This disenchantment arises because of the stock market's erratic behaviour and the belief by some executives that their level of work and the market price of the shares are not well correlated. As a result, there has been a substantial increase in the use of plans where executives receive common shares (or cash) if specified performance criteria are attained during the performance period (generally three to five years).

The **performance criteria** employed usually are increases in return on assets or equity, growth in sales, growth in earnings per share (EPS), or a combination of these factors. A performance-type plan's measurement date is the date of exercise because neither the number of shares that will be issued nor cash that will be paid out when performance is achieved is known at the date of grant. The compensation cost is allocated to the periods involved in much the same manner as with stock appreciation rights; that is, the percentage approach is used.

Tandem or combination awards are popular with these plans; that is, the executive has the choice of selecting between a performance or stock option award. In these cases, the executive has the best of both worlds because if either the share price increases or the performance goal is achieved, the executive gains. Sometimes, the executive receives both types of plans, so that the monies received from the performance plan can finance the exercise price on the stock option plan.

Summary

A summary of various plans used to compensate key executives and the major characteristics of each is provided below.

Summary of Compensation Plans				
Type of Plan	Measurement Date	Measurement of Compensation	Allocation Period	Allocation Method
Stock option	Grant	Market price less exercise price	Service	Percentage approach for service period
Stock appreciation rights	Exercise	Market price less exercise price	Service	Straight-line
Performance-type plan	Exercise	Market value of shares issued	Service	Percentage approach for service period

Objective 6

Identify the conceptual issues involved with stock compensation plans.

Conceptual Issues Involving Stock Compensation Plans

Much debate exists concerning the proper accounting and reporting for stock compensation plans. Two primary conceptual questions that must be resolved before acceptable accounting standards may be adopted are discussed in the following sections.

Alternative Dates. What date should be used to measure total compensation cost? Many accountants favour the *date of grant* because the company foregoes an alternative use of shares on that date. Others believe that some other date such as the date the *option becomes vested or exercised* is more appropriate.

The date the option becomes vested is favoured by some because at that date the employee has performed the option contract, and the company is obligated to issue shares at the option price. Others state that the excess of the market price over the option price at the date the option becomes vested is still an incomplete valuation that understates the value of the option, particularly when this option may be held for several years before expiring. They believe that only at the date that the *option is exercised* is the final value of the employee's services recognizable. In short, the commitment to transfer cash or shares to employees under a plan is only a contingency until the date of exercise, when the amount of the transfer will be known.

Valuation. A second issue relates to how the option should be valued, assuming the measurement date is the date of grant. One group believes that an attempt should be made to value the *option* itself. They note that an option to buy shares at a price equal to or below the market price has value and cannot be considered worthless. Because there is no risk of loss to the executive and a possibility, if not a probability, of great gain, the option may possess value that is greater than the spread between the option price and the market price at the date of the grant. Similarly, others argue that although services are normally valued at the cost of the assets given in exchange for them, the *fair value of the services received* is also a proper and acceptable basis of valuation. Using this approach, an attempt is made to determine what type of cash trade-off the executives make receiving an option for shares in lieu of a straight cash distribution. By imputing this cash trade-off, the total amount of compensation may be determined.[12]

Others stress that the approaches described above are too subjective and argue for the approach adopted by the profession in the United States, namely, that compensation expense be measured by the difference between the market price and the option price at the *date of grant*. This argument is based on the premise that the only objective and verifiable amount that can be determined at the date of grant is the spread between the market and option prices. Many are unhappy with this approach because little or no compensation is recorded for many stock option plans (e.g., incentive stock option plans report zero compensation expense).

Finally, it is sometimes argued that *no compensation expense should be reported* at all because no cost to the entity results from the issuance of additional shares; the cost to the shareholders is the possible dilution of their interest in the entity, and accountants should ignore this factor in their accounting. In the authors' opinion, this does not appear to be a reasonable approach because a cost is involved to the existing shareholders that should be considered a cost of operating the enterprise.

Disclosure of Compensation Plans. Disclosure of type and amount of compensation received by Canadian executives is not specifically required by the *CICA Handbook*. In a few provinces such information is required under securities legislation. Consequently, details about executive compensation are more difficult to obtain in Canada than in the United States. Users of financial statements could benefit from increased disclosure that would help them find answers to such questions as: Is the salary reasonable? Does the compensation package provide the proper types of incentives to executives? Will these plans lead to considerable dilution of existing shareholders' interest? Will these plans have an effect on corporate behaviour?

The answers to such questions are difficult because measurement of these plans is somewhat imprecise. Disclosure therefore plays an important role in helping users of the financial statements better understand these plans and their possible effects. Regardless of the basis used in valuing stock options, rights, and other types of awards, full disclosure should be made about the status of these

---

[12] For an interesting discussion of an attempt to value options, see Clifford W. Smith, Jr., and Jerold L. Zimmerman, "Valuing Employee Stock Option Plans Using Option Pricing Models," *Journal of Accounting Research* (Autumn 1976), pp. 357–364.

plans at the end of the period, including the number of shares under option and the option price. As to options exercised during the period, disclosure should be made of the number of shares involved and the option price used for exercise. Presented below is the disclosure of Canadian Occidental Petroleum Ltd.'s stock option plan as shown in their 1991 financial statements.

Note 8 (c) Stock options

Options to purchase common shares have been granted to certain officers and key employees. Under the stock option plan, options granted are contingent on continued employment and are exercisable on a cumulative basis until the year 2001.

(thousands of common shares)	1991	1990
Beginning of year	533	447
Options granted	130	139
Options exercised at option prices from $5.06 to $21.00	(68)	(42)
Options cancelled	(3)	(11)
End of year	592	533

The outstanding options at December 31, 1991 were granted at prices from $5.06 to $21.00 per common share. Of the options granted, as at December 31, 1991, options to purchase 310,180 common shares were available to be exercised at prices from $5.06 to $21.00 per common share. At December 31, 1991, 206,680 common shares were reserved for granting of additional options.

SECTION 2: COMPUTING EARNINGS PER SHARE

Earnings-per-share information is frequently reported in the financial press and is widely used by shareholders and potential investors in evaluating the profitability of a company. **Earnings per share** indicates the income earned by each common share. Thus, *earnings per share is reported only for common shares*. For example, if Oscar Limited has net income of $300,000 and a weighted average of 100,000 common shares outstanding for the year, earnings per share is $3.00 ($300,000 ÷ 100,000).

Because of the importance of earnings-per-share information, most companies are required to report this information either in the income statement or in the notes. Exceptions to this rule include government-owned companies, wholly owned subsidiaries, and companies with only a few shareholders. Generally, earnings-per-share information is reported below Net Income in the income statement. For Oscar Limited, the presentation would be as follows.

Net income	$300,000
Earnings per share	**$3.00**

When the income statement contains intermediate components of income, earnings per share should be disclosed for each component. The example at the top of page 835 is representative.

These disclosures enable the user of the financial statements to recognize the effects of income from continuing operations on EPS, as distinguished from income or loss from irregular items.[13]

---

[13] Reporting per-share amounts for gain or loss on discontinued operations and gain or loss on extraordinary items is optional. The reason is that a financial statement user can determine these amounts if the other per-share data are provided.

Earnings per share:	
Income from continuing operations	**$4.00**
Loss from discontinued operations, net of tax	0.60
Income before extraordinary item	**3.40**
Extraordinary gain, net of tax	1.00
Net income	**$4.40**

EARNINGS PER SHARE: SIMPLE CAPITAL STRUCTURE

A corporation's capital structure is regarded as **simple** if it consists only of common shares or includes no potentially dilutive convertible securities, options, warrants, or other rights that on conversion or exercise could in the aggregate dilute earnings per common share. A capital structure is regarded as **complex** if it includes securities that could have a dilutive effect on earnings per common share. The computation of earnings per share for a simple capital structure involves two items (other than net income)—preferred dividends and the weighted-average number of common shares outstanding.

Objective 7

Compute earnings per share in a simple capital structure.

Preferred Dividends

As indicated earlier, earnings per share relates to earnings per common share. When a company has both common and preferred shares outstanding, the *current year dividends on preferred shares is subtracted from net income to arrive at income available to common shareholders*. The formula for computing earnings per share is stated as follows.

$$\frac{\text{Net Income} - \text{Preferred Dividends}}{\text{Weighted Average of Shares Outstanding}} = \text{Earnings Per Share}$$

In reporting earnings-per-share information, preferred dividends should be subtracted from each of the intermediate components of income (income from continuing operations and income before extraordinary items) and finally from net income to arrive at income available to common shareholders. If preferred dividends are declared and a net loss occurs, the *preferred dividend is added to the loss* for the purposes of computing the loss per share. If the preferred shares are cumulative and the dividend is not declared in the current year, an *amount equal to the dividend that should have been declared for the current year only* should be subtracted from net income or added to net loss. Dividends in arrears for previous years should have been included in the previous year's computations.

WEIGHTED-AVERAGE NUMBER OF SHARES OUTSTANDING

In all computations of earnings per share, the weighted average of shares outstanding during the period constitutes the basis for the per-share amounts reported. Shares issued or retired during a period are weighed by the fraction of the period in which they were outstanding. The rationale for this approach is to find the equivalent number of whole shares outstanding for the year. To illustrate, assume that Stallone Limited has the changes in its common shares outstanding for the period as shown at the top of page 836.

To compute the weighted-average number of shares outstanding, the computation shown in the second box on page 836 is made. As illustrated, 90,000 shares were outstanding for three months, which translated into 22,500 whole shares for the entire year. Because additional shares were issued on April 1, the shares outstanding change and these shares must be weighted for the time outstanding.

Date	Share Changes	Shares Outstanding
Jan. 1	Beginning balance	90,000
Apr. 1	Issued 30,000 shares for cash	30,000
		120,000
July 1	Purchased 39,000 shares	39,000
		81,000
Nov. 1	Issued 60,000 shares for cash	60,000
Dec. 31	Ending balance	141,000

| | (A) | (B) | (C) Weighted |
Dates Outstanding	Shares Outstanding	Fraction of Year	Shares (A × B)
Jan. 1–Apr. 1	90,000	3/12	22,500
Apr. 1–July 1	120,000	3/12	30,000
July 1–Nov. 1	81,000	4/12	27,000
Nov. 1–Dec. 31	141,000	2/12	23,500
Weighted-average number of shares outstanding			**103,000**

When 39,000 shares were reacquired on July 1, the shares outstanding were reduced and again a new computation was made to determine the proper weighted shares outstanding.

Stock Dividends and Stock Splits

When **stock dividends** and **stock splits** occur, computation of the weighted-average number of shares requires restatement of the shares outstanding before the stock dividend or split. For example, assume that a corporation had 100,000 shares outstanding on January 1 and issued a 25% stock dividend on June 30. For purposes of computing a weighted average for the current year, the additional 25,000 shares outstanding as a result of the stock dividend are assumed to have been outstanding since the beginning of the year; the weighted average for the year would be 125,000 shares.

The issuance of a stock dividend or stock split requires retroactive restatement, but the issuance or reacquisition of shares for cash does not. Why? The reason is that stock splits and stock dividends do not increase or decrease the net assets of the enterprise; only additional shares are issued and, therefore, the weighted-average shares must be restated. Conversely, the issuance or purchase of shares for cash changes the amount of net assets. As a result, the company either earns more or less in the future as a result of this change in net assets. Stated another way, a stock dividend or split does not change the shareholders' total investment—it only increases (unless it is a reverse split) the number of common shares representing the investment. To illustrate how a stock dividend affects the computation of the weighted-average number of shares outstanding, assume that Rambo Limited has the changes as shown at the top of page 837 in its common shares during the year. The computation of the weighted-average number of shares outstanding would be as shown in the second box on page 837.

The shares outstanding prior to the stock dividend must be restated. The shares outstanding from January 1 to June 1 are adjusted for the stock dividend, so that these shares are stated on the same basis as shares issued subsequent to the stock dividend. Shares issued after the stock dividend

Date	Share Changes	Shares Outstanding
Jan. 1	Beginning balance	100,000
Mar. 1	Issued 20,000 shares for cash	20,000
		120,000
June 1	60,000 additional shares (50% stock dividend)	60,000
		180,000
Nov. 1	Issued 30,000 shares for cash	30,000
Dec. 31	Ending balance	210,000

	(A)	(B)	(C)	(D)
				Weighted
Dates	Shares		Fraction of	Shares
Outstanding	Outstanding	Restatement	Year	(A × B)
Jan. 1–Mar. 1	100,000	1.50	2/12	25,000
Mar. 1–June 1	120,000	1.50	3/12	45,000
June 1–Nov. 1	180,000		5/12	75,000
Nov. 1–Dec. 31	210,000		2/12	35,000
Weighted average number of shares outstanding				**180,000**

do not have to be restated because they are on the new basis. The stock dividend simply restates existing shares. The same type of treatment is required for a stock split.

If a stock dividend or stock split occurs after the end of the year but before the financial statements are issued, the weighted-average number of shares outstanding for the year (and any other years presented in comparative form) must be restated. For example, assume that Hendricks Limited computes its weighted-average number of shares to be 100,000 for the year ended December 31, 1994. On January 15, 1995, before the financial statements are issued, the company splits its shares three for one. In this case, the weighted-average number of shares used in computing earnings per share for 1994 would be 300,000 shares. If earnings-per-share information for 1993 is provided as comparative information, it also must be adjusted for the stock split.

Comprehensive Illustration

Bannerman Limited has income before extraordinary items of $580,000 and an extraordinary gain, net of tax, of $240,000. In addition, it has declared a dividend on its 100,000 preferred shares of $1 each. Bannerman Limited also has the changes shown at the top of page 838 on its common shares outstanding during 1994.

To compute the earnings-per-share information, the weighted-average number of shares outstanding is determined as shown in the second box on page 838.

In computing the weighted-average number of shares, the shares issued on December 31, 1994 are ignored because they have not been outstanding during the year. The weighted-average number of shares is then divided into income before extraordinary items and net income to determine earnings per share. Bannerman Limited's preferred dividends of $100,000 are subtracted from income before extraordinary items ($580,000) to arrive at income before extraordinary items available to common shareholders of $480,000 ($580,000 − $100,000). Deducting the preferred dividends from

Date	Share Changes	Shares Outstanding
Jan. 1	Beginning balance	180,000
May 1	Purchased 30,000 shares for cash	30,000
		150,000
July 1	300,000 additional shares (3-for-1 stock split)	300,000
		450,000
Dec. 31	**Issued 50,000 shares for cash**	50,000
Dec. 31	Ending balance	500,000

	(A)	(B)	(C)	(D)
Dates Outstanding	Shares Outstanding	Restatement	Fraction of Year	Weighted Shares (A × B × C)
Jan. 1–May 1	180,000	3	4/12	180,000
May 1–Dec. 31	150,000	3 1	8/12	300,000
Weighted-average number of shares outstanding				480,000

the income before extraordinary items has the effect of also reducing net income without affecting the amount of the extraordinary item. The final amount is referred to as income available to common shareholders.

	(A)	(B)	(C)
	Income Information	Weighted Shares	Earnings Per Share (A/B)
Income before extraordinary items available to common shareholders	$480,000	480,000	**$1.00**
Extraordinary gain (net of tax)	240,000	480,000	0.50
Income available to common shareholders	$720,000	480,000	**$1.50**

Disclosure of the per-share amount for the extraordinary item is optional. Income and per-share information reported would be as shown on page 839.

as shown on page 839.

Objective 8

Explain the concept of dual presentation.

EARNINGS PER SHARE: COMPLEX CAPITAL STRUCTURE

One problem with a simple EPS computation is that it fails to recognize the potentially dilutive impact of dilutive securities on earnings per share. **Dilutive securities** present a serious problem in determining the proper earnings per share because conversion or exercise may have an adverse effect on earnings per share. This adverse effect can be significant and, more importantly, unexpected unless financial statements call attention to the potential dilutive effect in some manner.

Income before extraordinary item	$580,000
Extraordinary gain, net of tax	240,000
Net income	$820,000
Earnings per share:	
Income before extraordinary item	**$1.00**
Extraordinary item, net of tax	**0.50**
Net income	**$1.50**

Because of the increasing use of dilutive securities in the 1960s, the profession can no longer ignore the significance of these securities and, therefore, has required additional earnings-per-share disclosures for firms having complex capital structures. A **complex capital structure** exists when a corporation has any debt or equity securities that may be converted, options, warrants, or other rights that on conversion or exercise could dilute earnings per share.

A complex capital structure requires a dual presentation of earnings per share. These two presentations are referred to as basic earnings per share and fully diluted earnings per share. **Basic earnings per share** is based on the number of common shares outstanding. **Fully diluted earnings per share** indicates the dilution of earnings per share that would have occurred if all contingent issuances of common shares that would have reduced earnings per share had taken place. Because of computational rules, fully diluted earnings per share are always less (less income per share or more loss per share) than basic EPS.

Materiality and Anti-Dilution

A company may have dilutive securities but still not have to report fully diluted earnings per share. Many corporations have potential dilution that is not material. In defining materiality, some Canadian accountants use the *3% materiality threshold* applicable in the United States. Any corporation whose capital structure has potential dilution of less than 3% of earnings per common share reports only basic earnings per share.

To illustrate, Murphy Limited has basic earnings per share of $2.00, ignoring all dilutive securities in its capital structure. If the possible conversion or exercise of the dilutive securities in the aggregate reduces earnings per share to $1.94 (97% × $2) or below, it is necessary to present both basic and fully diluted earnings per share (dual presentation), Otherwise, the company reports basic earnings per share at $2.00 without additional disclosure. It is to be assumed that the weighted-average number of shares is the basis and that potential dilution, if any exists, is less than 3%. In computing the 3% dilution factor, the aggregate of all dilutive securities should be considered.

Whether the capital structure is simple or complex, earnings-per-share data should be shown before and after extraordinary items where applicable. In addition, when the income statement includes a disposal of a business segment, the *CICA Handbook* recommends reporting results of continuing operations separately from the results of operations of the segment disposed of.[14] Also, earnings-per-share amounts must be shown for all periods presented; all prior period earnings-per-share amounts presented should be restated for stock dividends and stock splits. When results of operations of a prior period have been restated as a result of a prior period adjustment, the earnings-per-share data shown for the prior period should also be restated. The effect of the restatement, expressed in per-share terms, should be disclosed in the year of restatement.

Basic Earnings Per Share

Basic earnings per share must be computed and presented for all enterprises except for business enterprises that do not have share capital, government-owned companies, wholly owned subsidiaries,

---

[14] *CICA Handbook* (Toronto: CICA), Section 3500, par. .12.

and companies with only a few shareholders. If a corporation has more than one class of common shares (i.e. shares having equal participation rights after prescribed dividends), it is necessary to compute and report separate basic earnings-per-share amounts for each class.

When common shares are issued on conversion of debt or senior shares, the shares issued are considered to have been outstanding from the date when interest or dividends cease to be legally due on the securities converted. For example, if a firm had 100,000 shares outstanding on January 1 and on August 1 an additional 10,000 shares were issued as a result of bond conversions, the bond indenture specifies that interest on bonds converted will be paid to the regular interest payment date (June 30 and December 31) preceding the date of conversion. In this case the weighted-average number of common shares for the year would be 105,000 (100,000 + 10,000/2).

Another case in which the date of issue of common shares may not be the same as the date used in determining the term outstanding involves shares issued to effect a merger or an acquisition. If common shares are issued to effect a merger or an acquisition that is accounted for as a purchase, the shares so issued are considered to be outstanding from the date that earnings of the investee first accrue to the investor. If the merger is accounted for as a pooling of interests, the shares issued will be treated as outstanding, retroactive to the beginning of the period since the earnings are also included from that date.

Adjusted Basic Earnings Per Share

In the computation of basic earnings per share, common shares issued during the year as a result of conversions of senior shares or debt are considered to be outstanding for only that portion of the year subsequent to the termination of the firm's obligation for interest or dividends. When such conversions take place during a fiscal period, firms are required to provide an additional earnings-per-share amount. This additional per-share figure is known as **adjusted basic earnings per share**. Adjusted basic earnings per share is computed in the same way as basic earnings per share, except that the shares issued in the conversion are treated as if they had been outstanding from the beginning of the year.

Income Available to Common Shares

As previously emphasized, earnings per share is computed by dividing the amount of net income (or loss) available to common shareholders by the weighted-average number of common shares outstanding. The **income available to common shareholders** is determined by deducting dividends on senior shares from the reported income. If the senior shares are noncumulative, dividends declared should be deducted from reported income. When senior shares include cumulative preferreds, it is necessary to deduct the amount of dividends prescribed, whether paid or not. For example, a firm reports $100,000 net income for a year during which it had 60,000 common shares outstanding; 10,000, $1.00 ordinary preferred; and 20,000, $1.00 cumulative preferred. Assuming that dividends of $0.50 per share were paid on both ordinary and cumulative preferred shares, the amount of income available to common shareholders would be $75,000 ($100,000 − $5,000 paid on ordinary preferred and $20,000 prescribed on the cumulative preferred).

Fully Diluted Earnings Per Share

Firms having complex capital structures must present appropriate fully diluted earnings-per-share amounts if the potential dilution is material. Potential earnings-per-share dilution exists whenever a firm has convertible senior shares or debt outstanding or has issued stock rights, options, or warrants. The purpose of reporting fully diluted earnings per share is to disclose the maximum possible reduction in earnings per share that could take place if all qualifying issuable common shares were issued.

Computing fully diluted earnings per share involves a hypothetical calculation. The weighted-average number of common shares used in this calculation includes both issued and contingently issuable common shares. Issuable common shares include only those that are issuable under outstanding conversion privileges and/or options and warrants within a 10-year period from the balance sheet date. The term during which these issuable common shares are considered to be outstanding is the shorter of the full fiscal period or, if less than one year, the term during which the underlying security or option has been outstanding.

In addition to changing the weighted-average number of common shares outstanding, it is necessary to recognize the income effect of the issuable common shares. If common shares are issuable as a result of outstanding convertible preferred, the income effect is equal to the dividends applicable to the convertible preferred. That is, if the holders of the convertible preferred shares converted their shares to common, the income available to common shareholders would now be increased by the amount of the dividends that would have otherwise been allocated to preferred shares. When the income effect involves an income statement item such as interest expense on convertible bonds, the amount of the adjustment is the amount by which the after-tax income would be increased. For example, if holders of convertible bonds exercised their conversion privilege, income available to common shareholders would be increased by the amount of interest that would have been paid on the bonds, less the amount by which income tax expense would be increased due to the reduction in interest expense.

Convertible Securities

Convertible securities that affect the calculation of fully diluted earnings per share include convertible senior shares and debt. Any outstanding rights to convert either senior shares or debt into common shares within a *10-year term* that would result in dilution (reduction) of earnings per share should be included in the calculation of fully diluted earnings per share. As emphasized above, the number of issuable common shares outstanding as a result of the related convertible security is included in the computation of the weighted-average number of common shares outstanding. Income is adjusted to reflect, on a pro forma basis, the changes that would occur if the conversion privileges had been exercised at the beginning of the year or date of issue, whichever is later.

As an example, Marshy Field Limited has net income for the year of $310,000 and an average number of common shares outstanding during the period of 100,000. The company has two convertible debenture bond issues outstanding. One (outstanding at the beginning of the current year) is a 10% issue sold at 100 (total of $1,000,000) and convertible into 40,000 common shares. The other is a 15% issue sold at 100 (total of $1,000,000) on April 1 of the current year and convertible into 64,000 common shares. In addition, the firm has 50,000 noncumulative, $1.00 convertible (one preferred for one common) preferred shares outstanding. Due to a cash shortage, dividends of only $0.75 per share were declared and paid during the current year. Assume that the tax rate at present is 40%.

	Number of Shares	Net Income
Marshy Field Ltd.		
Computation of Earnings Per Share		
Net income		$310,000
Common shares	100,000	
Deduct:		
Preferred dividends declared (50,000 × $0.75)		37,500
Income available to common	100,000	$272,500
Basic earnings per share ($272,500/100,000)		$2.73
From above	100,000	$272,500
		(Continued)

	Number of shares	Net Income
Add assumed conversions:		
Convertible preferred		
Dividends (50,000 × $0.75)		37,500
Number of shares	50,000	
10% convertible debentures:		
Interest net of tax ($1,000,000 × [0.10 × 0.6])		60,000
Number of shares	40,000	
15% convertible debentures:		
Interest net of tax ($1,000,000 × [0.15 × 0.6]) × 9/12		67,500
Number of shares (64,000 × 9/12)	48,000	
Totals	238,000	$437,500
Fully diluted earnings per share		$1.84

Options and Warrants

Stock options and warrants outstanding and their equivalents (if exercisable within the 10-year limit) are included in fully diluted earnings-per-share computations unless their effect on EPS is anti-dilutive (i.e. increase EPS). Stock purchase contracts, stock subscriptions not fully paid, deferred compensation packages providing for the issuance of common shares, and convertible securities that allow or require the payment of cash at issuance are treated as options and warrants. The number of common shares issuable on exercise of outstanding options, warrants, and their equivalents are included in the weighted-average number of common shares for the calculation of fully diluted earnings per share.

These calculations are based on the assumption that the options and/or warrants are exercised at the beginning of the year (or date of issue if later) and the proceeds from the exercise of the options and warrants are invested in operating assets of the firm. The amount assumed to be invested, in turn, earns an assumed return that would increase the amount of income available to the common shareholders. The appropriate rate of return (net of tax) is left to the professional judgement of the accountant.

To illustrate the computation of fully diluted earnings per share when stock options and/or warrants are outstanding at the year end, assume that Kubitz Industries Limited has net income for the period of $220,000. The average number of common shares outstanding for the period was 50,000 shares. Options to purchase 5,000 common shares at a price of $10 per share were outstanding at the end of the year. Of the 5,000 options, 4,000 were outstanding at the beginning of the year and 1,000 were issued on October 1 of the current year. Kubitz's average rate of return on assets over the past three years has been 25% before income taxes of 40%.

Kubitz Industries Limited
Computation of Earnings Per Share

	Number of Shares	Net Income
Net income		$220,000
Common shares	50,000	
Basic earnings per share		$4.40
From above	50,000	$220,000

(Continued)

Issuable common shares—stock options:			
Outstanding one year 4,000 × 1		4,000	
Outstanding three months 1,000 × 3/12		250	
Imputed earnings on option proceeds:			
Proceeds 4,000 × $10	$40,000		
Imputed earnings $40,000 × 0.25	10,000		
Less income taxes @ 40%	4,000		6,000
Proceeds 1,000 × $10	$10,000		
Imputed earnings $10,000 × 0.25	2,500		
Less income taxes @ 40%	1,000		
Net earnings for 12 months	1,500		
Imputed earnings for three months			
$1,500 × 3/12			375
Totals		54,250	$226,375
Fully diluted earnings per share			$4.17

In most cases, holders of convertible securities, options, rights, and warrants are protected against a dilution of the number of shares to which they are entitled in the event of either a stock split or a stock dividend. This protection is an anti-dilution clause that provides for a proportionate increase (decrease) in the conversion ratio or the number of shares that may be acquired with each option or warrant. For example, a convertible bond with an original exchange ratio of 20 common shares for each $1,000 bond would, if so specified in an anti-dilution clause, have an exchange ratio of 40 to 1 after a 2-for-1 stock split.

Anti-Dilution

When determining whether fully diluted earnings per share should be reported, all dilutive securities must be considered. In addition, any of the securities that are anti-dilutive should be excluded and cannot be used to offset dilutive securities. Anti-dilutive securities are securities that would create an increase in earnings per share (or a reduction in net loss per share). For example, convertible debt is anti-dilutive whenever interest (net of tax) on the debt expressed in per-share terms (based on number of common shares issuable on conversion) is greater than basic earnings per share. With options or warrants, whenever the imputed earnings (net of tax) expressed in per-share terms (number of shares issuable under the associated options or warrants) are greater than basic earnings per share, they are considered anti-dilutive. A test for anti-dilution must be made before including any item in the fully diluted earnings-per-share calculation. This test involves simply comparing the per-share effect of each potentially dilutive item with the basic earnings per share. If the per-share amount of the potentially dilutive item is greater than the basic earnings per share (less than net loss per share), then the item is anti-dilutive and must be omitted from the fully diluted earnings per share.

To illustrate, assume that the conversion ratio for Marshy Field's preferred shares is four preferred for each common. The number of issuable common shares would be 12,500 (50,000 ÷ 4) and the income effect would remain $37,500. The per-share effect of the preferred would be $3.00 ($37,500 ÷ 12,500). Since this amount ($3.00) is greater than the basic earnings per share ($2.73) (see page 841), including these convertible preferred shares in the calculation of fully diluted earnings per share would increase rather than reduce earnings per share. Such securities (anti-dilutive) should be omitted from the computation of fully diluted earnings per share. The test for anti-dilution is more complex than implied by the above illustration and is discussed later in this chapter.

Pro Forma Earnings Per Share

When transactions affecting common shares occur subsequent to the date of the balance sheet, earnings-per-share figures previously computed may not be relevant to users' needs. In these cases, pro forma earnings-per-share amounts must be disclosed in a note to the financial statements. Pro forma basic earnings per share should be computed following any one of the following three types of transactions occurring subsequent to the date of the balance sheet.[15]

1. Issuance of common shares when the proceeds are to be used to retire senior shares or debt outstanding at the date of the balance sheet.

2. Common shares issued on the conversion of senior shares or debt outstanding at the balance sheet.

3. When common shares are issued in a reorganization.

The effect of the foregoing transactions on basic earnings per share is given retroactive recognition to the beginning of the current period or, if later, at the date of issuance of the senior shares or debt.

Type (2) transactions would have been anticipated in fully diluted earnings per share and therefore are not used in computing pro forma fully diluted earnings per share. However, if type (1) or (3) transactions occur, then pro forma fully diluted earnings per share must be computed and disclosed in a note to the financial statements. Neither pro forma basic nor pro forma fully diluted earnings per share need to be reported for any prior periods. In addition, it is not necessary to report pro forma earnings figures that are not materially different from the basic and fully diluted earnings-per-share amounts.

Earnings-Per-Share Presentations and Disclosures

If a corporation's capital structure is complex, the earnings-per-share presentations would be as follows.

Objective 9

Explain the disclosures and presentations of earnings per share.

Net Income Per Common Share	
Basic	$3.30
Fully diluted	$2.70

When the income of a period includes special transactions, per-share amounts (where applicable) should be shown for income before extraordinary items and net income. Reporting per-share amount for gain or loss on extraordinary items is optional. A presentation reporting extraordinary items is illustrated below.

Net Income Per Common Share	
Basic earnings per common share:	
Income before extraordinary item	$3.80
Extraordinary item	0.80
Net income	$3.00
Fully diluted earnings per common share:	
Income before extraordinary item	$3.35
Extraordinary item	0.65
Net income	$2.70

Earnings-per-share amounts must be shown for all periods presented and all prior period earnings-per-share amounts presented should be restated for stock dividends and stock splits. When the results of operations of a prior period have been restated as a result of a prior period adjustment, the earnings-per-share data shown for the prior periods should be restated. The effect of the restatement should be disclosed in the year of restatement.

---

[15] *Ibid.*, par. .39.

Some Canadian firms are required to report in jurisdictions outside of Canada. In these cases, the firms must disclose the earnings-per-share amounts required in Canada as well as those, if different, required in the foreign country.

Comprehensive Illustration

The following comprehensive illustration demonstrates how the methods for computing earnings per share would be handled in a complex situation. This section of the balance sheet of Rhode Limited is presented for analysis; assumptions related to the capital structure follow.

Rhode Limited
Selected Balance Sheet Information
At December 31, 1994

Long-term debt:		
Notes payable, 7.2%	$ 500,000	
4% convertible debentures	1,500,000	
5% convertible debentures	2,500,000	$ 4,500,000
Shareholders' equity:		
$5 cumulative convertible preferred, no-par value, authorized 100,000 shares, issued 25,000 shares	2,500,000	
Common shares, no-par value, authorized 5,000,000 shares, issued 500,000 shares	500,000	
Contributed surplus	2,500,000	
Retained earnings (includes 1994 income of $1,000,000)	9,000,000	14,500,000
		$19,000,000

Notes and Assumptions
December 31, 1994

1. Options, exercisable at any time after July 1, 1997, were granted to purchase 50,000 common shares at $20 per share on July 2, 1994.

2. Warrants to purchase 100,000 common shares at $25 per share were issued in 1992. These warrants may be exercised at any time after January 1, 1999.

3. 4% and 5% convertible debentures are convertible into common shares at $25 per share (40 shares for each $1,000 bond).

4. $5 cumulative convertible preferred shares are convertible at the rate of four shares of common for each share of preferred ($25 conversion price).

5. All debt was issued at face value and all preferred was issued at $100 per share.

6. Except for the stock options in item 1 and the convertible debentures in item 11, all debt and securities were outstanding at the beginning and end of the year.

7. The average applicable income tax rate is 40%.

8. 25,000 common shares were issued January 25, 1995 for $26 per share. The proceeds of this issue were used to retire 550, $1,000, 5% convertible debentures.

9. On February 10, 1995, prior to issuance of the financial statements, directors of Rhode Limited voted to split the common shares two for one.

10. Net income for the year of $1,000,000 did not include any extraordinary items.

11. Holders of 1000, 4% convertible debentures exercised their conversion rights on September 30, 1994.

12. Rhode earns approximately 8% after taxes on net assets.

The computation of earnings-per-share amounts in accordance with Section 3500 of the *CICA Handbook* is as follows.

Computation of Earnings Per Share

	No. of Shares	Income	Per-Share Amount
Basic earnings per share (Exhibit 1)	940,000	$ 875,000	$0.93
Dilutive securities:			
4% convertible debentures (Exhibit 2)	180,000	54,000	0.30
5% convertible debentures (Exhibit 3)	200,000	75,000	0.375
Convertible preferred shares (Exhibit 4)	200,000	125,000	0.625
Stock options (Exhibit 5)	—	—	—
Stock warrants (Exhibit 6)	—	—	—
Fully diluted earnings per share	1,520,000	$1,129,000	$0.74
Adjusted basic earnings per share (Exhibit 10)	1,000,000	$ 893,000	$0.89

The following exhibits illustrate the computations for arriving at basic and fully diluted earnings per share. Exhibit 1 shows the calculation of basic earnings per share.

Exhibit 1
Computation of Basic Earnings Per Share

Net income as reported	$1,000,000
Deduct dividends prescribed on cumulative preferred shares (25,000 × $5.00)	125,000
Income attributed to common shares	$ 875,000
Common shares outstanding:	
For 12 months (500,000 − 40,000)	460,000
For 3 months (1,000 × $1,000)/$25 = 40,000	
40,000 × 3/12 =	10,000
Total	470,000
Adjustment for 2-for-1 stock split	× 2
Weighted-average number of common shares outstanding	940,000
Basic earnings per share ($875,000/940,000)	$0.93

Exhibit 2 illustrates the calculation of the earnings-per-share effect of the 4% convertible debentures. Exhibit 3 presents the calculations of the pro forma earnings-per-share effect of the conversion of the 5% convertible debentures at January 1, 1994. Exhibit 4 illustrates the computation of the pro forma earnings-per-share effect of the conversion of the convertible preferred shares.

Exhibit 2
4% Convertible Debentures

Pro forma income effect of conversion:	
Interest expense reduction ($1,500,000 × 0.04) +	
($1,000,000 × 0.04) × 9/12	$ 90,000
Less income tax expense increase ($90,000 × 0.4)	36,000
Net increase in net income that would have	
occurred had conversion occurred Jan. 1, 1994	$ 54,000
Number of common shares issuable on conversion	
($1,500,000/$25) + ($1,000,000/$25 × 9/12)	90,000
Adjustment for 2-for-1 stock split	× 2
Total issuable common shares	180,000
Earnings-per-share effect of possible conversion	
($54,000/180,000)	$0.30

Exhibit 3
5% Convertible Debentures

Pro forma income effect of conversion:	
Interest expense reduction ($2,500,000 × 0.05)	$125,000
Less income tax expense increase ($125,000 × 0.4)	50,000
Net increase in net income that would have occurred	
had conversion taken place January 1, 1994	$ 75,000
Number of common shares issuable on conversion:	
($2,500,000/$25)	100,000
Adjustment for 2-for-1 stock split	× 2
Total issuable common shares	200,000
Pro forma earnings-per-share effect of conversion	
($75,000/200,000)	$0.375

Exhibit 4
Convertible Preferred Shares

Income effect of conversion:	
Dividends prescribed (25,000 × $5.00)	$125,000
Number of common shares issuable on conversion:	
(25,000 × 4)	100,000
Adjustment for 2-for-1 stock split	× 2
Issuable common shares	200,000
Earnings-per-share effect of conversion	
($125,000/200,000)	$0.625

Exhibit 5 shows the earnings-per-share effect of the exercise of the stock options on the date of issue (July 1, 1994).

Exhibit 5

Stock Options

Income that would have been earned on the proceeds from exercise of the options from date of issue to December 31, 1994 (50,000* × $20* × .08 × 6/12)	$40,000
Issuable common shares 50,000 × 6/12	25,000
Adjustable for 2-for-1 stock split	× 2
Issuable common shares	50,000
Earnings-per-share effect of exercise of stock options ($40,000/50,000)	$0.80

*At the time of the stock split, the number of shares issuable under the options would be increased proportionately and the option price would be reduced to prevent dilution of the value of the options. (Options would be increased to 100,000 shares and the price would be reduced to $10 per share.)

Exhibit 6 illustrates the calculation of the earnings-per-share effect of potential issuance of shares to holders of stock warrants. Notice that these are considered potentially dilutive securities since they may be exercised within the 10-year limit.

Exhibit 6

Stock Warrants

Imputed income on proceeds from exercise of stock warrants ($12.50* × 200,000*) × 0.08	$200,000
Number of common shares issuable on exercise of warrants	100,000
Adjustment for stock split	× 2
Total number of shares issuable	200,000
Earnings-per-share effect of exercise of stock warrants ($200,000/200,000)	$1.00

*Adjusted for stock split

Exhibits 2 through 6 show the calculations of the per-share effect of various potentially dilutive securities. Only those that cause reductions to basic earnings per share should be included in the calculation of fully diluted earnings per share. To determine which dilutive securities to include in the fully diluted earnings-per-share amount, it is necessary to rank the pro forma per-share effects starting with the most dilutive. Fully diluted earnings per share is then computed by progressively including the dilutive securities until the lowest per-share amount is determined. Any dilutive securities that cause this lowest possible amount to increase should be omitted from the calculation when determining the fully diluted earnings per share to be reported in the financial statements. This procedure is illustrated in Exhibit 7.

The issuance of common shares subsequent to the end of the fiscal period and the proceeds used to retire debt necessitates computation and disclosure of pro forma basic and fully diluted earnings per share. These calculations are illustrated in Exhibits 8 and 9.

When conversions of senior shares or debt occur during the fiscal period, adjusted basic earnings per share should be calculated as though the conversion had taken place at the beginning of the period. This calculation is presented in Exhibit 10.

Exhibit 7
Fully Diluted Earnings Per Share

	No. of Shares	Income	Earnings Per Share
Basic earnings per share (Exhibit 1)	940,000	$ 875,000	$0.93
4% debentures (Exhibit 2)	180,000	54,000	
Subtotal	1,120,000	929,000	0.829
5% debentures (Exhibit 3)	200,000	75,000	
Subtotal	1,320,000	1,004,000	0.761
Convertible preferred (Exhibit 4)	200,000	125,000	
Subtotal	1,520,000	1,129,000	0.743
Stock options (Exhibit 5)	50,000	40,000	
Subtotal	1,570,000	1,169,000	0.745*
Stock warrants (Exhibit 6)	200,000	200,000	
Total	1,770,000	$1,369,000	0.773*

*Earnings per share increases; therefore, stock options and warrants are anti-dilutive and should be omitted from calculation of fully diluted earnings per share.

Exhibit 8
Pro Forma Basic Earnings Per Share

Net income attributed to common shares (Exhibit 1)		$875,000
Add: Interest expense reduction from debt		
retired January 25, 1995 ($550,000 × 0.05)	$27,500	
Less income tax (27,500 × 0.4)	11,000	16,500
Pro forma income available to common shares		$891,500
Weighted-average number of common shares outstanding (Exhibit 1)		940,000
Add: Common shares issued January 25, 1995		50,000
Pro forma weighted-average number of common shares outstanding during 1994		990,000
Pro forma basic earnings per share ($891,500/990,000)		$0.90

Exhibit 9
Pro Forma Diluted Earnings Per Share

Pro forma available to common (Exhibit 8)		$ 891,500
Add: Income attributed to assumed conversions:		
4% convertible debentures (Exhibit 2)		54,000
5% convertible debentures (Exhibit 3)	$ 75,000	
Less after-tax interest on debentures retired January 25, 1995 (Exhibit 8)	16,500	58,500
Convertible preferred shares (Exhibit 4)		125,000
Total		$1,129,000

(Continued)

Weighted-average number of common shares:		
Pro forma basic (Exhibit 8)		990,000
4% convertible debentures (Exhibit 2)		180,000
5% convertible debentures (Exhibit 3)	200,000	
Less debentures retired January 25, 1995		
(550,000/25 adjusted for stock split)	44,000	156,000
Convertible preferred shares (Exhibit 4)		200,000
Total		1,526,000
Pro forma fully diluted earnings per share		
($1,129,000/1,526,000)		$0.74

Exhibit 10
Adjusted Basic Earnings Per Share

Income attributed to common shares (Exhibit 1)		$ 875,000
Add income effect of shares issued September 30 on		
conversion of 4% debentures (1,000,000 × 0.04 × 9/12)		30,000
Deduct increases in income tax ($30,000 × 0.4)		(12,000)
Net income available to common shareholders		$ 893,000
Weighted-average number of common shares outstanding		
(Exhibit 1)		940,000
Add shares issued September 30 on conversion		
restated to January 1 (40,000 × 9/12)	30,000	
Adjustment for stock split	× 2	60,000
Weighted-average number of common shares		
for adjusted basic earnings per share		1,000,000
Adjusted basic earnings per share ($893,000/1,000,000)		$0.89

Summary

Computation of earnings per share has become a complex issue. Many accountants take strong exception to some of the arbitrary rules contained in Section 3500 of the *CICA Handbook*. The situation facing accountants in this area is a difficult one because many securities, although technically not common shares, have the basic characteristics of common shares. In addition, many companies have issued these types of securities rather than common shares in order to avoid an adverse effect on the earnings-per-share figure. Section 3500 of the *Handbook* was issued as an attempt to develop credibility in reporting earnings-per-share data.

FUNDAMENTAL CONCEPTS

1. Dilutive securities are securities that are not common shares in form, but enable their holders to obtain common shares on exercise or conversion.

2. Accounting for convertible debt involves recognizing, measuring, and reporting issues at the time of issuance, conversion, and retirement.

(Continued)

3. At the date of issue, the recording of convertible debt follows that of a straight debt issue. At the time of conversion, the shares issued could be recorded (1) at the market price of the shares or bonds or (2) at the book value of the bonds.

4. Any additional consideration used to induce conversion of convertible securities is recorded as an expense of the current period and not as a reduction of equity.

5. When convertible debt is retired, the profession accounts for the difference between the cash acquisition price and the carrying amount as a gain or loss in the period of retirement.

6. Because preferred shares are considered a part of equity rather than debt, the book value method is employed at the time of conversion.

7. The proceeds from the sale of debt with detachable stock warrants are allocated between the two securities, whereas the proceeds from sale of debt with nondetachable warrants are recorded entirely as debt.

8. Employee stock option plans can be either compensatory or noncompensatory. Compensatory stock options require the measurement and recognition of compensation expense.

9. Compensation expense in a stock option plan is measured by the excess of market value of the shares over option price on the measurement date (usually the date of grant).

10. Compensation expense is allocated to the periods during which the qualifying service is rendered. The value of the options is recorded as an element of contributed surplus.

11. Stock appreciation rights (SARs) are compensatory plans that require recognition of compensation expense based on estimates from the grant to the exercise date (which is also the measurement date).

12. Performance-type compensation plans are accounted for in the same manner as SARs because the exact number of shares that will be issued or the cash that will be paid out when performance is achieved is not known at the date of grant.

13. Earnings per share (EPS) on common shares must be disclosed either as part of the income statement or in the notes. Companies with dilutive securities generally must report (1) earnings per common share and (2) fully diluted earnings per share.

14. The weighted-average number of shares outstanding during the period is the basis for per-share amounts reported. Shares issued or retired during a period are weighted by the fraction of the period in which they were outstanding.

15. Basic earnings per share is the amount of income attributed to each common share of outstanding. It is computed by dividing the income available to common shareholders (net income minus dividends paid on noncumulative preference shares and dividends prescribed on cumulative preference shares) by the weighted-average number of common shares outstanding during the period.

16. Fully diluted earnings per share represents the lowest possible earnings-per-share amount (largest possible loss) that could have been reported if all potentially issuable common shares had been issued during the year.

17. Basic and fully diluted earnings per share should be reported for net income and income before extraordinary items.

18. When common shares have been issued during the year as a result of conversions of senior shares or debt, adjusted basic earnings per share should be reported. Adjusted basic earnings per share indicates the amount that basic earnings per share would have been if the conversions had taken place at the beginning of the year.

19. If common shares are issued after the end of the current year and before the financial statements have been issued and the proceeds used to retire senior shares or debt, pro forma basic and pro forma fully diluted earnings per share should be disclosed.

20. Anti-dilutive securities should be ignored in all calculations and should not be considered in computing fully diluted earnings per share.

—— QUESTIONS ——

1. What were some of the major reasons for the increased merger activity in the early 1980s? Why might this increased activity have led to the issuance of dilutive securities?

2. Discuss the similarities and the differences between convertible debt and debt issued with stock purchase warrants.

3. What accounting treatment is required for convertible debt? What accounting treatment is required for debt issued with stock purchase warrants?

4. Roth Ltd. offered holders of its 1,000 convertible bonds a premium of $150 per bond to induce conversion into common shares. On conversion of all bonds, Roth Ltd. recorded the $150,000 premium as a reduction of Contributed Surplus. Comment on Roth's treatment of the $150,000 "sweetener."

5. Explain how the conversion feature of convertible debt has a value (a) to the issuer and (b) to the purchaser.

6. What are the arguments for giving separate accounting recognition to the conversion feature of debentures?

7. Assume that no value is assigned to the conversion feature on issue of the debentures. Assume further that four years after issue, debentures with a face value of $1,000,000 and book value of $960,000 are tendered for conversion into 8,000 common shares immediately after an interest payment date, when the market price of the debentures is $104 and the common shares are selling at $14 per share. The company records the conversion as follows:

Bonds Payable	1,000,000	
Discount on Bonds Payable		40,000
Common Shares (no-par value)		960,000

Discuss the propriety of this accounting treatment.

8. On July 1, 1994, Pat Delaney Corporation issued $3,000,000 of 9% bonds payable in 20 years. The bonds include detachable warrants giving the bondholder the right to purchase for $30 one no-par value common share at any time during the next 10 years. The bonds were sold for $3,000,000. The value of the warrants at the time of issuance was $200,000. Prepare the journal entry to record this transaction.

9. What are stock rights? How does the issuing company account for them?

10. What are the advantages to an executive of receiving an incentive stock option? Why do some accountants believe that the present accounting for these options is inappropriate?

11. Jason Sherwin Limited has an employee stock purchase plan that permits all full-time employees to purchase 10 common shares on the third anniversary of their employment and an additional 10 shares on each subsequent anniversary date. The purchase price is set at the market price on the date purchased and no commission is charged. Discuss whether this plan would be considered compensatory.

12. What date or event does the profession believe should be used in determining the value of a stock option? What arguments support this position? What criticism may be brought against the date or event advocated by the profession?

13. What support can be offered for dates other than the date of grant to determine the value of a stock option?

14. What is the advantage to an executive of a stock appreciation rights (SARs) plan? How is compensation expense measured in a SARs plan?

15. At December 31, 1994, Pearson Limited had 600,000 common shares issued and outstanding. Of these, 400,000 had been issued and outstanding throughout the year and 200,000 were issued on October 1, 1994. Net income for 1994 was $3,000,000 and dividends declared on noncumulative preferred were $400,000. Compute Pearson's earnings per common share (round to the nearest penny).

16. Define the following terms:
    (a) Potentially dilutive security.
    (b) Fully diluted earnings per share.
    (c) 3% test for dilution.
    (d) Complex capital structure.
    (e) Basic earnings per share.

17. Earnings per share can affect market prices of common shares. Can market prices affect earnings per share? Explain.

18. What is meant by the term "anti-dilution"? Give an example.

19. How is anti-dilution determined when multiple securities are involved?

——————— CASES ———————

(WARRANTS ISSUED WITH BONDS AND CONVERTIBLE BONDS)   Incurring long-term debt with **C17-1** an arrangement whereby lenders receive an option to buy common shares during all or a portion of the time during which the debt is outstanding is a frequent corporate financing practice. In some situations, the result is achieved through the issuance of convertible bonds; in others, the debt instruments and the warrants to buy shares are separate.

Instructions

(a) 1. Describe the differences that exist in current accounting for original proceeds of the issuance of convertible bonds and of debt instruments with separate warrants to purchase common shares.

  2. Discuss the underlying rationale for the differences described in (1) above.

  3. Summarize the arguments that have been presented in favour of accounting for convertible bonds in the same manner as for debt with separate warrants.

(b) At the start of the year, Regina Limited issued $18,000,000 of 12% notes, along with warrants to buy 1,200,000 shares of its no-par value common shares at $18 each. The notes mature over the next 10 years, starting one year from the date of issuance with annual maturities of $1,800,000. At the time, Regina had 9,600,000 common shares outstanding and the market price was $23 per share. The company received $20,040,000 for the notes and the warrants. For Regina Limited, 12% was a relatively low borrowing rate. If offered alone, at this time, the notes would have been issued at a 22% discount. Prepare the journal entry (or entries) for the issuance of the notes and warrants for the cash consideration received.

(AICPA adapted)

(CONVERTIBLE BONDS)   On February 1, 1991, Mahoney Company sold its five-year, $1,000 par value, **C17-2** 8% bonds, which were convertible at the option of the investor into Mahoney Company common shares at a ratio of 10 shares for each bond. The convertible bonds were sold by Mahoney Company at a discount. Interest is payable annually each February 1. On February 1, 1994, Sally Wong Company, an investor in the Mahoney Company convertible bonds, tendered 1,000 bonds for conversion into 10,000 of Mahoney Company's common shares that had a market value of $120 per share at the date of the conversion.

Instructions

How should Mahoney Company account for the conversion of the convertible bonds into common shares under both the book value and market value methods? Discuss the rationale for each method.

(AICPA adapted)

(STOCK WARRANTS: VARIOUS TYPES)   For various reasons, a corporation may issue warrants to pur- **C17-3** chase common shares at specified prices that, depending on the circumstances, may be less than, equal to, or greater than the current market price. For example, warrants may be issued:

  1. To existing shareholders on a pro rata basis.

  2. To certain key employees under an incentive stock option plan.

  3. To purchasers of the corporation's bonds.

Instructions

For each of the three examples of how stock warrants are used:

(a) Explain why they are used.

(b) Discuss the significance of the price (or prices) at which the warrants are issued (or granted) in relation to (1) the current market price of the company's shares and (2) the length of time over which they can be exercised.

(c) Describe the information that should be disclosed in financial statements, or notes thereto, that are prepared when stock warrants are outstanding in the hands of the three groups listed above.

(AICPA adapted)

C17-4 (STOCK OPTIONS AND STOCK APPRECIATION RIGHTS)   In 1991, Schneider Ltd. adopted a plan to give additional incentive compensation to its dealers to sell its principal product, fire extinguishers. Under the plan, Schneider transferred 9,000 shares of no-par value common shares to a trust, with the provision that Schneider would have to forfeit interest in the trust and no part of the trust fund could ever revert to Schneider. Shares were to be distributed to dealers on the basis of their share of fire extinguisher purchases from Schneider (above certain minimum levels) over the three-year period ending June 30, 1994.

In 1991, the shares were closely held. The book value of the shares was $7.90 per share as of June 30, 1991, and in 1991 additional shares were sold to existing shareholders for $8 per share. On the basis of this information, market value of the shares was determined to be $8 each.

In 1991, when the shares were transferred to the trust, Schneider charged Prepaid Expenses for $72,000 ($8 per-share market value) and credited Share Capital for $72,000. The prepaid expense was charged to operations over a three-year period ended June 30, 1994.

Schneider sold a substantial number of its shares to the public in 1993 at $60 per share.

In July 1994, all shares in the trust were distributed to the dealers. The market value of the shares at date of distribution from the trust had risen to $110 per share. Schneider obtained a tax deduction equal to that market value for the tax year ended June 30, 1995.

Instructions

(a) How much should be reported as selling expense in each of the years noted above?

(b) Schneider is also considering other types of option plans, such as a stock appreciation rights (SARs) plan. What is a stock appreciation right plan? What is a potential disadvantage of a SARs plan from the viewpoint of the company?

C17-5 (STOCK OPTIONS)   On December 12, 1991, the board of directors of McClure Company authorized a grant of options to company executives for the purchase of 20,000 common shares at $50 anytime during 1994 if the executives are still employed by the company. The closing price of McClure common shares was $55 on December 12, 1991, $51 on January 2, 1994, and $49⅛ on December 31, 1994. None of the options was exercised.

Instructions

(a) Prepare a schedule presenting the computation of the compensation cost that should be attributed to the options of McClure Company.

(b) Assume that the market price of McClure common rose to $58 (instead of declining to $51) on January 2, 1994, and that all options were exercised on that date. Would the company incur a cost for executive compensation? Why?

(c) Discuss the arguments for measuring compensation from executive stock options in terms of the spread between:

1. Market price and option price when the grant is made.

2. Market price and option price when the options are first exercisable.

3. Market price and option price when the options are exercised.

4. Cash value of the executives' services estimated at date of grant and the amount of their salaries.

(AICPA adapted)

(EPS: PREFERRED DIVIDENDS, OPTIONS, AND CONVERTIBLE DEBT)   Earnings per share (EPS)   **C17-6**
is the most featured single financial statistic about modern corporations. Daily published quotations of stock prices have recently been expanded to include, for many securities, a "times earnings" figure that is based on EPS. Stock analysts often focus their discussions on the EPS of the corporations they study.

Instructions

(a) Explain how dividends or dividend requirements on any class of preferred stock that may be outstanding affect the computation of EPS.

(b) The calculation of various EPS amounts requires the identification of issuable common shares:

1. What items are considered issuable common shares?

2. Describe the circumstances under which the potential impact of an outstanding convertible security on EPS would not be included in the calculation.

(AICPA adapted)

(EPS CONCEPTS AND PROFESSIONAL PRONOUNCEMENTS)   Earnings per share (EPS) amounts   **C17-7**
were calculated and reported in various ways on an optional basis prior to 1969. The *CICA Handbook*, Section 3500, "Earnings Per Share," issued in 1970, required that EPS be reported and prescribed how these amounts would be computed and disclosed.

The Accounting Standards Board requires that firms having a simple capital structure present a single EPS amount and those with complex capital structures provide a dual EPS presentation.

Instructions

(a) Explain why the existence of convertible securities and other financing instruments necessitated the reporting requirements for EPS prescribed by the *CICA Handbook*, Section 3500.

(b) Much of the effort involved in reporting EPS concerns the identification of issuable common shares:

1. What items are considered issuable common shares?

2. Describe the circumstances under which a convertible security would not be assumed to be converted in the computation of EPS.

(CMA adapted)

(EPS CONCEPTS AND EFFECT OF TRANSACTIONS ON EPS)   Fernandez Corporation, a new audit   **C17-8**
client of yours, has not reported earnings-per-share data in its annual reports to shareholders in the past. The treasurer, Spencer Martin, requests that you furnish information about the reporting of earnings-per-share data in the current year's annual report in accordance with generally accepted accounting principles.

Instructions

(a) Define the term "earnings per share" as it applies to a corporation with a capitalization structure composed of only one class of common shares. Explain how earnings per share should be computed and how the information should be disclosed in the corporation's financial statements.

(b) Discuss the treatment, if any, that should be given to each of the following items in computing earnings per common share for financial statement reporting:

1. Outstanding preferred shares issued at $46 with a $40 liquidation right.

2. The exercise at a price below market value but above book value of a common stock option issued during the current fiscal year to officers of the corporation.

3. The replacement of a machine immediately prior to the close of the current fiscal year at a cost 20% above the original cost of the replaced machine. The new machine will perform the same function as the old machine that was sold for its book value.

4. The declaration of current dividends on cumulative preferred shares.

5. The acquisition of some of the corporation's outstanding common shares during the current fiscal year. The shares were classified as treasury shares.

6. A two-for-one stock split of common shares during the current fiscal year.

7. An appropriation created out of retained earnings for a contingent liability from a possible lawsuit.

———————— EXERCISES ————————

E17-1 **(CONVERSION OF BONDS)**   Aubrey, Ltd. issued $4,000,000 of 11%, 10-year convertible bonds on June 1, 1993 at 98 plus accrued interest. The bonds were dated April 1, 1993, with interest payable April 1 and October 1. Bond discount was amortized semiannually on a straight-line basis.

On April 1, 1994, $1,500,000 of these bonds were converted into 30,000 no-par value common shares. Accrued interest was paid in cash at the time of conversion.

Instructions

(a) Prepare the entry to record the interest expense at October 1, 1993. Assume that accrued interest payable was credited when the bonds were issued. (Round to the nearest dollar.)

(b) Prepare the entry(ies) to record the conversion on April 1, 1994. (Book value method is used.) Assume that the entry to record amortization of the bond discount and interest payment has been made.

E17-2 **(ISSUANCE AND CONVERSION OF BONDS)**   For each of the unrelated transactions described below, present the entry(ies) required and record each transaction.

1. Grandgeorge Limited issued $20,000,000 par value, 10% convertible bonds at 99. If the bonds had not been convertible, the company's investment banker estimates they would have been sold at 94. Expenses of issuing the bonds were $70,000.

2. Hoosier Limited issued $20,000,000 par value, 10% bonds at 98. One detachable stock purchase warrant was issued with each $100 par value bond. At the time of issuance, the warrants were selling for $5.

3. On July 1, 1994, Tracey Company called its 11% convertible debentures for retirement. The $10,000,000 par value bonds were converted into 1,000,000 no-par value common shares. On July 1, there was $55,000 of unamortized discount applicable to the bonds, and the company paid an additional $75,000 to the bondholders to induce conversion of all the bonds. The company recorded the conversion using the book value method.

E17-3 **(CONVERSION OF BONDS)**   Vargo Company has bonds payable outstanding in the amount of $500,000 and the Premium on Bonds Payable account has a balance of $5,000. Each $1,000 bond is convertible into 20 no-par preferred shares.

Instructions

(a) Assuming that the bonds are quoted on the market at 102 and that the preferred shares may be sold on the market at $50⅞, make the entry to record the conversion of the bonds to preferred shares. (Use the market value approach.)

(b) Assuming that the book value method is used, what entry would be made?

(CONVERSION OF BONDS)   On January 1, 1993, when its no-par value common shares were selling for   **E17-4**
$80 per share, Plato Ltd. issued $10,000,000 of 8% convertible debentures due in 20 years. The conversion
option allowed the holder of each $1,000 bond to convert the bond into five shares of the corporation's no-par
common. The debentures were issued for $10,600,000. The present value of the bond payments at the time of
issuance was $8,500,000 and the corporation believed that the difference between the present value and the
amount paid was attributable to the conversion feature. On January 1, 1994, the corporation's common shares
were split two for one. On January 1, 1995, when the corporation's shares were selling for $135 per share, holders
of 30% of the convertible debentures exercised their conversion options. The corporation used the straight-line
method for amortizing any bond discounts or premiums.

Instructions

(a)   Prepare in general journal form the entry to record the original issuance of the convertible debentures.

(b)   Prepare in general journal form the entry to record the exercise of the conversion option, using the book value
method. Show supporting computations in good form.

(CONVERSION OF BONDS)   The December 31, 1993 balance sheet of Kehler Ltd. includes the following: **E17-5**

10% Callable, Convertible Bonds Payable (semiannual		
interest dates April 30 and October 31; convertible		
Into 6 no-par value common shares per $1,000 of bond		
principal; maturity date April 30, 1999)	$500,000	
Discount on Bonds Payable	10,880	$489,120

On March 5, 1994, Kehler Ltd. called all of the bonds as of April 30 for the principal plus interest through
April 30. By April 30, all bondholders had exercised their conversion rights as of the interest payment date.
Consequently, on April 30, Kehler Ltd. paid the semiannual interest and issued common shares for the bonds.
The discount was amortized on a straight-line basis. Kehler used the book value method.

Instructions

Prepare the entry(ies) to record the interest expense and conversion on April 30, 1994. Reversing entries were
made on January 1, 1994. (Round to the nearest dollar.)

(CONVERSION OF BONDS)   On January 1, 1993, Gottlieb Limited issued $4,000,000 of 10-year, 10%   **E17-6**
convertible debentures at 102. Interest is to be paid semiannually on June 30 and December 31. Each $1,000
debenture can be converted into eight of Gottlieb Limited's no-par common shares after December 31, 1994.

On January 1, 1995, $400,000 of debentures are converted into common shares, which were then selling
at $110. An additional $400,000 of debentures are converted on March 31, 1995. The market price of the
common shares is then $116. Accrued interest at March 31 will be paid on the next interest date.

Bond premium is amortized on a straight-line basis.

Instructions

Make the necessary journal entries for:

(a)   December 31, 1994.   (c)   March 31, 1995.

(b)   January 1, 1995.   (d)   June 30, 1995.

Record the conversions under both the fair market value method and the book value method.

E17-7 **(ISSUANCE OF BONDS WITH WARRANTS)** Homer Iliad Inc. has decided to raise additional capital by issuing $170,000 face value of bonds with a coon rate of 10%. In discussions with their investment consultants, it was determined that to help the sale of the bonds, detachable stock warrants should be issued at the rate of 10 warrants for each $1,000 bond sold. The value of the bonds without the warrants is considered to be $136,000, and the value of the warrants in the market is $24,000. The bonds sold in the market at issuance for $156,000.

Instructions

(a) What entry should be made at the time of the issuance of the bonds and warrants?

(b) If the warrants were nondetachable, would the entries be different? Discuss.

E17-8 **(ISSUANCE OF BONDS WITH DETACHABLE WARRANTS)** On September 1, 1994, Archimedes Limited sold at 104 (plus accrued interest) 4,000 of its 10%, 10-year, $1,000 face value, nonconvertible bonds with detachable stock warrants. Each bond carried two detachable warrants; each warrant was for one share of no-par common, at a specified option price of $15 per share. Shortly after issuance, the warrants were quoted on the market for $3 each. No market value could be determined for the bonds above. Interest was payable on December 1 and June 1. Bond issue costs of $40,000 were incurred.

Instructions

Prepare in general journal format the entry to record the issuance of the bonds.

(AICPA adapted)

E17-9 **(USE OF PROPORTIONAL AND INCREMENTAL METHOD)** Presented below are two independent situations:

1. On March 15, 1994, Erickson Limited issued $3,000,000 of 11% nonconvertible bonds at 109. Each $1,000 bond was issued with 50 detachable stock warrants, each of which entitled the bondholder to purchase, for $45, one of Erickson's no-par common shares. On March 15, 1994, the market value of Erickson common was $41 per share and the market value of each warrant was $6. Prepare the journal to record this transaction.

2. On February 1, 1994, Kurtz Ltd. issued $4,000,000, 10-year, 12% bonds for $4,200,000. Each $1,000 bond had two detachable warrants, each permitting the purchase of one of Kurtz's no-par common shares for $62. Immediately after the bonds were issued, Kurtz's securities had the following market values:

Common shares, no-par value	$ 58
Warrant	10
12% bond without warrant	1,040

Instructions

Prepare the journal entry to record this transaction. (Round all computations to the nearest dollar.)

E17-10 **(ISSUANCE AND EXERCISE OF STOCK OPTIONS)** On November 1, 1992, Tolstoi Company adopted a stock option plan that granted options to key executives to purchase 30,000 shares of the company's no-par value common shares. The options were granted on January 2, 1993 and were exercisable two years after date of grant if the grantee was still an employee of the company; the options expired six years from date of grant. The option price was set at $40; market price at the date of the grant was $48 a share.

All of the options were exercised during the year 1995: 20,000 on January 3 when the market price was $67 and 10,000 on May 1 when the market price was $77 a share.

Instructions

(a) Compute the value of the stock option and the corresponding amount of executive compensation.

(b) Prepare journal entries relating to the stock option plan for the years 1993, 1994, and 1995. Assume that the employee performs services equally in 1993 and 1994.

(ISSUANCE, EXERCISE, AND TERMINATION OF STOCK OPTIONS) On January 1, 1992, Sands **E17-11** Inc. granted stock options to officers and key employees for the purchase of 20,000 of the company's no-par value common shares at $25 each. The options were exercisable within a five-year period beginning January 1, 1994 by grantees still in the employ of the company, and they expire December 31, 1998. The market price of Sands' common was $32 per share at the date of grant. Sands prepared a formal journal entry to record this award. The service period for this award was two years.

On April 1, 1993, 2,000 option shares were terminated when the employees resigned from the company. The market value of the common was $35 per share on this date.

On March 31, 1994, 12,000 option shares were exercised when the market value of the common was $40 per share.

Instructions

Prepare journal entries to record issuance of the stock options, termination of the stock options, exercise of the stock options, and charges to compensation expense for the years ended December 31, 1992, 1993, and 1994.

(AICPA adapted)

(ISSUANCE, EXERCISE, AND TERMINATION OF STOCK OPTIONS) On November 2, 1990, the **E17-12** shareholders of Bolivar Limited voted to adopt a stock option plan for Bolivar's key officers. According to terms of the option agreement, the officers of the company could purchase 50,000 shares of no-par common during 1993 and 60,000 shares during 1994. The shares that were purchasable during 1993 represented executive compensation for 1991 and 1992, and those purchasable during 1994 represented such compensation for 1991, 1992, and 1993. If options for shares were not exercised during either year, they lapsed as of the end of that year.

Options were granted to the officers of Bolivar on January 1, 1991, and at that time the option price was set for all shares at $30. During 1993, all options were exercised. During 1994, however, options for only 40,000 shares were exercised. The remaining options lapsed because the executives decided not to exercise. The market prices of Bolivar common at various dates are as follows.

Dates	Market Price of Bolivar's Common
Option agreement accepted by shareholders	$33
Options granted	36
Options exercised in 1992	38
Options exercised in 1993	34

Instructions

Make any necessary journal entries related to this stock option for the years 1990 through 1994. (Bolivar closes its books on December 31.)

(STOCK APPRECIATION RIGHTS) On December 31, 1992, Beckman Limited issues 150,000 stock **E17-13** appreciation rights to its officers, entitling them to receive cash for the difference between the market price of its shares and a pre-established price of $10. The market price fluctuates as follows: 12/31/93: $14; 12/31/94: $8; 12/31/95: $20; 12/31/96: $18. The service period is four years and the exercise period is seven years.

Instructions

(a) Prepare a schedule that shows the amount of compensation expense that can be allocated to each year affected by the stock appreciation rights plan.

(b) Prepare the entry at 12/31/96 to record compensation expense, if any, in 1996.

(c) Prepare the entry on 12/31/96 assuming that all 150,000 SARs are exercised by all of the eligible officers.

E17-14 **(STOCK APPRECIATION RIGHTS)** Enright Limited establishes a stock appreciation rights program that entitles its new president, Erin Lindsay, to receive cash for the difference between the market price of the shares and a pre-established price of $30 (also market price) on December 31, 1993 on 40,000 SARs. The date of grant is December 31, 1993 and the required employment (service) period is four years. President Lindsay exercises all of the SARs in 1999. The market value of the stock fluctuates as follows: 12/31/94: $36; 12/31/95: $39; 12/31/96: $45; 12/31/97: $36; 12/31/98: $48.

Instructions

(a) Prepare a five-year (1994–1998) schedule of compensation expense pertaining to the 40,000 SARs that were granted to Lindsay.

(b) Prepare the journal entry for compensation expense in 1994, 1997, and 1998 relative to the 40,000 SARs.

E17-15 **(WEIGHTED-AVERAGE NUMBER OF SHARES)** Rosetta Ltd. uses a calendar year for financial reporting. The company is authorized to issue 9,000,000 no-par value common shares. At no time has Rosetta issued any potentially dilutive securities. Listed below is a summary of Rosetta's common share activities:

1. Number of common shares issued and outstanding at
   December 31, 1992 — 2,000,000

2. Shares issued as a result of a 10% stock dividend on
   September 30, 1993 — 200,000

3. Shares issued for cash on March 31, 1994 — 1,900,000
   Number of common shares issued and outstanding at
   December 31, 1994 — 4,100,000

4. A 2-for-1 stock split of Rosetta's common shares took place on March 31, 1995.

Instructions

(a) Compute the weighted-average number of common shares used in computing earnings per common share for 1993 on the 1994 comparative income statement.

(b) Compute the weighted-average number of common shares used in computing earnings per common share for 1994 on the 1994 comparative income statement.

(c) Compute the weighted-average number of common shares to be used in computing earnings per common share for 1994 on the 1995 comparative income statement.

(d) Compute the weighted-average number of common shares to be used in computing earnings per common share for 1995 on the 1995 comparative income statement.

(CMA adapted)

E17-16 **(EPS: SIMPLE CAPITAL STRUCTURE)** On January 1, 1994, the Sonetag Corp. had 480,000 shares of common stock outstanding. During 1994, it had the following transactions that affected the common stock account:

February 1   Issued 120,000 shares

March 1   Issued a 20% stock dividend

(Continued)

May 1	Acquired 96,000 shares of treasury stock
June 1	Issued a 3-for-1 stock split
October 1	Reissued 48,000 shares of treasury stock

Instructions

(a) Determine the weighted-average number of shares outstanding as of December 31, 1994.

(b) Assume that Sonetag Corp. earned net income of $3,456,000 during 1994. In addition, it had 100,000 shares of $9, no-par, nonconvertible, noncumulative preferred stock outstanding for the entire year. Because of liquidity considerations, however, the company did not declare and pay a preferred dividend in 1994. Compute earnings per share for 1994, using the weighted-average number of shares determined in part (a).

(c) Assume the same facts as in part (b), except that the preferred stock was cumulative. Compute earnings per share for 1994.

(d) Assume the same facts as in part (b), except that net income included an extraordinary gain of $864,000 and a loss from discontinued operations of $432,000. Both items are net of applicable income taxes. Compute earnings per share for 1994.

(EPS: SIMPLE CAPITAL STRUCTURE) Caruso Limited had 200,000 common shares outstanding on **E17-17** December 31, 1994. During 1995, the company issued 8,000 shares on May 1 and retired 14,000 shares on October 31. For 1995, Caruso Limited reported net income of $253,750 after a casualty loss of $44,660 (net of tax). *page 736*

Instructions

What earnings-per-share data should be reported in the financial statements, assuming that the casualty loss is extraordinary?

(EPS: SIMPLE CAPITAL STRUCTURE) Isaac Newton Inc. presented the following data: **E17-18**

Net income	$2,500,000
Preferred shares: 60,000 no-par shares outstanding no-par,	
$8 cumulative, not convertible	6,000,000
Common shares: Shares outstanding 1/1	670,500
Issued for cash, 5/1	300,000
Acquired treasury shares for cash, 8/1 - *treat as cancelled.*	150,000
2-for-1 stock split, 10/1	

Instructions

Compute earnings per share.

(EPS: SIMPLE CAPITAL STRUCTURE) A portion of the combined statement of income and retained **E17-19** earnings of Newton Ltd. for the current year is as follows:

Income before extraordinary item	$15,150,000
Extraordinary loss, net of applicable	
income tax (Note 1)	1,237,500
Net income	13,912,500
Retained earnings at beginning of year	82,997,500
	96,910,000

(Continued)

Dividends declared:		
On preferred shares: $6.00 per share	$ 300,000	
On common shares: $1.75 per share	14,875,000	15,175,000
Retained earnings at end of year		$81,735,000

Note 1. During the year, Newton Ltd. suffered a major casualty loss of $1,237,500 after applicable income tax reduction of $1,875,000.

pg 836

At the end of the current year, Newton Ltd. has outstanding 8,500,000 shares of no-par common and 50,000 shares of $6 preferred.

On April 1 of the current year, Newton Ltd. issued 1,000,000 common shares for $32 per share to help finance the casualty.

Instructions

Compute the earnings per share on common for the current year as it should be reported to shareholders.

E17-20 **(EPS: SIMPLE CAPITAL STRUCTURE)**   On January 1, 1994, Lemon Industries had shares outstanding as follows.

$6 cumulative preferred, no-par value, issued and outstanding 10,000 shares	$1,000,000
Common no-par value, issued and outstanding 215,000 shares	2,150,000

To acquire the net assets of three smaller companies, Lemon authorized the issuance of an additional 160,000 common shares. The acquisitions took place as follows.

Date of Acquisition		Shares Issued
Company A	April 1, 1994	50,000
Company B	July 1, 1994	80,000
Company C	October 1, 1994	30,000

On May 14, 1994, Lemon realized a $90,000 (before taxes) gain on the expropriation of investments originally purchased in 1983.

On December 31, 1994, Lemon recorded net income of $300,000 before tax and exclusive of the gain.

Instructions

Assuming a 40% tax rate, compute the earnings-per-share data that should appear on the financial statements of Lemon Industries as of December 31, 1994. Assume that the expropriation is extraordinary.

E17-21 **(EPS: SIMPLE CAPITAL STRUCTURE)**   At January 1, 1994, Wingfield Company's outstanding shares included:

280,000 shares of no-par value, $3.50 cumulative preferred
900,000 shares of no-par value common

Net income for 1994 was $2,631,650. No cash dividends were declared or paid during 1994. On February 15, 1995, however, all preferred dividends in arrears were paid, together with a 5% stock dividend on common shares. There were no dividends in arrears prior to 1994.

On April 1, 1994, 450,000 common shares were sold for $10 per share and on October 1, 1994, 110,000 common shares were purchased for $20 per share and held as treasury shares.

Instructions

Compute earnings per share for 1994. Assume that financial statements for 1994 were issued in March 1995.

(EPS WITH CONVERTIBLE BONDS, VARIOUS SITUATIONS) In 1993, Cinque Enterprises issued, **E17-22** at par, 60, $1,000, 8% bonds; each bond was convertible into 100 common shares. Cinque had revenues of $15,800 and expenses other than interest and taxes of $8,400 for 1994 (assume that the tax rate is 40%). Throughout 1994, 2,000 common shares were outstanding; none of the bonds were converted or redeemed.

Instructions

(a) Compute earnings per share for 1994.

(b) Assume the same facts as those assumed for (a), except that the 60 bonds were issued on September 1, 1994 (rather than in 1993), and none had been converted or redeemed.

(c) Assume the same facts as assumed for (a), except that 20 of the 60 bonds were actually converted on July 1, 1994.

(EPS WITH CONVERTIBLE BONDS) On June 1, 1992, Bonaparte Limited and Versailles Limited merged **E17-23** to form Decipher Ltd. A total of 800,000 shares were issued to complete the merger. The new corporation reports on a calendar-year basis.

On April 1, 1994, the company issued an additional 300,000 shares for cash. All 1,100,000 shares were outstanding on December 31, 1994.

Decipher Ltd. also issued $600,000 of 20-year, 8% convertible bonds at par on July 1, 1994. Each $1,000 bond converts to 50 common shares at any interest date. None of the bonds has been converted to date.

Decipher Ltd. is preparing its annual report for the fiscal year ending December 31, 1994. The annual report will show earnings-per-share figures based on a reported after-tax net income of $1,435,000 (the tax rate is 40%).

Instructions

Determine for 1994:

(a) The number of shares to be used for calculating:

1. Basic earnings per share.

2. Fully diluted earnings per share.

(b) The earnings figures to be used for calculating:

1. Basic earnings per share.

2. Fully diluted earnings per share.

(CMA adapted)

(BASIC AND FULLY DILUTED EPS) The Simon Corporation issued 10-year, $5,000,000 par, 8% callable **E17-24** convertible subordinated debentures on January 2, 1994. The bonds have a par value of $1,000, with interest payable annually. The current conversion ratio is 14:1, and in two years it will increase to 18:1. At the date of issue, the bonds were sold at 98. Bond discount is amortized on a straight-line basis. Simon's effective tax is 35%. Net income in 1994 was $9,500,000, and the company had 2,000,000 common shares outstanding during the entire year.

Instructions

(a) Prepare a schedule to compute basic and fully diluted earnings per share.

(b) Discuss how the schedule would differ if the security was convertible preferred shares.

E17-25 **(EPS WITH OPTIONS, VARIOUS SITUATIONS)** Petry Limited had the following capital structure at the end of 1993.

Debt: – 20-year, 8% bonds, $1,000 face value, convertible to 2 common shares any time after June 30, 2014	$2,000,000
Equity: – Preferred shares, no-par value, $6 cumulative and convertible to 2 common shares each at any time. Outstanding 10,000 shares	$ 360,000
– Common shares, no-par value, 50,000 outstanding	$ 250,000
– 5,000 warrants outstanding, one warrant and $60 may be exchanged for one common share	

On April 1, 1994, the company issued the following security:

– 10-year, 10% bonds, $1,000 face value, convertible into 4 common shares each at any time after June 30, 1999.	$ 100,000

Net income for 1994 was $600,000. The company has earned a 15% return before tax on net assets for the last five years. The company's current tax rate is 40%.

Instructions

Calculate the required earnings-per-share amounts for the company for 1994. Show your calculations.

E17-26 **(EPS WITH OPTIONS)** Venzuela Ltd. indicates that its net income for 1994 is $18,039,132, which includes a gain on casualty (net of tax) of $1,566,000. Its capital structure includes some common shares reserved under employee stock options (109,000 shares). The common shares outstanding for the year remain at 5,800,000. The controller, Bruce Springsteen, asks your advice concerning the earnings-per-share figure that they should present.

Instructions

What would you tell the controller? (Assume that the gain is extraordinary.)

E17-27 **(EPS WITH CONTINGENT ISSUANCE AGREEMENT)** Windsor Ltd. recently purchased Holiday Limited, a large western home painting corporation. One of the terms of the merger was that if Holiday's income for 1994 was $125,000 or more, 10,000 additional shares would be paid to Holiday's shareholders in 1995. Holiday's income for 1993 was $135,000.

Instructions

(a) Would the contingent shares have to be considered in Windsor's 1993 earnings-per-share computations?

(b) Assume the same facts, except that the 10,000 shares were contingent on Holiday's achieving a net income of $150,000 in 1994. Would the contingent shares have to be considered in Windsor's earnings-per-share computations?

(EPS WITH WARRANTS)   Howat Corporation earned $228,900 during a period when it had an average of **E17-28** 100,000 common shares outstanding. The company earns 15% after tax on its assets. Also outstanding were 15,000 warrants that could be exercised to purchase one common share for $10 for each warrant exercised.

Instructions

(a)   Are the warrants dilutive?

(b)   Compute basic earnings per share.

(c)   Compute fully diluted earnings per share.

(ETHICAL ISSUES, PERFORMANCE-BASED COMPENSATION)   The executive officers of **E17-29** ComputerTech Corporation have a performance-based compensation plan. The performance criteria of this plan is linked to growth in earnings-per-share. When annual earnings-per-share growth is 12%, executives earn 100% of the shares; if growth is 16%, executives earn 125%. If earnings-per-share growth is lower than 8%, executives receive no additional compensation.

In 1994, William Mattson, the controller of ComputerTech, reviews year-end estimates of bad debt expense and warranty expense. He calculates the EPS growth at 15%. Arnold Schwarz, a member of the executive group, remarks over lunch that the estimate of bad debt expense may be decreased so that EPS growth will be 16.1%. Mattson is not sure that he should do this because he believes that the current estimate of bad debts is sound. On the other hand, he recognizes that a great deal of subjectivity is involved in the computation.

Instructions

(a)   What, if any, is the ethical dilemma for Mattson?

(b)   Should Mattson's knowledge of the compensation plan be a factor that influences his estimate?

(c)   How would you respond to Schwarz's request?

———— **PROBLEMS** ————

(ENTRIES FOR VARIOUS DILUTIVE SECURITIES)   The shareholders' equity section of Risling Ltd. **P17-1** at the beginning of the current year appears below:

Common shares, no-par value, authorized 1,000,000	
shares, 300,000 shares issued and outstanding	$3,600,000
Retained earnings	570,000

During the current year the following transactions occurred:

1.   The company issued to the shareholders 100,000 rights. Ten rights are needed to buy one share at $32. The rights were void after 30 days. The market price of the shares at this time was $34 per share.

2.   The company sold to the public a $200,000, 10% bond issue at par. The company also issued with each $100 bond one detachable stock purchase warrant, which provided for the purchase of common at $30 per share. Shortly after issuance, similar bonds without warrants were selling at 94 and the warrants at $8.

3.   All but 8,000 of the rights issued in (1) were exercised in 30 days.

4.   At the end of the year, 80% of the warrants in (2) had been exercised and the remaining were outstanding and in good standing.

5.   During the current year, the company granted stock options for 5,000 common shares to company executives. The market price of the shares on that date was $38 and the option price was $30. The options were to expire at year end and were considered compensation for the current year.

6. All but 1,000 shares related to the stock option plan were exercised by year end. The expiration resulted because one of the executives failed to fulfil an obligation related to the employment contract.

Instructions

(a) Prepare general journal entries for the current year to record the transactions listed above.

(b) Prepare the shareholders' equity section of the balance sheet at the end of the current year. Assume that retained earnings at the end of the current year was $750,000.

P17-2 **(ENTRIES FOR CONVERSION, AMORTIZATION, AND INTEREST OF BONDS)**   Calorie Counter Ltd. issued $1,500,000 of convertible 10-year bonds on July 1, 1993. The bonds provide for 12% interest payable semiannually on January 1 and July 1. Expense and discount in connection with the issue was $36,000, which is being amortized monthly on a straight-line basis.

The bonds are convertible after one year into 8 shares of Calorie Counter Ltd.'s no-par value common shares for each $1,000 of bonds.

On August 1, 1994, $150,000 of bonds were turned in for conversion into common shares. Interest has been accrued monthly and paid as due. At the time of conversion any accrued interest on bonds being converted was paid in cash.

Instructions

Rounding to the nearest dollar, prepare the journal entries to record the conversion, amortization, and interest in connection with the bonds as of:

(a) August 1, 1994 (assume the book value method is used).

(b) August 31, 1994.

(c) December 31, 1994, including closing entries for the end of the year.

(AICPA adapted)

P17-3 **(STOCK OPTION PLAN)**   ISU Company adopted a stock option plan on November 30, 1992 that designated 70,000 shares of no-par value common as available for the granting of options to officers of the corporation, at a price of $10 per share. The market value was $13 per share on November 30, 1992.

On January 2, 1993, options to purchase 28,000 shares were granted to president Gene Rozanski—16,000 for services to be rendered in 1993 and 12,000 for services to be rendered in 1994. Also on that date, options to purchase 14,000 shares were granted to vice-president Gary Fish—7,000 for services to be rendered in 1993 and 7,000 for services to be rendered in 1994. The market value was $14 per share on January 2, 1993. The options were exercisable for a period of one year following the year in which the services were rendered.

In 1994, neither the president nor the vice-president exercised the options because the market price of the shares was below the exercise price. The market value was $9 per share on December 31, 1994, when the options for 1993 services lapsed.

On December 31, 1995, both Rozanski and Fish exercised their options for 12,000 and 7,000 shares, respectively, when the market price was $16 per share.

Instructions

(a) Prepare the necessary journal entries in 1992 when the stock option plan was adopted, in 1993 when options were granted, in 1994 when options lapsed, and in 1995 when options were exercised.

(b) What disclosure of the stock option plan should appear in the financial statements at December 31, 1992? At December 31, 1993? Assume that the stock options outstanding or exercised at any time are a significant financial item.

(SHAREHOLDERS' EQUITY DISCLOSURE AND EPS WITH CONVERTIBLE SECURITIES) P17-4

Tunnel Construction Company had the following account titles on its December 31, 1994 trial balance:

> $12 cumulative convertible preferred shares
> Common shares, no-par value
> Retained earnings

The following additional information about the Tunnel Construction Company was available for the year ended December 31, 1994:

1. 2,000,000 preferred shares were authorized, of which 1,000,000 were outstanding. All 1,000,000 shares outstanding were issued on January 2, 1991 for $110 per share. The preferred shares are convertible into common shares on a one-for-one basis until December 31, 2000; thereafter, the preferred shares cease to be convertible and are callable at $110 per share by the company. No preferred shares have been converted into common, and there were no dividends in arrears at December 31, 1994.

2. The common shares have been issued at various amounts since incorporation in 1976. Of the 5,000,000 shares authorized, there were 4,000,000 outstanding at January 1, 1994.

3. The company has an employee stock option plan under which certain key employees and officers may purchase common shares at 100% of the market price at the date of the option grant. All options are exercisable in instalments of one-third each year, commencing one year after the date of the grant, and expire if not exercised within four years of the grant date. On January 1, 1994, options for 80,000 shares were outstanding at prices ranging from $47 to $83 per share. Options for 22,000 shares were exercised at $47 to $79 per share during 1994. No options expired during 1994 and additional options for 16,000 shares were granted at $86 per share during the year. The 74,000 options outstanding at December 31, 1994 were exercisable at $54 to $86 per share; of these, 32,500 were exercisable at that date at prices ranging from $54 to $79 per share.

4. The company also has an employee stock purchase plan under which the company pays one-half and the employee pays one-half of the market price of the shares at the date of the subscription. During 1994, employees subscribed to 70,000 shares at an average price of $87 per share. All 70,000 shares were paid for and issued late in September 1994.

5. On December 31, 1994, a total of 450,000 common shares were set aside for the granting of future stock options and for future purchases under the employee stock purchase plan.

6. The only changes in the shareholders' equity for 1994 were those described above, 1994 net income, and cash dividends paid.

Instructions

(a) Prepare the shareholders' equity section of the balance sheet of Tunnel Construction Company at December 31, 1994 and substitute, where appropriate, "X" for unknown dollar amounts. Use good form and provide full disclosure. Write appropriate footnotes as they should appear in the published financial statements.

(b) Explain how the amount of the denominator should be determined to compute basic earnings per share for presentation in the financial statements. Be specific as to the handling of each item. If additional information is needed to determine whether an item should be included or excluded or the extent to which an item should be included, identify the information needed and how the item would be handled if the information were known. Assume Tunnel Construction Company had substantial net income for the year ended December 31, 1994.

(AICPA adapted)

(SIMPLE EPS AND EPS WITH STOCK OPTIONS) As auditor for Morris & Associates, you have been **P17-5** assigned to check Travel World Corporation's computation of earnings per share for the current year. The controller, Jason Sherwin, has supplied you with the following computations.

Net income	$3,461,500
Common shares issued and outstanding:	
Beginning of year	1,285,000
End of year	1,200,000
Average	1,242,500
Earnings per share:	

$$\frac{\$3,461,500}{1,242,500} = \$2.79 \text{ per share}$$

You have developed the following additional information:

1. There are no other equity securities in addition to the common shares.

2. There are no options or warrants outstanding to purchase common shares.

3. There are no convertible debt securities.

4. Activity in common shares during the year was as follows:

Outstanding Jan. 1	1,285,000
Treasury shares acquired Oct. 1	(250,000)
	1,035,000
Shares reissued Dec. 1	165,000
Outstanding Dec. 31	1,200,000

Instructions

(a) On the basis of the information above, do you agree with the controller's computation of earnings per share for the year? If you disagree, prepare a revised computation of earnings per share.

(b) Assume the same facts as those in (a), except that options had been issued to purchase 175,000 shares of common at $10 per share. These options were outstanding at the beginning of the year and none had been exercised or cancelled during the year. The company earns a rate of return of 10% after taxes. Prepare a computation of earnings per share.

P17-6   **(SIMPLE EPS: TWO-YEAR PRESENTATION)**   Jackson Corporation is preparing the comparative financial statements for the annual report to its shareholders for fiscal years ended May 31, 1993 and May 31, 1994. The income from operations for each year was $1,600,000 and $2,000,000, respectively. In both years, the company incurred a 10% interestexpense on $2,400,000 of debt, an obligation that requires interest-only payments for five years. The company experienced a loss of $500,000 from a fire in its Dartmouth facility in February 1994, which was determined to be an extraordinary loss. The company uses a 40% effective tax rate for income taxes.

    The capital structure of Jackson Corporation on June 1, 1992 consisted of 2,000,000 common shares outstanding and 20,000, $4 cumulative preferred shares of no-par value. There were no preferred dividends in arrears and the company had not issued any convertible securities, options, or warrants.

    On October 1, 1993, Jackson sold an additional 500,000 common shares at $20 per share. Jackson distributed a 20% stock dividend on the common shares outstanding on January 1, 1994. On December 1, 1994, Jackson was able to sell an additional 800,000 common shares at $22 per share. These were the only common share transactions that occurred during the two fiscal years.

Instructions

(a) Identify whether the capital structure at Jackson Corporation is a simple or complex capital structure, and explain why.

(b) Determine the weighted-average number of shares that Jackson Corporation would use in calculating earnings per share for the fiscal year ended:

1. May 31, 1993.

2. May 31, 1994.

(c) Prepare, in good form, a comparative income statement, beginning with income from operations, for Jackson Corporation for the fiscal years ended May 31, 1993 and May 31, 1994. This statement will be included in Jackson's annual report and should display the appropriate earnings-per-share presentations.

(CMA adapted)

(EPS COMPUTATION OF BASIC AND FULLY DILUTED EPS)   Ed Halvorson of the controller's office **P17-7** of Dalmeny Corporation is given the assignment of determining the basic and fully diluted earnings-per-share values for the year ending December 31, 1994. Halvorson has compiled the following information:

1. The company is authorized to issue 12,000,000 no-par value common shares. As of December 31, 1993, 4,000,000 shares had been issued and were outstanding.

2. A total of 800,000 shares of an authorized 1,200,000 convertible preferred shares had been issued on July 1, 1993. The shares were issued at $25 each, and they have a cumulative dividend of $2 per share. The shares are convertible into common at the rate of one share of convertible preferred for one share of common. The rate of conversion is to be automatically adjusted for stock splits and stock dividends. Dividends are paid quarterly on September 30, December 31, March 31, and June 30.

3. Dalmeny Corporation is subject to a 40% income tax rate.

4. The after-tax net income for the year ended December 31, 1994 was $14,554,000.

The following specific activities took place during 1994:

1. January 1: A 5% common stock dividend was issued. The dividend had been declared on December 1, 1993 to all shareholders of record on December 29, 1993.

2. April 1: A total of 200,000 shares of the $2 convertible preferred was converted into common. The company issued new common shares and retired the preferred shares. This was the only conversion of the preferred during 1994.

3. July 1: A two-for-one split of common became effective on this date. The board of directors had authorized the split on June 1.

4. August 1: A total of 300,000 common shares was issued to acquire a factory building.

5. November 1: A total of 24,000 common shares was purchased on the open market at $9 per share. These shares were to be held as treasury shares and were still in the treasury as of December 31, 1994.

6. Cash dividends to common shareholders were declared and paid as follows:

   (a)   April 15: $0.30 per share.

   (b)   October 15: $0.20 per share.

7. Cash dividends to preferred shareholders were declared and paid as scheduled.

Instructions

(a)   Determine the number of shares used to compute basic earnings per share for the year ended December 31, 1994.

(b)   Determine the number of shares used to compute fully diluted earnings per share for the year ended December 31, 1994.

(c) Compute the adjusted net income to be used as the numerator in the basic earnings-per-share calculation for the year ended December 31, 1994.

P17-8 **(EPS WITH STOCK DIVIDEND AND EXTRAORDINARY ITEMS)** Bluefish Limited is preparing the comparative financial statements to be included in the annual report to shareholders. Bluefish employs a fiscal year ending May 31.

Income from operations before income taxes for Bluefish was $1,420,000 and $650,000, respectively, for fiscal years ended May 31 of both 1994 and 1993. Bluefish experienced an extraordinary loss of $520,000 because of an earthquake on March 3, 1994. A 40% combined income tax rate pertains to any and all of Bluefish Limited's profits, gains, and losses.

Bluefish's capital structure consists of preferred and common shares. The company has not issued any convertible securities or warrants and there are no outstanding stock options.

Bluefish issued 50,000 no-par value, $6 cumulative preferred shares in 1980. All of these shares are outstanding and no preferred dividends are in arrears.

There were 1,500,000 no-par value common shares outstanding on June 1, 1992. On September 1, 1992, Bluefish sold an additional 500,000 common shares at $17 each. Bluefish distributed a 20% stock dividend on the common shares outstanding on December 1, 1993. These were the only common share transactions during the past two fiscal years.

Instructions

(a) Determine the weighted-average number of common shares that would be used in computing earnings per share on the current comparative income statement for:

1. The year ended May 31, 1993.

2. The year ended May 31, 1994.

(b) Starting with income from operations before income taxes, prepare a comparative income statement for the years ended May 31 of both 1994 and 1993. The statement will be part of Bluefish Limited's annual report to shareholders and should include appropriate earnings-per-share presentation.

(c) The capital structure of a corporation is the result of its past financing decisions. Furthermore, the earnings-per-share data presented on a corporation's financial statements are dependent on the capital structure.

1. Explain why Bluefish Limited is considered to have a simple capital structure.

2. Describe how earnings-per-share data would be presented for a corporation that has a complex capital structure.

P17-9 **(COMPREHENSIVE EPS CALCULATION WITH COMPLICATING FEATURES)** The controller of Hamilton Corporation has requested assistance in determining income, basic earnings per share, and fully diluted earnings per share for presentation in the company's income statement for the year ended September 30, 1994. As currently calculated, the company's net income is $850,000 for fiscal year 1993–1994. The controller has indicated that the income figure might be adjusted for the following transactions that were recorded by charges or credits directly to retained earnings (the amounts are net of applicable income taxes):

1. The sum of $350,000, applicable to a breached 1990 contract, was received as a result of a lawsuit. Prior to the award, legal counsel was uncertain about the outcome of the suit.

2. A gain of $280,000 was realized from an expropriation of property (extraordinary).

3. A "gain" of $165,000 was realized on the sale of treasury shares.

4. A special inventory write-off of $210,000 was made, of which $140,000 applied to goods manufactured prior to October 1, 1993.

Your working papers disclose the following opening balances and transactions in the company's share capital accounts during the year:

1. Common shares (at October 1, 1993, average issue price $10, authorized 450,000 shares; effective December 1, 1993, authorized 900,000 shares):

    > Balance, October 1, 1993: Issued and outstanding 100,000 shares
    > December 1, 1993: 100,000 shares issued in a 2-for-1 stock split
    > December 1, 1993: 420,000 shares issued at $39 per share

2. Treasury shares, common:

    > March 1, 1994: Purchased 60,000 shares at $37.25 per share
    > April 1, 1994: Sold 60,000 shares at $40 per share

3. Stock purchase warrants, Series A (initially, each warrant was exchangeable with $60 for one common share; effective December 1, 1993, each warrant became exchangeable for two common shares at $30 per share):

    > October 1, 1993: 40,000 warrants issued at $6 each

4. Stock purchase warrants, Series B (each warrant is exchangeable with $45 for one common share):

    > April 1, 1994: 30,000 warrants authorized and issued at $10 each

5. First mortgage bonds, 9%, due 2009 (nonconvertible; priced to yield 8% when issued):

    > Balance, October 1, 1993: Authorized, issued, and outstanding—the face value of $2,100,000

6. Convertible debentures, 7%, due 2013 (initially, each $1,000 bond was convertible at any time until maturity into 12½ common shares; effective December 1, 1993, the conversion rate became 25 shares for each bond):

    > October 1, 1993: Authorized and issued at their face value (no premium or discount) of $3,600,000

Instructions

(a) Prepare a schedule computing net income as it should be presented in the company's income statement for the year ended September 30, 1994.

(b) Assuming that net income after income taxes for the year was $3,702,600 and that there were no extraordinary items, prepare a schedule computing (1) the basic earnings per share and (2) the fully diluted earnings per share that should be presented in the company's income statement for the year ended September 30, 1994. A supporting schedule computing the numbers of shares to be used in these computations should also be prepared. (Assume an income tax rate of 40% and that the company earns 20% after tax on assets.)

(AICPA adapted)

(COMPREHENSIVE EPS CALCULATION WITH COMPLICATING FEATURES)   The shareholders' **P17-10** equity section of Reinhard Company's balance sheet as of December 31, 1994 contains the following:

$2 cumulative convertible preferred shares (no-par value authorized 1,500,000 shares, issued 1,400,000, converted to common 800,000, and outstanding 600,000 shares; liquidation value, $30 per share, aggregating $19,500,000)	$15,000,000
Common shares, authorized, 15,000,000 shares; issued and outstanding, 9,200,000 shares	2,300,000

(Continued)

Contributed surplus	30,500,000
Retained earnings	45,050,000
Total shareholders' equity	$92,850,000

On April 1, 1994, Reinhard Company acquired the business and assets and assumed the liabilities of Stein Corporation in a transaction accounted for as a pooling of interests. For each of Stein Corporation's 2,400,000 common shares outstanding, the owner received one Reinhard common share. (**Hint:** In a pooling of interests, shares are considered outstanding for the entire year.)

Included in the liabilities of Reinhard Company are 10% convertible subordinated debentures issued at their face value of $20,000,000 in 1993. The debentures are due in 2010 and until then are convertible into Reinhard Company common at the rate of six common shares for each $100 debenture. To date, none of these has been converted.

On April 2, 1994, Reinhard Company issued 1,400,000 convertible preferred shares at $40 per share. Quarterly dividends to December 31, 1994 have been paid on these shares. The preferred shares are convertible into common at the rate of two common shares for each preferred share. On October 1, 1994, 200,000 shares and on November 1, 1994, 600,000 preferred shares were converted into common.

During July 1993, Reinhard Company granted options to its officers and key employees to purchase 600,000 of the company's common shares at a price of $20 per share. The options do not become exercisable until 1995.

Reinhard Company's consolidated net income for the year ended December 31, 1993 was $11,400,000. The provision for income taxes was computed at a rate of 40%. The company earns 20% after tax on its assets.

Instructions

(a) Prepare a schedule that shows for 1994 the computation of:

1. The weighted-average number of shares for computing basic earnings per share.

2. The weighted-average number of shares for computing fully diluted earnings per share.

(b) Prepare a schedule that shows for 1994 the computation to the nearest cent of:

1. Baic earnings per share.

2. Fully diluted earnings per share.

(AICPA adapted)

P17-11 (**BASIC AND FULLY DILUTED EARNINGS PER SHARE**)   Selected accounts from the general ledger of Mitosis Company Ltd. as of December 31, 1994, are presented below:

Bonds payable, 9½%; each $1,000 bond is convertible into 200 common shares	$40,000
Bonds payable, 10½%; each $1,000 bond is convertible into 150 common shares	$200,000
Common shares, no-par value, authorized 500,000 shares; issued and outstanding throughout the period, 80,000	$680,000
Stock dividend issued December 31, 1994, 40,000 shares (not included in the 80,000 shares above)	340,000
Retained earnings (includes effect of dividends on all shares)	$480,000

The 1994 income included the following:

Income before extraordinary items	$125,000
Extraordinary gain	12,000
Net income	137,000

In addition, there were 8,000 stock options outstanding. Each option, together with $40 cash, may be exchanged for one common share. These options may not be exercised until after December 31, 2007. The company's income is taxed at 40%.

Instructions

(a) Calculate basic earnings per share for 1994.

(b) Calculate fully diluted earnings per share for 1994, on net income only.

(c) What effect does the existence of stock options have on the calculation of earnings-per-share figures for 1994?

(BASIC AND FULLY DILUTED EARNINGS PER SHARE) Zakreski Limited had the following capital **P17-12** structure at December 31, 1994.

	1994	1993
Number of common shares	336,000	300,000
Number of nonconvertible preferred shares	10,000	10,000
Amount of 8% convertible bonds	$1,000,000	$1,000,000

The following additional information is available:

1. On September 1, 1994, Zakreski sold 36,000 additional common shares. ✓

2. Net income for the year 1994 was $750,000. ✓

3. During 1994, dividends in the amount of $3.00 per share were paid on the preferred shares. ✓

4. Each $1,000 bond can be converted into 40 common shares. ✓

5. There were unexercised stock options, outstanding since 1989, that allow holders to purchase 30,000 common shares at $22.50 per share. ✓

6. Warrants to purchase 20,000 common shares at $38 per share were outstanding at the end of 1994. ✓

7. The company's income for the current year is taxed at a 40% rate. Management believes that the company's before-tax rate of return on investments is 14%.

(CMA adapted)

Instructions

Prepare the basic and fully diluted earnings-per-share figures for 1994.

─── FINANCIAL REPORTING PROBLEM ───

Refer to the financial statements and notes of Moore Corporation presented in Appendix 5A and answer the following questions.

1. At December 31, 1991, Moore Corporation had outstanding 1,744,250 options granted under a long-term incentive plan. How might these options affect the calculation of various earnings-per-share amounts?

2. Explain how the lapsing of 8,100 options during 1991 would affect expense and shareholders' equity.

3. How many options were granted in 1991? How would the granting of these options affect income for the year?

Investments: Temporary and Long-Term

To engage in the production and sale of goods or services, a business enterprise must invest funds in many types of assets: monetary assets—cash and receivables; productive tangible assets—inventories, plant and equipment, and land; and intangible assets—patents, licences, trademarks, and goodwill. Sound financial management requires not only that cash and other assets be available when needed in the business *but also that cash and near cash assets not immediately needed in the conduct of regular operations be invested advantageously in a variety of securities and other income-producing assets*. In many cases, *investments produce considerable revenue in addition to that derived from regular operations*.

Accounting for investments involves classification (current or noncurrent), measurement (valuation), and disclosure (accounting methods used). These problems are compounded by the complexity and diversity of the underlying financial instruments.[1] Innovative and complex securities[2] that are currently used for investment purposes must be accounted for according to their substance rather than legal form. The terms "debt" and "equity" are used here to denote the substance of a financial instrument that, for simplicity, will be the same as the form of the underlying security. This chapter, which covers accounting for both temporary and long-term investments, is divided into three sections: (1) temporary (short-term) investments, (2) long-term investments, and (3) cash surrender value of life insurance and special-purpose funds. The appendix to this chapter covers changes from and to the equity method of accounting for investments in shares.

SECTION 1
TEMPORARY INVESTMENTS

Temporary investments ordinarily consist of **short-term paper** (certificates of deposit, treasury bills, and commercial paper), **marketable debt securities** (government and corporate bonds), and **marketable equity securities** (preferred and common shares) acquired with cash not immediately needed in operations. The investments are held temporarily in place of cash and are capable of prompt liquidation when current financing needs make such conversion desirable. Temporary investments should be:

1. Readily marketable.

2. Intended to be converted into cash as needed within one year or the operating cycle, whichever is longer.

---

[1] A financial instrument is defined as "any contract that gives rise to both a . . . financial asset of one entity and a . . . financial liability or equity instrument of another entity" in "Financial Instruments," *Exposure Draft of the Accounting Standards Board* (Toronto: CICA, September 1991), par. .005(a).

[2] These are securities that are either debt or equity (or a combination) in legal form but, in substance, represent the opposite. For example, preferred shares that must be redeemed are legally considered equity but possess the substance of debt.

Readily marketable means that the security can be sold quite easily. If the shares are closely held (not publicly traded), there may be no market, or a limited market at best, for the security and its classification as a long-term investment may be more appropriate. Intent to convert is an extremely difficult principle to apply in practice. Generally, **intention to convert** is substantiated when the invested cash is considered a contingency fund to be used whenever a need arises or when investment is made from cash temporarily idle because of the seasonality of the business. In classifying investments, management's expressed intent should be supported by evidence, such as the history of investment activities, events subsequent to the balance sheet date, and the nature and purpose of the investment.

In contrast, long-term investments are purchased as part of some long-range program or plan, such as for long-term appreciation in the price of the security, ownership for control purposes, or maintaining or enhancing supplier or customer relationships.

ACCOUNTING FOR TEMPORARY INVESTMENTS

Objective 1

Describe the accounting for temporary investments in debt and equity securities.

Temporary investments consist of **marketable equity securities** and **marketable debt securities**. Accounting for these two kinds of investments differs as a result of the way that income is earned on each. Most equity securities generate dividend income, debt securities earn interest, and both types give rise to market gains or losses.

An **equity security** is "any contract that evidences a residual interest in the assets of an entity after deducting all of its liabilities."[3] Such securities include ownership shares (e.g., common and preferred) or the right to acquire (e.g., warrants, rights, and call options) or dispose of (e.g., put options) ownership shares in an enterprise at fixed or determinable prices. An equity security does not normally have a maturity date nor does it guarantee a return on the investment to the owner. Treasury shares and mandatorily redeemable preferred shares are excluded from the definition of equity security. **Marketable** means that the security is readily tradeable on a market at a minimal cost and without undue delay.

Acquisition of Marketable Securities

Marketable Equity Securities. Investments in marketable equity securities, like other assets, are recorded at cost when acquired. *Cost includes the purchase price and incidental acquisition costs such as brokerage commissions and taxes.* "Cost" generally refers to the purchase price plus other direct costs of acquisition such as brokers' commissions, legal fees, and taxes. The term "cost" is also used to refer to the current carrying value of a security that has been written down to recognize an impairment that is not a temporary decline in its value. In addition, when a security is transferred between current and noncurrent classifications, it is assigned a new "cost" basis that is also referred to as cost.

Marketable Debt Securities. The acquisition of debt securities is recorded at cost, which includes taxes and brokerage commissions, if any. If the debt securities are bonds purchased between interest dates, the interest accruing to the date of purchase is segregated from the acquisition cost and classified appropriately. For example, Western Publishing Limited invested some of its excess cash in the bond market by purchasing $100,000 face value 10% bonds at 86% of face value on April 1, 1994, interest payable semiannually on July 1 and January 1. The brokerage commission associated with this purchase was $1,720. The cash outlay is as shown below.

Purchase price of bonds ($100,000 × 86%)	$86,000
Commission	1,720
Cost of bonds acquired	87,720
Accrued interest January 1 to April 1 ($100,000 × 10% × 3/12)	2,500
Cash payment (due to the vendor)	$90,220

---

[3] *Exposure Draft*, "Financial Instruments," September 1991, par. .005(d).

The journal entry to record this transaction is:

April 1, 1994

Temporary Investments (or Marketable Securities)	87,720	
Interest Revenue (or Accrued Interest Receivable)	2,500	
Cash		90,220

Generally, the discount or premium on temporary bond investments is not recorded in the accounts and not amortized because the investment is ordinarily not expected to be held to maturity. The journal entry to record the receipt of interest as of July 1 is as follows:

July 1, 1994

Cash	5,000	
Interest Revenue		5,000

Accounting for Changes in Market Value

A single share or unit of a marketable security has a **market price** that, when multiplied by the number of shares or units of that specific security, produces the aggregate market price referred to as the **market value**. The market price generally changes as transactions involving the security occur. The central issue for many years has been: To what extent should the financial statements reflect the changes in market value of marketable securities that are held as temporary investments?

The CICA resolved this issue in relation to marketable securities by requiring that *when the market value of temporary investments has declined below the carrying value, they should be carried at market value.*[4] (Losses associated with write-downs to the lower of cost and market are not allowable for tax purposes.) Valuing securities at the lower of cost and market *may be applied to the entire portfolio or to each security in the portfolio*. When it is applied to the entire portfolio, then the amount by which aggregate cost exceeds market value (the net unrealized loss) of the short-term marketable equity securities portfolio should be accounted for as a "valuation allowance" and the unrealized loss reported in the determination of net income for the period. If, on the other hand, the lower of cost and market method of valuation is applied to each security, then the sum of individual security excesses of cost over market value is reported as a valuation allowance. Further, realized gains and losses and changes in the valuation allowance for a portfolio of temporary investments should be used in the determination of net income of the period in which they occur. These valuation adjustments are recorded as part of the adjustment process whenever statements are to be prepared. In subsequent periods, recoveries of market value may be recognized to the extent that the market valuation does not exceed the lesser of original cost and original cost adjusted for any impairment. In substance, this procedure involves adjusting carrying values down to market at each reporting date, and up only to the extent that previous write-downs to market have been recovered. Thus, unrealized losses and recoveries on short-term marketable securities flow through the income statement.[5] The following discussion illustrates application of the lower of cost and market method to marketable securities portfolios that are classified as current assets.

---

[4] *CICA Handbook* (Toronto: CICA), Section 3010, par. .06.

[5] Specialized industries (investment companies, brokers and dealers in securities, stock life insurance companies, and fire and casualty insurance companies) that carry marketable equity securities at market do not have to follow lower of cost or market. As indicated earlier, the accounting treatment for noncurrent marketable equity securities is different and is discussed in Section 2 of this chapter.

Illustration: 1993. National Service Corporation made the following purchases of marketable securities as temporary investments during the year 1993, which is the first year in which National invested in marketable securities:

February 23, 1993: Purchased 10,000 shares of Northeast Industries, Inc. common at a market price of $51.50 per share plus brokerage commissions[6] of $4,400 (total cost, $519,400; average cost per share, $519,400/10,000 = $51.94).

April 10, 1993: Purchased 10,000 shares of Bell Soup Co. common at a market price of $31.50 per share plus brokerage commissions of $2,500 (total cost, $317,500; average cost per share, $317,500/10,000 = $31.75).

August 3, 1993: Purchased 5,000 shares of Reggies Pulp Co. common at a market price of $28 per share plus brokerage commissions of $1,350 (total cost, $141,350; average cost per share, $141,350/5,000 = $28.27).

October 1, 1993: Purchased $100,000, 12% Cook Co. bonds at 92 plus brokerage commissions of $1,530 and accrued interest. Interest is payable on January 1 and July 1.

Each of the equity purchases above is recorded at total acquisition cost (market price plus commissions) by a debit to Marketable Securities and a credit to Cash. The purchase of the bonds is recorded by debiting Marketable Securities $93,530 and Interest Revenue (or Accrued Interest Receivable) $3,000, and crediting Cash for $96,530.

During the year National made the following security sale:

September 23, 1993: Sold 5,000 shares of Northeast Industries, Inc. common at a market price of $58 per share less brokerage commissions of $2,780 (proceeds, $287,220).

The entry to record this sale would be as follows:

Cash [(5,000 × $58) − $2,780]	287,220	
Marketable Securities (5,000 × $51.94)		259,700
Gain on Sale of Securities		27,520

On December 31, 1993, National Service Corporation determined the carrying value of its portfolio in short-term marketable equity securities to be as shown below.

Short-term marketable securities	Face Value or # of Shares	Cost	Unrealized Market	Gain (Loss)
		December 31, 1993		
Northeast Industries, Inc.	$ 5,000	$259,700	$275,000	$ 15,300
Cook Co. bonds	100,000	93,530	92,500	(1,030)
Bell Soup Co.	10,000	317,500	304,000	(13,500)
Reggies Pulp Co.	5,000	141,350	104,000	(37,350)
Total of portfolio		$812,080	$775,500	$(36,580)
Balance required in the valuation allowance				$(36,580)

---

[6] Brokerage commissions are incurred both when buying and selling securities; such commissions generally range between 1% and 3% of trade value on lots of 1,000 or less and $12.50 to $30.00 per hundred shares on lots of between 1,000 and 100,000 shares.

Applying the lower of cost and market method to National's securities portfolio results in a carrying value of $775,500. The net unrealized loss of $36,580 represents the aggregate excess of cost over the market value of National's portfolio of marketable securities classified as current assets. The unrealized loss of $36,580 is recorded as follows:

December 31, 1993

Unrealized Loss on Valuation of Marketable Securities	36,580	
Allowance for Excess of Cost of Marketable		
Securities Over Market Value		36,580
(To recognize a loss equal to the excess of cost		
over market value of marketable equity securities)		

The loss account appears on the income statement in the Other Expenses and Losses section and therefore would be included in income before extraordinary items in National's 1993 financial statements. The allowance account appears on the balance sheet among current assets as an asset valuation (contra) account deducted from the portfolio cost of $812,080 to produce a carrying amount of its portfolio of $775,500.

Illustration: 1994. During 1994, National made the following sale and purchase of marketable securities:

March 22, 1994: Sold 5,000 shares of Reggies Pulp Co. common at a market price of $17.50 per share less brokerage commissions of $1,590 (proceeds, $85,910).

July 2, 1994: Purchased 10,000 shares of James Bay Gas & Electric common at a market price of $20.25 per share plus brokerage commissions of $2,300 (total cost, $204,800).

On December 31, 1994, National Service Corporation determined the carrying value of its portfolio in short-term marketable securities to be as follows.

	December 31, 1993		
Short-term marketable securities	Cost	Market	Unrealized Gain (Loss)
Northeast Industries, Inc.	$259,700	$312,500	$52,800
Cook Co. Bonds	93,530	93,000	(530)
Bell Soup Co.	317,500	327,500	10,000
James Bay Gas & Electric	204,800	202,500	(2,300)
Total of portfolio	$875,530	$935,500	$59,970
Balance required in the valuation allowance			$ –0–

Applying the lower of cost and market method to National's portfolio at December 31, 1994 results in a carrying value of $875,530 and elimination of the balance in the valuation allowance account of $36,580. The adjustment of the valuation allowance is recorded as follows:

December 31, 1994

Allowance for Excess of Cost of Marketable		
Securities Over Market Value	36,580	
Recovery of Unrealized Loss on Valuation of		
Marketable Securities		36,580

(Continued)

(To record a reduction in the valuation allowance
due to increase in market value of the marketable
securities portfolio classified as current assets)

The Recovery of Unrealized Loss on Valuation of Marketable Securities $36,580 is reported in the Other Revenues and Gains section and therefore would be included in income before extraordinary items on National's 1994 income statement.

Note that the *recovery is recognized only to the extent that unrealized losses were previously recognized*. That is, the write-down of $36,580 in 1993 representing net unrealized losses may be reversed but only to the extent that the resulting carrying value of the portfolio does not exceed original cost or, in other words, to the extent that a balance exists in the valuation allowance account at the date of write-up. Also, *note that the valuation is applied to the total portfolio and not to individual securities*.

Under this approach, the reversal of the write-down does not represent a recognition of an unrealized gain. The unrealized gain is the excess of market value over cost, or the $59,970 net difference between aggregate cost and aggregate market value of National's portfolio on December 31, 1994. The write-down is viewed as establishing a valuation allowance representing the estimated reduction in the realizable value of the portfolio, and subsequent market increases are viewed as having reduced or eliminated the requirements for such an allowance. In other words, the reversal of the write-down represents a change in an accounting estimate of an unrealized loss.[7]

If National's investment portfolio of short-term marketable securities had suffered an additional loss of market value during 1994 instead of the increase described above, a loss would have been charged to 1994 expense. It follows that the valuation allowance would have been increased (credited) by the amount of the additional write-down.

Reclassification. If a marketable security is *transferred from the current to the noncurrent portfolio*, or vice versa, the security should be transferred at the lower of its cost and market value at the date of transfer. If market value is less than cost, the market value becomes the new cost basis, and the difference is accounted for as if it was a realized loss and included in the determination of net income.[8] This procedure has the effect of accounting for an unrealized loss at the date of transfer in the same manner as if it had been realized, thusreducing the incentive to manipulate income by transferring securities between the current and noncurrent portfolios.

For example, if National Service Corporation on December 31, 1993 had reclassified the Bell Soup Co. securities from current to noncurrent, the *unrealized* loss of $13,500 ($317,500 − $304,000, page 878) would have been recorded as a *realized* loss of $13,500, along with the following reclassification:

December 31, 1993

Long-Term Investments	304,000	
Loss on Reclassification of Securities	13,500	
Marketable Securities—Current		317,500

Of course, if this reclassification had taken place, the unrealized loss (as well as the allowance) at December 31, 1993 would have been $23,080 ($36,580 − $13,500) instead of $36,580.

Disposition of Temporary Investments

Temporary investments in marketable securities are sold when cash needs develop or when good investment management dictates a change in the securities held. The owner who sells the securities incurs costs such as brokerage commissions and receives only the net proceeds for the sale. The difference between the net proceeds from the sale of a marketable security and its cost represents

---

[7] This method has been adopted in the United States by *FASB Statement No. 12*, par. 29(c).
[8] *Ibid.*, par. 10.

the **realized gain or loss**. At the date of sale, no regard is given to unrealized losses or recoveries or the amount accumulated in the valuation allowance account because the valuation allowance relates to the total portfolio and not to specific security holdings.

For example, in the previous illustration National Service Corporation sold 5,000 shares of Northeast Industries, Inc. common on September 23, 1993 for $58 per share, incurring $2,780 in brokerage commissions. The gain on the sale is computed as follows.

Gross selling price of 5,000 shares @ $58	$290,000
Less: Commissions	2,780
Net proceeds from sale	287,220
Cost of 5,000 shares ($519,400/2)	259,700
Gain on sale	$ 27,520

The sale is recorded as follows:

September 23, 1993

Cash	287,220	
Marketable Securities		259,700
Realized Gain on Sale of Marketable Securities		27,520
(To record sale of 5,000 shares of Northeast Industries common held as a temporary investment at a gain)		

National Service Corporation also sold 5,000 shares of Reggies Pulp Co. on March 22, 1994 for $17.50 per share, incurring $1,590 in brokerage commissions. The loss on the sale is computed as shown below.

Cost of 5,000 shares ($28.27 × 5,000)		$141,350
Gross proceeds from sale ($17.50 × 5,000)	$87,500	
Less commissions	1,590	
Net proceeds from sale		85,910
Loss on sale		$ 55,440

As in the 1993 security sale, the amount of net proceeds from the 1994 sale of securities is compared with the original cost to determine the gain or loss and recorded as follows:

March 22, 1994

Cash	85,910	
Realized Loss on Sale of Marketable Securities	55,440	
Marketable Securities		141,350
(To record the sale of 5,000 shares of Reggies Pulp Co. common held as a temporary investment)		

When marketable debt securities are sold, the difference between the cost (or carrying value) and the selling price is recorded as a gain or loss. For example, if National Service Corporation sold the Cook Company bonds (that it acquired on October 1, 1993) on November 1, 1994 at 98 plus accrued interest, the computation of the gain would be as follows (assume that commissions associated with the sale are $1,870).

Selling price of bonds ($100,000 × .98)	$98,000
Less commissions	(1,870)
Net proceeds	96,130
Carrying amount of bonds	93,530*
Gain on sale of bonds	$ 2,600

*Discount is not amortized on bonds held as temporary investments.

The journal entry to record this transaction is:

November 1, 1994

Cash	100,130	
Interest Revenue (100,000 × .12 × 4/12)		4,000
Marketable Securities		93,530
Gain on Sale of Temporary Investment		2,600

The gain on sale enters into the determination of income from continuing operations before extraordinary items. In cases where there are numerous purchases of similar securities, the average cost flow assumption must be applied to match the proper cost with the proceeds of sale.

The presence or absence of realized gains or losses recorded since the last portfolio valuation as a result of sales of marketable securities has no effect on the method of computing the lower of cost and market for the remaining portfolio at the end of the period.

Even if a current marketable security is not sold but a decline in its market value is judged to be a permanent impairment, the market value becomes the new cost basis for inclusion in the year-end portfolio evaluation.

Valuation at Market

The use of the lower of cost and market and discontinuance of original cost as the carrying amount of a current asset portfolio of marketable securities is quite firmly established in Canadian practice.[9] Using original cost as the basis when the market value of the portfolio is lower has the effect of deferring unrealized losses on the basis of the expectation of a future recovery in market value, which may or may not occur.

However, some accountants are unhappy with Section 3010 of the *CICA Handbook*. They argue that market value, whether higher or lower than cost, should be recognized in the accounts. It is considered inconsistent to reduce the carrying value of the securities to an amount below cost without increasing their carrying value when market value is above cost. *Market value proponents indicate that gains or losses develop when the value of the investments changes and not when the investments are sold.* Recognition of losses only is conservative and does not reflect the underlying economics when prices increase. Because of this situation, management can to some extent manipulate net income by determining when securities are sold to realize gains. For example, an enterprise whose earnings are low in one year might sell some securities that have appreciated in past years to offset the low income figure from current operations.

A major objection to the use of market value is that fluctuations in earnings result as the market price of the equity securities changes. To illustrate, at one time Leaseway Transportation estimated that the use of market value in one year would have reduced earnings 28%, but that the

---

[9] The use of market values for temporary investments has been proposed in CICA *Exposure Draft*, "Financial Instruments," September 1991. If this proposal is adopted as a *Handbook* section, temporary investments would be reported at market value on each balance sheet date. Gains and losses in market values would be recognized in income each year.

use of market value a year later would have increased earnings approximately 21%. Most companies dislike these types of fluctuations in earnings because they have little control over these changes and are apprehensive of adverse effects on company share prices.

Recognition of impairment as opposed to improvement in the carrying amount of a securities portfolio is still the dominant attitude of accounting. As a result, it is not surprising that the profession adopted a compromise position between market valuation and historical cost (lower of cost and market). The following rationale was given for not using market value alone as the determinant of carrying value: "Consideration of that alternative would raise pervasive issues concerning the valuation of other types of assets, including the concept of historic cost versus current or realizable value."[10]

FINANCIAL STATEMENT DISCLOSURE OF TEMPORARY INVESTMENTS

Cash, the most liquid asset, is listed first in the current asset section of the balance sheet. All unrestricted cash, whether on hand (including petty cash) or on deposit at a financial institution, is presented as a single item, using the caption "Cash."

Temporary investments in marketable securities usually rank next to cash in liquidity and should be listed in the current asset section of the balance sheet, immediately after Cash. Marketable securities that are held for other than liquidity and temporary investment purposes should not be classified as current assets but as long-term investments.

As of the date of *each balance sheet* presented, the aggregate cost (carrying value) and the aggregate market value of marketable equity securities should be disclosed either in the body of the financial statements or in the accompanying notes. When classified balance sheets are presented, the aggregate cost and the aggregate market value should be disclosed, segregated between current and noncurrent assets.

Further, *significant* reductions in market value arising *after* the date of the financial statements but prior to their issuance that are applicable to marketable securities in the portfolio should be disclosed.

To illustrate, we will use the data from National Service Corporation's December 31, 1993 and December 31, 1994 portfolio valuations presented on pages 878 and 879, respectively. National's marketable equity securities might be presented in the financial statements and the notes thereto as shown on page 884.

> **Objective 2**
>
> Explain the disclosure requirements for temporary investments.

SECTION 2
LONG-TERM INVESTMENTS

This section is devoted primarily to long-term investments in corporate securities: bonds of various types, preferred shares, and common shares. Numerous other items are commonly classified as long-term investments: funds for bond retirement, share redemption, and other special purposes; investments in notes receivable, mortgages, and similar debt instruments; and miscellaneous items such as advances to affiliates, cash surrender value of life insurance policies, interests in estates and trusts, equity in joint ventures and partnerships, and real estate held for appreciation or future use. Some of these items are also discussed. Long-term investments are usually presented on the balance sheet just below current assets in a separate section called Long-Term Investments, Investments and Funds, or just Investments.

Although many reasons prompt a corporation to invest in the securities of another corporation, the ***primary motive is to enhance its own income***. A corporation may thus enhance its income (1) directly through the receipt of dividends or interest from the investment or through appreciation in the market value of the securities, or (2) indirectly by creating and ensuring desirable operating

---

[10] *FASB Statement No. 12*, par. 29(a).

Balance Sheet

	December 31	
	1994	1993
Current assets:		
Marketable securities, carried at lower of cost and market (Note 2)	$875,530	$775,500

Income Statement

	Year Ended December 31	
	1994	1993
Income from operations	$ XXX	$ XXX
Other revenues and gains:		
Realized gain on sale of marketable securities		27,520
Recovery of unrealized loss on valuation of marketable securities	36,580	
Other expenses and losses:		
Realized loss on sale of marketable securities	55,440	
Unrealized loss on valuation of marketable securities		36,580
Income before extraordinary items	$ XXXXX	$ XXXXX

Note 2—**Marketable Securities.** Marketable securities are carried at the lower of cost and market at the balance sheet date; that determination is made by aggregating all current marketable securities. Marketable securities included in current assets had a market value at December 31, 1994 of $935,500 and a cost at December 31, 1993 of $812,080.

relationships among companies to improve income performance. Frequently, the most permanent investments are those for improving income performance. Benefits to the investors are derived from the influence or control that may be exercised over a major supplier, customer, or otherwise related company. As an illustration, at one time Sears, Roebuck held large stock interests in several of its leading suppliers: 22% of Kellwood, 31% of DeSoto, 40% of Roper, and 59% of Universal Rundle Co.

INVESTMENTS IN BONDS

Objective 3

Describe the accounting for long-term investments in bonds.

Accounting for bonds as a long-term liability was presented in Chapter 14. In this chapter, the focus is on accounting for these same securities from the investor's viewpoint. The types and characteristics of bonds that may be purchased are presented on pages 677–678; you should reread that discussion as background for this chapter. The variety in these features, along with the variability in interest rates, permits investors to shop for exactly the investment that satisfies their safety, yield, and marketability preferences.

Accounting for Bond Acquisitions

Investment in bonds should be recorded on the date of acquisition at cost, which includes brokerage fees and any other costs incidental to the purchase. *The cost or purchase price of a bond investment is its market value, which is determined by the market's appraisal of the risk involved and consideration of the stated interest rate in comparison with the prevailing market (yield) rate of interest for that type of security.* The cash amount of interest to be received periodically is fixed by the stated rate of interest on the face value (also called principal, par, or maturity value). If the rate of return desired by the investors is exactly equal to the stated rate, *the bond will sell at its face amount.* If investors demand a higher yield than the stated rate offers, *the bond will sell at a discount.* Purchasing the bond at an amount below the face amount, or at a discount, equates the yield on the bond with the market rate of interest. If the market rate of interest is below the stated rate, *investors will pay a premium*, more than maturity value, for the bond. The relationship between bond market values and interest rates is similar to that discussed in Chapter 14 under the heading "Valuation of Bonds Payable," pages 679–681.

If bonds are *purchased between interest payment dates*, the investor must pay the owner the *market price plus the interest accrued* since the last interest payment date. The investor will collect this interest plus the additional interest earned by holding the bond until the next interest date. For example, assume the purchase on June 1 of bonds having a $100,000 face value and paying an annual rate of 12% interest on April 1 and October 1, at 97. The entry to record purchase of the bonds and accrued interest is as follows:

Investment in Bonds ($100,000 × .97)	97,000	
Interest Revenue (or Accrued Interest		
Receivable ($100,000 × .12 × 2/12)	2,000	
Cash		99,000

On October 1 the investor will receive interest of $6,000, consisting of $2,000 paid at date of acquisition and $4,000 earned for holding the bond for four months.

Investments acquired at par, at a discount, or at a premium are generally recorded in the accounts at cost, including brokerage and other fees but excluding the accrued interest; generally they are not recorded at maturity value. The use of a separate discount or premium account as a valuation account is acceptable procedure, but in practice it has not been widely used.

If the discount of $3,000 was recorded separately and the bond recorded at maturity value, the entry to record the investment in bonds would be as follows:

Investment in Bonds	100,000	
Interest Revenue	2,000	
Discount on Investment in Bonds		3,000
Cash		99,000

When the investment is recorded, net of the discount, at $97,000 as in the first example, the discount is amortized by debit entries recorded directly to the Investment in Bonds account. When the investment is recorded at maturity value at $100,000 as in the second example, the discount is amortized by debiting the Discount on Investment in Bonds account. Both methods produce exactly the same net results on the financial statements. The remaining illustrations record the investment net of discount or premium.

Computing Prices of Bond Investments

Theoretically, the market price of a bond is the present value of its maturity amount plus the present value of its interest payments, both discounted at the market rate of interest. Using this as a basis, the price that should be paid for $10,000 of 8% bonds, interest payablesemiannually, and maturing in six years with a 10% effective annual yield, is computed as shown at top of page 886.

Amortization of Bond Premium and Bond Discount

As discussed in Chapter 14, there are two widely used methods of amortizing bond premium and bond discount: (1) the **straight-line method** and (2) the **effective interest method** (also called the present value or compound interest or effective yield method).

Objective 4

Apply the methods of amortization for bond premium and discount.

Purchase price = PV of maturity amount plus PV of interest payments

$$= \$10,000 \times p_{\overline{12}|5\%} + \$400 \times P_{\overline{12}|5\%}$$

$$= (\$10,000 \times .55684, \text{ Table A-2}) + (\$400 \times 8.86325, \text{ Table A-4})$$

$$= \$5,568.40 + \$3,545.30$$

$$= \$9,113.70$$

Both methods of amortizing bond discount and premium are illustrated below. The write-off of discount on bond investments is sometimes referred to as discount "accumulation" instead of "amortization."

Straight-Line Amortization of Premium. Assume that on March 1, 1994, bonds having a face value of $50,000, bearing 8% interest payable January 1 and July 1 are purchased for $53,008 plus accrued interest. The bonds mature January 1, 2002. The entry on March 1, 1994 is:

Investment in Bonds	53,008	
Interest Revenue (or Accrued Interest Receivable)	667	
Cash		53,675

The accrued interest of $666.67 represents interest at 8% for two months on $50,000, the par value of the bonds purchased ($50,000 × 8% × 2/12).

When six months' interest is received on July 1, 1994, premium allocatable to four months is written off under the straight-line method by a credit to the Investment account, and Interest Revenue is reduced accordingly. The premium amortized would be 4/94 of $3,008, or $128, because the bonds have been held for four months and because there are 94 months from the date of purchase to maturity date. The entry on July 1, 1994, therefore, is:

Cash	2,000	
Investment in Bonds ($3,008 × 4/94)		128
Interest Revenue [($50,000 × .08 × 6/12) − $128]		1,872

The Interest Revenue account now has a balance of $1,872 less $667, or $1,205. This represents the revenue earned on the bonds during the four months from March 1 to July 1. This amount is analysed as shown below.

Interest received on July 1, 1994, 8% × $50,000 × 6/12	$2,000
Deduct interest accrued on March 1, 1994, date of purchase of bonds, 8% × $50,000 × 2/12	667
Interest received that is applicable to the 4 months from March 1 to July 1	1,333
Deduct premium amortized for 4 months, 4/94 × $3,008	128
Revenue earned during the 4 months	**$1,205**

On December 31, 1994, an adjusting entry would be made to accrue six months' interest and to amortize the premium applicable to six months:

Interest Receivable on Bonds ($50,000 × .08 × 6/12)	2,000	
Investment in Bonds ($3,008 × 6/94)		192
Interest Revenue		1,808

The $192 credit to the Investments account represents the premium amortization for the six months from July 1 to December 31, or 6/94 of $3,008. The credit to Interest Revenue, $1,808, represents the difference between the interest receivable of $2,000 and the premium amortized of $192, or the net amount taken up as revenue for the six months ended December 31, 1994. The total interest revenue in 1994 from this investment in bonds is $3,013 ($1,205 + $1,808).

During the next year and during each succeeding year, a premium of $384, representing 12/94 of the total premium paid, will be amortized. Thus, by the maturity date the entire amount of the premium will have been removed from the Investment account, and the bonds will be carried on the books at face value at that time. The entry to be made at the maturity date of the bonds will therefore be:

Cash	50,000	
Investment in Bonds		50,000

In the entries shown above, the premium is amortized simultaneously with the interest received or accrued. They do not have to be combined into one entry, however, or entered at the same time. The entries for interest received or receivable are made at the proper times, independently of the entries for premium amortization. The proper amount of premium may be amortized at the end of each fiscal year or at any other acceptable time by debiting Interest Revenue and crediting Investment in Bonds. Using the figures from the example above, the recognition of accrued interest and amortization of premium in separate entries would be as follows:

Interest Receivable on Bonds	2,000	
Interest Revenue		2,000
Interest Revenue	192	
Investment in Bonds		192

Separate entries are convenient when reversing entries are used because the entry for accrued interest will be reversed but no reversing entry is needed for premium amortization.

Amortization (Accumulation) of Discount. If bonds are purchased at a discount (below par), the discount amortized is added to the interest revenue. Assume that bonds with a par value of $50,000, bearing 8% interest payable January 1 and July 1, and maturing January 1, 2002, are purchased on March 1, 1994 for $46,992 plus accrued interest. In other words, assume that they are purchased at a discount of $3,008 instead of a premium of $3,008 as above. Because they have 94 months yet to run, the discount to be amortized for each month is 1/94 of $3,008, or $32. The entry to record the purchase is:

Investment in Bonds	46,992	
Interest Revenue ($50,000 × .08 × 2/12)	667	
Cash		47,659

When six months' interest is received on July 1, 1994, the entry is:

Cash	2,000	
Investment in Bonds ($3,008 × 4/94)	128	
Interest Revenue		2,128

In this case, the Investment account is debited and the credit to Interest Revenue is the total of the interest received and the discount amortized. If bonds are purchased at a discount, the discount amortized is debited to the asset account; by maturity date, the book value of the bonds will be at par. Thus, bonds purchased at a premium are written down to par through amortization of premium, and bonds purchased at a discount are written up to par through amortization of the discount.

Effective Interest Method. As discussed in Chapter 14, when a premium or discount is amortized under the straight-line method, the rate of return is not the same year after year. Although the interest received is constant from period to period, the carrying amount of the bond is either increasing or decreasing by the amount of the discount or premium amortization. *The straight-line method produces a constant revenue but produces a variable rate of return on the book value of the invest-*

ment. Although the effective interest method results in a varying amount being recorded as interest revenue from period to period, its virtue is that it produces a constant rate of return on the book value of the investment from period to period.

The straight-line method is the more popular method because (1) it is simple to apply, (2) it avoids the computations necessary under the effective interest rate method, and (3) it produces results not significantly different from the effective interest earned, unless the maturity date is many years distant or the premium or discount is exceptionally large. The effective interest method is preferable; however, the straight-line method may be used if the results obtained are not significantly different from those produced by the effective interest method.

The effective interest method is applied to bond investments in a fashion similar to that described for bonds payable. The effective interest rate or yield is computed at the time of investment and is applied to its beginning carrying amount (book value) for each interest period. The investment carrying amount is *increased* by the amortized discount or *decreased* by the amortized premium in each period.

To illustrate, assume that the Robinson Company is the purchaser of 8% bonds of Evermaster Corporation on January 1, 1994, paying $92,278. The bonds mature January 1, 1999; interest is payable each July 1 and January 1. The discount of $7,722 ($100,000 minus $92,278) provided an effective annual interest yield rate of 10%. The following schedule discloses the effect of the discount amortization on the interest revenue recorded each period, using the effective interest method.

Schedule of Interest Revenue and Bond Discount Amortization: Effective Interest Method
8% Bonds Purchased to Yield 10%

Date	Debit Cash	Credit Interest Revenue	Debit Bond Investment*	Carrying Value of Bonds
Jan. 1, 1994				$ 92,278
July 1, 1994	$ 4,000a	$ 4,614b	$ 614c	92,892d
Jan. 1, 1995	4,000	4,645	645	93,537
July 1, 1995	4,000	4,677	677	94,214
Jan. 1, 1996	4,000	4,711	711	94,925
July 1, 1996	4,000	4,746	746	95,671
Jan. 1, 1997	4,000	4,783	783	96,454
July 1, 1997	4,000	4,823	823	97,277
Jan. 1, 1998	4,000	4,864	864	98,141
July 1, 1998	4,000	4,907	907	99,048
Jan. 1, 1999	4,000	4,952	952	100,000
	$40,000	$47,722	$7,722	

a$4,000 = $100,000 × .08 × 6/12
b$4,614 = $92,278 × .10 × 6/12
c$614 = $4,614 − $4,000
d$92,892 = $92,278 + $614

*Or debit Discount on Investment in Bonds if the investment is carried at maturity value.

The journal entry to record the receipt of the first semiannual interest payment on July 1, 1994 (as shown on the schedule) is as follows.

Cash	4,000	
Investment in Bonds	614	
Interest Revenue		4,614

Sale of Bond Investments Before Maturity Date

If bonds carried as long-term investments are sold before the maturity date, entries must be made to amortize the discount or premium to the date of sale and to remove the book value of the bonds sold from the Investment account.

Assume that the bonds described on page 887 are sold on April 1, 2000 at 99½ *plus accrued interest*. Discount has been amortized at the rate of $32 per month from March 1, 1994 through the last closing date, December 31, 1999. An entry is made to amortize discount for the three months that have expired in 2000:

Investment in Bonds	96	
Interest Revenue		96

The entry to record the sale is:

Cash [($50,000 × .995) + ($50,000 × .08 × 3/12)]	50,750	
Interest Revenue ($50,000 × .08 × 3/12)		1,000
Investment in Bonds		49,328
Gain on Sale of Bond Investment		422

The credit to Interest Revenue represents accrued interest for three months, for which the purchaser pays cash. The debit to Cash represents the selling price of the bonds, $49,750, plus the accrued interest of $1,000. The credit to the Investment account represents the book value of the bonds on the date of the sale, and the credit to Gain on Sale of Bond Investment represents the excess of the selling price over the book value of the bonds. The computation of the latter two credits is shown below.

Selling price of bonds (exclusive of accrued interest)		$49,750
Deduct book value of bonds on April 1, 2000:		
Cost	$46,992	
Add discount amortized for the period from		
March 1, 1994 to April 1, 2000, 73/94 × $3,008	2,336	49,328
Gain on sale		**$ 422**

LONG-TERM INVESTMENTS IN SHARES

Shares may be acquired on the market from a firm's shareholders, from the issuing corporation, or from stockbrokers. When shares are purchased outright for cash, the full cost includes the purchase price of the security plus brokers' commissions and other fees incidental to the purchase. If shares are *acquired on margin* (the margin representing borrowings from the broker), the share purchase should be recorded at its full cost and a liability recognized for the unpaid balance. A *share subscription* or agreement to buy the shares of a corporation is recognized by a charge to an asset account for the security to be received and a credit to a liability account for the amount to be paid. Any interest on an obligation arising from a share purchase should be recognized as expense.

Shares acquired in *exchange for noncash consideration* (property or services) should be recorded at (1) the fair market value of the consideration given or (2) the fair market value of the shares received, whichever is more clearly determinable. The absence of clearly determinable values for the property or services or a market price for the security acquired may require the use of appraisals or estimates to arrive at a cost.

The purchase of two or more classes of securities for a *lump sum price* calls for the allocation of the cost to the different classes in some equitable manner. If market prices are available for each class of security, the lump sum cost may be apportioned on the basis of the *relative market values*. If the market price is available for one security but not for the other, the market price may be assigned to the one and the cost excess to the other. If market prices are not available at the date of acquisition of several securities, it may be necessary to defer cost apportionment until evidence of at least one value becomes available. In some instances, cost apportionment may have to wait until one of the securities is sold. In such cases, the proceeds from the sale of the one security may be subtracted from the lump sum cost, leaving the residual cost to be assigned as the cost of the other.

Accounting for numerous purchases of securities requires that information regarding the cost of individual purchases be preserved, as well as the dates of purchases and sales. Average cost should be used for multiple purchases of the same security.

Effect of Ownership Interest

Objective 5

Explain the effect of ownership interest on the accounting for long-term investments in shares.

The accounting treatment of an investment in shares of another corporation is based on the nature of the relationship between the **investor** and the **investee**. These relationships are divided into three categories based on the degree of control or influence that the investor is able to exercise over the strategic operating, investing, and financing policies of the investee. These are: (1) control, (2) significant influence, and (3) no significant influence.

The degree of control or influence held by the investor is evidenced by many factors such as representation on the board of directors, economic dependency, and commonality of human resources. Since representation on the board of directors is generally determined by the voting shareholders, the ownership of voting shares has become an important criterion in assessing the degree of control held by the investor.

The complexities of determining the degree of control held is simplified in the following discussion by the assumption that the proportion of voting shares held is the only relevant factor. Thus, the three following categories of shareholdings exist:

1. Holdings of more than 50% (consolidated statements)—investor has controlling interest.

2. Holdings between 20% and 50% if investor has significant influence (equity method).

3. Holdings of less than 20% if investor does not have significant influence (cost method)—investor has passive interest.

Controlling Interest. When one corporation acquires a voting interest of more than 50% or otherwise controls another corporation, the investor corporation is referred to as the **parent** and the investee corporation as the **subsidiary**. The investment in the common shares of the subsidiary is presented as a long-term investment on the separate financial statements of the parent.

Consolidated financial statements are, however, generally prepared instead of separate financial statements for the parent and the subsidiary, in which the parent treats the subsidiary as an investment. Consolidated financial statements disregard the distinction between separate legal entities and treat the parent and subsidiary corporations as a single economic entity. When and how to prepare consolidated financial statements are discussed extensively in advanced accounting. Whether or not consolidated financial statements are prepared, the investment in the subsidiary is generally accounted for on the parent's books using the **equity method**, as explained in this chapter.

Significant Influence. Although an investor corporation may hold an interest of less than 50% in an investee corporation and thus does not possess legal control, it "may be able to exercise significant influence over strategic operating, investing and financing decisions of an investee."[11] To provide a

---

[11] *CICA Handbook*, Section 3050, par. .04.

guide for accounting for investors when 50% or less of the voting interest is held and to develop an operational definition of "significant influence," the CICA adopted this statement:

> The ability to exercise significant influence may be indicated by, for example, representation on the board of directors, participation in policy making processes, material intercompany transactions, interchange of managerial personnel, or provision of technical information. If the investor holds less than 20% of the voting interest in the investee, it should be presumed that the investor does not have the ability to exercise significant influence, unless such influence is clearly demonstrated. On the other hand, the holding of 20% or more of the voting interest in the investee does not in itself confirm the ability to exercise significant influence. A substantial or majority ownership by another investor would not necessarily preclude an investor from exercising significant influence.[12]

Judgement is frequently required in determining whether an investment of 20% or more results in "significant influence" over the policies of an investee.

To achieve a reasonable degree of uniformity in application of the significant influence criterion, the profession concludes that an investment (direct or indirect) of 20% or more of the voting shares of an investee should lead to a presumption that, in the absence of evidence to the contrary, an investor has the ability to exercise significant influence over an investee.

In instances of significant influence (generally an investment of 20% or more), the investor is required to account for the investment using the **equity method**.

Lack of Significant Influence. When the investor lacks significant influence over the investee, presumably less than a 20% interest, the investment is to be accounted for using the **cost method**. The following pages discuss and illustrate the two methods of accounting for long-term investments: (1) the cost method and (2) the equity method.

Cost Method

Under the **cost method**, a long-term investment is originally recorded and reported at acquisition cost, which includes brokerage commission plus all other costs incidental to the purchase. It continues to be carried and reported at cost in the Investment account until it is either partially or entirely disposed of, or until some fundamental change in conditions makes it clear that the value originally assigned can no longer be justified. Ordinary cash dividends received by the investor are recorded as investment revenue. However, when the dividends received by the investor in subsequent periods exceed its share of the investee's earnings for such periods (i.e. a liquidating dividend), they should be accounted for as a reduction of the investment carrying amount (return of capital), rather than as investment revenue.

Objective 6

Apply the cost and equity methods for long-term investments in shares.

To illustrate, assume that Queco, Inc. purchases an investment in Ontco Mining Company for $60,000 on December 31, 1993. In 1994, Ontco has no income but declares and pays a dividend of $3,000 to Queco. The entry to record this transaction is as follows:

Cash	3,000	
Investment in Ontco Shares		3,000

The cost method is applicable to investments when:

1. Significant influence does not exist.

2. The investee holds either significant influence or owns more than 50% of the voting shares of the investee and earnings are not likely to accrue to the investor.

---

[12] *Ibid.*

Equity Method

Under the **equity method**, a substantive economic relationship is acknowledged between the investor and the investee. The investment is originally recorded at the cost of the shares acquired but is subsequently adjusted each period for changes in the net assets of the investee. That is, the *investment's carrying amount is periodically increased (decreased) by the investor's proportionate share of the earnings (losses) of the investee and decreased by all dividends received by the investor from the investee.* The equity method gives recognition to the fact that investee earnings increase investee net assets that underlie the investment, and that investee losses and dividends decrease these net assets.

To illustrate the cost and equity methods, assume that Maxi Company purchases a 20% interest in Mini Company. For purposes of applying the cost method in this illustration, assume that Maxi does not have the ability to exercise significant influence; where the equity method is applied, assume that the 20% interest permits Maxi to exercise significant influence. The entries are shown below.

Entries Under Cost and Equity Methods

Cost Method		Equity Method	

On January 2, 1993, Maxi Company acquired 48,000 shares (20%) of Mini Company common shares at a cost of $10 each.

Investment in			Investment in		
Mini Company	480,000		Mini Company	480,000	
Cash		480,000	Cash		480,000

For the year 1993, Mini Company reported net income of $200,000; Maxi Company's share is 20% or $40,000.

No entry		Investment in		
		Mini Company	40,000	
		Revenue From Investment		40,000

On January 28, 1994, Mini Company announced and paid a cash dividend of $100,000; Maxi Company received 20%, or $20,000.

Cash	20,000		Cash	20,000	
Revenue From			Investment in		
Investment		20,000	Mini Company		20,000

For the year 1994, Mini reported a net loss of $50,000; Maxi Company's share is 20%, or $10,000.

No entry		Loss on Investment	10,000	
		Investment in		
		Mini Company		10,000

Under the equity method, Maxi Company reports as revenue its share of net income reported by Mini Company; the cash dividends received from Mini Company are recorded as a decrease in the investment carrying value. As a result, the investor should record its share of the net income of the investee in the year when it is earned. In this case, the investor can ensure that any net asset increases resulting from net income will be paid as dividends if desired. To wait until a dividend is received ignores the fact that the investor is better off if the investee has earned income.

Using dividends as a basis for recognizing income poses an additional problem. For example, assume that the investee reports a net loss but the investor exerts influence to force a dividend payment from the investee. In this case, the investor reports income, even though the investee is experiencing a loss. *In other words, if dividends are used as a basis for recognizing income, the economics of the situation are not properly reported.*

The difference between the cost and equity method can be significant. For example, at one time McCloth Steel Corporation reported that the use of the equity method had increased its income before taxes for the year by 55% or $3.5 million.

Expanded Illustration of Equity Method. Under the equity method, periodic investor revenue consists of the investor's proportionate share of investee earnings (adjusted to eliminate intercompany gains and losses) and *amortization of the difference between the investor's initial cost and the investor's proportionate share of the underlying book value of the investee at date of acquisition*. And, if the investee's net income includes extraordinary items, the investor treats a proportionate share of the extraordinary items as an extraordinary item, rather than as ordinary investment revenue before extraordinary items.

Assume that on January 1, 1994, Investor Company purchased 250,000 shares of Investee Company's 1,000,000 outstanding common shares for $8,500,000. Investee Company's total net assets or book value was $30,000,000 at the date of Investor Company's 25% investment. Investor Company thereby paid $1,000,000 [$8,500,000 − .25 ($30,000,000)] in excess of book value. It was determined that $600,000 of this is attributable to its share of *undervalued depreciable assets* of Investee Company and $400,000 to *unrecorded goodwill*. Investor Company estimated the average remaining life of the undervalued assets to be 10 years and decided on a 40-year amortization period for goodwill (the maximum length of time allowed). For the year 1994, Investee Company reported net income of $2,800,000, which included an extraordinary loss of $400,000 and paid dividends at June 30, 1994 of $600,000 and at December 31, 1994 of $800,000. The following entries would be recorded on the books of Investor Company to report its long-term investment using the equity method:

January 1, 1994

Investment in Investee Company Shares	8,500,000	
Cash		8,500,000
(To record the acquisition of 250,000		
common shares of Investee Company, a 25% interest)		

June 30, 1994

Cash	150,000	
Investment in Investee Company Shares		150,000
(To record dividend received		
($600,000 × .25) from Investee Company)		

The entries on December 31, however, are more complex. In addition to the dividend payment, Investor Company must recognize its share of Investee Company's net income. Because Investee Company's income includes both an ordinary and extraordinary component, both of these components must be recorded by Investor Company. Furthermore, Investor Company paid more than the book value for Investee Company's net assets. As a result, this additional cost must be allocated to the proper accounting period:

December 31, 1994

Investment in Investee Company Shares ($2,800,000 × .25)	700,000	
Loss From Investment (extraordinary) ($400,000 × .25)	100,000	
Revenue From Investment (ordinary)		800,000
(To record share of Investee Company ordinary income		
($3,200,000 × .25) and extraordinary loss ($400,000 × .25))		

December 31, 1994

Cash	200,000	
Investment in Investee Company Shares		200,000
(To record dividend received ($800,000 × .25)		
from Investee Company)		

(Continued)

December 31, 1994

Revenue From Investment (ordinary)	70,000	
Investment in Investee Company Shares		70,000

(To record amortization of investment cost in excess
of book value represented by:

Undervalued depreciable assets: $600,000/10	=	$60,000
Unrecorded goodwill: $400,000/40	=	10,000
Total		$70,000)

The investment in Investee Company is presented in the December 31, 1994 balance sheet of Investor Company at a carrying value of $8,780,000 computed as follows.

Investment in Investee Company		
Acquisition cost Jan 1, 1994	$8,500,000	
Plus: Share of 1994 income before extraordinary item	800,000	$9,300,000
Less: Share of extraordinary loss	100,000	
Dividends received June 30 and Dec. 31	350,000	
Amortization of undervalued depreciable assets	60,000	
Amortization of unrecorded goodwill	10,000	520,000
Carrying value Dec. 31 1994		**$8,780,000**

In the preceding illustration, the investment cost exceeded the underlying book value. In some cases, an investor may acquire an investment at a *cost less than the underlying book value*. In such cases, specific assets are assumed to be overvalued and, if depreciable, the excess of the investee's book value over the investor's acquisition cost is amortized into investment revenue over the remaining lives of the assets. Investment revenue is increased under the presumption that the investee's net income as reported is actually understated because the investee is charging depreciation on overstated asset values.

Investee Losses Exceed Carrying Amount. If an investor's share of the investee's losses exceeds the carrying amount of the investment, the question arises as to whether the investor should recognize additional losses. Ordinarily, the investor should discontinue applying the equity method and not recognize additional losses.

If the investor's potential loss is not limited to the amount of its original investment (by guarantee of the investee's obligations or other commitment to provide further financial support), however, or if imminent return to profitable operations by the investee appears to be assured, it is appropriate for the investor to recognize additional losses.

Change in Method From and To the Equity Method. If the investor's level of influence or ownership falls below that necessary for continued use of the equity method, a change must be made to the cost method. Also, an investment in common shares of an investee that has been accounted for by the cost method may become qualified for use of the equity method by the increase in the level of ownership or influence. Both of these situations are discussed and illustrated in the appendix to this chapter.

Disclosures Required Under the Equity Method. The significance of an investment to the investor's financial position and operating results should determine the extent of disclosures. The following disclosures in the investor's financial statements are generally applicable to the equity method:

1. The name of each investee and the investor's proportionate interest in each.

2. The accounting policies of the investor with respect to investments.

3. The difference, if any, between the amount of the cost of the investment at the date of acquisition and the amount of underlying equity in the net assets of the investee.

4. When investments of 20% or more interest are in the aggregate material in relation to the financial position and operating results of an investor, it may be necessary to present summarized information concerning assets, liabilities, and results of operations of the investee, either individually or in groups, as appropriate.

5. Quoted market value and the carrying value(s) of marketable securities.

Applicability of Methods

In summary, application of the cost and equity methods for long-term investments in shares is as follows.

Nature of Investment	Method
Investment in excess of 50% of voting equity and earnings likely to accrue to investor (Consolidated statements will be prepared)	Cost or Equity
Investment in excess of 50% of voting equity and earnings not likely to accrue to investor	Cost
Investment in excess of 20% of voting equity, except when evidence exists of an inability to exercise significant influence	Equity
Investment in excess of 20% of voting equity and earnings of investee not likely to accrue to investor	Cost
Investment is less than a 20% interest in voting equity and evidence exists of an ability to exercise significant influence; earnings likely to accrue to investor	Equity
Investment is less than a 20% interest in voting equity and no evidence of an ability to exercise significant influence exists	Cost
Investment in nonequity or nonmarketable securities	Cost

Even in cases of investments in excess of a 50% voting interest in common shares, certain conditions may militate against the use of the equity method (e.g., foreign subsidiaries operating under conditions of exchange restrictions, governmental controls, or other uncertainties).

On January 27, 1991, Algonquin Mercantile Corporation reported its long-term investments in Note 3 as shown at the top of page 896.

Market Value Method

Although the profession has as yet not sanctioned the market value method of accounting for long-term investments, the profession did give credence to it by discussing it at considerable length in an Exposure Draft issued in July 1986. Under the market value method, the investor recognizes both dividends received and changes in market prices of the shares of the investee company as earnings or losses from the investment. Dividends received are accounted for as part of revenue from the investment. In addition, the investment account is adjusted for changes in the market value of the investee's shares. The change in market value since the preceding reporting date is included in the results of operations of the investor.

Reporting of investments in common shares at market value is considered by some accountants to meet most closely the objective of reporting the economic consequences of holding the investment. Although the market value method provides the best presentation of investments in some

	January 27, 1991	
	Book Value	Trading Value
Listed shares:		
Consolidated Enfield Corporation	$3,361,988	$2,091,903
Unlisted shares	10,000	
	$3,371,988	

The investment in Consolidated Enfield Corporation of 1,494,217 common shares represents approximately 14% of the issued and outstanding common shares. On June 28, 1990, the shareholders of the Enfield Corporation Limited approved a one for five consolidation of its common shares and as a result were required to change its name to Consolidated Enfield Corporation. The number of shares owned by the company as of March 31, 1990 have been adjusted to reflect this share consolidation. On January 27, 1991, this investment was written down to its estimated realizable value. The trading values referred to above do not necessarily reflect the realizable values of these investments.

situations, the profession has concluded that further study will be necessary before the market value method is used as the sole basis.

Effect of Methods on Financial Statements

The following schedule compares the various methods of accounting for long-term investments in shares in terms of their effects on the financial statements.

Comparison of the Effects of Methods of Accounting for Long-Term Investments in Shares[13]

	Balance Sheet	Income Statement
Cost Method	Investments are carried at acquisition cost.	Dividends are recognized as revenue.
Equity Method	Investments are carried at cost, are periodically adjusted by the investor's share of the investee's earnings or losses, and are decreased by all dividends received from the investee.	Revenue is recognized to the extent of the investor's share of investee earnings or losses reported subsequent to the date of investment (adjusted by amortization of the difference between cost and underlying book value).
Market Value Method	Investments are carried at market value.	Cash dividends received, plus or minus the changes in market price during the period, are recognized as revenue.

---

[13] Adapted and updated from Copeland, Strawser, and Binns, "Accounting for Investments in Common Stock," *Financial Executive* (February 1972), p. 37.

SPECIAL ISSUES RELATED TO INVESTMENTS

Presented below are five special issues related to accounting for investments:

1. Impairment of value.

2. Market value information.

3. Revenue from investments in shares.

4. Dividends received in shares.

5. Stock rights.

Objective 7

Discuss special issues related to investments.

Impairment of Value

Every investment, whether current or noncurrent, debt or equity, or a hybrid (both debt or equity, such as a convertible bond) should be evaluated at each reporting date to determine if it has suffered a loss in value that is other than temporary. A bankruptcy or a significant liquidity crisis being experienced by an investee are examples of situations that suggest that a loss in value to the investor may be permanent. If the decline is judged to be permanent, the cost basis of the individual security is written down to a new cost basis. The amount of nontemporary write-down is accounted for as a *realized loss*. The new cost basis is not changed for subsequent recoveries in market value.[14]

In judging whether a decline in market value below cost at the balance sheet date is other than temporary, a gain or loss realized on subsequent disposition or changes in market price occurring after the date of the financial statements, but prior to their issuance, should certainly be taken into consideration.

Market Value Information

Theoretical Issues. Many accountants argue that the market value of an investment is the attribute that is of most relevance to the company and to those interested in the company. Stating investments at market value instead of historical cost gives a better indication of the current status and prospects of the company. Shareholders are better able to evaluate managerial decisions regarding investments; creditors are better able to evaluate the solvency of the enterprise; and management is better able to evaluate the results of holding securities as well as the results of selling them.

In applying market value accounting, the investor company generally recognizes both the dividend and interest received and changes in the market prices of the shares and bonds held as part of income or loss in the current period. The notion that net income is the change in net assets for the period underlies this position.

Opponents of market value accounting contend that market value information is *subjective* and therefore *not verifiable*, especially for large holdings of restricted securities or securities that are not actively traded. In addition, some accountants make a distinction between marketable equity securities and marketable debt securities. Some are *reluctant to value marketable debt securities* at market prices because they have a defined value if held to maturity. Finally, *fluctuations in earnings* result as the market price of the investment changes. Most companies dislike undue fluctuations in earnings because they have little control over them.

Note that market value proponents do not believe that a lower of cost and market value is acceptable. It is considered inconsistent to reduce the carrying amount of securities to an amount below cost without increasing the carrying amount when market value is above cost. Recognition of

---

[14] The adoption of newly proposed standards for accounting for impairments in value of noncurrent investments would permit recognition of recoveries in value if there is evidence that the increase will persist for the foreseeable future. (CICA *Exposure Draft*, "Financial Instruments," September 1991).

losses only is conservative and does not reflect the underlying economics when prices increase. Lower of cost and market allows management to some extent to manipulate net income by determining when securities are sold to realize gains (often referred to as gains trading or cherry picking). An enterprise whose earnings are low in one year might sell some securities that have appreciated in past years to offset the low income amount from current operations.

Current Practice. Lower of cost and market is required in accounting for temporary investments. Certain specialized industries such as investment companies, brokers and dealers in securities, stock life insurance companies, and fire and casualty insurance companies carry marketable equity securities at market value. The rationale is that these companies are continually trading in these securities and, therefore, market value information is necessary, useful, and easily verified.

Revenue From Investments in Shares

Revenue recognized from investments, whether under the cost, equity, or market value method, should be included in the income statement of the investor. Under the cost method, dividends received (or receivable if declared but unpaid) are reported as investment revenue. Under the equity method, if the investee has extraordinary and prior period items reported during the period, the investor should report in a similar manner its proportionate share of the ordinary income, of the extraordinary items, and prior period adjustments, unless separation into these components is considered immaterial.

The gains or losses on sales of investments also are factors in determining the net income for the period. The gain or loss resulting from the sale of long-term investments, unless it is the result of a major casualty, an expropriation, or the introduction of a new law prohibiting its ownership (which may be viewed as unusual and nonrecurring), is reported as part of current income from operations and is not an extraordinary item.

Dividends that are paid in some form of assets other than cash are called **property dividends**. In such instances, the fair market value of the property received becomes the basis for debiting an appropriate asset account and crediting Dividend Revenue.

Occasionally an investor receives a dividend that is in part, or entirely, a **liquidating dividend**.[15] The investor should reduce the Investment account for the amount of the liquidating portion of the dividend and credit Dividend Revenue for the balance.

Dividends Received in Shares

If the investee corporation declares a dividend distributable in its own shares of the same class, instead of in cash, each shareholder owns a larger number of shares but retains the same proportionate interest in the firm as before. The issuing corporation has distributed no assets; it has merely transferred a specified amount of retained earnings to share capital, thus indicating that this amount will not provide a basis in the future for cash dividends.

Shares received as a result of a stock dividend or stock split do not constitute revenue to the recipients, because their interest in the issuing corporation is unchanged and the issuing corporation has not distributed any of its assets. *The recipient of such additional shares would make no formal entry*, but should make a memorandum entry and record a notation in the Investment account to show that additional shares have been received.

Although no dollar amount is entered at the time of the receipt of these shares, the fact that additional shares have been received must be considered in computing the carrying amount of any shares sold subsequently. The cost of the original shares purchased (plus the effect of any adjustments under the equity method) now constitutes the total carrying amount of both those shares and the additional shares received, because no price was paid for the additional shares. The carrying amount

---

[15] A company can receive a dividend from preacquisition retained earnings of the investee, which the investor should treat as a liquidating dividend. From the investee's point of view, however, it is not a liquidating dividend.

per share is computed by dividing the total shares into the carrying amount of the original shares purchased.

To illustrate, assume that 100 common shares of Flemal Limited are purchased for $9,600, and that two years later Flemal issues to shareholders one additional share for every two shares held; 150 shares that cost a total of $9,600 are then held. Therefore, if 60 shares are sold for $4,300, the carrying amount of the 60 shares would be computed as shown below, assuming that the investment has been accounted for under the cost method.

Cost of 100 shares originally purchased	$9,600
Cost of 50 shares received as stock dividend	–0–
Carrying amount of 150 shares held	$9,600

Carrying amount per share is $9,600/150, or $64
Carrying amount of 60 shares sold is 60 × $64, or $3,840

The entry to record the sale is:

Cash	4,300	
Investments in Shares		3,840
Gain on Sales of Investments		460

A total of 90 shares is still retained and they are carried in the Investment account at $9,600 − $3,840, or $5,760. Thus the carrying amount for those shares remaining is also $64 per share, or a total of $5,760 for the 90 shares.

Stock Rights

When a corporation is about to offer for sale additional shares of an issue already outstanding, it may forward to present holders of that issue certificates permitting them to purchase additional shares in proportion to their present holdings. These certificates represent rights to purchase additional shares and are called **stock rights**. In rights offerings, rights generally are issued on the basis of one right per share, but it may take one or many rights to purchase one new share.

The certificate representing the stock rights, called a **warrant**, states the number of shares that the holder of the right may purchase and also the price at which they may be purchased. If this price is less than the current market value of such shares, the rights have an intrinsic value, and from the time they are issued until they expire, they may be purchased and sold like any other security.

Stock rights have three important dates: (1) the date the rights offering is announced, (2) the date as of which the certificates or rights are issued, and (3) the date the rights expire. From the date the right is announced until it is issued, the share of stock and the right are not separable, and the share is described as **rights-on**; after the certificate or right is received and up to the time it expires, the share and right can be sold separately. A share sold separately from an effective stock right is sold **ex-rights**.

When a right is received, the shareholders have actually received nothing that they did not have before, because the shares already owned brought them the right; they have received no distribution of the corporation assets. The carrying amount of the original shares held is now the carrying amount of those shares plus the rights and should be allocated between the two on the basis of their total market values at the time the rights are received. If the value allocated to the rights is maintained in a separate account, an entry would be made debiting Investment in Stock Rights and crediting Investment.

Disposition of Rights. The investor who receives rights to purchase additional shares has three alternatives:

1. To exercise all or some of the rights by purchasing additional shares.

2. To sell the rights.

3. To permit them to expire without selling or using them.

If the investor buys additional shares, the carrying amount of the original shares allocated to the rights becomes a part of the carrying amount of the new shares purchased; if the investor sells the rights, the allocated carrying amount compared with the selling price determines the gain or loss on sale; and if the investor permits the rights to expire, a loss is suffered and the investment should be reduced accordingly. The following example illustrates the problem involved.

Shares owned before issuance of rights—100.
Cost of shares owned—$50 per share for a total cost of $5,000.
Rights received—one right for every share owned, or 100 rights; two
    rights are required to purchase one new share at $50.
Market values at date rights issued: Shares—$60 per share
                                        Rights—$3 per right

Total market value of shares (100 × $60)	$6,000
Total market value of rights (100 × $3)	300
Combined market value	$6,300

Cost allocated to shares: $\dfrac{\$6,000}{\$6,300} \times \$5,000 = \$4,761.90$

Cost allocated to rights: $\dfrac{\$300}{\$6,300} \times \$5,000 = \underline{\quad 238.10}$

$\underline{\underline{\$5,000.00}}$

Cost allocated to each share: $\dfrac{\$4,761.90}{100} = \$47.619$

Cost allocated to each right: $\dfrac{\$238.10}{100} = \$2.381$

The reduction in the carrying amount of the shares from $5,000 to $4,761.90 and the acquisition of the rights with an allocated cost of $238.10 would be recorded as follows:

Investment in Stock Rights	238.10	
Investment in Shares		238.10

Entries for Stock Rights. Rights may be sold, used to purchase additional shares, or permitted to expire. If 40 rights to purchase 20 shares are sold at $3.00 each, the entry is:

Cash	120.00	
Investment in Stock Rights		95.24
Gain on Sale of Investments		24.76

The amount removed from the Investment in Stock Rights account is the amount allocated to 40 rights, 40 × $2.381.

If rights to purchase 20 shares are exercised and 20 additional shares are purchased at the offer price of $50, the entry is:

Investment in Shares	1,095.24	
Cash		1,000.00
Investment in Stock Rights		95.24

If any shares are sold in the future, their cost should be considered to be $48.81 each—the average cost of all of the shares owned immediately before the sale, as computed below.

If the remaining 20 rights are permitted to expire, the amount allocated to these rights should be removed from the general ledger account by this entry:

Loss on Expiration of Stock Rights	47.62	
Investment in Stock Rights		47.62

The information relating to these investment accounts is shown below.

	Investment in Shares			Investment in Rights		
	Shares	Cost	Cost Per Share	Rights	Cost	Cost Per Right
Purchase of original shares @ $50 per share	100	$5,000.00	$50.00			
Cost allocated to rights received		(238.10)	47.62	100	$238.10	$2.38
Purchase of shares by exercise of rights	20	1,095.24	54.76	(40)	(95.24)	2.38
Subtotal	120	5,857.14	48.81	60	142.86	2.38
Sale of shares	(10)	(488.10)	48.81			
Subtotal	110	5,369.04	48.81			
Sale of rights				(40)	(95.24)	2.38
Subtotal				20	47.62	2.38
Expiration of rights				(20)	(47.62)	2.38
Total	110	$5,369.04	48.81	–0–	–0–	–0–

SECTION 3
CASH SURRENDER VALUE AND FUNDS
CASH SURRENDER VALUE OF LIFE INSURANCE

Objective 8

Explain the accounting for cash surrender value.

There are many different kinds of insurance. The kinds usually carried by businesses include (a) casualty insurance, (b) liability insurance, and (c) life insurance. Certain types of **life insurance** constitute an investment, whereas casualty insurance and liability insurance do not. The three common types of life insurance policies that companies often carry on the lives of their principal officers are (a) **ordinary life**, (b) **limited payment**, and (c) **term insurance**. During the period that ordinary life and limited payment policies are in force, there is a cash surrender value and a loan value. Term insurance ordinarily has no cash surrender value or loan value.

If the insured officers or their heirs are the beneficiaries of the policy, the premiums paid by the company represent expense to the company and, for income tax purposes, may represent income to the officer insured. In this case, the cash surrender value of the policy does not represent an asset to the company.

If the company, however, is the beneficiary and has the right to cancel the policy at its own option, the cash surrender value of the policy or policies is an asset of the company. Accordingly, part of the premium paid is not expense because the cash surrender value increases each year. Only the difference between the premium paid and the increase in cash surrender value represents expense to the company.

For example, if Zima Corporation pays an insurance premium of $2,300 on a $100,000 policy covering its president and, as a result, the cash surrender value of the policy increases from $15,000 to $16,400 during the period, the entry to record the premium payment is:

Life Insurance Expense	900	
Cash Surrender Value of Life Insurance	1,400	
Cash		2,300

If the insured officer died halfway through the most recent period of coverage for which the $2,300 premium payment was made, the following entry would be made (assuming cash surrender value of $15,700 and refund of a pro rata share of the premium paid):

Cash [$100,000 + (½ of $2,300)]	101,150	
Cash Surrender Value of Life Insurance		16,400
Life Insurance Expense (½ × $900)		450
Gain on Life Insurance Coverage ($100,000 − $15,700)		84,300

The gain on life insurance coverage is not generally reported as an extraordinary item because it is considered to be a "normal" business transaction.

The cash surrender value of such life insurance policies should be reported in the balance sheet as a long-term investment, inasmuch as it is unlikely that the policies will be surrendered and cancelled in the immediate future. The premium is not deductible for tax purposes, however, and the proceeds of such policies are not taxable as income.

To illustrate a disclosure in this area, Alico, Inc. recently reported information related to its cash surrender value as follows.

Other investments (note 4)	
Cash surrender value of life insurance	448,000

Note 4. The company purchased, as owner and beneficiary, individual life insurance policies on the lives of such officers and employees as a means of funding substantially all of such additional benefits. The company's accounting policy with respect to such insurance coverage is to charge operations with the annual premium cost, net of increase in cash surrender value.

FUNDS

Assets may be set aside in special funds for specific purposes and, therefore, become unavailable for ordinary operations of the business. In this way, the assets segregated in the special funds are available when needed for the intended purposes.

There are two general types of funds: (1) those in which cash is set aside to meet specific current obligations and (2) those that are not directly related to current operations and therefore are in the nature of long-term investments.

Several funds of the first type, discussed in preceding chapters, include the following:

Objective 9

Identify and explain the accounting for funds.

Fund	Purpose
Petty Cash	Payment of small expenditures, in currency
Payroll Cash Account	Payment of salaries and wages
Dividend Cash Account	Payment of dividends
Interest Fund	Payment of interest on long-term debt

In general, these funds are used to handle more conveniently and more expeditiously the payments of certain current obligations, to maintain better control over such expenditures, and to divide adequately the responsibility for cash disbursements. These funds are ordinarily shown as current assets (as part of Cash, if immaterial) because the obligations to which they relate are ordinarily current liabilities.

Funds of the second type are similar to long-term investments, as they do not relate directly to current operations. They are ordinarily shown in the long-term investments section of the balance sheet or in a separate section if relatively large in amount. The more common funds of this type and the purpose of each are listed below:

Fund	Purpose
Sinking Fund	Payment of long-term indebtedness
Plant Expansion Fund	Purchase or construction of additional plant
Stock Redemption Fund	Retirement of share capital (usually preferred shares)
Contingency Fund	Payment of unforeseen obligations

Because the cash set aside will not be needed until some time in the future, it is usually invested in securities so that revenue may be earned on the fund assets. The assets of a fund may or may not be placed in the hands of a trustee. If appointed, the trustee becomes the custodian of the assets, accounts to the company for them, and reports fund revenues and expenses.

Entries for Funds

To keep track of the assets, revenues, and expenses of funds, it is desirable to maintain separate accounts. For example, if a fund is kept for the redemption of a preferred share issue that was issued with a redemption provision after a certain date, the following accounts might be kept:

Share Redemption Fund Cash
Share Redemption Fund Investments
Share Redemption Fund Revenue
Share Redemption Fund Expense
Gain on Sale of Share Redemption Fund Investments
Loss on Sale of Share Redemption Fund Investments

When cash is transferred from the regular cash account, perhaps periodically, the entry is:

Share Redemption Fund Cash	30,000	
Cash		30,000

Securities purchased by the fund are recorded at cost:

Share Redemption Fund Investments	27,000	
Share Redemption Fund Cash		27,000

If securities purchased for the fund are to be held temporarily, they would be treated in the accounts in the same manner as temporary investments, described earlier in this chapter. If they are to be held for a long period of time, they are treated in accordance with the entries described for long-term investments. In both cases, the securities purchased are recorded at cost when acquired, but in the case of bonds purchased as long-term investments for the fund, premium or discount should be amortized.

If we assume that the entry above records the purchase at a premium of 10-year bonds of a par value of $25,000 on April 1, the issue date, and that the bonds bear interest at 8%, the entry for the receipt of semiannual interest on October 1 is:

Share Redemption Fund Cash	1,000	
Share Redemption Fund Revenue		1,000

At December 31, entries are made to record amortization of premium for nine months and to accrue interest on the bonds for three months:

Share Redemption Fund Revenue	150	
Share Redemption Fund Investments		150
(To record amortization of premium for		
9 months, 9/12 of 1/10 of $2,000)		
Accrued Interest on Stock Redemption Fund Investments	500	
Share Redemption Fund Revenue		500
(To record accrued interest for		
3 months, 3/12 of 8% of $25,000)		

Expenses of the fund paid are recorded by debiting Share Redemption Fund Expense and crediting Share Redemption Fund Cash.

When the investments held by the fund are disposed of, the entries to record the sale are similar to regular disposals of investments. Any revenue and expense accounts set up to record fund transactions should be closed to Income Summary at the end of the accounting period and reflected in earnings of the current period. The entry for retirement of the preferred shares is:

Preferred Shares	500,000	
Share Redemption Fund Cash		500,000

Any balance remaining in the Share Redemption Fund Cash account is transferred back to a general cash account.

In some cases, a company purchases its own shares or bonds when it is using a share redemption fund or sinking fund. In these situations, the treasury shares should be deducted from common shares (or the shareholders' equity section) and treasury bonds should be deducted from bonds payable. Dividend revenue or interest revenue should not be recorded for these securities.

Funds and Reserves Distinguished

Although funds and reserves (appropriations) are not similar, they are sometimes confused because they may be related and often have similar titles. *A simple distinction may be drawn: A fund is always an asset and always has a debit balance; a reserve (if used only in the limited sense recommended) is an appropriation of retained earnings, always has a credit balance, and is never an asset.*

The distinction is illustrated by reconsidering the entries made in connection with a stock redemption fund discussed earlier. The fund was originally established by the following entry.

| Share Redemption Fund Cash | 30,000 | |
| Cash | | 30,000 |

Some of this cash was used to purchase investments; the assets of the fund were then cash and investments. Ultimately, the investments were sold and the stock redemption fund cash was used to retire the preferred shares.

If the company chose to do so, it could establish an appropriation for stock redemption at the same time to reduce the retained earnings apparently available for dividends. Appropriated retained earnings is established by periodic transfers from retained earnings, as follows:

| Retained Earnings | 30,000 | |
| Appropriation for Share Redemption | | 30,000 |

It will have a credit balance and will be shown in the shareholders' equity section of the balance sheet. When the shares are retired by payment of cash from the stock redemption fund, the appropriation is transferred back to retained earnings:

| Appropriation for Share Redemption | 500,000 | |
| Retained Earnings | | 500,000 |

The foregoing discussion indicates that the fund was an asset accumulated to retire shares and had a debit balance; the appropriation was a subdivision of retained earnings and had a credit balance. The fund was used to redeem the shares; the appropriation was transferred back to retained earnings.

SUMMARY

The Investment section of a balance sheet can comprise many different items. The major equity and debt securities and their accounting treatment are summarized below.

Security	Method
Current Assets:	
Marketable securities	Lower of Cost and Market
Nonmarketable securities	Cost
Noncurrent Assets:	
Investment in common shares in excess of 50% voting equity interest	Equity
Investment in common shares of 20%–50% of voting equity interest	Equity
Investment is less than 20% voting equity interest in the form of marketable equity securities	Lower of Cost and Market
Nonmarketable equity securities	Cost
Marketable or nonmarketable debt securities	Unamortized Cost

Investments over 50% are usually consolidated, but on the parent company's books the equity method is generally used. The presumption is that investments of 20% or more exercise significant influence and investments less than 20% do not. Cash surrender value of life insurance and various types of funds, such as a stock redemption fund or bond sinking fund are also reported in the Investment section.

FUNDAMENTAL CONCEPTS

1. Temporary investments usually include short-term paper, marketable debt securities, and marketable equity securities. To be classified as current assets, such investments must be (1) readily marketable and (2) intended to be converted into cash within one year or the operating cycle, whichever is longer.

2. Temporary investments are aggregated (as a portfolio) and generally reported at the lower of the aggregated cost and market value determined at the balance sheet date.

3. The amount by which the aggregate cost of temporary investments exceeds market value is accounted for as a valuation allowance. The unrealized loss is reported in the income statement. Recoveries of previously recognized unrealized loses on temporary investments also flow through the income statement.

4. If a temporary investment is transferred from the current to the noncurrent portfolio, or vice versa, the security should be transferred at the lower of its cost and market value at the date of the transfer. Any loss should be accounted for as if realized.

5. If the market rate of interest is below a bond's stated rate, the bond will sell at a premium, whereas if the market rate is higher than the bond's stated rate, the bond will sell at a discount.

6. Two widely used methods of amortizing bond premium and discount are (1) the straight-line method and (2) the effective interest method. The effective interest method is the better method because it produces a constant rate of return on the book value of the investment from period to period.

7. An investment of more than 50% in the voting shares of another corporation results in a controlling interest, so the preparation of consolidated statements is generally appropriate.

8. An investment of between 20% and 50% of the voting shares of another corporation usually results in significant influence that is accounted for by using the equity method.

9. An investment of less than 20% of the voting shares of another corporation is generally a passive interest and the use of the cost method is appropriate.

10. Under the equity method, the investment's carrying amount is periodically increased (decreased) by the investor's proportionate share of the earnings (losses) of the investee and decreased by all dividends received by the investor from the investee.

11. The investor who receives rights to purchase additional shares may (1) exercise the rights by purchasing additional shares, (2) sell the rights, or (3) permit them to expire without selling or using them.

12. When the company is the beneficiary and has the right to cancel the life insurance policy at its own option, the cash surrender value of the policy is an asset of the company; only the difference between the premium paid and the increase in the cash surrender value represents an expense to the company.

13. Funds and reserves (appropriations) are not the same. A fund is always an asset and always has a debit balance; a reserve or appropriation of retained earnings always has a credit balance and is never an asset.

APPENDIX 18A
Changing From and To the Equity Method

If the investor level of influence or ownership falls below that necessary for continued use of the equity method, a change must be made to the cost method. The earnings or losses that were previously recognized by the investor under the equity method should remain as part of the carrying amount of the investment, with no retroactive restatement to the new method.

To the extent that dividends received by the investor in subsequent periods exceed its share of the investee's earnings for such periods (all periods following the change in method), they should be accounted for as a reduction of the investment carrying amount, rather than revenue.

For example, using the data from the Investee/Investor illustration on pages 893–894, assume that on January 2, 1994, Investee Company sold an additional 1,500,000 of its own common shares to the public, thereby reducing Investor Company's ownership from 25% to 10%, and that the net income (or loss) and dividends of Investee Company for the years 1994 through 1996 are shown below.

Year	Investor's Share of Investee Income (Loss)	Investee Dividends Received by Investor
1994	$600,000	$ 400,000
1995	350,000	400,000
1996	–0–	210,000
Totals	$950,000	$1,010,000

Assuming a change from the equity method to the cost method as of January 2, 1994, Investor Company's reported investment in Investee Company and its reported income would be as shown below.

Year	Dividend Revenue Recognized	Cumulative Excess of Share of Earnings Over Dividends Received	Investment at December 31
1994	$400,000	$200,000[a]	$8,780,000
1995	400,000	150,000[b]	8,780,000
1996	150,000	(60,000)[c]	8,780,000 − $60,000

[a]$600,000 − $400,000 = $200,000
[b]($350,000 − $400,000) + $200,000 = $150,000
[c]$150,000 − $210,000 = ($60,000)

The following entries would be recorded by Investor Company to recognize the above dividends and earnings data for the three years subsequent to the change in methods:

1994 and 1995

Cash	400,000	
Revenue From Investment		400,000
(To record dividend received from		
Investee Company)		

1996

Cash	210,000	
Investment in Investee Company		60,000
Revenue From Investment		150,000

(Continued)

(To record dividend revenue from Investee Company in
1996 and to recognize cumulative excess of dividends
received over share of Investee earnings in periods
subsequent to change from equity method)

When a change is made from the equity method to the cost method, *the cost basis for accounting purposes is the carrying amount of the investment at the date of the change.* In addition, amortizing the excess of acquisition price over the proportionate share of book value acquired attributable to undervalued depreciable assets and unrecorded goodwill ceases when the change of methods occurs. In other words, the net method is applied in its entirety once the equity method is no longer appropriate.

CHANGE TO THE EQUITY METHOD

Transactions and events may occur that require an investor to change to the equity method of accounting for an investment that was previously properly accounted for under the cost method. Such a change is not considered to be a change in accounting policy and must, therefore, be applied prospectively.[16]

For example, on January 2, 1993, Amsted Ltd. purchased 10% of Cable Company's outstanding common shares for $500,000 cash. On that date, the net assets of Cable Company had a book value of $3,000,000. On January 2, 1995, Amsted Ltd. purchased an additional 20% of Cable Company's common shares for $1,200,000 cash when the book value of Cable's net assets was $4,000,000. Now, having a 30% interest, Amsted Ltd. must use the equity method. The net income reported by Cable Company and the Cable Company dividends received by Amsted during the period 1993 through 1994 were as follows:

Year	Cable Company Net Income	Cable Co. Dividends Paid to Amsted
1993	$ 500,000	$ 20,000
1994	1,000,000	30,000
1995	1,200,000	120,000

The journal entries recorded from January 2, 1993 through December 31, 1994 relative to Amsted's investment in Cable, reflecting the data above and a change from the cost method to the equity method, are as follows:

January 2, 1993

Investment in Cable Company Shares	500,000	
Cash		500,000

(To record the purchase of a 10%
interest in Cable Company)

December 31, 1993

Cash	20,000	
Dividend Revenue		20,000

(To record the receipt of cash
dividends from Cable Company)

December 31, 1994

Cash	30,000	
Dividend Revenue		30,000

(To record the receipt of cash
dividends from Cable Company)

(Continued)

---

[16] *CICA Handbook,* Section 1506, par. .04.

January 2, 1995

Investment in Cable Company Shares	1,200,000	
Cash		1,200,000
(To record the purchase of an additional interest in Cable Company)		

Note: All **asterisked** questions, cases, exercises, and problems relate to material contained in the appendix to this chapter.

——— QUESTIONS ———

1. In what way may the accounting treatment of marketable debt securities differ from that accorded marketable equity securities (both classified as current assets)?

2. Define "marketable equity securities" and explain how to account for them when they are a current asset.

3. What disclosure is required for current marketable securities in either the financial statements or the accompanying notes?

4. Why is market value proposed as a substitute for cost in valuing marketable securities?

5. Distinguish between the nature of temporary and long-term investments. Give two examples of each type. Is it possible for securities of the same kind to be carried by one company as a long-term investment and by another as a short-term investment? Explain.

6. Where on the balance sheet are long-term investments customarily presented? Identify six items customarily classified as long-term investments.

7. For what reasons would a company purchase bonds and shares of another company?

8. What purpose does the variety in bond features (types and characteristics) serve?

9. Distinguish between bond maturity value, bond market value, bond face value, bond par value, and bond principal value.

10. What factors cause a difference between the stated interest rate and the yield interest rate?

11. What are the problems of accounting for bond investments between interest dates?

12. Kimmel Ltd. has both short-term and long-term debt securities. If the market value of these securities exceeds their carrying amount, at what amount should these assets be reported at the end of the year?

13. On July 1, 1994, Chen Ltd. purchased $1,000,000 of Swift Inc. 8% bonds due on July

1, 2004. Chen expects to hold the bonds until maturity. The bonds, which pay interest semiannually on January 1 and July 1, were purchased for $875,000 to yield 10%. Determine the amount of interest revenue Chen should report on its income statement for the year ended December 31, 1994.

14. Distinguish between the effective interest method and the straight-line method relative to the effect of each on net income over the life of a bond investment. What are the merits of each method?

15. What is the cost of a long-term investment in bonds? What is the cost of a long-term investment in shares?

16. Contrast the accounting treatment of a premium or discount on long-term bond investments with the treatment of a premium or discount on a long-term bond debt. How is the premium or discount handled relative to a temporary investment?

17. On what basis should shares acquired in exchange for noncash consideration be recorded?

18. Kernan purchased 1,000 of $1,000 face amount, 20-year bonds from Noble Inc. on June 30, 1994 for $1,020,000. Each bond carries five detachable stock purchase warrants, each of which entitles the holder to purchase one Noble common share for $60. On June 30, 1994, the market price of Noble's common shares was $50 per share and $5 per warrant. At what amount should Kernan report the carrying amount of the bonds in its June 30, 1990 balance sheet?

19. Name three methods of accounting for long-term investments in shares subsequent to the date of acquisition. When is each method applicable?

20. What constitutes "significant influence" when an investor's financial interest is below the 50% level?

21. Distinguish between the cost and equity method of accounting for long-term investments in shares subsequent to the date of acquisition.

22. When the equity method is applied, what disclosures should be made in the investor's financial statements?

23. Distinguish between the accounting treatment for Marketable Securities—Current and Marketable Securities—Noncurrent.

24. Sack Co. uses the cost method to account for investments in common shares. What accounting should be made for dividends received in excess of Sack's share of investee's earnings subsequent to the date of investment?

25. Patrick Inc. uses the equity method to account for investments in Korman common shares. The purchase price paid by Patrick implies a fair value of Korman's depreciable assets in excess of Korman's net asset carrying values. How should Patrick account for this excess?

26. How is a stock dividend accounted for by the recipient? How is a stock split accounted for by the recipient?

27. What three dates are significant in relation to stock rights? What are the alternatives available to the recipient of stock rights?

28. Jantzen Ltd. owns 300 of Doris Corporation's common shares, acquired on June 10, 1994 at a total cost of $11,000. On December 2, 1995, Jantzen receives 300 stock rights from Doris. Each right entitles the holder to acquire one share for $45. The market price of Doris' shares on this date, ex-rights, was $50, and the market price of each right was $5. Jantzen sells its rights on the same date for $5 per right less a $90 commission. Determine the gain on sale of the rights by Jantzen.

29. In applying the equity method, what recognition, if any, does the investor give to the excess of its investment cost over its proportionate share of the investee book value at the date of acquisition? What recognition, if any, is given if the investment cost is less than the underlying book value?

30. Delaney Limited has an investment carrying value (equity method) on its books of $170,000, representing a 40% interest in Norton Company, which suffers a $600,000 loss this year. How should Delaney Limited handle its proportionate share of Norton's loss?

31. Distinguish between a fund and a reserve.

32. What are the two general types of funds? Give three examples of each type of fund.

*33. Mohs Inc. gradually acquired stock in Stein Corp. (a nonsubsidiary) until its ownership exceeded 20%. How should this investment be recorded and reported after the last purchase?

CASES

C18-1   **(ISSUES RAISED ABOUT TEMPORARY INVESTMENTS)**   You have just started work for Duff Ltd. as part of the controller's group involved in current financial reporting problems. Rhoda Clements, controller for Duff, is interested in your accounting background because the company has experienced a series of financial reporting surprises over the last few years. Recently, Clements has learned from the company's auditors that a section of the *CICA Handbook* may apply to its investment in securities. She assumes that you are familiar with these requirements and asks how the following situations should be reported in the financial statements.

Situation I. Temporary investments in debt securities in the current asset section have a market value of $3,000 lower than cost.

Situation II. A marketable security whose market value is currently less than cost is classified as current but is to be reclassified as noncurrent.

Situation III. A marketable security, whose market value is currently less than cost, is classified as noncurrent but is to be reclassified as current.

Situation IV. A company's current portfolio of marketable securities consists of the common shares of one company. At the end of the prior year, the market value of the security was 50% of original cost and this reduction in market value was properly reflected in a valuation allowance account. However, at the end of the current year, the market value of the security has appreciated to twice the original cost. The security is still considered current at year end.

Situation V. The company has purchased some convertible debentures that it plans to hold for less than a year. At the end of the company's fiscal year, market value of the convertible debenture is $8,000 below its cost.

Instructions

What is the effect on classification, carrying value, and earnings for each of these situations? Assume that these situations are unrelated.

(MARKET VALUE ACCOUNTING FOR INVESTMENTS) The president of Comtel Ltd. is concerned **C18-2** about a proposed accounting change related to investments in marketable securities. The proposal is that all marketable securities be presented at market value on the balance sheet and the changes that occur in market value be reflected in income in the current period. The president agrees that market value on the balance sheet may be more useful to the investor, but he sees no reason why changes in market value should be reflected in income of the current year.

James Clarke, controller of Comtel Ltd., is also unhappy about the proposal and has recommended the following alternatives:

1. Recognize realized gains and losses from changes in market value in income and report unrealized gains and losses in a special balance sheet account on the equity side of the balance sheet.

2. Report realized and unrealized gains and losses from market value changes in a statement separate from the income statement or as direct charges and credits to a shareholders' equity account.

3. Recognize gains and losses from changes in market value in income based on long-term yield; for example, use the past performance of the enterprise over several years (a 10-year period has been suggested) to determine an average annual rate of yield because of an increase in value.

To the president of Comtel Ltd., these recommendations seem more reasonable.

Instructions

(a) Is the use of a market value or fair value basis of accounting for all marketable securities a desirable and feasible practice? Discuss.

(b) Do you believe the president is correct in stating that one of the alternatives is a better approach to recognition of income in accounting for marketable securities?

(LOWER OF COST AND MARKET: MARKETABLE EQUITY SECURITIES) Badger Limited has **C18-3** followed the practice of valuing its temporary investments in marketable equity securities at the lower of cost and market. At December 31, 1994, its account Investment in Marketable Equity Securities had a balance of $40,000, and the account Allowance for Excess of Cost of Marketable Equity Securities Over Market Value had a balance of $2,000. Analysis disclosed that on December 31, 1993, the facts relating to the securities were as follows.

	Cost	Market	Allowance Required
Mendota Corp. Shares	$20,000	$19,000	$1,000
Waubesa Company Shares	10,000	9,000	1,000
Monona Company Shares	20,000	20,600	–0–
	$50,000		$2,000

During 1994, Waubesa Company shares were sold for $9,200, the difference between the $9,200 and the "new adjusted basis" of $9,000 being recorded as a "Gain on Sale of Securities." The market price of the shares on December 31, 1994 was: Mendota Corp. Shares—$19,900; Monona Company Shares—$20,500.

Instructions

(a) What justification is there for the use of the lower of cost and market in valuing marketable equity securities?

(b) Did Badger Limited properly apply this rule on December 31, 1993? Explain.

(c) Did Badger Limited properly account for the sale of the Waubesa Company shares? Explain.

(d) Are there any additional entries necessary for Badger Limited at December 31, 1994 to reflect the facts on the balance sheet and income statement in accordance with generally accepted accounting principles? Explain.

(AICPA adapted)

C18-4 (MARKETABLE SECURITIES: CURRENT AND NONCURRENT)   Concordia Ltd. has both a current and noncurrent marketable equity securities portfolio. At the beginning of the year, the aggregate market value of each portfolio exceeded its cost. During the year, Concordia sold some securities from each portfolio. At the end of the year, the aggregate cost of each portfolio exceeded its market value.

Concordia also had long-term investments in various bonds, all of which were purchased for face value. During the year, some of these bonds held by Concordia were called prior to their maturity by the bond issuer. Three months before the end of the year, additional similar bonds were purchased for face value plus two months' accrued interest.

Instructions

(a) 1. How should Concordia account for the sale of securities from each portfolio? Why?

      2. How should Concordia account for the marketable equity securities portfolios at year end? Why?

(b) How should Concordia account for the disposition prior to their maturity of the long-term bonds called by their issuer? Why?

(c) How should Concordia report the purchase of the additional similar bonds at the date of the acquisition? Why?

(AICPA adapted)

C18-5 (FINANCIAL STATEMENT EFFECT OF MARKETABLE EQUITY SECURITIES)   Presented below are four unrelated situations involving marketable equity securities:

Situation I. A marketable security, whose market value is currently less than cost, is classified as noncurrent but is to be reclassified as current.

Situation II. A company's noncurrent portfolio of marketable securities consists of the common shares of one company. At the end of the prior year, the market value of the security was 50% of original cost and this effect was reflected in a valuation allowance account. However, at the end of the current year, the market value of the security has appreciated to twice the original cost. The security is still considered noncurrent at year end.

Situation III. A noncurrent securities portfolio with an aggregate market value in excess of cost includes one particular security whose market value has declined to less than one-half of the original cost. The decline in value is considered to be other than temporary.

Situation IV. The statement of financial position of a company does not classify assets and liabilities as current and noncurrent. The portfolio of marketable securities includes securities normally considered current that have a net cost in excess of market value of $12,000. The remainder of the portfolio has a net market value in excess of cost of $29,000.

Instructions

What is the effect on classification, carrying value, and earnings for each of these situations? Complete your response to each situation before proceeding to the next situation.

(MARKETABLE EQUITY SECURITIES: CURRENT AND NONCURRENT) The *CICA Handbook*, **C18-6**
Sections 3010 and 3050, prescribes accounting procedures for temporary and long-term investments, respectively. An important part of these sections concerns the distinction between noncurrent and current classification of investments.

Instructions

(a) Why does a company maintain an investment portfolio of current and noncurrent securities?

(b) What factors should be considered in determining whether investments in marketable securities should be classified as current or noncurrent, and how do these factors affect the accounting treatment for unrealized losses?

(MARKETABLE EQUITY SECURITIES, INCLUDING RECLASSIFICATION) Sylvan Limited pur- **C18-7**
chased marketable securities at a cost of $300,000 on February 1, 1993. When the securities were purchased, the company intended to hold the investment for more than one year. Therefore, the investment was classified as a noncurrent asset in the company's annual report for the year ended December 31, 1993 and stated at its then market value of $250,000.

On September 30, 1990, when the investment had a market value of $261,000, management reclassified the investment as a current asset because the company intended to sell the securities within the next 12 months. The market value of the investment was $273,000 on December 31, 1994.

The presentation of investments in marketable securities on a company's financial statement is affected by management's intentions regarding how long the investments are to be held and by the reporting requirements specified in the *CICA Handbook*.

Instructions

(a) Explain how the difference between cost and market value of the investment in marketable securities would be reflected in the financial statements of Sylvan Limited prepared for the fiscal year ending December 31, 1993, when the investment was classified as a noncurrent asset.

(b) The consequence of management's decision to recognize the investment in marketable securities as short term and reclassify it as a current asset was recorded in the accounts. At what amount would the investment be recorded on September 30, 1994, the date of this decision?

(c) How would the investment in marketable securities be reported in the financial statements of Sylvan Limited as of December 31, 1994 so that the company's financial position and operations for the year 1994 would reflect and report properly the reclassification of the investment from a noncurrent asset to a current asset? Be sure to indicate the affected accounts, the related dollar amounts, and the note disclosures, if any.

(CMA adapted)

(INVESTMENT IN LIFE INSURANCE POLICY) In the course of your examination of the financial **C18-8**
statements of Bartlett Limited as of December 31, 1994, the following entry came to your attention:

January 4, 1994

Receivable From Insurance Company	1,000,000	
Cash Surrender Value of Life Insurance Policies		136,000
Retained Earnings		159,000
Donated Capital From Life Insurance Proceeds		705,000
(Disposition of the proceeds of the life insurance		
policy on Mr. Bartlett's life. Mr. Bartlett died on		
January 1, 1994)		

You are aware that Mr. Tom Bartlett, an officer-shareholder in the small manufacturing firm, insisted that the corporation's board of directors authorize the purchase of an insurance policy to compensate for any loss of earning potential on his death. The corporation paid $295,000 in premiums prior to Mr. Bartlett's death, and was the sole beneficiary of the policy. At the date of death, there had been no premium prepayment and no rebate was due. In prior years, cash surrender value in the amount of $136,000 had been recorded in the accounts.

Instructions

(a) What is the cash surrender value of a life insurance policy?

(b) How should the cash surrender value of a life insurance policy be classified in the financial statements while the policy is in force? Why?

(c) Comment on the propriety of the entry recording the insurance receivable.

C18-9 (BASIC INVESTMENT CONCEPTS AND CLASSIFICATION OF SINKING FUND)

Part A. To manufacture and sell its products, a company must invest in inventories, plant and equipment, and other operating assets. In addition, a manufacturing company often finds it desirable or necessary to invest a portion of its available resources, either directly or through the operation of special funds, in shares, bonds, and other securities.

Instructions

(a) List the reasons why a manufacturing company might invest funds in shares, bonds, and other securities.

(b) What are the criteria for classifying investments as current or noncurrent assets?

Part B. Because of favourable market prices, the trustee of Gail Andersen Company's bond sinking fund invested the current year's contribution to the fund in the company's own bonds. The bonds are being held in the fund without cancellation. The fund also includes cash and securities of other companies.

Instructions

Describe three methods of classifying the bond sinking fund on the balance sheet of Gail Andersen Company. Include a discussion of the propriety of using each method.

C18-10 (CLASSIFICATION OF SINKING FUND)

Gibson Inc. administers the sinking fund applicable to its own outstanding long-term bonds. The following four proposals relate to the accounting treatment of sinking fund cash and securities:

1. To mingle sinking fund cash with general cash and sinking fund securities with other securities, and to show both as current assets on the balance sheet.

2. To keep sinking fund cash in a separate bank account and sinking fund securities separate from other securities, but on the balance sheet to treat cash as a part of the general cash and the securities as part of general investments, both being shown as current assets.

3. To keep sinking fund cash in a separate bank account and sinking fund securities separate from other securities, but to combine the two accounts on the balance sheet under one caption, such as Sinking Fund Cash and Investments, which will be listed as a noncurrent asset.

4. To keep sinking fund cash in a separate bank account and sinking fund securities separate from other securities, and to identify each separately on the balance sheet among the current assets.

Instructions

Identify the proposal that is most appropriate. Give the reasons for your selection.

(CHANGE FROM COST TO EQUITY)   For the past five years, RMT Ltd. has maintained an investment *C18-11 (properly accounted for and reported on) in Beloit Co., amounting to 10% interest in the voting common shares of Beloit Co. The purchase price was $1,050,000 and the underlying net equity in Beloit at the date of purchase was $930,000. On January 2 of the current year, RMT purchased an additional 20% of the voting common shares of Beloit for $2,400,000; the underlying net equity of the additional investment at January 2 was $2,000,000. Beloit has been profitable and has paid dividends annually since RMT's initial acquisition.

Instructions

Discuss how this increase in ownership affects the accounting for and reporting on the investment in Beloit Co. Include in your discussion adjustments, if any, to the amount shown prior to the increase in investment to bring the amount into conformity with generally accepted accounting principles. Also include how current and subsequent periods would be reported on.

(AICPA adapted)

(ETHICAL ISSUES, SALE OF MARKETABLE SECURITIES)   Clark Manufacturing holds a portfolio of C18-12 shares as a short-term marketable security. The market value of the portfolio is greater than its original cost, even though some holdings have decreased in value. Hector Gonzales, the financial vice-president, and Arthur Vanderbilt, the controller, are considering the sale of a part of this stock portfolio. Gonzales wants to sell only those holdings that have increased in value, in order to increase net income this year. Vanderbilt disagrees and wants to sell securities that have recently declined in value. He contends that the company is having a good earnings year and therefore the losses will help to smooth the income this year. As a result, the company will have built up gains for future periods when the company may not be as profitable.

Instructions

Is there an ethical issue in this discussion?

———————— **EXERCISES** ————————

(MARKETABLE EQUITY SECURITIES ENTRIES)   Colonial Limited has the following portfolio of mar- E18-1 ketable securities at the beginning of 1994.

	Cost	Market
London common (5,000 shares)	$225,000	$200,000
Fontaine, Inc. common (3,500 shares)	133,000	140,000
Kellmore nonredeemable preferred (2,000 shares)	180,000	179,000

In 1994, the London shares were sold at a price of $53 per share. In addition, 3,000 shares of Forrest common were acquired at $59.50 per share. The year-end market prices per share were: Fontaine, $32; Kellmore, $95; and Forrest, $44. All of the marketable securities are current assets.

Instructions

(a) Prepare the journal entries to record the sale, purchase, and adjusting entries related to the marketable securities in 1994.

(b) How would the entries in (a) change (if at all) if the marketable securities were long term?

(c) How would the entries in (a) change if the preferred shares were redeemable?

E18-2 **(MARKETABLE EQUITY SECURITIES ENTRIES)** Jackson Company has the following securities in its short-term portfolio of marketable securities on December 31, 1993. All of the securities were purchased in 1993.

	Cost	Market
1,500 shares of Canadian Pacific, common	$ 75,000	$ 69,000
5,000 shares of Northern Telecom, common	180,000	175,000
400 shares of Bell Canada, preferred	60,000	61,600
	$315,000	$305,600

In 1994, Jackson completed the following securities transactions:

March 1   Sold 1,500 shares of Canadian Pacific, common, at $45 less fees of $1,200.

April 1   Bought 700 shares of Stelco, common, at $75 plus fees of $1,300.

August 1   Transferred the Bell Canada, preferred, from the short-term portfolio to the long-term portfolio when the shares were selling at $145 per share.

Jackson Company's short-term portfolio of marketable securities appeared as follows on December 31, 1994.

	Cost	Market
5,000 shares of Northern Telecom, common	$180,000	$205,000
700 shares of Stelco, common	53,800	50,400
	$233,800	$255,400

Instructions

Prepare the general journal entries for Jackson Company for:

(a)   The 1993 adjusting entry.

(b)   The sale of the Canadian Pacific shares.

(c)   The purchase of the Stelco shares.

(d)   The transfer of the Bell Canada shares from the short-term to the long-term portfolio.

(e)   The 1994 adjusting entry for the short-term portfolio.

E18-3 **(MARKETABLE SECURITIES ENTRIES: RECLASSIFICATION)** Gordon Inc. purchased marketable securities at a cost of $340,000 on March 1, 1993. When the securities were purchased, the company intended to hold the investment for more than one year. Therefore, the investment was classified as a noncurrent asset in the company's annual report for the year ended December 31, 1993 and stated at its then market value of $290,000.

On September 30, 1994, when the investment had a market value of $310,000, management reclassified the investment as a current asset because the company intended to sell the securities within the next 12 months. The market value of the investment was $330,000 on December 31, 1994.

Instructions

(a)   What effect does management's decision to recognize the investment in marketable securities as short term and reclassify it as a current asset have on the accounts? At what amount would the investment be recorded on September 30, 1994, the date of this decision?

(b) How would the investment in the marketable securities be reported in the financial statements of Gordon Inc. as of December 31, 1994 so that the company's financial position and operations for the year 1994 would reflect and report properly the reclassification of the investment from a noncurrent asset to a current asset? Be sure to indicate the affected accounts, the related dollar amounts, and the disclosures, if any.

(CMA adapted)

(VALUATION OF TEMPORARY INVESTMENTS)   At the end of its first year of operations, Gilbert   **E18-4**
Limited had a current marketable securities portfolio with a cost of $600,000 and a market value of $650,000.
At the end of its second year of operations, Gilbert Limited had a current marketable securities portfolio with a cost of $550,000 and a market value of $510,000. No securities were sold during the first year. One security with a cost of $80,000 and a market value of $70,000 at the end of the first year was sold for $105,000 during the second year.

Instructions

How should Gilbert Limited report the above facts in its balance sheets and income statements for both years? Discuss the rationale for your answer.

(AICPA adapted)

(MARKETABLE DEBT SECURITIES ENTRIES)   The following information relates to the investments   **E18-5**
of the Lakeside Company in debt securities:

1. On February 1, the company purchased 9% marketable bonds of Crandall Ltd. having a par value of $500,000 at 97 plus accrued interest. Interest is payable April 1 and October 1.

2. On April 1, semiannual interest is received.

3. On July 1, 12% marketable bonds of Quincy, Inc. were purchased. These bonds, with a par value of $200,000, were purchased at 100 plus accrued interest. Interest dates are June 1 and December 1.

4. On September 1, bonds of a par value of $100,000, purchased on February 1, are sold at 99 plus accrued interest.

5. On October 1, semiannual interest is received.

6. On December 1, semiannual interest is received.

7. On December 31, the market value of the bonds purchased February 1 and July 1 are 95 and 94, respectively.

Instructions

(a) Prepare any journal entries you consider necessary, including year-end entries (December 31), assuming that the cost basis is used (i.e. the investment is noncurrent).

(b) If the investments were classified as current, how would the journal entries differ from those in (a)?

(MARKETABLE DEBT SECURITIES ENTRIES)   Robson Inc. frequently invests cash that is not imme-   **E18-6**
diately needed for operations in marketable debt securities. These temporary investments are generally held for a period of several months. The company had adopted the lower of cost and market method on an aggregate basis in accounting for its marketable debt securities. The following transactions occurred over a period of two years.

May 1   12% marketable bonds of a par value of $300,000, with interest payable June 1 and December 1, are purchased at 98 plus accrued interest.

June 1   Semiannual interest is received.

Aug. 1   Bonds of a par value of $70,000, purchased on May 1, are sold at 96½ plus accrued interest.

Dec. 1   Semiannual interest is received.

      31   Entry is made to accrue the proper amount of interest.

      31   The bonds are listed on the market at 94.

June 1   Semiannual interest is received (assume that reversing entries were made on 1/1).

Nov. 15   The remaining bonds of a par value of $230,000 are sold at 97 plus accrued interest.

Dec. 31   The allowance is closed out because no temporary securities are now held.

Instructions

Prepare entries to record the transactions above.

E18-7   **(BOND AMORTIZATION AND LCM ENTRY)**   The following data show the long-term investments of Carey Ltd. on June 30, 1994, the end of its fiscal year. These investments were purchased during the current year on the dates and at the costs shown:

Feb. 1	Prostaff Company $1,000, 11% bonds. Interest payable March 1 and September 1. 50 bonds. Due March 1, 1996.	$ 53,000
Mar. 30	Denson Company common shares, no par, 4,000 shares (5% of the outstanding shares).	45,400
May 1	Rickety, Inc. $1,000, 10% bonds. Interest payable September 1 and March 1. 25 bonds. Due September 1, 1997.	22,600
		$121,000

Instructions

(a)   If amortization of premium or discount is recorded once a year on June 30, what entry would be necessary on June 30, 1994? (Apply the straight-line method.)

(b)   What entry (if any) would be necessary if the investments were classified as current and the market values were as follows on June 30:

Prostaff Company	$ 52,000
Denson Company	41,200
Rickety, Inc.	26,000
	$119,200

E18-8   **(ENTRIES FOR INVESTMENTS IN BONDS)**   The transactions that follow related to bonds purchased by Victoria Limited.

Apr. 1, 1994   Bonds of Pacioli Company of a par value of $40,000 are purchased as a long-term investment at 96 plus accrued interest. The bonds bear interest at 9% payable annually on Dec. 1, and they mature Dec. 1, 2000.

Dec. 1   Interest of $3,600 is received on the Pacioli Company bonds. (Do not amortize discount at this time.)

Dec. 31   The proper amount of interest is accrued, and the entry is made to amortize the proper amount of discount for 1994.

June 1, 1995   Bonds of a par value of $10,000 are sold at 97 plus accrued interest. Assume that reversing entries are made January 1.

Instructions

Prepare journal entries required by Victoria Limited to record the above transactions, using straight-line amortization.

(BOND AMORTIZATION AND LCM ENTRY FOR EQUITY INVESTMENT) On December 31, **E18-9** 1993, Hamsmith Limited owns long-term investments purchased on the dates and at the costs shown below:

Jan. 10, 1993	A Company common, no par, 1,000 shares	$ 46,000
Mar. 20	B Company preferred, no par, 300 shares	60,600
Apr. 1	C Company $1,000, 11% bonds due April 1, 2003, interest payable April 1 and October 1; 25 bonds	27,400
June 1, 1994	D Company $1,000, 12% bonds due June 1, 1998, interest payable December 1 and June 1; 22 bonds	20,800
		$154,800

Instructions

(a) Prepare the entry to record amortization of discount or premium on December 31, 1993. Assume that the company records amortization of discount and premium only at the end of each year, using the straight-line method.

(b) Prepare the entry to record amortization of discount or premium on December 31, 1994.

(c) The market value of the securities as of December 31, 1994 is as follows:

A Company common shares (representing a 2% interest)	$ 49,000
B Company preferred shares (representing a 5% interest)	52,600
C Company bonds	25,300
D Company bonds	23,000
	$149,900

What entry, if any, would you recommend be made with respect to this information, and what disclosures, if any, should be made in the financial statements?

(EFFECTIVE INTEREST BOND AMORTIZATION) On January 1, 1994, Cullen Limited purchases **E18-10** $300,000 of Bloyd Company 8% bonds for $231,180. The interest is payable semiannually on June 30 and December 31 and the bonds mature in 10 years. The purchase price provides a yield of 12% on the investment.

Instructions

(a) Prepare the journal entry on January 1, 1994 to record the purchase of the investment (record the investment at gross or maturity value).

(b) Prepare the journal entry on June 30, 1994 to record the receipt of the first interest payment and any amortization, using the straight-line method.

(c) Prepare the journal entry on June 30, 1994 to record the receipt of the first interest payment and any amortization, using the effective interest method.

E18-11 **(PURCHASE AND SALE OF BONDS)**   On June 1, 1993, Doyle Inc. purchased as a long-term investment 600 of the $1,000 face value, 8% bonds of Universal Corporation for $553,668. The bonds were purchased to yield 10% interest. Interest is payable semiannually on December 1 and June 1. The bonds mature on June 1, 1998. Doyle uses the effective interest method of amortization. On November 1, 1994, Doyle sells the bonds for $588,000. This amount includes the appropriate accrued interest. (Round computations to nearest dollar.)

Instructions

Prepare a schedule showing the income or loss, before income taxes, from the bond investment that Doyle should record for the years ended December 31 of both 1993 and 1994.

(CMA adapted)

E18-12 **(EQUITY METHOD WITH REVALUED ASSETS)**   On January 1, 1994, Filley Company purchased 2,500 Pricer Ltd. common shares (25%) for $350,000. Additional information related to the identifiable assets and liabilities of Pricer Ltd. at the date of acquisition is as follows.

	Cost	Market
Assets not subject to depreciation	$ 500,000	$ 500,000
Assets subject to depreciation (10 years remaining)	800,000	860,000
Total identifiable assets	$1,300,000	$1,360,000
Liabilities	$ 100,000	$ 100,000

During 1994, Pricer Ltd. reported the following information on its income statement:

Income before extraordinary item	$200,000
Extraordinary gain (net of tax)	80,000
Net income	$280,000
Dividends declared and paid by Pricer Ltd. during 1994	$120,000

Instructions

(a) Prepare the journal entry to record the purchase by Filley Company of Pricer Ltd. on January 1, 1994.

(b) Prepare the journal entries to record Filley's equity in the net income and dividends of Pricer Ltd. for 1994. Depreciable assets are depreciated on a straight-line basis and goodwill is amortized over 20 years.

E18-13 **(EQUITY METHOD WITH REVALUED ASSETS)**   On January 1, 1994, Fernandez Inc. purchased 40% of the common shares of Erin Ltd. for $400,000. The balance sheet reported the following information related to Erin Ltd. at the date of acquisition:

Assets not subject to depreciation	$200,000
Assets subject to depreciation (10-year life remaining)	600,000
Liabilities	100,000

Additional Information

1. Both book value and fair value are the same for assets not subject to depreciation and the liabilities.

2. The fair market value of the assets subject to depreciation is $680,000.

3. The company depreciates its assets on a straight-line basis; intangible assets are amortized over five years.

4. Erin Ltd. reports net income of $150,000 and declares and pays dividends of $100,000 in 1994.

Instructions

(a) Prepare the journal entry to record Fernandez's purchase of Erin Ltd.

(b) Prepare the journal entries to record Fernandez's equity in the net income and dividends of Erin Ltd. for 1994.

(c) Assume the same facts as above, except that Erin's net income includes an extraordinary loss (net of tax) of $30,000. Prepare the journal entries to record Fernandez's equity in the net income and dividends of Erin Ltd. for 1994.

(SALE AFTER STOCK SPLIT; COST AND EQUITY) Price Company purchased 30,000 common shares **E18-14** (a 30% interest) of Waterhouse Company at $18 per share on January 2, 1993. During 1993, Waterhouse Company reported net income of $200,000 and paid dividends of $60,000. On January 2, 1994, Price received 10,000 common shares as a result of a stock split by Waterhouse Company.

Instructions

(a) Prepare the entry to record the sale of 1,000 shares at $14 per share by Price Company on January 3, 1994, applying the cost method of accounting for the investment (assume a lack of significant influence).

(b) Prepare the entry to record the sale of 1,000 shares at $14 per share on January 3, 1994, applying the equity method in accounting for the investment. Assume the acquisition cost approximated the book value acquired on January 2, 1993.

(INVESTMENT ACCOUNTED FOR UNDER THE EQUITY METHOD) On July 1, 1994, Ace Com- **E18-15** pany purchased for cash 50% of the outstanding common shares of Bethel Company. Both Ace Company and Bethel Company have a December 31 year end. Bethel Company, whose common shares are actively traded in the over-the-counter market, reported its total net income for the year to Ace Company and also paid cash dividends on November 15, 1994 to Ace Company and its other shareholders.

Instructions

How should Ace Company report the above facts in its December 31, 1994 balance sheet and its income statement for the year then ended? Discuss the rationale for your answer.

(AICPA adapted)

(DETERMINE PROPER INCOME REPORTING) Presented below are three independent situations that **E18-16** you are to solve:

1. Village Green Inc. received dividends from its investments in common shares during the year ended December 31, 1994, as follows:

   (a) A cash dividend of $10,000 is received from Gary Corporation. (Village Green owns a 2% interest in Gary.)

   (b) A cash dividend of $60,000 is received from Mid-Plains Corporation. (Village Green owns a 30% interest in Mid-Plains.) A majority of Village Green's directors are also directors of Mid-Plains Corporation.

(c) A stock dividend of 300 shares from Petty Inc. was received on December 10, 1994, on which date the quoted market value of Petty's shares was $10 each. Village Green owns less than 1% of Petty's common shares.

Determine how much dividend income Village Green should report in its 1994 income statement.

2. On January 3, 1994, Perly Co. purchased as a long-term investment 5,000 Bonton Co. common shares for $79 per share, which represents a 2% interest. On December 31, 1994, the market price of the shares was $83 each. On March 3, 1995, it sold all 5,000 Bonton shares for $100 each. The company regularly sells securities of this type. The income tax rate is 35%. Determine the amount of gain or loss on disposal that should be reported on the income statement in 1995.

3. Morgan owns a 4% interest in Canton Corporation, which declared a cash dividend of $600,000 on November 27, 1994 to shareholders of record on December 16, 1994, payable on January 6, 1995. In addition, on October 15, 1993, Morgan received a liquidating dividend of $9,000 from Silver Mining Company. Morgan owns 6% of Silver Mining. Determine the amount of dividend income Morgan should report on its financial statements for 1993.

E18-17 **(ENTRIES FOR STOCK RIGHTS)** On January 10, 1993, Missle Company purchased 240 of Patriot Corporation's common shares, no-par value (a 3% interest), for $24,000, as a long-term investment. On July 12, 1993, Missle Corporation announced that one right would be issued for every two shares held.

July 30, 1993 Rights to purchase 120 shares at $100 per share are received. The market value of the shares is $120 each and the market value of the rights is $30 each.

Aug. 10 The rights to purchase 50 shares are sold at $28 per right.

Aug. 11 The additional 70 rights are exercised, and 70 shares are purchased at $100 each.

Nov. 15 50 shares are sold at $130 each.

Instructions

Prepare general journal entries on the books of Missle Company for the foregoing transactions.

E18-18 **(ENTRIES FOR STOCK RIGHTS)** Voss Company purchases 240 common shares of Cadlac Inc. on February 17. The no-par shares, costing $27,300, are to be a long-term investment for Voss Company.

1. On June 30, Cadlac Inc. announces that rights are to be issued. One right will be received for every two shares owned.

2. The rights mentioned in (1) are received on July 15; 120 shares may be purchased with these rights plus $100 per share. The shares are currently selling for $120 each. Market value of the stock rights is $20 per right.

3. On August 5, 70 rights are exercised and 70 shares are purchased at $100 each.

4. On August 12, the remaining stock rights are sold at $22 each.

5. On September 29, Voss Company sells 50 shares at $125 each.

Instructions

Prepare necessary journal entries for the five numbered items above.

E18-19 **(INVESTMENT IN LIFE INSURANCE POLICY)** Cheryl Company pays the premiums on two insurance policies on the life of its president, Sue Cheryl. Information concerning premiums paid in 1994 follows.

Beneficiary	Face	Prem.	Dividends Cr. to Prem.	Prem.	Cash Surrender Value Net 1/1/94	12/31/94
1. Cheryl Co.	$250,000	$8,500	$2,940	$5,560	$35,000	$37,700
2. President's spouse	75,000	3,000		3,000	9,000	9,750

Instructions

(a)   Prepare entries in journal form to record the payment of premiums in 1994.

(b)   If the president died in January 1995 and the beneficiaries are paid the face amounts of the policies, what entry would Cheryl Company make?

(ENTRIES AND DISCLOSURE FOR BOND SINKING FUND)   The general ledger of Vic Sommerfeld **E18-20** Company shows an account for Bonds Payable with a balance of $2,000,000. Interest is payable on these bonds semiannually. Of the $2,000,000, bonds in the amount of $100,000 were recently purchased at par by the sinking fund trustee and are held in the sinking fund as an investment of the fund. The annual rate of interest is 11%.

Instructions

(a)   What entry or entries should be made by Vic Sommerfeld Company to record payment of the semiannual interest? (The company makes interest payments directly to bondholders.)

(b)   Illustrate how the bonds payable and the sinking fund accounts should be shown in the balance sheet. Assume that the sinking fund investments other than Vic Sommerfeld Company's bonds amount to $506,000, and that the sinking fund cash amounts to $21,000.

(ENTRIES FOR PLANT EXPANSION FUND, NUMBERS OMITTED)   The transactions given below **E18-21** relate to a fund being accumulated by Roeming Company over a period of 20 years for the construction of additional buildings:

1.   Cash is transferred from the general cash account to the fund.

2.   Preferred shares of Habitat Limited are purchased as an investment of the fund.

3.   Bonds of J. Mullins Corporation are purchased between interest dates at a discount as an investment of the fund.

4.   Expenses of the fund are paid from the fund cash.

5.   Interest is collected on J. Mullins Corporation bonds.

6.   Bonds held in the fund are sold at a gain between interest dates.

7.   Dividends are received on Habitat Limited preferred shares.

8.   Common shares held in the fund are sold at a loss.

9.   Cash is paid from the fund for building construction.

10.   The cash balance remaining in the fund is transferred to general cash.

Instructions

Prepare journal entries to record the miscellaneous transactions listed above, with amounts omitted.

*E18-22 **(CHANGE FROM EQUITY TO COST)**   Land Corp. was a 30% owner of Jensen Limited, holding 210,000 of Jensen's common shares on December 31, 1993. The investment account had the following entries:

Investment in Jensen

1/1/92 Cost	$3,180,000	12/6/92 Dividend received	$150,000
12/31/92 Share of income	390,000	12/31/92 Amortization of	
12/31/93 Share of income	510,000	undervalued assets	30,000
		12/5/93 Dividend received	240,000
		12/31/93 Amortization of	
		undervalued assets	30,000

On January 2, 1994, Land sold 119,000 shares of Jensen for $3,250,000, thereby losing its significant influence. During the year 1994, Jensen experienced the following results of operations and paid the following dividends to Land.

	Jensen Income (Loss)	Dividends Paid to Land
1994	$300,000	$56,600

Instructions

(a)   What effect does the January 2, 1994 transaction have on Land's accounting treatment for its investment in Jensen?

(b)   Compute the carrying value of the investment in Jensen as of December 31, 1994.

——————— **PROBLEMS** ———————

P18-1   **(MARKETABLE EQUITY SECURITIES: ENTRIES AND PRESENTATION)**   Total Computers Ltd. invests its excess idle cash on March 2, 1993 in the following short-term marketable securities.

Security	Quantity	Per-Share Cost
Mableleen Limited, preferred	1,700 shares	$70
Atlantic Cement Ltd., common	3,000 shares	35
Pacific Electric Ltd., common	1,000 shares	50

The following data relate to the years 1993 and 1994:

For year 1993—Cash dividends received: Mableleen, $6.00 per share
Atlantic Cement, $1.00 per share
Pacific Electric, $2.50 per share

Dec. 31, 1993—Market values per share: Mableleen, $67
Atlantic Cement, $33
Pacific Electric, $52

Feb. 12, 1994—Sold all shares of Atlantic Cement at $41 per share.

Nov. 30, 1994—Purchased 1,500 shares of Mobil Company common for $66 each.

(Continued)

For the year 1994—Cash dividends received: Mableleen, $6.00 per share
Atlantic Cement, $0.25 per share
Pacific Electric, $3.00 per share
Mobil Company, $2.00 per share

Dec. 31, 1994—Market values per share: Mableleen, $80
Pacific Electric, $34
Mobil Company, $61

Instructions

(a) Prepare all of the journal entries to reflect the transactions and data above in accordance with professional pronouncements.

(b) Prepare the descriptions and amounts that should be reported on the face of Total Computers Ltd.'s comparative financial statements for 1993 and 1994.

(c) Draft the note that should accompany the 1993–1994 comparative statements relative to the marketable equity securities.

(MARKETABLE EQUITY SECURITIES: STATEMENT PRESENTATION)   Oakwood Ltd. invested its **P18-2** excess cash in temporary investments during 1992. As of December 31, 1992, the portfolio of short-term marketable securities consisted of the following common shares.

Security	Quantity	Total Cost	Total Market
Tinkers, Inc.	1,000 shares	$ 15,000	$ 19,000
Evers Corp.	2,000 shares	50,000	42,000
Chance Aircraft	2,000 shares	72,000	60,000
		$137,000	$121,000

Instructions

(a) What descriptions and amounts should be reported on the face of Oakwood's December 31, 1992 balance sheet relative to short-term investments?

On December 31, 1993, Oakwood's portfolio of short-term marketable securities consisted of the following common shares.

Security	Quantity	Total Cost	Total Market
Tinkers, Inc.	1,000 shares	$ 15,000	$20,000
Tinkers, Inc.	2,000 shares	38,000	40,000
Lakeshore Company	1,000 shares	16,000	12,000
Chance Aircraft	2,000 shares	72,000	22,000
		$141,000	$94,000

During the year 1993, Oakwood Ltd. sold 2,000 shares of Evers Corp. for $37,000 and purchased 2,000 more shares of Tinkers, Inc. and 1,000 shares of Lakeshore Company.

(b) What descriptions and amounts should be reported on the face of Oakwood's December 31, 1993 balance sheet? What descriptions and amounts should be reported to reflect Oakwood's 1993 income statement?

On December 31, 1994, Oakwood's portfolio of short-term marketable securities consisted of the following.

Security	Quantity	Total Cost	Total Market
Chance Aircraft	2,000 shares	$72,000	$82,000
Lakeshore Company	500 shares	8,000	6,000
		$80,000	$88,000

During the year 1994, Oakwood Ltd. sold 3,000 shares of Tinkers, Inc. for $39,500 and 500 shares of Lakeshore Company at a loss of $2,500.

(c)   What descriptions and amounts should be reported on the face of Oakwood's December 31, 1994 balance sheet? What descriptions and amounts should be reported to reflect the above in Oakwood's 1994 income statement?

(d)   Assuming that comparative financial statements for 1993 and 1994 are presented, draft the footnote necessary for full disclosure of Oakwood's transactions and position in marketable securities.

P18-3   **(APPLYING LOWER OF COST AND MARKET)**   GraNite is a medium-sized corporation specializing in quarrying stone for building construction. The company has long dominated the market, at one time achieving a 70% market penetration. During prosperous years, the company's profits, coupled with a conservative dividend policy, resulted in funds being available for outside investment. Over the years. GraNite has had a policy of investing idle cash in equity securities. In particular, GraNite has made periodic investments in the company's principal supplier, Mark Industries. Although the firm currently owns 12% of the outstanding common shares of Mark Industries, GraNite does not have significant influence over the operations of Mark Industries.

Kristine Risling has recently joined GraNite as assistant controller, and her first assignment is to prepare the 1994 year-end adjusting entries for the accounts that are valued by the lower of cost and market rule for financial reporting purposes. Risling has gathered the following information about GraNite's pertinent accounts:

GraNite has short-term investments in the marketable securities of Ajax Motors and Morgan Electric. During this fiscal year, GraNite purchased 100,000 shares of Ajax Motors for $1,400,000; these shares currently have a market value of $1,600,000. GraNite's investment in Morgan Electric has not been as profitable; the company acquired 50,000 shares of Morgan in April 1994 at $20 per share, a purchase that currently has a value of $600,000.

Prior to 1994, GraNite invested $22,500,000 in Mark Industries and has not changed its holdings this year. This long-term investment in Mark Industries was valued on the company's 1993 Statement of Financial Position at $21,500,000. GraNite's 12% ownership of Mark Industries has a current market value of $22,200,000

Instructions

(a)   Prepare the appropriate adjusting entries for GraNite as of December 31, 1994 to reflect the application of the lower of cost and market rule for the temporary investments described above.

(b)   Describe how the results of the valuation adjustments made in (a) would be reflected in the body of and/or footnotes to GraNite's 1994 financial statements.

(CMA adapted)

P18-4   **(LOWER OF COST AND MARKET AND EQUITY METHOD)**   Zoe Incorporated is a publicly traded company that manufactures products to clean and demagnetize video and audio tape recorders and players. The company grew rapidly during its first 10 years and made three public offerings during this period. During its rapid growth period, Zoe acquired common shares of Guttman Inc. and Cairo Importers. In 1983, Zoe acquired 25% of Guttman's common shares for $588,000 and properly accounts for this investment using the equity method. For its fiscal year ended November 30, 1994, Guttman Inc. reported net income of $240,000 and paid dividends of $100,000. In 1985, Zoe acquired 10% of Cairo Importers' common shares for $204,000 and properly accounts for this investment using the cost method. Zoe has a policy of investing idle cash in marketable equity securities. The following data pertain to the securities in Zoe's investment portfolio.

Marketable Equity Securities at November 30, 1993

Security	Total Cost	Total Market
Horton Electric	$326,000	$314,000
Edwards Inc.	184,000	181,000
Evert Company	96,000	98,000
	606,000	593,000
Cairo Importers	204,000	198,000
	$810,000	$791,000

Marketable Equity Securities at November 30, 1994

Security	Total Cost	Total Market
Horton Electric	$326,000	$323,000
Edwards Inc.	184,000	180,000
Rogers Limited	105,000	108,000
	615,000	611,000
Cairo Importers	204,000	205,000
	$819,000	$816,000

On November 14, 1994, Amanda McElroy was hired by Zoe as assistant controller. Her first assignment was to propose the entries to record the November activity and the November 30, 1994 year-end adjusting entries for the investments in marketable equity securities and the long-term investment in common shares. Using Zoe's ledger of investment transactions and the data given above, McElroy proposed the following entries and submitted them to Able Gance, controller, for review.

Entry 1 (November 8, 1994)

Cash	$ 99,500	
Marketable Equity Securities: Evert Company		$ 98,000
Realized Gain on Sale of Marketable Equity Securities		1,500
(To record the sale of Evert Company shares for $99,500)		

Entry 2 (November 26, 1994)

Marketable Equity Securities: Rogers Limited	$105,000	
Cash		$105,000
(To record the purchase of Rogers Limited common shares for 102,200 plus brokerage fees of $2,800)		

Entry 3 (November 30, 1994)

Unrealized Loss on Valuation of Marketable Equity Securities	$ 3,000	
Allowance for Excess of Cost of Marketable Equity Securities Over Market Value		$ 3,000
(To recognize a loss equal to the excess of cost over market value of marketable equity securities)		

Entry 4 (November 30, 1994)

Cash	$ 37,000	
Dividend Revenue		$ 37,000

(Continued)

(To record dividends received from marketable
equity securities)

Guttman Inc.	$25,000
Cairo Importers	9,000
Horton Electric	3,000

Entry 5 (November 30, 1994)

Investment in Guttman Inc.	$ 60,000	
Investment income		$ 60,000

(To record share of Guttman Inc. income under the
equity method, $240,000 × .25)

Instructions

(a) Distinguish between the characteristics of temporary investments and long-term investments, and explain how a particular security may be properly classified as a temporary investment in one company and a long-term investment in another company.

(b) The journal entries proposed by Amanda McElroy will establish the value of Zoe Incorporated's equity investments to be reported on the company's external financial statements. Review each of the journal entries proposed by McElroy and indicate whether or not it is in accordance with the applicable reporting standards. If an entry is incorrect, prepare the correct entry or entries that should have been made.

(c) Because Zoe Incorporated owns more than 20% of Guttman Inc., Able Gance has adopted the equity method to account for the investment in Guttman Inc. Under what circumstances would it be inappropriate to use the equity method to account for a 25% interest in the common shares of Guttman Inc.?

(AICPA adapted)

P18-5 **(MARKETABLE SECURITIES: ENTRIES AND PRESENTATION)** Microline Limited has a policy of investing any cash not needed for immediate use in marketable securities. Microline usually invests in debt securities but occasionally invests in high-yield shares. On December 31, 1994, the portfolio of marketable securities contained the following.

	Cost	Market
80—9½% Province of Alberta, serial bonds, maturity July 1, 1995, interest payable January 1 and July 1 (face value, $1,000)	97½	96½
160—12% Evans Produce bonds, interest payable March 1 and September 1 (face value, $1,000)	93½	84¼
100—15% Sure Grow Lawn Turf bonds, interest payable February 1 and August 1 (face value, $1,000)	100½	99½

Microline had the following transactions in marketable securities during 1995:

Jan. 1   Received the semiannual interest on Province of Alberta bonds.

Feb. 1   Received the semiannual interest on Sure Grow Lawn Turf bonds.

Feb. 10   Purchased 600 no-par common shares of Ontario Bell Co. at $26 plus $150 in brokerage fees.

Mar. 1   Received the semiannual interest on Evans Produce bonds.

Mar. 15   Sold the Sure Grow Lawn Turf bonds at 102½ plus accrued interest less brokerage fees of $400.

(Continued)

Mar. 31   Received the first quarterly dividend of $1.50 per share from Ontario Bell Co.

Apr. 24   Purchased 1,500 Hydro Power Co. $5, preferred shares at $52 plus brokerage fees of $400.

June 30   Received the semiannual dividend on Hydro Power Co. preferred shares and quarterly dividend of $1.00 per share from Ontario Bell Co.

July 1   Received the semiannual interest on the Province of Alberta bonds and the maturity value.

July 15   Purchased 500, 12% Metro Toronto serial bonds, with a maturity date of May 15, 1999, at 96½ plus brokerage fees of $800. The bonds pay interest semiannually on May 15 and November 15 (face value, $1,000).

July 31   Purchased 400 Uranium Unlimited Inc. common shares at $67 each plus brokerage fees of $200.

Aug. 7   Sold 200 Ontario Bell Co. shares at $25 less brokerage fees of $80.

Sept. 1   Received the semiannual interest payment on Evans Produce bonds.

Sept. 30   Received the quarterly dividend of $1.00 from Ontario Bell Co.

Nov. 15   Received the semiannual interest payment on Metro Toronto serial bonds.

Dec. 10   Received a 15% common stock dividend from Uranium Unlimited Co.

Dec. 31   You determine the closing market values to be:

Evans Produce Bonds	81½
Sure Grow Lawn Turf Bonds	103
Metro Toronto Bonds	97
Hydro Power Co. $5 Preferred Shares	50
Ontario Bell Co. Common Shares	24
Uranium Unlimited Inc. Common Shares	69

Instructions

(a)   Prepare general journal entries for the transactions listed above in marketable securities and year-end adjusting entries, assuming Microline Limited reports all securities at the lower of cost and market in the aggregate. Microline does not use reversing entries. (All computations should be to the nearest dollar.)

(b)   Prepare the balance sheet presentation of marketable securities at December 31, 1995 for (a).

(EQUITY VS. COST METHOD OF ACCOUNTING FOR INVESTMENTS)   On December 31, 1992,   **P18-6**
Chef's Food Company acquired 75,000 of Lassie Corporation's common shares as a long-term investment at a cost of $30 each; the purchase represented 30% of Lassie Corporation's outstanding shares. The cost of the shares to Chef's Food Company represented 30% of the book value of Lassie's net assets, which was also 30% of the fair value of the net assets.

On May 1, 1993, Lassie Corporation paid a cash dividend of $1.50 per common share.

For the year 1993, Lassie Corporation reported net income of $450,000; the market value of the investment was $2,025,000 at December 31, 1993.

On May 1, 1994, Lassie Corporation paid a dividend of $0.50 per share. For the year 1994, Lassie Corporation reported a net income of $600,000; the market value of the investment was $2,175,000 at December 31, 1994.

Instructions

(a)   Prepare the journal entries necessary to record the transactions listed above on Chef's Food Company's books, assuming that the investment in Lassie Corporation does not represent a significant influence and, therefore, is accounted for under the cost method. December 31 is Chef's Food Company's year end.

(b) Prepare the journal entries necessary to record the transactions on Chef's Food Company's books, assuming that the investment in Lassie Corporation is carried on the equity basis.

(c) What is the carrying value of the investment in Lassie Corporation shares on January 1, 1995 under the equity method?

P18-7 (EFFECTIVE INTEREST VS. STRAIGHT-LINE BOND AMORTIZATION) On January 1, 1993, Brooks Company acquires $150,000 of Handel Products, Inc. 9% bonds at a price of $139,192. The interest is payable each December 31 and the bonds mature January 1, 1995. The investment will provide Brooks Company with a 12% yield.

Instructions

(a) Prepare a three-year schedule of interest revenue and bond discount amortization, applying the straight-line method.

(b) Prepare a three-year schedule of interest revenue and bond discount amortization, applying the effective interest method.

(c) Prepare the journal entry for the interest receipt of December 31, 1994 and the discount amortization under the straight-line method.

(d) Prepare the journal entry for the interest receipt of December 31, 1994 and the discount amortization under the effective interest method.

P18-8 (EQUITY VS. COST; EXCESS OF COST OVER BOOK VALUE) On January 1, 1994, Cat Corp. bought 3,000 of Mouse Company's common shares at $20 each. At that time, Mouse Company's balance sheet showed total assets of $200,000, liabilities of $40,000, common shares (10,000 issued) of $100,000, and retained earnings of $60,000. The difference between book value acquired and the purchase price was attributable to assets having a remaining life of 10 years.

At the end of 1994, Mouse Company reported net income of $30,000 and paid cash dividends of $9,000 on December 31, 1994. The market value of Mouse Company shares was $13 at December 31, 1994.

On January 1, 1995, Cat Corp. sold 1,000 of the Mouse Company shares at the market price of $25 each.

Instructions

(a) Prepare journal entries to record the events noted above and relevant data on the books of Cat Corp., assuming that it is unable to exercise significant influence over Mouse Company during 1994 and, therefore, applies the cost method.

(b) Prepare journal entries to record the events above and relevant data on the books of Cat Corp., applying the equity method. (Round to nearest dollar.)

P18-9 (ENTRIES FOR LONG-TERM EQUITY INVESTMENTS) Keniston Wildcats Corp. makes the following long-term investments during 1993.

Security	Quantity	Percent Interest	Per-Share Cost
Paduca Forms Company	3,000 shares	2	$80
London Grader Corp.	8,000 shares	16	20
Knoblett Development Inc.	3,000 shares	4	36

The following information concerning these investments relates to 1993 and 1994:

1. For the year 1993—Cash dividends received:
   Paduca Forms $4.00 per share
   London Grader $1.00 per share
   Knoblett Development $1.50 per share

2. Market values per share, 12/31/93:
   Paduca Forms $74
   London Grader $23
   Knoblett Development $28

3. For the year 1994—Cash dividends received:
   Paduca Forms $4.00 per share
   London Grader $0.50 per share
   Knoblett Development $1.70 per share

4. On Sept. 30, 1994, the investment in London Grader was reclassified to current asset status when its market value per share was $17.

5. Market value per share, 12/31/94:
   Paduca Forms $68
   Knoblett Development $46

Instructions

(a) Prepare all of the journal entries to reflect the transactions above and related data in accordance with professional standards.

(b) Prepare the descriptions and amounts that should be reported on the face of Keniston Wildcat Corp.'s comparative financial statements for 1993 and 1994 relative to these long-term investments.

(c) Draft the note that should accompany the 1993–1994 comparative statements relative to the noncurrent equity securities.

(ENTRIES FOR LONG-TERM INVESTMENTS) Karen Rostad Corp. carried an account in its general **P18-10** ledger called Investments, which contained the following debits for investment purchases, and no credits:

Feb. 1, 1993   Player Company common, no par, 200 shares $ 36,400

Apr. 1   Government of Canada bonds, 11%, due April 1, 2003,
               interest payable April 1 and October 1; 100 bonds
               of $1,000 par each (current asset)   123,000

July 1   Vicq Steel Company 12% bonds, par $50,000, dated
               March 1, 1993, purchased at 104 plus accrued
               interest, interest payable annually on March 1,
               due March 1, 2013 (noncurrent asset)   54,000

Instructions

(a) Prepare the entries necessary to classify the amounts into proper accounts, assuming that the Government of Canada bonds are the only temporary investments.

(b) Prepare the entry to record the accrued interest and amortization of premium on December 31, 1993, using the straight-line method.

(c) The market values of the securities on December 31, 1993 were:

Player Company common	$ 33,800	(1% interest)
Government of Canada bonds	124,700	
Vicq Steel Company bonds	58,600	

What entry or entries, if any, would you recommend be made?

(d) The Government of Canada bonds were sold on July 1, 1994 for $124,200 plus accrued interest. Give the proper entry.

(e) Twenty additional shares of Player Company common were received on July 15, 1994 as a stock dividend, and on July 31, 1994, 30 shares of Player Company common were sold at $180 per share. What entries would be made for these two transactions?

P18-11 (STOCK RIGHTS: COMPREHENSIVE)   Discorama Company holds 300 of Ryan Shay Inc. common shares that it purchased for $32,589 as a long-term investment. On January 15, 1994, Ryan Shay Inc. announced that one right will be issued for every four shares held.

Instructions

(a) Prepare entries on Discorama Company's books for the transactions below that occurred after the date of this announcement. Show all computations in good form.

1. For $11,500, 100 shares are sold rights-on.

2. Rights to purchase 50 additional shares at $100 per share are received. The market value on this date is $105 per share and the market value of the rights is $6 per right.

3. The rights are exercised, and 50 additional shares are purchased at $100 per share.

4. At $106 each, 100 of the original shares held are sold (use average cost).

(b) If the rights had not been exercised but instead had been sold at $6 per right, what would have been the amount of the gain or loss on the sale of the rights?

(c) If the shares purchased through the exercise of the rights are later sold at $107 each, what is the amount of the gain or loss on the sale?

(d) If the rights had not been exercised but had been allowed to expire, what would be the proper entry?

P18-12 (MARKETABLE SECURITIES, CURRENT AND NONCURRENT COMPREHENSIVE)   At December 31, 1993, Cheng Ltd. properly reported as current assets the following temporary investments:

Bea Corp., 1,500 shares, $2.40 convertible preferred	$ 60,000
Cha, Inc., 5,000 common shares	50,000
Dey Co., 2,000 common shares	55,000
Marketable equity securities at cost	$165,000
Less valuation allowance	7,000
Marketable equity securities at market	$158,000

On January 2, 1994, Cheng purchased 100,000 of Eddie Corporation's common shares for $1,700,000, representing 30% of Eddie's outstanding common shares and an underlying equity of $1,400,000 in Eddie's net assets at January 2. Cheng, which had no other financial transactions with Eddie during 1994, amortized goodwill over a 30-year period. As a result of Cheng's 30% ownership of Eddie, Cheng had the ability to exercise significant influence over Eddie's financial and operating policies.

During 1994, Cheng disposed of the following securities:

Jan. 18   Sold 2,500 shares of Cha for $12 per share.

June 1   Sold 500 shares of Dey, after a 10% stock dividend, for $22 per share.

Oct. 1   Converted 500 shares of Bea's preferred into 1,500 shares of Bea's common shares, when the market price was $60 per share for the preferred and $21 per share for the common.

The following 1994 dividend information pertains to the shares held by Cheng:

Feb. 14   Dey issued a 10% stock dividend when the market price of Dey's common was $22 per share.

Apr. 5 and   Bea paid dividends of $1.20 per share on its $2.40 preferred shares to shareholders of record on March 9 and
Oct. 5   September 9, respectively. Bea did not pay any dividends on its common shares during 1994.

June 30   Cha paid a $1.25 per share dividend on its common shares.

Mar. 1   Eddie paid quarterly dividends of $0.50 per share on each of these dates.

June 1,   Eddies' net income for the year ended December 31, 1994 was $1,100,000.
Sept. 1
and Dec. 1

At December 31, 1994, Cheng's management intended to hold the Eddie shares as a long-term investment, with the remaining investments considered as temporary. Market prices per share of the marketable equity securities were as follows.

	At December 31	
	1994	1993
Bea Corp.—preferred	$56	$42
Bea Corp.—common	20	18
Cha, Inc.—common	11	11
Dey Co.—common	22	20
Eddie Corp.—common	16	18

All of the foregoing shares are listed on major stock exchanges. Declines in market value from cost would not be considered as permanent declines.

Instructions

(a) Prepare a schedule of Cheng's *current* marketable securities at December 31, 1994, including any information necessary to determine the related valuation allowance and unrealized gross gains and losses.

(b) Prepare a schedule to show the carrying amount of Cheng's *noncurrent* marketable equity securities at December 31, 1994.

(c) Prepare a schedule showing all income, gains, and losses (realized and unrealized) relating to Cheng's investments for the year ended December 31, 1994.

(AICPA adapted)

(ENTRIES FOR SINKING FUND)   The transactions given below relate to a sinking fund for retirement of **P18-13** long-term bonds of Hilltop Corp.:

1. In accordance with the terms of the bond indenture, cash in the amount of $150,000 is transferred, at the end of the first year, from the regular cash account to the sinking fund.

2. Eau Claire Company 10% bonds of a par value of $50,000, maturing in five years, are purchased for $48,000.

3. 500 shares of Mankato Company $4 no-par preferred are purchased at $53 per share.

4. Annual interest of $5,000 is received on Eau Claire Company bonds. (Amortize the proper amount of discounting, using straight-line amortization.)

5. Sinking fund expenses of $450 are paid from sinking fund cash.

6. SFU Company 9% bonds with interest payable February 1 and August 1 are purchased on April 15 at par value of $60,000 plus accrued interest.

7. Dividends of $2,000 are received on Mankato Company preferred.

8. All the SFU Company bonds are sold on September 1 at 101 plus accrued interest. Assume interest collected August 1 was properly recorded.

9. Investments carried in the fund at $1,583,000 are sold for $1,528,000.

10. The fund contains cash of $1,622,000 after disposing of all investments and paying all expenses. Of this amount, $1,600,000 is used to retire the bonds payable at maturity date.

11. The remaining cash balance is returned to the general account.

Instructions

Prepare the journal entries required by Hilltop Corp. for the above transactions.

*P18-14(COST TO EQUITY METHOD WITH GOODWILL)   On January 1, Faye Inc. paid $700,000 for 10,000 voting common shares of Wolf Company, which was a 10% interest in Wolf. At that date, the net assets of Wolf totalled $6,000,000. The fair values of all of Wolf's identifiable assets and liabilities were equal to their book values. Faye does not have the ability to exercise significant influence over the operating and financial policies of Wolf. Faye received dividends of $1.00 per share from Wolf on October 1, 1993. Wolf reported net income of $500,000 for the year ended December 31, 1993.

On July 1, 1994, Faye paid $2,325,000 for 30,000 additional common voting shares of Wolf Company, which represented a 30% investment in Wolf. The fair values of all of Wolf's identifiable assets net of liabilities were equal to their book values of $6,550,000. As a result of this transaction, Faye had the ability to exercise significant influence over the operating and financial policies of Wolf. Faye received dividends of $1.00 per share from Wolf on April 1, 1994 and $1.50 per share on October 1, 1994. Wolf reported net income of $550,000 for the year ended December 31, 1994, and $300,000 for the six months ended December 31, 1994. Faye Inc. amortized goodwill over a 30-year period.

Instructions

(a) Prepare a schedule showing the income or loss before income taxes for the year ended December 31, 1993 that Faye should report from its investment in Wolf in its income statement issued in March 1994.

(b) During March 1995, Faye issues comparative financial statements for 1993 and 1994. Prepare schedules showing the income or loss before income taxes for the years ended December 31, 1993 and 1994 that Faye should report from its investment in Wolf.

(AICPA adapted)

*P18-15(CHANGE FROM COST TO EQUITY METHOD)   On January 3, 1992, Cajun Company purchased for $500,000 cash a 10% interest in Summerset Corp. On that date, the net assets of Summerset had a book value of $3,750,000. The excess of cost over the underlying equity in net assets was attributable to undervalued depreciable assets having a remaining life of 10 years from the date of the Cajun purchase.

On January 2, 1994, Cajun purchased an additional 30% of Summerset's common shares for $1,545,000 cash when the book value of Summerset's net assets was $4,150,000. The excess was attributable to depreciable assets having a remaining life of eight years.

During 1992, 1993, and 1994 the following occurred.

	Summerset Net Income	Dividends Paid by Summerset to Cajun
1992	$350,000	$15,000
1993	400,000	20,000
1994	500,000	60,000

Instructions

On the books of Cajun Company, prepare all journal entries in 1992, 1993, and 1994 that relate to its investment in Summerset Corp., reflecting the data above and a change from the cost method to the equity method.

───── FINANCIAL REPORTING PROBLEM ─────

Strand Inc., a chemical processing company, has been operating profitably for many years. On March 1, 1994, Strand purchased 50,000 First Executive Company shares for $2,000,000. The 50,000 shares represented 40% of First's outstanding common shares. Both Strand and First operate on a fiscal year ending August 31.

For the fiscal year ended August 31, 1994, First reported net income of $900,000 earned ratably throughout the year. During November 1993 and February, May, and August 1994, First paid its regular quarterly cash dividend of $125,000.

Instructions

(a) What criteria should Strand consider in determining whether its investment in First should be classified as (1) a current asset (marketable security) or (2) a noncurrent asset (investment) in Strand's August 31, 1994 balance sheet? Confine your discussion to the decision criteria for determining the balance sheet classification of the investment.

(b) Assume that the investment should be classified as a long-term investment in the noncurrent asset section of Strand's balance sheet. The cost of Strand's investment equalled its equity in the recorded values of First's net assets; recorded values were not materially different from fair values (individually or collectively). For the fiscal year ended August 31, 1994, how did the net income reported and dividends paid by First affect the accounts of Strand (ignore income tax considerations)? Indicate each account affected, whether it increased or decreased, and explain the reason for the change in the account balance (such as Cash, Investment in First, etc.). Organize your answer in the following format.

Account Name	Increase or Decrease	Reason for Change in Account Balance

PERSPECTIVES

ON READING FINANCIAL STATEMENTS

Howie Anderson

Howie Anderson, still a Newfoundlander after 17 years away, is branch manager of the Sydney, New Glasgow, and Amherst, Nova Scotia offices of Midland Walwyn, a successful Canadian firm of stockbrokers.

Howie graduated with a double major in accounting and finance from Acadia University in 1980 and then spent a year travelling in Australia before coming back to Canada and joining Touche Ross & Co. (now Deloitte & Touche) to article for his CA designation. With his CA and a year's experience as a controller in the construction industry, Howie joined what was then Scotia Bond as chief financial officer.

Why did you become a broker and why the CA first?

I've always wanted to do this—to trade—ever since I was a kid. I was offered jobs as a stockbroker right out of university, but I asked myself, "Who's going to listen to a twenty-year old?" I figured that the CA designation would give me some credibility. My Dad, also a chartered accountant, had always said to me, "Get your CA and after that you will be able to do whatever you want to do!" I've often thought over the last 10 years, that if things don't work out as a broker, at least I'd always be able to go back and get a *real* job. This one has been a lot of fun, more like a hobby, actually!

I hear that you're a valuable commodity because you can read a set of financial statements. Surely, lots of people in your business can read financial statements!

People in the business come from a variety of backgrounds, but even those with basic accounting courses in their education seem to have been taught the components of the financial statements—they understand what inventory is, that it is valued at lower of cost and market, they understand receivables and recognize that they are carried at no greater than net realizable value, that most other assets are carried at cost—but a lot of people don't seem to be able to put it all together, to make the transition to determine what a company is really worth. I got more of this integration in my professional accounting education.

What do you look for when you read a company's financial statements?

I usually start with the balance sheet. Normally, I don't read the information in the annual report which precedes the financial statements until after I've looked at the numbers because you can get a slanted view of what has happened. The annual report is a public relations document in many respects. However, you do get some useful insights from the MD&A (management discussion and analysis) because this is mandated by the Ontario Securities Commission and there is a requirement that it be more factual.

On the balance sheet, I start with the net common equity as reported and adjust this total by subtracting any assets which don't have real tangible value, and I look closely to see what "other assets" is made up of if this category of asset is significant. Are there large intercompany receivables, goodwill, or deferred taxes? I look for "soft" assets that may not be worth as much as book value, and, if so, I deduct their carrying value from the net equity figure I started with.

I go to the notes to the financial statements because there is a lot of good information buried there. Often, the segmented information note provides clues to asset values which are higher than book value. Companies which generate higher than average operating cash flows from a particular segment's operating assets tend to have hidden value which is not on the balance sheet. I add this hidden value to the company's net equity, divide the total by the number of shares outstanding and this gives me an estimate of the value of a share of the company's stock. If the shares are trading below this number, it's a buy; if the shares are selling higher than this value, I'll expect the market price to fall in the future so I'll recommend a "sell" if the stock is already held, or a "short sale" to profit from the expected decline in price.

I always look at the income statement too, zeroing in on the components of net income and the margins, the relationship between marketing and administrative expenses to total revenue. I want to know if the company's additional efforts, represented by increased marketing costs for example, are paying off in terms of higher sales. A computer software development company for the PC industry was expected by everybody to do very well. When met with increased competition, the company increased their marketing expenses by close to 100%, but they didn't manage to increase their sales at all. So this gives you a clue. That's all you're doing, looking for clues.

So you read the notes carefully?

Yes, there is a lot of information buried in the notes. By "buried" I don't mean hidden purposely, because the information is clearly provided. The note on accounting principles may tell you that the company is depreciating their capital assets at very low rates, or at very high rates. There is a lot of latitude in calculating the amount of depreciation, like in the oil and gas industry. That's why analysts look at cash flow multiples in the oil and gas industry instead of net income.

So, I look for information in the notes, and often find that things are much better than at first glance.

It's a matter of taking the time to read through the information provided.

What about the liability side of the balance sheet?

I guess the major one here is the pension liability, but it's not as bad as we're led to believe. I find the biggest adjustments relate to asset values.

What else?

Equally important is to keep up-to-date on news releases and to incorporate the new with what you already know about a company.

What about market efficiency?

The markets in Canada aren't as efficient as they are in the U.S. If the *Financial Times* comes out with a good story about a company on Sunday, you can go into the office and buy the stock Monday morning. By the time other people receive their subscriptions to the papers on Monday afternoon or Tuesday morning, the market has reacted to the new information. That's when it's time to get out. On the basis of information in the Sunday papers, we bought an energy stock on Monday morning at $1.35. The stock went to $1.65 later on Monday afternoon and then to $1.80 the next day.

Are you a heavy reader?

I read four or five newspapers a day and subscribe to the Dow Wire Service for instant news delivered right to the monitor on my desk. I pick up the weekend papers rather than having them delivered by subscription. Getting the news and reacting to it on a timely basis is crucial to playing the market.

Do you remember your Intermediate Accounting course?

Very clearly, and I use what I learned there every day. It is the course where I really caught the grasp of accounting. If you come into the course with a good understanding of how the statements are related to one another, Intermediate allows you to interpret what the individual numbers mean. Students who tried to memorize the material ran into real problems. If you can understand the big picture and work backwards from there, the details make sense. It was the best course I ever took as far as accounting goes; it put everything in perspective.

What about the future?

For now, I'd just like to continue doing what I'm doing. It's fun. I like talking to my clients, doing my own research, and keeping up on the news. I like to trade. I love what I'm doing now!

5

Issues Related to Selected Topics

CHAPTER 19

Accounting for Corporate Income Tax

■—■

Objective 1

Define taxable income, accounting income, tax differences, interperiod tax allocation, and intraperiod tax allocation.

Income of an incorporated business is generally subject to federal and provincial income taxes (proprietorships and partnerships are not subject to income taxes as separate entities). In computing income taxes payable, corporations must complete tax returns, including a statement showing the amount of net income subject to tax. This **taxable income** (*the amount on which taxes paid is based*) in the tax return is computed in accordance with prescribed tax regulations and rules. **Accounting income**[1] (*the amount on which tax expense is based*) in the income statement is, however, measured in accordance with generally accepted accounting principles (GAAP). Therefore, differences between taxable income and accounting income may exist because the basic objectives, rules, and principles of measuring taxable income are different from those of measuring accounting income.

Differences between taxable income and accounting income, called **tax differences**, give rise to important issues regarding financial statement reporting. Our interest in examining these differences is to determine their effect on the measurement of income tax expense and related balance sheet accounts for corporations.

This chapter deals primarily with **interperiod tax allocation**, which is the *accounting for tax differences between periods*. The *accounting requirements for tax allocation within a period*, called **intraperiod tax allocation**, are reviewed briefly at the end of the chapter because they were discussed in Chapter 4.

OBJECTIVES RELATED TO THE DETERMINATION OF ACCOUNTING INCOME AND TAXABLE INCOME

Objective 2

Appreciate the differences between the objectives of determining accounting income and taxable income.

A major cause of problems in accounting for income taxes is that the objectives of reporting income on financial statements to shareholders and others are not the same as the objectives for determining taxable income reported to the government.

Determination of income for financial statement purposes is based on the belief that revenues should be recognized when the criteria for revenue recognition are met (revenue realization principle) and expenses should be charged to the period in which related revenues are recognized (matching principle). In this framework, income taxes are considered a cost incurred in the process of earning income. The underlying objective of such an income determination is to provide relevant information to assist owners and others in making decisions.

From a company's point of view, determination of taxable income should rest on the objective of minimizing the present value of income taxes paid over the life of the company. This is accomplished by excluding all revenues and including all expenses permitted within the law when deter-

---

[1] *CICA Handbook* (Toronto: CICA), Section 3470, defines "accounting income" as "the net income for the period, shown in the financial statements prepared for submission to the shareholders, before the provision for income taxes (including any income taxes applicable to discontinued operations and extraordinary items) but after excluding items that are non-taxable or non-deductible for income tax purposes on a once-and-for-all basis. Similarly, the term 'accounting loss' is used in this Section to mean the converse of accounting income." This definition is used throughout this chapter.

mining taxable income, regardless of their recognition for purposes of determining accounting income (avoidance but not evasion of tax). Furthermore, to be consistent with this objective, a company should calculate taxable income in a manner that would defer payment of taxes into the future rather than pay them in the present period. Therefore, for purposes of taxable income determination, this would mean deferring the inclusion of revenues or gains to future years and including all expenses and losses in the present year when such options exist under tax laws. Because these calculation principles are different from generally accepted accounting principles, the result can be a difference between taxable income and accounting income.

NATURE OF DIFFERENCES BETWEEN TAXABLE INCOME AND ACCOUNTING INCOME

Differences between taxable income and accounting income as determined under Canadian GAAP arise from two sources: (1) permanent differences and (2) timing differences.

Permanent Differences

Permanent differences refer to (1) items that appear on the income statement prepared under GAAP but *never* enter into the determination of taxable income and (2) items that enter into the determination of taxable income but are *never* reported on an income statement. Such differences arise from tax laws that (a) exclude certain accounting revenues from taxation (e.g., dividends received from another Canadian corporation; life insurance proceeds received on the death of an insured company officer), (b) exclude certain accounting expenses as tax deductions (e.g., premiums paid on company officers' life insurance; membership fees for dining, sporting, and recreation organizations), and (c) allow certain deductions that are not taken into the determination of reported income (e.g., resource allowances; earned depletion allowances). When permanent difference items are reported in accounting income, they are simply treated as nontaxable or nondeductible items in the determination of the amount of tax expense. If a permanent difference item is on the tax return, it is used to calculate tax expense to be reported in the income statement even though the item itself is not in the statement.

> *When only permanent differences exist, both the tax payable and the tax expense for the period are equal to the tax rate multiplied by the taxable income.* For example, assume that taxable income was $100,000 and income before tax to be reported was $98,000, the difference being due to a permanent difference expense item appearing in the latter. If the statutory tax rate was 45%, both the tax payable and the tax expense would be $45,000 as shown below.

Objective 3

Understand the nature of permanent differences and how they affect the determination of tax expense.

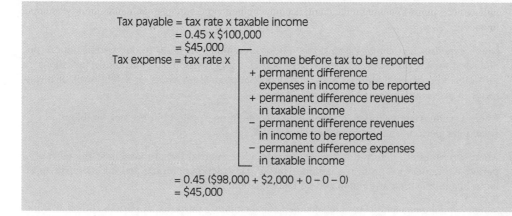

It should be recognized that when permanent differences exist, the **effective tax rate** of 46% in this example (tax expense of $45,000 divided by reported income before tax of $98,000) would not correspond to the 45% statutory tax rate. Disclosure of such discrepancies is required in the financial statements of enterprises that trade securities in a public market or file annually with a securities commission and is deemed desirable for other enterprises.[2] The following excerpt from a financial statement of Hudson's Bay Company illustrates how this type of disclosure can be made.

Hudson's Bay Company
(from the notes to the January 31, 1993 financial statements)

5. INCOME TAXES

The average statutory Canadian income tax rates for the years ended January 31, 1993 and January 31, 1992 were 43.2% and 42.6%, respectively. The following schedule reconciles nominal tax provisions at these rates with the amounts provided in the Consolidated Statements of Earnings.

	Year Ended January 31,	
	1993 $000's	1992 $000's
Earnings before income taxes	199,473	139,516
Nominal income tax provision at average statutory Canadian income tax rates	86,172	59,434
Increase (decrease) in income taxes resulting from:		
Large corporations tax	5,612	5,048
Tax rates in other jurisdictions	(576)	(8,557)
Capital gains and losses	(2,369)	(1,917)
Adjustments to prior years' taxes	(2,196)	(843)
Non deductible costs	1,255	4,150
Transactions with affiliate	(5,148)	(579)
Provision for income taxes per Consolidated Statements of Earnings	82,750	56,736

Timing Differences

Objective 4

Understand the nature of timing differences and appreciate the implications for accounting for tax expense.

A **timing difference** *exists when an item of revenue, expense, gain, or loss is included in the computation of accounting income in one period but is included in the computation of taxable income in another period.*

Timing differences **originate** in one period*or more* and **reverse** or "turn around" in one or more subsequent periods. The *CICA Handbook* identifies five situations from which timing differences arise:

1. where expenses are claimed for tax purposes in one period but are not charged against income for accounting purposes until some later period, e.g., capital cost allowances in excess of depreciation charged, and certain other costs which are sometimes deferred in the accounts but claimed immediately for taxes, such as exploration and development costs, start-up costs, past service pension contributions, and accounting and legal expenses in connection with bond financing;

2. where expenses are charged against income for accounting purposes in one period but are not deducted for tax purposes until some later period, e.g., provisions for warranties, provisions for deferred compensation payments, and depreciation of fixed assets or write-downs of inventories in excess of amounts allowed for tax purposes;

3. where revenues are included in accounting income in one period but are not taxable until some later period, e.g., profit on instalment sales;

4. where revenues are deferred in the accounts to a later period but are taxable in the current period, e.g., unearned profits on certain types of construction contracts and intercompany profits in inventories that are eliminated on consolidation;

5. where capital gains and losses are recorded for accounting purposes in periods different from those in which they are recognized for tax purposes.[3]

---

[2] *Ibid.*, par. .33.
[3] *Ibid.*, par. .06.

To illustrate timing differences, assume that Baker Ltd. bought a Class 10 (capital cost allowance (CCA) rate of 30%) asset on January 10, 1994 at a cost of $100,000.[4] While the company deducted the maximum allowed CCA for tax purposes, the asset was depreciated over a period of 10 years for financial reporting purposes using the straight-line method. The appropriate depreciation and CCA expense charges year by year would be as follows.

	Amount of Expense	
Year	CCA for Tax Purposes	Depreciation for Accounting Purposes
1994	$15,000*	$ 10,000
1995	25,500	10,000
1996	17,850	10,000
1997	12,495	10,000
1998	8,746	10,000
1999	6,123	10,000
2000	4,286	10,000
2001	3,000	10,000
2002	2,100	10,000
2003	1,470	10,000
Total	$96,570 **	$100,000

* For the first year of ownership, CCA equals one-half of the CCA rate times the undepreciated capital cost. Thereafter, CCA equals the CCA rate times the undepreciated capital cost.
** Assume the asset class continues even though this asset may be disposed of after 10 years.

As a result of using CCA for determining taxable income rather than straight-line depreciation amounts, the company will pay less tax in the early years of the asset's life (1994–1997, when timing differences originate) but, if other things remain constant, more tax in later years (1998–2003, when the originating timing differences reverse).

By carrying this illustration a step further, the results of this practice become clearer. Assume that Baker Ltd. has gross revenue of $300,000, expenses other than depreciation of $250,000, and an income tax rate of 45% on its taxable income. The following schedule presents partial income statements for tax and accounting purposes for 1994, 1997, 1998, and 2003, assuming that tax expense reported equals the taxes payable as determined by the tax return (i.e. that there is no interperiod tax allocation).

Baker Ltd.
Partial Income Statement
(Without Interperiod Tax Allocation)

	For Tax Purposes	For Accounting Purposes
1994		
Income before CCA or depreciation and taxes	$50,000	$50,000
CCA or depreciation	15,000	10,000
Income before taxes	$35,000	$40,000
Income tax payable and expense	$15,750	$15,750
Net income reported		$24,250
Effective tax rate		39.4%

(Continued)

[4] See Chapter 11 for the capital cost allowance technique.

<u>1997</u>

Income before CCA or depreciation and taxes	$50,000	$50,000
CCA or depreciation	12,495	10,000
Income before taxes	$37,505	$40,000
Income tax payable and expense	$16,877	$16,877
Net income reported		$23,123
Effective tax rate		42.2%

<u>1998</u>

Income before CCA or depreciation and taxes	$50,000	$50,000
CCA or depreciation	8,746	10,000
Income before taxes	$41,254	$40,000
Income tax payable and expense	$18,564	$18,564
Net income reported		$21,436
Effective tax rate		46.4%

<u>2003</u>

Income before CCA or depreciation and taxes	$50,000	$50,000
CCA or depreciation	1,470	10,000
Income before taxes	$48,530	$40,000
Income tax payable and expense	$21,838	$21,838
Net income reported		$18,162
Effective tax rate		54.6%

Owners and prospective investors acquainted only with the information found in the "accounting" income statement may derive an erroneous impression of the company's profitability. Although the underlying economic activity of the company is the same each year, the reported income after taxes is declining each year. Furthermore, the effective tax rate on accounting income (income taxes divided by accounting income before tax) is increasing each year. Because of this, accounting issues exist regarding the appropriate amount of income tax expense to be reported in the income statement.

POSSIBLE WAYS TO ACCOUNT FOR TIMING DIFFERENCES: THE THEORY

In this section, issues regarding the determination of tax expense and related balance sheet accounts are identified and possible solutions examined. This framework provides a background for understanding the Canadian practice of accounting for timing differences on a comprehensive allocation basis using the deferral method. In subsequent sections, the application of this approach is illustrated.

Taxes Payable Approach Versus Tax Allocation Approach

Given the existence of timing differences, the determination of the provision for income taxes (i.e. income tax expense) to be reported in the income statement could follow at least two basic approaches: (1) the taxes payable approach or (2) the tax allocation approach.

    The **taxes payable approach** *reports as tax expense the amount payable based on taxable income determined in the tax return.* The previous example (without interperiod tax allocation) illustrates this approach. Reasons supporting this approach are:

1. Since it is taxable income and not accounting income that attracts taxation, the taxes actually payable for the period represent the appropriate cost to be allocated to that period.

2. It is unnecessary to provide for income taxes for which there is no legal liability at the end of the financial period.

3. While timing differences in one period may give rise to the reverse situation in some future period, the date of the reversal may be indefinitely postponed and, accordingly, there is no necessity to provide for an amount that may never become payable.

Objective 5

Understand the taxes payable approach and the tax allocation approach, and know that the latter is used in Canadian GAAP.

4. Even where the taxes may become payable in some future period, it is usually difficult to estimate the future tax effects with any degree of accuracy.[5]

As indicated by the previous example, application of the taxes payable approach can lead to erroneous impressions regarding an enterprise's profitability—although the underlying economic activity remains unchanged, net income after taxes declines and the effective tax rate increases each year. The fundamental reason for this is that the income tax expense reported is not totally related (matched) to the revenues and expenses reported in accounting income because of timing differences. Therefore, assuming that income taxes are a cost incurred to earn net income, this approach violates the basic concept that costs incurred to earn income should be charged to the period in which the related revenues are reported.[6]

The tax allocation approach is designed to overcome this limitation through associating the income tax expense with related accounting income. In essence, this is a method of interperiod tax allocation that applies the notion of "let the tax follow the income" (a notion equally applicable to intraperiod tax allocation). Under the **tax allocation approach**, *tax expense is related to accounting income when such tax expense differs from actual taxes paid because of the differences in the timing of revenue or expense recognition*.

While recognizing the arguments for the taxes payable approach, the Accounting Standards Board concluded that interperiod tax allocation is the appropriate basis to account for timing differences.[7] The basic reasons given to support this recommendation were:

1. The incidence of income taxes on specific transactions should be recorded in the period in which the transactions are recognized for accounting purposes.

2. Income fluctuations that may arise on the taxes payable basis because of wide variations from period to period in the relationship between accounting income and the provision for income taxes are avoided.[8]

Given that tax allocation is to be employed when accounting for timing differences, *the result will be that the amount of income tax payable for a period will not likely be equal to the income tax expense reported in the financial statements of the period.* Two issues require resolution regarding differences between the tax expense and the tax payable:

1. To what extent should timing differences be recognized (comprehensive allocation versus partial allocation)?

2. How should the amount of the difference be determined and reported (the deferral method versus the liability method)?

Comprehensive Allocation Versus Partial Allocation

As a practical matter, **recurring timing differences** between taxable income and accounting income could give rise to an indefinite postponement of tax. An example of a recurring timing difference

---

[5] *CICA Handbook*, Section 3470, par. .09.

[6] The legitimacy of this assumption relies on acceptance of the **proprietary theory** of accounting, which conceives of a business in terms of its benefits to owners. As such, payments to others (e.g., interest to debtors and taxes to governments) are costs incurred to generate benefits of ownership. The proprietary theory is the commonly held view. The **entity theory** of accounting is an alternative. It conceives of the business as a distinct entity in itself for which there are separate stakeholder groups (i.e. creditors, debtors, governments, owners). As such, payments to these stakeholders are considered as distributions of income of the entity. Consequently, interest and taxes would not be expenses to be matched against revenues in the determination of income.

[7] *CICA Handbook*, Section 3470, par. .13. Exception to this requirement is permitted for certain regulated and similar enterprises. *Financial Reporting in Canada—1991* (Toronto: CICA, 1991) indicated that in 1990, 295 of the 300 surveyed companies reported accounts dealing with timing differences. Of these, 277 reported use of the tax allocation basis.

[8] *Ibid.*, par. .08.

Objective 6

Understand the differences between comprehensive allocation and partial allocation, and know that the former is used in Canada.

arises from the use of capital cost allowance calculations for tax purposes by a company that uses straight-line depreciation for accounting purposes. As long as the CCA is greater than the depreciation expense, taxable income will be less than accounting income and the difference between tax payable and tax expense will accumulate. Indeed, if a company acquires depreciable assets faster than it retires them, the difference between tax payable and tax expense could take a very long time to reverse. Because of uncertainties related to the tax consequences of recurring timing differences, two concepts exist regarding the extent to which tax allocation may be applied: comprehensive allocation or partial allocation.

Under **comprehensive allocation**, *interperiod tax allocation is applied to all timing differences*. Supporters of this view believe that reported income tax expense should reflect the tax effects of all timing differences included in accounting income, regardless of the period in which the related income taxes are actually paid. Consequently, differences between tax expense and tax payable should be recognized when all timing differences originate, even if their reversal in future periods will be offset by new originating differences at that time.

Supporters of **partial allocation** contend that, *unless differences between tax payable and tax expense are expected to reverse within a relevant period of time, they should not affect reported income*. Consequently, interperiod tax allocation is not appropriate for recurring timing differences that result in an indefinite postponement of tax. Under this view, the presumption is that reported tax expense would be the same as the tax payable for a period, even if recurring timing differences existed. Accordingly, only *nonrecurring* material differences between taxes payable and accounting tax expense should be recognized. These should be recognized and allocated between periods only if they are reasonably expected to reverse within a relatively short period of time. An example of a nonrecurring difference would be an *isolated* instalment sale in which the gross profit is reported for accounting purposes when cash is collected and for tax purposes at the date of sale.

The supporters of comprehensive allocation contend that partial allocation is a departure from accrual accounting because it emphasizes cash outlays for taxes, whereas comprehensive allocation results in a thorough and consistent matching of revenues and expenses.

While the *CICA Handbook* recommends interperiod tax allocation, there is no explicit recommendation regarding partial versus comprehensive allocation. Implicitly, however, comprehensive allocation appears to be suggested. This is because the *Handbook* states that tax allocation should be used when there are timing differences between accounting income and taxable income. As previously indicated, accounting income is defined, for purposes of Section 3470, as income in the financial statements before provision for income taxes (including any income taxes applicable to discontinued operations and extraordinary items) but after excluding permanent differences. Under such a definition, accounting income reflects a comprehensive concept because all timing differences are included.

Deferral Method Versus Liability Method

Objective 7

Understand the differences between the deferral method and the liability method, and know that the former is applied in Canada.

The preceding discussion indicates that timing differences between taxable income and accounting income should be accounted for using interperiod tax allocation, likely employing a comprehensive approach. Given this, additional questions relate to which tax rates will be used to measure the effects of timing differences (i.e. rates applicable to the year of the originating timing difference or the years in which reversals are expected to occur) and how resulting accounts and amounts are to be presented in the financial statements. There are two different methods that provide different answers to these questions: (1) the deferral method and (2) the liability method.[9]

Deferral Method. Under the **deferral method**, *the measurement of future income tax (difference between tax payable and tax expense) is based on the tax rate in effect during the year when a*

---

[9] Our intention here is to recognize these two methods and identify the basic differences between them in terms of measurements and reporting (accounts used). As the deferral method is used in Canada, details pertaining to its application are examined later through examples. A third method, called the "net of tax" method, also exists. It is not used to any extent and is beyond the scope of our coverage.

timing difference originates. As such, income tax expense is usually determined by multiplying the tax rate of the current year by the accounting income. Tax payable is determined by multiplying the current year's tax rate by the taxable income. The difference is a "balancing" amount placed in a balance sheet account for future income tax. This amount is equal to the difference between the accounting income and taxable income multiplied by the year's tax rate. Balances for future income taxes are not adjusted for anticipated future years' tax rates, enacted changes in tax rates, or the imposition of new taxes.

This method emphasizes an **income statement perspective** because the resulting measure of income tax expense is based on what would have to be paid on the current year's accounting income if there were no timing differences. However, under the deferral method, a balance in a balance sheet account for future income tax may not represent the actual amount of taxes payable or recoverable in future periods when timing differences reverse (i.e. they are not based on tax rates that will be in effect when the reversals occur).

In the deferral method, future income tax amounts calculated on originating timing differences are recorded in a Deferred Income Taxes (DIT) account, not a future income tax liability or asset account. A credit balance in a DIT account would technically not be a liability because it would not measure appropriately the future expected cash outflow. This expected cash outflow could only be appropriately determined by multiplying originating timing differences by the tax rate expected in the year of their reversal. For similar reasons, a debit balance in a DIT account would technically not be an asset as defined in the conceptual framework. Because of this, classification of a DIT account in the balance sheet is a problem. If a DIT account has a credit balance, many report it as a unique item between total liabilities and shareholders' equity. Others simply ignore the rigour of the definition of a liability and show a DIT credit balance within the applicable current or noncurrent liability category. A debit balance in a DIT account, while not meeting the definition of an asset, would likely be classified as a current or noncurrent asset or shown in a separate category in the asset section labelled Deferred Amounts.

Liability Method. Under the **liability method** (also called the asset-liability method or accrual method), the *measurement of future income tax is based on the tax rates that will be in effect during the periods in which timing differences reverse.* Consequently, the amount placed in the balance sheet account for future income tax is determined by multiplying originating differences by the tax rate expected in the year of their reversal. Income tax payable is determined in the usual way. The result of these measurements gives rise to the income tax expense to be reported for a period (i.e. a "balancing" amount). Ordinarily, the most reasonable assumption about future tax rates is that the current tax rate will continue. However, if a rate change is known (enacted) at the time of the initial computation, the anticipated rate is used under the liability method. Also, since the initial computation is an estimate, it is subject to future adjustment if tax rates change or new taxes are imposed.

Because this method concentrates on measuring liability or asset amounts, classification of these amounts as a liability or asset is appropriate. However, since the measurements are based on tax payments or recoveries that will occur in the future, many believe that it would be appropriate to determine and report them at their present value (i.e. discount them). This method is considered a **balance sheet approach** that emphasizes the usefulness of that statement in evaluating financial position and predicting cash flows.

In Canada, the deferral method has been, and continues to be, the recommended practice in the *CICA Handbook*. In the late 1980s, however, various events in the world were taking place that suggested this could change. In the United States, the Financial Accounting Standards Board (FASB) had been working for several years on implementing the liability method on a comprehensive basis. Also, the International Accounting Standards Committee (IASC) appeared to be favouring the liability method. Consequently, for Canada to be "in tune" with these developments, the AcSB issued an *Exposure Draft* on corporate income tax reporting, recommending that the *CICA Handbook* be changed so that the liability method rather than the deferral method be used. During the exposure period and while the AcSB was considering its action, the FASB experienced considerable difficulty and delay in implementing its standard and the IASC delayed its consideration of the issue. Within Canada, differing opinion existed as to how to account for timing difference and the issuance of the *Exposure Draft* generated a variety of contradicting responses to the AcSB's proposed change.[10] The result was that, in 1990, the AcSB decided to discontinue work on the corporate income tax project.

The FASB, however, resolved concerns regarding the use of the liability method in 1992 and this method is now U.S. practice.[11] The liability method is also applied in Australia, the United Kingdom, Mexico, and other countries.[12] Also, in 1992, the IASC revived accounting for income taxes as a high priority project. Given these developments, the AcSB incorporated into a five-year plan the intent to issue an *Exposure Draft* regarding corporate income taxes in 1994.[13] This action is likely to have considerable consequences on how such taxes are accounted for in Canada. Because of the inability to predict these consequences at the time of writing, the balance of this chapter examines the measurement and reporting issues associated with current *CICA Handbook* recommendations that are based on comprehensive tax allocation using the deferral method.

In summary, the following schematic is useful for considering the various approaches to accounting for corporate income tax. The boldfaced words indicate current *CICA Handbook* conclusions as to Canadian GAAP.

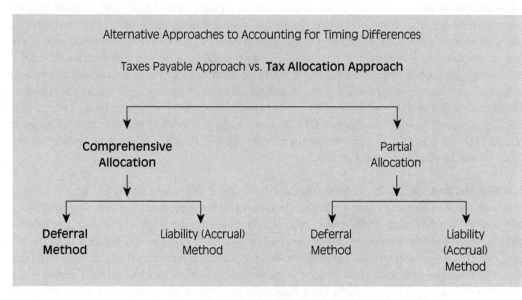

APPLYING COMPREHENSIVE TAX ALLOCATION USING THE DEFERRAL METHOD

As stated earlier, if interperiod allocation procedures are not employed, the amounts of income tax expense and income taxes payable are the same. With interperiod tax allocation, the amounts reported for income tax expense and income taxes payable are different. As a result, accounting tax expense

---

[10] Rosalind M. Callard, "Down for the Count," *CA Magazine*, October 1990, pp. 47–50. This article reported that the more than 280 responses to the *Exposure Draft* appeared to be evenly divided among retaining the deferral method, adopting the liability method, changing to the liability method with discounting, and changing to the taxes payable method.

[11] "Accounting for Income Taxes," *Statement of Financial Accounting Standards No. 109* (Stamford, CT: FASB, 1992).

[12] Darroch A. Robertson, "Deferred but not forgotten," *CA Magazine*, January 1993, pp. 54–60. This article identifies the history, basic issues, and requirements in different countries and then summarizes some research regarding accounting for income taxes.

[13] At the time of writing this book, the AcSB had just undertaken work on a project (a preliminary step to an *Exposure Draft*) dealing with corporate income taxes, based on the principle that income tax effects should be recognized on a comprehensive basis and calculated using the liability method.

is debited to Income Tax Expense, the taxes due and payable are credited to Income Tax Payable, and the difference between these two amounts is debited (or credited) to an account titled Deferred Income Taxes. In the period or periods in which timing differences reverse, the amount accumulated in Deferred Income Taxes is reduced, as it absorbs the difference between reported tax expense and the tax actually payable for those later years.

Objective 8

Know how to apply comprehensive tax allocation using the deferral method in various situations.

Example 1: Interperiod Tax Allocation When Tax Expense Is Initially Greater Than Tax Payable

To illustrate comprehensive interperiod tax allocation accounting, the information presented previously for Baker Ltd. will be used. The income tax expense reported in the income statement each year would be $18,000. This is determined by multiplying the tax rate (45%) by the accounting income ($40,000: the $50,000 income before taxes and depreciation less the depreciation expense of $10,000). The tax payable equals the tax rate multiplied by the taxable income. The difference between the tax expense and the tax payable from 1994 through 2003 is shown below.

Baker Ltd.
Tax Expense versus Tax Payable

Year	Tax Expense	Tax Payable	Difference Expense – Payable
1994	$18,000	$15,750	$ 2,250
1995	18,000	11,025	6,975
1996	18,000	14,468	3,532
1997	18,000	16,877	1,123
1998	18,000	18,564	(564)
1999	18,000	19,745	(1,745)
2000	18,000	20,571	(2,571)
2001	18,000	21,150	(3,150)
2002	18,000	21,555	(3,555)
2003	18,000	21,838	(3,838)

During the first four years, the tax expense is greater than the tax payable and the difference is credited to the Deferred Income Taxes account as indicated in the following entries.

	1994	1995	1996	1997
Income Tax Expense	18,000	18,000	18,000	18,000
Income Tax Payable	15,750	11,025	14,468	16,877
Deferred Income Taxes	2,250	6,975	3,532	1,123

At the end of four years, the Deferred Income Taxes account has four credit entries, as follows.

Deferred Income Taxes

	1994	2,250
	1995	6,975
	1996	3,532
	1997	1,123

A credit balance in Deferred Income Taxes is presented in the balance sheet, likely under a liability classification or as a unique item between liabilities and shareholders' equity.

During the next six years, the income statement will continue to show income of $40,000 before taxes and a tax expense of $18,000. Tax payable, however, is greater than this tax expense. Therefore, for each of these years, the Deferred Income Taxes account is debited for the difference between the expense and payable amount, as illustrated below for the years 1998, 1999, and 2003.

	1998	1999	2003
Income Tax Expense	18,000	18,000	18,000
Deferred Income Taxes	564	1,745	3,838
Income Tax Payable	18,564	19,745	21,838

At the end of 2003, the Deferred Income Taxes account is as follows.

Deferred Income Taxes

1998	564	1994	2,250
1999	1,745	1995	6,975
2000	2,571	1996	3,532
2001	3,150	1997	1,123
2002	3,555		
2003	3,838		

Balance 1,543 Dr.

The $1,543 debit balance at the end of 2003 resulted from the fact that application of the CCA method left some undepreciated capital cost for tax purposes. The disposition of the Deferred Income Taxes balance depends on the nature of disposition of the undepreciated capital cost.

Thus, by this allocation of income taxes, the income tax expense during each period is unaffected by the decision to use CCA for income tax purposes. The temporary tax advantage, although of real significance for financial reasons, has no influence on reported net income, which would be $22,000 per year. The calculation of tax payable is unaffected by the allocation of tax expense to periods based on accounting income.

Partial income statements for tax and accounting purposes for 1994, 1997, 1998, and 2003 based on interperiod tax allocation notions are presented on page 951. These should be compared to the statements without allocation as presented on pages 943–944. Note that the *tax effect of a timing difference in any year is found by computing income taxes both with and without the timing difference*. The difference in the computations is the amount debited or credited to the Deferred Income Taxes account.

This example illustrated the accounting for interperiod tax allocation in the situation where the tax expense is initially greater than the tax payable. The cause of the difference was that the depreciation expense included in the determination of accounting income was initially less than the CCA deducted for tax purposes. Similar results in terms of originating deferred income tax credits and their reversals occur for other timing differences that result in accounting income being greater than taxable income (i.e. when accounting revenues are greater than or accounting expenses are less than those in taxable income).

Baker Ltd.
Partial Income Statement
(With Interperiod Tax Allocation – Accounting Income
Initially Exceeds Taxable Income)

	For Tax Purposes	For Accounting Purposes
1994		
Income before CCA or depreciation and taxes	$50,000	$50,000
CCA or depreciation	15,000	10,000
Income before taxes	$35,000	$40,000
Income tax payable	$15,750	
Income tax expense		$18,000
Net income reported		$22,000
Effective tax rate		45%
1997		
Income before CCA or depreciation and taxes	$50,000	$50,000
CCA or depreciation	12,495	10,000
Income before taxes	$37,505	$40,000
Income tax payable	$16,877	
Income tax expense		$18,000
Net income reported		$22,000
Effective tax rate		45%
1998		
Income before CCA or depreciation and taxes	$50,000	$50,000
CCA or depreciation	8,746	10,000
Income before taxes	$41,254	$40,000
Income tax payable	$18,564	
Income tax expense		$18,000
Net income reported		$22,000
Effective tax rate		45%
2003		
Income before CCA or depreciation and taxes	$50,000	$50,000
CCA or depreciation	1,470	10,000
Income before taxes	$48,530	$40,000
Income tax payable	$21,838	
Income tax expense		$18,000
Net income reported		$22,000
Effective tax rate		45%

Example 2: Interperiod Tax Allocation When Tax Expense Is Initially Less Than Tax Payable

When an originating timing difference results in taxable income being greater than accounting income (i.e. when accounting revenues are less than or accounting expenses are greater than those in taxable income), the tax expense is less than the tax payable. Accounting for product warranties can serve as an example. In order to match expenses against revenues, accounting income includes warranty expense reflecting the estimated costs to be incurred under warranty contracts related to sales of the current period. However, warranty costs can be deducted only as they are incurred for purposes of determining taxable income. Consequently, when the expense recognized in accounting income is greater than the actual costs incurred for the period, the amount of tax payable exceeds the amount of tax expense and the difference is debited to Deferred Income Taxes. The Deferred

Income Taxes account is credited in later periods when the actual warranty costs are greater than the expense recognized in the accounting income.

To illustrate, we will return to the Baker Ltd. example. ***To avoid the complication*** of having two sources of timing differences to account for, ***we will initially assume that depreciation expense in accounting income equals the capital cost allowance each year***. Also, assume that the company has included a $20,000 product warranty expense in its annual total expenses of $250,000. The actual warranty costs allowed for purposes of determining taxable income from 1994 through 1998 are $10,000, $15,000, $25,000, $28,000, and $21,000, respectively. The following schedule shows the determination of tax expense, tax payable, and deferred tax amounts for 1994 through 1998.

Baker Ltd.
Interperiod Tax Allocation — Accounting Income
Initially Less Than Taxable income

	1994	1995	1996	1997	1998
Income Tax Expense Calculations:					
Gross Revenue	$300,000	$300,000	$300,000	$300,000	$300,000
Expenses, including $20,000 for warranties	250,000	250,000	250,000	250,000	250,000
Depreciation (equals CCA)	15,000	25,500	17,850	12,495	8,746
Accounting Income Before Tax	$ 35,000	$ 24,500	$ 32,150	$ 37,505	$ 41,254
Income Tax Expense (45%)	**15,750**	**11,025**	**14,468**	**16,877**	**18,564**
Income Tax Payable Calculation:					
Accounting Income Before Tax	$ 35,000	$ 24,500	$ 32,150	$ 37,505	$ 41,254
Adjustment for Timing Differences					
Add: Warranty Expense	20,000	20,000	20,000	20,000	20,000
Deduct: Actual Warranty Costs	(10,000)	(15,000)	(25,000)	(28,000)	(21,000)
Taxable Income	$45,000	$29,500	$27,150	$29,505	$ 40,254
Income Tax Payable (45%)	**20,250**	**13,275**	**12,218**	**13,277**	**18,114**
Deferred Income Taxes:					
Tax Expense — Tax Payable	($4,500)	($2,250)	$ 2,250	$ 3,600	$ 450

The entries to record the tax expense for the first two years are as follows.

	1994		1995	
Income Tax Expense	15,750		11,025	
Deferred Income Taxes	4,500		2,250	
Income Tax Payable		20,250		13,275

For the next three years the entries are as shown below.

	1996		1997		1998	
Income Tax Expense	14,468		16,877		18,564	
Income Tax Payable		12,218		13,277		18,114
Deferred Income Taxes		2,250		3,600		450

At the end of 1998, the Deferred Income Taxes account is as follows.

Deferred Income Taxes			
1994	4,500		
1995	2,250		
		1996	2,250
		1997	3,600
		1998	450

As this account has a debit balance each year, it will likely be shown in the balance sheet under an asset classification.

Originating and Reversing Differences: Additional Clarification

As implied earlier, an **originating difference** *is the initial timing difference between accounting income and taxable income, whether the accounting income exceeds, or is exceeded by, taxable income.* Depending on whether taxable income exceeds accounting income or vice versa in a year of origination, an originating difference may result in either a debit or credit to Deferred Income Taxes. When the direction of timing differences in subsequent years is the same as that of the initial timing difference, they are also referred to as originating differences (i.e. they increase existing balances in the Deferred Income Taxes account). A **reversing difference,** on the other hand, *occurs when timing differences that originated in prior periods are eliminated and the tax effect is removed from the Deferred Income Taxes account.* As a result, a reversing difference may result in a debit or credit, depending on the originating difference.

In Example 1 for Baker Ltd., the originating differences occur in the years 1994 through 1997 when credits flow into the Deferred Income Taxes account because tax expense is initially greater than tax payable in each year. Reversing differences occur from 1998 through 2003 when the Deferred Income Taxes account is debited and the built-up credit balance is reduced.

In Example 2 for Baker Ltd., the originating differences in 1994 and 1995 result in debits to the Deferred Income Taxes account because the tax expense is initially less than tax payable. In this example, the reversing differences occur from 1996 through 1998 when the built-up debit balance in the Deferred Income Taxes account is credited.

From these examples, it can be seen that *an originating difference can start either as a credit or debit to Deferred Income Taxes and continues as an originating difference as long as the original balance established in the first period increases. Reversing differences occur when the balance in Deferred Income Taxes is reduced.*

Example 3: Interperiod Tax Allocation When More Than One Timing Difference Exists

In typical situations, many timing differences of various types occur causing tax expense to differ from tax payable. While the basic calculations previously illustrated apply to such situations, it is desirable to keep track of the nature of each timing difference (by source and whether it is an originating or reversing difference) in order to be able to meet financial statement presentation requirements and to apply prescribed accounting procedures when tax rates change from year to year. These aspects are examined shortly. To conclude this set of examples, however, the following illustration indicates a basic approach to compiling information when two or more timing differences exist.

This example combines the previous two illustrations regarding Baker Ltd. Here it is assumed that timing differences between accounting income and taxable income for a year arise because (1) depreciation expense is not equal to CCA (using Example 1 amounts) *and* (2) warranty expense is not equal to actual warranty costs (using Example 2 amounts). Accordingly, the tax expense, tax payable, and deferred tax amounts for 1994 through 1998 are determined as shown below.

Baker Ltd.
Interperiod Tax Allocation —Two Timing Differences Exist

	1994	1995	1996	1997	1998
Income Tax Expense Calculation:					
Accounting Income Before Tax*	$40,000	$40,000	$40,000	$40,000	$40,000
Income Tax Expense (45%)	18,000	18,000	18,000	18,000	18,000

* Revenue of $300,000 less expenses of $250,000 (including warranty expense of $20,000) less depreciation of $10,000.

	1994	1995	1996	1997	1998
Income Tax Payable Calculation:					
Accounting Income Before Tax	$40,000	$40,000	$40,000	$40,000	$40,000
Adjustments for Timing Differences					
Warranties:					
Add: Warranty Expense	$20,000	$20,000	$20,000	$20,000	$20,000
Deduct: Actual Costs	(10,000)	(15,000)	(25,000)	(28,000)	(21,000)
Net Adjustment for Warranties	$10,000	$ 5,000	($5,000)	($8,000)	($1,000)
Deprecation:					
Add: Depreciation Expense	$10,000	$10,000	$10,000	$10,000	$10,000
Deduct: CCA	(15,000)	(25,500)	(17,850)	(12,495)	(8,746)
Net Adjustment for Depreciation	($5,000)	($15,500)	($7,850)	($2,495)	$1,254
Taxable Income	$45,000	$29,500	$27,150	$29,505	$40,254
Income Tax Payable (45%)	20,250	13,275	12,218	13,277	18,114
Deferred Income Taxes:					
Due to Timing Differences on:					
Warranties	($4,500)	($2,250)	$ 2,250	$ 3,600	$ 450
Depreciation	2,250	6,975	3,532	1,123	(564)
Total	($2,250)	$ 4,725	$ 5,782	$ 4,723	($ 114)

The information presented in this schedule is used to make the entries related to income taxes. These entries, however, may include a Deferred Income Taxes account for each of the items causing the timing differences. If only one account is used, the effect of the two timing differences would be combined and the different nature of each would be lost. This can create problems regarding requirements for financial statement presentation, as discussed in the following section.

Financial Statement Presentation: Balance Sheet

Objective 9

Know how deferred income taxes amounts are reported in the balance sheet.

Example 1 in the previous section illustrated a situation in which the Deferred Income Taxes account had a credit balance because the originating timing difference resulted in income tax expense exceeding income tax payable. It was stated that such credit balances are likely reported in the balance sheet under a liability classification, or at least not in the shareholders' equity section. Example 2 resulted in the Deferred Income Taxes account having a debit balance due to the nature of the originating timing difference. It was stated that such debit balances are likely shown under an asset classification in the balance sheet. The questions remain as to which classification (current or noncurrent) would apply and whether the debit and credit balance consequences of various types of timing differences can be netted into a single account. To answer these questions, the *CICA Handbook* makes the following recommendations:

1. Accumulated tax allocation credits and/or debits should be segregated in the balance sheet as current or noncurrent according to the classification of the assets and liabilities to which they relate.

2. Current accumulated tax allocation debits or credits should be shown in current assets or current liabilities.

3. Noncurrent accumulated tax allocation debits or credits should be shown as a deferred charge or as a deferred credit outside shareholders' equity.[14]

The critical distinction in these recommendations is that of classifying amounts between current and noncurrent portions of the balance sheet. Where both debit and credit tax allocation amounts are classified as current, it is acceptable to report the net amount as either a current asset or liability. Similarly, the net amount for noncurrent amounts is all that needs to be shown.[15]

In Example 1, the credit balance in Deferred Income Taxes is shown in the balance sheet as a noncurrent liability (i.e. outside shareholders' equity) because it relates to timing differences regarding a noncurrent asset's cost allocation. Assuming the warranty contracts are for a year or less, the Deferred Income Taxes account debit balance in Example 2 is classified as a current asset on the balance sheet because it relates to a current liability (liability under product warranties). Using these conclusions regarding Example 3, the annual balance sheets would present two accounts for Deferred Income Taxes: one shown as a noncurrent liability for the credit balance resulting from differences between depreciation expense and CCA, and one shown as a current asset for the debit balance resulting from the timing differences on the warranties. Because of the requirement for separate classification, separate Deferred Income Taxes accounts may be used. If this is done by Baker Ltd. in Example 3, the journal entries for 1994 through 1998 are as follows.

	1994	1995	1996	1997	1998
Income Tax Expense	18,000	18,000	18,000	18,000	18,000
Deferred Income Taxes — Warranties	4,500	2,250	2,250	3,600	450
Deferred Income Taxes — Depreciation		2,250	6,975	3,532	1,123	564
Income Tax Payable	20,250	13,275	12,218	13,277	18,114

Alternatively, if it is assumed that the warranty liability is noncurrent, the resulting debit balance for the related deferred taxes account could be netted against the deferred tax credit balance related to depreciation. Thus, a noncurrent asset for deferred taxes in the amount of $2,250 ($4,500 related to warranties less $2,250 related to depreciation) would be shown in the 1994 balance sheet.

Financial Statement Presentation: Income Statement

The *CICA Handbook* recommends that the amount by which the current income tax provision (expense) is increased or decreased as a result of tax deferrals should be disclosed.[16] This may be done by stating the amount in the statement of changes in financial position, by showing the current and deferred portions of the income tax expense in the income statement, or by means of a note.

Using the data for Baker Ltd. in Example 3, the required disclosure can be accomplished in the 1994 income statement as shown at the top of page 956.

The use of a note to fulfil this requirement is illustrated by the excerpt from a financial statement of Northern Telecom Limited, which reported provisions for income taxes in its income statements for 1992, 1991, and 1990 of $208.0 million, $195.3 million, and $158.4 million, respectively. This also serves as an example of how differences between the statutory tax rate and a company's effective tax rate may be disclosed and reconciled, a requirement noted earlier in the discussion of permanent differences.

[14] *CICA Handbook*, Section 3470, pars. .24, .26, .27.

[15] *Ibid.*, pars. .23, .25.

[16] *Ibid.*, par. .29.

Objective 10

Know how income tax expense is disclosed on the income statement to indicate the components related to amounts currently payable and amounts deferred.

Baker Ltd.
Partial Income Statement
for the Year Ended December 31, 1994

Income Before Income Taxes		$40,000
Income Tax Expense		
Current*	$20,250	
Deferred	(2,250)	18,000
Net Income		$22,000

*This is the amount payable or paid for the year.

Northern Telecom Limited
(from the notes of the December 31, 1992 financial statements)

4. Provision for Income Taxes

	1992	1991	1990
The following is a reconciliation of income taxes calculated at the Canadian combined federal and provincial income tax rate to the provision for income taxes included in the consolidated statement of operations:			
Income taxes at Canadian rate	**$320.4**	$297.9	$259.0
Reduction of Canadian taxes applicable to:			
Research and development incentives	**(66.1)**	(69.1)	(61.1)
Manufacturing profits	**(7.1)**	(5.6)	(8.5)
Difference between Canadian rate and rates applicable to United States and other subsidiaries	**(47.1)**	(54.2)	(31.7)
Other	**7.9**	26.3	.7
Provision for income taxes	**$208.0**	$195.3	$158.4

	1992	1991	1990
Details of Northern Telecom's income taxes were:			
Earnings before income taxes			
Canadian	**$221.4**	$157.3	$201.6
United States and other	**534.9**	552.9	417.0
	$756.3	$710.2	$618.6
Provision for income taxes			
Canadian	**$ 19.3**	$ 32.5	$ 25.7
United States and other	**188.7**	162.8	132.7
	$208.0	$195.3	$158.4
Provision for income taxes			
Current	**$189.4**	$188.3	$186.1
Deferred	**18.6**	7.0	(27.7)
	$208.0	$195.3	$158.4

The deferred portion of the provision for income taxes results from the recognition of certain revenues and expenses in the financial statements in different periods from those for income tax purposes. The following is a summary of the components:

	1992	1991	1990
Investment and other tax credits	**$(41.8)**	$(49.9)	$(54.4)
Depreciation	**(16.5)**	(1.9)	(16.5)
Contracts in progress and other income items	**5.2**	3.7	(11.4)
Utilization of recorded tax benefits	**45.4**	45.6	68.1
Other	**26.3**	9.5	(13.5)
	$18.6	$7.0	$(27.7)

INTERPERIOD TAX ALLOCATION: SOME PRACTICAL PROBLEMS

The preceding examples were fairly straightforward in that there were few timing differences between taxable income and accounting income. It was relatively easy to determine the exact tax effect, the build-up of the deferral, and the reversal or turnaround for each timing difference. This method is called the **individual item basis**.

In practice, however, it is typical for a corporation to have a multitude of items that contribute to timing differences. Because of the volume of records that must be kept, it becomes impractical to identify, follow, and account for each transaction. To simplify computation of the tax effects of numerous timing differences, *similar* items may be grouped. When this is done, a company is said to be applying the **group-of-similar-items basis**. Items are considered similar when there is a common underlying reason for the timing difference resulting from each item. For example, a company may have several capital assets on which it takes capital cost allowance for tax purposes but depreciates on a straight-line basis when determining accounting income.

When groups of similar items are used and tax rates do not change or timing differences for all assets in the group are originating, the aggregate (net) of the timing differences in the group can serve as the basis of accounting for deferred income tax amounts. In such circumstances, the amount of the change in deferred taxes for a year is simply the current year's tax rate multiplied by the aggregate timing difference. Determining the change in deferred taxes in this manner is not appropriate, however, when there are tax rate changes and originating differences are reversing. This is because multiplying the current year's tax rate by the amount of the reversal can give a significantly different result than that obtained by multiplying the same amount by the tax rate existing when the timing difference originated. Accordingly, in a discussion paragraph pertaining to reversing differences, the *CICA Handbook* states:

> Where the difference between accounting and taxable income in a period gives rise to a transfer to income from the tax allocation balance accumulated in prior periods, such transfer will be computed at the rate of accumulation. Where there are practical difficulties in identifying the specific components, the transfer may be calculated at the effective average rate of accumulation, i.e. the proportion that the accumulated deferred credit or charge bears to the accumulated difference between taxable and accounting income. This calculation might be made either by types of differences or in the aggregate.[17]

Two alternative methods exist regarding how amounts can be calculated within the context of this guidance: the gross change method and the net change method.

Gross Change Method

Under the **gross change method**, *the tax effects of timing differences originating on items in the group in the current period are computed at current tax rates. Reversals of timing differences that originated in prior periods on items in the group are removed from the Deferred Income Taxes account at the applicable prior tax rates.* To facilitate the computations, the following steps are used:

1. Separate all timing differences, whether originating or reversing, into groups of similar items. For example, group all instalment sales transactions or all depreciation items.

2. Classify the items within each group as either originating or reversing.

3. Determine the tax effect of the **aggregate originating differences** within a particular group by using the current tax rates.

4. Determine the tax effect of the **aggregate reversing differences** in the group by using the applicable prior tax rates (that is, the rates in effect when the differences originated).

5. For each group, the difference between (3) and (4) constitutes the amount of change in the Deferred Income Taxes account for the period.

Since it is unlikely that all of the reversing timing differences in a particular group originated at the same tax rate, it is necessary to select an appropriate tax rate to be applied to these timing differences in the periods they reverse. In practice, either a FIFO flow assumption or an average rate assumption may be used. If the **FIFO basis** is employed, a record must be maintained for all of

<aside>
Objective 11

Recognize that the group-of-similar-items basis rather than the individual item basis is used when there are many items contributing to timing differences.

Objective 12

Understand how the gross change method is applied when the group-of-similar-items basis is used.
</aside>

---

[17] *CICA Handbook*, Section 3470, par. .18.

the originating differences and the rates at which they originated. As these timing differences reverse, the *first-in differences are the amounts first reversed.* If an **average rate basis** is used, the *tax effect of the reversing differences is determined by multiplying the reversing differences in a group by the weighted-average tax rate in effect during prior periods.* This weighted-average tax rate is equal to the total deferred taxes divided by the total timing differences as they existed for the group at the beginning of the period. For each group, a different weighted-average tax rate may be appropriate.

Net Change Method

Objective 13

Understand how the net change method is applied when the group-of-similar-items basis is used.

The net change method is similar to the gross change method in that all timing differences are separated into groups of similar items. It is different in that tax effects are not computed separately for the originating items and the reversing items within a particular group. Rather, the total amount of items having reversing differences within the group is offset against the total amount of items having originating differences to determine the net difference. If the total originating amount is greater than the total reversing amount, a **net originating difference** results and the *tax effect is determined by multiplying the current tax rate by the net amount.* If the reversing amount is greater than the originating amount, a **net reversing difference** results and the *tax effect is determined using tax rates derived by either the FIFO basis or average rate basis.*

Illustration of Gross Change and Net Change Methods

To illustrate these methods and the differences between them, assume that Magic Corp. determines its 1994 accounting income before taxes to be $118,000. The company is subject to a 46% tax rate and the following differences exist between its income before taxes and taxable income for 1994:

1. Dividend revenue of $12,000 received from Canadian corporations is not subject to tax and, therefore, is a permanent difference.

2. Capital cost allowance taken is $10,000 greater than depreciation expense. This is an originating difference that results in tax expense exceeding tax payable.

3. There is $7,000 gross profit from instalment sales for tax purposes that was recognized in prior years for accounting purposes. This, therefore, is a reversing difference that has the effect of reducing tax expense relative to tax payable.

The reconciliation of Magic Corp.'s income before taxes to taxable income and the computation of tax payable is as follows.

Magic Corp. Reconciliation and Computation of Income Tax Payable — 1994	
Income before taxes	$118,000
Permanent difference	
Dividend from Canadian corporations (tax exempt)	(12,000)
Timing differences:	
Originating – CCA in excess of depreciation	(10,000)
Reversing – taxable gross profit on instalment sales	
in excess of accounting gross profit on instalment sales	7,000
Taxable income	$103,000
Tax rate	46%
Income tax payable	$ 47,380

Magic Corp. maintained the record of timing differences and deferred taxes for prior years that appears at the top of page 959.

Computations of deferred taxes and tax expense for 1994 under the gross change (FIFO and average rate basis) and the net change method are shown in the second box on page 959.[18]

---

[18] All items related to timing differences are treated as belonging to a single group in this example. Because there is a net originating difference under the net change method in this illustration, the current tax rate is applied.

Magic Corp.
Summary of Prior Years' Timing Differences

Year	Timing Difference	Tax Rate	Deferred Taxes
1991	$ 6,000	50%	$3,000
1992	5,000	44%	2,200
1993	3,000	47%	1,410
	$14,000		$6,610

The weighted-average tax rate in prior years was 47.2% ($6,610 ÷ $14,000).

Magic Corp.
Computation of Deferred Taxes and Tax Expense — 1994

	Gross Change Method		Net Change Method
	FIFO	Average	
Income tax payable	$47,380 cr.	$47,380 cr.	$47,380 cr.
Tax effect of timing differences: Originating:			
$10,000 x 46%	$ 4,600 cr.	$ 4,600 cr.	
Reversing:			
$6,000 x 50% (from 1991)	3,000 dr.		
1,000 x 44% (from 1992)	440 dr.		
7,000 x 47.2% (average)		3,304 dr.	
Net originating difference:			
($10,000 – $7,000) x 46%			$ 1,380 cr.
Deferred income taxes	$ 1,160 cr.	$ 1,296 cr.	$ 1,380 cr.
Income tax expense (to balance)	$48,540 dr.	$48,676 dr.	$48,760 dr.

The **income tax payable** is unaffected whether the gross change or the net change method is employed. If the tax rate was the same in all periods, the tax expense and the deferred income tax amounts would also be unaffected by the choice of methods. But because of tax rate changes, the methods produce different results.

The *CICA Handbook* does not recommend one method and, therefore, the choice of which to use rests on judgement. The net change method is easier to apply. The gross change method may be viewed as preferable because it accounts for reversing differences on items in a group at the rate at which they were accumulated earlier than does the net change method.

Different Tax Rates Being Applied to Different Components of Income

The accounting implications of changes in tax rates from year to year can be handled by the gross change or net change methods. An additional accounting problem occurs, however, when components of income are taxed at different rates. This exists when tax laws have provisions for graduated rate schedules, special capital gains tax rates, investment tax credits, foreign tax credits, and carryovers for certain losses and expenses. To solve this problem, the **with and without technique** is used in conjunction with the gross or net change method. This technique is discussed in Appendix 19A.

The Problem of Understandability

The foregoing material described issues regarding application of accounting procedures to measure and disclose amounts for income tax expense and deferred income taxes. Comprehensive tax allocation using the deferral method is done to appropriately match income tax expense to the revenues, expenses, gains, and losses recognized in a period under generally accepted accounting principles. While this is a legitimate objective of financial reporting, it has resulted in accounts and amounts being reported that are often misunderstood.

For example, Statistics Canada information indicates that Deferred Income Taxes credit balances on balance sheets of Canadian corporations exceed $32 billion. This reflects the fact that, over the years, corporations have reported tax expense on their income statements in an amount exceeding the taxes actually paid by over $32 billion. Because of this, politicians and others have incorrectly criticized Canadian corporations on the grounds that they have somehow put off paying the amount shown as deferred income taxes. The implication is that, if not for some mystical accounting and tax breaks, this amount would have flowed into government coffers and significantly reduced the deficit.

Such thinking is incorrect because it does not reflect an understanding of the nature of the different principles used to measure accounting income and taxable income. The principles and methods used to determine taxable income and applicable tax rates are based on the wisdom of governments. Corporations follow these rules when determining income tax payable. Because the accrual accounting system is based on different principles and methods, accounting income and related tax expense are not the same as taxable income and tax payable.

ACCOUNTING FOR INCOME TAX LOSSES AND LOSS CARRYOVERS

Objective 14

Understand that a loss for tax purposes may be carried back to recover taxes paid in previous years and/or carried forward to reduce taxes that would otherwise be paid in future years.

A **loss for income tax purposes** occurs in a year when tax-deductible expenses and losses exceed taxable revenues and gains. An inequitable tax burden would result if companies were taxed during profitable periods without receiving any tax relief during periods of losses. Therefore, tax laws permit taxpayers to use a tax loss of one year to offset taxable income of other years. This income-averaging provision is accomplished through the *carryback and carryforward of income tax losses*. Under this provision, a company pays no income taxes for a year in which it incurs a loss for tax purposes. In addition, it may utilize the loss for tax purposes in either or both of the following ways.

Loss Carryback. A corporation may elect to carry the loss back against taxable income of any or all of the immediately preceding three years, receiving refunds for income taxes paid in those years.[19]

Loss Carryforward. A corporation may elect to carry the loss forward to any or all of the immediate seven years following the year of the loss, using it to offset taxable income and thereby reducing or eliminating taxes that would otherwise be payable in those years. The following diagram illustrates these, assuming a tax loss in 1994.

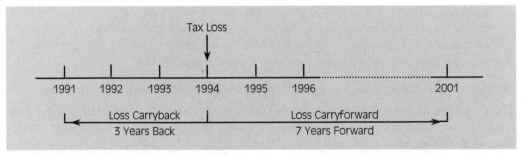

The decision of how to use a tax loss will depend on such factors as its size, results of the previous years' operations, past and anticipated future tax rates, and other factors in which manage-

---

[19] The number of years for which losses may be carried back or forward is stipulated by tax laws. These provisions change from time to time. Provisions existing in 1993 were the basis of years used in this text.

ment sees the greatest tax advantage.[20] Companies that have suffered substantial losses are often attractive candidates for takeover because the acquirer may be able to use these losses to reduce its income taxes. In a sense, companies that have suffered substantial losses may be worth more "dead" than "alive" because of the economic value related to the tax benefit that may be derived from the losses by other companies.

The following discussion examines the accounting treatments of loss carrybacks and carryforwards, *initially assuming the absence of timing differences between accounting and tax amounts*. After these procedures are examined, implications of loss carrybacks and carryforwards on accounting for deferred income taxes are examined.

Loss Carryback Illustrated

If a corporation suffers a tax loss in a period following periods of taxable income, a refund of the prior years' taxes may be claimed. In such cases, the accounting treatment as stated in the *CICA Handbook* is quite clear:

> Where a loss for tax purposes gives rise to a recovery of income taxes of the previous period, such recovery should be reflected in the income statement for the period of the loss either before "income (loss) before discontinued operations and extraordinary items" or, if it relates to discontinued operations or an extraordinary item, as a deduction therefrom.[21]

To illustrate the accounting procedures for tax loss carrybacks, assume that Groh Inc. experienced the following.

Year	Taxable Income (Loss)	Tax Rate	Tax Paid
1990	$ 75,000	30%	$22,500
1991	50,000	35%	17,500
1992	100,000	30%	30,000
1993	200,000	40%	80,000

In 1994, Groh Inc. incurs a $500,000 tax loss that it elects to carry back. The carryback may be applied to any or all of the preceding three years. Assume that management decides to carry it back to 1991 and subsequent years in order. Accordingly, Groh would file amended tax returns for each of the years 1991, 1992, and 1993, receiving a refund of $127,500 ($17,500 + $30,000 + $80,000) for taxes paid in those years. For accounting purposes, the $127,500 represents the *tax effect of the loss carryback*. Note that the tax rate in effect during the year(s) to which the loss carryback is taken, not the tax rate of the year of the loss, is used to determine the tax effect.

Since the tax loss gives rise to a refund that is both measurable and currently realizable, the associated tax benefit is recognized in 1994, the loss period. The following journal entry is made for 1994:

Income Tax Refund Receivable	127,500	
Refund of Income Taxes Due to		
‑ Loss Carryback (Income Tax Expense)		127,500

Objective 15

Know how to account for a loss carryback.

The account debited is reported on the balance sheet as a current asset at December 31, 1994. The account credited is reported on the income statement for 1994 as follows.

Groh Inc.
Partial Income Statement for 1994
(Recognition of Loss Carryback in the Loss Year)

Loss before income taxes	$(500,000)
Less: Refund of income taxes due to loss carryback	127,500
Net loss	$(372,500)

Since the $500,000 tax loss for 1994 exceeds the $350,000 total taxable income from the three preceding years, the remaining $150,000 loss remains to be carried forward.

Loss Carryforward Illustrated

Objective 16

Know how to account for a loss carry-forward when there is or there is not virtual certainty of realizing tax benefits from the loss.

If a tax loss is not fully absorbed through a carryback, or if it is decided not to carry the loss back, it can be carried forward for up to seven years. Because loss carryforwards are used to offset future taxable income, *the tax effect of a loss carryforward represents future tax savings.* Realization of the future tax benefit is dependent on future earnings, the prospect of which may be highly uncertain.

An accounting issue, then, is whether the tax effect of a loss carryforward should be recognized in the loss year when the potential benefits arise or in future years when the benefits are actually realized. To resolve this issue, the *CICA Handbook* has specified the accounting and reporting treatment for loss carryforwards under two conditions. These conditions reflect the degree of uncertainty (virtual certainty or not virtual certainty) associated with the earning of taxable income in the future from which the tax effects of the carryforwards can be realized.

Accounting for Loss Carryforward When Virtual Certainty of Realizing Future Tax Benefits Exists. **Virtual certainty** exists when all three of the following conditions exist:

1. The loss results from an identifiable and nonrecurring cause.

2. A record of profitability has been established over a long period by the corporation or a predecessor business, with any occasional losses being more than offset by income in subsequent years.

3. There is assurance beyond any reasonable doubt that future taxable income will be sufficient to offset the loss carryforward and will be earned during the carryforward period prescribed by the tax laws. In assessing its ability to earn sufficient future taxable income to offset the loss, a corporation may recognize that it can maximize its taxable income during the loss carryforward period by not claiming certain deductions allowable for tax purposes (e.g., capital cost allowances). This will result either in a reduction of accumulated deferred income tax credits or in the recording of deferred income tax debits during the carryforward period.[22]

When these conditions are met, the tax saving on the loss carryforward is recognized in the year of the loss. An asset (Estimated Future Tax Benefits From Loss Carryforward) is debited and an income statement item (Reduction of Loss Due to Tax Carryforward Benefits) is credited. The income statement account is shown in the calculation of "income (loss) before discontinued opera-

---

[22] *Ibid.*, par. .43. In the discussion of virtual certainty situations (par. .45), the *Handbook* states that the tax benefit should be calculated on the basis of the known enacted tax rates of relevant future periods. If there are no enacted tax rate changes for future years, the current year's tax rate would be used in the calculation.

tions and extraordinary items" or, if it relates to discontinued operations or an extraordinary item, as a deduction therefrom.[23]

To illustrate, assume that Norton Inc. suffers a $200,000 net operating loss in 1994 when the tax rate is (and is expected to continue at) 40%. Furthermore, assume that management decides the full amount of the loss is to be carried forward. If realization of the future tax savings is "virtually certain," Norton Inc. will recognize the tax carryforward as an *asset* (future tax benefit) and reduce the current operating loss by the amount of the tax benefit of the loss carryforward. The tax benefit of $80,000 ($200,000 × 40%) is recorded in 1994 through this journal entry:

Estimated Future Tax Benefits From Loss Carryforward	80,000	
Reduction of Loss Due to Tax Carryforward Benefits		80,000

The lower portion of the income statement for 1994 is as follows.

Operating loss before income tax effect	$200,000
Less: Reduction of loss due to tax carryforward benefits	80,000
Net loss	$120,000

If, in 1995, Norton Inc. earns $600,000 income before taxes, the following entry is recorded in 1995, assuming a 40% tax rate:

Income Tax Expense	240,000	
Estimated Future Tax Benefits From Loss Carryforward		80,000
Income Taxes Payable		160,000

The lower portion of the 1995 income statement is as follows.

Income before taxes	$600,000
Less: Income tax expense	240,000
Net income	$360,000

In situations where a company discovers that virtual certainty no longer exists, any tax benefit of a loss carryforward previously recorded is written off.[24]

Accounting for Loss Carryforward When Virtual Certainty of Realizing Future Tax Benefits Does Not Exist. If the criteria for virtual certainty of realizing future tax benefits are not met, any potential tax benefit of a loss carryforward is not recognized in the loss year. Instead, it is recognized in future periods when the tax savings are realized.[25] The amounts of any loss carryforwards for tax purposes not recognized in the loss period, along with the expiration period of the loss carryforwards, are disclosed in a note to the financial statements.[26] From this disclosure the financial statement user can determine the amount of income that may be recognized in the future on which no income tax will be paid.

Using the information from the Norton Inc. example, but now assuming the criteria for virtual certainty are not met, no entry is made regarding income taxes in 1994. For 1994, the company simply reports a net operating loss of $200,000 on its income statement. An accompanying note

---

[23] *Ibid.*, par. .46.
[24] *Ibid.*, par. .50.
[25] *Ibid.*, par. .56.
[26] *Ibid.*, par. .54.

would state that the loss can be carried forward for seven years for tax purposes. If Norton Inc. then experiences a $600,000 pretax income in 1995, the following entry is recorded:

Income Tax Expense	240,000	
Tax Reduction Due to Loss Carryforward		80,000
Income Taxes Payable		160,000

The lower portion of the 1995 income statement is as follows.[27]

Income before income taxes		$600,000
Income taxes	$240,000	
Less: Tax reduction due to loss carryforward	80,000	160,000
Net income		$440,000

Accounting treatments similar to those illustrated above would occur beyond 1995 if the 1995 income was not sufficient to absorb the entire amount of the loss carryforward.

LOSS CARRYBACKS AND CARRYFORWARDS INTEGRATED WITH INTERPERIOD INCOME TAX ALLOCATION

Objective 17

Understand and appreciate the accounting for situations that integrate deferred income taxes with loss carrybacks and carryforwards.

Interperiod tax allocation for timing differences should continue to be employed by a corporation through loss and loss carryback or carryforward periods.[28] Accounting for these situations can be very complex. The following examples are designed to introduce the basic concepts, but they are limited as to the variety of possible circumstances.

Example 1. Assume that Brooke Corp. began operations in 1993. For that year, the following schedule reflects pertinent information regarding its operations, given a 40% tax rate.

Brooke Corp.
Data for 1993

Accounting income (including $12,000 depreciation expense)		$50,000
Timing difference:		
CCA in excess of depreciation		10,000
Taxable income		$40,000
Taxes payable (40%)		16,000
Journal entry:		
Income Tax Expense	20,000	
Income Tax Payable		16,000
Deferred Income Taxes		4,000

In 1994, the company incurs an accounting loss of $62,000, including depreciation of $12,000. Although $20,000 CCA could be taken in 1994, management chooses not to take any CCA during that year. Because of this decision, the tax loss for 1994 is $50,000 and a timing difference for

---

[27] Prior to 1990, recognition of a tax benefit from a loss carryforward that was not recorded in the year of the loss was reported as an extraordinary item. Given the 1989 revision of criteria to be met for an item to be extraordinary, Section 3480, par. .04 of the *CICA Handbook* now explicitly states that tax reductions on the utilization of prior period losses are not extraordinary.

[28] *CICA Handbook*, Section 3470, par. .36.

depreciation expense exceeding CCA by $12,000 results. (Note that not taking CCA this year means it could still be taken in future years.)

Assuming that Brooke Corp. decides to carry back the 1994 loss and recover the $16,000 taxes paid in 1993, the following entry is made:

Income Tax Refund Receivable	16,000	
Refund of Income Taxes Due to Loss Carryback		16,000

An additional element entering into this situation is that the company may refile prior years' tax returns amending (changing) the amount taken for CCA. This would occur if such an action was advantageous to the company. While a refiling associated with a loss carryback cannot result in the company obtaining a refund in excess of the taxes paid in prior years, it may be advantageous in terms of reinstating CCA taken previously to undepreciated capital cost, which could then be taken in future years to reduce taxable income. Reducing the CCA taken in previous tax returns would, however, necessitate adjusting the Deferred Income Taxes credit build-up from the excess CCA over depreciation in the prior years.

To illustrate, assume that Brooke Corp. does refile its 1993 tax return, on which it reduces the CCA taken by $10,000 (the full timing difference in 1993). The amended return shows taxable income of $50,000. However, the full $50,000 tax loss in 1994 totally offsets this taxable income, and no additional tax is payable for 1993. Therefore, the $16,000 tax paid is still refunded and the full loss would be carried back. After refiling, the $10,000 CCA could be taken in future years. This, however, means that the Deferred Income Taxes credit recorded in 1993 is no longer applicable (the depreciation expense and CCA for 1993 are the same after refiling). Consequently, the deferred taxes have to be adjusted. In this regard, the *CICA Handbook* states:

> Where the recomputation of taxable income for the previous period results in an adjustment to accumulated deferred income taxes, such adjustment should be reflected in the income statement for the period of the loss.[29]

Therefore, the following entry is made:

Deferred Income Taxes	4,000	
Deferred Income Tax Recoverable in the Future		4,000

The credited account is shown in the income statement as a deferred tax recoverable item, as illustrated on page 966. The Deferred Income Taxes account now has a zero balance.

The fact that depreciation expense of $12,000 is included in the 1994 income determination but no CCA was taken in calculating the tax loss for the year means that there is a timing difference in the loss year. The accounting loss is greater than the tax loss because the former includes an expense not included in the latter. Accounting for this difference depends on expectations as to whether the timing difference will reverse—that the company will eventually have taxable income. (Note that the period for reversal of a timing difference is not limited, as is the case for a loss carryforward.) When there is "reasonable assurance" that the timing difference will reverse, then the tax effect of the difference is recorded in the year of the loss.[30] Such an entry for Brooke Corp. in 1994 is:

Deferred Income Taxes	4,800	
Deferred Income Tax Recoverable in the Future		4,800
(Timing difference of $12,000 × tax rate of 40%)		

---

[29] *Ibid.*, par. .42.

[30] *Ibid.*, par. .52. The phrase "reasonable assurance" is used in the *Handbook* to describe the level of expectation regarding the likelihood of the timing difference reversing. This is different from the "virtual certainty" required to recognize the tax benefits of a loss carryforward in the loss year. Consequently, there can be reasonable assurance that the timing difference will reverse when there is no virtual certainty of realizing loss carryforward benefits. The criteria for "reasonable assurance" to exist are not specified in the *Handbook*.

When there is not reasonable assurance that there will be sufficient income in the future to absorb the reversal, deferred income tax debits are not recognized.[31]

Assuming reasonable assurance regarding a reversal, the partial 1994 income statement for Brooke Corp. is as shown below.

Brooke Corp.
Partial Income Statement
For the Year Ended December 31, 1994

Net loss before depreciation		$50,000
Depreciation expense		12,000
Net loss before income taxes		$62,000
Deduct:		
Current refund due to loss carryback	$16,000	
Deferred income taxes recoverable in the future ($4,000 + $4,800)	8,800	24,800
Net loss		$37,200

Example 2. For various reasons, a corporation may not be able to, or may choose not to, carry back a loss or portion thereof. In such circumstances, the previously discussed recommended accounting practice concerning loss carryforwards would apply. Additionally, timing differences in the loss year may have to be accounted for.

Assume, for example, that Brooke Corp. decides not to carry back its 1994 loss or to refile its tax return of 1993, as was the case in Example 1. Therefore, the question becomes: How will the company account for the loss carryforward and the timing difference in 1994?

Assuming virtual certainty of the tax benefits from the carryforward and reasonable assurance that the timing difference will reverse, the following entries are made:[32]

Estimated Future Tax Benefits—Loss Carryforward	20,000	
Reduction of Loss Due to Tax Carryforward Benefit		20,000
($50,000 tax loss × 40% tax rate)		
Deferred Income Taxes	4,800	
Deferred Income Tax Recoverable in the Future		4,800
($12,000 excess depreciation over CCA × 40% tax rate)		

If virtual certainty does not exist but reasonable assurance that timing differences would reverse is present, then only the second entry is made. If both virtual certainty and reasonable assurance do not exist, then deferred income tax debits are not recognized. Since the Deferred Income Taxes account has a credit balance of only $4,000 resulting from 1993, this is the maximum amount by which it can be debited under such circumstances.

INTRAPERIOD TAX ALLOCATION

Tax allocation is the process of matching tax expense with reported income. **Interperiod tax allocation** involves determination of the *amount* of tax expense to be reported in a particular accounting period; this is done by matching tax expense to accounting income. **Intraperiod tax allocation** involves determination of the *format* to be used in disclosing tax expense within a particular period;

---

[31] *Ibid.*, par. .52.

[32] Because Brooke Corp. began operation in 1993, the criteria for virtual certainty would not be met. However, the assumption of virtual certainty is made to simplify the points being illustrated.

this is done by apportioning reported taxes to the related components of reported items in financial statements (see Chapter 4 to review the basics of intraperiod tax allocation). Thus, intraperiod tax allocation means assigning tax expense to income from continuing operations, discontinued operations, and extraordinary items in the income statement. Additionally, it requires that prior period adjustments, corrections of errors made in previous periods, and adjustments for changes in accounting policies accounted for on a retroactive basis be reported net of their income tax consequences in the statement of retained earnings.

The amount of income tax expense allocated to the results of continuing operations is that which would result based on only the revenues, expenses, gains, and losses included in the determination of income from continuing operations. Assuming that all items are taxed at the same rate, any difference between the income tax expense applicable to continuing operations and the total income tax expense is allocated to remaining items. For example, assume that Cole Co. Ltd. has income from continuing operations of $1,000,000, an extraordinary gain of $300,000, and no timing or permanent differences exist. The current tax rate is 34%. In this case, the amount of income tax expense is $442,000 ($1,300,000 × 34%). This tax is first allocated to the income from continuing operations and then the remainder is allocated to the extraordinary gain as follows.

Total income tax expense	$442,000
Tax consequence associated with income from operations ($1,000,000 × 34%)	340,000
Remainder to extraordinary item	$102,000

Income taxes are reported in the income statement as follows.

Income from continuing operations	$1,000,000
Income tax expense	340,000
Income before extraordinary item	$ 660,000
Extraordinary gain (net of $102,000 tax)	198,000
Net income	$ 858,000

This example is simplified in that the same tax rate applies to each of these items. To illustrate a more complex situation, assume that Schroeder Inc. has the following:

1. The company's pretax accounting income and taxable income are the same. The tax rate is 40%.

2. The company's loss from continuing operations is $500,000. A loss carryback would give rise to a $100,000 refund of taxes paid on $250,000 of taxable income from continuing operations during the carryback years.

3. The company also has an extraordinary gain of $900,000.

4. Income tax payable and income tax expense are $160,000 computed as shown below.

Loss from continuing operations	$(500,000)
Extraordinary gain	900,000
Taxable income	$ 400,000
Tax rate	40%
Income tax payable and income tax expense	$ 160,000

Objective 18

Know the difference between interperiod and intraperiod tax allocation and understand how to apply intraperiod tax allocation.

Income tax expense is allocated between the pretax loss from continuing operations and the extraordinary gain as follows.

Total income tax expense	$ 160,000
Tax consequences associated with the loss from continuing operations	(100,000)
Tax related to extraordinary item	$ 260,000

In this example, the benefit attributable to the loss from continuing operations is limited to the assumed carryback that the company would have realized in the absence of the extraordinary gain. The benefit ($100,000) plus the tax payable ($160,000) is allocated to the extraordinary item.

If there was a timing difference between the amount of an extraordinary item for tax and accounting purposes, the related tax effects are shown with the extraordinary item in the income statement.

Similar concepts apply to accounting for the tax consequences related to any discontinued operations reported in the income statement and adjustments to previously reported balances in retained earnings when intraperiod tax allocation is employed.

CONCLUDING COMMENT

Interperiod tax allocation is one of the most challenging and complex areas in accounting. Many complications encountered in practice have not been discussed in this chapter. For example, when considering the tax effects of a loss carryforward, it was assumed that the current year's tax rate was the same as the tax rate expected to exist when the benefits of the loss are realized. The examples regarding the integration of loss carryforwards or carrybacks and interperiod allocation for timing differences, while reasonably complex, only scratched the surface of possible situations. Additionally, accounting for the tax effects of capital losses relative to taxable capital gains has not been covered. Therefore, while many basic aspects have been examined, much remains if one is to acquire a complete and comprehensive understanding of interperiod tax allocation accounting.

FUNDAMENTAL CONCEPTS

1. Because the objectives and principles for determining accounting income and taxable income differ, the amounts are likely to differ. The nature of the item causing the difference can be one of two types: permanent difference or timing difference.

2. Permanent differences are items that enter into the calculation of either accounting income or taxable income, but never into both. When such differences occur in accounting income, they are simply treated as nontaxable or nondeductible when determining tax expense reported on the income statement. If they are part of the taxable income calculation, they are used to calculate the tax expense reported even though the items are not shown on the income statement.

3. Timing differences result when revenue, gain, expense, or loss items are included in either the accounting income or taxable income of a period and in the taxable income or accounting income, respectively, of a subsequent period. That is, they originate in one period and reverse in a future period.

(Continued)

4. The tax effects of timing differences are accounted for using interperiod tax allocation. The *CICA Handbook* currently recommends that comprehensive allocation (rather than partial allocation) be applied, using the deferral method (rather than the liability method). As such, tax expense is based on accounting income whereas tax payable is based on taxable income. The tax effects of all timing differences originating in a year are measured using the current year's tax rate. An alternative to interperiod allocation is the taxes payable approach, which would result in reporting a tax expense equal to tax payable, but this is not recommended in the *CICA Handbook*.

5. Application of interperiod tax allocation gives rise to deferred income taxes being reported in the balance sheet. The amount reflects the cumulative tax effects (originating and reversing) of the timing differences associated with the balance sheet classification (current or noncurrent) of the item (asset or liability) that caused the deferred taxes.

6. Disclosure of the portion of income tax expense related to current taxes payable and to deferred amounts is necessary. This may be accomplished by showing the current and deferred portion of tax expense in the body of the income statement, through a note, or by stating the increase or decrease in deferred taxes in the statement of changes in financial position.

7. The existence of a large number of timing differences and/or tax rate changes over the years complicates the accounting for deferred taxes. The gross change method or the net change method may be used in such situations.

8. Tax rates may be expected to change over the years. Present recommendations in the *CICA Handbook* state that deferred tax amounts are to be determined using the tax rate existing in the year of origination, and are not to be adjusted for future years' expected or actual tax rate changes (the deferral method). Recognizing expected and actual tax rate changes when recording originating amounts or adjusting deferred tax balances (the liability method) is an alternative approach not currently recommended.

9. Tax laws permit tax losses to be carried back or forward for purposes of determining taxes recoverable from previous years or payable in future years.

10. Carryback of a loss results in a refund of taxes paid in previous years. The refund due to the loss carryback is reported in the income statement.

11. Accounting for a loss carryforward depends on whether or not there is virtual certainty of realizing tax savings during the loss carryforward period. If "virtual certainty" exists, the future tax benefit is recorded and reported in the income statement of the year of the loss. Otherwise, the benefit (except for implications regarding deferred tax amounts) is not recognized in the loss year but is recognized in the year the tax saving is realized. Amounts and expiration dates of loss carryforwards not recognized in the accounts should be disclosed through a note to the financial statements.

12. Loss carrybacks and carryforwards and implications for determining amounts in tax returns (e.g., CCA taken) often affect deferred income tax amounts. The circumstances of such situations are varied and often complex. Examples integrating the consequences of loss carrybacks and carryforwards with deferred income tax accounts illustrated basic accounting procedures associated with such situations.

13. Intraperiod tax allocation refers to the recommended practice of apportioning reported taxes to the related components of income (i.e. from continuing operations, discontinued operations, and extraordinary items) and any adjustments to previously reported retained earnings (i.e. from prior period adjustments, correction of errors, or retroactive adjustments for changes in accounting policies).

APPENDIX 19A
The With and Without Technique

The examples in the chapter illustrate the deferred tax computation as simply the current tax rate multiplied by the timing difference. This is referred to as the **"short-cut method."** In practice, however, owing to the interplay of such items as graduated tax rates, special tax rates, investment tax credits, and foreign tax credits, the deferred tax is frequently computed using the **"with and without timing differences technique."** The with and without technique is not an alternative to the gross change or the net change methods, but is used in conjunction with one of these methods. When the net change method is used, the following steps are involved in applying the with and without technique:

1. Compute the *income tax payable* on taxable income. Taxable income is equal to accounting income adjusted for any permanent differences and for all timing differences. All special tax rates and credits are applied in the determination of income tax payable. This represents the "with" portion of the computation (that is, *with* adjustment for timing differences).

2. Compute the income tax that would have been paid on accounting income. Recall that accounting income, for purposes of this chapter, is the net income for the period to be reported in the financial statements after excluding permanent difference items. All special tax rates and credits are applied to accounting income *as if they were taxable income* on which tax would be paid. This represents the "without" portion of the computation (that is, *without* adjustment for timing differences).

3. The difference between (1) the income tax payable *with* adjustment for timing differences and (2) the pro forma tax *without* adjustment for timing differences represents the current tax effect of net timing differences. It is debited (or credited) to the Deferred Income Taxes account.

To illustrate, the following schedule presents data and the computation of taxes payable for a hypothetical corporation that has the first $25,000 of income taxed at a rate of 22% and additional amounts subject to a 48% rate.

Computation of Tax Payable		
	1993	1994
Accounting income	$50,000	$35,000
Timing difference —		
Excess of CCA over book depreciation	(20,000)	(15,000)
Taxable income	$30,000	$20,000
Taxes currently payable (computed on taxable income)	$ 5,500[a]	$ 4,400[b]
	$ 2,400[c]	
Tax payable	$ 7,900	$ 4,400

[a] $25,000 x 22%
[b] $20,000 x 22%
[c] $ 5,000 x 48%

Based on these data, the deferred tax provisions for 1993 and 1994 are computed as follows using the with and without technique:

1. Tax computed on accounting income *with* timing difference:

	1993		1994	
Tax Bracket	Income (With)	Tax Payable	Income (With)	Tax Payable
$0–$25,000	$25,000 x 22% = $5,500		$20,000 x 22% = $4,400	
Over $25,000	5,000 x 48% = 2,400		–0– x 48% = –0–	
	$30,000	$7,900	$20,000	$4,400

2. Tax computed on accounting income *without* timing difference:

| | 1993 | | 1994 | |
| | Income | Tax | Income | Tax |
Tax Bracket	(Without)	Expense	(Without)	Expense
$0–$25,000	$25,000 × 22% =	$ 5,500	$25,000 × 22% =	$ 5,500
Over $25,000	25,000 × 48% =	12,000	10,000 × 48% =	4,800
	$50,000	$17,500	$35,000	$10,300

3. Deferred tax provision:

	1993	1994
$17,500 – $7,900 (tax expense minus tax payable)	$9,600	
$10,300 – $4,400 (tax expense minus tax payable)		$5,900

Under the short-cut method, the deferred tax would have been computed in 1993 as $9,600 ($20,000 × 48%) and in 1994 as $7,200 ($15,000 × 48%); 1993 would be correct but not 1994. The amount deferred in 1994 is not 48% of the timing difference, as happened to be the case in 1993. Owing to the interplay of the different tax rates applied to different portions of income, the deferral is at an effective rate for 1994 of somewhere between 22% and 48%. This illustrates that the short-cut method of applying the current tax rate to the amount of timing differences should be used only when special tax rates or credits will not apply.

Note: All **asterisked** questions, cases, exercises, and problems relate to material contained in the appendix to this chapter.

––––––––– QUESTIONS –––––––––

1. In what basic ways do the objectives of determining taxable income differ from the objectives of measuring accounting income?

2. As controller for Toon Products Co. Ltd., you are asked to meet with the board of directors to discuss the company's reporting of income tax. Several members of the board express concern over the fact that the company is reporting a larger amount of income tax expense on its published income statements than is to be paid to the government according to the company's income tax return for that same year.
   (a) Explain to the board members the accounting rationale for this discrepancy.
   (b) How might this difference between tax paid and tax expense have arisen?

3. Explain what a permanent difference is. Give three examples.

4. Explain what a timing difference is. Give three examples.

5. What is meant by the "taxes payable basis"? What arguments support its use?

6. What is the rationale for allocating income taxes between periods?

7. Comprehensive allocation and partial allocation are two concepts that exist regarding the extent to which interperiod tax allocation could be applied. Explain what is meant by each. What is the *CICA Handbook* position regarding which should be used?

8. The deferral method and the liability method represent alternative approaches to interperiod tax allocation. Explain what is meant by each and identify the one recommended in the *CICA Handbook*.

9. How are deferred charges (debits) and deferred credits, arising under the deferral method for income tax allocation, treated on the balance sheet?

10. Explain the "individual-item basis" of interperiod tax allocation.

11. What are the steps involved in applying the "gross change method"?

12. Explain the "net change method" of applying interperiod income tax allocation.

13. Differentiate between "carrybacks" and "carryforwards." Which can be accounted for with the greater certainty when they arise? Why?

14. What are the alternative ways of accounting for a tax loss carryforward? What are the circumstances that determine the alternative to be applied?

*15. Explain what is meant by the "short-cut method" and the "with and without timing differences technique" for determining deferred tax amounts. Under what circumstances would the latter method be superior to the former?

CASES

C19-1 (DEFERRED INCOME TAXES: DEPRECIATION VERSUS CCA) In its financial statements for 1994, the Clear Water Company Ltd. reports an item: Deferred Income Taxes, $225,000. The president in his letter to shareholders states that this is in connection with a capital cost allowance allowed by the federal government.

Instructions

(a) Explain the nature of this item and the accounting theory related to reporting such an item on the financial statements.

(b) Assuming that straight-line depreciation with no salvage value is used for financial statement purposes, give the journal entries that were probably made to record Deferred Income Taxes, and the entries that will affect this account in future years. Amounts for the journal entries need not be given. Assume that the direction of the difference between CCA and book depreciation reverses in the sixth year and that the life of the assets involved is 15 years.

C19-2 (JUSTIFYING DEFERRED TAXES) The president of Fish Carriers Ltd. is very upset with the accounting treatment of deferred taxes. "We wrote off the deferred tax balance this year because it doesn't mean anything. In fact, our banker adds the accumulated deferred tax balance to retained earnings when he reviews our annual financing proposals. I just couldn't think of any reason why we should pay someone to calculate deferred taxes when no one uses them."

Instructions

Discuss the president's comments.

(CICA, UFE adapted)

C19-3 (DEFERRED INCOME TAXES: CAUSES AND REPORTING)
Part A. This year, Pine Co. Ltd. has each of the following items in its income statement:

1. Gross profits on instalment sales.

2. Revenues on long-term construction contracts.

3. Estimated cost of product warranty contracts.

4. Premiums on officers' life insurance, with Pine as beneficiary.

Instructions

(a) Under what conditions will deferred income taxes need to be reported in the financial statements?

(b) Specify whether or not deferred income taxes will need to be recognized for each of the previous items, and indicate the rationale for such recognition.

Part B. Mary Corp.'s president has heard that deferred income taxes can be variously classified in the balance sheet.

Instructions

Identify the conditions under which deferred income taxes will be classified as a noncurrent item in the balance sheet. What justification exists for such classification?

(AICPA adapted)

(INTRAPERIOD AND INTERPERIOD TAX ALLOCATION: THEORY)   Income tax allocation is an **C19-4** integral part of generally accepted accounting principles. The applications of intraperiod tax allocation (within a period) and interperiod tax allocation (among periods) are both required.

Instructions

(a) Explain the need for *intraperiod* tax allocation (covered in Chapter 4).

(b) Accountants who favour *interperiod* tax allocation argue that income taxes are an expense rather than a distribution of earnings. Explain the significance of this argument.

(c) Indicate and explain whether each of the following *independent* situations will be treated as a timing difference or a permanent difference.

1. Estimated warranty costs (covering a three-year warranty) are expensed for accounting purposes at the time of sale but deducted for income tax purposes when incurred.

2. Depreciation for accounting income and capital cost allowance for taxable income differ.

3. A company properly uses the equity method to account for its 30% investment in a non-Canadian company. The investee pays dividends that are 10% of its annual earnings. Only dividends received are taxable.

(d) Discuss the nature of the deferred income tax accounts and possible classifications in a company's balance sheet.

(DEFERRAL METHOD VERSUS LIABILITY METHOD)   During 1994, Crystal Corp. incurred interest **C19-5** cost of $600,000 during construction of a new office building, which was completed on December 31. For tax purposes, the interest cost is deductible in 1994. For accounting purposes, the interest is capitalized and amortized over the 15-year life of the building, using the straight-line method. Based on a 1994 tax rate of 40%, Crystal's accountant estimates that the company will enjoy an immediate tax saving of $240,000. He contends that recognition of an immediate deferred tax credit for the full $240,000 will distort the company's debt ratios, since payment of any additional future taxes depends on such uncertain factors as the company's future earnings and tax rates. He believes that use of the deferral method of interperiod tax allocation would be misleading to financial statement users, since the $600,000 timing difference is a "semipermanent difference" that will take 15 years to fully reverse. He thinks that the liability method is more appropriate for semipermanent differences such as this, and that the tax effect should be discounted to its present value.

Instructions

(a) Describe the difference between the deferral method and the liability method of interperiod tax allocation.

(b) Assuming accounting income of $2,000,000, prepare the journal entry needed to record income taxes for 1994 under the deferral method.

(c) Assuming annual accounting income of $2,000,000 and a 40% tax rate, prepare the annual journal entry to record income taxes during the 15 years subsequent to 1994 under the deferral method.

(d) Assuming that the liability method of interperiod tax allocation is appropriate, what is the journal entry to record the 1994 income taxes? Assume that discounting is applied, a 10% discount factor is used, a 40% tax rate is appropriate, and accounting income is $2,000,000.

——————— EXERCISES ———————

E19-1 **(PERMANENT VERSUS TIMING DIFFERENCES; ORIGINATING EFFECT ON DEFERRED TAXES)**   Listed below are 18 items that are treated differently for accounting and tax purposes:

1. Excess of capital cost allowance over depreciation.

2. Tax-exempt interest income.

3. Excess of depletion allowance for tax purposes over depletion expense for accounting income determination.

4. Excess of charge to tax return over charge to books for estimated uncollectibles.

5. Excess of accrued pension expense over amount paid.

6. Excess of fair market value of a charitable contribution (deductible for taxes) over cost (charged to expense).

7. Instalment sales income for accounting purposes exceeds taxable income from instalment sales.

8. Expenses incurred in obtaining tax-exempt income.

9. A trademark acquired directly from the government is amortized more rapidly for tax purposes than it is expensed for accounting purposes.

10. Prepaid advertising is deducted as an expense for tax purposes but set up as a prepaid asset on the books.

11. Premiums paid on life insurance of officers (the corporation is the beneficiary).

12. Receipt of tax-free dividends from a Canadian corporation.

13. Proceeds of life insurance policies on lives of officers.

14. Estimated future warranty costs that are expensed for accounting purposes but are not deductible for tax purposes until they are incurred.

15. Excess of research and development cost per tax return over book amount.

16. Charitable contributions—excess of accounting amount over tax limitation.

17. Fine for polluting.

18. Income discovered after closing but included in the tax return.

Instructions

Indicate whether each item results in a *permanent* difference or a *timing* difference and whether any *originating* difference results in a debit or a credit to deferred taxes.

(TAX ALLOCATION ENTRIES)   Following is information about Garden Inc.   **E19-2**

	1992	1993	1994
Accounting income	$80,000	$95,000	$60,000
Taxable income	70,000	70,000	80,000

Instructions

(a) Assuming a tax rate of 45% and that the differences between accounting and taxable income are entirely the result of timing differences, prepare the journal entries at the end of each year to reflect income tax allocation.

(b) Assume the same facts as in (a) except that in 1993 the accounting income includes $10,000 for dividends received from Canadian corporations (tax-exempt). Prepare any journal entries that would be different from those in (a).

(TAX ALLOCATION ENTRIES)   The accounting income of Purple Inc. has differed from that of its taxable **E19-3** income throughout each of the last four years as follows.

Year	Accounting Income	Taxable Income	Tax Rate
1991	$270,000	$180,000	50%
1992	300,000	225,000	40%
1993	330,000	270,000	45%
1994	360,000	480,000	40%

Accounting income for each year includes an expense of $20,000 that is not deductible for tax purposes (it is a permanent difference).

Instructions

Prepare journal entries to reflect income tax allocation in all four years, using the deferral method. Assume that the reversing difference in 1994 is accounted for using the gross change method on a FIFO basis.

(CLASSIFICATION AND PRESENTATION OF TIMING DIFFERENCES)   At December 31, 1994 **E19-4** Cats Corp.'s Deferred Income Taxes account has a $375,000 credit balance consisting of the following items.

Timing Difference	Resulting Balance in Deferred Taxes
1. Excess of capital cost allowance over accounting depreciation.	$410,000 cr.
2. Accrual, for accounting purposes, of estimated warranty costs that are expected to be paid in 1995. For tax purposes, such costs are deductible in the year paid.	110,000 dr.
3. Capitalization, for accounting purposes, of interest and property taxes incurred during construction of a building in 1994. The expenditures were deducted on the 1994 tax return.	75,000 cr.
Total	$375,000 cr.

Instructions

Indicate the manner in which deferred taxes will be presented on Cats Corp.'s December 31, 1994 balance sheet.

E19-5 **(TAX ALLOCATION ENTRIES: DEPRECIATION VERSUS CCA)** The income statements of Baker Inc. for a three-year period provide the following data:

	1992	1993	1994
Income before depreciation	$180,000	$170,000	$200,000
Depreciation (asset with 3-year life, no salvage value)	30,000	30,000	30,000
Accounting income after depreciation	$150,000	$140,000	$170,000

A 40% tax rate is applicable to all three years. The capital cost allowance method is used for tax purposes, with a CCA rate of 50%. The asset class will continue after three years.

Instructions

Prepare the journal entry for each year to record the income tax expense and the income tax payable.

E19-6 **(CLASSIFICATION OF DEFERRED TAXES)** George's Imports Co. Ltd., which sells furniture on instalment plans, records sales on the accrual basis for financial reporting purposes but on the instalment method for tax purposes. As a result, $35,000 of deferred income taxes have been accrued at December 31, 1994. In accordance with industry practice, instalment accounts receivable from customers are shown as current assets.

At December 31, 1994, George's Imports Co. Ltd. has recorded a $50,000 deferred income tax debit arising from an accrual of noncurrent deferred compensation expense that is *not* tax-deductible until paid.

Also at December 31, 1994, George's Imports has accrued $32,500 of deferred income taxes resulting from the use of capital cost allowance for tax purposes and straight-line depreciation for financial reporting purposes.

Instructions

How will the deferred income taxes be classified on George's Imports Co. Ltd.'s December 31, 1994 balance sheet?

(AICPA adapted)

E19-7 **(TAX ALLOCATION ENTRIES: ORIGINATING AND REVERSING)** Spartan Corporation has an item costing $90,000 that is expensed for tax purposes in 1994 but is amortized over three years (1994, 1995, 1996) for accounting purposes. The tax rate is 40% in the year of origination, 1994, and 30% in the years of turnaround, 1995 and 1996. The accounting and tax data for the three years are shown below.

	Financial Accounting	Tax Return
1994 (40% tax rate)		
Income before timing difference	$100,000	$100,000
Timing difference	30,000	90,000
Income after timing difference	$ 70,000	$ 10,000
1995 (30% tax rate)		
Income before timing difference	$100,000	$100,000
Timing difference	30,000	–0–
Income after timing difference	$ 70,000	$100,000
1996 (30% tax rate)		
Income before timing difference	$100,000	$100,000
Timing difference	30,000	–0–
Income after timing difference	$ 70,000	$100,000

Instructions

Prepare the journal entries to record the income tax expense and the deferred income taxes at the end of each year, applying the individual item basis and the deferral method.

(DEFERRED TAX COMPUTATIONS)   During the audit of Taco Sales Co. Ltd., the following information   **E19-8**
was obtained:

1.

Year	Amount Due Per Tax Return
1994	$80,000
1995	$65,000

2.   On January 1, 1994, equipment costing $110,000 was purchased. The equipment had a life of five years and a salvage value of $10,000. Capital cost allowance was taken for income tax purposes and the straight-line depreciation method was used for accounting purposes. The appropriate CCA rate was 30%.

3.   In January 1995, $75,000 was collected in advance rental of a building for a three-year period. The entire $75,000 was reported as taxable income in 1995 but $50,000 was reported as unearned revenue in 1995 for accounting purposes.

4.   The tax rate was 45% in both years.

5.   The client company used the deferral method of income tax allocation.

Instructions

(a)   Determine the balance in the Deferred Income Taxes account at the end of 1994 and whether it is a debit or a credit.

(b)   Determine the balance in the Deferred Income Taxes account at the end of 1995 and whether it is a debit or a credit.

(GROSS AND NET CHANGE METHODS: ENTRIES)   Bear Co. Ltd. uses capital cost allowance for tax   **E19-9**
purposes and straight-line depreciation for accounting purposes. In the current year, 1994, the tax rate is 40%. The rate in all prior years was 35%. Accounting income is $800,000 in 1994, when originating timing differences are $100,000 and reversing timing differences are $80,000. *Taxable income is $780,000.*

Instructions

(a)   Compute the change in deferred taxes under (1) the gross change method and (2) the net change method.

(b)   Prepare the journal entry to record the taxes payable, the tax expense, and the deferred taxes for 1994 under (1) the gross change method and (2) the net change method.

(GROSS AND NET CHANGE METHODS: ENTRIES)   Aero Corp. leases equipment under five-year **E19-10**
leases that require each year's rent be paid in advance. At the beginning of the current year there was $400,000 of deferred rental income that, for accounting purposes, was earned during the year. During the year, $600,000 of taxable rent was collected, of which $350,000 was earned, leaving a balance of $250,000 in the deferred rental income account. The tax rate in the current year is 40%; in prior years, it was 45%.

Instructions   *a) The co. maintains a separate schedule of timing differences for each years' deferred until income.*
Compute the income tax expense for the current year and the ending balance in deferred taxes using (a) the gross change method and (b) ~~the net change method~~. Accounting income before taxes was $1,200,000.

E19-11 (GROSS AND NET CHANGE METHODS: ENTRIES) Taxable income and accounting income would be identical for Blades Corp. except for its treatments of gross profits on instalment sales and estimated costs of warranties. The following income computations have been prepared.

Taxable Income	1992	1993	1994
Excess of Revenues Over Expenses	$200,000	$140,000	$170,000
Instalment Gross Profit Collected	16,000	16,000	16,000
Cost of Warranties	(5,000)	(5,000)	(5,000)
Taxable Income	$211,000	$151,000	$181,000

Accounting Income	1992	1993	1994
Excess of Revenues Over Expenses	$200,000	$140,000	$170,000
Instalment Gross Profit—Earned	48,000	–0–	–0–
Estimated Cost of Warranties	(15,000)	–0–	–0–
Income Before Taxes	$233,000	$140,000	$170,000

The tax rates in effect were: 1992, 40%; 1993 and 1994, 50%.

Instructions

(a) Assuming that instalment sales are one group and warranties are another group, prepare the journal entries to record income tax expense, deferred income taxes, and income tax payable for each of the three years, using the gross change method, FIFO basis.

(b) Would the journal entries in (a) be different if the net change method, FIFO basis for net reversing differences was used? Explain.

E19-12 (LOSS CARRYBACKS AND CARRYFORWARDS) Small Company Ltd. experienced the following income (loss) amounts for both accounting and tax purposes.

Year	Income (Loss)	Tax Rate
1990	$10,000	45%
1991	40,000	45%
1992	30,000	45%
1993	(120,000)	40%
1994	90,000	40%

The company utilizes the loss carryback provision of tax laws for the maximum period allowable before considering loss carryforwards.

Instructions

(a) Prepare the journal entries for the years 1990 through 1994 to reflect tax expense and the allocation of loss carrybacks and carryforwards, assuming that in 1993 Small Company Ltd. is not virtually certain of future earnings against which to offset the loss.

(b) Prepare the journal entries for 1993 and 1994, assuming that Small Company Ltd. is virtually certain of future earnings against which to offset any loss, given that the loss is carried back to the maximum extent possible.

(LOSS CARRYBACKS AND CARRYFORWARDS: ENTRIES AND REPORTING) Diet Corporation **E19-13** experienced accounting income and taxable income from 1989 through 1994 as follows.

Year	Income (Loss)	Tax Rate
1989	$20,000	20%
1990	40,000	40%
1991	16,000	40%
1992	64,000	45%
1993	(160,000)	30%
1994	50,000	30%

The company follows a policy of carrying back a loss against taxable income for the maximum allowable three years, applying the loss to the earliest year possible first.

Instructions

(a) What entry for income taxes would have been recorded in 1993 if there was no virtual certainty that taxable income would be reported in the next seven years?

(b) What entry for income taxes would have been recorded in 1993 if taxable income was assured with virtual certainty in the next seven years?

(c) Indicate what the bottom portion of the income statement in 1994 would look like, assuming that the situation in (b) existed in 1993.

(LOSS CARRYBACKS AND CARRYFORWARDS WITH DEFERRED TAX ASPECTS) Lobster Corp. **E19-14** began operations in 1993. For that year (ended December 31) there was a credit balance of $12,000 in the Deferred Income Taxes account as determined below:

Accounting income	$200,000
Excess CCA over depreciation	25,000
Taxable income	$175,000
Tax payable (48%)	$ 84,000

Journal entry:

Income Tax Expense	96,000	
Income Tax Payable		84,000
Deferred Income Taxes		12,000

For 1994, the company incurred a tax loss of $180,000, excluding $25,000 CCA that management decided would not be claimed in that year. Depreciation expense of $10,000 was reported in the income statement, resulting in an accounting loss of $190,000. Management refiled the tax return for 1993, reducing by $5,000 the CCA claimed for that year and claiming the full available refund of $84,000 taxes that had been paid.

Instructions

(a) Give the 1994 journal entries to account for the loss and management's actions. Assume that reasonable assurance exists regarding timing difference reversals.

(b) Beginning with the accounting loss, show the partial income statement for 1994.

E19-15 (LOSS CARRYBACKS AND CARRYFORWARDS WITH DEFERRED TAX ASPECTS) Assume the circumstances presented in E19-14, except that management decides not to amend the 1993 CCA amount taken but to carry forward the $5,000 remaining from the $180,000 tax loss after claiming a refund.

Instructions

Give the 1994 journal entries related to the loss and management's actions, as well as a partial income statement beginning with the accounting loss. Assume that for any tax benefit of a loss carryforward there is:

(a) Virtual certainty (assumed for exercise even though criteria are not met).

(b) No virtual certainty.

E19-16 (INTERPERIOD AND INTRAPERIOD TAX ALLOCATION) Bart Ltd. was formed on January 2, 1994. The general ledger accounts of Bart Ltd. for the year ended December 31, 1994, before consideration of income tax expense, include the following.

	Debit	Credit
Sales		$1,000,000
Dividend Revenue From ABC Ltd., a Subsidiary of Bart Ltd. (Note 1)		80,000
Cost of Goods Sold	$500,000	
Depreciation Expense (Note 2)	100,000	
Administration Expenses	52,000	
Warranty Expense (Note 3)	40,000	
Life Insurance Expense (Note 4)	10,000	
Expropriation Loss (Note 5)	40,000	
Other Expenses	8,000	
	$750,000	$1,080,000

Additional Information:

Note 1   Intercorporate dividends are not taxable. ✓

Note 2   The company adopted straight-line depreciation for reporting purposes but is claiming the maximum capital cost allowance for tax purposes. The 1994 capital cost allowance claim is $200,000.

Note 3   The company provides a 12-month warranty on its sales. Actual (tax-deductible) expenditures made in 1994 under its warranty are $30,000. Warranty expense for accounting income purposes is determined using accrual concepts.

Note 4   Premiums paid on life insurance policies are not deductible for income tax purposes. ✓

Note 5   This loss is fully deductible for tax purposes and is extraordinary. ✓

Instructions

(a) Prepare the journal entry to record the income tax provision (expense) for 1994. Assume an income tax rate of 40%.

(b) Prepare the 1994 income statement for Bart Ltd. using appropriate intraperiod and interperiod tax presentation.

(Contributed by Gerry Woudstra, NAIT)

(WITH AND WITHOUT TECHNIQUE) Assume the following for VR Company Limited: ***E19-17**

Accounting income	$400,000
Taxable income	180,000

Tax rates:	
$0–$100,000	25%
Over $100,000	40%

Accounting income includes $60,000 of tax-exempt interest on community bonds. Depreciation expense computed using capital cost allowance for tax purposes exceeds the amount computed under the straight-line method (used for financial accounting purposes) by $160,000.

Instructions

Using the with and without technique, determine the amount of income tax expense to be reported on the income statement, differentiating between the portion that is current and that which is deferred.

(WITH AND WITHOUT TECHNIQUE) The income of the Simpson's Co. Ltd. for the year is as follows: ***E19-18**

Accounting income	$115,000
Taxable income	142,000

The accounting and taxable income figures include a $25,000 gain on the sale of land, which is taxed at a special capital gain rate of 25%. The difference between accounting income and taxable income is a result of accruing warranty expense for accounting purposes but deducting it for tax purposes only when paid. The following tax rates are in effect for the noncapital gain income:

$0–$100,000	22%
Over $100,000	46%

Instructions

(a) Prepare the journal entry to record the tax payable, tax expense, and deferred tax for the year using the with and without technique.

(b) If the short-cut method was used, what would be the amount of the deferred tax?

--------- PROBLEMS ---------

(TAX ALLOCATION COMPUTATIONS: MISCELLANEOUS TAX DIFFERENCES) The current **P19-1**
year's accounting income for Dome Inc. is $1,960,000. The following identify sources of differences between this amount and taxable income:

1. Capital cost allowance exceeds book depreciation expense by $110,000 in the current year.

2. Officer life insurance expense is $5,000 for the year but is not deductible for tax purposes. The expense amount is the difference between the premium paid ($7,000) and the increase in the cash value of the policy ($2,000).

3. Rents of $6,000, applicable to next year, were collected in December and deferred for financial statement purposes but are taxable in the year received.

4. In a previous year, the company established an allowance for product warranty expense. A summary of the current year's transactions follows.

Balance at January 1	$ 96,300
Provision for the year	35,600
	$131,900
Payments made on product warranties	26,000
Balance at December 31	$105,900

Instructions

(a) Compute the current year's income tax payable, income tax expense, and deferred income tax provision. Assume a 40% tax rate and apply the individual item basis.

(b) Draft the income statement for the current year beginning with Income Before Income Taxes and identifying the current and deferred components of the tax expense.

P19-2 **(BASIC DEFERRED TAX COMPUTATIONS AND ENTRIES)**   The following facts apply to the Thorn Company Ltd. for the calendar year 1994:

1. Assets are purchased at the beginning of 1994 at a cost of $120,000, 10-year life, no salvage value. The capital cost allowance rate for tax purposes is 25%, but the company uses the straight-line method for financial reporting purposes.

2. Warranty expense of $16,800 provided for accounting purposes is not deductible for tax purposes until warranty costs are incurred.

3. Accounting income before taxes includes $24,000 related to construction contracts still in process that are accounted for by using the percentage-of-completion method for accounting purposes and the completed-contract method for tax purposes.

4. Amortization of goodwill in the amount of $2,000 is not deductible for tax purposes.

5. Included in accounting income is $9,000 of tax-exempt dividends received from Canadian corporations.

6. Accounting income is $150,000.

Instructions

Calculate the income tax payable and the income tax expense for 1994. Assume that the income tax rate is 45%.

P19-3 **(BASIC DEFERRED TAX COMPUTATIONS AND CLASSIFICATIONS)**   The Fragrance Co. Ltd. began operations on January 3, 1994. Taxable income and accounting income would be identical except for the following items.

Item	Revenue (Expense) Reported on 1994 Income Statement	Revenue (Expense) Reported on 1994 Tax Return
1. Depreciation: Difference due to using CCA for tax purposes and straight-line method for accounting purposes.	$(90,000)	$(140,000)
2. Rental fees collected in advance: Recognized in entirety on 1994 tax return. $70,000 will be earned in 1995.	170,000	240,000

(Continued)

3. Prepaid advertising expenditures
   for 1995 ad campaign: Deferred for
   accounting purposes and deducted as
   an expense in 1994 for tax purposes.   –0–   (20,000)

The income tax rate is 40% for 1994.

Instructions

(a) Determine the balance in Fragrance Co. Ltd.'s Deferred Income Taxes account at December 31, 1994.

(b) Show how the deferred taxes should be presented on Fragrance's December 31, 1994 balance sheet.

(BASIC DEFERRED TAX COMPUTATIONS) The following information is obtained from the records of **P19-4**
M. Ducks Company Ltd.

Year	Accounting Income	CCA Over (Under) Book Depreciation	Taxable Income	Tax Paid at 40%
1989	$ 20,000	$ 20,000	–0–	–0–
1990	60,000	20,000	$ 40,000	$ 16,000
1991	120,000	100,000	20,000	8,000
1992	170,000	120,000	50,000	20,000
1993	80,000	(60,000)	140,000	56,000
1994	10,000	(200,000)	210,000	84,000
	$460,000	$ –0–	$460,000	$184,000

Instructions

For each of the years identified, determine the amount for each column in the following schedule.

Year	Income Tax Expense	Income Tax Payable	Increase (Decrease) in Deferred Tax	Balance in Deferred Tax

**(TAX ALLOCATION COMPUTATIONS: GROSS CHANGE METHOD, INCOME STATEMENT P19-5
DISCLOSURE)** You have been assigned to determine Cabins Inc.'s provision for income taxes for 1993 and
1994. Based on a review of the working papers, you developed the following information.

Reconciliation of Accounting Income to Taxable Income	1993	1994
	($ in thousands)	
Accounting income	$130	$910
Permanent accounting/tax differences:		
Amortization of goodwill in excess of allowed amount	70	80
Accounting income after adjustment for permanent tax differences	$200	$990

(Continued)

Accounting/tax timing differences:		
Excess of CCA over depreciation expense	(400)	(200)
Provision for loss on sale of plant—booked in 1993		
but sold in 1994	200	(200)
Provision for warranties:		
Provided during year	500	
Paid during year		(300)
Taxable income	$500	$290
Income tax rates	38%	50%

Instructions

Compute the provision for income taxes and net income for both years by drafting the lower portion of the comparative income statement beginning with Income Before Taxes and presenting the portion of the tax expense that is currently payable and the amount due to increase or decrease in the deferral. Apply the gross change method.

P19-6 **(DEFERRED TAXES: GROSS CHANGE AND NET CHANGE METHODS)**   The following information about Ragweed Inc. is provided:

1. In 1993, $80,000 was collected in rent; for accounting purposes, the entire amount was reported as revenue in 1994. In 1994, $95,000 was collected in rent; of this amount, $30,000 was reported as unearned revenue in 1994. For tax purposes, the rent is reported as revenue in the year of collection. ✓

2. On January 1, 1990, the company purchased a machine costing $240,000. The machine has a salvage value of $15,000 and a useful life of five years. The straight-line method of depreciation is used for accounting purposes and the capital cost allowance method is used for income tax purposes. The capital cost allowance on this machine was $30,000 for 1994. ✓

3. On January 1, 1994, equipment was purchased at a cost of $180,000. The equipment has no salvage value and a useful life of six years. The straight-line method of depreciation is used for accounting purposes and the capital cost allowance (rate 50%) method for tax purposes. ✓

4. The tax rate for years prior to 1994 was 40%; for 1994, the tax rate is 50%.

5. Accounting income of $700,000 for 1994 includes tax-exempt dividend revenue of $22,500. ✓

6. On the 1994 tax return, the company reported $45,000 of gross profit from instalment sales. This profit was reported in 1993 for accounting purposes. ✓

7. The balance (credit) in the Deferred Income Taxes account as of December 31, 1993 was $180,000.

Instructions

Assuming that there are three groups of similar items: (1) machinery and equipment, (2) rent, and (3) instalment sales, compute:

(a) The tax expense for 1994 and the balance in the Deferred Income Taxes account at December 31, 1994, using the net change method. *[handwritten: gross]*   *[handwritten: Assume that on Jan. 1/94 the NBV is greater than ✓ UCC of machine.]*

(b) The tax expense for 1994 and the balance in the Deferred Income Taxes account at December 31, 1994, using the net change method.

P19-7 **(LOSS CARRYFORWARD: ENTRIES AND INCOME STATEMENT PRESENTATION)**   Bark Co. Ltd. had an accounting loss of $600,000 for the year ending December 31, 1993. There were no timing differences during 1993. During 1994, the company had taxable income (equal to its accounting income) of $800,000. Assume the tax rate for 1993 and 1994 was 40%.

Instructions

(a) Assume there is no carryback of the loss for tax purposes and there is no virtual certainty of realizing any tax benefit from a carryforward of the 1993 loss. Should income occur in the future when the loss can be carried forward for tax purposes, the company will use such provisions. Accordingly, prepare (1) the journal entries for 1993 and 1994 regarding the recording of income taxes and (2) a comparative partial income statement for the years ending December 31, 1993 and 1994. Start the statement with Income (Loss) Before Income Taxes.

(b) Provide answers as asked for in (a), except now assume that tax benefits from carryforward of the 1993 loss are virtually certain.

(LOSS CARRYBACKS AND CARRYFORWARDS, INTERPERIOD TAX ALLOCATION, AND **P19-8**
STATEMENT PRESENTATION)   Mex Corp. began operations in 1992. The following summarizes differences between accounting income and taxable income for 1992 and 1993 and the resulting deferred income tax entries.

	1992	1993
Accounting income	$100,000	$120,000
Excess CCA over depreciation	20,000	30,000
Taxable income	$ 80,000	$ 90,000
Tax payable (40% rate)	$ 32,000	$ 36,000

Journal Entries:	1992		1993	
Income Tax Expense	40,000		48,000	
Tax Payable		32,000		36,000
Deferred Income Taxes		8,000		12,000

The tax rate of 40% is expected to continue.

Part A. Assume that the company incurred a tax loss of $200,000 in 1994 without including any of the maximum allowable CCA of $25,000 in its determination (because of the loss, management decided that no CCA would be taken in 1994). The accounting loss was $230,000 because it included $30,000 depreciation expense. Furthermore, the company decided to refile for 1992 and 1993 in order to amend the amount of CCA taken in those years, so that the full amount of the loss could be carried back to those years and the reduction in the CCA taken for those years would be available in the future. There was reasonable assurance that any timing difference involved would reverse in the future.

Instructions

(a) Give the journal entries for 1994 to account for the loss and the related management actions.

(b) Beginning with the accounting loss, present the remaining portion of the 1994 income statement.

Part B. Assume the same circumstances as Part A except that the company, while claiming the full possible refund of 1992 and 1993 taxes, decided it would not refile to change the CCA claimed in previous years.

Instructions

Give (1) the journal entries for 1994 to account for the loss and related management actions and (2) the partial income statement beginning with the accounting loss, assuming that the portion of the loss not carried back will be carried forward and that:

(a) There is virtual certainty of realizing its tax benefits (assumed for this problem even though criteria are not met).

(b) There is no virtual certainty.

Part C. Assume that the tax loss in 1994 was $300,000 (excluding CCA as stated in Part A). Management decided to obtain a refund of taxes paid in 1992 and 1993 as well as refile in order to amend the CCA taken in those years, so that the full amount of the excess CCA over depreciation would be recovered. Any remaining portion of the loss will be carried forward.

Instructions

Give (1) the 1994 journal entries to account for the loss and (2) the partial income statement beginning with the accounting loss, assuming that for any loss carryforward amount there is:

(a) Virtual certainty (assumed for this problem even though criteria are not met).

(b) No virtual certainty.

P19-9 **(COMPREHENSIVE PROBLEM: TAX ALLOCATION)** Grain-Keep Corp. manufactures, constructs, and sells silos. The company was organized and began operations on January 1, 1992. A silo sells for a gross profit of $120,000. One-third of the total sales price is collected in the first year and one-third in each of the following two years. Twelve silos were sold in 1992, 18 in 1993, and 20 in 1994.

There have been no bad debts and none are expected. Gross profit is recognized in the year of sale for accounting purposes but for tax purposes is recognized in the year in which the cash is received. Instalment accounts receivable are considered a current asset.

The company's plant and equipment, acquired on January 1, 1992, cost $2,700,000 and are depreciated over a nine-year life, with no salvage value. A capital cost allowance rate of 25% is used for tax purposes and the straight-line method is used for accounting purposes. The company owns $200,000 of 10% government bonds, the interest on which is nontaxable. Accounting income for 1994 is $1,000,000.

Instructions

(a) Prepare the necessary journal entry to record income taxes for 1994 under the deferral method. The tax rate has been 40% since the company was organized.

(b) Assume that there was an $899,250 credit balance in the Deferred Income Taxes account at December 31, 1993. Of this amount, $768,000 credit relates to the instalment sales and the remainder to the depreciation. Compute the balance in Deferred Income Taxes at December 31, 1994. Indicate the section(s) of the balance sheet where it would be shown.

(c) Prepare the necessary journal entry to record income taxes for 1994 under the deferral method, assuming that the tax rate changed to 30% for 1994. The gross change method is to be used.

P19-10 **(COMPREHENSIVE PROBLEM ON TAX ALLOCATION)** Your firm has been appointed to examine the financial statements of Fine Flowers Ltd. (FFL) for the two years ended December 31, 1994. FFL was formed on January 2, 1983.

Early in the engagement, you learn that the controller is unfamiliar with income tax accounting and that no tax allocations have been recorded.

During the examination, considerable information was gathered from the accounting records and client employees regarding interperiod tax allocation. This information is as follows (with dollar amounts rounded to the nearest $1,000):

1. FFL uses the bad debt direct write-off method for tax purposes and the full accrual method for accounting purposes. The balance of the Allowance for Doubtful Accounts account at December 31, 1992 was $124,000. Following is a schedule of accounts written off and the corresponding year(s) in which the related sales were made.

Year(s) in Which Sales Made	Year in Which Accounts Written Off	
	1994	1993
1992 and prior	$39,600	$58,000
1993	14,400	—
1994	—	—
	$54,000	$58,000

The following is a schedule of changes in the Allowance for Doubtful Accounts account for the two years ended December 31, 1993 and 1994.

	Year Ended December 31	
	1994	1993
Balance at beginning of year	$132,000	$124,000
Accounts written off during the year	(54,000)	(58,000)
Bad debt expense for the year	76,000	66,000
Balance at end of year	$154,000	$132,000

2. Following is a reconciliation between net income per books and taxable income.

		Year Ended December 31	
		1994	1993
(a)	Net income per books	$ 666,200	$ 525,600
(b)	Income tax payable during year	364,600	473,600
(c)	Taxable income not recorded on the books this year: Deferred sales commissions	20,000	
(d)	Expenses recorded on the books this year not deducted on the tax return:		
	(i) Allowance for doubtful receivables	22,000	8,000
	(ii) Amortization of goodwill	16,000	16,000
(e)	Total of items (a) through (d)	$1,088,800	$1,023,200
(f)	Income recorded on the books this year not included on the tax return: Tax-exempt dividends from Canadian corporations	10,000	
(g)	Deductions on the tax return not charged against accounting income this year: CCA in excess of depreciation	167,400	76,000
(h)	Total of items (f) and (g)	$ 177,400	$ 76,000
(i)	Taxable income (line (e) less line (h))	$ 911,400	$ 947,200

3. Assume that the effective tax rates are as follows: 1992 and prior years: 60%; 1993: 50%; 1994: 40%.

4. In December 1994, FFL entered into a contract to distribute engineering products for Green Manufacturer Inc. The contract took effect December 31, 1994 and $20,000 of advance commissions on the contract were received and deposited on that date. Because the commissions had not been earned, they were accounted for as a deferred credit (i.e. liability) on the December 31, 1994 balance sheet.

5. Goodwill represents the excess of cost over fair value of the net tangible assets of a retiring competitor that were acquired for cash on January 2, 1989. The original balance was $160,000.

Instructions

(a) Prepare (1) a schedule calculating the amount of the timing differences between income tax payable and accounting income tax expense for 1993 and 1994 and (2) a schedule to derive the balance of deferred income taxes at December 31, 1993 and 1994. Round all calculations to the nearest $1,000. (Use the gross change method.)

(b) Independent of your solution to (a) and assuming data shown below, prepare the partial income statements beginning with accounting income before income tax for the years ended December 31, 1994 and 1993.

	1994	1993
Accounting income	$960,800	$931,200
Taxes payable currently	364,600	473,600
Deferred tax accounting change—Dr. (Cr.)	(56,200)	49,000
Balance of deferred tax at end of year—Dr. (Cr.)	(88,400)	(32,200)

P19-11 (COMPREHENSIVE PROBLEM: TAX ALLOCATION, INTERPERIOD AND INTRAPERIOD, STATEMENT PRESENTATION) The following information relates to Sunlight Inc., a Canadian public company, for the year ended December 31, 1994:

1. The company's accounting income before depreciation expense, taxes, and extraordinary items was $2,000,000. ✓

2. Depreciation expense for 1994 was $200,000, computed in accordance with generally accepted accounting principles. The company takes maximum capital cost allowance for tax purposes and in 1994 this amounted to $280,000. ✓

3. The following items were included in determining the company's net income before depreciation expense, taxes, and extraordinary items:

    (a) Nontaxable dividends in the amount of $100,000 were received from Canadian corporations. ✓

    (b) Dues paid to various social clubs totalled $20,000. This amount will never be deductible for tax purposes. ✓

    (c) An expense of $23,000 for the termination of redundant employees was recorded to recognize the expected settlement to be made with these employees. This amount will not be deductible for tax purposes until it is paid in ~~1997~~. *1995.* ✓

4. The company had an extraordinary gain of $100,000. Only three-quarters of this gain is taxable. ✓

5. During 1994, the company experienced a litigation gain of $85,000. This gain resulted from a lawsuit initiated by the company in 1992 and is fully taxable. It is accounted for as a prior period adjustment to retained earnings. ✓

6. The company is subject to a 40% tax rate.

7. The company's retained earnings at December 31, 1993 was $2,000,000.

8. The company paid $50,000 dividends during the year.

Instructions

(a) Prepare the journal entry for all income taxes for the year ending December 31, 1994.

(b) Prepare a partial income statement for the company for 1994, beginning with income before income tax and extraordinary items.

(c) Prepare a statement of retained earnings for the year ended December 31, 1994.

(d) Assume that on December 31, 1993 there were no deferred tax balances in the balance sheet of the company. Indicate the amount or amounts that would be disclosed in the December 31, 1994 balance sheet.

(Contributed by Gerry Woudstra, NAIT)

CHAPTER 20

Accounting for Pension Costs

◼

Since the late 1800s, many business organizations have been concerned with providing for the retirement of their employees. During recent decades a marked increase in this concern has resulted in the establishment of private pension plans in most large companies and in medium- and small-sized ones.

The substantial growth of these plans, both in numbers of employees covered and in dollar amounts of retirement benefits, has increased the significance of pension cost in relation to the financial position, results of operations, and cash flows. Generally accepted accounting principles for accounting by employers for pensions are provided in the *CICA Handbook*, Section 3460. It has been a much debated subject and many aspects of this section are still controversial.

TYPES OF PENSION PLANS

Objective 1

Identify types of pension plans and their characteristics.

A **pension plan** is an arrangement whereby an employer promises to provide benefits (payments) to employees after they retire for services they provided while employed. The two most common types of pension arrangements are defined contribution plans and defined benefit plans.

Defined Contribution Plan

In a **defined contribution plan**, the employer agrees to contribute to a pension trust a certain sum each period based on a formula. This formula may consider such factors as age, length of employee service, employer's profits, and compensation level. Only the employer's contribution is defined; no promise is made regarding the ultimate benefits paid out to the employees.

The size of the pension benefit that the employee finally collects under the plan depends on the amounts originally contributed to the pension trust, the income accumulated in the trust, and the treatment of forfeitures of funds caused by early terminations of other employees. The amounts originally contributed are usually turned over to an **independent third party trustee** who acts on behalf of the beneficiaries—participating employees. The trustee assumes ownership of the pension assets and is accountable for their investment and distribution. The trust is separate and distinct from the employer.

The accounting for a defined contribution plan is straightforward. The employee gets the benefit of gain or the risk of loss from assets contributed to the pension plan. The employer's responsibility is simply to make a contribution each year based on the formula established in the plan. As a result, the employer's annual cost (pension expense) is the amount that it is obligated to contribute to the pension trust. A liability is reported on the employer's balance sheet only if the contribution has not been made in full, and an asset is reported only if more than the required amount has been contributed.

When a defined contribution plan is initiated or amended, the employer may be obligated to make contributions for employee services rendered prior to the date of the initiation or amendment. This obligation is referred to as **past service cost**. Amounts arising as past service costs are amortized as part of the annual pension expense. Differences between the annual amortization amount and the amount contributed to the pension fund will be reported as either an asset or a liability.

The only disclosure required of employers under a defined contribution plans is "the present value of required future contributions in respect of past service."[1] In addition, firms may wish to disclose a description of the plan, including employee groups covered, the basis for determining contributions, and the nature and effect of significant matters affecting comparability from period to period.

Defined Benefit Plan

A **defined benefit plan** defines the benefits that the employee will receive at the time of retirement. The formula that is typically used provides for the benefits to be a function of the employee's years of service and the employee's compensation level when he or she nears retirement. It is necessary to determine what the contribution should be today to meet the pension benefit commitments that will arise at retirement. Many different contribution approaches could be used. Whatever funding method is employed, it should provide enough money at retirement to meet the benefits defined by the plan.

The employees are the beneficiaries of a defined contribution trust, but the employer is the beneficiary of a defined benefit trust. The trust's primary purpose under a defined benefit plan is to safeguard the assets and to invest them so that there will be enough to pay the employer's obligation to the employees when they retire. *In form*, the trust is a separate entity; *in substance*, the trust assets and liabilities belong to the employer. That is, *as long as the plan continues, the employer is responsible for the payment of the defined benefits (without regard to what happens in the trust)*. Any shortfall in the accumulated assets held by the trust must be made up by the employer. Any excess accumulated in the trust can be recaptured by the employer, either through reduced future funding or through a reversion of funds.[2]

The accounting for a defined benefit plan is complex. Because the benefits are defined in terms of uncertain future variables, an appropriate funding pattern must be established to assure that enough funds will be available at retirement to provide the benefits promised. This funding level depends on a number of factors such as turnover, mortality, length of employee service, compensation levels, and interest earnings.

Employers are at risk because they must be sure to make enough contributions to meet the cost of the benefits that are defined in the plan. The expense recognized each period is not necessarily equal to the cash contribution. Similarly, the liability is controversial because its measurement and recognition relate to unknown future variables.

Of the two plans, the most attractive type to employees is the defined benefit plan because it provides more protection. Unfortunately, the accounting issues related to this type of plan are complex. *Our discussion in the following sections deals primarily with defined benefit plans.*

EMPLOYER VERSUS PLAN ACCOUNTING

The subject of pension accounting may be divided and separately treated as **accounting for the employer** and **accounting for the pension fund**. The company or employer is the organization sponsoring the pension plan. It incurs the cost and makes contributions to the pension fund. The fund or plan is the entity that receives the contributions from the employer, administers the pension assets, and makes the benefit payments to the pension recipients (retired employees). The diagram that follows shows the three entities involved in a pension plan and indicates the flow of cash among them.

Objective 2

Distinguish between accounting for the employer's pension plan and accounting for the pension fund.

---

[1] *CICA Handbook* (Toronto: CICA), Section 3460, par. .74.

[2] The ownership of pension fund surpluses has been the subject of litigation. Ontario Hydro and Gainers Ltd. were both prevented from using pension plan surplus funds for operating purposes.

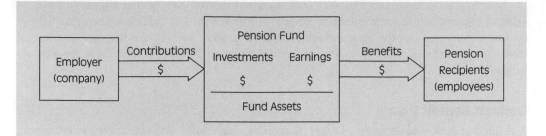

The pension plan above is being *funded*:[3] that is, the employer (company) sets funds aside for future pension benefits by making payments to a funding agency that is responsible for accumulating the assets of the pension fund and for making payments to the recipients as the benefits become due. In an insured plan, the funding agency is an insurance company; in a trust fund plan, the funding agency is a trustee.

Some plans are **contributory**; the employees bear part of the cost of the stated benefits or voluntarily make payments to increase their benefits. Other plans are **noncontributory**, the employer bearing the entire cost. Companies generally design **registered pension plans** in accord with income tax requirements that permit deductibility of the employer's contributions to the pension fund (within certain limits) and tax-free status of earnings on the pension fund assets.

The need for proper administration of and sound accounting for pension funds becomes apparent when one appreciates the size of these funds. For example, the companies listed below recently had pension fund assets and related shareholders' equity as follows.

Company	Size of the Pension Fund	Total Shareholders' Equity
TransCanada Pipelines Ltd.	$ 188,000,000	$2,098,200,000
Power Corporation of Canada	508,059,000	2,236,659,000
Northern Telecom Limited	3,100,100,000	4,121,400,000

The fund should have separate legal and accounting identity for which a set of books is maintained and financial statements are prepared. Maintaining books and records and preparing financial statements for the fund, known as "accounting for employee benefit plans," is not the subject of this chapter.[4] Instead this chapter is devoted to the pension accounting and reporting problems of the employer as the sponsor of a pension plan.

THE ROLE OF ACTUARIES IN PENSION ACCOUNTING

Because the problems associated with pension plans involve complicated actuarial considerations, actuaries are engaged to ensure that the plan is appropriate for the employee group covered.[5]

---

[3] When used as a verb, fund means to pay to a funding agency (as to fund future pension benefits or to fund pension cost). Used as a noun, it refers to assets accumulated in the hands of a funding agency (trustee) for the purpose of meeting pension benefits when they become due.

[4] Section 4100 of the *CICA Handbook* prescribes accounting standards for accounting for pension plans.

[5] An actuary's primary purpose is to ensure that the company has established an appropriate funding pattern to meet its pension obligations. This computation entails the development of a set of assumptions and continued monitoring of these assumptions to assure their realism. That the general public has little understanding of what an actuary does is illustrated by the following excerpts from *The Wall Street Journal*: "A polling organization once asked the general public what an actuary was and received among its more coherent responses the opinion that it was a place where you put dead actors."

Actuaries are individuals who are trained through a long and rigorous certification program to assign probabilities to future events and their financial effects. The insurance industry employs actuaries to assess risks and to advise on the setting of premiums and other aspects of insurance policies. Employers rely heavily on actuaries for assistance in developing, implementing, and funding pension plans.

It is actuaries who make predictions (actuarial assumptions) of mortality rates, employee turnover, interest and earnings rates, early retirement frequency, future salaries, and any other factors necessary to operate a pension plan. They assist by computing the various measures that affect the financial statements, such as the pension obligation, the annual cost of servicing the plan, and the cost of amendments to the plan. In summary, accounting for defined benefit pension plans is highly reliant upon information and measurements provided by actuaries.

THE PENSION OBLIGATION (LIABILITY)

In accounting for pension plans, the question eventually arises, "What is the amount of the employer's liability and the amount of the pension obligation that should be reported in the financial statements?" Attempting to answer this question has produced much controversy. Most agree that an employer's **pension obligation** is the deferred compensation obligation it has to the employees for their service under the terms of the pension plan, but there are alternative ways of measuring it.[6]

Alternative Measures of the Liability

One measure of the obligation is to base it only on the benefits vested to the employees. **Vested benefits** are those that the employee is entitled to receive even if the employee renders no additional services under the plan. Under most pension plans a certain minimum number of years of service to the employer is required before an employee achieves vested benefits status. The **vested benefits pension obligation** is computed using current salary levels and includes only vested benefits.

Another measure of the obligation is to base the computation of the deferred compensation amount on all years of service performed by employees under the plan—both vested and nonvested—using *current salary levels*. This measurement of the pension obligation is called the **accumulated benefit obligation**.

A third measure bases the computation of the deferred compensation amount on both vested and nonvested service *using future salaries*. This measurement of the pension obligation is called the **projected benefit obligation**.[7] Because future salaries are expected to be higher than current salaries, this approach results in the largest measurement of the pension obligation.

The choice between these measures is critical because it affects the amount of the pension liability and the annual pension expense reported. The diagram on page 994 illustrates the differences in these three measurements. Regardless of the approach used, the estimated future benefits to be paid are discounted to present value.

Which of these approaches did the profession adopt? *In general, the profession adopted the projected benefit obligation, which is the present value of vested and nonvested benefits accrued to date based on employees' future salary levels.*

> #### Objective 3
> Explain alternative measures for valuing the obligation.

---

[6] When the phrase "present value of benefits" is used throughout this chapter, it really means the actuarial present value of benefits. Actuarial present value is the amount payable adjusted to reflect the time value of money and the probability of payment (by means of decrements for events such as death, disability, withdrawals, or retirement) between the present date and the expected date of payment. For simplicity, the term "present value" (instead of "actuarial present value") will be used.

[7] The *CICA Handbook* uses the phrase "accrued benefits" to denote the actuarial present value of the pension obligation. Since a projected benefit actuarial method must be used for this calculation, the amount of the accrued benefits is a "projected benefit" obligation. For clarity, "projected benefit obligation" (instead of accrued benefits) will be used.

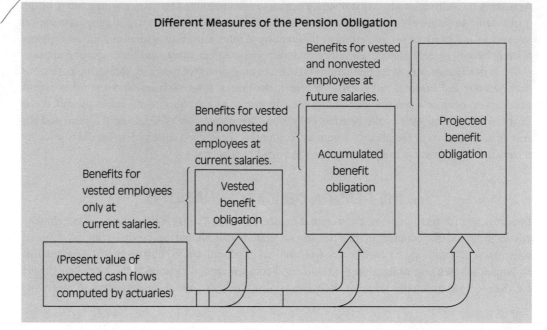

Those critical of the projected benefit obligation argue that using future salary levels is tantamount to adding future obligations to existing ones. Those in favour of the projected benefit obligation contend that a promise by an employer to pay benefits based on a percentage of the employees' future salary is far different from a promise to pay a percentage of their current salary, and such a difference should be reflected in the pension liability and the pension expense.

Capitalization Versus Noncapitalization

Noncapitalization, often referred to as **off-balance-sheet financing**, is achieved when the balance sheet reports an asset or liability for the pension plan arrangement only if the amount funded during the year by the employer is different from the amount reported by the employer as pension expense for the year. As the employees work during each year, the employer incurs pension cost and becomes obligated to fund that amount by making cash payments to the pension fund (viewed as a third-party trust). When the trust pays benefits to retirees, the employer records no entries because its own assets or liabilities are not reduced.

The accounting profession has been tending toward a **capitalization approach**, supporting the economic *substance* of the pension plan arrangement over its legal form. Under this view the employer has a liability for pension benefits that it has promised to pay for employee services already performed. As pension expense is incurred—as the employees work—the employer's liability increases. Funding the plan has no effect on the amount of the liability; only the employer's promises and the employee's services affect the liability. The pension liability is reduced through the payment of benefits to retired employees.

Under a defined benefit plan, if additional funds are necessary to meet the pension obligation, the source is the employer. From the capitalization point of view, underfunding does not increase the liability, and funding more than the amount expensed does not create a prepaid expense. Capitalization means measuring and reporting in the financial statements a fair representation of the employers' pension assets and liabilities.

The Accounting Standards Board adopted a noncapitalization approach. Accounting for pensions as outlined in Section 3460 and demonstrated in the balance of this chapter is not perfectly logical, totally complete, or conceptually sound. The fault is not entirely that of the Accounting

Standards Board. Because of the financial complexity of defined benefit pensions, many well-intentioned, competent people cannot agree on the nature of such an arrangement and what exists in it. As a result, they are unlikely to agree on how to account for it. Because of the difficulties in gaining a consensus among the Board members and support from preparers as well as users of financial statements, Section 3460 has a number of compromises that make it less than ideal. In its defence, however, Section 3460 is an improvement over previous accounting pronouncements and represents a first step toward a conceptually sound approach to employers' accounting for pension plans.

COMPONENTS OF PENSION EXPENSE

There is broad agreement that pension cost should be accounted for on the *accrual basis*. The profession recognizes that **accounting for pension plans requires measurement of the cost and its identification with appropriate time periods**. The determination of pension cost, however, is extremely complicated because it is a function of the following components:

> *Objective 4*
>
> Identify the components of pension expense.

> *Know for exam.*

Service Cost. The expense caused by the increase in pension benefits payable (the projected benefit obligation) to employees because of their services rendered during the current year. Actuaries compute **service cost** as the present value of the new benefits earned by employees during the year.

Interest on the Liability. Because a pension is a deferred compensation arrangement, there is a time value of money factor. As a result, it is recorded on a discounted basis. **Interest expense accrues each year on the projected benefit obligation just as it does on any discounted debt**. The accountant receives help from the actuary in selecting the interest rate.

Expected Return on Plan Assets. The return expected to be earned by the accumulated pension fund assets in a particular year is relevant in measuring the net cost to the employer of sponsoring an employee pension plan. Therefore, **annual pension expense should be adjusted for interest and dividends that are expected to flow into the fund as well as increases and decreases in the market value of the fund assets.**

Amortization of Unrecognized Past Service Cost. Plan initiation or amendment often includes provisions to increase benefits for service provided in prior years. Because plan amendments are granted with the expectation that the employer will realize economic benefits in future periods, **the cost (past service cost) of providing these retroactive benefits is generally considered to be allocated to pension expense in the future**, specifically to the remaining service years of the affected employees. The amount of past service cost is computed by the actuary.

Amortization of Experience Gains and Losses. Experience gains and losses arise from two sources: (1) projected obligations that do not materialize and, consequently, do not agree with the obligation determined using year-end assumptions, and (2) when the expected return on plan assets is not equal to the actual return accomplished. As indicated earlier, a set of assumptions are used to estimate the pension obligation and the fund balance. If these assumptions are proven to be inaccurate by later events such as changes in service lives, adjustments are needed. That is, the experience gains and losses that develop as a result of the difference between actual and expected experience must be accounted for.

In summary, then, the components of pension expense and their effect are as follows:

Service cost (increases pension expense).

Interest on the liability (increases pension expense).

Expected return on plan assets (decreases pension expense).

Amortization of past service cost (generally increases pension expense).

Amortization of experience gains and losses (increases or decreases pension expense).

The components of pension expense are exhibited in the following diagram.

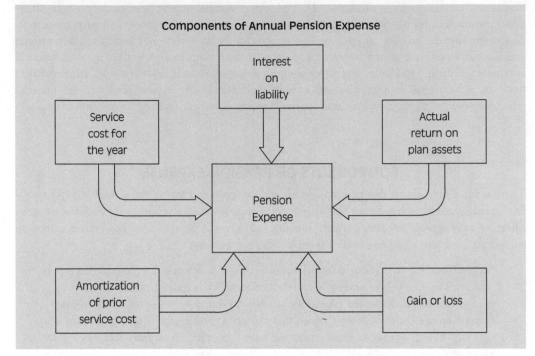

Service Cost

In Section 3460 of the *CICA Handbook*, the Accounting Standards Board states that the service cost component recognized in a period ***should be determined as the actuarial present value of benefits attributed by the pension benefit formula to employee service during the period.*** The actuary predicts the additional benefits that must be paid under the plan's benefit formula as a result of the employees' current year's service and then discounts the cost of those future benefits back to their present value.

The Board also concluded that ***future compensation levels had to be considered in measuring the present obligation and periodic pension expense if the plan benefit formula incorporated them.*** In other words, the present obligation resulting from a promise to pay a benefit of 1% of an employee's *final pay* is different from an employer's promise to pay 1% of *current pay*. To ignore this fact would be to ignore an important aspect of pension expense. Thus, the **projected benefit actuarial method** is the approach adopted by the AcSB.

Some object to this determination on the basis that a company should have more freedom to select an expense recognition pattern. Others believe that incorporating future salary increases into current pension expense is accounting for events that have not happened yet. They argue that if the plan were terminated today, only liabilities for benefits earned by service to date would have to be paid. ***Nevertheless the Board indicated that the projected benefit obligation provided a more realistic measure on a going concern basis of the employer's obligation under the plan and, therefore, should be used as the basis for determining service cost.***

Interest on the Liability

The second component of pension expense is interest on the liability. As indicated earlier, a pension is a deferred compensation arrangement under which this element of wages is deferred and an obligation is created. Because the obligation is not paid until maturity, it is measured on a discounted basis and accrues interest due to the passage of time over the life of the employee. ***The interest component for the period is computed on the projected benefit obligation outstanding during the period.*** The AcSB did not address the question of how often to compound the interest cost. To simplify the illustrations and problem materials, a simple interest computation is used, applying it to the beginning-of-the-year balance of the projected benefit liability.

How is the interest rate determined? The Board stated that the assumed discount rate should *reflect management's best estimates*. In determining these rates, it would be appropriate for management to look to available information about rates implicit in current prices of annuity contracts that could be used to effect settlement of the obligation. (Under an annuity contract, an insurance company unconditionally guarantees to provide specific pension benefits to specific individuals in return for a fixed consideration or premium.) Other rates of return on high-quality fixed-income investments might also be employed.

Expected Return on Plan Assets

Pension plan assets are usually investments in shares, bonds, other securities, and real estate that are held to earn a reasonable return, generally at a minimum of risk. Pension plan assets for a period are increased by employer contributions and returns on plan assets, and they are decreased by benefits paid to retired employees. As indicated, the return earned on these assets increases the fund balance and correspondingly reduces the employer's net cost of providing employees' pension benefits. The return will likely fluctuate from year to year as a result of changes in economic conditions. Pension plan asset investments are long term in nature and, as a result, the periodic amount contributed to the fund is based on expected long-term yields. Consequently, for the purpose of determining periodic pension expense the expected long-term return is used. As will be discussed later, the variance between the yearly actual return and the expected return is also included in periodic pension expense.

Plan assets for purposes of applying the rate of return are investments that have been segregated and restricted to provide for pension claims. Plan assets include contributions made by the employer and contributions made by employees when a contributory plan of some type is involved. Plan assets cannot normally be withdrawn from the plan. Pension assets that are still under the control of the company are not considered plan assets. That is, if the company may use these assets as it desires, the company has not funded the pension plan. Pension assets must be segregated in a trust or effectively restricted to be considered plan assets. Receivables from the employer should not be considered plan assets for purposes of applying interest because the employer has not provided the funds on which to earn interest.

ILLUSTRATIVE ACCOUNTING ENTRIES

Before covering in detail the other more complex pension expense components (amortization of unrecognized past service cost and amortization of experience gains and losses), the basic accounting entries for the first three components (service cost, interest, and expected returns on plan assets) will be illustrated. Several significant items of the pension plan are unrecognized in the accounts and in the financial statements. Among the compromises the AcSB made in issuing Section 3460 was the nonrecognition (noncapitalization) of the following pension items:

1. Projected benefit obligation.

2. Pension plan assets.

3. Unrecognized past service cost.

4. Unrecognized experience gain or loss.

As discussed later, the employer is required to disclose in the notes to the financial statements the first two of the four above noncapitalized items, but they are not recognized in the body of the financial statements. In addition, the exact amount of these items must be known at all times because they are used in the computation of annual pension expense. Therefore, in order to track these off-balance-sheet pension items, memo entries and accounts have to be maintained outside the formal general ledger accounting system. As an example of how this could be done, a work sheet unique to pension accounting will be utilized to record both the formal entries and the memo entries to keep track of all the employer's relevant pension plan items and components.[8]

The format of the work sheet is shown below.

Objective 5

Develop a facility to utilize a work sheet to develop the employer's pension plan entries.

	General Journal Entries			Memo Record	
		Pension Work Sheet			
Items	Annual Pension Expense	Cash	Prepaid/ Accrued Cost	Projected Benefit Obligation	Plan Assets

The left-hand "General Journal Entries" columns of the work sheet record entries in the formal general ledger accounts. The right-hand "Memo Record" columns maintain balances on the un-recognized (noncapitalized) pension items. On the first line of the work sheet, the beginning balances (if any) are recorded. Subsequently, transactions and events related to the pension plan are recorded, using debits and credits and using both sets of records as if they were one for recording the entries. For each transaction or event, the debits must equal the credits.

1994 ENTRIES AND WORK SHEET

To illustrate the use of the work sheet and how it helps in accounting for a pension plan, assume that on January 1, 1994, Zarle Company adopts *Handbook* Section 3460 to account for its defined benefit pension plan. The following facts apply to the pension plan for the year 1994:

Plan assets, January 1, 1994, are $100,000.

Projected benefit obligation, January 1, 1994, is $100,000.

Annual service cost for 1994 is $9,000.

Interest rate on the liability for 1994 is 10%.

Expected earnings on plan assets for 1994 is 10%.

Contributions (funding) in 1994 are $8,000.

Benefits paid to retirees in 1994 are $7,000.

Using the date presented above, the following work sheet presents the beginning balances and all of the pension entries recorded by Zarle Company in 1994. The beginning balances for the projected benefit obligation and the pension plan assets are recorded on the first line of the work sheet in the memo record. They are not recorded in the formal general journal and, therefore, are not reported as a liability and an asset in the financial statements of Zarle Company. These two significant pension items are off-balance-sheet amounts that affect pension expense but are not recorded as assets and liabilities in the employer's books.

---

[8] The use of this pension entry work sheet is recommended and illustrated by Paul B.W. Miller, "The new Pension Accounting (Part 2)," *Journal of Accountancy* (February 1987), pp. 86–94.

Zarle Company
Pension Work Sheet: 1994

Items	General Journal Entries			Memo Record	
	Annual Pension Expense	Cash	Prepaid/ Accrued Cost	Projected Benefit Obligation	Plan Assets
Balance, Jan. 1, 1994				100,000 Cr.	100,000 Dr.
(a) Service cost	9,000 Dr.			9,000 Cr.	
(b) Interest cost	10,000 Dr.			10,000 Cr.	
(c) Expected return	10,000 Cr.				10,000 Dr.
(d) Contributions		8,000 Cr.			8,000 Dr.
(e) Benefits				7,000 Dr.	7,000 Cr.
Journal entry for 1994	9,000 Dr.	8,000 Cr.	1,000 Cr.		
Balance, Dec. 31, 1994			1,000 Cr.	112,000 Cr.	111,000 Dr.

Entry (a) records the service cost component, which increases pension expense $9,000 and increases the liability (projected benefit obligation) $9,000. Entry (b) accrues the interest expense component, which increases both the liability and the pension expense by $10,000 (the beginning projected benefit obligation multiplied by the interest rate of 10%). Entry (c) records the expected return on plan assets, which increases the plan assets and decreases the pension expense. Entry (d) records Zarle Company's contribution (funding) of assets to the pension fund; cash is decreased $8,000 and plan assets are increased $8,000. Entry (e) records the benefit payments made to retirees, which results in equal $7,000 decreases to the plan assets and the projected benefit obligation.

The "journal entry" on December 31, which is the adjusting entry made to formally record the pension expense in 1994, is as follows:

1994

Pension Expense	9,000	
Cash		8,000
Prepaid/Accrued Pension Cost		1,000

The credit to Prepaid/Accrued Pension Cost for $1,000 represents the difference between the 1994 service cost of $9,000 and the amount funded of $8,000. Prepaid/Accrued Pension Cost (credit) is a liability because the plan is underfunded by $1,000. The Prepaid/Accrued Pension Cost account balance of $1,000 also equals the net of the balances in the memo accounts. This reconciliation of the off-balance-sheet items with the prepaid/accrued pension cost reported in the balance sheet is shown on page 1000.

If the net of the memo record balances is a credit, the reconciling amount in the prepaid/ accrued cost column will be a credit equal in amount. If the net of the memo record balances is a debit, the prepaid/accrued cost amount will be a debit equal in amount. The work sheet is designed to produce this reconciling feature which will be useful later in preparing the notes related to pension disclosures.

Reconciliation Schedule: December 31, 1994	
Projected benefit obligation (Credit)	$(112,000)
Plan assets at fair value (Debit)	111,000
Prepaid/accrued pension cost (Credit)	**$ (1,000)**

In this illustration, the debit to Pension Expense exceeds the credit to Cash, resulting in a credit to Prepaid/Accrued Pension Cost—the recognition of a liability. If the credit to Cash exceeded the debit to Pension Expense, Prepaid/Accrued Pension Cost would be debited—the recognition of an asset.

AMORTIZATION OF UNRECOGNIZED PAST SERVICE COST (PSC)

Objective 6

Describe the amortization of unrecognized past service costs.

When a defined benefit plan is either initiated (adopted) or amended, credit is often given to employees for years of service provided prior to the date of initiation or amendment. As a result of these credits for past services, the projected benefit obligation is usually greater than it was before. In many cases, the increase in the projected benefit obligation is substantial. One question that arises is whether an expense and related liability for these **past service costs (PSC)** should be fully reported at the time the plan is initiated or amended. The AcSB has taken the position that no expense for these costs should be recognized at the time of the plan's adoption or amendment. The Board rationale is that the employer will not provide credit for past years of service unless it expects to receive benefits in the future. As a result, *the retroactive benefits should not be recognized as pension expense entirely in the year of initiation or amendment but should be recognized during the service periods of those employees who are expected to receive benefits under the plan (the remaining service life of the covered active employees).*

The cost of the retroactive benefits (including benefits that are granted to existing retirees) is the increase in the projected benefit obligation at the date of initiation or amendment. The amount of the past service cost is computed by an actuary. Amortization of the unrecognized past service cost is an accounting function performed with the assistance of an actuary.

The method used to amortize past service costs should be systematic and rational. The straight-line, declining-balance, and years-of-service methods would be acceptable methods. The straight-line method is simplest and will be used in the following illustrations.

To illustrate the amortization of the unrecognized past service cost, assume that Zarle Company's defined benefit pension plan covers 170 employees. In its negotiations with its employees, Zarle Company amends its pension plan on January 1, 1995 and grants past service benefits to its employees. The Company's actuaries determine that the resulting increase in the projected benefit obligation is $80,000. The employees are grouped according to expected years of service and the average remaining service life is computed as follows.

Group	Number of Employees	Expected Remaining Years of Service	Total
A	40	1	40
B	20	2	40
C	40	3	120
D	50	4	200
E	20	5	100
	170		500

Expected average remaining service life (EARSL) = 500 ÷ 170 = 2.94

The annual amortization of the unrecognized past service cost would be $27,211 ($80,000 ÷ 2.94) in 1995, $27,211 in 1996, and $25,578 ($27,211 × .94) in 1997.

If the full capitalization of all elements of the pension plan had been adopted, the past service cost would have been capitalized as an intangible asset and amortized over its useful life. The intangible asset comes from the assumption that the cost of additional pension benefits increases loyalty and productivity (and reduces turnover) among the affected employees. However, past service cost is accounted for off-balance-sheet and may be called **unrecognized past service cost**. Although not recognized on the balance sheet, past service cost is a factor in computing pension expense.

1995 ENTRIES AND WORK SHEET

Continuing the Zarle Company illustration into 1995, we note that the January 1, 1995 amendment to the pension plan grants to employees past service benefits having a present value of $80,000. The annual amortization amounts, as computed in the previous section ($27,211 for 1995), are employed in this illustration. The following facts apply to the pension plan for the year 1995:

On January 1, 1995, Zarle Company grants past service benefits having a present value of $80,000.

Annual service cost of 1995 is $9,500.

Interest on the pension obligation is 10%.

Expected return on plan assets for 1995 is $10%.

Annual contributions (funding) are $20,000.

Benefits paid to retirees in 1995 are $8,000.

Amortization of past service cost (PSC) is $27,211.

The work sheet at the top of page 1002 presents all of the pension entries and information recorded by Zarle Company in 1995. The first line of the work sheet shows the beginning balances of the Prepaid/Accrued Pension Cost account and the memo accounts. Entry (f) records Zarle Company's granting of past service cost by adding $80,000 to the projected benefit obligation and to the unrecognized (noncapitalized) past service cost. Entries (g), (h), (i), (k), and (l) are similar to the corresponding entries in 1994. Entry (j) records the 1995 amortization of unrecognized past service cost be debiting Pension Expense by $27,211 and crediting the new Unrecognized Past Service Cost account by the same amount.

The journal entry on December 31 to formally record the pension expense for 1995 is as follows:

1995

Pension Expense	44,811	
Cash		20,000
Prepaid/Accrued Pension Cost		24,811

Because the expense exceeds the funding, the Prepaid/Accrued Pension Cost account is credited for the $24,811 difference and is a liability. In 1995, as in 1994, the balance of the Prepaid/Accrued Pension Cost account ($25,811) is equal to the net of the balances in the memo accounts as shown in the reconciliation schedule on page 1002.

Zarle Company
Pension Work Sheet: 1995

Items	General Journal Entries			Memo Record		
	Annual Pension Expense	Cash	Prepaid/ Accrued Cost	Projected Benefit Obligation	Plan Assets	Unrecognized Past Service Cost
Balance, Dec. 31, 1994			1,000 Cr.	112,000 Cr.	111,000 Dr.	
(f) Prior Service Cost				80,000 Cr.		80,000 Dr.
Balance, Jan. 1, 1995			1,000 Cr.	192,000 Cr.	111,000 Dr.	80,000 Dr.
(g) Service cost	9,500 Dr.			9,500 Cr.		
(h) Interest cost	19,200 Dr.			19,200 Cr.		
(i) Expected return	11,100 Cr.				11,100 Dr.	
(j) Amortization of PSC	27,211 Dr.					27,211 Cr.
(k) Contributions		20,000 Cr.			20,000 Dr.	
(l) Benefits				8,000 Dr.	8,000 Cr.	
Journal entry for 1995	44,811 Dr.	20,000 Cr.	24,811 Cr.			
Balance, Dec. 31, 1995			25,811 Cr.	212,700 Cr.	134,100 Dr.	52,789 Dr.

Reconciliation Schedule: December 31, 1995

Projected benefit obligation (Credit)	$(212,700)
Plan assets at fair value (Debit)	134,100
Funded status (unfunded projected benefit obligation)	(78,600)
Unrecognized past service cost (Debit)	52,789
Prepaid/accrued pension cost (Credit)	$ (25,811)

EXPERIENCE GAINS AND LOSSES

Objective 7

Explain the accounting procedure for recognizing experience gains and losses.

Of great concern to companies that have pension plans are the uncontrollable and unexpected swings in pension expense that could be caused by (1) sudden and large changes in the market value of plan assets and (2) changes in actuarial assumptions that affect the amount of the projected benefit obligation. If these gains or losses were to have a full impact on the financial statements in the period of realization or incurrence, substantial fluctuations in pension expense would result. Therefore, the profession decided to reduce the volatility associated with pension expense by **smoothing techniques** that dampen the fluctuations.

Asset Experience Gains and Losses

One component of pension expense, expected return on plan assets, reduces pension expense. A large change in the actual return can substantially affect pension expense for the year. Assume a company has used 8% as an expected return on plan assets while the actual return accomplished is 40%. Should this substantial and perhaps one-time event affect current pension expense?

Actuaries ignore current fluctuations when they develop a funding pattern to pay expected benefits in the future. They develop an **expected rate of return** and multiply it by the assets in the pension fund to arrive at an **expected return on plan assets**. This return is then used to determine funding patterns and, in part, pension expense.

The Board adopted the actuary's approach to dampen wide swings that might occur in the actual return. That is, the expected return on plan assets is to be included as a component of pension expense, not the actual return in a given year. To achieve this goal, the expected rate of return (the actuary's rate) is multiplied by the market-related values of plan assets. The *market-related asset value is a calculated value that recognizes changes in fair value in a systematic and rational manner over not more than five years.*[9]

What happens to the difference between the expected return and the actual return is referred to as **experience gains and losses**. Asset experience gains (occurring when actual return is greater than expected return) and asset losses (occurring when actual return is less than expected return) are not recorded in the general ledger.

The annual amount of asset gain or loss is determined at the end of each year by comparing the expected balance of plan assets with their market-related values. The expected balance at year end is the opening balance plus contributions and expected return minus benefits paid. In the preceding example, the expected balance of Zarle's pension fund assets at the end of 1995 was $134,100. If the market-related value of the plan assets was $135,000, then there would be an experience gain of $900 ($135,000 − $134,100).

Liability Experience Gains and Losses

In estimating the projected benefit obligation (the liability), actuaries make assumptions about such items as mortality rate, retirement rate, turnover rate, disability rate, and salary amounts. Any change in these actuarial assumptions changes the amount of the projected benefit obligation. Seldom does actual experience coincide exactly with actuarial predictions. These unexpected gains or losses from changes in the projected benefit obligation are referred to as **liability experience gains and losses**.

Liability experience gains result when the expected balance of the projected benefit obligation differs from the currently computed actuarial amount. For example, the expected projected benefit obligation of Zarle Company was $212,700 at December 31, 1995. If the company's actuaries using December 31, 1995 estimates computed a projected benefit obligation of $213,500, then the company would have suffered a liability experience loss of $800 ($213,500 − $212,700).

Amortization of Experience Gains and Losses

Once the net experience gains and losses (net of asset and liability gains and losses) have been identified and measured, the problem becomes one of determining how they should affect the computation of pension expense. The profession requires that these gains and losses be amortized over an "appropriate" period of time which is generally the expected average remaining service life of the employee group.

Experience gains and losses are generally amortized in the current period only if, as of the *beginning of the year*, there is an unamortized gain or loss. That is, if no unamortized gain or loss existed at the beginning of the period, usually there will be no recognition of gains or losses in the current period. The reasons for this delayed recognition are that the gains and losses are long term in nature and it is more convenient to begin amortization in the fiscal period following their occurrence.

To illustrate the amortization of unrecognized experience gains or losses, assume the following information for Soft-White.

---

[9] Different ways of calculating market-related value may be used for different classes of assets (for example, an employer might use fair value for bonds and a five-year-moving-average for equities), but the manner of determining market-related value should be applied consistently from year to year for each asset class.

Soft-White Ltd.
Calculation of Net Experience Losses (Gains)
Fund Assets

	1994	1995	1996
Fund assets (first of year)	$2,190,000	$2,850,000	$3,795,000
Expected return on fund assets	219,000	285,000	379,500
Funding contributions (end of year)	590,000	625,000	648,000
Projected asset value	2,999,000	3,760,000	4,822,500
Market-related asset value	2,850,000	3,795,000	4,950,000
Experience loss (gain)	$ 149,000	$ (35,000)	$ (127,500)

Pension Obligation

	1994	1995	1996
Pension obligation (first of year)	$2,190,000	$2,950,000	$3,800,000
Past service cost (plan amendment)	–0–	–0–	900,000
Interest (10%)	219,000	295,000	470,000
Accrual for service (at end of year)	590,000	625,000	648,000
Expected obligation	2,999,000	3,870,000	5,818,000
Year-end obligation (as determined by actuary)	2,950,000	3,800,000	5,990,000
Experience loss (gain)	$ (49,000)	$ (70,000)	$ 172,000

Net Experience Loss (Gain)

	1994	1995	1996
Fund assets	$ 149,000	$ (35,000)	$ (127,500)
Pension obligation	(49,000)	(70,000)	172,000
Net experience loss (gain)	$ 100,000	$ (105,000)	$ 44,500

If the expected average remaining service life is 5.5 years, the schedule to amortize the net experience loss is as follows.

Soft-White Ltd.
Amortization of Experience Loss (Gain)

	1994	1995	1996
Opening balance	$ –0–	$100,000	$(23,182)
Experience loss (gain)	100,000	(105,000)	44,500
Amortization of 1994 loss*		(18,182)	(18,182)
Amortization of 1995 gain**			19,090
Closing balance	$100,000	$(23,182)	$ 22,226

*$100,000/5.5
**($105,000)/5.5

As indicated in the above schedule, the loss recognized in 1995 increases pension expense by $18,182. This amount is small compared to the total loss of $100,000 and indicates that the amortization approach (rather than immediate recognition) dampens the effects of these gains and losses on pension expense (reduces volatility). The rationale for this approach is that gains and losses from refinements in estimates over time will offset one another. It therefore seems reasonable that gains and losses should not be recognized fully as a component of pension expense in the period in which they arise.

However, gains and losses that arise from a pension plan settlement or curtailment should be recognized immediately. A plan settlement occurs "when an employer legally discharges the obligation for accrued pension benefits."[10] This may be done by transferring assets to the beneficiaries of the plan or by transferring the obligation to an unrelated third party. A curtailment, on the other hand, "occurs when the expected years of future service to be rendered by the existing employee group is reduced significantly or when benefits will not be earned by employees for some or all future periods."[11] In addition to recognizing gains and losses from settlements or curtailments immediately, any related unamortized experience gains and losses should be charged to expense.

1996 ENTRIES AND WORK SHEET

Continuing the Zarle Company illustration into 1996, the following facts apply to the pension plan:

Annual service cost for 1996 is $13,000.

Interest on accrued benefits is 10%; expected earnings rate is 10%.

Expected return on plan assets for 1996 is $13,410.

Actual return on plan assets for 1996 is $12,000 (i.e. plan assets at market-related values at December 31, 1996 are $159,600).

Amortization of past service cost in 1996 is $27,211.

Annual funding contribution (funding) is $24,000.

Benefits paid to retirees in 1996 are $10,500.

Changes in actuarial assumptions establish the end-of-year projected benefit obligation at $265,000.

The work sheet shown on page 1006 presents all of the pension entries and information recorded by Zarle Company in 1996. On the first line of the work sheet are recorded the beginning balances that relate to the pension plan. In this case, the beginning balances for Zarle Company are the ending balances from the 1995 pension work sheet on page 1002.

Entries (m), (n), (o), (p), (q), and (r) are similar to the corresponding entries explained in 1994 or 1995. Entries (o) and (t) are related. The recording of the expected return in entry (o) has been illustrated in both 1994 and 1995. In both 1994 and 1995, it was assumed that the actual return on plan assets was equal to the expected return on plan assets. In 1996 the expected return of $13,410 (the expected rate of 10% times the beginning-of-the-year plan assets balance of $134,100) is higher than the actual return of $12,000. The resulting asset loss of $1,410 ($13,410 − $12,000) is not recognized in the company's accounts.

Entry (s) records the change in the projected benefit obligation resulting from a change in actuarial assumptions. As indicated, the actuary has now computed the ending balance to be $265,000. Given that the memo record balance at December 31 is $236,470 ($212,700 + $13,000 + $21,270 − $10,500), a difference of $28,530 ($265,000 − $236,470) is indicated. This $28,530 increase in the employer's liability is an experience loss that is deferred by debiting it to the Unrecognized Experience Gain or Loss account.

---

[10] *CICA Handbook*, Section 3460, par. .03(l).

[11] *Ibid.*, par. .03(m).

Zarle Company
Pension Work Sheet: 1996

Items	General Journal Entries			Memo Record			
	Annual Pension Expense	Cash	Prepaid/ Accrued Cost	Projected Benefit Obligation	Plan Assets	Unrecognized Past Service Cost	Unrecognized Experience Gain or Loss
Balance, Dec. 31, 1995			25,811 Cr.	212,700 Cr.	134,100 Dr.	52,789 Dr.	
(m) Service Cost	13,000 Dr.			13,000 Cr.			
(n) Interest cost	21,270 Dr.			21,270 Cr.			
(o) Expected return	13,410 Cr.				13,410 Dr.		
(p) Amortization of PSC	27,211 Dr.					27,211 Cr.	
(q) Contributions		24,000 Cr.			24,000 Dr.		
(r) Benefits				10,500 Dr.	10,500 Cr.		
(s) Liability loss				28,530 Cr.			28,530 Dr.
(t) Asset loss					1,410 Cr.		1,410 Dr.
Journal entry for 1996	48,071 Dr.	24,000 Cr.	24,071 Cr.				
Balance, Dec. 31, 1996			49,882 Cr.	265,000 Cr.	159,600 Dr.	25,578 Dr.	29,940 Dr.

The journal entry on December 31 to formally record pension expense for 1996 is as follows:

1996

Pension Expense	48,071	
Cash		24,000
Prepaid/Accrued Pension Cost		24,071

As illustrated in the work sheets of 1994 and 1995, the balance of the Prepaid/Accrued Pension cost account at December 31, 1996 of $49,882 is equal to the net of the balances in the memo accounts as shown below.

Reconciliation Schedule: 1996

Projected benefit obligation (Credit)	$(265,000)
Plan assets at market-related value (Debit)	159,600
Funded status	(105,400)
Unrecognized past service cost (Debit)	25,578
Unrecognized experience loss (Debit)	29,940
Prepaid/accrued pension cost (Credit)	$ (49,882)

Objective 8

Describe the reporting requirements for pension plans in financial statements

FINANCIAL STATEMENT PRESENTATION

Within the Financial Statements. As already indicated, if the amount paid (credit to Cash) by the employer to the pension trust is less than the annual provision (debit to Pension Expense), a credit balance accrual in the amount of the difference arises. This accrued pension cost usually appears in the long-term liability section and is described as Accrued Pension Cost.

If the cash paid (amount funded) to the pension trust during the period is greater than the amounts expensed, a deferred charge equal to the difference arises. This deferral should be reported as Deferred Pension Expense in the deferred charges section of the balance sheet.

Under present GAAP, unexpensed past service cost is not reported as a liability. Past service cost, although measured by employee service in years prior to the incurrence of the cost, is considered an expense of periods subsequent to the plan initiation or amendment. Although some argue that unfunded past service cost should be recognized as a liability on the date that the benefits are granted, past service cost is not presently considered to have accounting significance until it is recognized as expense under appropriate accrual accounting.

Within the Footnotes. Because company pension plans are frequently important to an understanding of financial position and results of operations, the following information, if not disclosed in the body of the financial statements, may be disclosed in the notes. These notes are particularly important for pensions because of the compromises and complexities that are involved in establishing the recognition of financial statement amounts. For defined benefit plans, the *Handbook* requires disclosure of "the actuarial present value of accrued pension benefits attributed to services rendered up to the reporting date and the value of pension fund assets."[12] Companies having defined contribution plans are only required to disclose the amount of the required contribution for the period.[13] Other details may be disclosed at the discretion of management. The general disclosures and the rationale for each are provided below to illustrate the information that firms may wish to include in the notes to the financial statements:

1. A general description of the plan including employee groups covered, type of benefit formula, funding policy, type of assets held, and the nature and effect of significant matters affecting comparability of information for all periods presented.

    Rationale. Because the measurement of pension expense is based on the benefit formula, a description of the plan and the benefit formula is useful. Furthermore, disclosure of funding policies and types of assets held helps in determining cash flows and their likelihood as well as highlighting the difference between cash flow and pension expense. Finally, significant events affecting the plan are noted so the financial statement reader can better predict these effects on long-term trends of the plan.

2. Pension expense for the period.

    Rationale. Information about the calculation of the amount helps users to better understand how pension expense is determined. Thus, changes in the expense from one period to the next are better explained.

3. The value of pension fund assets, the actuarial present value of accumulated pension obligations, and the date of the most recent actuarial valuation.

    Rationale. The funded status of the plan is of obvious importance. In addition, some believe that the unfunded accumulated benefit obligation is a liability. In this disclosure, a reader can determine this amount.

In summary, mandatory disclosures are minimal, when compared to the information which may be useful. One factor that has made pension reporting difficult to understand in the past has been the lack of consistent terminology. Furthermore, a substantial amount of offsetting was done to arrive at pension expense. These required and suggested disclosures should take some of the mystery out of pension reporting, particularly when a large cost or asset has been offset by a revenue or liability to produce small reported net amounts.

Note disclosures vary significantly in practice from minimal presentation of pension assets and obligation to very detailed descriptions and schedules. A good example of the latter is found in

---

[12] *CICA Handbook*, Section 3460, par. .60.

[13] *Ibid.*, par. .65.

Canadian Occidental Petroleum Ltd.'s 1991 Annual Report shown below. It provides an illustration of the components of pension expense disclosure and the reconciliation schedule.

Canadian Occidental Petroleum Ltd.

Note 10. Employee Pension Plan

CanadianOxy maintains a non-contributory defined benefit plan which covers substantially all of its employees. The pension costs for this plan are determined by independent actuarial valuations and are funded in accordance with federal and provincial government regulations by contributions to a trust fund which is administered by an independent trustee. Assets of the pension fund are invested in investment funds, consisting primarily of equities, fixed income bonds and real estate, and guaranteed investment contracts.

Pension expense has been determined as follows:

	1991	1990	1989
Cost of benefits earned by employees during the year	$3,006	$2,475	$2,289
Current year's interest cost on benefits earned	3,506	3,095	2,713
Total benefit earned for current year	6,512	5,570	5,002
Less return on pension plan assets:			
Actual	3,827	3,626	5,539
Deferred (a)	(709)	(404)	(2,746)
Less amortization of deferred items (b)	(91)	300	186
Net pension expense	$3,485	$2,048	$2,023

(a)   Represents the difference between the estimated and actual return on pension plan assets.

(b)   The gain at transition, past service costs, and past experience gains (losses) are amortized on a straight-line basis over the expected remaining average service life of the employees in the pension plan.

The following table sets forth the funded status of the pension plan and the amounts both recognized and unrecognized in CanadianOxy's Consolidated Balance Sheet at December 31, 1991 and 1990.

	1991	1990
Pension plan assets at fair value	$53,312	$45,741
Actuarial present value of benefit obligations:		
Benefits based on service to date and present pay levels		
Vested	$42,645	$34,041
Non-vested	142	290
Accumulated benefit obligation	42,787	34,331
Additional benefits related principally to projected pay increases	11,649	10,529
Total projected benefit obligation based on service to date	$54,436	$44,860
Excess (deficiency) of pension plan assets over projected benefit obligation	$ (1,124)	$ 881
Fund requirements in (excess) deficiency of recognized book provision	(332)	3,483
Total pension plan assets and book provision in excess (deficiency) of projected benefit obligation	$ (1,456)	$ 4,364

(Continued)

The excess consists of:

Unamortized gain at transition	$ 1,302	$ 1,421
Unamortized past service costs	(1,281)	(1,377)
Unamortized past net experience gains (losses)	(1,477)	4,320
	$ (1,456)	$ 4,364

The assumptions used in the determination of the projected benefit obligation and pension expense are as follows:

	1991	1990
Discount rate	7.0%	7.5%
Long-term annual rate of return on pension plan assets	7.0%	7.5%

In addition, the Company has a non-contributory executive benefit plan which provides supplemental benefits to the extent that the benefits under the pension plan are limited by statutory guideline.

The plans provide benefits based on length of service and final average earnings.

1997 ENTRIES AND WORK SHEET: A COMPREHENSIVE ILLUSTRATION

Incorporating the amortization of experience gains and losses and the required disclosure, the Zarle Company pension plan accounting is continued based on the following facts for 1997:

Service cost for 1997 is $16,000.

Interest on accrued benefits is 10%; expected rate of return is 10%.

Actual return on plan assets for 1997 is $11,460.

Amortization of past service cost in 1997 is $25,578.

Annual contributions (funding) are $27,000.

Benefits paid to retirees in 1997 are $18,000.

Accumulated benefit obligation is $263,000 at the end of 1997.

Average service life of all covered employees is 20 years.

To facilitate accumulation and recording components of pension expense and maintenance of the unrecognized amounts related to the pension plan, the work sheet shown at the top of page 1010 is prepared from the basic date presented above. Beginning-of-the-year 1997 account balances are the December 31, 1996 balances from the 1996 work sheet on page 1006.

Work Sheet Explanations and Entries. Entries (aa) through (gg) are similar to the corresponding entries previously explained in the prior years' work sheets with the exception of entry (gg). Entry (gg) results from amortizing the 1997 opening balance ($29,940) of unrecognized experience losses. This amount is amortized over the expected 20-year remaining service life of the employees from January 1, 1997.

The journal entry to formally record pension expense for 1997 is as follows:

1997

Pension Expense	53,615	
Cash		27,000
Prepaid/Accrued Pension Cost		26,615

	Zarle Company Pension Work Sheet: 1997						
	General Journal Entries			Memo Record			
Items	Annual Pension Expense	Cash	Prepaid/ Accrued Cost	Projected Benefit Obligation	Plan Assets	Unrecognized Past Service Cost	Unrecognized Experience Gain or Loss
Balance, Dec. 31, 1996			49,882 Cr.	265,000 Cr.	159,600 Dr.	25,578 Dr.	29,940 Dr.
(aa) Service cost	16,000 Dr.			16,000 Cr.			
(bb) Interest cost	26,500 Dr.			26,500 Cr.			
(cc) Expected return	15,960 Cr.				15,960 Dr.		
(dd) Amortization of PSC	25,578 Dr.					25,578 Cr.	
(ee) Contributions		27,000 Cr.			27,000 Dr.		
(ff) Benefits				18,000 Dr.	18,000 Cr.		
(gg) Amortization of loss	1,497 Dr.						1,497 Cr.
(hh) Liability gain				26,500 Dr.			26,500 Cr.
(jj) Asset loss					4,500 Cr.		4,500 Dr.
Journal entry for 1997	53,615 Dr.	27,000 Cr.	26,615 Cr.				
Balance, Dec. 31, 1997			76,497 Cr.	263,000 Cr.	180,060 Dr.	–0–	6,443 Dr.

Financial Statement Presentation. The financial statements of Zarle Company at December 31, 1997 present the following items relative to its pension plan.

Zarle Company
Balance Sheet
As at December 31, 1997

Assets	Liabilities	
	Accrued pension cost	$76,497

Zarle Company
Income Statement
For the Year Ended December 31, 1997

Operating expenses
  Pension expense* $53,615

*Pension expense is frequently reported as "employee benefits."

Zarle Company
Statement of Changes in Financial Position
For the Year Ended December 31, 1997

Cash flow from operating activities
  Net income (assumed) $905,000
  Adjustments to reconcile net income to
    cash provided by operating activities:
      Increase in accrued pension liability   26,615

Note Disclosure. The note disclosure by Zarle Company of the pension plan for 1997 might appear as follows.

Notes to the financial statements

Note D. The company maintains a defined benefit final average pension plan covering substantially all of its employees. The plan provides pension benefits based on length of service and final average earnings.

      Reports of the company's actuaries based on management's projections of compensation levels at estimated retirement dates indicate that the present value of the projected pension benefits and the net assets available to provide for these benefits as of December 31 are as follows:

	1993	1996
Accrued pension benefits	$263,000	$265,000
Pension fund assets (at market value)	180,600	159,600

The pension expense of $53,615 includes the amortization of past service costs and experience gains and losses. Past service costs are being amortized on a straight-line basis over a 3-year period and experience gains and losses are amortized over a 20-year period.

The cumulative difference between the amounts expensed and the funding contributions has been reflected in the balance sheet as long-term items. The amounts recorded are 1993—$76,497 (accrual); 1996—$49,882 (accrual).

TRANSITION: A SPECIAL IMPLEMENTATION PROBLEM

Because the amendments to Section 3460 involved such significant changes in pension reporting, the AcSB decided to delay its adoption so that companies could adjust to the new reporting system. As a result, companies on a calendar year reporting basis did not have to follow the requirements until 1988.

    When a company switches over to the new reporting system, an important factor to be considered is the transition amount that will occur. That is, the excess of the projected benefit obligation over the fair value of the pension plan assets must be determined and amortized in the future. This transition amount is amortized over EARSL of the employees participating in the plan.

    To illustrate, assume that Swingline Ltd. decides to adopt the requirements of Section 3460 in 1988. At the beginning of the year, its projected benefit obligation is $900,000 and the fair value of its pension plan assets is $750,000. The computation of the transition amount is as follows.

Projected benefit obligation	$900,000
Pension plan assets (at market related value)	750,000
Unrecognized net obligation	$150,000

This amount is not recorded as a liability. The periodic amortization over EARSL of the initial unrecognized net liability is included in pension expense.

MULTI-EMPLOYER PLANS

Multi-employer pension plans are plans sponsored by two or more different employers. They are often negotiated as part of labour union contracts in the trucking, coal mining, construction, and entertainment industries. Although a multi-employer plan may have the characteristics of a defined benefit plan, every employer participating in the plan may not have access to the necessary actuarial amounts. In these cases, the employer would account for the pension plan as if it were a defined contribution plan.

PENSION TERMINATIONS

Some employees believe that employers are simply treating pension plans like company piggy banks, to be raided at will. This refers to the practice by some companies that have pension plan assets in excess of projected benefit obligations—paying off the obligation and pocketing the difference. Generally, provincial laws prevent companies from recapturing excess assets unless they pay participants what is owed to them and then terminate the plan. As a result, companies sometimes buy annuities to pay off the pension claimants and use the excess funds for other corporate purposes.[14]

The accounting issue that arises from these terminations is whether a gain should be recognized by the corporation when these assets revert back to the company. This issue is complex because, in some cases, a new defined benefit plan is started after the old one has been eliminated. Therefore some contend that there has been no change in substance, but one in form.

The profession requires recognition in earnings of a net gain or loss when the employer settles (or curtails) a pension obligation either by lump-sum cash payments to participants or by purchase of annuity contracts. In other words, gains or losses arising as a result of plan settlements or curtailments are recognized immediately as unusual or extraordinary items.

POST-EMPLOYMENT BENEFITS

Post-employment benefits (other than pensions) can be defined as all forms of benefits, such as health insurance, life insurance, and disability benefits, provided to a former employee. Although these types of costs have generally been charged on a pay-as-you-go basis, some argue that these benefits are similar to pensions and should be accrued and funded prior to the time the employee retires. With the escalating costs of these benefits to retirees, these costs can be substantial. These benefits should be treated as contingencies, that is, accrued and reported as a liability if likely to occur and reasonably estimable. If material but not reasonably estimable, disclosure in the notes to the financial statements is required. However, if the amount is immaterial, no disclosure is required.

TERMINATION BENEFITS PAID TO EMPLOYEES

It is not unusual for an employer to offer for a short period of time special benefits to its employees to induce termination or early retirement. These special termination or early retirement benefits

---

[14] A real question exists as to whom the pension fund money belongs to; that is, some argue that the excess funds are for the employees, not for the employer. In addition, given that the funds have been reverting to the employer, critics charge that cost-of-living increases and the possibility of other increased benefits in the future will be reduced, because companies will be reluctant to use those excess funds to pay for such increases.

can take the form of lump sum payments, periodic future payments, or both. The payments may be made directly from the employer's assets, an existing pension fund, a new employee benefit plan, or a combination thereof. Some accountants believe that the cost of such special termination benefits should be recognized as an expense of future periods, whereas others believe that the costs of those benefits should be expensed immediately.

A recordable liability exists if the following two conditions are met:

1. The employee(s) accept the offer.

2. The amount can be reasonably estimated.

Included in the amount recognized should be (1) any lump-sum cash payments, (2) the present value of any expected future payments, and (3) if reliably measurable, the effect of the special termination benefit offer on previously accrued pension expense.

CONCLUDING OBSERVATIONS

Frequently the financial press reports in depth on some issue related to pension plans in Canada. The AcSB in its revision of Section 3460 has attempted to clarify many of the accounting issues which should help users who wish to understand the implications of a company's pension plans.

Critics still argue, however, that much remains to be done. One issue in particular is the delayed recognition of certain events. The delayed recognition features adopted by the Board mean that changes in pension plan obligations (such as for plan amendments) and changes in the value of plan assets are not recognized immediately but are systematically incorporated over subsequent periods.

However, the Board recognizes this deferring, noting that the delayed recognition feature for certain events excludes the most current and most relevant information from the balance sheet. However, as indicated, it is possible to find information about the excess of plan assets over the projected benefit obligation and vice versa in the notes to the financial statements.

FUNDAMENTAL CONCEPTS

1. A pension plan is an arrangement whereby an employer promises income benefits for employees after they retire. Two common types are defined contribution and defined benefit plans. Defined benefit plans provide the most difficulty from an accounting standpoint.

2. Under a defined benefit plan, the trust is a separate entity in form; in substance, the trust is an integral part of the employer's assets and liabilities. The employer is responsible for the eventual payment of the defined benefits.

3. An actuary's primary purpose is to suggest an adequate funding plan to the employer company. Actuaries have devised a number of actuarial funding methods to determine the periodic contributions that the employers might make to the pension fund to ensure that funds are available to meet the retirees' claim to benefits. In addition, actuaries provide the information about the plan, including service cost, past service cost, vested, accumulated, and projected benefit obligation values.

4. Three possible measures of the pension benefit obligation are: vested, accumulated, and projected. The projected benefit obligation is the measure generally adopted for accounting purposes. It is the present value of vested and nonvested benefits accrued to date based on employees' future salary levels.

5. The components of pension expense are: (1) service cost, (2) interest cost, (3) expected return on plan assets, (4) amortization of past service cost, (5) amortization of experience gains and losses, (6) amortization of the transition amount.

6. A discount rate (estimated by management) should be used to compute the present value of the projected benefit obligation. A market-related asset value is multiplied by the expected rate of return on plan assets for purposes of computing pension expense.

(Continued)

7. At the time of plan change (initiation or amendment of a plan), an expense and related liability are not recognized for past service cost immediately. Retroactive benefits are not recognized as pension expense entirely in the period of amendment but should be recognized during the service period of those employees who are expected to receive benefits under the plan.

8. Gains and losses are adjustments made to reflect (1) deviations between estimated conditions and actual experience and (2) revisions in the underlying assumptions. To eliminate wide fluctuations in pension expense caused by these gains and losses, the profession requires amortization over the estimated remaining service life of the employee group.

9. Unique to pension accounting is keeping track of the unrecognized (noncapitalized), off-balance-sheet elements of the pension plan, such as the projected benefit obligation, the plan assets, the unrecognized past service cost, and unrecognized experience gains and losses.

10. In the usual situation, an accrued pension cost (liability) or deferred pension cost (asset) will be reported on the balance sheet when funding is different from the amount of expense recognized.

11. The disclosures related to defined benefit pension plans may be extensive. These disclosures provide descriptive information on employees covered, value of assets held, and the amount of the projected benefit obligation. In addition, the components of pension expense may be disclosed along with schedules highlighting components of the pension obligation. A reconciliation from the funded status of the pension plan to its balance sheet liability or asset may also be included.

QUESTIONS

1. What is a private pension plan? How does a contributory pension plan differ from a noncontributory plan?

2. Differentiate between a defined contribution pension plan and a defined benefit pension plan. Explain how the employer's obligation differs between the two types of plans.

3. Differentiate between "accounting for the employer" and "accounting for the pension fund."

4. The meaning of the term "fund" depends on the context in which it is used. Explain its meaning when it is used as a noun. Explain its meaning when it is used as a verb.

5. What is the role of an actuary relative to pension plans? What are actuarial assumptions?

6. What factors must be considered by the actuary in measuring the amount of pension benefits under a defined benefit plan?

7. Name three approaches to measuring the benefits from a pension plan and explain how they differ.

8. Distinguish between the noncapitalization approach and the capitalization approach with regard to accounting for pension plans? Which approach does the *CICA Handbook* adopt?

9. Explain how the cash basis of accounting for pension plans differs from the accrual basis accounting for pension plans. Why is cash basis accounting generally considered unacceptable for pension plan accounting?

10. Identify the five components that comprise pension expense. Briefly explain the nature of each component.

11. What is service cost and what is the basis of its measurement?

12. In computing the interest component of pension expense, what interest rates may be used?

13. What is meant by "past service cost"? When is past service cost recognized as pension expense?

14. What are "experience gains and losses" as related to pension plans?

15. If pension expense recognized in a period exceeds the current amount funded by the employer, what kind of account arises and how should it be reported in the financial statements? If the reverse occurs—that is, current funding by the employer exceeds the amount recognized as pension expense—what kind of account arises and how should it be reported?

16. Given the following items and amounts, compute the actual return on plan assets: market-

related value of plan assets at the beginning of the period, $9,200,000; benefits paid during the period, $1,400,000; contributions made during the period, $1,000,000; and market-related value of the plan assets at the end of the period, $10,000,000.

17. How does an "asset gain or loss" develop in pension accounting? How does a "liability gain or loss" develop in pension accounting?

18. At the end of the current period, Warren Ltd. had an accumulated benefit obligation of $400,000, pension plan assets (at market-related value) of $300,000, and a balance in deferred pension cost of $35,000. Assuming that Warren Ltd. follows Section 3460 of the *CICA Handbook*, what are the accounts and amounts that will be reported on the company's balance sheet as pension assets or pension liabilities?

19. At the end of the current year, Barry Dubray Co. has unrecognized past service cost of $9,000,000. Should the unrecognized past service cost be reported on the balance sheet?

20. Determine the meaning of the following terms:
    (a) Contributory plan.
    (b) Vested benefits.
    (c) Retroactive benefits.

21. One disclosure required by *CICA Handbook* Section 3460 is that "an enterprise should disclose separately the actuarial present value of accrued pension benefits attributed to services rendered up to the reporting date and the value of pension fund assets." Section 3460 also suggests that companies may wish to disclose additional information such as, "description of the plan, pension expense for the period, the amount of deferred charge or accrual for pension costs, the basis of valuing pension fund assets, the salary and interest assumptions." What is the rationale for this disclosure?

22. Of what value to the financial statement reader is the schedule reconciling the funded status of the plan with amounts reported in the employer's balance sheet?

23. What is a multi-employer plan? What accounting questions arise when a company is involved with one of these plans?

24. A headline in *The Wall Street Journal* stated "Firms Increasingly Tap Their Pension Funds to Use Excess Assets." What is the accounting issue related to the use of these "excess assets" by companies?

25. What are post-employment benefits? What is the present accounting treatment for these costs?

26. Why didn't the AcSB cover both types of post-retirement benefits—pensions and health care— in the earlier pension accounting standard?

CASES

(PENSION TERMINOLOGY AND THEORY) Many business organizations have been concerned with **C20-1** providing for the retirement of employees since the late 1800s. During recent decades, a marked increase in this concern has resulted in the establishment of private pension plans in most large companies and in many medium- and small-sized ones.

The substantial growth of these plans, both in numbers of employees covered and in amounts of retirement benefits, has increased the significance of pension cost in relation to the financial position and results of operations of many companies. In examining the costs of pension plans, an accountant encounters certain terms. The elements of pension costs that the terms represent must be dealt with appropriately if generally accepted accounting principles are to be reflected in the financial statements of entities with pension plans.

Instructions

(a) Define a private pension plan. How does a contributory pension plan differ from a noncontributory plan?

(b) Differentiate between "accounting for the employer" and "accounting for the pension fund."

(c) Explain the terms "funded" and "pension liability" as they relate to:

   1. The pension fund.

   2. The employer.

(d) 1. Discuss the theoretical justification for accrual recognition of pension costs.

2. Discuss the relative objectivity of the measurement process of accrual versus cash (pay-as-you-go) accounting for annual pension costs.

(e) Distinguish among the following as they relate to pension plans:

1. Service cost.

2. Past service costs.

3. Actuarial funding methods.

4. Vested benefits.

C20-2 (PENSION TERMINOLOGY)   The following items appear on Paul Reist Company's financial statements.

1. Under the caption Assets:
Deferred pension cost.

2. Under the caption Liabilities:
Accrued pension cost.

3. On the Income Statement:
Pension Expense

Instructions

With regard to "Pension costs and obligations," explain the significance of each of the items above on corporate financial statements. (**Note:** All items set forth above are not necessarily to be found on the statements of a single company.)

C20-3 (BASIC TERMINOLOGY)   In examining the costs of pension plans, an accountant encounters certain terms. The elements of pension costs that the terms represent must be dealt with appropriately if generally accepted accounting principles are to be reflected in the financial statements of entities with pension plans.

Instructions

(a) 1. Discuss the theoretical justification for accrual recognition of pension costs.

2. Discuss the relative objectivity of the measurement process of accrual versus cash (pay-as-you-go) accounting for annual pension costs.

(b) Explain the following terms as they apply to accounting for pension plans:

1. Market-related asset value.

2. Actuarial funding methods.

3. Projected benefit obligation.

(c) What information should be disclosed about a company's pension plans in its financial statements and its notes?

C20-4 (BASIC CONCEPTS OF PENSION REPORTING)   Marion Burke, president of Express Mail Ltd., is discussing the possibility of developing a pension plan for its employees with Mark Sullivan, controller, and James Salamon, assistant controller. Their conversation is as follows.

Marion Burke: If we are going to compete with our competitors, we must have a pension plan to attract talented employees.

Mark Sullivan: I must warn you, Marion, that a pension plan will take a large bite out of our income. The only reason why we have been so profitable is the lack of a pension cost in our income statement. In some of our competitors' cases, pension expense is 30% of pretax income.

James Salamon: Why do we have to worry about a pension cost now anyway? Benefits do not vest until after 10 years of service. If they do not vest, then we are not liable. We should not have to report an expense until we are legally liable to provide benefits.

Marion Burke: But, James, the employees would want credit for past service with full vesting 10 years after starting service, not 10 years after the plan. How would we allocate the large past service cost?

James Salamon: Well, I believe that the past service cost is a cost of providing a pension plan for employees forever. It is an intangible asset that will not diminish in value because it will increase the morale of our present and future employees and provide us with a competitive edge in acquiring future employees.

Marion Burke: I hate to disagree, but I believe the past service cost is a benefit only to the present employees. This past service is directly related to the composition of the employee group at the time the plan is initiated and is in no way related to any intangible benefit received by the company because of the plan's existence. Therefore, I propose that the past service cost be amortized over the expected average remaining service life (EARSL) of the existing employee group.

Mark Sullivan (Somewhat perturbed): But what about the income statement? You two are arguing theory without consideration of our income figure.

Marion Burke: Settle down, Mark.

Mark Sullivan: Sorry, perhaps James' approach to resolving this problem is the best one. I am just not sure.

Instructions

(a) Assuming that Express Mail Ltd. establishes a pension plan, how should their liability for pensions be computed in the first year?

(b) How should pension expense be computed each year?

(c) Assuming that the pension fund is set up in a trustee relationship, should the assets of the fund be reported on the books of Express Mail Ltd.?

(d) What interest rate factor should be used in the present value computations?

(e) How should experience gains and losses be reported?

(MAJOR PENSION CONCEPTS)   Barlex Corporation is a medium-sized manufacturer of paperboard containers and boxes. The corporation sponsors a noncontributory, defined benefit pension plan that covers its 250 employees. Alex Nowicki has recently been hired as president of Barlex Corporation. While reviewing last year's financial statements with Susan Kimpton, controller, Nowicki expressed confusion about several of the items in the footnote to the financial statements relating to the pension plan. In part, the footnote reads as follows: **C20-5**

> **Note J.** The company has a defined benefit pension plan covering substantially all of its employees. The benefits are based on years of service and the employee's compensation during the last four years of employment. The company's funding policy is to contribute annually the maximum amount allowed under the federal tax code. Contributions are intended to provide for benefits expected to be earned in the future as well as those earned to date.

Effective for the year end December 31, 1988, Barlex Corporation adopted the provisions of *CICA Handbook*, Section 3460—Pension Costs and Obligations. The net periodic pension expense on Barlex Corporation's comparative income statement was $36,000 in 1994 and $28,840 in 1993.

The following are selected figures from the plan's funded status and amount recognized in Barlex Corporation's Statement of Financial Position at December 31, 1993 ($000 omitted):

Actuarial present value of benefit obligations:	
Accumulated benefit obligation	
(including vested benefits of $318)	$(435)
Projected benefit obligation	$(600)
Plan assets at fair value	525
Projected benefit obligation in	
excess of plan assets	$ (75)

Given that Barlex Corporation's workforce has been stable for the last six years, Nowicki could not understand the increase in the net periodic pension expense. Kimpton explained that the net periodic pension expense consists of several elements, some of which may decrease the net expense.

Instructions

(a) The determination of the net periodic pension expense is a function of five elements. List and briefly describe each of the elements.

(b) Describe the major difference and the major similarity between the accumulated benefit obligation and the projected benefit obligation.

(c) 1. Explain why pension gains and losses are not recognized on the income statement in the period in which they arise.

     2. Briefly describe how pension gains and losses are recognized.

(CMA adapted)

C20-6 (IMPLICATIONS OF *HANDBOOK* SECTION 3460) Sally Groft and Kathy Dahl have to do a class presentation on the new pension pronouncement "Pension Costs and Obligations." In developing the class presentation, they decided to provide the class with a series of questions related to pensions and then discuss the answers in class. Given that the class has all read *Handbook* Section 3460, they felt that this approach would provide a lively discussion. Here are the situations:

1. In an article in *Business Week*, it was reported that the discount rates used by the largest 200 companies for pension reporting ranged from 5% to 11%. How can such a situation exist, and does the new pension pronouncement alleviate this problem?

2. An article indicated that when *Handbook* Section 3460 became effective, it caused an increase in the liability for pensions for approximately 20% of companies. Why might this situation occur?

3. A recent article noted that while "smoothing" is not necessarily an accounting virtue, pension accounting has long been recognized as an exception—an area of accounting in which at least some dampening of market swings is appropriate. This is because pension plans are managed so that their performance is insulated from the extremes of short-term market swings. A pension expense that reflects the volatility of market swings might, for that reason, convey information of little relevance. Are these statements true?

4. At the end of 1987, funds of many companies held assets twice as large as they need to fund their pension plans. Are these assets reported on the balance sheet of these companies per the pension pronouncement? If not, where are they reported?

5. Understanding the impact of the changes required in pension reporting requires detailed information about its pension plan(s) and an analysis of the relationship of many factors, particularly:

(a)   the transition amount and the date of initial application.

(b)   the type of plan(s) and any significant amendments.

(c)   the plan participants.

(d)   the funding status.

(e)   the actuarial funding method and assumptions currently used.

What impact does each of these items have on financial statement presentation?

(SPECIAL REPORTING ISSUES RELATED TO POST-RETIREMENT BENEFITS)   A September 17,   **C20-7**
1992 *Wall Street Journal* article discussed a $1.8 billion charge to income made by General Electric for post-
retirement benefit costs. It was attributed to previously unrecognized health care and life insurance cost. As
financial vice-president and controller for Alco, Inc., you found this article interesting because the president
recently expressed concern about the company's rising health costs. The president was particularly concerned
with health care cost premiums being paid for retired employees. He wondered what charge Alco, Inc. will have
to take for its post-retirement benefit program.

Instructions

As financial vice-president and controller of Alco, Inc., explain why the charge was made against General Electric's
income. What alternatives are available for Alco, Inc. to report and/or disclose obligations for post-retirement
benefits?

———— **EXERCISES** ————

(COMPUTATION OF PENSION EXPENSE)   Tony Ltd. provides the following information about its   **E20-1**
defined benefit pension plan for the year 1994:

Service cost	$ 90,000
Projected benefit obligation at Jan. 1, 1994	800,000
Actual and expected return on plan assets	16,000
Amortization of past service cost	12,000
Amortization of experience loss	3,000
Interest on liability	10%

Instructions

Compute the pension expense for the year 1994.

(COMPUTATION OF PENSION EXPENSE)   Quality Print Ltd. provides the following information about   **E20-2**
its defined benefit pension plan for the year ~~1990:~~ *1994.*

Service cost	$ 95,000 ✓
Contribution to the plan	115,000 ✓
Past service cost amortization	10,000 ✓
Actual and expected return on plan assets	70,000 ✓
Benefits paid	50,000 ✓
Accrued pension cost liability at Jan. 1, 1994	7,000 ✓
Plan assets at Jan. 1, 1994	743,000 ✓
Projected benefit obligation at Jan. 1, 1994	900,000 ✓
Unrecognized past service cost balance at Jan. 1, 1994	150,000 ✓
Interest on pension obligation	10% ✓

Instructions

Compute the pension expense for the year 1994.

E20-3 **(PREPARATION OF PENSION WORK SHEET WITH RECONCILIATION)**   Using the information in E20-2, prepare a pension work sheet, inserting January 1, 1994 balances, showing December 31, 1994 balances and the journal entry recording pension expense.

E20-4 **(BASIC PENSION WORK SHEET)**   The following facts apply to the pension plan of Browning Ltd. for the year 1994:

Plan assets, Jan. 1, 1994	$485,000
Projected benefit obligation, Jan. 1, 1994	485,000
Settlement rate	8.5%
Annual pension service cost	34,000
Contributions (funding)	30,000
Actual return on plan assets	42,605
Benefits paid to retirees	21,400

Instructions

Using the preceding data, compute pension expense for the year 1994. As part of your solution, prepare a pension work sheet that shows the journal entry for pension expense for 1994 and the year-end balances in the related pension accounts.

E20-5 **(APPLICATION OF YEARS-OF-SERVICE METHOD)**   Magic Wand Card Company has five employees participating in its defined benefit pension plan. Expected years of future service for these employees at the beginning of 1994 are as follows.

Employee	Future Years of Service
Tom	2
Carole	3
Greg	5
Kate	5
Mike	5

On January 1, 1994, the company amended its pension plan, increasing its projected benefit obligation by $80,000.

Instructions

Compute the amount of past service cost amortization for the years 1994, 1995, 1996, 1997, and 1998 using the straight-line method over the expected average service life when setting up appropriate schedules.

E20-6 **(COMPUTATION OF ACTUAL RETURN)**   Bishop Importers provides the following pension plan information:

Market-related value of pension plan assets, Jan. 1, 1994	$2,400,000
Market-related value of pension plan assets, Dec. 31, 1994	2,600,000
Contributions to the plan in 1994	350,000
Paid to retirees in 1994	450,000

Instructions

From the data above, compute the actual return on the plan assets for 1994.

(BASIC PENSION WORK SHEET)   The following defined pension data of E. Merz Ltd. apply to the year   **E20-7**
1994:

Projected benefit obligation, 1/1/94 (before amendment)	$538,800
Plan assets, 1/1/94	536,200
Prepaid/accrued pension cost (credit)	2,600
On Jan. 1, 1994, E. Merz Ltd., through plan amendment, grants past service benefits having a present value of	100,000
Rate of return on plan assets and discount rate	9%
Annual pension service cost	48,000
Contributions (funding)	45,000
Actual return on plan assets	52,280
Benefits paid to retirees	40,000
Past service cost amortization for 1994	17,000

Instructions

For 1994 for E. Merz Ltd. prepare a pension work sheet that shows the journal entry for pension expense and the year-end balances in the related pension accounts.

(APPLICATION OF THE CORRIDOR APPROACH)   Paradise Limited has beginning-of-the-year present   **E20-8**
values for its projected benefit obligation and market-related values for its pension plan assets.

	Projected Benefit Obligation	Plan Assets Value
1992	$2,200,000	$1,900,000
1993	2,400,000	2,600,000
1994	2,900,000	2,600,000
1995	3,900,000	3,000,000

The average remaining service life per employee in 1992 and 1993 is 10 years and in 1994 and 1995 is 12 years. The experience gain or loss that occurred during each year is as follows: 1992, $280,000 loss; 1993, $90,000 loss; 1994, $12,000 loss; and 1995, $25,000 gain (in working the solution, the unrecognized gains and losses must be aggregated to arrive at year-end balances).

Instructions

Compute the amount of experience gain or loss amortized and charged to pension expense in each of the four years, setting up an appropriate schedule.

(DISCLOSURES: PENSION EXPENSE AND RECONCILIATION SCHEDULE)   Round Table Enter-   **E20-9**
prises provides the following information relative to its defined benefit pension plan.

Balances or Values at December 31, 1994

Projected benefit obligation	$2,753,000
Market-related value of plan assets	2,278,329
Unrecognized past service cost	205,000
Unrecognized experience loss (Jan. 1, 1994 balance, –0–)	45,680
Accrued pension cost liability	223,991
Other pension plan data:	
Service cost for 1994	$ 95,000
Unrecognized past service cost amortization for 1994	48,000
Actual return on plan assets in 1994	140,000
Expected return on plan assets in 1994	185,680
Interest on Jan. 1, 1994 projected benefit obligation	253,000
Contributions to the plan in 1994	92,329
Benefits paid	160,000

Instructions

(a) Prepare the note disclosing the components of pension expense for the year 1994.

(b) Prepare a schedule reconciling the funded status of the plan with the amounts reported in the December 31, 1994 financial statements.

E20-10 (PENSION WORK SHEET WITH RECONCILIATION SCHEDULE) B. Rodier Ltd. sponsors a defined benefit pension plan for its employees. On January 1, 1994, the following balances relate to this plan:

Plan assets	$450,000
Projected benefit obligation	575,000
Prepaid/accrued pension cost (credit)	25,000
Unrecognized prior service cost	100,000

As a result of the operation of the plan during 1994, the following additional data are provided by the actuary:

Service cost for 1994	$85,000
Discount rate	9%
Accrual return on plan assets in 1994	52,000
Amortization of prior service cost	19,000
Expected return on plan assets	47,000
Experience loss from change in projected benefit obligation,	
due to change in actuarial predictions	76,000
Contributions in 1994	99,000
Benefits paid retirees in 1994	81,000

Instructions

(a) Using the data above, compute pension expense for B. Rodier Ltd. for the year 1994 by preparing a pension work sheet that shows the journal entry for pension expense and the year-end balances in the related pension accounts.

(b) At December 31, 1994, prepare a schedule reconciling the funded status of the plan with the pension amount reported on the balance sheet.

(PENSION EXPENSE, JOURNAL ENTRIES, STATEMENT PRESENTATION) The Rocky Pizza **E20-11** Company sponsors a defined benefit pension plan for its employees. The following data relate to the operation of the plan for the year 1994:

1. The actuarial present value of future benefits earned by employees for services rendered in 1994 amounted to $60,000 using the projected benefits approach pro rated on years of service.

2. The company's funding policy requires a contribution to the pension trustee amounting to $155,000 for 1994.

3. As of January 1, 1994, the company had an accrued benefit obligation of $1,100,000. The pension asset market value was $800,000. The expected return on plan assets and the interest rate for the accrued benefits were both 9%.

4. Amortization of unrecognized past service cost was $40,000 in 1994.

Instructions

(a) Determine the amounts of the components of pension expense that should be recognized by the company in 1994.

(b) Prepare the journal entries to record pension expense and the employer's contribution to the pension trustee in 1994.

(PENSION EXPENSE, JOURNAL ENTRIES, STATEMENT PRESENTATION) Hurka Ltd. received **E20-12** the following information from its pension plan trustee concerning the operation of the company's defined benefit pension plan for the year ended December 31, 1994.

	January 1, 1994	December 31, 1994
Accrued benefit obligation	$2,200,000	$2,275,000
Market-related value of pension assets	900,000	1,250,000
Actuarial (gains) losses	–0–	(230,000)

The service cost component of pension expense for employee services rendered in the current year amounted to $85,000 and the amortization of unrecognized past service cost was $125,000. The company's actual funding (contributions) of the plan in 1994 amounted to $260,000. The expected return on plan assets and the interest rate were both 10%.

Instructions

(a) Determine the amounts of the components of pension expense that should be recognized by the company in 1994.

(b) Prepare the journal entries to record pension expense and the employer's contribution to the pension plan in 1994.

(COMPUTATION OF ACTUAL RETURN, GAINS AND LOSSES, PAST SERVICE COST, PENSION E20-13 EXPENSE, AND RECONCILIATION) Henry Smits Ltd. sponsors a defined benefit pension plan. The corporation's actuary provides the following information about the plan.

	January 1, 1994	December 31, 1994
Projected benefit obligation —*9 AAP*	$2,800	$3,750
Plan assets (market-related value)	1,900	2,800
Interest rate and expected rate of return		10%
Deferred/(Accrued) pension cost	–0–	?

(Continued)

Unamortized past service cost	900	?
Service cost for the year 1994		400
Contributions (funding) in ~~1990~~ *1994*		800
Benefits paid in 1994		300

The average remaining service life is 20 years.

Instructions

(a) Compute the actual return on the plan assets in 1994.

(b) Compute the amount of the experience gain or loss as of December 31, 1994 (assume the January 1, 1994 balance was zero).

(c) Compute the amount of experience gain or loss amortization for 1994.

(d) Compute the amount of past service cost amortization for 1994.

(e) Compute the pension expense for 1994.

(f) Prepare a schedule reconciling the plan's funded status with the amounts reported on the December 31, 1994 balance sheet.

E20-14 **(WORK SHEET FOR E20-14)**   Using the information in E20-13 about Henry Smits Ltd.'s defined benefit pension plan, prepare a 1994 pension work sheet with supplementary schedules of computations. Prepare the journal entries at December 31, 1994 to record pension expense and the funding payment.

E20-15 **(PENSION EXPENSE, JOURNAL ENTRIES)**   Harmon Workshop Inc. initiated a noncontributory-defined benefit pension plan for its 100 employees on January 1, 1993. Employment levels have remained constant and are expected to be stable in the future. All these employees are expected to receive benefits under the plan. It is calculated that the expected average remaining service life of the employees is 25 years. On December 31, 1993, the company's actuary submitted the following information:

Present value of future benefits attributed by the pension	
plan formula to employee services rendered in the current year	$140,000
Accrued benefit obligation	100,000
Employer's funding contribution for 1993 (made on Dec. 31, 1993)	150,000
Interest rate used in actuarial computations	8%
Expected return on plan assets	8%

During 1994, the company amended the pension plan by granting credit for past services performed prior to January 1, 1994, the date of the plan amendment. The plan amendment increased unrecognized past service cost by $120,000, which is to be amortized based on the expected average remaining service life of the employees. The company's accountants calculated the pension expense that is to be recognized in 1994 at $170,031.

Instructions

(Round to the nearest dollar.)

(a) Calculate the amount of the pension expense to be recognized in 1993. Explain.

(b) Prepare the journal entries to record pension expense and the employer's funding contribution for 1993.

(c) Describe how the company's accountants calculated the $170,031 as the pension expense to be recognized in 1994. Indicate each of the five components that make up the total amount to be recognized.

(PENSION EXPENSE, STATEMENT PRESENTATION) Golden Foods Company obtained the follow- **E20-16** ing information from the insurance company that administers the company's employee-defined benefit pension plan.

	For Year Ended December 31,		
	1993	1994	1995
Plan assets (at market value)	$270,000	$388,000	$586,000
Pension expense	95,000	128,000	140,000
Employer's funding contribution	110,000	160,000	125,000
Past service cost not yet recognized in earnings	494,230	451,365	420,438

Prior to 1993, cumulative pension expense recognized equal cumulative contributions. The company has decided to adopt the recommendations of the *CICA Handbook*, Section 3460, "Pension costs and obligations" beginning with the 1993 financial statements.

Instructions

(a) Prepare the journal entries to record pension expense and the employer's funding contribution for the years 1993, 1994, and 1995.

(b) Indicate the pension-related amounts that would be reported on the company's income statement and balance sheet for 1993, 1994, and 1995.

(JOURNAL ENTRIES, BALANCE SHEET ITEMS) Presented below is partial information related to the **E20-17** pension fund of Buttler Inc.

Funded Status (end of year)	1993	1994	1995
Plan assets at market	$1,300,000	$1,650,000	$1,800,000
Projected benefit obligation	1,600,000	1,910,000	2,500,000
Amounts to be recognized (Accrued)/Prepaid pension cost at beginning of year	–0–	25,000	22,000
Pension expense	250,000	268,000	310,000
Contribution	275,000	265,000	275,000
(Accrued)/prepaid pension cost at end of year	$ 25,000	$ 22,000	$ (13,000)

Instructions

(a) What pension-related amounts are reported on the balance sheet of Buttler Inc. for 1993, 1994, and 1995?

(b) What are the journal entries made to record pension expense in 1993, 1994, and 1995?

(RECONCILIATION SCHEDULE AND UNRECOGNIZED LOSS) Presented below is partial infor- **E20-18** mation related to Sharon Costume Company at December 31, 1994:

Market-related asset value	$700,000
Projected benefit obligation	950,000

(Continued)

Past service cost not yet recognized in pension expense	120,000
Unamortized experience gains and losses	–0–

Instructions

(a) Present a schedule reconciling the funded status with the asset/liability reported on the balance sheet.

(b) Assume the same facts as in (a) except that Sharon Costume Company has an experience loss of $18,000 during 1993. (Assume that EARSL is 10 years.)

(c) Explain the rationale for the treatment of the unrecognized loss and the past service cost not yet recognized in pension expense.

E20-19(AMORTIZATION OF EXPERIENCE GAIN OR LOSS, PENSION EXPENSE COMPUTATION) The actuary for the pension plan of Bailey Limited calculated the following net gains and losses.

	Net Gain or Loss

For the Year Ended December 31,	(Gain) or Loss
1993	$320,000
1994	480,000
1995	(240,000)
1996	(290,000)

Bailey Limited has a stable labour force of 400 employees who are expected to receive benefits. It is anticipated that the expected average remaining service life is 25 years. All these employees are expected to receive benefits under the plan. The company has elected to apply the recommendations of *CICA Handbook*, Section 3460, "Pension cost and obligation" beginning in 1993. As a result, the beginning balance of unrecognized net gain or loss is zero on January 1, 1993. (Assume that EARSL remains constant.)

Instructions

Prepare a schedule which reflects the amount of experience gain or loss amortized as a component of net periodic pension expense for each of the years 1993, 1994, 1995, and 1996.

E20-20(AMORTIZATION OF EXPERIENCE GAIN OR LOSS) Contour Company sponsors a defined benefit pension plan for its 500 employees. The company's actuary provided the following information about the plan.

	January 1,	December 31,	
	1993	1993	1994
Projected benefit obligation	$2,900,000	$3,750,000	$4,400,000
Plan assets at market value	1,700,000	2,600,000	3,100,000
Experience (gain) or loss	–0–	(110,000)	(24,000)
Discount rate		11%	8%
Expected asset return rate		10%	10%

The company anticipates that the expected average remaining service life of the employees is 10.5 years. All these employees are expected to receive benefits under the plan. The service cost component of net periodic pension expense for employee services rendered amounted to $400,000 in 1993 and $475,000 in 1994.

Instructions

(a) Compute the amount of the initial transition amount at January 1, 1993, assuming Contour wishes to follow *CICA Handbook*, Section 3460.

(b) Prepare a schedule which reflects the amount of unrecognized experience gain or loss to be amortized as a component of net periodic pension expensed for 1993 and 1994.

(c) Determine the total amount of net periodic pension expense to be recognized by the company in 1993 and 1994.

———— PROBLEMS ————

(TWO-YEAR WORK SHEET AND RECONCILIATION SCHEDULE) On January 1, 1994, Bob Bun- **P20-1** don Company had the following defined benefit pension plan balances:

Projected benefit obligation	$4,200,000
Fair value of plan assets	$4,200,000

The interest rate applicable to the pension obligation is 10%. On January 1, 1995, the company amends its pension agreement so that past service costs of $600,000 are created. Other data related to the pension plan are:

	1994	1995
Service costs	$150,000	$170,000
Unrecognized past service cost amortization	–0–	90,000
Contributions (funding) to the plan	150,000	184,658
Benefits paid	220,000	280,000
Actual return on plan assets	252,000	250,000
Expected return on plan assets	6%	8%

Instructions

(a) Prepare a pension work sheet for the pension plan for 1994 and 1995.

(b) As of December 31, 1995, prepare a schedule reconciling the funded status with the reported accrued pension cost.

(THREE-YEAR WORK SHEET, JOURNAL ENTRIES, AND RECONCILIATION SCHEDULES) **P20-2** Hisle Company adopts acceptable accounting for its defined benefit pension plan on January 1, 1994, with the following beginning balances: plan assets, $220,000; projected benefit obligation, $220,000. Other data relative to three years of operation of the plan are as follows.

	1994	1995	1996
Annual service cost	$17,000	$ 20,000	$ 28,000
Interest rate on accrued benefits and fund assets	10%	10%	10%
Actual return on plan assets	19,000	24,200	25,000
Annual funding (contributions)	17,000	43,000	48,000
Benefits paid	14,000	16,400	21,000

(Continued)

Unrecognized past service cost (plan amended, Jan. 1, 1995)		165,000	
Change in actuarial assumptions establishes a Dec. 31, 1996 projected benefit obligation of:			520,000
EARSL	10 years	10 years	10 years

Instructions

(a) Prepare a pension work sheet presenting all three years' pension balances and activities.

(b) Prepare the journal entries (from the work sheet) to reflect all pension plan transactions and events at December 31 of each year.

(c) At December 31 each year, prepare a schedule reconciling the funded status of the plan with the pension amounts reported in the financial statements.

P20-3 **(PENSION EXPENSE, JOURNAL ENTRIES, AMORTIZATION OF EXPERIENCE LOSS, REC- ONCILIATION SCHEDULE)** Samuels Company sponsors a defined benefit plan for its 100 employees. On January 1, 1993 (the date the company starts following Section 3460 of the *CICA Handbook*), the company's actuary provided the following information:

Unrecognized past service cost	$150,000
Pension plan assets (market-related asset value)	210,000
Accumulated benefit obligation	260,000
Projected benefit obligation	360,000

The average remaining service life for the participating employees is 10.5 years. All employees are expected to receive benefits under the plan. On December 31, 1993, the actuary calculated that the present value of future benefits earned for employee services rendered in the current year amounted to $60,000; the projected benefit obligation was $460,000; and the market-related asset value is $260,000. The expected return on plan assets and interest on the accrued benefits were both 10%. The actual return on plan assets is $12,000. The company's current year's contribution to the pension plan amounted to $75,000. No benefits were paid during the year.

Instructions

(Round to the nearest dollar.)

(a) Determine the components of pension expense that the company would recognize in 1993. (With only one year involved, you need not prepare a work sheet.)

(b) Prepare the journal entries to record the pension expense and the company's funding of the pension plan in 1993.

(c) Compute the amount of the 1993 increase/decrease in unrecognized experience gains or losses and the amount to be amortized in 1993 and 1994.

(d) Prepare a schedule reconciling the funded status of the plan with the pension amounts reported in the financial statements as of December 31, 1993.

P20-4 **(PENSION EXPENSE, ACTUAL RETURN COMPUTATION, FINANCIAL STATEMENT PRES- ENTATION, COMPUTATION OF EXPERIENCE GAIN OR LOSS, RECONCILIATION SCHEDULE)** Sesame Company sponsors a defined benefit pension plan for its 50 employees. On January 1, 1994 the company's actuary calculated the following:

Projected benefit obligation	$1,500,000
Plan assets (at market-related value)	800,000
Unamortized past service cost	400,000

The average remaining service life of the participating employees is 13 years. All employees are expected to receive benefits under the plan. The actuary calculated the present value of future benefits attributed to employees' services in the current year to be $65,000. A 10% interest rate is assumed for the actuarial computations. The expected return on plan assets is 11%. The company's funding contribution to the pension plan for 1994 was $135,000. The status of the pension plan's operations at December 31, 1994 is as follows:

Projected benefit obligation	$1,710,000
Pension plan assets (at market-related value)	960,000
Benefit payments	–0–

Instructions

(Round to the nearest dollar; with only one year involved, you need not prepare a work sheet.)

(a) Determine the amounts of the components of pension expense that should be recognized by the company in 1994.

(b) Prepare the journal entries to record pension expense and the employer's funding contribution for 1994.

(c) Indicate the pension-related amounts that would be reported on the company's income statement and balance sheet for the year 1994.

(d) Compute the amount of the 1994 increase/decrease in unamortized experience gains or losses and the amount to be amortized in 1994 and 1995.

(e) Prepare a schedule reconciling the funded status of the plan with the pension amounts reported in the financial statements as of December 31, 1994.

(COMPUTATION OF PENSION EXPENSE, AMORTIZATION OF EXPERIENCE GAIN OR LOSS, P20-5 AND JOURNAL ENTRIES FOR THREE YEARS) Bluemint Toothpaste Company initiates a defined benefit pension plan for its 50 employees on January 1, 1994. The insurance company which administers the pension plan provides the following information for the years 1994, 1995, and 1996.

	For Year Ended December 31,		
	1994	1995	1996
Plan assets (market-related value)	$50,000	$85,000	$170,000
Projected benefit obligation	55,000	91,550	303,194
Employer's funding contribution			
(made at end of year)	50,000	60,000	95,000

There were no balances as of January 1, 1994 when the plan was initiated. The actual and expected return on plan assets was 10% over the three-year period but the interest rate used in computing the projected benefit obligation was 13% in 1994, 11% in 1995, and 8% in 1996. The service cost component of net periodic pension expenses amounted to the following: 1994, $55,000; 1995, $85,000; and 1996, $115,000. The average remaining service life of the employee group was 13 years. No benefits were paid in 1994; $30,000 benefits were paid in 1995, $18,500 benefits were paid in 1996 (all benefits paid at end of year).

Instructions

(a) Calculate the amount of net periodic pension expense that the company would recognize in 1994, 1995, and 1996.

(b) Prepare the journal entries to record net periodic pension expense and the employer's funding contribution for the years 1994, 1995, and 1996.

P20-6 (COMPUTATION OF UNAMORTIZED PRIOR SERVICE COST AMORTIZATION, PENSION EXPENSE, JOURNAL ENTRIES, EXPERIENCE GAIN OR LOSS, AND RECONCILIATION SCHEDULE) Cramer Ltd. has sponsored a noncontributory-defined benefit pension plan for its employees since 1979. Prior to 1994, cumulative net pension expense recognized equalled cumulative contributions to the plan. Other relevant information about the pension plan on January 1, 1994 is as follows:

1. The company has 200 employees who are expected to receive benefits under the plan. The expected average remaining service life of the employees is 13 years.

2. The accrued benefit obligation amounted to $5,200,000 and the market-related value of plan assets was $3,000,000. Unamortized past service cost was $2,200,000.

On December 31, 1994, the accrued benefit obligation was $4,950,000. The market related value of plan assets was $3,790,000. A 10% interest rate and a 10% expected asset return rate was used in the actuarial present value computations in the pension plan. The present value of benefits attributed by the pension benefit formula to employee service in 1994 amounted to $250,000. The employer's contribution to the plan assets amounted to $585,000 in 1994.

Instructions

(a) Prepare a schedule, based on the expected future years of employee service, showing the unrecognized past service cost that would be amortized as a component of pension expense for 1994, 1995, and 1996.

(b) Compute pension expense for the year 1994.

(c) Prepare the journal entries required to report the accounting for the company's pension plan for 1994.

(d) Prepare a schedule reconciling the funded status of the plan with the pension amounts reported in the financial statements as of December 31, 1994.

P20-7 (PENSION WORK SHEET) Vince O'Reilly Corp. sponsors a defined benefit pension plan for its employees. On January 1, 1994, the following balances relate to this plan:

Plan assets (fair value)	$520,000
Projected benefit obligation	706,700
Prepaid/accrued pension cost (credit)	14,700
Unamortized past service cost	81,000
Unamortized experience gain or loss (debit)	91,000

As a result of the operation of the plan during 1994, the actuary provided the following additional data at December 31, 1994:

Service cost for 1994	$ 98,000
Expected return on assets	10%
Actual return on assets in 1994	48,000

(Continued)

Amortization of past service cost	20,000
Contributions in 1994	128,000
Benefits paid retirees in 1994	85,000
Average remaining service life of active employees	10 years
Expected and actual interest on obligation	9%

Instructions

Using the preceding data, compute pension expense for Vince O'Reilly Corp. for the year 1994 by preparing a pension work sheet that shows the journal entry for prepaid expense and any accrued pension cost. (Amortize the unrecognized gain or loss.) Use the market-related asset value to compute the expected return.

(COMPREHENSIVE TWO-YEAR WORK SHEET)   Brian Limited sponsors a defined benefit pension plan **P20-8** for its employees. The following data relate to the operation of the plan for the years 1993 and 1994.

	1993	1994
Projected benefit obligation, Jan. 1	$638,100	
Plan assets (fair value), Jan. 1	402,300	
Prepaid/Accrued pension cost (credit), Jan. 1	77,400	
Unamortized past service cost, Jan. 1	158,400	
Service cost	39,000	$ 48,000
Expected rate of return	10%	10%
Actual return on plan assets	36,000	66,000
Amortization of past service cost	62,400	52,800
Annual contributions	72,000	81,000
Benefits paid retirees	31,500	54,000
Increase in projected benefit obligation due to		
changes in actuarial assumptions	85,590	–0–
Average service life of all employees		20 years
Vested benefit obligation at Dec. 31		464,000

Instructions

(a)   Prepare a pension work sheet presenting both years 1993 and 1994 and accompanying computations.

(b)   Prepare the journal entries (from the work sheet) to reflect all pension plan transactions and events at December 31 of each year.

(c)   At December 31, 1994, prepare a schedule reconciling the funded status of the pension plan with the pension amounts reported in the financial statements.

(COMPREHENSIVE PENSION WORK SHEET)   Al Zelony was recently promoted to assistant controller **P20-9** of Haber Corporation, having previously served Haber as a staff accountant. One of the responsibilities of his new position is to prepare the annual pension accrual. Julius Berger, the corporate controller, provided Zelony with last year's workpapers and information from the actuary's annual report. The pension work sheet for the prior year is presented below.

| | Journal Entry | | | | Memo Records | |
	Pension Expense	Cash	Prepaid (Accrued) Cost	Projected Benefit Obligation	Plan Assets	Unamortized Past Service Cost
6-1-92[1]				$(20,000)	$20,000	
Service cost[1]	$1,800			(1,800)		
Interest[2]	1,200			(1,200)		
Actual return[3]	(1,600)				1,600	
Contribution[1]		$(1,000)			1,000	
Benefits paid[1]				900	(900)	
Prior service cost[4]				(2,000)		$2,000
Journal entry	$1,400	$(1,000)	$(400)			
May 31, 1993 balance			$(400)	$(24,100)	$21,700	$2,000

[1]Per actuary's report.

[2]Beginning projected benefit obligation × discount rate of 6%.

[3]Expected return was $1,600 (beginning plan assets × expected return of 8%).

[4]A plan amendment that granted employees retroactive benefits for work performed in earlier periods took effect on May 31, 1993. The amendment increased the May 31, 1993 projected benefit obligation by $2,000. No amortization was recorded in the fiscal year ended May 31, 1993.

Pertinent information from the actuary's report for the year ended May 31, 1994 is presented below. The report indicated no actuarial gains or losses in the fiscal year ended May 31, 1994.

Contribution	$ 100
Service cost	$ 2,400
Expected interest on obligation	6%
Accumulated benefits obligation 5-31-93	$21,000
Accumulated benefits obligation 5-31-94	$27,000
Expected and actual return on plan assets	$ 1,736
Benefits paid	$ 500
Average remaining service life	10 years
Fair value plan assets 5-31-93	$21,700
Fair value plan assets 5-31-94	$23,036

When briefing Zelony, Berger indicated that the past service cost is to be amortized over the average remaining service life.

Instructions

(a) Prepare the pension work sheet for Haber Corporation for the year ended May 31, 1994.

(b) Prepare the journal entries required to reflect the accounting for Haber Corporation's pension plan for the year ended May 31, 1994.

(CMA adapted)

──────── **FINANCIAL REPORTING PROBLEM** ────────

Refer to the financial statements and other documents of Moore Corporation Limited presented in Appendix 5A and answer the following questions:

1. What kinds of pension plans does Moore offer to its employees? How are the funding policies determined for each of these pension plans?

2. What were the amounts of Moore's prepaid pension cost and accrued pension cost at the end of 1991 and 1992? How did the Corporation report the prepaid and accrued pension cost?

3. What were the amounts of net periodic pension cost for Moore's pension plans for the years 1990 and 1991? What was the discount rate used to determine the projected benefit obligation for 1991? What was the expected long-term rate of return for plan assets?

Accounting for Leases

■

A lease is a contractual agreement between a **lessor** and a **lessee** that gives the lessee the right to use specific property, owned by the lessor, for a specific period of time in return for stipulated, and generally periodic, cash payments (rents). An essential element of the lease agreement is that the lessor conveys less than the total interest in the property. Because of the financial, operating, and risk advantages that the lease arrangement provides, many businesses lease substantial amounts of property, both real and personal, as an alternative to ownership.

Over the past two and a half decades, leasing has grown tremendously in popularity and today it is the fastest-growing form of capital investment. Instead of borrowing money to buy an airplane, a computer, a nuclear core, or a satellite, a company leases it. Even gambling casinos lease their slot machines. Airlines and railroads lease huge amounts of equipment; many hotel and motel chains lease their facilities; and most retail chains lease the bulk of their retail premises and warehouses.

The increased significance and prevalence of lease arrangements in recent years have intensified the need for uniform accounting and complete informative reporting of these transactions.[1]

LEASE PROVISIONS

Because a lease is a contract, the provisions agreed to by the lessor and lessee may vary widely and be limited only by their ingenuity. The **duration** (lease term) of the lease may be from a few moments to the entire expected economic life of the asset. The **rental payments** may be level from year to year, increasing in amount, or decreasing. The rents may be predetermined or may vary with sales, the prime interest rate, the consumer price index, or some other factor. In most cases the rent is set to enable the lessor to recover the cost of the asset plus a fair return over the life of the lease.

The **obligations for taxes, insurance, and maintenance** (executory costs) may be assumed by either the lessor or the lessee, or they may be divided. **Restrictions** comparable to those in bond indentures may limit the lessee's activities relative to dividend payments or the incurrence of further debt and lease obligations. The lease contract may be **noncancellable** or may grant the right to **early termination** on payment of a set scale of prices plus a penalty. In case of **default**, the lessee may be liable for all future payments at once, receiving title to the property in exchange, or the lessor may enjoy the prerogative to sell and to collect from the lessee all or a portion of the difference between the sale price and the lessor's unrecovered cost.

Alternatives of the lessee at termination of the lease may range from none to the right to purchase the leased asset at the fair market value or the right to renew or buy at a nominal price.[2]

ADVANTAGES OF LEASING

Although the lease arrangement is not without its disadvantages, the growth in its use suggests that leasing often has a genuine advantage over owning property. Some of the commonly discussed advantages to the lessee of leasing include the following.

---

[1] The popularity and general applicability of leasing are evidenced by the fact that 223 of 300 companies surveyed by the CICA in 1990 disclosed either capitalized or noncapitalized lease data. *Financial Reporting in Canada—1991* (Toronto: CICA, 1991).

[2] John H. Myers, "Reporting of Leases in Financial Statements, *Accounting Research Study No. 4* (New York: AICPA, 1964), pp. 10–11.

1. **100% financing at fixed rates.** Leases are often executed without requiring any money down from the lessee, which helps to conserve scarce cash—an especially desirable feature for new and developing companies. In addition, lease payments often remain fixed, which protects the lessee against inflation and increases in the cost of money. The following comment regarding a conventional loan is typical: "Our local bank finally came up to 80% of the purchase price but wouldn't go any higher, and they wanted a floating interest rate. We just couldn't afford the down payment and we needed to lock in a final payment rate we knew we could live with."

2. **Protection against obsolescence.** Leasing equipment reduces risk of obsolescence to the lessee, and in many cases passes the risk in residual value to the lessor. For example, Syntex Corp. (pharmaceutical maker) leases Wang computers. Syntex is permitted under the lease agreement to turn in an old computer for a new model at any time, cancelling the old lease and writing a new one. The cost of the new lease is added to the balance due on the old lease, less the old computer's trade-in value. As the treasurer of Syntex remarked, "Our instinct is to purchase. But if a new computer comes along in a short time, then leasing is just a heck of a lot more convenient than purchasing."

3. **Flexibility.** Lease agreements may contain less restrictive provisions than other debt agreements. Innovative lessors can tailor a lease agreement to the lessee's special needs. For instance, rental payments can be structured to meet the timing of cash revenues generated by the equipment, so that payments are made when the equipment is productive.

4. **Less costly financing.** Some companies find leasing cheaper than other forms of financing. For example, start-up companies in depressed industries or companies in low tax brackets may lease as a way of claiming tax benefits that might otherwise be lost. Investment tax credits and capital cost allowance deductions are of no benefit to companies that have little if any taxable income. Through leasing, these tax benefits are used by the leasing companies or financial institutions, which can pass some of these tax benefits back to the user of the asset in the form of lower rental payments.

5. **Off-balance-sheet financing.** Certain leases do not add debt on a balance sheet or affect financial ratios, and may add to borrowing capacity.[3] Off balance sheet financing is critical to some companies. For instance, the balance sheet of Chart House, Inc., which operated over 500 restaurants in the United States, showed long-term debt of $127 million and total shareholders' equity of $88 million. Therefore, Chart House's debt-to-equity ratio was a high but manageable 1.4 to 1. But the company also had lease obligations chiefly for restaurant land; the future rental payments related to those noncancellable operating leases was $125 million. Add the capitalized value of these payments to the long-term debt and Chart House's debt-to-equity ratio climbed well over 2 to 1. In the late seventies, Safeway Stores was first required to capitalize lease commitments with a present value of $748 million on a balance sheet showing only $131 million in long-term debt. Or, consider what the situation of Glosser Bros., Inc., a retail department store chain, would be if it had to capitalize its future minimum lease commitments on noncancellable leases of $70 million on its balance sheet showing less than $4 million of long-term debt and $32 million of equity.

CONCEPTUAL NATURE OF A LEASE

If Echo Bay Mines Ltd. borrows $15,000,000 on a 10-year note from the Royal Bank of Canada to purchase a Boeing 727 jet plane, it is clear that an asset and related liability should be reported on Echo Bay's balance sheet at that amount. If Echo Bay purchases the 727 jet for $15,000,000 directly

---

[3] As demonstrated later in this chapter, certain types of lease arrangements need not be capitalized on the balance sheet. The liability section is frequently relieved of large future lease commitments that, if recorded, would adversely affect the debt-to-equity ratio. The reluctance to record lease obligations as liabilities is one of the primary reasons that capitalized lease accounting is resisted and circumvented by lessees.

from Boeing through an instalment purchase over 10 years, it is equally clear that an asset and related liability should be reported. However, if Echo Bay leases the Boeing 727 for 10 years through a noncancellable lease transaction with payments of the same amount as the instalment purchase transaction, differences of opinion start to develop over how this and other types of lease transactions should be reported. The various views of accounting for leases are as follows:

Do Not Capitalize Any Leased Assets. Because the lessee does not have ownership of the property, capitalization under this view is considered inappropriate. Furthermore, a lease is an "executory" contract requiring continuing performance by both parties. Because other executory contracts (such as purchase commitments and employment contracts) are not capitalized at present, leases should not be capitalized.

Capitalize Those Leases Similar to Instalment Purchases. Accountants should report transactions in accordance with their economic substance; therefore, if instalment purchases are capitalized, so also should leases that have similar characteristics. For example, in the illustration above, Echo Bay is committed to the same payments over a 10-year period for either a lease or an instalment purchase; lessees simply make rental payments, while owners make mortgage payments. Why shouldn't the financial statements report these transactions in the same manner?

Capitalize All Long-Term Leases. Under this approach, the only requirement for capitalization is the long-term right to use the property. This property rights approach capitalizes all long-term leases.[4]

Capitalize Firm Leases Where the Penalty for Nonperformance Is Substantial. A final approach is to capitalize only firm (noncancellable) contractual rights and obligations. "Firm" means that it is unlikely that performance under the lease can be avoided without a severe penalty.[5]

In short, the various viewpoints range from no capitalization to capitalization of all leases. The CICA apparently agrees with the capitalization approach when it is similar to an instalment purchase, noting that *a lease that transfers substantially all of the benefits and risks of ownership of property should be capitalized*.

This viewpoint leads to three basic conclusions: (1) the characteristics that indicate that substantially all of the benefits and risks of ownership have been transferred must be identified; (2) the same characteristics should apply consistently to the lessee and the lessor; (3) those leases that do *not* transfer substantially all of the benefits and risks of ownership are **operating leases** and should not be capitalized but rather accounted for as rental payments and receipts.

By capitalizing the present value of the future rental payments, the *lessee* records an asset and a liability at an amount generally representative of the asset's market value or purchase price. The *lessor*, having transferred substantially all of the benefits and risks of ownership, recognizes a sale by removing the asset from the balance sheet and replacing it with a receivable. The typical journal entries for the lessee and the lessor, assuming that equipment is leased and is capitalized, appear as shown below.

Lessee			Lessor		
Leased Equipment	XXX		Lease Receivable (net)	XXX	
Lease Obligation		XXX	Equipment		XXX

---

[4] See, for example, *Accounting Research Study No. 4*, which advocated this position.

[5] Yuji Ijiri, "Recognition of Contractual Rights and Obligations," *Research Report* (Stamford, CT: FASB, 1980).

Having capitalized the asset, the lessee records the depreciation. The lessor and lessee treat the rental payments as consisting of interest and principal.

If the lease is not capitalized, no asset is recorded by the lessee and no asset is removed from the lessor's books. When a lease payment is made, the lessee records rental expense and the lessor recognizes rental revenue.

The remainder of this chapter presents the different types of leases and the specific criteria, accounting rules, and disclosure requirements set forth by the CICA in accounting for leases.

ACCOUNTING BY LESSEES

In attempting to standardize accounting for leases, the CICA tried to determine when the risks and benefits of ownership transfer. If conditions are similar to an instalment purchase, in effect, the lessee should capitalize the lease and the lessor should remove the asset from its balance sheet. If the transaction does not meet certain criteria, the lease should not be capitalized. Therefore, from the standpoint of the lessee, all leases may be classified for accounting purposes as follows:

1. Operating leases (noncapitalization method).

2. Capital leases (capitalization method).

If at the date of the lease agreement (inception of the lease)[6] the lease meets _one or more_ of the following three criteria, the lessee shall classify and account for the arrangement as a **capital lease:**[7]

> *Objective 2*
>
> Describe the lessee accounting criteria and procedures for capitalizing leases.

Capitalization Criteria (Lessee)

1. There is reasonable assurance that the lessee will obtain ownership of the leased property by the end of the lease term.

2. The lease term is such that the lessee will receive substantially all of the economic benefits expected to be derived from the use of the leased property over its life span. This is usually assumed to occur if the lease term is 75% or more of the economic life of the leased property.

3. The present value of the minimum lease payments (excluding executory costs) is equal to substantially all (usually 90% or more) of the fair value of the leased property.

Leases that do not meet any of the three criteria listed above are classified and accounted for by the lessee as **operating leases.** The flow chart on page 1038 shows that a lease meeting any one of the three criteria above results in the lessee having a capital lease.

EXAMINATION OF CAPITALIZATION CRITERIA

The three capitalization criteria applicable to lessees are controversial and can be difficult to apply in practice. They are discussed in detail in the following pages.

Transfer of Ownership Test

If the lease transfers ownership of the asset to the lessee, it is a capital lease. This criterion is not controversial and is easily implemented in practice.

---

[6] *CICA Handbook* (Toronto: CICA), Section 3065, par. .03(k).
[7] *Ibid.*

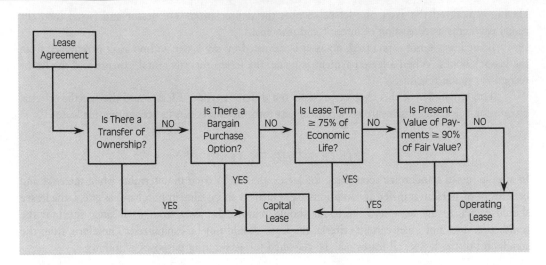

The transfer of ownership may be facilitated at the end of the lease term without additional consideration or through a bargain purchase option. A **bargain purchase option** is a provision allowing the lessee to purchase the leased property for a price that is significantly lower than the property's expected fair value at the date the option becomes exercisable. At the inception of the lease, the difference between the option price and the expected fair market value must be large enough to make exercise of the option reasonably assured.

For example, assume that you are to lease a car for $350 per month for 40 months with an option to purchase for $100 at the end of the 40-month period. If the estimated fair value of the car is $4,000 at the end of 40 months, the $100 option to purchase is clearly a bargain and, therefore, capitalization is required. In other cases, the criterion may not be as easy to apply, and to determine now that a certain future price is a bargain can be difficult.

Economic Life Test (75% Test)

If the lease period equals or exceeds 75% of the asset's economic life, it follows that most of the risks and rewards of ownership are transferred to the lessee and, therefore, capitalization is appropriate. However, determining the lease term and economic life of the asset may be troublesome.

The lease term is generally considered the fixed, noncancellable term of the lease. However, this period can be extended if a bargain renewal option is provided in the lease agreement. A **bargain renewal option** is a provision allowing the lessee to renew the lease for a rental that is lower than the expected fair rental at the date the option becomes exercisable. At the inception of the lease, the difference between the renewal rental and the expected fair rental must be great enough to make the exercise of the option to renew reasonably assured.

For example, if a computer is leased for three years at a rental of $100 per month, and then subsequently can be leased for $10 per month for another two years, it clearly is a bargain renewal option and the lease term is considered to be five years. However, as with bargain purchase options, it is sometimes difficult to determine what is a bargain.[8]

Determining estimated economic life can also pose problems, especially if the leased item is a specialized item or has been used for a significant period of time. For example, determining the economic life of a nuclear core is extremely difficult because it is subject to much more than normal wear and tear.

---

[8] The original lease term is also extended for leases having the following: substantial penalties for nonrenewal; periods for which the lessor has the option to renew or extend the lease; renewal periods preceding the date on which a bargain purchase option becomes exercisable; and renewal periods where any lessee guarantees of the lessor's debt are expected to be in effect or in which there will be a loan outstanding from the lessee to the lessor.

Recovery of Investment Test (90% Test)

If the present value of the minimum lease payments equals or exceeds 90% of the fair market value of the asset, then the leased asset should be capitalized. The rationale for this test is that if the present value of the minimum lease payments is reasonably close to the market price of the asset, the asset is being purchased.

In determining the present value of the minimum lease payments, three important concepts are involved: (1) minimum lease payments, (2) executory costs, and (3) discount rate.

Minimum Lease Payments. These are payments that the lessee is obligated to make or can be expected to make in connection with the leased property. Minimum lease payments include the following:

1. **Minimum Rental Payments.** Minimum payments the lessee is obligated to make to the lessor under the lease agreement. In some cases, the minimum rental payments may be equal to the minimum lease payments. However, the minimum lease payments may also include a guaranteed residual value (if any), penalty for failure to renew, or a bargain purchase option (if any), as noted below.

2. **Guaranteed Residual Value.** The residual value is the estimated fair (market) value of the leased property at the end of the lease term. The lessor often transfers the risk of loss to the lessee or to a third party through a guarantee of the estimated residual value. The **guaranteed residual value** is (1) the certain or determinable amount at which the lessor has the right to require the lessee to purchase the asset or (2) the amount that the lessee or the third-party guarantor guarantees the lessor will realize. If it is not guaranteed in full, the **unguaranteed residual value** is "that portion of the residual value of leased property which is not guaranteed or is guaranteed solely by a party related to the lessor."[9]

3. **Penalty for Failure to Renew or Extend the Lease.** The amount payable that is required of the lessee if the agreement specifies that the lease must be extended or renewed and the lessee fails to do so.

4. **Bargain Purchase Option.** As indicated earlier, an option given to the lessee to purchase the equipment at the end of the lease term at a price that is fixed sufficiently below the expected fair value, so that at the inception of the lease, purchase appears to be reasonably assured.

Executory costs (defined below) are not included in the lessee's computation of the present value of the minimum lease payments.

Executory Costs. Like most assets, leased tangible assets require the incurrence of insurance, maintenance, and tax expenses (called **executory costs**) during their economic life. If the lessor retains responsibility for the payment of these ownership-type costs, a portion of each lease payment that represents executory costs *should be excluded* in computing the present value of the minimum lease payments because this portion of the lease payment does not represent payment on or a reduction of the obligation. If the portion of the minimum lease payments representing executory costs is not determinable from the provisions of the lease, an estimate of the amount must be made. Many lease agreements, however, specify that these executory costs be assumed by the lessee; in these cases, the rental payments can be used without adjustment in the present value computation.

Discount Rate. The lessee computes the present value of the minimum lease payments using the **lessee's incremental borrowing rate**, which is defined as: "The interest rate that, at the inception of the lease, the lessee would have incurred to borrow, over a similar term and with similar security for the borrowing, the funds necessary to purchase the leased asset."[10] For example, assume that

---

[9] *CICA Handbook*, Section 3065, par. .03(t).

[10] *Ibid.*, par. .03(p).

Mortensen Ltd. decides to lease computer equipment for a five-year period at a cost of $10,000 per year. To determine whether the present value of these payments is less than 90% of the fair value of the property, the lessee discounts this amount using its incremental borrowing rate. The determination of the incremental borrowing rate will often require judgement because it is based on a hypothetical purchase of the property.

However, there is one exception to this rule. If (1) the lessee knows the **implicit rate computed by the lessor** and (2) it is less than the lessee's incremental borrowing rate, then the lessee must use the implicit rate. The **interest rate implicit in the lease** is the discount rate that, when applied to the minimum lease payments and the unguaranteed residual value accruing to the lessor, causes the aggregate present value to be equal to the fair value of the leased property to the lessor.[11]

The purpose of this exception is twofold. First, the implicit rate of the lessor is generally a *more realistic rate* to use in determining the amount (if any) to report as the asset and related liability for the lessee. Second, the guideline is provided to ensure that the lessee *does not use an artificially high incremental borrowing rate* that would cause the present value of the minimum lease payments to be less than 90% of the fair market value of the property and thus make it possible to avoid capitalization of the asset and related liability. The lessee may argue that it cannot determine the implicit rate of the lessor and therefore the higher rate should be used. However, in many cases, the implicit rate used by the lessor can be approximated. The determination of whether a reasonable estimate could be made will require judgement, particularly where the result from using the incremental borrowing rate comes close to meeting the 90% test. Because the *lessee may not capitalize the leased property at more than its fair value* (as discussed later), the lessee is prevented from using an excessively low discount rate.

Asset and Liability Accounted for Differently

In a capital lease transaction, the lessee is using the lease as a source of financing. The lessor finances the transaction (provides the investment capital) through the leased asset and the lessee makes rent payments, which actually are instalment payments. Therefore, over the life of the property rented, *the rental payments to the lessor constitute a payment of principal plus interest.*

Asset and Liability Recorded. Under the capital lease method, the lessee treats the lease transaction as if an asset was being purchased in a financing transaction in which an asset is acquired and an obligation is created. The lessee records a capital lease as an asset and a liability at the lower of (1) the present value of the minimum lease payments (excluding executory costs) and (2) the fair market value of the leased asset at the inception of the lease. The rationale for this approach is that the leased asset should not be recorded for more than its fair market value.

Depreciation (Amortization) Period. One troublesome aspect of accounting for the amortization (depreciation) of the capitalized leased asset relates to the period of amortization. For example, if the lease agreement satisfies criterion (1) (that is, transfers ownership of the asset to the lessee or contains a bargain purchase option), the leased asset is depreciated in a manner consistent with the lessee's normal depreciation policy for owned assets, *using the economic life of the asset.*

On the other hand, if the lease does not transfer ownership or does not contain a bargain purchase option, the leased asset is depreciated over the *term of the lease*. In this case, the leased asset reverts to the lessor after a certain period of time.

Effective Interest Method. Throughout the term of the lease, the *effective interest method* is used to allocate each lease payment between principal and interest. This method produces a constant rate of interest in each period on the obligation's outstanding balance.

The discount rate used by the lessee in determining the present value of the minimum lease payments must be used by the lessee in applying the effective interest method to capital leases.

---

[11] *Ibid.*, par. .03(m).

Depreciation Method. Although the amount initially capitalized as an asset and recorded as an obligation are computed at the same present value, the ***depreciation (amortization) of the asset and the discharge of the obligation are independent accounting processes*** during the term of the lease. The lessee should depreciate the leased asset by applying conventional depreciation methods: straight-line, sum-of-the-years'-digits, declining balance, units-of-production, etc. The selection of a depreciation method should be in line with the objectives of income measurement and asset valuation.

The CICA uses the term "amortization" more frequently than the term "depreciation" in recognition of intangible leased property rights. The authors prefer the term "depreciation" as a description of the write-off of the costs of the expired services of a tangible asset.

Capitalized Lease Method Illustrated (Lessee)

Lessor Company and Lessee Company sign a lease agreement dated January 1, 1994 that calls for Lessor Company to lease equipment to Lessee Company beginning January 1, 1994. The lease agreement contains the following terms and provisions:

1. The term of the lease is five years and the lease agreement is noncancellable, requiring equal rental payments of $25,981.62 at the beginning of each year (annuity due basis).

2. The equipment has a fair value at the inception of the lease of $100,000, an estimated economic life of five years, and no residual value.

3. Lessee Company pays all of the executory costs directly to third parties except for the property taxes of $2,000 per year, which are included in the annual payments.

4. The lease contains no renewal options and the equipment reverts to Lessor Company at the termination of the lease.

5. Lessee Company's incremental borrowing rate is 11% per year.

6. Lessee Company depreciates on a straight-line basis similar equipment that it owns.

7. Lessor Company set the annual rental to ensure a rate of return on its investment of 10% per year; this fact is known to Lessee Company.[12]

The lease meets the criteria for classification as a capital lease because (1) the lease term of five years, being equal to the equipment's estimated economic life of five years, satisfies the 75% test and (2) the present value of the minimum lease payments ($100,000, as computed below) exceeds 90% of the fair value of the property ($100,000).

The minimum lease payments are $119,908.10 ($23,981.62 × 5) and the amount capitalized as leased assets is computed as the present value of the minimum lease payments (excluding executory costs—property taxes—of $2,000) as follows.

Capitalized amount = ($25,981.62 − $2,000) × present value of an annuity due of
$1 for 5 periods at 10%
(Table A-5)

= $23,981.62 × 4.16986

= **$100,000**

---

[12] If Lessee Company had an incremental borrowing rate of, for example, 9% (lower than the 10% rate used by Lessor Company) and it had not known the rate used by Lessor Company, the present value computation would yield a capitalized amount of $101,675.35 ($23,981.62 × 4.23972). Because this amount exceeds the $100,000 fair value of the equipment, Lessee Company would have to capitalize the $100,000 and use 10% as its effective rate for amortization of the lease obligation.

The lessor's implicit interest rate of 10% is used instead of the lessee's incremental borrowing rate of 11% because (1) it is lower and (2) the lessee has knowledge of it.

The entry to record the capital lease on Lessee Company's books on January 1, 1994 is:

Leased Equipment Under Capital Leases	100,000	
Obligations Under Capital Leases		100,000

Note that the preceding entry records the obligation at the net amount of $100,000 (the present value of the future rental payments) rather than at the gross amount of $119,908.10 ($23,981.62 × 5).

The journal entry to record the *first lease payment on January 1, 1994* is as follows:

Property Tax Expense	2,000.00	
Obligations Under Capital Leases	23,981.62	
Cash		25,981.62

Each lease payment of $25,981.62 consists of three elements: (1) a reduction in the lease obligation, (2) a financing cost (interest expense), and (3) executory costs (property taxes). The total financing cost (interest expense) over the term of the lease is the difference between the present value ($100,000) of the lease payments and the actual cash disbursed, net of executory costs ($119,908.10), or $19,908.10. Therefore, the annual interest expense is a function of the outstanding obligation, as illustrated in the following schedule.

Lessee Company
Lease Amortization Schedule
(Annuity due basis)

Date	Annual Lease Payment	Executory Costs	Interest (10%) on Unpaid Obligation	Reduction of Lease Obligation	Balance of Lease Obligation
	(a)	(b)	(c)	(d)	(e)
Jan. 1/94					$100,000.00
Jan. 1/94	$ 25,981.62	$ 2,000.00	–0–	$ 23,981.62	76,018.38
Jan. 1/95	25,981.62	2,000.00	$ 7,601.84	16,379.78	59,638.60
Jan. 1/96	25,981.62	2,000.00	5,963.86	18,017.76	41,620.84
Jan. 1/97	25,981.62	2,000.00	4,162.08	19,819.54	21,801.30
Jan. 1/98	25,981.62	2,000.00	2,180.32*	21,801.30	–0–
	$129,908.10	$10,000.00	$19,908.10	$100,000.00	

(a) Lease payment as required by lessor.
(b) Executory costs included in rental payment.
(c) Ten percent of the preceding balance of (e) except for Jan. 1, 1994; since this is an annuity due, no time has elapsed at the date of the first payment and no interest has accrued.
(d) (a) minus (b) and (c).
(e) Preceding balance minus (d).
*Rounded by 19 cents.

At December 31, 1994, Lessee Company's fiscal year end, *accrued interest* is recorded as follows:

Interest Expense	7,601.84	
Interest Payable		7,601.84

Depreciation of the leased equipment over its lease term of five years, applying Lessee Company's normal depreciation policy (straight-line method), results in the following entry on December 31, 1994:

Depreciation Expense—Leased Equipment	20,000	
Accumulated Depreciation—Leased Equipment		
($100,000 ÷ 5 years)		20,000

At December 31, 1994, the assets recorded under capital leases are separately identified on the lessee's balance sheet. Similarly, the related obligations are separately identified. The portion due within one year or the operating cycle, whichever is longer, is classified with current liabilities and the rest with noncurrent liabilities. For example, the current portion of the December 31, 1994 total obligation of $76,018.38 in the lessee's amortization schedule is the amount of the reduction in the obligation in 1995, or $16,379.78. The liability section as it relates to lease transactions at December 31, 1994 would appear as follows.

Current Liabilities	
Interest Payable	$ 7,601.84
Obligation Under Capital Leases	16,379.78
Noncurrent Liabilities	
Obligations Under Capital Leases	$59,638.60

The journal entry to record the lease payment of January 1, 1995 is as follows:

Property Tax Expense	2,000.00	
Interest Expense (or Interest Payable)	7,601.84	
Obligations Under Capital Leases	16,379.78	
Cash		25,981.62

Entries through 1998 would follow the pattern above. Other executory costs (insurance and maintenance) assumed by Lessee Company would be recorded in a manner similar to that used to record any other operating costs incurred on assets owned by Lessee Company.

On expiration of the lease, the amount capitalized as leased equipment is fully amortized and the lease obligation is fully discharged. If not purchased, the equipment would be returned to the lessor, and the leased equipment and related accumulated depreciation accounts would be removed from the books.[13] If the equipment is purchased at termination of the lease at a price of $5,000, and the estimated life of the equipment is changed from five to seven years, the following entry might be made:

Equipment ($100,000 + $5,000)	105,000	
Accumulated Depreciation—Capital Leases	100,000	
Leased Equipment Under Capital Leases		100,000
Accumulated Depreciation—Equipment		100,000
Cash		5,000

Operating Method (Lessee)

Under the **operating method,** rent expense (and a compensating liability) accrues day by day to the lessee as the property is used. The lessee assigns rent to the periods benefiting from the use of the

---

[13] If the lessee purchases a leased asset during the term of a capital lease, it may be accounted for as a renewal or an extension of a capital lease. This is done by adjusting the carrying value of the asset for any difference between the agreed purchase price and the carrying amount of the lease obligation at the purchase date.

asset and ignores, in the accounting, any commitments to make future payments. Appropriate accruals or deferrals are made if the accounting period ends between cash payment dates. For example, assume that the capital lease illustrated above did not qualify as a capital lease and was therefore accounted for as an operating lease. The first-year charge to operations would have been $25,981.62, the amount of the rental payment. The journal entry to record this payment on January 1, 1994 would be as follows:

| Rent Expense | 25,981.62 | |
| Cash | | 25,981.62 |

The rented asset, as well as any long-term liability for future rental payments, is not reported on the balance sheet. Rent expense would be reported on the income statement. In addition, note disclosure is required for operating leases that have initial lease terms in excess of one year. An illustration of the type of note disclosure required for an operating lease (as well as other types of leases) is provided later in this chapter.

Comparison of Capital Lease With Operating Lease

Objective 3

Contrast the operating and capitalization methods of recording leases.

As indicated above, if the lease had been accounted for as an operating lease, the first-year charge to operations would have been $25,981.62, the amount of the rental payment. Treating the transaction as a capital lease, however, resulted in a first-year charge of $29,601.84: depreciation of $20,000 (assuming straight-line), interest expense of $7,601.84 (per schedule on page 1042), and executory costs of $2,000. The schedule below shows that while the *total* charges to operations are the same over the lease term whether the lease is accounted for as a capital lease or as an operating lease, under the capital lease treatment the charges are higher in the earlier years and lower in the later years.[14]

Lessee Company
Schedule of Charges to Operations
Capital Lease vs. Operating Lease

| | Capital Lease Charges | | | | Operating Lease | |
Year	Depreciation	Executory Costs	Interest	Total Charge	Charge	Difference
1994	$ 20,000	$ 2,000	$ 7,601.84	$ 29,601.84	$ 25,981.62	$ 3,620.22
1995	20,000	2,000	5,963.86	27,963.86	25,981.62	1,982.24
1996	20,000	2,000	4,162.08	26,162.08	25,981.62	180.46
1997	20,000	2,000	2,180.32	24,180.32	25,981.62	(1,801.30)
1998	20,000	2,000	—	22,000.00	25,981.62	(3,981.62)
	$100,000	$10,000	$19,908.10	$129,908.10	$129,908.10	$ –0–

If an accelerated method of depreciation is used, the differences between the amount charged to operations under the two methods would be even larger in the earlier and later years.

In addition, using the capital lease approach would have resulted in an asset and related liability of $100,000 being initially reported on the balance sheet; no such asset or liability would be reported under the operating method. Therefore, the following occurs if a capital lease instead of an operating

---

[14] The higher charges in the early years are one reason lessees are reluctant to adopt the capital lease accounting method. Lessees (especially those of real estate) claim that it is really not more costly to operate the leased asset in the early years than in the later years; thus, they advocate an even charge similar to that produced by the operating method.

lease is employed: (1) an increase in the amount of reported debt (both short term and long term), (2) an increase in the amount of total assets (specifically long-lived assets), and (3) a lower income early in the life of the lease and, therefore, lower retained earnings. Thus, many companies believe that capital leases have a detrimental impact on their financial position as their debt-to-total-equity ratio increases and their rate of return on total assets decreases. As a result, the business community resists capitalizing leases.

Whether their resistance is well founded is a matter of conjecture. From a cash flow point of view, the company is in the same position whether the lease is accounted for as an operating or a capital lease. The reasons managers often argue against capitalization are: (1) it can more easily lead to violation of loan covenants, (2) it can affect the amount of compensation received by owners (for example, a stock compensation plan tied to earnings), and (3) it can lower rates of return and increase debt to equity relationships, thus making the company less attractive to present and potential investors.[15]

ACCOUNTING BY LESSORS

Leasing's advantages to the lessee were discussed earlier in this chapter. Three important benefits are available to the lessor:

1. **Interest Revenue.** Leasing is a form of financing; therefore, financial institutions and leasing companies find leasing attractive because it provides competitive interest margins.

2. **Tax Incentives.** In many cases, companies cannot use the tax benefit, but leasing provides them with an opportunity to transfer such tax benefits to another party in return for a lower rental rate on the leased asset. To illustrate, Boeing Aircraft recently sold one of its 767 jet planes to a wealthy investor who did not need the plane but could use the tax benefit. The investor then leased the plane to a foreign airline, which cannot use the tax benefits. Everyone gains. Boeing is able to sell its 767, the investor receives the tax benefits, and the foreign airline finds a cheaper way to acquire a 767.[16]

3. **High Residual Value.** Another advantage of leasing is the reversion of the property to the lessor at the end of the lease term. Residual values can produce very large profits. For example, Citicorp at one time assumed that the commercial aircraft it was leasing to the airline industry would have a residual of 5% of its purchase price. It turned out that the planes were worth 150% of their cost—a handsome price appreciation. Even though three years later these same planes slumped to 80% of their cost, the appreciation was still far more than 5%.

Economics of Leasing

The lessor determines the amount of the rental, basing that amount on the rate of return—the **implicit rate**—needed to justify leasing the asset. The factors considered in establishing the rate of return are the credit standing of the lessee, the length of the lease, the status of the residual value (guaranteed versus unguaranteed), and so on. In the Lessor Company/Lessee Company example that starts on page 1041, the implicit rate of the lessor was 10%, the cost of the equipment to the lessor was $100,000 (also the fair market value), and the estimated residual value was zero. Lessor Company determined the amount of the rental payment in the following manner.

---

[15] A recent study indicates that management's behaviour did change as a result of the profession's requirements to capitalize certain leases. For example, many companies restructure their leases to avoid capitalization; others increase their purchases of assets instead of leasing; and others, faced with capitalization, postpone their debt offerings or issue stock instead. However, it is interesting to note that the study found no significant effect on stock or bond prices as a result of capitalization of leases. A. Rashad Abdel-khalik, "The Economic Effects on Leases of FASB Statement No. 13, Accounting for Leases," *Research Report* (Stamford, CT: FASB, 1981).

[16] Some would argue that there is a loser—the government. The tax benefits enable the profitable investor to reduce or eliminate taxable income.

Cost of leased equipment	$100,000.00
Less present value of residual value	–0–
Amount to be recovered by lessor through lease payments	$100,000.00
Five beginning-of-the-year lease payments	
to yield a 10% return ($100,000 ÷ 4.16986)	**$ 23,981.62**

If a residual value was involved (whether guaranteed or not), the lessor would not have to recover as much from the rental payments. Therefore, the rental payments would be less (this is illustrated later on page 1054).

Classification of Leases by the Lessor

Objective 4

Identify the classifications of leases for the lessor.

From the standpoint of the *lessor*, all leases may be classified for accounting purposes as follows:

1. Operating leases.
2. Direct financing leases.
3. Sales-type leases.

If at the date of the lease agreement (inception) the lessor is party to a lease that meets *one or more* of the following three Group I criteria and *both* of the following Group II criteria, the lessor shall classify and account for the arrangement as a **direct financing lease** or a **sales-type lease**.[17] (Note that the Group I criteria are identical to the criteria that must be met for a lease to be classified as a capital lease by a lessee, as per page 1037.)

Capitalization Criteria (Lessor)

Group I
1. There is reasonable assurance that the lessee will obtain ownership of the leased property by the end of the lease term.
2. The lease term is such that the lessee will receive substantially all of the economic benefits expected to be derived from the use of the leased property over its lifespan. This is usually assumed to occur if the lease term is 75% or more of the economic life of the leased property.
3. The present value of the minimum lease payments (excluding executory costs) is equal to substantially all (usually 90% or more) of the fair value of the leased property.

Group II
1. The credit risk associated with the lease is normal when compared to the risk of collection of similar receivables.
2. The amounts of any unreimbursable costs that are likely to be incurred by the lessor under the lease can be reasonably estimated.[18]

Why the Group II requirements? The answer is that the profession wants to make sure that the lessor has really transferred the risks and benefits of ownership. If collectibility of payments is not predictable or if performance by the lessor is incomplete, then it is inappropriate to remove this leased asset from the lessor's books.

---

[17] *CICA Handbook*, Section 3065, par. .09.

[18] *Ibid.*, par. .07.

Computer leasing companies at one time used to buy IBM equipment, lease it, and remove the leased assets from their balance sheets. In leasing the asset, the computer lessors stated that they would be willing to substitute new IBM equipment if obsolescence occurred. However, when IBM introduced a new computer line, IBM refused to sell it to the computer leasing companies. As a result, a number of computer leasing companies could not meet their contracts with their customers and were forced to take back the old equipment. What the computer leasing companies had taken off the books now had to be reinstated. Such a case demonstrates one reason for Group II requirements.

The difference for the lessor between a direct financing lease and a sales-type lease is the presence or absence of a manufacturer's or dealer's profit (or loss). A sales-type lease involves a manufacturer's or dealer's profit, but a direct financing lease does not. The profit (or loss) to the lessor is the difference between the fair value of the leased property at the inception of the lease and the lessor's cost or carrying amount (book value). Normally, sales-type leases arise when manufacturers or dealers use leasing as a means of marketing their products. For example, a computer manufacturer will lease its computer equipment to businesses and institutions. Direct financing leases generally result from arrangements with lessors that are primarily engaged in financing operations, such as lease-finance companies, banks, insurance companies, and pension trusts. However, a lessor need not be a manufacturer or dealer to realize a profit (or loss) at the inception of the lease that requires application of the sales-type lease accounting.

All leases that do not qualify as direct financing or sales-type leases are classified and accounted for by the lessors as operating leases. The following flow chart shows the circumstances under which a lease is classified as operating, direct financing, or sales-type for the lessor.

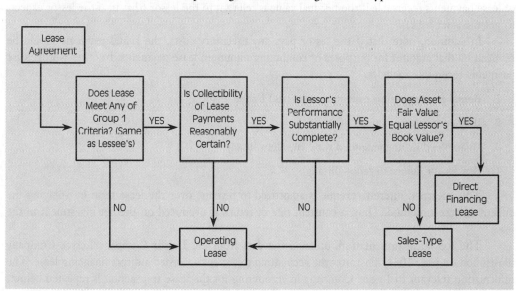

As a consequence of the additional Group II criteria for lessors, it is possible that a lessor that does not meet both criteria will classify a lease as an *operating* lease, while the lessee will classify the same lease as a *capital* lease. In such an event, both the lessor and lessee will carry the asset on their books and both will depreciate the capitalized asset.

For purposes of comparison with the lessee's accounting, only the operating and direct financing leases will be illustrated in the following section. The more complex sales-type lease will be discussed later in the chapter.

Direct Financing Method (Lessor)

Leases that are in substance the financing of an asset purchase by a lessee require the lessor to substitute a "lease payments receivable" for the leased asset. The information necessary to record a direct financing lease is as follows.

Objective 5

Describe the lessor's accounting for direct financing leases.

Direct Financing Terms

1. **Gross Investment (Lease Payments Receivable).** The minimum lease payments plus any unguaranteed residual value accruing to the lessor at the end of the lease term.[19]
2. **Unearned Finance (Interest) Revenue.** The difference between the gross investment (the receivable) and the fair market value of the property.[20]
3. **Net Investment.** The gross investment (the receivable) less the unearned interest (finance) revenue included therein.

The computation of the gross investment (lease payments receivable) is often confusing because of uncertainty about how to account for residual values. Remember that the term "minimum lease payments" includes:

1. Rental payments (excluding executory costs).

2. Bargain purchase option (if any).

3. Guaranteed residual value (if any).

4. Penalty for failure to renew (if any).

When "lease payments receivable" is defined as minimum lease payments plus unguaranteed residual value, it simply means that residual value, whether guaranteed or unguaranteed, is included as part of lease payments receivable if the residual value is relevant to the lessor (that is, if the lessor expects to get the asset back).

In addition, note that if the lessor pays any executory costs, the rental payment should be reduced by that amount for purposes of computing minimum lease payments. In other words, lease payments receivable includes:

1. Rental payments (less executory costs paid by the lessor).

2. Bargain purchase options (if any).

3. Guaranteed or unguaranteed residual values (if any).

4. Penalty for failure to renew (if any).

The unearned interest revenue is amortized to revenue over the lease term by applying the effective interest method. Thus, a constant rate of return is produced on the net investment in the lease.

The following presentation, utilizing the data from the Lessor Company/Lessee Company illustration on page 1041, illustrates the accounting treatment accorded a direct financing lease. The information relevant to Lessor Company in accounting for the lease transaction is repeated below.

1. The term of the lease is five years, beginning January 1, 1994, noncancellable, and requires equal rental payments of $25,981.62 at the beginning of each year; payments include $2,000 of executory costs (property taxes).

2. The equipment has a cost of $100,000 to Lessor Company, a fair value at the inception of the lease of $100,000, an estimated economic life of five years, and no residual value.

---

[19] Initially, the unguaranteed residual value could be classified in a separate account. If the unguaranteed residual value is included in the Lease Payments Receivable account, it would be reclassified by the lessor at the end of the lease term if not purchased by the lessee.

[20] In a direct financing lease, the cost or carrying amount of the asset should be used instead of fair market value. In most cases, however, cost or carrying amount is equal to fair market value. The use of fair market value will simplify subsequent discussion in this area. Note that significant differences between cost or carrying amount and fair market value exist for sales-type leases.

3. No initial direct costs were incurred in negotiating and closing the lease transaction.

4. The lease contains no renewable options and the equipment reverts to Lessor Company at the termination of the lease.

5. Collectibility is reasonably assured and no additional costs (with the exception of the property taxes being collected from the lessee) are to be incurred by Lessor Company.

6. Lessor Company sets the annual rentals to ensure a rate of return of 10% (implicit rate) on its investment as follows and as shown previously on page 1046.

Cost of leased asset	$100,000.00
Less: Present value of residual value	–0–
Amount to be recovered by lessor through lease payments	$100,000.00
Five periodic lease payments: $100,000 ÷ 4.16986[a]	**$ 23,981.62**

[a]PV of an annuity due of 1 for 5 years at 10% (Table A-5)

The lease meets the criteria for classification as a direct financing lease because (1) the lease term exceeds 75% of the equipment's estimated economic life, (2) the present value of the minimum lease payments exceeds 90% of the equipment's fair value, (3) collectibility of the payments is reasonably assured, and (4) there are no further costs to be incurred by Lessor Company. It is not a sales-type lease because there is no difference between the fair value ($100,000) of the equipment and the lessor's cost ($100,000).

The lease payments receivable (gross investment) is calculated as follows.

Lease payments receivable = Minimum lease payments minus executory costs
paid by lessor plus unguaranteed residual value
= [($25,981.62 – $2,000) × 5] + $0
= **$119,908.10**

The unearned interest income is computed as the difference between the lease payment receivable and the lessor's cost or carrying amount of the leased asset, as shown below.

Unearned interest income = Lease payments receivable minus asset fair
market value
= $119,908.10 – $100,000
= **$19,908.10**

The net investment in this direct financing lease is $100,000: the gross investment of $119,908.10 minus the unearned interest revenue of $19,908.10.

The lease of the asset, the resulting receivable, and the unearned interest income are recorded January 1, 1994 (the inception of the lease) as follows:

Lease Payments Receivable	119,908.10	
Equipment		100,000.00
Unearned Interest Revenue—Leases		19,908.10

The unearned interest income is classified on the balance sheet as a deduction from the lease payments receivable if the receivable is reported gross. Generally, the lease payments receivable,

although *recorded* at the gross investment amount, is *reported* in the balance sheet at the "net investment" amount (gross investment less unearned interest revenue) and entitled "Net investment in
capital leases." It is classified as current or noncurrent, depending on when the net investment is to
be recovered.

The leased equipment with a cost of $100,000, which represents Lessor Company's invest-
ment, is replaced with a net lease receivable. In a manner similar to the lessee's treatment of interest,
Lessor Company applies the effective interest method and recognizes interest revenue as a function
of the unrecovered net investment, as illustrated below.

Lessor Company
Lease Amortization Schedule
(Annuity due basis)

Date	Annual Lease Payment	Executory Costs	Interest (10%) on Unpaid Obligation	Reduction of Lease Obligation	Balance of Lease Obligation
	(a)	(b)	(c)	(d)	(e)
Jan. 1/94					$100,000.00
Jan. 1/94	$ 25,981.62	$ 2,000.00	–0–	$ 23,981.62	76,018.38
Jan. 1/95	25,981.62	2,000.00	$ 7,601.84	16,379.78	59,638.60
Jan. 1/96	25,981.62	2,000.00	5,963.86	18,017.76	41,620.84
Jan. 1/97	25,981.62	2,000.00	4,162.08	19,819.54	21,801.30
Jan. 1/98	25,981.62	2,000.00	2,180.32*	21,801.30	–0–
	$129,908.10	$10,000.00	$19,908.10	$100,000.00	

(a) Annual rental that provides a 10% return on net investment.
(b) Executory costs included in rental payment.
(c) Ten percent of the preceding balance of (e) except for Jan. 1, 1994.
(d) (a) minus (b) and (c).
(e) Preceding balance minus (d).
*Rounded by 19 cents.

On January 1, 1994, the journal entry to record receipt of the first year's lease payment is as
follows:

Cash	25,981.62	
Lease Payments Receivable		23,981.62
Property Tax Expense/Property Taxes Payable		2,000.00

On December 31, 1994, the interest revenue earned during the first year is recognized through the
following entry:

Unearned Interest Revenue—Leases	7,601.84	
Interest Revenue—Leases		7,601.84

At December 31, 1994, the net investment under capital leases is reported in the lessor's
balance sheet among current assets or noncurrent assets or both. The portion due within one year
or the operating cycle, whichever is longer, is classified as a current asset and the balance with
noncurrent assets.

The total investment at December 31, 1994 is equal to $83,620.22 (the balance at January 1,
1994, $76,018.38, plus interest receivable for 1994 of $7,601.84). The current portion is the net
investment to be received in 1994, $16,379.78, plus the interest of $7,601.84. The remainder,

$59,638.60 (Lease Payments Receivable of $71,944.86 [$23,981.62 × 3] minus Unearned Interest Revenue of $12,306.26 [$5,963.86 + $4,162.08 + $2,180.32]), should be reported in the noncurrent asset section.

The asset section as it relates to lease transactions at December 31, 1994 would appear as follows.

Current assets:	
Net investment in capital leases	$23,981.62
Noncurrent assets (investments):	
Net investment in capital leases	$59,638.60

The following entries record receipt of the second year's lease payment and recognition of the interest earned:

January 1, 1995

Cash	25,981.62	
Lease Payments Receivable		23,981.62
Property Tax Expense		2,000.00

December 31, 1995

Unearned Interest Revenue—Leases	5,963.86	
Interest Revenue—Leases		5,963.86

Journal entries through 1998 would follow the same pattern except that no entry would be recorded in 1998 (the last year) for earned interest. Because the receivable is fully collected by January 1, 1998, no balance (investment) is outstanding during 1998 to which Lessor Company could attribute any interest. On expiration of the lease (whether an ordinary annuity or an annuity due situation), the gross receivable and the unearned interest revenue would be fully written off. *Lessor Company recorded no depreciation.* If the equipment is sold to Lessee Company for $5,000 on expiration of the lease, Lessor Company would recognize disposition of the equipment as follows:

Cash	5,000	
Gain on Sale of Equipment Leased		5,000

Classification of Lease Obligation/Net Investment (Ordinary Annuity)

The classification of the lease obligation/net investment was presented in the previous section in an annuity due situation. As indicated on page 1042, the lessee's current liability is the payment ($23,981.62) to be made on January 1 of the next year. Similarly, on page 1050, the lessor's current asset is the amount to be collected ($23,981.62) on January 1 of the next year. In both of these annuity due instances, the balance sheet date is December 31 and the due date of the lease payment is January 1 (less than one year), so that the present value ($23,981.62) is the same as the rental payment ($23,981.62).

What happens if the situation is an ordinary annuity rather than an annuity due situation? For example, assume that the rent is to be paid at the end (December 31) of the next year rather than at the beginning (January 1) of the next year. *CICA Handbook* Section 3065 does not indicate how to measure the current and noncurrent amounts; it requires that "any portion of lease obligations payable within a year out of current funds should be included in current liabilities."[21] The most

---

[21] *CICA Handbook*, Section 3065, par. .23.

common method of measuring the current liability portion in ordinary annuity leases is the change in the present value method.[22]

To illustrate the change in the present value method, assume an ordinary annuity situation with the same facts as the Lessee Company/Lessor Company case, excluding the $2,000 of executory costs. Because the rents are paid at the end of the period instead of at the beginning, the five rents are set at $26,379.73 to have an effective interest rate of 10%. The ordinary annuity amortization schedule appears as follows.

Lessee Company/Lessor Company
Lease Amortization Schedule
(Ordinary annuity basis)

Date	Annual Lease Payment	Interest (10%)	Reduction of Principal	Balance of Lease Obligation/ Net Investment
Jan. 1/94				$100,000.00
Dec. 31/94	$ 26,379.73	$10,000.00	$ 16,379.73	83,620.27
Dec. 31/95	26,379.73	8,362.03	18,017.70	65,602.57
Dec. 31/96	26,379.73	6,560.26	19,819.47	45,783.10
Dec. 31/97	26,379.73	4,578.31	21,801.42	23,981.68
Dec. 31/98	26,379.73	2,398.05	23,981.68	–0–
	$131,898.65	$31,898.65	$100,000.00	

The current portion of the lease obligation/net investment under the *change in the present value method* as of December 31, 1994 would be $18,017.70 ($83,620.27 − $65,602.57), and as of December 31, 1995, it would be $19,819.47 ($65,602.57 − $45,783.10). The portion of the lease obligation/net investment that is not current is classified as such; that is, $65,602.57 is the noncurrent portion at December 31, 1994.

Thus, both the annuity due and the ordinary annuity situations report the reduction of principal for the next period as a current liability/current asset. In the annuity due situation, interest is accrued during the year but is not paid until the next period. As a result, in the annuity due situation a current liability/current asset arises for both the principal reduction and the interest that was incurred/earned in the preceding period.

In the ordinary annuity situation, the interest accrued during the period is also paid in the same period; consequently, only the principal reduction is shown as a current liability/current asset.

Operating Method (Lessor)

Under the **operating method**, each rental receipt of the lessor is recorded as rental revenue. The leased asset is depreciated in the normal manner, with the depreciation expense of the period matched against the rental revenue. The amount of revenue recognized in each accounting period is a level amount (straight-line basis) regardless of the lease provisions, unless another systematic and rational basis is more representative of the time pattern in which the benefit is derived from the leased asset. In addition to the depreciation charge, maintenance costs and the costs of any other services rendered under the provisions of the lease that pertain to the current accounting period are charged to expense.

To illustrate the operating method, assume that the direct financing lease illustrated above did not qualify as a capital lease and was therefore accounted for as an operating lease. The entry to

---

[22] For additional discussion on this approach and possible alternatives, see R.J. Swieringa, "When Current is Noncurrent and Vice Versa!" *The Accounting Review* (January 1984), pp. 123–130.

record the cash rental payment, assuming the $2,000 was for property tax expense, would be as follows:

Cash	25,981.62	
Rental Revenue		25,981.62

Depreciation is recorded by the lessor as follows (assuming the straight-line method, a cost basis of $100,000, and a five-year life):

Depreciation—Expense—Leased Buildings	20,000	
Accumulated Depreciation—Leased Buildings		20,000

If property taxes, insurance, maintenance, and other operating costs during the year are the obligation of the lessor, they are recorded as expenses chargeable against the gross rental revenues.

If the lessor owned plant assets that it used in addition to those leased to others, the leased building would be separately classified in an account such as Property Leased to Others or Investment in Leased Property. If significant in amount or in terms of activity, the rental revenues and accompanying expenses are separated in the income statement from sales revenue and cost of goods sold.

SPECIAL ACCOUNTING PROBLEMS

The features of lease arrangements that provide unique accounting problems include:

1. Residual values.
2. Sales-type leases.
3. Bargain purchase options.
4. Initial direct costs.
5. Sale leaseback.

> **Objective 6**
>
> Identify special features of lease arrangements that cause unique accounting problems.

Residual Values

To this point, there has been little discussion of residual values so that the basic accounting issues related to lessee and lessor accounting could be developed. It should be emphasized that accounting for residual values is complex and will provide you with the greatest challenge in understanding lease accounting.

Meaning of Residual Value. The residual value is the *estimated fair value* of the leased asset at the end of the lease term. Frequently, a significant residual value exists at the end of the lease term, especially when the economic life of the leased asset exceeds the lease term. If title does not pass automatically to the lessee or a bargain purchase option (criterion 1) does not exist, the lessee returns physical custody of the asset to the lessor at the end of the lease term.[23]

Guaranteed Versus Unguaranteed. The residual value may be unguaranteed or guaranteed by the lessee. If the lessee, for example, agrees to make up any deficiency below a stated amount that the lessor realizes in residual value at the end of the lease term, that stated amount is the **guaranteed residual value**.

The guaranteed residual value is employed in lease arrangements for two reasons. One is a business reason: it protects the lessor against any loss in estimated residual value, thereby ensuring the lessor of the desired rate of return on investment. The second is an accounting benefit that you will learn from the discussion at the end of this chapter.

Rental Payments. A guaranteed residual value has more assurance of realization than does an unguaranteed residual value. As a result, the lessor may adjust rental rates because the certainty of

> **Objective 7**
>
> Describe the effect of residual values, guaranteed and unguaranteed, on lease accounting.

[23] When the lease term and the economic life are not the same, the residual value and the salvage value of the asset will probably differ. For simplicity, we will assume that residual value and salvage value are the same, even when the economic life and lease term vary.

recovery has been increased. After this rate has been established, it makes no difference from an accounting point of view whether the residual value is guaranteed or unguaranteed. The net investment to be recorded by the lessor (once the rate is set) will be the same.

Assume the same data as in the Lessee Company/Lessor Company illustrations except that a residual value of $5,000 is estimated at the end of the five-year lease term. In addition, a 10% return on investment (ROI) is assumed;[24] whether the residual value is guaranteed or unguaranteed, Lessor Company would compute the amount of the lease payments as follows.

Lessor's Computation of Lease Payments (10% ROI)	
(Annuity due basis, including residual value)	
Guaranteed or Unguaranteed Residual Value	
Cost of leased asset to lessor	$100,000.00
Less: Present value of residual value	
($5,000 × 0.62092, Table A-2)	3,104.60
Amount to be recovered by lessor through lease payments	$ 96,895.40
Five periodic lease payments ($96,895.40 ÷ 4.16986, Table A-5)	**$ 23,237.09**

The foregoing lease payment amount should be contrasted to the lease payments of $23,981.62 as computed on page 1046, where no residual value existed. The payments are less because the lessor's recoverable amount of $100,000 is reduced by the present value of the residual value.

Lessee Accounting for Residual Value. Whether the estimated residual value is guaranteed or unguaranteed is of both economic and accounting consequence to the lessee. The accounting difference is the fact that the term **minimum lease payments**, the basis for capitalization, includes the guaranteed residual value but excludes the unguaranteed residual value. Since the lessee assumes no responsibility for the condition of the leased asset on termination of the lease when the residual value is unguaranteed, no liability is recorded.

Guaranteed Residual Value (Lessee Accounting). A guaranteed residual value affects the lessee's computation of the minimum lease payments and, therefore, the amounts capitalized as a leased asset and a lease obligation. In effect, it is an additional lease payment that will be paid in property or cash, or both, at the end of the lease term. Using the rental payments as computed by the lessor above, the minimum lease payments are $121,185.45 ([$23,237.09 × 5] + $5,000). The capitalized present value of the minimum lease payments (excluding executory costs) is computed as shown below.

Lessee's Capitalized Amount (10% Rate)	
(Annuity due basis, including *guaranteed* residual value)	
Present value of five annual rental payments of	
$23,237.09 × 4.16986 (Table A-5)	$ 96,895.40
Present value of guaranteed residual value of $5,000	
due five years after date of inception: ($5,000 × 0.62092)	3,104.60
Lessee's capitalized amount	**$100,000.00**

---

[24] Technically, the rate of return demanded by the lessor would be different, depending on whether the residual value was guaranteed or unguaranteed. We are ignoring this difference in subsequent sections to simplify the illustrations.

Lessee Company's schedule of interest expense and amortization of the $100,000 lease obligation that produces a $5,000 final guaranteed residual value final payment at the end of five years is shown below.

Lessee Company
Lease Amortization Schedule
(Annuity due basis, *guaranteed* residual value—GRV)

Date	Lease Payment Plus GRV	Executory Costs	Interest (10%) on Unpaid Obligation	Reduction of Lease Obligation	Lease Obligation
	(a)	(b)	(c)	(d)	(e)
Jan. 1/94					$100,000.00
Jan. 1/94	$ 25,237.09	$ 2,000.00	$ –0–	$ 23,237.09	76,762.91
Jan. 1/95	25,237.09	2,000.00	7,676.29	15,560.80	61,202.11
Jan. 1/96	25,237.09	2,000.00	6,120.21	17,116.88	44,085.23
Jan. 1/97	25,237.09	2,000.00	4,408.52	18,828.57	25,256.66
Jan. 1/98	25,237.09	2,000.00	2,525.67	20,711.42	4,545.24
Dec. 31/98	5,000.00*		454.76**	4,545.24	–0–
	$131,185.45	$10,000.00	$21,185.45	$100,000.00	

(a) Annual lease payment as required by lease.
(b) Executory costs included in rental payment.
(c) Preceding balance of (e) × 10%, except January 1, 1994.
(d) (a) minus (b) and (c).
(e) Preceding balance minus (d).
*Represents the guaranteed residual value.
**Rounded by 24 cents.

The journal entries (page 1058) to record the leased asset and obligation, depreciation, interest, property tax, and lease payments are then made on the basis that the residual value is guaranteed. The format of these entries is the same as illustrated earlier, but the amounts are different because of the guaranteed residual value. The leased asset is recorded at $100,000 and is depreciated over five years. Assuming that the straight-line method is used, the depreciation expense each year is $19,000 ([$100,000 − $5,000] ÷ 5 years).

At the end of the lease term, before the lessee transfers the asset to the lessor, the lease asset and obligation accounts have the following balances.

Leased equipment under capital leases	$100,000	Obligations under capital leases	$5,000
Less accumulated depreciation—capital leases	95,000		
	$ 5,000		

If, at the end of the lease, the fair market value of the leased property is less than $5,000, Lessee Company may have to record a loss. Assume that Lessee Company depreciated the leased asset down to its residual value of $5,000 but that the fair market value of the asset at December 31, 1998 was $3,000. In this case, the Lessee Company would have to report a loss of $2,000. The following journal entry would be made, assuming cash was paid to make up the residual value deficiency:

Loss on Capital Lease	2,000.00	
Interest Expense (or Interest Payable)	454.76	
Obligations Under Capital Lease	4,545.24	
Accumulated Depreciation—Capital Lease	95,000.00	
Leased Equipment Under Capital Lease		100,000.00
Cash		2,000.00

If the fair market value exceeds $5,000, a gain may be recognized. Gains on guaranteed residual values may be apportioned to the lessor and lessee in whatever ratio the parties initially agreed.

If the lessee depreciated the total cost of the asset ($100,000), a misstatement would occur; that is, the carrying amount of the asset at the end of the lease term would be zero, but the obligation under the capital lease would be stated as $5,000. Thus, if the asset was worth $5,000, the lessee would end up reporting a gain of $5,000 at the time the asset is transferred to the lessor. As a result, depreciation is overstated and net income is understated in 1994 through 1997, but in the last year (1998), net income would be overstated.

Unguaranteed Residual Value (Lessee Accounting). An unguaranteed residual value from the lessee's viewpoint is the same as no residual value in terms of its effect on the lessee's method of computing the minimum lease payments and the capitalization of the leased asset and the lease obligation. Assume the same facts as those above except that the $5,000 residual value is *unguaranteed instead of guaranteed*. The amount of the annual lease payments would be the same ($23,237.09) because whether the residual value is guaranteed or unguaranteed, Lessor Company's amount to be recovered through lease rentals is the same: $96,895.40. The minimum lease payments are $116,185.45 ($23,237.09 × 5). Lessee Company would capitalize the following amount.

Lessee's Capitalized Amount (10% Rate)	
(Annuity due basis including *unguaranteed* residual value)	
Present value of five annual rental payments of	
$23,237.09 × 4.16986 (Table A-5)	$96,895.40
Unguaranteed residual value of $5,000 (not capitalized by lessee)	–0–
Lessee's capitalized amount	**$96,895.40**

The Lessee Company's schedule of interest expense and amortization of the lease obligation of $96,895.40, assuming an unguaranteed residual value of $5,000 at the end of five years, is as shown at the top of page 1057. The journal entries (page 1058) to record the leased asset and obligation, depreciation, interest, property tax, and payments on the lease obligation are then made on the basis that the residual value is unguaranteed. The format of these entries is the same as illustrated earlier. Note that the leased asset is recorded at $96,895.40 and is depreciated over five years. Assuming that the straight-line method is used, the depreciation expense each year is $19,379.08 ($96,895.40 ÷ 5 years). At the end of the lease term, before the lessee transfers the asset to the lessor, the balances in the accounts shown in the second box on page 1057 result.

Assuming that the residual had a fair market value of $3,000, no loss would be reported in this situation. Assuming that the leased asset has been fully depreciated and that the lease obligation

Lessee Company
Lease Amortization Schedule (10%)
(Annuity due basis, *unguaranteed* residual value)

Date	Annual Lease Payments	Executory Costs	Interest (10%) on Unpaid Obligation	Reduction of Lease Obligation	Lease Obligation
	(a)	(b)	(c)	(d)	(e)
Jan. 1/94					$96,895.40
Jan. 1/94	$ 25,237.09	$ 2,000.00	–0–	$23,237.09	73,658.31
Jan. 1/95	25,237.09	2,000.00	$ 7,365.83	15,871.26	57,787.05
Jan. 1/96	25,237.09	2,000.00	5,778.71	17,458.38	40,328.67
Jan. 1/97	25,237.09	2,000.00	4,032.87	19,204.22	21,124.45
Jan. 1/98	25,237.09	2,000.00	2,112.64*	21,124.45	–0–
	$126,185.45	$10,000.00	$19,290.05	$96,895.40	

(a) Annual lease payment as required by lease.
(b) Executory costs included in rental payment.
(c) Preceding balance of (e) × 10%.
(d) (a) minus (b) and (c).
(e) Preceding balance minus (d).
*Rounded by 19 cents.

Leased equipment under capital leases	$96,895	Obligations under capital lease	$–0–
Less accumulated depreciation— capital leases	96,895		
	$ –0–		

has been fully amortized, no entry is required at the end of the lease term, except to remove the asset from the books.

If the lessee depreciated the asset down to its unguaranteed residual value, a misstatement would occur; that is, the carrying amount of the leased asset would be $5,000 at the end of the lease, but the obligation under the capital lease would be stated as zero before the transfer of the asset. Thus, the lessee would end up reporting a loss of $5,000 when it transferred the asset to the lessor. Depreciation would be understated and net income overstated in 1994 through 1997, but in the last year (1998), net income would be understated because of the loss recorded.

Lessee Entries Involving Residual Values. The entries by Lessee Company for both a guaranteed and an unguaranteed residual value are shown in comparative form at the top of page 1058.

Lessor Accounting for Residual Value. As indicated earlier, the net investment to be recovered by the lessor is the same whether the residual value is guaranteed orunguaranteed. The lessor works on the assumption that the residual value will be realized at the end of the lease term whether guaranteed or unguaranteed. The lease payments required by the lessor to earn a certain return on investment are the same ($23,237.09) whether the residual value is guaranteed or unguaranteed.

Lessee Company
Entries for Guaranteed and Unguaranteed Residual Values

Guaranteed Residual Value			Unguaranteed Residual Value		
Capitalization of Lease Jan 1/94					
Leased Equipment Under			Leased Equipment Under		
Capital Leases	100,000.00		Capital Leases	96,895.40	
Obligations Under			Obligations Under		
Capital Leases		100,000.00	Capital Leases		96,895.40
First Payment Jan 1/94					
Property Tax Expense	2,000.00		Property Tax Expense	2,000.00	
Obligations Under			Obligations Under		
Capital Leases	23,237.09		Capital Leases	23,237.09	
Cash		25,237.09	Cash		25,237.09
Adjusting Entry for Accrued Interest Dec. 31/94					
Interest Expense	7,676.29		Interest Expense	7,365.83	
Interest Payable		7,676.29	Interest Payable		7,365.83
Entry to Record Depreciation Dec. 31/94					
Depreciation Expense—			Depreciation Expense—		
Capital Leases	19,000.00		Capital Leases	19,379.08	
Accumulated Depreciation—			Accumulated Depreciation—		
Capital Leases		19,000.00	Capital Leases		19,379.08
([$100,000 − $5,000] ÷ 5 years)			($96,895.40 ÷ 5 years)		
Second Payment Jan. 1/95					
Property Tax Expense	2,000.00		Property Tax Expense	2,000.00	
Obligations Under			Obligations Under		
Capital Leases	15,560.80		Capital Leases	15,871.26	
Interest Expense			Interest Expense		
(or Interest Payable)	7,676.29		(or Interest Payable)	7,365.83	
Cash		25,237.09	Cash		25,237.09

Using the Lessee Company/Lessor Company data and assuming a residual value (either guaranteed or unguaranteed) of $5,000 and the classification of the lease as a direct financing lease, the following necessary amounts are computed.

$$\text{Gross investment} = (\$23,237.09 \times 5) + \$5,000 = \$121,185.45$$
$$\text{Unearned interest revenue} = \$121,185.45 - \$100,000 = \$21,185.45$$
$$\text{Net investment} = \$121,185.45 - \$21,185.45 = \$100,000$$

The schedule for amortization with guaranteed or unguaranteed residual value is the same, as shown at the top of page 1059.

Using the amounts computed above, the entries in the second box on page 1059 would be made by Lessor Company during the first year for this direct financing lease. These entries may be compared to those of Lessee Company on page 1055.

Objective 8

Describe the lessor's accounting for sales-type leases.

Sales-Type Lease (Lessor)

As already indicated, the primary difference between a direct financing lease and a sales-type lease is the manufacturer's or dealer's profit (or loss). A diagram illustrating these relationships is shown at the top of page 1060.

The information necessary to record the sales-type lease is as shown in the second box on page 1060.

Lessor Company

Lease Amortization Schedule

(Annuity due basis, *guaranteed* or *unguaranteed* residual value)

Date	Annual Lease Payment Plus Residual Value	Executory Costs	Interest (10%) on Net Investment	Net Investment Recovery	Net Investment
	(a)	(b)	(c)	(d)	(e)
Jan. 1/94					$100,000.00
Jan. 1/94	$ 25,237.09	$ 2,000.00	–0–	$ 23,237.09	76,762.91
Jan. 1/95	25,237.09	2,000.00	$ 7,676.29	15,560.80	61,202.11
Jan. 1/96	25,237.09	2,000.00	6,120.21	17,116.88	44,085.23
Jan. 1/97	25,237.09	2,000.00	4,400.52	18,820.57	25,250.60
Jan. 1/98	25,237.09	2,000.00	2,525.67	20,711.42	4,545.24
Dec. 31/98	5,000.00*		454.76**	4,545.24	–0–
	$131,185.45	$10,000.00	$21,185.45	$100,000.00	

(a) Annual lease payment as required by lease.

(b) Executory costs included in rental payment.

(c) Preceding balance of (e) × 10%, except January 1, 1994

(d) (a) minus (b) and (c).

(e) Preceding balance minus (d).

*Represents the guaranteed residual value.

**Rounded by 24 cents.

Lessor Company

Lessor Entries for Either Guaranteed or Unguaranteed Residual Value

Inception of Lease Jan. 1/94

Lease Payments Receivable	121,185.45	
Equipment		100,000.00
Unearned Interest Revenue—Leases		21,185.45

First Payment Received Jan. 1/94

Cash	25,237.09	
Lease Payments Receivable		23,237.09
Property Tax Expense/Property Tax Payable		2,000.00

Adjusting Entry for Accrued Interest Dec. 31/94

Unearned Interest Revenue—Leases	7,676.29	
Interest Revenue—Leases		7,676.29

The gross investment and the unearned interest revenue account are the same whether a guaranteed or an unguaranteed residual value is involved.

When recording sales revenue and cost of goods sold, there is a difference in accounting for guaranteed and unguaranteed residual values. The guaranteed residual value can be considered part

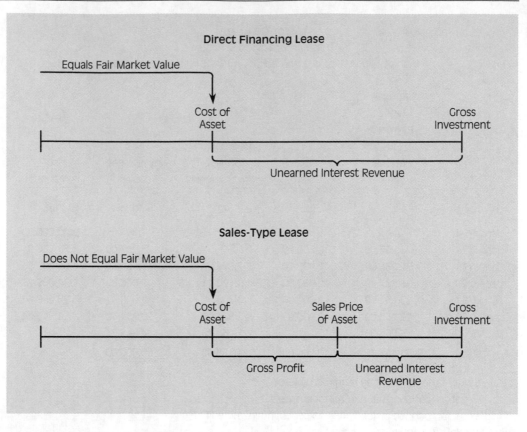

Sales-Type Lease Terms

1. **Gross investment** (also "lease payments receivable"). The minimum lease payments plus the unguaranteed residual value.

2. **Unearned interest revenue.** The gross investment less the fair market value of the asset.

3. **Sales price of the asset.** The present value of the minimum lease payments.

4. **Cost of goods sold.** The cost of the asset to the lessor, less the present value of any unguaranteed residual value.

[handwritten: same as on page 1048.]

of sales revenue because the lessor knows that the entire asset has been sold. There is certainty that the unguaranteed residual portion of the asset has been "sold" (i.e., will be realized); therefore, sales and cost of goods sold are recognized only for the portion of the asset for which realization is assured. However, *the gross profit amount on the sale of the asset is the same whether a guaranteed or unguaranteed residual value is involved.*

To illustrate a sales-type lease with a guaranteed residual value and a sales-type lease with an unguaranteed residual value, assume the same facts as in the preceding direct financing lease situation (pages 1048–1049). The estimated residual value is $5,000 (the present value of which is $3,104.60) and the leased equipment has an $85,000 cost to the dealer, Lessor Company. At the end of the lease term assume that the fair market value of the residual value is $3,000. The amounts relevant to a sales-type lease are computed as shown at the top of page 1061.

The profit recorded by Lessor Company at the point of sale is the same, $15,000, whether the residual value is guaranteed or unguaranteed, but the sales revenue and cost of goods sold amounts are different.

	Sales-Type Lease	
	Guaranteed Residual Value	Unguaranteed Residual Value
Gross investment	$121,185.45	Same
	([$23,237.09 × 5] + 5,000)	
Unearned interest revenue	$21,185.45	Same
	($121,185.45 − $100,000)	
Sales price of the asset	$100,000.00	$96,895.40
	($96,895.40 + $3,104.60)	
Cost of goods sold	$85,000.00	$81,895.40
		($85,000.00 − $3,104.60)
Gross profit	$15,000.00	$15,000.00
	($100,000 − $85,000)	($96,895.40 − $81,895.40)

The entries to record this transaction on January 1, 1994 and the receipt of the residual value at the end of the lease term are shown at the top of page 1062.

The *estimated unguaranteed residual value* in a sales-type lease (and a financing-type lease) must be reviewed periodically. If the estimate of the unguaranteed residual value declines, the accounting for the transaction must be revised using the changed estimate. The decline represents a reduction in the lessor's net investment and is recognized as a loss in the period in which the residual estimate is reduced. Upward adjustments in estimated residual values are not recognized.

Bargain Purchase Option (Lessee)

A bargain purchase option allows the lessee to purchase the leased property for a future price that is substantially lower than the property's expected future fair value. The price is so favourable at the lease's inception that the future exercise of the option appears to be reasonably assured. If a bargain purchase option exists, *the lessee must increase the present value of the minimum lease payments by the present value of the option price*.

For example, assume that Lessee Company in the illustration on page 1055 had an option to buy the leased equipment for $5,000 at the end of the five-year lease term, when the fair value is expected to be $18,000. The significant difference between the option price and the fair value creates a bargain purchase option, and exercising the option is reasonably assured. The computations— (1) the amount of the five lease payments necessary for the lessor to earn a 10% return on net investment, (2) the amount of the minimum lease payments, (3) the amount capitalized as leased assets and lease obligation, and (4) the amortization of the lease obligation—are affected by a bargain purchase option as they were by a guaranteed residual value. Therefore, the computations and amortization schedule that would be prepared for this $5,000 bargain purchase option are identical to those shown on page 1055 for the $5,000 guaranteed residual value.

The only difference between the accounting treatment given a bargain purchase option and a guaranteed residual value of identical amounts and circumstances is in the computation of the annual depreciation. In the case of a guaranteed residual value, the lessee depreciates the asset over the lease life, while in the case of a bargain purchase option, the lessee uses the economic life of the asset.

Initial Direct Costs (Lessor)

Initial direct costs are of two types. The first, **incremental direct costs**, are costs incurred in originating a lease arrangement and paid to independent third parties. Examples would include cost of independent appraisal of collateral used to secure a lease or a broker's fee for finding the lessee.

Lessor Company

Entries for Guaranteed and Unguaranteed Residual Values

Guaranteed Residual Value			Unguaranteed Residual Value		
To record sales-type lease at inception (January 1, 1994):					
Cost of Goods Sold	85,000.00		Cost of Goods Sold	81,895.40	
Lease Payments			Lease Payments		
Receivable	121,185.45		Receivable	121,185.45	
Sales Revenue		100,000.00	Sales Revenue		96,895.40
Unearned Interest Revenue		21,185.45	Unearned Interest Revenue		21,185.45
Inventory		85,000.00	Inventory		85,000.00
To record receipt of the first lease payment (January 1, 1994):					
Cash	25,237.09		Cash	25,237.09	
Lease Payments Receivable		23,237.09	Lease Payments Receivable		23,237.09
Property Tax Expense/			Property Tax Expense/		
Property Tax Payable		2,000.00	Property Tax Payable		2,000.000
To recognize interest revenue earned during the first year (December 31, 1994):					
Unearned Interest			Unearned Interest		
Revenue	7,676.29		Revenue	7,676.29	
Interest Revenue		7,676.29	Interest Revenue		7,676.29
(See lease amortization schedule, page 1059.)					
To record receipt of second lease payment (January 1, 1995):					
Cash	25,237.09		Cash	25,237.09	
Lease Payments Receivable		23,237.09	Lease Payments Receivable		23,237.09
Property Tax Expense/			Property Tax Expense/		
Property Tax Payable		2,000.00	Property Tax Payable		2,000.00
To recognize interest revenue earned during the second year (December 31, 1995):					
Unearned Interest			Unearned Interest		
Revenue	6,120.21		Revenue	6,120.21	
Interest Revenue		6,120.21	Interest Revenue		6,120.21
To record receipt of residual value at end of the leased term (December 31, 1998):					
Inventory	3,000.00		Inventory	3,000.00	
Cash	2,000.00		Loss on Capital Lease	2,000.00	
Lease Payments Receivable		5,000.00	Lease Payments Receivable		5,000.00

The second type, **internal direct costs,** are costs directly related to specified activities performed by the lessor on a given lease. Examples of such activities are evaluating the prospective lessee's financial condition; evaluating and recording guarantees, collateral, and other security arrangements; negotiating lease terms and preparing and processing lease documents; and closing the transaction. The costs directly related to an employee's time spent on a specific lease transaction may also be considered initial direct costs.

Initial direct costs should not include **internal indirect costs** related to activities performed by the lessor for advertising, servicing existing leases, and establishing and monitoring credit policies; nor should they include costs for supervising and administration. In addition, expenses such as rent and depreciation are not considered to be initial direct costs.

For *operating leases,* the lessor should defer initial direct costs and allocate them over the lease term in proportion to the recognition of rental income. In a *sales-type lease* transaction, the lessor expenses the initial direct costs in the year of incurrence; that is, they are expensed in the period in which the profit on the sale is recognized.

In a *direct financing lease,* however, initial direct costs should be added to the net investment in the lease and amortized over the life of the lease as a yield adjustment. In addition, the unamortized deferred initial direct costs that are part of the lessor's investment in the direct financing lease must be disclosed. If the carrying value of the asset in the lease is $4,000,000 and the lessor incurs initial direct costs of $35,000, the net investment in the lease would then be $4,035,000. The yield would be adjusted to ensure proper amortization of this amount over the life of the lease and would be lower than the initial rate of return.

Sale-Leaseback

Sale-leaseback describes a transaction in which the owner of property (seller-lessee) sells the property to another and simultaneously leases it back from the new owner. The use of the property is generally continued without interruption.

For example, a company buys land, constructs a building to its specifications, sells the property to an investor, and then immediately leases it. The advantage of a sale-leaseback from the seller's viewpoint usually involves financing considerations. If the purchase of equipment has already been financed, a sale-leaseback can allow the seller to refinance at lower rates, assuming that rates have decreased. In addition, a sale-leaseback can provide another source of additional working capital, particularly when liquidity is a problem.

To the extent that the seller-lessee's *use* of the asset sold continues after the sale, the sale-leaseback is really a form of financing and, therefore, no gain or loss should be recognized on the transaction. In short, the seller-lessee is simply borrowing funds. On the other hand, if the seller-lessee gives up the right to the use of the asset sold, the transaction is in substance a sale, and gain or loss recognition is appropriate. Trying to ascertain when the lessee has given up the use of the asset is difficult, however, and complex rules have been formulated to identify this situation.[25] To understand the profession's position in this area, the basic accounting for the lessee and lessor are discussed below.

Lessee. If the lease meets one of the three criteria for treatment as a capital lease (see page 1037), **the *seller-lessee accounts for the lease as a capital lease*.** Any profit or loss experienced by the seller-lessee from the sale of the assets that are leased back under a capital lease should be deferred and amortized over the lease term (or the economic life, if criterion 1 is satisfied) in proportion to the amortization of the leased assets.[26] If Lessee, Inc. sells equipment having a book value of $580,000 and a fair value of $623,110 to Lessor, Inc. for $623,110 and leases the equipment back for $50,000 per year for 20 years, the profit of $43,110 should be amortized over the 20-year period at the same rate that the $623,110 is depreciated.

Objective 9

Describe the lessee's accounting for sale-leaseback transactions.

If none of the capital lease criteria are satisfied, **the *seller-lessee accounts for the transaction as a sale and the lease as an operating lease*.** Under an operating lease, such profit or loss should be deferred and amortized in proportion to the rental payments over the period of time the assets are expected to be used by the lessee. If the leased asset is land only, the amortization shall be on a straight-line basis over the lease term.

The profession requires, however, that when the fair value of the asset is *less* than the book value (carrying amount), a loss must be recognized immediately up to the amount of the difference between the book value and fair value. For example, if Lessee, Inc. sells equipment having a book value of $650,000 and a fair value of $623,110, the difference of $26,890 should be charged to a loss account.[27]

Lessor. If the lease meets one of the criteria in Group I and both of the criteria in Group II (see page 1046), the purchaser-lessor records the transaction as a purchase and a direct financing lease. If the lease does not meet the criteria, the purchaser-lessor records the transaction as a purchase and an operating lease.

[25] Sales and leaseback of real estate are often accounted for differently. A discussion of the issues related to these transactions is beyond the scope of this textbook.
[26] *CICA Handbook*, Section 3065, par. .68.
[27] *Ibid.*, par. .70.

Sale-Leaseback Illustration. To illustrate the accounting treatment accorded a sale-leaseback transaction, assume that Lessee Corp. on January 1, 1994 sells aircraft having a carrying amount on its books of $75,500,000 to Lessor Corp. for $80,000,000, and immediately leases the aircraft back under the following conditions:

1. The term of the lease is 15 years, noncancellable, requiring equal rental payments of $10,487,443 at the beginning of each year.

2. The aircraft has a fair value of $80,000,000 on January 1, 1994 and an estimated economic life of 15 years.

3. Lessee Corp. pays all executory costs.

4. Lessee Corp. depreciates similar aircraft that it owns on a straight-line basis over 15 years.

5. The annual payments assure the lessor a 12% return.

6. The incremental borrowing rate of Lessee Corp. is 12%.

This lease is a capital lease to Lessee Corp. because the lease term exceeds 75% of the estimated life of the aircraft and the present value of the lease payments exceeds 90% of the fair value of the aircraft to the lessor. Assuming that collectibility of the lease payments is reasonably predictable and no important uncertainties exist in relation to unreimbursable costs yet to be incurred by the lessor, Lessor Corp. should classify this lease as a direct financing lease.

The typical journal entries to record the transactions relating to this lease for both Lessee Corp. and Lessor Corp. for the first year are presented on page 1065.

LEASE ACCOUNTING: THE UNSOLVED PROBLEM

As indicated at the beginning of this chapter, lease accounting is a much abused area in which strenuous efforts are being made to circumvent *CICA Handbook* Section 3065. In practice, the accounting rules for capitalizing leases have been rendered partially ineffective by the strong desires of lessees to resist capitalization. Leasing generally involves large dollar amounts that, when capitalized, materially increase reported liabilities and adversely affect the debt-to-equity ratio. Lease capitalization is also resisted because charges to expense made in the early years of the lease term are higher under the capital lease method than under the operating method, frequently without tax benefit. As a consequence, much effort has been devoted to beating the profession's lease capitalization rules.[28]

To avoid leased asset capitalization, lease agreements are designed, written, and interpreted so that none of the three capitalized lease criteria are satisfied from the lessee's viewpoint. Devising lease agreements in such a way has not been too difficult when the following specifications are met:

1. Make certain that the lease does not specify the transfer of title to the property to the lessee.

2. Do not write in a bargain purchase option.

3. Set the lease term at something less than 75% of the estimated economic life of the leased property.

4. Arrange for the present value of the minimum lease payments to be less than 90% of the fair value of the leased property.

---

[28] Richard Dieter, "Is Lessee Accounting Working?" *The CPA Journal* (August 1979), pp. 13–19. This article provides interesting examples of abuses of U.S. Statement No. 13, discusses the circumstances that led to the current situation, and proposes a solution for the confusion.

Entries for Sale-Leaseback

Lessee Corp.	Lessor Corp.

Sale of Aircraft by Lessee to Lessor Corp., Jan. 1, 1994

Cash	80,000,000		Aircraft	80,000,000	
Aircraft		75,500,000	Cash		80,000,000
Unearned Profit on					
Sale-Leaseback		4,500,000	Lease Payments		
			Receivable	157,311,645	
Leased Aircraft Under			Aircraft		80,000,000
Capital Leases	80,000,000		Unearned Interest		
Obligations Under			Revenue—Leases		77,311,645
Capital Lease		80,000,000	($10,487,443 × 15 = $157,311,645)		

First Lease Payment, Jan. 1, 1994

Obligations Under			Cash	10,487,443	
Capital Leases	10,487,443		Lease Payments		
Cash		10,487,443	Receivable		10,487,443

Incurrence and Payment of Executory Costs by Lessee Corp. Throughout 1994

Insurance, Maintenance,		(No entry)	
Taxes, etc.	XXX		
Cash or Accounts			
Payable		XXX	

Depreciation Expense on the Aircraft, Dec. 31, 1994

Depreciation Expense	5,333,333	(No entry)
Accumulated Depreciation—		
Capital Leases	5,333,333	
($80,000,000 ÷ 15)		

Amortization of Profit on Sale-Leaseback by Lessee Corp., Dec. 31, 1994

Unearned Profit on		(No entry)
Sale-Leaseback	300,000	
Depreciation Expense	300,000	
($4,500,000 ÷ 15)		

Note: A case might be made for crediting Revenue instead of Depreciation Expense.

Interest for 1994, Dec. 31, 1994

Interest Expense—			Unearned Interest		
Capital Leases	8,341,507		Revenue	8,341,507	
Interest Payable		8,341,507	Interest Revenue—		
			Lease		8,341,507[a]

[a]**Partial Lease Amortization Schedule**

Date	Annual Rental Payment	Interest (12%)	Reduction of Balance	Balance
Jan. 1/94				$80,000,000
Jan. 1/94	$10,487,443	–0–	$10,487,443	69,512,557
Jan. 1/95	10,487,443	$8,341,507	$ 2,145,936	67,366,621

But the real challenge lies in disqualifying the lease as a capital lease to the lessee while having the same lease qualify as a capital (sales or financing) lease to the lessor. Unlike lessees, lessors try to avoid having lease arrangements classified as operating leases.[29]

Avoiding the first two criteria is relatively simple, but it takes a little ingenuity to avoid the "90% recovery test" for the lessee while satisfying it for the lessor. Two factors involved in this effort are: (1) the use of the incremental borrowing rate by the lessee when it is higher than the implicit interest rate of the lessor, by making information about the implicit rate unavailable to the lessee, and (2) residual value guarantees.

The lessee's use of the higher interest rate is probably the more popular subterfuge. While lessees are knowledgeable about the fair value of the leased property and, of course, the rental payments, they generally are not aware of the estimated residual value used by the lessor. Therefore, the lessee does not know exactly the lessor's implicit rate and is therefore free to use its own incremental borrowing rate.

The residual value guarantee is the other unique, yet popular device used by the lessees and lessors. In fact, a whole new industry has emerged to circumvent symmetry between the lessee and the lessor in accounting for leases. The residual value guarantee has spawned numerous companies whose principal or sole function is to guarantee the residual value of leased assets. For a fee, these "third-party guarantors" (insurers) assume the risk of deficiencies in leased asset residual value.

Because the guaranteed residual value is included in the minimum lease payments for the lessor, the 90% recovery of fair market value test is satisfied and the lease is a nonoperating lease to the lessor. Because the residual value is guaranteed by a third party, the minimum lease payments of the lessee do not include the guarantee. Thus by merely transferring some of the risk to a third party, lessees can alter substantially the accounting treatment by converting what would otherwise be capital leases to operating leases.

Much of this circumvention is encouraged by the nature of the criteria set out in *CICA Handbook* Section 3065. Accounting standard-setting bodies continue to have poor experience with arbitrary break points or other size and percentage criteria, such as "90% of," "75% of," etc. Some accountants believe that a more workable solution would be to require capitalization of all leases that extend for some defined period (such as one year) on the basis that the lease has acquired an asset (a property right) and a corresponding liability, rather than on the basis that the lease transfers substantially all of the risks and rewards of ownership.

REPORTING LEASE DATA IN FINANCIAL STATEMENTS

Disclosures Required of the Lessee

Objective 10

Describe the disclosure requirements for leases.

The CICA requires that the following information on leases be disclosed in the lessee's financial statements or in the notes:

Lessee's Disclosures

1. For *capital leases*:

   a. The gross amount of assets recorded under capital leases and related accumulated amortization as of the date of each balance sheet presented, in aggregate and, preferably, by major category.

   b. Future minimum lease payments as of the date of the latest balance sheet presented, in the aggregate and for each of the five succeeding fiscal years, with a separate deduction

---

[29] The reason is that most lessors are financial institutions and do not want these types of assets on their balance sheets. Furthermore, the capital lease transaction from the lessor's standpoint provides higher income flows in the earlier periods of the lease.

for amounts included in the minimum lease payments representing executory costs and imputed interest.

   c. The portion, if any, of the lease obligations that is payable within one year out of current funds should be reported as a current liability.

   d. Periodic interest expense related to lease obligations may be disclosed either separately or included in interest on long-term indebtedness.

   e. It may be desirable to disclose separately total contingent rentals (rentals based on a factor other than the passage of time) as well as the amount of future minimum rentals receivable from noncancellable subleases.

2. For *operating leases*:

   a. The future minimum lease payments both in aggregate and for each of the five succeeding years.

   b. A description of any other commitments under operating leases.[30]

Disclosures Required of the Lessor

The CICA requires that lessors disclose the following information in either the financial statements or in the accompanying notes.

Lessor's Disclosures

1. For *operating leases*:

   a. The cost of property held for leasing and the amount of accumulated depreciation.

   b. Rental income from operating leases.

   c. Minimum future rentals both in aggregate and for each of the five succeeding years are not explicitly required but are desirable.

2. For *sales-type and direct financing leases*:

   a. The lessor's net investment in sales-type and direct financing leases; it may also be desirable to present the components of the net investment, namely:
     i. Future minimum lease payments receivable.
     ii. Unguaranteed residual values.
     iii. Unearned finance income.
     iv. Executory costs included in the minimum lease payments receivable.

   b. Future minimum lease payments to be received for each of the five succeeding fiscal years as of the date of the balance sheet presented.

   c. Total contingent rentals included in income.[31]

Illustrated Disclosures

The financial statement excerpts on page 1068 from the 1991 annual report of Potash Corporation of Saskatchewan Inc. present the statement and note disclosures typical of a lessee having capital leases.

[30] *CICA Handbook*, Section 3065, par. .54.
[31] *Ibid.*, par. .??.

Potash Corporation of Saskatchewan Inc.

	1991	1990
Assets:		
Fixed assets (Note 6)	$1,106,879	$1,131,192
Current Liabilities:		
Current obligations under capital leases (Note 11)	6,947	6,179
Long-Term Debt:		
Obligations under capital leases (Note 11)	$ 76,346	$ 83,293

Note 1: Significant Accounting Policies

Leases

Leases entered into are classified as either capital or operating leases. Leases that transfer substantially all of the benefits and risks of ownership of property to the Company are accounted for as capital leases. At the time a capital lease is entered into, an asset is recorded together with the related long-term obligation. Equipment acquired under capital leases is being depreciated on the same basis as other fixed assets. Gains or losses resulting from sale-leaseback transactions are deducted from the cost of equipment under capital lease and amortized on the same basis as the related asset. Rental payments under operating leases are charged to expense as incurred.

Note 6: Fixed Assets

	Cost	Accumulated Depreciation	Net Book Value
Land and improvements	$ 64,198	$ 12,888	$ 51,310
Buildings and improvements	435,073	82,070	353,003
Machinery and equipment	744,086	264,085	480,001
Mine development costs	176,025	36,464	139,561
Equipment under capital lease	107,928	24,924	83,004
	$1,527,310	$420,431	$1,106,879

Note 11: Lease Commitments

The company has long-term lease agreements for buildings, equipment, and rail cars, the latest of which expires in 2005. Future minimum lease payments under these capital and operating leases will be approximately as follows:

	Operating	Capital
1992	$13,006	$ 16,859
1993	8,714	16,859
1994	6,784	16,859
1995	5,526	16,842
1996	3,487	16,807
Subsequent years	14,036	41,638
		125,864
Less amount representing interest at 12.1%		42,571
Present value of minimum capital lease payments		83,293
Current obligation		6,947
Long-term portion		$ 76,346

(Continued)

Note 15: Interest Expense	1991	1990
Interest on:		
Long-term debt	$ 733	$ 705
Short-term debt	3,695	9,814
Obligations under capital leases	10,596	11,266
	$15,024	$ 21,785

The following note from the 1991 annual report of Du Pont Canada Inc. illustrates the disclosures of a lessee having only operating leases.

Operating Lease Disclosures
Du Pont Canada Inc. (Lessee)

Note 11—Commitments and Contingent Liabilities
The Company's future minimum lease payments under operating leases are as follows:

Years ending December 31

1992	$ 8,334
1993	9,048
1994	2,175
1995	1,836
1996	1,516
Remainder	4,276
	$27,185

FUNDAMENTAL CONCEPTS

1. Leasing has been a popular method of acquiring the use of assets because it (1) is 100% financing at fixed rates, (2) provides protection against obsolescence, (3) is more flexible than other financing arrangements, (4) can be less costly than other forms of financing, and (5) can be a means of off-balance-sheet financing.

2. Lease capitalization is advocated when the lease transfers substantially all of the benefits and risks of ownership of property from the lessor to the lessee.

3. Lessees classify leases as either capital leases or operating leases. In a capital lease the lessee, by capitalizing the present value of the future rental payments, records an asset and a liability at an amount generally representative of the asset's market value or purchase price. Operating leases result in the recognition of only rent expense as it accrues.

4. To be a capital lease, it must satisfy one or more of the following four criteria: (1) the lease transfers ownership, (2) the lease contains a bargain purchase option, (3) the lease term is equal to 75% or more of the estimated economic life of the leased asset, and (4) the present value of the minimum lease payments equals or exceeds 90% of the fair market value of the leased asset.

5. Minimum lease payments include (1) the rental payments made by the lessee over the lease term, (2) the amount of any guaranteed residual value, (3) the amount payable for failure to renew the lease, and (4) any bargain purchase option.

(Continued)

6. Under a capital lease, lessees record depreciation by applying any acceptable method and recognize interest expense by using the effective interest method.

7. Lessors classify leases as either operating leases or as one of two types of capital leases—direct financing leases or sales-type leases.

8. In addition to satisfying one of the four criteria mentioned for lessees (transfer of ownership, bargain purchase option, and the 75% and 90% rules), lessors must meet two other criteria to capitalize a lease: (1) collectibility of the rental payments must be reasonably predictable and (2) future costs are reasonably predictable or lessor's performance is substantially complete.

9. Lessors continue to depreciate assets under operating leases and recognize rental revenue as it accrues.

10. Lessors recognize only interest revenue for direct financing leases, but they recognize a manufacturer's or dealer's profit and interest revenue for sales-type leases.

11. Lessees capitalize guaranteed residual values but not unguaranteed residual values. To lessors, the net investment to be recovered is the same whether the residual value is guaranteed or unguaranteed.

12. If a sale-leaseback transaction qualifies as a capital lease, the seller-lessee accounts for the transaction as a sale and for the lease as a capital lease, whereas the purchaser-lessor records the transaction as a purchase and a direct financing lease.

13. The CICA requires extensive disclosure of details pertaining to capitalized leases. These include, among other items, assets held or leased under capital leases and future minimum lease payments (receivable) both in aggregate for the lease term and detailed for each of the five years following the date of the financial statements.

APPENDIX 21A

Illustration of Different Lease Arrangements

To illustrate a number of concepts discussed in this chapter, assume that Morgan Bakeries is involved in four different lease situations, as described below. These leases are noncancellable and in no case does Morgan receive title to the properties leased during or at the end of the lease term. All leases start on January 1, 1994, with the first rental due at the beginning of the year. The additional information is as shown below.

Lessor	Harmon Ltd.	Arden's Oven Co.	Mendota Truck Co.	Appleland Computer
Type of property	Cabinets	Oven	Truck	Computer
Yearly rental	$6,000.00	$15,000.00	$5,582.62	$3,557.25
Lease term	20 years	10 years	3 years	3 years
Estimated economic life	30 years	25 years	7 years	5 years
Purchase option	None	$75,000 at end of 10 years $4,000 at end of 15 years	None	$3,000 at end of 3 years, which approximates fair market value.
Renewal option	None	5-year renewal option at $15,000 per year	None	1 year at $1,500; no penalty for nonrenewal
Fair market value at inception of lease	$60,000.00	$120,000.00	$20,000.00	$10,000.00
Cost of asset to lessor	$60,000.00	$120,000.00	$15,000.00	$10,000.00
Residual value				
Guaranteed	–0–	–0–	$7,000.00	–0–
Unguaranteed	$5,000.00	–0–	–0–	$3,000.00
Incremental borrowing rate of lessee	12%	12%	12%	12%
Executory costs paid by	Lessee $300 per year	Lessee $1,000 per year	Lessee $500 per year	Lessor Estimated to be $500 per year
Present value of minimum lease payments Using incremental borrowing rate of lessee	$50,194.68	$115,153.35	$20,000.00	$8,224.16
Using implicit rate of lessor	Not known	Not known	Not known	Known by lessee: $8,027.48
Fair market value at end of lease	$5,000.00	$80,000 at end of 10 years $60,000 at end of 15 years	Not available	$60,000 at end of 15 years

Harmon Ltd.

The following is an analysis of the Harmon Ltd. lease:

1. **Transfer of title?** No.

2. **Bargain purchase option?** No.

3. **Economic life test (75% test).** The lease term is 20 years and the estimated economic life is 30 years. Thus it does *not* meet the 75% test.

4. **Recovery of investment test (90% test):**

Fair market value	$60,000	Rental payments	$ 6,000
Rate	90%	PV of annuity due for 20 years at 12%	× 8.36578
	$54,000		$50,194.68

Because the present value of the minimum lease payments is less than 90% of the fair market value, the 90% test is not met. Both Morgan and Harmon should account for this lease as an operating lease, as indicated by the entries shown below for January 1, 1994.

Morgan Bakeries (Lessee)			Harmon Ltd. (Lessor)		
Rental expense	6,000		Cash	6,000	
Cash		6,000	Rental revenue		6,000

Arden's Oven Co.

The following is an analysis of the Arden's Oven Co. lease:

1. **Transfer of title?** No.

2. **Bargain purchase option?** The $75,000 option at the end of 10 years does not appear to be sufficiently lower than the expected fair value of $80,000 to be reasonably assured that it will be exercised. However, the $4,000 at the end of 15 years when the fair value is $60,000 does appear to be a bargain. From the information given, criterion 1 is therefore met.

3. **Economic life test (75% test):** Given that a bargain purchase option exists, the lease term is the initial lease period of 10 years plus the 5-year renewal option, since it precedes a bargain purchase option. Even though the lease term is now 15 years, this test is still not met because 75% of the economic life of 25 years is 18.75 years.

4. **Recovery of investment test (90% test):**

Fair market value	$120,000	Rental payments (1–10)	$ 15,000.00
Rate	90%	PV of annuity due for 15 years	
90% of fair market value	$108,000	at 12%	× 7.62817
		PV of rental payments	$114,422.55
		PV of bargain purchase option:	
		($4,000 × 0.18270 = $730.80)	
		PV of rental	$114,422.55
		PV of bargain purchase option	730.80
		PV of minimum lease payments	$115,153.35

The present value of the minimum lease payments is greater than 90% of the fair market value; therefore, the 90% test *is* met. Morgan Bakeries should account for this as a capital lease because both criteria 2 and 4 are met. Assuming that Arden's implicit rate is the same as Morgan's incremental borrowing rate, the following entries are made on January 1, 1994.

Morgan Bakeries (Lessee)			Arden's Oven Co. (Lessor)		
Leased Asset—Oven	115,153.35		Lease Payments		
Obligation Under			Receivable	$229,000*	
Capital Lease		115,153.35	Asset—Oven		120,000
			Unearned Interest		
			Revenue		109,000
			*([$15,000 × 15] + $4,000)		

Morgan Bakeries would depreciate the lease asset over its economic life of 25 years, given the bargain purchase option. Arden does not use sales-type lease accounting because the fair market value and the cost of the asset are the same at the inception of the lease.

Mendota Truck Co.

The following is an analysis of the Mendota Truck Co. lease:

1. **Transfer of title?** No.

2. **Bargain purchase option?** No.

3. **Economic life test (75% test):** The lease term is three years and the estimated economic life is seven years. Thus it does *not* meet the 75% test.

4. **Recovery of investment test (90% test):**

Fair market value	$20,000	Rental payments	$ 5,582.62
Rate	90%	PV on annuity due for	
Adjusted fair market value	$18,000	3 years at 12%	× 2.69005
		PV of rental payments	$15,017.54*
		(*adjusted for .01 due to rounding)	
		Guaranteed residual value	$ 7,000.00
		PV of 1 for 3 years at 12%	× 0.71178
		PV of guaranteed residual value	$ 4,982.46
		PV of rental payments	$15,017.54
		PV of guaranteed residual value	4,982.46
		PV of minimum lease payments	$20,000.00

The present value of the minimum lease payments is greater than 90% of the fair market value; therefore, the 90% test *is* met. Assuming that Mendota Truck Co.'s implicit rate is the same as Morgan's incremental borrowing rate, the following entries are made on January 1, 1994.

Morgan Bakeries (Lessee)			Mendota Truck (Lessor)		
Leased Asset	20,000.00		Lease Payments		
Lease Obligation		20,000.00	Receivable	23,747.86*	
			Cost of Goods Sold	15,000.00	
			Asset—Truck		15,000.00
			Sales		20,000.00
			Unearned Interest		
			Revenue		3,747.86
			*([$5,582.62 × 3] + $7,000)		

The leased asset is depreciated over three years to its guaranteed residual value.

Appleland Computer

The following is an analysis of the Appleland Computer lease:

1. **Transfer of title?** No.

2. **Bargain purchase option?** No. The option to purchase at the end of three years at appropriate fair market value is clearly not a bargain.

3. **Economic life test (75% test):** The lease term is three years and no bargain renewal period exists. Therefore, the 75% test is *not* met.

4. **Recovery of investment test (90% test):**

Fair market value	$10,000	Rental payments	$3,557.25
Rate	90%	Less executory costs	500.00
90% of fair market value	$ 9,000	and profit thereon	$3,057.25
		PV of annuity due for 3 years at 12%	× 2.69005
		PV of minimum lease payments using incremental borrowing rate	$8,224.16

The present value of the minimum lease payments using the incremental borrowing rate is $8,224.16; using the implicit rate, it is $8,027.48. The lessee uses the lower $8,027.48 when comparing to the adjusted fair market value. However, the present value of the minimum lease payments is lower than the adjusted fair market value, and therefore the recovery of investment test is *not* met.

The following entries are therefore made on January 1, 1994, indicating an operating lease.

Morgan Bakeries (Lessee)			Appleland Computer (Lessor)		
Rental Expense	3,557.25		Cash	3,557.25	
Cash		3,557.25	Rental Revenue		3,557.25

If the lease payments had been $3,557.25 with no executory costs involved, this lease arrangement would have qualified for capital lease accounting treatment.

APPENDIX 21B
Real Estate Leases

Special problems can arise when leases involve land, or land and buildings, or equipment as well as real estate.

Land

If land is the sole item of property leased, the *lessee* should account for the lease as a capital lease only if criterion 1 is met; that is, if the lease transfers ownership of the property or contains a bargain purchase option. Otherwise, it is accounted for as an operating lease. Although the lease is classified as a capital lease when ownership of the land is expected to pass to the lessee, this is an asset that is not normally depreciated. The *lessor* accounts for a land lease either as a sales-type or direct financing lease, whichever is appropriate, provided the lease transfers ownership or contains a bargain purchase option and meets both the collectibility and uncertainties tests—otherwise the operating method is used.

Land and Building

If both land and building are involved and the lease transfers ownership or contains a bargain purchase option, the capitalized value of the land and the building should be separately classified by the *lessee*. The present value of the minimum lease payments is allocated between land and building in proportion to their fair values at the inception of the lease. The *lessor* accounts for the lease as a single unit, either as a sales-type, direct financing, or an operating lease, as appropriate.

When both land and building are involved and the lease does not transfer ownership or contain a bargain purchase option, the accounting treatment is dependent on the proportion of land to building. If the fair value of the land is "minor" in relation to the total fair value of the leased property, both lessee and lessor consider the land and the building as a single unit. However, if the fair value of the land at the inception of the lease is "significant" in relation to the total fair value of the leased property, the land and building are considered separately by both lessee and lessor. The lessee accounts for the building as a capital lease and the land as an operating lease if one of the two remaining criteria (2 and 3) is met. If none of the criteria are met, the lessee uses the operating method on the land and building. The lessor accounts for the building as a sales-type or direct financing lease, as appropriate, and the land element separately as an operating lease.

Real Estate and Equipment

If a lease involves both real estate and equipment, the portion of the lease payments applicable to the equipment should be estimated by whatever means are appropriate and reasonable. The equipment then should be treated separately for purposes of applying the criteria and accounted for separately according to its classification by both lessees and lessors.

Note: All **asterisked** questions, cases, exercises, and problems relate to material contained in the appendices to this chapter.

———— QUESTIONS ————

1. Daniel Ltd. is expanding its operations and is in the process of selecting the method of financing this program. After some investigation, the company determines that it may (1) issue bonds and with the proceeds purchase the needed assets or (2) lease the assets on a long-term basis. Without knowing the comparative costs involved, answer these questions:
   (a) What might be the advantages of leasing the assets instead of owning them?
   (b) What might be the disadvantages of leasing the assets instead of owning them?
   (c) In what way will the balance sheet be differently affected by leasing the assets as opposed to issuing bonds and purchasing the assets?

2. King Corp. is considering leasing a significant number of assets. The president, Patty Lewis, is attending an informal meeting in the afternoon with a potential lessor. Because her legal advisor cannot be reached, she has called on you, the controller, to brief her on the general provisions of lease agreements to which she should give consideration in such preliminary discussions with a possible lessor. Identify the general provisions of the lease agreement that the president should be told to include in the discussion with the potential lessor.

3. Identify the two recognized lease accounting methods for lessees and distinguish between them.

4. P. Bradley Company rents a warehouse on a month-to-month basis for the storage of its excess inventory. Periodically the company must rent space whenever its production greatly exceeds actual sales. For several years, the company officials have discussed building their own storage facility, but this enthusiasm wavers when sales increase sufficiently to absorb the excess inventory. What is the nature of this type of lease arrangement and what accounting treatment should be accorded it?

5. Why are present value concepts appropriate and applicable in accounting for financing-type lease arrangements?

6. Differentiate between the "lessee's incremental borrowing rate" and the "lessor's implicit rate" in accounting for leases, indicating when one or the other should be used.

7. Outline the accounting procedures involved in applying the operating method by a lessee.

8. Outline the accounting procedures involved in applying the capital lease method by a lessee.

9. Identify the lease classifications for lessors and the criteria that must be met for each classification.

10. Outline the accounting procedures involved in applying the direct financing method.

11. Outline the accounting procedures involved in applying the operating method by a lessor.

12. Jamieson Limited is a manufacturer and lessor of computer equipment. What should be the nature of its lease arrangements with lessees if the company wishes to account for its lease transactions as sales-type leases?

13. Okamota Corporation's lease arrangements qualify as sales-type leases at the time of entering into the transactions. How should the corporation recognize revenues and costs in these situations?

14. Dawn Coe, M.D. (lessee), has a noncancellable 20-year lease with Lupul Realty, Inc. (lessor) for the use of a medical building. Taxes, insurance, and maintenance are paid by the lessee in addition to the fixed annual payments, of which the present value is equal to the fair market value of the leased property. At the end of the lease period, title to the property becomes the lessee's on payment of a nominal price. Considering the terms of the lease described above, comment on the nature of the lease transaction and the accounting treatment that should be accorded it by the lessee.

15. The residual value is the estimated fair value of the leased property at the end of the lease term.
    (a) Of what significance is (1) an unguaranteed and (2) a guaranteed residual value in the lessee's accounting for a capitalized lease transaction?
    (b) Of what significance is (1) an unguaranteed and (2) a guaranteed residual value in the lessor's accounting for a direct financing lease transaction?

16. How should changes in the estimated residual value be handled by the lessor?

17. Describe the effect of a bargain purchase option on accounting for a capital lease transaction by a lessee.

18. What are initial direct costs and how are they accounted for?

19. What is the nature of a sale-leaseback transaction?

20. What disclosures should be made by a lessee if the leased assets and the related obligation are not capitalized?

*21. Assume that Cathy Goering leases land for agricultural purposes. What criteria are applied to determine whether capital or operating lease treatment is applied?

--- CASES ---

C21-1 **(LESSEE ACCOUNTING AND REPORTING)** On January 1, 1994, Evans Company entered into a noncancellable lease for a machine to be used in its manufacturing operations. The lease transfers ownership of the machine to Evans by the end of the lease term. The term of the lease is eight years. The minimum lease payment made by Evans on January 1, 1994 was one of eight equal annual payments. At the inception of the lease, the criteria established for classification as a capital lease by the lessee were met.

Instructions

(a) What is the theoretical basis for the accounting standard that requires certain long-term leases to be capitalized by the lessee? Do not discuss the specific criteria for classifying a specific lease as a capital lease.

(b) How should Evans account for this lease at its inception and determine the amount to be recorded?

(c) What expenses related to this lease will Evans incur during the first year of the lease and how will they be determined?

(d) How should Evans report the lease transaction on its December 31, 1994 balance sheet?

(AICPA adapted)

(LESSOR AND LESSEE ACCOUNTING AND DISCLOSURE) B. Shapiro Corp. entered into a lease **C21-2** arrangement with Wildcat Leasing Corporation for a certain machine. Wildcat's primary business is leasing and it is not a manufacturer or dealer. Shapiro will lease the machine for a period of three years, which is 50% of the machine's economic life. Wildcat will take possession of the machine at the end of the initial three-year lease and lease it to another smaller company that does not need the most current version of the machine. Shapiro does not guarantee any residual value for the machine and will not purchase the machine at the end of the lease term.

Shapiro's incremental borrowing rate is 16% and the implicit rate in the lease is 14.5%. Shapiro has no way of knowing the implicit rate used by Wildcat. Using either rate, the present value of the minimum lease payments is between 90% and 100% of the fair value of the machinery at the date of the lease agreement.

Shapiro has agreed to pay all executory costs directly and no allowance for these costs is included in the lease payments.

Wildcat is reasonably certain that Shapiro will pay all lease payments. Because Shapiro has agreed to pay all executory costs, there are no important uncertainties regarding costs to be incurred by Wildcat. Assume that no indirect costs are involved.

Instructions

(a) With respect to Shapiro (the lessee), answer the following:

1. What type of lease has been entered into? Explain the reason for your answer.

2. How should Shapiro compute the appropriate amount to be recorded for the lease or asset acquired?

3. What accounts will be created or affected by this transaction and how will the lease or asset and other costs related to the transaction be matched with earnings?

4. What disclosures must Shapiro make regarding this lease or asset?

(b) With respect to Wildcat (the lessor), answer the following:

1. What type of leasing arrangement has been entered into? Explain the rason for your answer.

2. How should this lease be recorded by Wildcat and how are the appropriate amounts determined?

3. How should Wildcat determine the appropriate amount of earnings to be recognized from each lease payment?

4. What disclosures must Wildcat make regarding this lease?

(AICPA adapted)

(LESSEE CAPITALIZATION CRITERIA) On January 1, Lia Company, a lessee, entered into three non- **C21-3** cancellable leases for brand new equipment, Lease J, Lease K, and Lease L. None of the three leases transfers ownership of the equipment to Lia at the end of the lease term. For each of the three leases, the present value at the beginning of the lease term of the minimum lease payments, excluding that portion of the payments representing executory costs such as insurance, maintenance, and taxes to be paid by the lessor, is 75% of the fair value of the equipment. The following information is peculiar to each lease.

1. Lease J does not contain a bargain purchase option; the lease term is equal to 80% of the estimated economic life of the equipment.

2. Lease K contains a bargain purchase option; the lease term is equal to 50% of the estimated economic life of the equipment.

3. Lease L does not contain a bargain purchase option; the lease term is equal to 50% of the estimated economic life of the equipment.

Instructions

(a) How should Lia Company classify each of the three leases above, and why? Discuss the rationale for your answer.

(b) What amount, if any, should Lia record as a liability at the inception of the lease for each of the three leases above?

(c) Assuming that the minimum lease payments are made on a straight-line basis, how should Lia record each minimum lease payment for each of the three leases above?

(AICPA adapted)

C21-4 **(COMPARISON OF DIFFERENT TYPES OF ACCOUNTING BY LESSEE AND LESSOR)**
Part 1. Capital leases and operating leases are the two classifications of leases described in the *CICA Handbook* from the standpoint of the *lessee*.

Instructions

(a) Describe how a capital lease would be accounted for by the lessee both at the inception of the lease and during the first year of the lease, assuming the lease transfers ownership of the property to the lessee by the end of the lease.

(b) Describe how an operating lease would be accounted for by the lessee both at the inception of the lease and during the first year of the lease, assuming equal monthly payments are made by the lessee at the beginning of each month of the lease. Describe the change in accounting, if any, when rental payments are not made on a straight-line basis.

Do *not* discuss the criteria for distinguishing between capital leases and operating leases.

Part 2. Sales-type leases and direct financing leases are two of the classifications of leases described in the *CICA Handbook* from the standpoint of the *lessor*.

Instructions

Compare and contrast a sales-type lease with a direct financing lease as follows:

(a) Gross investment in the lease.

(b) Amortization of unearned interest revenue.

(c) Manufacturer's or dealer's profit.

Do *not* discuss the criteria for distinguishing between the leases described above and operating leases.

(AICPA adapted)

C21-5 **(LESSEE CAPITALIZATION OF BARGAIN PURCHASE OPTION)**   Norman Corporation is a diversified company with nationwide interests in commercial real estate developments, banking, copper mining, and metal fabrication. The company has offices and operating locations in major cities throughout Canada. Corporate headquarters for Norman Corporation is located in a metropolitan area of a western province, and executives connected with various phases of company operations travel extensively. Corporate management is currently evaluating the feasibility of acquiring a business aircraft that can be used by company executives to expedite business travel to areas not adequately served by commercial airlines. Proposals for either leasing or purchasing a suitable aircraft have been analysed and the leasing proposal is considered to be more desirable.

The proposed lease agreement involves a twin-engine turboprop Viking that has a fair market value of $900,000. This plane would be leased for a period of 10 years beginning January 1, 1994. The lease agreement is cancellable only on accidental destruction of the plane. An annual lease payment of $127,600 is due on January 1 of each year; the first payment is to be made January 1, 1994. Maintenance operations are strictly scheduled by the lessor, and Norman Corporation will pay for these services as they are performed. Estimated annual maintenance costs are $6,200. The lessor will pay all insurance premiums and local property taxes, which amount to a combined total of $3,600 annually and are included in the annual lease payment of $127,600. On expiration of the 10-year lease, Norman Corporation can purchase the Viking for $40,000. The estimated useful life of the plane is 15 years, and its salvage value in the used plane market is estimated to be $100,000 after 10 years. The salvage value probably will never be less than $75,000 if the engines are overhauled and maintained as prescribed by the manufacturer. If the purchase option is not exercised, possession of the plane will revert to the lessor, and there is no provision for renewing the lease agreement beyond its termination on December 31, 2003.

Norman Corporation can borrow $900,000 under a 10-year term loan agreement at an annual interest rate of 12%. The lessor's implicit interest rate is not expressly stated in the lease agreement, but this rate appears to be approximately 8%, based on 10 net rental payments of $124,000 per year and the initial market value of $900,000 for the plane. On January 1, 1994, the present value of all net rental payments and the purchase option of $40,000 is $800,000, using the 12% interest rate. The present value of all net rental payments and the $40,000 purchase option on January 1, 1994 is $920,000, using the 8% interest rate implicit in the lease agreement. The financial vice-president of Norman Corporation has established that this lease agreement is a capital lease, as defined in Section 3065 of the *CICA Handbook*, "Accounting for Leases."

Instructions

(a) What is the appropriate amount that Norman Corporation should recognize for the leased aircraft on its balance sheet after the lease is signed?

(b) Without prejudice to your answer to (a), assume that the annual lease payment is $127,600 as stated in the text, that the appropriate capitalized amount for the leased aircraft is $900,000 on January 1, 1994, and that the interest rate is 9%. How will the lease be reported in the December 31, 1994 balance sheet and related income statement? (Ignore any income tax implications.)

(CMA adapted)

(SALE-LEASEBACK) On January 1, 1994, Metcalf Company sold equipment for cash and leased it back. As **C21-6** seller-lessee, Metcalf retained the right to substantially all of the remaining use of the equipment.

The term of the lease is eight years. There is a gain on the sale portion of the transaction. The lease portion of the transaction is classified appropriately as a capital lease.

Instructions

(a) What is the theoretical basis for requiring lessees to capitalize certain long-term leases? Do *not* discuss the specific criteria for classifying a lease as a capital lease.

(b) 1. How should Metcalf account for the sale portion of the sale-leaseback transaction at January 1, 1994?

2. How should Metcalf account for the leaseback portion of the sale-leaseback transaction at January 1, 1994?

(c) How should Metcalf account for the gain on the sale portion of the sale-leaseback transaction during the first year of the lease? Why?

(AICPA adapted)

(ETHICAL ISSUE: LEASE AGREEMENTS) Amboy Corporation entered into a lease agreement for **C21-7** 10 photocopy machines for its corporate headquarters. The lease agreement qualifies as an operating lease in all terms except there is a bargain purchase option. After the five-year lease term, the corporation can purchase each copier for $1,000, when the anticipated market value is $2,500.

Mark Althaus, the financial vice-president, thinks the financial statements must necessarily recognize the lease agreement as a capital lease because of the bargain purchase agreement. The controller, Alicia Greenberg, disagrees: "Although I don't know much about the copiers themselves, there is a way to avoid recording the lease liability." She argues that the corporation might claim that copier technology advances rapidly and that by the end of the lease term the machines will most likely not be worth the $1,000 bargain price.

Instructions

(a) What ethical issue is at stake?

(b) Should the controller's argument be accepted if she does not really know much about copier technology? Would it make a difference if the controller was knowledgeable about the pace of change in copier technology?

(c) What would you do?

––––––––––– EXERCISES –––––––––––

E21-1 **(LESSEE ENTRIES: BASIC CAPITAL LEASE)**   Hoch Company enters into a lease agreement on July 1, 1994 for the purpose of leasing a machine to be used in its manufacturing operations. The following data pertain to this agreement:

1. The term of the noncancellable lease is three years, with no renewal option and no residual value at the end of the lease term. Payments of $98,700.80 are due on July 1 of each year, beginning July 1, 1994.

2. The fair value of the machine on July 1, 1994 is $290,000. The machine has a remaining economic life of five years, with no salvage value. The machine reverts to the lessor on the termination of the lease.

3. Hoch Company elects to depreciate the machine on the straight-line method.

4. Hoch Company's incremental borrowing rate is 10% per year, and it has no knowledge of the implicit rate computed by the lessor.

Instructions

Prepare the journal entries on the books of the lessee that relate to the lease agreement through June 30, 1997. The accounting period of Hoch Company ends on December 31. (Assume that reversing entries are made.)

E21-2 **(LESSEE COMPUTATIONS AND ENTRIES: CAPITAL LEASE WITH GUARANTEED RESIDUAL VALUE)**   Faldo Company leases an automobile with a fair value of $7,850 from Wheaton Motors, Inc. on the following terms:

1. Noncancellable term of 50 months.

2. Rental of $180 per month (at end of each month; present value at 1% per month is $7,055).

3. Estimated residual value after 50 months is $1,100 (the present value at 1% per month is $669). Faldo Company guarantees the residual value of $1,100.

4. Estimated economic life of the automobile is 60 months.

5. Faldo Company's incremental borrowing rate is 12% a year (1% per month). Wheaton's implicit rate is unknown.

Instructions

(a) What is the nature of this lease to Faldo Company?

(b) What is the present value of the minimum lease payments?

(c) Record the lease on Faldo Company's books at the date of inception.

(d) Record the first month's depreciation on Faldo Company's books (assume straight line).

(e) Record the first month's lease payment.

(LESSEE ENTRIES: CAPITAL LEASE WITH EXECUTORY COSTS AND UNGUARANTEED **E21-3** **RESIDUAL VALUES)** On January 1, 1994, Watson Paper Co. signs a 10-year noncancellable lease agreement to lease a storage building from Player Storage Company. The following information pertains to this lease agreement:

1. The agreement requires equal annual rental payments of $70,054.49 beginning January 1, 1994.

2. The fair value of the building on January 1, 1994 is $440,000.

3. The building has an estimated economic life of 12 years with an unguaranteed residual value of $10,000. Watson Paper Co. depreciates similar buildings on the straight-line method.

4. The lease is nonrenewable. At the termination of the lease, the building reverts to the lessor.

5. Watson Paper's incremental borrowing rate is 12% per year. The lessor's implicit rate is not known by Watson Paper Co.

6. The yearly rental payment includes $525 of executory costs related to taxes on the property.

Instructions

Prepare the journal entries on the lessee's books to reflect the signing of the lease agreement and to record the payments and expenses related to this lease for the years 1994 and 1995. Watson Paper's corporate year end is December 31.

(LESSOR ENTRIES: DIRECT FINANCING LEASE WITH BARGAIN PURCHASE OPTION) **E21-4** Palmer Leasing Company signs a lease agreement on January 1, 1994 to lease electronic equipment to Nicklaus Company at cost. The term of the noncancellable lease is two years and payments are required at the end of each year. The following information relates to this agreement:

1. Nicklaus Company has the option to purchase the equipment for $10,000 on termination of the lease.

2. The equipment has a cost of $160,000 to Palmer Leasing Company; the useful economic life is two years, with a salvage value of $10,000.

3. Nicklaus Company is required to pay $5,000 each year to the lessor for executory costs.

4. Palmer Leasing Company wants to earn a return of 10% on its investment.

5. Collectibility of the payments is reasonably predictable and there are no important uncertainties surrounding the costs yet to be incurred by the lessor.

Instructions

(a) Prepare the journal entries on the books of Palmer Leasing Company to reflect the payments received under the lease and to recognize income for the years 1994 and 1995.

(b) Assuming that Nicklaus Company exercises its option to purchase the equipment on December 31, 1995, prepare the journal entry to reflect the sale on Palmer's books.

E21-5 **(TYPE OF LEASE: AMORTIZATION SCHEDULE)** Finch Leasing Company leases a new machine that has a cost and fair value of $101,250 to Woosman Corporation on a three-year noncancellable contract. Woosman Corporation agrees to assume all risks of normal ownership, including such costs as insurance, taxes, and maintenance. The machine has a three-year useful life and no residual value. The lease was signed on January 1, 1994; Finch Leasing Company expects to earn a 9% return on its investment; and the annual rentals are payable on each December 31.

Instructions

(a) Discuss the nature of the lease arrangement and the accounting method each party to the lease should apply.

(b) Prepare an amortization schedule that would be suitable for both lessor and lessee and would cover all of the years involved.

E21-6 **(LESSOR ENTRIES: SALES-TYPE LEASE)** Trevino Company leases a car at fair value to Nancy Lopez on January 1, 1994. The term on the noncancellable lease is four years. The following information about the lease is provided:

1. Title to the car passes to the lessee on termination of the lease. Residual value is estimated at $1,000 at the end of the lease.

2. The fair value of the car is $17,657. The car is carried in Trevino's inventory at $12,000. The car has an economic life of five years.

3. Trevino Company wants a rate of return of 9% on its investment.

4. Collectibility of the lease payments is reasonably predictable. There are no important uncertainties surrounding the amount of costs yet to be incurred by the lessor.

5. Equal annual lease payments are due at the beginning of each lease year.

Instructions

(a) Prepare a lease amortization schedule for Trevino Company for the four-year lease term.

(b) What type of lease is this? Discuss.

(c) Prepare the journal entries in 1994, 1995, and 1996 to record the lease agreement, the receipt of lease payments, and the recognition of income.

E21-7 **(LESSEE ENTRIES WITH BARGAIN PURCHASE OPTION)** The following facts pertain to a noncancellable lease agreement between Romero Leasing Company and Crenshaw Company, a lessee:

Inception date	May 1, 1994
Annual lease payment due at the beginning of	
each year, beginning with May 1, 1994	$18,589.67
Bargain purchase option price at end of lease term	$ 4,000.00
Lease term	5 years
Economic life of leased equipment	10 years
Lessor's cost	$65,000.00
Fair value of asset at April 1, 1994	$80,000.00
Lessor's implicit rate	10%
Lessee's incremental borrowing rate	10%

The collectibility of the lease payments is reasonably predictable and there are no important uncertainties surrounding the costs yet to be incurred by the lessor. The lessee assumes responsibility for all executory costs.

Instructions

(Round all numbers to the nearest cent.)

(a) Discuss the nature of this lease to Crenshaw Company.

(b) Discuss the nature of this lease to Romero Leasing Company.

(c) Prepare a lease amortization schedule for Crenshaw Company for the five-year lease term.

(d) Prepare the journal entries on the lessee's books to reflect the signing of the lease agreement and to record the payments and expenses related to this lease for the years 1994 and 1995. Crenshaw's annual accounting period ends on December 31. Reversing entries are used by Crenshaw.

(LESSOR ENTRIES WITH BARGAIN PURCHASE OPTION) Refer to the lease agreement between **E21-8** Romero Leasing Company and Crenshaw Company described in E21-7.

Instructions

Based on the data in E21-7, do the following for the lessor, rounding all numbers to the nearest cent:

(a) Compute the amount of gross investment at the inception of the lease.

(b) Compute the amount of net investment at the inception of the lease.

(c) Prepare a lease amortization schedule for Romero Leasing Company for the five-year term.

(d) Prepare the journal entries to reflect the signing of the lease agreement and to record the receipts and income related to this lease for the years 1994, 1995, and 1996. The lessor's accounting period ends on December 31. Reversing entries are not used by Romero.

(COMPUTATION OF RENTAL: JOURNAL ENTRIES FOR LESSOR) Wadkins Leasing Company **E21-9** signs an agreement on January 1, 1994 to lease equipment to Irwin Company. The following information relates to this agreement:

1. The term of the noncancellable lease is six years, with no renewal option. The equipment has an estimated economic life of six years.

2. The cost of the asset to the lessor is $240,000. The fair value of the asset at January 1, 1994 is $240,000.

3. The asset will revert to the lessor at the end of the lease term, at which time the asset is expected to have a residual value of $43,250, none of which is guaranteed.

4. Irwin Company assumes direct responsibility for all executory costs.

5. The agreement requires equal annual rental payments, beginning on January 1, 1994.

6. Collectibility of the lease payments is reasonably predictable. There are no important uncertainties surrounding the amount of costs yet to be incurred by the lessor.

Instructions

(Round all numbers to the nearest cent.)

(a) Assuming the lessor desires a 10% rate of return on its investment, calculate the amount of the annual rental payment required.

(b) Prepare an amortization schedule that would be suitable for the lessor for the lease term.

(c) Prepare all of the journal entries for the lessor for 1994 and 1995 to record the lease agreement, the receipt of lease payments, and the recognition of income. Assume the lessor's annual accounting period ends on December 31.

E21-10 **(AMORTIZATION SCHEDULE AND JOURNAL ENTRIES FOR LESSEE)** Hammond Leasing Company signs an agreement on January 1, 1994 to lease equipment to Peete Company. The following information relates to this agreement:

1. The term of the noncancellable lease is five years, with no renewal option. The equipment has an estimated economic life of five years.

2. The fair market value of the asset at January 1, 1994 is $80,000.

3. The asset will revert to the lessor at the end of the lease term, at which time the asset is expected to have a residual value of $7,000, none of which is guaranteed.

4. Peete Company assumes direct responsibility for all executory costs, which include the following annual amounts: $900 to Frontier Insurance Company for insurance, $2,000 to County of Appleton for property taxes.

5. The agreement requires equal annual rental payments of $18,142.95 to the lessor, beginning January 1, 1994.

6. The lessee's incremental borrowing rate is 12%. The lessor's implicit rate is 10% and is known to the lessee.

7. Peete Company uses the straight-line depreciation method for all equipment.

8. Peete uses reversing entries when appropriate.

Instructions

(Round all numbers to the nearest cent.)

(a) Prepare an amortization schedule that would be suitable for the lessee for the lease term.

(b) Prepare all of the journal entries for the lessee for 1994 and 1995 to record the lease agreement, the lease payments, and all expenses related to this lease. Assume the lessee's annual accounting period ends on December 31.

E21-11 **(ACCOUNTING FOR AN OPERATING LEASE)** On January 1, 1994, Azinger Co. leased a building to Aoki Inc. The relevant information related to the lease is as follows:

1. The lease arrangement is for 10 years.

2. The leased building cost $4,000,000 and was purchased for cash on January 1, 1994.

3. The building is depreciated on a straight-line basis. Its estimated economic life is 50 years.

4. Lease payments are $200,000 per year and are made at the end of the year.

5. Property tax expense of $40,000 and insurance expense of $8,000 on the building were incurred by Azinger in the first year. Payment on these two items was made at the end of the year.

6. Both the lessor and the lessee are on a calendar-year basis.

Instructions

(a) Prepare the journal entries that Azinger Co. should make in 1994.

(b) Prepare the journal entries that Aoki Inc. should make in 1994.

(c) If Azinger paid $30,000 to a real estate broker on January 1, 1994 as a fee for finding the lessee, how much should be reported as an expense for this item in 1994 by Azinger Co.?

(ACCOUNTING FOR AN OPERATING LEASE)   On January 1, 1994, a machine was purchased for **E21-12** $800,000 by Nelson Co. The machine is expected to have an eight-year life, with no salvage value. It is to be depreciated on a straight-line basis. The machine was leased to Geiberger Inc. on January 1, 1994 at an annual rental of $180,000. Other relevant information is as follows:

1. The lease term is for three years.

2. Nelson incurred maintenance and other executory costs of $20,000 in 1994 related to this lease.

3. The machine could have been sold by Nelson for $840,000 instead of leasing it.

4. Geiberger is required to pay a rent security deposit of $35,000 and to prepay the last month's rent of $15,000.

Instructions

(a)   How much should Nelson Co. report as income before income tax on this lease for 1994?

(b)   What amount should Geiberger Inc. report for rent expense for 1994 on this lease?

(OPERATING LEASE FOR LESSEE AND LESSOR)   On February 20, 1994, Archer, Inc. purchased a **E21-13** machine for $1,620,000 for the purpose of leasing it. The machine is expected to have a 10-year life, no residual value, and will be depreciated on the straight-line basis. The machine was leased to Dent Company on March 1, 1994 for a four-year period at a monthly rental of $20,000. There is no provision for the renewal of the lease or purchase of the machine by the lessee at the expiration of the lease term. Archer paid $36,000 of commissions associated with negotiating the lease in February 1994.

Instructions

(a)   What expense should Dent record as a result of the facts above for the year ended December 31, 1994? Show supporting computations in good form.

(b)   What income or loss before income taxes should Archer record as a result of the facts above for the year ended December 31, 1994? (**Hint:** Amortize commissions over the life of the lease.)

(AICPA adapted)

(SALE AND LEASEBACK)   On January 1, 1994, Conrad Corporation sells a computer to Liquidity Finance **E21-14** Co. for $680,000 and immediately leases the computer back. The relevant information is as follows:

1. The computer was carried on Conrad's books at a value of $600,000.

2. The term of the noncancellable lease is 10 years; title will transfer to Conrad.

3. The lease agreement requires equal rental payments of $110,666.81 at the end of each year.

4. The incremental borrowing rate of Conrad Corporation is 12%. Conrad is aware that Liquidity Finance Co. sets the annual rental to ensure a rate of return of 10%.

5. The computer has a fair value of $680,000 on January 1, 1994 and an estimated economic life of 10 years.

6. Conrad pays executory costs of $6,200 per year.

Instructions

Prepare the journal entries for both the lessee and the lessor for 1994 to reflect the sale and leaseback agreement. No uncertainties exist and collectibility is reasonably certain.

E21-15 (LESSEE-LESSOR, SALE-LEASEBACK)   Presented below are four independent situations.

(a) On December 31, 1994, Hill Inc. sold computer equipment to Coody Co. and immediately leased it back for 10 years. The sales price of the equipment was $500,000, its carrying amount was $410,000, and its estimated remaining economic life was 12 years. Determine the amount of deferred revenue to be reported from the sale of the computer equipment on December 31, 1994.

(b) On December 31, 1994, Barber Co. sold a machine to Charles Co. and simultaneously leased it back for one year. The sale price was $480,000, the carrying amount was $430,000, and the machine had an estimated remaining useful life of 14 years. The present value of the rental payments for the one-year term is $35,000. At December 31, 1994, how much should Barber report as deferred revenue from the sale of the machine?

(c) On January 1, 1994, Beard Corp. sold an airplane with an estimated useful life of 10 years. At the same time, Beard leased back the plane for 10 years. The sales price of the airplane was $500,000; the carrying amount, $390,000; and the annual rental, $73,975.22. Beard intended to depreciate the lease asset using the sum-of-the-years'-digits depreciation method. Discuss how the gain on the sale should be reported at the end of 1994 in the financial statements.

(d) On January 1, 1994, Crampton Co. sold equipment with an estimated useful life of five years. At the same time, Crampton leased back the equipment for two years under a lease classified as an operating lease. The sales price (fair market value) of the equipment was $212,700, the carrying amount was $310,000, the monthly rental under the lease was $6,000, and the present value of the rental payments was $115,753. For the year ended December 31, 1994, determine which items would be reported on its income statement for the sale-leaseback transaction.

PROBLEMS

P21-1 (BASIC LESSEE COMPUTATIONS AND ENTRIES: CAPITAL LEASE)   Beck, Inc. agrees to rent Floyd Winery Corporation the equipment that it requires to expand its production capacity to meet customers' demands for its products. The lease agreement calls for five annual lease payments of $100,000 at the end of each year. On the date the capital lease begins, the lessee recognizes the existence of leased assets and the related lease obligation at the present value of the five annual payments discounted at a rate of 12%, $360,478. The lessee uses the effective interest method of reducing lease obligations. The leased equipment has an estimated useful life of five years and no residual value. Floyd Winery uses the sum-of-the-years'-digits method on similar equipment that it owns.

Instructions

(a) What would be the total amount of the reduction in the lease obligation of the lessee during the first year? The second year?

(b) Prepare the journal entry made by Floyd Winery Corporation (lessee) on the date the lease begins.

(c) Prepare the journal entries to record the lease payment and interest expense for both the first and second years.

(d) Prepare the journal entry at the end of the first full year to recognize depreciation of the leased equipment.

P21-2 (OPERATING LEASE: LESSEE–LESSOR ENTRIES)   Stewart Company leased a new crane to Strange Company under a five-year noncancellable contract starting January 1, 1994. Terms of the lease required payments of $22,000 each January 1, starting January 1, 1994. Stewart would pay insurance, taxes, and maintenance charges on the crane, which has an estimated life of 12 years, a fair value of $160,000, and a cost to Stewart Company of $160,000. The estimated fair value of the crane is expected to be $66,000 at the end of the lease term. No bargain purchase or renewal options were included in the contract. Both Stewart and Strange adjust and close books annually at December 31. Collectibility was reasonably certain and no uncertainties existed relative to unreimbursable lessor costs. Strange's incremental borrowing rate was 10% and Stewart's implicit interest rate of 9% was unknown to Strange.

Instructions

(a) Identify the type of lease involved and give reasons for your classification. Discuss the accounting treatment that should be applied by both the lessee and lessor.

(b) Prepare all of the entries related to the lease contract and leased asset for the year 1994 for the lessee and lessor, assuming:

1. Insurance, $2,900.

2. Taxes, $300.

3. Maintenance, $1,100.

4. Straight-line depreciation and salvage value, $10,000.

(c) Discuss what should be presented in the balance sheet and income statement and related notes of both the lessee and the lessor at December 31, 1994.

(LESSEE–LESSOR ENTRIES, BALANCE SHEET PRESENTATION: SALES-TYPE LEASE) Central **P21-3** Alberta Railroad and Electro-Motive Corporation enter into an agreement that requires Electro-Motive to build three diesel-electric engines to Central Alberta's specifications. On completion of the engines, Central Alberta has agreed to lease them for a period of 10 years and to assume all costs and risks of ownership. The lease is noncancellable, becomes effective on January 1, 1994, and requires annual rental payments of $700,000 due each January 1, beginning in 1994.

Central Alberta's incremental borrowing rate is 10% and the implicit interest rate used by Electro-Motive and known to Central Alberta is 8%. The total cost of building the three engines is $4,100,000. The economic life of the engines is estimated to be 10 years, with residual value set at zero. The railroad depreciates similar equipment on a straight-line basis. At the end of the lease, the railroad assumes title to the engines. Collectibility is reasonably certain and no uncertainties exist relative to unreimbursable lessor costs.

Instructions

(Round all numbers to the nearest dollar.)

(a) Discuss the nature of this lease transaction from the viewpoint of both lessee and lessor.

(b) Prepare the journal entry or entries to record the transaction on January 1, 1994 on the books of the Central Alberta Railroad.

(c) Prepare the journal entry or entries to record the transaction on January 1, 1994 on the books of the Electro-Motive Corporation.

(d) Prepare the journal entries for both the lessee and the lessor to record the first rental payment on January 1, 1994.

(e) Prepare the journal entries to record interest expense (revenue) for both the lessee and lessor at December 31, 1994. (Prepare a two-year lease amortization schedule.)

(f) Show the items and amounts that would be reported on the balance sheet (not notes) at December 31, 1994 for both the lessee and the lessor.

(BALANCE SHEET AND INCOME STATEMENT DISCLOSURE: LESSEE) The following facts per- **P21-4** tain to a noncancellable lease agreement between Ozaki Leasing Company and Renz Company, a lessee, for a computer system.

Inception date	September 1, 1994
Lease term	6 years
Economic life of leased equipment	6 years
Fair value of asset at September 1, 1994	$200,000.00
Residual value at end of lease term	–0–
Lessor's implicit rate	10%
Lessee's incremental borrowing rate	10%
Annual lease payment due at the beginning of each year, beginning with September 1, 1994	$41,746.77

The collectibility of the lease payments is reasonably predictable and there are no important uncertainties surrounding the costs yet to be incurred by the lessor. The lessee assumes responsibility for all executory costs, which amount to $4,000 per year and are to be paid each September 1, beginning September 1, 1994. This $4,000 is not included in the rental payment of $41,746.77. The asset will revert to the lessor at the end of the lease term. The straight-line depreciation method is used for all equipment.

The following amortization schedule has been prepared correctly for use by both the lessor and the lessee in accounting for this lease. The lease is to be accounted for properly as a capital lease by the lessee and as a direct financing lease by the lessor.

Date	Annual Lease Payment/ Receipt	Interest (10%) on Unpaid Obligation/ Net Investment	Reduction of Lease Obligation/ Net Investment	Balance of Lease Obligation/ Net Investment
9/01/94				$200,000.00
9/01/94	$ 41,746.77		$ 41,746.77	158,253.23
9/01/95	41,746.77	$15,825.32	25,921.45	132,331.78
9/01/96	41,746.77	13,233.18	28,513.59	103,818.19
9/01/97	41,746.77	10,381.82	31,364.95	72,453.24
9/01/98	41,746.77	7,245.32	34,501.45	37,951.79
9/01/99	41,746.77	3,794.98*	37,951.79	–0–
	$250,480.62	$50,480.62	$200,000.00	

*Rounding error is 20 cents.

Instructions

(Round all numbers to the nearest cent.)

(a) Assuming the lessee's accounting period ends on August 31, answer the following questions with respect to this lease agreement:

    1. What items and amounts will be shown on the lessee's income statement for the year ending August 31, 1995?

    2. Where and what items and amounts will be shown on the lessee's balance sheet at August 31, 1995?

    3. What items and amounts will be shown on the lessee's income statement for the year ending August 31, 1996?

    4. Where and what items and amounts will be shown on the lessee's balance sheet at August 31, 1996?

(b) Assuming the lessee's accounting period ends on December 31, answer the following questions with respect to this lease agreement.

1. What items and amounts will be shown on the lessee's income statement for the year ending December 31, 1994?

2. Where and what items and amounts will be shown on the lessee's balance sheet at December 31, 1994?

3. What items and amounts will be shown on the lessee's income statement for the year ending December 31, 1995?

4. Where and what items and amounts will be shown on the lessee's balance sheet at December 31, 1995?

(BALANCE SHEET AND INCOME STATEMENT DISCLOSURE: LESSOR) Assume the same information as for Problem 21-4. **P21-5**

(a) Assuming the lessor's accounting period ends on August 31, answer the following questions with respect to this lease agreement:

1. What items and amounts will be shown on the lessor's income statement for the year ending August 31, 1995?

2. Where and what items and amounts will be shown on the lessor's balance sheet at August 31, 1995?

3. What items and amounts will be shown on the lessor's income statement for the year ending August 31, 1996?

4. Where and what items and amounts will be shown on the lessor's balance sheet at August 31, 1996?

(b) Assuming the lessor's accounting period ends on December 31, answer the following questions with respect to this lease agreement:

1. What items and amounts will be shown on the lessor's income statement for the year ending December 31, 1994?

2. mWhere and what items and amounts will be shown on the lessor's balance sheet at December 31, 1994?

3. What items and amounts will be shown on the lessor's income statement for the year ending December 31, 1995?

4. Where and what items and amounts will be shown on the lessor's balance sheet at December 31, 1995?

(LESSEE ENTRIES WITH RESIDUAL VALUE) The following facts pertain to a noncancellable lease agreement between Ballantyne Leasing Company and Kite Company, a lessee: **P21-6**

Inception date	January 1, 1994
Annual lease payment due at the beginning of each year, beginning with January 1, 1994	$92,773.52
Residual value of equipment at end of lease term, guaranteed by the lessee	$45,000.00
Lease term	6 years
Economic life of leased equipment	6 years
Fair value of asset at January 1, 1994	$450,000.00
Lessor's implicit rate	12%
Lessee's incremental borrowing rate	12%

The lessee assumes responsibility for all executory costs, which are expected to amount to $4,000 per year. The asset will revert to the lessor at the end of the lease term. The lessee has guaranteed the lessor a residual value of $45,000. The lessee uses the straight-line depreciation method for all equipment.

Instructions

(Round all numbers to the nearest cent.)

(a) Prepare an amortization schedule that would be suitable for the lessee for the lease term.

(b) Prepare all of the journal entries for the lessee for 1994 and 1995 to record the lease agreement, the lease payments, and all expenses related to this lease. Assume the lessee's annual accounting period ends on December 31 and reversing entries are used when appropriate.

P21-7 **(LESSEE ENTRIES AND BALANCE SHEET PRESENTATION: CAPITAL LEASE)** Levi Steel Company as lessee signed a lease agreement for equipment for five years, beginning December 31, 1993. Annual rental payments of $40,000 are to be made at the beginning of each lease year (December 31). The taxes, insurance, and maintenance costs are the obligation of the lessee. The interest rate used by the lessor in setting the payment schedule is 10%; Levi's incremental borrowing rate is 12%. Levi is unaware of the rate being used by the lessor. At the end of the lease, Levi has the option to buy the equipment for $1, considerably below its then-estimated fair value. The equipment has an estimated useful life of eight years. Levi uses the straight-line method of depreciation on similar owned equipment.

Instructions

(Round all numbers to the nearest dollar.)

(a) Prepare the journal entry or entries, with explanations that should be recorded on December 31, 1993 by Levi. (Assume no residual value.)

(b) Prepare the journal entry or entries, with explanations, that should be recorded on December 31, 1994 by Levi. (Prepare the lease amortization schedule for all five payments.)

(c) Prepare the journal entry or entries, with explanations, that should be recorded on December 31, 1995 by Levi.

(d) What amounts would appear on the December 31, 1995 balance sheet of Levi relative to the lease arrangement?

P21-8 **(LESSEE ENTRIES AND BALANCE SHEET PRESENTATION: CAPITAL LEASE)** On January 1, 1994, Swiss Cheese Company contracts to lease equipment for five years, agreeing to make a payment of $84,500 (including the executory costs of $4,500) at the beginning of each year, starting January 1, 1994. The taxes, insurance, and maintenance costs, estimated at $4,500 per year, are the obligations of the lessee. The leased equipment is to be capitalized at $333,589. The asset is to be amortized on a double-declining balance basis and the obligation is to be reduced on an effective interest basis. Swiss Cheese Company's incremental borrowing rate is 12%, and the implicit rate in the lease is 10%, which is knownby Swiss Cheese. Title to the equipment transfers to Swiss Cheese when the lease expires. The asset has an estimated useful life of five years and no residual value.

Instructions

(Round all numbers to the nearest dollar.)

(a) Explain the probable relationship of the $333,589 amount to the lease arrangement.

(b) Prepare the journal entry (or entries) that should be recorded on January 1, 1994 by Swiss Cheese Company.

(c) Prepare the journal entry to record depreciation of the leased asset for the year 1994.

(d) Prepare the journal entry to record the interest expense for the year 1994.

(e) Prepare the journal entry to record the lease payment of January 1, 1995, assuming reversing entries are not made.

(f) What amounts will appear on the lessee's December 31, 1994 balance sheet relative to the lease contract?

P21-9 **(LESSEE ENTRIES: CAPITAL LEASE WITH MONTHLY PAYMENTS)** Reid, Inc. was incorporated in 1993 to operate as a computer software service firm, with an accounting fiscal year ending August 31. Reid's primary product is a sophisticated on-line, inventory-control system; its customers pay a fixed fee plus a usage charge for using the system.

Reid has leased a large, BIG-I computer system from the manufacturer. The lease calls for a monthly rental of $70,000 for the 144 months (12 years) of the lease term. The estimated useful life of the computer is 15 years.

Each scheduled monthly rental payment includes $10,000 for full-service maintenance on the computer to be performed by the manufacturer. All rentals are payable on the first day of the month, beginning with August 1, 1994, the date the computer was installed and the lease agreement was signed.

The lease is noncancellable for its 12-year term, and it is secured only by the manufacturer's chattel lien on the BIG-I system. Reid can purchase the BIG-I system from the manufacturer at the end of the 12-year lease term for 75% of the computer's fair value at that time.

This lease is to be accounted for as a capital lease by Reid, and it will be depreciated by the straight-line method with no expected salvage value. Borrowed funds for this type of transaction would cost Reid 12% per year (1% per month). Following is a schedule of the present value of $1 for selected periods discounted at 1% per period when payments are made at the beginning of each period.

Periods (months)	Present Value of $1/Period Discounted at 1%/Period
1	1.000
2	1.990
3	2.970
143	76.658
144	76.899

Instructions

Prepare, in general journal form, all entries Reid should have made in its accounting records during August 1994 relating to this lease. Give full explanations and show supporting computations for each entry. August 31, 1994 is the end of Reid's fiscal accounting period and it will be preparing financial statements on that date. Do not prepare closing entries.

(AICPA adapted)

(LESSEE ENTRIES: CAPITAL LEASE WITH GUARANTEED RV, COMPREHENSIVE) Morgan P21-10

Dairy leases its milking equipment from Murdoch Finance Company under the following lease terms:

1. The lease term is 10 years, noncancellable, and requires equal rental payments of $25,250, due at the beginning of each year starting January 1, 1994.

2. The equipment has a fair value at the inception of the lease (January 1, 1994) of $185,078, an estimated economic life of 10 years, and a residual value (which is guaranteed by Morgan Dairy) of $20,000.

3. The lease contains no renewal options and the equipment reverts to Murdoch Finance Company on termination of the lease.

4. Morgan Dairy's incremental borrowing rate is 9% per year; the implicit rate is also 9%.

5. Morgan Dairy depreciates similar equipment that it owns on a straight-line basis.

6. Collectibility of the lease payments is reasonably predictable and there are no important uncertainties surrounding the costs yet to be incurred by the lessor.

Instructions

(a) Describe the nature of the lease and, in general, discuss how the lessee and lessor should account for the lease transaction.

(b) Prepare the journal entries at January 1, 1994 for both parties.

(c) Prepare the journal entries at December 31, 1994 (both the lessee's and lessor's year end).

(d) Prepare the journal entries at January 1, 1995 for the lessor and lessee. (Assume no reversing entries are needed).

(e) What would have been the amount to be capitalized by the lessee on the inception of the lease if:

   1. The residual value of $20,000 had been guaranteed by a third party, not the lessee?

   2. The residual value of $20,000 had not been guaranteed at all?

(f) On the lessor's books, what would be the amount recorded as the net investment at the inception of the lease assuming:

   1. The residual value of $20,000 had been guaranteed by a third party?

   2. The residual value of $20,000 had not been guaranteed at all?

(g) Suppose the useful life of the milking equipment has been 20 years. How large would the residual value have to be at the end of 10 years in order for the lessee to qualify for the operating method? (Assume that the residual value would be guaranteed by a third party.) **Hint:** The lessee's annual payments will be appropriately reduced as the residual value increases. *On Dec. 31, 2003, residual value is #4,000. Morgan returns equipment & makes good on residual value guarantee. Prepare all J.E. for this date.*

P21-11 (LESSOR COMPUTATIONS AND ENTRIES: SALES-TYPE LEASE WITH UNGUARANTEED RV)

Grady Company manufactures a desk-type computer with an estimated economic life of 12 years and leases it to Nocturnal Airlines for a period of 10 years. The normal selling price of the equipment is $210,485, and its unguaranteed residual value at the end of the lease term is estimated to be $20,000. Nocturnal will make annual payments of $30,000 at the beginning of each year and will pay all maintenance, insurance, and taxes. Grady incurred costs of $170,000 in manufacturing the equipment and $6,000 in negotiating and closing the lease. Grady has determined that the collectibility of the lease payments is reasonably predictable, that there will be no additional costs incurred, and that the implicit interest rate is 10%.

Instructions

(Round all numbers to the nearest dollar.)

(a) Discuss the nature of this lease in relation to the lessor and compute the amount of each of the following items:

   1. Gross investment.

   2. Unearned income.

   3. Sales price.

   4. Cost of sales.

(b) Prepare a 10-year lease amortization schedule.

(c) Prepare all of the lessor's journal entries for the first year.

P21-12 (LESSEE COMPUTATIONS AND ENTRIES: CAPITAL LEASE WITH UNGUARANTEED RESIDUAL VALUE)

Assume the same data as in Problem 21-11, with Nocturnal Airlines having an incremental borrowing rate of 10%.

Instructions

(Round all numbers to the nearest dollar.)

(a) Discuss the nature of this lease in relation to the lessee and compute the amount of the initial obligation under capital leases.

(b) Prepare a 10-year lease amortization schedule.

(c) Prepare all of the lessee's journal entries for the first year.

(LESSOR COMPUTATIONS: UNEARNED REVENUE RECOGNIZED USING SUM-OF-THE-P21-13 MONTH'S-DIGITS) During 1994, We-Lease-It Leasing Co. began leasing equipment to small manufacturers. Below is information regarding leasing arrangements:

1. We-Lease-It Leasing Co. leases equipment with terms from three to five years, depending on the useful life of the equipment. At the expiration of the lease, the equipment will be sold to the lessee at 10% of the lessor's cost, the expected salvage value of the equipment.

2. The amount of the lessee's monthly payment is computed by multiplying the lessor's cost of the equipment factor applicable to the term of lease.

Term of Lease	Payment Factor
3 years	3.32%
4 years	2.63%
5 years	2.22%

3. The excess of the gross contract receivable for equipment rentals over the cost (reduced by the estimated salvage value at the termination of the lease) is recognized as revenue over the term of the lease under the sum-of-the-years'-digits method computed on a monthly basis.

4. The following leases were entered into during 1994.

Machine	Dates of Lease	Period of Lease	Machine Cost
Die	7/1/94–6/30/98	4 years	$160,000
Press	9/1/94–8/31/97	3 years	$100,000

Instructions

(a) Prepare a schedule of gross contracts receivable for equipment rentals at the dates of the lease for the die and press machines.

(b) Prepare a schedule of unearned lease income at December 31, 1994 for each machine lease.

(c) Prepare a schedule computing the present dollar value of lease payments receivable (gross investment) for equipment rentals at December 31, 1994. (The present dollar value of the "lease receivables for equipment rentals" is the outstanding amount of the gross lease receivables less the unearned lease income included therein.) Without prejudice to your solution to (b), assume that the unearned lease income at December 31, 1994 was $68,000.

(AICPA adapted)

(BASIC LESSEE ACCOUNTING WITH DIFFICULT PV CALCULATION) In 1993, McCumberP21-14 Express Company negotiated and closed a long-term lease contract for newly constructed truck terminals and freight storage facilities. The buildings were erected to the company's specifications on land owned by the company. On January 1, 1994, McCumber Express Company took possession of the leased properties. On January 1, 1994 and 1995, the company made cash payments of $1,050,000 that were recorded as rental expenses.

Although the terminals have a composite useful life of 40 years, the noncancellable lease runs for 20 years from January 1, 1994, with a bargain purchase option available on expiration of the lease.

The 20-year lease is effective for the period January 1, 1994 through December 31, 2013. Advance rental payments of $900,000 are payable to the lessor on January 1 of each of the first 10 years of the lease. Advance rental payments of $320,000 are due on January 1 for each of the last 10 years of the lease. The company has an option to purchase all of these leased facilities for $1 on December 31, 2013. It also must make annual payments to the lessor of $50,000 for property taxes and $100,000 for insurance. The lease was negotiated to assure the lessor a 6% rate of return.

Instructions

(Round all computations to the nearest dollar.)

(a) Prepare a schedule to compute for McCumber Express Company the discounted present value of the terminal facilities and related obligation at January 1, 1994.

(b) Assuming that the discounted present value of terminal facilities and related obligation at January 1, 1994 was $8,400,000, prepare journal entries for McCumber Express Company to record:

1. Cash payment to the lessor on January 1, 1996.

2. Amortization of the cost of the leased properties for 1996 using the straight-line method and assuming a zero salvage value.

3. Accrual of interest expense at December 31, 1996.

Selected present value factors are as follows.

Periods	For an Ordinary Annuity of $1 @ 6%	For $1 @ 6%
1	0.943396	0.943396
2	1.833393	0.889996
8	6.209794	0.627412
9	6.801692	0.591898
10	7.360087	0.558395
19	11.158117	0.330513
20	11.469921	0.311805

(AICPA adapted)

P21-15(COMPUTATION OF ANNUAL RENTALS AND OTHER AMOUNTS FOR LESSOR AND LESSEE) Riel Corporation, a lessor of office machines, purchased a new machine for $600,000 on December 31, 1994, which was delivered the same day (by prior arrangement) to O'Hara Company, the lessee. The following information relating to the lease transaction is available:

1. The leased asset has an estimated useful life of five years, which coincides with the lease term.

2. At the end of the lease term, the machine will revert to Riel, at which time it is expected to have a residual value of $60,000 (none of which is guaranteed by O'Hara).

3. Riel's implicit interest rate (on its net investment) is 8%, which is known by O'Hara.

4. O'Hara's incremental borrowing rate is 10% at December 31, 1994.

5. Lease rental consists of five equal annual payments, the first of which is paid on December 31, 1994.

6. The lease is appropriately accounted for as a direct financing lease by Riel and as a capital lease by O'Hara. Both lessor and lessee are calendar-year corporations and depreciate all fixed assets on the straight-line basis.

Instructions

(Round all numbers to the nearest dollar.)

(a) Compute the annual rental under the lease.

(b) Compute the amounts of the gross lease rentals receivable and the unearned interest revenue that Riel should disclose at the inception of the lease on December 31, 1994.

(c) What expense should O'Hara record for the year ended December 31, 1995?

(AICPA adapted)

(LESSOR COMPUTATIONS AND ENTRIES: SALES-TYPE LEASE WITH GUARANTEED RESID- P21-16 UAL VALUE) Jacobson Inc. manufactures an X-ray machine with an estimated life span of 12 years and leases it to Lutheran Hospital for a period of 10 years. The normal selling price of the machine is $343,734 and its guaranteed residual value at the end of the lease term is estimated to be $15,000. The hospital will pay rents of $50,000 at the beginning of each year and all maintenance, insurance, and taxes. Jacobson Inc. incurred costs of $260,000 in manufacturing the machine and $7,000 in negotiating and closing the lease. Jacobson Inc. has determined that the collectibility of the lease payments is reasonably predictable, there will be no additional costs incurred, and the implicit interest rate is 10%. *initial direct costs – $7000 negotiating & closing.*

Instructions

(Round all numbers to the nearest dollar.)

(a) Discuss the nature of this lease in relation to the lessor and compute the amount of each of the following items:

1. Gross investment

3. Sales price.

2. Unearned interest revenue.

4. Cost of sales.

(b) Prepare a 10-year lease amortization schedule.

(c) Prepare all of the lessor's journal entries for the first year.

(LESSEE COMPUTATIONS AND ENTRIES: CAPITAL LEASE WITH GUARANTEED RESIDUAL P21-17 VALUE) Assume the same data as in P21-16 and that Lutheran Hospital has an incremental borrowing rate of 10%.

Instructions

(Round all numbers to the nearest dollar.)

(a) Discuss the nature of this lease in relation to the lessee and compute the amount of the initial obligation under capital leases.

(b) Prepare a 10-year lease amortization schedule.

(c) Prepare all of the lessee's journal entries for the first year.

22

Accounting Changes and Error Analysis

◼

Headlines depicting accounting-initiated changes and other events such as the following appear in the financial press:

"Accounting change aids White Farm"
"Aeronautical company revises estimates of service lives of Boeing 747s"
"Deficit would have been $20 million more if firm hadn't altered accounting"
"AT&T hit by accounting change"
"Thompson taking $170-million charge"

Why do these changes in accounting occur? First, the accounting profession may mandate the use of a new accounting method or principle. For example, in 1990 the CICA for the first time required accruals for site-restoration costs. Second, changing economic conditions may cause a company to change its methods of accounting. Third, changes in technology and in operations may require a company to revise the service lives, depreciation method, or the expected residual value of depreciable assets. AT&T changed its estimates and depreciation methods as a result of the changes in its competitive environment and in telecommunications technology. Whatever the cause, changes in accounting should result in more useful information for decision making. Accountants must determine whether such changes are appropriate and, if made, how they should be reported to facilitate analysis and understanding of financial statements.

While the qualitative characteristics of *usefulness* may be enhanced by changes in accounting, the characteristics of *comparability* and *consistency* may be adversely affected. Comparative financial statements and historical five- and ten-year summaries can be particularly affected by changes in accounting. Proper treatment and full disclosure should enable readers of financial statements to comprehend and assess the effects of such changes.

When accounting errors are discovered, the accountant faces similar problems. How should accounting errors be corrected and disclosed so that the usefulness of the financial information is enhanced? In this chapter we discuss the different types of accounting changes and error corrections and the procedures for handling them in the financial statements.

ACCOUNTING CHANGES

Before the 1980 issuance of *CICA Handbook* Section 1506, "Accounting Changes," companies had considerable flexibility and were able to use alternative accounting treatments for essentially equivalent situations. When steel companies changed their methods of depreciating plant assets from accelerated depreciation to straight-line depreciation, the effect of the change was presented in many different ways. The cumulative difference between the depreciation charges that had been recorded and those that would have been recorded under the new method could have been reported in the income statement of the period of the change. Or the change could have been ignored and the undepreciated asset balance simply depreciated on a straight-line basis in the future. Or companies could simply have restated the prior periods on the basis that the straight-line approach had always been used. When such alternatives exist, comparability of the statements between periods and between companies is diminished and useful historical trend data are obscured.

The profession's first step in this area was to establish categories for the different types of changes and corrections that occur in practice.[1]

Types of Accounting Changes

1. **Change in accounting policy**. A change from one generally accepted accounting principle to another generally accepted accounting principle; for example, a change in the method of depreciation from declining balance to straight-line depreciation of plant assets.

2. **Change in accounting estimate**. A change that occurs as a result of new information or as additional experience is acquired. An example is a change in the estimate of the service lives of depreciable assets.

3. **Change in reporting entity**. A change from reporting as one type of entity to another; for example, changing specific subsidiaries that constitute the group of companies for which consolidated financial statements are prepared.

> **Objective 1**
>
> Identify the types of and justifications for accounting changes.

Correction of an Error in Previously Issued Financial Statements
(not an accounting change)

Errors in financial statements that occur as a result of mathematical mistakes, mistakes in the application of accounting principles, or oversight or misuse of facts that existed at the time financial statements were prepared; for example, the incorrect application of the retail inventory method for determining final inventory value.

Changes were classified into these categories because the individual characteristics of each category necessitate different methods of recognizing these changes in the financial statements. Each of these items is discussed separately to investigate its unusual characteristics and to determine how each item should be reported in the accounts and how the information should be disclosed in comparative statements.

CHANGES IN ACCOUNTING POLICY

A change in accounting policy involves a change from one generally accepted accounting principle to another.

1. Changing the basis of inventory pricing from average cost to FIFO.

2. Changing the method of depreciation on plant assets from accelerated to straight-line or vice versa.

3. Changing the accounting for construction contracts from the completed contract method to the percentage-of-completion method.

> **Objective 2**
>
> Describe the accounting for changes in accounting principles.

A careful examination must be made in each circumstance to ensure that a change in principle has actually occurred. *A change in accounting principle is not considered to result from the adoption of a new principle in recognition of events that have occurred for the first time or that were previously immaterial.* For example, when a depreciation method that is adopted for *newly* acquired plant assets is different from the method or methods used for previously recorded assets of a similar class, a change in accounting principle has *not* occurred. Certain marketing expenditures that were previously immaterial and expensed in the period incurred may now be material and acceptably deferred and amortized without a change in accounting principle occurring.

Finally, *if the accounting principle previously followed was not acceptable or if the principle was applied incorrectly, a change to a generally accepted accounting principle is considered a correction of an error.* A switch from the cash basis of accounting to the accrual basis is considered a

---

[1] *CICA Handbook* (Toronto: CICA), Section 1506.

correction of an error. If the company deducted residual value when computing declining balance depreciation on plant assets and later recomputed depreciation without deduction of estimated residual, an error is corrected.

Three approaches have been suggested for reporting changes in accounting policies in the accounts:

Retroactive. The cumulative effect of the use of the new method on the financial statements at the beginning of the period is computed. A retroactive adjustment of the financial statement is then made, recasting the financial statements of prior years on a basis consistent with the newly adopted principle. Advocates of this position argue that only with restatement of prior periods can changes in accounting principles lead to comparable financial statements. If this approach is not used, the year previous to the change will be on the old method; the year of the change will reflect the entire cumulative adjustment in income; and the following year will present financial statements on the new basis without the cumulative effect of the change. The question is how can public confidence in financial statements be maintained when the periods are not on a comparable basis? Consistency is considered essential to providing meaningful earnings-trend data and other financial relationships necessary to evaluate a business.

Current. The cumulative effect of the use of the new method on the financial statements at the beginning of the period is computed. This adjustment is then reported in the current year's income statement as a special item between the captions Extraordinary Items and Net Income. Advocates of this position argue that restating financial statements for prior years results in a loss of confidence by investors in financial reports. How will a present or prospective investor react when told that the earnings computed five years ago are now entirely different? Restatement, if permitted, also might upset many contractual and other arrangements that were based on the old figures. For example, profit-sharing arrangements computed on the old basis might have to be recomputed and completely new distributions made, which might create numerous legal problems. Many practical difficulties also exist: the cost of restatement may be excessive, or restatement may be impossible on the basis of data available.

Prospective. No change is made in previously reported results. Opening balances are not adjusted and no attempt is made to allocate charges or credits for prior events. Advocates of this position argue that once management presents financial statements based on acceptable accounting principles to investors and to others, these statements are final because management cannot change prior periods by adopting a new principle. According to this line of reasoning, the cumulative adjustment in the current year is not appropriate because this approach would reflect in net income an amount that has little or no relationship to the current year's income or economic events.

Before the adoption of *Handbook* Section 1506, all three of the above approaches were used. Section 1506, however, settled this issue by establishing guidelines depending on the type of change in accounting principle involved. We have classified these changes in accounting policy into three categories:

1. Retroactive-with-restatement method accounting change.

2. Retroactive-without-restatement method accounting change.

3. Prospective method accounting change.

Retroactive-With-Restatement Method Accounting Change

The general requirement established by the profession was that the *retroactive method with restatement of prior periods should be used to account for changes in accounting policy*. The general requirements are as follows:

1. The newly adopted accounting policy should be applied retroactively.

2. Financial statement amounts for prior periods included for comparative purposes should be restated to give effect to the new accounting policy.

3. The effect of the change on significant items such as net income, earnings per share, and working capital for the current year as well as for prior periods should be disclosed along with a brief description of the change.

To illustrate, assume that Lang Ltd. decided at the beginning of 1994 to change from the declining balance method of depreciation to the straight-line method for financial reporting on its plant assets (assume that this change is not being made as a result of changed circumstances, experience, or new information). For tax purposes, the company has claimed capital cost allowance that is coincidentally equal to the amount of the declining balance depreciation, and this relationship will continue. The assets originally cost $120,000 in 1992 and have an estimated useful life of 10 years. The data assumed for this illustration are as shown below.

Year	Declining Balance Depreciation	Straight-Line Depreciation	Difference	Tax Effect 40%	Effect on Income (net of tax)
1992	$24,000	$12,000	$12,000	$4,800	$ 7,200
1993	19,200	12,000	7,200	2,880	4,320
Cumulative effect			$19,200	$7,680	$11,520
1994	$15,360	$12,000	$ 3,360	$1,344	$ 2,016

The entry made to record this change in accounting policy in 1994 should be:

Accumulated Depreciation	19,200	
Deferred Income Tax		7,680
Retained Earnings—Cumulative Effect of		
Change in Accounting Policy—Depreciation		11,520

The debit of $19,200 to Accumulated Depreciation is the excess of the declining balance depreciation over the straight-line depreciation. The Deferred Income Tax of $7,680 is recorded to reflect interperiod tax allocation procedures. Prior to the change in accounting principle, depreciation and capital cost allowance were the same. However, if the straight-line method had been employed for book purposes in previous years, the excess of capital cost allowance over book depreciation would have created credits to Deferred Income Tax totalling $11,520. The cumulative effect on retained earnings at the beginning of the year in which the change was made results from the difference between declining balance and straight-line depreciation, reduced by the tax on that difference.

The information presented in the *original* income statements prior to the change for 1992 and 1993 is summarized below.

Lang Ltd.
Summarized Comparative Income Statements
for the Years 1993 and 1992

	1993	1992
Income before extraordinary item (assumed)	$120,000	$111,000
Extraordinary item (assumed)	(30,000)	10,000
Net income	$ 90,000	$121,000

(Continued)

Earnings per share		
Basic earnings per share (100,000 shares)		
Income before extraordinary item	$1.20	$1.11
Extraordinary item	(0.30)	0.10
Net income	$0.90	$1.21

Lang's two-year comparative income statements for 1994 and 1993 following the change in depreciation method would appear as follows.

Lang Ltd.
Summarized Comparative Income Statements
for the Years 1994 and 1993

	1994	1993
Income before extraordinary item (assumed)	$135,000	$124,320*
Extraordinary item (assumed)	18,000	(30,000)
Net income	$153,000	$ 94,320
Earnings per share		
Basic earnings per share (100,000 shares)		
Income before extraordinary item	$1.35	$1.24
Extraordinary item	0.18	(0.30)
Net income	$1.53	$0.94

*Restated ($120,000 + $4,320)

The statement of retained earnings for 1993 would reflect the portion of the cumulative effect of the accounting change not included in the 1993 comparative income statement (the portion attributed to 1992). The same method would be used for 1994, as illustrated in the comparative statement of retained earnings shown below.

It should be noted that only the financial statements presented for comparison purposes are restated to show the effect of the change. Any change attributable to those periods prior to the

Lang Ltd.
Comparative Statement of Retained Earnings
for the Years 1994 and 1993

	1994	1993
Balance at beginning of year	$483,800	$450,000
As previously reported (assumed)		
Retroactive change in accounting policy (Note 2)	11,520	7,200
As restated	$495,320	$457,200
Net income	153,000	94,320
	$648,320	$551,520
Dividends	63,000	56,200
Balance at end of year	$585,320	$495,320

(Continued)

Note 2—Change in Depreciation Method for Plant Assets. In 1994, depreciation of plant equipment is computed by use of the straight-line method. In prior years, beginning in 1992, depreciation of plant and equipment was computed by the declining balance method. The straight-line method has been applied retroactively to equipment acquisitions of prior years. The effect of the change in 1994 was to increase net income by approximately $2,016 (or two cents per share). The 1993 comparative income statement has been retroactively restated to reflect the effect of the change on 1993 net income (an increase of $4,320, or approximately four cents per share). Income for 1993 and prior periods would have been increased by $11,520 (or 12 cents per share).

earliest comparative period presented is shown as an adjustment to beginning retained earnings. Other balance sheet accounts affected by the change should also be restated.

Retroactive-Without-Restatement Method Accounting Change

Retroactive restatement requires the use of information that may, in some cases, be unreasonably difficult to obtain. For example, if a construction firm wishes to change from the completed-contract method of accounting for long-term projects to the percentage-of-completion method, it would be necessary to obtain the estimated completion costs for each uncompleted project at various preceding year ends. In such cases where the total cumulative effect of a change in accounting policy may be determined but the effect on individual prior periods cannot be reasonably determined, the *Handbook* permits retroactive adjustment without restatement of prior periods' financial statements.

To illustrate the retroactive-without-restatement method, assume that Denson Construction Limited has accounted for its income from long-term construction contracts using the completed-contract method. In 1994, the company changed to the percentage-of-completion method because the management believed that it provided a more appropriate measure of the income earned. For tax purposes (assume a 40% rate), the company has employed the completed-contract method and plans to continue using this method in the future. The following information is available for analysis.

| | Pretax Income From | | Difference in Income | | |
| | Percentage-of-Completion | Completed-Contract | Difference | Tax Effect 40% | Income Effect (net of tax) |
Year					
Prior to 1993	$600,000	$400,000	$200,000	$80,000	$120,000
In 1993	180,000	160,000	20,000	8,000	12,000
Total: Beginning of 1994	$780,000	$560,000	$220,000	$88,000	$132,000
In 1994	$200,000	$190,000	$ 10,000	$ 4,000	$ 6,000

The entry to record the change in 1994 would be:

Construction in Progress	220,000	
Deferred Income Tax		88,000
Retained Earnings		132,000

The Construction in Progress account is increased by $220,000, representing the increase in the inventory under the new method. The Deferred Income Tax account is used to recognize interperiod tax allocation. If, in previous years, the percentage-of-completion method had been employed for accounting purposes while the completed-contract method was used for tax purposes, a difference of $220,000 between book income and taxable income would have developed, on which $88,000 of tax would have been deferred. The adjustment for the cumulative effect of the accounting change would be reported in the statement of retained earnings as follows.

Statement of Retained Earnings

	1994	1993
Balance at beginning of year, as previously reported	$1,696,000	$1,600,000
Add: Adjustment for the cumulative effect on prior years of applying retroactively the new method of accounting for long-term contracts (Note A)	132,000	120,000
Balance at beginning of year, as restated	$1,828,000	1,720,000
Net income (assumed)	120,000	108,000
Balance at end of year	$1,948,000	$1,828,000

Note A—Change in Method of Accounting for Long-Term Contracts. The company has accounted for revenue and costs for long-term contracts by the percentage-of-completion method in 1994, whereas in all prior years, revenue and costs were determined by the completed-contract method. The new method of accounting for long-term contracts was adopted to recognize. . .[state justification for change in accounting policy]. . . and financial statements of prior periods have not been restated to apply the new method retroactively. For income tax purposes, the completed-contract method has been continued. The effect of the accounting change on income of 1994 was an increase of $6,000, net of related taxes, and on income of prior periods an increase of $132,000, net of related taxes.

Note that the foregoing example is similar to the case involving restatement of prior periods' financial statements. The journal entries to record the accounting change are similar since the cumulative effect of the change on Retained Earnings is recorded as an adjustment to beginning Retained Earnings. The only difference between retroactive adjustment with restatement and without restatement is in the printed financial statements. Restatement provides financial statement readers with amounts that would have been reported had the new policy been adopted at an earlier date. On the other hand, retroactive adjustment without restatement leaves the comparative financial statements as originally reported and presents the cumulative effect of the change as an adjustment to beginning Retained Earnings. In both examples, as required by Section 1506 of the *Handbook*, the effect of the change on the current year's income is disclosed in the note.

Prospective Method Accounting Change

Retroactive application of a change in an accounting policy may not be possible in some cases because it would be extremely difficult to obtain the necessary financial data. This situation could arise, for example, on the adoption of a new *Handbook* recommendation or legislative requirement of such a nature that the cumulative effect of the necessary accounting change could not be determined without incurring unreasonable cost or using imprecise data. In these rare circumstances, it is permissible to make the required or desired accounting change in the current year without restating the beginning Retained Earnings.

As an example, suppose that a new *Handbook* section requires capitalization of interest on certain long-term construction projects. Those firms having assets that have been constructed in the past and that now qualify for interest capitalization would find it extremely difficult to determine the adjusted cost and accumulated depreciation necessary to apply the method retroactively. In these cases, the *Handbook* permits prospective application of the accounting change. That is, the new accounting policy would be applied in the current and future years.

CHANGES IN ACCOUNTING ESTIMATES

The preparation of financial statements requires an estimate of the effects of future conditions and events. Future conditions and events and their effects cannot be perceived with certainty; therefore, estimating requires the exercise of judgement. Accounting estimates will change as new events occur, as more experience is acquired, or as additional information is obtained. The following are examples of items that require estimates:

Objective 3

Describe the accounting for changes in estimates.

1. Uncollectible receivables.

2. Inventory obsolescence.

3. Useful lives and residual values of assets.

4. Periods benefited by deferred costs.

5. Liabilities for warranty costs and income taxes.

6. Recoverable mineral reserves.

Changes in estimates must be handled prospectively;[2] that is, no changes should be made in previously reported results. Opening balances are not adjusted and no attempt is made to "catch up" for prior periods. Financial statements of prior periods are not restated and pro forma amounts for prior periods are not reported. Instead, the effects of all changes in estimates are accounted for in (1) the period of change if the change affects that period only or (2) the period of change and future periods if the change affects both. As a result, changes in estimates are viewed as normal recurring corrections and adjustments that are the natural result of the accounting process; therefore, retroactive treatment is prohibited.

The circumstances related to a change in estimate are different from those surrounding a change in accounting policy. If changes in estimates were handled on a retroactive or catch-up basis, continual adjustments of prior years' income would occur. It seems proper to accept the view that because new conditions or circumstances exist, the revision fits the new situation and should be handled in the current and future periods.

To illustrate, Salamon Ltd. purchased a building for $300,000 that was originally estimated to have a life of 15 years and no residual value. Depreciation has been recorded for five years on a straight-line basis. On January 1, 1994, the estimate of the useful life of the asset is revised, so that the asset is considered to have a total life of 25 years. Assume, for simplicity, that depreciation and capital cost allowance are the same. The amounts at the beginning of the sixth year are as follows.

Building	$300,000
Less: Accumulated Depreciation—Building	100,000
Book Value of Building	$200,000

The entry to record depreciation for the year 1994 is:

Depreciation Expense	10,000	
Accumulated Depreciation—Building		10,000

The $10,000 depreciation charge is computed as follows.

$$\text{Depreciation Charge} = \frac{\text{Book Value of Asset}}{\text{Remaining Service Life}} = \frac{\$200,000}{25 \text{ Years} - 5 \text{ Years}}$$

---

[2] *CICA Handbook*, Section 1506, par. .25.

The following disclosure of a change in estimated useful lives and residual value appeared in the 1990 annual report of Atco Ltd.

> Change in accounting estimate
> Note 9. Property, plant and equipment (in part)
> Effective January 1, 1990, the Corporation revised the estimated useful life of its space rental assets from ten to fifteen years. The effect of this change has been applied prospectively and increased earnings in 1990 by $3,025,000 ($.10 per share).

Differentiating between a change in an estimate and a change in an accounting policy is sometimes difficult. Is it a change in policy or a change in estimate when a company changes from deferring and amortizing certain costs to expensing them as incurred? *Whenever it is difficult to determine whether a change in policy or a change in estimate has occurred, it is considered to be the latter.* The profession has clarified this problem slightly by recommending that whenever a change is attributed to "changed circumstances, experience, or new information" it should be treated as a change in estimate.[3]

A similar problem occurs in differentiating between a change in estimate and a correction of an error, although the answer is more clear cut. How do we determine whether the information was overlooked in earlier periods (an error) or whether the information is now available for the first time (change in estimate)? Proper classification is important because corrections of errors have a different accounting treatment from that given changes in estimates. The general rule is that *careful estimates that later prove to be incorrect should be considered changes in estimate*. Only when the estimate was obviously computed incorrectly because of lack of expertise or in bad faith should the adjustment be considered an error. There is no clear demarcation line here and the accountant must use good judgement in light of all the circumstances.

A CHANGE IN REPORTING ENTITY

Objective 4

Identify changes in a reporting entity.

Circumstances often arise such that the entity's financial statements for the current period actually represent the activities of a different entity from that reported on in the prior period. As examples, when two firms merge, forming a single continuing entity as a result of a transaction known as a **pooling of interests**, or when a significant business segment is discontinued, the continuing entity is different from the reporting entity of the prior year. Such circumstances are collectively referred to in this book as a **change in the reporting entity**.[4]

An accounting change resulting in financial statements that are actually the statements of a different entity should be reported by (1) restating the financial statements of all prior periods presented to show the financial information for the new reporting entity for all periods (retroactive-with-restatement) or (2) by reporting the activities of the new entity prospectively from the date of acquisition (disposal) and presenting supplementary pro forma information in a note (prospective).

When a business combination transaction is accounted for as a pooling of interests, "the results of operations for the period in which the combination occurs and for all prior periods should be reflected on a combined basis."[5] Thus, a change in the reporting entity caused by a pooling of interests must be disclosed by retroactive application with restatement of all prior periods.

---

[3] *Ibid.*, par. .23.

[4] The *CICA Handbook* does not define a change in a reporting entity. However, Sections 1580 and 3475 prescribe reporting and disclosure procedures for circumstances in which there has been a substantial change in the entity.

[5] *CICA Handbook*, Section 1580, par. .69.

When an acquisition of another firm has been accounted for as a purchase transaction and the financial statements are consolidated following the acquisition, the resulting change in the reporting entity is disclosed on a prospective basis. That is, the statements of the current and future periods reflect the effect of the change. In addition, if the acquisition takes place on a date other than the beginning of the fiscal period, the acquiring firm must present supplementary information showing on a pro forma basis the amount of income that would have been earned had the acquisition taken place at the beginning of the fiscal period.

If a firm disposes of an investment in a firm previously included in the consolidated financial statements, then income from the remaining or continuing operations should be presented on a pro forma basis. The reason for this requirement is that projections of future income are facilitated by data about the earnings of that portion of the accounting entity that is expected to continue operations in the future.

In summary, a change in a reporting entity attributed to a pooling of interests requires retroactive restatement of the financial statements, while a change in a reporting entity resulting from either acquisitions or disposals of subsidiaries is disclosed on a prospective basis with supplementary pro forma information containing the full year's earnings of the continuing entity.

REPORTING A CORRECTION OF AN ERROR

CICA Handbook Section 1506 also discusses how a correction of an error should be handled in the financial statements. No business, large or small, is immune from errors. The risk of material errors, however, may be reduced through the installation of good internal controls and the application of sound accounting procedures. The following are examples of accounting errors:

Objective 5

Describe the accounting for correction of errors.

1. A change from an accounting principle that is *not* generally accepted to an accounting principle that is acceptable. The rationale is that the prior periods were incorrectly presented because of the application of an improper accounting principle—for example, a change from the cash basis of accounting to the accrual basis.

2. Mathematical mistakes that result from adding, subtracting, and so on. An illustration is the incorrect totalling of the inventory count sheets in computing the inventory value.

3. Changes in estimates that occur because the estimates are not prepared in good faith. For example, the adoption of a clearly unrealistic depreciation rate.

4. An oversight such as the failure to accrue or defer certain expenses and revenues at the end of the period.

5. A misuse of facts, such as the failure to use salvage value in computing the depreciation base for the straight-line approach.

6. The incorrect classification of a cost as an expense instead of as an asset and vice versa.

As soon as they are discovered, errors must be corrected by proper entries in the accounts and reflected in the financial statements. ***The profession requires that correction of an error be treated as a prior period adjustment***, be recorded in the year in which the error is discovered, and be reported in the financial statements as an adjustment to the beginning balance of retained earnings. If comparative statements are presented, the prior statements affected should be restated to correct for the error. The disclosures need not be repeated in the financial statements of subsequent periods.

To illustrate, in 1994 the bookkeeper for Selectric Company discovered that in 1993 the company failed to record in the accounts $20,000 of depreciation expense on a newly constructed building. The capital cost allowance is correctly included in the tax return. Because of numerous timing differences, reported net income for 1993 was $150,000 and taxable income was $110,000. The following entry was made for income taxes (assume a 40% effective tax rate in 1993):

Income Tax Expense	60,000	
Income Tax Payable		44,000
Deferred Income Tax		16,000

As a result of the $20,000 omission error in 1993:

Depreciation expense (1993) *was* understated	$20,000
Accumulated depreciation *is* understated	20,000
Income tax expense (1993) *was* overstated ($20,000 × 40%)	8,000
Net income (1993) *was* overstated	12,000
Deferred income tax *is* overstated ($20,000 × 40%)	8,000

The entry made in 1994 to correct the omission of $20,000 of depreciation in 1993 would be as follows:

1994 Correcting Entry

Retained Earnings	12,000	
Deferred Income Tax	8,000	
Accumulated Depreciation—Buildings		20,000

The journal entry to record the correction of the error is the same whether single-period or comparative financial statements are prepared; however, presentation on the financial statements will differ. If single-period (noncomparative) statements are presented, the error should be reported as an adjustment to the opening balance of retained earnings of the period in which the error is discovered, as shown below.

Retained Earnings, January 1, 1994:		
As previously reported		**$350,000**
Correction of an error (depreciation)	**$20,000**	
Less applicable income tax reduction	**8,000**	**(12,000)**
Adjusted balance of retained earnings January 1, 1994		**338,000**
Add net income 1994		400,000
Retained earnings December 31, 1994		$738,000

If comparative financial statements are prepared, adjustments should be made to correct the amounts for all affected accounts reported in the statements for all periods reported. The data for each year being presented should be restated to the correct basis, and any catch-up adjustment should be shown as a prior period adjustment to retained earnings for the earliest period being reported. For example, in the case of Selectric Company, the error of omitting the depreciation of $20,000 in 1993, which was discovered in 1994, results in the restatement of the 1993 financial statements when presented in comparison with those of 1994. The following accounts in the 1993 financial statements (presented in comparison with those of 1994) would have been restated as follows.

In the balance sheet:

Accumulated Depreciation—Buildings	$20,000	increase
Deferred Income Tax	$ 8,000	decrease
Retained Earnings, Ending Balance	$12,000	decrease

In the income statement:

Depreciation Expense—Buildings	$20,000	increase
Tax Expense	$ 8,000	decrease
Net Income	$12,000	decrease

In the statement of retained earnings:

Retained Earnings, Ending Balance	$12,000 decrease
(due to lower net income for the period)	

The 1994 financial statements in comparative form with those of 1993 are prepared as if the error had not occurred. As a minimum, such comparative statements in 1994 would include a note calling attention to restatement of the 1993 statements and disclosing the effect of the correction on income before extraordinary items, net income, and the related per-share amounts.

SUMMARY OF ACCOUNTING CHANGES AND CORRECTION OF ERRORS

The development of guidelines in reporting accounting changes and corrections has helped in resolving several significant and long-standing accounting problems. Yet, because of diversity in situations and characteristics of the items encountered in practice, the application of professional judgement is of paramount importance. In applying these guides, the primary objective is to serve the user of the financial statements; achieving such service requires accuracy, full disclosure, and an absence of misleading implications. The principal distinction and treatments presented in the earlier discussion are summarized below.

1. **Changes in accounting policy (General Rule).** Employ the retroactive-with-restatement approach by:

    (a) Reporting current and future results on the new basis.

    (b) Restating all prior period financial statements presented for comparison.

    (c) Describing in a note the change and its effect on the current period's financial statements.

2. **Changes in accounting policy (Exceptions).** Employ the retroactive-without-restatement approach by:

    (a) Reporting the current and future results on the new basis.

    (b) Reporting the cumulative effect of the adjustment in the statement of retained earnings as an adjustment to the beginning balance.

    (c) Describing in a note the change and the effect of the change on the current year's net income.

    Employ the prospective approach by:

    (a) Reporting the current and future results on the new basis.

    (b) Disclosing the effect of the change on the current year's income.

3. **Changes in estimate.** Employ the prospective approach by:

    (a) Reporting current and future results on the new basis.

    (b) Presenting prior period financial statements as previously reported.

    (c) Making no adjustment to current period opening balances for purposes of catch-up and making no pro forma presentations.

(Continued)

4. **Changes in entity**. Employ the retroactive-with-restatement approach (pooling of interests) by:

   (a) Restating the financial statements of all prior periods presented.

   (b) Disclosing in the year of change the effect on net income for all prior periods presented.

   (c) Describing in a note the details of the entity acquired or disposed of.

   Employ the prospective approach with pro forma information (purchases or disposals of subsidiaries) by:

   (a) Reporting current financial statements on the new basis.

   (b) Providing pro forma supplementary information of the new income for the full year from the continuing entity.

5. **Errors**. Employ the retroactive-with-restatement approach by:

   (a) Correcting all prior period statements presented.

   (b) Restating the beginning balance of retained earnings for the first period presented when the error effects extend to a period prior to that one.

   (c) Describing in a note the error, its effect on the current and prior year's financial statements, and that prior period financial statements have been restated.

Changes in accounting principles are considered appropriate when the enterprise considers that the alternative generally accepted accounting principle that is adopted is preferable to the existing one. Preferability among accounting principles should be determined on the basis of whether the new principle constitutes an improvement in financial reporting, not on the basis of the effect on income and taxes alone. But it is not always easy to determine what is an improvement in financial reporting. *How does one measure preferability or improvement?* One enterprise might argue that a change in accounting principle from FIFO to LIFO inventory valuation better matches current costs and current revenues. Conversely, another enterprise might change from LIFO to FIFO because it wishes to report a more realistic balance sheet amount for inventory. How does an accountant determine which is the better of these two arguments? It appears that the auditor should have some standard or objective as a basis for determining the method that is preferable. Because no universal standard or objective is generally accepted, the problem of determining preferability continues to be a difficult one.

MOTIVATIONS FOR CHANGE

Objective 6

Identify economic motives for changing accounting methods.

Difficult as it is to determine which accounting standards have the strongest conceptual support, other complications make the process even more complex. These complications stem from the fact that managers (and others) have a self-interest in how the financial statements make the company look. Managers naturally wish to show their financial performance in the best light. A favourable profit picture can influence investors and a strong liquidity position can influence creditors. *Too* favourable a profit picture, however, can provide union negotiators with ammunition during collective bargaining negotiations. Also, if the federal government has established price controls, managers might believe that lower-trending profits might persuade the regulatory authorities to grant their company a price increase. Hence, managers might have varying profit motives depending on economic times and whom they seek to impress.

Recent research has provided additional insight into why companies may prefer certain accounting methods. Some of these reasons are as follows.

1. **Political costs**. As companies become larger and more politically visible, politicians and regulators devote more attention to them. Many suggest that these politicians and regulators can "feather their own nests" by imposing regulations on these organizations for the benefit of their own constituents. Thus, the larger the firm, the more likely it is to become subject to regulations such as the anti-combines regulation and the more likely it is to be required to pay higher taxes. Therefore, companies that are politically visible may attempt to report income numbers that are low to avoid the scrutiny of regulators. By reporting low income numbers, companies hope to reduce their exposure to the perception of monopoly power. In addition, other constituents such as labour unions may be less willing to ask for wage increases if reported income is low. Thus, researchers have found that the larger the company, the more likely it is to adopt income-decreasing approaches in selecting accounting methods.[6]

2. **Capital structure**. A number of studies have indicated that the capital structure of the company can affect the selection of accounting methods. For example, a company with a high debt-to-equity ratio is more likely to be constrained by debt covenants. That is, a company may have a debt covenant indicating that it cannot pay any dividends if retained earnings fall below a certain level. As a result, this type of company is more likely to select accounting methods that will increase net income. For example, one group of writers indicated that a company's capital structure affected its decision whether to expense or capitalize interest.[7] Others indicated that full cost accounting was selected instead of successful efforts by companies that have high debt-to-equity ratios.[8]

3. **Bonus payments**. If bonus payments paid to management are tied to income, it has been found that management will select accounting methods that maximize its bonus payments. Thus, in selecting accounting methods, management does concern itself with the effect of accounting income changes on its compensation plans.[9]

4. **Smooth earnings**. Substantial increases in earnings attract the attention of politicians, regulators, and competitors. In addition, large increases in income create problems for management because the same results are difficult to achieve the following year. Compensation plans may adjust to these higher numbers and therefore make it difficult for management to achieve its profit goals and receive its bonus compensation the following year. Conversely, large decreases in earnings might be viewed as a signal that the company is in financial trouble. Furthermore, substantial decreases in income raise concerns on the part of shareholders, lenders, and other interested parties about the competency of management. Thus, companies have an incentive to manage earnings. Management therefore believes that a steady 10% growth per year is much better than a 30% growth one year and a 10% decline the next.[10] In other words, management usually prefers a gradually increasing income report (often referred to as income smoothers) and sometimes changes accounting methods to ensure such a result.

Management pays careful attention to the accounting it follows and often changes accounting methods for economic rather than conceptual reasons. As indicated throughout this textbook, such arguments have come to be known as "economic consequences arguments," since they focus on the

---

[6] Ross Watts and Jerold Zimmerman, "Towards a Positive Theory of the Determination of Accounting Standards," *The Accounting Review* (January 1978).

[7] R.M. Bowen, E.W. Noreen, and J.M. Lacy, "Determinants of the Corporate Decision to Capitalize Interest," *Journal of Accounting and Economics* (August 1981).

[8] See, for example, Dan. S. Dhaliwal, "The Effect of the Firm's Capital Structure on the Choice of Accounting Methods," *The Accounting Review* (January 1980); and W. Bruce Johnson and Ramachandran Ramanan, "Discretionary Accounting Changes from 'Successful Efforts' to 'Full Cost Methods' 1970–76," *The Accounting Review* (January 1988). The latter study found that firms that changed to full cost were more likely to exhibit higher levels of financial risk (leverage) than firms that retained successful efforts.

[9] See, for example, Mark Zmijewski and Robert Hagerman, "An Income Strategy Approach to the Positive Theory of Accounting Standard Setting/Choice," *Journal of Accounting and Economics* (1985).

[10] O. Douglas Moses, "Income Smoothing and Incentives: Empirical Tests Using Accounting Changes," *The Accounting Review* (April 1987). Findings provide evidence that smoothers are associated with firm size, the existence of bonus plans, and the divergence of actual earnings from expectations.

supposed impact of accounting on the behaviour of investors, creditors, competitors, or governments, or on the behaviour of the managers of the reporting companies themselves, rather than addressing the conceptual justification for accounting standards.[11]

To counter these pressures, standard setters have declared, as part of their conceptual framework, that they will assess the merits of proposed standards from a position of neutrality. That is, the soundness of standards should not be evaluated on the grounds of their possible impact on behaviour. It is not the Accounting Standards Board's place to choose standards according to the kinds of behaviour they wish to promote and the kinds they wish to discourage. At the same time, it must be admitted that some standards *will* often have the effect of influencing behaviour. Yet their justification should be conceptual; standards should not be judged in terms of their impact.

ERROR ANALYSIS

Objective 7

Analyse the effect of errors.

As indicated earlier, material errors are unusual in large corporations because internal control procedures coupled with the diligence of the accounting staff are ordinarily sufficient to find any major errors in the system. Smaller businesses may face a different problem. These enterprises may not be able to afford an internal audit staff nor to implement the necessary control procedures to ensure that accounting data are always recorded accurately.[12]

In practice, firms do not correct for errors discovered that do not have a significant effect on the presentation of the financial statements. For example, the failure to record accrued wages of $5,000 when the total payroll for the year is $1,750,000 and net income is $940,000 is not considered significant and no correction is made. Obviously, defining materiality is difficult, and accountants must rely on their experience and judgement to determine whether adjustment is necessary for a given error. *All errors discussed in this section are assumed to be material and to require adjustment.* Also, all of the tax effects are ignored in this section.

The accountant must answer three questions in error analysis:

1. What type of error is involved?

2. What entries are needed to correct for the error?

3. How are financial statements to be restated once the error is discovered?

As indicated earlier, the profession requires that errors be treated as prior period adjustments and reported in the current year as adjustments to the beginning balance of Retained Earnings. If comparative statements are presented, the prior statements affected should be restated to correct for the error.

Three types of errors can occur; because each type has its own peculiarities, it is important to differentiate among them.

Balance Sheet Errors

Balance sheet errors affect only the presentation of an asset, liability, or shareholders' equity account. Examples are the classification of a short-term receivable as part of the investment section; the classification of a note payable as an account payable; and the classification of plant assets as inventory. Reclassification of the item to its proper position is needed when the error is discovered. If com-

---

[11] Economic consequences arguments—and there are many of them—are manipulation through the use of lobbying and other forms of pressure brought on standard setters. We have seen examples of these arguments in the oil and gas industry about successful efforts versus full cost, in the technology area with the issue of mandatory expensing of all research and most development costs, and so on.

[12] See Mark L. DeFord and James Jiambalvo, "Incidence and Circumstances of Accounting Errors," *The Accounting Review* (July 1991) for examples of different types of errors and why these errors might have occurred.

parative statements that include the error year are prepared, the balance sheet for the error year is restated correctly.

Income Statement Errors

Income statement errors affect only the presentation of the nominal accounts in the income statement. Errors involve the improper classification of revenues or expenses, such as recording interest revenue as part of sales; purchases as bad debt expense; and depreciation expense as interest expense. An income statement error has no effect on the balance sheet and no effect on net income; a reclassification entry is needed when the error is discovered, if it is discovered in the year it is made. If the error occurred in prior periods, no entry is needed at the date of discovery because the accounts for the current year are correctly stated and accounting records have been closed for the previous years. If comparative statements that include the error year are prepared, the income statement for the error year is restated correctly.

Balance Sheet and Income Statement Errors

The third type of error involves both the balance sheet and income statement. For example, assume that accrued wages payable were overlooked by the bookkeeper at the end of the accounting period. The effect of this error is to understate expenses, understate liabilities, and overstate net income for that period of time. This type of error affects both the balance sheet and the income statement and is classified in the following two ways—counterbalancing and noncounterbalancing.

Counterbalancing errors are errors that will be offset or corrected over two periods. In the previous illustration, the failure to record accrued wages is considered a counterbalancing error because over a two-year period the error will no longer be present. In other words the failure to record accrued wages in the previous period means: (1) wages expense is understated; (2) net income for the first period is overstated; and (3) accrued wages payable (a liability) is understated. In the next period, net income is understated; accrued wages payable (a liability) is correctly stated; and wages expense is overstated. For the *two years combined*: (1) total wage expense is correct; (2) net income is correct, and (3) accrued wages payable at the end of the second year is correct. Most errors in accounting that affect both the balance sheet and income statement are counterbalancing errors.

Noncounterbalancing errors are errors that are not offset in the next accounting period; for example, the failure to capitalize equipment that has a useful life of five years. If we expense this asset immediately, expenses will be overstated in the first period but understated in the next four periods. At the end of the second period, the effect of the error is not fully offset. Net income is correct in the aggregate only at the end of five years, because the asset is fully depreciated at this point.

Accountants define counterbalancing errors as errors that correct themselves over two periods, whereas noncounterbalancing errors are those that take longer than two periods to correct themselves. Only in rare circumstances is an error never reversed; for example, when land is initially expensed. Because land is not depreciable, theoretically the error is never offset unless the land is sold.

Counterbalancing Errors

The usual types of counterbalancing errors are illustrated on the following pages. In studying these illustrations, a number of points should be remembered. First, determine whether or not the books have been closed for the period in which the error is found:

1. **The books have been closed**:

    (a) If the error is already counterbalanced, no entry is necessary.

    (b) If the error is not yet counterbalanced, an entry is necessary to adjust the present balance of retained earnings and the other balance sheet account(s) affected.

2. **The books have not been closed**:

    (a) If the error is already counterbalanced and we are in the second year, an entry is necessary to correct the current period income statement item(s) and to adjust the beginning balance of Retained Earnings.

    (b) If the error is not yet counterbalanced, an entry is necessary to adjust the beginning balance of Retained Earnings and to correct the current period income statement item and any other balance sheet account(s) affected.

Second, if comparative statements are presented, restatement of the amounts for comparative purposes is necessary. This situation occurs even if a correcting journal entry is not required. To illustrate, assume that Sanford's Cement Co. failed to accrue income in 1991 when earned, but recorded the income in 1992 when received. The error was discovered in 1994. No entry is necessary to correct for this error because the effects have been counterbalanced by the time that the error was discovered in 1994. However, if comparative financial statements for 1991 through 1994 are presented, the accounts and related amounts for the years 1991 and 1992 should be restated correctly for financial reporting purposes.

Failure to Record Accrued Wages. On December 31, 1993, accrued wages in the amount of $1,500 were not recognized. The entry in 1994 to correct this error, assuming that the books have not been closed for 1994, is:

Retained Earnings	1,500	
Wages Expense		1,500

The rationale for this entry is as follows:

1. Wages that should have been accrued in 1993 were paid in 1994 and an additional debit of $1,500 was made to the 1994 Wages Expense, which is therefore overstated by $1,500.

2. Because 1993 accrued wages were not recorded as Wages Expense in 1993, net income for 1993 was overstated by $1,500 and, as a consequence, the Retained Earnings account was overstated by $1,500.

If the books have been closed for 1994, no entry would be made because the error was counterbalanced.

Failure to Record Prepaid Expenses. In January 1993, Hurley Enterprises purchased a two-year insurance policy costing $1,000; Insurance Expense was debited and Cash was credited. No adjusting entries were made at the end of 1993.

    The entry on December 31, 1994 to correct this error, assuming that the books were not closed for 1994, would be:

Insurance Expense	500	
Retained Earnings		500

If the books have been closed for 1994, no entry would be made because the error has been counterbalanced.

Overstatement of Prepaid Revenue. On December 31, 1993, Hurley Enterprises received $50,000 as a prepayment for renting certain office space for the following year. The entry made at the time of receipt of the rent payment was a debit to Cash and a credit to Rent Revenue. No adjusting entry was made as of December 31, 1993. The entry on December 31, 1994 to correct this error, assuming that the books have not been closed for 1994, would be:

Retained Earnings	50,000	
Rent Revenue		50,000

If the books have been closed for 1994, no entry would be made because the error has been counterbalanced.

Overstatement of Accrued Revenue. On December 31, 1993, Hurley Enterprises accrued as interest revenue $8,000 that applied to 1994. The entry made on December 31, 1993 was to debit Accrued Interest Receivable and credit Interest Revenue. The entry on December 31, 1994 to correct this error, assuming that the books have not been closed for 1994, would be:

Retained Earnings	8,000	
Interest Revenue		8,000

If the books have been closed for 1994, no entry would be made because the error has been counterbalanced.

Understatement of Ending Inventory. On December 31, 1993, the physical count of the inventory was understated by $25,000 because the inventory crew failed to count one warehouse of merchandise. The entry on December 31, 1994 to correct this error, assuming that the books have not been closed for 1994, would be:

Inventory (beginning income statement)	25,000	
Retained Earnings		25,000

If the books have been closed for 1994, no entry would be made because the error has been counterbalanced.

Overstatement of Purchases. Hurley Enterprise's accountant recorded a purchase of merchandise for $9,000 in 1993 that applied to 1994. The physical inventory for 1993 was correctly stated. The entry on December 31, 1994 to correct this error, assuming that the books have not been closed for 1994, would be:

Purchases	9,000	
Retained Earnings		9,000

If the books have been closed for 1994, no entry would be made because the error has been counterbalanced.

Overstatement of Purchases and Inventories. Sometimes both the physical inventory and the purchases are incorrectly stated. Assume, as in the previous illustration, that purchases for 1993 were overstated by $9,000 and that inventory was overstated by the same amount. The entry on December 31, 1994 to correct this error, assuming that the books have not been closed for 1994, would be:

Purchases	9,000	
Inventory		9,000[a]

[a]The net income for 1993 is correctly computed because the overstatement of Purchases was offset by the overstatement of ending inventory in the Cost of Goods Sold computation.

If the books have been closed for 1994, no entry would be made because the error is counterbalanced.

Noncounterbalancing Errors

Because noncounterbalancing errors do not counterbalance over a two-year period, the entries are more complex and correcting entries are needed, even if the books have been closed.

Failure to Record Depreciation. Assume that Hurley Enterprises purchased a machine for $10,000 on January 1, 1993 and it had an estimated useful life of five years. The accountant incorrectly expensed this machine in 1993. The error was discovered in 1994. If we assume that the company desired to use straight-line depreciation on this asset, the entry on December 31, 1994 to correct this error, given that the books have not been closed, would be:

Machinery	10,000	
Depreciation Expense	2,000	
Retained Earnings		8,000[a]
Accumulated Depreciation		4,000[a]

[a]Computations:
Retained Earnings

Overstatement of expense in 1993	10,000
Proper depreciation for 1993 (20% × $10,000)	(2,000)
Retained earnings understated as of Dec. 31, 1993	$ 8,000

Accumulated Depreciation

Accumulated depreciation (20% × $10,000 × 2)	$ 4,000

If the books have been closed for 1994, the entry is:

Machinery	10,000	
Retained Earnings		6,000[a]
Accumulated Depreciation		4,000

[a]Computations:
Retained Earnings

Retained earnings understated as of Dec. 31, 1993	$ 8,000
Proper depreciation for 1994 (20% × $10,000)	(2,000)
Retained earnings understated as of Dec. 31, 1994	$ 6,000

Failure to Adjust for Bad Debts. Companies sometimes use a specific charge-off method in accounting for bad debt expense when a percentage of sales is more appropriate. Adjustments are often made to change from the specific write-off to some type of allowance method. Assume that Hurley Enterprises has recognized bad debt expense because the debts have actually become uncollectible as follows.

	1993	1994
From 1993 sales	$550	$690
From 1994 sales		700

Hurley estimates that an additional $1,400 will be charged off in 1995: $300 applicable to 1993 Sales and $1,100 to 1994 Sales. The entry on December 31, 1994, assuming that the books have not been closed for 1994, would be:

Bad Debt Expense	410[a]	
Retained Earnings	990[a]	
Allowance for Doubtful Accounts		1,400

[a]Computations:
Allowance for doubtful accounts: Additional $300 for 1993 sales and $1,100 for 1994 sales.

Bad debts and retained earnings balance:

	1993	1994
Bad debts expense charged for	$1,240[b]	$ 700
Additional bad debts anticipated	300	1,100

(Continued)

Proper bad debt expense	1,540	1,800
Charges currently made to each period	(550)	(1,390)
Bad debt adjustment	$ 990	$ 410

ᵇ$550 + $690 = $1,240

If the books have been closed for 1994, the entry would be:

Retained Earnings	1,400	
Allowance for Doubtful Accounts		1,400

Comprehensive Illustration: Numerous Errors

In some circumstances, a combination of errors rather than one error occurs. A work sheet is therefore prepared to facilitate the analysis. To demonstrate the use of a work sheet, the following problem is presented for solution. The mechanics of the work sheet preparation should be obvious from the solution format.

The income statements of the Hudson Company for the three years ended December 31 indicate the following net incomes:

1992	$17,400
1993	20,200
1994	11,300

An examination of the accounting records of the Hudson Company for these years indicates that several errors were made in arriving at the net income amounts reported. The following errors were discovered:

1. Wages earned by workers but not paid at December 31 were consistently omitted from the records. The amounts omitted were:

December 31, 1992	$1,000
December 31, 1993	1,400
December 31, 1994	1,600

    These amounts were recorded as expenses when paid in the year following that in which they were earned.

2. The merchandise inventory on December 31, 1992 was overstated by $1,900 as the result of errors made in the footings and extensions on the inventory sheets.

3. Unexpired insurance of $1,200, applicable to 1994, was expensed on December 31, 1993.

4. Interest receivable in the amount of $240 was not recorded on December 31, 1993.

5. On January 2, 1993, a piece of equipment costing $3,900 was sold for $1,800. At the date of sale, the equipment had accumulated depreciation pertaining to it of $2,400. The cash received was recorded as Miscellaneous Revenue in 1993. In addition, depreciation was recorded for this equipment in both 1993 and 1994 at the rate of 10% of cost.

Instructions. Prepare a schedule showing the corrected net income amounts for the years ended December 31, 1992, 1993, and 1994. Each correction of the amount originally reported should be clearly labelled. In addition, indicate the balance sheet accounts affected as of December 31, 1994.

Correcting entries *if the books have not been closed* on December 31, 1994 would be:

1. 1992 error has been counterbalanced—no entry necessary.

Retained Earnings	1,400	
Wages Expense		1,400

    (To correct improper charge of 1993 wages to expense for 1994)

(Continued)

Wages Expense	1,600	
Wages Payable		1,600

(To record proper wages expense for 1994)

2. No entry—counterbalanced.

3. Insurance Expense	1,200	
Retained Earnings		1,200

(To record proper insurance expense for 1994)

4. Interest Revenue	240	
Retained Earnings		240

(To correct improper credit to interest revenue in 1994)

5. Retained Earnings	1,500	
Accumulated Depreciation	2,400	
Machinery		3,900

(To record write-off of machinery in 1993 and
adjustment of retained earnings. Proceeds from sale $1,800—
gain, $300)

Accumulated Depreciation	780	
Depreciation Expense		390
Retained Earnings		390

(To correct improper charge for depreciation expense
in 1993 and 1994)

If the books have been closed:

1. Retained Earnings	1,600	
Wages Payable		1,600

(To record proper wage expense for 1994)

2., 3., 4. No entry.

5. Retained Earnings	1,500	
Accumulated Depreciation	2,400	
Machinery		3,900

(To record write-off of machinery in 1993 and adjustment
of retained earnings)

Accumulated Depreciation	780	
Retained Earnings		780

(To correct improper charge for depreciation expense
in 1993 and 1994)

	Work Sheet Analysis of Changes in Net Income				Balance Sheet Correction at December 31, 1994		
	1992	1993	1994	Totals	Debit	Credit	Account
Net income as reported	17,400	20,200	11,300	48,900			
Wages unpaid, Dec. 31/92	(1,000)	1,000		–0–			
Wages unpaid, Dec. 31/93		(1,400)	1,400	–0–			
Wages unpaid, Dec. 31/94			(1,600)	(1,600)		1,600	Wages Payable
Inventory overstatement, Dec. 31/92	(1,900)	1,900		–0–			

(Continued)

Unexpired insurance, Dec. 31/93	1,200	(1,200)	–0–			
Interest receivable, Dec. 31/93	240	(240)	–0–			
Correction for entry made on sale of equipment, Jan. 2/93a		(1,500)	(1,500)	2,400	3,900	Accumulated Depreciation Machinery
Overcharge of depreciation, 1993	390		390	390		Accumulated Depreciation
Overcharge of depreciation, 1994			390	390	390	
Corrected net income	14,500	22,030	10,050	46,580		

aCost	$3,900
Accumulated depreciation	2,400
Book value	1,500
Proceeds from sale	1,800
Gain on sale	300
Income reported	(1,800)
Adjustment	(1,500)

Preparation of Comparative Statements

Discussion of error analysis up to now has been concerned with the identification of the type of error involved and the accounting for its correction in the accounting records. The correction of the errors should be presented on comparative financial statements. In addition, five- or ten-year summaries are often given for the interested financial reader.

The work sheet on page 1118 illustrates how a typical year's financial statements are restated, given many different errors. Dick & Wally's Outlet is a small retail outlet in the town of Prescott. Lacking expertise in accounting, the owners did not keep adequate records; as a result, many errors occurred in recording the accounting information. These errors are listed below:

1. The bookkeeper inadvertently failed to record a cash receipt of $1,000 on the sale of merchandise in 1994.

2. Accrued wages expense at the end of 1993 was $2,500; at the end of 1994, $3,200. The company did not accrue for wages; all wages are charged to administrative expense.

3. The beginning inventory was understated by $5,400 because goods in transit at the end of last year were not counted. The proper purchase entry had been made.

4. No allowance had been set up for estimated uncollectible receivables. It is decided to set up such an allowance for the estimated probable losses as of December 31, 1994 for 1993 accounts of $700, and for 1994 accounts of $1,500. It is also decided to correct the charge against each year so that it shows the losses (actual and estimated) relating to that year's sales. Accounts have been written off to bad debt expense (selling expense) as follows.

	In 1993	In 1994
1993 Accounts	$400	$2,000
1994 Accounts		1,600

5. Unexpired insurance not recorded at the end of 1993, $600; at the end of 1994, $400. All insurance expense is charged to administrative expense.

6. An account payable of $6,000 should have been a note payable.

7. During 1993, an asset that cost $10,000 and had a book value of $4,000 was sold for $7,000. At the time of sale, Cash was debited and Miscellaneous Revenue was credited for $7,000.

8. As a result of the last transaction, the company overstated depreciation expense (an administrative expense) in 1993 by $800 and in 1994 by $1,200.

9. In a physical count, the company determined the final inventory to be $40,000.

Presented below is a work sheet that begins with the unadjusted trial balance of Dick & Wally's Outlet; the correcting entries and their effect on the financial statements can be determined by examining the work sheet.

Dick & Wally's Outlet
Work Sheet Analysis to Adjust Financial Statements for the Year 1994

	Trial Balance Unadjusted		Adjustments		Income Statement Adjusted		Balance Sheet Adjusted	
	Debit	Credit	Debit	Credit	Debit	Credit	Debit	Credit
Cash	3,100		(1) 1,000				4,100	
Accounts Receivable	17,600						17,600	
Notes Receivable	8,500						8,500	
Inventories, Jan. 1, 1994	34,000		(3) 5,400		39,400			
Property, Plant and Equip.	112,000			(7) 10,000ᵃ			102,000	
Accumulated Depreciation		83,500	(7) 6,000ᵃ					
			(8) 2,000					75,500
Investments	24,300						24,300	
Accounts Payable		14,500	(6) 6,000					8,500
Notes Payable		10,000		(6) 6,000				16,000
Share Capital		43,500						43,500
Retained Earnings		20,000	(4) 2,700ᵇ	(3) 5,400				
			(7) 4,000ᵃ	(5) 600				
			(2) 2,500	(8) 800				17,600
Sales		94,000		(1) 1,000		95,000		
Purchases	21,000				21,000			
Selling Expenses	22,000			(4) 500ᵇ	21,500			
Administrative Expenses	23,000		(2) 700	(5) 400				
			(5) 600	(8) 1,200	22,700			
Totals	265,500	265,000						
Wages Payable				(2) 3,200				3,200
Allowance for Doubtful Accounts				(4) 2,200ᵇ				2,200
Unexpired Insurance			(5) 400				400	
Inventory, Dec. 31, 1994						(9) 40,000	(9) 40,000	
Net Income					30,400			30,400
Totals			31,300	31,300	135,000	135,000	196,900	196,900

Computations:

ᵃMachinery		ᵇBad Debts		1992	1993
Proceeds from sale	$7,000	Bad debts charged for		$2,400	$1,600
Book value of machinery	4,000	Additional bad debts anticipated		700	1,500
Gain on sale	3,000			3,100	3,100
Income credited	7,000	Charges currently made to each year		(400)	(3,600)
Retained earnings adjustment	$4,000	Bad debt adjustment		$2,700	$ (500)

FUNDAMENTAL CONCEPTS

1. The three different types of accounting changes are (1) changes in accounting policy, (2) changes in accounting estimate, and (3) changes in accounting entity.

2. Accounting changes may be handled retroactively with restatement, retroactively without restatement, or prospectively (only current and future periods are affected).

3. Changes in accounting policy involve a change from one generally accepted accounting principle to another generally accepted accounting principle. If the accounting principle previously followed was not acceptable or if the principle was applied incorrectly, a change to a generally accepted accounting principle is considered a correction of an error.

4. The general requirement for changes in accounting policy is that the cumulative effect of the change (net of tax) be shown as an adjustment of the opening retained earnings.

5. Changes in accounting estimates are handled prospectively; that is, only the current and future periods affected by a change are adjusted.

6. Changes in the reporting entity as a result of a pooling of interests transaction are reported by restating the financial statements of all prior periods presented. Changes in the reporting entity resulting from a purchase transaction are reported prospectively.

7. Errors result from mathematical mistakes, oversight or misuse of facts, or incorrect application of accounting principles.

8. Corrections of errors are accounted for in a manner similar to a prior period adjustment. The effects of errors are reported by restating all prior period statements presented.

9. Error analysis involves identifying the type of error, making the proper correcting entries, and properly restating the prior period financial statements.

—— QUESTIONS ——

1. In recent years, various Canadian business publications have indicated that many companies have changed their accounting principles. What are the major reasons for companies to change accounting methods?

2. State how each of the following items is reflected in the financial statements:
   (a) Change from straight-line method of depreciation to sum-of-the-years'-digits.
   (b) Change from FIFO to LIFO method for inventory valuation purposes.
   (c) Charge for failure to record depreciation in a previous period.
   (d) Litigation won in current year, related to prior period.
   (e) Change in the realizability of certain receivables.
   (f) Write-off of receivables.
   (g) Change from the percentage-of-completion to the completed-contract method for reporting net income.

3. What are the advantages of employing the retroactive-with-restatement approach for handling changes in accounting principles?

4. Define a change in estimate and provide an illustration. When is a change in accounting estimate affected by a change in accounting principle?

5. Richard Siu Inc. has followed the practice of capitalizing certain marketing costs and amortizing these costs over their expected life. In the current year, the company determined that the future benefits from these costs were doubtful. Consequently, the company adopted the policy of expensing these costs as incurred. How should this accounting change be reported in the comparative financial statements?

6. Indicate how the following items are recorded in the accounting records in the current year:
   (a) Large write-off of goodwill.
   (b) A change in depreciating plant assets from accelerated to the straight-line method.
   (c) Large write-off of inventories because of obsolescence.
   (d) Change from the cash basis to accrual basis of accounting.
   (e) Change from average cost to FIFO method for inventory valuation purposes.

   (f) Change in the estimate of service lives for plant assets.

7. Ellithorpe Construction Co. had followed the practice of expensing all materials assigned to a construction job without recognizing any salvage inventory. On December 31, 1994, it was determined that salvage inventory should be valued at $59,000. Of this amount, $27,000 arose during the current year. How does this information affect the financial statements to be prepared at the end of 1994?

8. Maureen Ltd. wishes to change from the sum-of-the-years'-digits to the straight-line depreciation method for financial reporting purposes. The auditor indicates that a change would be permitted only if it is to a preferable method. What difficulties develop in assessing preferability?

9. How should consolidated financial statements be reported this year when statements of individual companies were presented last year?

10. Rachel Fenton controlled four domestic subsidiaries and one foreign subsidiary. Prior to the current year, Rachel had excluded the foreign subsidiary from consolidation. During the current year, the foreign subsidiary was included in the financial statements. How should this change in accounting principle be reflected in the financial statements?

11. Allman Ltd., a closely held corporation, is in the process of preparing financial statements to accompany an offering of its common shares. The company at this time has decided to switch from the accelerated depreciation to the straight-line method of depreciation to better represent its financial operations. How should this change in accounting principle be reported in the financial statements?

12. Discuss and illustrate how a correction of an error in previously issued financial statements should be handled.

13. Prior to 1994, O'Shea Ltd. excluded manufacturing overhead costs from work-in-process and finished goods inventory. These costs have been expensed as incurred. In 1994, the company decided to change its accounting methods for manufacturing inventories to full costing by including these costs as product costs. Assuming that these costs are material, how should this change be reflected in the financial statements for 1994 and 1993?

14. Jan Way Corp. failed to record accrued salaries for 1991, $2,000; 1992, $2,100; and 1993, $4,200. What is the amount of the overstatement or understatement of Retained Earnings at December 31, 1994?

15. In January 1993, installation costs of $10,000 on new machinery were charged to Repair Expense. Other costs of this machinery of $30,000 were correctly recorded and have been depreciated using the straight-line method with an estimated life of 10 years and no residual value. At December 31, 1994, it is decided that the machinery has a useful life of 20 years, starting with January 1, 1994. What entry(ies) should be made in 1994 to correctly record transactions related to machinery, assuming that the machinery has no residual value? The books have not been closed for 1994 and depreciation expense has not yet been recorded for 1994.

16. On January 2, 1994, $100,000 of 11%, 20-year bonds were issued for $98,000. The $2,000 discount was charged to Interest Expense. The bookkeeper, Mike Mahar, recorded interest only on the interest payment dates of January 1 and July 1. What is the effect of this error on reported net income for 1994, assuming straight-line amortization of the discount? What entry is necessary to correct for this error, assuming that the books are not closed for 1994?

17. An account payable of $11,000 for merchandise purchased on December 23, 1994 was recorded in January 1995. This merchandise was not included in inventory at December 31, 1994. What effect does this error have on reported net income for 1994? What entry should be made to correct this error, assuming that the books are not closed for 1994?

18. Equipment was purchased on January 2, 1994 for $15,000, but no portion of the cost has been charged to depreciation. The corporation wishes to use the straight-line method for these assets, which have been estimated to have a life of 10 years and no residual value. What effect does this error have on net income in 1994? What entry is necessary to correct this error, assuming that the books are not closed for 1994?

--------- CASES ---------

C22-1 **(ANALYSIS OF VARIOUS ACCOUNTING CHANGES AND ERRORS)** Amarada Ltd. has recently hired a new independent auditor who says she wants "to get everything straightened out." Consequently, she has proposed the following accounting changes in connection with Amarada's 1994 financial statements.

1. At December 31, 1993, the client had a receivable of $900,000 from Reenie, Inc. on its balance sheet. Reenie, Inc. has gone bankrupt, and no recovery is expected. The client proposes to write off the receivable as a prior period item.

2. The auditor proposes the following changes in depreciation policies:

   (a) For office furniture and fixtures, she proposes a change from a 10-year useful life to an eight-year life. If this change had been made in prior years, retained earnings at December 31, 1993 would have been $250,000 less. The effect of the change on 1994 income alone would be a reduction of $50,000.

   (b) For Amarada's manufacturing assets, the auditor proposes to change from double-declining balance depreciation to straight-line. If straight-line depreciation had been used for all prior periods, retained earnings would have been $380,800 greater at December 31, 1993. The effect of the change on 1994 income alone would be a reduction of $4,800.

   (c) For Amarada's equipment in the leasing division, the auditor proposes to adopt the sum-of-the-years'-digits depreciation method. Amarada has never used SYD before. The first year that Amarada operated a leasing division was 1994. If straight-line depreciation was used, 1994 income would be $90,000 greater.

3. In preparing it's 1993 statements, one of Amarada's bookkeepers overstated ending inventory by $250,000 because of a mathematical error. The auditor proposes to treat this item as a prior period adjustment.

4. In the past, Amarada has spread preproduction costs in its furniture division over five years. Because its latest furniture is of the "fad" type, it appears that the largest volume of sales will occur during the first two years after introduction. Consequently, the auditor proposes to amortize preproduction costs on a per-unit basis, which will result in expensing most of such costs during the first two years after the furniture's introduction. If the new accounting method had been used prior to 1994, retained earnings at December 31, 1993 would have been $400,000 less.

5. For the nursery division, the auditor proposes to switch from FIFO to average-cost inventories as it is believed that average-cost will provide a better matching of current costs with revenues. The effect of making this change on 1994 earnings would be an increase of $310,000. The auditor says that the effect of the change on December 31, 1993 retained earnings cannot be determined.

6. To achieve a better matching of revenues and expenses in Amarada's building construction division, the auditor proposes to switch from the completed-contract method of accounting to the percentage-of-completion method. Had the percentage-of-completion method been employed in all prior years, retained earnings at December 31, 1993 would have been $1,250,000 greater.

Instructions

(a) For each of the changes described above decide whether:

   1. The change involves an accounting principle, accounting estimate, or correction of an error.

   2. Restatement of opening retained earnings is required.

(b) What would be the proper adjustment to the December 31, 1993 retained earnings? What would be the effect of the new policies on the 1994 income statement?

(ANALYSIS OF VARIOUS ACCOUNTING CHANGES AND ERRORS) Various types of accounting C22-2
changes can affect the financial statements of a business enterprise differently. Assume that the following list describes changes that have a material effect on the financial statements for the current year of your business enterprise:

1. A change from the completed-contract method to the percentage-of-completion method of accounting for long-term construction-type contracts.

2. A change in the estimated useful life of previously recorded fixed assets based on newly acquired information.

3. A change from deferring and amortizing preproduction costs to recording such costs as expenses when incurred because future benefits of the costs have become doubtful. The new accounting method was adopted in recognition of the change in estimated future benefits.

4. A change from including the employer share of CPP premiums with Payroll Expenses to including it with Retirement Benefits on the income statement.

5. Correction of a mathematical error in inventory pricing made in a prior period.

6. A change from prime costing to full absorption costing for inventory valuation.

7. A change from presentation of statements of individual companies to presentation of consolidated statements.

8. A change in the method of accounting for leases for tax purposes to conform with the financial accounting method. As a result, both deferred and current taxes payable changed substantially.

9. A change from the FIFO method of inventory pricing to the average-cost method of inventory pricing.

Instructions

Identify the type of change that is described in each item above and indicate whether the prior year's financial statements should be restated when presented in comparative form with the current year's statements. Ignore possible pro forma effects.

C22-3 **(ANALYSIS OF THREE ACCOUNTING CHANGES AND ERRORS)** Listed below are three independent, unrelated sets of facts relating to accounting changes.

Situation I. Algonquin Company is in the process of having its first audit. The company's policy with regard to recognition of revenue is to use the instalment method. However, *CICA Handbook* Section 3400 permits the use of the instalment method of revenue recognition in circumstances that are not present here. Algonquin's president, Tom Zarle, is willing to change to an acceptable method.

Situation II. A company decides in January 1994 to adopt the straight-line method of depreciation for plant equipment. The straight-line method will be used for new acquisitions as well as for previously acquired plant equipment for which depreciation had been provided on an accelerated basis.

Situation III. A company determined that the depreciable lives of its fixed assets are too long at present to fairly match the cost of the fixed assets with the revenue produced. The company decided at the beginning of the current year to reduce the depreciable lives of all of its existing fixed assets by five years.

Instructions

For each of the situations described, provide the information indicated below:

(a) Type of accounting change.

(b) Manner of reporting the change under current generally accepted accounting principles including a discussion, where applicable, of how amounts are computed.

(c) Effect of the change on the balance sheet and income statement.

C22-4 **(ANALYSIS OF VARIOUS ACCOUNTING CHANGES AND ERRORS)** Scott Gilbert, controller of Chippewa Corp., is aware that a new *CICA Handbook* section on accounting changes has been issued. After reading the section, he is confused and is not sure what action should be taken on the following items related to Chippewa Corp. for the year 1994:

1. In 1994, Chippewa decided to change the company's policy on accounting for certain marketing costs. Previously, the company had chosen to defer and amortize all marketing costs over at least five years because Chippewa believed that a return on these expenditures did not occur immediately. Recently, however, the time differential has considerably shortened, and Chippewa is now expensing the marketing costs as incurred.

2. In 1994, the company examined its entire policy relating to the depreciation of plant equipment. Plant equipment had normally been depreciated over a 15-year period, but recent experience has indicated that the company was incorrect in its estimates and that the assets should be depreciated over a 20-year period.

3. Cree Co., a division of Chippewa Corp., has consistently shown an increasing net income from period to period. On closer examination of their operating statement, it is noted that bad debt expense and inventory obsolescence charges are much lower than in other divisions. In discussing this with the controller of this division, it is learned that the controller has increased the net income each period by knowingly making low estimates related to the write-off of receivables and inventory.

4. In 1994, the company purchased new machinery that should increase production dramatically. The company has decided to depreciate this machinery on an accelerated basis, even though other machinery is depreciated on a straight-line basis.

5. All equipment sold by Chippewa is subject to a three-year warranty. It has been estimated that the expense ultimately to be incurred on these machines is 1% of sales. In 1994, because of a production breakthrough, it is now estimated that ½ of 1% of sales is sufficient. In 1992 and 1993, warranty expense was computed as $55,000 and $60,000, respectively. The company now believes that these warranty costs should be reduced by 50%.

6. In 1994, the company decided to change its method of inventory pricing from average-cost to the FIFO method. The effect of this change on prior years is to increase 1992 income by $60,000 and increase 1993 income by $20,000.

Instructions

Scott Gilbert has come to you, as his accountant, for advice about the situations above. Indicate the appropriate accounting treatment in each of these situations.

(COMPREHENSIVE ACCOUNTING CHANGES AND ERROR ANALYSIS) Sidney Manufacturing is **C22-5** preparing its year-end financial statements. The controller is confronted with several decisions about statement presentation with regard to the following items:

1. The vice-president of sales has indicated that one product line has lost its customer appeal and will be phased out over the next three years. Therefore, a decision has been made to lower the estimated lives on related production equipment from the remaining five years to three years.

2. Estimating the lives of new products in the Leisure Products Division has become very difficult due to the highly competitive conditions in this market. Therefore, the practice of deferring and amortizing preproduction costs has been abandoned in favour of expensing such costs as they are incurred.

3. The Hightone Building was converted from a sales office to offices for the accounting department at the beginning of this year. Therefore, the expense related to this building will now appear as an administrative expense rather than a selling expense on the current year's income statement.

4. When the year-end physical inventory adjustment was made for the current year, the prior year's physical inventory sheets for an entire warehouse were discovered to have been mislaid and excluded from last year's count.

5. The method of accounting used for financial reporting purposes for certain receivables has been approved for tax purposes during the current tax year by Revenue Canada. This change for tax purposes will cause both deferred and current taxes payable to change substantially.

6. Management has decided to switch from the FIFO inventory valuation method to the average-cost inventory valuation method for all inventories.

7. Sidney's Custom Division manufactures large-scale, custom-designed machinery on a contract basis. Management decided to switch from the completed-contract method to the percentage-of-completion method of accounting for long-term contracts.

Instructions

(a) *CICA Handbook* Section 1506, "Accounting Changes," identifies three types of accounting changes: changes in accounting policy, changes in accounting estimates, and changes due to error. For each of these three types of accounting changes:

1. Define the type of change.

2. Explain the general accounting treatment required according to *Handbook* Section 1506 with respect to the current year and prior years' financial statements.

3. Discuss the impact of the changes on the external auditor's report.

(b) For each of the seven changes Sidney Manufacturing has made in the current year, identify and explain whether the change is a change in accounting principle, in estimate, in entity, or due to error. If any of the changes is not one of these four types, explain why.

(CMA adapted)

──── EXERCISES ────

E22-1   **(ERROR AND CHANGE IN PRINCIPLE: DEPRECIATION)**   Narraganset Ltd. purchased equipment on January 1, 1991 for $440,000. At that time it was estimated that the machine would have a 10-year life and no residual value. On December 31, 1994, the firm's accountant found that the entry for depreciation expense had been omitted in 1992. In addition, management informed the accountant that it plans to switch to straight-line depreciation, starting with the year 1994. At present, the company uses the sum-of-the-years'-digits method for depreciating equipment.

Instructions

Assuming that this is a change in accounting policy, prepare the general journal entries the accountant should make at December 31, 1994. (Ignore tax effects.)

E22-2   **(CHANGE IN PRINCIPLE AND CHANGE IN ESTIMATE: DEPRECIATION)**   Resurrection, Inc. acquired the following assets in January of 1991:

Equipment, estimated service life, 5 years; residual value, $15,000	$525,000
Building, estimated service life, 30 years; no residual value	$693,000

The equipment has been depreciated using the sum-of-the-years'-digits method for the first three years, for financial reporting purposes. In 1994, the company decided to change the method of computing depreciation to the straight-line method for the equipment, but no change was made in the estimated service life or residual value. It was also decided to change the total estimated service life of the building from 30 years to 45 years, with no change in the estimated residual value. The building is depreciated on the straight-line method.

The company has 100,000 common shares outstanding. Results of operations for 1994 and 1993 are shown below.

	1994	1993
Net income (depreciation for 1994 has been computed on the straight-line basis for both the equipment and buildings[a])	$375,000	$400,000
Income per share	$3.75	$4.00

[a]It should be noted that the computation for depreciation expense for 1994 and 1993 for the building was based on the original estimate of service life of 30 years.

Instructions

(a) Compute the effect of the change in accounting principle to be reported in the restated statement of retained earnings for 1994, and prepare the journal entry to record the change. (Ignore tax effects.)

(b) Present comparative data for the years 1993 and 1994, starting with the income before the effect of accounting change. Prepare pro forma data. Do not prepare the footnote. (Ignore tax effects.)

(CHANGE IN PRINCIPLE AND CHANGE IN ESTIMATE: DEPRECIATION) Sauk Corporation **E22-3** owns equipment that originally cost $300,000 and had an estimated useful life of 20 years. The equipment had no expected residual value.

The two requirements below are independent and must be considered as entirely separate from each other.

Instructions

(a) After using the double-declining balance method for two years, the company decided to switch to the straight-line method of depreciation. Prepare the general journal entry(ies) necessary in the third year to properly account for (1) the change in accounting principle and (2) depreciation expense. (Ignore income tax effects and assume that this is a change in policy and not a change in estimate.)

(b) After using the straight-line method for two years, the company determined that the useful life of the equipment is 27 years (7 more than the original estimate). Prepare the general journal entry(ies) necessary to properly account for the depreciation expense in the third year.

(CHANGE IN ESTIMATE: DEPRECIATION) Susquehenna Co. purchased equipment for $460,000 that **E22-4** was estimated to have a useful life of 10 years, with a residual value of $10,000 at the end of that time. Depreciation has been entered for eight years on a straight-line basis. In 1994, it was determined that the total estimated life should be 15 years, with a salvage value of $9,000 at the end of that time.

Instructions

(a) Prepare the entry (if any) to correct the prior years' depreciation.

(b) Prepare the entry to record depreciation for 1994.

(CHANGE IN PRINCIPLE: DEPRECIATION) Warman Industries changed from the double-declining **E22-5** balance to the straight-line method in 1994 on all of its plant assets. For tax purposes, assume that the amount of CCA is higher than the double-declining balance depreciation for each of the three years. The appropriate information related to this change is as follows.

Year	Double-Declining Balance Depreciation	Straight-Line Depreciation	Difference
1992	$250,000	$125,000	$125,000
1993	225,000	125,000	100,000
1994	202,500	125,000	77,500

Net income for 1993 was reported at $270,000 and for 1994, $300,000, excluding any adjustment for the effect of a change in depreciation methods. The straight-line method of depreciation was employed in computing net income for 1994. (Assume that this may be accounted for as a change in policy.)

Instructions

(a) Assuming a tax rate of 45%, what is the amount of the cumulative effect adjustment in 1994?

(b) Prepare the journal entry(ies) to record the cumulative effect adjustment in the accounting records.

E22-6 (CHANGE IN POLICY: DEPRECIATION)   At the end of fiscal year 1994, management of Moncton Manufacturing Company has decided to change its depreciation method from the double-declining balance method to the straight-line method for financial reporting purposes. For federal income taxes, the company must continue to use the CCA method. The income tax rate for all years is 35%. At the end of fiscal 1994, the company has 200,000 common shares issued and outstanding. Information regarding depreciation expense and income after income taxes is as follows.

Depreciation expense to date under:

	Straight-Line	Double-Declining Balance
Pre-1993	$400,000	$950,000
1993	150,000	260,000
1994	160,000	275,000

Reported income after income taxes:

1993	$1,200,000
1994	1,450,000

Instructions

(a) Prepare the journal entries to record the change in accounting method in 1994 and indicate how the change in depreciation method would be reported in the 1994 statement of retained earnings. Also, indicate how earnings per share would be disclosed. (**Hint:** Adjust Deferred Income Tax account.)

(b) Show the amount of depreciation expense to be reported in 1994.

E22-7 (CHANGE IN PRINCIPLE: LONG-TERM CONTRACTS)   Kickapoo Construction Company changed from the completed-contract to the percentage-of-completion method of accounting for long-term construction contracts during 1994. For tax purposes, the company employs the completed-contract method and will continue this approach in the future. The appropriate information related to this change is as follows.

	Pretax Income from:		
	Percentage-of-Completion	Completed-Contract	Difference
1993	$780,000	$590,000	$190,000
1994	700,000	480,000	220,000

Instructions

(a) Assuming that the tax rate is 30%, what is the amount of net income that would be reported in 1994?

(b) What entry(ies) are necessary to adjust the accounting records for the change in accounting principle?

E22-8 (VARIOUS CHANGES IN PRINCIPLE: INVENTORY METHODS)   Following is the net income of Huron Instrument Co., a private corporation, computed under the two inventory methods, using a periodic system.

	FIFO	Average-Cost
1991	$25,000	$23,000
1992	30,000	25,000
1993	29,000	27,000
1994	34,000	30,000

Instructions

(a) Assume that in 1994 Huron decided to change from the FIFO method to the average-cost method of pricing inventories. Prepare the journal entry necessary for the change that took place during 1994, and show all of the appropriate information needed for reporting on a comparative basis.

(b) Assume that in 1994 Huron, which had been using the average-cost method since incorporation in 1991, changed to the FIFO method of pricing inventories. Prepare the journal entry necessary for the change, and show all of the appropriate information needed for reporting on a comparative basis.

(CHANGE IN PRINCIPLE: FIFO TO AVERAGE-COST)   Mohegan Industries utilizes periodic inventory   **E22-9**
procedures and on Dec. 31, 1994 decides to change from FIFO to average-cost. The following information is available in the company records.

		Units	Unit Cost
1993:	Beginning Inventory	3,000	$21
	Purchases: #1	5,000	24
	#2	4,000	30
	#3	6,000	32
	#4	5,000	34
	#5	5,000	36
	Ending Inventory	8,000	
1994:	Beginning Inventory	8,000	
	Purchases: #1	2,000	45
	#2	5,000	48
	#3	5,000	50
	#4	7,000	54
	#5	3,000	56
	Ending Inventory	11,000	

Instructions

(a) State the value at which Mohegan Industries reports the ending inventory for 1994.

(b) Indicate what additional disclosures are necessary for this change (both within the body of the financial statements and in notes). Assume a 40% tax rate.

(ERROR CORRECTION ENTRIES)   The first audit of the books of Menominee Company was made for   **E22-10**
the year ended December 31, 1994. In examining the books, the auditor found that certain items had been overlooked or incorrectly handled in the last three years. These items are:

1. At the beginning of 1992, the company purchased a machine for $500,000 (residual value of $50,000) that had a useful life of five years. The bookkeeper used straight-line depreciation but failed to deduct the residual value in computing the depreciation base for the three years.

2. At the end of 1993, the company failed to accrue sales salaries of $45,000.

3. A tax lawsuit that involved the year 1992 was settled late in 1994. It was determined that the company owed an additional $80,000 in taxes related to 1992. The company did not record a liability in 1992 or 1993 because the possibility of loss was considered remote, and charged the $80,000 to a loss account in 1994.

4. Menominee Company purchased another company early in 1992 and recorded goodwill of $600,000. Menominee had not amortized goodwill since its value had not diminished.

5. In 1994, the company changed its basis of inventory pricing from FIFO to average-cost. The cumulative effect of this change decreased the income of prior years by $75,000. The company debited this cumulative effect to Retained Earnings. Average-cost was used in computing income in 1994.

6. In 1994, the company wrote off $85,000 of inventory considered to be obsolete; this loss was charged directly to Retained Earnings.

Instructions

Prepare the journal entries necessary in 1994 to correct the books, assuming that the books have not been closed. The proper amortization period for goodwill is 40 years. Disregard effects of corrections on income tax.

E22-11 (CHANGE IN PRINCIPLE AND ERROR: FINANCIAL STATEMENTS) Presented below are the comparative statements for Seneca Company Ltd.

	1994	1993
Sales	$340,000	$270,000
Cost of sales	200,000	142,000
Gross profit	140,000	128,000
Expenses	88,000	50,000
Net income	$ 52,000	$ 78,000
Retained earnings (Jan. 1)	$125,000	$ 72,000
Net income	52,000	78,000
Dividends	(30,000)	(25,000)
Retained earnings (Dec. 31)	$147,000	$125,000

The following additional information is provided:

1. In 1994, Seneca Inc. decided to switch its depreciation method from sum-of-the-years'-digits to the straight-line method. The differences in the two depreciation methods for the assets involved are as follows.

	1994	1993
Sum-of-the-years'-digits	$40,000[a]	$50,000
Straight-line	25,000	25,000

[a]The 1994 income statement contains depreciation expense of $40,000.

2. In 1994, the company discovered that the ending inventory for 1993 was overstated by $12,000; ending inventory for 1994 was correctly stated.

Instructions

(a) Prepare the revised income and retained earnings statement for 1993 and 1994, assuming comparative statements (ignore income tax effects). Do not prepare notes or pro forma amounts.

(b) Prepare the revised income and retained earnings statement for 1994, assuming a noncomparative presentation (ignore income tax effects).

Do not prepare footnotes.

(ERROR ANALYSIS AND CORRECTING ENTRY) You have been engaged to review the financial state-**E22-12** ments of Oneida Corporation. In the course of your examination, you conclude that the bookkeeper hired during the current year is not doing a good job. You notice a number of irregularities as follows:

1. Year-end wages payable of $3,000 were not recorded because the bookkeeper thought that "they were immaterial."

2. Accrued vacation pay for the year of $25,000 was not recorded because the bookkeeper had "never heard that you should do it."

3. Insurance for a 12-month period purchased on November 1 of this year was charged to insurance expense in the amount of $2,400 because "the amount of the cheque is about the same every year."

4. Reported sales revenue for the year is $2,120,000. This includes all sales taxes collected for the year. The sales tax rate is 6%. Because the sales tax is forwarded to the provincial minister of revenue, the Sales Tax Expense account is debited because the bookkeeper thought that "the sales tax is a selling expense." At the end of the current year, the balance in the Sales Tax Expense account is $105,000.

Instructions

Prepare the necessary correcting entries (assuming that Oneida uses a calendar-year basis).

(ERROR ANALYSIS AND CORRECTING ENTRY) The reported net incomes for the first two years of **E22-13** Mohawk Products, Inc. were as follows: 1993: $147,000; 1994: $185,000. Early in 1995, the following errors were discovered:

1. Depreciation of equipment for 1993 was overstated $9,000.

2. Depreciation of equipment for 1994 was understated $39,000.

3. December 31, 1993 inventory was understated $50,000.

4. December 31, 1994 inventory was overstated $16,000.

Instructions

Prepare the correcting entries necessary when these errors are discovered. Assume that the books are closed. Ignore income tax considerations.

(ERROR ANALYSIS) Calcutta Tool Company's December 31 year-end financial statements contained the **E22-14** following errors.

	December 31, 1993	December 31, 1994
Ending inventory	$9,600 understated	$8,100 overstated
Depreciation expense	$2,300 understated	—

An insurance premium of $63,000 was prepaid in 1993 covering the years 1993, 1994, and 1995. The entire amount was charged to expense in 1993. In addition, on December 31, 1994, fully depreciated machinery was sold for $18,000 cash, but the entry was not recorded until 1995. There were no other errors during 1993 or 1994, and no corrections have been made for any of the errors. Ignore income tax considerations.

Instructions

(a) Compute the total effect of the errors on 1994 net income.

(b) Compute the total effect of the errors on the amount of Calcutta's working capital at December 31, 1994.

(c) Compute the total effect of the errors on the balance of Calcutta's retained earnings at December 31, 1994.

E22-15 **(ERROR ANALYSIS: CORRECTING ENTRIES)** A partial trial balance of Cayuga Corporation is as follows on December 31, 1994.

	Dr.	Cr.
Supplies on hand	$ 2,700	
Accrued salaries and wages		$ 1,500
Accrued interest on investments	5,100	
Prepaid insurance	90,000	
Unearned rental income		–0–
Accrued interest payable		15,000

Additional adjusting data:

1. A physical count of supplies on hand on December 31, 1994 totalled $1,000.

2. Through oversight, the accrued salaries and wages account was not changed during 1994. Accrued salaries and wages on 12/31/94 amounted to $4,200.

3. The accrued interest on the investments account was also left unchanged during 1994. Accrued interest on investments amounts to $4,300 on 12/31/94.

4. The unexpired portions of insurance policies totalled $64,500 as of December 31, 1994.

5. $30,000 was received on January 1, 1994 for the rent of a building for both 1994 and 1995. The entire amount was credited to rental income.

6. Depreciation for the year was erroneously recorded as $2,500 rather than the correct figure of $25,000.

7. A further review of depreciation calculations of prior years revealed that depreciation of $6,000 was not recorded. It was decided that this oversight should be corrected by a prior period adjustment.

Instructions

(a) Assuming that the books have not been closed, what are the adjusting entries necessary at December 31, 1994? Ignore income tax considerations.

(b) Assuming that the books have been closed, what are the adjusting entries necessary at December 31, 1994? Ignore income tax considerations.

E22-16 **(ERROR ANALYSIS)** The before-tax income for Iroquis Co. for 1993 was $98,000 and $75,400 for 1994. However, the accountant noted that the following errors had been made:

1. Sales for 1993 included amounts of $37,000 that had been received in cash during 1993, but for which the related products were delivered in 1994. Title did not pass to the purchaser until 1994.

2. The inventory on December 31, 1993 was understated by $8,700.

3. The bookkeeper in recording interest expense for both 1993 and 1994 on bonds payable made the following entry on an annual basis:

Interest Expense	15,000	
Cash		15,000

The bonds have a face value of $250,000 and pay a stated interest rate of 6%. They were issued at a discount of $15,000 on January 1, 1993 to yield an effective interest rate of 7%. (Assume that the effective yield method should be used.)

4. Ordinary repairs to equipment had been erroneously charged to the Equipment account during 1993 and 1994: $8,500 in 1993 and $9,400 in 1994. The company applies a rate of 10% to the balance in the Equipment account at the end of the year in its determination of depreciation charges.

Instructions

Prepare a schedule showing the determination of corrected net income for 1993 and 1994.

(ERROR ANALYSIS) When the records of Cherokee Corporation were reviewed at the close of 1994, the **E22-17** errors listed below were discovered. For each item, indicate by a check mark in the appropriate column whether the error resulted in an overstatement, an understatement, or had no effect on net income for the years 1993 and 1994.

	1993			1994		
Item	Over-statement	Under-statement	No Effect	Over-statement	Under-statement	No Effect
1. Failure to record amortization of patent in 1994.						
2. Failure to record accrued interest on notes payable in 1993; amount was recorded when paid in 1994.						
3. Failure to reflect supplies on hand on balance sheet at end of 1993.						
4. Failure to record the correct amount of ending 1993 inventory. The amount was understated because of an error in calculation.						

(Continued)

5. Failure to record merchandise purchased in 1993. Merchandise was also omitted from ending inventory in 1993 but was not yet sold.						

E22-18 (ERROR AND CHANGES IN PRINCIPLE AND ESTIMATE: ENTRIES)   Presented below is the net income related to Chicksaw, Inc.

1994	1993	1992
$186,000	$142,000	$224,000

Assume that depreciation entries for 1994 have not been recorded. The following information is also available:

1. Chicksaw purchased a truck on January 1, 1991 for $50,000, with a $5,000 residual value and a five-year life. The company debited an expense account and credited cash on the purchase date.

2. During 1994, Chicksaw changed from the straight-line method of depreciation for its building to the double-declining method. The following computations present depreciation on both bases (assume a change in policy).

	1994	1993	1992
Straight-line	$30,000	$30,000	$30,000
Double-declining	54,150	57,000	60,000

3. Early in 1994, Chicksaw determined that a piece of equipment purchased in January 1991 at a cost of $27,000, with an estimated life of five years and residual value of $2,000, is now estimated to continue in use until December 31, 1998 and will have a $1,000 residual value. Chicksaw has been using straight-line depreciation.

4. Chicksaw won a court case in 1994 related to a patent infringement in 1991. Chicksaw will collect its $20,000 settlement of the suit in 1995. The company had not recorded any entries related to this suit in previous periods.

5. Chicksaw, in reviewing its provision for uncollectibles during 1994, has determined that 1% of sales is the appropriate amount of bad debt expense to be charged to operations. The company had used ½ of 1% as its rate in 1993 and 1992, when the expense had been $10,000 and $7,000, respectively. The company would have recorded $9,000 of bad debt expense on December 31, 1994 under the old rate. An entry for bad debt expense in 1994 has not been recorded.

Instructions

For each of the foregoing accounting changes, errors, or prior period adjustments, present the journal entry(ies) that Chicksaw would have made to record them during 1994, assuming that the books have not been closed. If no entry is required, write "None." Ignore income tax considerations.

— PROBLEMS —

P22-1 (CHANGE IN ESTIMATE, PRINCIPLE, AND ERROR CORRECTION)   Choctaw Company reported net income of $640,000 for 1993. Its preliminary calculation of net income for 1994 shows $900,000. The books are still open for 1994. Additional information is as follows.

1. On January 1, 1993, Choctaw purchased equipment for $880,000. Choctaw estimated its useful life to be 10 years, with a zero residual value. Choctaw uses sum-of-the-years'-digits depreciation. Based on new information available at the end of 1994, Choctaw now estimates the asset's useful life should total eight years. Depreciation expense based on a 10-year useful life has already been recorded in 1994.

2. In reviewing the December 31, 1994 inventory, Choctaw discovered errors in its inventory-taking procedures that caused inventories for the last three years to be incorrect. Inventory at the end of 1992 was overstated $11,000; at the end of 1993, it was overstated $20,000; and at the end of 1994, it was understated $15,000. Choctaw uses a periodic inventory system and does not have a Cost of Goods Sold account. All information used to compute cost of goods sold is compiled in the Income Summary account. At the end of 1994, entries were made to remove the beginning inventory amount from the Inventory account (with a corresponding debit to Income Summary) and to establish the ending inventory amount in the Inventory account (with a corresponding credit to Income Summary). The Income Summary account is still open.

3. Choctaw has failed to accrue wages payable at the end of each of the last three years, as follows:

December 31, 1992	$2,000
December 31, 1993	9,000
December 31, 1994	3,000

4. Choctaw has two large blast furnaces that it uses in its manufacturing process. These furnaces must be periodically relined. Furnace A was relined in January 1988 at a cost of $300,000 and again in January 1993 at a cost of $400,000. Furnace B was relined for the first time in January 1994 at a cost of $480,000. All of these costs were charged to Maintenance Expense as incurred.

5. Since a relining will last for five years, a better matching of revenues and expenses would have resulted if the cost of the relining was capitalized and depreciated over five years on a straight-line basis. A full year's depreciation will be taken in the year of relining. This change meets the requirements for a change in accounting principle.

Instructions

(a) Prepare the journal entries necessary at December 31, 1994 to record the corrections and changes above. The books are still open for 1994. Income tax effects may be ignored.

(b) Choctaw plans to issue comparative (1994 and 1993) financial statements. Starting with $900,000 for 1994 and $640,000 for 1993, prepare a schedule to derive the correct net incomes for 1994 and 1993 to be shown in these statements. Income tax effects may be ignored.

(COMPREHENSIVE ACCOUNTING CHANGE AND ERROR ANALYSIS PROBLEM) On December- **P22-2** ber 31, 1994, before the books were closed, the management and accountants of Creed, Inc. made the following determinations about three depreciable assets:

1. Depreciable asset A was purchased January 2, 1991. It originally cost $495,000 and, for depreciation purposes, the straight-line method was originally chosen. The asset was originally expected to be useful for 10 years and have a zero residual value. In 1994, the decision was made to change the depreciation method from straight-line to sum-of-the-years'-digits, and the estimates relating to useful life and residual value remained unchanged (assume a change in policy).

2. Depreciable asset B was purchased January 3, 1990. It originally cost $120,000 and, for depreciation purposes, the straight-line method was chosen. The asset was originally expected to be useful for 15 years and have a zero residual value. In 1994, the decision was made to shorten the total life of this asset to 9 years and to estimate the residual value at $8,000.

3. Depreciable asset C was purchased January 5, 1990. The asset's original cost was $70,000 and this amount was entirely expensed in 1990. This particular asset has a 10-year useful life and no residual value. The straight-line method was chosen for depreciation purposes.

Additional Information:

1. Income in 1994 before depreciation expense amounted to $410,000.

2. Depreciation expense on assets other than A, B, and C totalled $55,000 in 1994.

3. Income in 1993 was reported at $380,000.

4. Ignore all income tax effects.

5. 100,000 common shares were outstanding in 1993 and 1994.

Instructions

(a) Prepare all necessary entries in 1994 to record these determinations.

(b) Prepare comparative income statements for Creed, Inc. for 1993 and 1994.

(c) Prepare comparative retained earnings statements for Creed, Inc. for 1993 and 1994. The company had retained earnings of $200,000 at December 31, 1992.

P22-3 **(COMPREHENSIVE ACCOUNTING CHANGE AND ERROR ANALYSIS PROBLEM)**   Natchez Ltd. was organized in early 1991 to manufacture and sell hosiery. At the end of its fourth year of operation, the company has been fairly successful, as indicated by the following reported net incomes.

1991	$180,000[a]	1993	245,000
1992	200,000[b]	1994	316,000

[a]Includes a $14,000 increase because of change in bad debt experience rate.
[b]Includes extraordinary gain of $40,000.

The company has decided to expand operations and has applied for a sizeable bank loan. The bank officer has indicated that the records should be audited and presented in comparative statements to facilitate analysis by the bank. Natchez, therefore, hired the auditing firm of Check, Doublecheck & Co. and has provided the following additional information:

1. In early 1992, Natchez changed its estimate from 2% to 1% on the amount of bad debt expense to be charged to operations. Bad debt expense for 1991, if a 1% rate had been used, would have been $14,000. The company, therefore, restated its net income of 1991.

2. In 1994, the auditor discovered that the company had changed its method of inventory pricing from average-cost to FIFO. The effect on the income statements for the previous years is as follows.

	1991	1992	1993	1994
Net income unadjusted— average-cost basis	$180,000	$200,000	$245,000	$316,000
Net income unadjusted— FIFO basis	195,000	205,000	255,000	300,000
	$ 15,000	$ 5,000	$ 10,000	($ 16,000)

3. In 1992, the company changed its method of depreciation from the accelerated method to the straight-line approach. The company used the straight-line method in 1992. The effect on the income statement for the previous year is as follows.

	1991
Net income unadjusted (accelerated method)	$180,000
Net income unadjusted (straight-line method)	190,000
	$ 10,000

4. In 1994, the auditor discovered that:

   (a) The company incorrectly overstated the ending inventory by $15,000 in 1993.

   (b) A dispute developed in 1992 with Revenue Canada over the deductibility of entertainment expenses. In 1991, the company was not permitted these deductions, but a tax settlement was reached in 1994 that allowed these expenses. As a result of the court's finding, tax expenses in 1994 were reduced by $60,000.

Instructions

(a) Indicate how each of these changes or corrections should be handled in the accounting records. Ignore income tax considerations.

(b) Present comparative income statements for the years 1991 through 1994, starting with income before extraordinary items. Ignore income tax considerations.

(CHANGE IN PRINCIPLE [FIFO TO AVERAGE-COST]: INCOME STATEMENTS) The management of Samantha Instrument Company has concluded, with the concurrence of its independent auditors, that results of operations would be more fairly presented if Samantha changed its method of pricing inventory from FIFO to average-cost in 1994. Given below is the five-year summary of income and a schedule of what the inventories might have been if stated on the average-cost method. **P22-4**

Samantha Instrument Company
Statement of Income and Retained Earnings
For the Years Ended May 31

	1990	1991	1992	1993	1994
Sales	$13,964	$15,506	$16,673	$18,221	$18,898
Cost of goods sold:					
Beginning inventory	1,000	1,100	1,000	1,115	1,237
Purchases	13,000	13,900	15,000	15,900	17,100
Ending inventory	(1,100)	(1,000)	(1,115)	(1,237)	(1,369)
Total	12,900	14,000	14,885	15,778	16,968
Gross profit	1,064	1,506	1,788	2,443	1,930
Administrative expenses	700	763	832	907	989
Income before taxes	364	743	956	1,536	941
Income taxes (50%)	182	372	478	768	471
Net income	182	371	478	768	470
Retained earnings—beginning	1,206	1,388	1,759	2,237	3,005
Retained earnings—ending	$ 1,388	$ 1,759	$ 2,237	$ 3,005	$ 3,475
Earnings per share	$ 1.82	$ 3.71	$ 4.78	$ 7.68	$ 4.70

Schedule of Inventory Balances Using Average-Cost Method
Years Ended May 31

1989	1990	1991	1992	1993	1994
$1,010	$1,124	$1,101	$1,270	$1,500	$1,720

Instructions

Prepare comparative statements for the five years, assuming that Samantha changed its method of inventory pricing to average-cost. Indicate the effects on net income and earnings per share for the years involved. (All amounts except EPS are rounded up to the nearest dollar.)

P22-5 **(FINANCIAL STATEMENT EFFECT OF CHANGES IN PRINCIPLE AND ESTIMATE)** Shawnee Corporation has decided that in the preparation of its 1994 financial statements, two changes will be made from the methods used in prior years:

1. **Depreciation.** Shawnee has always used the CCA method for tax and financial reporting purposes but has decided to change during 1994 to the straight-line method for financial reporting only. Assume that the CCA method for tax and reporting purposes has been the same in the past. The effect of this change is as follows.

	Excess of CCA Depreciation Over Straight-Line Depreciation
Prior to 1993	$1,365,000
1993	120,000
1994	100,000
	$1,585,000

Depreciation is charged to cost of sales and to selling, general, and administrative expenses on the basis of 75% and 25%, respectively.

2. **Bad debt expense.** In the past Shawnee has recognized bad debt expense equal to 1.5% of net sales. After careful review, it has been decided that a rate of 1.75% is more appropriate for 1994. Bad debt expense is charged to selling, general, and administrative expenses.

   The following information is taken from preliminary financial statements, prepared before giving effect to the two changes.

Shawnee Corporation
Condensed Balance Sheet
December 31, 1994
With Comparative Figures for 1993

	1994	1993
Assets		
Current assets	$43,561,000	$43,900,000
Plant assets, at cost	45,792,000	43,974,000
Less accumulated depreciation	23,761,000	22,946,000
	$65,592,000	$64,928,000
Liabilities and Shareholders' Equity		
Current liabilities	$21,124,000	$23,650,000
Long-term debt	15,154,000	14,097,000
Share capital	11,620,000	11,620,000
Retained earnings	17,694,000	15,561,000
	$65,592,000	$64,928,000

Shawnee Corporation
Income Statement
For the Year Ended December 31, 1994
With Comparative Figures for 1993

	1994	1993
Net sales	$80,520,000	$78,920,000
Cost of goods sold	(54,847,000)	(53,074,000)
	25,673,000	25,846,000
Selling, general, and administrative expenses	(19,540,000)	(18,411,000)
	6,133,000	7,435,000
Other income (expense), net	(1,198,000)	(1,079,000)
Income before income taxes	4,935,000	6,356,000
Income taxes	(1,974,000)	(2,542,400)
Net income	$ 2,961,000	$ 3,813,600

There have been no timing differences between any book and tax items prior to the changes above. The tax rate is 40%.

Instructions

For the items listed below, compute the amounts that would appear on the comparative (1994 and 1993) financial statements of Shawnee Corporation after adjustment for the two accounting changes. Show amounts for both 1994 and 1993 and prepare supporting schedules as necessary.

(a) Accumulated depreciation.

(b) Deferred income taxes (cumulative).

(c) Selling, general, and administrative expenses.

(d) Current portion of federal income tax expense.

(e) Deferred portion of federal income tax expense.

(f) Retained earnings

(g) Net income.

(ERROR CORRECTIONS) You have been assigned to examine the financial statements of Shiro Company **P22-6** for the year ended December 31, 1994. You discover the following situations:

1. Depreciation of $3,000 for 1994 on delivery vehicles was not recorded.

2. The physical inventory count on December 31, 1993 improperly excluded merchandise costing $19,000 that had been temporarily stored in a public warehouse. Shiro uses a periodic inventory system.

3. The physical inventory count on December 31, 1994 improperly included merchandise with a cost of $8,000 that had been recorded as a sale on December 27, 1994 and held for the customer to pick up on January 4, 1995.

4. A collection of $6,000 on account from a customer received on December 31, 1994 was not recorded until January 2, 1995.

5. In 1994, the company sold for $3,500 fully depreciated equipment that originally cost $22,000. The company credited the proceeds from the sale to the Equipment account.

6. During November 1994, a competitor company filed a patent-infringement suit against Shiro, claiming damages of $250,000. The company's legal counsel has indicated that an unfavourable verdict is probable and a reasonable estimate of the court's award to the competitor is $150,000. The company has not reflected nor disclosed this situation in the financial statements.

7. Shiro has a portfolio of temporary investments reported as a short-term investment at the lower of cost and market. Information on cost and market value is as follows.

	Cost	Market
December 31, 1993	$84,000	$86,000
December 31, 1994	$84,000	$81,000

8. At December 31, 1994, an analysis of payroll information shows accrued salaries of $12,400. The Accrued Salaries Payable account had a balance of $17,000 at December 31, 1994, which was unchanged from its balance at December 31, 1993.

9. A large piece of equipment was purchased on January 3, 1994 for $32,000 and was charged to Repairs Expense. The equipment is estimated to have a service life of eight years and no residual value. Shiro normally uses the straight-line depreciation method for this type of equipment.

10. A $15,000 insurance premium paid on July 1, 1993 for a policy that expires on June 30, 1996 was charged to insurance expense.

11. A trademark was acquired at the beginning of 1993 for $60,000. No amortization has been recorded since its acquisition. The maximum allowable amortization period is to be used.

Instructions

Assume that the trial balance has been prepared but the books have not been closed for 1994. Assuming all amounts are material, prepare journal entries showing the adjustments that are required. Ignore income tax considerations.

P22-7 **(ERROR CORRECTIONS AND CHANGES IN PRINCIPLE)**   Tuscarora Company is in the process of adjusting and correcting its books at the end of 1994. In reviewing its records, the following information is compiled:

1. On January 1, 1993, Tuscarora implemented a stock appreciation right (SAR) plan for its top executives. The plan was to run from January 1, 1992 through December 31, 1994. This period was the intended service period and the date of exercise was December 31, 1994. At December 31, 1994 (the measurement date), the executives were to receive in cash the appreciation in the market value of the shares over the three-year period. Using the market prices of the shares at the end of 1992 and 1993, respectively, Tuscarora estimated compensation expense of $32,800 for 1992 and $49,700 for 1993. At December 31, however, the market price of the stock was below its price at January 1, 1992.

2. Tuscarora has failed to accrue sales commissions payable at the end of each of the last two years, as follows.

December 31, 1993	$4,000
December 31, 1994	$5,600

3. In reviewing the December 31, 1994 inventory, Tuscarora discovered errors in its inventory-taking procedures that have caused inventories for the last three years to be incorrect, as follows:

December 31, 1992	Understated	$16,000
December 31, 1993	Understated	$21,000
December 31, 1994	Overstated	$ 7,000

Tuscarora has already made an entry to establish the incorrect December 31, 1994 inventory amount.

4. At December 31, 1994, Tuscarora decided to change its depreciation method on its office equipment from double-declining balance to straight-line. Assume that tax CCA is higher than the double-declining depreciation taken for each period. The following information is available (the tax rate is 30%).

	Double-Declining Balance	Straight-Line	Pretax Difference	Tax Effect	Difference, Net of Tax
Prior to 1994	$70,000	$40,000	$30,000	$9,000	$21,000
1994	12,000	10,000	2,000	600	1,400

Tuscarora has already recorded the 1994 depreciation expense using the double-declining balance method.

5. Before 1994, Tuscarora accounted for its income from long-term construction contracts on the percentage-of-completion basis (while using the completed-contract method for tax purposes). Early in 1994, Tuscarora changed to the completed-contract basis on its books so that it would be using the same method for its books as it uses for tax purposes. Income for 1994 has been recorded using the completed-contract method. The income tax rate is 30%. The following information is available.

	Pretax Income	
	Percentage-of-Completion	Completed-Contract
Prior to 1994	$150,000	$100,000
1994	60,000	20,000

Instructions

Prepare the journal entries necessary at December 31, 1994 to record the above corrections and changes. The books are still open for 1994. Tuscarora has not yet recorded its 1994 income tax expense and payable amounts so current year tax effects may be ignored. Prior year tax effects must be considered in (4) and (5).

(COMPREHENSIVE ERROR ANALYSIS) On March 5, 1994, you were hired by Powhatan, Inc., a closely **P22-8** held company, as a staff member of its newly created internal auditing department. While reviewing the company's records for 1992 and 1993, you discover that no adjustments have yet been made for the items listed below:

1. Interest income of $17,000 was not accrued at the end of 1992. It was recorded when received in February 1993.

2. A word processor costing $14,000 was expensed when purchased on July 1, 1992. It is expected to have a four-year life with no residual value. The company typically uses straight-line depreciation for all fixed assets.

3. Research costs of $45,000 were incurred early in 1992. They were capitalized and were to be amortized over a three-year period. Amortization of $15,000 was recorded for 1992 and $15,000 for 1993.

4. On January 2, 1992, Powhatan leased a building for five years at a monthly rental of $8,000. On that date, the company paid the following amounts, which were expensed when paid.

Security deposit	$32,000
First month's rent	8,000
Last month's rent	8,000
	$48,000

5. The company received $60,000 from a customer at the beginning of 1992 for services that it is to perform evenly over a three-year period beginning in 1992. None of the amount received was reported as unearned revenue at the end of 1992.

6. Merchandise inventory costing $18,000 was in the warehouse at December 31, 1992, but was incorrectly omitted from the physical count at that date.

Instructions

Indicate the effect of any errors on the net income figure reported on the income statement for the year ending December 31, 1992 and the retained earnings figure reported on the balance sheet at December 31, 1993. Assume that all amounts are material and ignore income tax effects. Using the following format, enter the appropriate dollar amounts in the appropriate columns. Consider each item independently of the other items. It is unnecessary to total the columns on the grid.

	Net Income for 1992		Retained Earnings at 12/31/93	
Item	Understated	Overstated	Understated	Overstated

(CIA adapted)

P22-9 **(ERROR ANALYSIS)**   Arapaho Corporation has used the accrual basis of accounting for several years. A review of the records, however, indicates that some expenses and revenues have been handled on a cash basis because of errors made by an inexperienced bookkeeper. Income statements prepared by the bookkeeper reported $36,000 net income for 1993 and $40,000 net income for 1994. Further examination of the records reveals that the following items were handled improperly:

1. Rent was received from a tenant in December 1993; the amount, $2,000, was recorded as income at that time even though the rental pertained to 1994.

2. Wages payable on December 31 have been consistently omitted from the records of that date and have been entered as expenses when paid in the following year. The amounts of the accruals recorded in this manner were:

December 31, 1992	$1,100
December 31, 1993	1,500
December 31, 1994	1,050

3. Invoices for office supplies purchased have been charged to expense accounts when received. Inventories of supplies on hand at the end of each year have been ignored, and no entry has been made for them.

December 31, 1992	$1,300
December 31, 1993	740
December 31, 1994	1,500

Instructions

Prepare a schedule that will show the corrected net income for the years 1993 and 1994. All items listed should be labelled clearly.

(ERROR ANALYSIS AND CORRECTING ENTRIES) Cheyenne Corporation is in the process of nego- **P22-10** tiating a loan for expansion purposes. Cheyenne's books and records have never been audited and the bank has requested that an audit be performed. Cheyenne has prepared the following comparative financial statements for the years ended December 31, 1994 and 1993.

Balance Sheet

As of December 31, 1994 and 1993

	1994	1993
Assets		
Current assets:		
Cash	$163,000	$ 82,000
Accounts receivable	392,000	296,000
Allowance for doubtful accounts	(37,000)	(18,000)
Marketable securities, at cost	78,000	78,000
Merchandise inventory	207,000	202,000
Total current assets	$803,000	$640,000
Plant assets:		
Property, plant, and equipment	167,000	169,500
Accumulated depreciation	(121,600)	(106,400)
Total fixed assets	45,400	63,100
Total assets	$848,400	$703,100
Liabilities and Shareholders' Equity		
Liabilities:		
Accounts payable	$121,400	$196,100
Shareholders' equity:		
Common shares, no-par value,		
authorized 50,000 shares; issued		
and outstanding, 20,000 shares	260,000	260,000
Retained earnings:	467,000	247,000
Total shareholders' equity	727,000	507,000
Total liabilities and shareholders' equity	$848,400	$703,100

Statement of Income

For the Years Ended December 31, 1994 and 1993

	1994	1993
Sales	$1,000,000	$900,000
Cost of sales	430,000	395,000
Gross profit	570,000	505,000
Operating expenses	210,000	205,000

(Continued)

Administrative expenses	140,000	105,000
Total expenses	350,000	310,000
Net income	$ 220,000	$195,000

During the course of the audit, the following additional facts were determined:

1. An analysis of collections and losses on accounts receivable during the past two years indicates a drop in anticipated losses due to bad debts. After consultation with management, it was agreed that the loss experience rate on sales should be reduced from the recorded 2% to 1%, beginning with the year ended December 31, 1994.

2. An analysis of temporary investments revealed that this portfolio consisted entirely of short-term investments in marketable equity securities that were acquired in 1993. The total market valuation for these investments as of the end of each year was as follows.

December 31, 1993	$82,000
December 31, 1994	$64,000

3. The merchandise inventory at December 31, 1993 was overstated by $8,900 and the merchandise inventory at December 31, 1994 was overstated by $13,400.

4. On January 2, 1993, equipment costing $30,000 (estimated useful life of five years and residual value of $3,000) was incorrectly charged to operating expenses. Cheyenne records depreciation on the straight-line method. In 1994 fully depreciated equipment (with no residual value) that originally cost $17,500 was sold as scrap for $2,800. Cheyenne credited the proceeds of $2,800 to the equipment account.

5. An analysis of 1992 operating expenses revealed that Cheyenne charged to expense a three-year insurance premium of $4,260 on January 15, 1993.

Instructions

(a) Prepare the journal entries to correct the books at December 31, 1994. The books for 1994 have not been closed. Ignore income taxes.

(b) Prepare a schedule showing the computations of corrected net income for the years ended December 31, 1994 and 1993, assuming that any adjustments are to be reported on comparative statements for the two years. The first items on your schedule should be the net income for each year. Ignore income taxes. (Do not prepare financial statements.)

(AICPA adapted)

P22-11 (ERROR ANALYSIS AND CORRECTING ENTRIES) You have been asked by a client to review the records of Arikara Company, a small manufacturer of precision tools and machines. Your client is interested in buying the business, and arrangements have been made for you to review the accounting records. Your examination reveals the following:

1. Arikara Company commenced business on April 1, 1991 and it has been reporting on a fiscal year ending March 31. The company has never been audited but the annual statements prepared by the bookkeeper reflect the following income before closing and before deducting income taxes.

Year Ended March 31	Income Before Taxes
1992	$ 73,600
1993	114,400
1994	107,580

2. A relatively small number of machines have been shipped on consignment. These transactions have been recorded as ordinary sales and billed as such. On March 31 of each year, machines billed and in the hands of consignees amounted to:

1992	$ 6,500
1993	None
1994	10,400

Sales price was determined by adding 30% to cost. Assume that the consigned machines are sold the following year.

3. On March 30, 1993, two machines were shipped to a customer on a C.O.D. basis. The sale was not entered until April 5, 1993, when cash was received for $7,000. The machines were not included in the inventory at March 31, 1993. (Title passed on March 30, 1993.)

4. All machines are sold subject to a five-year warranty. It is estimated that the expense ultimately to be incurred in connection with the warranty will amount to ½ of 1% of sales. The company has charged an expense account for warranty costs incurred. Sales per books and warranty costs were as follows.

Year Ended March 31	Sales	Warranty Expense for Sales Made in 1992	1993	1994	Total
1992	$ 940,000	$760			$ 760
1993	1,010,000	360	$1,310		1,670
1994	1,795,000	320	1,620	$1,910	3,850

5. A review of the corporate minutes reveals that the manager is entitled to a bonus of ½ of 1% of the income before deducting income taxes and the bonus. The bonuses have never been recorded or paid.

6. Bad debts have been recorded on a direct write-off basis. Experience of similar enterprises indicates that losses will approximate ¼ of 1% of sales. Bad debts written off were as shown below.

	Bad Debts Incurred on Sales Made In 1992	1993	1994	Total
1992	$750			$ 750
1993	800	$ 520		1,320
1994	350	1,800	$1,700	3,850

7. The bank deducts 6% on all contracts financed. Of this amount, ½% is placed in a reserve to the credit of Arikara Company that is refunded to Arikara as finance contracts are paid in full. The reserve established by the bank has not been reflected in the books of Arikara. The excess of credits over debits (net increase) to the reserve account with Arikara on the books of the bank for each fiscal year were as follows.

1992	$ 3,000
1993	3,900
1994	5,100
	$12,000

8.   Commissions on sales have been entered when paid. Commissions payable on March 31 of each year were:

1992	$1,400
1993	800
1994	1,120

Instructions

(a)   Present a schedule showing the revised income before taxes for each of the years ended March 31, 1992, 1993, and 1994. Make computations to the nearest whole dollar.

(b)   Prepare the journal entry or entries you would give the bookkeeper to correct the books. Assume the books have not yet been closed for the fiscal year ended March 31, 1994. Disregard correction of income taxes.

(AICPA adapted)

PERSPECTIVES

ON TAXATION

Dan Thornton

Dan Thornton is a Professor at Queen's University, School of Business. He has won both the Canadian Academic Accounting Association's <u>Award for Distinguished Contribution to Accounting Thought</u> (1987) and the Association's <u>L.S. Rosen Outstanding Educator Award</u> (1989). He serves on the editorial board of <u>Contemporary Accounting Research</u> and is editor of <u>CA Magazine</u>'s education department. He has also appeared as an expert accounting witness for The Department of Justice, Taxation.

Your first degree is in the Sciences. In fact, you made the Dean's List. What made you decide to pursue a career in accounting?

My first job was as a research chemist, in the experimental research department of Dow Chemical. Every afternoon we would take a fifteen-minute break and go to the cafeteria. The president of the company sat with me on several occasions and talked about what it was like to run a company like that. You can imagine how impressed I was! I wanted to be like him, so I applied to the MBA program at Western, intending to follow in his footsteps.

I soon developed an affection for financial economics. I thought that obtaining a CA designation would be a good way of seeing how the concepts were applied in practice.

Why did your interests turn to taxation?

Actually, I've always been interested in taxation, but mainly in how it interfaces with other business disciplines.

Like most research professors, I was raised on a strict diet of perfect markets. "Let us assume there are no market imperfections such as taxes or transaction costs," my professors would begin. Later, working in the public accounting profession, I saw that often, investment and financing decisions were made because of taxes. When I began teaching both finance and accounting at The University of Toronto, I soon realized that assuming away transaction costs usually amounted to presuming that information was costless, so there could be no market for accountants (including me). I decided that I had to try to incorporate both taxes and transaction costs in my teaching and research—not only to be "relevant" to the profession, but also to be intellectually honest with myself about what I was doing.

In your recently published book, *Managerial Tax Planning: A Canadian Perspective*, you contend that the government is "an uninvited partner to every business transaction conducted" in Canada. Could you elaborate?

Once the managerial orientation to tax planning is adopted, it follows that the fiscal branch of the government is best viewed as an uninvited partner in all business ventures, an uninvited party to every contract undertaken by business.

Partnership agreements entail commitments to share profits. This implies that while the partners share the rewards of the business, they also share the risks. Such is the government's relationship with business. If a business earns no profits, the government collects no taxes. All else being equal, the more profitable the business is, the more taxes the government collects. Just as partners have been known to cheat each other, taxpayers are prosecuted each year for evading the taxes that they rightfully owe their partner, the government. Though partners sometimes behave altruistically toward each other, more commonly they take from the business everything they are legally entitled to, according to the partnership agreement. So it is with taxpayers, who strive to pay the government only what is required according to The Income Tax Act, and no more. Indeed governments and courts of law, worldwide, have repeatedly enunciated the principle that taxpayers need not pay more than the minimum amount of tax. When taxpayers do pay more tax than is absolutely necessary, according to strict reading of the partnership agreement, the government does not go out of its way to apprise them of the "loopholes" that they missed. This behaviour is consistent with that of business partners who look after their own interests first.

Partners usually ask public accountants to audit (or review) their financial statements, to ensure that the profits have been determined correctly, according to the terms of the partnership agreement. Audits are also thought to deter partners from cheating each other, were they so inclined. Likewise, the government can have its own auditors scrutinize taxpayers' financial statements periodically, the object being to see whether the taxpayers have reckoned their taxable incomes according to The Income Tax Act. Like their private-sector counterparts, tax audits also deter cheating. Though only a few businesses are subjected to tax audits every year, one never knows when his or her business will be among the few. If the penalties for tax evasion are set high enough, even a small probability of being audited will suffice to encourage compliance with the Act.

A final advantage of adopting the government-as-a-business-partner perspective in managerial tax planning is that it illuminates certain ethical issues that should concern every manager. First, it makes clear that the objective of managerial tax planning is not to look for "loopholes" in the tax legislation. Exploiting such loopholes, if they can be found at all, implies that managers are thwarting certain objectives that the government wishes to achieve though they are complying with the strict letter of the law. In other words, the

managers are not treating their business partner ethically. Moreover, partners have long memories. Canadian courts have traditionally interpreted The Income Tax Act quite literally. Recently, however, the issue of "substance over form" has gained currency, and the government has enacted certain anti-avoidance rules. This means that the government has the power to "undo," retroactively, a business transaction whose sole purpose was to avoid taxes. Thus, loophole-hunting may be just as short-sighted as it is unethical. Myopia is inconsistent with the multiperiod focus of managerial tax planning.

In light of the importance of taxes, what do you see as the accountant's role?

Taxation is not a subject that should be relegated to accounting alone. All business students should study how their most important business partner is going to treat them, both on the job and in their personal lives!

Given the complexities and changing nature of The Tax Act, does an accountant need to be thoroughly immersed to offer sound advice to a firm's management?

If tax planning is considered as part of business strategy, the objective is to take taxes fully into account, as if the government were another party, an uninvited party, to the planning meeting. The name of the Managerial Tax Planning game is "Maximize wealth, including that of the uninvited party; then divide it up

fairly and ethically." There will always be a need for specialists — lawyers and accountants—to interpret the finer details of the tax law.

Given Canada's tax environment and the increasingly globalized nature of business, how well-prepared will Canadian accountants be to effectively advise and interpret the tax policies and legislation of international trading partners?

Canada's tax laws are more like the rest of the world's than like those of the U.S. mainly because personal and corporate taxes are partially integrated in Canada; i.e., shareholders get tax credits for all or part of the tax that their corporations pay. For instance, England has an "advance corporations tax" which is analogous to Canada's "dividend gross-up and credit system." Canada, like many other countries, taxes people on the basis of residency, whereas the U.S. taxes people on the basis of their citizenship, no matter where they reside.

Any final words of advice that you'd offer to accountants at the beginning of their careers?

Don't even try to "think like an accountant," whatever that means. Concentrate on getting a broad liberal education, so that you can see where the accounting profession fits in the general scheme of things. Paradoxically, by doing this, you will be well on your way to becoming an excellent accountant.

6

Preparation and Analysis of Financial Statements

Statement of Changes in Financial Position

◼

How did Imperial Oil Ltd. finance the large investment it made to acquire Texaco Canada? How did Campeau Corp. finance the $6.58 billion required to purchase Federated Department Stores Inc.? How will de Havilland finance the new Dash 8 aircraft that it is building for the airline industry? How was Sears Industries Inc. able to purchase long-term assets in the same year that it sustained a net loss? How much of Marriott's hotel expansion program was financed through net cash flow from operating activities? How much through borrowing? How much through issuance of shares?

These types of questions are often asked by investors, creditors, and internal management personnel who are interested in the financial operations of a business enterprise. An examination of the balance sheet, income statement, and statement of retained earnings, however, often fails to provide ready answers to such questions. That is why companies are required to prepare a fourth primary financial statement, the **statement of changes in financial position**.

EVOLUTION OF A NEW STATEMENT

Objective 1

Describe the evolution and purpose of the statement of changes in financial position.

The evolution of the statement of changes in financial position is an interesting example of how the needs of financial statement users are met. The statement originated as a simple analysis called the "Where-Got and Where-Gone Statement" that consisted of nothing more than a listing of the increases or decreases in the company's balance sheet items. After some years, the title of this statement was changed to the "funds statement." In 1961, the AICPA, recognizing the significance of this statement, sponsored research in this area that resulted in the publication of *Accounting Research Study No. 2*, entitled, "'Cash Flow' Analysis and the Funds Statement."[1] This study recommended that the funds statement be included in all annual reports to the shareholders and that it be covered by the auditor's opinion.

Prior to 1974, this statement was known as the "Statement of Source and Applications of Funds." In 1974, the CICA revised and expanded Section 1540 of the *Handbook* that deals with this statement. In the revision, the statement was given the title "Statement of Changes in Financial Position." The objective of this statement was to provide information on how the activities of the enterprise had been financed and how its **financial resources** had been used during the period covered by the statement. Accordingly, the statement summarized the sources and uses of funds; namely, details of how funds were acquired by the company (through borrowings, sales of assets, etc.) and how the company used these funds (to retire debt, to purchase assets, etc.). In preparing the statement, companies were permitted to use various definitions of "funds," such as cash, quick assets, or working capital.

In September 1985, an important revision to Section 1540 was released. In this revision, the objective was changed to "provide information about the operating, financing, and investing activities of an enterprise and the effects of those activities on **cash resources**."[2] The change in emphasis

---

[1] Perry Mason, "'Cash Flow' Analysis and the Funds Statement," *Accounting Research Study No. 2* (New York: AICPA, 1961).

[2] *CICA Handbook* (Toronto: CICA), Section 1540, par. .01.

from providing information about changes in financial resources to providing information about changes in cash resources has important implications for accountants. Under the new section, information about inflows and outflows of cash and cash equivalents is required. Although the *Handbook* does not explicitly require all firms to present a statement of changes in financial position with their financial statements, it is required of companies that operate under the jurisdiction of the Canada Business Corporations Act.[3]

REASONS FOR CHANGE TO THE CASH BASIS

Why the sudden change in the financial reporting environment? One major reason is that investors and analysts are concerned that *accrual accounting has become far removed from the underlying cash flows of the enterprise.*[4] They contend that accountants are using too many arbitrary allocation devices (deferred taxes, depreciation, amortization of intangibles, accrual of revenues, etc.) and are therefore computing a net income figure that no longer provides an acceptable indicator of the enterprise's earning power. Similarly, *because financial statements take no cognizance of inflation, many look for a more concrete standard, such as cash flow, to evaluate operating success or failure.* In addition, others contend that the *working capital concept does not provide as useful information about liquidity and financial flexibility as does the cash basis.* Frequently, receivable and inventory mismanagement leads to a lack of liquidity that a statement focusing on working capital would not uncover.

Finally, a statement of cash flows is useful to management and short-term creditors in *assessing the enterprise's ability to meet cash operating needs.* The chairman of one bank noted, "Well, assets give you a warm feeling, but they don't generate cash. The first question I would ask any borrower these days is, 'What is your breakeven cash flow?' That's the one thing we can't find out from your audit reports and it is the single most important question we ask."

PURPOSE OF THE STATEMENT OF CHANGES IN FINANCIAL POSITION

The primary purpose of the statement of changes in financial position is to provide information about the cash receipts and cash payments of an entity during a period.[5] A secondary objective is to provide information about the investing and financing activities of the entity during the period. According to the Accounting Standards Board, the information provided in a statement of changes in financial position, if used with related disclosures and information in the other financial statements, should help investors, creditors, and others to:

1. Evaluate the liquidity and solvency of an enterprise.

2. Assess the enterprise's ability to generate cash from internal sources, to repay debt, to make investments, and to make distributions to owners.[6]

The statement of changes in financial position reports cash receipts, cash payments, and the net change in cash (and equivalents) resulting from the operating, investing, and financing activities of an enterprise during a period, in a format that reconciles the beginning and ending cash balances.

---

[3] *Financial Reporting in Canada—1987* (Toronto: CICA, 1987), for example, indicates that 299 of 325 companies presented a statement of changes in financial position in 1986.

[4] See "Where's the Cash?" *Forbes* (April 8, 1985), p. 120. Three reasons cited for the rising importance of cash flow analysis are: (1) the high and continuing debt levels of many companies, (2) the trend over the past 20 years toward capitalizing and deferring more expenses, and (3) a wave of corporate bankruptcies in the early 1980s.

[5] The basis recommended by *CICA Handbook* Section 1540 for the statement of changes in financial position is actually "cash and cash equivalents." **Cash equivalents** include cash net of short-term borrowings and temporary investments.

[6] *CICA Handbook*, Section 1540, par. .01.

The statement of changes in financial position thus helps to indicate how it is possible to report a net loss and still make a large capital expenditure or pay dividends. Or it will tell whether the company issued or retired debt or common shares, or both, during the period.

Reporting the net increase or decrease in cash is considered useful because investors, creditors, and other interested parties want to know and can generally comprehend what is happening to a company's most liquid resource—its cash. A statement of changes in financial position is useful because it provides answers to the following simple but important questions about the enterprise:

1. Where did the cash come from during the period?

2. What was the cash used for during the period?

3. What was the change in the cash balance during the period?

CLASSIFICATION OF CASH FLOWS

Objective 2

Identify the major classifications of cash flows.

The statement of changes in financial position classifies cash receipts and cash payments into operating, investing, and financing activities. Transactions and events characteristic of each kind of activity are as follows:

1. **Operating activities** involve the cash effects of transactions that enter into the determination of net income, such as cash receipts from sales of goods and services and cash payments for acquisitions of inventory and expenses.

2. **Investing activities** generally involve long-term assets and include (a) making and collecting loans and (b) acquiring and disposing of investments and productive long-lived assets.

3. **Financing activities** involve liability and owners' equity items and include (a) obtaining cash through the issuance of debt and repaying the amounts borrowed and (b) obtaining capital from owners and providing them with a return on their investment.

The following schedule lists typical receipts and payments of a business enterprise that are classified according to operating, investing, and financing activity classifications.

Operating
Cash inflows
   From sale of goods or services.
   From returns on loans (interest) and on equity securities (dividends).
Cash outflows
   To suppliers for inventory.
   To employees for services.
   To government for taxes.
   To lenders for interest.
   To others for expenses.
Investing
Cash inflows
   From sale of property, plant, and equipment.
   From sale of debt or equity securities of other entities.
   From collection of principal on loans to other entities.
Cash outflows
   To purchase property, plant, and equipment.
   To purchase debt or equity securities of other entities.
   To make loans to other entities.

(Continued)

Financing

  Cash inflows

    From sale of own equity securities.

    From issuance of debt (bonds and notes).

  Cash outflows

    To shareholders as dividends.*

    To redeem long-term debt or reacquire share capital.

*Some accountants classify the payment of dividends as an operating activity.

Some cash flows relating to investing or financing activities are classified as operating activities. For example, receipts of investment income (interest and dividends) and payments of interest to lenders are classified as operating activities. Conversely, some cash flows relating to operating activities are classified as investing or financing activities. For example, the cash received from the sale of property, plant, and equipment at a gain, although reported in the income statement, is classified as an investing activity and the effects of the related gain would not be included in net cash flow from operating activities. Likewise, a gain or loss on the payment (extinguishment) of debt would generally be part of the cash outflow related to the repayment of the amount borrowed and therefore is a financing activity.

FORMAT OF STATEMENT OF CHANGES IN FINANCIAL POSITION

The three activities discussed in the preceding section constitute the general format of the statement of changes in financial position. The cash flows from the operating activities section always appears first, followed by the investing and financing activities sections. Also, individual inflows and outflows from investing and financing activities are reported separately. Thus, the cash outflow from the purchase of property, plant, and equipment is reported separately from the cash inflow from the sale of property, plant, and equipment. Similarly, the cash inflow from the issuance of debt securities is reported separately from the cash outflow from the retirement of debt. Not reporting them separately obscures the investing and financing activities of the enterprise and makes it more difficult to assess future cash flows.

The skeleton format of the statement of changes in financial position is as shown below.

[Company Name]
Statement of Changes in Financial Position
[Period Covered]

Cash flows from operating activities		
Net income		XXX
Add (deduct) items not affecting cash		
[List of individual items]	XX	XXX
Net cash flow from operating activities		XXX
Cash flows from investing activities		
[List of individual inflows and outflows]	XX	
Net cash provided (used) by investing activities		XXX
Cash flows from financing activities		
[List of individual inflows and outflows]	XX	
Net cash provided (used) by financing activities		XXX
Net increase (decrease) in cash		XXX

PREPARATION OF THE STATEMENT

Unlike the other major financial statements, the statement of changes in financial position is not prepared from the adjusted trial balance. The information to prepare this statement usually comes from three sources:

Comparative balance sheets provide the amount of the changes in assets, liabilities, and equities from the beginning to the end of the period.

Current income statement data help the reader determine the amount of cash provided by or used by operations during the period.

Selected transaction data from the general ledger provide additional detailed information needed to determine how cash was provided or used during the period.

Preparing the statement of changes in financial position from the data sources above involves three major steps:

1. **Determine the change in cash and cash equivalents**. This procedure is straightforward because the difference between the beginning and the ending cash and cash equivalent balances can easily be computed from an examination of the comparative balance sheets.

2. **Determine the net cash flow from operating activities**. This procedure is complex; it involves analysing not only the current year's income statement but also comparative balance sheets as well as selected transaction data.

3. **Determine cash flows from investing and financing activities**. All other changes in the balance sheet accounts must be analysed to determine their effect on cash.

FIRST ILLUSTRATION: 1992

To illustrate a statement of changes in financial position, we will use the *first year of operations* for Tax Consultants Ltd. The company started on January 1, 1992, when it issued 60,000 no-par value common shares for $60,000 cash. It rented its office space, furniture, and equipment, and performed tax consulting services throughout the first year. The comparative balance sheets at the beginning and end of the year 1992 appear as follows.

Tax Consultants Ltd.
Comparative Balance Sheets

Assets	Dec. 31, 1992	Jan. 1, 1992	Change: Increase/Decrease
Cash	$49,000	$–0–	$49,000 Increase
Accounts receivable	36,000	–0–	36,000 Increase
Total	$85,000	$–0–	
Liabilities and Shareholders' Equity			
Accounts payable	$ 5,000	$–0–	$ 5,000 Increase
Common shares	60,000	–0–	60,000 Increase
Retained earnings	20,000	–0–	20,000 Increase
Total	$85,000	$–0–	

The income statement and additional information for Tax Consultants Ltd. are as follows.

Tax Consultants Ltd.
Income Statement
for the Year Ended December 31, 1992

Revenues	$125,000
Operating expenses	85,000
Income before income taxes	40,000
Income tax expense	6,000
Net income	$ 34,000

Additional information:
Examination of selected data indicates that a dividend of $14,000 was paid during the year.

To prepare a statement of changes in financial position, the first step, *determining the change in cash*,[7] is a simple computation. Tax Consultants Ltd. had no cash on hand at the beginning of the year 1992, but $49,000 was on hand at the end of 1992; thus, the change in cash for 1992 was an increase of $49,000. The other two steps are more complex and involve additional analysis.

Determine Net Cash Flow From Operating Activities

A useful starting point in *determining net cash flow from operating activities* is to understand why net income must be converted. Under generally accepted accounting principles, most companies use the accrual basis of accounting, which requires that revenue be recorded when earned and that expenses be recorded when incurred. Earned revenues may include credit sales that have not been collected in cash and expenses incurred that may not have been paid in cash. Thus, under the accrual basis of accounting, net income will not indicate the net cash flow from operating activities.

To arrive at net cash flow from operating activities, it is necessary to report revenues and expenses on a **cash basis**. This is done by eliminating the effects of income statement transactions that did not result in a corresponding increase or decrease in cash. The relationship between net income and net cash flow from operating activities is graphically depicted as follows.

Objective 3

Differentiate between net income and net cash flows from operating activities.

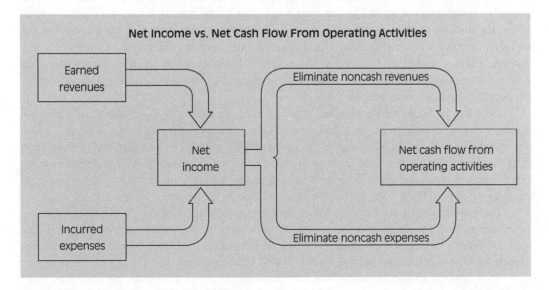

Net Income vs. Net Cash Flow From Operating Activities

---

[7] The company does not have any cash equivalents such as marketable securities or short-term notes.

In this chapter, we use the term "net income" to refer to accrual-based net income. The conversion of net income to net cash flow from operating activities may be done through either a direct method or an indirect method as explained in the following discussion.

Objective 4

Contrast the direct and indirect methods of calculating net cash flow from operating activities.

Direct Method. Under the **direct method** (or income statement method), cash receipts and cash disbursements from operating activities are determined. The difference between these amounts is the net cash flow from operating activities. In other words, the direct approach deducts from operating cash receipts the operating cash disbursements. The direct method results in the presentation of a condensed cash receipts and cash disbursements statement.

As indicated by the accrual-based income statement, Tax Consultants Ltd. reported revenues of $125,000. However, because the company's accounts receivable increased during 1992 by $36,000, only $89,000 ($125,000 − $36,000) in cash was collected on these revenues. Similarly, Tax Consultants Ltd. reported operating expenses of $85,000, but accounts payable increased during the period by $5,000. Assuming that these payables related to operating expenses, cash payments for operating expenses were $80,000 ($85,000 − $5,000). Because no taxes payable exist at the end of the year, the $6,000 income tax expense for 1992 must have been paid in cash during the year. Then the computation of net cash flow from operating activities is as follows.

Direct Approach: Computation of Net Cash Flow From Operating Activities	
Cash collected from revenues	$89,000
Cash payments for expenses	(80,000)
Cash payments for income taxes	(6,000)
Net cash provided by operating activities	**$ 3,000**

"Net cash provided by operating activities" is the equivalent of cash-basis net income ("net cash used by operating activities" would be equivalent to cash-basis net loss).

Indirect Method. Another method, referred to as the **indirect method** (or reconciliation method), is simply to start with net income and convert it to net cash flow from operating activities. In other words, *the indirect method adjusts net income for items that affected reported net income but did not affect cash*. That is, noncash charges in the income statement are added back to net income and noncash credits are deducted to compute net cash flow from operating activities. Explanations for the two adjustments to net income in this example, namely, the increases in accounts receivable (net) and accounts payable, are as follows.

Increase in Accounts Receivable. When accounts receivable increase during the year, revenues on an accrual basis are higher than revenues on a cash basis because goods sold on account are reported as revenues. In other words, operations of the period led to increased revenues, but not all of these revenues resulted in an increase in cash. Some of the increase in revenues resulted in an increase in accounts receivable. To convert net income to net cash flow from operating activities, the increase of $36,000 in accounts receivable must be deducted from net income.

Increase in Accounts Payable. When accounts payable increase during the year, expenses on an accrual basis are higher than they are on a cash basis because expenses are incurred for which payment has not taken place. To convert net income to net cash flow from operating activities, the increase of $5,000 in accounts payable must be added to net income.

As a result of the accounts receivable and accounts payable adjustments, net cash flow from operating activities is determined to be $3,000 for the year 1992. This computation is shown as follows.

**Indirect Method: Computation of Net Cash Flow
From Operating Activities**

Net income		$34,000
Add (deduct) items not affecting cash		
Increase in accounts receivable	$(36,000)	
Increase in accounts payable	5,000	(31,000)
Net cash provided by operating activities		**$ 3,000**

Note that net cash flow from operating activities is the same whether the direct or the indirect approach is used.

Determine Cash From Investing and Financing Activities

Once the net cash flow from operating activities is computed, the next step is to determine whether any other changes in balance sheet accounts caused an increase or decrease in cash. For example, an examination of the remaining balance sheet accounts shows that both common shares and retained earnings have increased. The increase in common shares of $60,000 resulted from the issuance of common shares for cash. The issuance of common shares is a receipt of cash from a financing activity and is reported as such in the statement of changes in financial position. The retained earnings increase of $20,000 is caused by two items:

1. Net income of $34,000 increased retained earnings.

2. Dividends declared of $14,000 decreased retained earnings.

Net income has been converted into net cash flow from operating activities as explained earlier. The additional data indicate that the dividend was paid. Dividend payments are viewed by some as a financing activity and by others as an operating activity. As a result, dividends are sometimes included with operating activities and sometimes with financing activities. Occasionally, dividends are shown on a separate line following operating activities. In this and other examples, dividend payments are reported as a cash outflow classified as a financing activity.

Statement of Changes in Financial Position: 1992

We are now ready to prepare the statement of changes in financial position. The statement starts with the operating activities section. Either the direct or indirect method may be used to report net cash flow from operating activities. The indirect approach, more extensively employed in practice, is used throughout this chapter. (You should use the indirect method in doing homework assignments unless instructed otherwise.) The statement of changes in financial position for Tax Consultants Ltd. is as follows.

Objective 5

Determine net cash flows from investing and financing activities.

Objective 6

Prepare a statement of changes in financial position.

Tax Consultants Ltd.
Statement of Changes in Financial Position
for the Year Ended December 31, 1992

Cash flows from operating activities		
Net income		$34,000
Add (deduct) items not affecting cash		
Increase in accounts receivable	$(36,000)	
Increase in accounts payable	5,000	(31,000)
Net cash flow from operating activities		3,000

(Continued)

Cash flows from financing activities	
Issuance of common shares	$ 60,000
Payment of cash dividends	(14,000)
Cash provided by financing activities	46,000
Net increase in cash	$49,000
Cash, January 1, 1992	–0–
Cash, December 31, 1992	$49,000

As indicated, the increase of $60,000 in common shares results in cash inflow from a financing activity. The payment of $14,000 in cash dividends is classified as a use of cash from a financing activity. The increase in cash of $49,000 reported in the statement of changes in financial position agrees with the increase of $49,000 shown as the change in the cash account in the comparative balance sheets.

SECOND ILLUSTRATION: 1993

Tax Consultants Ltd. continued to grow and prosper during its second year of operations. Land, building, and equipment were purchased, and its revenues and earnings increased substantially over the first year. Presented below is information related to the second year of operations for Tax Consultants Ltd.

Tax Consultants Ltd.
Comparative Balance Sheets
as at December 31, 1993 and 1992

Assets	1993	1992	Change: Increase/Decrease
Cash	$ 37,000	$49,000	$ 12,000 Decrease
Accounts receivable	26,000	36,000	10,000 Decrease
Prepaid expenses	6,000	–0–	6,000 Increase
Land	70,000	–0–	70,000 Increase
Building	200,000	–0–	200,000 Increase
Accumulated depreciation—building	(11,000)	–0–	11,000 Increase
Equipment	68,000	–0–	68,000 Increase
Accumulated depreciation—equipment	(10,000)		10,000 Increase
Total	$386,000	$85,000	
Liabilities and Shareholders' Equity			
Accounts payable	$ 40,000	$ 5,000	$ 35,000 Increase
Bonds payable	150,000	–0–	150,000 Increase
Common shares	60,000	60,000	–0–
Retained earnings	136,000	20,000	116,000 Increase
Total	$386,000	$85,000	

Tax Consultants Ltd.
Income Statement
for the Year Ended December 31, 1993

Revenues		$492,000
Operating expenses (excluding depreciation)	$269,000	
Depreciation expense	21,000	290,000
Income from operations		202,000
Income tax expense		68,000
Net income		$134,000

Additional information:

(a) In 1993, the company paid a cash dividend of $18,000.

(b) The company obtained $150,000 cash through the issuance of long-term bonds.

(c) Land, building, and equipment were acquired for cash.

To prepare a statement of changes in financial position from this information, the first step is to *determine the change in cash*. As indicated from the information presented, cash decreased $12,000 ($49,000 − $37,000). The second and third steps are discussed in the next paragraphs.

Determine Net Cash Flow From Operating Activities: Indirect Method

Using the indirect method, net income of $134,000 on an accrual basis is adjusted to arrive at net cash flow from operating activities. Explanations for the adjustments to net income are as follows.

Decrease in Accounts Receivable. When accounts receivable decrease during the period, revenues on a cash basis are higher than revenues on an accrual basis, because cash collections are higher than revenues reported on an accrual basis. To convert net income to net cash flow from operating activities, the decrease of $10,000 in accounts receivable must be added to net income.

Increase in Prepaid Expenses. When prepaid expenses (assets) increase during a period, expenses on an accrual-basis income statement are lower than they are on a cash-basis income statement. Expenditures (cash payments) have been made in the current period, but expenses (as charges to the income statement) have been deferred to future periods. To convert net income to net cash flow from operating activities, the increase of $6,000 in prepaid expenses must be deducted from net income. An increase in prepaid expenses results in a decrease in cash during the period.

Increase in Accounts Payable. Like the increase in 1992, the 1993 increase of $35,000 in accounts payable must be added to net income to convert to net cash flow from operating activities. A greater amount of expense was incurred than cash disbursed.

Depreciation Expense (Increase in Accumulated Depreciation). The purchase of depreciable assets is shown as a use of cash in the investing section in the year of acquisition. The depreciation expense of $21,000 (also represented by the increase in accumulated depreciation) is a noncash charge that is added back to net income to arrive at net cash flow from operating activities. The $21,000 is the sum of depreciation on the building of $11,000 and the depreciation on the equipment of $10,000.

Other charges to expense for a period that do not require the use of cash, such as the amortization of intangible assets and depletion expense, are treated in the same manner as depreciation. Depreciation and similar noncash charges are frequently listed in the statement as the first adjustments to net income.

As a result of the foregoing items, net cash flow from operating activities is $194,000 as computed in the following manner.

Computation of Net Cash Flow From Operating Activities

Net income		$134,000
Add (deduct) items not affecting cash		
Decrease in accounts receivable	$10,000	
Increase in prepaid expenses	(6,000)	
Increase in accounts payable	35,000	
Depreciation expense	21,000	60,000
Net cash flow from operating activities		**$194,000**

Determine Cash Flows From Investing and Financing Activities

After you have determined the items affecting cash provided by operating activities, the next step involves analysing the remaining changes in balance sheet accounts.

Increase in Land. As indicated from the change in the land account, land was purchased for $70,000 during the period. This transaction is an investing activity that is reported as a use of cash.

Increase in Building and Related Accumulated Depreciation. As indicated in the additional data and from the change in the building account, an office building was acquired using $200,000 cash. This transaction is a cash outflow reported in the investing section. The accumulated depreciation account increase of $11,000 is fully explained by the depreciation expense entry for the period. As indicated earlier, the reported depreciation expense has no effect on cash.

Increase in Equipment and Related Accumulated Depreciation. An increase in equipment of $68,000 resulted because equipment was purchased for cash. This transaction should be reported as an outflow of cash from an investing activity. The increase in Accumulated Depreciation—Equipment was explained by the depreciation expense entry for the period.

Increase in Bonds Payable. The Bonds Payable account increased $150,000. Cash received from the issuance of these bonds represents an inflow of cash from a financing activity.

Increase in Retained Earnings. Retained earnings increased $116,000 during the year. This increase can be explained by two factors: (1) net income of $134,000 increased retained earnings and (2) dividends of $18,000 decreased retained earnings. Payment of the dividends is a financing activity that involves a cash outflow.

Statement of Changes in Financial Position: 1993

Combining the foregoing items, a statement of changes in financial position for 1993 for Tax Consultants Ltd., using the indirect method to compute net cash flow from operating activities, shows the following data.

Tax Consultants Ltd.
Statement of Changes in Financial Position
for the Year Ended December 31, 1993

Cash flows from operating activities		
Net income		$134,000
Add (deduct) items not affecting cash		
Depreciation expense	$ 21,000	
Decrease in accounts receivable	10,000	
Increase in prepaid expenses	(6,000)	
Increase in accounts payable	35,000	60,000
Net cash provided by operating activities		194,000

(Continued)

Cash flows from investing activities

Purchase of land	(70,000)	
Purchase of building	(200,000)	
Purchase of equipment	(68,000)	
Cash used by investing activities		(338,000)
Issuance of bonds	$150,000	
Payment of cash dividends	(18,000)	
Cash provided by financing activities		132,000
Net decrease in cash		$ (12,000)
Cash, January 1, 1993		49,000
Cash, December 31, 1993		$ 37,000

THIRD ILLUSTRATION: 1994

This third illustration covering the 1994 operations of Tax Consultants Ltd. is slightly more complex; it again uses the indirect approach to compute and present net cash flow from operating activities.

Tax Consultants Ltd. experienced continued success in 1994 and expanded its operations to include the sale of selected lines of computer software that is used in tax return preparation and tax planning. Thus, inventory is one of the new assets appearing in its December 31, 1994 balance sheet. The comparative balance sheets, income statement, and selected data for 1994 are as follows.

Tax Consultants Ltd.
Comparative Balance Sheets
as at December 31, 1994 and 1993

Assets	1994	1993	Change: Increase/Decrease
Cash	$ 54,000	$ 37,000	$ 17,000 Increase
Accounts receivable	68,000	26,000	42,000 Increase
Prepaid expenses	4,000	6,000	2,000 Decrease
Inventories	54,000	–0–	54,000 Increase
Land	45,000	70,000	25,000 Decrease
Building	200,000	200,000	–0–
Accumulated depreciation—building	(21,000)	(11,000)	10,000 Increase
Equipment	193,000	68,000	125,000 Increase
Accumulated depreciation—equipment	(28,000)	(10,000)	18,000 Increase
Total	$569,000	$386,000	
Liabilities and Shareholders' Equity			
Accounts payable	$ 33,000	$ 40,000	$ 7,000 Decrease
Bonds payable	110,000	150,000	40,000 Decrease
Common shares	220,000	60,000	160,000 Increase
Retained earnings	206,000	136,000	70,000 Increase
Total	$569,000	$386,000	

Tax Consultants Ltd.
Income Statement
for the Year Ended December 31, 1994

Revenues		$890,000
Cost of goods sold	$465,000	
Operating expenses	221,000	
Interest expense	12,000	
Loss on sale of equipment	2,000	700,000
Income from operations		190,000
Income tax expense		65,000
Net income		$125,000

Additional information:

(a) Operating expenses include depreciation expense of $33,000 and amortization of prepaid expenses of $2,000.

(b) Land was sold at its book value for cash.

(c) Cash dividends of $55,000 were paid in 1994.

(d) Interest expense of $12,000 was paid in cash.

(e) Equipment with a cost of $166,000 was purchased for cash. Equipment with a cost of $41,000 and a book value of $36,000 was sold for $34,000 cash.

(f) Bonds were redeemed at their book value for cash.

(g) Common shares were issued for cash.

The first step in the preparation of the statement of changes in financial position is to *determine the change in cash*. As is shown in the comparative balance sheet, cash increased $17,000 in 1994. The second and third steps are discussed below.

Determine Net Cash Flow From Operating Activities: Indirect Method

Explanations for the adjustments to net income of $125,000 are as follows.

Increase in Accounts Receivable. The increase in accounts receivable of $42,000 represents recorded accrual-basis revenues in excess of cash collections in 1994; the increase is deducted from net income to convert from the accrual basis to the cash basis.

Increase in Inventories. The increase in inventories of $54,000 represents an operating use of cash for which an expense was not incurred. This amount is therefore deducted from net income to arrive at cash flow from operations. In other words, when inventory purchased exceeds inventory sold during a period, cost of goods sold on an accrual basis is lower than on a cash basis.

Decrease in Prepaid Expenses. The decrease in prepaid expenses of $2,000 represents a charge to the income statement for which there was no cash outflow in the current period. The decrease is added back to net income to arrive at net cash flow from operating activities.

Decrease in Accounts Payable. When accounts payable decrease during the year, cost of goods sold and expenses on a cash basis are higher than they are on an accrual basis because on a cash basis the goods and expenses are recorded as expense when paid. To convert net income to net cash flow from operating activities, the decrease of $7,000 in accounts payable must be deducted from net income.

Depreciation Expense (Increase in Accumulated Depreciation). Accumulated Depreciation—Building increased $10,000 ($21,000 − $11,000). The Building account did not change during the period, which means that $10,000 of depreciation was recorded in 1994.

Accumulated Depreciation—Equipment increased by $18,000 ($28,000 − $10,000) during the year. But Accumulated Depreciation—Equipment was decreased by $5,000 as a result of the sale during the year. Thus, depreciation expense for the year was $23,000. The reconciliation of Accumulated Depreciation—Equipment is as follows.

Beginning balance	$10,000
Add depreciation for 1994	23,000
	33,000
Deduct accumulated depreciation on sold equipment	5,000
Ending balance	$28,000

The total depreciation of $33,000 ($10,000 + $23,000) charged to the income statement must be added back to net income in our determination of net cash flow from operating activities.

Loss on Sale of Equipment. Equipment having a cost of $41,000 and a book value of $36,000 was sold for $34,000. As a result, the company reported a loss of $2,000 on the sale. To arrive at net cash flow from operating activities, it is necessary to add back to net income the loss on the sale of the equipment. The reason is that the loss is a noncash charge to the income statement; it did not reduce cash but it did reduce net income.

From the foregoing items, the operating activities section of the statement of changes in financial position is prepared as follows.

**Computation of Net Cash Flow From
Operating Activities**

Net income		$125,000
Add (deduct) items not affecting cash		
Depreciation expense	$33,000	
Increase in accounts receivable	(42,000)	
Increase in inventories	(54,000)	
Decrease in prepaid expenses	2,000	
Decrease in accounts payable	(7,000)	
Loss on sale of equipment	2,000	(66,000)
Net cash flow from operating activities		$ 59,000

Determine Cash Flows From Investing and Financing Activities

By analysing the remaining changes in the balance sheet accounts, cash flows from investing and financing activities can be identified.

Land. Land decreased $25,000 during the period. As indicated from the information presented, land was sold for cash at its book value. This transaction is an investing activity that is reported as a $25,000 source of cash.

Equipment. An analysis of the equipment account is shown at the top of page 1162. Equipment with a fair value of $166,000 was purchased for cash. This is an investing transaction that is reported as a cash outflow. The sale of the equipment for $34,000 is an investing activity but one that generates a cash inflow.

Bonds Payable. Bonds payable decreased $40,000 during the year. As indicated from the additional information, bonds were redeemed at their book value. This financing transaction used $40,000 cash.

Beginning balance	$ 68,000
Purchase of equipment	166,000
	234,000
Sale of equipment	41,000
Ending balance	$193,000

Common Shares. The common share account increased $160,000 during the year. As indicated by the additional information, common shares of $160,000 were issued. This is a financing transaction that provided cash of $160,000.

Retained Earnings. Retained earnings changed $70,000 ($206,000 − $136,000) during the year. The $70,000 change in retained earnings is the result of net income of $125,000 from operating activities and the financing activity of paying cash dividends of $55,000.

Preparation of the 1994 Statement (Indirect Approach)

The following statement of changes in financial position is prepared by combining the foregoing items.

Tax Consultants Ltd.
Statement of Changes in Financial Position
for the Year Ended December 31, 1994

Cash flows from operating activities		
Net income		$125,000
Add (deduct) items not affecting cash		
Depreciation expense	$ 33,000	
Increase in accounts receivable	(42,000)	
Increase in inventories	(54,000)	
Decrease in prepaid expenses	2,000	
Decrease in accounts payable	(7,000)	
Loss on sale of equipment	2,000	(66,000)
Net cash flow from operating activities		59,000
Cash flows from investing activities		
Sale of land	25,000	
Sale of equipment	34,000	
Purchase of equipment	(166,000)	
Cash used by investing activities		(107,000)
Cash flows from financing activities		
Redemption of bonds	$ (40,000)	
Issue of common shares	160,000	
Payment of cash dividends	(55,000)	
Cash provided by financing activities		65,000
Net increase in cash		$ 17,000
Cash, January 1, 1994		37,000
Cash, December 31, 1994		$ 54,000

SOURCES OF INFORMATION FOR STATEMENT OF CHANGES IN FINANCIAL POSITION

The following are important points to remember in the preparation of the statement of changes in financial position:

Objective 7

Identify sources of information for a statement of changes in financial position.

1. Comparative balance sheets provide the basic information from which the report is prepared. Additional information obtained from analyses of specific accounts is also included.

2. An analysis of the Retained Earnings account is necessary. The net increase or decrease in Retained Earnings without any explanation is a meaningless amount in the statement, because it might represent the effect of net income, dividends declared, appropriations of retained earnings, and prior period adjustments.

3. The statement includes all changes that have passed through cash or have resulted in an increase or decrease in cash.

4. Write-downs, amortization charges, and similar "book" entries, such as depreciation of plant assets, are considered as neither inflows nor outflows of cash because they have no effect on cash. To the extent that they have entered into the determination of net income, however, they must be added back or subtracted from net income to arrive at net cash flow from operating activities.

NET CASH FLOW FROM OPERATING ACTIVITIES: INDIRECT VERSUS DIRECT METHOD

As we discussed previously, the two different methods available to adjust income from operations on an accrual basis to net cash flow from operating activities are the indirect (reconciliation) approach and the direct (income statement) method.

Indirect Method

For consistency and comparability and because it is the most widely used method in practice, we used the indirect method in the previous illustrations. We determined net cash flows from operating activities by adding back to or deducting from net income those items that had no effect on cash. The second box on page 1164 presents more completely the common types of adjustments that are made to net income to arrive at net cash flow from operating activities. The additions and deductions listed in the box reconcile net income to net cash flow from operating activities, illustrating the reason for referring to the indirect method as the reconciliation method.

Direct Method

Under the direct method, the statement of changes in financial position reports net cash flow from operating activities as major classes of operating cash receipts (e.g., cash collected from customers and cash received for interest and dividends) and cash disbursements (e.g., cash paid to suppliers for goods, to employees for services, to creditors for interest, and to government for taxes).

The direct method is illustrated here in more detail to help you understand the difference between accrual-based income and net cash flow from operating activities and to illustrate the data needed to apply the direct approach. For example, assume that Farmer Company has the following selected balance sheet information.

	1994	1993
Cash	$ 54,000	$ 48,000
Receivables	60,000	68,000
	(Continued)	

Inventory	110,000	112,000
Prepaid expenses	9,000	8,000
Accounts payable	75,000	87,000
Taxes payable	8,000	3,000

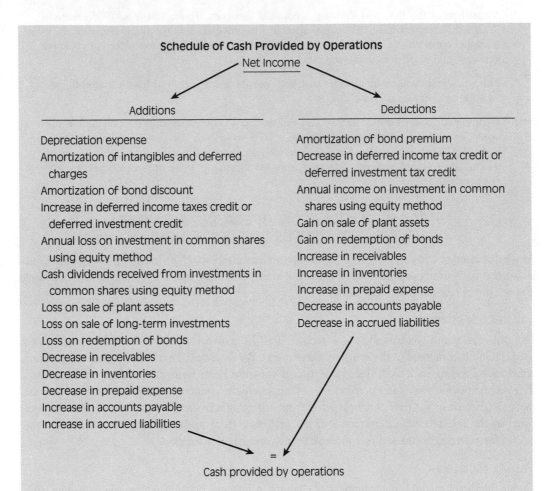

Schedule of Cash Provided by Operations

Net Income

Additions

Depreciation expense
Amortization of intangibles and deferred
  charges
Amortization of bond discount
Increase in deferred income taxes credit or
  deferred investment credit
Annual loss on investment in common shares
  using equity method
Cash dividends received from investments in
  common shares using equity method
Loss on sale of plant assets
Loss on sale of long-term investments
Loss on redemption of bonds
Decrease in receivables
Decrease in inventories
Decrease in prepaid expense
Increase in accounts payable
Increase in accrued liabilities

Deductions

Amortization of bond premium
Decrease in deferred income tax credit or
  deferred investment tax credit
Annual income on investment in common
  shares using equity method
Gain on sale of plant assets
Gain on redemption of bonds
Increase in receivables
Increase in inventories
Increase in prepaid expense
Decrease in accounts payable
Decrease in accrued liabilities

=

Cash provided by operations

Farmer Company's income statement and additional information are as shown below.

Sales	$232,000
Cost of goods sold	94,000
Gross profit	138,000
Selling and administrative expenses	70,000
Income before income taxes	68,000
Income tax expense	12,000
Net income	$ 56,000

(Continued)

Additional information:

(a) Receivables relate to sales and accounts payable relate to cost of goods sold.

(b) Depreciation of $4,000 and prepaid expenses both relate to selling and administrative expenses.

The adjustments to arrive at net cash flow from operating activities are as follows:

Cash Sales. Sales on an accrual basis are $232,000. If receivables have decreased $8,000 ($68,000 − $60,000) during the year, cash collections are higher than accrual-basis sales. The decrease in receivables must be added to accrual-basis sales to determine cash sales, as follows:

Sales	$232,000
Add decrease in receivables	8,000
Cash sales	$240,000

Cash Purchases. To determine cash purchases, it is first necessary to determine purchases for the year. Inventory decreased during the year, which means that goods from prior periods rather than current year purchases were used as cost of goods sold. As a result, the decrease in inventory is deducted from cost of goods sold to arrive at purchases. This computation is as follows:

Cost of goods sold	$94,000
Deduct decrease in inventories	(2,000)
Purchases	$92,000

After purchases on an accrual basis are computed, cash purchases are determined by finding the change in accounts payable. Accounts payable has decreased $12,000 ($87,000 − $75,000), which means that more cash was paid this period for goods than is reported under accrual accounting. Cash purchases are therefore determined as follows:

Purchases	$ 92,000
Add decrease in accounts payable	12,000
Cash purchases	$104,000

Cash Selling and Administrative Expenses. The selling and administrative expenses are stated at $70,000. Selling and administrative expenses, however, include a noncash charge related to depreciation of $4,000. In addition, prepaid expenses (assets) increased $1,000 ($9,000 − $8,000) and this amount must be added to selling and administrative expenses. The computation of cash selling and administrative expenses is as follows:

Selling and administrative expenses	$70,000
Deduct depreciation expense	(4,000)
	66,000
Add increase in prepaid expenses	1,000
Cash selling and administrative expenses	$67,000

Cash Income Taxes. Income taxes on the accrual basis are $12,000. Taxes payable, however, have increased $5,000 ($8,000 − $3,000), which means that a portion of the taxes have not been paid. As a result, income taxes paid are less than income taxes reported on an accrual basis. This computation is as follows:

Income taxes	$12,000
Deduct increase in taxes payable	(5,000)
Cash income tax expense	$ 7,000

The computations illustrated here are summarized in the following schedule.

Farmer Company
Schedule of Changes From the Accrual-
to the Cash-Basis Income Statement
(Direct Approach)

Accrual-Basis			Adjustment	Add (Subtract)	Cash-Basis
Sales	$232,000	+	Decrease in receivables	$ 8,000	$240,000
Cost of goods sold	94,000	−	Decrease in inventories	(2,000)	
		+	Decrease in accounts payable	12,000	104,000
Selling and administrative expenses	70,000	−	Depreciation expense	(4,000)	
		+	Increase in prepaid expenses	1,000	67,000
Income tax expense	12,000	−	Increase in taxes payable	(5,000)	7,000
Total expenses	176,000				178,000
Net income	$ 56,000		Net cash provided by operating activities		$ 62,000

Presentation of the direct method for reporting net cash flow from operating activities takes the form of a condensed cash-basis income statement, as presented below.

Farmer Company
Statement of Changes in Financial Position (Partial)
(Direct Approach)

Cash flows from operating activities		$240,000
Cash received from customers		
Cash paid to suppliers	$104,000	
Selling and administrative expenses paid	67,000	
Selling and administrative expenses paid	7,000	
Cash paid for taxes		178,000
Net cash provided by operating activities		**$ 62,000**

If Farmer Company uses the direct method to present the net cash flow from operating activities, it may wish to provide in a separate schedule the reconciliation of net income to net cash provided by operating activities. The reconciliation assumes the identical format and content of the indirect method of presentation, as shown below.

Reconciliation of net income to net cash provided by operating activities		
Net income		$56,000
Adjustments to reconcile net income to net cash provided by operating activities:		
Depreciation expense	$ 4,000	
Decrease in receivables	8,000	
Decrease in inventory	2,000	
Increase in prepaid expenses	(1,000)	
Decrease in accounts payable	(12,000)	
Increase in taxes payable	5,000	6,000
Net cash provided by operating activities		**$62,000**

The reconciliation may be presented at the bottom of the statement of changes in financial position when the direct method is used.

Evaluation of Direct and Indirect Methods

The direct and indirect methods have advantages and disadvantages that have produced controversy among users and preparers of financial statements. Some management personnel have argued against the direct method while some commercial lending officers have expressed a strong preference for the direct method.

Direct Method. The principal advantage of the direct method is that *it shows operating cash receipts and payments*. That is, it is more consistent with the objective of a statement of changes in financial position—to provide information about cash receipts and cash payments—than the indirect method, which does not report operating cash receipts and payments.

Supporters of the direct method contend that knowledge of the specific sources of operating cash receipts and the purposes for which operating cash payments were made in past periods is useful in estimating future operating cash flows. Furthermore, information about amounts of major classes of operating cash receipts and payments is more useful than information about only their arithmetic sum the net cash provided (used) by operating activities—in assessing an enterprise's ability to (1) generate sufficient cash from internal sources, (2) repay debt obligations, (3) reinvest, and (4) make distributions to its owners.[8]

Many corporate providers of financial statements say that they do not currently collect information in a manner that allows them to determine amounts such as cash received from customers or cash paid to suppliers directly from their accounting systems. But supporters of the direct method contend that the incremental cost of assimilating such operating cash receipts and payments data is not significant.

Indirect Method. The principal advantage of the indirect method is that *it focuses on the difference between net income and net cash flow from operating activities*. That is, it provides a useful link between the statement of cash flows and the income statement and the balance sheet.

Many providers of financial statements contend that it is less costly to adjust net income to net cash flow from operating activities (indirect) than it is to report gross operating cash receipts and payments (direct). Because the indirect method was used almost exclusively in the past, users are more familiar with it. Supporters of the indirect method also state that the direct method, which effectively reports income statement information on a cash basis rather than an accrual basis, may erroneously suggest that net cash flow from operating activities is as good as, or better than, net income as a measure of performance.

SPECIAL PROBLEMS IN STATEMENT ANALYSIS

Some of the special problems related to preparing the statement of changes in financial position were discussed in connection with the preceding illustrations. Other problems that arise with some frequency in the preparation of this statement may be categorized as follows:

Objective 8

Identify special problems in preparing a statement of changes in financial position.

1. Adjustments similar to depreciation.

2. Accounts receivable (net).

3. Cash equivalent items.

4. Net losses.

5. Gains.

---

[8] *CICA Handbook*, Section 1540, par. .01.

6. Stock options.

7. Pensions.

8. Extraordinary items.

9. Significant noncash transactions.

Adjustments Similar to Depreciation

Depreciation expense is the most common adjustment to net income that is made to arrive at net cash flow from operating activities, but there are numerous other noncash expense or revenue items. Examples of expense items that must be added back to net income are the **amortization of intangible assets** such as goodwill and patents, and the **amortization of deferred costs** such as bond issue costs. These charges to expense involve cash outlays made in prior periods that are being amortized currently and reduce net income without affecting cash in the current period. Also, **amortization of bond discount or premium** on long-term bonds payable affects the amount of interest expense, but neither changes cash. As a result, amortization of these items should be added back to or subtracted from net income to arrive at net cash flow from operating activities. In a similar manner, **changes in deferred income taxes** affect net income but have no effect on cash.

Another common adjustment to net income is **a change related to an investment in common shares** when the income or loss is accrued under the equity method. For example, General Motors Corporation's equity in undistributed earnings of unconsolidated subsidiaries increased by approximately $111 million. Such an increase, however, is not a cash inflow; hence, it was deducted from net income to arrive at net cash flow from operating activities. If a company receives a dividend from its equity investee, cash provided from the dividend is recorded as a reduction of the Investment account; an adjustment to net income is necessary, since the cash dividend received is considered operating activity cash inflow.

Accounts Receivable (Net)

Up to this point, we have assumed that no allowance for doubtful accounts—a contra account—was needed to offset accounts receivable. However, if an allowance for doubtful accounts is needed, how does it affect the determination of net cash flow from operating activities? For example, assume that Redmark Ltd. reports net income of $40,000 and has the following balances related to accounts receivable.

	1994	1993	Change: Increase/Decrease
Accounts receivable	$105,000	$90,000	$15,000 Increase
Allowance for doubtful accounts	10,000	4,000	6,000 Increase
Accounts receivable (net)	$ 95,000	$86,000	

The proper reporting treatment using the indirect and direct methods is illustrated in the following sections.

Indirect Method. Because an increase in the Allowance for Doubtful Accounts is caused by a charge to bad debts expense, an increase in the Allowance for Doubtful Accounts should be added back to net income to arrive at net cash flow from operating activities. One method for presenting this information in a statement of cash flows is as follows.

Redmark Ltd.
Partial Statement of Changes in Financial Position
for the Year 1994

Cash flows from operating activities		
Net income		$40,000
Add (deduct) items not affecting cash		
Increase in accounts receivable	**$(15,000)**	
Increase in allowance for doubtful accounts	**6,000**	(9,000)
		$31,000

As indicated, the increase in the Allowance for Doubtful Accounts balance is caused by a charge to bad debts expense for the year. Because bad debts expense is a noncash charge, it must be added back to net income in arriving at net cash flow from operating activities. Instead of separately analysing the allowance account, a shortcut approach is to net the allowance balance against the receivable balance and compare the change in accounts receivable on a net basis. This presentation would be as follows.

Redmark Ltd.
Partial Statement of Changes in Financial Position
for the Year 1994

Cash flows from operating activities	
Net income	$40,000
Add (deduct) items not affecting cash	
Increase in accounts receivable (net)	(9,000)
	$31,000

This shortcut procedure works also if the change in the allowance account was caused by a write-off of accounts receivable. In this case, both the Accounts Receivable and the Allowance for Doubtful Accounts are reduced and no effect on cash flows occurs. Because of its simplicity, you should use the net approach in your homework assignments.

Direct Method. If the direct method is used, the Allowance for Doubtful Accounts should *not* be netted against the Accounts Receivable. To illustrate, assume that Redmark Ltd.'s net income of $40,000 comprises the following items.

Redmark Ltd.
Income Statement
for the Year 1994

Sales		$100,000
Expenses:		
Salaries	$46,000	
Utilities	8,000	
Bad debts	6,000	60,000
Net income		$ 40,000

If the $9,000 increase in accounts receivable (net) is deducted from sales for the year, cash sales would be reported at $91,000 ($100,000 − $9,000) and cash payments for operating expenses at

$60,000. Both items are misstated because cash sales should be reported at $85,000 ($100,000 − $15,000) and total cash payments for operating expenses should be reported at $54,000 ($60,000 − $6,000). The proper presentation is as follows.

Redmark Ltd.
Partial Statement of Changes in Financial Position
for the Year 1994

Cash flows from operating activities		
Cash received from customers		$85,000
Salaries paid	$46,000	
Utilities paid	8,000	54,000
Net income		$31,000

An added complication develops when accounts receivable are written off. Simply adjusting sales for the change in accounts receivable will not provide the proper amount of cash sales. The reason is that the write-off of the accounts receivable is not a cash collection. Thus, an additional adjustment is necessary.

Cash Equivalent Items

Up to this point, we have considered only changes to cash. The statement of changes in financial position, as emphasized earlier, focuses on liquid financial resources that are readily available to the enterprise. These highly liquid financial resources include cash and temporary investments (marketable securities) minus short-term borrowings.

Cash, term deposits, temporary investments, and short-term borrowings are combined under the heading Cash and Cash Equivalents in the statement. Transactions involving these accounts (i.e. obtaining or repaying short-term loans, acquiring or disposing of temporary investments) would not be reported as financing or investing activities. Gains or losses on disposals of temporary investments represent an increase or decrease in the amount of cash and cash equivalents. Therefore, no adjustment for these gains or losses is necessary.

Net Losses

If an enterprise reports a net loss instead of a net income, the net loss must be adjusted for those items that do not result in a cash inflow or outflow. The net loss after adjusting for the charges or credits not affecting cash may result in a negative or a positive cash flow from operating activities. For example, if the net loss was $50,000 and the total amount of charges to be added back was $60,000, then net cash flow from operating activities is $10,000, as shown in the following computation.

**Computation of Net Cash Flow From
Operating Activities
(Cash Inflow)**

Net loss		$(50,000)
Add (deduct) items not affecting cash		
Depreciation of plant assets	$55,000	
Amortization of patents	5,000	60,000
Net cash flow from operating activities		$ 10,000

If the company experiences a net loss of $80,000 and the total amount of the charges to be added back is $25,000, the presentation appears as follows.

Computation of Net Cash Flow From Operating Activities (Cash Outflow)	
Net loss	$(80,000)
Add (deduct) items not affecting cash	
Depreciation of plant assets	25,000
Net cash flow from operating activities (decrease)	$(55,000)

Although it is not illustrated in this chapter, a negative cash flow may result even if the company reports a net income.

Gains

In the third illustration (1994) of Tax Consultants Ltd., the company experienced a loss of $2,000 from the sale of equipment. This loss was added to net income to compute net cash flow from operating activities because *the loss is a noncash charge in the income statement*. If a gain from a sale of equipment is experienced, it too requires that net income be adjusted. Because the gain is reported in the statement of changes in financial position as part of the cash proceeds from the sale of equipment under investing activities, *the gain is deducted from net income to avoid double counting*—once as part of net income and again as part of the cash proceeds from the sale.

Stock Options

If a company has a stock option plan, compensation expense will be recorded during the period(s) in which the employee performs the services. Although compensation expense is debited, deferred compensation expense is credited, with cash being unaffected by the amount of the expense. Therefore, net income has to be increased by the amount of compensation expense in computing net cash flow from operating activities.

Pensions

If a company has an employee pension plan, it is likely that the pension expense recorded during a period will be either higher or lower than the amount of cash funded. In these circumstances, net income must be adjusted by the difference between cash paid and the expense reported in computing net cash flow from operating activities.

Extraordinary Items

Cash flows from extraordinary transactions and other events, the effects of which are included in net income but which are not related to operations, should be reported either as investing activities or as financing activities. For example, if a municipality expropriated land owned by Tax Consultants Ltd., paying compensation of $40,000 in cash for the land that originally cost $35,000, Tax Consultants would have recognized a $3,000 ($5,000 gain less $2,000 of taxes) extraordinary gain. In the statement of changes in financial position, the $3,000 gain would be ignored in the operating activity section. The $38,000 ($40,000 cash received minus $2,000 cash paid for taxes) would be reported as a financing activity as follows.

> Cash flows from financing activities
> Expropriation of land—extraordinary gain of $3,000
> (net of $2,000 tax) $38,000

Note that in the above example, the net cash received is reported as a financing activity at $38,000. Under both the direct method and the indirect method, the total amount of income taxes is disclosed.

Significant Noncash Transactions

Because the statement of changes in financial position reports the effects of operating, investing, and financing activities only in terms of cash flows, some significant noncash transactions and other events that are investing or financing activities could be omitted from the body of the statement. Among the more common of these noncash transactions that should be reported or disclosed in some manner are the following:

1. The acquisition of assets by assuming liabilities (including capital lease obligations) or by the issuance of equity securities.

2. Exchanges of nonmonetary assets.

3. Refinancing of long-term debt.

4. Conversion of debt or preferred shares to common shares.

5. The issuance of equity securities to retire debt.

These transactions are similar to a cash inflow with a simultaneous cash outflow and should be reported in the statement of changes in financial position. If material in amount, they should be shown as both cash inflows and outflows in the financing and investing activities sections, with an appropriate reference to show that they are related.

Certain other significant noncash transactions or other events are generally not reported in conjunction with the statement of changes in financial position. Examples of these types of transactions are **stock dividends, stock splits, and appropriations of retained earnings**. These items represent neither financing nor investing activities, but are generally reported in conjunction with the statement of retained earnings or schedules and notes pertaining to changes in capital accounts.

COMPREHENSIVE ILLUSTRATION: USE OF A WORK SHEET

Objective 9

Explain the use of a work sheet in preparing a statement of changes in financial position.

When numerous adjustments are necessary or other complicating factors are present, *many account-ants prefer to use a work sheet to assemble and classify the data that will appear on the statement of changes in financial position*. The work sheet (a spreadsheet, when using computer software) is merely a device that aids in the preparation of the statement; its use is optional. The skeleton format of the work sheet for preparation of the statement of changes in financial position using the indirect approach is shown in the example on page 1173.

The following guidelines are important in using a work sheet:

1. In the balance sheet accounts section, accounts with debit balances are listed separately from those with credit balances. This means, for example, that Accumulated Depreciation is listed under credit balances and not as a contra account under debit balances. The beginning and ending balances of each account are entered in the appropriate columns. The transactions that caused the change in the account balance during the year are entered; each line pertaining to a balance sheet account should balance across. That is, the beginning balance plus or minus the reconciling item(s) must equal the ending balance. When this agreement exists for all balance sheet accounts, all changes in account balances have been reconciled.

XYZ Limited
Statement of Changes in Financial Position
for the Year Ended . . .

Balance Sheet Accounts	End of Last Year Balances	Reconciling Items		End of Current Year Balances
		Debits	Credits	
Debit balance accounts	XX	XX	XX	XX
	XX	XX	XX	XX
Totals	XXX			XXX
Credit balance accounts	XX	XX	XX	XX
	XX	XX	XX	XX
Totals	XXX			XXX
Statement of Changes in Financial Position				
Operating activities				
Net income		XX		
Adjustments		XX	XX	
Investing activities				
Receipts and payments		XX	XX	
Financing activities				
Receipts and payments		XX	XX	
Totals		XXX	XXX	
Increase (decrease) in cash		(XX)	XX	
Totals		XXX	XXX	

2. The bottom portion of the work sheet consists of the operating, investing, and financing activities sections. Accordingly, it provides the information necessary to prepare the formal statement of changes in financial position. Inflows of cash are entered as debits in the reconciling columns and outflows of cash are entered as credits in the reconciling columns. Thus, in this section, the sale of equipment for cash at book value is entered as a debit under inflows of cash from investing activities. Similarly, the purchase of land for cash is entered as a credit under outflows of cash from investing activities.

3. The reconciling items shown in the work sheet are not entered in any journal or posted to any account. They do not represent either adjustments or corrections of the balance sheet accounts. They are used only to facilitate the preparation of the statement of changes in financial position.

Preparation of the Work Sheet

The preparation of a work sheet involves a series of prescribed steps. The steps in this case are:

1. Enter the balance sheet accounts and their beginning and ending balances in the balance sheet accounts section.

2. Enter the data that explain the changes in the balance sheet accounts (other than cash) and their effects on the statement of changes in financial position in the reconciling columns of the work sheet.

3. Enter the increase or decrease in cash on the cash line and at the bottom of the work sheet. This entry should enable the totals of the reconciling columns to be in agreement.

To illustrate procedures for preparing the work sheet, the following comprehensive illustration is presented for Satellite Manufacturing Limited. Again, the indirect method serves as the basis for the computation of net cash provided by operating activities. The financial statements and other data related to Satellite Manufacturing Limited are presented with the balance sheet and the statement of income and retained earnings shown on the following pages. Additional explanations related to preparation of the work sheet are provided throughout the discussion that follows the financial statements.

Satellite Manufacturing Limited
Comparative Balance Sheets
December 31, 1994 and 1993

	1994	1993	Difference: Incr. or Decr.
Assets			
Cash	$ 59,000	$ 66,000	$ 7,000 Decr.
Accounts receivable (net)	104,000	51,000	53,000 Incr.
Inventories	493,000	341,000	152,000 Incr.
Prepaid expenses	16,500	17,000	500 Decr.
Investments in shares of Porter Co. (equity method)	18,500	15,000	3,500 Incr.
Land	131,500	82,000	49,500 Incr.
Equipment	187,000	142,000	45,000 Incr.
Accumulated depreciation—equipment	(29,000)	(31,000)	2,000 Decr.
Buildings	262,000	262,000	—
Accumulated depreciation—buildings	(74,100)	(71,000)	3,100 Incr.
Goodwill	7,600	10,000	2,400 Decr.
Total Assets	$1,176,000	$884,000	
Liabilities			
Accounts payable	$ 132,000	$131,000	$ 1,000 Incr.
Accrued liabilities	43,000	39,000	4,000 Incr.
Income taxes payable	3,000	16,000	13,000 Decr.
Notes payable (long term)	60,000	—	60,000 Incr.
Bonds payable	100,000	100,000	—
Premium on bonds payable	7,000	8,000	1,000 Decr.
Deferred income tax	9,000	6,000	3,000 Incr.
Total Liabilities	$ 354,000	$300,000	
Shareholders' Equity			
Common shares	$ 247,000	$ 88,000	$159,000 Incr.
Retained earnings	592,000	496,000	96,000 Incr.
Treasury shares	(17,000)	—	17,000 Incr.
Total Shareholders' Equity	$ 822,000	$584,000	
Total Liabilities and Shareholders' Equity	$1,176,000	$884,000	

Satellite Manufacturing Limited
Combined Statement of Income and Retained Earnings
for the Year Ended 1994

Net sales		$524,500
Other revenue		3,500
Total revenues		$528,000
Expense		
Cost of goods sold		$310,000
Selling and administrative expense		47,000
Other expense and losses		12,000
Total expenses		$369,000
Income before income tax and extraordinary item		$159,000
Income tax		
Current	47,000	
Future	3,000	50,000
Income before extraordinary item		$109,000
Gain on expropriation of land (net of tax)		8,000
Net income		$117,000
Retained earnings, January 1		496,000
Less:		
Cash dividends	6,000	
Stock dividend	15,000	21,000
Retained earnings, December 31		$592,000
Per share:		
Income before extraordinary items		$1.98
Extraordinary item		0.15
Net income		$2.13

Additional information:

(a) Other income of $3,500, represents Satellite's equity share in the net income of Porter Company, an equity investee. Satellite owns 22% of Porter Company.

(b) Land in the amount of $60,000 was purchased through the issuance of a long-term note; in addition, certain parcels of land were expropriated, resulting in an $8,000 gain, net of $2,500 tax.

(c) An analysis of the equipment account and related accumulated depreciation indicates the following:

	Equipment Dr./(Cr.)	Accum. Dep. Dr./(Cr.)	Gain or Loss
Balance at end of 1993	$142,000	$(31,000)	
Purchase of equipment	53,000		
Sale of equipment	(8,000)	2,500	$1,500 L
Depreciation for the period		(11,500)	
Major repair charged to accumulated depreciation		11,000	
Balance at end of 1994	$187,000	$(29,000)	

(Continued)

(d) The changes in the Accumulated Depreciation—Building, Goodwill, Premium on Bonds Payable, and Deferred Income Tax accounts—resulted from income tax accrual, depreciation, and amortization entries.

(e) An analysis of the share capital accounts in shareholders' equity discloses the following:

	Common Shares
Balance at end of 1993	$ 88,000
Issuance of 2% stock dividend	15,000
Sale of shares for cash	144,000
Balance at end of 1994	$247,000

(f) Interest paid (net of amount capitalized) is $9,000; income tax amount paid is $62,000.

Analysis of Transactions

The following discussion provides an explanation of the individual adjustments that appear on the work sheet on pages 1179 through 1181. Because cash (there are no cash equivalents) is the basis for analysis, the cash account will be reconciled last. Because income is the first item that appears on the statement of changes, it will be analysed first.

Change in Retained Earnings. Net income for the period is $117,000; the entry for it on the work sheet is as follows:

(1)

Operating—Income Before Extraordinary Item	109,000	
Investing—Expropriation of Land	8,000	
Retained Earnings		117,000

Net income is reported at the bottom of the work sheet and is the starting point for preparation of the statement of changes in financial position.

Retained earnings was also affected by a stock dividend and a cash dividend. The retained earnings statement reports a stock dividend of $15,000. The work sheet entry for this transaction is as follows:

(2)

Retained Earnings	15,000	
Common Shares		15,000

The issuance of stock dividends is not a cash operating, investing, or financing item; therefore, *although this transaction is entered on the work sheet for reconciling purposes, it is not reported in the statement of changes in financial position*.

The cash dividend of $6,000 represents a financing activity cash outflow. The following work sheet entry is made:

(3)

Retained Earnings	6,000	
Financing—Cash Dividends		6,000

The beginning and ending balances of retained earnings are reconciled by the entry of the three items above.

Accounts Receivable (Net). The increase in accounts receivable (net) of $53,000 represents adjustments that did not result in cash inflows during 1994; as a result, the increase of $53,000 would be deducted from income. The following work sheet entry is made:

(4)

Accounts Receivable (Net)	53,000	
Operating—Increase in Accounts Receivable		53,000

Inventories. The increase in inventories of $152,000 represents an operating use of cash. The incremental investment in inventories during the year reduces cash without increasing cost of goods sold. The work sheet entry is made as follows:

(5)

Inventories	152,000	
Operating—Increase in Inventories		152,000

Prepaid Expenses. The decrease in prepaid expenses of $500 represents a charge in the income statement for which there was no cash outflow in the current period. It should be added back to income through the following entry:

(6)

Operating—Decrease in Prepaid Expenses	500	
Prepaid Expenses		500

Investment in Shares of Porter Co. The investment in the common shares of Porter Co. increased $3,500, which reflects Satellite's share of the income earned by its equity investee during the current year. Although revenue, and therefore income per the income statement, was increased $3,500 by the accounting entry that recorded Satellite's share of Porter Co.'s net income, no cash (dividend) was provided. The following work sheet entry is made:

(7)

Investment in Shares of Porter Co.	3,500	
Operating—Equity in Earnings of Porter Co.		3,500

Land. Land in the amount of $60,000 was purchased through the issuance of a long-term note payable. This transaction did not affect cash, but it is considered a significant noncash investing/financing transaction that should be reported as both an investing and a financing transaction. Two entries are necessary to record this transaction on the work sheet:

(8)

Land	60,000	
Investing—Purchase of Land		60,000
Financing—Issue of Note Payable	60,000	
Note Payable		60,000

In addition to the noncash transaction involving the issuance of a note to purchase land, the land account was decreased by the expropriation proceedings. The work sheet entry to record the receipt of $18,500 for land having a book value of $10,500 is as follows:

(9)

Investing—Expropriation of Land (Book Value)	10,500	
Land		10,500

The extraordinary gain of $8,000 is deducted from net income in reconciling net income to net cash flow from operating activities because the transaction that gave rise to the gain is an item for which the cash effect is already classified as an investing cash inflow. The Land account is now reconciled.

Equipment and Accumulated Depreciation. An analysis of the Equipment account and Accumulated Depreciation shows that a number of transactions have affected these accounts. Equipment in the amount of $53,000 was purchased during the year. The entry to record this transaction on the work sheet is as follows:

(10)

Equipment	53,000	
Investing—Purchase of Equipment		53,000

In addition, equipment with a book value of $5,500 was sold at a loss of $1,500. The entry to record this transaction on the work sheet is as follows:

(11)

Investing—Sale of Equipment	4,000	
Operating—Loss on Sale of Equipment	1,500	
Accumulated Depreciation—Equipment	2,500	
Equipment		8,000

The proceeds from the sale of the equipment provided cash of $4,000. In addition, the loss on the sale of the equipment reduced the income but did not affect cash; therefore, it must be added back to income to accurately report cash provided by operations.

Depreciation on the equipment was reported at $11,500 and should be presented on the work sheet in the following manner:

(12)

Operating—Depreciation Expense—Equipment	11,500	
Accumulated Depreciation—Equipment		11,500

The depreciation expense is added back to net income because it reduced income but did not affect cash.

Finally, a major repair to equipment in the amount of $11,000 was charged to Accumulated Depreciation—Equipment. Because this expenditure required cash, the following work sheet entry is made:

(13)

Accumulated Depreciation—Equipment	11,000	
Investing—Major Repairs of Equipment		11,000

The balances in the Equipment and related Accumulated Depreciation accounts are reconciled after adjustment for the foregoing items.

Building Depreciation and Amortization of Goodwill. Depreciation expense on the buildings of $3,100 and amortization of goodwill of $2,400 are both expenses in the income statement that reduced net income but did not require cash outflows in the current period. The following work sheet entry is made:

(14)

Operating—Depreciation Expense—Buildings	3,100	
Operating—Amortization of Goodwill	2,400	
Accumulated Depreciation—Buildings		3,100
Goodwill		2,400

Other Noncash Charges or Credits. An analysis of the remaining accounts indicates that changes in the Accounts Payable, Accrued Liabilities, Income Taxes Payable, Premium on Bonds Payable, and Deferred Income Tax balances resulted from charges or credits to net income that did not affect cash. Each of these items should be individually analysed and entered in the work sheet. We have summarized in the following compound entry to the work sheet these noncash, income-related items:

(15)

Income Taxes Payable	13,000	
Premium on Bonds Payable	1,000	

(Continued)

Operating—Increase in Accounts Payable	1,000	
Operating—Increase in Accrued Liabilities	4,000	
Operating—Increase in Deferred Income Tax	3,000	
Operating—Decrease in Income Taxes Payable		13,000
Operating—Amortization of Bond Premium		1,000
Accounts Payable		1,000
Accrued Liabilities		4,000
Deferred Income Tax		3,000

Common Shares and Related Accounts. A comparison of the common share balances shows that transactions during the year affected these accounts. First, a stock dividend of 2% was issued to shareholders. As indicated in the discussion of work sheet entry (2) on page 1176, no cash was provided or used by the stock dividend transaction. In addition to the shares issued via the stock dividend, Satellite issued common shares at $16 each. The work sheet entry to record this transaction is as follows:

(16)

Financing—Issue of Common Shares	144,000	
Common Shares		144,000

Also, the company purchased its own common shares in the amount of $17,000. The work sheet entry to record this transaction is as follows:

(17)

Treasury Shares	17,000	
Financing—Purchase of Treasury Shares		17,000

Final Reconciling Entry. The final entry to reconcile the change in cash and to balance the work sheet is as follows:

(18)

Decrease in Cash	7,000	
Cash		7,000

The amount is the difference between the cash balance at the beginning of the year and at the end of the year.

Once it has been determined that the differences between the beginning and ending balances per the work sheet columns have been accounted for, the reconciling transactions columns can be totalled; these column totals should balance. The statement of changes in financial position can be prepared entirely from the items and amounts that appear at the bottom of the work sheet under "Statement of Changes Effects."

Satellite Manufacturing Limited
Work Sheet for Preparation of Statement of Changes in Financial Position
for the Year Ended 1994

	Balance 12/31/93	Reconciling Items—1994 Debits	Reconciling Items—1994 Credits	Balance 12/31/94
Debits:				
Cash	$ 66,000		(18) $ 7,000	$ 59,000
Accounts receivable (net)	51,000	(4) $ 53,000		104,000
Inventories	341,000	(5) 152,000		493,000
				(Continued)

Prepaid expenses	17,000			(6)	500	16,500
Investment (equity method)	15,000	(7)	3,500			18,500
Land	82,000	(8)	60,000	(9)	10,500	131,500
Equipment	142,000	(10)	53,000	(11)	8,000	187,000
Buildings	262,000					262,000
Goodwill	10,000			(14)	2,400	7,600
Treasury shares	–0–	(17)	17,000			17,000
Total debits	$986,000					$1,296,100

Credits:

Accumulated depreciation—equipment	$ 31,000	(11) (13)	2,500 11,000	(12)	11,500	$ 29,000
Accumulated depreciation—buildings	71,000			(14)	3,100	74,100
Accounts payable	131,000			(15)	1,000	132,000
Accrued liabilities	39,000			(15)	4,000	43,000
Income taxes payable	16,000	(15)	13,000			3,000
Notes payable (long term)	–0–			(8)	60,000	60,000
Bonds payable	100,000					100,000
Premium on bonds payable	8,000	(15)	1,000			7,000
Deferred income tax	6,000			(15)	3,000	9,000
Common shares	88,000			(16) (2)	144,000 15,000	247,000
Retained earnings	496,000	(2) (3)	15,000 6,000	(1)	117,000	592,000
Total credits	$986,000					$1,296,100

Statement of Changes Effects:

Operating activities:

Income before extraordinary item	(1)	109,000		
Increase in accounts receivable			(4)	53,000
Increase in inventories			(5)	152,000
Decrease in prepaid expense	(6)	500		
Equity in earnings of Porter Co.			(7)	3,500
Loss on sale of equipment	(11)	1,500		
Depreciation expense—equipment	(12)	11,500		
Depreciation expense—buildings	(14)	3,100		
Amortization of goodwill	(14)	2,400		
Increase in accounts payable	(15)	1,000		
Increase in accrued liabilities	(15)	4,000		
Deferred income tax	(15)	3,000		
Decrease in income taxes payable			(15)	13,000
Amortization of bond premium			(15)	1,000

Investing activities:

Expropriation of land (gain)	(1)	8,000		
Expropriation of land (book value)	(9)	10,500		
Purchase of land through issuance of note payable			(8)	60,000
Purchase of equipment			(10)	53,000
Sale of equipment	(11)	4,000		
Major repairs of equipment			(13)	11,000

(Continued)

Financing activities:				
Payment of cash dividend			(3)	6,000
Issue of common shares	(16)	144,000		
Issuance of note payable to				
purchase land	(8)	60,000		
Purchase of treasury shares			(17)	17,000
		$749,500		$756,500
Decrease in cash	(18)	7,000		
Totals		$756,500		$756,500

Preparation of Statement

Presented below is a formal statement of changes in financial position prepared from the data compiled in the lower portion of the work sheet.

Satellite Manufacturing Limited
Statement of Changes in Financial Position
for the Year Ended December 31, 1994

Cash flows from operating activities:		
Income before extraordinary item		$109,000
Add (deduct) items not affecting cash		
Depreciation expense	$ 14,600	
Amortization of goodwill	2,400	
Amortization of bond premium	(1,000)	
Equity in earnings of Porter Co.	(3,500)	
Loss on sale of equipment	1,500	
Increase in deferred income tax	3,000	
Increase in accounts receivable (net)	(53,000)	
Increase in inventories	(152,000)	
Decrease in prepaid expenses	500	
Increase in accounts payable	1,000	
Increase in accrued liabilities	4,000	
Decrease in income taxes payable	(13,000)	(195,500)
Net cash flow from operating activities		(86,500)
Cash flows from investing activities:		
Proceeds from expropriation of land	$ 18,500	
Purchase of land by issuance of note payable	(60,000)	
Purchase of equipment	(53,000)	
Sale of equipment	4,000	
Major repairs of equipment	(11,000)	
Net cash used by investing activities		(101,500)
Cash flows from financing activities:		
Payment of cash dividend	$ (6,000)	
Purchase of treasury shares	(17,000)	
Issue of note to purchase land	60,000	
Issue of common shares	144,000	
Net cash provided by financing activities		181,000
Net decrease in cash		$ (7,000)

USEFULNESS OF THE STATEMENT OF CHANGES IN FINANCIAL POSITION

The information in a statement of changes in financial position should help investors, creditors, and others to assess the following:

1. ***The entity's ability to generate future cash flows.*** A primary objective of financial reporting is to provide information that makes it possible to predict the amounts, timing, and uncertainty of future cash flows. By examining relationships between items such as net income and net cash flow from operating activities, or net cash flow from operating activities and increases or decreases in cash, it is possible to make better predictions of the amounts, timing, and uncertainty of future cash flows than is possible using accrual-basis data only.

2. ***The entity's ability to pay dividends and meet obligations.*** Simply put, if a company does not have adequate cash, employees cannot be paid, debts settled, dividends paid, or equipment acquired. A statement of changes in financial position indicates how cash is used and where it comes from. Employers, creditors, shareholders, and customers should be particularly interested in this statement because it alone shows the flows of cash in a business.

3. ***The reasons for the difference between net income and net cash flow from operating activities.*** The net income number is important because it provides information on the success or failure of a business enterprise from one period to another. But some people are critical of the accrual-basis net income because estimates must be made to arrive at it. As a result, the reliability of the number is often challenged. Such is not the case with cash. Thus, many readers of the financial statement want to know the reasons for the difference between net income and net cash flow from operating activities. Then they can assess for themselves the reliability of the income number.

4. ***The cash and noncash investing and financing transactions during the period.*** By examining a company's investing activities (purchase and sales of assets other than products) and its financing transactions (borrowings and repayments of borrowings, investments by owners and distribution to owners), a financial statement reader can better understand why assets and liabilities increased or decreased during the period. For example, the following questions might be answered:
   How did cash increase when there was a net loss for the period?
   How were the proceeds of the bond issue used?
   How was the expansion in plant and equipment financed?
   Why were dividends not increased?
   How was the retirement of debt accomplished?
   How much money was borrowed during the year?
   Is cash flow greater or less than net income?

FUNDAMENTAL CONCEPTS

1. In 1985, *CICA Handbook* Section 1540 required the inclusion of a statement of changes in financial position, in the primary financial statements along with the balance sheet, income statement, and statement of retained earnings. This change reflected the growing importance of cash flow information to financial statement users.

2. The statement of changes in financial position classifies cash receipts and cash payments into the categories of operating, investing, and financing activities.

3. The operating section reports the cash effects of transactions that affect net income. The net cash flow from operating activities can be computed using the direct approach, where cash receipts and cash disbursements from operating activities are compared, or by using the indirect approach, which adjusts net income for items that affect net income but do not affect cash.

4. The investing section reports cash flows resulting from changes in assets, other than operating items; the financing section reports cash flows resulting from changes in liabilities and shareholders' equity, other than operating items.

(Continued)

5. The information needed to prepare the statement of changes in financial position comes from three sources: comparative balance sheets, current income statement, and selected transaction data. Three steps are involved in the preparation: determine the change in cash and cash equivalents, the cash flow from operating activities, and the cash flow from investing and financing activities.

6. When computing the net cash flow from operating activities, three types of adjustments are made to net income: changes in current assets and current liabilities, depreciation expense and similar items, and gains or losses on the sale of assets.

7. Under the direct approach, cash revenues and cash expenses are computed directly so that cash provided from revenue-earning activities and cash expended for operating purposes may be reported.

8. Some changes in current assets and current liabilities are not net income adjustments because they do not affect net income. Examples are transactions involving short-term investments, short-term nontrade notes payable, and dividends payable.

9. Significant noncash transactions that are financing and/or investing activities are reported as if they involve cash. For example, a cash inflow and an equal cash outflow is reported so that the nature of the resulting change in resources is disclosed.

10. Two devices are available for assembling and classifying transactions and changes in account balances in order to prepare the statement of changes in financial position: the work sheet and T-accounts. The latter are discussed in the appendix to this chapter.

11. The statement of changes in financial position is useful in helping to assess (1) the entity's ability to generate future cash flows, (2) the entity's ability to pay dividends and meet obligations, (3) the reasons for the difference between net income and net cash flow from operating activities, and (4) the cash and noncash investing and financing transactions during the period.

The T-Account Approach to Preparation of the Statement of Changes in Financial Position

Many accountants find the work-sheet approach to preparing a statement of changes in financial position time-consuming and cumbersome. In some cases, the detail of a work sheet is not needed and time does not permit for preparation of one. Therefore, the **T-account approach** to preparing a statement of changes in financial position has been devised. This procedure provides a quick and systematic method of accumulating the appropriate information to be presented in the formal statement of changes in financial position. The T-accounts used in this approach are not part of the general ledger or any other ledger; they are developed only for use in this process.

To illustrate the T-account approach, this appendix will use the Satellite Manufacturing Ltd. information previously presented.

T-ACCOUNT ILLUSTRATION

When the T-account approach is employed, the net change in cash for the period is computed by comparing the beginning and ending balances of the Cash account. After the net change is computed, a T-account for Cash is prepared and the net change in cash is entered at the top of this account on the left if cash increased, and on the right if it decreased (see the T-account illustration on pages 1186–1187). The T-account is then structured into six separate classifications: **Increases**—(1) Operating, (2) Investing, and (3) Financing, on the left; and **Decreases**—(4) Operating, (5) Investing, and (6) Financing, on the right. T-accounts are then set up for all noncash items that have had activity during the period, with the net change entered at the top of each account. The objective of the T-account approach is to explain the net change in cash through the various changes that have occurred in the noncash accounts. The Cash T-account acts as a summarizing account. Most of the changes in the noncash items are explained through the Cash account. Significant financial transactions that did not affect cash are not recorded in the Cash account but are entered in their respective noncash accounts for purposes of reconciling the net changes in these accounts.

To illustrate, a complete version of the T-account approach is presented on the following pages. The following items caused the change in cash (you should trace each entry to the accounts that are presented following the entries):

1. Net income for the period, composed of income before extraordinary item of $109,000 and an extraordinary gain of $8,000 (net of tax), increased Retained Earnings $117,000. In general journal form, the entry to report this increase and the extraordinary item would be:

Cash—Operations	109,000	
Cash—Investing	8,000	
Retained Earnings		117,000

2. The Retained Earnings account also discloses stock dividends of $15,000. Because this transaction does not affect cash and it is not reported in the statement of changes in financial position, the following entry would be made:

Retained Earnings	15,000	
Common Shares		15,000

3. Further analysis of the Retained Earnings account indicates that a cash dividend of $6,000 was declared during the current period. The entry to record the transaction would be:

Retained Earnings	6,000	
Cash—Financing		6,000

Note that the net change in the retained earnings balance of $96,000 is now reconciled. This reconciliation procedure is basic to the T-account approach because it ensures that all appropriate transactions have been considered.

4. The equity in the earnings of Porter Co. must be subtracted from income before extraordinary item because this income item does not increase cash. The journal entry to recognize this equity in the earnings of Porter Co. is as follows:

Investment in Porter Co. Shares	3,500	
Cash—Operations		3,500

5. A note of $60,000 was issued to purchase land. Although this transaction did not affect cash, it is a significant financial transaction that should be reported. The transaction is therefore assumed both to have increased cash and to have decreased cash in order to report this amount in the Cash account. The following entry would be made:

Land	60,000	
Cash—Investing		60,000
Cash—Financing	60,000	
Note Payable		60,000

An alternative to this approach is simply to adjust the Land and Note Payable accounts, noting that in a formal preparation of a statement of changes in financial position, this transaction must be reported.

6. In addition, land with a book value of $10,500 was expropriated. The entry to record this transaction is as follows:

Cash—Investing	10,500	
Land		10,500

Note that adding the $10,500 book value of this expropriation to the $8,000 extraordinary gain (before tax of $2,000) provides total cash of $18,500 related to the expropriation.

7. Equipment and the related Accumulated Depreciation account indicate that a number of financial transactions affected these accounts. The first transaction is the purchase of equipment, which is recorded as follows:

Equipment	53,000	
Cash—Investing		53,000

8. In addition, equipment with a book value of $5,500 was sold at a loss of $1,500. The entry to record this transaction is as follows:

Cash—Investing	4,000	
Cash—Operations	1,500	
Accumulated Depreciation—Equipment	2,500	
Equipment		8,000

Note that the loss on the sale of the equipment has reduced net income but has not affected cash. The loss must therefore be added back to net income to accurately report net cash flow from operating activities.

9. Depreciation on the equipment of $11,500 must be recorded as follows:

Cash—Operations	11,500	
Accumulated Depreciation—Equipment		11,500

10. The major repair reduced cash, so the necessary journal entry is as follows:

Accumulated Depreciation—Equipment	11,000	
Cash—Investing		11,000

The Equipment account and related Accumulated Depreciation account are now reconciled.

11. Analysis of the remaining *noncurrent accounts* indicates changes in Accumulated Depreciation—Building, Premium on Bonds Payable, and Deferred Income Tax that must be accounted for in determining the net cash flow from operating activities. The compound entry to record these transactions is as follows:

Cash—Operations	3,100	
Cash—Operations	2,400	
Cash—Operations	3,000	
Premium on Bonds Payable	1,000	
Accumulated Depreciation—Buildings		3,100
Goodwill		2,400
Deferred Income Tax		3,000
Cash—Operations		1,000

12. Analysis of the *current accounts* exclusive of cash indicates an increase in Accounts Receivable (net), an increase in Inventories, a decrease in Prepaid Expenses, an increase in Accounts Payable, an increase in Accrued Liabilities, and a decrease in Income Taxes Payable. All of these changes must be accounted for in determining the net cash flows from operating activities. The compound entry to record these changes is as follows:

Cash—Operations	500	
Cash—Operations	1,000	
Cash—Operations	4,000	
Accounts Receivable (net)	53,000	
Inventories	152,000	
Income Taxes Payable	13,000	
Prepaid Expenses		500
Accounts Payable		1,000
Accrued Liabilities		4,000
Cash—Operations		53,000
Cash—Operations		152,000
Cash—Operations		13,000

13. Examination of the Common Share accounts indicates that in addition to the stock dividend (transaction 2), common shares were issued at $16 per share. The entry to record this transaction is as follows:

Cash—Financing	144,000	
Common Shares		144,000

14. The company also purchased treasury shares, which is recorded as follows:

Treasury Shares	17,000	
Cash—Financing		17,000

After the entries above are posted to the appropriate accounts, the Cash account (below) is used as the basis for preparing the statement of changes in financial position. The debit side of the Cash account contains the cash provided and the credit side contains the cash used. The difference between the two sides of the working capital account should reconcile to the increase or decrease in cash. The completed statement of changes in financial position is presented on page 1181.

Cash

Increases			Decreases		
			Net change	7,000	
Operating Activities:			Operating Activities:		
1. Income before extraordinary item	109,000		4. Equity in earnings of Porter Co.	3,500	
8. Loss on sale of equipment	1,500		11. Bond premium amortization	1,000	
9. Depreciation expense	11,500		12. Accounts receivable (net)	53,000	
11. Depreciation expense	3,100		12. Inventories	152,000	
11. Goodwill amortization	2,400		12. Income taxes payable	13,000	
12. Deferred income tax	3,000			222,500	
12. Prepaid expenses	500				
12. Accounts payable	1,000				
12. Accrued liabilities	4,000				
	136,000				

(Continued)

Investing Activities:		Investing Activities:	
1. Expropriation of land	8,000	5. Purchase of land through	
6. Expropriation of land	10,500	issuance of note	60,000
8. Sale of equipment	4,000	7. Purchase of equipment	53,000
	22,500	10. Major repair of equipment	11,000
			124,000

Financing Activities:		Financing Activities:	
5. Issue of note to purchase land	60,000	3. Cash dividends paid	6,000
13. Issue of common shares	144,000	14. Purchase of treasury shares	17,000
	204,000		23,000

Accounts Receivable (Net)

Net change	53,000		
12. Increase	53,000		

Inventories

Net change	152,000		
12. Increase	152,000		

Prepaid Expenses

		Net change	500
		12. Decrease	500

Investment in Shares of Porter Co. (Equity Method)

Net change	3,500		
4. Equity in earnings	3,500		

Land

Net change	49,500		
5. Purchase of land	60,000	6. Expropriation	10,500

Equipment

Net change	45,000		
7. Purchase	53,000	8. Sale of equipment	8,000

Accumulated Depreciation—Equipment

Net change	2,000		
8. Sale of equipment	2,500	9. Depreciation expense	11,500
10. Major repair	11,000		
	13,500		

(Continued)

Accumulated Depreciation—Buildings

	Net change	3,100
	11. Depreciation expense	3,100

Goodwill

	Net change	2,400
	11. Amortization of goodwill	2,400

Accounts Payable

	Net change	1,000
	12. Increase	1,000

Accrued Liabilities

	Net change	4,000
	12. Increase	4,000

Income Taxes Payable

Net change	13,000		
12. Decrease	13,000		

Notes Payable

	Net change	60,000
	5. Issuance of note	60,000

Premium on Bonds Payable

Net change	1,000		
11. Bond premium amortization	1,000		

Deferred Income Tax

	Net change	3,000
	11. Increase	3,000

Common Shares

	Net change	159,000
	2. Stock dividend	15,000
	13. Issue of common shares	144,000

Retained Earnings

		Net change	96,000
2. Stock dividend	15,000	1. Net income	117,000
3. Cash dividend	6,000		
	21,000		

(Continued)

Treasury Shares

Net change	17,000
14. Purchase of treasury shares	17,000

SUMMARY OF T-ACCOUNT APPROACH

Shortcut approaches are often used with the T-account approach. For example, the journal entries may not be prepared because the transactions are obvious. Also, only the noncash T-accounts that have a number of changes, such as Equipment, Accumulated Depreciation—Equipment, and Retained Earnings, need to be presented in T-account form. Other more obvious changes in noncash items can be determined simply by examining the comparative balance sheet and other related data. The T-account approach provides certain advantages over the work-sheet method in that (1) a statement usually can be prepared much faster using the T-account method and (2) the use of the T-account method helps in understanding the relationship between cash and noncash items. Conversely, when highly complex problems exist, the work sheet provides a more orderly and systematic approach to preparing the statement of changes in financial position. In addition, in practice the work sheet is used extensively to ensure that all items are properly accounted for.

The following steps are used in the T-account approach:

1. Determine the increase or decrease in cash for the year.

2. Post the increase or decrease to the Cash T-account and establish six classifications within this account: Increases—Operating, Investing, and Financing, and Decreases—Operating, Investing, and Financing.

3. Determine the increase or decrease in each noncash account. Accounts that have no change can be ignored unless two transactions have occurred in the same account of the same amount, which is highly unlikely. A shortcut approach is to prepare T accounts only for noncash accounts that have a number of transactions. All other changes can be immediately posted to the Cash account after examining the additional information related to the changes in the balance sheet for a period.

4. Reconstruct entries in noncash accounts and post them to the noncash account affected.

5. Using the postings from the Cash T-account, prepare the formal statement of changes in financial position.

———— QUESTIONS ————

1. Why has the statement of changes in financial position become a popular type of financial statement?

2. What is the purpose of the statement of changes in financial position? What information does it provide?

3. Differentiate between investing activities, financing activities, and operating activities.

4. What are the major sources of cash (inflows) in a statement of changes in financial position? What are the major uses (outflows) of cash?

5. Unlike the other major financial statements, the statement of changes in financial position is not prepared from the adjusted trial balance. From what sources does the information to prepare this statement come, and what information does each source provide?

6. Why is it necessary to convert accrual-based net income to a cash basis when preparing a statement of changes in financial position?

7. Differentiate between the direct method and the indirect method by discussing each method.

8. Pam Larsen Company reported net income of $3.5 million in 1994. Depreciation for the year was $520,000, accounts receivable increased $350,000, and accounts payable increased $500,000. Compute net cash flow from operating activities using the indirect method.

9. Karen Fior Ltd. reported sales on an accrual basis of $100,000. If accounts receivable increased $30,000 and the allowance for doubtful accounts increased $12,000 after a write-off of $8,000, compute cash sales.

10. Your roommate is puzzled. During the last year, the company in which he/she is a shareholder reported a net loss of $654,127, yet its cash increased $324,585 during the same period of time. Explain to your roommate how this situation could occur.

11. The board of directors of Linda Mitchell Corp. declared cash dividends of $260,000 during the

current year. If dividends payable was $81,000 at the beginning of the year and $70,000 at the end of the year, how much cash was paid in dividends during the year?

12. Kathy Graham Ltd. reported sales of $2 million for 1994. Accounts receivable decreased $308,000 and accounts payable increased $200,000. Compute cash sales, assuming that the receivable and payable transactions related to operations.

13. The net income for Ray Knopka Company for 1994 was $320,000. During 1994, depreciation on plant assets was $90,000, amortization of goodwill was $40,000, and the company incurred a loss on sale of plant assets of $25,000. Compute net cash flow from operating activities.

14. Each of the following items must be considered in preparing a statement of changes in financial position for Bud Jorgensen Inc. for the year ended December 31, 1994. State where it is to be shown in the statement, if at all.
    (a) Plant assets that 6½ years before had cost $20,000 and were being depreciated on a straight-line basis over 10 years, with no estimated residual value, were sold for $6,000.
    (b) During the year, 10,000 common shares were issued for $40 per share.
    (c) Uncollectible accounts receivable in the amount of $22,000 were written off against the Allowance for Doubtful Accounts.
    (d) The company sustained a net loss for the year of $50,000. Depreciation amounted to $22,000 and a gain of $7,000 was realized on the sale of equity securities (noncurrent) for $38,000 cash.

15. Classify the following items as (1) operating—add to net income, (2) operating—deduct from net income, (3) investing, (4) financing, or (5) significant noncash investing and financing activities.

    (a) Purchase of equipment.
    (b) Redemption of bonds.
    (c) Sale of building.
    (d) Depreciation.
    (e) Exchange of equipment for furniture.
    (f) Issuance of shares.
    (g) Amortization of intangible assets.
    (h) Purchase of treasury shares.
    (i) Issuance of bonds for land.
    (j) Payment of dividends.
    (k) Increase in interest receivable on notes receivable.
    (l) Pension expense exceeds amount funded.

16. Heather Remmers and Julie Countryman were discussing the presentation format of the statement of changes in financial position of Amy Boardman's Co. The amount of $200,000 appeared under the section headed "Investing Activities" as a purchase of land and a similar amount appeared under "Financing Activities" as an issuance of shares for land. Give three other examples of significant noncash transactions that would be reported in the statement of changes in financial position.

17. During 1994, Tillie Reichenbacher Company redeemed $2,000,000 of bonds payable for $1,700,000 cash. Indicate how the transaction would be reported on a statement of changes in financial position, if at all.

18. What are some of the arguments in favour of using the indirect (reconciliation method) as opposed to the direct method for reporting a statement of changes in financial position?

19. Why is it desirable to use a work sheet when preparing a statement of changes in financial position? Is a work sheet required to prepare a statement of changes in financial position?

20. Of what use is the statement of changes in financial position?

———— CASES ————

C23-1 **(ANALYSIS OF IMPROPER SCFP)**   The following statement was prepared by Charlie Hodgins Corporation's accountant.

Charlie Hodgins Corporation
Statement of Sources and Application of Cash
for the Year Ended September 30, 1994

Sources of cash
    Net income $ 85,000

(Continued)

Depreciation and depletion	70,000
Increase in long-term debt	189,000
Common shares issued under employee option plans	16,000
Changes in current receivables and inventories, less current liabilities (excluding current maturities of long-term debt)	14,000
	$374,000
Application of cash	
Cash dividends	$ 50,000
Expenditure for property, plant, and equipment	224,000
Investments and other uses	20,000
Change in cash	80,000
	$374,000

The following additional information relating to Charlie Hodgins Corporation is available for the year ended September 30, 1994:

1. The corporation received $16,000 in cash from its employee stock option plans, and wage and salary expense attributable to the option plans was an additional $22,000.

2.

Expenditures for property, plant, and equipment	$250,000
Proceeds from retirements of property, plant, and equipment	26,000
Net expenditures	$224,000

3. A stock dividend of 10,000 common shares was distributed to common shareholders on April 1, 1994 when the per-share market price was $7.

4. On July 1, 1994, when its market price was $6 per share, 16,000 Hodgins Corporation common shares were issued in exchange for 4,000 preferred shares.

5.

Depreciation expense	$ 65,000
Depletion expense	5,000
	$ 70,000

6.

Increase in long-term debt	$620,000
Retirement of debt	431,000
Net increase	$189,000

Instructions

(a) In general, what are the objectives of a statement of the type shown above for the Charlie Hodgins Corporation? Explain.

(b) Identify the weaknesses in the form or format of the Charlie Hodgins Corporation's statement of changes in financial position without reference to the additional information.

(c) For each of the six items of additional information for the statement of changes in financial position, indicate the preferred treatment and explain why the suggested treatment is preferable.

(AICPA adapted)

(SCFP THEORY AND ANALYSIS OF IMPROPER SCFP) Bev Brennan and Walter Mennear are examining the following statement of changes in financial position for Schewe's Clothing Store, showing its first year in operations.   **C23-2**

Schewe's Clothing Store

Statement of Changes in Financial Position

for the Year Ended January 31, 1994

Sources of cash	
From sales of merchandise	$362,000
From sale of share capital	440,000
From sale of investment	80,000
From depreciation	70,000
From issuance of note for truck	30,000
From interest on investments	8,000
Total sources of cash	$990,000
Uses of cash	
For purchase of fixtures and equipment	$340,000
For merchandise purchased for resale	253,000
For operating expenses (including depreciation)	160,000
For purchase of investment	85,000
For purchase of truck by issuance of note	30,000
For purchase of treasury shares	10,000
For interest on note	3,000
Total uses of cash	$881,000
Net increase in cash	$109,000

Bev claims that Schewe's statement of changes in financial position is an excellent portrayal of a superb first year, with cash increasing $109,000. Walter replies that it was not a superb year, that the year was an operating failure, that the statement was incorrectly presented, and that $109,000 is not the actual increase in cash.

Instructions

(a) With whom do you agree, Bev or Walter? Explain your position.

(b) Using the data provided, prepare a statement of changes in financial position in proper form. The only noncash items in the income statement are depreciation and the loss from the sale of the investment.

C23-3 (SCFP THEORY AND ANALYSIS OF TRANSACTIONS)   LaGrange Company is a young and growing producer of electronic measuring instruments and technical equipment. You have been retained by LaGrange as advisor in the preparation of a statement of changes in financial position using the indirect method. For the fiscal year ended October 31, 1994, you have obtained the following information concerning certain events and transactions of LaGrange:

1. The amount of reported earnings for the fiscal year was $800,000, which included a deduction for an extraordinary loss of $85,000 (see item 5).

2. Depreciation expense of $325,000 was included in the earnings statement.

3. Uncollectible accounts receivable of $40,000 were written off against the allowance for doubtful accounts. Also, $48,000 of bad debts expense was included in determining income for the fiscal year, and the same amount was added to the allowance for doubtful accounts.

4. A gain of $6,000 was realized on the sale of a machine; it originally cost $75,000, of which $30,000 was undepreciated on the date of sale.

5. On April 1, 1994, lightning caused an uninsured inventory loss of $85,000 ($140,000 loss, less reduction in income taxes of $55,000). This extraordinary loss was included in determining income as indicated in item 1.

6. On July 3, 1994, building and land were purchased for $600,000; LaGrange gave a payment of $75,000 cash, $200,000 market value of its unissued common shares, and a $325,000 mortgage.

7. On August 3, 1994, $800,000 face value of LaGrange's 10% convertible debentures were converted into no-par value common shares. The bonds were originally issued at face value.

Instructions

Explain whether each of the seven numbered items above is a source or use of cash and explain how it should be disclosed in LaGrange's statement of changes in financial position for the fiscal year ended October 31, 1994. If any item is neither a source nor a use of cash, explain why it is not and indicate the disclosure, if any, that should be made of the item in LaGrange's statement of changes in financial position for the fiscal year ended October 31, 1994.

(ANALYSIS OF TRANSACTIONS' EFFECT ON SCFP)   Each of the following items must be considered **C23-4** in preparing a statement of changes in financial position for Adams Fashions Inc. for the year ended December 31, 1994:

1. Fixed assets that 6½ years before had cost $20,000 and were being depreciated on a 10-year basis, with no estimated residual value, were sold for $6,250.

2. During the year, goodwill of $10,000 was completely written off to expense.

3. During the year, 500 common shares were issued for $32 per share.

4. The company sustained a net loss for the year of $2,100. Depreciation amounted to $2,000 and patent amortization was $400.

5. An appropriation for contingencies in the amount of $80,000 was created by a charge against Retained Earnings.

6. Uncollectible accounts receivable in the amount of $2,000 were written off against the Allowance for Doubtful Accounts.

7. Investments (noncurrent) that cost $12,000 when purchased four years earlier were sold for $11,000.

8. Bonds payable with a par value of $24,000 on which there was an unamortized bond premium of $2,000 were redeemed at 103. The gain was credited to income.

Instructions

For each item, state where it is to be shown in the statement and then illustrate how you would present the necessary information, including the amount. Consider each item to be independent of the others. Assume that correct entries were made for all transactions as they took place.

(PURPOSE AND ELEMENTS OF SCFP)   In 1974, the CICA's Accounting Research Committee issued a **C23-5** replacement to *Handbook* Section 1540 on the Statement of Source and Application of Funds. The new section expanded the funds statement to include noncash exchanges (e.g., issue of common shares for plant and equipment). The statement could show either changes in cash, working capital, or quick assets.

In 1985, Section 1540 was revised again. This revision required that changes in cash and cash equivalents be reported. In addition, the statement should present information for operating activities, financing activities, and investing activities.

Instructions

(a) By citing problems inherent in the statement of changes in financial position based on the source and application of funds, explain at least three reasons for developing the statement of cash flows.

(b) Explain the purposes of the statement of changes in financial position.

(c) List and describe the three categories of activities that must be reported in the statement of changes in financial position.

(d) Identify and describe the two methods that are allowed for reporting cash flows from operations.

(e) Describe the financial statement presentation of noncash investing and financing transactions. Include in your description an example of a noncash investing and financing transaction.

——————— EXERCISES ———————

E23-1 **(SCFP: INDIRECT AND DIRECT METHODS)** Condensed financial data of Navajo Company for 1993 and 1994 are presented below.

Navajo Company
Comparative Balance Sheet Data
as of December 31, 1994 and 1993

	1994	1993
Cash	$1,700	$1,150
Receivables	1,750	1,300
Inventory	1,650	1,900
Plant assets	1,950	1,700
Accumulated depreciation	(1,200)	(1,150)
Long-term investments	1,300	1,400
	$7,150	$6,300
Accounts payable	$1,200	$ 900
Accrued liabilities	400	300
Bonds payable	1,200	1,500
Share capital	1,900	1,700
Retained earnings	2,450	1,900
	$7,150	$6,300

Navajo Company
Income Statement
for the Year Ended December 31, 1994

Sales		$6,900
Cost of goods sold		4,700
Gross margin		2,200
Operating expenses:		
Selling expense	$450	
Administrative expense	650	

(Continued)

Depreciation expense	50	1,150
Net income		1,050
Cash dividends		500
Income retained in business		$ 550

Additional Information

There were no gains or losses in any noncurrent transactions during 1994.

Instructions

(a) Prepare a statement of changes in financial position using the indirect method.

(b) Prepare a statement of changes in financial position using the direct method (do not prepare the reconciliation schedule).

(SCFP: INDIRECT AND DIRECT METHODS) Condensed financial data of Yuma Company for the years **E23-2** ended December 31, 1994 and December 31, 1993 are presented below.

Yuma Company
Comparative Position Statement Data
as of December 31, 1994 and 1993

	1994	1993
Cash	$160,800	$ 38,400
Receivables	123,200	49,000
Inventories	112,500	61,900
Investments (long term)	90,000	97,000
Plant assets	240,000	212,500
	$726,500	$458,800
Accounts payable	$100,000	$ 62,200
Mortgage payable	50,000	80,000
Accumulated depreciation	30,000	52,000
Common shares	175,000	131,100
Retained earnings	371,500	133,500
	$726,500	$458,800

Yuma Company
Income Statement
for the Year Ended December 31, 1994

Sales	$440,000	
Interest and other revenue	43,000	$483,000
Less:		
Cost of goods sold	130,000	
Selling and administrative expenses	10,000	
Depreciation	42,000	
Income taxes	25,000	

(Continued)

Interest charges	6,000	
Loss on sale of plant assets	12,000	225,000
Net income		258,000
Cash dividends		20,000
Income retained in business		$238,000

Additional Information

New plant assets costing $110,000 were purchased during the year. Investments were sold at book value.

Instructions

(a) Prepare a statement of changes in financial position using the indirect method.

(b) Prepare a statement of changes in financial position using the direct method (do not prepare a reconciliation schedule).

E23-3 **(SCFP: INDIRECT AND DIRECT METHODS)**   Taos Limited, a greeting card company, had the following statements prepared as of December 31, 1994.

Taos Limited
Comparative Balance Sheet
as of December 31, 1994 and 1993

	12/31/94	12/31/93
Cash and short-term investments	$ 41,000	$ 27,000
Accounts receivable	56,000	49,000
Inventories	40,000	60,000
Prepaid rent	5,000	4,000
Printing equipment	160,000	130,000
Accumulated depreciation—equipment	(35,000)	(25,000)
Goodwill	46,000	50,000
Total assets	$313,000	$295,000
Accounts payable	$ 62,000	$ 50,000
Income taxes payable	4,000	5,000
Wages payable	8,000	4,000
Long-term loans payable	60,000	70,000
Common shares	130,000	130,000
Retained earnings	49,000	36,000
Total liabilities and equity	$313,000	$295,000

Taos Limited
Income Statement
for the Year Ending December 31, 1994

Sales	$338,150
Cost of goods sold	175,000

(Continued)

Gross margin	163,150
Operating expenses	120,000
Operating income	43,150
Interest expense	9,400
Income before tax	33,750
Income tax expense	10,750
Net income	$ 23,000

Additional Information

1. Dividends in the amount of $10,000 were declared and paid during 1994.

2. Depreciation expense and amortization expense are included in operating expenses.

Instructions

(a) Prepare a statement of changes in financial position using the direct method (do not prepare a reconciliation schedule).

(b) Prepare a statement of changes in financial position using the indirect method.

(SCFP: INDIRECT AND DIRECT METHODS)   Shoshoni Inc. had the following information available at **E23-4** the end of 1994.

Shoshoni Inc.
Comparative Balance Sheet
as of December 31, 1994 and 1993

	12/31/94	12/31/93
Cash	$ 78,000	$ 40,000
Accounts receivable	84,000	136,000
Inventory	106,000	127,000
Prepaid expenses	6,000	9,000
Land	160,000	90,000
Building	750,000	750,000
Accumulated depreciation—building	(235,000)	(200,000)
Equipment	516,000	436,000
Accumulated depreciation—equipment	(146,000)	(110,000)
Total assets	$1,319,000	$1,278,000
Accounts payable	$ 149,600	$ 112,000
Accrued liabilities	44,000	36,000
Income taxes payable	–0–	12,000
Interest payable	9,000	6,000
Long-term notes payable	170,000	175,000
Common shares	800,000	730,000
Retained earnings	146,400	207,000
Total liabilities and equity	$1,319,000	$1,278,000

Shoshoni Inc.
Income Statement
for the Year Ended December 31, 1994

Sales	$570,000
Cost of goods sold	(317,600)
Gross margin	252,400
Operating expenses	(296,000)
Operating income	(43,600)
Financial:	
Interest revenue	3,000
Interest expense	(20,000)
Net loss	$(60,600)

Depreciation expense is included in operating expenses.

Instructions

(a) Prepare a statement of changes in financial position using the direct method (do not prepare a reconciliation schedule).

(b) Prepare a statement of changes in financial position using the indirect method.

E23-5 **(SCFP: INDIRECT METHOD)** Presented below are data taken from the records of Klamath Company.

	December 31, 1994	December 31, 1993
Cash	$ 15,000	$ 8,000
Current assets other than cash	81,000	55,000
Long-term investments	10,000	58,000
Plant assets	370,000	215,000
	$476,000	$336,000
Accumulated depreciation	$ 20,000	$ 40,000
Current liabilities	35,000	22,000
Bonds payable	80,000	–0–
Share capital	254,000	254,000
Donated capital	31,000	–0–
Retained earnings	56,000	20,000
	$476,000	$336,000

Additional Information

1. Securities carried at a cost of $48,000 on December 31, 1993 were sold in 1994 for $39,000. The loss was incorrectly charged directly to Retained Earnings. *It would have washed out by year end so not relevant.*

2. Plant assets that cost $50,000 and were 80% depreciated were sold during 1994 for $8,000. The loss was incorrectly charged directly to Retained Earnings. *Assume E.O.*

3. Net income as reported on the income statement for the year was $67,000. *56,000 (errors have been corrected)*

4. Dividends paid amounted to $20,000.

5. Depreciation charged for the year was $20,000.

6. Land was donated to Klamath Company by the city. The land was worth $31,000. (Assume credit to Donated Capital is correct.)

Instructions

Prepare a statement of changes in financial position for the year 1994 (indirect method).

(SCFP: INDIRECT AND DIRECT METHODS) Comparative balance sheets at December 31, 1994 and **E23-6** 1993 for Rick Folkerson's Pottery are presented below.

	1994	1993
Cash	$ 70,000	$ 48,000
Receivables	58,000	66,000
Inventory	100,000	112,000
Prepaid expenses	9,000	8,000
Plant assets	314,000	240,000
Accumulated depreciation	(66,000)	(41,000)
Patents	30,000	40,000
	$515,000	$473,000
Accounts payable	$ 85,000	$105,000
Accrued liabilities	65,000	63,000
Mortgage payable	—	70,000
Preferred shares	128,000	—
Common shares	200,000	200,000
Retained earnings	37,000	35,000
	$515,000	$473,000

Additional Information

1. The only entries in the Retained Earnings account are for dividends paid in the amount of $20,000 and for the net income for the year.

2. The income statement for 1994 is as follows:

Sales	$124,000
Cost of sales	84,000
Gross profit	40,000
Operating expenses	18,000
Net income	$ 22,000

3. The only entry in the Accumulated Depreciation account is the depreciation expense for the period. Depreciation and patent amortization are included in cost of sales in the income statement.

Instructions

From the information above, prepare a statement of changes in financial position:

(a) Use the indirect method.

(b) Use the direct method.

E23-7   **(SCFP: INDIRECT METHOD AND BALANCE SHEET)**   Kitimat Inc. had the following condensed balance sheet at the end of operations for 1993.

Kitimat Inc.

Balance Sheet

December 31, 1993

Cash	$ 8,500	Current liabilities	$ 15,000
Current assets other than cash	29,000	Long-term notes payable	25,500
Investments	20,000	Bonds payable	25,000
Plant assets (net)	67,500	Share capital	75,000
Land	40,000	Retained earnings	24,500
	$165,000		$165,000

During 1994, the following occurred:

1. A tract of land was purchased for $9,000.

2. Bonds payable in the amount of $15,000 were retired at par.

3. An additional $10,000 in common shares was issued.

4. Dividends totalling $11,000 were paid to shareholders.

5. Net income for 1994 was $35,250 after allowing depreciation of $11,250.

6. Land was purchased through the issuance of $25,000 in bonds.

7. Kitimat Inc. sold part of its investment portfolio (noncurrent) for $12,875. This transaction resulted in a gain of $875 for the firm. The company often sells and buys securities of this nature.

8. Both current assets (other than cash) and current liabilities remained at the same amount.

Instructions

(a) Prepare a statement of changes in financial position for 1994 using the indirect method.

(b) Prepare the condensed balance sheet for Kitimat Inc. as it would appear at December 31, 1994.

E23-8   **(WORK-SHEET ANALYSIS OF SELECTED ACCOUNTS)**   The 1994 accounts below appear in the ledger of Algonquin Company.

	Retained Earnings	Dr.	Cr.	Bal.
Jan. 1	Credit Balance			$ 42,000
Aug. 15	Dividends (Cash)	$18,000		24,000
Dec. 31	Net Income for 1994		$35,000	59,000

	Machinery	Dr.	Cr.	Bal.
Jan. 1	Debit Balance			$140,000
Aug. 3	Purchase of Machinery	$62,000		202,000

(Continued)

		Dr.	Cr.	Bal.
Sept. 10	Cost of Machinery Constructed	48,000		250,000
Nov. 15	Machinery Sold		$56,000	194,000

	Accumulated Depreciation— Machinery	Dr.	Cr.	Bal.
Jan. 1	Credit Balance			$ 84,000
Apr. 8	Extraordinary Repairs	$21,000		63,000
Nov. 15	Accumulated Depreciation on Machinery Sold	25,200		37,800
Dec. 31	Depreciation for 1994		$18,000	55,800

Instructions

From the information given, prepare entries in journal form for all adjustments that should be made on a work sheet for a statement of changes in financial position. The loss on sale of equipment (Nov. 15) was $16,800.

(WORK-SHEET ANALYSIS OF SELECTED TRANSACTIONS) The transactions below took place dur- **E23-9** ing the year 1994:

1. Convertible bonds payable of a par (and market) value of $300,000 were exchanged for unissued common shares with a market value of $300,000.

2. The net income for the year was $90,000.

3. Depreciation charged on the building was $30,000.

4. Organization costs in the amount of $10,000 were written off during the year as a charge to expense.

5. Some old office equipment was traded in on the purchase of some dissimilar office equipment and the following entry was made:

Office Equipment	5,000	
Accum. Depreciation—Office Equipment	3,000	
Office Equipment		4,000
Cash		3,400
Gain on Disposal of Plant Assets		600

The gain on disposal of plant assets was credited to current operations as ordinary income.

6. Dividends in the amount of $20,000 were declared. They are payable in January of next year.

7. The Appropriations for Bonded Indebtedness in the amount of $300,000 was returned to Retained Earnings during the year because the bonds were retired during the year.

Instructions

Show by journal entries the adjustments that would be made on a work sheet for a statement of changes in financial position.

(WORK-SHEET PREPARATION) Following is the comparative balance sheet for Waubonsee Corporation. **E23-10**

	Dec. 31, 1994	Dec. 31, 1993
Cash	$ 15,500	$ 20,000
Short-term investments	26,000	20,000
Accounts receivable	43,000	45,000
Allowance for doubtful accounts	(1,800)	(2,000)
Prepaid expenses	4,200	2,500
Inventories	81,500	65,000
Land	50,000	50,000
Buildings	125,000	73,500
Accumulated depreciation—buildings	(30,000)	(23,000)
Equipment	53,000	47,000
Accumulated depreciation—equipment	(19,000)	(16,500)
Delivery equipment	39,000	39,000
Accumulated depreciation—delivery equipment	(22,000)	(20,500)
Patents	15,000	–0–
	$379,400	$300,000
Accounts payable	$ 26,000	$ 16,000
Short-term notes payable	4,000	6,000
Accrued payables	3,000	5,000
Mortgage payable	73,000	53,000
Bonds payable	50,000	65,000
Capital shares	150,000	103,500
Retained earnings	73,400	51,500
	$379,400	$300,000

Dividends in the amount of $35,000 were declared and paid in 1994.

Instructions

From this information, prepare a work sheet for a statement of changes in financial position. Make reasonable assumptions as appropriate. (**Hint**: Combine cash, short-term investments, and short-term notes payable into one account called Cash and Cash Equivalents.)

E23-11 **(SCFP: INDIRECT AND DIRECT METHODS)**   Kishwaukee Co. has recently decided to go public and has hired you as its independent public accountant. The enterprise is anxious to have a statement of changes in financial position prepared. Financial statements of Kishwaukee Co. for 1994 and 1993 are provided below.

Comparative Balance Sheets as of:

		12/31/94		12/31/93
Cash		$ 25,000		$ 13,000
Accounts receivable		29,000		14,000
Inventory		26,000		35,000
Property, plant, and equipment	$60,000		$78,000	
Less accumulated depreciation	(20,000)	40,000	(24,000)	54,000
		$120,000		$116,000

(Continued)

Accounts payable	$ 34,000	$ 23,000
Short-term notes payable (trade)	25,000	30,000
Bonds payable	37,000	33,000
Common shares	6,000	14,000
Retained earnings	18,000	16,000
	$120,000	$116,000

Income Statement
for the Year Ended December 31, 1994

Sales		$220,000
Cost of sales		170,000
Gross profit		50,000
Selling expenses	$ 18,000	
Administrative expenses	16,000	34,000
Income from operations		16,000
Interest expense		5,000
Income before taxes		11,000
Income taxes		3,300
Net income		$ 7,700

The following additional data were provided:

1. Dividends for the year 1994 were $2,200.

2. During the year, equipment was sold for $8,500. This equipment cost $18,000 originally and had a book value of $12,000 at the time of sale. The loss on the sale was incorrectly charged to Retained Earnings.

3. All depreciation expense is in the selling expense category.

Instructions

Prepare a statement of changes in financial position using (a) the indirect method and (b) the direct method. All sales and purchases are on account.

(SCHEDULE OF NET CASH FLOW FROM OPERATING ACTIVITIES: INDIRECT METHOD) E23-12

Clarence Hawkins Ltd. reported $150,000 of net income for 1994. The accountant, in preparing the statement of changes in financial position, noted several items that might affect cash flows from operating activities. These items are listed below:

1. During 1994, Hawkins purchased 100 treasury shares at a cost of $20 per share. These shares were then resold at $25 per share.

2. During 1994, Hawkins sold 100 shares of IBM common at $200 per share. The acquisition cost of these shares was $150 per share. This investment was shown on Hawkins' December 31, 1993 balance sheet as a noncurrent asset at cost.

3. During 1994, Hawkins changed from the straight-line method to the double-declining balance method of depreciation for its machinery. The debit to the Retained Earnings account was $14,000, net of tax.

4. During 1994, Hawkins revised its estimate for bad debts. Before 1994, Hawkins' bad debts expense was 1% of its net sales. In 1994, this percentage was increased to 2%. Net sales for 1994 were $500,000, and net accounts receivable decreased by $12,000 during 1994.

5. During 1994, Hawkins issued 500 of its no-par common shares for a patent. The market value of the shares on the date of the transaction was $23 per share.

6. Depreciation expense for 1994 is $38,000.

7. Hawkins Co. holds 40% of the Seabrook Company's common shares as a long-term investment. Seabrook Company reported $26,000 of net income for 1994.

8. Seabrook Company paid a total of $2,000 of cash dividends in 1994.

9. A comparison of Hawkins' December 31, 1993 and December 31, 1994 balance sheets indicates that the credit balance in Deferred Income Tax (classified as a long-term liability) decreased $4,000.

10. During 1994, Hawkins declared a 10% stock dividend. One thousand no-par value common shares were distributed. The market price at date of issuance was $20 per share.

Instructions

Prepare a schedule that shows net cash flow from operating activities using the indirect method. Assume that no items other than those listed above affected the computation of 1994 net cash flow from operating activities.

E23-13 **(SCFP: DIRECT METHOD)**   Somonauk Company has not yet prepared a formal statement of changes in financial position for the 1994 fiscal year. Comparative statements of financial position as of December 31, 1993 and 1994, and a statement of income and retained earnings for the year ended December 31, 1994 are presented below.

Somonauk Company
Statement of Income and Retained Earnings
Year Ended December 31, 1994
($000 omitted)

Sales		$3,760
Expenses		
Cost of goods sold	$1,401	
Salaries and benefits	725	
Heat, light, and power	75	
Depreciation	80	
Property taxes	18	
Patent amortization	25	
Miscellaneous expense	10	
Interest	30	2,364
Income before income taxes		1,396
Income taxes		556
Net income		840
Retained earnings—Jan. 1, 1994		310
		1,150
Stock dividend declared and issued		600
Retained earnings—Dec. 31, 1994		$ 550

Somonauk Company
Statement of Financial Position
December 31
($000 omitted)

Assets	1994	1993
Current assets		
Cash	$ 383	$ 150
Accounts receivable	740	500
Inventory	720	560
Total current assets	1,843	1,210
Long-term assets		
Land	142	70
Buildings and equipment	940	600
Accumulated depreciation	(200)	(120)
Patents (less amortization)	105	130
Total long-term assets	987	680
Total assets	$2,830	$1,890
Liabilities and Shareholders' Equity		
Current liabilities		
Accounts payable	$ 740	$ 660
Taxes payable	40	20
Total current liabilities	780	680
Term notes payable—due 1998	200	200
Total liabilities	980	880
Shareholders' equity		
Common shares	1,300	700
Retained earnings	550	310
Total shareholders' equity	1,850	1,010
Total liabilities and shareholders' equity	$2,830	$1,890

Instructions

Prepare a statement of changes in financial position that reconciles the changes in cash balance. Use the direct method. Changes in accounts receivable relate to sales and cost of sales. Taxes Payable relates only to income taxes.

(CMA adapted)

——————— PROBLEMS ———————

(SCFP: INDIRECT METHOD)   The manager of Blackhawk Limited has reviewed the annual financial statements for the year 1994 and is unable to determine from a reading of the balance sheet the reasons for the cash flows during the year. You are given the following comparative balance sheet information of Blackhawk Limited.

P23-1

	12/31/94	12/31/93	Increase (Decrease)
Land	$ 138,000	$ 218,000	$ (80,000)
Machinery	485,000	200,000	285,000
Tools	40,000	70,000	(30,000)
Bond investment	20,000	15,000	5,000
Inventories	157,000	207,000	(50,000)
Goodwill	–0–	14,000	(14,000)
Buildings	810,000	550,000	260,000
Accounts receivable	292,000	92,000	200,000
Notes receivable—trade	96,000	176,000	(80,000)
Cash in bank	–0–	8,000	(8,000)
Cash on hand	7,000	1,000	6,000
Unexpired insurance—machinery	700	1,400	(700)
Unamortized bond discount	2,000	2,500	(500)
	$2,047,700	$1,554,900	$ 492,800
Share capital	$ 900,000	$ 400,000	$ 500,000
Bonds payable	180,000	130,000	50,000
Accounts payable	36,000	32,000	4,000
Bank overdraft	3,000	–0–	3,000
Notes payable—trade	11,500	16,800	(5,300)
Accrued interest	9,000	6,000	3,000
Accrued taxes	4,000	3,000	1,000
Allowance for doubtful accounts	4,700	2,300	2,400
Accumulated depreciation	300,400	181,000	119,400
Retained earnings	599,100	783,800	(184,700)
	$2,047,700	$1,554,900	$ 492,800

You are advised that the following transactions took place during the year:

1. The income statement for the year 1994 was:

Sales (net)		$1,276,300
Operating charges:		
Material and supplies	$250,000	
Direct labour	210,000	
Manufacturing overhead	181,500	
Depreciation	158,900	
Selling expenses	245,000	
General expenses	230,000	
Interest expense (net)	15,000	
Unusual items:		
Write-off of goodwill	14,000	
Write-off of land	80,000	
Loss on machinery	6,600	1,391,000
Net loss		$ (114,700)

2. A 5% cash dividend was declared and paid on the outstanding shares at January 1, 1994.

3. There were no purchases or sales of tools. The cost of tools used is in Depreciation.

4. Common shares were issued during the year at $90.

5. Old machinery that cost $16,100 was scrapped and written off the books. Accumulated depreciation on such equipment was $9,500.

Instructions

Prepare a statement of changes in financial position. Use the indirect method. All sales and purchases of inventory are made on account.

(BALANCE SHEET; SCFP: INDIRECT METHOD; NET CASH FLOWS FROM OPERATING **P23-2** **ACTIVITIES: DIRECT METHOD)**   The balance sheet of Shabbona Limited at December 31, 1993 is as follows.

Shabbona Limited
Balance Sheet
December 31, 1993

Cash			$ 189,000
Receivables			258,000
Inventories			174,000
Prepaid expenses			28,000
Total current assets			649,000
Investments (long term)			102,000
Land		$ 46,000	
Buildings	$570,000		
Less accumulated depreciation	110,000	460,000	
Equipment	385,000		
Less accumulated depreciation	180,000	205,000	711,000
Patents			121,000
			$1,583,000
Accounts payable			$ 60,000
Notes payable			120,000
Taxes payable			188,000
Total current liabilities			368,000
Bonds payable			500,000
Preferred shares		$400,000	
Common shares		300,000	
Retained earnings		15,000	715,000
			$1,583,000

Shabbona Limited's management predicts the following transactions for 1994:

Sales (accrual basis)	$5,000,000
Payments for salaries, purchases, interest, taxes, etc. (cash basis)	4,500,000
Decrease in prepaid expenses	7,000
Increase in receivables	110,000
Increase in inventories	35,000

(Continued)

Depreciation:	
Buildings	55,000
Equipment	80,000
Patent amortization	11,000
Increase in accounts payable	25,000
Increase in taxes payable	90,000
Reduction in bonds payable	500,000
Sales of investments (all those held 12/31/93)	120,000
Issuance of common shares	100,000

Instructions

(a) Prepare a balance sheet as it will appear December 31, 1994 if all of the anticipated transactions work out as expected.

(b) Prepare a statement of changes in financial position for 1994, assuming that the expected 1994 transactions are all completed. Use the indirect method.

(c) Compute net cash flow from operating activities, using the direct method.

P23-3 **(CASH COMPUTATIONS; SCFP: INDIRECT METHOD; NET CASH FLOW FROM OPERATING ACTIVITIES: DIRECT METHOD)** The following financial data were furnished to you by Cree Limited:

1. A six-month note payable for $60,000 was issued toward the purchase of new equipment.

2. The long-term note payable requires the payment of $20,000 per year plus interest until paid.

3. Treasury shares were sold for $4,500 more than cost.

4. All dividends were paid by cash.

5. All purchases and sales were on account.

6. The sinking fund will be used to retire the long-term bonds.

7. Equipment with an original cost of $54,000 was sold for $32,000.

8. Selling and General Expenses includes the following expenses:

Expired insurance	$ 4,000
Building depreciation	10,000
Equipment depreciation	15,500
Bad debts expense	12,000
Interest expense	18,000

Cree Limited
Comparative Trial Balances
at Beginning and End of Fiscal Year Ended October 31, 1994

	October 31, 1994	Increase	Decrease	November 1, 1993
Cash	$ 336,000	$221,000		$115,000
Accounts receivable	146,000	46,000		100,000
Inventories	291,000		$ 9,000	300,000
Unexpired insurance	7,000	3,000		4,000

(Continued)

Long-term investments at cost	10,000		30,000	40,000
Sinking fund	90,000	10,000		80,000
Land and building	195,000			195,000
Equipment	220,000	100,000		120,000
Discount on bonds payable	8,400		2,400	10,800
Treasury shares at cost	5,600		4,600	10,200
Cost of goods sold	420,000			
Selling and general expense	153,000			
Income tax	34,000			
Loss on sale of equipment	12,000			
Total debits	$1,928,000			$975,000
Allowance for doubtful accounts	$ 10,000	$ 5,000		$ 5,000
Accumulated depreciation—building	30,000	10,000		20,000
Accumulated depreciation—equipment	33,000	5,500		27,500
Accounts payable	130,000	25,000		105,000
Accrued expenses payable	20,000	5,000		15,000
Taxes payable	33,000	23,000		10,000
Unearned revenue	6,000		9,000	15,000
Note payable—long-term	40,000		20,000	60,000
Bonds payable—long-term	250,000			250,000
Share capital—common	401,000	125,500		275,500
Appropriation for sinking fund	90,000	10,000		80,000
Unappropriated retained earnings	90,000		22,000	112,000
Sales	753,000			
Gain on sale of investments (ordinary)	42,000			
Total credits	$1,928,000			$975,000

Forget chapter content & calculate amounts required

Instructions

(a) Prepare schedules computing:

    1. Collections of accounts receivable.
    2. Payments of accounts payable.

(b) Prepare a statement of changes in financial position for Cree Limited using the indirect method.

(c) Prepare a cash flow from the operating activities section, using the direct method.

(SCFP: DIRECT METHOD) Simonole Company had the following information available at the end **P23-4** of 1994.

Simonole Company
Comparative Balance Sheet
as of 12/31/94 and 12/31/93

	12/31/94	12/31/93
Cash and term deposits	$ 35,000	$ 34,000

(Continued)

Accounts receivable	14,500	12,950
Inventory	42,000	35,000
Prepaid rent	3,000	12,000
Prepaid insurance	2,100	900
Office supplies	1,000	750
Land	125,000	175,000
Building	350,000	350,000
Accumulated depreciation	(105,000)	(87,500)
Equipment	528,000	400,000
Accumulated depreciation	(130,000)	(112,000)
Patent	45,000	50,000
Total assets	$910,600	$871,100
Accounts payable	$ 37,000	$ 42,000
Taxes payable	5,000	4,000
Wages payable	3,500	3,000
Long-term notes payable	60,000	70,000
Bonds payable	400,000	400,000
Premium on bonds payable	20,303	25,853
Common shares	261,500	237,500
Retained earnings	123,297	88,747
Total liabilities and equity	$910,600	$871,100

Simonole Company

Income Statement

for the Year Ended December 31, 1994

Sales revenue		$1,159,248
Cost of goods sold		(747,915)
Gross margin		411,333
Operating expenses		
Selling expenses	$ 79,200	
Administrative expenses	156,700	
Depreciation/amortization expense	40,500	
Total operating expenses		(276,400)
Income from operations		134,933
Other revenues/expenses		
Gain on sale of land	12,000	
Dividend revenue	6,400	
Interest expense	(51,750)	(33,350)
Income before taxes		101,583
Income tax expense (40%)		(39,033)
Net income		62,550
Dividends to common shareholders		(28,000)
To retained earnings		$ 34,550

Instructions

Prepare a statement of changes in financial position for Simonole Company using the direct method, accompanied by a reconciliation schedule.

(SCFP: INDIRECT METHOD) The comparative balance sheets for Seneca Limited show the following **P23-5** information.

	December 31	
	1994	1993
Cash	$ 38,500	$13,000
Accounts receivable	12,250	10,000
Inventory	12,000	9,000
Investments, long term	–0–	3,000
Building	–0–	29,750
Equipment	40,000	20,000
Patent	5,000	6,250
Totals	$107,750	$91,000
Allowance for doubtful accounts	$ 3,000	$ 4,500
Accumulated depreciation on equipment	2,000	4,500
Accumulated depreciation on building	–0–	6,000
Accounts payable	5,000	3,000
Dividends payable	–0–	6,000
Notes payable, short-term (nontrade)	3,000	4,000
Long-term notes payable	31,000	25,000
Common shares	43,000	33,000
Retained earnings	20,750	5,000
	$107,750	$91,000

Additional data related to 1994 are as follows:

1. Equipment that had cost $11,000 and was 40% depreciated at time of disposal was sold for $2,500.

2. $10,000 of the long-term note payable was paid by issuing common shares.

3. The only cash dividends paid were $6,000.

4. On January 1, 1994, the building was completely destroyed by a flood. Insurance proceeds on the building were $37,000.

5. Investments (long term) were sold at $2,500 above their cost.

6. Cash of $15,000 was paid for the acquisition of equipment.

7. A long-term note for $16,000 was issued for the acquisition of equipment.

8. Interest of $2,000 and income taxes of $5,000 were paid in cash.

Instructions

Prepare a statement of changes in financial position. Flood damage is unusual and infrequent in that part of the country. (**Hint**: The short-term note is a cash equivalent.)

(SCFP: INDIRECT AND DIRECT METHODS) Sauk Winches & Hoists Inc. had the following infor- **P23-6** mation available at the end of 1994.

Sauk Winches & Hoists Inc.
Comparative Balance Sheet
as of December 31, 1994 and 1993

	12/31/94	12/31/93
Cash	$ 46,000	$ 30,000
Accounts receivable	340,000	296,000
Short-term investments	350,000	325,000
Prepaid insurance	16,000	22,000
Merchandise inventory	400,000	350,000
Office supplies	4,000	7,000
Long-term investments (equity)	775,000	700,000
Land	650,000	500,000
Building	1,300,000	1,300,000
Accumulated depreciation—building	(400,000)	(360,000)
Equipment	500,000	550,000
Accumulated depreciation—equipment	(155,000)	(135,000)
Goodwill	63,000	65,000
Total assets	$3,889,000	$3,650,000
Accounts payable	$ 95,000	$ 70,000
Taxes payable	26,000	15,000
Accrued liabilities	47,000	40,000
Dividends payable	–0–	80,000
Long-term notes payable	45,000	50,000
Bonds payable	1,000,000	1,000,000
Discount on bonds payable	(50,750)	(64,630)
Preferred shares	720,000	600,000
Common shares	1,150,000	1,150,000
Retained earnings	876,750	749,630
Treasury shares (common, at cost)	(20,000)	(40,000)
Total liabilities and equity	$3,889,000	$3,650,000

Sauk Winches & Hoists Inc.
Income Statement
for the Year Ended December 31, 1994

Sales revenue		$1,007,500
Cost of goods sold		403,000
Gross profit		604,500
Selling/administrative expenses		222,000
Income from operations		382,500
Other revenues/expenses		
Long-term investment revenue	$115,000	
Short-term investment dividend	15,000	
Gain on sale of equipment	15,000	145,000
Interest expense		(99,000)

(Continued)

Income before taxes	428,500
Income tax expense	(154,000)
Net income	274,500
Dividends (current year)	(150,000)
Increase in retained earnings	$ 124,500

Additional Information

1. In early January, equipment with a book value of $45,000 was sold for a gain.

2. Long-term investments are carried under the equity method. Sauk's share of investee income totalled $115,000 in 1994. Sauk received dividends from its long-term investments totalling $40,000 during 1994.

Instructions

(a) Prepare a statement of changes in financial position using the direct method.

(b) Prepare a statement of changes in financial position using the indirect method.

(SCFP: INDIRECT METHOD) You have completed the field work in connection with your audit of Susquehanna Limited for the year ended December 31, 1994. The following schedule shows the balance sheet accounts at the beginning and end of the year.   **P23-7**

	Dec. 31, 1994	Dec. 31, 1993	Increase or (Decrease)
Cash	$ 267,100	$ 298,000	$ (30,900)
Accounts receivable	499,424	353,000	146,424
Inventory	731,700	610,000	121,700
Prepaid expenses	12,000	8,000	4,000
Investment in subsidiary	114,000	–0–	114,000
Cash surrender value of life insurance	2,304	1,800	504
Machinery	187,000	190,000	(3,000)
Buildings	545,200	407,900	137,300
Land	52,500	52,500	–0–
Patents	75,000	64,000	11,000
Goodwill	40,000	50,000	(10,000)
Bond discount and expense	4,502	–0–	4,502
	$2,530,730	$2,035,200	$495,530
Accrued taxes payable	$ 95,250	$ 79,600	$ 15,650
Accounts payable	299,280	280,000	19,280
Dividends payable	70,000	–0–	70,000
Bonds payable—8%	125,000	–0–	125,000
Bonds payable—12%	–0–	100,000	(100,000)
Allowance for doubtful accounts	35,300	40,000	(4,700)
Accumulated depreciation—building	423,200	400,000	23,200
Accumulated depreciation—machinery	173,000	130,000	43,000
Premium on bonds payable	–0–	2,400	(2,400)
Common shares	1,286,200	1,453,200	(167,000)
Appropriation for plant expansion	10,000	–0–	10,000

(Continued)

Retained earnings—unappropriated	13,500	(450,000)	463,500
	$2,530,730	$2,035,200	$495,530

Statement of Retained Earnings

Jan. 1, 1994	Balance (deficit)	$(450,000)
Mar. 31, 1994	Net income for first quarter of 1994	25,000
Apr. 1, 1994	Transfer from common shares	425,000
	Balance	–0–
Dec. 31, 1994	Net income for last three quarters of 1994	93,500
	Dividend declared—payable January 20, 1995	(70,000)
	Appropriation for plant expansion	(10,000)
	Balance	$ 13,500

Your working papers contain the following information:

1. On April 1, 1994, the existing deficit was written off against share capital created by reducing the stated value of the no-par shares.

2. On November 1, 1994, 29,600 no-par shares were issued for $258,000.

3. A patent was purchased for $21,000.

4. During the year, machinery that had a cost basis of $16,400 and on which there was accumulated depreciation of $5,200 was sold for $7,000. No other plant assets were sold during the year.

5. The 12%, 20-year bonds were dated and issued on January 2, 1982. Interest was payable on June 30 and December 31. They were sold originally at 106. These bonds were retired at 102 (net of tax) plus accrued interest on March 31, 1994.

6. The 8%, 40-year bonds were dated January 1, 1994 and were sold on March 31 at 97 plus accrued interest. Interest is payable semiannually on June 30 and December 31. Expense of issuance was $839.

7. Susquehanna Limited acquired 70% control in the Subsidiary Company on January 2, 1994 for $100,000. The income statement of the Subsidiary Company for 1994 shows a net income of $20,000.

8. Extraordinary repairs to buildings of $8,000 were charged to Accumulated Depreciation—Building.

9. Interest paid in 1994 was $10,500 and income taxes paid were $34,000.

Instructions

From the information above prepare a statement of changes in financial position. A work sheet is not necessary but the principal computations should be supported by schedules or skeleton ledger accounts.

P23-8 **(SCFP: INDIRECT METHOD)**   Presented below are comparative balance sheet accounts of Choctaw Corporation at December 31, 1994 and 1993.

			Increase or (Decrease)
	1994	1993	
Assets			
Cash	$ 313,000	$ 195,000	$118,000

(Continued)

Marketable equity securities, at cost	175,000	175,000	—
Allowance to reduce marketable equity			
securities to market	(13,000)	(24,000)	11,000
Accounts receivable, net	418,000	440,000	(22,000)
Inventories	595,000	525,000	70,000
Land	390,000	170,000	220,000
Plant and equipment	765,000	690,000	75,000
Accumulated depreciation	(199,000)	(145,000)	(54,000)
Goodwill, net	57,000	60,000	(3,000)
Total assets	$2,501,000	$2,086,000	$415,000

Liabilities and Shareholders' Equity

Current portion of long-term note	$ 150,000	$ 150,000	$ —
Accounts payable and accrued liabilities	594,000	475,000	119,000
Note payable, long term	300,000	450,000	(150,000)
Deferred income tax	44,000	32,000	12,000
Bond payable	190,000	160,000	30,000
Common shares, no par value	889,000	660,000	229,000
Retained earnings	334,000	195,000	139,000
Treasury shares, at cost	—	(36,000)	36,000
Total liabilities and shareholders' equity	$2,501,000	$2,086,000	$415,000

Additional Information

1. On January 20, 1994, Choctaw issued 10,000 shares of its common shares for land having a fair value of $220,000.

2. On February 5, 1994, Choctaw reissued all of its treasury shares for $45,000.

3. On May 15, 1994, Choctaw paid a cash dividend of $58,000 on its common shares.

4. On August 8, 1994, equipment was purchased for $140,000.

5. On September 1, 1994, twenty $1,000 bonds were issued at face value.

6. On September 30, 1994, equipment was sold for $40,000. The equipment cost $65,000 and had a carrying amount of $37,000 on the date of sale.

7. Deferred income tax represents timing differences relating to the use of CCA for income tax reporting and the straight-line method for financial reporting.

8. Net income for 1994 was $197,000.

9. Income taxes paid were $70,000; interest paid was $63,000.

Instructions

Prepare a statement of changes in financial position using the indirect method. (Marketable equity securities are cash equivalents.)

(SCFP: INDIRECT METHOD)   Following are the 1994 financial statements of Powhatan Corporation.   **P23-9**

Balance Sheets

$ in millions	December 31 1994	December 31 1993
Assets		
Current assets:		
Cash	$ 13.4	$ 7.5
Receivable (net of allowance for doubtful accounts of $5.0 million in 1994 and $4.6 million in 1993)	246.6	213.2
Inventories		
Finished goods	86.7	84.7
Raw materials and supplies	115.7	123.8
Prepaid expenses	6.2	6.7
Total current assets	468.6	435.9
Property, plant, and equipment:		
Plant and equipment	2,358.8	2,217.7
Less: Accumulated depreciation	(993.4)	(890.1)
	1,365.4	1,327.6
Timberland—net	171.3	169.5
Total property, plant, and equipment—net	1,536.7	1,497.1
Other assets	74.7	34.7
Total assets	$2,080.0	$1,967.7
Liabilities and Shareholders' Investment		
Current liabilities:		
Current maturities of long-term debt	$ 13.2	$ 10.5
Bank overdrafts	25.5	20.2
Accounts payable	102.2	91.3
Accrued liabilities		
Payrolls and employee benefits	73.5	73.9
Interest and other expenses	44.3	29.4
Federal income taxes	17.4	12.7
Total current liabilities	276.1	238.0
Long-term liabilities:		
Deferred income tax	333.6	280.0
4.75% to 11.25% revenue bonds with maturities to 2013	174.6	193.4
Other revenue bonds at variable rates with maturities to 2020	46.3	26.6
7⅞% sinking fund debentures due 1999	19.5	21.0
8.70% sinking fund debentures due 2014	75.0	75.0
9½% convertible subordinated debentures due 2014	—	38.9
9¾% notes due 1996	50.0	50.0
Promissory notes	—	60.2
Mortgage debt and miscellaneous obligations	25.7	21.7
Other long-term liabilities	21.8	—
Total long-term liabilities	746.5	766.8

(Continued)

Shareholders' investment:

Common shares (60,000,000 shares authorized, 26,661,770 and 25,265,921 shares outstanding as of December 31, 1994 and 1993)	247.4	196.9
Reinvested earnings	810.0	766.0
Total shareholders' investment	1,057.4	962.9
Total liabilities and shareholders' investment	$2,080.0	$1,967.7

Statement of Income and Reinvested Earnings

$ in millions, except per-share amounts	1994
Income	
Net sales	$2,039.2
Cost of sales	1,637.8
Gross margin	401.4
Selling, general, and administrative expense	(182.6)
Provision for reduced operations	(41.0)
Operating income	177.8
Interest on long-term debt	(33.5)
Other income—net	2.2
Pretax income	146.5
Income taxes	(61.2)
Net income	$ 85.3
Earnings per share	$ 3.20
Reinvested earnings	
Reinvested earnings at beginning of year	$ 766.0
Add: Net Income	85.3
	851.3
Deduct: Dividends:	
Common shares ($1.57 per share in 1994)	41.3
Reinvested earnings at end of year	$ 810.0

Additional Information

1. Depreciation and cost of timberland harvested was $114.6 million.

2. The provision for reduced operations included a decrease in cash of $15.9 million.

3. Purchases of plant and equipment were $176.5 million, and purchases of timberland were $45 million.

4. Sales of plant and equipment resulted in cash inflows of $2.2 million. All sales were at book value.

5. The changes in long-term liabilities are summarized below:

Increase in deferred income tax	$ 53.6
New borrowings	63.2
Debt retired by cash payments	(86.5)
Debt converted into shares	(37.4)
Reclassification of current maturities	(13.2)
Decrease in long-term liabilities	$(20.3)

6. The increase in common shares results from the issuance of shares for debt conversion, $37.4 million, and shares issued for cash, $13.1 million.

7. Interest paid during 1994 was $21.2 million and income tax paid was $2.9 million.

Instructions

Prepare a statement of changes in financial position for the Powhatan Corporation using the indirect method.

P23-10(SCFP: INDIRECT METHOD; NET CASH FLOW FROM OPERATING ACTIVITIES: DIRECT METHOD) Comparative balance sheet accounts of Shawnee Inc. are presented below.

Shawnee Inc.
Comparative Balance Sheet Accounts
December 31, 1994 and 1993

	December 31	
Debit Accounts	1994	1993
Cash	$ 44,250	$ 33,750
Accounts receivable	69,500	60,000
Merchandise inventory	29,000	24,000
Investments (long-term)	22,250	37,500
Machinery	32,000	18,750
Buildings	67,500	56,250
Land	7,500	7,500
Totals	$272,000	$237,750
Credit Accounts		
Allowance for doubtful accounts	$ 2,250	$ 1,500
Accumulated depreciation—machinery	5,625	2,250
Accumulated depreciation—buildings	13,500	9,000
Accounts payable	30,000	24,750
Accrued payables	3,375	2,625
Long-term note payable	26,000	30,000
Common shares	150,000	125,000
Retained earnings	41,250	42,625
Totals	$272,000	$237,750

Additional Data (ignore taxes)

1. Net income for the year was $45,250.

2. Cash dividends declared during the year were $21,625.

3. A 20% stock dividend was declared during the year. $25,000 of retained earnings was capitalized.

4. Investments that cost $20,000 were sold during the year for $24,000.

5. Machinery that cost $3,750, on which $750 of depreciation had accumulated, was sold for $2,200.

Shawnee's 1994 income statement follows (ignore taxes).

Sales		$540,000
Less cost of goods sold		377,500
Gross margin		162,500
Less operating expenses (includes $8,625 depreciation and $1,000 bad debts)		120,450
Income from operations		42,050
Other: Gain on sale of investments	$4,000	
Loss on sale of machinery	(800)	3,200
Net income		$ 45,250

Instructions

(a) Compute net cash flow from operating activities using the direct method.

(b) Prepare a statement of changes in financial position using the indirect method.

(SCFP: DIRECT AND INDIRECT METHODS, FROM COMPARATIVE FINANCIAL STATE-P23-11 MENTS)   Illini Company, a major retailer of bicycles and accessories, operates several stores and is a publicly traded company. The comparative statement of financial position and income statement for Illini as of May 31, 1994 are shown below. The company is preparing its statement of cash flows.

Illini Company
Statement of Financial Position
for the Year Ended May 31, 1994 and 1993

	5/31/94	5/31/93
Current assets		
Cash	$ 43,250	$ 20,000
Accounts receivable	70,000	50,000
Merchandise inventory	210,000	250,000
Prepaid expenses	9,000	7,000
Total current assets	332,250	327,000
Plant assets		
Plant assets	600,000	510,000
Less: Accumulated depreciation	150,000	125,000
Net plant assets	450,000	385,000
Total assets	$782,250	$712,000
Current liabilities		
Accounts payable	$123,000	$115,000
Salaries payable	47,250	72,000
Interest payable	27,000	25,000
Total current liabilities	197,250	212,000
Long-term debt		
Bonds payable	70,000	100,000
Total liabilities	267,250	312,000

(Continued)

Shareholders' equity		
Common shares	370,000	280,000
Retained earnings	145,000	120,000
Total shareholders' equity	515,000	400,000
Total liabilities and shareholders' equity	$782,250	$712,000

Illini Company

Income Statement

for the Year Ended May 31, 1994

Sales	$1,255,250
Cost of merchandise sold	712,000
Total contribution	543,250
Expenses	
Salary expense	252,100
Interest expense	75,000
Other expenses	8,150
Depreciation expense	25,000
Total expenses	360,250
Operating income	183,000
Income tax expense	43,000
Net income	$ 140,000

The following is additional information concerning Illini's transactions during the year ended May 31, 1994:

1. All sales during the year were made on account.

2. All merchandise was purchased on account, comprising the total accounts payable account.

3. Plant assets costing $90,000 were purchased by paying $40,000 in cash and issuing 5,000 common shares.

4. The Other Expenses are related to prepaid items.

5. All income taxes incurred during the year were paid during the year.

6. In order to supplement its cash, Illini issued 4,000 common shares at $10 each.

7. There were no penalties assessed for the retirement of bonds.

8. Cash dividends of $115,000 were declared and paid at the end of the fiscal year.

Instructions

(a) Compare and contrast the direct method and the indirect method for reporting cash flows from operating activities.

(b) Prepare a statement of cash flows for Illini Company for the year ended May 31, 1994, using the direct method. Be sure to support the statement with approriate calculations. (A reconciliation of net income to net cash is not required.)

(c) Using the indirect method, calculate only the net cash flow from operating activities for Illini Company for the year ended May 31, 1994.

———— FINANCIAL REPORTING PROBLEM ————

Refer to the financial statements and other documents of Moore Corporation Limited presented in Appendix 5A and answer the following questions.:

1. Which method of computing net cash provided by operating activities did Moore use? What were the amounts of cash provided by operations for the years 1990 and 1991? Which item was responsible for the significant increase in cash provided by operations in 1991? Why was there such an increase?

2. What was the most significant item in the cash provided by (used for) the investment activities section? Which items in the cash provided by (used for) the financing activities section were directly related to the item identified above (that is, in the investment activities section)?

3. Where is the Gain on Sale of Assets reported in Moore's statement of changes in financial position? How does it appear in that section of the statement of changes?

4. Where is Deferred Income Tax reported in Moore's statement of cash flows? Why does it appear in that section of the statement of cash flows?

Basic Financial Statement Analysis

—◼—

As stated in Chapter 1, the *objective of financial statements* is to "communicate information that is useful to investors, creditors and other users in making resource allocation decisions and/or assessing management stewardship."[1] Thus far in this book we have examined (1) how accountants identify the economic transactions and events to be reported in financial statements, (2) how measurements are derived, and (3) how such items and measurements are disclosed in the body of the statements or related notes. Communication, however, means more than just preparing and sending out financial statements. **Communication** presumes understanding of the statements by users and accountants so that the information can be analysed and interpreted in a meaningful way. The objective of this chapter is to describe and illustrate some basic techniques of financial statement analysis as well as to consider the limitations of such analysis.

ROLE OF FINANCIAL STATEMENT ANALYSIS IN DECISION MAKING

Objective 1

Understand
the role of
financial state-
ment analysis
in helping vari-
ous users of
financial state-
ments evaluate
risk and reduce
uncertainty
regarding their
decisions.

In Chapter 1, it was indicated that *several distinct groups could use information in financial statements to help them make decisions*. Each group, however, has its own perspective and types of decisions with which it is primarily concerned. **Short-term creditors**, such as banks and suppliers, are primarily interested in a company's ability to pay its currently maturing obligations. **Bondholders** are concerned with the risk associated with the company's ability to pay the principal when due as well as periodic interest. **Owners and financial analysts** also are interested in aspects of importance to creditors and bondholders. Additionally, they wish to assess a company's long-run profitability in order to evaluate their investment or recommendations for investment.[2] **Union leaders** need information to determine a company's "ability to pay" when negotiating wages and benefits.

A company's **management** has responsibility to these and other stakeholders. As such, it must carefully monitor and manage operations with which these groups are concerned. Also, the financial statements are a primary means by which management communicates financial information regarding

---

[1] *CICA Handbook* (Toronto: CICA), Section 1000, par. .15.

[2] Two major viewpoints exist regarding the usefulness of financial statement (ratio) analysis to existing and potential shareholders of companies that trade shares through a well-organized market (i.e. stock exchange). The **capital market approach** is based on the hypothesis that such markets are efficient because a share's price incorporates all publicly available information (including that in financial statements) at any point in time. Therefore, analysing financial statements with the intent to identify over- or under-valued shares is not a useful exercise. Rather, investors should concentrate on the return from ownership of shares in an investment portfolio. Alternatively, the **fundamental analysis approach** assumes that financial statement analysis can provide information useful for identifying over- or under-valued shares. While considerable research has provided support for the capital markets approach, many believe that a combination of both approaches is useful. Even under the capital markets approach, someone (e.g., financial analysts) must analyse financial statement information in order to see that it is incorporated into market prices. Fundamental financial statement analysis also remains useful for investors in less than efficient market situations (e.g., private companies, proprietorships, partnerships) and for parties other than shareholders that have questions to be answered about a company. In this chapter, we consider financial statement analysis techniques associated with a fundamental analysis approach. Techniques and concepts of a capital markets approach are commonly examined in finance or more advanced accounting courses.

the results of their decisions. Consequently, the possible results of a contemplated decision on financial statements and ratios developed from these statements are often important factors in making the decision.[3]

Regardless of the perspective or the type of decision, an underlying objective of a decision maker is to evaluate risk. **Risk** may be thought of as *the possibility of loss resulting from a decision*.[4] A major factor contributing to risk is uncertainty. **Uncertainty** is the *doubt experienced about the best action to take*.[5] It can be caused by factors such as naïvete, lack of information, or the simple fact that future events are unpredictable. Therefore:

> Risk is compounded by uncertainty, but reduced by decision-relevant information which enables enterprises, investors and creditors to take appropriate action to either avoid risky situations or obtain fair compensation for risk taking.[6]

Acquisition and use of decision-relevant information is, therefore, an important factor in evaluating risk. Information about a particular company, the industry in which it operates, and the general state of the economy is all likely to have some relevance when making decisions about the company. Such information can come from a variety of sources, including financial magazines and newspapers, economic forecasts, speeches by top executives, credit rating organizations, financial analysts, reports filed with a securities commission, or personal or business acquaintances. Added to this list is financial statements. Therefore, while the authors concentrate on financial statement analysis as a means of deriving decision-relevant information, it is important to appreciate that many other sources of such information are considered when making decisions.

A GENERAL PERSPECTIVE ON FINANCIAL STATEMENT ANALYSIS

Financial statements include the balance sheet, income statement, statement of retained earnings, statement of changes in financial position, and cross-referenced notes to these statements. Generally, an auditor's report accompanies the statements. An **auditor's report** provides the opinion of an independent professional accountant as to whether the statements present information fairly and in accordance with generally accepted accounting principles. If the statements satisfy these requirements an **unqualified opinion** is given. When the requirements of fairness and/or conformity to GAAP are not satisfied, the auditor must explain why. The seriousness of the problem determines whether a **qualified opinion**, **adverse opinion**, or **denial of opinion** will be given in the auditor's report. Consequently, when carrying out financial statement analysis, an initial action would be to examine the auditor's report to determine if there are any basic problems with the information in the financial statements. In some circumstances, an auditor's report may not accompany the financial statements. This fact should alert the user of the statements to discover why and to be particularly cautious when using the financial statements as a source of information for decision making.

Awareness of particular accounting policies and methods used by a company to recognize items and measure amounts reported is also important to interpreting and understanding the results of financial statement analysis. Whether interest related to financing assets constructed or development of research is capitalized or expensed, the method for amortizing long-lived assets, how inventory is valued, and the method used to recognize revenue on long-term contracts are examples of where companies may choose different accounting policies. The particular choice can have a significant effect on whether items and amounts are reported, how they are measured, where they are reported,

Objective 2

Appreciate the importance of an auditor's report, awareness of accounting policies used by a company, and having a logical approach when conducting financial statement analysis.

---

[3] In addition to annual financial statements, management typically has internal financial reports prepared regularly. Day-to-day information regarding cash flows, gross margins, variances from plans, etc., is used extensively for internal planning and control purposes.

[4] J.E. Boritz, *Approaches to Dealing with Risk and Uncertainty* (Toronto: CICA, 1990), p. xv. We have adapted the specific definition given by Boritz.

[5] *Ibid.*

[6] *Ibid.*

and trends over time for a given company. Also, if the financial statement analysis involves inter-company comparison, the use of different policies by the companies must be taken into consideration.

Recognizing that awareness of accounting policies is important, the *CICA Handbook* requires that a "clear and concise description of significant accounting policies . . . should be included as an integral part of the financial statements."[7] Companies typically disclose these policies in the first note to the financial statements or in a separate summary. Therefore, in addition to examining the auditor's report, reading the disclosure regarding accounting policies is an important preparatory step to conducting financial statement analysis and interpreting the results.

Within this general context, specific information from financial statements can be obtained by examining relationships between items on the statements (ratios, percentages) and identifying trends in these relationships (comparative analysis). Such an examination is called **financial statement analysis**.

A problem with learning how to analyse statements is that the means may become an end in itself. There are thousands of possible relationships that could be calculated and trends identified. If one knows only how to calculate ratios and trends without realizing how such information can be used, little is accomplished. Therefore, a logical approach to financial statement analysis is necessary. Such an approach may consist of the following steps:

1. ***Know the questions for which you want to find answers***. As indicated earlier in this chapter, there are various groups with different types of interests in a company. Depending on the perspective of the user, particular questions of interest to them can be identified.

2. ***Know the questions that particular ratios and comparisons are able to help answer***. These will be discussed in the remainder of this chapter.

3. ***Match 1 and 2 above***. By such a matching, the statement analysis will have a logical direction and purpose.

Several caveats must be mentioned. ***Financial statements report on the past***. As such, analysis of this data is an examination of the past. Whenever such information is incorporated into a decision-making (future-oriented) process, a critical assumption is that the past is a reasonable basis for predicting the future. This is usually a reasonable approach, but the limitations associated with it should be recognized.

Also, ***while ratio and trend analyses will help identify strengths and weaknesses of a company, such analyses will not likely reveal why things are as they are***. Ratios and trends may serve as "red flags" indicating problem areas. Finding answers about "why" usually requires an in-depth analysis and an awareness of many factors about a company that are not reported in the financial statements—for instance, the impact of inflation, actions of competitors, technological developments, or a strike at a major supplier's or buyer's business.

Another point is that a ***single ratio by itself is not likely to be very useful***. For example, a current ratio of 2:1 (current assets are twice current liabilities) may be viewed as satisfactory. If, however, the industry average is 3:1, such a conclusion may be questioned. Even given this industry average, one may conclude that the particular company is doing well if the ratio last year was 1.5:1. Consequently, to derive meaning from ratios, some standard against which to compare them is needed. Such a standard may come from industry averages, past years' amounts, a particular competitor, or planned levels.

Finally, ***awareness of the limitations of accounting numbers used in an analysis*** is important. For example, the implications of different acceptable accounting policies on statements, ratios, and trends, particularly regarding comparability among companies and between a company and an industry average, must always be recognized. Understanding the many accounting issues and alternatives (many of which have been considered throughout this book) provides a background against which

---

[7] *CICA Handbook*, Section 1505, par. .04.

the limitations of accounting numbers can be more fully appreciated. More will be said about some of the limitations and their consequences later in this chapter.

BASIC TECHNIQUES OF FINANCIAL ANALYSIS

Various techniques are used in the analysis of financial statement data to bring out the comparative and relative significance of the financial information presented. These include *ratio analysis*, *comparative analysis*, *percentage analysis*, and *examination of related data* (i.e. in notes and other sources). It is difficult to say that one technique is more useful than another because every situation faced by the analyst is different, and the answers needed are often obtained only on close examination of the interrelationships among all the data provided. Therefore, knowledge of a variety of techniques and well-established relationships in the data is important to reaching informed conclusions when performing a comprehensive analysis. The nature of these techniques and relationships is examined in the remainder of this chapter.

RATIO ANALYSIS

Ratio analysis is the usual starting point in deriving information desired by the analyst. A **ratio** is simply *an expression of the relationship between two numbers* drawn or derived from the financial statements. Ratios can be classified as follows.[8]

Objective 3

Identify major types of ratios and know what each is attempting to measure.

Liquidity Ratios. Measures of the enterprise's short-run ability to pay its maturing obligations.
Activity Ratios. Measures of how efficiently the enterprise is using the assets employed.
Profitability Ratios. Measures of the degree of success or failure of a given enterprise or division for a given period of time.
Coverage Ratios. Measures of the degree of protection for long-term creditors and investors.

The calculation[9] and use of these ratios will be illustrated through a case example adopted from the annual report of a large concern that we have disguised under the name of Anetek Corporation.

Anetek Corporation is a worldwide enterprise offering more than 1,400 products and services. Anetek employees number some 50,000 in 48 countries. The comparative consolidated income statement and balance sheet shown on page 1226 are the basis for the ratios to be calculated. The numbers used in the ratios, like the numbers used in the financial statements, have the last three digits (000) omitted.

Liquidity Ratios

The ability of a firm to meet its current debts is important in evaluating its financial position. For example, Anetek has current liabilities of $575,000. Can these current obligations be met when due? Certain basic ratios can be computed that provide some guidance for determining the enterprise's short-term debt-paying ability.

---

[8] Other terms may be used to categorize these ratios. For example, liquidity ratios are sometimes referred to as solvency ratios, activity ratios as turnover or efficiency ratios, and coverage ratios as leverage or capital structure ratios.

[9] The definitions and calculations for the various ratios to be illustrated are fairly commonly used. However, alternative definitions exist of what is included in any particular ratio. Consequently, when using ratios prepared by others (e.g., published industry averages being used for making comparisons to a company's calculated ratios), close attention should be given to the description of how these ratios were determined.

Anetek Corporation
Income Statement
For the Year Ended December 31
(in thousands of dollars)

	1994	1993
Sales and other revenue:		
Net sales	$1,600,000	$1,350,000
Interest revenue	25,000	20,000
Other revenue	50,000	30,000
Total revenue	$1,675,000	$1,400,000
Cost and other charges:		
Cost of goods sold	$1,000,000	$ 850,000
Depreciation and amortization	150,000	150,000
Selling and administrative expenses	225,000	150,000
Interest expense	50,000	25,000
Total	$1,425,000	$1,175,000
Income before taxes	$ 250,000	$ 225,000
Income taxes	100,000	75,000
Net income	$ 150,000	$ 150,000
Earnings per share*	$ 5.00	$ 5.00

*Additional information:
Number of shares outstanding in 1994 is 30 million.
Market price of Anetek's shares at end of 1994 is $60 each.
Cash dividend per share in 1994 is $2.25.

Anetek Corporation
Balance Sheet*
December 31, 1994 and 1993
(in thousands of dollars)

	1994	1993
Assets		
Current assets:		
Cash	$ 40,000	$ 25,000
Marketable securities (at cost)	100,000	75,000
Accounts receivable	350,000	300,000
Inventories (at lower of cost and market)	310,000	250,000
Total current assets	$ 800,000	$ 650,000
Investments (at cost)	$ 300,000	$ 325,000
Fixed assets:		
Property, plant, and equipment (at cost)	$2,000,000	$1,900,000
Less: accumulated depreciation	(900,000)	(800,000)
	$1,100,000	$1,100,000

(Continued)

*The notes and some detail that accompanied this statement are excluded for purposes of simplicity and brevity.

Goodwill	$ 50,000	$ 25,000
Total assets	$2,250,000	$2,100,000

Liabilities and Shareholders' Equity

Current liabilities:		
Accounts payable	$ 125,000	$ 100,000
Notes payable	250,000	200,000
Accrued and other liabilities	200,000	150,000
Total current liabilities	$ 575,000	$ 450,000
Long-term debt:		
Bonds and notes payable	725,000	782,500
Total liabilities	$1,300,000	$1,232,500
Shareholders' equity:		
Common shares	$ 150,000	$ 150,000
Contributed surplus	550,000	550,000
Retained earnings	250,000	167,500
Total shareholders' equity	$ 950,000	$ 867,500
Total liabilities and shareholders' equity	$2,250,000	$2,100,000

1. Current Ratio. The current ratio is the relationship of total current assets to total current liabilities. Although the quotient is the dollars of current assets available to cover each dollar of current debt, it is most frequently expressed as a coverage of so many times. Sometimes it is called the working capital ratio, because working capital is the excess of current assets over current liabilities. The computation of the 1994 current ratio for Anetek is as shown below.

Objective 4

Identify liquidity ratios, know how they are calculated, and appreciate the questions they can help answer.

$$\text{Current Ratio} = \frac{\text{Current Assets}}{\text{Current Liabilities}} = \frac{\$800,000}{\$575,000} = 1.39 \text{ times}$$

$$\text{Industry Average}^{10} = 2.30 \text{ times}$$

The current ratio of 1.39 to 1 compared with the industry average of 2.3 to 1 indicates that Anetek's safety factor to meet maturing short-term obligations is noticeably low. Does the relatively low current ratio indicate the existence of a liquidity problem? Or, considering that the ratio is greater than 1 to 1, is the situation well in hand? The current ratio is only one measure of determining liquidity and it does not answer all of the liquidity questions. How liquid are the receivables and inventory? What effect does the omission of the inventory have on the analysis of liquidity? To help answer these and other questions, additional analysis of other related data is required.

2. Acid-Test Ratio. A satisfactory current ratio does not disclose the fact that a portion of the current assets may be tied up in slow-moving inventories. With inventories, especially raw material and work in process, there is a question of how long it will take to transform them into the finished product

---

[10] The industry average ratios are taken from Dun and Bradstreet, Inc., *Key Business Ratios in 25 Lines*, and Leo Troy's *The Almanac of Business and Industrial Financial Ratios*. The industry average ratios provide a basis for comparison with other companies in the same industry. One of the problems of using industry average as a basis for comparison is determining the particular industry with which comparison should be made. This is a problem because a company's operations may span several industries, yet the financial statements consolidate all the operations. A partial solution is achieved because companies provide information on their major business segments. Such reporting is examined in Chapter 25.

and what ultimately will be realized on the sale of the merchandise. Also, different companies may be using different inventory valuation methods. Elimination of the inventories, along with any prepaid expenses, from the current assets might provide better information for the short-term creditor. Many analysts favour a "quick" or "acid-test" ratio that relates total current liabilities to cash, marketable securities, and receivables. The acid-test ratio is computed for Anetek as follows.

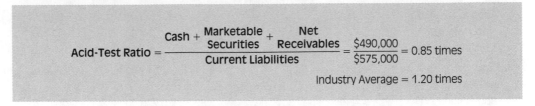

$$\text{Acid-Test Ratio} = \frac{\text{Cash} + \text{Marketable Securities} + \text{Net Receivables}}{\text{Current Liabilities}} = \frac{\$490,000}{\$575,000} = 0.85 \text{ times}$$

Industry Average = 1.20 times

The acid-test ratio for Anetek as compared with the industry average is low. This suggests that Anetek may have difficulty in meeting its short-term obligations unless the firm is able to obtain additional current assets through conversion of some of its long-term assets, through additional financing, or through profitable operating results.

3. Defensive-Interval Ratio. Neither the current ratio nor the acid-test ratio gives a complete explanation of the current debt-paying ability of the company. The matching of current assets with current liabilities assumes that the current assets will be employed to pay off the current liabilities. Some analysts argue that a better measure of liquidity is provided by the defensive-interval ratio. The defensive-interval ratio is computed by dividing defensive assets (cash, marketable securities, and net receivables) by projected daily expenditures for operations. This ratio measures the time span a firm can operate on present liquid assets without resorting to funds that would be generated by future operations or other sources (e.g., sale of fixed assets, issuance of shares). Projected daily expenditures are computed by dividing cost of goods sold plus selling and administrative expenses and other ordinary cash expenses by 365 days.[11] The defensive-interval measure for Anetek is shown below.

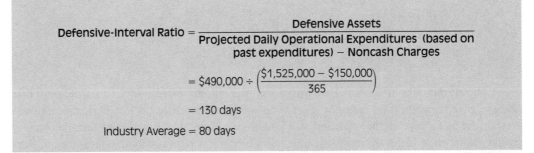

$$\text{Defensive-Interval Ratio} = \frac{\text{Defensive Assets}}{\text{Projected Daily Operational Expenditures (based on past expenditures)} - \text{Noncash Charges}}$$

$$= \$490,000 \div \left(\frac{\$1,525,000 - \$150,000}{365} \right)$$

$$= 130 \text{ days}$$

Industry Average = 80 days

Whether this ratio provides a better measure of liquidity than the current ratio or acid-test ratio is difficult to evaluate, but it does provide another useful tool for analysing the liquidity position of the enterprise. This ratio establishes a safety factor or margin for the analyst in determining the capability of the company to meet its basic operational costs. It would appear that 130 days provides the company with a relatively high degree of protection and tends to offset somewhat the weakness indicated by the low current and acid-test ratios. Despite this, an overall conclusion from the foregoing analysis would be that Anetek's management and creditors should be concerned about the company's liquidity position.

---

[11] Alternatively, and as shown in the example, projected daily expenditures may be determined by dividing 365 into total expenses reported, less any noncash charges such as depreciation and provisions for any known changes in planned operations from previous periods. Income tax expense has been included in the illustration to determine total expenses for the year.

Activity Ratios

Another way of evaluating liquidity is to determine how quickly certain assets can be turned into cash. How liquid, for example, are the receivables and inventory? Calculation of activity ratios helps to provide answers. Activity ratios express the relationship between the results of organizational activity (e.g., net sales) and the amount of an asset or combination of assets used to achieve the results. Since an activity ratio is a measure of output (results) divided by a measure of input (resources), it provides information regarding how efficiently an enterprise is utilizing its assets. Activity ratios are also called turnover ratios because the resulting number represents how many times a particular asset or combination of assets has been turned over during the period (i.e. how many times the inventory balance has sold). Activity ratios are computed for Anetek on the basis of receivables, inventories, and total assets.

> **Objective 5**
>
> Identify activity ratios, know how they are calculated, and appreciate the questions they can help answer.

4. Receivables Turnover. The receivables turnover ratio is computed by dividing net sales by average receivables outstanding during the year. Theoretically, the numerator should include only net credit sales. This information is frequently not available, however, and if the relative amounts of charge and cash sales remain fairly constant, the trend indicated by the ratio will still be valid. Average receivables outstanding can be computed by dividing the total of beginning and ending balances of net trade receivables by 2.[12] This simple average is a reasonable reflection of the net receivables balance throughout the year unless seasonal factors are significant.

$$\text{Accounts Receivable Turnover} = \frac{\text{Net Sales}}{\text{Average Trade Receivables (net)}}$$

$$= \$1,600,000 \div \left(\frac{\$350,000 + \$300,000}{2}\right)$$

$$= 4.92 \text{ times or every 74 days}[13] \text{ (365 days/4.92)}$$

$$\text{Industry Average} = 7.15 \text{ times or every 51 days}$$

This information provides some indication of the quality of the receivables and also an idea of how successful the firm is in collecting its outstanding receivables. The faster this turnover, the more credence the current ratio and acid-test ratio have in the financial analysis. For management purposes, an aging schedule should also be prepared to determine how long the receivables have been outstanding. It is possible that the receivables turnover is quite satisfactory, but this situation may have resulted because certain receivables have been collected quickly whereas others have been outstanding for a relatively long period.

In Anetek's case, the receivables turnover appears low. Dividing 365 days by the turnover provides a measure (74 days for Anetek) of the **average number of days to collect accounts receivable**. The lower the turnover, the longer this period of time. As a general rule, the time allowed for payment by the selling terms should not be exceeded by more than 10 or 15 days.

5. Inventory Turnover. Inventory turnover is computed by dividing the average inventory into the cost of goods sold. The inventory turnover ratio for Anetek is shown at the top of page 1230.

The inventory turnover measures how quickly inventory is sold. Dividing 365 days by the inventory turnover indicates the **average number of days it takes to sell inventory** (or **average number of days' sales for which inventory is on hand**). Generally, the higher the inventory

---

[12] If a beginning balance is not available, an average cannot be determined and, therefore, the ending balance is used to calculate the ratio.

[13] Often the receivables turnover is transformed to an average collection period. In this case, 4.92 is divided into 365 days to obtain 74 days. Several figures other than 365 could be used here; a common alternative is 360 days. Because the industry average was based on 365 days, we used this figure in our computations.

$$\text{Inventory Turnover} = \frac{\text{Cost of Goods Sold}}{\text{Average Inventory}} = \frac{\$1,000,000}{\dfrac{\$310,000 + \$250,000}{2}}$$

= 3.57 times or every 102 days (365 days/3.57)

Industry Average = 4.62 times or every 79 days

turnover, the better the enterprise is performing. It is possible, however, that an enterprise is incurring high "stockout costs" because not enough inventory is available.

The inventory turnover ratio is useful because it provides a signal of possible problems, such as whether obsolete inventory is present or pricing problems exist. In Anetek's case, the turnover ratio is lower than the industry average, indicating that some slow-moving inventory exists. Remember that this ratio is an average, which means that many goods may be turning over quite rapidly whereas others may have failed to sell at all. In addition, it was assumed that an average of the beginning and ending inventory was representative of the average for the year. If this situation is not correct,[14] additional computations could be made by management but, because of the lack of information on fluctuations in inventory during the year, could not be made by others.

Because inventory is stated at cost, it should be divided into cost of sales (a cost figure) instead of into sales, which includes some margin of profit. Occasionally, analysts use net sales when the cost of goods sold is not reported. While such a calculation may reveal trends over time if the underlying gross margin rate is fairly stable, it is not a true inventory turnover. For example, it would not be useful for determining the number of days that inventory is on hand.

The method of inventory valuation can affect the computed inventory turnover and the current ratio. The analyst should be aware of the different valuations that can be used in costing inventory (i.e. FIFO, Average-Cost, LIFO) and the effect these different valuation procedures might have on the ratios.

From the accounts receivable and inventory turnover information, a total conversion period can be determined. The **total conversion period** is the average number of days it takes from acquiring inventory to collecting cash from its sale.[15] It is calculated by adding the average number of days it takes to sell inventory to the average number of days to collect accounts receivable. For Anetek, the total conversion period is 176 days (102 + 74). Examining the conversion period and its two components can be useful in identifying differences between companies or between years for the same company when evaluating the efficiency of marketing, credit granting, and collection policies.

6. Asset Turnover. The asset turnover ratio is determined by dividing average total assets into net sales for the period. The asset turnover for Anetek is as follows.

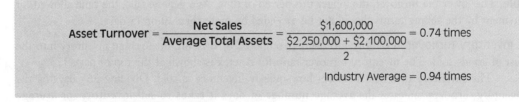

$$\text{Asset Turnover} = \frac{\text{Net Sales}}{\text{Average Total Assets}} = \frac{\$1,600,000}{\dfrac{\$2,250,000 + \$2,100,000}{2}} = 0.74 \text{ times}$$

Industry Average = 0.94 times

[14] Year-end inventory may not be representative of that held during the year because the year end occurs at the low point in a company's annual operating cycle. Also, inventory clearance sales just prior to a year end can result in the year-end inventory amount being substantially lower than is the normal amount during the year.
[15] The conversion period is sometimes referred to as the operating cycle, which is the span of time from the spending of cash to acquire inventory to the collection of cash from sales of that inventory. The operating cycle could, however, be shorter than the conversion period if inventory is bought on credit.

If this turnover ratio is high, the implication is that the company is using its assets efficiently to generate sales. (A turnover of 0.74 indicates that for each $1 of assets, $0.74 of net sales revenue is earned.) If the turnover ratio is low, it could signal that the company's management should be considering how to use assets more efficiently or, possibly, that some should be disposed of.

A problem with this turnover is that it places a premium on using old assets because their book value is low. In addition, this ratio can be significantly affected by the depreciation method employed by the company. For example, a company that employs an accelerated method of depreciation will have a higher turnover than a company using straight-line, all other factors being equal. For these reasons, this ratio should be interpreted in the context of the underlying accounting policies being employed.

Profitability Ratios

Profitability ratios indicate how well the enterprise has operated during the year. These ratios help to answer such questions as: Was the net income adequate? What rate of return does it represent? What is the rate of net income earned for assets invested in operating segments or other defined areas of activity? What percentage of income was paid in dividends? What amount was earned by different equity claimants? Generally, the ratios are computed either on the basis of sales or on an investment base such as total assets. Profitability is frequently used as a significant test for evaluating management effectiveness.

7. Profit Margin on Sales. The profit margin on sales is computed by dividing net income by net sales for the period. Anetek's ratio is shown below.

$$\text{Profit Margin on Sales} = \frac{\text{Net Income}}{\text{Net Sales}} = \frac{\$150,000}{\$1,600,000} = 9.4\%$$

$$\text{Industry Average} = 6\%$$

This ratio indicates that Anetek is achieving an above-average rate of profit on each dollar of sales. It provides some indication of the buffer available in case of higher costs or lower sales in the future.

8. Rate of Return on Assets. While the profit margin discloses useful information, it does not answer the important question of how profitable the enterprise was for the given time period. This can be examined by relating profit margin on each dollar of sales to the volume of sales per dollar invested in the company (asset turnover). The resulting relationship is called the rate of return on assets and can be determined as follows.

$$\text{Rate of Return on Assets} = \text{Profit Margin on Sales} \times \text{Asset Turnover}$$

$$\text{Rate of Return on Assets} = \frac{\text{Net Income}}{\text{Net Sales}} \times \frac{\text{Net Sales}}{\text{Average Total Assets}}$$

$$= \frac{\$150,000}{\$1,600,000} \times \frac{\$1,600,000}{\frac{\$2,250,000 + \$2,100,000}{2}}$$

$$= 6.9\%$$

$$\text{Industry Average} = 5.6\%$$

Rather than multiply the profit margin by the asset turnover, the rate of return on assets can be computed by simply dividing net income by average total assets, as follows.

Objective 6

Identify profitability ratios, know how they are calculated, and appreciate the questions they can help answer.

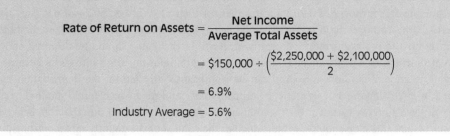

$$\text{Rate of Return on Assets} = \frac{\text{Net Income}}{\text{Average Total Assets}}$$

$$= \$150,000 \div \left(\frac{\$2,250,000 + \$2,100,000}{2}\right)$$

$$= 6.9\%$$

$$\text{Industry Average} = 5.6\%$$

While this calculation is a simpler and more direct means of determining the rate of return on assets, examining the profit margin and asset turnover components of the ratio is likely to reveal important information that is otherwise not evident. For example, Anetek's relatively high profit margin (compared to the industry) has more than offset its lower-than-average asset turnover, resulting in a rate of return on assets (6.9% under either calculation) that is above the average for the industry. Anetek's management appears to have established a policy of setting higher prices for its products (assuming costs are fairly similar across the industry) and accepting a lower volume of sales relative to assets invested.

Analysis of profit margin and asset turnover is, therefore, helpful in determining the particular strategies of companies within an industry when attempting to understand and evaluate rates of return on assets. Many enterprises have a small profit margin on sales and a high turnover (grocery and discount stores), whereas other enterprises have a relatively high profit margin but a low turnover (jewellery and furniture stores). Even companies in the same type of business may follow different strategies. For example, in the restaurant business, McDonald's follows a strategy of charging relatively low prices to obtain a high volume of sales. A high-class restaurant follows a strategy of charging higher prices, realizing volume may be lower than that generated by McDonald's. Both types of strategies can prove to be successful in terms of overall profitability. The significant point is that many factors contribute to the overall profitability of a company. One of the more interesting and often-used applications of this point is called the du Pont system of financial control.[16] In this system, ratios can be defined in enough detail to give the analyst the desired information. The basic components of this system are shown in the following diagram.

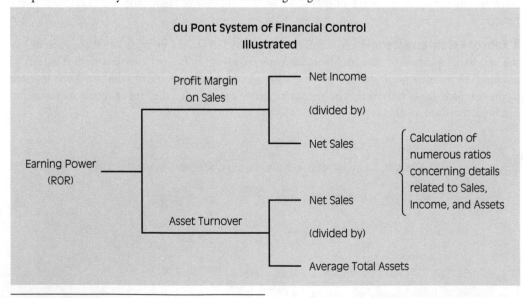

du Pont System of Financial Control Illustrated

---

[16] Descriptions of this system are given in T.C. Davis, *How the du Pont Organization Appraises Its Performance*, Financial Management Series, No. 94 (New York: American Management Association Treasurer's Dept., 1950); and C.A. Kline, Jr. and H.L. Hissler, "The Du Pont Chart System for Appraising Operating Performance," *NACA Bulletin* (August 1953), pp. 1595–1619.

Because of a belief that operating activities should be separated from financing activities when analysing a company, many contend that a better measure of the rate of return earned on the assets results from the use of net income before subtraction of any interest charge.[17] This ratio is computed by dividing net income plus interest expense (net of tax) by average total assets. Interest expense (net of tax), including discount amortization, is added back to income because the interest represents a cost of financing the assets, not operating them. The result is a rate of return on assets that is independent of how they are financed. The ratio for Anetek is as follows.

$$\text{Rate of Return on Assets (after eliminating interest expense and related tax savings)} = \frac{\text{Net Income} + \text{Interest Expense} - \text{Tax Savings[18]}}{\text{Average Total Assets}}$$

$$= \frac{\$150,000 + \$50,000 - 0.40(\$50,000)}{\dfrac{\$2,250,000 + \$2,100,000}{2}}$$

$$= 8.3\%$$

9. Rate of Return on Common Shareholders' Equity. This widely used ratio is defined as net income after interest, taxes, and preferred dividends (i.e. the income available specifically to common shareholders) divided by average common shareholders' equity. Anetek's ratio is computed in this manner.

$$\text{Rate of Return on Common Shareholders' Equity} = \frac{\text{Net Income} - \text{Preferred Dividends}}{\text{Average Common Shareholders' Equity}}$$

$$= \$150,000 \div \left(\frac{\$950,000 + \$867,500}{2}\right)$$

$$= 16.5\%$$

$$\text{Industry Average} = 9.5\%$$

Whether the rate of return on total assets or the rate of return on common shareholders' equity is a better measure of performance is difficult to evaluate. For example, the three merchandising companies listed below all have a comparable return on shareholders'equity; however, they differ considerably in their return on invested capital (total assets less current liabilities).[19]

Comparison of Different Types of Profitability Indices

	Rate of Return	
	on Invested Capital	on Shareholders' Equity
Thomson Corp.	7.78%	8.89%
Hydro-Québec	2.13	8.43
Maple Leaf Foods Inc.	15.45	8.77

[17] For example, public utility companies often compute their rate of return using this approach.
[18] The tax savings is computed by multiplying the interest expense by the effective tax rate. The effective tax rate, if not reported, may be approximated by dividing the income tax expense by income before taxes.
[19] *The Financial Post 500* (Toronto: The Financial Post, 1992), p. 92.

If an analyst was to look at only one of these profitability ratios, the ranking of Thomson Corp. and Maple Leaf Foods Inc. would be just the opposite to the ranking obtained from using the other ratio. Therefore, to evaluate the companies, both ratios should be considered. Additionally, the reason for the different rankings should be examined. In many cases, the differences are related to the degree of leverage (amount of debt in the capital structure) employed by the companies and the extent to which their trading on equity is favourable or unfavourable.

Financial Leverage. The expression "using financial leverage" or "trading on the equity" describes the practice of using borrowed money at fixed interest rates or issuing preferred shares with constant dividend amounts in hope of obtaining a higher rate of return from the use of the money acquired. Because these sources of financing are given a prior claim on some or all of the corporate assets, the advantage to common shareholders mustcome from borrowing at a lower rate of interest than the rate of return obtained by the corporation on its assets. If this can be done, the capital obtained from bondholders or preferred shareholders earns enough to pay the interest or preferred dividends and leave a margin for the common shareholders. When this condition exists, favourable use of financial leverage or trading on the equity at a profit occurs.

A comparison of the rate of return on total assets with the rate of return on common shareholders' equity indicates the profitability of trading on the equity in any given case. To illustrate, Anetek's rate of return on total assets is 6.9%, whereas the rate of return on the shareholders' equity is 16.5%. Anetek used financial leverage favourably. In essence, the liability claimants were paid a lower rate than 6.9%. Anetek is a very highly leveraged company that has achieved an excellent rate of return on common equity by using its debt effectively. A similar conclusion applies to Du Pont Canada Inc. that, in its summary of financial information, showed a rate of return on common shareholders' equity from 2.6% to 7.8% greater than the rate of return on capital employed for each year from 1986 to 1991. A word of caution—using financial leverage is a two-way street: just as a company's ownership gains can be magnified, so also can losses be magnified. In 1985, Du Pont reported a substantial loss, yet it still had to pay its interest commitments on long-term debt.

10. Earnings Per Share. Earnings per share is the only ratio that must be disclosed in the financial statements of most corporations.[20] It is one of the most frequently used ratios, yet it is one of the most deceptive. If no dilutive securities are present in the capital structure, then earnings per share is computed simply by dividing net income minus preferred dividends by the weighted-average number of common shares outstanding. If, however, convertible securities, stock options, warrants, or other dilutive securities are included in the capital structure, (1) basic earnings per common share and (2) fully diluted earnings-per-share figures would have to be examined.[21] The computation for Anetek is as shown below.

$$\text{Earnings Per Share} = \frac{\text{Net Income} - \text{Preferred Dividends}}{\text{Weighted-Average Number of Shares Outstanding}} = \frac{\$150,000 - 0}{30,000} = \$5.00$$

Because no dilutive securities that are common share equivalents or potentially dilutive securities are present in Anetek's capital structure, fully diluted earnings-per-share amounts are not calculated.

---

[20] *CICA Handbook*, Section 3500, par. .06. Excluded from this recommendation are businesses that do not have share capital, government-owned companies, wholly owned subsidiaries, and companies with few shareholders.
[21] See Chapter 17 for a discussion of how dilutive securities should be handled to compute fully diluted earnings per share.

Certain problems exist when using the earnings-per-share ratio. For example, earnings per share can be increased simply by reducing the number of shares outstanding through purchase and cancellation. In addition, the earnings-per-share figure fails to recognize the probable increasing base of the shareholders' investment. That is, earnings per share, all other factors being equal, will probably increase year after year if the corporation reinvests earnings in the business because a larger earnings figure should be generated without a corresponding increase in the number of shares outstanding. Because even well-informed investors attach such importance to earnings per share, caution must be exercised and the figure should not be given more emphasis than it deserves.

11. Price Earnings Ratio. The price earnings (P/E) ratio is an oft-quoted statistic used by analysts in discussing the investment potential of a given enterprise. It is computed by dividing the market price of a share by the earnings per share. For Anetek, the ratio is as follows.

$$\text{Price Earnings Ratio} = \frac{\text{Market Price Per Share}}{\text{Earnings Per Share}} = \frac{\$60}{\$5} = 12 \text{ times}$$

Some companies have high P/E multiples, while others have low multiples. For instance, Alberta Energy Company Ltd. in 1991 had a P/E ratio of 118.25 while the Bank of Nova Scotia had a P/E ratio of 5.43. The reason for such differences is linked to several factors: relative risk, stability of earnings, trends in earnings, and the market's perception of the company's growth potential.

The inverse of the price earnings ratio (earnings per share divided by market price per share) provides a measure of the **rate of return on the market value of the share**. For Anetek, this would be 8.33%.

12. Payout Ratio. The payout ratio is the ratio of cash dividends to net income. If preferred shares are outstanding, this ratio is computed for common shareholders by dividing cash dividends paid to common shareholders by income available to common shareholders. Given that Anetek's cash dividends are $67,500, the payout ratio is as shown below.

$$\text{Payout Ratio} = \frac{\text{Cash Dividends}}{\text{Net Income} - \text{Preferred Dividends}} = \frac{\$67,500}{\$150,000 - 0} = 45\%$$

It is important to investors seeking continuous cash flow that a fairly substantial payout ratio exist; however, speculators view appreciation in the value of shares as more important. Generally, growth companies are characterized by low payout ratios because they reinvest most of their earnings. For example, Anetek has a rather high payout ratio when compared with Cambior Inc., which paid out approximately 31% of earnings in 1991, but a relatively low ratio when compared with Bruncor Inc.'s payout of approximately 76% of net earnings to common shareholders in 1991.

Another closely related ratio that is often used is the **dividend yield**—the cash dividend per share divided by the market price per share. The cash dividend per share for Anetek is $2.25, so the dividend yield is 3.75% ($2.25/$60). This ratio affords investors some idea of the rate of return that will be received in cash dividends from their investment. In 1991, Canadian Pacific Forest Products Limited shareholders experienced a modest yield of 1.4%, while the Bank of Nova Scotia shareholders obtained a dividend yield of approximately 6.6%.

Coverage Ratios

Coverage ratios are computed to help in predicting the long-run solvency of a company. These ratios are of interest primarily to bondholders and other long-term debtors who need some indication of the measure of protection available to them. In addition, they indicate part of the risk involved in investing in common shares. The more debt there is in a company's capital structure, the more uncertain is the return to common shareholders.

13. Debt to Total Assets. This ratio (also referred to as the debt to total financing ratio) provides creditors with some idea of a corporation's ability to withstand losses without impairing the interests of creditors. From the creditor's point of view, a low ratio of debt (total liabilities) to total assets is desirable. The lower this ratio the more "buffer" there is available to creditors before the corporation becomes insolvent. The ratio for Anetek is as follows.

$$\text{Debt to Total Assets} = \frac{\text{Debt}}{\text{Total Assets}} = \frac{\$1,300,000}{\$2,250,000} = 58\%$$

$$\text{Industry Average} = 38\%$$

There are other ratios that provide information similar to that given by this ratio. These include the ratio of debt to shareholders' equity, the ratio of shareholders' equity to the sum of debt and shareholders' equity, or the ratio of long-term debt to total assets less current liabilities. Essentially, these ratios provide guidance to answer the question: How well protected are the creditors in the case of possible insolvency of the enterprise?[22] The information conveyed through these ratios can have a definite effect on the company's ability to obtain additional financing. Anetek is highly leveraged compared to the industry average. Further growth through debt financing could prove to be costly because debtors would require a high interest rate to compensate for the relatively higher risk.

14. Times Interest Earned. The times interest earned ratio is computed by dividing income before interest charges and taxes by the interest charge. This ratio stresses the importance of a company covering all interest charges. Note that the times interest earned ratio uses income before interest and income taxes because this amount represents the amount of income available to cover interest. Income taxes are paid only after interest charges have been met. The ratio for Anetek is computed as follows.

$$\text{Times Interest Earned} = \frac{\text{Income Before Taxes and Interest Charges}}{\text{Interest Charges}} = \frac{\$300,000}{\$50,000} = 6 \text{ times}$$

In this case Anetek's interest coverage appears to be adequate.

If a company pays preferred dividends, the number of *times preferred dividends were earned* is computed by dividing the net income for the year by the annual preferred dividend requirements.

15. Book Value Per Share. A much-used basis for evaluating net worth is found in the book value or equity value per share. Book value per share is the amount each share would receive if the company were liquidated *on the basis of amounts reported on the balance sheet*. The figure loses much of its relevance if the valuations on the balance sheet do not approximate fair market value of the assets. It is computed by (1) allocating the shareholders' equity among the various classes of shares and (2) dividing the amount allocated to a class by the number of shares outstanding in that class. The book value per common share for Anetek is shown at the top of page 1237.

Preferred shares are not a part of the capital structure of Anetek. When this type of security is present, an analysis of the covenants involving the preferred shares should be studied. If preferred

---

[22] Additional protection, of course, is afforded through specified liens and collateral and through contractual restrictive covenants.

$$\text{Book Value Per Share} = \frac{\text{Common Shareholders' Equity}}{\text{Outstanding Shares}} = \frac{\$950,000}{30,000} = \$31.67$$

dividends are in arrears, the preferred shares are participating, or the preferred shares have a redemption or liquidating value higher than their carrying amount, retained earnings must be allocated between the preferred and common shareholders. To illustrate, assume the following situation.

Shareholders' equity	Preferred	Common
Preferred shares, $5 dividend per share	$300,000.00	
Common shares		$400,000.00
Contributed surplus		37,500.00
Retained earnings		162,582.00
Totals	$300,000.00	$600,082.00
Shares outstanding	3,000	4,000
Book value per share	$ 100.00	$ 150.02

In the computation, it is assumed that no preferred dividends are in arrears and that the preferred shares are not participating. Now assume that the same facts exist except that the $5 preferred is cumulative, participating up to $8 per share, and that dividends for the previous three years are in arrears. The book value of each class of shares is then computed as follows, assuming that no action has yet been taken concerning dividends for the current year.

Shareholders' equity	Preferred	Common
Preferred shares,[23] $5	$300,000.00	
Common shares		$400,000.00
Contributed surplus		37,500.00
Retained earnings:		
Dividends in arrears		
(3 years at $15,000 per year)	45,000.00	
Current year dividends		
($5 per share)	15,000.00	20,000.00
Participating—Additional $3 per share	9,000.00	12,000.00
Remainder to common		61,582.00
Totals	$369,000.00	$531,082.00
Shares outstanding	3,000	4,000
Book value per share	$ 123.00	$ 132.77

16. Cash Flow From Operations Per Share. This is a popular yet not well understood ratio. It is computed by dividing cash flow from operations by the number of common shares outstanding. The cash flow from operations per share for Anetek is as follows.

---

[23] If the preferred shares have a liquidating preference as to assets, this is considered in determining book value. For example, if the preferred shareholders receive $360,000 at liquidation instead of $300,000, an additional $60,000 is allocated to the preferred.

$$\text{Cash Flow From Operations Per Share} = \frac{\text{Cash Flow From Operations}}{\text{Outstanding Shares}}$$

$$= \frac{\$300,000^{24}}{30,000} = \$10.00$$

This ratio does measure cash flow from operations per share but it has serious faults that can lead to its misinterpretation. It does not provide a measure of all cash flowing through the organization since it incorporates only cash from operations. Additionally, it has nothing to do with cash available to a shareholder at any point in time. It does not reflect the profitability of the company on a per-share basis (this is the purpose of earnings per share). Until the ratio is better understood and its usefulness determined, employing it as an aspect of financial statement analysis must be done with care.

Many companies disclose a cash flow per share in the financial statements, although such disclosure is not required by the *CICA Handbook*. Recognizing that there are problems associated with this ratio, the CICA's Emerging Issues Committee issued an *Abstract* to guide presentation of cash flow per-share information if it is provided.[25] The Committee concluded that the cash flow per share should be shown on the statement of changes in financial position or a note cross-referenced thereto. Not putting it on the income statement would help avoid any implication that it is a summary statistic reflecting profitability of the company. Additionally, information should be provided to clearly identify items from the statement of changes in financial position that are included in the cash flow when calculating the ratio. Our example used only cash flow from operations, but other sources of cash flow (i.e. from investing and financing decisions) could be used. To clarify the calculation for our example, we therefore specifically called the ratio Cash Flow From Operations Per Share rather than Cash Flow Per Share. The Emerging Issues Committee clearly stated that the term "cash flow per share" should be used only if all cash flows from operating, investing, and financing activities are included.

Summary of Ratios and Implications From Analysis

A summary of the financial ratios examined in this chapter, their formulas, and their calculation using data for Anetek Corporation is presented on page 1239.

Given the preceding analysis and comparisons made to the industry averages, the following general conclusions may be reached regarding Anetek. The liquidity ratios signal some problems may exist in terms of the company's ability to pay creditors when due. Without addressing this potential problem, the company may defer paying creditors beyond due dates and, possibly, be unable to take advantage of cash discounts. If the problem becomes serious, creditors may require down payments or security for their deliveries, or may not be willing to sell to Anetek. The activity ratios for receivables and inventory confirm possible liquidity problems and the conversion period is considerably longer than the industry average. The turnover ratios indicate that, relative to sales, the company appears to have excess investment in receivables, inventory, and total assets. This suggests the company should address its credit granting and collection policies and determine if and why it may have more inventory than required. Increased efficiency in these areas could result in more cash being available to pay bills when due.

---

[24] Cash flow from operations can be obtained from the Statement of Changes in Financial Position and is determined as described in Chapter 23. In our example, the $300,000 cash flow from operations resulted from simply adding the $150,000 noncash expense for depreciation and amortization to the net income of $150,000. As such, the $300,000 does not adjust for changes in noncash current assets and current liabilities as they affect operations.
[25] "Presentation of Cash Flow Per Share Information," *Abstract of Issue Discussed* by the Emerging Issues Committee (Toronto: CICA, November 20, 1992). In the United States, the FASB has a standard specifically stating that cash flow per share may not be presented in financial statements.

Anetek Corporation
Summary of Financial Ratios

Ratio	Formula for Computation	Computation
I. Liquidity		
1. Current ratio	$\dfrac{\text{Current assets}}{\text{Current liabilities}}$	$\dfrac{\$800,000}{\$575,000} = 1.39$ times
2. Quick or acid-test ratio	$\dfrac{\text{Cash, marketable securities, and receivables}}{\text{Current liabilities}}$	$\dfrac{\$490,000}{\$575,000} = 0.85$ times
3. Defensive-interval ratio	$\dfrac{\text{Defensive assets}}{\dfrac{\text{Projected daily expenditures minus noncash charges}}{365}}$	$\dfrac{\$490,000}{\dfrac{\$1,525,000 - \$150,000}{365}} = 130$ days
II. Activity		
4. Receivables turnover	$\dfrac{\text{Net sales}}{\text{Average trade receivables (net)}}$	$\dfrac{\$1,600,000}{\dfrac{\$350,000 + \$300,000}{2}} = 4.92$ times, every 74 days
5. Inventory turnover	$\dfrac{\text{Cost of goods sold}}{\text{Average inventory}}$	$\dfrac{\$1,000,000}{\dfrac{\$310,000 + \$250,000}{2}} = 3.57$ times, every 102 days
6. Asset turnover	$\dfrac{\text{Net sales}}{\text{Average total assets}}$	$\dfrac{\$1,600,000}{\dfrac{\$2,250,000 + \$2,100,000}{2}} = 0.74$ times
III. Profitability		
7. Profit margin on sales	$\dfrac{\text{Net income}}{\text{Net sales}}$	$\dfrac{\$150,000}{\$1,600,000} = 9.4\%$
8. Rate of return on assets	$\dfrac{\text{Net income}}{\text{Average total assets}}$	$\dfrac{\$150,000}{\dfrac{\$2,250,000 + \$2,100,000}{2}} = 6.9\%$
9. Rate of return on common shareholders' equity	$\dfrac{\text{Net income minus preferred dividends}}{\text{Average common shareholders' equity}}$	$\dfrac{\$150,000}{\dfrac{\$950,000 + \$867,500}{2}} = 16.5\%$
10. Earnings per share	$\dfrac{\text{Net income minus preferred dividends}}{\text{Weighted-average number of shares outstanding}}$	$\dfrac{\$150,000}{30,000} = \$5.00$
11. Price earnings ratio	$\dfrac{\text{Market price per share}}{\text{Earnings per share}}$	$\dfrac{\$60}{\$5} = 12$ times
12. Payout ratio	$\dfrac{\text{Cash dividends}}{\text{Net income}}$	$\dfrac{\$67,500}{\$150,000} = 45\%$
IV. Coverage		
13. Debt to total assets	$\dfrac{\text{Debt}}{\text{Total assets or equities}}$	$\dfrac{\$1,300,000}{\$2,250,000} = 58\%$
14. Times interest earned	$\dfrac{\text{Income before interest charges and taxes}}{\text{Interest charges}}$	$\dfrac{\$300,000}{\$50,000} = 6$ times
15. Book value per share	$\dfrac{\text{Common shareholders' equity}}{\text{Outstanding shares}}$	$\dfrac{\$950,000}{30,000} = \$31.67$
16. Cash flow per share	$\dfrac{\text{Cash flow from operations}}{\text{Outstanding shares}}$	$\dfrac{\$150,000 + \$150,000}{30,000} = \$10.00$

In terms of profitability, Anetek is doing relatively well. The apparent strategy of selling at a higher margin and incurring a lower asset turnover compared to the industry has resulted in a rate of return on assets above the industry average. Potential improvement may arise, however, if the company was able to reduce the investment in assets yet maintain the same margin on sales. The possibility of doing this is signalled by the ratio analysis, but actually achieving it requires considerable assessment of various possible actions by management. Clearly the company is using leverage favourably. The coverage ratios indicate, however, that Anetek's use of debt to finance its assets is considerably in excess of the industry average. The shareholder's exposure to risks should profitability decline is, therefore, greater.

As these summary comments suggest, ratio analysis provides signalling information on financial strengths and weaknesses of a company. It does not provide answers as to why or what will be done to overcome the weaknesses and maintain the strengths.

LIMITATIONS OF RATIO ANALYSIS

Objective 8

Know sources of uncertainty for decision makers when using financial statement information and the related limitations of ratio analysis.

Earlier, it was stated that an underlying objective of decision makers is to evaluate risk. Uncertainty is the major factor contributing to risk. Uncertainty is reduced and, therefore, awareness of risk is enhanced by decision-relevant information. We have argued that information in financial statements and ratio analysis based on this information can be decision-relevant and, consequently, useful in reducing uncertainty. Even so, a decision maker should be aware that there are significant limitations regarding financial statement information and ratio analysis.

A CICA *Research Study* identified the following four sources of uncertainty as being important when considering the usefulness of financial statement information to a decision maker:[26]

1. *Uncertainty about the nature and role of financial statements*. Misunderstanding the nature, purpose, terminology used, and method of preparation of financial statements can lead users to misinterpret and/or place inappropriate reliance on the information. An important component of the conceptual framework, discussed in Chapter 2, was the notion of user understandability to be assumed by preparers of financial statements. It is assumed that users have a reasonable understanding of business and economic activities and accounting, as well as a willingness to study information with reasonable diligence. This source of uncertainty indicates that accountants can have difficulty recognizing the problems for users to appropriately understand what is reported and/or how it is reported.

2. *Uncertainty about the nature of business operations portrayed in the financial statements*. The unpredictability of business activities due to factors such as economic environment, technology, and competitors' actions causes uncertainty. Knowledge of the type of business activities carried out is important in determining the extent of the uncertainties that characterize these activities. It is within such a knowledge base that analysis of financial information becomes most meaningful. At present, a description of the nature of a company's operations and the related risks and uncertainties is not provided in financial statements.

3. *Uncertainty due to limitations of financial statement measurements and disclosures*. The conceptual framework, *CICA Handbook* recommendations, and accounting practice dictate that various principles must be followed and methods used. Uncertainty occurs when there is recognition that the resulting measurements and disclosures are not well understood or are thought to be incomplete or to lack relevance in a particular decision context. Ignoring or not being aware of these concerns can lead to inappropriate conclusions based on financial statement analysis.

4. *Uncertainty about management's motives and intentions*. Management is responsible for determining the accounting policies and methods used to prepare the financial statements. Choice of a policy or method should be based on reflecting underlying economic reality. This source of uncertainty suggests, however, that users may suspect that management's choices are more motivated by a need to report a smooth growth in income or to "bury" or not disclose

---

[26] J.E. Boritz, *Approaches to Dealing with Risk and Uncertainty*, pp. 44–45.

information the users believe is important. To date, only the methods and policies chosen have to be disclosed in financial statements, not the underlying assumptions on which the choice is based.

Generally, the first, second, and fourth sources of uncertainty reflect an underlying limitation in that ***there is a substantial amount of important information that is not provided in a company's financial statements***. Therefore, since ratio analysis is based on what is in financial statements, any conclusions from such analysis are subject to this limitation. Competitors' actions, technological developments, industry changes, management changes, union activities, government actions, and the state of the economic environment are examples of events that are often critical to the success of a company but are not disclosed in financial statements. They occur continuously and information regarding them must come from careful analysis of reports in the media, speeches by knowledgeable persons, presentations in annual and other reports outside the financial statements, and other sources.

The third source of uncertainty—limitations regarding measurements and disclosures that are in financial statements—has a direct relationship to limitations of using ratios. Because a ratio can be computed precisely, it is easy to attach a high degree of reliability and significance to it. However, it must be remembered that ratios are only as good as the data on which they are based and the information with which they are compared.

One important limitation of ratios is that they are ***based on historical cost, which can lead to distortions in measuring performance***. By failing to incorporate changing price information, some believe that inaccurate assessments of an enterprise's financial condition and performance result. To illustrate, Kerr Addison Mines Limited, in its 1991 statements, carried its investment in the common shares of Noranda Inc. at the cost of $117,609,000, although the fair market value of the investment was $138,000,000. Such significant information tends to be obscured when computing and using ratios based on the historical cost amounts in the body of the statements.

Also, financial statement users must remember that ***where estimated items (such as amortization, site restoration costs, bad debts) are significant, ratios lose some of their credibility***. In analysing ratios, the user should be cognizant of the uncertainty surrounding the computation of net income and the consequences on balance sheet amounts. "The physicist has long since conceded that the location of an electron is best expressed by a probability curve. Surely an abstraction like earnings per share is even more subject to the rules of probability and risk."[27]

Probably the greatest criticism of ratio analysis is the ***difficult problem of achieving comparability among companies in a given industry***. Achieving comparability among companies that apply different accounting policies is difficult and requires that the analyst (1) identify basic differences existing in their accounting and (2) adjust the balances to achieve comparability. Basic differences in accounting can involve any of the following areas:

1. Inventory valuation (FIFO, LIFO, average-cost).

2. Amortization methods, particularly the use of straight-line versus accelerated methods.

3. Capitalization versus expensing of certain costs such as interest on self-constructed assets or development of research ideas.

4. Pooling versus purchase in accounting for business combinations.

5. Capitalization of leases versus noncapitalization.

6. Investments in common shares carried at cost, equity, and sometimes market.

7. Differing treatments of pension and other post-retirement costs.

8. Disclosure of off-balance-sheet financing.

The use of alternative but acceptable policies and methods can make a significant difference in the ratios computed. Several studies have analysed the impact of different accounting methods on

---

[27] Richard E. Cheney, "How Dependable Is the Bottom Line?" *The Financial Executive* (January 1971), p. 12.

financial statement analysis. The differences in income that can develop are staggering in some cases, depending on the company's accounting policies.[28] Decision makers may find it difficult to grasp all of these differences but must be aware of the potential pitfalls if they are to be able to make the appropriate adjustments.

In addition to the limitations mentioned above, one should always be aware that "financial ratio analysis, as a quantitative approach, may appear to be easily learned and applied, but there are pitfalls to be avoided:"[29]

1. If historical analysis covers an insufficient number of years, the analyst may misinterpret trends and current performance.

2. Failing to use an average or weighted average where applicable can distort ratios.

3. Selecting an inappropriate comparison basis (e.g., noncomparable industries) can result in potentially misleading conclusions.

4. The nature and size of the business, geographic location, business practices, and other factors may introduce differences in the comparative analysis that may affect the result.

REPORTING RATIOS: SOME ISSUES

Computation of ratios requires that the necessary information be provided in the financial statements. For example, because rate of return on assets or shareholders' equity is often computed, it follows that sufficient data should be provided in the financial statements to enable its calculation. In fact, some argue that the profession should simply require the reporting of the more common ratios in the financial statements rather than leaving the computation to the analyst. Many companies do report ratios in their five- or ten-year summaries of financial information, but this is not part of the formal financial statements.

Objective 9

Recognize issues associated with requiring ratios to be reported in financial statements.

Whether the Accounting Standards Board should establish standards for reporting of ratios is debatable. In fact, the *CICA Handbook* is already involved in establishing standards in the area of ratios, given its requirement that EPS information be disclosed. Because EPS is the only required ratio, many believe that undue emphasis is given to it. To discourage this emphasis and to enhance financial reporting, some argue that additional ratio information, such as rate of return on assets or equity, should be presented.

Others, however, believe that the AcSB should not be involved in developing standards related to the determination and presentation of ratios. A basic concern is how far the profession should go if such a responsibility was assumed. That is, where does financial reporting end and financial analysis begin? Another reason for the profession's reluctance to mandate disclosures is that research regarding the use and usefulness of summary indicators is still limited and, generally, inconclusive. For example, several studies using a combination of ratios to predict bankruptcy have been partially successful, whereas attempts to predict profitability from ratio analysis have met with failure. Ratios also have been used to predict other types of events, such as bank lending decisions, credit ratings, and mergers and acquisitions, although success has been limited in these areas.[30]

---

[28] Examples of such studies are: Curtis L. Norton and Ralph E. Smith, "A Comparison of General Price Level and Historical Cost Financial Statements in the Prediction of Bankruptcy," *The Accounting Review* (January 1979), pp. 72–87; and Thomas A. Nelson, "Capitalizing Leases—The Effect on Financial Ratios," *Journal of Accountancy* (July 1963), pp. 49–58.

[29] Joseph E. Palmer, "Financial Ratio Analysis," *CPA/MAS Technical Consulting Practice Aid No. 3* (New York: AICPA, 1983), pp. 3–4.

[30] Paul Frishkoff, "Reporting of Summary Indicators: An Investigation of Research and Practice," *Research Report* (Stamford, CT: FASB, 1981); William H. Beaver, "Financial Ratios as Predictors of Failure," Empirical Research in Accounting, Selected Studies, 1966, *Journal of Accounting Research*, pp. 71–127; and William H. Beaver, "Alternative Accounting Measures as Predictors of Failures," *The Accounting Review* (January 1968), pp. 113–122. See also E.B. Deakin, "Discriminate Analysis of Predictors of Business Failure," *Journal of Accounting Research* (Spring 1972), pp. 167–179 and Robert Libby, "Accounting Ratios and the Prediction of Failure: Some Behavioural Evidence," *Journal of Accounting Research* (Spring 1975), pp. 150–161.

COMPARATIVE OR TREND ANALYSIS

In comparative analysis, the same information for two or more different dates or periods is presented so that like items may be compared. Ratio analysis provides only a single snapshot, the analysis being for one given point in, or period of, time. In a comparative analysis, an analyst can concentrate on a given item and determine whether it appears to be growing or diminishing year by year and the proportion of such change to related items. Comparative analysis is the same thing as trend analysis.

The *CICA Handbook* states that "when it is meaningful, financial statements should be prepared on a comparative basis showing the figures for the corresponding preceding period."[31] Generally, companies present comparative financial statements.[32] In addition, many companies include in their

Objective 10

Describe and know how to apply comparative analysis.

Anetek Corporation
Condensed Comparative Statements
(in millions of dollars, except where noted)

Income	1994	1993	1992	1991	1990	10 Years Ago 1984	20 Years Ago 1974
Sales and other revenue:							
Net sales	$1,600.0	$1,350.0	$1,309.7	$1,176.2	$1,077.5	$ 636.2	$ 170.7
Other revenue	75.0	50.0	39.4	34.1	24.6	9.0	3.7
Total	$1,675.0	$1,400.0	$1,349.1	$1,210.3	$1,102.1	$ 645.2	$ 174.4
Costs and other charges:							
Cost of sales	$1,000.0	$ 850.0	$ 827.4	$ 737.6	$ 684.2	$ 386.8	$ 111.0
Depreciation and depletion	150.0	150.0	122.6	115.6	98.7	82.4	14.2
Selling and administrative expenses	225.0	150.0	144.2	133.7	126.7	66.7	10.7
Interest expense	50.0	25.0	28.5	20.7	9.4	8.9	1.8
Taxes on income	100.0	75.0	79.5	73.5	68.3	42.4	12.4
Total	$1,525.0	$1,250.0	$1,202.2	$1,081.1	$ 987.3	$ 587.2	$ 150.1
Net income for the year	$ 150.0	$ 150.0	$ 146.9	$ 129.2	$ 114.8	$ 58.0	$ 24.3
Other Statistics							
Earnings per share on common shares (in dollars)*	$ 5.00	$ 5.00	$ 4.90	$ 3.58	$ 3.11	$ 1.66	$ 1.06
Cash dividends per share paid to shareholders on common shares (in dollars)*	2.25	2.15	1.95	1.79	1.71	1.11	.25
Cash dividends declared on common shares	67.5	64.5	58.5	64.6	63.1	38.8	5.7
Stock dividend at approximate market value				46.8		27.3	
Taxes (major)	144.5	125.9	116.5	105.6	97.8	59.8	17.0
Wages paid	389.3	325.6	302.1	279.6	263.2	183.2	48.6
Cost of employee benefits	50.8	36.2	32.9	28.7	27.2	18.4	4.4
Number of employees at year end (thousands)	47.4	36.4	35.0	33.8	33.2	26.6	14.6
Additions to property	306.3	192.3	241.5	248.3	166.1	185.0	49.0

* Adjusted for stock splits and stock dividends.

---

[31] *CICA Handbook*, Section 1500, par. .09.

[32] *Financial Reporting in Canada—1991* (Toronto: CICA, 1991) reported that all 300 of the surveyed companies provided comparative figures for the immediate preceding fiscal period in their 1991 financial statements.

annual reports five- or ten-year summaries of pertinent data that permit the reader to examine and analyse trends. An illustration of a five-year condensed statement with additional supporting data as presented by Anetek Corporation is shown on page 1243.

PERCENTAGE AND COMMON-SIZE ANALYSIS

Objective 11

Describe and know how to apply percentage or common-size analysis.

Analysts also use percentage analysis to help them evaluate an enterprise. Percentage analysis consists of reducing a series of related amounts to a series of percentages of a given base. All items in an income statement are frequently expressed as a percentage of net sales; a balance sheet may be analysed on the basis of total assets. Converting absolute dollar amounts to percentages is helpful in evaluating the relative size of items in a given year's financial statements and can facilitate comparison of amounts or changes in amounts over time. It is also very helpful for comparing companies of different size. To illustrate, the following is a comparative percentage analysis of the change in expenses in Anetek's income statement for the last two years.

Anetek Corporation				
	1994	1993	Difference	% Change Inc. (dec.)
Cost of sales	$1,000.0	$850.0	$150.0	**17.6%**
Depreciation and amortization	150.0	150.0	–0–	**–0–**
Selling and administrative expenses	225.0	150.0	75.0	**50.0**
Interest expense	50.0	25.0	25.0	**100.0**
Taxes	100.0	75.0	25.0	**33.3**

This approach, normally called **horizontal analysis,** indicates the proportionate change over a period of time. It is especially useful in evaluating a trend situation because absolute changes are often deceiving.

Another approach, called **vertical analysis**, is the proportional expression of each item on a financial statement in a given period to a base figure. For example, Anetek's income statement using this approach with net sales as the base figure appears on page 1245.

Reducing all of the dollar amounts to a percentage of a base amount is frequently called **common-size analysis** because all of the statements and all of the years are reduced to a common size; that is, all of the elements within each statement are expressed in percentages of some common number. Common-size (percentage) analysis is the analysis of the composition of each of the financial statements.

For the balance sheet, common-size analysis answers such questions as: What is the distribution of equities between current liabilities, long-term debt, and owners' equity? What is the mix of assets (percentage-wise) with which the enterprise has chosen to conduct its business? What percentage of current assets is in inventory, receivables, and so forth?

The income statement lends itself to an analysis because each item in it is related to a common amount, usually net sales. It is useful to know what proportion of each sales dollar is absorbed by the various costs and expenses incurred by the enterprise during a period or over several periods.

Common-size analysis may be used for comparing one company's statements over different years to detect trends not evident from the comparison of absolute amounts. Also, common-size analysis facilitates intercompany comparisons regardless of their size because the financial statements are recast into a comparable common-size format.

Anetek Corporation
Income Statement
(in millions of dollars)

	1994 Amount	Percentage of Total Revenue
Net sales	$1,600	100.0%
Other revenue	75	4.7
Total revenue	$1,675	104.7%
Less:		
Cost of goods sold	$1,000	62.5%
Depreciation and amortization	150	9.4
Selling and administrative expenses	225	14.1
Interest expense	50	3.1
Income tax	100	6.2
Total expenses	$1,525	95.3%
Net income	$ 150	9.4%

FUNDAMENTAL CONCEPTS

1. Decision makers want to evaluate risks associated with their alternative choices. Risk is compounded by uncertainty but reduced by decision-relevant information. Such information is provided in financial statements and by related financial statement analysis.

2. Basic financial statement analysis involves examining relationships between items on the statements (ratio and percentage analysis) and identifying trends in these relationships (comparative analysis).

3. Analysis is used to evaluate the past (feedback value) and help predict the future (predictive value). Ratio analysis identifies strengths and weaknesses of a company, but it may not reveal why things are as they are. Although single ratios are helpful, they should be compared with those from industry averages, particular other companies, past years, planned amounts, and the like for maximum usefulness.

4. The reasons for analysing financial statements vary and depend on the objectives of the interested party. Short-term creditors, bondholders, shareholders, management, and other groups employ financial statement analysis to help answer questions of particular concern to them. Therefore, the choice of ratios and their comparisons should be directly related to the questions being addressed.

5. Liquidity ratios help assess the short-run ability of an enterprise to pay its maturing obligations. Liquidity ratios include the current ratio, acid-test ratio, and defensive-interval ratio.

6. Activity ratios, also called turnover ratios, are designed to help assess how efficiently an enterprise is using its assets. Such ratios include the receivables turnover, inventory turnover, and asset turnover.

7. Profitability ratios help assess the degree of success or failure of an enterprise to generate revenues adequate to cover its costs of operations and provide a return on investment. Rate of return on assets and on common shareholders' equity are particularly relevant in this regard. Assessing rate of return in terms of profit margin and asset turnover reveals significant insight into an enterprise's strategy regarding profitability. Earnings per share, price earnings ratio, and payout ratio are other ratios used.

8. Coverage ratios help assess the degree of protection for, and risk attached to, long-term creditors and investors. Coverage ratios include debt to total assets, times interest earned, book value per share, and cash flow from operations per share.

(Continued)

9. While ratio analysis is useful, its limitations must be recognized. These include the fact that ratios are traditionally based on historical cost numbers and that many ratios use estimated amounts in their calculation. A significant criticism is that comparison of ratios between different enterprises is very difficult because each may be using different accounting policies and procedures.

10. With the exception of earnings per share, accounting standards do not require that any ratios be reported in the financial statements.

11. Comparative or trend analysis is the comparison of like items for two or more accounting periods. From such analysis, trend relationships are identified.

12. Percentage analysis or common-size analysis consists of reducing a series of absolute dollar amounts to a series of percentages of a given base. Horizontal analysis provides the percentage change in an item over time and vertical analysis expresses each item on a financial statement as a percentage of a base amount.

——— QUESTIONS ———

1. A close friend of yours, who has not had any experience in business, receives financial statements from companies in which he has minor investments. He asks you what he needs to know to interpret and evaluate the financial statement data that he is receiving. What would you tell him?

2. The controller of a large chemical company has requested you to include in your report certain balance sheet and income statement ratios so that comparisons may be made. Indicate the types or categories of ratios that might be provided and explain their significance.

3. Of what significance is the current ratio? If this ratio is too low, what may it signify? Can this ratio be too high? Explain.

4. How does the acid-test ratio differ from the current ratio? How are they similar? Of what benefit is the defensive-interval ratio?

5. Answer each of the questions in the following unrelated situations.
   (a) The current ratio of a company is 5:1 and its acid-test ratio is 1:1. If the inventories and prepaid items amount to $600,000, what is the amount of current liabilities?
   (b) A company had an average inventory last year of $200,000 and its inventory turnover was 5.0 times. If sales volume and unit cost remain the same this year as last and inventory turnover is 8.0 times this year, what will average inventory have to be during the current year?
   (c) A company has current assets of $90,000 (of which $40,000 is inventory and prepaid items) and current liabilities of $30,000. What is the current ratio? What is the acid-test ratio? If the company borrows $15,000 cash from a bank on a 120-day loan, what

will its current ratio be? What will the acid-test ratio be?
   (d) A company has current assets of $600,000 and current liabilities of $240,000. The board of directors declares a cash dividend of $180,000. What is the current ratio after the declaration, but before payment? What is the current ratio after the payment of the dividend?

6. Steeple Inc.'s budgeted sales and cost of goods sold for the coming year are $144,000,000 and $90,000,000, respectively. Short-term interest rates are expected to average 10%. If Steeple can increase inventory turnover from its present level of 9 times per year to a level of 12 times per year, compute its expected interest savings for the coming year.

7. One member of the board of directors suggests that the corporation maximize its use of financial leverage (trading on equity); that is, using shareholders' equity as a basis for borrowing additional funds at a lower rate of interest than the expected earnings from the use of the borrowed funds.
   (a) Explain how a change in income tax rates affects use of financial leverage.
   (b) Explain how the use of financial leverage affects earnings per common share.
   (c) Under what circumstances should a corporation seek to use its financial leverage to a substantial degree?

8. In calculating inventory turnover, why is cost of goods sold used as the numerator? As the inventory turnover increases, what increasing risk may the business be assuming?

9. What is the relationship of the asset turnover ratio to the rate of return on assets?

10. Of what importance are the following ratios in financial analysis?
    (a) Shareholders' equity to total assets or equities.
    (b) Debt to total assets or equities.
    (c) Times interest earned.
    (d) Ratio of plant assets to long-term liabilities.

11. Explain the meaning of the following:
    (a) Payout ratio.
    (b) Earnings per share.
    (c) Dividend yield.
    (d) Price earnings ratio.

12. Rambo Co. Ltd.'s net accounts receivable were $1,000,000 at December 31, 1994 and $1,200,000 at December 31, 1995. Net cash sales for 1995 were $400,000. The accounts receivable turnover for 1995 was 5.0. Determine Rambo's total net sales for 1995.

13. What is meant by book value of assets or equities? Of what significance are preferred shares in the computation of book value per common share?

14. Presently, the profession requires that earnings per share be disclosed on the face of the income statement or in a note cross-referenced to this statement. What are some disadvantages of reporting ratios in the financial statements?

15. Discuss the limitations of single-year statements relative to comparative statements for purposes of analysis and interpretation.

16. Comparative balance sheets and comparative income statements that show a firm's financial history for each of the last 10 years may be misleading. Discuss the factors or conditions that might contribute to misinterpretations. Include a discussion of the limitations caused because the financial statements are based on the historical cost principle.

17. Explain the meaning of the following:
    (a) common-size or percentage analysis,
    (b) vertical analysis, (c) horizontal analysis.

18. Distinguish between ratio analysis and percentage analysis relative to the interpretation of financial statements. What is the value of these two types of analysis?

19. A student who had just completed an introductory finance course commented, "We didn't use ratio analysis; our instructor indicated that ratio analysis was no longer fashionable." Discuss.

CASES

(DISCUSSION OF BOOK VALUE PER SHARE)   The owners of Cullen Inc., a closely held corporation,   **C24-1** have offered to sell their 100% interest in the company's common shares at an amount equal to their book value. They will retain their interest in the company's preferred shares.

The president of Agassi Ltd., your client, would like to combine the operations of Cullen Inc. with the Publishing Division, and she is seriously considering having Agassi Ltd. buy the common shares of Cullen Inc. She questions the use of "book value" as a basis for the sale, however, and has come to you for advice.

Instructions

Draft a report to your client. Your report should cover the following points:

(a) Explain the significance of book value in establishing a value for a business that is expected to continue in operation indefinitely.

(b) Why should your client consider Cullen Inc.'s accounting policies and methods in her evaluation of the company's reported book value? List the areas of accounting policy and methods relevant to this evaluation.

(c) What factors, other than book value, should your client recognize in determining a basis for the sale?

(AICPA adapted)

(RATIO ANALYSIS AND LIMITATIONS)   As a consultant for Scrubs Inc., you have been requested to   **C24-2** develop some key ratios from the comparative financial statements. This information is to be used to convince creditors that Scrubs Inc. is solvent (able to pay bills when due) and to support the use of going-concern valuation procedures in the financial statements. The data requested and the computations developed from the financial statements follow.

	1994	1993
Current ratio	2.6 times	2.1 times
Acid-test ratio	0.8 times	1.3 times
Property, plant, and equipment to shareholders' equity	2.5 times	2.2 times
Sales to shareholders' equity	2.4 times	2.7 times
Net income	Up 32%	Down 9%
Earnings per share	$3.30	$2.50
Book value per share	Up 6%	Up 9%

Instructions

(a) Scrubs' management asks you to prepare brief comments stating how each of these items supports the solvency and going-concern valuation of the business. The management wishes to use these comments to support a presentation to its creditors. You are to prepare the comments as requested, giving the implications and the limitations of each item separately and then the collective inference that may be drawn from them about Scrubs' solvency and going-concern potential.

(b) Having completed the requirement requested in (a), prepare a brief listing of additional ratio-analysis-type data for Scrubs that you think its creditors are going to ask for to supplement the data provided in (a). Explain why you think the additional data will be helpful to these creditors in evaluating Scrubs' solvency.

(c) What warnings should you offer these creditors about the limitations of ratio analysis for the purposes stated here?

C24-3 **(ANALYSIS OF ALTERNATIVE SOURCES OF FUNDS)** The Budget Committee of Emerson Limited was established to appraise and screen departmental requests for plant expansions and improvements at a time when these requests totalled $11,200,000. The committee then sought your advice and help in establishing the minimum performance standards that it should demand of these projects in the way of anticipated rates of return before interest and taxes.

Emerson Limited is a closely held family corporation in which the shareholders exert an active and unified influence on the management. At this date, the company has no long-term debt and has 1,000,000 common shares outstanding that were sold at $20 per share. It is currently earning $5 million (income before interest and taxes) per year. The applicable tax rate is 40%.

If the projects under consideration are approved, management is confident that the $11,200,000 of required funds can be obtained either:

1. By borrowing, via an issue of $11,200,000, 11%, 20-year bonds.

2. By equity financing, via an issue of 560,000 common shares to the general public. It is expected that the ownership of these 560,000 shares will be widely dispersed and scattered.

The company has been earning an after-tax net income of $3,000,000 per year, which provides slightly more than 14% return on a capitalized value per share of $21. The management and the dominant shareholders consider this rate of earnings to result in a fair price earnings ratio (7 times earnings) as long as the company remains free of long-term debt. A lowering of the price earnings ratio to 6 times earnings constitutes an adequate adjustment to compensate for the risk of carrying $11,200,000 of long-term debt. They believe that this reflects, and is consistent with, current market appraisals.

Instructions

(a) Prepare a schedule in columnar form to determine the minimum earnings before interest and taxes required under each financing alternative so that the present capitalized value per share of $21 is maintained. (**Hint:** Begin with the capitalized value per share and work in reverse to determine the required earnings for each alternative.)

(b) What minimum rate of return before interest and taxes on new investment is necessary for each alternative to maintain the present capitalized value per share of $21?

(c) Which alternative financing plan would you recommend? Why? (**Hint:** Determine the rate of return before interest and taxes on shareholders' capitalized value of investment prior to any expansion and compare it with the answers to (b).)

(AICPA adapted)

(DIVIDEND POLICY ANALYSIS)   Alcott Inc. went public three years ago (early 1992). The board of direc-   **C24-4** tors will be meeting shortly (early 1995) to decide on a dividend policy. In the past, growth has been financed primarily through the retention of earnings. A stock or a cash dividend has never been declared. Presented below is a brief financial summary of Alcott Inc.'s operations.

	($000 omitted)				
	1994	1993	1992	1991	1990
Sales	$20,000	$16,000	$14,000	$6,000	$4,000
Net income	$ 2,900	$ 1,600	$ 800	$ 900	$ 250
Average total assets	$22,000	$19,000	$11,500	$4,200	$3,000
Current assets	$ 8,000	$ 6,000	$ 3,000	$1,200	$1,000
Working capital	$ 3,600	$ 3,200	$ 1,200	$ 500	$ 400
Common shares:					
Number of shares outstanding (000)	2,000	2,000	2,000	20	20
Average market price	$9	$6	$4	—	—

Instructions

(a) Suggest at least 10 factors to be considered by the board of directors in establishing a dividend policy.

(b) Compute the rate of return on assets, profit margin on sales, earnings per share, price earnings ratio, and current ratio for each of the five years for Alcott Inc.

(c) Comment on the appropriateness of declaring a cash dividend at this time, using the ratios computed in (b) as a major factor in your analysis.

(ETHICAL ISSUE: RATIO ANALYSIS)   John McElroy, the financial vice-president, and Scott Stuart, the   **C24-5** controller, of Armbruster Manufacturing are reviewing the financial ratios of the company for the years 1993 and 1994. The financial vice-president notes that the profit margin on sales ratio has increased from 6% to 12%, a hefty gain. McElroy is in the process of issuing a media release that emphasizes the efficiency of Armbruster Manufacturing in controlling cost. Scott Stuart knows that the difference in ratios is due primarily to an earlier company decision to reduce the estimates of warranty and bad debts expense for 1994. The controller, not sure of his supervisor's motives, hesitates to suggest to McElroy that the company's improvement is unrelated to efficiency in control of cost. To complicate matters, the media release is scheduled to take place in a few days.

Instructions

(a) What, if any, is the ethical dilemma in this situation?

(b) Should Stuart, the controller, remain silent? Give reasons.

(c) What stakeholders might be affected by McElroy's media release?

(d) Give your opinion on the following statement and cite reasons: "Because McElroy, the vice-president, is most directly responsible for the media release, Stuart has no real responsibility in this matter."

C24-6 **(ANALYSIS AND INTERPRETATION OF FINANCIAL STATEMENT INFORMATION)** Bagel Co. Ltd. declared bankruptcy in 1994. The company's financial statements for the three most recent years are as follows.

Financial Statements (figures are in 000s)

	1991	1992	1993
Income Statement			
Sales	$5,000	$5,200	$5,500
Cost of goods sold	3,000	3,100	4,000
Gross profit	$2,000	$2,100	$1,500
Operating expenses	1,150	1,300	1,400
Operating income	$ 850	$ 800	$ 100
Interest expense	150	250	400
Income before taxes	$ 700	$ 550	$ (300)
Income tax	210	150	–0–
Net income	$ 490	$ 400	$ (300)
Common share dividends	$ 200	$ 200	$ –0–
Assets			
Cash	$ 500	$ 100	$ 10
Marketable securities	400	100	–0–
Accounts receivable	100	300	500
Inventories	300	210	100
Total current assets	$1,300	$ 710	$ 610
Land and buildings	$2,000	$3,000	$4,000
Machinery and equipment	500	800	1,500
Other	300	600	500
Less: Accumulated depreciation	1,000	1,400	1,800
Net fixed assets	$1,800	$3,000	$4,200
Total assets	$3,100	$3,710	$4,810
Liabilities and Shareholders' Equity			
Accounts payable	$ 100	$ 50	$ 20
Notes payable	100	150	150
Accruals	200	100	180
Total current liabilities	$ 400	$ 300	$ 350
Long-term debt	$1,000	$1,510	$2,860
Common shares	$ 710	$ 710	$ 710
Contributed surplus	300	300	300
Retained earnings	690	890	590
Total shareholders' equity	$1,700	$1,900	$1,600
Total liabilities and shareholders' equity	$3,100	$3,710	$4,810

Instructions

(a)   Using the financial statements provided, identify causes of the firm's financial difficulties.

(b)   Using the financial statements provided, explain how the company could have either avoided these financial difficulties or resolved the difficulties as they developed.

(RATIOS, ANALYSIS, AND EVALUATING PLANS)   Aurora Limited is a manufacturer of highly specialized products for networking video-conferencing equipment. Production of specialized units are, to a large extent, performed under contract, with standard units manufactured to marketing projections. Maintenance of customer equipment is an important area of customer satisfaction. With the recent downturn in the computer industry, the video-conferencing equipment segment has suffered, causing a slide in Aurora's performance. Aurora's income statement for the fiscal year ended October 31, 1994 is presented below.

C24-7

Aurora Limited
Income Statement
For the Year Ended October 31, 1994
($000 omitted)

Net sales	
Equipment	$6,000
Maintenance contracts	1,800
Total net sales	$7,800
Expenses	
Cost of goods sold	$4,600
Customer maintenance	1,000
Selling expense	600
Administrative expense	900
Interest expense	150
Total expenses	$7,250
Income before income taxes	$ 550
Income taxes	220
Net income	$ 330

Aurora's return on sales before interest and taxes was 9% in fiscal 1994, while the industry average was 12%. Aurora's total asset turnover was three times, and its return on average assets before interest and taxes was 27%, both well below the industry average. To improve performance and raise these ratios nearer to, or above, industry averages, Greg Christiansen, Aurora's president, established the following goals for fiscal 1995:

- Return on sales before interest and taxes   11%

- Total asset turnover   4 times

- Return on average assets before interest and taxes   35%

To achieve Christiansen's goals, Aurora's management team took into consideration the growing international video-conferencing market and proposed the following actions for fiscal 1995:

1.   Increase equipment sales prices by 10%.

2.   Increase the cost of each unit sold by 3% for needed technology and quality improvements, and increased variable costs.

3.   Increase maintenance inventory by $250,000 at the beginning of the year and add two maintenance technicians at a total cost of $130,000 to cover wages and related travel expenses. These revisions are intended to improve customer service and response time. The increased inventory will be financed at an annual interest rate of 12%; no other borrowings or loan reductions are contemplated during fiscal 1995. All other assets will be held to fiscal 1995 levels.

4. Increase selling expenses by $250,000 but hold administrative expenses at 1994 levels.

5. The effective rate for 1995 income taxes is expected to be 40%, the same as 1994.

It is expected that these actions will increase equipment unit sales by 6%, with a corresponding 6% growth in maintenance contracts.

Instructions

(a) Prepare a pro forma income statement for Aurora Limited for the fiscal year ending October 31, 1995, on the assumption that the proposed actions are implemented as planned and that the increased sales objectives will be met. (All numbers should be rounded to the nearest thousand; i.e. $000 omitted.)

(b) Calculate the following ratios for Aurora Limited for fiscal year 1995 and determine whether Greg Christiansen's goals will be achieved:

1. Return on sales before interest and taxes.

2. Total asset turnover.

3. Return on average assets before interest and taxes.

(c) Discuss the limitations and difficulties that can be encountered in using ratio analysis, particularly when making comparisons to industry averages.

—————— EXERCISES ——————

E24-1 **(RATIO COMPUTATION)** Financial information for Soderberg Co. Ltd. is presented below.

	12/31/94	12/31/93
Assets		
Cash	$ 140,000	$ 165,000
Receivables (net)	340,000	198,000
Inventories	1,350,000	980,000
Short-term investments	200,000	600,000
Prepaid items	40,000	60,000
Land	580,000	400,000
Building and equipment (net)	2,000,000	1,760,000
	$4,650,000	$4,163,000
Equities		
Accounts payable	$ 730,000	$ 543,000
Notes payable	400,000	150,000
Accrued liabilities	100,000	100,000
Bonds payable due 1996	700,000	820,000
Common shares	2,000,000	2,000,000
Retained earnings	720,000	550,000
	$4,650,000	$4,163,000

Soderberg Co. Ltd.
Comparative Income Statement
Years Ended December 31, 1994 and 1993

	1994	1993
Sales	$4,400,000	$3,900,000
Cost of goods sold	3,080,000	2,925,000
Gross profit	$1,320,000	$ 975,000
Operating expenses	520,000	450,000
Net income	$ 800,000	$ 525,000

Instructions

From these data compute as many ratios presented in the chapter, for both years, as possible. Assume that the ending account balances for 1993 are representative of that year unless the information provided indicates differently. The beginning inventory for 1993 was $720,000.

(RATIO COMPUTATIONS, ANALYSIS, AND EFFECT OF TRANSACTIONS)   Crane Boat Ltd.'s con- **E24-2** densed financial statements provide the following information.

Balance Sheet

	Dec. 31, 1994	Dec. 31, 1993
Cash	$ 52,000	$ 60,000
Accounts receivable (net)	198,000	80,000
Marketable securities (short term)	80,000	40,000
Inventories	400,000	360,000
Prepaid expenses	3,000	7,000
Total current assets	$ 733,000	$ 547,000
Property, plant, and equipment (net)	857,000	853,000
Total assets	$1,590,000	$1,400,000
Current liabilities	$ 240,000	$ 160,000
Bonds payable	400,000	400,000
Common shareholders' equity	950,000	840,000
Total liabilities and shareholders' equity	$1,590,000	$1,400,000

Income Statement
For the Year Ended 1994

Sales	$1,640,000
Cost of goods sold	(800,000)
Gross profit	$ 840,000
Selling and administrative expense	(440,000)
Interest expense	(40,000)
Net income	$ 360,000

Instructions

(a) Determine the following:

    1. Current ratio at December 31, 1994.

    2. Acid-test ratio at December 31, 1994.

    3. Accounts receivable turnover for 1994.

    4. Inventory turnover for 1994.

    5. Rate of return on assets for 1994.

    6. Rate of return on common shareholders' equity for 1994.

(b) Prepare a brief evaluation of the financial condition of Crane Boat Ltd. and of the adequacy of its profits.

(c) Indicate for each of the following transactions whether the transaction would improve, weaken, or have no effect on the current ratio of Crane Boat Ltd. at December 31, 1994:

    1. Write off an uncollectible account receivable, $3,000.

    2. Purchase for $30,000 cash the outstanding bonds payable.

    3. Pay $30,000 on notes payable (short term).

    4. Collect $25,000 on accounts receivable.

    5. Buy equipment on account.

    6. Give an existing creditor a short-term note in settlement of account.

E24-3 **(COMPARISON OF ALTERNATIVE FORMS OF FINANCING)** Shown below is the equity section of the balance sheet for Rock Inc. and Haven Inc. Each has assets totalling $4,200,000.

Rock Inc.		Haven Inc.	
Current liabilities	$ 300,000	Current liabilities	$ 600,000
Long-term debt, 10%	1,200,000	Common shares ($20 per	
Common shares ($20 per		share)	2,900,000
share)	2,000,000	Retained earnings	700,000
Retained earnings	700,000		$4,200,000
	$4,200,000		

For the last two years each company has earned the same income before interest and taxes.

	Rock Inc.	Haven Inc.
Income before interest and taxes	$1,200,000	$1,200,000
Interest expense	120,000	–0–
	$1,080,000	$1,200,000
Income taxes (40%)	432,000	480,000
Net income	$ 648,000	$ 720,000

Instructions

(a) Which company is more profitable in terms of return on total assets?

(b) Which company is more profitable in terms of return on shareholders' equity?

(c) Which company has the greater net income per share? Why?

(d) From the point of view of income, is it advantageous to the shareholders of Rock Inc. to have the long-term debt outstanding? Why?

(PREPARATION OF WORKING CAPITAL SECTION OF BALANCE SHEET FROM RATIOS)   You **E24-4** have been engaged to perform management consulting services for Wolbaum Inc. One aspect of the engagement is to project working capital requirements. The sales forecast is $12 million for 1994. Target ratios for this year are as follows:

Cost of sales	60% of sales	Cash	2½% of sales
Inventory turnover	6 times	Prepaid expenses	2% of sales
Receivables turnover	10 times	Accrued expenses	3% of sales

In addition, accounts payable are projected to be $550,000 at the end of 1994. Assume that the beginning and ending accounts receivable and inventory balances will not change.

Instructions

Prepare the projected working capital section of the balance sheet for December 31, 1994.

(COMPUTATION AND ANALYSIS OF INVENTORY TURNOVER)   The controller of Wendel Com- **E24-5** pany Ltd. finds that, although the company continues to earn about the same net income year after year, the rate of return on shareholders' equity is decreasing. Most of the profits remain in the business, so total assets are increasing year by year. As a recently hired accountant, you are requested to assist the controller in locating the difficulty and to suggest remedial measures. You obtain the following information.

	Inventory Dec. 31	Cost of Goods Sold
1991	$456,000	$3,120,000
1992	545,000	2,960,000
1993	601,000	3,000,000
1994	689,000	3,160,000

Instructions

(a) What conclusions can be reached on the basis of this information only?

(b) What further investigation does it suggest? State how you would proceed.

(c) If your conclusions are confirmed in the additional investigation, what recommendations would you make concerning remedial measures?

E24-6 **(FINANCIAL LEVERAGE ANALYSIS)** Following is information related to TJVB Inc.

Operating income	$ 532,150
Bond interest expense	135,000
	$ 397,150
Income taxes	158,860
Net income	$ 238,290
Bonds payable	$1,000,000
Common shares	875,000
Appropriation for contingencies	75,000
Retained earnings, unappropriated	300,000

Instructions

Is TJVB Inc. using financial leverage favourably? Explain.

E24-7 **(RATIO COMPUTATION AND ANALYSIS; LIQUIDITY)** As loan analyst for Monopoly Bank, you have been presented with the following information.

Assets	Herman Co. Ltd.	Melville Co. Ltd.
Cash	$ 120,000	$ 320,000
Receivables	220,000	302,000
Inventories	570,000	518,000
Total current assets	$ 910,000	$1,140,000
Other assets	500,000	612,000
Total assets	$1,410,000	$1,752,000
Liabilities and Shareholders' Equity		
Current liabilities	$ 350,000	$ 350,000
Long-term liabilities	400,000	500,000
Share capital and retained earnings	660,000	902,000
Total liabilities and shareholders' equity	$1,410,000	$1,752,000
Annual sales	$ 930,000	$1,500,000
Rate of gross profit on sales	30%	40%

Each of these companies has requested a loan of $50,000 for six months, with no collateral offered. Inasmuch as your bank has reached its quota for loans of this type, only one of these requests is to be granted.

Instructions

Which of the two companies, as judged by the information given above, would you recommend as the better risk and why? Assume that the ending account balances are representative of the entire year.

E24-8 **(ANALYSIS OF GIVEN RATIOS)** Stowe Co. Ltd. is a wholesale distributor of professional equipment and supplies. The company's sales have averaged about $1,000,000 annually for the three-year period 1992–1994. The firm's total assets at the end of 1994 amounted to $900,000.

The president of Stowe has asked the controller to prepare a report that summarizes the financial aspects of the company's operations for the past three years. This report will be presented to the board of directors at its next meeting.

In addition to comparative financial statements, the controller has decided to present a number of financial ratios that can assist in the identification and interpretation of trends. At the request of the controller, the accounting staff has calculated the following ratios for the three-year period.

	1992	1993	1994
Current ratio	1.80	1.89	2.01
Acid-test (quick) ratio	1.04	0.99	0.87
Accounts receivable turnover	8.75	7.71	6.51
Inventory turnover	4.91	4.32	3.45
Percentage of total debt to total assets	51.0%	46.0%	41.0%
Percentage of long-term debt to total assets	31.0%	27.0%	24.0%
Sales divided by fixed assets (fixed asset turnover)	1.58	1.69	1.79
Sales as a percentage of 1992 sales	100.0%	103.0%	107.0%
Gross profit percentage	36.0%	35.1%	34.5%
Net income to sales	6.9%	7.0%	7.2%
Return on total assets	7.7%	7.7%	7.8%
Return on shareholders' equity	13.6%	13.1%	12.7%

In the preparation of his report, the controller has decided first to examine the financial ratios independently of any other data to determine if the ratios themselves reveal any significant trends over the three-year period.

Instructions

(a) The current ratio is increasing while the acid-test (quick) ratio is decreasing. Using the ratios provided, identify and explain the contributing factor(s) for this apparently divergent trend.

(b) In terms of the ratios provided, what conclusion(s) can be drawn regarding the company's use of financial leverage during the 1992–1994 period?

(c) Using the ratios provided, what conclusion(s) can be drawn regarding the company's net investment in plant and equipment?

(CMA adapted)

(RATIO COMPUTATIONS AND ANALYSIS) Technotron is a manufacturer of electronic components and **E24-9** accessories with total assets of $20,000,000. Selected financial ratios for Technotron and the industry averages for firms of similar size are presented below.

	Technotron			1994 Industry Average
	1992	1993	1994	
Current ratio	2.09	2.29	2.55	2.24
Quick ratio	1.15	1.12	1.18	1.22
Inventory turnover	2.40	2.18	1.99	3.50
Net sales to shareholders' equity	2.71	2.80	3.00	2.85
Net income to shareholders' equity	0.14	0.15	0.17	0.11
Total liabilities to shareholders' equity	1.41	1.37	1.44	0.95

Technotron is being reviewed by several entities whose interests vary, and the company's financial ratios are a part of the data being considered. Each of the parties listed on the next page must recommend an action based on its evaluation of Technotron's financial position.

- Dominion Bank. The bank is processing Technotron's application for a new five-year term note. Dominion has been Technotron's banker for several years, but must re-evaluate the company's financial position for each major transaction.

- Tekneeks Co. Ltd. Tekneeks is a new supplier to Technotron and must decide on the appropriate credit terms to extend to the company.

- Tom & Diane. As a brokerage firm specializing in the shares of electronics firms that are sold over-the-counter, Tom & Diane must decide if it will include Technotron in a new fund being established for sale to Tom & Diane's clients.

- Working Capital Management Committee. This is a committee of Technotron's management personnel, chaired by the chief operating officer. The committee is charged with the responsibility of periodically reviewing the company's working capital position, comparing actual data against budgets, and recommending changes in strategy as needed.

Instructions

(a) Describe the analytical use of each of the six ratios identified.

(b) For each of the four entities described, identify two financial ratios from those ratios presented that would be most useful as a basis for its decision regarding Technotron.

(c) Discuss what the financial ratios presented in the question reveal about Technotron. Support your answer by citing specific ratio levels and trends as well as the interrelationships between these ratios.

(CMA adapted)

─────── **PROBLEMS** ───────

P24-1 **(EFFECT OF TRANSACTIONS ON FINANCIAL STATEMENTS AND RATIOS)** The transactions identified below relate to Cooper Inc. You are to assume that on the date on which each of the transactions occurred, the corporation's accounts showed only common shares outstanding, a current ratio of 2.7:1, and a substantial net income for the year to date (before giving effect to the transaction concerned). On that date, the book value per share was $151.53.

Each numbered transaction is to be considered completely independently of the others, and its related answer should be based on the effect(s) of that transaction alone. Assume that all transactions occurred during 1994 and that the amount involved in each case was sufficiently material to distort reported net income if improperly included in the determination of net income. Assume further that each transaction was recorded in accordance with generally accepted accounting principles.

For each of the numbered transactions you are to decide whether it:

(a) Increased the corporation's 1994 net income.

(b) Decreased the corporation's 1994 net income.

(c) Increased the corporation's total retained earnings directly (i.e. not via net income).

(d) Decreased the corporation's total retained earnings directly.

(e) Increased the corporation's current ratio.

(f) Decreased the corporation's current ratio.

(g) Increased each shareholder's proportionate share of total shareholders' equity.

(h) Decreased each shareholder's proportionate share of total shareholders' equity.

(i) Increased each shareholder's equity per share (book value).

(j)   Decreased each shareholder's equity per share (book value).

(k)   Had none of the foregoing effects.

Instructions

List the numbers 1 through 8. Select as many letters as you deem appropriate to reflect the effect(s) of each transaction as of the date of the transaction by printing beside the transaction number the letter(s) that identifies that transaction's effect(s).

Transactions

1.   The corporation sold, at a profit, land and a building that had been idle for some time. Under the terms of the sale, the corporation received a portion of the sales price in cash immediately, the balance maturing at six-month intervals.

2.   In January, the board directed the write-off of certain patent rights that had suddenly and unexpectedly become worthless.

3.   The corporation wrote off all of the unamortized discount and issue expense applicable to bonds that it refinanced in 1994.

4.   The board of directors authorized the write-up of certain fixed assets to values established in a competent appraisal.

5.   The corporation called in all its outstanding shares and exchanged them for new shares on a two-for-one basis.

6.   The corporation paid a cash dividend that had been recorded as a liability in the accounts at the time of declaration.

7.   Litigation involving Cooper Inc. as defendant was settled in the corporation's favour, with the plaintiff paying all court costs and legal fees. The corporation had appropriated retained earnings in 1991 as a special contingency for this court action, and the board directed abolition of the appropriation. (Indicate the effect of reversing the appropriation only.)

8.   The corporation received a cheque for the proceeds of an insurance policy from the company with which it was insured against theft of trucks. No entries concerning the theft had been made previously, and the proceeds reduced but did not completely cover the loss.

(AICPA adapted)

(RATIO COMPUTATIONS)   Zany Ltd. is listed on the Toronto Stock Exchange. The market value of its   **P24-2** common shares was quoted at $57 per share at December 31, 1994 and 1993. Zany's balance sheet at December 31, 1994 and 1993 and statement of income and retained earnings for the years then ended are presented below.

Zany Ltd.
Balance Sheet

	December 31	
	1994	1993
Assets		
Current assets:		
Cash	$ 12,100,000	$ 3,600,000
Marketable securities, at cost that		
approximates market	13,000,000	11,000,000

(Continued)

Accounts receivable, net of allowance for doubtful accounts	123,000,000	141,000,000
Inventories, lower of cost and market	192,000,000	148,000,000
Prepaid expenses	2,500,000	2,400,000
Total current assets	$342,600,000	$306,000,000
Property, plant, and equipment, net of accumulated depreciation	339,000,000	338,000,000
Investments, at equity	2,000,000	3,000,000
Long-term receivables	14,000,000	18,000,000
Goodwill and patents, net of accumulated amortization	6,000,000	6,500,000
Other assets	7,000,000	8,500,000
Total assets	$710,600,000	$680,000,000

Liabilities and Shareholders' Equity

Current liabilities:		
Notes payable	$ 10,000,000	$ 20,000,000
Accounts payable	45,000,000	48,000,000
Accrued expenses	31,500,000	27,000,000
Income taxes payable	1,000,000	1,000,000
Payments due within one year on long-term debt	6,500,000	7,000,000
Total current liabilities	$ 94,000,000	$103,000,000
Long-term debt	$257,000,000	$255,000,000
Shareholders' equity:		
Common shares, authorized 20,000,000 shares; 10,000,000 issued and outstanding December 31, 1994 (8,000,000 December 31, 1993)	$ 10,000,000	$ 8,000,000
Preferred shares, $10 dividend, cumulative, $100.00 liquidating value; authorized 75,000 shares; issued and outstanding, 60,000 shares	6,000,000	6,000,000
Contributed surplus	124,000,000	124,000,000
Retained earnings	219,600,000	184,000,000
Total shareholders' equity	$359,600,000	$322,000,000
Total liabilities and shareholders' equity	$710,600,000	$680,000,000

Zany Ltd.
Statement of Income and Retained Earnings

	Year ended December 31	
	1994	1993
Net sales	$800,000,000	$600,000,000
Costs and expenses:		
Cost of goods sold	$600,000,000	$400,000,000

(Continued)

Selling, general, and administrative expenses	66,000,000	60,000,000
Other, net	7,000,000	6,000,000
Total costs and expenses	$673,000,000	$466,000,000
Income before income taxes	$127,000,000	$134,000,000
Income taxes	50,800,000	53,600,000
Net income	$ 76,200,000	$ 80,400,000
Retained earnings at beginning of period	184,000,000	114,200,000
Dividends on common shares	(40,000,000)	(10,000,000)
Dividends on preferred shares	(600,000)	(600,000)
Retained earnings at end of period	$219,600,000	$184,000,000

Instructions

Using this information, compute the following for 1994 only:

(a) Current (working capital) ratio.

(b) Quick (acid-test) ratio.

(c) Number of days' sales in average receivables, assuming a business year consisting of 300 days and all sales on account.

(d) Inventory turnover.

(e) Book value per common share, assuming that there is no dividend arrearage on the preferred shares.

(f) Earnings per common share.

(g) Price earnings ratio on common shares.

(h) Dividend payout ratio on common shares.

(HORIZONTAL AND VERTICAL ANALYSIS) Presented below are comparative balance sheets for the **P24-3** Tater Co. Ltd.

Tater Co. Ltd.
Comparative Balance Sheet
December 31, 1994 and 1993

	1994	1993
Assets		
Cash	$ 160,000	$ 275,000
Accounts receivable (net)	230,000	155,000
Investments	280,000	150,000
Inventories	960,000	980,000
Prepaid expenses	25,000	25,000
Fixed assets	2,685,000	1,950,000
Accumulated depreciation	(1,000,000)	(750,000)
	$3,340,000	$2,785,000
Liabilities and Shareholders' Equity		
Accounts payable	$ 80,000	$ 75,000

(Continued)

Accrued expenses	140,000	200,000
Bonds payable	500,000	190,000
Share capital	2,100,000	1,770,000
Retained earnings	520,000	550,000
	$3,340,000	$2,785,000

Instructions

(a) Prepare a comparative balance sheet of Tater Co. Ltd. showing the percentage of each item to the total assets.

(b) Prepare a comparative balance sheet of Tater Co. Ltd. showing the dollar change and the percentage change for each item.

(c) Of what value is the information provided in (a)?

(d) Of what value is the information provided in (b)?

P24-4 **(RATIO COMPUTATIONS AND ADDITIONAL ANALYSIS)** Ferber Corporation Ltd. was formed five years ago through a public subscription of common shares. Wendy Dahl, who owns 15% of the common shares, was one of the organizers of Ferber and is its current president. The company has been successful but currently is experiencing a shortage of funds. On June 10, 1994, Dahl approached the Commerce Bank, asking for a 24-month extension on two $35,000 notes, which are due on June 30, 1994 and September 30, 1994. Another note of $6,000 is due on December 31, 1995 but she expects no difficulty in paying this note on its due date. Dahl explained that Ferber's cash flow problems are due primarily to the company's desire to finance a $300,000 plant expansion over the next two fiscal years through internally generated funds.

The commercial loans officer of the bank requested financial reports for the last two fiscal years. These reports are reproduced below.

Ferber Corporation Ltd.
Statement of Financial Position
March 31

	1993	1994
Assets		
Cash	$ 12,500	$ 18,200
Notes receivable	132,000	148,000
Accounts receivable (net)	125,500	131,800
Inventories (at cost)	75,000	95,000
Plant & equipment (net of depreciation)	1,395,500	1,449,000
Total assets	$1,740,500	$1,842,000
Liabilities and Shareholders' Equity		
Accounts payable	$ 91,000	$ 69,000
Notes payable	61,500	76,000
Accrued liabilities	6,000	9,000
Common shares (130,000 shares issued and outstanding)	1,300,000	1,300,000
Retained earnings*	282,000	388,000
Total liabilities and shareholders' equity	$1,740,500	$1,842,000

*Cash dividends were paid at the rate of $1.00 per share in fiscal year 1993 and $2.00 per share in fiscal year 1994.

Ferber Corporation Ltd.
Income Statement
For the Fiscal Years Ended March 31

	1993	1994
Sales	$2,700,000	$3,000,000
Cost of goods sold*	1,425,000	1,530,000
Gross margin	$1,275,000	$1,470,000
Operating expenses	780,000	860,000
Income before income taxes	$ 495,000	$ 610,000
Income taxes (40%)	198,000	244,000
Net income	$ 297,000	$ 366,000

*Depreciation charges on the plant and equipment of $100,000 and $102,500 for fiscal years ended March 31, 1993 and 1994, respectively, are included in cost of goods sold.

Instructions

(a) Compute the following for Ferber Corporation Ltd.:

1. Current ratio for fiscal years 1993 and 1994.

2. Acid-test (quick) ratio for fiscal years 1993 and 1994.

3. Inventory turnover for fiscal year 1994.

4. Return on assets for fiscal years 1993 and 1994. (Assume total assets were $1,688,500 at 3/31/92.)

5. Percentage change in sales, cost of goods sold, gross margin, and net income after taxes from fiscal year 1993 to 1994.

(b) Identify and explain what other financial reports and/or financial analyses might be helpful to the commercial loans officer in evaluating Dahl's request for a time extension on Ferber's notes.

(c) Assume that the percentage changes experienced in fiscal year 1994 as compared with fiscal year 1993 for sales, cost of goods sold, gross margin, and net income after taxes will be repeated in each of the next two years. Is Ferber's desire to finance the plant expansion from internally generated funds realistic? Discuss.

(d) Should the Commerce Bank grant the extension on Ferber's notes, considering Dahl's statement about financing the plant expansion through internally generated funds? Discuss.

(CMA adapted)

(RATIO ANALYSIS: ALTERNATIVE FINANCING PLANS) Oliver Inc. is planning to invest $12,000,000 **P24-5** in an expansion program that is expected to increase income before interest and taxes by $2,200,000. The company currently is earning $2.80 per share on 1,000,000 common shares outstanding. The capital structure prior to the investment is:

Debt	$ 25,000,000
Equity	75,000,000
	$100,000,000

The expansion can be financed by sale of 300,000 shares at $40 net each or by issuing long-term debt at an 8% interest cost. The company's recent income statement was as follows.

Sales	$100,000,000
Variable costs	$ 65,000,000
Fixed costs	29,000,000
	$ 94,000,000
Income before interest and taxes	$ 6,000,000
Interest	2,000,000
Income before income taxes	$ 4,000,000
Income taxes (30%)	1,200,000
Net income	$ 2,800,000

Instructions

(a) Assuming that the company maintains its current income and achieves the anticipated income from the expansion, what will be the earnings per share (1) if the expansion is financed by debt? (2) if the expansion is financed by equity?

(b) At what level of income before interest and taxes will the earnings per share under either alternative be the same amount?

(c) The choice of financing alternatives influences the earnings per share. The choice might also influence the earnings multiple (price to earnings ratio) used by the "market." Discuss the factors inherent in the choice between the debt and equity alternatives that might influence the earnings multiple. Be sure to indicate the direction in which these factors might influence the earnings multiple.

(CMA adapted)

P24-6 (RATIO ANALYSIS: ALTERNATIVE FINANCING PLANS) Sidewinder Inc. has been operating successfully for a number of years. The balance sheet of the company as of December 31, 1994, is presented below.

Sidewinder Inc.
Balance Sheet
December 31, 1994

Assets			Equities		
Current assets			**Current liabilities**		
Cash		$ 50,000	Notes payable		$ 80,000
Accounts receivable (net)		125,000	Accounts payable		97,000
Notes receivable		60,000	Taxes payable		61,000
Inventories		270,000	Total current liabilities		$ 238,000
Prepaid items		20,000			
Total current assets		$ 525,000	**Long-term liabilities**		
			Long-term bank loan,		
Fixed assets			due in 1998, 10% interest		190,000
Land	$ 50,000		**Shareholders' equity**		
Building (net)	256,000		Common shares		
Equipment (net)	400,000		(35,000 issued)	$350,000	
Total fixed assets		706,000	Retained earnings	453,000	803,000
		$1,231,000			$1,231,000

The balance sheet indicates that the bulk of the company's growth has been financed by the common shareholders, because $453,000 of past net income of the company has been retained and is now invested in various operating assets. For the last three years, the company has earned an average net income of $85,000 after interest ($21,000) and taxes ($61,000).

The board of directors has been considering an expansion of operations. Estimations indicate that the company can double its volume of operations with an additional investment of about $900,000. Of this amount, $600,000 would be used to add to the present building, to purchase new equipment, and to reorganize certain operations. The remaining amount would be needed for working capital—inventories and higher receivables. Competitive conditions are such that the added volume can probably be sold at the existing prices and that the total income from all operations before taxes and interest will be $320,000. The tax rate of about 36% on income after interest will continue. Three alternative plans for financing the expansion are under consideration:

1. Sell enough additional shares to raise $900,000. For this purpose, it is estimated that the shares would sell at $30 each.

2. Sell 20-year bonds at 12% interest, totalling $790,000. In addition, sell 10,000 shares at a price of $30 per share. Use part of the proceeds to pay off the present long-term bank loan.

3. Sell 20-year bonds at 12% interest, totalling $900,000. Use part of the proceeds to pay off present long-term bank loan. The remaining funds are to be provided by short term creditors. The cost of these remaining funds (in interest and discounts not taken) is estimated at $27,000 a year.

Assume that the financing alternative selected will take place immediately.

Instructions

(a) 1. Compute the current ratio under each plan and compare it with the present current ratio.

2. Compute earnings per share under each plan and compare with the present earnings per share.

3. Compute the rate of return on common shareholders' equity under each plan and compare with the present return.

4. Compute the ratio of debt to total equity under each plan and compare it with the present ratio.

(b) Which alternative financing plan do you recommend? Why?

(RATIO COMPUTATIONS AND PREPARATION OF STATEMENTS) Gatzke Ltd. has, in recent **P24-7** years, maintained the following relationships among the data on its financial statements:

1.	Gross profit rate on net sales	32%
2.	Profit margin on net sales	8%
3.	Rate of selling expenses to net sales	16%
4.	Accounts receivable turnover	8 per year
5.	Inventory turnover	10 per year
6.	Acid-test ratio	2 to 1
7.	Current ratio	3 to 1
8.	Quick asset composition: 7% cash, 28% marketable securities, 65% accounts receivable	
9.	Asset turnover	2 per year
10.	Ratio of total assets to intangible assets	25 to 1
11.	Ratio of accumulated depreciation to cost of fixed assets	1 to 4

12. Ratio of accounts receivable to accounts payable	2 to 1
13. Ratio of working capital to shareholders' equity	1 to 1.95
14. Ratio of total debt to shareholders' equity	1 to 3

The corporation had a net income of $520,000 for 1994 which resulted in earnings of $9.74 per common share. Additional information follows:

1. Share capital authorized, issued (all in 1986), and outstanding:
   Common, no-par value, issued at $11 per share.
   Preferred, $11 nonparticipating, no-par value, issued at $110 per share.

2. Market value per common share at December 31, 1994: $107.25

3. Preferred dividends paid in 1994: $33,000.

4. Times interest earned in 1994: 28.73.

5. The amounts of the following were the same at December 31, 1994 as at January 1, 1994: inventory, accounts receivable, 10% bonds payable—due 1996, and total shareholders' equity.

6. All purchases and sales were on account.

Instructions

(a) Prepare in good form the condensed (1) balance sheet and (2) income statement for the year ending December 31, 1994, presenting the amounts you would expect to appear on Gatzke's financial statements (ignoring income taxes). Major captions appearing on Gatzke's balance sheet are: Current Assets; Property, Plant, and Equipment; Intangible Assets; Current Liabilities; Long-Term Liabilities; and Shareholders' Equity. In addition to the accounts divulged in the problem, you should include accounts for Prepaid Expenses, Accrued Expenses, and Administrative Expenses.

(b) Compute the following for 1994 (show your computations):

    1. Rate of return on common shareholders' equity.

    2. Price earnings ratio for common shares.

    3. Dividends paid per common share.

    4. Dividends paid per preferred share.

    5. Dividend yield on common shares.

(AICPA adapted)

Full Disclosure in Financial Reporting

◼

Accountants have long recognized that attempting to present all essential information about an enterprise in a balance sheet, income statement, and statement of changes in financial position is an extremely difficult task. *CICA Handbook* Section 1000 notes that although financial reporting and financial statements have essentially the same objectives, some useful information is better provided in the financial statements and some is better provided by means of financial reporting other than financial statements. For example, earnings and cash flows are readily available in financial statements—but comparisons to other companies in the same industry might better be found in news articles or brokerage house reports.

Financial statements, notes to the financial statements, and supplementary information are areas directly affected by CICA standards. Other types of information found in the annual report, such as management's discussion and analysis, are not subject to CICA standards.

FULL DISCLOSURE PRINCIPLE

As indicated in Chapter 2, the profession has adopted a **full disclosure principle** that calls for financial reporting of any financial facts significant enough to influence the judgement of an informed

Objective 1

Review the full disclosure principle and describe problems of implementation.

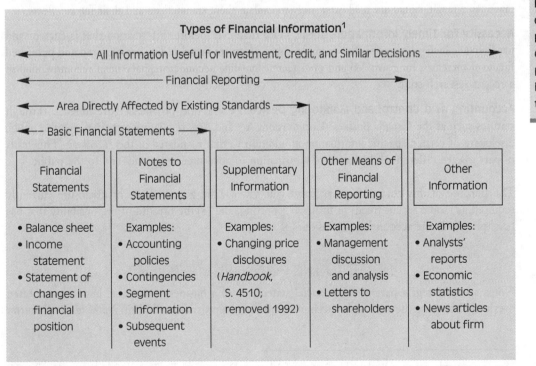

¹ Adapted from *Statement of Financial Accounting Concepts No. 5* (Stamford, CT: FASB, 1984).

reader. In some situations, the benefits from disclosure may be apparent but the costs uncertain, whereas in other instances the costs may be certain but the benefits of disclosure not as apparent.

The costs of disclosure cannot be dismissed. For example, an article in the financial press indicated that if segmented reporting were adopted, a company such as Fruehauf would have to increase its accounting staff 50%, from 300 to 450 individuals. In this case, the cost of disclosure is apparent but the benefits are less well defined. Some argue that reporting requirements are so detailed and substantial that users will have a difficult time absorbing the information; they charge the profession with engaging in **information overload.** Conversely, others contend that even more information is needed to assess an enterprise's financial position and earnings potential.

The difficulty of implementing the full disclosure principle is highlighted by such financial disasters as White Farm, W.T. Grant, or Canadian Commercial Bank. Was the information presented about these companies not comprehensible? Was it buried? Was it too technical? Was it properly presented and fully disclosed as of the financial statement date, but the situation later deteriorated? Or was it simply not there? No easy answers are forthcoming.

One problem is that the profession is still in the process of developing guidelines on whether a given transaction should be disclosed and what format this disclosure should take. Different users want different information, and it becomes exceedingly difficult to develop disclosure policies that meet their varied objectives.[2]

Increase in Reporting Requirements

Disclosure requirements have increased substantially in recent years. Each new *Handbook* section issued by the CICA, as illustrated throughout this textbook, has additional disclosure requirements for both financial and nonfinancial information. The reasons for this increase in disclosure requirements are varied; some of them are listed below.

Complexity of the Business Environment. The difficulty of distilling economic events into summarized reports has been magnified by the increasing complexity of business operations in such areas as leasing, business combinations, pensions, financing arrangements, revenue recognition, and deferred taxes. As a result, **notes** are used extensively to explain these transactions and their future effects.

Necessity for Timely Information. Today, more than ever before, information that is current and predictive is being demanded. For example, more complete **interim data** are required and published financial forecasts, long avoided and even feared by some accountants, have been recommended in a recent research study.[3]

Accounting as a Control and Monitoring Device. Federal and provincial governments, through statutes such as the Canada Business Corporations Act and Acts regulating securities, require public disclosure of certain specific information in addition to that mandated in the *Handbook*. This leads in part toward differential disclosure of information to government agencies and to the public.

The purpose of this chapter is to acquaint you with (1) the general types of disclosure currently required, (2) some recent trends in financial reporting, and (3) the breadth of responsibility that has been placed on the accounting profession.

NOTES TO THE FINANCIAL STATEMENTS

Objective 2

Explain the use of notes in financial statement preparation.

Notes are an integral part of the financial statements of a business enterprise, but they are often overlooked because they are highly technical and often appear in small print. *Notes to the financial*

---

[2] See, for example, Stephen Buzby, "The Nature of Adequate Disclosure," *The Journal of Accountancy* (April 1974) for an interesting discussion of issues related to disclosure.
[3] Robert H. Kidd, *Earnings Forecasts* (Toronto: CICA, 1976).

statements are the accountant's means of amplifying or explaining the items presented in the main body of the statements. Information pertinent to specific financial statement items can be explained in qualitative terms and supplementary data of a quantitative nature can be provided to expand the information in the financial statements. Restrictions imposed by financial arrangements or basic contractual agreements can also be explained in notes. Although notes may be technical and difficult to understand, they provide meaningful information for the user of the financial statements.

Accounting Policies

Accounting policies of a given entity are the specific accounting principles and methods currently employed and considered most appropriate to present fairly the financial statements of the enterprise. The profession, in *Handbook* Section 1505, concluded that information about the accounting policies adopted and followed by a reporting entity is essential for financial statement users in making economic decisions. It recommended that when financial statements are issued, *a statement identifying the accounting policies adopted and followed by the reporting entity should also be presented as an integral part of the financial statements.* The disclosure should be given in either a separate summary or as the first note to the financial statements. The Summary of Significant Accounting Policies should answer such questions as: What method of depreciation is used on plant assets? What valuation method is employed on inventories? What amortization policy is followed in regard to intangible assets?

Appendix 5A provides an illustration of note disclosure of accounting methods and other notes accompanying the audited financial statements of Moore Corporation Limited. An illustration from Doman Industries Limited is provided below.

Doman Industries Limited

1. Significant Accounting Policies

These consolidated financial statements have been prepared in accordance with accounting principles generally accepted in Canada and reflect the following accounting policies:

(a) Basis of Consolidation

The consolidated financial statements include the accounts of Doman Industries Limited (the "Company") and all of its subsidiaries individually and collectively referred to as "Doman."

(b) Inventories

Inventories, other than supplies which are valued at cost, are valued at the lower of cost and net realizable value.

(c) Investments

Investments in associated companies (those 20% to 50% owned where Doman has the ability to exercise significant influence) are accounted for using the equity method whereby Doman's share of their earnings and losses is included in earnings and its investments therein adjusted by a like amount. Dividends received are credited to the investment accounts.

Other investments are accounted for using the cost method whereby dividends are included in earnings when received.

(d) Property, Plant and Equipment

Property, plant and equipment, including those under capital leases, are stated at cost including capitalized interest and start-up costs incurred for major projects during the period of construction. Amortization of the pulpmills is provided on a unit-of-production basis over twenty-five years for the Port Alice mill and over forty years for the modernized Squamish mill. Amortization of the sawmills and equipment is provided for the period of operations on a straight-line basis over fifteen to twenty-five years

(Continued)

---

and over five to fifteen years, respectively. These rates reflect the estimated useful lives of the assets. Amortization of timberlands and logging roads is computed on the basis of the volume of timber cut.

(e) **Deferred Financing Costs**

Deferred costs are being amortized to earnings on a straight-line basis over the term of the related debt. The amount of the amortization is included in interest on long-term debt.

(f) **Foreign Currency Translation**

Transactions denominated in U.S. dollars have been translated into Canadian dollars at the approximate rate of exchange prevailing at the time of the transaction. Monetary assets and liabilities have been translated into Canadian dollars at the year-end exchange rate or at the forward contract rate of a hedged item. All exchange gains and losses are included in earnings, except for unrealized exchange gains and losses on translation of long-term debt which are deferred and amortized over the life of the debt.

(g) **Reforestation Obligation**

Timber is harvested under various licences issued by the province of British Columbia. The future estimated reforestation obligation is accrued and charged to earnings on the basis of the volume of timber cut.

(h) **Pension Costs**

Pension costs for hourly paid employees are charged to earnings as contributions become payable.

Pension costs for salaried employees are charged to earnings as they accrue. In determining pension expense, the initial past service liability on implementation of the pension plan, adjustments arising from changes in actuarial assumptions, and experience gains and losses are amortized on a straight-line basis over the expected average remaining service life of the employee groups. The assets of Doman's pension plan are valued at market values.

(i) **Income Taxes**

Doman uses the tax allocation method of accounting for income taxes whereby differences between the provision for income taxes on earnings for accounting purposes and the income taxes currently payable are shown as deferred income taxes.

Analysts examine carefully the summary of accounting policy section to determine whether the company is using conservative or liberal accounting practices. For example, amortizing intangible assets over 40 years (the maximum) or depreciating plant assets over an unusually long period of time is considered liberal. On the other hand, expensing interest on funds borrowed for the construction of new plant and equipment might be considered conservative by some.

Other Notes

Many of the notes to the financial statements are discussed throughout this textbook. Others will be discussed more fully in this chapter. The more common are as follows.

Inventory. The basis on which inventory amounts are stated (lower of cost and market) and the method used in determining cost (FIFO, average-cost, etc.) should also be reported. Manufacturers should report the inventory composition either in the balance sheet or in a separate schedule in the notes. Unusual or significant financing arrangements relating to inventories that may require disclosure include transactions with related parties, product financing arrangements, firm purchase commitments, and pledging of inventories as collateral.

(Continued)

Property, Plant, and Equipment. The basis of valuation for property, plant, and equipment should be stated: It is usually historical cost. Pledges, liens, and other commitments related to these assets should be disclosed. In the presentation of depreciation, the following disclosures should be made in the financial statements or in the notes: (1) depreciation expense for the period; (2) balances of major classes of depreciable assets, by nature and function, at the balance sheet date; (3) accumulated depreciation, either by major classes of depreciable assets or in total, at the balance sheet date; and (4) a general description of the method or methods used in computing depreciation with respect to major classes of depreciable assets.

Credit Claims. An investor normally finds it extremely useful to determine the nature and cost of creditorship claims. The liability section in the balance sheet can provide the major types of liabilities outstanding only in the aggregate. Note schedules regarding such obligations provide additional information about how the company is financing its operations, the costs that will have to be borne in future periods, and the timing of future cash outflows. Recall that the profession requires that financial statements disclose for each of the five years following the date of the financial statements the aggregate amount of maturities and sinking fund requirements for all long-term borrowings.

Equity Holders' Claims. Many companies present in the body of the balance sheet the number of shares authorized, issued, and outstanding for each type of equity security. Such data may also be presented in a note. Beyond that, the most common type of equity note disclosure relates to contracts and senior securities outstanding that might affect the various claims of the residual equity holders; for example, the existence of outstanding stock options, outstanding convertible debt, redeemable preferred shares, and convertible preferred shares. In addition, it is necessary to disclose to equity claimants certain types of restrictions currently in force. Generally, these types of restrictions involve the amount of earnings available for dividend distribution.

Contingencies and Commitments. An enterprise may have gain or loss contingencies that are not disclosed in the body of the financial statements. These contingencies may take a variety of forms such as litigation, debt and other guarantees, possible tax assessments, renegotiation of government contracts, sales of receivables with recourse, and so on. In addition, commitments that relate to dividend restrictions, purchase agreements (through-put and take-or-pay), hedge contracts, and employment contracts are also disclosed.

Income Taxes, Pensions, and Leases. Extensive disclosure is required in these areas. Chapters 19, 20, and 21 discuss each of these disclosures in detail. It should be emphasized that notes to the financial statements should be given a careful reading for information about off-balance-sheet commitments, future financing needs, and the quality of a company's earnings.

Changes in Accounting Principles. The profession defines various types of accounting changes and establishes guides for reporting each type. Either in the summary of significant accounting policies or in the other notes, changes in accounting principles (as well as material changes in estimates and corrections of errors) are discussed in Chapter 22.

Subsequent Events. Events or transactions that occur subsequent to the balance sheet date but prior to the issuance of the financial statements should be disclosed in the financial statements. Chapter 5 sets forth the criteria for the proper treatment of subsequent events.

The disclosures above have been discussed in earlier chapters. Three additional disclosures of significance (special transactions or events, segment reporting, and interim reporting) are illustrated in later sections of this chapter.

DISCLOSURE OF SPECIAL TRANSACTIONS OR EVENTS

Related party transactions, errors and irregularities, and subsequent events pose especially sensitive and difficult problems for the accountant. The accountant/auditor who has responsibility for reporting on these types of transactions has to be extremely careful that the rights of the reporting company and the needs of users of the financial statements are properly balanced.

Related party transactions arise when a business engages in transactions in which one of the transacting parties has the ability to influence significantly the policies of the other.[4] Transactions involving related parties cannot be presumed to be carried out on an arm's-length basis because the requisite conditions of competitive, free-market dealings may not exist. Transactions such as borrowing or lending money at abnormally low or high interest rates, real estate sales at amounts that differ significantly from appraisal value, exchanges of nonmonetary assets, and transactions involving enterprises that have no economic substance ("shell corporations") suggest that related parties may be involved.

The accountant is expected to report the economic substance rather than the legal form of these transactions and to make adequate disclosures. Section 3840 of the *CICA Handbook* requires the following disclosures of material related party transactions:

1. A description of the nature and extent of transactions.

2. A description of the relationship.

3. Amounts due to or from related parties as of the date of each balance sheet presented.[5]

An example of the disclosure of related party transactions is taken from the 1991 annual report of Canada Safeway Inc.

Note 10—Related Party Information

There are no material related party transactions during the years presented, except for purchases of merchandise inventories made by Safeway Inc. on behalf of the Company. During 1991 and 1990, such purchases were $103.0 million and $101.7 million, respectively. Amounts due to Parent of $5.6 million and $6.6 million at year-end 1991 and 1990, respectively, represent the unpaid balances from the purchase of merchandise inventories. In addition, Safeway Inc. provides the Company with certain management and administrative services. Amounts paid for such services were $3.1 million and $2.3 million in 1991 and 1990, respectively. The Company believes these related party transactions were entered into on terms that would exist in normal arm's-length transactions.

Errors are defined as unintentional mistakes, whereas **irregularities** (frauds) are intentional distortions of financial statements.[6] As indicated in earlier sections of this textbook, when errors are discovered, the financial statements should be corrected. The same treatment should be given to irregularities. The discovery of irregularities, however, gives rise to an entirely different set of suspicions, procedures, and responsibilities on the part of the accountant/auditor.

Many companies are involved in related party transactions; errors and illegal acts, however, are the exception rather than the rule. Disclosure plays a very important role in these areas because the transaction or event is more qualitative than quantitative and involves more subjective than objective evaluation. The users of the financial statements must be provided with some indication of the existence and nature of these transactions, where material, through disclosures, modifications in the auditor's report, or in reports of changes in auditors.

---

[4] *CICA Handbook* (Toronto: CICA), Section 3840.

[5] *Ibid.*, par. .13.

[6] *Ibid.*, Section 5135, par. .02.

Reporting for Diversified (Conglomerate) Companies

Objective 3

Describe the disclosure requirements for major segments of a business.

In the last two decades, business enterprises have at times had a tendency to diversify their operations. As a result, investors and investment analysts have sought more information concerning the details behind conglomerate financial statements. Particularly, they need income statement, balance sheet, and cash flow information on the *individual* segments that compose the *total* business income figure. An illustration of segmentation is presented in the following example of a hypothetical office equipment and auto parts company.

Office Equipment and Auto Parts Company
Income Statement Data
(in millions)

	Consolidated	Office Equipment	Auto Parts
Net sales	$78.8	$18.0	$60.8
Manufacturing costs:			
Inventories, beginning	12.3	4.0	8.3
Materials and services	38.9	10.8	28.1
Wages	12.9	3.8	9.1
Inventories, ending	(13.3)	(3.9)	(9.4)
	50.8	14.7	36.1
Selling and administrative expense	12.1	1.6	10.5
Total operating expenses	62.9	16.3	46.6
Operating income	15.9	1.7	14.2
Income taxes	(9.3)	(1.0)	(8.3)
Net income	$ 6.6	$ 0.7	$ 5.9

If only the consolidated figures are available to the analyst, much information regarding the composition of these figures is hidden in aggregated totals. There is no way to tell from the consolidated data the extent to which the differing product lines *contribute to the company's profitability, risk, and growth potential.*[7] For example, in the illustration above, if the office equipment segment is deemed to be a risky venture, the segmentation provides useful information for purposes of making an informed investment decision regarding the whole company.

Companies have been somewhat hesitant to disclose segmented data for the reasons listed below:

1. Without a thorough knowledge of the business and an understanding of such important factors as the competitive environment and capital investment requirements, the investor may find the segment information meaningless or even draw improper conclusions about the reported earnings of the segments.

2. Additional disclosure may harm reporting firms because it may be helpful to competitors, labour unions, suppliers, and certain government regulatory agencies.

3. Additional disclosure may discourage management from taking intelligent business risks because segments reporting losses or unsatisfactory earnings may cause shareholder dissatisfaction with management.

---

[7] One writer has shown that data provided on a segmental basis allow an analyst to predict future total sales and earnings better than data presented on a nonsegmental basis. See D.W. Collins, "Predicting Earnings with Sub-Entity Data: Some Further Evidence," *Journal of Accounting Research* (Spring 1976).

4. The wide variation among firms in the choice of segments, cost allocation, and other accounting problems limits the usefulness of segment information.

5. The investor is investing in the company as a whole and not in the particular segments, and it should not matter how any single segment is performing if the overall performance is satisfactory.

6. Certain technical problems, such as classification of segments and allocation of segment revenues and costs (especially "common costs"), are formidable.

On the other hand, advocates of segmented disclosures offer these reasons:

1. Segment information is needed by the investor to make an intelligent investment decision regarding a diversified company.

   (a) Sales and earnings of individual segments are needed to forecast consolidated profits because of the differences between segments in growth rate, risk, and profitability.

   (b) Segment reports disclose the nature of a company's business and the relative size of the components as an aid in evaluating the company's investment worth.

2. The absence of segmented reporting by a diversified company may put its unsegmented, single-product-line competitors at a competitive disadvantage because the conglomerate may obscure information that its competitors must disclose.

The advocates of segment disclosure appear to have a much stronger case. For example, many users indicate that segment data are the most informative financial information provided, aside from the basic financial statements. As a result, the CICA has issued extensive reporting guidelines in this area.

Professional Pronouncements

Recognizing the need for guidelines in the area of segment reporting, the profession issued *Handbook* Section 1700 in 1979. This standard, however, applies only to enterprises whose securities are traded in a public market or that are required to file financial statements annually with a securities commission. The basic requirements of this pronouncement are discussed below.

Accounting Principle Selection. *Segment information required to be reported must be prepared on the same accounting basis as that used in the enterprise's consolidated financial statements*. An exception is intersegment sales that are eliminated for consolidated purposes but are shown when individual segments are presented. **Intersegment sales** are transfers of products or services among segments of the enterprise. An example of segment disclosures required by the profession is shown for Inco Limited below.

The Company is engaged in two primary business segments, primary metals and alloys and engineered products, and has a variety of other interests which are included in other business. In its primary metals business segment the Company is a major producer of nickel, and an important producer of copper, cobalt and precious metals. In its alloys and engineered products business segment the Company is a major producer of high-nickel and other alloys and manufacturers high-performance alloy components for aerospace and other industrial applications. The Company's other business segment includes the operations of TVX Gold Inc. which is a medium-size gold company, the company's venture capital program, its metals reclamation operations, its mining equipment operations and its lightweight aggregates operations. Intersegment sales are generally made at approximate prices used for sales to unaffiliated companies. Nonoperating expenses which are not allocated to business segments include interest expense, general corporate income and expenses and currency translation adjustments. Other assets which are not allocated to business segments consist of corporate assets, principally cash, securities, deferred pension charges, and certain receivables and fixed assets.

(Continued)

The principal geographic areas in which the Company operates are Canada, the United States and Europe. The Company also operates in other geographic areas including Indonesia, Japan and other Asian countries. Sales between geographic areas are generally made at prevailing market prices, except that sales of primary metals from Canada to other primary metals affiliates are net of discounts. Total net sales in Canada include exports to the United States of $557 million in 1992, $632 million in 1991 and $631 million in 1990, and exports to Europe of $574 million in 1992, $722 million in 1991 and $842 million in 1990. Identifiable assets in the other geographic area at December 31 include $676 million in 1992, $687 million in 1991 and $689 million in 1990, relating to the Company's primary metals nickel operations in Indonesia.

Data by Business Segment	1992				
	Primary Metals	Alloy Products	Other	Elimin- ations	Total
Net sales to customers	$1,955	$557	$ 47	$ —	$2,559
Intersegment sales	102		7	(109)	—
Total net sales	$2,057	$557	$ 54	$(109)	$2,559
Operating earnings (loss)	$ 162	$ (29)	$ 16	$ 7	$ 156
Non-operating expenses					(134)
Earnings before income and mining taxes					$ 22
Capital expenditures	$ 211	$ 17	$ 6	$ —	$ 234
Depreciation and depletion	$ 219	$ 29	$ 5	$ —	$ 253
Identifiable assets at December 31	$3,062	$596	$357	$ (31)	$3,984
Other assets					$ 177
Total assets at December 31					$4,161

Data by Geographic Area	Canada	United States	Europe	Other	Total After Eliminations
Net sales to customers	$ 274	$852	$778	$655	$2,559
Sales between geographic areas	1,393	30	32	4	—
Total net sales	$1,667	$882	$810	$659	$2,559
Operating earnings (loss)	$ 60	$ (10)	$ 17	$ 84	$ 156
Identifiable assets at December 31	$2,349	$555	$314	$854	$3,984

Note that Inco Limited reports three segments: primary metals, alloy products, and other. Each segment follows the same accounting principles that are used to prepare the consolidated financial statements. *The profession also requires that the segment's revenues, operating profit (loss), and identifiable assets be reconciled to the consolidated financial statements. In addition, depreciation expense and the amount of capital expenditures must be reported for each segment.*

Selecting Reportable Segments. A number of methods might have been used by Inco Limited to identify its industry segments, such as the Statistics Canada Standard Industrial Classification Code, currently existing profit centres, or relating common risk factors to products or product groups. The CICA concluded that none of these methods by itself is universally applicable and that management should exercise its judgement in determining industry segments. The CICA, however, did indicate that there are three factors that should be seriously considered.[8]

1. **The nature of the product or service**. Related products or services have similar purposes or end uses. Thus, they may be expected to have similar rates of profitability, similar degrees of risk, and similar opportunities for growth.

2. **The nature of the production process**. Sharing of common or interchangeable facilities, equipment, labour force, or service group or use of the same or similar basic raw materials may suggest that products or services are related. Likewise, similar degrees of labour-intensiveness or similar degrees of capital-intensiveness may indicate a relationship among products or services.

3. **The nature of marketing methods**. Similarity of geographic marketing areas, types of customers, or marketing methods may indicate a relationship among products or services. The sensitivity of market price changes and to changes in general economic conditions may also indicate whether products or services are related or unrelated.

After the company decides on the segments it wishes to disclose, a quantitative test is made to determine whether the segment is significant enough to disclose. An industry segment is regarded as significant and therefore identified as a reportable segment, if it satisfies *one or more* of the following tests:

1. Its **revenue** (including both sales to unaffiliated customers and intersegment sales or transfers) is 10% or more of the combined revenue (sales to unaffiliated customers and intersegment sales or transfers) of all of the enterprise's industry segments.

2. The absolute amount of its **operating profit or operating loss** is 10% or more of the greater, in absolute amount, of:

   (a) either the combined operating profit of all industry segments that did not incur an operating loss or

   (b) the combined operating loss of all industry segments that did incur an operating loss.

3. Its **identifiable assets** are 10% or more of the combined identifiable assets of all industry segments.[9]

In applying these tests, two additional factors must be considered. First, segment data must explain a significant portion of the company's business. Specifically, the segmented results must equal or exceed 75% of the combined sales to unaffiliated customers for the entire enterprise. This test prevents a company from providing limited information on only a few segments and lumping all of the rest into one category.

Second, the profession recognized that reporting too many segments may overwhelm users with detailed information that may not be useful. Although the CICA did not issue any specific guidelines regarding how many segments are too many, this point is generally reached when a

---

[8] *CICA Handbook*, Section 1700, par. .17.
[9] *Ibid.*, par. .23.

company has 10 or more reportable segments. To illustrate these requirements, assume that a company has identified six possible reporting segments (000s omitted).

Segments	Total Revenue (Unaffiliated)	Operating Profit (Loss)	Identifiable Assets
A	$ 100	$10	$ 60
B	50	2	30
C	700	40	390
D	300	20	160
E	900	18	280
F	100	(5)	50
	$2,150	$85	$970

The respective tests may now be applied as follows:

Revenue test: 10% × $2,150 = $215; C, D, and E meet this test.

Operating profit (loss) test: 10% × $90 = $9 (note that the $5 loss is ignored); A, C, D, and E meet this test.

Identifiable assets test: 10% × $970 = $97; C, D, and E meet this test.

The reportable segments are therefore A, C, D, and E, assuming that these four segments have enough sales to meet the 75% of combined sales test. The 75% test is computed as follows:

75% of combined sales test: 75% × $2,150 = $1,612.50; the sales of A, C, D, and E total $2,000 ($100 + $700 + $300 + $900); therefore, the 75% test is met.

Information to Be Reported. As indicated above, the primary basis for segmenting the results of Inco Limited was by product line. The profession requires segmented information on other bases when appropriate. The three general areas are:

1. Service or product line.

2. Foreign geographic segments.

3. Export sales.

Geographic segment operating profit, revenues, and identifiable assets are reported when revenues of this type are 10% or more of total revenue or when total identifiable assets are more than 10% of the total assets of the firm. Export sales must be reported when a company derives 10% or more of its revenue from sales from this source. For example, Inco provides information about sales to customers, intercompany transfers between segments, operating earnings, and identifiable assets for each geographic segment. This information is extremely useful to investors who are concerned about the political and economic stability of a given geographic area.

   Export sales are sales to customers in foreign countries by Inco's domestic operation. Since Inco's shares are listed on U.S. stock exchanges, the company must report to the SEC. Consequently, export sales from the United States are also disclosed.

Continuing Controversy

The area of segment reporting is controversial from a number of perspectives. One frequent complaint is that this information is costly to develop. As a result, the Accounting Standards Committee of the CICA decided that nonpublic companies are not required to disclose segmental data. Conversely, others argue that segment reporting should be extended to interim reports. The following issues are still hotly debated.

Definition of a Segment. A general view that seems to prevail among accountants is that the enterprise should be free to select the breakdown that best represents the underlying activities of the business. The problem with using this procedure is that a great deal of subjectivity is involved in selecting the segments, which can lead to a lack of comparability over a period of time.

In addition to the problem of determining the basis for identifying the segments, there is the question of what percentage to use. As indicated earlier, a 10% factor is applied to one of the following items: revenue, income or loss, or identifiable assets. But these criteria are still subject to interpretation. In general, however, the disclosure requirements associated with *Handbook* Section 1700 appear quite reasonable and the flexibility afforded management seems desirable. Management is in the best position to judge which is the most meaningful breakdown of its divisional data; and with experimentation, useful information should be forthcoming.

Allocation of Common Costs. One of the critical problems in providing segmented income statements for conglomerate companies is the allocation of common costs. Common costs are those incurred for the benefit of more than one segment and whose interrelated nature prevents a completely objective division of costs among segments. For example, the president's salary is very difficult to allocate to various segments.

Many different bases for allocation have been suggested, such as sales, gross profit, assets employed, investment, and marginal income. The choice of basis is difficult because it can materially influence the relative profitability of the segments.

Transfer Pricing Problems. Transfer pricing is the practice of charging a price for goods "sold" between divisions or subsidiaries of a company, commonly called intracompany transfers. A transfer price system is used for several reasons, but the primary objective is to measure the performance and profitability of a given segment of the business in relation to other segments. In addition, a pricing system is needed to ensure control over the flow of goods through the enterprise.

Transfer pricing is not a problem of the same magnitude as common costs, but it still is very significant in many business enterprises. At present, different approaches to transfer pricing are used. Some firms transfer the goods at market prices; others use cost plus a fixed fee; and yet others use variable cost. In certain situations, the company lets the division bargain for the price of the item in question.

In evaluating a specific division, we must consider the transfer pricing problem. If, for example, Division A sells certain goods to Division B using a market price instead of cost, the operating results of both divisions are affected. Transfer pricing in many situations does not occur on an arm's-length basis and, therefore, the final results of a given division must be suspect. The basis of accounting for intersegment sales and transfers should be disclosed.

INTERIM REPORTS

Objective 4

Describe the accounting problems associated with interim reporting.

One further source of information for the investor is interim reports, which, as noted earlier, are reports that cover periods of less than one year. At one time, interim reports were referred to as the forgotten reports; such is no longer the case. The stock exchanges and the accounting profession have taken an active role in developing guidelines for the presentation of interim information. The CICA issued Section 1750 of the *Handbook* in 1971, which attempted to narrow the reporting alternatives related to interim reports. A recent annual report of Inco Limited, presented on page 1279, illustrates the disclosure of selected quarterly data.

Because of the short-term nature of these reports, however, there is considerable controversy as to the general approach that should be employed. One group (**discrete view**) believes that each interim period should be treated as a separate accounting period; deferrals and accruals would there-

Inco Limited					
(In thousands except per share amounts) 1992	First Quarter	Second Quarter	Third Quarter	Fourth Quarter	Full Year
Net sales	$679,844	$665,833	$601,282	$611,970	$2,558,929
Cost of sales and operating expenses	599,176	581,952	488,373	573,823	2,243,324
Earnings (loss) before income and mining taxes and minority interest	12,794	8,161	33,290	(32,025)	22,222
Net earnings (loss)	2,159	(1,432)	10,621	(28,960)	(17,612)
Net earnings (loss) per common share	$ (.01)	$ (.03)	$ .09	$ (.28)	$ (.21)
Dividends per common share	$ .25	$ .25	$ .25	$ .10	$ .85

fore follow the principles employed for annual reports. Accounting transactions should be reported as they occur and expense recognition should not change with the period of time covered. Another group (**integral view**) believes that the interim report is an integral part of the annual report and that deferrals and accruals should take into consideration what will happen for the entire year. In this approach, estimated expenses are assigned to parts of a year on the basis of sales volume or some other activity base. Atpresent, many companies follow the discrete approach for certain types of expenses and the integral approach for others.

Interim Reporting Requirements

Handbook *Section 1750 requires that the same accounting principles used for annual reports should be employed for interim reports.* Revenues should be recognized in interim periods on the same basis as they are for annual periods. For example, if the instalment sales method is used as the basis for recognizing revenue on an annual basis, then the instalment basis should also be applied to interim reports. Also, costs directly associated with revenues (product costs), such as material, labour and related fringe benefits, and manufacturing overhead, should be treated in the same manner for interim reports as for annual reports.

Companies generally should use the same inventory pricing methods (FIFO, weighted-average, etc.) for interim reports that they use for annual reports. Determination of the interim inventory valuation should include consideration of such factors as current market or replacement value as well as losses due to obsolescence, shrinkage, and theft. In addition, companies may use the retail inventory or gross profit methods of estimating interim inventory pricing.

Costs and expenses other than product costs, often referred to as period costs, are allocated among interim periods on the basis of an estimate of time expired, benefit received, or activity associated with the periods. Considerable latitude is exercised in accounting for these costs in interim periods, and many believe more definitive guidelines are needed. Regarding disclosure, the following interim data should be reported as a minimum:

1. Sales or gross revenue, investment income, amount charged for depreciation and amortization, interest expense, income taxes, income before extraordinary items, extraordinary items (net of income taxes), and net income.

2. Basic and fully diluted earnings per share.

3. Details of any significant changes in financial position, such as in working capital, fixed assets, long-term liabilities, and shareholders' equity.

4. Changes in accounting principles.

5. Subsequent events.

6. Other material matters not previously reported.[10]

The profession does not require companies to publish a balance sheet and a statement of changes in financial position. When this information is voluntarily presented, it should be presented in comparative form using consistent accounting policies. Thus, when accounting changes are made, retroactive restatement of both the current year's interim reports and any prior period interim data presented for comparison is required. To illustrate the type of summarized disclosure presented, an interim report for Industra Service Corporation for the first quarter of 1993 and 1992 is presented below.

CONSOLIDATED STATEMENT OF INCOME
Industra Service Corporation

	Three Months Ended March 31,	
	1993	1992
Contract Income	$22,167,820	$ 9,292,416
Cost of Contracts	18,602,702	7,225,063
Gross Profit	3,565,118	2,067,353
General and Administrative Expenses	2,683,480	1,805,109
Depreciation and Amortization	254,474	155,736
Interest (Note)	212,484	(133,612)
	3,150,438	1,827,233
Operating Income	414,680	240,120
Income Taxes	144,195	107,940
Income Before Minority Interest	270,485	132,180
Minority Interest	(12,322)	4,159
Net Income	$ 282,807	$ 128,021
Earnings Per Share		
Basic	$0.12	$0.05
Fully Diluted	$0.12	$0.05

The above statements have not been audited and are subject to year end adjustments.

---

[10] *CICA Handbook*, Section 1750, par. .06.

CONSOLIDATED SUMMARY BALANCE SHEET
Industra Service Corporation

	As at March 31,	
	1993	1992
ASSETS		
Current Assets	$24,517,592	$13,278,741
Other Assets	496,168	498,398
Property, Plant and Equipment	5,978,476	5,490,027
Intangible Assets	4,006,954	1,394,425
	$34,999,190	$20,661,591
LIABILITIES AND SHAREHOLDERS' EQUITY		
Current Liabilities	$18,170,447	$ 4,032,149
Long Term Liabilities	3,827,745	1,767,626
Minority Interest	381,063	85,850
Shareholders' Equity	12,619,935	14,775,966
	$34,999,190	$20,661,591

The above statements have not been audited and are subject to year end adjustments.

CONSOLIDATED STATEMENT OF CHANGES IN FINANCIAL POSITION
Industra Service Corporation

	Three Months Ended March 31,	
	1993	1992
Cash Provided By (Used In) Operating Activities		
Operations		
Net Income	$ 282,807	$ 128,021
Depreciation and Amortization	254,474	155,736
Deferred Income Taxes	109,688	278,440
Minority Interest	(12,322)	4,159
Other	—	13,494
	634,647	579,850
Working Capital Items	(2,942,483)	(407,318)
	(2,307,836)	172,532
Cash Provided By (Used In) Financing Activities		
Dividends	(49,240)	(98,120)
Payments on Term Debt	(391,824)	(81,458)
Share Capital Issued	29,280	—
	(411,784)	(179,578)

(Continued)

Cash Provided By (Used In) Investing Activities		
Purchase of Property, Plant and Equipment	(136,651)	(39,430)
Decrease in Other Assets	568	540
	(136,083)	(38,890)
Decrease In Cash	(2,855,703)	(45,936)
Bank Indebtedness at Beginning of Period	(5,719,534)	(551,690)
Bank Indebtedness at End of Period	$ (8,575,237)	$ (597,626)

The above statements have not been audited and are subject to year end adjustments.

NOTE TO CONSOLIDATED FINANCIAL STATEMENTS
Industra Service Corporation

	Three Months Ended March 31,	
Analysis of Interest:	1993	1992
Interest On Revolving Bank Loans	$ 120,155	$ 19,095
Interest On Term Debt	98,127	46,551
Interest And Other Income	(5,798)	(199,258)
Interest (Income) Expense	$ 212,484	$ (133,612)

The above statements have not been audited and are subject to year end adjustments.

Unique Problems of Interim Reporting

In *Handbook* Section 1750, the Committee indicated that it favoured the discrete approach. However, within this broad guideline, a number of unique reporting problems exist related to the following items.

Advertising and Similar Costs. The general guidelines are that costs such as advertising should be deferred in an interim period if the benefits extend beyond that period; otherwise, they should be expensed as incurred. But such a determination is difficult, and even if such costs are deferred, how should they be allocated between quarters? Because of the vague guidelines in this area, accounting for advertising varies widely. One method, for example, would involve charging advertising costs as a percentage of sales and adjusting to actual at year end, whereas under another acceptable method these costs would be charged to expense as incurred.

The same type of problem relates to such items as the employer's contributions to the Canada Pension Plan, research and development costs, major repairs, and tax loss carryback or carryforward. For example, should the company expense Canada Pension Plan contributions on the highly paid personnel early in the year when paid or allocate and spread them to subsequent quarters? Should a major repair that occurs later in the year be anticipated and allocated proportionately to earlier periods?

Expenses Subject to Year-End Adjustment. Allowance for bad debts, executive bonuses, pension costs, and inventory shrinkage are often not known with a great deal of certainty until year end. *These costs should be estimated and allocated in the best possible way to interim periods.* It should be emphasized that companies use a variety of allocation techniques to accomplish this objective.

Income Taxes. Not every dollar of corporate taxable income is assessed at the same tax rate if, for example, the company is eligible for the small business deduction. In these cases, certain corporations would be taxed at 21% less on the first $150,000 of income. As a result, there is a progressive aspect of business income taxes that poses a problem in preparing interim financial statements. Should the income to date be annualized and the proportionate income tax accrued for the period to date? Or should the first amount of income earned be taxed at the lower rate of tax applicable to such income? Section 1750 permits either method, with the stipulation that the method used be consistent from period to period.[11]

Extraordinary Items. Extraordinary items consist of unusual and nonrecurring material gains and losses. In the past, they were handled in interim reports in one of three ways: (1) absorbed entirely in the quarter in which they occurred; (2) prorated over the four quarters; or (3) disclosed only by note. *The required approach is to charge or credit the loss or gain in the quarter that it occurs instead of attempting some arbitrary multiple-period allocation.* This approach is consistent with the way in which extraordinary items are currently handled on an annual basis; no attempt is made to prorate the extraordinary items over several years. Some accountants favour the omission of extraordinary items from the quarterly net income because they believe that the inclusion of extraordinary items that may be large in proportion to interim results naturally distorts the predictive value of interim reports. Many accountants, however, consider this approach inappropriate because it deviates from the actual situation.

Earnings Per Share. Interim reporting of earnings per share has all of the problems inherent in computing and presenting annual earnings per share, and more. If shares are issued in the third period, EPS for the first two periods will not be indicative of year-end EPS. If an extraordinary item is present in one period and new equity shares are sold in another period, the EPS figure for the extraordinary item will change for the year. On an annual basis, only one EPS figure is associated with an extraordinary item and that figure does not change; the interim figure is subject to change. *For purposes of computing earnings per share and making the disclosure determinations required by Section 1750, each interim period should stand alone; that is, all applicable tests should be made for that single period.*

Seasonality. Seasonality occurs when sales are compressed into one short period of the year while certain costs are fairly evenly spread throughout the year. For example, the natural gas industry has its heavy sales in winter months, as contrasted with the beverage industry, which has its heavy sales in summer months.

The problem of seasonality is related to the matching concept in accounting. Expenses should be matched against the revenues they create. In a seasonal business, wide fluctuations in profits occur because off-season sales may not absorb the company's fixed costs (e.g., manufacturing, selling, and administrative costs that tend to remain fairly constant regardless of sales or production). To illustrate why seasonality is a problem, assume the following information.

Selling price per unit	$1
Annual sales for the period (projected and actual)	
100,000 units @ $1.00	$100,000
Manufacturing costs:	
Variable	$0.10 per unit
Fixed	$0.20 per unit or $20,000 for the year
Nonmanufacturing costs:	
Variable	$0.10 per unit
Fixed	$0.30 per unit or $30,000 for the year

---

[11] *CICA Handbook*, Section 1750, par. .17.

Sales for four quarters and the year (projected and actual) were as shown below.

		Percentage of Sales
1st Quarter	$ 20,000	20%
2nd Quarter	5,000	5
3rd Quarter	10,000	10
4th Quarter	65,000	65
Total for the Year	$100,000	100%

Under the present accounting framework, the income statements for the quarters might be presented as follows.

	1st Qtr.	2nd Qtr.	3rd Qtr.	4th Qtr.	Year
Sales	$20,000	$5,000	$10,000	$65,000	$100,000
Manufacturing costs:					
Variable	(2,000)	(500)	(1,000)	(6,500)	(10,000)
Fixed[a]	(4,000)	(1,000)	(2,000)	(13,000)	(20,000)
	14,000	3,500	7,000	45,500	70,000
Nonmanufacturing costs:					
Variable	(2,000)	(500)	(1,000)	(6,500)	(10,000)
Fixed[b]	(7,500)	(7,500)	(7,500)	(7,500)	(30,000)
Net income	$ 4,500	($4,500)	($ 1,500)	$31,500	$ 30,000

[a]The fixed manufacturing costs are inventoried so that equal amounts of fixed costs do not appear during each quarter.
[b]The fixed nonmanufacturing costs are not inventoried so that equal amounts of fixed costs appear during each quarter.

An investor who uses the first quarter's results can be misled. If the first quarter's earnings are $4,500, should this figure be multiplied by four to predict annual earnings of $18,000? Or, as the analysis suggests, inasmuch as $20,000 in sales is 20% of the predicted sales for the year, net income for the year should be $22,500 ($4,500 × 5). Either figure is obviously wrong, and after the second quarter's results occur, the investor may become even more confused.

The problem with the conventional approach is that the fixed nonmanufacturing costs are not charged in proportion to sales. Some enterprises have adopted a way of avoiding this problem by making all fixed nonmanufacturing costs follow the sales pattern, as shown on page 1285.

This approach solves some of the problems of interim reporting; sales in the first quarter are 20% of total sales for the year, and net income in the first quarter is 20% of total income. In this case, as in the previous example, the investor cannot rely on multiplying any given quarter by four, but can use comparative data or rely on some estimate of sales in relation to income for a given period.

The greater the degree of seasonality experienced by a company, the greater the possibility for distortion. Because no definitive guidelines are available for handling such items as the fixed nonmanufacturing costs, variability in income can be substantial. To alleviate this problem, the profession recommends that companies should present comparative financial information using consistent methods.

	1st Qtr.	2nd Qtr.	3rd Qtr.	4th Qtr.	Year
Sales	$20,000	$5,000	$10,000	$65,000	$100,000
Manufacturing costs:					
Variable	(2,000)	(500)	(1,000)	(6,500)	(10,000)
Fixed	(4,000)	(1,000)	(2,000)	(13,000)	(20,000)
	14,000	3,500	7,000	45,500	70,000
Nonmanufacturing costs:					
Variable	(2,000)	(500)	(1,000)	(6,500)	(10,000)
Fixed	(6,000)	(1,500)	(3,000)	(19,500)	(30,000)
Net income	$ 6,000	$1,500	$ 3,000	$19,500	$ 30,000

The two illustrations above highlight the difference between the *discrete* and *integral* viewpoints. The fixed nonmanufacturing expenses would be expensed as incurred under the discrete viewpoint, but under the integral method they would be charged to income on the basis of some measure of activity.

Continuing Controversy. The profession has developed some standards for interim reporting, but much still has to be done. As yet, it is unclear whether the discrete, integral, or some combination of these two methods will be proposed.

Discussion also persists concerning the independent auditor's involvement in interim reports. Many auditors are reluctant to express an opinion on interim financial information, arguing that the data are too tentative and subjective. Conversely, an increasing number of individuals advocates some type of examination of interim reports. Since there is no statutory responsibility for auditors to perform a review of such information, the auditor may, on request from the client, permit his or her name to be associated with the interim report if a limited review in accordance with *Handbook* Section 8200 has been made.

Analysts want financial information as soon as possible, before it becomes old news. We may not be far from a continuous database system where corporate financial records can be accessed by microcomputer as often as desired and the information put into the required format. Thus investors could learn about sales slippage, cost increases, or earnings changes as they happen, rather than wait until after the quarter has ended.

A steady stream of information from the company to the investor could be very positive because it might alleviate management's continual concern with short-run interim numbers. Today, many contend that management is too short-run oriented. The truth of this statement is echoed by the words of the president of a large company who decided to retire early: "I wanted to look forward to a year made up of four seasons rather than four quarters."

OTHER AREAS IN THE ANNUAL REPORT

Some other areas in the annual report that merit special attention are as follows:

1. Management's Responsibilities for Financial Statements.

2. Social Responsibility.

3. Auditor's Report.

Management's Responsibilities for Financial Statements

The public accounting profession has attempted for many years to educate the public to the fact that a company's management has the primary responsibility for the preparation, integrity, and objec-

Objective 5

Describe management's reporting responsibilities in annual reports.

tivity of the company's financial statements. Only recently have management letters acknowledging such responsibility appeared in annual reports to shareholders. Presented below is the management statement that served as a prelude to the 1992 annual report of The Oshawa Group Limited.

Responsibility for Financial Reporting

The management of The Oshawa Group Limited is responsible to the Board of Directors for the preparation and integrity of the consolidated financial statements and related information of the Company. These have been prepared in accordance with generally accepted accounting principles consistently applied and are based on management's best information and judgments.

   To provide assurance in fulfilling its responsibilities, management maintains appropriate accounting records which incorporate sound systems of internal control designed to safeguard the Company's assets and ensure proper accounting of all its business transactions.

   In support of carrying out these responsibilities management and the Directors have the assistance of the internal audit department, the external auditors and the Audit Committee of the Board all of whom review and report on such matters.

   The Company's external auditors, Arthur Andersen & Co. conduct an independent examination of accounting records, policies, procedures and internal controls in accordance with generally accepted auditing standards and express their opinion on the consolidated financial statements.

   The Audit Committee of the Board consisting of a majority of outside Directors meets with both Arthur Andersen & Co. and the Director of Internal Audit to review their audit findings. It then reports to the Board of Directors prior to the approval of the audited consolidated financial statements for publication.

"Allister P. Graham"
Chairman and Chief Executive Officer

"Robert E. Boyd, C.A.
Executive Vice President Finance
and Chief Financial Officer

Social Responsibility

The social responsibility of business has received a great deal of public attention in recent years. The public and local, provincial, and federal governments have urged that businesses make a more adequate response to current issues of social concern than they have in the past.

   The information related to social expenditures as presented in current annual reports is haphazard. Expenditures for the following types of items are generally considered "social awareness expenditures":

- Assistance to educational institutions.

- Contributions to charitable foundations.

- Aid to minority groups or enterprises.

- Aid to the unemployed and related programs.

Nova Corporation of Alberta, for example, disclosed the following regarding its social responsibility activities.

NOVA in the Community

NOVA is a consistent supporter of activities that improve the quality of life in communities in which it operates. Primary emphasis is directed to health and welfare, education and the environment.

In addition to cash donations, NOVA encourages employee volunteer activities and supports worthy organizations through methods such as the use of NOVA facilities or services. Many of these activities support community-based projects that provide benefits not available by other means.

In 1991, NOVA agreed to provide funding for a University Chair at the University of Calgary to focus on the related nature of health, safety and the environment as important issues for all students. A program will be developed as part of the management faculty and offered to students of all disciplines.

Other major initiatives included support for charities such as the United Way, litter clean-up campaigns in Alberta and Ontario, sponsorship of the Alberta Sport Council, and contributions to support the preservation of Native heritage through sponsorship at the Calgary Exhibition and Stampede.

As yet, no standards or requirements have been proposed for the measurement and reporting of the social responsibilities assumed by individual enterprises. To some investors, it is a matter of importance whether a company is adopting affirmative policies with regard to environmental matters or is simply doing the minimum to assure legal compliance. As indicated in Chapter 14, many companies have become concerned about the potentially large contingent liabilities related to hazardous waste because stricter laws are being enacted to control industrial waste.

Auditor's Report

Another important source of information that is often overlooked by investors in their examination of the financial statements is the auditor's report. An **auditor** is a professional who conducts an independent examination of the accounting data presented by the business enterprise. If the auditor is satisfied that the financial statements represent the financial position, results of operations, and changes in financial position fairly in accordance with generally accepted accounting principles, an unqualified opinion as shown below is expressed.[12]

Objective 6

Identify the major disclosures found in the auditor's report.

To the Shareholders, Federal Industries Ltd.

We have audited consolidated balance sheets of Federal Industries Ltd. at December 31, 1992 and 1991 and the consolidated statements of earnings, retained earnings, and changes in financial position for the years then ended. These financial statements are the responsibility of the Corporation's management. Our responsibility is to express an opinion on these financial statements based on our audits.

We conducted our audits in accordance with generally accepted auditing standards. Those standards require that we plan and perform an audit to obtain reasonable assurance whether the financial statements are free of material misstatement. An audit includes examining, on a test basis, evidence supporting the amounts and disclosures in the financial statements. An audit also includes assessing the accounting principles used and significant estimates made by management, as well as evaluating the overall financial position.

(Continued)

---

[12] This auditor's report is in exact conformance with the specifications contained in "The Auditor's Standard Report," *CICA Handbook*, Section 5400.

> In our opinion, these consolidated financial statements present fairly the financial position of the Corporation at December 31, 1992 and 1991 and the results of its operations and the changes in its financial position for the years then ended in accordance with generally accepted accounting principles.

In preparing this report, the auditor follows these reporting standards:

1. The report shall state whether the financial statements are presented in accordance with generally accepted accounting principles.

2. The report shall state whether such principles have been consistently observed in the current period in relation to the preceding period.

3. The report shall contain either an expression of opinion regarding the financial statements taken as a whole or an assertion to the effect that an opinion cannot be expressed. When an overall opinion cannot be expressed, the reasons therefor should be stated. In all cases where an auditor's name is associated with financial statements, the report should contain a clear-cut indication of the character of the auditor's examination, if any, and the degree of responsibility being taken.

4. Informative disclosures in the financial statements are to be regarded as reasonably adequate unless otherwise stated in the report.

In most cases, the auditor issues a standard, unqualified, or clean opinion; that is, the auditor expresses the opinion that the financial statements present fairly, in all material respects, the financial position, results of operations, and its changes in financial position in conformity with generally accepted accounting principles. Certain circumstances, although they do not affect the auditor's unqualified opinion, may require the auditor to add a reservation to the audit report. Some of the more important circumstances are as follows:

1. **Departure from generally accepted accounting principles**. Occurs when one or more of the following three conditions arise:

   (a) Application of an inappropriate accounting policy.

   (b) An item in the financial statements is inappropriately valued.

   (c) Inadequate disclosure.

2. **Limitation in the scope of the audit**. Refers to circumstances under which the auditor has been unable to complete all of the tests and other audit procedures considered necessary.

The reservation may take the form of a qualified opinion, an adverse opinion, or a denial of opinion. The magnitude of the effect of the circumstances above on the financial statements is a primary factor used by auditors in determining the type of reservation that is appropriate.

A **qualified opinion** contains an exception to the standard opinion; ordinarily, the exception is not of sufficient magnitude to invalidate the statements as a whole; if it were, an adverse opinion would be rendered. A qualified opinion states that, except for the effects of the matter to which the qualification relates, the financial statements present fairly, in all material respects, the financial position, results of operations, and changes in financial position in conformity with generally accepted accounting principles.

An **adverse opinion** is required in any report in which the exceptions to fair presentation are so material that, in the independent auditor's judgement, a qualified opinion is not justified. In such a case, the financial statements taken as a whole are not presented in accordance with generally accepted accounting principles. Adverse opinions are rare because most enterprises change their accounting to conform with the auditor's desires.

A **denial of an opinion** is appropriate when the auditor has gathered so little information from the financial statements that no opinion can be expressed.

The audit report should provide useful information to the investor. One investment banker noted, "Probably the first item to check is the auditor's opinion to see whether or not it is a clean one—in conformity with generally accepted accounting principles—or is qualified in regard to differences between the auditor and company management in the accounting treatment of some major item, or in the outcome of some major litigation."

REPORTING ON FINANCIAL FORECASTS AND PROJECTIONS

In recent years, the investing public's demand for more and better information has focused on disclosure of corporate expectations for the future.[13] These disclosures take one of two forms:[14]

> **Objective 7**
>
> Identify issues related to financial forecasts and projections.

1. A **forecast** is prospective financial results of operations, financial position, or changes in financial position that reflect management's expectations and plans for the period involved.

2. A **projection** is prospective financial results of operations, financial position, or changes in financial position based on one or more hypothetical assumption(s) and a course of action that are not necessarily the most likely in the circumstances.

As indicated above, the difference between a forecast and a projection is that a forecast attempts to provide information on what is expected to happen, whereas a projection may provide information on what is not necessarily expected to happen.

Note that forecasts are the subject of intensive discussion with journalists, corporate executives, financial analysts, accountants, and others making their views known. Predictably, there are strong arguments on either side. Listed below are some of the arguments.

Arguments for requiring published forecasts:

1. Investment decisions are based on future expectations; therefore, information about the future facilitates better decisions.

2. Forecasts are already circulated informally, but are uncontrolled, frequently misleading, and not available equally to all investors. This confused situation should be brought under control.

3. Circumstances now change so rapidly that historical information is no longer adequate for prediction.

Arguments against requiring published forecasts:

1. No one can foretell the future. Therefore, forecasts, while conveying an impression of precision about the future, will inevitably be wrong.

---

[13] Some areas in which companies are using financial information about the future are equipment lease-versus-buy analysis, analysis of a company's ability to successfully enter new markets, and examining merger and acquisition opportunities. In addition, forecasts and projections are also prepared for use by third parties in public offering documents (requiring financial forecasts), tax-oriented investments, and financial feasibility studies. Use of forward-looking data has been enhanced by the increased capability of the microcomputer to analyse, compare, and manipulate large quantities of data.

[14] "Future-Oriented Financial Information," *CICA Accounting Standards Committee, Re-exposure Draft*, August 1988.

2. Organizations will strive only to meet their published forecasts, not to produce results that are in the stockholders' best interest.

3. When forecasts are not proved to be accurate, there will be recriminations and probably legal actions.

4. Disclosure of forecasts will be detrimental to organizations because it will fully inform not only investors, but also competitors (foreign and domestic).[15]

The Accounting Standards Board has issued a standard (*Handbook*, Section 4250) entitled "Future-Oriented Financial Information." Important components of this section are that it requires accountants to provide (1) a cautionary note stating that the actual results for the period may be different from the forecast, (2) a clear indication as to whether the information is a forecast or a projection, and (3) disclosure about the assumptions and hypotheses used.[16]

Experience in the United States and the United Kingdom

The United Kingdom has permitted financial forecasts for years and the results have been fairly successful. A typical British forecast adapted from a construction company's report to support a public share offering is as follows.

Profits have grown substantially over the past 10 years and directors are confident of being able to continue this expansion. . . While the rate of expansion will be dependent on the level of economic activity in Ireland and in England, the group is well structured to avail itself of opportunities as they arise, particularly in the field of property development, which is expected to play an increasingly important role in the group's future expansion.

Profits before taxation for the half year ended 30th June 1993 were 402,000 pounds. On the basis of trading experiences since that date the present level of sales and completions, the directors expect that in the absence of unforeseen circumstances, the group's profits before taxation for the year to 31st December 1993 will be not less than 960,000 pounds . . .

No dividends will be paid in respect of the year December 31, 1993. In a full financial year, on the basis of the above forecasts (not including full year profits) it would be the intention of the board, assuming current rates of tax, to recommend dividends totalling 40% (of after-tax profits), of which 15% payable would be as an interest dividend in November 1994 and 25% as a final dividend in June 1995.

In the United States, the legal environment is not as favourable toward publication of financial forecasts. A general narrative-type forecast would be preferred over the more quantitative British forecast. The following illustrates a forecast that a U.S. company might issue.

On the basis of promotions planned by the company for the second half of fiscal 1994, net earnings for that period are expected to be approximately the same as those for the first half of fiscal 1995, with net earnings for the third quarter expected to make the predominant contribution to net earnings for the second half of 1995.

---

[15] Joseph P. Cummings, *Financial Forecasts and the Certified Public Accountant* (New York: Peat, Marwick, Mitchell & Co., November 30, 1972).

[16] *CICA Handbook*, Section 4250, pars. .24 and .32.

Questions of Liability

What happens if a company does not meet its forecasts? Are the company and the auditor going to be sued? If a company, for example, projects an earnings increase of 15% and achieves only 5%, should the shareholder be permitted to have some judicial recourse against the company? One possible solution to this problem would require passage of "safe harbour" legislation that would protect companies that have used "good faith" and "reasonable assumptions" in their forecasting.

In addition to the question of liability, several other issues must be resolved before earnings projections should be made mandatory. The role and responsibility of independent public accountants as attestors of forecasts must be determined. Should forecasts consist of general expectations or of detailed disclosures? Should a single value ($1.50) or a range of values ($1.50 ± $.20) be presented? What should be the length of the period to be forecasted?

Financial forecasts provide such highly relevant investment information that the demand for them will not subside. Although there are some disadvantages to the requirement of forecasts, these are outweighed by the advantages. The authors believe that the publication of forecasts is a natural and inevitable extension of corporate disclosure.

CRITERIA FOR MAKING ACCOUNTING AND REPORTING CHOICES

Throughout this textbook and especially in this chapter, we have stressed the need to provide information that is useful to predict the amount, timing, and uncertainty of future cash flows. To achieve this objective, accountants must make judicious choices between alternative accounting concepts, methods, and means of disclosure. There are many choices among acceptable alternatives that accountants are required to make.

As indicated in Chapter 1, accounting is greatly influenced by its environment. Because accounting does not exist in a vacuum, it seems unrealistic to assume that alternative presentations to certain transactions and events will be eliminated entirely. Nevertheless, we are hopeful that the profession, through the development of a conceptual framework, will be able to focus on the needs of financial statement users and eliminate diversity where appropriate. Concepts statements (e.g., the FASB's conceptual framework) on objectives of financial reporting, elements of financial statements, qualitative characteristics of accounting information, and potential statements on reporting, recognition, and measurement are important steps in the right direction. Nevertheless, the profession must continue its efforts to develop a sound foundation on which accounting standards and practice can be built.

FUNDAMENTAL CONCEPTS

1. Financial statements, notes to the financial statements, and supplementary information are areas directly affected by CICA standards. In addition, financial reporting includes other types of information found in the annual report.

2. Disclosure requirements have increased because of (1) the complexity of the business environment, (2) the necessity for timely information, and (3) the use of accounting as a control and monitoring device.

3. If only the consolidated figures are available to the user, much information regarding the composition of these figures is hidden in aggregated amounts. There is no way to tell from the consolidated data the extent to which the differing product lines contribute to the company's profitability, risk, and growth potential. As a result, segment information is required by the profession in certain situations.

4. The same accounting principles used for consolidated data should be used for segment data. Segment data may be prepared for a service or product line, foreign operations, or export sales.

5. Interim reports cover periods of one year or less. Two viewpoints exist regarding interim reports. One view (discrete view) believes that each interim period should be treated as a separate accounting period. Another view (integral view) is that the interim report is an integral part of the annual report and that deferrals and accruals should take into consideration what will happen for the entire year.

(Continued)

6. Publication of financial forecasts has not been incorporated into the formal reporting requirements, although the matter is being discussed in the profession. One of the main problems deterring the presentation of forecasts is the nature and extent of liability assumed by the company and its auditors for the accuracy of the forecast.

7. Management has primary responsibility for the financial statements and this responsibility is often indicated in a letter to shareholders in the annual report.

8. Certain supplementary information is often presented with financial statements to help users understand relationships such as the effect of changing prices on the firm.

9. An important source of information is the auditor's report. In most cases, the auditor issues a standard, unqualified, or clean opinion. There are situations, however, in which the auditor is required to (1) express a qualified opinion, (2) express an adverse opinion, or (3) deny an opinion.

APPENDIX 25A
Accounting for Changing Prices

One assumption made in accounting is that the monetary unit remains stable over a period of time. But is that assumption realistic? Consider the classic story about the individual who went to sleep and woke up 10 years later. Hurrying to a telephone, she got through to her broker and asked what her formerly modest stock portfolio was worth. She was told that she was a multimillionaire—her Xerox Canada shares were worth $5 million and her BCE Inc. shares were up to $10 million. Elated, she was about to inquire about her other holdings, when the telephone operator cut in with "Your time is up. Please deposit $100,000 for the next three minutes."[17]

What this little story demonstrates is that prices can and do change over a period of time, and that one is not necessarily better off when this happens. Although the example above is extreme, consider some more realistic data that compare prices in 1984 with what was expected in 1994, assuming that prices increased either an average of 6% or 13% per year.

Examples of Changing Prices			
	1984	1994	
Assumed Average Price Increase		6%	13%
University, yearly average cost	$ 3,350.00	$ 6,000.00	$ 11,400.00
Average taxi ride, Toronto (before tip)	2.95	5.30	10.00
Slice of pizza	.65	1.20	2.25
First-class postage stamp	.30	.54	.93
Run-of-the-mill suburban $150,000 house, Vancouver	150,000.00	270,000.00	510,000.00
McDonald's milk shake	.75	1.35	2.55

Despite the inevitability of changing prices during a period of inflation, the accounting profession still follows the stable monetary unit assumption in the preparation of a company's primary financial statements. While admitting that some changes in prices do occur, the profession believes that the unit of measure (e.g., the dollar) has remained sufficiently constant over time to provide meaningful financial information.

The profession, however, at one time encouraged the disclosure of certain price-level-adjusted data in the form of supplemental information. The two most widely used approaches to show the effects of changing prices on a company's financial statement are (1) constant dollar accounting and (2) current cost accounting.

CONSTANT DOLLAR ACCOUNTING

The real value of the dollar is determined by the goods or services for which it can be exchanged. This real value is commonly called **purchasing power**. As the company experiences **inflation** (rising price levels) or **deflation** (falling price levels), the amount of goods or services for which a dollar can be exchanged changes; that is, the purchasing power of the dollar changes from one period to the next.

Constant dollar accounting restates financial statement items into dollars that have equal purchasing power. As one executive of Shell Oil Company explained, "Constant dollar accounting is a restatement of the traditional financial information into a common unit of measurement." In other words, constant dollar accounting changes the unit of measurement; it does not, however, change the underlying accounting principles used to report historical cost amounts. Constant dollar accounting is cost-based.

Through constant dollar restatement, financial data are rendered comparable; thus, important trends can be detected. For example, a newspaper article recently lamented the fact that family incomes after taxes ($42,612) were only slightly

---

[17] Adapted from *Barron's*, January 28, 1980, p. 27.

higher than they were in 1976 ($42,495) after adjusting for inflation. This information suggests that the standard of living in Canada is holding constant at best.

Price-Level Indices

To restate financial information into constant dollars, it is necessary to measure a change in the price of a "basket of goods" from one period to the next. Developing this basket of goods is a complex process and involves judgement in selecting the most appropriate items to be part of this market basket. Fortunately, the government puts together a number of different baskets of goods and computes indices for them. One of the most popular, and the one that accountants use, is the Consumer Price Index (CPI). The CPI reflects the average change in the retail prices of a fairly broad group of consumer goods.

The procedure for restating reported historical cost dollars, which vary in purchasing power, to dollars of constant purchasing power is relatively straightforward. The restatement is accomplished by multiplying the amount to be restated by a fraction, the numerator of which is the index for current prices and the denominator of which is the index for prices that prevailed at the date related to the amount being restated. The denominator is often referred to as the base year. The formula is as follows.

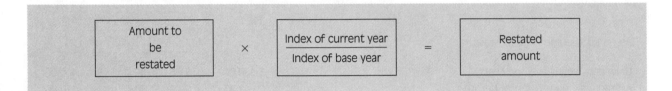

To illustrate how this restatement process works, assume that land was purchased in 1987 for $100,000 and another parcel of land was purchased in 1991 for $80,000. If the price-level index was 100 in 1987, 120 in 1990, and 180 in 1994, the land parcels would be restated to the 1994 price level as follows.

$$\text{1987 purchase} \quad \$100,000 \times \frac{180}{100} = \$180,000$$

$$\text{1991 purchase} \quad \$\ 80,000 \times \frac{180}{120} = \underline{\ 120,000}$$

Land as restated $\qquad \underline{\underline{\$300,000}}$

The land is restated to $300,000 in terms of 1994 dollars using the 1994 index of 180 as the numerator for both parcels and the base year indices of 100 and 120 as the denominators. If historical cost dollars are not restated, dollars of different purchasing power are added together and the total dollar amount is not meaningful.

Monetary and Nonmonetary Items

In preparing constant dollar statements, it is essential to distinguish between monetary and nonmonetary items. **Monetary items** are contractual claims to receive or pay a fixed amount of cash. Monetary assets include cash, accounts and notes receivable, and investments that pay a fixed rate of interest and will be repaid at a fixed amount in the future. Monetary liabilities include accounts and notes payable, accruals such as wages and interest payable, and long-term obligations payable in a fixed amount of cash.

All assets and liabilities not classified as monetary items are classified as nonmonetary for constant dollar accounting purposes. **Nonmonetary items** are items whose prices in terms of the monetary unit change in proportion to changes in the general price level. Examples of nonmonetary assets are inventories; property, plant, and equipment; and intangible assets. Most liabilities are monetary items, while owners' equity items are usually nonmonetary. The following chart indicates some major monetary and nonmonetary items.

Monetary Items	Nonmonetary Items
Cash	Inventories
Notes and accounts receivable	Investments in common shares
Investments that pay a fixed rate	Property, plant, and equipment
of interest	Intangible assets
Notes and accounts payable	Share capital

Effects of Holding Monetary and Nonmonetary Items

Holders of monetary assets lose during inflation because a given amount of money buys progressively fewer goods and services. Conversely, liabilities such as accounts payable and notes payable held during a period of inflation become less burdensome because they are payable in dollars of reduced general purchasing power. The gains or losses that result from holding monetary items during periods of price changes are often referred to as **purchasing power gains and losses**. As one company explained in its annual report, "If the company's equity is invested in monetary assets, the purchasing power of its equity is gradually eroded at a rate equal to inflation."

To illustrate the effects of holding monetary and nonmonetary items in a period of inflation, assume that Helio Company has the following balance sheet at the beginning of the year.

Helio Company
Balance Sheet
(Beginning of Period)
Price Index = 100

Cash	$1,000		Share capital	$4,000
Inventory	3,000			
Total assets	$4,000		Total equity	$4,000

If the general price level doubles during the year and no transactions take place, then for the company to be in the same economic position at the end of the year as it was at the beginning, it should have the balance sheet shown below.

Helio Company
Balance Sheet
(End of Period)
Price Index = 200

Cash	$2,000		Share capital	$8,000
Inventory	6,000			
Total assets	$8,000		Total equity	$8,000

As illustrated, all items should have doubled if the company is to be in the same economic position. However, only nonmonetary items (inventory and share capital) can be doubled. Helio still has only $1,000 in cash; therefore, it has experienced a purchasing power loss by holding cash during a period of inflation. Helio's balance sheet presented on a constant dollar basis would appear as shown at the top of page 1296.

As noted, Helio Company has experienced a purchasing power loss of $1,000, which is shown as a reduction of retained earnings.

Helio Company
Balance Sheet
(End of Period)
Price Index = 200

Cash	$1,000	Share capital	$8,000
Inventory	6,000	Retained earnings	(1,000)
Total assets	$7,000	Total equity	$7,000

In summary, because monetary assets and liabilities are already stated in terms of current purchasing power in the historical cost balance sheet, they appear at the same amounts in statements adjusted for general price-level changes. The fact that the end-of-the-current-year amounts are the same in historical dollar statements as in constant dollar statements does not obscure the fact that purchasing power gains or losses result from holding them during a period of general price-level change. Conversely, nonmonetary items are reported at different amounts in the constant dollar statements than they are in the historical cost statements, when there is a change in the general price level. As a result, both the inventory and the share capital are adjusted to recognize changes in the purchasing power of the dollar.

Constant Dollar Illustration

To illustrate the preparation of financial statements on a constant dollar basis, assume that Hartley Company starts business on December 31, 1993 by issuing common shares for $190,000 cash. Land costing $80,000 is purchased immediately. During 1994, the company reports $190,000 of sales, cost of goods sold of $100,000, and operating expenses of $20,000. The income statement for Hartley Company on an historical cost basis is as follows.

Hartley Company
Income Statement (Historical Cost)
for the Year Ended December 31, 1994

Sales	$190,000
Cost of goods sold	100,000
Gross profit	90,000
Operating expenses	20,000
Net income	$ 70,000

The comparative balance sheets on an historical cost basis are as follows.

Hartley Company
Balance Sheet (Historical Cost)
December 31

Assets

	1994	1993
Cash	$145,000	$110,000
Inventory	35,000	—
Land	80,000	80,000
Total assets	$260,000	$190,000

(Continued)

Liabilities and Shareholders' Equity		
Common shares	$190,000	$190,000
Retained earnings	70,000	—
Total liabilities and shareholders' equity	$260,000	$190,000

The relevant price indices for use in preparing constant dollar financial statements are presented below. These price indices are magnified here to illustrate their effect.

	Price Indices
December 31, 1993	100
1994 average	160
December 31, 1994	200

Constant Dollar Income Statement. When a constant dollar income statement is prepared, revenues and expenses are restated to end-of-year dollars. The difference between restated revenues and expenses is reported as income (loss) before purchasing power gain (loss). The purchasing power gain (loss) is then added (deducted) to produce Constant Dollar Net Income (Loss).

Revenues and expenses are usually assumed to occur evenly throughout the period. Therefore, the historical dollar amounts are multiplied by the restatement ratio, of which the numerator is the end-of-year index and the denominator is the average index. The constant dollar income statement for Hartley Company is provided below (the explanations highlighted are not part of the formal statement; they are provided to explain how the statement is prepared).

Hartley Company
Constant Dollar Income Statement
for the Year Ended December 31, 1994

Sales	$237,500	$190,000 \times \dfrac{200}{160}$
Cost of goods sold	125,000	$100,000 \times \dfrac{200}{160}$
Gross profit	112,500	
Operating expenses	25,000	$\ 20,000 \times \dfrac{200}{160}$
Income before purchasing power loss	87,500	
Purchasing power loss	(118,750)	**(Per computation on page 1298)**
Constant dollar net loss	$ (31,250)	

Restatement of the items above is explained below:

- **Sales.** Because sales were spread evenly over the year, the average index is used in the computation to restate sales to end-of-year dollars.

- **Cost of Goods Sold.** The cost of goods sold of $100,000 consists of two amounts, purchases of $135,000 less ending inventory of $35,000. Because the costs of purchases and ending inventories were spread evenly over the year, the average index is used in the computation to restate cost of goods sold to end-of-year dollars.

- **Operating Expenses.** Because operating expenses were spread evenly over the year, the average index is used in the computation to restate operating expenses to end-of-year dollars.

- **Purchasing Power Loss**. Computation of the purchasing power gain (loss) on monetary items requires a reconciliation of the beginning and ending balances of each monetary item for the period. A restatement ratio is then applied to the beginning balance and each reconciling amount. Hartley Company has only one monetary item, cash. Because prices are rising, it will experience a purchasing power loss for 1994. The computation of the loss is shown below.

Computation of Purchasing Power Loss

	1994 Historical	× Restatement Ratio =	Restated to 12/31/94 Dollars
Cash:			
Beginning balance	$ 110,000	$\frac{200}{100}$	$ 220,000
Add: Sales	190,000	$\frac{200}{160}$	237,500
Deduct: Purchases	(135,000)	$\frac{200}{160}$	(168,750)
Operating expenses	(20,000)	$\frac{200}{160}$	(25,000)
Total restated dollars			263,750
Ending balance	$ 145,000		145,000
Purchasing power loss			$(118,750)

The first column of this schedule provides a reconciliation of the beginning and ending cash balances. Note that the purchases amount is determined by adding ending inventory ($35,000) to cost of goods sold ($100,000) for Hartley Company. The restatement ratio for the beginning cash balance is based on the price index at the beginning of the year (100). The other ratios are based on the average price index during the year (160). The total restated dollars, $263,750, indicates how much cash the company should have to stay even with the price increases that have occurred. This amount is then compared with the historical cost ending balance to determine the amount of the purchasing power gain or loss. In this case, Hartley should have $263,750; it has only $145,000. Therefore, it has experienced a purchasing power loss of $118,750.

Constant Dollar Balance Sheet. When a constant dollar balance sheet is prepared, all monetary items are stated in end-of-year dollars and therefore do not need adjustment. Nonmonetary items, however, must be restated to end-of-year dollars. The constant dollar balance sheet for Hartley Company is provided at the top of page 1299 (the explanations highlighted are not part of the formal statement; they are provided to help you understand how the statement is prepared). Restatement of the balance sheet items is explained as follows:

- **Cash**. Cash is a monetary item; therefore, no restatement is necessary.

- **Inventory**. Inventory is a nonmonetary item and therefore it must be restated. Because inventory was purchased evenly throughout the year, the $35,000 must be multiplied by the ratio of the ending index, 200, to the index at the time the inventory was purchased, which was the average for the year of 160.

- **Land**. Land is a nonmonetary item; therefore, it must be restated. Because land was purchased at the end of the preceding year, the $80,000 must be multiplied by the ratio of the ending index to the index at the time the land was purchased, which was 100.

- **Common Shares**. Share capital is a nonmonetary item; therefore, restatement is necessary. Because share capital was issued at the end of the preceding year, the $190,000 must be multiplied by the ratio of the ending index, 200, to the index at the time the shares were issued, which was 100.

Hartley Company
Constant Dollar Balance Sheet
December 31, 1994

Assets

Cash	$145,000	(Same as historical cost)
Inventory	43,750	$35,000 \times \dfrac{200}{160}$
Land	160,000	$80,000 \times \dfrac{200}{100}$
Total assets	$348,750	

Liabilities and Shareholders' Equity

Common shares	$380,000	$190,000 \times \dfrac{200}{100}$
Retained earnings	(31,250)	(See constant dollar income statement)
Total liabilities and shareholders' equity	$348,750	

- **Retained Earnings.** Since no balance existed in retained earnings at the beginning of the year, the retained earnings in constant dollars includes only the constant dollar net loss for the current period of $31,250. Thus, Hartley Company on a constant dollar basis reports a negative retained earnings after its first year of operations.

Advantages and Disadvantages of Constant Dollar Accounting

Constant dollar financial statements have been discussed widely within both the accounting profession and the business and financial community and lauded by many as a means of overcoming reporting problems during periods of inflation or deflation. The following arguments have been submitted in support of preparing such statements:

1. Constant dollar accounting provides management with an *objectively* determined quantification of the impact of inflation on its business operations.

2. Constant dollar accounting eliminates the effects of inflation from financial information by requiring each enterprise to follow the same objective procedure and use the same price-level index, thereby *preserving comparability of financial statements among firms*.

3. Constant dollar accounting *enhances comparability among the financial statements of a single firm* by eliminating differences due to price-level changes and thereby improves trend analysis.

4. Constant dollar accounting eliminates the effects of price-level changes without having to develop a new structure of accounting; that is, it *preserves the historical cost-based accounting system* that is currently used and understood.

5. Constant dollar accounting *eliminates the necessity of and attraction to the "piecemeal" approaches* used in combating the effects of inflation on financial statements, namely, LIFO inventory costing and accelerated depreciation of property, plant, and equipment.

In spite of widespread publicity, discussion, and authoritative support both inside and outside the accounting profession, the preparation and public issuance of constant dollar financial statements up to this point have been negligible, probably because of the following disadvantages said to be associated with constant dollar financial statements:

1. The additional *cost* of preparing constant dollar statements is not offset by the benefit of receiving sufficient relevant information.

2. Constant dollar financial statements will cause *confusion* and will be misunderstood by users.

3. Restating the "value" of nonmonetary items at historical cost adjusted for general price-level changes *is no more meaningful than historical cost alone*, that is, it suffers all of the shortcomings of the historical cost method.

4. The reported purchasing power gain from monetary items is *misleading* because it does not necessarily represent successful management or provide funds for dividends, plant expansion, or other purposes.

5. Constant dollar accounting *assumes that the impact of inflation falls equally* on all business and on all classes of assets and costs, which is not true.

Probably the greatest deterrent to adoption of constant dollar accounting in the past has been *what it is not*: constant dollar accounting is not present value, net realizable value, and not current cost accounting, and therein lies much of the opposition to its use.

CURRENT COST ACCOUNTING

The price of a specific item may be affected not only by general inflation but also by individual market forces. For example, in a recent six-year period, certain items changed more or less than the general price level. To illustrate, during this period of time, the cost of a local telephone call increased 150%, guaranteed overnight mail delivery increased 4,575%, a gallon of gasoline decreased over 30%, and a flawless one-carat diamond decreased over 70%. Thus, changes in the specific price of items may be very different from the change in the general price level.

A popular means to measure the change in a specific price is current cost. **Current cost** is the cost of replacing the identical asset owned. Current cost may be approximated by reference to current catalogue prices or by applying a specific index to the book value of the asset. Unlike the constant dollar approach, which is simply a restatement of historical dollars into constant purchasing power, the current cost approach changes the basis of measurement from historical cost to current value.

Current Cost Adjustments

When current cost statements are prepared, it is also necessary to distinguish between monetary and nonmonetary items. Monetary items are stated at their current cost in the historical cost financial statements. As a result, no adjustment is necessary to items such as cash, accounts receivable, notes payable, or accounts payable when preparing a current cost balance sheet. A purchasing power gain or loss on the monetary items is not computed under current cost accounting because the measuring unit, the dollar, is not considered to have changed from one period to the next.

Conversely, nonmonetary items as a rule must be adjusted at year end. The current cost of nonmonetary items tends to change over time. For example, land held over a period of time will usually experience some type of price change. The same is true of other nonmonetary items such as inventory; property, plant, and equipment; and intangible assets.

When a nonmonetary item is restated, a holding gain or loss arises and must be reported on the financial statements. A **holding gain (loss)** is an increase or decrease in an item's value while it is held by the company. For example, if the current cost of land is $20,000 on January 1, 1994 and $32,000 on December 31, 1994, the company has a holding gain on this land of $12,000, computed as follows.

Current cost of land, December 31, 1994	$32,000
Current cost of land, January 1, 1994	20,000
Holding gain on land	$12,000

Revenues and expenses appearing on a current cost income statement are the same as the historical cost amounts, because at the time they are earned or incurred they represent current cost. A major exception is the cost of goods sold, which will be explained later.

To illustrate the preparation of financial statements on a current cost basis, assume that Sensor, Inc. started business on December 31, 1993 by selling common shares for $90,000. Land costing $40,000 was purchased immediately. During the next year, the company reported $160,000 of sales revenue, cost of goods sold of $75,000, and operating expenses of $25,000. The income statement for Sensor, Inc. on an historical cost basis appears as follows.

Sensor, Inc.
Income Statement (Historical Cost)
for the Year Ended December 31, 1994

Sales	$160,000
Cost of goods sold	75,000
Gross profit	85,000
Operating expenses	25,000
Net income	$ 60,000

The comparative balance sheets on an historical cost basis are as follows.

Sensor, Inc.
Balance Sheet (Historical Cost)
December 31

Assets

	1994	1993
Cash	$ 30,000	$50,000
Inventory	80,000	—
Land	40,000	40,000
Total assets	$150,000	$90,000

Liabilities and Shareholders' Equity

Share capital	$ 90,000	$90,000
Retained earnings	60,000	—
Total liabilities and shareholders' equity	$150,000	$90,000

The relevant current cost amounts for the income statement and balance sheet items for 1994 are as follows.

Income Statement		Balance Sheet	
Sales	$160,000	Cash	$ 30,000
Cost of goods sold	95,000	Inventory	105,000
Operating expenses	25,000	Land	48,000
		Share capital	90,000

Current Cost Income Statement

In a current cost income statement, two income numbers are reported. The first, **current cost income from operations**, is sales revenues less the current cost of goods sold plus operating expenses. This amount is the income a company has earned after providing for the replacement of assets used in operations.

The second income number, **current cost net income**, measures the total income of a company from one period to the next. Thus, holding gains (losses) are added (deducted) to current cost income from operations to arrive at this number. The current cost income statement for Sensor, Inc. follows. (The explanations highlighted are not part of the formal statement; they are provided to explain how the statement is prepared.)

Sensor, Inc.
Current Income Statement
for the Year Ended December 31, 1994

Sales	$160,000	(Same as historical cost)
Cost of goods sold	95,000	(Restated to current cost)
Gross profit	65,000	
Operating expenses	25,000	(Same as historical cost)
Current cost income from operations	40,000	
Holding gain	53,000	(Increase in current cost)
Current cost net income	$ 93,000	

The preceding items are explained below:

- **Sales and Operating Expenses.** Sales and operating expenses are already stated at their current cost amounts on historical cost statements; therefore, no adjustment is needed for these items.

- **Cost of Goods Sold.** Goods are sold at varying times of the year. At the time these goods are sold, the current cost of the inventory sold must be determined. The historical cost of goods sold and the current cost of goods sold are usually different.

- **Total Holding Gain.** The holding gain for Sensor comprises three items, as shown below.

Current cost of goods sold	$ 95,000	
Historical cost of goods sold	75,000	
		$20,000
Current cost of inventory	105,000	
Historical cost of inventory	80,000	
		25,000
Current cost of land	48,000	
Historical cost of land	40,000	
		8,000
Total holding gain		$53,000

Recall that a holding gain is an increase in an item's value from one period to the next. If the item is sold during the period, however, the holding gain (loss) is computed only to the point of sale. Thus, the inventory sold, as reported in the current cost of goods sold amount, had increased $20,000. Also, inventory on hand and land experienced holding gains of $25,000 and $8,000, respectively. Holding gains or losses indicate how effective management is in acquiring and holding assets.

Current Cost Balance Sheet

The preparation of a current cost balance sheet is relatively straightforward. Monetary items are not adjusted because they are already stated at current cost. Similarly, capital equity is not adjusted because its balance represents the current cost of capital stock. All other nonmonetary items must be adjusted to current cost. The current cost balance sheet for Sensor, Inc. is shown on page 1303. (The explanations highlighted are not part of the formal statement; they are provided to explain how the statement is prepared.) As indicated from the statement, retained earnings is determined by adding the current cost net income amount to the beginning balance of retained earnings.

Sensor, Inc.
Current Cost Balance Sheet
December 31, 1994

Assets

Cash	$ 30,000	(Same as historical cost)
Inventory	105,000	(Restated to current cost)
Land	48,000	(Restated to current cost)
Total assets	$183,000	

Liabilities and Shareholders' Equity

Share capital	$ 90,000	(Same as historical cost)
Retained earnings	93,000	(From current cost income statement)
Total liabilities and shareholders' equity	$183,000	

Advantages and Disadvantages of Current Cost

A distinct advantage that current cost has over both historical cost and constant dollar accounting is that specific changes (up and down) in individual items are considered. While the general level of prices may be increasing, prices of specific items may be decreasing. Such items as calculators, tennis balls, watches, microwave ovens, and television sets, for example, have decreased in price, whereas the general level of prices has increased. Constant dollar accounting using a general price index does not make an allowance for these changes in prices as effectively as a current cost system does. The major arguments for the use of a current cost approach are:

1. *Current cost provides a better measure of efficiency*. If, for example, depreciation is based on current costs, not historical costs, a better measure of operating efficiencies is obtained. For example, assume that you are a new manager in an operation that includes a number of assets purchased recently at current prices, and your performance is compared with that of someone in a similar job elsewhere who is using similar assets that were purchased five years ago when the prices were substantially lower. You probably would contend that the five-year-old assets should be revalued because the other manager will show a lower depreciation charge and higher net income than you will.

2. *Current cost is an approximation of the service potential of the asset*. It is difficult if not impossible to determine the present discounted values of specific cash flows that will occur from the use of certain assets, but current cost frequently is a reasonable approximation of this value. As the current cost increases, the implication is that the enterprise has a holding gain (an increase from one period to another in the current cost of that item) because the aggregate value of the asset's service potential has increased.

3. *Current cost provides for the maintenance of physical capital*. Assume that an asset is purchased for one dollar, sold for two dollars, and replaced for two dollars. How much income should be reported and how much tax should be paid? Under traditional accounting procedures, one dollar of income would be earned (which is subject to tax and a claim for dividend distribution). If current cost is used, however, no income exists to be taxed and claims for dividend distribution would probably be fewer.

4. *Current cost provides an assessment of future cash flows*. Information on current cost margins may be useful for assessing future cash flows when the selling price of a product is closely related to its current cost. In addition, reporting holding gains (losses) may help in assessing future cash flows.

The major arguments against current cost adjustments are:

1. *The use of current cost is subjective because it is difficult to determine the exact current cost of all items at any point in time*. A good second-hand market for all types of assets does not exist. In most cases, the asset is not replaced with an identical asset; it is replaced with a better one, a faster one, an improved one, an altogether different one, or not replaced at all.

2. *The maintenance of physical capital is not the accountant's function*. It is generally conceded that it is management's function to ensure that capital is not impaired.

3. *Current cost is not always an approximation of the fair market value*. An asset's value is a function of the future cash flows generated by it. Current cost, however, does not necessarily measure an increase in the service potential of that asset.

One final comment—many of the arguments above also apply to a **current cost/constant dollar system** (a full illustration is not provided in the chapter). Additional arguments for a current cost/constant dollar system are: (1) it stabilizes the measuring unit and provides current, comparable data and (2) it provides more information than either other system alone. Holding gains and losses adjusted for inflation or deflation are reported, as well as the purchasing power gain or loss on net monetary items. Its potential disadvantages are: (1) cost of preparation and (2) information is not always better information because it may confuse readers or lead to information overload.

PROFESSION'S POSITION ON CHANGING PRICE INFORMATION

In September 1982, the CICA, in response to a perceived need for information on the effects of changing prices on financial statements, recommended that large publicly held companies disclose certain price-level-adjusted financial information. The required price-level-adjusted information was provided on an experimental basis and consisted of restated information from the primary financial statements to reflect changes in (1) general price levels (constant dollar data) and (2) specific price levels (current cost data).

A CICA survey of financial statement users, preparers, and auditors revealed that both the number of users and the extent of use of the data were limited. Many respondents commented that the price-level-adjusted data did not appear to have been used by the institutional investment community, bankers, or investors in general. Therefore, partly as a result of nonuse and partly as a result of prevailing low inflation rates, the accounting profession in 1987 was persuaded to cease requiring the disclosure of supplementary information on the effects of changing prices. Companies now are encouraged only to disclose price-level-adjusted information and are not discouraged from experimenting with different forms of disclosure.

Note: All **asterisked** questions, cases, exercises, and problems relate to material contained in the appendix to this chapter.

——————— QUESTIONS ———————
---

1. What are the major advantages of notes to financial statements? What type of items are usually reported in the notes?

2. What is the full disclosure principle in accounting? Why has disclosure increased substantially in the last 10 years?

3. The auditor for Gleim Ltd. is debating whether the major categories of property, plant, and equipment and related accumulated depreciation should be reported in a note or in the summary of significant accounting policies. What would be your recommendation? Why?

4. Sande Limited is liable for a 12% mortgage payable of $44,000, secured by land and buildings, which is payable in semiannual instalments (including principal and interest) of $6,000. Indicate the balance sheet presentation of long-term debt, current maturities, and, in general terms, the necessary disclosure.

5. At the beginning of 1993, Sun-Kist Ltd. entered into an eight-year, nonrenewable lease agreement. Provisions in the lease require the client to make substantial reconditioning and restoration expenditures at the end of the lease. What

disclosure do you believe is necessary for this type of situation?

6. A recent annual report of Cocina Industries states: "The company and its subsidiaries have long-term leases expiring on various dates after December 31, 1994. Amounts payable under such commitments, without reduction for related rental income, are expected to average approximately $5,711,000 annually for the next three years. Related rental income from certain subleases to others is estimated to average $3,094,000 annually for the next three years." What information is provided by this note?

7. What type of disclosure or accounting do you believe is necessary for the following items:

   (a) Because of a general increase in the number of labour disputes and strikes, both within and outside the industry, there is an increased likelihood that the client will suffer a costly strike in the near future?

   (b) A company reports an extraordinary item (net of tax) correctly on the income statement. No other mention is made of this item in the annual report?

(c) A company expects to recover a substantial amount in connection with a pending refund claim for a prior year's taxes. Although the claim is being contested, counsel for the company has confirmed the client's expectation of recovery?

8. An annual report of Ford Motor Company states:

> Net income a share is computed based upon the average number of all classes of capital shares outstanding. Additional common shares may be issued or delivered in the future on conversion of outstanding convertible debentures, exercise of outstanding employee stock options, and for payment of defined supplemental compensation. Had such additional shares been outstanding, net income a share would have been reduced by $0.10 in the current year and $0.03 in the previous year.
>
> As a result of capital stock transactions by the company during the current year, (primarily the purchase of Class A Stock from Ford Foundation), net income a share was increased by $0.06.

What information is provided by this note?

9. The following information was described in a note to the financial statements of Rochelle Packing Co.:

> During August Halco Products Corporation purchased 311,003 of the Company's common shares which constitutes approximately 35% of the shares outstanding. Halco has since obtained representation on the Board of Directors.
>
> An affiliate of Halco Products Corporation acts as a food broker for the Company in the greater Toronto marketing area. The commissions for such services after August amounted to approximately $20,000.

Why is this information disclosed?

10. What approaches might be employed to disclose social awareness expenditures?

11. What are diversified companies? What accounting problems are related to diversified companies?

12. Explain the following terms:
    (a) Identifiable assets.
    (b) Defined profit.

(c) Industry segment.
(d) Common cost.

13. The controller for Fedenia Ltd. recently commented: "If I have to disclose our segments individually, the only people who will gain are our competitors and the only people that will lose are our present shareholders." Evaluate this comment.

14. "The financial statements of a company are management's, not the accountant's." Discuss the implications of this statement.

15. Sylvia Reynolds, a student of Intermediate Accounting, was heard to remark after a class discussion on diversified reporting: "All this is very confusing to me. First we are told that there is merit in presenting the consolidated results and now we are told that it is better to show segmented results. I wish they would make up their minds." Evaluate this comment.

16. Karen Allman, a financial writer, noted recently: "There are substantial arguments for including earnings projections in annual reports and the like. The most compelling is that it would give anyone interested something now available to only a relatively select few, like large shareholders, creditors, and attentive bartenders." Identify some arguments against providing earnings projections.

17. The following recently appeared in the financial press: "Inadequate financial disclosure, particularly with respect to how management views the future and its role in the marketplace, has always been a stone in the shoe. After all, if you don't know how a company views the future, how can you judge the worth of its corporate strategy?" What are some arguments for reporting earnings forecasts?

18. What are interim reports? Why are balance sheets often not provided with interim data?

19. What are the accounting problems related to the presentation of interim data?

20. What approaches have been suggested to overcome the seasonal problem related to interim reporting?

21. What is the difference between an unqualified opinion or "clean" opinion and a qualified one?

*22. (a) What is meant by constant dollar accounting?
     (b) What is purchasing power?

*23. Distinguish between monetary items and nonmonetary items. Give two examples of each.

*24. Joe Plett, the president of Educator Publications Ltd., is confused. He does not understand how a purchasing power gain or loss can exist when monetary assets and liabilities are unadjusted in constant dollar financial statements. Explain why this treatment is proper.

*25. Flatware Limited purchased equipment in 1987 for $150,000. Flatware purchased another piece of equipment in 1993 for $70,000. If the price level index was 100 in 1987, 125 in 1993, and 130 in 1994, what would be the restated amount of the equipment in 1994 dollars?

*26. How are income statement items restated on a constant dollar income statement?

*27. What is current cost accounting? How does it differ from constant dollar accounting?

*28. Are both purchasing power gain or loss and holding gain or loss to be recognized when using current cost accounting? Explain.

*29. A company had land that cost $100,000. It had a current cost of $130,000 on December 31, 1994. The company also had a cash balance of $30,000 throughout the year. What was the holding gain on the land for 1994?

*30. What information does current cost income from operations and current cost net income provide to the financial statement user?

*31. What is the accounting profession's position on reporting changing price information?

CASES

C25-1 (GENERAL DISCLOSURES; INVENTORIES; PROPERTY, PLANT, AND EQUIPMENT)   Holiday Corporation is in the process of preparing its annual financial statements for the fiscal year ended April 30, 1994. The company manufactures plastic, glass, and paper containers for sale to food and drink manufacturers and distributors.

Holiday Corporation maintains separate control accounts for its raw materials, work in process, and finished goods inventories for each of the three types of containers. The inventories are valued at the lower of cost and market.

The company's property, plant, and equipment are classified in the following major categories: land, office buildings, furniture and fixtures, manufacturing facilities, manufacturing equipment, leasehold improvements. All fixed assets are carried at cost. The depreciation methods employed depend on the type of asset (its classification) and when it was acquired.

Holiday Corporation plans to present the inventory and fixed asset amounts in its April 30, 1994 balance sheet as shown below:

Inventories	$4,814,200
Property, plant, and equipment (net of depreciation)	$6,310,000

Instructions

What information regarding inventories and property, plant, and equipment must be disclosed by Holiday Corporation in the audited financial statements issued to shareholders, either in the body or the notes, for the 1993–1994 fiscal year?

(CMA adapted)

C25-2 (DISCLOSURES REQUIRED IN VARIOUS SITUATIONS)   Roman Inc. produces electronic components for sale to manufacturers of radios, television sets, and phonographic systems. In connection with her examination of Roman's financial statements for the year ended December 31, 1994, Ann Stedry, CA, completed field work two weeks ago. Ms. Stedry is now evaluating the significance of the following items prior to preparing her auditor's report. Except as noted, none of these items have been disclosed in the financial statements or notes.

Item 1. A 10-year loan agreement, which the company entered into three years ago, provides that dividend payments may not exceed net income earned after taxes subsequent to the date of the agreement. The balance of retained earnings at the date of the loan agreement was $420,000. From that date through December 31, 1994, net income after taxes totalled $570,000 and cash dividends totalled $320,000. On the basis of these data, the staff auditor assigned to this review concluded that there was no retained earnings restriction at December 31, 1994.

Item 2. Recently, Roman interrupted its policy of paying cash dividends quarterly to its shareholders. Dividends were paid regularly through 1993, discontinued for all of 1994 to finance equipment for the company's new plant, and resumed in the first quarter of 1995. In the annual report, dividend policy is to be discussed in the president's letter to shareholders.

Item 3. A major electronics firm has introduced a line of products that will compete directly with Roman's primary line, now being produced in the specially designed new plant. Because of manufacturing innovations, the competitor's line will be of comparable quality but priced 50% below Roman's line. The competitor announced its new line during the week following completion of field work. Ms. Stedry read the announcement in the newspaper and discussed the situation by telephone with Roman executives. Roman will meet the lower prices, which are high enough to cover variable manufacturing and selling expenses, but will permit recovery of only a portion of fixed costs.

Item 4. The company's new manufacturing plant building, which cost $2,400,000 and has an estimated life of 25 years, is leased from Maritime National Bank at an annual rental of $600,000. The company is obligated to pay property taxes, insurance, and maintenance. At the conclusion of its 10-year noncancellable lease, the company has the option of purchasing the property for $1.00. In Roman's income statement, the rental payment is reported on a separate line.

Instructions

For each of the items above, discuss any additional disclosures in the financial statements and footnotes that the auditor should recommend to her client. (The cumulative effect of the four items should not be considered.)

(CORRECTION OF VARIOUS NOTES) You are completing an examination of the financial statements of **C25-3** Portico Manufacturing Corporation for the year ended February 28, 1994. Portico's financial statements have not been examined previously. The controller of Portico has given you the following draft of proposed footnotes to the financial statements.

Portico Manufacturing Corporation
Notes to Financial Statements
Year Ended February 28, 1994

Note 1. With the approval of the minister of finance, the company changed its method of accounting for inventories from the first-in method to the average-cost method on March 1, 1993. In the opinion of the company, the effects of this change on the pricing of inventories and cost of goods manufactured were not material in the current year but are expected to be material in future years.

Note 2. The investment property was recorded at cost until December 1993, when it was written up to its appraisal value. The company plans to sell the property in 1994 and an independent real estate agent in the area has indicated that the appraisal price can be realized. Pending completion of the sale, the amount of the expected gain on the sale has been recorded in an unearned income account.

Note 3. The stock dividend described in our May 24, 1993 letter to shareholders has been recorded as a 110 for 100 stock split-up. Accordingly, there were no changes in the shareholders' equity account balances from this transaction.

Instructions

For each of the notes above, discuss the note's adequacy and needed revisions, if any, of the financial statements or the note.

C25-4 **(DISCLOSURES REQUIRED IN VARIOUS SITUATIONS)**   You have completed your audit of Carol Limited and its consolidated subsidiaries for the year ended December 31, 1994 and were satisfied with the results of your examination. You have examined the financial statements of Carol Limited for the past three years. The corporation is now preparing its annual report to shareholders. The report will include the consolidated financial statements of Carol Limited and its subsidiaries and your short-form auditor's report. During your audit the following matters came to your attention:

1. A vice-president who is also a shareholder resigned on December 31, 1994 after an argument with the president. The vice-president is soliciting proxies from shareholders and expects to obtain sufficient proxies to gain control of the board of directors so that a new president will be appointed. The president plans to have a note to the financial statements prepared that will include information of the pending proxy fight, management's accomplishments over the years, and an appeal by management for the support of shareholders.

2. The corporation decides in 1994 to adopt the straight-line method of depreciation for plant equipment. The straight-line method will be used for new acquisitions as well as for previously acquired plant equipment for which depreciation had been provided on an accelerated basis.

3. Revenue Canada is currently examining the corporation's 1991 federal income tax return and is questioning the amount of a deduction claimed by the corporation's domestic subsidiary for a loss sustained in 1991. The examination is still in process, and any additional tax liability is indeterminable at this time. The corporation's tax counsel believes that there will be no substantial additional tax liability.

Instructions

(a)   Prepare the notes, if any, that you would suggest for the items listed above.

(b)   State your reasons for not making disclosure by note for each of the listed items for which you do not prepare a note.

(AICPA adapted)

C25-5 **(DISCLOSURES, CONDITIONAL AND CONTINGENT LIABILITIES)**   Presented below are three independent situations.

Situation I. A company offers a one-year warranty for the product that it manufactures. A history of warranty claims has been compiled and the probable amount of claims related to sales for a given period can be determined.

Situation II. Subsequent to the date of a set of financial statements, but prior to the issuance of the financial statements, a company enters into a contract that will probably result in a significant loss to the company. The amount of the loss can be reasonably estimated.

Situation III. A company has adopted a policy of recording self-insurance for any possible losses resulting from injury to others by the company's vehicles. The premium for an insurance policy for the same risk from an independent insurance company would have an annual cost of $4,000. During the period covered by the financial statements, there were no accidents involving the company's vehicles that resulted in injury to others.

Instructions

Discuss the accrual or type of disclosure necessary (if any) and the reason(s) why such disclosure is appropriate for each of the three independent sets of information above.

(AICPA adapted)

C25-6 **(SEGMENT REPORTING: THEORY)**   Following are excerpts from the financial statements of Vender Corporation International.

Note 7. Major Segments of Business

VCI conducts funeral service and cemetery operations in Canada and the United States. Floral and dried whey operations (which operate principally in Canada) are included as Other. Substantially all revenues of VCI's major segments of business are from unaffiliated customers. Segment information for fiscal 1994, 1993, and 1992 is as follows:

	Funeral	Cemetery	Other	Corporate	Consolidated
		(Thousands)			
Revenues:					
1994	$302,000	$ 83,000	$31,000	$ —	$416,000
1993	245,000	61,000	18,000	—	324,000
1992	208,000	42,000	10,000	—	260,000
Operating income:					
1994	$ 79,000	$ 18,000	$ 4,000	$(36,000)	$ 65,000
1993	64,000	12,000	800	(28,000)	48,800
1992	54,000	6,000	600	(21,000)	39,600
Capital expenditures:*					
1994	$ 26,000	$ 9,000	$ 2,300	$ 400	$ 37,700
1993	68,000	60,000	2,800	1,500	132,300
1992	14,000	8,000	100	600	22,700
Depreciation and amortization:					
1994	$ 13,000	$ 2,400	$ 400	$ 1,400	$ 17,200
1993	10,000	1,400	200	700	12,300
1992	8,000	1,000	100	600	9,700
Identifiable assets:					
1994	$334,000	$162,000	$10,000	$114,000	$620,000
1993	322,000	144,000	8,000	52,000	526,000
1992	223,000	78,000	4,500	34,000	339,500

*Includes $4,520,000, $111,480,000, and $1,294,000 for the years ended April 30, 1994, 1993, and 1992, respectively, for purchases of businesses.

Instructions

(a) What are the criteria used to determine whether a business segment for a product or service must be disclosed?

(b) What are the major items for products or services that must be disclosed in reporting segments of a business?

(c) Comment on when segments of a business for a product or service do not have to be disclosed.

(SEGMENT REPORTING: THEORY) In 1979, the Accounting Standards Committee issued guidelines for companies grappling with the problem of dividing up their businesses into industry segments for their annual reports. An industry segment may bedefined as a part of an enterprise engaged in providing a product or service or a group of related products or services primarily to unaffiliated customers for a profit.   **C25-7**

Although conceding that the process is a "subjective talk" that "to a considerable extent, depends on the judgment of management," the Accounting Standards Committee said companies should consider the nature of the products, the nature of their production, and their markets and marketing methods to determine whether products and services should be grouped together or in separate industry segments.

Instructions

(a) What does financial reporting for segments of a business enterprise involve?

(b) Identify the reasons for requiring financial data to be reported by segments.

(c) Identify the possible disadvantages of requiring financial data to be reported by segments.

(d) Identify the accounting difficulties inherent in segment reporting.

C25-8 (SEGMENT REPORTING: THEORY)   The most recently published statement of consolidated income of Hosig Industries, Inc. appears below.

Hosig Industries, Inc.

Statement of Consolidated Income

for the Year Ended March 31, 1994

Net sales	$130,200,000
Other revenue	1,500,000
Total revenue	131,700,000
Cost of products sold	91,540,000
Selling and administrative expenses	28,100,000
Interest expense	1,000,000
Total cost and expenses	120,640,000
Income before income taxes	11,060,000
Income taxes	3,318,000
Net income	$ 7,742,000

Karen Mortensen, a representative of a firm of security analysts, visited the central headquarters of Hosig Industries to obtain more information about the company's operations.

In the annual report, Hosig's president stated that Hosig was engaged in the pharmaceutical, food-processing, toy-manufacturing, and metal-working industries. Ms. Mortensen complained that the published income statement was of limited utility in her analysis of the firm's operations. She said that Hosig should have disclosed separately the profit earned in each of its component industries. Further, she maintained that several items appearing on the statement of consolidated retained earnings should have been included on the income statement: a gain of $1,780,000 on the sale of the furniture division in early March of the current year and an assessment for additional income taxes of $495,000 resulting from an examination of the returns covering the years ended March 31, 1992 and 1993 (normally recurring).

Instructions

(a) Explain what is meant by a "conglomerate" company.

(b) 1. Discuss the accounting problems involved in measuring net profit by industry segments within a company.

   2. With reference to Hosig Industries' statement of consolidated income, identify the specific items where difficulty might be encountered in measuring profit by each of its industry segments, and explain the nature of the difficulty.

(c) 1. What criteria should be applied in determining whether a gain or loss should be excluded from the determination of net income?

   2. What criteria should be applied in determining whether a gain or loss that is properly includable in the determination of net income should be included in the results of ordinary operations or shown separately as an extraordinary item after all other items of revenue and expense?

3. How should the gain on the sale of the furniture division and the assessment of additional taxes each be presented in Hosig's financial statements?

(AICPA adapted)

(DISCLOSURE OF SOCIALLY RESPONSIBLE ACTIVITIES) In an annual report of Republic Steel, **C25-9** the following was reported:

> In the Toronto District, a major improvement in air emission control was made possible by the completion of the first phase of construction of a giant suppressed combustion pollution control system for the basic oxygen furnaces.
>
> The system, believed to be the first of its type ever installed on an existing steelmaking complex, replaces a bank of electrostatic precipitators which will be used to control other emissions that occur in the steelmaking process. The total system is expected to become fully operational this spring.

Instructions

(a) Do you believe that Republic should disclose information of this nature?

(b) How might an enterprise measure its socially responsible activities?

(ETHICAL ISSUE: FULL DISCLOSURE) Jan Larsen, the controller of Blue Ridge Furniture Company, **C25-10** and Ernest Robson, her assistant, are preparing the year-end financial statements. Robson wants to disclose the cost of marketable securities as a parenthetical note on the balance sheet. Larsen—concerned about the decline in market value compared to cost of these securities—does not want to call attention to this decline. She wants to bury the information in a note to the financial statements.

Instructions

(a) What ethical issue is posed by the choice between these two forms of disclosure?

(b) Are the interests of different stakeholders in conflict in the choice between the two methods of accounting reports?

(c) Which method would you choose, and why?

(INTERIM REPORTING) Ramon Corporation, a publicly traded company, is preparing the interim financial **C25-11** data that it will issue to its shareholders at the end of the first quarter of the 1993–1994 fiscal year. Ramon's financial accounting department has compiled the following summarized revenue and expense data for the first quarter of the year:

Sales	$60,000,000
Cost of goods sold	36,000,000
Variable selling expenses	2,000,000
Fixed selling expenses	3,000,000

Included in the fixed selling expenses was the single lump sum payment of $2,000,000 for television advertisements for the entire year.

Instructions

(a) Ramon Corporation must issue its quarterly financial statements in accordance with generally accepted accounting principles regarding interim financial reporting.

1. Explain whether Ramon should report its operating results for the quarter as if the quarter was a separate reporting period in and of itself, or as if the quarter was an integral part of the annual reporting period.

2. State how the sales, cost of goods sold, and fixed selling expenses would be reflected in Ramon Corporation's quarterly report prepared for the first quarter of the 1993–1994 fiscal year. Briefly justify your presentation.

(b) What financial information, as a minimum, must Ramon Corporation disclose to its shareholders in its quarterly reports?

(CMA adapted)

C25-12 (TREATMENT OF VARIOUS INTERIM REPORTING SITUATIONS)   The following statements have been excerpted from paragraphs .13 and .14 of *CICA Handbook* Section 1750, "Interim Financial Reporting to Shareholders."

Interim financial reports should present information with respect to the results of operations of a company for a specified period rather than a proration of expected results for the annual period. Consistent with this position, the interim financial reports have to be prepared on the same basis as annual statements.

The preparation of financial data should be based on accounting principles and practices consistent with those used in the preparation of annual financial statements.

Instructions

Listed below are six independent cases on how accounting facts might be reported on an individual company's interim financial reports. For each of these cases, state whether the method proposed to be used for interim reporting would be acceptable under generally accepted accounting principles applicable to interim financial data. Support each answer with a brief explanation.

1. Field Company takes a physical inventory at year end for annual financial statement purposes. Inventory and cost of sales reported in the interim quarterly statements are based on estimated gross profit rates because a physical inventory would result in a cessation of operations. Field Company does have reliable perpetual inventory records.

2. Fischer Company is planning to report one-fourth of its pension expense each quarter.

3. Gansner Company wrote inventory down to reflect the lower of cost and market in the first quarter. At year end, the market exceeds the original acquisition cost of this inventory. Consequently, management plans to write the inventory back up to its original cost as a year-end adjustment.

4. Rice Company realized a large gain on the sale of investments at the beginning of the second quarter. The company wants to report one-third of the gain in each of the remaining quarters.

5. Downs Company has estimated its annual audit fee. They plan to prorate this expense equally over all four quarters.

6. Sanborn Company was reasonably certain they would have an employee strike in the third quarter. As a result, they shipped heavily during the second quarter but plan to defer the recognition of the sales in excess of the normal sales volume. The deferred sales would be recognized as sales in the third quarter, when the strike would likely be in progress. Sanborn Company management thought this was more nearly representative of normal second- and third-quarter operations.

(CMA adapted)

C25-13 (FINANCIAL FORECASTS)   Recently, an accountant and a financial analyst were discussing the problem of corporate forecasts. The accountant noted that Section 4250 of the *CICA Handbook* established standards for reporting "future-oriented financial information." Despite these standards, there is some concern among accountants over possible liability if forecasted results do not materialize.

The analyst responded by saying that "no one expects accountants to be able to forecast accurately" and that "the courts would certainly not hold them liable." In fact, a "safe harbour" rule would protect accountants, providing that the forecasts were made on a reasonable basis and in good faith.

Instructions

(a) What are the arguments for preparing profit forecasts?

(b)   What is the purpose of a "safe harbour" rule?

(c)   Why are corporations concerned about presenting profit forecasts?

(TREATMENT OF VARIOUS INTERIM REPORTING ITEMS)   Love Manufacturing Company, a Brit-**C25-14**
ish Columbia corporation listed on the Vancouver Stock Exchange, budgeted activities for 1994 as follows.

	Amount	Units
Net sales	$9,000,000	1,000,000
Cost of goods sold	5,400,000	
Gross margin	$3,600,000	
Selling, general, and administrative expenses	2,100,000	
Operating income	$1,500,000	
Nonoperating revenues and expenses	–0–	
Income before income taxes	$1,500,000	
Estimated income taxes (current and deferred)	600,000	
Net income	$ 900,000	
Earnings per common share	$9.75	

Love has operated profitably for many years and has experienced a seasonal pattern of sales volume and production similar to those below forecasted for 1994. Sales volume is expected to follow a quarterly pattern of 10%, 20%, 35%, 35%, respectively, because of seasonality of the industry. Also, owing to production and storage capacity limitations, it is expected that production will follow a pattern of 20%, 25%, 30%, 25% per quarter, respectively.

At the conclusion of the first quarter of 1994, the controller of Love prepared and issued the following interim report for public release.

	Amount	Units
Net sales	$ 900,000	100,000
Cost of goods sold	540,000	100,000
Gross margin	$ 360,000	
Selling, general, and administrative expenses	412,500	
Operating loss	$ (52,500)	
Loss from warehouse fire	(262,500)	
Loss before income taxes	$(315,000)	
Estimated income taxes	–0–	
Net loss	$(315,000)	
Loss per common share		$(3.15)

The following additional information is available for the first quarter just completed but was not included in the public information released:

1. Assume that the warehouse fire loss met the conditions of an extraordinary loss. The warehouse had an undepreciated cost of $480,000; $217,500 was recovered from insurance on the warehouse. No other gains or losses are anticipated this year from similar events or transactions, and Love had no similar losses in preceding years; thus, the full loss will be deductible as an ordinary loss for income tax purposes.

2. The company uses a standard cost system in which standards are set at currently attainable levels on an annual basis. At the end of the first quarter, there was underapplied fixed factory overhead (volume variance) of $75,000 that was treated as an asset at the end of the quarter. Production during the quarter was 200,000 units, of which 100,000 were sold.

3. The selling, general, and administrative expenses were budgeted on a basis of $1,350,000 fixed expenses for the year plus $0.75 variable expenses per unit of sales.

4. The effective income tax rate is expected to average 40% of earnings before income taxes during 1994. There are no permanent differences between pretax accounting earnings and taxable income.

5. Earnings per share were computed on the basis of 100,000 common shares outstanding. Love has only one class of shares issued, no long-term debt outstanding, and no stock option plan.

Instructions

(a) Without reference to the specific situation described above, what are the standards of disclosure for interim financial data (published interim financial reports) for publicly traded companies? Explain.

(b) Identify the weaknesses in form and content of Love's interim report without reference to the additional information.

(c) For each of the five items of additional information, indicate the preferable treatment for each item for interim reporting purposes and explain why that treatment is preferable.

(AICPA adapted)

C25-15 (DISCLOSURES AND AUDITOR'S OPINION; LIMITED PROFITABILITY PROSPECTS) Koch Enterprises acquired a large tract of land in a small town approximately 16 km from Capital City. The company executed a firm contract on November 15, 1993 for the construction of a 1.6-km race track, together with related facilities. The track and facilities were completed December 15, 1994. On December 31, 1994, a 15% instalment note of $210,000 was issued, along with other consideration in settlement of the construction contract. Instalments of $70,000 fall due on December 31 of each of the next three years. The company planned to pay the notes from cash received from operations and from sale of additional common shares.

The company adopted the double-declining balance method of computing depreciation. No depreciation was taken in 1994 because all racing equipment was received in December after the completion of the track and facilities.

The land on which the racing circuit was constructed was acquired at various dates for a total of $81,000, and its approximate market value on December 31, 1994 was $100,000.

Through the sale of tickets to spectators, parking fees, concession income, and income from betting, company officials anticipated that approximately $275,000 is taken in during a typical year's racing season. Cash expenses for a racing season were estimated at $173,000.

You have made an examination of the financial condition of Koch Enterprises as of December 31, 1994. The balance sheet as of that date and statement of operations follow.

Koch Enterprises
Balance Sheet
December 31, 1994

Assets

Cash		$ 11,000
Accounts receivable		12,000
Prepaid expenses		9,000
Property (at cost)		
Land	$ 81,000	
Grading and track improvements	86,000	

(Continued)

Grandstand	200,000	
Buildings	76,000	
Racing equipment	56,000	499,000
Organization costs		1,000
Total assets		$532,000

Liabilities and Shareholders' Equity

Accounts payable	$ 32,000
Instalment note payable—15%	210,000
Shareholders' equity	
Common shares, no-par value; authorized,	
200,000; issued and outstanding, 121,500 shares	121,500
Contributed surplus	188,500
Retained earnings (deficit)	(20,000)
Total liabilities and shareholders' equity	$532,000

Koch Enterprises
Statement of Income
for the Period From Inception, December 1, 1991
to December 31, 1994

Income	
Profit on sales of land	$10,000
Other	2,000
	12,000
General and administrative expenses	32,000
Net loss for the period	$20,000

On January 15, 1995, legislation that declared betting to be illegal was enacted by the provincial government. A discussion with management on January 17 about the effect of the legislation revealed that revenue would be reduced to approximately $80,000 and cash expenses would be reduced to one-third the original estimate.

Instructions

(Disregard federal income tax implications.)

(a) Prepare the explanatory notes to accompany the balance sheet.

(b) What opinion do you believe the auditor should render? Discuss.

(AICPA adapted)

(INFLATION ACCOUNTING METHODS) A business entity's financial statements could be prepared by *C25-16 using historical cost or current value as a basis. In addition, the basis could be stated in terms of unadjusted dollars or dollars restated for changes in purchasing power. The various permutations of these two separate and distinct areas are shown in the following matrix.

	Unadjusted Dollars	Dollars Restated for Changes in Purchasing Power
Historical cost	1	2
Current value	3	4

Block 1 of the matrix represents the traditional method of accounting for transactions in accounting today, wherein the absolute (unadjusted) amount of dollars given up or received is recorded for the asset or liability obtained (**relationship between resources**). This method assumes the validity of the accounting concepts of going-concern and stable monetary unit. Any gain or loss (including holding and purchasing power gains or losses) resulting from the sale or satisfaction of amounts recorded under this method is deferred in its entirety until sale or satisfaction.

Instructions

For each of the remaining matrix blocks (2, 3, and 4) respond to the following questions. *Limit your discussion to nonmonetary assets only.*

(a) How will this method of recording assets affect the relationship between resources and the standard of comparison?

(b) What is the theoretical justification for using each method?

(c) How will each method of asset valuation affect the recognition of gain or loss during the life of the asset and ultimately from the sale or abandonment of the asset? Your response should include a discussion of the timing and magnitude of the gain or loss and conceptual reasons for any difference from the gain or loss computed using the traditional method.

(AICPA adapted)

*C25-17 (ACCOUNTING FOR CHANGING PRICES) Sally Groft Corp., a wholesaler with large investments in plant and equipment, began operations in 1949. The company's history has been one of expansion in sales, production, and physical facilities. Recently, some concern has been expressed that the conventional financial statements do not provide sufficient information for decisions by investors. After consideration of proposals for various types of supplementary financial statements to be included in the 1994 annual report, management has decided to present a balance sheet as of December 31, 1994 and a statement of income and retained earnings for 1994, both restated for changes in the general price level.

Instructions

(a) On what basis can it be contended that Groft's conventional statements should be restated for changes in the general price level?

(b) Distinguish between financial statements restated for general price-level changes and current value financial statements.

(c) Distinguish between monetary and nonmonetary assets and liabilities as the terms are used in constant dollar accounting. Give examples of each.

(d) Outline the procedures Groft should follow in preparing the proposed supplementary statements.

(e) Indicate the major similarities and differences between the proposed supplementary statements and the corresponding conventional statements.

(f) Assuming that in the future Groft will want to present comparative supplementary statements, can the 1994 supplementary statements be presented in 1995 without adjustment? Explain.

(AICPA adapted)

*C25-18 (ACCOUNTING FOR CHANGING PRICES) The general purchasing power of the dollar has declined considerably because of inflation in recent years. To account for this changing value of the dollar, many accountants suggest that financial statements be adjusted for general price-level changes. Three independent, unrelated statements regarding general price-level-adjusted financial statements follow. Each statement contains some fallacious reasoning.

Statement I. The accounting profession has not seriously considered price-level-adjusted financial statements before because the rate of inflation usually has been so small from year to year that the adjustments would have been immaterial in amount. Price-level-adjusted financial statements represent a departure from the historical cost basis of accounting. Financial statements should be prepared on the basis of facts, not estimates.

Statement II. When adjusting financial data for general price-level changes, a distinction must be made between monetary and nonmonetary assets and liabilities that, under the historical cost basis of accounting, have been identified as "current" and "noncurrent." When using the historical cost basis of accounting, no purchasing power gain or loss is recognized in the accounting process; but when financial statements are adjusted for general price-level changes, a purchasing power gain or loss will be recognized on monetary and nonmonetary items.

Statement III. If financial statements were adjusted for general price-level changes, depreciation charges in the income statement would permit the recovery of dollars of current purchasing power and, thereby, equal the cost of new assets to replace the old ones. General price-level-adjusted data would yield statement-of-financial-position amounts closely approximating values. Furthermore, management can make better decisions if constant dollar financial statements are published.

Instructions

Evaluate each of the independent statements and identify the areas of fallacious reasoning in each. Explain why the reasoning is incorrect. Complete your discussion of each statement before proceeding to the next statement.

(AICPA adapted)

———— **EXERCISES** ————

(CONSTANT DOLLAR INDEX USE) Cockburn Co. has made the following purchases of property, plant, *E25-1 and equipment since its formation in 1988.

Year	Price-Level Index	Item	Cost
1988	100	Land	$140,000
1988	100	Building	200,000
1988	100	Machinery	80,000
1990	120	Office Equipment	25,000
1992	125	Machinery	30,000
1994	150	Office Equipment	8,000

The price-level index for 1995 is 160.

Instructions

Restate the above items in terms of 1995 dollars. Round to two decimals.

(CONSTANT DOLLAR INCOME STATEMENT) Stipe, Inc. had the following income statement data *E25-2 for 1994:

Sales	$240,000
Cost of goods sold	168,000
Gross profit	72,000
Operating expenses	34,000
Net income	$ 38,000

The following price levels were observed during the year:

	Price Index
December 31, 1994	150
1994 average	125
December 31, 1993	100

Instructions

Determine Stipe's constant dollar income before purchasing power gain or loss for 1994.

*E25-3 (CONSTANT DOLLAR: PURCHASING POWER COMPUTATION)   Presented below is comparative financial statement information for Steve Gilmour Corp. for the years 1994 and 1993.

	December 31, 1994	December 31, 1993
Cash	$ 88,000	$ 57,000
Inventory	40,000	25,000
Sales	230,000	200,000
Cost of goods sold	150,000	132,000
Operating expenses	34,000	30,000

The following price level indexes were observed during the year.

	Price Index
December 31, 1994	140
1994 average	125
December 31, 1993	100

Instructions

Determine Gilmour's purchasing power gain or loss for 1994. Assume that all transactions involved cash.

*E25-4 (CONSTANT DOLLAR FINANCIAL STATEMENTS)   Berry Corp. in its first year of operations reported the following financial information for the year ended December 31, 1994, before closing:

Cash	$ 85,500	Retained earnings	$ 67,500
Inventory	42,000	Sales	215,000
Land	90,000	Cost of goods sold	122,500
Capital share	150,000	Operating expenses	25,000

The following price-level indices were observed during the year.

	Price Index
December 31, 1994	121
1994 average	110
January 1, 1994	100

Berry experienced a purchasing power loss of $15,150 during 1994. Land was purchased and common shares issued on January 1, 1994. No inventory was on hand at the beginning of the year.

Instructions

Prepare the following financial statements for Berry Corp.:

(a) Constant dollar income statement for the year ended December 31, 1994.

(b) Constant dollar balance sheet on December 31, 1994.

(CURRENT COST INCOME STATEMENT) Rockford Co. reported the following financial information *E25-5 for 1994, its first year of operations.

Rockford Co.
Income Statement
for the Year Ended December 31, 1994

Sales	$290,000
Cost of goods sold	197,200
Gross profit	92,800
Operating expenses	41,300
Net income	$ 51,500

Rockford Co.
Balance Sheet
December 31, 1994

Assets		Liabilities and Shareholders' Equity	
Cash	$ 40,000	Common shares	$270,000
Inventory	95,000	Retained earnings	40,000
Land	175,000	Total liabilities and	
Total assets	$310,000	shareholders' equity	$310,000

Current cost information for 1993 is as follows:

Sales	$290,000	Inventory	$107,000
Cost of goods sold	215,000	Land	190,000
Operating expenses	41,300	Common shares	270,000
Cash	40,000		

Instructions

(a) Determine Rockford's holding gain or loss for 1994 on a current cost basis.

(b) Prepare Rockford's current cost income statement for 1994.

(DETERMINE CURRENT COST INCOME COMPONENTS) Sandley Chemical, Inc. is experimenting *E25-6 with the use of current costs. In 1994, the company purchased inventory that had a cost of $50,000, of which $30,000 was sold by year end at a sales price of $45,000. It was estimated that the current cost of the inventory at the date of sale was $33,000 and the current cost of the ending inventory at December 31, 1994 was $26,000. Operating expenses were $10,000.

Instructions

(a) Determine current cost income from operations.

(b) Determine current cost net income.

*E25-7 (CONSTANT DOLLAR PURCHASING POWER COMPUTATION) Assume that the Corrine Company has the following net monetary assets (monetary assets less monetary liabilities) at the beginning and the end of 1994.

	1/1/94	12/31/94
Net monetary assets	$300,000	$200,000

Transactions causing a change in net monetary assets during the period were incurrence and payments of accounts payable, collections of accounts receivable, and purchases and sales of merchandise during the period. All of these transactions occurred evenly throughout the year. Assume the following price-level indices:

January 1, 1994	120
Average for the year	150
December 31, 1994	160

Instructions

(Round all computations to the nearest dollar.)

(a) What is the amount of purchasing power gain or loss from holding the January 1 balance of net monetary items throughout the year?

(b) What is the amount of purchasing power gain or loss from holding net monetary items?

(c) Explain why the company had a purchasing power gain or loss.

*E25-8 (CONSTANT DOLLAR FINANCIAL STATEMENTS) The income statement for 1994 and the balance sheet on December 31, 1994 for Jackson Cage Co. appear below.

Jackson Cage Co.
Income Statement
for the Year Ended December 31, 1994

Sales	$341,600
Cost of goods sold	246,000
Gross profit	95,600
Operating expenses	30,400
Net income	$ 65,200

Jackson Cage Co.
Balance Sheet
December 31, 1994

Assets		Liabilities and Shareholders' Equity	
Cash	$ 59,000	Notes payable	$ 40,400
Accounts receivable	47,100	Accounts payable	61,000
Inventory	75,600	Common shares	300,000
Land	316,500	Retained earnings	96,800
Total assets	$498,200	Total liabilities and	
		shareholders' equity	$498,200

Additional Information

1. The relevant price indices are as follows:

January 1, 1989	105
June 30, 1991	112
August 31, 1993	120
December 31, 1994	168
Average for 1994	140

2. The company was founded on January 1, 1989. All common shares were issued at that time.

3. One-fifth of the land was acquired on August 31, 1993; the remainder of the land was acquired on January 1, 1989.

4. A purchasing power loss of $20,400 was computed for 1994.

Instructions

(a) Prepare a constant dollar income statement for Jackson Cage for the year ended December 31, 1994.

(b) Prepare a constant dollar balance sheet for Jackson Cage on December 31, 1994. (**Hint**: Retained earnings is a balancing item.)

(**CURRENT COST FINANCIAL STATEMENTS**) Bill's Fisheries Co. income statement for 1994 and ***E25-9** balance sheet on December 31, 1994, its first year of operations, are presented below.

Bill's Fisheries
Income Statement
for the Year Ended December 31, 1994

Sales	$795,000
Cost of goods sold	550,000
Gross profit	245,000
Operating expenses	57,000
Net income	$188,000

Bill's Fisheries Co.
Balance Sheet
December 31, 1994

Assets		Liabilities and Shareholders' Equity	
Cash	$ 74,000	Notes payable	$ 42,000
Accounts receivable	91,000	Accounts payable	63,000
Inventory	187,000	Common shares	559,000
Land	450,000	Retained earnings	188,000
Goodwill	50,000	Total liabilities and	
Total assets	$852,000	shareholders' equity	$852,000

The current cost of the following items on December 31, 1994 is as follows:

Inventory	$200,000
Land	495,000
Goodwill	20,000
Cost of goods sold	585,000

Instructions

(a) Prepare a schedule to show the total holding gain (loss) for Bill's Fisheries for 1994.

(b) Prepare a current cost income statement for Bill's Fisheries for the year ended December 31, 1994.

(c) Prepare a current cost balance sheet for Bill's Fisheries on December 31, 1994.

*E25-10 (CURRENT COST FINANCIAL STATEMENTS)   Hoyt Enterprises is considering the adoption of a current cost system. Presented below is Hoyt's balance sheet based on historical cost at the end of its first year of operations.

Hoyt Enterprises
Balance Sheet
December 31, 1994

Assets		Liabilities and Shareholders' Equity	
Cash	$25,000	Accounts payable	$ 9,000
Inventory	42,000	Common shares	50,000
Land	16,000	Retained earnings	24,000
	$83,000		$83,000

The following additional information is presented:

1. Cost of goods sold on an historical cost basis is $54,000; on a current cost basis, $58,000.

2. No dividends were paid in the first year of operations.

3. Ending inventory on a current cost basis is $46,000; land on a current cost basis is $22,000 at the end of the year.

4. Operating expenses for the first year were $19,000.

Instructions

(a)   Prepare an income statement for the current year on (1) an historical cost basis and (2) a current cost basis.

(b)   Prepare a balance sheet for the current year on a current cost basis.

(c)   Assume that the general price level at the beginning of the year was 100, the average for the year was 160, and the ending 200. Also assume that revenues were earned and costs were incurred uniformly during the year. The land was purchased and the capital stock was issued at the beginning of the year.

   Determine the following:

1.   Income before purchasing power gain or loss on a constant dollar income statement for 1994.

2.   Amount reported for land on a constant dollar balance sheet at December 31, 1994.

3.   Amount reported for cash on a constant dollar balance sheet at December 31, 1994.

─────────── **FINANCIAL REPORTING PROBLEM** ───────────

Refer to the financial statements and other documents of Moore Corporation Limited in Appendix 5A and answer the following questions:

1.   What were the major operations Moore selected to report separately in its Notes to Financial Statements? What were the items reported?

2.   What were the items disclosed in the interim reports for Moore?

PERSPECTIVES

ON ETHICS

Ross Denham

Ross Denham is a Professor of Financial Accounting Theory and related courses which include a heavy component of ethics, at the University of Alberta, where he is currently acting Chair of the department. He has, in addition to his academic posts, served as Director General, Audit Operations with the Office of the Auditor General of Canada. He has recently written a brochure entitled Ethics and You: A Pocket Guide for the Institute of Chartered Accountants of Alberta.

Your pamphlet begins with a quotation from Moliere, "It is not alone what we do, but also what we do not do, for which we are accountable." Why?

I think the quote illustrates the all encompassing scope of ethics and the impact ethics have on all aspects of our lives.

What do most people mean by ethics?

Ethics is a very broad subject, embracing morals, laws, personal beliefs, philosophical approaches, and religious teachings. Ethics are the application of all of these in specific situations. Ideally, ethics guide the level of trust in our business and personal dealings and convey behavioural expectations against which we evaluate each other. Ethical dilemmas arise when expected norms are not met.

The issue of ethics has had a lot of attention lately within academic and popular media. Is there an ethical crisis within the business community?

No, not really. Transgressions of trust have always been around. I believe that the attention reflects an increased awareness and sensitivity to ethical situations. We may be seeing greater levels of public reaction because there is heightened scrutiny of business and government, and the public is naturally expressing its anger over the revealed violations of trust and breaking of professional norms. I feel that this heightened awareness is a good thing that will help maintain ethical standards.

As your students graduate and enter the accounting profession, what sorts of ethical dilemmas are they likely to encounter?

That depends somewhat on their career directions—whether they choose to become public accountants or if they work for other organizations. It's hard to illustrate all types of situations, but I can give you a range.

Confidentiality is very important in all cases. What happens when you learn, through working on one case, of information that may be relevant to another? Can you apply this information to the benefit of the second? Generally not, but in some situations the details of the case may require a cross over of information. This can tie in with another major problem area, conflicts of interest.

Another situation students may be exposed to is cheating on expense accounts. Can you create a fictitious client to explain an unusually expensive dinner expense? Do you turn a blind eye? (Which, by the way, can create another dilemma.)

Nepotism also occurs. It is not uncommon for people to advance within organizations for their connections more than their merits.

Maintaining the integrity of financial information is critical and there may be occasions when accountants are asked to "window dress" information so as to de-emphasize some aspect of a situation. An example would be where the survival of the institution is at stake and reporting of the bad news is postponed in hopes that by doing so the institution can weather the storm until circumstances improve. However, there are implications concerning the organization's responsibility to its shareholders, clients, and creditors as well as to maintaining its own integrity.

Are these situations generally black and white issues?

Again, that depends. Most situations are not and require professional judgment. I try to explain this to my students by describing a continuum.

On the extreme left is clearly illegal activity; insider trading, fraudulent activity, embezzlement, and the like. Moving toward the right are clearly prohibited, yet not necessarily illegal actions, for example, sexual harassment, and possibly churning accounts in a portfolio management situation. At the extreme right are those situations that require the most judgment, such as where conflicts of interest arise, especially where the available courses of action can be defended to a certain degree.

Do ethical dilemmas, particularly the ones you described, confront new entries to the professions more so than experienced practitioners?

Not at all. Ethical situations are incredibly varied. Fortunately, as professionals mature, they hone their judgment skills and should be better equipped to address the situations.

Given the variety of situations that accountants can find themselves confronted by, what sorts of measures have the associations or other organizations taken to support practitioners in making appropriate decisions?

There have been a number of initiatives taken at a variety of levels. Associations, firms, and many organizations have codes of conduct

that deal primarily with maintaining the reputation of the organization by describing appropriate methods of dealing with others. In Alberta, the CAs have taken a stand, with the President making a point to address issues of ethics at public speaking engagements. The focus is on the importance of maintaining your personal reputation and, by extension, the organization's reputation through making the appropriate ethical decisions. Rebuilding a lost reputation is no mean feat.

By way of support mechanisms, most firms have established codes of conduct to guide employees in their decision making. Some large corporations, such as Shell or Syncrude Canada, have designated individuals with powers to address ethical problems and implement changes to prevent dilemmas from arising or recurring. Most organizations, however, do not, and employees must rely upon their professional judgment.

What guidelines would you recommend for practitioners confronted by an ethical dilemma for which the answer is not necessarily clear?

This may sound obvious, but I think it is exceptionally valuable. When confronted by an ethical dilemma, people should begin by asking themselves a series of deliberative

questions to explore the situation: What is the problem? Make sure you clearly define the problem and understand precisely what the dilemma is. Whose interests are foremost? (Personal, the corporation's, or a third party.) What standards apply to this situation? What is the impact of this situation on others? What are the various courses of action? Are the courses of action acceptable or legal? Am I comfortable with the required course of action?

As I indicated earlier, most firms have an established code of conduct or due process, based on accounting standards, which should provide direction in the vast majority of cases. To deviate from a firm's due process is a serious matter, and I'd recommend that before doing so, individuals be aware of why they are deviating and of the possible impact.

Any final advice for students about to enter a very competitive job market and who will, undoubtedly, encounter ethical dilemmas?

Yes. I've referred to the relationship between being ethical and reputation once or twice already. Some time ago I came across an anonymous quotation that summarizes that relationship nicely: When wealth is lost, nothing is lost; when health is lost, something is lost; when character is lost, all is lost.

Appendix: Accounting and the Time Value of Money

A prime purpose of financial accounting is to provide information that is useful in making business and economic decisions. Certainly the relationship between time and money is central to economic decision making. It would seem reasonable, then, to expect that any accounting system that has decision usefulness as a primary goal should have a rational basis for reflecting the time value of money in the values it assigns to assets and liabilities—that is, should provide monetary measurements that are interpretable in present value terms.[1]

Would you like to be a millionaire? If you are 20 years old now, can save $100 every month and can invest those savings to earn an after-tax rate of return of 1% per month (over 12% per year), you could be a millionaire before you are 59 years old. Or if you could invest just $10,000 today at that same interest rate, you would have over a million dollars by age 59. Such is the power of *interest*, especially when it is energized with a generous dosage of *time*.[2]

Business enterprises both invest and borrow large sums of money. The common characteristic in these two types of transactions is the **time value of the money** (i.e. the interest factor involved). The timing of the returns on the investment has an important effect on the worth of the investment (asset), and the timing of debt repayments has an effect on the value of the commitment (liability). Business people have become acutely aware of this timing factor and invest and borrow only after carefully analysing the relative values of the cash outflows and inflows.

Accountants are expected to make and understand the implications of value measurements. To do so, they must understand and be able to measure the *present value* of future cash inflows and outflows. This measurement requires an understanding of compound interest, annuities, and present value concepts. Therefore, the basic objectives of this appendix are to discuss and illustrate the essentials of these concepts and provide some accounting and business-related examples in which they are applied.

APPLICATIONS OF TIME VALUE CONCEPTS

Compound interest, annuities, and application of present value concepts are relevant to making measurements and disclosures when accounting for various financial statement elements. The following are some examples examined in this book and the chapters in which they appear:

> **Objective 1**
>
> Identify accounting topics where time value of money is used.

---

[1] J. Alex Milburn, *Incorporating the Time Value of Money Within Financial Accounting* (Toronto: CICA, 1988), p. 1. This is an excellent study regarding financial accounting and present value measurements. Its objective is to "develop proposals for reflecting the time value of money more fully within the existing financial accounting framework so as to enable a substantive improvement in the usefulness and credibility of financial statements" (p. 1). While we, the authors, accept the basic premise of this study, it is not our intention to examine the model and suggested changes to current financial accounting that are presented. The purpose of this appendix is more basic—to examine the time value of money and show how it can be incorporated in making measurements.

[2] As another example of how interest can multiply dollars quickly, Sidney Homer (author of *A History of Interest Rates*) indicated, "$1,000 invested at a mere 8% for 400 years would grow to $23 quadrillion—$5 million for every human on earth." But, "the first 100 years are the hardest." (*Forbes*, July 14, 1986).

1. **Notes.** Valuing receivables and payables that carry no stated interest rate or a different than market interest rate (Chapters 7 and 14).

2. **Leases.** Valuing assets and obligations to be capitalized under long-term leases and measuring the amount of the lease payments and annual leasehold amortization (Chapter 21).

3. **Amortization of Premiums and Discounts.** Measuring amortization of premium or discount on both bond investments and bonds payable (Chapters 14 and 18).

4. **Pensions and Other Post-Retirement Benefits.** Measuring service cost components of employers' post-retirement benefits expense and benefit obligations (Chapter 20).

5. **Capital Assets.** Determining the value of assets acquired under deferred-payment contracts (Chapter 10).

6. **Sinking Funds.** Determining the contributions necessary to accumulate a fund for debt retirements (Chapter 14).

7. **Business Combinations.** Determining the value of receivables, payables, liabilities, accruals, and commitments acquired or assumed in a "purchase" (Chapter 18).

8. **Depreciation.** Measuring depreciation charges under the sinking fund and the annuity methods (Chapter 11).

9. **Instalment Contracts.** Measuring periodic payments on long-term sales or purchase contracts (Chapters 6 and 14).

In addition to accounting and business applications, compound interest, annuity, and present value concepts have applicability to personal finance and investment decisions. In purchasing a home, planning for retirement, and evaluating alternative investments, you need to understand time value of money concepts.

NATURE OF INTEREST

Interest *is payment for the use of money*. It is the excess cash received or paid over and above the amount lent or borrowed (**principal**). For example, if the Corner Bank lends you $1,000 with the understanding that you will repay $1,150, the excess over $1,000, or $150, represents interest expense to you and interest revenue to the bank.

The amount of interest to be paid is generally stated as a rate over a specific period of time. For example, if you use the $1,000 for one year before repaying $1,150, the rate of interest is 15% per year ($150/$1,000). The custom of expressing interest as a rate is an established business practice.[3] In fact, business managers make investing and borrowing decisions on the basis of the rate of interest involved rather than on the actual dollar amount of interest to be received or paid.

The rate of interest is commonly expressed as it is applied to a one-year time period. Interest of 12% represents a rate of 12% per year unless stipulated otherwise. The statement that a corporation will pay bond interest of 12%, payable semiannually, means a rate of 6% every six months, not 12% every six months.

How is the *rate* of interest determined? One of the most important factors is the level of **credit risk** (risk of nonpayment) involved. Other factors being equal, the higher the credit risk, the higher the interest rate. Every borrower's risk is evaluated by the lender. A low-risk borrower like Canadian Pacific Ltd. may obtain a loan at or slightly below the going market "prime" rate of interest. You or the neighbourhood delicatessen, however, will probably be charged several percentage points above the prime rate.

---

[3] Federal and provincial legislation requires the disclosure of the effective interest rate on an *annual basis* in contracts. That is, instead of or in addition to stating the rate as "1% per month," it must be stated as "12% per year" if it is simple interest or "12.68% per year" if it is compounded monthly.

Another important factor is **inflation** (change in the general purchasing power of the dollar). Lenders desire to protect the purchasing power of the future cash flows they will receive (interest payments and return of the principal). If inflation is expected to be significant in the future, lenders will require a higher number of dollars (i.e. a higher interest rate) in order to offset their anticipation that the purchasing power of these dollars will be reduced.

In addition to receiving compensation for risk and expected inflation, lenders also desire a **pure** or **real return** from letting someone else use their money. This real return reflects the amount the lender would charge if there were no possibility of default or expectation of inflation.

The *amount* of interest related to any financing transaction is a function of three variables:

1. **Principal**—the amount borrowed or invested.

2. **Interest Rate**—a percentage of the outstanding principal.

3. **Time**—the number of years or portion of a year that the principal is outstanding.

Simple Interest

Simple interest *is computed on the amount of the principal only*. It is the return on (or growth of) the principal for one time period. Simple interest[4] is commonly expressed as:

$$\text{Interest} = p \times i \times n$$

Where

$$p = \text{principal}$$
$$i = \text{rate of interest for a single period}$$
$$n = \text{number of periods}$$

Objective 2

Distinguish between simple and compound interest.

To illustrate, if you borrowed $1,000 for a three-year period, with a simple interest rate of 15% per year, the total interest you would pay would be $450, computed as follows:

$$\text{Interest} = (p)\,(i)\,(n)$$
$$= (\$1,000)\,(.15)\,(3)$$
$$= \$450$$

Compound Interest

John Maynard Keynes, the legendary English economist, supposedly called it magic. Mayer Rothschild, the founder of the famous European banking firm, is said to have proclaimed it the eighth wonder of the world. Today people continue to extol its wonder and its power.[5] The object of their affection is compound interest.

Compound interest *is computed on the principal* and *any interest earned that has not been paid*. To illustrate the difference between simple interest and compound interest, assume that you deposit $1,000 in the Last Canadian Bank where it earns simple interest of 9% per year, and you deposit another $1,000 in the First Canadian Bank where it earns annually compounded interest of 9%. Also assume that in both cases you do not withdraw any interest until three years from the date of deposit. The calculation of interest to be received is shown at the top of page A-4.

Note that simple interest uses the initial principal of $1,000 to compute the interest in all three years, while compound interest uses the accumulated balance (principal plus interest to date) at each year end to compute interest in the succeeding year. Obviously, if you had a choice between

---

[4] Simple interest is also expressed as i (interest) $= P$ (principal) $\times R$ (rate) $\times T$ (time).

[5] Here is an illustration of the power of time and compounding interest on money. In 1626, Peter Minuit bought Manhattan Island from the Manhattoe Indians for $24 worth of trinkets and beads. If the Indians had taken a boat to Holland, invested the $24 in Dutch securities returning just 6% per year, and kept the money and interest invested at 6%, by 1971 they would have had $13 billion, enough to buy back all the land on the island and still have a couple of billion dollars left (*Forbes*, June 1, 1971). By 1988, 362 years after the trade, the $24 would have grown to approximately $34.6 billion—$29 trillion had the interest rate been 8%.

SIMPLE INTEREST VS. COMPOUND INTEREST

		Last Canadian Bank			First Canadian Bank	
	Simple Interest Calculation	Simple Interest	Accumulated Year-End Balance	**Compound** Interest Calculation	Compound Interest	Accumulated Year-End Balance
Year 1	$1,000.00 × 9%	$ 90.00	$1,090.00	$1,000.00 × 9%	$ 90.00	$1,090.00
Year 2	1,000.00 × 9%	90.00	1,180.00	1,090.00 × 9%	98.10	1,188.10
Year 3	1,000.00 × 9%	90.00	1,270.00	1,188.00 × 9%	106.93	1,295.03
		$270.00				$295.03

$25.03
Difference

investing at simple interest or at compound interest, you would choose compound interest, all other things—especially risk—being equal. In the example, compounding provides $25.03 of additional interest income.

Compound interest is generally applied in business situations. Financial managers view and evaluate their investment opportunities in terms of a series of periodic returns, each of which can be reinvested to yield additional returns. Simple interest is applicable only to short-term investments and debts that are due within one year.

Compound Interest Tables

Five different compound interest tables are presented at the end of this appendix (see pages A-25–A-29). These tables are the source for various "interest factors" used in solving problems involving interest illustrated in this appendix and throughout the book. The titles of these five tables and their contents are:

1. **Future Amount of 1**. Contains the amounts to which $1.00 will accumulate if deposited now at a specified rate and left for a specified number of periods. (Table A-1)

2. **Present Value of 1**. Contains the amounts that must be deposited now at a specified rate of interest to equal $1.00 at the end of a specified number of periods. (Table A-2)

3. **Future Amount of an Ordinary Annuity of 1**. Contains the amounts to which periodic rents of $1.00 will accumulate if the rents are invested at the *end* of each period at a specified rate of interest for a specified number of periods. (Table A-3)

4. **Present Value of an Ordinary Annuity of 1**. Contains the amounts that must be deposited now at a specified rate of interest to permit withdrawals of $1.00 at the *end* of regular periodic intervals for the specified number of periods. (Table A-4)

5. **Present Value of an Annuity Due of 1**. Contains the amounts that must be deposited now at a specified rate of interest to permit withdrawals of $1.00 at the *beginning* of regular periodic intervals for the specified number of periods. (Table A-5)

The excerpt at the top of page A-5 illustrates the general format and content of these tables. It is from Table A-1, "Future Amount of 1," which indicates the amount to which a dollar accumulates at the end of each of five periods at three different rates of compound interest.

Interpreting the table, if $1.00 is invested for three periods at a compound interest rate of 9% per period, it will amount to $1.30 (1.29503 × $1.00), the **compound future amount.** If $1.00 is invested at 11%, at the end of four periods it amounts to $1.52. If the investment is $1,000 instead of $1.00, it will amount to $1,295.03 ($1,000 × 1.29503) if invested at 9% for three periods or $1,518.07 if invested at 11% for four periods.

Throughout the foregoing discussion (and most of the discussion that follows) the use of the term *periods* instead of *years* is intentional. While interest is generally expressed as an annual rate, the compounding period is often shorter. Therefore, the annual interest rate must be converted to correspond to the length of the period. To convert the "annual interest rate" into the "compounding

Objective 3

Learn how to use appropriate compound interest tables.

Future Amount of 1 at Compound Interest
(Excerpt from Table A-1)

Period	9%	10%	11%
1	1.09000	1.10000	1.11000
2	1.18810	1.21000	1.23210
3	1.29503	1.33100	1.36763
4	1.41158	1.46410	1.51807
5	1.53862	1.61051	1.68506

period interest rate," *divide the annual rate by the number of compounding periods per year*. In addition, the number of periods is determined by *multiplying the number of years involved by the number of compounding periods per year*.

To illustrate, assume that $1.00 is invested for six years at 8% annual interest compounded quarterly. Using Table A-1, the amount to which this $1.00 will accumulate is determined by reading the factor that appears in the 2% column (8% ÷ 4) on the 24th row (6 years × 4), namely 1.60844, or approximately $1.61.

Because interest is theoretically earned (accruing) every second of every day, it is possible to calculate interest that is compounded continuously but, as a practical matter, most business transactions assume interest to be compounded no more frequently than daily.

How often interest is compounded can make a substantial difference in the rate of return achieved. For example, 9% interest compounded daily provides a 9.42% annual yield, or a difference of .42%. The 9.42% is referred to as the **effective yield** or **rate**[6] whereas the 9% annual interest rate is called the **stated, nominal, coupon,** or **face rate.** When the compounding frequency is greater than once a year, the effective interest rate is greater than the stated rate.

FUNDAMENTAL VARIABLES

The following four variables are fundamental to all compound interest problems:

1. **Rate of Interest**. This rate, unless otherwise stated, is an annual rate that must be adjusted to reflect the length of the compounding period less than a year.

2. **Number of Time Periods**. This is the number of compounding periods for which interest is to be computed.

3. **Future Amount**. The value at a future date of a given sum or sums invested assuming compound interest.

4. **Present Value**. The value now (present time) of a future sum or sums discounted assuming compound interest.

The relationship of these four variables is depicted in the *time diagram* on page A-6.

In some cases all four of these variables are known, but in many business situations at least one is unknown. Frequently, the accountant is expected to determine the unknown amount or amounts. To do this, a time diagram can be very helpful in understanding the nature of the problem and finding a solution.

Objective 4

Identify variables fundamental to solving interest problems.

---

[6] The formula for calculating the effective rate in situations where the compounding frequency (f) is more than once a year is as follows:

$$\text{Effective rate} = (1 + i)^f - 1$$

where i = the interest rate per compounding period.

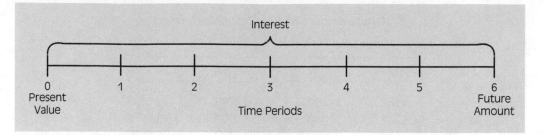

The remainder of the appendix covers the following six major time value of money concepts. Both formula and interest table approaches are used to illustrate how problems may be solved:

1. Future amount of a single sum.

2. Present value of a single sum.

3. Future amount of an ordinary annuity.

4. Future amount of an annuity due.

5. Present value of an ordinary annuity.

6. Present value of an annuity due.

SINGLE SUM PROBLEMS

Objective 5

Solve future
and present
value of single-
sum problems.

Many business and investment decisions involve a single amount of money that either exists now or will exist in the future. Single sum problems can generally be classified into one of the following two categories:

1. Determining the *unknown future amount* of a known single sum of money that is invested for a specified number of periods at a specified interest rate.

2. Determining the *unknown present value* of a known single sum of money that is discounted for a specified number of periods at a specified interest rate.

Future Amount of a Single Sum

The "amount" of a sum of money is the future value of that sum when left to accumulate for a certain number of periods at a specified rate of interest per period.

The amount to which 1 (one) will accumulate may be expressed as a formula:

$$a_{\overline{n}|i} = (1 + i)^n$$

where

$a_{\overline{n}|i}$ = future amount of 1
i = rate of interest for a single period
n = number of periods

To illustrate, assume that \$1.00 is invested at 9% interest compounded annually for three years. The amounts to which the \$1.00 will accumulate at the end of each year are:

$$a_{\overline{1}|9\%} = (1 + .09)^1 \text{ for the end of the first year.}$$
$$a_{\overline{2}|9\%} = (1 + .09)^2 \text{ for the end of the second year.}$$
$$a_{\overline{3}|9\%} = (1 + .09)^3 \text{ for the end of the third year.}$$

These compound amounts accumulate as follows.

Period	Beginning-of-Period Amount	×	Multiplier $(1 + i)$	=	End-of-Period Amount*	Formula $(1 + i)^n$
1	1.00000		1.09		1.09000	$(1.09)^1$
2	1.09000		1.09		1.18810	$(1.09)^2$
3	1.18810		1.09		1.29503	$(1.09)^3$

*These amounts appear in Table A-1 in the 9% column.

To calculate the *future value of any single amount*, multiply the future amount of 1 factor by that amount.

$$a = p(a_{\overline{n}|i})$$

where

a = future amount

p = beginning principal or sum (present value)

$a_{\overline{n}|i}$ = $(1 + i)^n$ = future amount of 1 for n periods at i%

For example, what is the future amount of $50,000 invested for five years at 11% compounded annually? In time-diagram form, this investment situation is as follows.

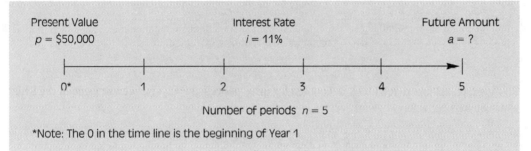

This investment problem is solved as follows:

$$a = p(a_{\overline{n}|i})$$
$$= \$50,000(a_{\overline{5}|11\%})$$
$$= \$50,000\ (1.68506)$$
$$= \$84,253.$$

The future amount of 1 factor of 1.68506 is that which appears in Table A-1 in the 11% column and 5-period row.

To illustrate a more complex business situation, assume that at the beginning of 1994 Ontario Hydro Corp. deposits $250 million in an escrow account with Canada Trust Company as a commitment toward a small nuclear power plant to be completed December 31, 1997. How much will be on deposit at the end of four years if interest is compounded semiannually at 10%?

With a known present value of $250 million, a total of eight compounding periods (4 × 2), and an interest rate of 5% per compounding period (.10 ÷ 2), this problem can be time-diagrammed and the future amount determined as follows.

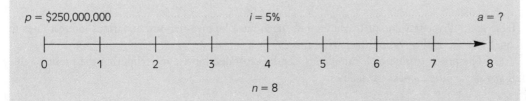

$$a = \$250{,}000{,}000\ (a_{\overline{8}|5\%})$$
$$= \$250{,}000{,}000\ (1.47746)$$
$$- \$369{,}365{,}000$$

The deposit of \$250 million will accumulate to \$369,365,000 by December 31, 1997. The future amount of 1 factor is found in Table A-1 (5% column and the 8-period row).

Present Value of a Single Sum

A previous example showed that \$50,000 invested at an annually compounded interest rate of 11% will be worth \$84,253 at the end of five years. It follows that \$84,253 to be received five years from now is presently worth \$50,000 given an 11% interest rate (i.e. \$50,000 is the present value of this \$84,253). The **present value** is the amount that must be invested now to produce a known future amount. The *present value is always a smaller amount than the known future amount because interest is earned and accumulated on the present value to the future date*. In determining the future amount we move forward in time using a process of **accumulation**, while in determining present value we move backward in time using the process of **discounting**.

The present value of 1 (one) may be expressed as a formula:

$$p_{\overline{n}|i} = 1\ /\ a_{\overline{n}|i} = \frac{1}{(1+i)^n}$$

where

$p_{\overline{n}|i}$ = present value of 1 for n periods at i%.

$a_{\overline{n}|i}$ = $(1+i)^n$ = future amount of 1 for n periods at i%.

To illustrate, assume that \$1.00 is discounted for three periods at 9%. The present value of the \$1.00 is discounted each period as follows:

$$p_{\overline{1}|9\%} = 1/(1+.09)^1 \text{ for the first period}$$
$$p_{\overline{2}|9\%} = 1/(1+.09)^2 \text{ for the second period}$$
$$p_{\overline{3}|9\%} = 1/(1+.09)^3 \text{ for the third period}$$

Therefore, the \$1.00 is discounted as follows.

Discount Periods	Future Amount	$\div$	Divisor $(1+i)^n$	$=$	Present Value*	Formula $1/(1+i)^n$
1	1.00000		1.09		.91743	$1/(1.09)^1$
2	1.00000		$(1.09)^2$		.84168	$1/(1.09)^2$
3	1.00000		$(1.09)^3$		.77218	$1/(1.09)^3$

*These amounts appear in Table A-2 in the 9% column.

Table A-2, "Present Value of 1," shows how much must be invested now at various interest rates to equal 1 at the end of various periods of time.

The present value of 1 formula $p_{\overline{n}|i}$ can be expanded for use in computing the present value of *any single future amount* as follows:

$$p = a(p_{\overline{n}|i})$$

where

p = present value of a single future amount

a = future amount

$p_{\overline{n}|i} = \dfrac{1}{(1+1)^n}$ = present value of 1 for n periods at $i\%$

To illustrate the use of this formula, assume that your favourite uncle proposes to give you $4,000 for a trip to Europe when you graduate three years from now. He will finance the trip by investing a sum of money now at 8% compound interest that will accumulate to $4,000 upon your graduation. The only conditions are that you graduate and that you tell him how much to invest now.

To impress your uncle you might set up the following time diagram and solve the problem as follows.

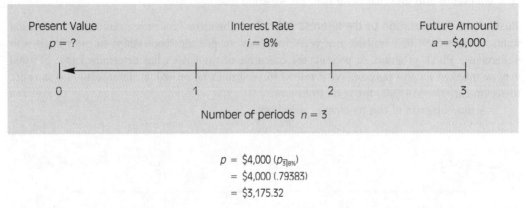

$$p = \$4,000\ (p_{\overline{3}|8\%})$$
$$= \$4,000\ (.79383)$$
$$= \$3,175.32$$

Advise your uncle to invest $3,175.32 now to provide you with $4,000 upon graduation. To satisfy your uncle's other condition, you must simply pass this course and many more. Note that the present value factor of .79383 is found in Table A-2 (8% column, 3-period row).

Single Sum Problems: Solving for Other Unknowns

In computing either the future amount or the present value in the previous single sum illustrations, both the number of periods and the interest rate were known. In business situations, both the future amount and the present value may be known and either the number of periods or the interest rate may be unknown. The following two illustrations demonstrate how to solve single sum problems when there is either an unknown number of periods (n) or an unknown interest rate (i). These illustrations show that if any three of the four values (future amount, a; present value, p; number of periods, n; interest rate, i) are known, the one unknown can be derived.

Illustration: Computation of the Number of Periods. The local Big Sisters and Big Brothers associations in Regina want to accumulate $70,000 for the construction of a day-care centre. If at the beginning of the current year the associations are able to deposit $47,811 in a building fund that earns 10% interest compounded annually, how many years will it take for the fund to accumulate to $70,000?

In this situation, the present value ($47,811), future amount ($70,000), and interest rate (10%) are known. A time diagram of this investment is as follows.

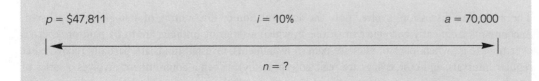

The unknown number of periods can be determined using either the future amount or present value approaches as shown below:

Future Amount Approach	Present Value Approach
$a = p(a_{\overline{n}|10\%})$	$p = a(p_{\overline{n}|10\%})$
$\$70{,}000 = \$47{,}811(a_{\overline{n}|10\%})$	$\$47{,}811 = \$70{,}000(p_{\overline{n}|10\%})$
$a_{\overline{n}|10\%} = \dfrac{\$70{,}000}{\$47{,}811} = 1.46410$	$p_{\overline{n}|10\%} = \dfrac{\$47{,}811}{\$70{,}000} = .68301$

Using the future amount of 1 factor of 1.46410, refer to Table A-1 and read down the 10% column to find that factor in the 4-period row. Thus, it will take four years for the $47,811 to accumulate to $70,000. Using the present value of 1 factor of .68301, refer to Table A-2 and read down the 10% column to also find that factor is in the 4-period row.

Illustration: Computation of the Interest Rate. The Canadian Academic Accounting Association wants to have $141,000 available five years from now to provide scholarships to individuals who undertake a Ph.D. program. At present, the executive of the CAAA has determined that $80,000 may be invested for this purpose. What rate of interest must be earned on the investments in order to accumulate the $141,000 five years from now?

A time diagram of this problem is as follows.

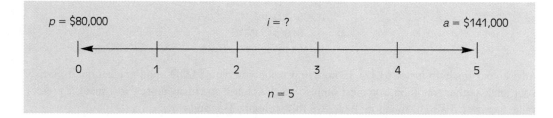

Given that the present value, future amount, and number of periods are known, the unknown interest rate can be determined using either the future amount or present value approaches as shown below:

Future Amount Approach	Present Value Approach
$a = p(a_{\overline{5}|})$	$p = a(p_{\overline{5}|})$
$\$141{,}000 = \$80{,}000\,(a_{\overline{5}|})$	$\$80{,}000 = \$141{,}000\,(P_{\overline{5}|})$
$a_{\overline{5}|} = \$141{,}000 \, / \, \$80{,}000$	$p_{\overline{5}|} = \$80{,}000 \, / \, \$141{,}000$
$= 1.7625$	$= 0.5674$

Using the future amount of 1 factor of 1.7625, refer to Table A-1 and read across the 5-period row to find a close match of this future amount factor in the 12% column. Thus, the $80,000 must be invested at 12% to accumulate to $141,000 at the end of five years. Using the present value of 1 factor of 0.5674 and Table A-2, reading across the 5-period row shows this factor in the 12% column.

ANNUITIES

The preceding discussion involved only the accumulation or discounting of a single principal sum. Accountants frequently encounter situations in which a series of amounts are to be paid or received over time (e.g., when loans or sales are paid in instalments, invested funds are partially recovered at regular intervals, and cost savings are realized repeatedly). When a commitment involves a series of equal payments made at equal intervals of time, it is called an annuity. By definition, an **annuity** requires that (1) the *periodic payments or receipts* (called **rents**) *always be the same amount*, (2) the *interval between such rents always be the same*, and (3) the *interest be compounded once each interval*.

The **future amount of an annuity** *is the sum of all the rents plus the accumulated compound interest on them*. Rents may, however, occur at either the beginning or the end of the periods. To distinguish annuities under these two alternatives, an annuity is classified as an **ordinary annuity** *if the rents occur at the end of each period*, and as an **annuity due** *if the rents occur at the beginning of each period*.

Future Amount of an Ordinary Annuity

One approach to calculating the future amount of an annuity is to determine the future amount of each rent in the series and then aggregate these individual future amounts. For example, assume that $1 is deposited at the *end* of each of five years (an ordinary annuity)and earns 12% interest compounded annually. The future amount can be computed as follows using the "Future Amount of 1," for each of the five $1 rents.

<table>
<tr><td colspan="8" align="center">End of Period in Which $1.00 is to Be Invested</td></tr>
<tr><td></td><td></td><td></td><td></td><td></td><td></td><td>Amount at End</td></tr>
<tr><td>Present</td><td>1</td><td>2</td><td>3</td><td>4</td><td>5</td><td>of Year 5</td></tr>
<tr><td></td><td>$1.00 ───────────────────►</td><td></td><td></td><td></td><td></td><td>$1.57352</td></tr>
<tr><td></td><td></td><td>$1.00 ──────────────►</td><td></td><td></td><td></td><td>1.40493</td></tr>
<tr><td></td><td></td><td></td><td>$1.00 ─────────►</td><td></td><td></td><td>1.25440</td></tr>
<tr><td></td><td></td><td></td><td></td><td>$1.00 ───►</td><td></td><td>1.12000</td></tr>
<tr><td></td><td></td><td></td><td></td><td></td><td>$1.00</td><td>1.00000</td></tr>
<tr><td colspan="6" align="right">Total (future amount of an ordinary annuity of $1.00 for 5 periods at 12%)</td><td>**$6.35285**</td></tr>
</table>

Although the foregoing procedure for computing the future amount of an ordinary annuity produces the correct answer, it is cumbersome if the number of rents is large. A more efficient way of determining the future amount of an ordinary annuity of 1 is by applying the following formula:

$$A_{\overline{n}|i} = \frac{(1 + i)^n - 1}{i}$$

where

$A_{\overline{n}|i}$ = future amount of an ordinary annuity of 1 for n periods at i rate of interest

n = number of compounding periods

i = rate of interest per period

Using this formula, Table A-3 has been developed to show the "Future Amount of an Ordinary Annuity of 1" for various interest rates and investment periods. The top box on page A-12 is an excerpt from this table. Interpreting the table, if $1.00 is invested at the end of each year for four years at 11% interest compounded annually, the amount of the annuity at the end of the fourth year will be $4.71 (4.70973 × $1.00). The $4.71 is made up of $4 of rent payments ($1 at the end of each of the 4 years) and compound interest of $0.71.

Objective 6

Solve future amount of ordinary and annuity due problems.

Future Amount of an Ordinary Annuity of 1
(Excerpt from Table A-3)

Period	10%	11%	12%
1	1.00000	1.00000	1.00000
2	2.10000	2.11000	2.12000
3	3.31000	3.34210	3.37440
4	4.64100	4.70973	4.77933
5	6.10510	6.22780	6.35285*

*Note that this factor is the same as the sum of the future amounts of 1 factors shown in the previous schedule.

The $A_{\overline{n}|i}$ formula can be expanded to determine the future amount of an ordinary annuity as follows:

$$A = R\,(A_{\overline{n}|i})$$

where

A = future amount of an ordinary annuity

R = periodic rents

$A_{\overline{n}|i} = \dfrac{(1+i)^n - 1}{i} = \begin{array}{l}\text{future amount of an ordinary annuity}\\\text{of 1 for } n \text{ periods at } i\%\end{array}$

To illustrate, what is the future amount of five $5,000 deposits made at the end of each of the next five years, earning interest at 12%? The time diagram and solution for this problem are as follows.

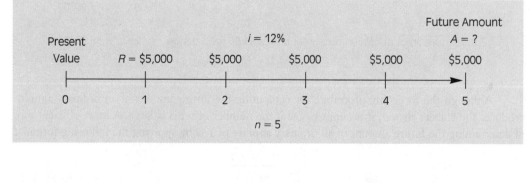

$A = R\,(A_{\overline{n}|i})$

$\quad = \$5,000\ (A_{\overline{5}|12\%})$

$\quad = \$5,000\ (6.35285)$

$\quad = \$31,764.25$

The future amount of an ordinary annuity of 1 factor of 6.35285 is found in Table A-3 (12% column, 5-period row).

To illustrate these computations in a business situation, assume that Lightning Electronics Limited's management decides to deposit $75,000 at the end of each six-month period for the next three years for the purpose of accumulating enough money to meet debts that mature in three years. What is the future amount that will be on deposit at the end of three years if the annual interest rate is 10%? The time diagram and solution are as follows.

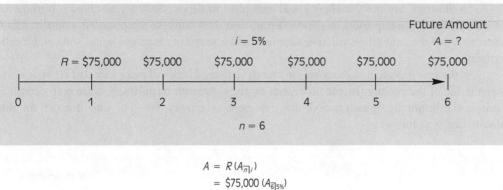

$$A = R(A_{\overline{n}|i})$$
$$= \$75{,}000\,(A_{\overline{6}|5\%})$$
$$= \$75{,}000\,(6.80191)$$
$$= \$510{,}143.25$$

Thus, six deposits of $75,000 made at the end of every six months and earning 5% per period will grow to $510,143.25 at the time of the last deposit.

Future Amount of an Annuity Due

The preceding analysis of an *ordinary annuity* was based on the fact that the *periodic rents* occur at the *end* of each period. An **annuity due** is based on the fact that the *periodic rents* occur at the *beginning* of each period. This means an annuity due will accumulate interest during the first period whereas an ordinary annuity will not. Therefore, the significant difference between the two types of annuities is in the number of interest accumulation periods involved. The distinction is shown graphically below.

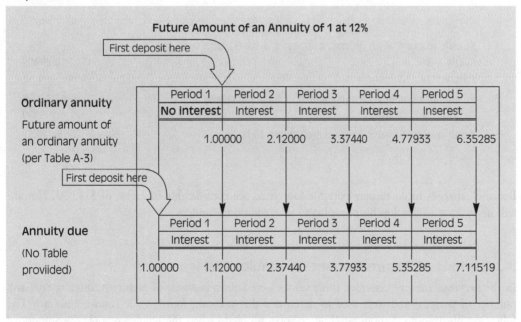

Because the cash flows from the annuity due come exactly one period earlier than for an ordinary annuity, the future value of the annuity due of 1 factor is exactly 12% higher than the ordinary annuity factor. Therefore, *to determine the future value of an annuity due of 1 factor, multiply the corresponding future value of the ordinary annuity of 1 factor by one plus the interest rate*. For example, to determine the future value of an annuity due of 1 factor for five periods at 12% compound interest, simply multiply the future value of an ordinary annuity of 1 factor for five periods (6.35285) by one plus the interest rate (1 + .12) to arrive at the future value of an annuity due of 1, 7.1159 (6.35285 × 1.12).

To illustrate, assume that Hank Lotadough plans to deposit $800 a year on each birthday of his son Howard, starting today, his tenth birthday, at 12% interest compounded annually. Hank wants to know the amount he will have accumulated for university expenses by his son's eighteenth birthday.

As the first deposit is made on his son's tenth birthday, Hank will make a total of eight deposits over the life of the annuity (assume no deposit on the eighteenth birthday). Because each deposit is made at the beginning of each period, they represent an annuity due. The time diagram for this annuity due is as follows.

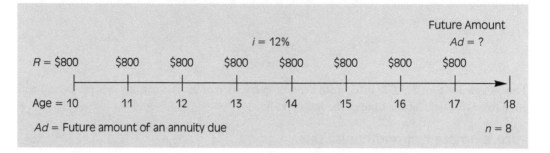

Referring to Table A-3, "Future Amount of an Ordinary Annuity of 1," for eight periods at 12%, a factor of 12.29969 is found. This factor is then multiplied by (1 + .12) to arrive at the future amount of an annuity due of 1 factor. As a result, the accumulated amount on his son's eighteenth birthday is computed as follows.

1.	Future amount of an ordinary annuity of 1 for 8 periods at 12% (Table A-3)	12.29969
2.	Factor (1 + .12)	× 1.12
3.	Future amount of an annuity due of 1 for 8 periods at 12%	13.77565
4.	Periodic deposit (rent)	× $800
5.	Accumulated amount on son's eighteenth birthday	$11,020.52

Because expenses to go to university for four years are considerably in excess of $11,000, Howard will likely have to develop his own plan to save additional funds.

Illustrations of Future Amount of Annuity Problems

In the previous annuity examples, three values were known (amount of each rent, interest rate, and number of periods) and were used to determine the unknown fourth value (future amount). The following illustrations demonstrate how to solve problems when the unknown is (1) the amount of the rents or (2) the number of rents in ordinary annuity situations.

Illustration: Computing the Amount of Each Rent. Assume that you wish to accumulate $14,000 for a down payment on a condominium apartment five years from now and that you can earn an annual return of 8% compounded semiannually during the next five years. How much should you deposit at the end of each six-month period?

The $14,000 is the future amount of ten (5 × 2) semiannual end-of-period payments of an unknown amount at an interest rate of 4% (8% ÷ 2). This problem is time-diagrammed as follows.

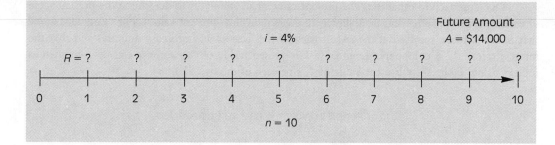

Using the formula for the future amount of an ordinary annuity, the amount of each rent is determined as follows:

$$A = R(A_{\overline{n}|i})$$
$$\$14{,}000 = R(A_{\overline{10}|4\%})$$
$$\$14{,}000 = R(12.00611)$$
$$\frac{\$14{,}000}{12.00611} = R$$
$$R = \$1{,}166.07$$

Thus, you must make 10 semi-annual deposits of $1,166.07 each in order to accumulate $14,000 for your down payment. The future amount of an ordinary annuity of 1 factor of 12.00611 is provided in Table A-3 (4% column, 10-period row).

Illustration: Computing the Number of Periodic Rents. Suppose that your company wants to accumulate $117,332 by making periodic deposits of $20,000 at the end of each year that will earn 8% compounded annually. How many deposits must be made?

The $117,332 represents the future amount of $n(=?)$ $20,000 deposits at an 8% annual rate of interest. The time diagram for this problem is as follows.

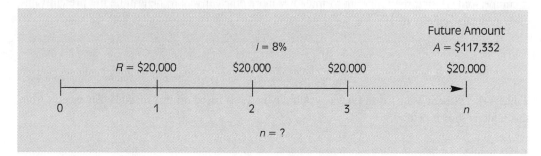

Using the future amount of an ordinary annuity formula, the factor of 1 is determined as follows:

$$A = R(A_{\overline{n}|i})$$
$$\$117{,}332 = \$20{,}000\,(A_{\overline{n}|8\%})$$
$$A_{\overline{n}|8\%} = \frac{\$117{,}332}{\$20{,}000} = 5.86660$$

Using Table A-3 and reading down the 8% column, 5.86660 is in the 5-period row. Thus, five deposits of $20,000 each must be made.

Present Value of an Ordinary Annuity

The present value of an annuity may be viewed as the *single amount* that, if invested now at compound interest, would provide for a series of withdrawals of a certain amount per period for a specific number of future periods. In other words, the present value of an ordinary annuity is the present value of a series of rents to be withdrawn at the end of each equal interval.

Objective 7

Solve present value of ordinary and annuity due problems.

One approach to calculating the present value of an annuity is to determine the present value of each rent in the series and then aggregate these individual present values. For example, assume that $1.00 is to be received at the *end* of each of five periods (an ordinary annuity) and that the interest rate is 12% compounded annually. The present value of this annuity can be computed as follows using Table A-2, "Present Value of 1," for each of the five $1 rents.

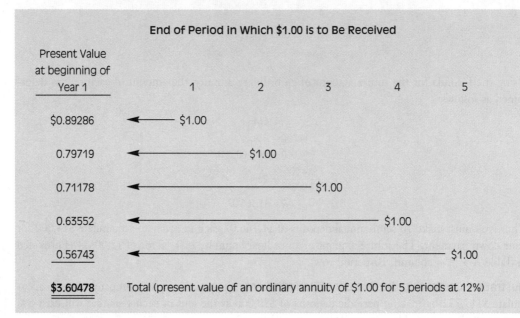

End of Period in Which $1.00 is to Be Received

Present Value at beginning of Year 1	1	2	3	4	5
$0.89286	← $1.00				
0.79719	←	$1.00			
0.71178	←		$1.00		
0.63552	←			$1.00	
0.56743	←				$1.00
$3.60478	Total (present value of an ordinary annuity of $1.00 for 5 periods at 12%)				

This computation indicates that if the single sum of $3.60 is invested today at 12% interest for five periods, $1.00 can be withdrawn at the end of each period for five periods. This procedure is cumbersome. Using the following formula is a more efficient way to determine the present value of an ordinary annuity of 1:

$$P_{\overline{n}|i} = \frac{1 - \dfrac{1}{(1 + i)^n}}{i}$$

Table A-4, "Present Value of an Ordinary Annuity of 1," is based on this formula. An excerpt from this table is shown below.

Present Value of an Ordinary Annuity of 1
(Excerpt from Table A-4)

Period	10%	11%	12%
1	0.90909	0.90090	0.89286
2	1.73554	1.71252	1.69005
3	2.48685	2.44371	2.40183
4	3.16986	3.10245	3.03735
5	3.79079	3.69590	**3.60478***

*Note that this factor is equal to the sum of the present value of 1 factors shown in the previous schedule.

The formula for the present value of any ordinary annuity of any rent value is as follows:

$$P = R(P_{\overline{n}|i})$$

where

P = present value of an ordinary annuity

R = periodic rent (ordinary annuity)

$$P_{\overline{n}|} = \frac{1 - \dfrac{1}{(1+i)^n}}{i} = \text{present value of an ordinary annuity of 1 for } n \text{ periods at } i\%$$

To illustrate, what is the present value of rental receipts of $6,000 each to be received at the end of each of the next five years when discounted at 12%? This problem is time-diagrammed and solved as shown below. The present value of the five ordinary annuity rental receipts of $6,000 each is $21,628.68. The present value of the ordinary annuity of 1 factor, 3.60478, is from Table A-4 (12% column, 5-period row).

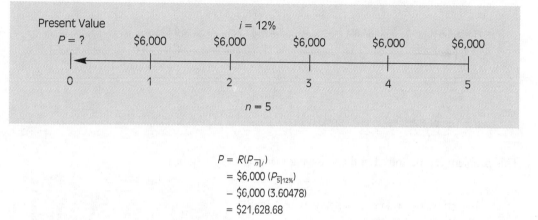

$$P = R(P_{\overline{n}|i})$$
$$= \$6,000 \, (P_{\overline{5}|12\%})$$
$$= \$6,000 \, (3.60478)$$
$$= \$21,628.68$$

Present Value of an Annuity Due

In the discussion of the present value of an ordinary annuity, the final rent was discounted back the same number of periods that there were rents. In determining the present value of an annuity due, there is always one fewer discount periods. This distinction is shown graphically below.

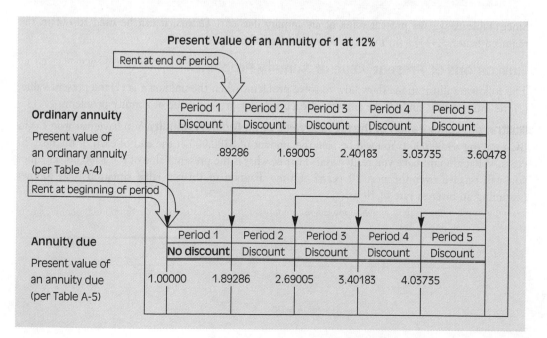

Because each cash flow (rent) comes exactly one period sooner in the present value of an annuity due, the present value of the cash flows is exactly 12% higher than the present value of an ordinary annuity. Thus, ***the present value of an annuity due of 1 factor can be found by multiplying the present value of an ordinary annuity of 1 by one plus the interest rate.*** For example, to determine the present value of an annuity due of 1 factor for five periods at 12% interest, take the present value of an ordinary annuity of 1 factor for five periods at 12% interest (3.60478) and multiply it by 1.12 to arrive at the present value of an annuity due of 1, 4.03735 (3.60478 × 1.12). Table A-5 provides present value of annuity due of 1 factors.

To illustrate, assume that Space Odyssey Inc. rents a communications satellite for four years with annual rental payments of $4.8 million to be made at the beginning of each year. Assuming an annual interest rate of 11%, what is the present value of the rental obligations?

This problem is time-diagrammed as follows.

Present Value

$Pd = ?$ $i = 11\%$

$R = \$4.8M$ $\$4.8M$ $\$4.8M$ $\$4.8M$

```
|◄──────────────────────────────────────────────|
0        1           2           3           4
```

$n = 4$

Pd = The present value of an annuity due

This problem can be solved in the following manner.

1.	Present value of an ordinary annuity of 1 for 4 periods at 11% (Table A-4)	3.10245
2.	Factor (1 + .11)	× 1.11
3.	Present value of an annuity due of 1 for 4 periods at 11%	3.44371
4.	Periodic deposit (rent)	× $4,800,000
5.	Present value of payments	$ 16,529,808

Since Table A-5 gives present value of an annuity due of 1 factors, it can be used to obtain the required factor 3.44371 (in the 11% column, 4-period row).

Illustrations of Present Value of Annuity Problems

The following illustrations show how to solve problems when the unknown is (1) the present value, (2) the interest rate, and (3) the amount of each rent for present value of annuity problems.

Illustration: Computation of the Present Value of an Ordinary Annuity. You have just won Lotto BC totalling $4,000,000. You will be paid the amount of $200,000 at the end of each of the next 20 years. What amount have you really won? That is, what is the present value of the $200,000 cheques you will receive over the next 20 years? A time diagram of this enviable situation is as follows (assuming an interest rate of 10%).

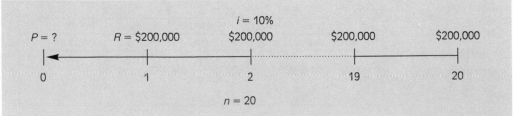

$i = 10\%$

$P = ?$ $R = \$200,000$ $\$200,000$ $\$200,000$ $\$200,000$

```
|◄──────|───────────┆·········|·········┆───────|
0        1           2           19          20
```

$n = 20$

The present value is determined as follows:

$$P = R(P_{\overline{n}|i})$$
$$= \$200,000 \, (P_{\overline{20}|10\%})$$
$$= \$200,000 \, (8.51356)$$
$$= \$1,702,712$$

As a result, if Lotto BC deposits $1,702,712 now and earns 10% interest, it can draw $200,000 a year for twenty years to pay you the $4,000,000.

Illustration: Computation of the Interest Rate.
Many shoppers make purchases by using a credit card. When you receive an invoice for payment, you may pay the total amount due or pay the balance in a certain number of payments. For example, if you receive an invoice from VISA with a balance due of $528.77 and are invited to pay it off in twelve equal monthly payments of $50.00 each with the first payment due one month from now, what rate of interest are you paying?

The $528.77 represents the present value of the twelve $50 payments at an unknown rate of interest. This situation is time diagrammed and the interest rate is determined as follows.

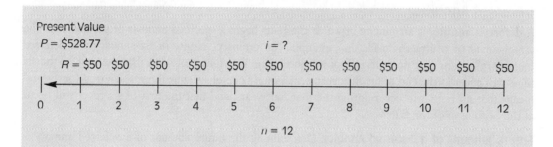

$$P = R(P_{\overline{n}|i})$$
$$\$528.77 = \$50 \, (P_{\overline{12}|i})$$
$$P_{\overline{12}|i} = \frac{\$528.77}{\$50} = 10.5754$$

Referring to Table A-4 and reading across the 12-period row, the 10.57534 factor is in the 2% column. Since 2% is a monthly rate, the nominal annual rate of interest is 24% (12 × 2%) and the effective annual rate is 26.82413% $[(1 + .02)^{12} - 1]$. At such a high rate of interest, you are better off paying the entire bill now if possible.

Illustration: Computation of a Periodic Rent.
Vern and Marilyn have saved $18,000 to finance their daughter Dawn's university education. The money has been deposited with the National Trust Company and is earning 10% interest compounded semiannually. What equal amounts can Dawn withdraw at the end of every six months during the next four years while she attends university and exhausts the fund with the last withdrawal? This problem is time-diagrammed as follows.

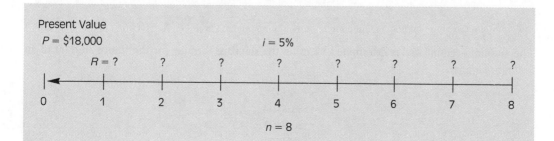

The answer is not determined simply by dividing $18,000 by 8 withdrawals because that ignores the interest earned on the money remaining on deposit. Given that interest is compounded semiannually at 5% (10% ÷ 2) for eight periods (4 years × 2) and using the present value of an ordinary annuity formula, the amount of each withdrawal is determined as follows:

$$P = R(P_{\overline{n}|i})$$
$$\$18,000 = R(P_{\overline{8}|5\%})$$
$$\$18,000 = R(6.46321)$$
$$R = \$2,784.99$$

COMPLEX SITUATIONS

It is often necessary to use more than one table to solve time-value problems. Two common situations will be illustrated to demonstrate this point:

1. Deferred annuities.

2. Bond problems.

Deferred Annuities

A **deferred annuity** is an annuity in which the rents begin a specified number of periods after the arrangement or contract is made. For example, "an ordinary annuity of six annual rents deferred four years" means that no rents will occur during the first four years and that the first of the six rents will occur at the end of the fifth year. "An annuity due of six annual rents deferred four years" means that no rents will occur during the first four years, and that the first of six rents will occur at the beginning of the fifth year.

Future Amount of a Deferred Annuity. Determining the future amount of a deferred annuity is relatively straightforward. Because there is no accumulation or investment on which interest accrues during the deferred periods, the future amount of a deferred annuity is the same as the future amount of an annuity not deferred.

To illustrate, assume that Sutton Co. Ltd. plans to purchase a land site in six years for the construction of its new corporate headquarters. Because of cash flow problems, Sutton is able to budget deposits of $80,000 only at the end of the fourth, fifth, and sixth years, which are expected to earn 12% annually. What future amount will Sutton have accumulated at the end of the sixth year?

A time diagram of this situation is as follows.

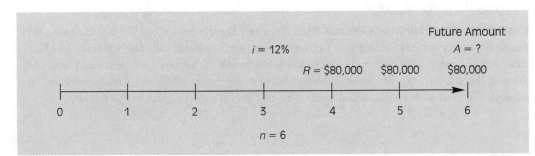

The amount accumulated is determined by using the standard formula for the future amount of an ordinary annuity:

$$A = R(A_{\overline{n}|i})$$
$$= \$80,000 (A_{\overline{3}|12\%})$$
$$= \$80,000 (3.37440)$$
$$= \$269,952$$

Present Value of a Deferred Annuity. In determining the present value of a deferred annuity, recognition must be given to the facts that no rents occur during the deferral period and that the future actual rents must be discounted for the entire period.

For example, Tom Whiz has developed and copyrighted a software computer program that is a tutorial for students in introductory accounting. He agrees to sell the copyright to Campus Micro Systems for six annual payments of $5,000 each, the payments to begin five years from today. The annual interest rate is 8%. What is the present value of the six payments?

This situation is an ordinary annuity of six payments deferred four periods and can be time-diagrammed as follows.

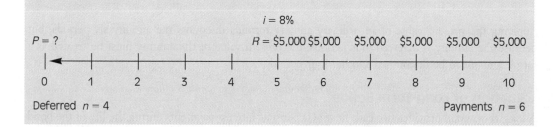

Two options are available to solve this problem. The first is to use only Table A-4 as follows.

1.	Each periodic rent	$5,000
2.	Present value of an ordinary annuity of 1 for total periods (10) [number of rents (6) plus number of deferred periods (4)] at 8%	6.71008
3.	Less: Present value of an ordinary annuity of 1 for the number of deferred periods (4) at 8%	3.31213
4.	Difference	× 3.39795
5.	Present value of 6 rents of $5,000 deferred 4 periods	$16,989.75

The subtraction of the present value of an ordinary annuity of 1 for the deferred periods eliminates the nonexistent rents during the deferral period and converts the present value of an ordinary annuity of 1 for 10 periods to the present value of 6 rents of 1, deferred 4 periods.

Alternatively, the present value of the six rents may be computed using both Tables A-2 and A-4. The first step is to determine the present value of an ordinary annuity for the number of rent payments involved using Table A-4. This step provides the present value of the ordinary annuity as at the beginning of the first payment period (this is the same as the present value at the end of the last deferral period). The second step is to discount the amount determined in step 1 for the number of deferral periods using Table A-2. Application of this approach is as follows:

$$\text{Step 1: } P = R(P_{\overline{n}|i})$$
$$= \$5,000(P_{\overline{6}|8\%})$$
$$= \$5,000 \,(4.62288) \text{ Table A-4 (Present Value of an Ordinary Annuity)}$$
$$= \$23,114.40$$

$$\text{Step 2: } p = a(p_{\overline{n}|i}) \text{ ("}a\text{" is the amount "}P\text{" determined in Step 1)}$$
$$= \$23,114.40 \,(p_{\overline{4}|8\%})$$
$$= \$23,114.40 \,(.73503) \text{ Table A-2 (Present Value of a Single Sum)}$$
$$= \$16,989.77$$

A time diagram reflecting the completion of this two-step approach is as follows.

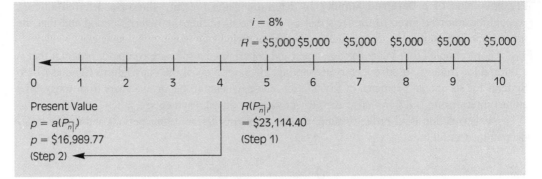

Applying the present value of an ordinary annuity formula discounts the annuity six periods, but because the annuity is deferred four periods, the present value of the annuity must be treated as a future amount to be discounted another four periods.[7]

Valuation of Long-Term Bonds

A long-term bond provides two cash flows: (1) periodic interest payments during the life of the bond and (2) the principal (face value) paid at maturity. At the date of issue, bond buyers determine the present value of these two cash flows using the market rate of interest.

The periodic interest payments represent an annuity while the principal represents a single sum. The current market value of the bonds is the combined present values of the interest annuity and the principal amount.

To illustrate, Servicemaster Inc. issues $100,000 of 9% bonds due in five years with interest payable annually at year end. The current market rate of interest for bonds of similar risk is 11%. What will the buyers pay for this bond issue?

The time diagram depicting both cash flows is shown below.

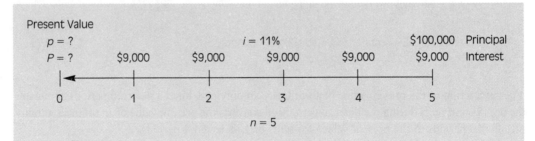

The present value of the two cash flows is computed as follows.

1.	Present value of the principal: $a(p_{\overline{5}|11\%}) = \$100,000\,(.59345) =$	$59,345.00
2.	Present value of interest payments: $R(P_{\overline{5}|11\%}) = \$9,000\,(3.69590)$	33,263.10
3.	Combined present value (market price)	$92,608.10

---

[7] Deferred annuity contracts are common in professional sports. For example, Rich Gossage's contract when he signed as a pitcher with the San Diego Padres was for him to be paid $240,000 a year from 1990 to 2006 and $125,000 from 2007 to 2016 in addition to salary and bonuses over the first five or six years. The deferred payouts from 1990 through 2016 total $5.33 million, but the present value of this deferred annuity was estimated at $1.5 million when the contract was signed.

By paying $92,608.10 at date of issue, the buyers of the bonds will realize an effective yield of 11% over the 5-year term of the bonds.

INTERPOLATION OF TABLES TO DERIVE INTEREST RATES

Throughout the previous discussion, the illustrations were designed to produce interest rates and factors that could be found in the tables. Frequently it is necessary to interpolate to derive the exact or required interest rate. **Interpolation** is used to calculate a particular unknown value that lies between two values given in a table. The following examples illustrate interpolation using Tables A-1 and A-4.

Example 1. If $2,000 accumulates to $5,900 after being invested for 20 years, what is the annual interest rate on the investment?

Dividing the future amount of $5,900 by the investment of $2,000 gives $2.95 which is the amount to which $1.00 will grow if invested for 20 years at the unknown interest rate. Using Table A-1 and reading across the 20-period line, the value 2.65330 is found in the 5% column and the value 3.20714 is in the 6% column. The factor 2.95 is between 5% and 6%, which means that the interest rate is also between 5% and 6%. By interpolation, the rate is determined to be 5.536% as follows (i = unknown rate and d = difference between 5% and i).

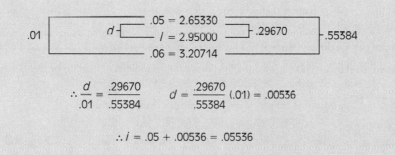

$$\therefore \frac{d}{.01} = \frac{.29670}{.55384} \qquad d = \frac{.29670}{.55384}(.01) = .00536$$

$$\therefore i = .05 + .00536 = .05536$$

Example 2. You are offered an annuity of $1,000 a year beginning one year from now for 25 years for investing $7,000 cash today. What rate of interest is your investment earning?

Dividing the investment of $7,000 by the annuity of $1,000 gives a factor of 7, which is the "present value of an ordinary annuity of 1" for 25 years at an unknown interest rate. Using Table A-4 and reading across the 25-period line, the value 7.84314 in the 12% column and the value 6.46415 is in the 15% column. The factor 7 is between 12% and 15%, which means that the unknown interest rate is also between 12% and 15%. By interpolation, the rate is determined to be 13.834% as follows (i = unknown rate and d = difference between 12% and i).

```
           ┌──── .12 = 7.84314 ────┐
  .03 ┤  d ┤                       ├ .84314 ┐
       │    └──── i = 7.00000 ─────┘        ├ 1.37899
           └──── .15 = 6.46415 ────────────┘
```

$$\therefore \frac{d}{.03} = \frac{.84314}{1.37899} \qquad d = \frac{.84314}{1.37899}(.03) = .01834$$

$$\therefore i = .12 + d = .12 + .01834 = .13834$$

Interpolation assumes that the change between any two values in a table is linear. Although such an assumption is incorrect, the margin of error is generally insignificant if the table value ranges are not too wide.

FUNDAMENTAL CONCEPTS

The following list of terms and their definitions is provided as a summarization and review of the essential items presented in this appendix:

1. **Simple Interest.** Interest is computed only on the principal, regardless of interest that may have accrued in the past.

2. **Compound Interest.** Interest is computed on the unpaid interest of past periods as well as on the principal.

3. **Rate of Interest.** Interest is usually expressed as an annual rate, but when the interest period is shorter than one year, the interest rate for the shorter period must be determined.

4. **Annuity.** A series of payments or receipts (called rents) which occur at equal intervals of time. The types of annuities are:

    (a) **Ordinary Annuity.** Each rent is payable (receivable) at the end of a period.

    (b) **Annuity Due.** Each rent is payable (receivable) at the beginning of a period.

5. **Future Amount.** Value at a later date of a given sum that is invested at compound interest.

    (a) **Future Amount of 1** (or amount of a given sum). The future value of $1.00 (or a single given sum) at the end of n periods at i compound interest rate (Table A-1).

    (b) **Future Amount of an Annuity.** The future value of a series of rents invested at compound interest; it is the accumulated total that results from a series of equal deposits at regular intervals invested at compound interest. Both deposits and interest increase the accumulation.

        (1) **Future Amount of an Ordinary Annuity.** The future value on the date of the last rent (Table A-3).

        (2) **Future Amount of an Annuity Due.** The future value one period after the date of the last rent. When an annuity due table is not available, use Table A-3 with the following formula:

$$\text{Amount of annuity due of 1 for } n \text{ rents} = \text{Amount of ordinary annuity of 1 for } n \text{ rents} \times (1 + \text{interest rate}).$$

6. **Present Value.** The value at an earlier date (usually now) of a given sum discounted at compound interest.

    (a) **Present Value of 1** (or present value of a single sum). The present value (worth) of $1.00 due n periods hence, discounted at i compound interest (Table A-2).

    (b) **Present Value of an Annuity.** The present value (worth) of a series of rents discounted at compound interest; it is the present sum when invested at compound interest that will permit a series of equal withdrawals at regular intervals.

        (1) **Present Value of an Ordinary Annuity.** The value now of $1.00 to be received or paid each period (rents) for n periods, discounted at i compound interest (Table A-4).

        (2) **Present Value of an Annuity Due.** The value now of $1.00 to be received or paid at the beginning of each period (rents) for n periods, discounted at i compound interest (Table A-5). To use Table A-4 for an annuity due, apply this formula:

$$\text{Present value of an annuity due of 1 for } n \text{ rents} = \text{Present value of ordinary annuity of 1 for } n \text{ rents} \times (1 + \text{interest rate}).$$

Table A-1 Future Amount of 1 (Future Amount of a Single Sum)

$$a_{\overline{n}|_i} = (1 + i)^n$$

(n) periods	2%	2½%	3%	4%	5%	6%	8%	9%	10%	11%	12%	15%
1	1.02000	1.02500	1.03000	1.04000	1.05000	1.06000	1.08000	1.09000	1.10000	1.11000	1.12000	1.15000
2	1.04040	1.05063	1.06090	1.08160	1.10250	1.12360	1.16640	1.18810	1.21000	1.23210	1.25440	1.32250
3	1.06121	1.07689	1.09273	1.12486	1.15763	1.19102	1.25971	1.29503	1.33100	1.36763	1.40493	1.52088
4	1.08243	1.10381	1.12551	1.16986	1.21551	1.26248	1.36049	1.41158	1.46410	1.51807	1.57352	1.74901
5	1.10408	1.13141	1.15927	1.21665	1.27628	1.33823	1.46933	1.53862	1.61051	1.68506	1.76234	2.01136
6	1.12616	1.15969	1.19405	1.26532	1.34010	1.41852	1.58687	1.67710	1.77156	1.87041	1.97382	2.31306
7	1.14869	1.18869	1.22987	1.31593	1.40710	1.50363	1.71382	1.82804	1.94872	2.07616	2.21068	2.66002
8	1.17166	1.21840	1.26677	1.36857	1.47746	1.59385	1.85093	1.99256	2.14359	2.30454	2.47596	3.05902
9	1.19509	1.24886	1.30477	1.42331	1.55133	1.68948	1.99900	2.17189	2.35795	2.55803	2.77308	3.51788
10	1.21899	1.28008	1.34392	1.48024	1.62889	1.79085	2.15892	2.36736	2.59374	2.83942	3.10585	4.04556
11	1.24337	1.31209	1.38423	1.53945	1.71034	1.89830	2.33164	2.58043	2.85312	3.15176	3.47855	4.65239
12	1.26824	1.34489	1.42576	1.60103	1.79586	2.01220	2.51817	2.81267	3.13843	3.49845	3.89598	5.35025
13	1.29361	1.37851	1.46853	1.66507	1.88565	2.13293	2.71962	3.06581	3.45227	3.88328	4.36349	6.15279
14	1.31948	1.41207	1.51259	1.73168	1.97993	2.26090	2.93719	3.34173	3.79750	4.31044	4.88711	7.07571
15	1.34587	1.44830	1.55797	1.80094	2.07893	2.39656	3.17217	3.64248	4.17725	4.78459	5.47357	8.13706
16	1.37279	1.48451	1.60471	1.87298	2.18287	2.54035	3.42594	3.97031	4.59497	5.31089	6.13039	9.35762
17	1.40024	1.52162	1.65285	1.94790	2.29202	2.69277	3.70002	4.32763	5.05447	5.89509	6.86604	10.76126
18	1.42825	1.55966	1.70243	2.02582	2.40662	2.85434	3.99602	4.71712	5.55992	6.54355	7.68997	12.37545
19	1.45681	1.59865	1.75351	2.10685	2.52695	3.02560	4.31570	5.14166	6.11591	7.26334	8.61276	14.23177
20	1.48595	1.63862	1.80611	2.19112	2.65330	3.20714	4.66096	5.60441	6.72750	8.06231	9.64629	16.36654
21	1.51567	1.67958	1.86029	2.27877	2.78596	3.39956	5.03383	6.10881	7.40025	8.94917	10.80385	18.82152
22	1.54598	1.72157	1.91610	2.36992	2.92526	3.60354	5.43654	6.65860	8.14028	9.93357	12.10031	21.64475
23	1.57690	1.76461	1.97359	2.46472	3.07152	3.81975	5.87146	7.25787	8.95430	11.02627	13.55235	24.89146
24	1.60844	1.80873	2.03279	2.56330	3.22510	4.04893	6.34118	7.91108	9.84973	12.23916	15.17863	28.62518
25	1.64061	1.85394	2.09378	2.66584	3.38635	4.29187	6.84847	8.62308	10.83471	13.58546	17.00000	32.91895
26	1.67342	1.90029	2.15659	2.77247	3.55567	4.54938	7.39635	9.39916	11.91818	15.07986	19.04007	37.85680
27	1.70689	1.94780	2.22129	2.88337	3.73346	4.82235	7.98806	10.24508	13.10999	16.73865	21.32488	43.53532
28	1.74102	1.99650	2.28793	2.99870	3.92013	5.11169	8.62711	11.16714	14.42099	18.57990	23.88387	50.06561
29	1.77584	2.04641	2.35657	3.11865	4.11614	5.41839	9.31727	12.17218	15.86309	20.62369	26.74993	57.57545
30	1.81136	2.09757	2.42726	3.24340	4.32194	5.74349	10.06266	13.26768	17.44940	22.89230	29.95992	66.21177
31	1.84759	2.15001	2.50008	3.37313	4.53804	6.08810	10.86767	14.46177	19.19434	25.41045	33.55511	76.14354
32	1.88454	2.20376	2.57508	3.50806	4.76494	6.45339	11.73708	15.76333	21.11378	28.20560	37.58173	87.56507
33	1.92223	2.25885	2.65234	3.64838	5.00319	6.84059	12.67605	17.18203	23.22515	31.30821	42.09153	100.69983
34	1.96068	2.31532	2.73191	3.79432	5.25335	7.25103	13.69013	18.72841	25.54767	34.75212	47.14252	115.80480
35	1.99989	2.37321	2.81386	3.94609	5.51602	7.68609	14.78534	20.41397	28.10244	38.57485	52.79962	133.17552
36	2.03989	2.43254	2.88928	4.10393	5.79182	8.14725	15.96817	22.25123	30.91268	42.81808	59.13557	153.15185
37	2.08069	2.49335	2.98523	4.26809	6.08141	8.63609	17.24563	24.25384	34.00395	47.52807	66.23184	176.12463
38	2.12230	2.55568	3.07478	4.43881	6.38548	9.15425	18.62528	26.43668	37.40434	52.75616	74.17966	202.54332
39	2.16474	2.61957	3.16703	4.61637	6.70475	9.70351	20.11530	28.81598	41.14479	58.55934	83.08122	232.92482
40	2.20804	2.68506	3.26204	4.80102	7.03999	10.28572	21.72452	31.40942	45.25926	65.00087	93.05097	267.86355

Table A-2 Present Value of 1 (Present Value of a Single Sum)

$$P_{\overline{n}|i} = \frac{1}{(1+i)^n} = (1+i)^{-n}$$

(n) periods	2%	2½%	3%	4%	5%	6%	8%	9%	10%	11%	12%	15%
1	.98039	.97561	.97087	.96156	.95238	.94340	.92593	.91743	.90909	.90090	.89286	.86957
2	.96117	.95181	.94260	.92456	.90703	.89000	.85734	.84168	.82645	.81162	.79719	.75614
3	.94232	.92860	.91514	.88900	.86384	.83962	.79383	.77218	.75132	.73119	.71178	.65752
4	.92385	.90595	.88849	.85480	.82270	.79209	.73503	.70843	.68301	.65873	.63552	.57175
5	.90583	.88385	.86261	.82193	.78353	.74726	.68058	.64993	.62092	.59345	.56743	.49718
6	.88797	.86230	.83748	.79031	.74622	.70496	.63017	.59627	.56447	.53464	.50663	.43233
7	.87056	.84127	.81309	.75992	.71068	.66056	.58349	.54703	.51316	.48166	.45235	.37594
8	.85349	.82075	.78941	.73069	.67684	.62741	.54027	.50187	.46651	.43393	.40388	.32690
9	.83676	.80073	.76642	.70259	.64461	.59190	.50025	.46043	.42410	.39092	.36061	.28426
10	.82035	.78120	.74409	.67556	.61391	.55839	.46319	.42241	.38554	.35218	.32197	.24719
11	.80426	.76214	.72242	.64958	.58468	.52679	.42888	.38753	.35049	.31728	.28748	.21494
12	.78849	.74356	.70138	.62460	.55684	.49697	.39711	.35554	.31863	.28584	.25668	.18691
13	.77303	.72542	.68095	.60057	.53032	.46884	.36770	.32618	.28966	.25751	.22917	.16253
14	.75788	.70773	.66112	.57748	.50507	.44230	.34046	.29925	.26333	.23199	.20462	.14133
15	.74301	.69047	.64186	.55526	.48102	.41727	.31524	.27454	.23939	.20900	.18270	.12289
16	.72845	.67362	.62317	.53391	.45811	.39365	.29189	.25187	.21763	.18829	.16312	.10687
17	.71416	.65720	.60502	.51337	.43630	.37136	.27027	.23107	.19785	.16963	.14564	.09293
18	.70016	.64117	.58739	.49363	.41552	.35034	.25025	.21199	.17986	.15282	.13004	.08081
19	.68643	.62553	.57029	.47464	.39573	.33051	.23171	.19449	.16351	.13768	.11611	.07027
20	.67297	.61027	.55368	.45639	.37689	.31180	.21455	.17843	.14864	.12403	.10367	.06110
21	.65978	.59539	.53755	.43883	.35894	.29416	.19866	.16370	.13513	.11174	.09256	.05313
22	.64684	.58086	.52189	.42196	.34185	.27751	.18394	.15018	.12285	.10067	.08264	.04620
23	.63416	.56670	.50669	.40573	.32557	.26180	.17032	.13778	.11168	.09069	.07379	.04017
24	.62172	.55288	.49193	.39012	.31007	.24698	.15770	.12641	.10153	.08170	.06588	.03493
25	.60953	.53939	.47761	.37512	.29530	.23300	.14602	.11597	.09230	.07361	.05882	.03038
26	.59758	.52623	.46369	.36069	.28124	.21981	.13520	.10639	.08391	.06631	.05252	.02642
27	.58586	.51340	.45019	.34682	.26785	.20737	.12519	.09761	.07628	.05974	.04689	.02297
28	.57437	.50088	.43708	.33348	.25509	.19563	.11591	.08955	.06934	.05382	.04187	.01997
29	.56311	.48866	.42435	.32065	.24295	.18456	.10733	.08216	.06304	.04849	.03738	.01737
30	.55207	.47674	.41199	.30832	.23138	.17411	.09938	.07537	.05731	.04368	.03338	.01510
31	.54125	.46511	.39999	.29646	.22036	.16425	.09202	.06915	.05210	.03935	.02980	.01313
32	.53063	.45377	.38834	.28506	.20987	.15496	.08520	.06344	.04736	.03545	.02661	.01142
33	.52023	.44270	.37703	.27409	.19987	.14619	.07889	.05820	.04306	.03194	.02376	.00993
34	.51003	.43191	.36604	.26355	.19035	.13791	.07305	.05340	.03914	.02878	.02121	.00864
35	.50003	.42137	.35538	.25342	.18129	.13011	.06763	.04899	.03558	.02592	.01894	.00751
36	.49022	.41109	.34505	.24367	.17266	.12274	.06262	.04494	.03235	.02335	.01691	.00653
37	.48061	.40107	.33498	.23430	.16444	.11579	.05799	.04123	.02941	.02104	.01510	.00568
38	.47119	.39128	.32523	.22529	.15661	.10924	.05369	.03783	.02674	.01896	.01348	.00494
39	.46195	.38174	.31575	.21662	.14915	.10306	.04971	.03470	.02430	.01708	.01204	.00429
40	.45289	.37243	.30656	.20829	.14205	.09722	.04603	.03184	.02210	.01538	.01075	.00373

Table A-3 Future Amount of an Ordinary Annuity of 1

$$A_{\overline{n}|i} = \frac{(1 + i)^n - 1}{i}$$

(n) periods	2%	2½%	3%	4%	5%	6%	8%	9%	10%	11%	12%	15%
1	1.00000	1.00000	1.00000	1.00000	1.00000	1.00000	1.00000	1.00000	1.00000	1.00000	1.00000	1.00000
2	2.02000	2.02500	2.03000	2.04000	2.05000	2.06000	2.08000	2.09000	2.10000	2.11000	2.12000	2.15000
3	3.06040	3.07563	3.09090	3.12160	3.15250	3.18360	3.24640	3.27810	3.31000	3.34210	3.37440	3.47250
4	4.12161	4.15252	4.18363	4.24646	4.31013	4.37462	4.50611	4.57313	4.64100	4.70973	4.77933	4.99338
5	5.20404	5.25633	5.30914	5.41632	5.52563	5.63709	5.86660	5.98471	6.10510	6.22780	6.35285	6.74238
6	6.30812	6.38774	6.46841	6.63298	6.80191	6.97532	7.33592	7.52334	7.71561	7.91286	8.11519	8.75374
7	7.43428	7.54743	7.66246	7.89829	8.14201	8.39384	8.92280	9.20044	9.48717	9.78327	10.08901	11.06680
8	8.58297	8.73612	8.89234	9.21423	9.54911	9.89747	10.63663	11.02847	11.43589	11.85943	12.29969	13.72682
9	9.75463	9.95452	10.15911	10.58280	11.02656	11.49132	12.48756	13.02104	13.57948	14.16397	14.77566	16.78584
10	10.94972	11.20338	11.46338	12.00611	12.57789	13.18079	14.48656	15.19293	15.93743	16.72201	17.54874	20.30372
11	12.16872	12.48347	12.80780	13.48635	14.20679	14.97164	16.64549	17.56029	18.53117	19.56143	20.65458	24.34928
12	13.41209	13.79555	14.19203	15.02581	15.91713	16.86994	18.97713	20.14072	21.38428	22.71319	24.13313	29.00167
13	14.68033	15.14044	15.61779	16.62684	17.71298	18.88214	21.49530	22.95339	24.52271	26.21164	28.02911	34.35192
14	15.97394	16.51895	17.08632	18.29191	19.59863	21.01507	24.21492	26.01919	27.97498	30.09492	32.39260	40.50471
15	17.29342	17.93193	18.59891	20.02359	21.57856	23.27597	27.15211	29.36092	31.77248	34.40536	37.27972	47.58041
16	18.63929	19.38022	20.15688	21.82453	23.65749	25.67253	30.32428	33.00340	35.94973	39.18995	42.75328	55.71747
17	20.01207	20.86473	21.76159	23.69751	25.84037	28.21288	33.75023	36.97371	40.54470	44.50084	48.88367	65.07509
18	21.41231	22.38635	23.41444	25.64541	28.13238	30.90565	37.45024	41.30134	45.59917	50.39593	55.74972	75.83636
19	22.84056	23.94601	25.11687	27.67123	30.53900	33.75999	41.44626	46.01846	51.15909	56.93949	63.43968	88.21181
20	24.29737	25.54466	26.87037	29.77808	33.06595	36.78559	45.76196	51.16012	57.27500	64.20283	72.05244	102.44358
21	25.78332	27.18327	28.67649	31.96920	35.71925	39.99273	50.42292	56.76453	64.00250	72.26514	81.69874	118.81012
22	27.29898	28.86286	30.53678	34.24797	38.50521	43.39229	55.45676	62.87334	71.40275	81.21451	92.50258	137.63164
23	28.84496	30.58443	32.45288	36.61789	41.43048	46.99583	60.89330	69.53194	79.54302	91.14788	104.60289	159.27638
24	30.42186	32.34904	34.42647	39.08260	44.50200	50.81558	66.76476	76.78981	88.49733	102.17415	118.15524	184.16784
25	32.03030	34.15776	36.45926	41.64591	47.72710	54.86451	73.10594	84.70090	98.34706	114.41331	133.33387	212.79302
26	33.67091	36.01171	38.55304	44.31174	51.11345	59.15638	79.95442	93.32398	109.18177	127.99877	150.33393	245.71197
27	35.34432	37.91200	40.70963	47.08421	54.66913	63.70577	87.35077	102.72314	121.09994	143.07864	169.37401	283.56877
28	37.05121	39.85990	42.93092	49.96758	58.40258	68.52811	95.33883	112.96822	134.20994	159.81729	190.69889	327.10408
29	38.79223	41.85630	45.21885	52.96629	62.32271	73.63980	103.96594	124.13536	148.63093	178.39719	214.58275	377.16969
30	40.56808	43.90270	47.57542	56.08494	66.43885	79.05819	113.28321	136.30754	164.49402	199.02088	241.33268	434.74515
31	42.37944	46.00027	50.00268	59.32834	70.76079	84.80168	123.34587	149.57522	181.94343	221.91317	271.29261	500.95692
32	44.22703	48.15028	52.50276	62.70147	75.29883	90.88978	134.21354	164.03699	201.13777	247.32362	304.84772	577.10046
33	46.11157	50.35403	55.07784	66.20953	80.06377	97.34316	145.95062	179.80032	222.25154	275.52922	342.42945	644.66553
34	48.03380	52.61289	57.73018	69.85791	85.06696	104.18376	158.62667	196.98234	245.47670	306.83744	384.52098	765.36535
35	49.99448	54.92821	60.46208	73.65222	90.32031	111.43478	172.31680	215.71076	271.02437	341.58955	431.66350	881.17016
36	51.99437	57.30141	63.27594	77.59831	95.83632	119.12087	187.10215	236.12472	299.12681	380.16441	484.46312	1014.34568
37	54.03425	59.73395	66.17422	81.70225	101.62814	127.26812	203.07032	258.37595	330.03949	422.98249	543.59869	1167.49753
38	56.11494	62.22730	69.15945	85.97034	107.70955	135.90421	220.31595	282.62978	364.04543	470.51056	609.83053	1343.62216
39	58.23724	64.78298	72.23423	90.40915	114.09502	145.05846	238.94122	309.06646	401.44778	523.26673	684.01020	1546.16549
40	60.40198	67.40255	75.40126	95.02552	120.79977	154.76197	259.05652	337.88245	442.59256	581.82607	767.09142	1779.09031

Table A-4 Present Value of an Ordinary Annuity of 1

$$P_{\overline{n}|i} = \frac{1 - \dfrac{1}{(1+i)^n}}{i} = \frac{1 - P_{\overline{n}|i}}{i}$$

(n) periods	2%	2½%	3%	4%	5%	6%	8%	9%	10%	11%	12%	15%
1	.98039	.97561	.97087	.96154	.95238	.94340	.92593	.91743	.90909	.90090	.89286	.86957
2	1.94156	1.92742	1.91347	1.88609	1.85941	1.83339	1.78326	1.75911	1.73554	1.71252	1.69005	1.62571
3	2.88388	2.85602	2.82861	2.77509	2.72325	2.67301	2.57710	2.53130	2.48685	2.44371	2.40183	2.28323
4	3.80773	3.76197	3.71710	3.62990	3.54595	3.46511	3.31213	3.23972	3.16986	3.10245	3.03735	2.85498
5	4.71346	4.64583	4.57971	4.45182	4.32948	4.21236	3.99271	3.88965	3.79079	3.69590	3.60478	3.35216
6	5.60143	5.50813	5.41719	5.24214	5.07569	4.91732	4.62288	4.48592	4.35526	4.23054	4.11141	3.78448
7	6.47199	6.34939	6.23028	6.00205	5.78637	5.58238	5.20637	5.03295	4.86842	4.71220	4.56376	4.16042
8	7.32548	7.17014	7.01969	6.73274	6.46321	6.20979	5.74664	5.53482	5.33493	5.14612	4.96764	4.48732
9	8.16224	7.97087	7.78611	7.43533	7.10782	6.80169	6.24689	5.99525	5.75902	5.53705	5.32825	4.77158
10	8.98259	8.75206	8.53020	8.11090	7.72173	7.36009	6.71008	6.41766	6.14457	5.88923	5.65022	5.01877
11	9.78685	9.51421	9.25262	8.76048	8.30641	7.88687	7.13896	6.80519	6.49506	6.20652	5.93770	5.23371
12	10.57534	10.25776	9.95400	9.38507	8.86325	8.38384	7.53608	7.16073	6.81369	6.49236	6.19437	5.42062
13	11.34837	10.98319	10.63496	9.98565	9.39357	8.85268	7.90378	7.48690	7.10336	6.74987	6.42355	5.58315
14	12.10625	11.69091	11.29607	10.56312	9.89864	9.29498	8.24424	7.78615	7.36669	6.98187	6.62817	5.72448
15	12.84926	12.38138	11.93794	11.11839	10.37966	9.71225	8.55948	8.06069	7.60608	7.19087	6.81086	5.84737
16	13.57771	13.05500	12.56110	11.65230	10.83777	10.10590	8.85137	8.31256	7.82371	7.37916	6.97399	5.95424
17	14.29187	13.71220	13.16612	12.16567	11.27407	10.47726	9.12164	8.54363	8.02155	7.54879	7.11963	6.04716
18	14.99203	14.35336	13.75351	12.65930	11.68959	10.82760	9.37189	8.75563	8.20141	7.70162	7.24967	6.12797
19	15.67846	14.97889	14.32380	13.13394	12.08532	11.15812	9.60360	8.95012	8.36492	7.83929	7.36578	6.19823
20	16.35143	15.58916	14.87747	13.59033	12.46221	11.46992	9.81815	9.12855	8.51356	7.96333	7.46944	6.25933
21	17.01121	16.18455	15.41502	14.02916	12.82115	11.76408	10.01680	9.29224	8.64869	8.07507	7.56200	6.31246
22	17.65805	16.76541	15.93692	14.45112	13.16800	12.04158	10.20074	9.44243	8.77154	8.17574	7.64465	6.35866
23	18.29220	17.33211	16.44361	14.85684	13.48857	12.30338	10.37106	9.58021	8.88322	8.26643	7.71843	6.39884
24	18.91393	17.88499	16.93554	15.24696	13.79864	12.55036	10.52876	9.70661	8.98474	8.34814	7.78432	6.43377
25	19.52346	18.42438	17.41315	15.62208	14.09394	12.78336	10.67478	9.82258	9.07704	8.42174	7.84314	6.46415
26	20.12104	18.95061	17.87684	15.98277	14.37519	13.00317	10.80998	9.92897	9.16095	8.48806	7.89566	6.49056
27	20.70690	19.46401	18.32703	16.32959	14.64303	13.21053	10.93516	10.02658	9.23722	8.45780	7.94255	6.51353
28	21.28127	19.96489	18.76411	16.66306	14.89813	13.40616	11.05108	10.11613	9.30657	8.60162	7.98442	6.53351
29	21.84438	20.45355	19.18845	16.98371	15.14107	13.59072	11.15841	10.19828	9.36961	8.65011	8.02181	6.55088
30	22.39646	20.93029	19.60044	17.29203	15.37245	13.76483	11.25778	10.27365	9.42691	8.69379	8.05518	6.56598
31	22.93770	21.39541	20.00043	17.58849	15.59281	13.92909	11.34980	10.34280	9.47901	8.73315	8.08499	6.57911
32	23.46833	21.84918	20.38877	17.87355	15.80268	14.08404	11.43500	10.40624	9.52638	8.76860	8.11159	6.59053
33	23.98856	22.29188	20.76579	18.14765	16.00255	14.23023	11.51389	10.46444	9.56943	8.80054	8.13535	6.60046
34	24.49859	22.72379	21.13184	18.41120	16.19290	14.36814	11.58693	10.51784	9.60858	8.82932	8.15656	6.60910
35	24.99862	23.14516	21.48722	18.66461	16.37419	14.49825	11.65457	10.56682	9.64416	8.85524	8.17550	6.61661
36	25.48884	23.55625	21.83225	18.90828	16.54685	14.62099	11.71719	10.61176	9.67651	8.87859	8.19241	6.62314
37	25.96945	23.95732	22.16724	19.14258	16.71129	14.73678	11.77518	10.65299	9.70592	8.89963	8.20751	6.62882
38	26.44064	24.34860	22.49246	19.36786	16.86789	14.84602	11.82887	10.69082	9.73265	8.91859	8.22099	6.63375
39	26.90259	24.73034	22.80822	19.58448	17.01704	14.94907	11.87858	10.72552	9.75697	8.93567	8.23303	6.63805
40	27.35548	25.10278	23.11477	19.79277	17.15909	15.04630	11.92461	10.75736	9.77905	8.95105	8.24378	6.64178

Table A-5 Present Value of an Annuity Due of 1

$$Pd_{\overline{n}|\,i} = \frac{1 - \dfrac{1}{(1+i)^{n-1}}}{i} = (1+i)\left(\frac{1 - P_{\overline{n}|i}}{i}\right) = (1+i)\,P_{\overline{n}|i}$$

(n) periods	2%	2½%	3%	4%	5%	6%	8%	9%	10%	11%	12%	15%
1	1.00000	1.00000	1.00000	1.00000	1.00000	1.00000	1.00000	1.00000	1.00000	1.00000	1.00000	1.00000
2	1.98039	1.97561	1.97087	1.96154	1.95238	1.94340	1.92593	1.91743	1.90909	1.90090	1.89286	1.86957
3	2.94156	2.92742	2.91347	2.88609	2.85941	2.83339	2.78326	2.75911	2.73554	2.71252	2.69005	2.62571
4	3.88388	3.85602	3.82861	3.77509	3.72325	3.67301	3.57710	3.53130	3.48685	3.44371	3.40183	3.28323
5	4.80773	4.76197	4.71710	4.62990	4.54595	4.46511	4.31213	4.23972	4.16986	4.10245	4.03735	3.85498
6	5.71346	5.64583	5.57971	5.45182	5.32948	5.21236	4.99271	4.88965	4.79079	4.69590	4.60478	4.35216
7	6.60143	6.50813	6.41719	6.24214	6.07569	5.91732	5.62288	5.48592	5.35526	5.23054	5.11141	4.78448
8	7.47199	7.34939	7.23028	7.00205	6.78637	6.58238	6.20637	6.03295	5.86842	5.71220	5.56376	5.16042
9	8.32548	8.17014	8.01969	7.73274	7.46321	7.20979	6.74664	6.53482	6.33493	6.14612	5.96764	5.48732
10	9.16224	8.97087	8.78611	8.43533	8.10782	7.80169	7.24689	6.99525	6.75902	6.53705	6.32825	5.77158
11	9.98259	9.75206	9.53020	9.11090	8.72173	8.36009	7.71008	7.41766	7.14457	6.88923	6.65022	6.01877
12	10.78685	10.51421	10.25262	9.76048	9.30641	8.88687	8.13896	7.80519	7.49506	7.20652	6.93770	6.23371
13	11.57534	11.25776	10.95400	10.38507	9.86325	9.38384	8.53608	8.16073	7.81369	7.49236	7.19437	6.42062
14	12.34837	11.98319	11.63496	10.98565	10.39357	9.85268	8.90378	8.48690	8.10336	7.74987	7.42355	6.58315
15	13.10625	12.69091	12.29607	11.56312	10.89864	10.29498	9.24424	8.78615	9.36669	7.98187	7.62817	6.72448
16	13.84926	13.38138	12.93794	12.11839	11.37966	10.71225	9.55948	9.06069	8.60608	8.19087	7.81086	6.84737
17	14.57771	14.05500	13.56110	12.65230	11.83777	11.10590	9.85137	9.31256	8.82371	8.37916	7.97399	6.95424
18	15.29187	14.71220	14.16612	13.16567	12.27407	11.47726	10.12164	9.54363	9.02155	8.54879	8.11963	7.04716
19	15.99203	15.35336	14.75351	13.65950	12.68959	11.82760	10.37189	9.75563	9.20141	8.70162	8.24967	7.12797
20	16.67846	15.97889	15.32380	14.13394	13.08532	12.15812	10.60360	9.95012	9.36492	8.83929	8.36578	7.19823
21	17.35143	16.58916	15.87747	14.59033	13.46221	12.46992	10.81815	10.12855	9.51356	8.96333	8.46944	7.25933
22	18.01121	17.18455	16.41502	15.02916	13.82115	12.76408	11.01680	10.29224	9.64869	9.07507	8.56200	7.31246
23	18.65805	17.76541	16.93692	15.45112	14.16300	13.04158	11.20074	10.44243	9.77154	9.17574	8.64465	7.35866
24	19.29220	18.33211	17.44361	15.85684	14.48857	13.30338	11.37106	10.58021	9.88322	9.26643	8.71843	7.39884
25	19.91393	18.88499	17.93554	16.24696	14.79864	13.55036	11.52876	10.70661	9.98474	9.34814	8.78432	7.43377
26	20.52346	19.42438	18.41315	16.62208	15.09394	13.78336	11.67478	10.82258	10.07704	9.42174	8.84314	7.46415
27	21.12104	19.95061	18.87684	16.98277	15.37519	14.00317	11.80998	10.92897	10.16095	9.48806	8.89566	7.49056
28	21.70690	20.46401	19.32703	17.32959	15.64303	14.21053	11.93518	11.02658	10.23722	9.54780	8.94255	7.51353
29	22.28127	20.96489	19.76411	17.66306	15.89813	14.40616	12.05108	11.11613	10.30657	9.60162	8.98442	7.53351
30	22.84438	21.45355	20.18845	17.98371	16.14107	14.59072	12.15841	11.19828	10.36961	9.65011	9.02181	7.55088
31	23.39646	21.93029	20.60044	18.29203	16.37245	14.76483	12.25778	11.27365	10.42691	9.69379	9.05518	7.56598
32	23.93770	22.39541	21.00043	18.58849	16.59281	14.92909	12.34980	11.34280	10.47901	9.73315	9.08499	7.57911
33	24.46833	22.84918	21.38877	18.87355	16.80268	15.08404	12.43500	11.40624	10.52638	9.76860	9.11159	7.59053
34	24.98856	23.29188	21.76579	19.14765	17.00255	15.23023	12.51389	11.46444	10.56943	9.80054	9.13535	7.60046
35	25.49859	23.72379	22.13184	19.41120	17.19290	15.36814	12.58693	11.51784	10.60858	9.82932	9.15656	7.60910
36	25.99862	24.14516	22.48722	19.66461	17.37419	15.49825	12.65457	11.56682	10.64416	9.85524	9.17550	7.61661
37	26.48884	24.55625	22.83225	19.90828	17.54685	15.62099	12.71719	11.61176	10.67651	9.87859	9.19241	7.62314
38	26.96945	24.95732	23.16724	20.14258	17.71129	15.73678	12.77518	11.65299	10.70592	9.89963	9.20751	7.62882
39	27.44064	25.34860	23.49246	20.36786	17.86789	15.84602	12.82887	11.69082	10.73265	9.91859	9.22099	7.63375
40	27.90259	25.73034	23.80822	20.58448	18.01704	15.94907	12.87858	11.72552	10.75697	9.93567	9.23303	7.63805

— QUESTIONS —

1. What is the time value of money? Why should accountants have an understanding of compound interest, annuities, and present value concepts?

2. What is the nature of interest? Distinguish between "simple interest" and "compound interest."

3. What are the components of an interest rate? Why is it important for accountants to understand these components?

4. Presented below are a number of values taken from compound interest tables involving the same number of periods and the same rate of interest. Indicate what each of these four values represent.
   (a) 7.36009
   (b) 1.79085
   (c) .55839
   (d) 13.18079

5. Harmon Co. deposits $18,000 in a money market certificate that provides interest of 12% compounded quarterly if the amount is maintained for three years. How much will Harmon have at the end of three years?

6. Phil Bayliss will receive $30,000 five years from today from a trust fund established by his mother. Assuming the interest rate is 12%, compounded semiannually, what is the present value of this amount today?

7. What are the primary characteristics of an annuity? Differentiate between an "ordinary annuity" and an "annuity due."

8. Norm Zelten Inc. owes $30,000 to Parton Company. How much would Zelten have to pay each year if the debt is to be retired through four equal payments made at the end of each year and the interest rate on the debt is 15%? (Round to two decimals.)

9. The Foxes are planning for a retirement home. They estimate they will need $130,000 four years from now to purchase this home. Assuming an interest rate of 10%, what amount must be deposited at the end of each of the four years to fund the home price? (Round to two decimal places.)

10. Assume the same situation as in question 9, except that the four equal amounts are deposited at the beginning of the period rather than at the end. In this case, what amount must be deposited at the beginning of each period? (Round to two decimals.)

11. Explain how the amount of an ordinary annuity interest table is converted to the amount of an annuity due interest table.

12. Explain how the present value of an ordinary annuity interest table is converted to the present value of an annuity due interest table.

13. In a book named *Treasure*, the reader has to figure out where a one kilogram, 24 kt gold horse has been buried. If the horse is found, a prize of $25,000 a year for twenty years is provided. The actual cost of the publisher to purchase an annuity to pay the prize is $210,000. What interest rate (to the nearest percent) was used to determine the amount of the annuity? (Assume end-of-year payments.)

14. Harried Enterprises leases property to Lia Inc. Because Lia Inc. is experiencing financial difficulty, Harried agrees to receive five rents of $8,000 at the end of each year, with the rents deferred three years. What is the present value of the five rents discounted at 12%?

15. Kell Inc. invests $20,000 initially, which accumulates to $38,000 at the end of five years. What is the annual interest rate earned on the investment? (**Hint**: Interpolation will be needed.)

16. Answer the following questions:
   (a) On May 1, 1994, Pat Company sold some machinery to Merlin Company on an instalment contract basis. The contract required five equal annual payments, with the first payment due on May 1, 1994. What present value concept is appropriate for this situation?
   (b) On June 1, 1994, Struthers Inc. purchased a new machine that it did not have to pay for until May 1, 1996. The total payment on May 1, 1996 will include both principal and interest. Assuming an interest rate of 12%, the cost of the machine will be the total payment multiplied by what time value of money concept?
   (c) Koppel Inc. wishes to know how much money it will have available in five years if five equal amounts of $30,000 are invested, with the first amount invested immediately. What interest table is appropriate for this situation?
   (d) Burrows invests in a "jumbo" $100,000 three-year certificate of deposit. What table will be used to determine the amount accumulated at the end of three years?

17. Recently Sally Hogan was interested in purchasing a Honda Acura. The salesperson indicated that the price of the car was either $25,000 cash or $6,400 at the end of each of five years. Compute the effective interest rate to the nearest percent that Hogan would have to pay if she chose to make the five annual payments.

18. A football player was reported to have received an $11 million contract. The terms were a signing bonus of $500,000 in 1991 plus $500,000 in 2001 through the year 2004. In addition, he was to receive a base salary of $300,000 in 1991 which was to increase $100,000 a year to the year 1995; in 1996 he was to receive $1 million a year which would increase $100,000 per year to the year 2000. Assuming that the appropriate interest rate was 9% and that each payment occurred on December 31 of the respective year, compute the present value of this contract as of December 31, 1991.

———— EXERCISES ————

(Interest rates are per annum unless otherwise indicated.)

(FUTURE AMOUNT AND PRESENT VALUE PROBLEMS) Presented below are three unrelated situations: **EA-1**

(a) Twig Company recently signed a 10-year lease for a new office building. Under the lease agreement, a security deposit of $10,000 was made which would be returned at the expiration of the lease with interest compounded at 6% per year. What amount will the company receive when the lease expires?

(b) Patterson Corporation, having recently issued a $10 million, 15-year bond issue, is committed to make annual sinking fund deposits of $300,000. The deposits are made on the last day of each year and yield a return of 10%. Will the fund at the end of 15 years be sufficient to retire the bonds? If not, what will the excess or deficiency be?

(c) Under the terms of his salary agreement, President Jed Sorensen has an option of receiving either an immediate bonus of $50,000 or a deferred bonus of $100,000, payable in 10 years. Ignoring tax considerations and assuming a relevant interest rate of 8%, which form of settlement should President Sorensen accept?

(COMPUTATION OF BOND PRICES) What will you pay for a $50,000 debenture bond that matures in 15 years and pays $5,000 interest at the end of each year if you want to earn a yield of: (a) 8%; (b) 10%; (c) 12%?   **EA-2**

(COMPUTATIONS FOR A RETIREMENT FUND) Mr. Bud Light, a super salesman contemplating retirement on his fifty-fifth birthday, plans to create a fund which will earn 8% and enable him to withdraw $15,000 per year on June 30, beginning in 1998 and continuing through 2001. Bud intends to make equal contributions to this fund on June 30 of each of the years 1994–1997.   **EA-3**

Instructions

(a) How much must the balance of the fund equal on June 30, 1997 in order for Bud Light to satisfy his objective?

(b) What is the required amount of each of Bud's contributions to the fund?

(UNKNOWN PERIODS AND UNKNOWN INTEREST RATE)   **EA-4**

(a) Ron Boyle wishes to become a millionaire. His money market fund has a balance of $83,905.43 and has a guaranteed interest rate of 10%.

Instructions

How many years must Ron leave the balance in the fund in order to get his desired $1,000,000?

(b) Lila Osage desires to accumulate $1,000,000 in 15 years using her money market fund balance of $122,894.51.

Instructions

At what interest rate must her investment compound annually?

EA-5 **(ANALYSIS OF ALTERNATIVES)** S.O. Easy, a manufacturer of low-sodium, low-cholesterol TV dinners, would like to increase its market share in Atlantic Canada. In order to do so, S.O. Easy has decided to locate a new factory in the Halifax area. S.O. Easy will either buy or lease a building depending upon which is more advantageous. The site location committee has narrowed down the options to the following three buildings:

Building A: Purchase for a cash price of $1,000,000, useful life 25 years.

Building B: Lease for 25 years with annual payments of $115,000 being made at the beginning of the year.

Building C: Purchase for $1,080,000 cash. This building is larger than needed; however, the excess space can be sublet for 25 years at a net annual rental of $12,000. Rental payments will be received at the end of each year. S.O. Easy has no aversion to being a landlord.

Instructions

In which building would you recommend that S.O. Easy locate assuming a 12% interest rate?

EA-6 **(FUTURE AMOUNT AND CHANGING INTEREST RATES)** Lisa Fleck intends to invest $10,000 in a trust on January 10 of every year, 1994 to 2008, inclusive. She anticipates that interest rates will change during that period of time as follows:

1/10/94–1/09/97	10%
1/10/97–1/09/04	11%
1/10/04–1/09/08	12%

How much will Lisa have in trust on January 10, 2008?

EA-7 **(AMOUNT NEEDED TO RETIRE SHARES)** Arrow Inc. is a computer software development company. In recent years, it has experienced significant growth in sales. As a result, the Board of Directors has decided to raise funds by issuing redeemable preferred shares to meet cash needs for expansion. On January 1, 1993, the company issued 100,000 redeemable preferred shares with the intent to redeem them on January 1, 2003. The redemption price per share is $25.

As the controller of the company, Dean Rask is asked to set up a plan to accumulate the funds that will be needed to retire the redeemable preferred shares in 2003. He expects that the company will have a surplus of funds of $120,000 each year for the next 10 years and decides to put these amounts into a sinking fund. Beginning January 1, 1994, the company will deposit $120,000 into the sinking fund annually for 10 years. The sinking fund is expected to earn 10% interest compounded annually. However, the sinking fund will not be sufficient for the redemption of the preferred shares. Therefore, Dean plans to deposit on January 1, 1998 a single amount into a savings account which is expected to earn 8% interest.

Instructions

What is the amount that must be deposited on January 1, 1998?

EA-8 **(COMPUTATION OF PENSION LIABILITY)** Homemaker Inc. is a furniture manufacturing company with 50 employees. Recently, after a long negotiation with the local union, the company decided to initiate a pension plan as a part of its compensation package. The plan will start on January 1, 1994. Each employee covered by the plan is entitled to a pension payment each year after retirement. As required by accounting standards, the controller of the company needs to report the projected pension obligation (liability). On the basis of a discussion with the supervisor of the Personnel Department and an actuary from an insurance company, the controller develops the following information related to the pension plan.

Average length of time to retirement	15 years
Expected life duration after retirement	10 years
Total pension payment expected each year for all retired employees.	
Payment made at the end of the year.	$700,000/year
The interest rate is 8%.	

Instructions

On the basis of the information given, determine the projected pension obligation.

(RETIREMENT OF DEBT)   Mike Bone borrowed $100,000 on March 1, 1994. This amount plus accrued **EA-9** interest at 12% compounded semiannually is to be repaid March 1, 2004. To retire this debt, Mike plans to contribute to a debt retirement fund five equal amounts starting March 1, 1999 and for the next four years. The fund is expected to earn 10% per annum.

Instructions

How much must Mike Bone contribute each year to provide a fund sufficient to retire the debt on March 1, 2004?

(PRESENT VALUE OF A BOND)   Your client, Wayne Inc., has acquired Housepent Manufacturing Com- **EA-10** pany in a business combination that is to be accounted for as a purchase transaction (at fair market value). Along with the assets of Housepent, Wayne assumed an outstanding liability for a debenture bond issue having a principal amount of $7,500,000 with interest payable semiannually at a rate of 9%. Housepent received $6,800,000 in proceeds from the issuance five years ago. The bonds are currently 20 years from maturity. Equivalent securities command a 12% current market rate of interest.

Instructions

Your client requests your advice regarding the amount to record for the acquired bond issue.

(LEAST COSTLY PAYOFF: ORDINARY ANNUITY)   Elliot Corporation has outstanding a contractual **EA-11** debt. The corporation has available two means of settlement: (1) it can make an immediate payment of $2,250,000 or (2) it can make annual payments of $250,000 for 15 years, each payment due on the last day of the year.

Instructions

Which method of payment do you recommend, assuming an expected effective interest rate of 8%?

(LEAST COSTLY PAYOFF: ANNUITY DUE)   Assuming the same facts as those in EA-11 except that the **EA-12** payments must begin now and be made on the first day of each of the 15 years, what payment method would you recommend?

(INTERPOLATING THE INTEREST RATE)   On July 17, 1994, Kris Blader borrowed $42,000 from his **EA-13** grandfather to open a clothing store. Starting July 17, 1995, Kris has to make 10 equal annual payments of $6,700 each to repay the loan.

Instructions

What interest rate is Kris Blader paying? (Interpolation is required.)

(INTERPOLATING THE INTEREST RATE)   As the purchaser of a new house, Sandra Hofer signed a **EA-14** mortgage note to pay the Canadian Bank $16,000 every six months for 20 years, at the end of which time she will own the house. At the date the mortgage was signed, the purchase price was $198,000 and Sandra made a down payment of $20,000. The first mortgage payment is to be made six months after the date the mortgage was signed.

Instructions

Compute the exact rate of interest earned by the bank on the mortgage. (Interpolate if necessary.)

———— PROBLEMS ————

PA-1 **(COMPUTATION OF PRESENT VALUE)** Answer each of these unrelated questions:

1. On January 1, 1994, Gizmo Corporation sold a building that cost $250,000 and that had accumulated depreciation of $100,000 on the date of sale. Gizmo received as consideration a $275,000 noninterest-bearing note due on January 1, 1997. There was no established exchange price for the building and the note had no ready market. The prevailing rate of interest for a note of this type on January 1, 1994 was 9%. At what amount should the gain from the sale of the building be reported?

2. On January 1, 1994, Gizmo Corporation purchased 100 of the $1,000 face value, 10% ten-year bonds of Heath Inc. The bonds mature on January 1, 2004 and pay interest annually beginning January 1, 1995. Gizmo Corporation purchased the bonds to yield 11%. How much did Gizmo pay for the bonds?

3. Gizmo Corporation bought a new machine and agreed to pay for it in equal annual instalments of $4,000 at the end of each of the next 10 years. Assuming an interest rate of 8% applies to this contract, how much should Gizmo record as the cost of the machine?

4. Gizmo Corporation purchased a tractor on December 31, 1994, paying $16,000 cash on that date and agreeing to pay $10,000 at the end of each of the next eight years. At what amount should the tractor be valued on December 31, 1994, assuming an interest rate of 12%?

5. Gizmo Corporation wants to withdraw $50,000 (including principal) from an investment fund at the end of each year for nine years. What is the required initial investment at the beginning of the first year if the fund earns 11%?

PA-2 **(FUTURE AMOUNTS OF ANNUITIES DUE)** Mack Aroni, a bank robber, is worried about his retirement. He decides to start a savings account. Mack deposits annually his net share of the "loot," which consists of $70,000 per year, for three years beginning January 1, 1992. Mack is arrested on January 4, 1994 (after making the third deposit) and spends the rest of 1994 and most of 1995 in jail. He escapes in September of 1995 and resumes his savings plan with semiannual deposits of $25,000 each beginning January 1, 1996. Assume that the bank's interest rate is 8% compounded annually from January 1, 1992 through January 1, 1995, and 10% compounded semiannually thereafter.

Instructions

When Mack retires on January 1, 1999 (six months after his last deposit), what will be the balance in his savings account?

PA-3 **(ANALYSIS OF ALTERNATIVES)** Cheapo Inc. has decided to surface and maintain for ten years a vacant lot next to one of its discount retail outlets to serve as a parking lot for customers. Management is considering the following bids involving two different qualities of surfacing for a parking area of 12,000 square metres:

Bid A. A surface that costs $8.25 per square metre. This surface will have to be replaced at the end of five years. The annual maintenance cost on this surface is estimated at 15 cents per square metre for each year except the last of its service. The replacement surface will be similar to the initial surface.

Bid B. A surface that costs $12.50 per square metre. This surface has a probable useful life of 10 years and will require annual maintenance in each year except the last year, at an estimated cost of 5 cents per square metre.

Instructions

Prepare computations showing which bid should be accepted by Cheapo Inc. You may assume that the cost of capital is 9%, that the annual maintenance expenditures are incurred at the end of each year, and that prices are not expected to change during the next ten years.

(ANALYSIS OF ALTERNATIVES) When James Baker died, he left his wife Tammy an insurance policy contract that permitted her to choose any one of the following four options:

PA-4

(a) $55,000 immediate cash.

(b) $3,600 every three months payable at the end of each quarter for five years.

(c) $20,000 immediate cash and $1,500 every three months for 10 years, payable at the beginning of each three-month period.

(d) $4,000 every three months for three years and $1,000 each quarter for the following 25 quarters, all payments payable at the end of each quarter.

Instructions

If money is worth 2½% per quarter, compounded quarterly, which option will you recommend that Tammy choose?

(COMPUTATION OF UNKNOWN PAYMENTS) Provide a solution to each of the following situations by computing the unknowns (use the interest tables):

PA-5

(a) Winona Potts invests in a $125,000 annuity insurance policy at 9% compounded annually on February 8, 1994. The first of 20 receipts from the annuity is payable to Winona 10 years after the annuity is purchased (February 8, 2004). What will be the amount of each of the 20 equal annual receipts?

(b) Bill Sullivan owes a debt of $40,000 from the purchase of his new sports car. The debt bears interest of 8% payable annually. Bill wishes to pay the debt and interest in eight annual instalments, beginning one year hence. What equal annual instalments will pay the debt and interest?

(c) On January 1, 1994, Bob Mackey offers to buy David Martin's used combine for $39,000, payable in 10 equal instalments, which are to include 9% interest on the unpaid balance and a portion of the principal, with the first payment to be made on January 1, 1994. How much will each payment be?

(PURCHASE PRICE OF A BUSINESS: DEFERRED ANNUITIES) During the past year, Shawna Leonard planted a new vineyard on 150 hectares of land which she leases for $30,000 a year. She has asked you to assist in determining the value of her vineyard operation.

PA-6

The vineyard will bear no grapes for the first five years (1–5). In the next five years (6–10), Shawna estimates that the vines will bear grapes that can be sold for $60,000 each year. For the next 20 years (11–30), she expects the harvest will provide annual revenues of $110,000. During the last 10 years (31–40) of the vineyard's life, she estimates that revenues will decline to $80,000 per year.

During the first five years the annual cost of pruning, fertilizing, and caring for the vineyard is estimated at $10,000; during the years of production, 6–40, these costs will rise to $15,000 per year. The relevant market rate of interest for the entire period is 12%. Assume that all receipts and payments are made at the end of each year.

Instructions

Rob Bryshun has offered to buy Shawna's vineyard business. On the basis of the current value of the business, what is the minimum price Shawna should accept?

PA-7 **(TIME VALUE CONCEPTS APPLIED TO SOLVE BUSINESS PROBLEMS)** Answer the following questions related to Lazybones Inc.:

1. Lazybones Inc. has $114,400 to invest. The company is trying to decide between two alternative uses of the funds. One alternative provides $16,000 at the end of each year for 12 years, and the other is to receive a single lump sum payment of $380,000 at the end of 12 years. Which alternative should Lazybones select? Assume the interest rate is constant over the entire investment.

2. Lazybones Inc. has just purchased a new computer. The fair market value of the equipment is $717,750. The purchase agreement specified an immediate down payment of $100,000 and semiannual payments of $80,000 beginning at the end of six months for five years. What interest rate, to the nearest percent, was used in discounting this purchase transaction?

3. Lazybones Inc. loaned $300,000 to Wright Corporation. Lazybones accepted a note due in seven years at 8% compounded semiannually. After two years (and receipt of interest for two years), Lazybones needed money and therefore sold the note to Royal Canadian Bank, which required interest on the note of 12% compounded semiannually. What amount did Lazybones receive from the sale of the note?

4. Lazybones Inc. wishes to accumulate $700,000 by December 31, 2004 to retire outstanding bonds. The company deposits $150,000 on December 31, 1994, which will earn interest at 10% per year compounded quarterly, to help in the debt retirement. The company wants to know what additional equal amounts should be deposited at the end of each quarter for 10 years to ensure that $700,000 is available at the end of 2004. (The quarterly deposits will also earn interest at a rate of 10%, compounded quarterly.) Round to even dollars.

PA-8 **(ANALYSIS OF BUSINESS PROBLEMS)** Dave Analyst is a financial executive with Peanuts Company. Although Dave has not had any formal training in finance or accounting, he has a "good sense" for numbers and has helped the company grow from a very small company ($1,000,000 sales) to a large operation ($90 million sales). With the business growing steadily, however, the company needs to make a number of difficult financial decisions in which Dave feels a little "over his head." He therefore decided to hire a new employee with facility in "numbers" to help him. As a basis for determining who to employ, he asked each prospective employee to prepare answers to questions relating to the following situations he has encountered recently. Here are the questions which you are asked to answer:

1. In 1993 Peanuts Company negotiated and closed a long-term lease contract for newly constructed truck terminals and freight storage facilities. The buildings were constructed on land owned by the company. On January 1, 1994, Peanuts Company took possession of the leased property. The 20-year lease is effective for the period January 1, 1994 through December 31, 2013. Rental payments of $800,000 are payable to the lessor (owner of facilities) on January 1 of each of the first 10 years of the lease term. Payments of $300,000 are due on January 1 for each of the last 10 years of the lease term. Peanuts has an option to purchase all the leased facilities for $1.00 on December 31, 2013. At the time the lease was negotiated, the fair market of the truck terminals and freight storage facilities was approximately $6,500,000. If the company had borrowed the money to purchase the facilities, it would have to pay 10% interest. Should the company have purchased rather than leased the facilities?

2. Last year the company exchanged some land for a noninterest-bearing note. The note was to be paid at the rate of $20,000 per year for nine years, beginning one year from the date of the exchange. The interest rate for the note was 11%. At the time the land was originally purchased, it cost $90,000. What is the fair value of the note?

3. The company has always followed the policy to take any cash discounts offered on goods purchased. Recently the company purchased a large amount of raw materials at a price of $800,000 with terms 1/10, n/30 on which it took the discount. If Peanuts' cost of funds was 10%, should the policy of always taking cash discount be continued?

PA-9 **(ANALYSIS OF LEASE VS. PURCHASE)** Helpless Inc. owns and operates a number of hardware stores on the Prairies. Recently the company has decided to locate another store in a rapidly growing area of Manitoba; the company is trying to decide whether to purchase or lease the building and related facilities.

Purchase. The company can purchase the site, construct the building, and purchase all store fixtures. The cost would be $1,650,000. An immediate down payment of $400,000 is required, and the remaining $1,250,000 would be paid off over five years at $300,000 per year (including interest). The property is expected to have a useful life of 12 years and then it will be sold for $400,000. As the owner of the property, the company will have the following out-of-pocket expenses each period:

Property taxes (to be paid at the end of each year)	$48,000
Insurance (to be paid at the beginning of each year)	27,000
Other (maintenance which primarily occurs at the end of each year)	16,000
	$91,000

Lease. Strongman Corp. Ltd. has agreed to purchase the site, construct the building, and install the appropriate fixtures for Helpless Inc. if Helpless will lease the completed facility for 12 years. The annual costs for the lease will be $250,000. The lease would be a triple-net lease, which means that Helpless will have no responsibility related to the facility over the 12 years. The terms of the lease are that Helpless would be required to make 12 annual payments (the first payment to be made at the time the store opens and then each following year). In addition, a deposit of $125,000 is required when the store is opened, which will be returned at the end of the twelfth year, assuming no unusual damage to the building structure or fixtures.

Currently the cost of funds for Helpless Inc. is 10%.

Instructions

Which of the two approaches should Helpless Inc. follow?

(PRESENT VALUE BUSINESS PROBLEMS) Presented below are a series of time value of money problems. Solve each of them. **PA-10**

(a) Your client, Young Chen, wishes to provide for the payment of an obligation of $250,000 due on July 1, 2002. Chen plans to deposit $20,000 in a special fund each July 1 for eight years, starting July 1, 1995. She also wishes to make a deposit on July 1, 1994 of an amount that, with its accumulated interest, will bring the fund up to $250,000 at the maturity of the obligation. She expects that the fund will earn interest at the rate of 8% compounded annually. Compute the amount to be deposited on July 1, 1994.

(b) On January 1, 1994, Kap Inc. initiated a pension plan under which each of its employees will receive a pension annuity of $10,000 per year beginning one year after retirement and continuing until death. Employee A will retire at the end of 2000 and, according to mortality tables, is expected to live long enough to receive eight pension payments. What is the present value of Kap Inc.'s pension obligation for employee A at the beginning of 1994 if the interest rate is 10%?

(c) Yurie Company purchases bonds from Erica Inc. in the amount of $400,000. The bonds are 10-year, 13% bonds that pay interest semiannually. After three years (and receipt of interest for three years), Yurie needs money and, therefore, sells the bonds to Korea Company, which demands interest at 16% compounded semiannually. What is the amount that Yurie will receive on the sale of the bonds?

INDEX

WE WANT TO HEAR FROM YOU!

By sharing your opinions about Intermediate Accounting 4/E, you will help us ensure that you are getting the most value for your textbook dollars. After you have used the book for a while, please fill out this form. Either fold, tape, and mail, or fax us toll free @ 1(800)565-6802!

Course name: _____   School name: _____

Your name: _____

I am using: ❏ Volume 1   ❏ Volume 2

1) Did you purchase this book (check all that apply):
   ❏ From your campus bookstore
   ❏ From a bookstore off-campus
   ❏ New   ❏ Used   ❏ For yourself
   ❏ For yourself and at least one other student

2) Was this text available at the bookstore when you needed it?
   ❏ Yes   ❏ No

3) Was the study guide available for purchase?
   ❏ Yes   ❏ No   ❏ Don't know
   If yes, did you purchase it?
   ❏ Yes   ❏ No   ❏ I intend to purchase it

4) How far along are you in this course (put an ✘ where you are now)?
   ❏ _____   ❏ _____   ❏
   Beginning   Midway   Completed

5) How much have you used this text (put an ✘ where appropriate)?
   ❏ _____   ❏ _____   ❏
   Skimmed   Read Half   Read entire book

6) Have you read the introductory material (i.e., the preface)?
   ❏ Yes   ❏ No   ❏ Parts of it

7) Even if you have only skimmed this text, please rate the following features:

Features:	Very valuable/effective	Somewhat valuable/effective	Not valuable/effective
Value as a reference			
Readability			
Design & illustrations			
Study & review material			
Problems & cases			
Relevant examples			
Overall perception			

8) What do you like most about this book?

_____

_____

_____

What do you like least?

_____

_____

_____

9) At the end of the semester, what do you intend to do with this text?
   ❏ Keep it   ❏ Sell it   ❏ Unsure

Thank you for your time and feedback!

🌀 WILEY

(fold here)

0108529899-M9W1L1-BR01

COLLEGE DIVISION
JOHN WILEY & SONS CANADA LTD
22 WORCESTER RD
PO BOX 56213 STN BRM B
TORONTO ON   M7Y 9C1

(tape shut)